213.50

Elsevier Science Ltd, The Boulevard, Langford Lane,
Kidlington, Oxford OX5 1GB, UK

Library of Congress Cataloging in Publication Data
Concise encyclopedia of language pathology/edited by
Franco Fabbro; consulting editor, R. E. Asher.
   p.   cm.
1. Language disorders—Encyclopedias. 2. Speech
disorders—Encyclopedias. I. Fabbro, F. II. Asher, R.
E.
[DNLM: 1. Language Disorders encyclopedias. 2.
Speech Disorders encyclopedias. 3. Language
encyclopedias. 4. Speech encyclopedias. WL 13 C744
1999]
RC423.C656 1999
616.8'55'003—dc21
DNLM/DLC   98–55691

British Library Cataloguing in Publication Data
Concise encyclopedia of language pathology
1. Language disorders—Encyclopedias   2. Speech
disorders—Encyclopedias
I. Fabbro, Franco
616.8'55'003

ISBN 0–08–043151–8 (HC)

Typeset by Polestar Digital Data Ltd., Glasgow, UK.
Printed and bound in Great Britain by Polestar Wheatons Ltd.,
Exeter, UK.

CONCISE
ENCYCLOPEDIA
OF
LANGUAGE
PATHOLOGY

Edited by

FRANCO FABBRO

Università di Trieste and
Istituto Scientifico 'E. Medea', Bosisio Parini, Italy

Consulting Editor

R. E. ASHER

University of Edinburgh, UK

1999

ELSEVIER

AMSTERDAM – LAUSANNE – NEW YORK – OXFORD – SHANNON – SINGAPORE – TOKYO

57873

CONCISE
ENCYCLOPEDIA
OF
LANGUAGE
PATHOLOGY

Contents

Editor's Preface

In the following pages I will explain the *objectives* I set myself when editing this book; I will also present its *contents* in a structured way to give readers a general overview; and lastly, I will indicate the possible *target readership* that may benefit from consulting, reading, and/or studying the book.

1. Objectives

Approximately half of the contributions to this book are updated entries from *The Encyclopedia of Language and Linguistics*, published by Pergamon in 1994. The remainder consist of new contributions specifically written for the present issue. When editing the *Concise Encyclopedia of Language Pathology* I attempted to comply with three principles, namely i) providing a systematic analysis of all main topics concerning speech and language pathology; ii) adopting an interdisciplinary approach to the various speech and language pathologies, and iii) using a style as concise and clear as possible and oriented towards clinical practice.

The topics dealt with in the book are grouped in six general sections. The first section (*Speech and Language in Normal Speakers*) presents and discusses the current knowledge on acoustics, anatomy, neurophysiology, and language psychology in adults along with speech and language acquisition in children. The second section (*General Aspects of Speech and Language Pathologies*) provides an explanation of the main models used in the study of language pathologies, and discusses the main acquired and developmental causes and some general statistics concerning language pathologies in the world. The third section focuses on *Developmental Speech and Language Pathologies*, presenting and discussing developmental dysarthrias, disorders of fluency, developmental language disorders, and major learning disabilities. Besides theoretical issues, special emphasis is laid on diagnosis and treatment of speech and language pathologies. The fourth section deals with *Acquired Speech Pathologies*, in particular with disorders of voice, acquired dysarthrias, and verbal apraxia. The fifth section (*Acquired Language Pathologies*) presents and discusses current knowledge on the various forms of aphasia in children and adults. In addition to the main concepts of neurolinguistics, this section describes aphasic syndromes, explores the role of subcortical structures in language processing, and addresses the issue of the relations between different memory systems and language as well as the issue of aphasia in multilinguals. It further deals with issues of verbal communication in patients with lesions to the right cerebral hemisphere. The final chapters of this section present the main techniques used in the rehabilitation of aphasia, and their effectiveness. The sixth section (*Language Pathology in Neuropsychiatric Disorders*) focuses on language disorders in autism and psychoses.

Many researchers and clinicians have become aware that research into speech and language pathology is increasingly concentrating on details while overlooking the overall picture. Several strategies are available to counteract this reductionist trend. For example, a possible solution consists in devising theoretical approaches that identify language as a function and thus developing a theory (a model) of such function (see, e.g., the logical models of language developed by Chomsky [1965, 1980], and the language organization models developed in the field of cognitive neuropsychology [Shallice 1988, McCarthy and Warrington 1990]). These theoretical approaches are very attractive, but sometimes they look at an issue from a single point of view. A somewhat harder and often less attractive, but probably more effective, way to gain an insight into speech and language pathologies is an interdisciplinary approach to language disorders. It basically consists in studying, observing, and storing information from different approaches with a view to employ, in a given clinical situation, those tools that apparently contribute to understanding, describing, diagnosing, and treating a given disorder in a more effective way. Insight into a given speech pathology requires taking into account all information on and approaches to it. The present volume touches on almost all approaches to the study of language and its pathologies, namely approaches based on acoustics, computer science, epidemiology, health policy, anatomy, neurophysiology, linguistics, psychology, psycholinguistics, sociolinguistics, neurology, neuropsychology related to the studies of neurology, cognitive neuropsychology, neurolinguistics, and psychiatry. An interdisciplinary approach to language definitely requires tolerance towards less known and less common approaches. Tolerance towards other customs and habits is a virtue which often contributes to widening our knowledge. Apart from an interdisciplinary approach, curiosity and a slightly 'subversive' attitude appear to be essential for the development of scientific knowledge (Kuhn 1962, Harrington 1987). Indeed, in my opinion, diagnosis and therapy, even though aiming at treating a specific verbal communication disorder, ought to be based on the widest possible knowledge in the field.

   The practical utility of an interdisciplinary approach to speech and language disorders is clear to all people working in this field. For example, not so long ago few neurologists knew basic concepts of linguistics (e.g., the concept of phonemes and of morphosyntactic aspects peculiar to a language) and the more general aspects of pragmatics. The situation has radically changed and today reviews of neurology (see *Brain, NeuroReport, Neurology, Archives of Neurology*) publish articles that, at interdisciplinary level (e.g., neurolinguistic level), deal with the description, diagnosis, and treatment of patients affected by neurological diseases associated with speech and language disorders. Whereas, at present, the practical utility of a linguistic and psychological approach to language is easily accepted, other approaches such as the acoustic, neurophysiological, and computer-based approaches are still somewhat disliked. However, recent studies based on interdisciplinary approaches such as acoustics, neurophysiology of cortical plasticity, and speech processing have allowed a better understanding of language comprehension deficits in some forms of developmental language disorders and acquired speech disorders, and have also led to the individuation of intervention tools that seem to be very promising (Tallal et al. 1996, Merzenich et al. 1996, Wright et al. 1997).

   A third objective of the *Concise Encyclopedia of Language Pathology* is to present the reader with the largest possible number of topics in an exhaustive, yet concise, style. Because each person looks at an issue from a personal point of view, I have attempted to edit a book on language pathologies that, while not overlooking theoretical aspects, strongly focuses on clinical practice.

2. Contents

Speech and Language in Normal Speakers
H. J. Wakita in *Acoustics of Speech* describes the physical characteristics of sounds and the mathematical and physical methods used to study sounds as well as the main acoustical methods of speech analysis and synthesis. S. Greenberg in *Auditory Models of Speech Processing* describes the major anatomical and physiological aspects of the auditory periphery (receptor cells, the basilar membrane, and the fibers of the auditory nerve) as well as the anatomical and functional organization of the cochlear nucleus and the central auditory mechanisms. In addition he addresses the role of the auditory systems for language comprehension in normal individuals and in individuals with moderate-to-severe hearing loss, thereby comparing the human auditory systems with computerized systems for speech recognition. Finally, this chapter also contains comments on the evolution of the auditory systems in mammals as related to the evolution of verbal communication in human beings. D. W. Massaro in *Speech Perception* introduces and describes the concept of

'perceptive unity of spoken language'; furthermore, the author presents and discusses the latest theories on word recognition and explores the role of context in language comprehension. J. C. Kahane in *Functional and Clinical Anatomy of the Speech Mechanism* provides a detailed description of the main organs involved in speech production (lungs, larynx, pharynx, tongue, nasal cavity, facial muscles, etc.), their development in children, and the effects on speech production following a lesion to these areas. H. Hirose in *Neuromuscular Aspects of Speech* analyses the main contributions of electromyography (EMG) to the study of language physiology as well as the study and differentiation of some speech pathologies (for instance, distinction between neurogenic and myogenic diseases).

V. L. Gracco and K. G. Munhall in *The Neurophysiology of Speech* highlight the importance of the vocal tract and of its dynamic in speech production. As to the neurophysiological organization of speech production, these authors maintain that it is accounted for by i) preprogrammed movement sequences (open loop systems), ii) afferent information coming from the vocal tract structures (close loop systems), and iii) a central rhythm generator. The chapter further contains a description of the main cortical structures (primary motor and sensory areas, supplementary motor area, premotor area, and posterior parietal regions) and of the subcortical structures (cerebellar cortex, deep cerebellar nucleus, thalamus and basal ganglia) as well as of their functioning in the process of speech production. M. A. Garman in *Psycholinguistics* presents the main theoretical and experimental research works carried out on the mental mechanisms subserving linguistic competence while analyzing the representation of linguistic sounds both at the acoustic and articulatory level and of the different writing systems at mental level. Finally he discusses how useful studying the biologic representation of language may be for the purpose of understanding the linguistic and psychological levels of language. H. L. Petrie in *Language Production* distinguishes the level of conceptualization (conscious) from the level of speech production (unconscious) during expression. The author presents and discusses a series of models of language production derived from the analysis of speech errors in normal subjects. P. W. Jusczyk in *Development of Language Perception in Infants* describes the ability of infants to discriminate sound properties of native and foreign languages during their first year of age. C. Stoel-Gammon in *Babbling in Hearing and Deaf Infants* presents the development stages of vocalization and speech production in normal and deaf children from birth to 15 months of age. C. Stoel-Gammon and L. Menn in *Acquisition of Phonemes* illustrate the main development stages of phonemic production in American children. The authors underline the fact that little girls acquire the ability to produce phonemes earlier than little boys, which must be taken into account in the assessment of developmental disorders of phonemic production.

M. D. Barrett in *Acquisition of Vocabulary* describes the stages of receptive and expressive vocabulary acquisition from birth to 30 months of age, and for each stage, the minimal performance in comprehension and production tasks. Children whose performance is below this minimal level must be accurately examined for a clinical assessment of their situation. H. Tager-Flusberg in *Acquisition of Grammar* explains the main stages of grammar development both at comprehension and production level. The author describes and discusses the main tools and methodologies used in the study of grammar acquisition. J. Oakhill in *Acquisition of Reading* explores the role of specific prerequisites that are necessary for children to learn how to read (e.g., metalinguistic awareness of words, syllables, and phonemes). Moreover, the author discusses the most common approaches used in the teaching of reading (global reading of words and letter-for-letter reading) and the role of language comprehension in reading. J. L. Locke in *Language Development and Brain Development* associates the various development stages of vocalization and speech with the development of the neural substrates underlying these functions. Latest studies show that before 20 months of age words and sentences are acquired as prosodic-articulatory units and processed by the 'minor' cerebral hemisphere (namely, the right hemisphere in more than 90% of the population). After 20 months, once a sufficient vocabulary has been acquired, the analytical and computational aspects of language start developing. The latter aspects are generally controlled by the left cerebral hemisphere.

B. Lindblom in *Biological Bases of Speech* provides an analysis of the biological bases accounting for language acquisition in humans. Actually, human beings are unique among Primates in that they can acquire language, most probably owing to the development of specific, adequate neural structures subserving phonological and syntactic competence and to a peculiar conformation of the vocal tract allowing the production of the speech sounds that are typical of human languages. J. Maxim in *Aging and Language* maintains that aging does not affect linguistic competence, but it slightly reduces performances related to expression and comprehension. Current studies have highlighted that normal aging tends to provoke a reduction in verbal short-term memory and episodic memory, whereas semantic memory and the morphosyntactic aspects of speech have a greater resistance to aging. O. Togeby in *Pragmatic Principles in Verbal Communication* explains the basic principles regulating human verbal communication, and specifically, metapragmatic principles, cooperation principles, and kindness and comprehension principles. Over the past few years, awareness of the fundamental importance of pragmatic competence with regard to verbal communication disorders (Joanette et al. 1990, Paradis 1998) has become stronger. This line of research is gaining ground in the fields of theoretical, applied and clinical linguistics, and neurolinguistics. W. Li and H. Zhu in *Sociolinguistics and Language Pathology* underscore that aspects of language assessment and rehabilitation are a specific sociolinguistic setting. In particular, the authors focus on a current issue, namely the use of standard language (used at school and by mass media) in the assessment and rehabilitation of patients who generally use nonstandard language.

General Aspects of Speech and Language Pathologies

J. M. Cooper in *Overview* and *Historical Perspective* outlines the most significant historical contributions to the study of language pathologies. The author identifies the main disciplines involved in the study and treatment of language pathologies and verbal communication disorders. In addition, he proposes a structured training for speech and language pathologists. D. Crystal in *Models* describes some of the most widely applied models in the study of speech and language pathologies (medical, psychological, linguistic, developmental), their practical utility, and their limits. Since each model tends to highlight some aspects at the expense of others, Crystal suggests the development of interactive models. B. M. Ansel and R. L. Ringel in *Acquired Causes* look at the causes of acquired communication disorders that almost exclusively depend on neurological diseases, and describe their development and the difficulties related to their treatment.

S. O. Richardson in *Developmental Causes* summarizes the most frequent and better-known causes of speech and language disorders during development, the most important of which are neurological causes, hearing disorders, mental retardness, anomalies in the organs of speech production, and some emotional and psychosocial factors. P. M. Enderby in *Incidence and Prevalence* explains some fundamental statistical data concerning verbal communication disorders. In the UK approximately 5% of the population is affected by a verbal communication disorder. In particular, 12% of children have verbal communication disorders, 6% have a specific language impairment, while 5% of children attending school have or have had a stuttering problem. K. G. Butler in *International Perspective* discusses training of speech and language therapists in the various continents and in particular in some Western countries. It has been estimated that more than 200 000 speech and language therapists are active worldwide and, according to the author, given the increasing number of people who know and speak more than one language it is imperative to train multilingual therapists.

Developmental Speech and Language Pathologies

E. Pizzuto and V. Volterra in *Deafness and Sign Language*, after introducing the various types and gravity of deafness, explain the linguistic, sociolinguistic, psychological, and neuropsychological aspects of sign language. In addition, they describe the complementary systems of communication in deaf people (e.g., finger spelling) and the role of sign language (L1) in the learning of writing and reading in a second language (L2), such as English. E. Davies in *Developmental Dysarthrias* illustrates a classificatory scheme for developmental dysarthrias in the light of the scheme proposed by some clinicians of the Mayo Clinic. The author also discusses the role of speech production disorders in the development of phonology in children with dysarthrias and describes some basic concepts useful for its diagnosis and treatment.

H. H. Gregory and C. B. Gregory in *Disorders of Fluency* describe the main characteristics of stuttering and cluttering in children. Stuttering affects 1% of children attending school, while it is estimated that 5% of the population have been through a short period of stuttering in their lives. Stuttering mainly affects males, its age of onset is between 18 months and 9 years of age, and it is often associated with language disorders. Cluttering is an intelligible and drawled speech articulation. It is a barely known verbal expression disorder which is often associated with a low IQ and electroencephalographic alterations. L. Rustin and F. Cook in *Disorders of Fluency: Intervention* present the general principles underlying the treatment of stuttering according to the age of the subjects. Therapy for early stutterers (2–7 years of age) mainly consists in giving advice to parents (e.g., speak slower, increase listening and attention towards children, be less authoritative). Periodic meetings are arranged with the child and his/her parents; only rarely are meetings arranged with the child alone. With regard to older children (8–14 years of age), either individual treatment or intensive group therapy (two weeks) are advisable. The aim is to reduce tension and increase fluency during verbal expression. Group therapy is preferable for adolescents (15–18 years of age). As with chronic adult stutterers, in this case too, treatments have been devised that make subjects under treatment 'speak more fluently' and/or 'stutter more fluently.'

A. Van Hout in *Learning Disabilities* defines specific learning disabilities (developmental dyslexia, developmental dysgraphia, developmental dyscalculia) and distinguishes them from learning retardation disorders, namely learning disorders which depend on developmental disorders of acquisition. The author thus provides a description of the main learning retardation disorders in children with attention-deficit hyperactivity disorder (ADHD), developmental language disorders, developmental dyspraxia, and visuospatial developmental disorders. Among the specific learning disabilities Van Hout describes developmental dysgraphias, which affect 5% of children, and developmental dyscalculias, which affect approximately 2% of children. S. L. James in *General Aspects of Developmental Language Disorders* focuses on the information necessary to identify children with specific language disorders (assessment of comprehension and verbal production as against the abilities shown by the control group), and describes the difficulties these children encounter at all linguistic levels (e.g., phonological, morphological, syntactic, and semantic levels). Furthermore, the author identifies populations of children with developmental language disorders (e.g., retarded children, children with emotional disorders, neurosensory deafness, learning disabilities, and children with specific language impairments). M. Korkman in *Specific Language Impairment: Subtypes and Assessment* provides a definition of such disorder in the acquisition of language (children with no apparent neurological disorders and without mental retardness) which affects 3–7% of children. Korkman looks at the possible mechanisms underlying this disorder, for example, difficulty in processing rapidly changing acoustic stimuli, in phonological decoding, in acquiring the procedures underlying morphosyntax as well as verbal working memory disorders, and articulatory and lexical access difficulties. Lastly, the author proposes some of the best-known classification schemes for language-specific disorders and a structured itinerary to reach a diagnosis. G. C. Bedi and E. Dorsett in *Developmental Disorders of Language: Evaluation of the Effectiveness of Intervention* present experimental procedures used to verify the effectiveness of a treatment in children with language-specific disorders. In addition, the authors describe various types of therapy that have proved to be effective, for example, training with synthesized and computer-processed verbal stimuli (slowing down and amplifying formant transition of stop phonemes), treatment based on imitation, 'modeling-based' treatment, and treatment based on conversional recasting. According to the authors, the most effective therapy is short-term and intensive.

M. J. Snowling in *Reading Difficulties* distinguishes children with difficulties in learning to read because they had a previous language-specific disorder from children with a specific learning disorder. The latter are children with normal IQ, who often have difficulty with phonemic segmentation, non-word repetition and lexical access. Some of them, when reading, also have difficulty in understanding complex morphosyntactic elements. J. Robertson and D. J. Bakker in *Classification of Developmental Dyslexia and Intervention*, after a historical introduction to the concept of developmental dyslexia, give an explanation of the main classification schemes for the various subtypes of dyslexia and their diagnostic and therapeutic validity. In particular, they describe and discuss the neuropsychological classification of dyslexia devised by Bakker which associates reading difficulties with an inappropriate involvement of the right cerebral hemisphere (L dyslexia) or the left cerebral hemisphere (P dyslexia) in the processes of reading. The authors then describe some of the most widely applied methods used in the treatment of reading-specific disorders.

Acquired Speech Pathologies

L. Mathieson in *Disorders of Voice* describes the main characteristics of voice disorders, namely the most frequent functional voice disorders, and those caused by organic pathologies and of endocrinological origin. The author also takes up the subject of dysphonias due to neoplastic pathologies of the larynx. H. Hirose in *Acquired Dysarthrias* introduces the concept of dysarthria (a motor disorder of speech production), and describes the main modalities for its assessment (perceptive assessment, acoustic analysis, and physiological assessment of altered articulatory movements). H. Ackermann in *Acquired Disorders of Articulation: Classification and Intervention*, after describing the most widely accepted classification schemes for dysarthria in the clinical setting, explains the symptomatology and pathophysiology of the main types of dysarthrias; such aspects, according to the author, allow for a more accurate diagnosis and a correct treatment. Lastly, he describes the main types of treatment for dysarthria (behavioral techniques, technological aids, pharmacotherapy, surgical techniques) and discusses their effectiveness. J. C. Rosenbek in *Verbal Apraxia* defines the concept of verbal apraxia distinguishing it from aphasia and dysarthria, describes the clinical characteristics of this disorder (random errors during speech production with spared verbal comprehension, writing and reading abilities), and points at the criteria used in the differential diagnosis of aphasia and dysarthria. Finally, the author describes the main types of treatment for such disorder.

Acquired Language Pathologies

Y. Lebrun in *Historical Perspectives of Aphasia* describes the fundamental stages of scientific thinking which led to the identification of the main aphasic syndromes (e.g., Broca's motor aphasia, Wernicke's sensory aphasia, conduction aphasia, and the various forms of transcortical aphasia). The author also gives an explanation of the concepts of crossed aphasia, anarthria, and word apraxia. J. C. Marshall and J. M. Gurd in *Neurolinguistics* illustrate the main development stages of neurolinguistic studies. The use of linguistic concepts and tools in the study of aphasic patients has led to the emergence of neurolinguistics. The authors illustrate the first pioneering studies on grammar errors (A. Pick), and phonological and phonetic errors (T. Alajouanine) in aphasic patients. They also look at the introduction and use of structuralist concepts (R. Jacobson, A. R. Luria) and generative-grammar concepts (D. Caplan and Y. Grodzinsky) in the study of aphasic disorders. J. M. Gurd and J. C. Marshall in *Language and the Brain* examine the main approaches used in the study of the cerebral representation of language. The most widely applied method still consists in the study of verbal communication abilities in patients with cortical and subcortical lesions. In recent years, the introduction of Positron Emission Tomography (PET) and functional Magnetic Resonance (fMRI) has led to the development of functional neuroanatomical studies allowing a better understanding of the neural structures underlying language.

C. Luzzatti in *Neurolinguistic Assessment of Aphasia* describes the origin and development of the main concepts of aphasiology on which basis the current classification scheme for aphasic syndromes has been developed. The author also looks at the techniques available for a neurolinguistic assessment of aphasia (analysis of spontaneous speech and assessment of linguistic skills), and the tests currently being used for the assessment of language disorders. R. Lesser in *Aphasia* describes a cognitive neuropsychological approach to the study of acquired language disorders. According to this model, language is supported by a set of functionally independent, yet interactive, modules. An aphasic disorder is thus due to the activity of normal and abnormal modules. D. Tranel and S. W. Anderson in *Syndromes of Aphasia* define the concept of 'aphasic syndrome' and underscore the utility of such taxonomy in the clinical practice. The study of aphasic syndromes is no longer considered as a tool to understand the cerebral organization of language; yet, it is still useful for making a diagnosis and a prognosis as well as deciding on a treatment, and assessing its effectiveness. The authors then provide a detailed description of the aphasic syndromes and the neural structures that are mainly involved in each of the syndromes described. S. F. Cappa and J. Abutalebi in *Subcortical Aphasia* focus on language disorders following lesions to the basal ganglia, the thalamus, and the white matter of the dominant hemisphere for language. Lesions to the left basal ganglia may determine a nonfluent output with semantic and verbal paraphasias, whereas lesions to the left thalamus may provoke fluent aphasias with semantic paraphasias and anomias. However, the extent of the involvement of subcortical structures in the organization of language is still under discussion, and, according to the authors, further investigation by means of neuroimaging techniques will be likely to allow a better understanding of the situation.

B. E. Murdoch in *Acquired Childhood Aphasia* describes the main clinical symptoms in children (mutism, nonfluent output, agrammatism). In recent years, cases of fluent aphasia (Wernicke's aphasia, transcortical sensory aphasia, conduction aphasia) have also been reported. Furthermore, it has been established that, irrespective of the age of onset and the site of the lesion, language recovery is rarely complete, and there are still consequences characterized by difficulties at school. The author then focuses on the main causes of aphasia in children (traumas, tumors, cerebrovascular disorders, infectious diseases, and epilepsy). Indeed, such causes have an effect both on symptomatology and prognosis. F. Fabbro in *Aphasia in Multilinguals*, after defining the concept of multilingualism, draws attention to the fact that more than half of the world's population is bilingual. Therefore, more than half of the aphasics in the world are likely to be bilingual aphasics. The author also describes pathological phenomena that are typical of aphasia in multilinguals (e.g., selective aphasia, alternating antagonism, switching disorders, mixing, and translation errors) and the main recovery patterns in bilinguals. Furthermore, he illustrates the results of neurophysiological and neuroimaging studies on the organization of the brain in bilinguals.

A. R. Butcher in *Phonological Disorders of Language* distinguishes phonological disorders (inability to recognize some phonological contrasts) from phonetic disorders (inappropriate production of the sounds of a language with preserved ability to recognize phonemic contrasts).

Patients with phonological disorders independent of production disorders show an inability to perceptively distinguish one or more phonemes. The author describes a classification scheme for the most frequent phonological disorders. W. D. Dressler in *Morphosyntactic Disorders of Language* describes the major morphosyntactic disorders in fluent and nonfluent aphasias, in developmental language disorders, and in dementias. The study of patients with morphosyntactic disorders, in particular of those who know languages rich in morphology, has lead to a better understanding of the typology of specific language disorders such as agrammatism and paragrammatism. M. J. Snowling and A. Edmundson in *Disorders of Reading and Writing* look at reading disorders according to the model developed by cognitive neuropsychology. Such an approach has allowed for the individuation of three main reading disorders: superficial dyslexia (letter-for-letter reading), deep dyslexia (production of semantic errors in reading), and phonological dyslexia (preserved reading of words with inability to read non-words). The authors apply this model to the study of acquired and developmental dyslexia.

R. Morris in *Language Dysfunction in Dementia* illustrates the main language disorders in patients with Alzheimer's disease. The most evident disorders impair lexical access (anomias and circumlocutions) and pragmatic aspects of verbal communication, whereas the phonological and syntactic levels appear to be more resistant to this type of dementia. D. Van Lancker in *The Right Hemisphere and Verbal Communication* presents and discusses those aspects of verbal communication processing in which the right hemisphere is involved (nonpropositional speech, prosody, concrete words with a highly emotional content, nonliteral language, and pragmatics). These aspects play an important role in verbal communication, which actually depends on the coordinated activity of both cerebral hemispheres. S. Aglioti in *Language and Memory Systems* describes the various human memory systems (working memory, declarative memory [episodic memory and semantic memory] and nondeclarative memory [e.g., procedural memory, priming, etc.]). According to the author, many memory systems are 'partially' involved in verbal functions. Aphasia may provoke a selective impairment of working memory systems (repetition difficulty), semantic memory systems (anomias, semantic paraphasias), or procedural memory systems (phonologic and syntactic disorders). Furthermore, in comparison with declarative memory, procedural memory shows a different resistance to neurological diseases (see Alzheimer's disease vs. Parkinson's disease). Various memory systems appear to be involved in the acquisition of the first language as against learning of a second language by formal methods and after 7 years of age.

G. Demeurisse in *Rehabilitation of Acquired Language Disorders* maintains that a fundamental prerequisite for the rehabilitation of aphasia is an accurate neurolinguistic assessment of the patient's residual communication abilities. The author thus describes the main rehabilitation techniques that are based on repeated linguistic and cognitive exercises, the implementation of strategies based on cognitive neuropsychology, techniques that tend to increase the communicative and pragmatic functions of the right hemisphere, techniques aiming at reducing stress and tension, and the use of drugs with a view to increase the effectiveness of language therapy. Finally, the author examines variables (such as site, extent, and type of the lesion) that influence the recovery of verbal functions. R. Whurr and M. Lorch in *Acquired Disorders of Language (Aphasia): Evaluation of the Effectiveness of Intervention* systematically describe the most relevant factors determining an improvement of verbal communication in patients with acquired brain lesions. The authors especially deal with the specific effects of language therapy. By means of a particular statistical analysis (meta-analysis) of literature data, they have shown the efficacy of the rehabilitation training carried out by specialized staff, particularly in severe aphasics. They too express the view that for the purpose of successfully evaluating the efficacy of a given rehabilitation treatment, it is necessary to accurately assess the patient's language before and after treatment.

Language Pathology in Neuropsychiatric Disorders

S. Baron-Cohen in *Autism* explains the key symptoms of this syndrome, namely an inability to develop normal social relations, language acquisition and verbal communication deficits, and a serious cognitive imagination deficit (inability to conceive other people's mental states). In particular, with regard to verbal communication, autistic children show serious pragmatic deficits (inability to understand and tell jokes, and to understand and convey irony, sarcasm, and metaphors) and a tendency to produce immediate or delayed echolalias. Y. Lebrun in *Mutism* distinguishes functional mutism (of psychological origin) from organic mutism. The most common forms of functional mutism are i) selective mutism, rather frequent in children, which manifests itself in specific circumstances and specific individuals or in particular environments; and ii) total mutism, often defined as 'hysteric mutism,' which can generally be observed in adults with psychopathological problems. On the other hand, a series of organic diseases may cause mutism, such as surgical operations to the vocal folds, global aphasia, anarthria, and lesions to the midbrain, the cerebellum, or both frontal lobes. In children, some forms of mutism may depend on severe developmental motor dysphasia. L. C. Sanfilippo and R. E. Hoffman in *Language Disorders in the Psychoses* define the main characteristics of the 'disorder of formal thinking' in psychotic patients (weakness of associations and derailment, tangentiality, circumstantiality, pressured speech, flight of ideas, alogia). The authors also present the main disorders affecting speech planning (vague anaphoric references, inability to follow the thread of ideas, etc.) as well as difficulties in the choice of words and semantic associations, grammar difficulties (grammar mistakes and/or reduction of syntactic complexity), and phonological disorders.

3. Target readership

In my opinion, operators in the field of diagnosis and treatment of speech and language disorders ought to have some basic knowledge on normal language processing, namely some knowledge on fundamental aspects of language acquisition and use, starting from acoustics to pragmatics and sociolinguistics. I find it useful that operators in this field have a general knowledge of all developmental and acquired speech and language pathologies. At the levels of application, diagnosis, and treatment, speech and language therapists are probably led to becoming specialized and operating in only one of the sectors and topics dealt with in the present volume. However, the fact that clinical and research activity is limited to only one sector does not necessarily imply that general knowledge must be likewise limited. This book is thus meant to provide an outline of the topics that ought to be known to all operators in the fields of research into, and diagnosis and treatment of speech and language disorders as well as verbal communication disorders.

My activity in the fields of study and my clinical research into, and treatment of, adults and children has given me the opportunity to meet many speech and language pathologists operating in Europe. I have found that often therapists were not updated on basic aspects of language in normal subjects. Furthermore, operators dealing with articulation disorders had often unclear ideas on language pathologies, and vice versa. Besides, there is a huge gap between therapists dealing with language disorders in developmental ages and those dealing with the same disorders in adults. It seems, therefore, that what is lacking in this clinical setting is an overview of normal and pathological aspects of language and verbal communication in children and adults. It is hoped that students, speech and language pathologists, and all people interested in these subjects will consider the *Concise Encyclopedia of Language Pathology* a useful tool for studying and exploring not only topics that are part of their day-to-day activity, but also those of related fields in which they are not (yet) directly involved.

Acknowledgments

It is true that without the respective contributions of the authors this work would not have been possible, however the two most precious and helpful people whom my deepest gratitude goes to are my wife Valeria Darò for her underlying organizational work and Michael Lax, Editor at Elsevier, for his impeccable coordination and supportive attitude throughout this joint enterprise.

Bibliography

Chomsky N 1965 *Aspects of the Theory of Syntax*. MIT Press, Cambridge, MA

Chomsky N 1980 *Rules and Representations*. Basil Blackwell, Oxford

Harrington A 1987 *Medicine, Mind, and the Double Brain*. Princeton University Press, Princeton, NJ

Kuhn T S 1962 *The Structure of Scientific Revolutions*. University of Chicago, Chicago, IL

Joanette Y, Goulet P, Hannequin D 1990 *Right Hemisphere and Verbal Communication*. Springer-Verlag, New York

McCarthy R A, Warrington E K 1990 *Cognitive Neuropsychology. A Clinical Introduction*. Academic Press, Orlando, FL

Merzenich M M, Jenkins W M, Johnston P, Schreiner C, Miller S L, Tallal P 1996 Temporal processing deficits of language-learning impaired children ameliorating by training. *Science*, **271**: 77–81

Paradis M 1998 *Pragmatics in Neurogenic Communication Disorders*. Pergamon, Oxford

Shallice T 1988 *From Neuropsychology to Mental Structure*. Cambridge University Press, Cambridge

Tallal P, Miller S L, Bedi G, Byma G, Wang X, Nagarajan S S, Schreiner C, Jenkins W M, Merzenich M M 1996 Language comprehension in language-learning impaired children improved with acoustically modified speech. *Science*, **271**: 81–84

Wright B A, Lombardino L J, King W M, Puranik C S, Leonard C M, Merzenich M M 1997 Deficits in auditory temporal and spectral resolution in language-impaired children. *Nature*, **387**: 176–178

Speech and Language in Normal Speakers

Acoustics of Speech

H. J. Wakita

Acoustic phonetics gives an account of speech manifested as 'sound': it shows how to describe and quantify sound as well as how the quality of the sound relates to the vocal-tract shape that produced it. This chapter gives first a general account of sound, then a more specific account of speech sounds.

1. Sound

In the general sense, sound is a pressure wave which consists of pulsations or vibrations of molecules of an elastic medium (gas, liquid, or solid). The term 'sound' denotes a physical disturbance of air particles caused by vibrating objects, for example, vocal cords, the diaphragm of an earphone or loudspeaker, bells, etc. Sound can also be generated by high-speed or unsteady airflow such as in the exhaust of jet engines, sirens, and fans. In these cases, it is the high energy level of the turbulence which causes the pressure disturbance or vibrating air particles resulting in aerodynamic sound.

Sound waves differ from vibratory motion of other kinds in two important respects. First, sound waves in free air are three-dimensional, that is, they propagate or spread out in all directions once they are generated, though not necessarily with equal efficiency in all directions. The popular example of wave motion that uses the notion of a stone cast into a body of quiescent water and the ripples spreading outward in two dimensions (on the surface only) is not really representative of a sound wave. The differences are major: the waves of sound spread in three dimensions in ever-enlarging spheres in the elastic medium that is in contact with the vibrating source of sound.

Second, sound in air is propagated as a longitudinal wave; that is, the motion of air molecules lies in the direction of propagation. Water ripples, however, are transverse waves: the vibrations of the water molecules are at right angles to the direction of propagation of the wave.

For the case of the sound wave, the movement of each air molecule is purely local, making small to-and-fro motions similar to the vibrating surface causing the displacement. The motion is transmitted to adjacent

air molecules where the action is repeated. The to-and-fro molecular motion must be clearly distinguished from the velocity of the wave traveling through the medium. The molecule does not travel along with the sound wave.

1.1 Frequency

The most common way to study a complex vibration is to decompose it into a number of the simplest regular vibrations, called 'sinusoidal' vibrations, one of which is shown in Fig. 1. Such a vibration of air might be caused by the diaphragm of a loudspeaker; the forward motion compresses the air, the rearward motion reduces the pressure. This motion results in the vibration of air particles; the amplitude of vibration is measured in terms of air pressure. The to-and-fro motion of the air molecules creates a series of compressions (increased pressure) and rarefactions (reduced pressure) of the normal or steady-state value of atmospheric pressure. Therefore, the waveform shows how the air pressure changes with time when it is measured at a given point. This sequence of one compression followed by one rarefaction is known as one cycle, and the number of times the sequence is repeated (the number of cycles) in one second is called the frequency.

A pressure wave having the amplitude versus time characteristics shown in Fig. 1 is a pure tone, that is, only one frequency is involved. Pure tones do not occur often in nature, but may be approximated by a

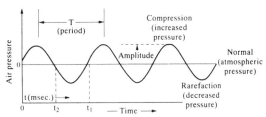

Figure 1. Sinusoidal wave: the waveform shows how the air pressure changes with time when it is measured at a given point.

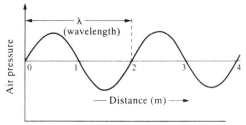

Figure 2. Sinusoidal wave: the waveform shows how the air pressure changes with distance from a given point at a given time.

siren or whistle. Most sounds are made up of combinations of tones of different frequencies which may have different amplitudes and which may or may not be harmonically related, (see Sect. 2.1).

As seen in Fig. 1, the changes of air pressure repeat regularly in the same fashion; thus, the wave is periodic. The reciprocal of frequency f is the period T in seconds:

$$f(Hz) = \frac{1}{T(sec)}$$

showing that frequency has the units of 1/seconds. T represents the time in seconds required to complete one cycle; thus, for example, the period of a 500 Hz wave is 1/500, or 0.002 seconds.

1.2 Wavelength and Speed of Sound

Fig. 2 shows a propagating sinusoidal sound wave in terms of the changes of air pressure at a distance along some straight line from a given point at a given time. This is different from Fig. 1 because the horizontal scale is in distance, not time. The length is equivalent to a period T in Fig. 1 and is now called a wavelength, λ. The wavelength of sound is the distance between corresponding points on two successive cycles.

The wavelength is obtained by dividing the distance that a sound propagates in a second by its frequency, which is the number of waveforms repeated in a second. Thus, the wavelength λ is given by:

$$\lambda(m) = \frac{c(m/sec)}{f(1/sec)} = cT(m)$$

where c denotes the sound velocity. The sound velocity in the air is approximately given by:

$$c(m/sec) = 0.6t(^{\circ}C) + 331(m/sec)$$

where t denotes the atmospheric temperature in centigrade. The frequency in this case shows how many waveform repetitions take place while the sound propagates in a second, and is given by:

$$f(Hz) = \frac{c(m/sec)}{\lambda(m)}$$

2. Phase Angle

There is another way of representing a sinusoidal wave. Consider a bead moving with a constant speed along a wire hoop with a certain radius. The location of the bead can be expressed in terms of its angle and the vertical distance from the baseline, as shown in Fig. 3. One cycle of motion of the bead concludes when it comes back to where it started, that is, when the angle becomes 360°. The same pattern is repeated as the bead keeps moving around the wire hoop. Sometimes it is necessary to describe the relative locations of two sinusoidal waves with identical frequencies. The term 'phase difference' is often used to describe the relative locations. An example is shown in Fig. 4; the phase difference between the two waves A and B is 90°; wave B lags 90° from wave A, or wave A leads 90° from wave B.

Three ways of representing the sinusoidal wave have been given: time versus amplitude, distance versus amplitude, and phase angle versus amplitude. These three representations are frequently used in the acoustics of speech.

2.1 Complex Waves

The sinusoidal wave plays an important role in understanding acoustic aspects of speech events, since it is the fundamental mode of any vibration. The most general motion of a vibrating surface is composed of

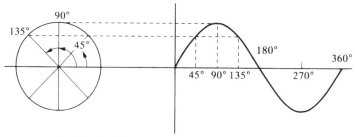

Figure 3. Phase angle representation of a sinusoidal wave; one cycle of motion of the bead in the hoop concludes when it comes back to where it started.

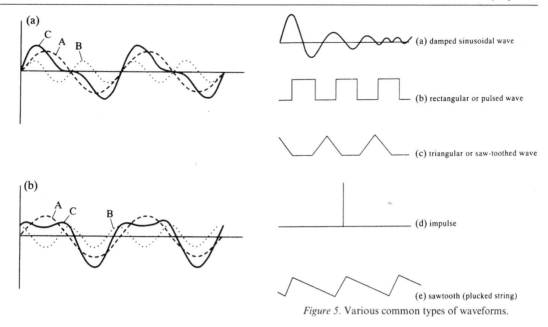

(a) damped sinusoidal wave

(b) rectangular or pulsed wave

(c) triangular or saw-toothed wave

(d) impulse

(e) sawtooth (plucked string)

Figure 5. Various common types of waveforms.

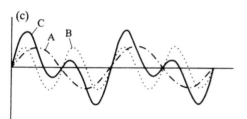

Figure 4. Complex waves: wave C is the sum of waves A and B.

the sum of a sinusoidal oscillation of the fundamental frequency F0, another at the second harmonic frequency 2F0, another at the third 3F0, etc. The fundamental mode repeats itself in $T0 = 1/F0$ seconds, the second harmonic mode repeats itself in $T1 = 1/2F0$, or $T0 = 2T1$ (that is, the second harmonic has twice the frequency and half the period of the fundamental), the third harmonic has three times the frequency and a third of the period, etc. The harmonic structure of the wave is very significant in determining the timbre or character of a sound. It is this timbre which allows one to distinguish different speech sounds.

It can be shown that any continuous waveform can be separated into a set of sinusoidal waves. The mathematical function that describes this is called the Fourier series. The amplitude and frequency of each wave and the relative phase differences do the trick. Simple examples are given in Fig. 4. In Fig. 4a, the frequency of wave B is twice that of A and the amplitude of wave B is half that of A. Wave C is the result of waves A and B added together; wave C can be

decomposed into the sinusoidal waves A and B. The component waves of complex waves are referred to as harmonics if they are integral multiples of the F0; thus, wave A is the first harmonic and wave B the second harmonic of the F0. Fig. 4b shows a different combination of two waves A and B. Although wave B is still the second harmonic of wave A, the result is a different complex wave C. In this case, wave B is shifted 90 degrees against wave B in Fig. 4a. One can observe how different resultant waveforms are obtained by changing the phase of one or both of the two component waves. If wave B has the same amplitude as wave A, and has the same phase as wave B in Fig. 4a, then yet another complex wave C is obtained as shown in Fig. 4c.

As given in the examples, any waveform which looks very complicated can be composed from a sufficient number of sinusoidal waves by adjusting the amplitude and phase of each wave in an appropriate manner. Other waveforms which often occur in acoustic studies are shown in Fig. 5.

Conversely, one may wish to decompose a complex wave into its sinusoidal structure rather than synthesize it. The same Fourier analysis may be used to accomplish this decomposition of a speech wave. It can be stated that any continuous waveform can be decomposed into a number of sinusoidal waves, although for very complex waveforms the number of frequencies required may approach infinity.

3. Fourier Transform and Spectrum

The simplest form of a sound wave is a sinusoid, but most sounds including speech have a much more

3

(a)

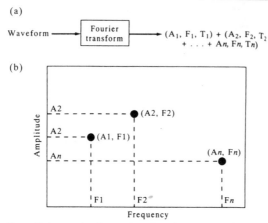

(b)

Figure 6. A mapping from a time-domain representation to a frequency-domain representation via the Fourier Transform.

complex waveshape. It also has been stated that any continuous waveform having finite energy can be formed by a suitable combination of sinusoidal waveforms. Mathematically, a sinusoidal wave is defined by its maximum amplitude A, a frequency F, and a phase P relative to the coordinate origin, thus it is represented as a set of three values $\{A, F, P\}$. Using this notation, a given waveform is decomposed into a set of $\{A, F, P\}$, that is, a set of sinusoidal waves. If one considers only the amplitude and the frequency, then the set of $\{A, F\}$ is called the amplitude spectrum of a given waveform, whereas the set of $\{F, P\}$ is called the phase spectrum. A graphical plot of the amplitude spectrum is schematically shown in Fig. 6. This transformation from a given waveform to a set of $\{A, F, P\}$ is called a Fourier transform. The Fourier transform constitutes a basis for spectral analysis and extraction of related speech parameters.

This distribution of sound energy with frequency is known as the sound spectrum. The method used to identify the frequency components of a noise, a musical tone, or other sound, is a spectral or frequency analysis. By this method, the frequency or frequency band and the amplitude of each are determined. The analyses may result in a line spectrum, a continuous spectrum, or a band spectrum.

3.1 Line Spectrum

In Fig. 7a, an example of a sinusoidal sound wave with a frequency F and the amplitude A is displayed as pressure versus time and pressure versus frequency graphs. Note that there is only one line on the frequency graph; it is positioned along the abscissa (the horizontal or frequency axis) at the value of the frequency. This sinusoidal wave should actually be plotted as a point at (F, A) in the frequency–amplitude display, but it is customary to represent the point by a line; thus, the name 'line spectrum' is given to this

representation. A pure-tone audiometer would generate such a single frequency, usually at intervals from 125 to 8000 Hz.

Fig. 7b shows the case of a slightly more complex waveform, that is, one composed of several sinusoidal waves. The basic wave form (or F0) repeats itself with period T seconds. The amplitude and frequency distribution of sound is shown by the spectrum. The frequency is represented by the position along the abscissa, and the amplitude of the sound at each frequency is shown by the height of the line above the abscissa. When the lines are integral multiples of the fundamental (i.e., one, two, three, etc. times the lowest frequency), these multiples are called overtones or harmonics.

3.2 Continuous Spectrum

In the two cases just discussed, sound energy existed only at discrete frequencies with no energy between frequencies. A continuous spectrum (Fig. 7c) implies a continuous distribution of sound energy over a band of frequencies; that is, some sound energy exists at each frequency within the band. Sounds of this kind are usually random, such as the roar from a waterfall or a jet airplane engine, implying the existence of energy at an infinite number of waves with different amplitudes. These are known as aperiodic sounds, that is, nonperiodic or not having a repetitive waveform. If the acoustic energy is distributed so that each cycle per second has equal energy, it is designated as 'white noise' by analogy to white light. If each cycle has slightly less energy than the preceding cycle, so that there is an equal amount of energy for each octave band (doubling of frequency), it is known as pink noise.

On occasion, as shown in Fig. 7d, one may observe a continuous spectrum combined with a line spectrum, such as a noisy fan having a characteristic whine, or a whistle in a noisy factory. Sometimes it is desirable to examine only the part of a continuous spectrum which contains the conspicuous line. For that, only a band of frequency containing such frequency components is examined.

4. Speech Sounds

Treated from the viewpoint of acoustics, a speech event is a vibration of air in a complex mode changing rapidly with time. In generating a voiced sound, vibration of air is caused by the closing and opening motion of the vocal cords sending out a train of air puffs into the vocal tract through the glottis. The vibration of air produced at the glottis is 'deformed' in various ways while propagating in the vocal tract toward the lips. Depending upon the different configurations of the vocal tract, different sounds are radiated from the lips. In the case of voiceless sounds, a turbulent flow of air is generated by making a constriction within the vocal tract but without involving

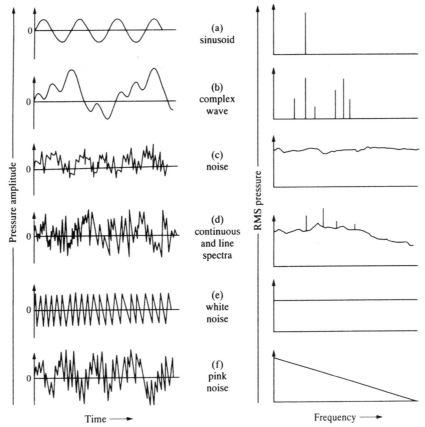

Figure 7. Various waveforms and their line spectra.

any vibratory motion of the glottis. The sound radiated from the mouth is then transmitted through the air to the ear of a listener, where it causes vibration which is physiologically processed by the auditory organs and finally perceived as sound. Thus, vibration plays an important role in the production and perception of speech. The acoustics of speech is a science which makes clear this intricate mechanism of the vibration event in order to obtain a better understanding of speech production and perception processes.

4.1 Waveforms

The vibratory motion of air is not visible to human eyes. Normally, the variation of air pressure is converted into a variation of electrical voltage by means of an electroacoustic transducer (e.g., a microphone) so that a replica of the variation of air pressure can be seen in terms of the variation of electrical voltage. As an example, a portion of an utterance, *Thieves who rob friends deserve jail,* is shown in Fig. 8. This was recorded at a point about 38 cm from the mouth of the speaker, and shows a period of only approximately

500 msec. Thus, the variation of air pressure can be visualized in terms of the variation of electrical voltage.

The task of acoustic phonetics is to attempt to discover the relation between such a display and the posited meaning-bearing structures of language, as well as those aspects of the speech signal which enable the identification of individual speakers, their regional dialect, sex, state of mind and health, and the acoustic environment in which they are speaking.

4.2 Filters

Sometimes it is desirable to alter the spectral envelope or eliminate some of the frequency components artificially. Systems having this function are called filters. Three types of filters are often used: a low-pass filter (LPF), a high-pass filter (HPF), and a band-pass filter (BPF). If a signal as shown in Fig. 9a is passed through each of these filters, the output spectra can be illustrated as shown in Figs. 9b, c, and d. The frequency components shown by the broken lines are eliminated by the filters. This effect of a filter system on the input spectrum is called the 'frequency characteristic' of the

5

(a)

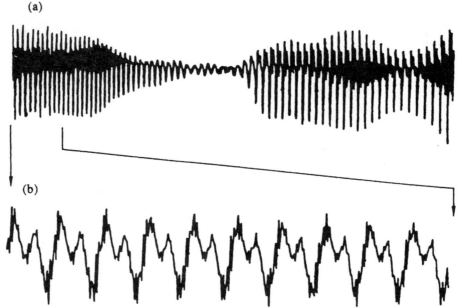

(b)

Figure 8. A portion of the waveform of the utterance *Thieves who rob friends deserve jail*; (a) The waveform for a portion ...*ieves who ro*... (about 500 msec); (b) Expanded waveform of the first 50 msec of the waveform in (a) above.

system, or the 'transfer function' of the system. These terms are frequently used for electroacoustic transducers and electrical devices such as microphones, loudspeakers, and amplifiers. Usually, it is desired in these devices that the frequency components of an input signal are not altered while the signal is transmitted through them.

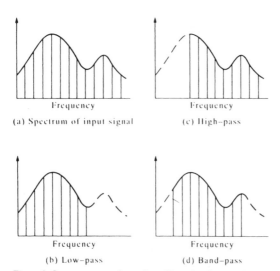

Figure 9. Output spectra from three filters for the same input.

4.3 Resonators

There is another kind of system, called a resonator, which emphasizes particular frequency components of a signal. The resonator is also considered to be a kind of filter if it has both input and output terminals. Its frequency characteristic is as shown in Fig. 10. The frequency characteristic of a resonator is usually specified by the frequency of the maximum amplitude, which is called the 'center frequency' or the 'resonance frequency.' The bandwidth of a resonance is defined as the frequency range where the amplitude of the frequency component is 3 dB (or less) below the amplitude of the center frequency, or, in other words, the frequency range around the center frequency where 50 percent of the power is included. If an impulse is used as an input to a resonator, the constant spectrum

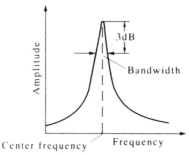

Figure 10. Frequency characteristics of a resonator.

of the input is deformed by the frequency characteristics of the resonator, and the output spectrum would look exactly as shown in Fig. 10; the output waveform will be a damped sinusoid. The output signal of a system when an impulse is applied as an input is called an 'impulse response.' Thus, the impulse response of a resonance system is a damped sinusoid. Since the frequency spectrum of an impulse is a constant for all the frequencies, the Fourier transform (i.e., the frequency spectrum) of an impulse response represents the transfer function (i.e., the frequency characteristics) of any filter system. The resonance system plays an important role in building a speech synthesizer as well as modeling the vocal system in understanding speech production.

5. Speech Production Model and Acoustic Features

Based on the various acoustic concepts described in the previous sections, a simple model of speech production can be made. The simplest model for producing the voiced sounds, such as vowels, is given in Fig. 11. The glottal wave caused by the vibration of the vocal cords is represented by the excitation source, and the vocal tract is regarded as an acoustic filter. The frequency characteristics of this filter are varied according to the shape of the air space in the vocal tract, which in turn is determined by the positions of the vocal organs such as the tongue, the jaw, the lips, and so on. By virtue of the vibration of the vocal cords, a train of air puffs is sent out into the vocal tract. While the train of air puffs travels through the vocal tract, the amplitudes of some of the frequency components are reduced and others are emphasized in a complex manner, depending on the vocal-tract configuration. A simple example is shown in Fig. 12. The input, Fig. 12a, shows the glottal wave which is roughly triangular-shaped, and Fig. 12b shows the output of the filter. It is to be noted how a relatively simple input waveform is changed into a complicated waveform by the vocal-tract filter. In terms of the changes of the power spectral envelope, Fig. 13a shows the spectral envelope of the excitation source and Fig. 13b shows the output spectral envelope of the excitation source changed by the frequency characteristics of the vocal-tract filter. To see the frequency characteristics of the vocal-tract filter more clearly, characteristics of the excitation source can be subtracted from the output spectral envelope if the amplitude is represented in decibels. The frequency characteristics of the vocal-tract filter thus obtained

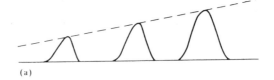

Figure 12. Waveforms of the filter input and output; (a) waveform of excitation source; (b) waveform of sound output.

are shown in Fig. 13c. This production model is called a source–filter model.

5.1 Excitation Source

Even such a simple model of speech production can explain many of the important properties of voiced sounds. Observe the waveforms in Fig. 12; the peaks in the excitation waveform are still preserved in the output waveform. These peaks show the number of repetitions of air puffs per second in the excitation source, which is called the fundamental frequency of the voice and is directly related to its pitch (the auditory sensation corresponding to F0). Usually, the average F0 of male voices is around 125 Hz, and that of female voices around 230 Hz. Another significant feature about the excitation waveform, as indicated by the dotted lines in Fig. 12, is the amplitude of the peaks. They are well reflected in the output waveform.

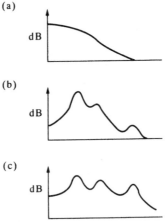

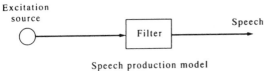

Speech production model

Figure 11. Speech production model.

Figure 13. Frequency characteristics (a) excitation source, (b) output, (c) filter.

Thus, the amplitude of the excitation source determines the power of speech and, hence, the loudness of the sound. These two quantities, the F0 and the amplitude, are considered to be the most important properties pertaining to the excitation source.

5.2 Spectral Characteristics and Formants

The significant property of the frequency characteristics of the filter in Fig. 13c is the conspicuous peaks. These peaks reflect the resonance characteristics of the vocal tract. The center frequency of each peak is called the 'formant frequency.' From lower to higher, they are called the first, second, and third formant frequencies, and so on. Since these peaks are due to the resonances of the vocal tract, each peak can be described by its center frequency and bandwidth. Thus, the frequency characteristics of the vocal-tract filter can be described by their formant frequencies and bandwidths. Each sound is characterized by the locations of the formant frequencies resulting from the vocal-tract configuration pertaining to the sound. Thus, formant frequency is known to be the most important acoustic property of a speech sound. Usually, the first three formant frequencies are dominant, and they are usually below 3500 Hz.

For the production of a fricative consonant, a noise source is assumed to be at the place of the consonantal constriction where turbulent noise is generated, plus a glottal excitation source if the consonant is voiced. For the production of nasal sounds, a nasal filter corresponding to the nasal tract is branched from the vocal-tract filter to account for the spectral dips due to the nasal tract. However, it is very difficult to separate the frequency characteristics of the nasal tract from those of the oral cavity. Acoustically, all the consonants are described by their overall frequency spectral characteristics.

6. Speech Analysis

In order to examine the acoustic properties of a particular sound, it is necessary to know how to obtain those properties in an efficient way. This has long been a primary topic for the speech researcher. In the early days, a technique of photographically recording speech waves was used to examine the F0 of the speech sound, and laborious calculations of Fourier transforms were tried by the use of a hand calculator in order to obtain the frequency spectrum of a sound. With the development of electronic techniques, various machines were developed to analyze speech. The sound spectrograph, among others, played (and in the 1990s is still playing) an important role in speech analysis. A great deal of speech information has been obtained with this machine by many researchers. Since the development of digital computers, especially since around 1970, highly sophisticated techniques have been applied to speech analysis, allowing fast and accurate computation. Digital computer techniques are especially suitable for processing large amounts of speech data.

6.1 Time–Frequency Representations

The sound spectrograph provides various data on speech sounds, such as formant structure, voicing, friction, stress, and fundamental frequency. It is, whether analog or digital, based mainly on a method for obtaining and displaying frequency spectra of speech sounds on time–frequency coordinates. The amplitude of the frequency components is shown as marks with varying degrees of darkness. Since formant frequencies are peaks in the frequency spectrum, they appear as darker marks in the spectrogram. Besides the formant structure of the sound, the duration of sounds, voiced and unvoiced portions, etc., can be either observed or measured from the spectrogram.

The traditional sound spectrograph used to be an analog device, but has been replaced by one based on digital techniques in which the Fourier transform is used as a major mathematical tool. With proper software, the spectrogram can be displayed on the monitor screen of a workstation or a personal computer.

The digital spectrograph based on the Fourier transform allows somewhat flexible control of the frequency resolution. The frequency resolution corresponding to the wideband or narrowband spectrogram can be controlled by changing the length of a waveform segment to which the Fourier transform is applied. The larger the length of the waveform segment, the better the frequency resolution. This relation is often referred to as the 'uncertainness of resolution.' Normally, satisfactory results are obtained for vowels by properly selecting the length of the segment for analysis, while consonants of short duration obviously lose the frequency resolution. Since the Fourier transform assumes a stationary signal for analysis, it suffers when used for the analysis of nonstationary signals or speech segments where the frequency components are changing. Various time–frequency representations with better frequency resolutions have been proposed, but none has been verified to be appropriate for speech analysis by the time of writing.

6.2 Formant Analysis

It is of utmost importance to know the formant structure of sounds in order to examine their acoustic properties. The development in computer techniques has made possible automatic tracking of formant frequencies, allowing fast and accurate analysis of a large amount of data, and thus the digital spectrograph is now widely used. The most efficient and promising computer methods, among others, are the cepstrum method and the linear prediction method, both of which are based on highly sophisticated mathematical procedures.

8

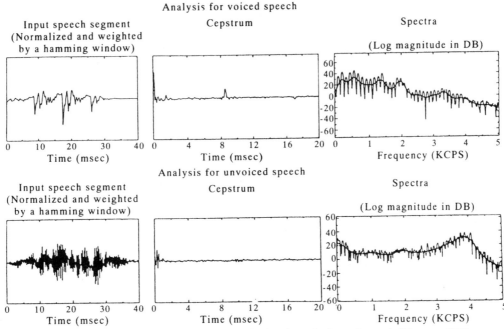

Analysis for voiced speech

Figure 14. Spectrum and cepstrum analysis of voiced and unvoiced speech sounds (Flanagan 1972).

In the cepstrum method, the frequency spectrum of a sound is computed by applying the Fourier transform to a segment of the corresponding speech wave. If the Fourier transform of the logarithm of the frequency spectrum itself is computed, a different kind of spectrum called a 'cepstrum' is obtained, which separates the vocal-tract characteristics from the excitation-source characteristics. The vocal cords' excitation appears at the high end of the cepstrum as rapidly varying periodic components, whereas the vocal-tract transmission function appears at the low end of it as slowly varying components having the formant information. If the Fourier transform is applied to the low end of the cepstrum, a smooth spectrum showing clear formant peaks is obtained. In Fig. 14, examples of cepstrum analysis of voiced and unvoiced sounds are shown. The formant information is locally separated from the fundamental frequency information in the cepstrum shown at the middle of the top row. The smoothed spectra are shown by the solid lines in the right-hand figures for voiced and voiceless sounds.

Another powerful method is linear prediction, in which the amplitude of a given speech sound is predicted by the past amplitude values of the sound. Unknown variables, called 'prediction coefficients,' are determined in such a way that the difference between the predicted and the actual values is minimized to a certain criterion. The prediction coefficients thus obtained are mathematically related to the formant frequencies, which can be computed in a very efficient manner. The linear prediction method is considered very reliable and accurate for obtaining formant frequencies of voiced, nonnasalized sounds, and the mathematical procedure is quite suitable for computer processing. An example of the result obtained for the utterance *I am now a man* is shown in Fig. 15. Although this method has a disadvantage for nasal sound analysis, since it neglects the antiresonance due to the nasal cavity which affects formant frequencies, it is an excellent method for automatically estimating the spectral envelope of various speech sounds.

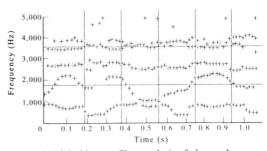

Figure 15. Digital inverse filter analysis of phrase: *I am now a man* (Markel 1972).

9

6.3 *Fundamental Frequency Analysis*

F0 can be calculated by measuring the time difference between two successive peaks in the sound wave and then computing the reciprocal of it. However, this procedure is extremely time-consuming. A faster method involves tracing the harmonics in a narrow-band spectrogram produced by the sound spectrograph. However, even this is not suitable for large amounts of speech data as would be required, for example, when compiling statistics on the fundamental frequencies of several speakers. In such cases, it is essential to use any of several methods which can be implemented on a digital computer.

One simple method is autocorrelation, which is, so to speak, a computerized 'peak-picking' method which extracts the periodicity of the sound wave by knowing peak locations in its autocorrelation function. A disadvantage of this method is that there is interaction between the source excitation and the first formant frequency, thus sometimes giving a false result. Experience shows, however, that such a case is not encountered frequently, and autocorrelation serves its purpose well.

The cepstrum method may be another choice which avoids this disadvantage, since the periodic component is completely separated from the vocal-tract characteristics in the cepstrum, as exemplified in Fig. 14. The linear prediction method is also a valuable tool for F0 analysis as well as formant analysis. The prediction error, after eliminating the combined characteristics of the glottal waveshape, the vocal tract, and the radiation, still preserves the information on source periodicity. Thus, one can extract this information from the prediction error by such a method as autocorrelation.

While formant frequencies are necessary for knowing the acoustic attributes of each sound, fundamental voice frequency, together with other acoustic properties such as voice intensity level and phonetic duration, gives information on the prosodic variation of the voice such as stress, intonation, individual voice characteristics, and emotional characteristics. Since the amplitude of the glottal wave is known to be proportional to voice intensity level, it is easily measured by an electronic device or computed by a digital computer.

Formant bandwidth is another acoustic parameter needed to specify the shape of the spectral envelope of a sound. Normally, formant bandwidth is obtained as the combined effects of the glottal wave, the vocal tract, and the radiation at the mouth. It is difficult to know the contribution of the vocal tract to formant bandwidths due to interactions with the glottal wave and the radiation.

7. **Basic Speech Production Models for Synthesis**

One way of testing whether these extracted acoustic properties are truly valid is to reconstruct the original speech sounds based on these properties. Also, how speech is produced in the human vocal tract can be examined by 'speech synthesis.' There are various ways to synthesize speech, depending upon the vocal-tract model chosen.

7.1 *Terminal Analog Model*

The simplest model of speech production is to regard the vocal tract as a filter which is excited by the glottal source. A speech synthesizer based on this simple model is called a 'terminal analog synthesizer.' Since the conspicuous peaks in the frequency characteristics of the vocal tract are due to its resonances, the filter in this model consists of several resonance circuits connected in series or in parallel.

A typical example of a terminal analog synthesizer is shown in Fig. 16. For synthesis of vowels, fundamental frequency F0 is produced by the pulse generator, and then formed into a triangular-shaped glottal wave by the pulse-forming circuit. The amplitude A0 of the glottal wave is also controlled. For vowels, only gate 1 is open, and the circuit in the top row corresponding to the vocal tract is excited. This circuit consists of six series-connected resonance circuits in which each resonant frequency corresponds to each formant frequency. The first three formants, F1, F2, and F3, are variable, whereas F4 and F5 are constant. KH is for the connection of higher formant frequencies and is fixed. By properly setting the variables for the values obtained from analysis, one can generate vowel sounds to see if the analysis was or was not valid by listening. For generation of voiced consonants, the same circuit is used. For some voiced consonants, noise and pulses are mixed to excite the vocal-tract circuit. Four resonant circuits (N1–N4) and an antiresonant circuit (N0) in the middle row correspond to the nasal cavity and are used for generation of nasal sounds. All the resonant frequencies are fixed in the nasal model. Two other resonant circuits (K1 and K2) and another antiresonance (K0) are used for synthesizing voiceless consonants with three frequencies and the noise amplitude as variables.

7.2 *Acoustic Tube Model*

In another type of speech synthesizer, the vocal tract is regarded as a nonuniform acoustic tube. Generally, two waves exist in the tube; one, the incident wave, advancing in a given direction; and the other, the reflected wave, advancing in the opposite direction. A traveling sound wave has both pressure and velocity; since they are related to each other, the velocity wave is considered for the sake of convenience. If the pressure wave varies sinusoidally, so does the velocity wave. Suppose one end of the tube is closed, and the tube is excited sinusoidally at the other end. Since the wave cannot move at the closed-end wall, the velocity there must always be zero. In Fig. 17, at the left, the velocity of the incident wave (solid line) and the reflected wave

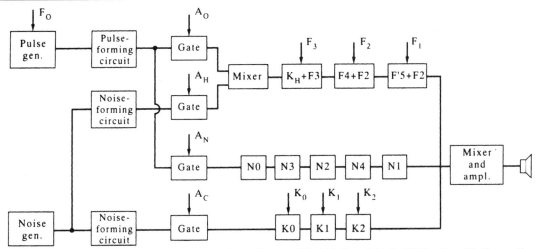

Figure 16. Terminal analog speech synthesizer (Hanley and Peters 1971: 115. Copyright © 1971 by Meredith Corporation. Reproduced by permission of Appleton-Century-Crofts, Educational Division, Meredith Corporation.)

(dotted line) are illustrated in successive times. The total velocity is illustrated at the right. Note that the velocity at the end wall is always zero. If the other end of the tube is also closed, then the velocity there must also be zero. Thus, only those velocity waves that are zero at both ends can be accommodated in the tube. For a tube of length L, the first three such waves are illustrated in Fig. 18. The wavelength of such waves is determined by the length of the tube.

Since wavelength is determined by the length of the tube, waves of other frequencies (i.e., other wavelengths) die out quickly, while waves of this particular length, or frequency, remain for a long time. A tube like this, that selectively accommodates such frequencies, is a 'resonator,' and the frequency of the wave remaining for a long time is called a 'resonant frequency' or a 'resonance.' The lowest resonant frequency is the first resonance, or first formant, and the next higher ones are the second, third, etc. In the above example, the first resonance is $c/2L$, where c is the speed of sound and L is the length of the tube. In this case, all the higher resonances are integer multiples of the first resonance. For instance, assuming that the speed of sound is 34 000 cm/sec, the resonant

Figure 17. Velocity waves at the closed end; (a) incident and reflected velocity waves; (b) velocity wave.

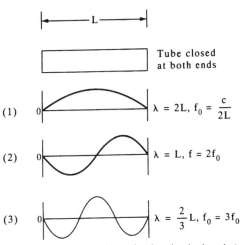

Figure 18. Velocity waves in a tube closed at both ends (c is a sound velocity).

11

frequencies of a tube 17 cm configured like that in Fig. 18 are 1000 Hz, 2000 Hz, 3000 Hz, and so on.

If a uniform tube is open at one end and closed at the other end, the velocity at the open end is known to become maximum. The first three waves in such a tube are illustrated in Fig. 19. The tube has different resonance frequencies which are also determined by the length of the tube L. In this case, the first formant is $c/4L$, and all the higher formants are odd multiples of it. For instance, the resonance frequencies for a tube of 17 cm are 500 Hz, 1500 Hz, 2500 Hz, 3500 Hz, and so on. When one considers the vocal tract as an acoustic tube, the resonant frequencies correspond to the formant frequencies which are resonance frequencies of the vocal tract, but they are not in simple relation any more because of a complex nonuniform shape. It is easy to understand from this model that a shorter vocal tract has higher resonant frequencies, that is, higher formant frequencies, which typically characterize the female and child voices.

The shape of the vocal tract in the speech synthesis model based on the nonuniform acoustic tube is represented by the cross-sectional area along its length. Since the vocal-tract shape is rather complicated to be expressed by a continuous mathematical function, it is usually approximated by a concatenation of cylindrical sections of equal length. The acoustic tube model is more closely related to the physiological process of speech production than a terminal analog synthesizer in the sense that the variables for this model are the cross-sectional area for each cylindrical section. In a terminal analog synthesizer, the individual resonance frequencies of the vocal tract are represented by single resonant circuits which are connected in series or in parallel. Instead of controlling the shape of the vocal tract, from which the resonant frequencies are derived, resonant frequencies (formants) and bandwidths are input directly.

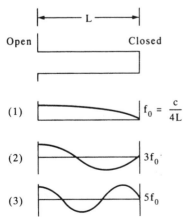

Figure 19. Waves in a tube open at one end and closed at the other end (c is a sound velocity).

Synthesis based on the acoustic tube model, however, has a problem in obtaining the data for real configurations of the vocal tract. A midsagittal X-ray photograph is usually used with palatography or a plaster cast of the mouth as a supplementary tool to obtain the parameters to determine the vocal-tract shape. However, it is not really practical to obtain the necessary articulatory data from X-rays, since the technique is so laborious and since extensive exposure to X-rays is dangerous to subjects. Newer imaging techniques such as ultrasound and nuclear magnetic imaging hold some promise, but are still too new at the time of writing to have impacted on speech synthesis.

7.3 Articulatory Model

In another type of speech synthesis which is most closely related to the physiological process of speech production, efforts are concentrated on the description of movements of speech articulators such as tongue, jaw, lips, etc. For this purpose, various techniques and mathematical models have been tried either to measure or to estimate the movements of those articulators. However, in the actual synthesis of speech, the result of the measurement must be interpreted in terms of the cross-sectional area along the vocal tract. Easy transformation from the movements of articulators to the vocal-tract area function has not yet been successfully worked out.

8. Acoustic Properties of Speech Sounds

8.1 Wave Types

Speech waveforms can be acoustically categorized according to the type of excitation source. Among voiced sounds, when only the laryngeal source is involved to produce a sound, the resultant waveform will usually have a quasiperiodic component in it. Vowel sounds, for example, have quasiperiodic waveforms. Some voiced sounds have irregular periodic waveforms which are produced by an irregular glottal pulsation. This occurs, for example, in creaky voice.

In contrast to the voiced sounds, a quasirandom waveform results when a turbulent noise source is active during the production of a sound. Such sounds as the voiceless fricatives and sibilants, and the whispered sounds, have quasirandom waveforms. A speech burst is another wave type resulting from a noise excitation which has the form of an impulse produced by release of a closure in the vocal tract, such as in the production of stop articulations. Since an impulse results in an oscillatory response, the resulting waveform usually consists of the superposition of a complex oscillatory waveform upon a quasirandom waveform caused by turbulent airflow during the release.

When no excitation source is active, the acoustic speech waveform is defined as quiescent, and all values of instantaneous amplitude are approximately zero. A quiescent speech wave is produced during a voiceless interval, for example, when the occlusion of a voiceless plosive takes place.

Some sounds are characterized by a composite form of more than one type of basic speech wave. The combined speech wave types do not always result in a simple superposition, but often result in a modulated waveform. Such is the case, for example, during the production of a voiced sibilant, in which the airflow against the edge of the teeth is normally periodically reduced or interrupted by the closure of the vocal folds.

8.2 Spectral Characteristics

Acoustic properties which appear in the waveforms are often not fully satisfactory to describe the various speech sounds. More consistent acoustic properties are observed in the frequency spectra of speech sounds. Acoustic parameters, such as formant frequencies, formant bandwidths, formant amplitudes, and fundamental frequency, are used as quantitative specifications of the acoustic speech wave. In the following subsections, spectral characteristics of vowel, fricative, sibilant, stop, sonorant, and nasal manners of articulation are described.

8.2.1 Vowels

The vowel sounds are produced by exciting the vocal tract with a train of air puffs caused by vocal-cord vibration. The vocal tract is configured such that the pharynx and mouth form a transmission path for the laryngeal excitation. The schematic configurations to show the position of the tongue for each of the eight vowel sounds /i, e, ε, a, ɑ, ɔ, o, u/ are shown in Fig. 20. These different configurations result in the different cross-sectional areas along the vocal tract for each vowel, thus causing different resonant frequencies for the different vowels. For an isolated sustained vowel

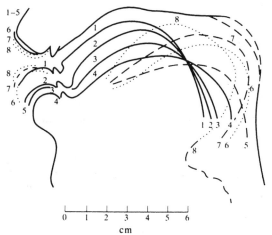

Figure 20. Tongue positions for eight vowel configurations (Ladefoged 1964).

utterance, the resulting waveform at the lips consists mainly of a quasiperiodic type of wave.

Results of extensive spectrographic measurements of the fundamental voice frequency and the formant frequencies of vowel utterances spoken by 76 different speakers are given in Table 1 in terms of averages of fundamental and formant frequencies and formant amplitudes for vowel sounds. The 76 speakers comprised 33 men, 28 women, and 15 children. The vowels were uttered in the context of 'hVd,' such as *heed, hid, head,* and so on. In general, children's formants are highest in frequency, women's are intermediate, and men's are lowest. More specifically, the first formants for children are about half an octave higher than those of men, and the second and third formants are also appreciably higher. These differences are due mainly to differences of vocal-tract length among men, women, and children; women and children have shorter vocal tracts than men (see *Functional and Clinical Anatomy of the Speech Mechanism*). From a uniform tube model, it is easily understood that a tube of shorter length has higher resonant frequencies. It should be noted that vowel sounds cannot be defined by the absolute values of formant frequencies. All three types of speakers are capable of producing the same highly intelligible vowel with different formant frequency structures. This fact led to the hypothesis that the relative values of the formant frequencies determine the phonetic value of vowel sounds. Although various attempts have been tried to prove this hypothesis, there seems to be no satisfactory result yet obtained. A distribution of vowels by 76 speakers on the F1–F2 plane is shown in Fig. 21. It is known that the first and second formants are the most significant for the differentiation of the vowels. The third formant provides a more precise characterization of a vowel's quality, although it does not necessarily separate those vowel areas that overlap each other.

Although less important to the definition of the phonetic quality of the vowels, the formant bandwidth has been measured in various ways. The formant bandwidth provides information for estimating the loss of sound energy involved in speech production. Such information is very useful, for instance, in the synthesis of high-quality speech. However, due to the difficulty of accurately measuring formant bandwidth, the results are not consistent among many studies. Table 2 shows the average bandwidths of three vowel formants measured by different (groups of) researchers and by different measuring techniques. In general, the formant bandwidth tends to become larger as the formant frequency increases.

The acoustic properties of the steady-state portion of vowels described above become complicated in connected speech, in which articulators are in continuous movement. The formant frequencies take different patterns depending on context, such as consonant–vowel (CV), consonant–vowel–consonant (CVC), etc.

Table 1. Averages of fundamental and formant frequencies and formant amplitudes of vowels by 76 speakers.

		i	I	ɛ	æ	ɑ	ɔ	ʊ	u	ʌ	ɜ
Fundamental frequencies (Hz)	M	136	135	130	127	124	129	137	141	130	133
	W	235	232	223	210	212	216	232	231	221	218
	Ch	272	269	260	251	256	263	276	274	261	261
Formant frequencies (Hz)	M	270	390	530	660	730	570	440	300	640	490
F^1	W	310	430	610	860	850	590	470	370	760	500
	Ch	370	530	690	1010	1030	680	560	430	850	560
	M	2290	1990	1840	1720	1090	840	1020	870	1190	1350
F^2	W	2790	2480	2330	2050	1220	920	1160	950	1400	1640
	Ch	3200	2730	2610	2320	1370	1060	1410	1170	1590	1820
	M	3010	2550	2480	2410	2440	2410	2240	2240	2390	1690
F^3	W	3310	3070	2990	2850	2810	2710	2680	2670	2780	1960
	Ch	3730	3600	3570	3320	3170	3180	3310	3260	3360	2160
	L^1	−4	−3	−2	−1	−1	0	−1	−3	−1	−5
Formant amplitudes (dB)	L^2	−24	−23	−17	−12	−5	−7	−12	−19	−10	−15
	L^3	−28	−27	−24	−22	−28	−34	−34	−43	−27	−20

(Peterson and Barney 1952: 183)

It happens quite often in CVC contexts that formant frequencies moving toward the steady-state values of the vowel from the initial consonant begin to move toward the final consonant before they reach the steady-state values of the vowel.

8.2.2 Consonants

It is more difficult to describe the acoustic properties of consonants, owing to their short durations, less steady state, lack of vowel like formant structure, context-dependency, and interspeaker variation, among other factors.

Although there have been a number of studies on acoustic properties of consonants, no sufficiently consistent acoustic properties have been obtained yet for many of the consonants. This subsection reviews some of the acoustical analyses of consonants.

8.2.2.1 Fricatives and Sibilants

For the production of voiceless fricatives and sibilants, a frictional airflow is caused by constriction in the vocal tract, and the resulting waveform becomes quasirandom. In the production of voiced fricatives and sibilants, the laryngeal voice source is active as well as the friction source, thus resulting in waveforms consisting of both quasirandom and quasiperiodic wave types. It is observed in general that the /s/ and /ʃ/ have the highest relative intensity and that the /f/ and /θ/ have the lowest, while /h/ is medium.

Frequency spectra of these sounds have energy components in a wide range of frequencies, normally up to as high as 10 kHz. However, due to large interspeaker variation, it is difficult to extract characteristics of each sound from the spectrum envelope to describe each phonetic value precisely. The energy contained in certain frequency bands has been found to be useful in discriminating these sounds. It is not clear, however, whether the fact is relevant to determination of the phonetic value of these sounds. Examples of frequency spectra for some of these sounds are shown in Fig. 22.

From theoretical considerations, it is anticipated that the vocal-tract configurations for these sounds produce formant frequencies and that the existence of a friction source at the constriction tends to produce antiresonances. Although some synthetic speech studies of voiceless fricatives based on this theoretical consideration have given good identification and spectral matching, more extensive study of fricatives and sibilants is needed.

In perceptual studies, it was found that /s/ and /ʃ/ are identified more correctly by their steady-state

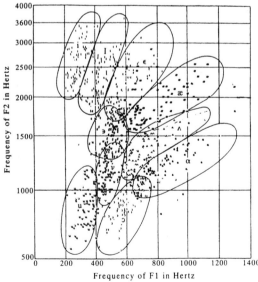

Figure 21. Frequency of second formant versus frequency of first formant for 10 vowels by 76 speakers (Peterson and Barney 1952: 176).

Table 2. Average half-power bandwidths of three vowel formants (Hz).

	Year	Number of Voices	Vowels	First formant	Second formant	Third formant
Steinberg	1934	1	7	83	118	...
Lewis	1936	1	5	39	51	80
Lewis and Tuthill	1940	6	2	45	50	93
Tarnóczy	1943	?	4–9	110	190	260
Bogert	1953	33	10	130	150	185
van den Berg	1955	1	11	54	66	89
House and Stevens	1958	3	8	54	65	70
New spectrogram measurements	1961	20	10	50	64	115
30 pps measurements	1961	2	12	47	75	106

(Dunn 1961: 1737)

portions, while the transitional portion is rather more important for the identification of /f/ and /θ/.

8.2.2.2 Stops

English stops are characterized by three phases: a period of overall low energy ('silence'), a burst which is an abrupt but brief increase in energy created by the release of air under pressure, and a period of formant transitions. Voiced stops are differentiated from voiceless by the presence during the initial silent phase of low-frequency, periodic energy below 300 Hz and by a somewhat lower-intensity stop burst due to the fact that there is typically less pressure built up behind the point of constriction (since airflow is impeded by the vibrating vocal cords). Voiceless stops are also often followed by a period of aspiration, from 10 to 100 msec in duration. Aspiration is characterized by low-amplitude aperiodic energy and concentrated in the regions of the second and higher formants of the following vowel. The formant transitions, that is, a period of from 30 to 80 msec where the formants move between values characteristic of the stop at the moment of release to values characteristic of the vowel, are created by the movement of the articulators between closed and open configurations.

Some spectral properties of stop bursts help to differentiate place of articulation. The bilabial stops, /p/ and /b/, have a primary concentration of energy between 500 Hz and 1500 Hz. The alveolar stops, /t/ and /d/, have a flat spectrum in which frequency components above 4000 Hz sometimes predominate, plus an energy concentration in the region of 1500–1800 Hz. The palatal or velar stops, /k/ and /g/, have strong energy concentrations between 4000 Hz and 1500 Hz, the lower energy peak being correlated with the frequency of formants two, three, or four of the adjacent vowel. It is also known that the voiced stops have a strong low-frequency component due to the active laryngeal source and have less strong high-frequency components than the voiceless stops.

When a stop is preceded or followed by a vowel, the transitional portion of the CV or VC utterance characterizes the formant structure of the sound. The transition of the second formant is known to be especially characteristic. For example, the first and second formant transitions of /b/, /d/, and /g/ when followed by the vowel /a/ are shown in Fig. 23. The second formant of /ba/ starts from a very low frequency and increases sharply toward the second formant of /a/. The second formant of /da/ starts from a

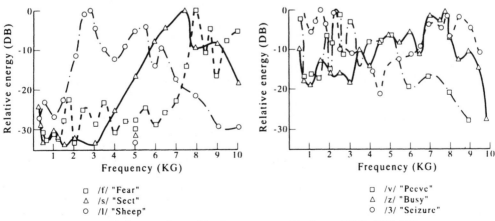

Figure 22. Spectra of some fricative consonants (Hughes and Halle 1956: 306).

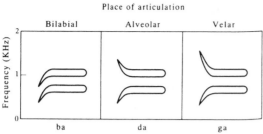

Figure 23. The transition of the first and the second formant frequencies of voiced stops followed by the vowel /a/.

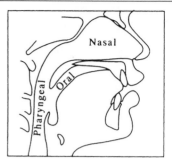

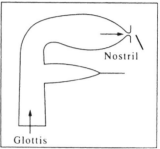

Figure 24. The upper figure is a tracing from a radiograph showing a midsagittal section of the vocal and nasal tracts during production of the nasal consonant /n/. The structure of the articulatory system is schematized in the lower figure as a joined three-tube model (Fujimura 1962: 1865).

frequency slightly higher than the second formant of /a/, whereas the second formant of /ga/ starts from a much higher frequency than the second formant of /a/. However, when these transitions are in the VCV context, they are affected by coarticulation with the first vowel.

8.2.2.3 Sonorants

The sonorant consonants of English—/w/, /j/, /r/, and /l/—are often called 'semivowels' since they have formant structures similar to those of vowels. Waveforms of these consonants are quasiperiodic. Acoustic properties of the sonorants are known only qualitatively, since the formant structures of these sounds are often influenced by the preceding or the succeeding sound, or according to position within an utterance.

Generally speaking, /w/ is similar to the vowel /u/, but has a lower first formant. For /j/, which is similar to /i/, the first formant is lower than that of /i/. For /r/ and /l/, the first and second formant frequencies are located fairly close to each other, and the third formant is relatively low in frequency.

Perceptually, the transition between a sonorant and the adjacent sound is also important. In this case, the duration of the transition is more influential than the rate of transition.

8.2.2.4 Nasals

Nasal consonants are normally characterized by opening the velum (thus making a passage to the nasal tract) and making an oral closure. The sound is radiated chiefly from the nostrils. The waveform is quasiperiodic, but its intensity is normally lower than that of vowels, due mainly to greater attenuation in the nasal tract and the small openings at the nostrils.

Theoretically, it is difficult to analyze the production of the nasal sounds, but some gross features of them can be estimated by schematizing the vocal-tract and nasal-tract configurations, as in Fig. 24. In this case, the closed oral cavity acts as a side branch of the pharyngeal–nasal passage. A side branch causes antiresonances which appear as dips in the output spectrum envelope. If a uniform side branch of length L_m is assumed, then the frequency of the first antiresonance is known to be $c/4L_m$, where c is, as above,

the speed of sound. All the other antiresonance frequencies are odd multiples of the first one. If a side branch is 7 cm long and a sound velocity is 34 000 cm/sec (which roughly corresponds to the production of /m/), then the first antiresonance frequency falls at approximately 1200 Hz. From this simple model, it is anticipated that the antiresonance frequency of /ŋ/ is higher than that of /n/ and that of /m/, since the lengths of the side branches for /m/, /n/, and /ŋ/ become shorter in this order.

Fig. 25 shows an example of a measured spectrum for the nasal consonant /m/ in real speech. In this example, the first antiresonance appears to be reflected by the relatively broad dip in the spectrum at approximately 1200 Hz. Antiresonances for /m/ are observed between 750 Hz and 1250 Hz, those for /n/ are observed between 1450 Hz and 2200 Hz, and those for /ŋ/ above 3000 Hz. Based on observation of the nasal spectra, together with other synthetic speech experiments, it is generally considered that the nasals /m/, /n/, and /ŋ/ are characterized by low, medium, and high antiresonances, respectively. The formants in the immediate vicinity of antiresonance are influenced appreciably, whereas other formants are relatively intact. On average, bandwidths of formants observed in nasal murmurs are comparable to, or greater than, those observed in vowels. Perceptual studies, however, have shown that highly intelligible nasals can be syn-

16

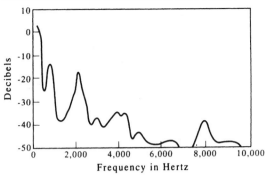

Figure 25. Measured spectrum for the nasal consonant /m/ in real speech (Flanagan 1972).

Bibliography

Dunn 1961 *J. Acoust. Soc. Amer.* **33:** 1737
Fant 1960 *Acoustic Theory of Speech Production.* Mouton, The Hague
Fant 1973 *Speech Sounds and Features.* MIT Press, Cambridge, MA
Flanagan J L 1972 *Speech Analysis, Synthesis, and Perception,* 2nd edn. Springer-Verlag, New York
Fujimura 1962 Analysis of nasal consonants. *Journal of the Acoustical Society of America.* **34:** 1865
Hanley, Peters 1971 In: Travis L E (ed.) *Handbook of Speech Pathology and Audiology.* Meredith Corporation, Des Moines, TA
Hughes, Halle 1956 *Journal of the Acoustical Society of America* **28:** 306
Ladefoged P 1964 *A Phonetic Study of West African Languages.* Cambridge University Press, Cambridge
Markel 1972 Digital inverse filtering, a new tool for format trajectory estimation. *IEEE Trans. And Electroacoust.* AU-**20:** 129–37
O'Shaughnessy D 1990 *Speech Communication, Human and Machine.* Addison-Wesley, Reading, MA
Peterson, Barney 1952 Control methods used in a study of vowels. *Journal of the Acoustical Society of America.* **24:** 176–183

thesized without antiresonance, and, thus, that the antiresonance may not be essential for the perception of nasals. In the study of the perception of some nasal–vowel and vowel–nasal sounds, it has been found that perception was more influenced by the transitions than by the steady state.

Auditory Models of Speech Processing

S. Greenberg

At first glance, auditory processing of speech appears to be a rather straightforward and simple process. The auditory periphery possesses the capability of spectrally analyzing incoming sound, and it is natural to assume that the ear's primary responsibility, as far as speech is concerned, is to construct and transmit a running spectrum of the signal on to higher, cortical centers for conversion into linguistic units. In this rather commonly held view (e.g., Klatt 1989; Pisoni 1982), the auditory periphery functions merely as a biological frequency analyzer, with little capability for intelligent processing or learning. In the 1990s knowledge concerning complex auditory processing is largely confined to such peripheral structures as the auditory nerve and cochlear nucleus, yet it is apparent that even at these caudal stations of the auditory pathway there exist powerful and elegantly designed systems to encode incoming speech and other biological sounds in a manner that provides a robust, reliable representation of the spectrotemporal properties most germane to the information-bearing elements of the signal under an exceedingly wide range of acoustic conditions. The importance of such adaptive processing is apparent to anyone who has ever experi-

enced a serious hearing loss. Although such listeners generally understand speech well in quiet, non-reverberant environments, their ability to comprehend verbal communication is seriously compromised in noisy conditions. It may be concluded from this that the auditory periphery, locus of most hearing pathology, functions as far more than a mere spectrum analyzer. It also serves as an automatic gain control, adjusting the neural activity to the background level, and contains powerful, effective noise-reduction circuitry which allows the meaningful elements of speech to be successfully decoded, even in the presence of spectrally overlapping, competing sounds. Although the means by which the ear accomplishes these feats are not known in detail, there is a growing body of evidence suggesting that much of this adaptive processing occurs in the inner ear and cochlear nuclei.

1. Relevance of Auditory Physiology to Speech Processing

The inferences that can be made about speech coding in the auditory pathway is limited by virtue of the fact that the overwhelming majority of physiological and anatomical studies have been performed, by necessity, on nonhumans, typically on cats and rodents. Because speech is a peculiarly human trait, that almost surely relies on neural circuitry unique to the species, caution must be exercised in extending the insights garnered from animal studies to the processing of speech in humans. Despite this limitation, several observations suggest that most of what is known about the mammalian auditory periphery in general applies to humans as well. The anatomy and physiology of this region (with the exception of the dorsal cochlear nucleus) is remarkably similar across the majority of mammalian species, including primates, and much of the functional capability dependent on these peripheral structures is comparable across species. Differences among mammalian hearing organs generally involve parameters of relatively minor relevance to speech coding, such as sensitivity to ultrasonic signals and very low frequencies (the ability to make fine discriminations in frequency is an exception).

Two additional caveats need to be made concerning the use of physiological data to infer the neural basis of human speech coding. Virtually all physiological studies are performed with the use of barbiturate anesthesia, which is known to alter certain neural circuits, particularly those of an inhibitory nature. Anesthesia probably has little or no effect on the response properties of cells in either the auditory nerve or ventral cochlear nucleus (Rhode and Kettner 1987). However, the response properties of dorsal cochlear nucleus cells are known to change in the presence of barbiturates (Rhode and Kettner 1987, Evans and Nelson 1973a, 1973b, Young and Brownell 1976). In addition, one of the major circuits mediating the automatic gain control of the cochlea, the crossed olivo-cochlear bundle, is also affected by anesthesia.

A second concern involves linking physiology, particularly that of the auditory periphery, to the complex pattern of behavior underlying the reception of speech. Many auditory nuclei and millions of nerve cells intervene between the auditory periphery and the ultimate destination of speech information in the cortical association areas of the parietal, temporal, and frontal lobes. For this reason it should be kept in mind that the representation of the speech signal developed in the periphery is a crude one, far removed from such abstract linguistic entities as 'phoneme' and 'distinctive feature.' And because of the complex interactions among the auditory nuclei, it would be rash to link a specific behavioral capability to a single anatomical locus or population of cells. Nevertheless, certain inferences can be made about the nature of the acoustic representation of speech, based on the physiological response properties in the auditory periphery, that are likely to pertain in the human and which have significant consequences for general properties of the sound patterns of language.

2. The Ear's Mission

The role of the auditory periphery has traditionally been viewed as a frequency analyzer, albeit of limited precision, providing a faithful representation of the spectrotemporal properties of the acoustic waveform for higher level processing in the central auditory pathway. According to Fourier theory, any waveform can be decomposed into a series of sinusoidal constituents, which mathematically describe the acoustic waveform. By this analytical technique it is possible to describe all speech sounds in terms of an energy distribution across frequency and time. For example, the Fourier spectrum of a typical vowel is composed of a series of sinusoidal components whose frequencies are integral multiples of a common (fundamental frequency), and whose amplitudes vary in accordance with the resonance (formant) pattern of the associated vocal tract configuration. The vocal tract transfer function modifies the glottal spectrum by selectively amplifying energy in certain regions of the spectrum. These regions of energy maxima are commonly referred to as 'formants.'

The spectra of nonvocalic sounds, such as stop consonants, affricates, and fricatives differ from vowels in a number of ways potentially significant for the manner in which they are encoded in the auditory periphery. These sounds typically exhibit formant patterns in which the energy peaks are considerably reduced relative to those of vowels. In certain segments, such as the stop release and frication, the energy distribution is rather diffuse, with only a crude delineation of the underlying formant pattern. In addition, many of these segments are 'voiceless,' their waveforms lacking a clear periodic quality which would reflect the vibration of the vocal folds. The amplitude of such consonantal segments is typically 30–50 dB SPL, up to 40 dB less intense than adjacent vocalic segments. In addition, the rate of spectral change is generally greater for consonants, and they are usually of brief duration compared to vocalic segments. These differences have significant consequences for the manner in which consonants and vowels are encoded in the auditory periphery.

The traditional view of the ear as a frequency analyzer is probably inadequate for describing the auditory periphery's ability to process speech. Under many conditions, the frequency selective properties of the auditory periphery appear to bear only a tangential relationship to its ability to convey important information concerning the speech signal, relying rather on the operation of integrative mechanisms to isolate the information-laden elements of the speech stream and provide a continuous 'event stream' from which to extract the underlying message.

Cocktail party devotees can attest to the fact that far more is involved in decoding the speech signal than merely computing a running spectrum. In such noisy conditions, a faithful representation of the spectrum may even hinder the ability to understand as a consequence of acoustic interference. It is likely that the auditory system uses specific strategies to focus on those elements of speech most likely to extract the meaningful components of the acoustic signal. Computing a running spectrum of the speech signal is a singularly inefficient means to accomplish this end, since much of the acoustics is extraneous to the message. Instead, the ear has developed the means to extract the information-laden components of the speech signal (and other biological communication sounds) that may only resemble slightly the Fourier spectral representation. Such strategies are discussed in Sects. 5 and 6.

3. Anatomy and Physiology of the Auditory Periphery

3.1 Origins of Cochlear Frequency Selectivity

Much of the ear's frequency selective capabilities stems from physiological mechanisms of the inner ear (Fig. 1), which contains three chambers, all of which are fluid filled. The middle chamber, known as the scala media, contains the anatomical structures of principal concern for acoustic transduction. At the bottom of this partition is the basilar membrane (BM), which underlies the organ of Corti containing the sensory hair cells, supporting cells, and tectorial membrane. The BM is tapered along its length, being relatively narrow and stiff at its base, and becoming progressively wider and more massive towards the apex. As a consequence of this taper, the stiffness of the BM varies by a factor of a hundred over its 35 mm length, with the basal (stiffest) portion responding most sensitively to very high frequencies and the apex being most sensitive to low frequencies (Fig. 2a). The motion of the BM conforms to that of a 'traveling wave.' For high frequencies (> 5 kHz) this wave motion will quickly reach a maximum near the base of the membrane and damp out quickly before traveling much further down the BM (Fig. 2b). In response to very low frequencies (< 1 kHz), the pattern of motion is rather different. The displacement of the BM is not confined to a restricted segment, but rather vibrates along much of its length, particularly at higher sound pressure levels typical of speech. At the place of resonance (i.e., peak response) the displacement amplitude will be maximum, but the motion does not diminish very rapidly as the wave proceeds towards the helicotrema at the apical end. Moreover, BM displacement in response to low-frequency signals can be of considerable magnitude across much of the cochlear partition at SPLs typical of speech. As a consequence of this asymmetrical characteristic of the traveling wave, the BM is sharply tuned (i.e., highly selective) to frequencies greater than 4 kHz, and is rather broadly tuned to most frequencies in the speech range. The tuning characteristics of neural elements all the way up the auditory pathway appears to stem from the mechanical tuning of the BM. This differential

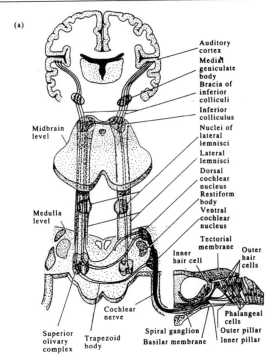

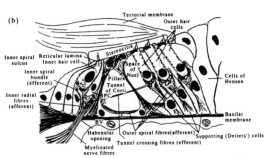

Figure 1. (a) Schematic illustration of the auditory pathway, from inner ear to auditory cortex. (Adapted from Flanagan 1972.) (b) The cochlear partition of the inner ear is shown in expanded detail. (Adapted by Pickles 1988 from an illustration in Ryan and Dallos 1984.)

tuning is of considerable significance for models of speech coding in the auditory periphery.

The motion of the basilar membrane acts to filter the input waveform, distributing its local pattern of vibration in accordance with the traveling wave. Thus, the pattern of BM motion at the base may differ considerably from that at the apex. As an example, consider the response of the BM to three different signals (Fig. 2b). An 8 kHz sinusoid results in a spatially discrete pattern of vibration, confined to the basal portion of the membrane. The BM moves up and down at a rate of 8 kHz along a relatively small portion of its extent, and otherwise is effectively immobile. Increas-

(a)

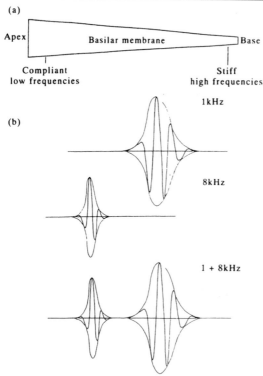

Apex
Basilar membrane
Base

Compliant
low frequencies

Stiff
high frequencies

(b)

1 kHz

8 kHz

1 + 8 kHz

Figure 2. (a) The width of the basilar membrane varies by a factor of four from base to apex, resulting in a stiffness gradient along its length that varies over a hundred fold. (b) As a consequence, the membrane is most sensitive at its base to high frequencies, and responds best to low frequencies at its apex. The locations of the traveling wave for two signals, 1 kHz and 8 kHz, are shown, as well as the pattern of motion for a signal comprised of both frequencies. The sound pressure level is moderate (ca. 50 dB) in order to delineate most clearly the different locations of maximal stimulation. (Traveling wave patterns adapted from Pfeiffer and Kim 1975.)

ing the amplitude of this signal to speech intensities (50–80 dB SPL) widens the area of response along the BM only slightly, consistent with the sharply tuned characteristic of the basal portion of the membrane. A 1 kHz signal will cause the BM to vibrate at that frequency. At very low intensities the vibration will be largely confined to the apical portion. At higher sound pressure levels, much of the membrane, including the base, will move in synchrony to the 1 kHz tone. The pattern of BM motion resulting from concurrent presentation of these signals will depend on both their relative and absolute amplitudes. If the intensity of the 1 kHz signal is relatively low the membrane will vibrate in two spatially discrete modes, each synchronized to one of the frequencies. Under these conditions, the mechanical response of the basilar membrane resolves, along its spatial extent, the particular vibratory motion associated with each spectral

component. At higher sound pressure levels BM motion becomes dominated by the response to the 1 kHz signal. Such nonlinear interactions are discussed in further detail in Sects. 5 and 6.

Traditional models of auditory frequency analysis assume that this sort of 'place' representation is the primary means by which spectral information is encoded in the cochlea and auditory nerve. The mechanical motion of the BM is transformed into nerve cell impulses ('spikes') by virtue of the membrane's coupling to the auditory nerve. The membrane's motion is converted into a modulation of the inner hair cell (IHC) receptor potential as a consequence of the shearing action between the reticular membrane and the tectorial membrane overlying the IHC cilia. This modulation of the receptor potential, in turn, modulates the release of chemical neurotransmitter, which is effective in depolarizing auditory nerve fibers (ANFs) innervating the cell. When the energy associated with a spectral component is high, the displacement of the BM, at its maximum, will be relatively large. In turn, the deflection of the ciliary bundle atop the IHC will also be large, resulting in large bursts of neurotransmitter release when the hair cell is depolarized. Up to a certain limit, the displacement of the BM, the deflection of IHC cilia, the magnitude of the receptor potential, the amount of neurotransmitter released and the rate of auditory nerve fiber discharge are all proportional to the amount of energy driving that portion of the cochlea. Under these conditions, it is possible, in principle, to encode the spectrum of speech and other complex sounds in terms of the amount of activity (measured in terms of ANF discharge) at each location, distributed along the cochlear partition. The conditions under which such isomorphic coding pertains are those in which the physiological elements of the system behave linearly, typically between threshold and 40 dB SPL. Thus, at low sound pressure levels it should be possible, in principle, to infer a sound's spectrum from the spatial pattern of neural activity in the auditory nerve, provided that the filtering action of the basilar membrane is sufficiently sharp to resolve individual frequency components contained in the input signal. This is the basis of the rate-place coding of the spectrum (see Sect. 5).

3.2 Significance of Cochlear Nonlinearities

At sound pressure levels characteristic of many speech sounds, the response of the cochlear partition to sound is highly nonlinear. The reasons for the nonlinear response are complex and not fully understood. A most important source of nonlinear response is the displacement behavior of the basilar membrane. Above approximately 50 dB SPL, the maximum amplitude of the BMs displacement is compressive, being less than proportional to input energy (Robles et al. 1986). In this range a doubling of sound pressure level (i.e., 6 dB) will result in perhaps only a 40 percent (3 dB) gain in BM displacement magnitude. This nonlinearity is frequency dependent. Thus, the amount of compression is greatest at that BM location being driven the hardest, and is least in regions driven by relatively low amounts of energy distant from the compressive segments. This frequency-dependent compression behavior has significant implications for speech processing, because it appreciably alters (broadens) the filtering performed by the cochlea, as described in Sect. 6.1.

A second source of nonlinearity is in the IHC transduction. Above 50 dB SPL, the behavior of the receptor potential also becomes compressive. Although some of this nonlinearity is a consequence of BM compression, there appears to be an additional mechanism operating to limit the magnitude of the receptor potential.

A third form of nonlinearity limits the rate at which auditory nerve fibers can discharge. Most fibers increase their firing rate with increases in intensity over a 20–30 dB change in intensity. Over this range the discharge rate of a fiber can increase from its background (spontaneous) level up to 200–250 spikes/s. With further increases in sound pressure level the fiber's discharge rate fails to increase, having reached its saturation point. The mechanisms underlying rate saturation are poorly understood and highly controversial. Some models favor a limitation on the IHCs ability to produce and/or release neurotransmitter as the primary cause ('presynaptic' mechanisms), while others are inclined to weight postsynaptic mechanisms, such as neurotransmitter uptake, more heavily. It is also possible that such rate saturation stems from the operation of pre- and postsynaptic mechanisms acting in concert. However, certain lines of evidence suggest that the postsynaptic mechanisms may be more important.

3.3 Spontaneous Activity

Most auditory nerve fibers discharge in the absence of external acoustic stimulation. This spontaneous activity is thought to reflect the random release of transmitter from the IHC and its uptake by associated ANFS. Sixty percent of the fibers have spontaneous rates (SR) between 18 and 120 spikes/s ('high SR' group). A smaller proportion (25 percent) have spontaneous rates between 0.5–18 spikes/s ('medium SR'). The remainder exhibit little or no spontaneous activity ('low SR'; Liberman 1978). The underlying basis of these different SR classes remains obscure. However, there are a number of morphological and physiological differences, segregating the three classes, of potential significance for speech coding. Because the low- and medium-SR fibers have many features in common, they will generally be discussed below as a single group, and referred to, in aggregate, as low-SR units.

Approximately 10 ANFS innervate each IHC in the human. Among each subpopulation the proportion of low, medium, and high-SR fibers will be roughly the same as for the auditory nerve as a whole (Liberman 1980; Liberman and Oliver 1984). Thus, whatever mechanism regulates spontaneous activity, it is unlikely to be exclusively presynaptic in nature. It is of interest that low- and medium-SR fibers innervate the modiolar side of the IHC, while most of their high-SR counterparts contact the IHC on the opposite, pillar side (ibid.). This spatial segregation of fibers is consistent with the possibility that much of the transmitter release comes from the modiolar side. The high-SR population is also distinguished from other fibers in that their postsynaptic terminals appear to be adapted for more rapid uptake of neurotransmitter.

In addition to these morphological differences, several functional properties distinguish the low- and high-SR groups. These pertain to response threshold, rapid adaptation, phase-locking, and suppression. High-SR fibers are typically 5–10 dB more sensitive than their low-SR counterparts (Liberman 1978, Geisler et al. 1985). Some low-SR fibers are as much as 20–30 dB less sensitive. Another difference concerns rapid adaptation. Adaptation refers to the decline in the instantaneous discharge rate over time. Among high-SR fibers, the instantaneous discharge rate is greatest at stimulus onset and declines very quickly over the following 10–15 msec. The initial decline is termed 'rapid' adaptation and is most pronounced in response to high-amplitude signals. The very lowest-SR fibers do not exhibit rapid adaptation, even at high signal intensities. Rapid adaptation for medium-SR units occurs at an intermediate level (Rhode and Smith 1985). A third distinction between low- and high-SR fibers concerns their ability to temporally encode low-frequency modulations. The low-SR group are generally superior in synchronizing their discharge activity to the modulating waveform (Miller and Sachs 1984, Greenberg 1986). The significance of this difference is discussed below. The dynamic range of response (the intensity range over which a fiber increases its firing rate) for low-SR fibers is often two to three times greater than for high-SR units (Sokolowski et al. 1989). Much of this extended dynamic range occurs at levels above 50 dB SPL, where the slope of the input-output function is relatively low. Low-SR units also exhibit more 'suppression' of their discharge rate than high-SR fibers (see Sect. 3.5).

3.4 Phase-locking

The modulation of neurotransmitter release by the IHC receptor potential has an important consequence for the coding of speech in the auditory periphery. At low frequencies, below 4–5 kHz, the receptor potential oscillation is large enough to modulate transmitter release in a manner that affects the temporal pattern of ANF discharge (Sellick and Russell 1978). In response to sinusoidal stimulation, transmitter release occurs only during a restricted portion (the 'rarefac-

21

tion phase') of the stimulus cycle. Because the probability of a fiber's discharge is highly correlated with transmitter release, the unit's firing pattern is itself modulated in a fashion analogous to (but differing in important ways from) the IHC receptor potential. The receptor potential modulation is of sufficient magnitude to produce a cadence of discharge activity in ANFS temporally synchronized to the driving waveform.

This 'phase-locked' ANF response provides a second means by which frequency is encoded in the auditory periphery. In the absence of phase-locking the probability of firing, relative to the cochlear-filtered waveform, is approximately uniform throughout. Under this condition, the firing probability is uncor-

related with the fine temporal structure of the driving signal, thus providing no temporal information with which to infer the spectrotemporal characteristics of the stimulating waveform. This uniform firing distribution (which is approximately described by a Poisson process), is characteristic of the ANF response to sinusoidal stimuli above 4–5 kHz. Contrast this pattern with that pertaining to lower frequency stimuli. For such signals, the probability of discharge is relatively high during a restricted time interval (or phase) of the stimulus cycle, and relatively low otherwise (Fig. 3). Under such conditions potentially important information concerning the spectrotemporal characteristics of the driving waveform are contained in the cadence of auditory nerve discharge. There is dis-

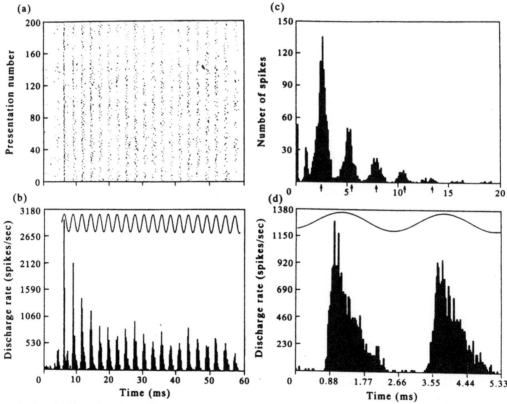

Figure 3. Phase locking of a primary-like unit recorded from the anteroventral cochlear nucleus of the cat, in response to a 375 Hz sinusoid presented at 70 dB SPL. Stimulus duration was 50 msec. Temporal response pattern is similar to that of an auditory-nerve fiber. (a) Dot raster display (in which each dot represents the occurrence of a discharge) shows the stochastic nature of the phase-locked response. Binwidth = 250 μsec. (b) Post-stimulus-time (PST) histogram shows the probability of response as a function of time from stimulus onset. In this instance the probability is indicated in units of instantaneous discharge rate. The average rate was approximately 160 spikes/sec. Sinusoidal function whose period is equivalent to that of the input signal is shown for reference. Note the rapid adaptation of the response over the initial 5–10 msec. Binwidth = 250 μsec. (c) Interval histogram spanning a time window of 20 msec. Arrows mark the stimulus period and integral multiples thereof. Binwidth = 100 μsec. (d) Period histogram binned over a time window of 5.33 msec (equivalent to two periods of the input signal). Binwidth = 26.7 μsec. The unit's discharge rate threshold was 25 dB SPL. Its spontaneous rate was 36 spikes/sec. Histograms are based on 200 stimulus repetitions. (From Greenberg 1988.)

cussion in Sects. 6 and 7 of how such phase-locked patterns could be utilized by higher auditory centers to decode important features of the acoustic signal.

3.5 Lateral Suppression

Under certain stimulus conditions, the discharge activity of single fibers actually diminishes in the presence of intense signals. In response to wideband noise, the firing rate of certain fibers, usually of low spontaneous rate, will first grow with increasing stimulus level, and then decrease with further increments of the noise level (Schalk and Sachs 1980). A second instance of suppression is in response to the concurrent presentation of two sinusoidal signals. The response (measured in terms of average firing rate) to a sinusoid presented at the fiber's most sensitive ('characteristic') frequency ('CF tone') will diminish upon presentation of a second tone (the 'suppressor'; Sachs and Kiang 1968). The effective frequency and intensity range of the suppressor tone is the suppression region. This area generally lies outside the range of frequencies and intensities effective in driving the fiber to single-tone stimuli (the 'excitation' region). Under most conditions, the suppressor needs to be at least 20 dB more intense than the CF signal to drive down the fiber's discharge rate. It is potentially significant that the spectral magnitude disparities required for suppression are commonplace in many speech sounds. Sachs and Young (1980) have demonstrated such suppression can occur in the auditory nerve in response to vowels.

The origins and functional consequences of this suppression remain obscure and controversial. Much of the suppression appears to be mechanical in origin, reflecting the nonlinear motion of the basilar membrane to complex signals. The low-SR fibers exhibit more rate suppression than high-SR units. One possibility is that the behavior of low-SR fibers more closely reflects the mechanical motion of the basilar membrane at high sound pressure levels (where the suppression would be most apparent) than their more sensitive high-SR counterparts (Sokolowski et al. 1989).

4. Physiology and Anatomy of the Cochlear Nucleus

Information in the auditory nerve is integrated and processed in the cochlear nucleus (CN), which consists of three principal divisions (anteroventral, posteroventral, and dorsal), each of which receives a strong, direct projection from the auditory nerve. Each division has its own distinctive 'personality,' both in terms of cytoarchitecture and the physiological response properties of cells that lie within its boundaries (Fig. 4). Moreover, each division has a unique set of projections to the upper auditory brainstem nuclei, and appear to behave as separate functional systems. Because of this anatomical and physiological diversity, as well as for reasons discussed

below, the cochlear nucleus is likely to represent the first locus in the auditory pathway where integrative operations concerned with extraction of biologically important acoustic features are performed.

4.1 Anteroventral Cochlear Nucleus

The anteroventral division (AVCN) is populated principally by 'primary-like' (PL) neurons, whose response properties closely resemble those of AN fibers. These cells project, via the trapezoid body, to the superior olivary complex (SOC), and are thought to play an important role in binaural analysis for the localization of sound (Erulkar 1972). A smaller population are stellate cells, which are physiologically identified as 'chopper' units (Rhode et al. 1983), and are discussed in relation to speech coding in Sect. 5.1.

4.2 Posteroventral Cochlear Nucleus

The posteroventral division (PVCN) contains relatively few PL units, but has a large concentration of chopper and 'onset' units. These neurons project through the intermediate acoustic stria (IAS) to the lateral lemniscus and inferior colliculus, nuclei of the upper auditory brainstem pathway. Although the function of this IAS projection is not as clearly defined as that of the AVCN-trapezoid body pathway, it appears to be involved in the coding of intensity and spectral information for complex sounds (Rhode and Smith 1986).

Choppers derive their name from their regularity of discharge. In response to high-frequency sinusoidal stimulation, these units discharge at a regular interval, independent of the stimulus frequency. This modal discharge interval typically ranges between 1.5–10 msec, with most choppers capable of discharging at rates up to 250–600 spikes/s. Choppers phase-lock to low-frequency sinusoidal and amplitude-modulated (AM) signals, but their ability to follow waveform modulations is generally limited to frequencies below 1 kHz (Rhode and Greenberg 1991). Choppers appear to receive extensive inhibitory input, which serves to enhance both the extent and magnitude of lateral suppression exhibited by these units relative to that observed in the auditory nerve. The manner in which this enhanced suppression could serve as an effective means to encode gross spectral contours in terms of rate-place activity is discussed in Sect. 5.1.

The other major physiological response class of the PVCN comprise the onset units, so named because of their tendency to discharge at the onset of stimulation with a high degree of probability and temporal precision, and thereafter diminish their responsiveness. Although the instantaneous discharge rate declines appreciably after the initial onset spike, the sustained firing level of most onset units is still relatively high. Their preferential response at stimulus onset pertains principally to signals whose frequencies are higher than 1.5–2 kHz. In response to low-

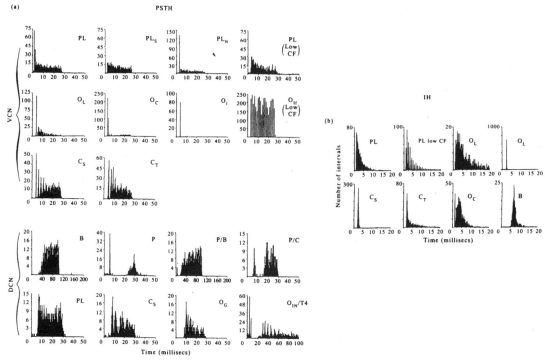

Figure 4. Representative sample of response patterns (PSTH) and interval histograms (IH) recorded from the cochlear nucleus in response to sinusoidal stimuli. PL = primary-like, PL$_s$ = low-SR PL, PL$_N$ = primary-like with notch, C$_S$ = sustained chopper, C$_T$ = transient chopper, O$_L$ = onset-locker, O$_I$ = onset-inhibitory, O$_C$ = onset-chopper, B = buildup, P = pauser, O$_G$ = onset-graded, P/B = pauser-buildup, P/C = pauser-chopper. Refer to Fig. 3 for explanation of PST and interval histograms.

frequency, sinusoidal, or amplitude-modulated signals many of these units phase-lock to the modulation frequency with a remarkably high degree of temporal precision (Rhode and Smith 1986, Greenberg and Rhode 1987, Rhode and Greenberg 1991).

Two major subclasses of onset unit may be distinguished in the PVCN, comprising 95 percent of the onset population. The onset-lockers (O$_L$) are, in all likelihood, giant 'octopus' cells concentrated in the octopus cell area (OCA) of the PVCN (Rhode et al. 1983). The other major subclass is the onset-choppers (O$_C$), which are probably large multipolar stellate cells (ibid.), principally found in the multipolar cell region adjacent to the OCA. All onset units are capable of phase-locking to low-frequency (<0.5 kHz) modulations in such a fashion that the cell fires virtually on every modulation cycle. This 'entrainment' phenomenon has potentially significant implications for both temporal and rate coding of frequency. The entrainment drives the sustained discharge rate up to very high rates, between 500–1100 spikes/s, well beyond that observed in response to a high-CF tone (ca. 200 spikes/s). In consequence, the neuron is likely to be considerably more responsive to low-frequency signals than to stimuli to which it is most sensitive. This is a potentially very significant property of onset units,

suggesting that they are optimized for processing of AM and low-frequency signals. It is thus not surprising that the tonotopic organization which so clearly characterizes the anteroventral division is not nearly so well defined in the PVCN (Adams 1991).

Onset-choppers physiologically differ from onset-lockers in two principal respects. First, O$_C$s are much more broadly tuned than O$_L$s. The tuning properties of O$_L$ units are roughly equivalent to that of AN fibers of comparable CF. Onset-choppers are, on average, twice as broadly tuned as O$_L$ units, meaning that the former are not very frequency selective, even at very low sound pressure levels, close to threshold (Rhode and Smith 1986). This property of O$_C$ units is probably a consequence of the spatial orientation of their dendritic arborization which lies at an angle relatively oblique with respect to the isofrequency contour of ANF projections. In consequence, these cells sample the output of AN fibers spanning a relatively broad range of characteristic frequencies, suggesting that these cells are optimized to integrate AN activity over a large frequency range (Fig. 5a).

One consequence of this broad tuning is that the discharge activity of a substantial proportion of the AN fiber projection will continue to grow with increasing sound pressure level, implying that O$_C$s have a much

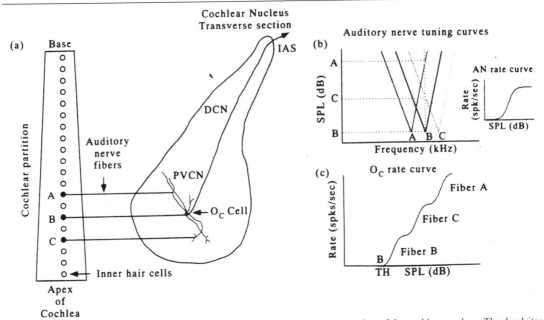

Figure 5. (a) An onset-chopper (multipolar stellate cell) is shown in transverse section of the cochlear nucleus. The dendrites of the cell span the CN from its ventral border to the granule cap region. AN fibers spanning a broad range of characteristic frequencies probably synapse on this cell. (b) Model accounting for the extended dynamic range of O_C cells. On account of receiving inputs across a wide frequency region, the rate-intensity function (c) of the unit does not typically saturate 20–30 dB above threshold as do other CN cell types and most AN fibers. Instead, the cell integrates the activity of unsaturated AN fibers, which are recruited as stimulus intensity is increased.

wider dynamic range than AN fibers and other CN unit types. Indeed this is the case. The dynamic range of most AN fibers lies between 20 and 30 dB, a range typical of most CN units as well, including O_Ls. In contrast, the discharge rate of O_Cs grows with increasing intensity over a 50–90 dB range, suggesting that these cells are optimized to encode changes in intensity over the full range of hearing sensitivity. A model for this extended dynamic range is illustrated in Fig. 5b, c. At each intensity level the cell receives a significant proportion of AN fiber input whose rate is unsaturated. The CF range from which this unsaturated projection originates will change as a function of stimulus intensity. At low SPLs the input will come principally from AN fibers most sensitive to the stimulus frequency. At higher intensities, at that point where the rate of the on-CF fiber projection is saturated, other, unsaturated AN fibers with CFs above, and especially below, the signal frequency, will dominate the afferent input activity to the O_Cs. The implications of O_Cs and O_Ls response patterns for speech coding are discussed in Sects. 5.1 and 6.2.

4.3 Dorsal Cochlear Nucleus (DCN)

The dorsal division is perhaps the most difficult region of the cochlear nucleus to describe and quantify in general terms. In contrast to the antero- and post-

eroventral divisions, which vary relatively little across mammalian species, there is appreciable diversity in the cytoarchitecture and morphology of the DCN, even among closely related species (Moore 1991). Significantly, the morphology of the human DCN differs dramatically from that of cats and rodents (ibid.), from which the bulk of physiological data derive. For this reason the DCN's role in speech processing is assessed with the utmost caution since much of the physiological data from animal studies may not pertain to the human. Despite the morphological diversity there are several properties of DCN physiology which appear to apply across most, if not all, mammalian species.

Virtually all DCN cells have a significant degree of inhibitory input. This inhibition is reflected in two principal response properties. The input-output function (rate-intensity curve) of most cells is highly non-monotonic. At low sound pressure levels the unit discharge rate grows with increasing intensity. However, at moderate-to-high SPLs the rate neither grows nor saturates, but actually declines with increasing intensity, often by an amount sufficient to completely shut down the cell at high SPLs. The basis of this decline in responsiveness is thought to lie in the complex interplay between excitatory and inhibitory inputs. At low SPLs, the excitatory, on-CF component of the ANF projection dominates the cell's discharge behavior. At increasing intensities the more diffusely organized inhibitory inputs come to play a more important role, overwhelming the excitatory component of the projection at higher SPLs. One consequence of this interplay is that many DCN cells respond weakly, if at all, to broadband noise, due to the prevalence of inhibitory inputs evoked by such signals (Young and Brownell 1976). Such response behavior may be useful for extracting biologically significant signals occurring in background noise (Rhode and Greenberg 1991). This possibility is considered in greater detail in Sect. 6.2.

A second manifestation of inhibition is observed in the magnitude and extent of lateral suppression observed in many DCN cells. The pauser-buildup (P/B) units of the dorsal division exhibit more suppression than any other CN unit type, including choppers. Moreover, the threshold of this suppression is very low, close to the cell's excitatory rate threshold, suggesting that these cells may be optimized to extract spectral contours of signals at relatively low and moderate intensities on the basis of rate-place information (Young et al. 1991). The implications of this behavior for speech coding is discussed in Sect. 5.1.

Most neurons in the DCN of the cat (the species in which most of the physiological research has been conducted) are fusiform cells, which correspond to the pauser-buildup response type (Rhode and Smith 1986b). The temporal course of their discharge is highly sensitive to stimulus intensity. At low SPLs the unit is often unresponsive until 20–100 ms after stimulus onset, increasing the magnitude of its discharge gradually over the next 100–150 ms (buildup pattern). At higher intensities such a unit may exhibit either a chopper or pauser response pattern. The latter is similar to a buildup pattern, except that the cell responds strongly at stimulus onset, and then shuts down for a variable interval ranging between 20–100 ms. Both the pauser and buildup patterns possess certain properties consistent with the temporal integration capabilities of human and animal listeners.

The functional role of the dorsal division remains an enigma. In terms of its extensive inhibitory input and intricate, complex intrinsic neural circuitry, the DCN possesses more of an affinity to upper brainstem and cortical auditory nuclei than to the ventral cochlear nucleus. The organization of its granule cell layer is reminiscent of the parallel and climbing fiber organization of the cerebellum (Mugnaini 1991), suggesting that the DCN may have the capability of dynamically modifying both its own and other regions' responses to sound. The DCN is also rich in zinc, a compound associated with long-term synaptic changes in other regions of the brain thought to be involved in learning (e.g., the hippocampus).

The DCN also appears to possess special noise-reduction circuitry that minimizes the effect of background sounds on the encoding of certain types of complex sounds, such as amplitude-modulated tones (Rhode and Greenberg 1991). Environmental background noise varies from location to location, and is highly dependent on the acoustic ecology of the species. For this reason it is possible that the variability observed in DCN morphology across mammalian species reflects the acoustic conditions under which different animals process sound. Because of short-term fluctuations in the sonic environment it may be useful to possess some means of dynamically modifying the noise-reduction circuitry of the DCN to optimize the signal-to-noise ratio of incoming acoustic information in 'real time.' If the DCN does function as a noise-reduction circuit its role in the processing of speech in humans should be particularly important.

5. Place Coding of the Spectrum in the Auditory Nerve and Cochlear Nucleus

5.1 Rate-place Information

The response properties of the auditory nerve have been discussed, so far, mostly in terms of single neural elements. However, the coding of speech and other complex sounds is based on the activity of thousands of nerve fibers whose tuning characteristics span a broad range in terms of frequency sensitivity, threshold, and selectivity. The ideal would be to extrapolate from what is known about the response of single fibers to sinusoidal signals and noise to predict the response of the auditory nerve, as a whole, to various speech sounds.

It is possible to infer the activity of the auditory nerve to speech by recording the response of hundreds of single fibers to the same stimulus. In the typical 'population' study the characteristic frequency and spontaneous activity of the fibers recorded is distributed in a fashion thought to accurately reflect the underlying statistics of the auditory nerve. In this manner, it is possible to infer how much information is contained in the distribution of activity across the tonotopic extent of the auditory nerve pertaining to the stimulus spectrum.

The representation of the spectrum for the steady-state vowel [ɛ], based on the distribution of average firing rate across the auditory nerve, is shown in Fig. 6 for three stimulus intensities (Sachs and Young 1979). At the lowest intensity, characteristic of very soft speech, the tonotopic distribution of firing rate approximates the gross spectral envelope of the vowel (Fig. 6b). This correspondence is expected, since the cochlea is operating within the quasi-linear portion of its range. At this intensity most ANFs fire at a rate roughly proportional to the cochlear-filtered energy level. Increasing the sound pressure level by 20 dB alters the distribution of discharge activity such that the spectral peaks are no longer so prominently resolved in the tonotopic place-rate profile (Fig. 6c). This is a consequence of the fact that the discharge of

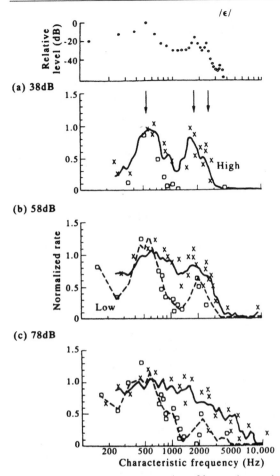

Figure 6. The rate-place representation of low-SR (squares) and high-SR (Xs) AN fibers, in response to the vowel /ɛ/, presented over a 40 dB range of sound pressure levels (1–3). The solid line indicates the average response for the high-SR units, and the dashed line shows the average or the low-SR population. (Adapted from Sachs 1984 and Handel's 1989 adaptation of an illustration from Sachs et al. 1982 (1–3).)

fibers with CFs near the formant peaks has saturated relative to those with CFs corresponding to the spectral troughs. As the stimulus intensity is raised still further, to a level typical of conversational speech, the ability to resolve the spectral peaks on the basis of place-rate information is compromised even further (Fig. 6d).

On the basis of such population profiles it is difficult to envision how the spectral profile of vowels and other speech sounds could be accurately and reliably encoded on the basis of place-rate information at all but the lowest stimulus intensities. However, a small proportion of AN fibers (15 percent), with spontaneous rates less than 0.5 spikes/s, may be capable of encoding the spectral envelope on the basis of rate-place information, even at the highest stimulus levels (Sachs et al. 1983, Blackburn and Sachs 1990). These fibers exhibit extended dynamic ranges and are most sensitive to the mechanical suppression behavior of the basilar membrane (Schalk and Sachs 1980, Sokolowski et al. 1989). Thus, the discharge rate of low-SR fibers, with CFs close to the formant peaks, will continue to grow at high sound pressure levels, and the activity of low-SR fibers responsive to the spectral troughs should, in principle, be suppressed by energy associated with the formants. However, such rate suppression also reduces the response to the second and third formants (Sachs and Young 1980), thereby decreasing the resolution of the spectral peaks in the rate-place profile at higher sound pressure levels. For this reason it is not clear that lateral suppression, by itself, actually functions to provide an adequate rate-place representation of speech and other spectrally complex signals in the auditory nerve.

The case for a rate-place code for vocalic stimuli is equivocal at the level of the auditory nerve. The discharge activity of a large majority of fibers is saturated at these levels in response to vocalic stimuli. Only a small proportion of AN fibers resolve the spectral peaks across the entire dynamic range of speech and the representation provided by these low-SR units is less than ideal, particularly at conversational intensity levels.

The rate-place representation of the spectrum may be enhanced in the cochlear nucleus and higher auditory stations relative to that observed in the auditory nerve. Such enhancement could be a consequence of preferential projection or through the operation of lateral inhibitory networks that sharpen still further the contrast between excitatory and background neural activity.

Many chopper units in the anteroventral cochlear nucleus respond to steady-state vocalic stimuli in a manner similar to that of low-SR AN fibers (Blackburn and Sachs 1990). The rate-place profile of these choppers exhibit clearly delineated peaks at CFs corresponding to the lower formant frequencies, even at 75 dB SPL (Blackburn and Sachs 1990). In principle, a spectral peak would act to suppress the activity of choppers with CFs corresponding to less intense energy, thereby enhancing the neural contrast between spectral maxima and minima. Blackburn and Sachs have proposed that such lateral inhibitory mechanisms may underlie the ability of AVCN choppers to encode the spectral envelope of vocalic stimuli at sound pressure levels well above those at which the average rate of the majority of ANFs saturate.

Winslow et al. (1987) have suggested that the low-SR fibers have an impact out of proportion to their numbers, preferentially innervating certain chopper unit populations in the ventral cochlear nucleus based on the anatomical studies of Rouiller and Ryugo (1984) and Fekete et al. (1982). Blackburn and Sachs (1990) and Sachs et al. (1991) have amended this hypothesis in accordance with more recent anatomical evidence, which indicate that most chopper units receive significant projections from all SR fiber classes (Rouiller et al. 1986). According to their 'selective listening' model, the activity of chopper units is dominated by the input of low threshold, high-SR AN fibers at low sound pressure levels, and by less sensitive, low-SR fibers at higher intensities.

This intensity-dependent domination of the chopper discharge behavior is, in their model, a consequence of the differential projection pattern of AN fibers. Low-SR fibers are presumed to innervate that portion of the cell closest to the soma (cell body) and the initial segment, while high-SR units contact the dendritic arborization distal from the stellate soma. At low SPLs only the high-SR fibers discharge. Their activity is integrated in the distal stellate dendritic complex and this neural energy propagates down the dendrites to the cell body to drive the chopper's response pattern. At higher intensities both high- and low-SR units fire. The activity of the high-SR population is 'blocked' from reaching the cell body by virtue of the discharge input of low-SR units, whose activity effectively controls the chopper response.

Although this 'shunting inhibition' model can qualitatively account for the ability of AVCN choppers to rate-place encode spectral peaks, there is, as yet, no anatomical or physiological evidence to support this conjecture. There is another means by which such selective listening could be accomplished without the operation of shunting inhibition. The ability of high-SR fibers to encode low-frequency amplitude modulation declines appreciably at moderate-to-high intensities (Rhode and Greenberg 1991), while the low-SR units are still capable of synchronizing their discharge to the modulation frequency (Young and Sachs 1979, Miller and Sachs 1984). In the absence of phase-locked behavior, choppers typically fire at a rate between 250–600 spikes/s in response to signals 30 dB or more above threshold. In response to low-frequency AM stimuli, choppers are capable of entraining their discharge to the modulation frequency. For vocalic stimuli with a low f_0 (ca.100 Hz), the effect of such synchronization will often be to lower the cell's discharge rate to a level below that typical of sustained chopper firing rates. As a consequence, the synchronization to f_0 observed in the AN fiber population (Young and Sachs 1979) could serve to sharpen the rate-place representation of the vocalic spectrum as well.

The evidence is stronger for a rate-place representation of certain consonantal segments. The amplitude of most voiceless consonants is sufficiently low (< 50 dB SPL) to evade the rate saturation attendant in the coding of vocalic signals. The spectra of plosive bursts, for example, is generally broadband, with several local maxima. Such spectral information is not likely to be temporally encoded due to its brief

duration and the lack of sharply defined peaks. Physiological studies have shown that such segments are adequately represented in the rate-place profile of all spontaneous rate groups across the tonotopic axis (e.g., Delgutte and Kiang 1984).

The place-rate representation in the auditory nerve may also be enhanced in the dorsal cochlear nucleus. Certain cells (with type II and IV receptive fields) in this region may be specialized to process spectral contours on the basis of rate-place information as a consequence of intrinsic neural circuitry (Young et al. 1991). Although this system may have evolved originally for localization of sound based on monaural cues (ibid.), it is likely that comparable inhibitory mechanisms operate at higher sound pressure levels typical of interspecific communication, and that such inhibitory processes may serve to enhance the rate-place representation of spectral contour information.

Certain phonetic parameters, such as voice-onset time, are signaled through absolute and relative timing of specific acoustic cues. Such cues are observable in the tonotopic distribution of ANF responses to the initial portion of these segments (Sachs et al. 1983, Delgutte and Kiang 1984). For example, the articulatory release associated with stop consonants has a broadband spectrum and a rather abrupt onset, which evokes a marked flurry of activity across a wide CF range of fibers. Another burst of activity occurs at the onset of voicing. Because the dynamic range of ANF discharge is much larger during the initial rapid adaptation phase (0–10 ms), there is relatively little or no saturation of discharge rate during this interval at high sound pressure levels (Sachs et al. 1983). In consequence, the onset spectra serving to distinguish the stop consonants (Blumstein and Stevens 1980) are adequately represented in the distribution of rate-place activity across the auditory nerve (Delgutte and Kiang 1984) over the narrow time window associated with articulatory release.

This form of rate information differs from the more traditional 'average' rate metric. The underlying parameter governing neural magnitude at onset is the probability of discharge over a very small time interval. This probability is usually converted into effective discharge rate. If the analysis window (i.e., binwidth) is sufficiently small (e.g., 100 μs) the apparent rate can be exceedingly high (up to 10 000 spikes/s). Such high onset rates reflect two properties of the neural discharge—the high probability of firing correlated with stimulus onset and the small degree of variance for this first spike latency. This measure of onset response magnitude is one form of 'instantaneous' rate. Instantaneous, in this context, refers to the spike rate measured over an interval corresponding to the analysis binwidth, which generally ranges between 10–1000 μs. This is in contrast to average rate which reflects the magnitude of activity occurring over the entire stimulus duration. Average rate is essentially an integrative measure of activity, which counts spikes over relatively long periods of time, and weights each point in time equally. Instantaneous rate emphasizes the clustering of spikes over small time windows, and is effectively a correlational measure of neural response. Activity which is highly correlated in time, upon repeated presentations will, over certain time intervals, have very high instantaneous rates of discharge. Conversely, poorly correlated response patterns will show much lower peak instantaneous rates, whose magnitudes are close to that of the average rate. The distinction between integrative and correlational measures of neural activity is of critical importance for understanding how information in the auditory nerve is processed by neurons in the higher stations of the auditory pathway. This distinction is considered in detail in Sects. 6.1 and 7.

5.2 Phase-place and Latency-place Information

In a linear system the phase characteristics of a filter are highly correlated with its amplitude response. On the skirts of the filter, where the amplitude response diminishes quickly, the phase of the output signal also changes rapidly. The phase response, by itself, can thus be used in such a system to infer the properties of the filter (Huggins 1952). For a nonlinear system, such as the cochlea, phase and latency (group delay) information may provide a more accurate estimate of the underlying filter characteristics than average discharge rate because latency and phase are not necessarily so sensitive to such nonlinearities as compression of the input-output response (saturation). Although the average rate of a fiber may not continue to change with increasing intensity, the unit's phase response may continue to do so, thus providing information concerning the input spectrum beyond what is available in the rate-place population profile at high sound pressure levels.

Several studies suggest that such phase and latency cues occur in the auditory nerve across a very broad range of intensities. A large phase transition is observed in the neural response distributed across AN fibers whose CFS span the lower tonotopic boundary of a dominant frequency component (Anderson et al. 1971), indicating that the high-frequency skirt of the cochlear filters is sharply tuned across intensity. A latency shift of the neural response is observed over a small range of fiber CFS. The magnitude of the shift can be appreciable, as much as half a cycle of the driving frequency (Anderson et al. 1971; Kitzes et al. 1978). For a 500 Hz signal this latency change would be on the order of 1 msec. Because this phase transition may not be subject to the same nonlinearities that result in discharge-rate saturation, fibers with CFS just apical to the place of maximal response can potentially encode a spectral peak in terms of the onset phase across a wide range of intensities.

Interesting variants of this response-latency model

have been proposed by Shamma (1985) and Deng et al. (1988). The phase transition for low-frequency signals should, in principle, occur throughout the entire response, not just at the beginning, as a result of AN fibers' phase-locking properties. They propose that such ongoing phase disparities are registered by some form of neural circuitry presumably located in the cochlear nucleus. The output of such networks would magnify activity in those tonotopic regions over which the phase and/or latency changes rapidly through some form of cross-frequency-channel correlation. In the Shamma model, the correlation is performed through the operation of a lateral inhibitory network, which subtracts the AN output of adjacent channels. The effect of this cross-channel subtraction is to null out activity for channels with similar phase and latency characteristics, leaving only that portion of the activity pattern where rapid phase transitions occur. The Deng model uses cross-channel correlation (i.e., multiplication) instead of subtraction to locate the response boundaries. Correlation magnifies the activity of channels with similar response patterns and reduces the output of dissimilar adjacent channels. Whether the cross-channel comparison is performed through subtraction, multiplication, or some other operation, the consequence of such neural computation is to provide 'pointers' to those tonotopic regions where a boundary occurs that might otherwise be hidden if analyzed solely on the basis of average rate. These pointers could, in principle, act in a manner analogous to 'peaks' in the excitation pattern.

5.3 Synchrony-place Information

Place and temporal models of frequency coding are generally discussed as if they are diametrically opposed perspectives. Traditionally, temporal models have de-emphasized tonotopic organization in favor of the fine-temporal structure of the neural response. However, place and temporal coding need not mutually exclude the other. The concept of the 'central' spectrum (Goldstein and Srulovicz 1977; Srulovicz and Goldstein 1983) attempts to reconcile the two approaches into a single theory of frequency coding. In this model, both place and temporal information are used to construct the peripheral representation of the spectrum. Timing information, as reflected in the interval histogram of AN fibers, is used to estimate the driving frequency. The model assumes that temporal activity is keyed to the tonotopic frequency representation. In some unspecified way, the system 'knows' what sort of temporal activity corresponds to each tonotopic location, analogous to 'matched' filters in systems engineering.

The central spectrum model is the intellectual antecedent of the peripheral representational model of speech proposed by Young and Sachs (1979). Their model is based on the auditory-nerve population response study discussed in Sect. 5.1 (Sachs and

Young 1979). As with place schemes in general, spectral frequency is mapped on to tonotopic place (i.e., fiber characteristic frequency), while the amplitude of each frequency is given by the magnitude of the neural response synchronized to that component by nerve fibers whose characteristic frequencies (CFs) lay within close proximity (1/4 octave). The resulting 'average localized synchronized rate' (ALSR) representation of the stimulus spectrum is illustrated in Fig. 7. The spectral peaks associated with the three lower formants (F_1, F_2, F_3) are clearly delineated in the ALSR representation, in marked contrast to the rate-place representation.

The mechanism underlying the ALSR representation is known as 'synchrony suppression' or 'synchrony capture.' At low sound pressure levels, temporal activity synchronized to a single low-frequency (<4 kHz) spectral component is generally restricted to a circumscribed tonotopic region close to that frequency. Increasing the sound pressure level results in a spread of the synchronized activity, particularly towards the region of high-CF fibers. In this instance,

the spread of temporal activity occurs in roughly tandem relation with the activation of fibers in terms of average discharge rate. At high sound pressure levels (ca.70–80 dB) a large majority of ANFs with CFs below 10 kHz are phase-locked to low-frequency components of the spectrum. This upward spread of excitation into the high-frequency portion of the auditory nerve is a consequence of the unique filter characteristics of high-CF mammalian nerve fibers. Although the filter function for such units is sharply bandpass within 20–30 dB of rate threshold, it becomes broadly tuned and low-pass at high sound pressure levels. This 'tail' component of the high-CF fiber frequency-threshold curve (FTC) renders such fibers extremely responsive to low-frequency signals at sound pressure levels typical of conversational speech (Fig. 8). The consequence of this low-frequency sensitivity, in concert with the diminished selectivity of low-CF fibers, is the orderly basal recruitment (toward the high-frequency end of the auditory nerve) of ANFs as a function of increasing sound pressure level.

Synchrony suppression is intricately related to the

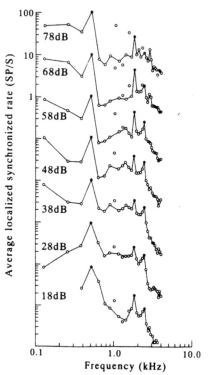

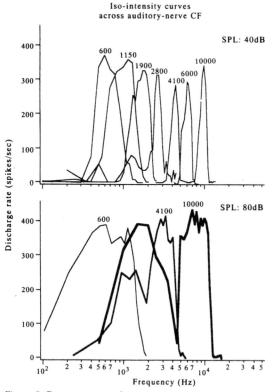

Figure 7. Average localized synchronized rate representation of cat AN fibers in response to the vowel [ɛ] across a 60 dB range of sound pressure levels. Spectrum of the stimulus is shown in Fig. 6a. Note the peaks in the ALSR representation corresponding to the lowest formant peaks. See Sect. 5.3 for detailed explanation of ALSR model. (From Young and Sachs 1981.)

Figure 8. Response areas for representative AN fibers at 40 and 80 dB SPL across a wide range of characteristic frequencies. At 40 dB the filtering is relatively linear and bandpass. At the higher SPL the filtering is skewed towards the low frequencies.

frequency selectivity of auditory-nerve fibers. At low sound pressure levels, most low-CF nerve fibers are phase-locked to components in the vicinity of their CF. At this amplitude, the magnitude of a fiber's response, measured in terms of either synchronized or average rate, is roughly proportional to the signal energy at the unit CF, resulting in rate-place and synchrony-place profiles relatively isomorphic to the input stimulus spectrum. At higher sound pressure levels, the average-rate response saturates across the tonotopic array of nerve fibers, resulting in a significant degradation of the rate-place representation of the formant pattern, as mentioned above. The distribution of temporal activity also changes, but in a somewhat different manner. The activity of fibers with CFs near the spectral peaks remain phase-locked to the formant frequencies. Fibers whose CFs lie in the spectral valleys, particularly between F_1 and F_2, become synchronized to a different frequency, most typically F_1.

The basis for this suppression of synchrony is as follows. The amplitude of components in the formant region (particularly F_1) are typically 20–40 dB greater than that of harmonics in the valleys. When the amplitude of the formant becomes sufficiently intense, its energy 'spills' over into neighboring frequency channels as a consequence of the broad tuning of low-frequency fibers referred to above. Because of the large amplitude disparity between spectral peak and valley, there is now more formant-related energy passing through the fiber's filter than energy derived from components in the CF region of the spectrum. Suppression of the original timing pattern actually begins when the amount of formant-related energy equals that of the original signal. Virtually complete suppression of the less intense signal results when the amplitude disparity is greater than 15 dB (Greenberg et al. 1986). In this sense, encoding frequency in terms of neural phase-locking acts to enhance the peaks of the spectrum at the expense of less intense components.

The result of this synchrony suppression is to reduce the amount of activity phase-locked to frequencies other than the formants. At higher sound pressure levels, the activity of fibers with CFs in the spectral valleys are indeed phase-locked, but to frequencies distant from their CFs. In the ALSR model the response of these units contribute to the auditory representation of the signal spectrum only in an indirect fashion, since the magnitude of temporal activity is measured only for frequencies near the fiber CF. In this model, only a small subset of ANFs, with CFs near the formant peaks, directly contribute to the auditory representation of the speech spectrum in the model.

5.4 Liabilities of Place Models

Place models of spectral coding do not function properly under intense background noise. Because the frequency parameter is coded through the spatial position of active neural elements, the representation of complex spectra is particularly vulnerable to extraneous interference (Greenberg 1988). Intense noise or competing sounds with significant energy overlapping frequency regions containing primary information have the capability of damaging the auditory representation of the spectrum. This vulnerability of place representations is particularly acute when the neural information is in the form of average rate. This is because there is no neural marker other than tonotopic affiliation which carries information about the frequency of the driving signal. In instances where both fore- and background signals are sufficiently intense it will be exceedingly difficult to distinguish that portion of the place representation driven by the target signal from that driven by the interfering sounds. In other words, there is no systematic way of separating the neural activity associated with each source purely on the basis of rate-place-encoded information.

The perceptual implications of a strictly rate-place model are counter-intuitive, for it is implied that the intelligibility of speech should decline with increasing sound pressure level above 40 dB. Above this level the rate-place representation of the vocalic spectrum for most AN fibers becomes much less well defined, and only the low-SR fiber population continues to encode the spectral envelope with any degree of precision. In actuality speech intelligibility is somewhat better above 60 dB, where the rate-place representation is not nearly so well delineated.

The ALSR model offers, at first glance, an appealing alternative to rate-based models, in that temporal information is more robust in the presence of noise. The ALSR model assumes the existence of a central mechanism which 'knows' the synchrony pattern appropriate to the CFs of the projecting fibers, and is capable of filtering out all other temporal activity. The ALSR approach requires that at some level of the auditory pathway a correlation be performed between the temporal activity and a neuron's filter characteristics near close to threshold. Physiological evidence for such a matched filter operation is entirely lacking, and it does not appear likely that any will be adduced in the near future. From a physiological perspective it is difficult to conceive of how such matched filtering would be implemented in the auditory pathway.

Another difficulty with place representations is their vulnerability to peripheral (i.e., cochlear) damage. Because the coding of frequency depends, in this representation, on the activity of discrete populations of nerve cells, significant damage to specific regions of the cochlea should result in the inability to encode whole regions of the spectrum. However, this does not occur except for frequency coding above 4 kHz (see Sect. 8 for further discussion on this topic).

6. Distributed Coding of the Spectrum in the Auditory Nerve and Cochlear Nucleus

6.1 Synchrony-distributed Information in the Auditory Nerve

The mechanism which underlies synchrony suppression also insures that temporal information pertaining to the formant peaks (particularly F_1) is distributed across auditory-nerve fibers spanning a broad tonotopic range under normal listening conditions. At low sound pressure levels formant-related synchrony is confined to fibers with CFs close to the spectral peaks of the vowel [ɛ] (Fig. 9). As the signal amplitude rises, so does the number of fibers synchronized to F_1 (Fig. 9a, 9b). At amplitude levels typical of conversational speech, most fibers with CFs below 10 kHz are synchronized to the first formant (Young and Sachs 1979). In the example shown, there is a gap in the tonotopic distribution of F_1 synchrony, centered at 1,800 Hz, the frequency of the second formant. This circumscribed population of fibers maintains its synchrony to F_2 by virtue of the relatively large amplitude of the second formant peak.

The broadening of AN fiber frequency selectivity is the primary basis of this wide distribution of F_1 synchrony. At conversational levels, the filtering of AN fibers becomes almost low-pass, in contrast to the sharply bandpass characteristic observed in response to signals below 60 dB SPL (Fig. 8). In consequence, low-frequency signals possess the capability of 'capturing' the activity of AN fibers most sensitive to much higher frequencies. Jenison et al. (1991) have accu-

rately simulated the tonotopic distribution of synchrony to the lower formants of vocalic stimuli using filter functions derived from the discharge-rate-based response areas (iso-intensity curves) of single AN fibers. In their simulation, the filter functions change as a function of tonotopic frequency and sound pressure level. Only at intensities 60 dB or greater is there observed a spreading of F_1 synchrony, analogous to that reported by Young and Sachs (1979).

It is perhaps not coincidental that the broadening of AN filtering is always towards the low-frequency portion of the spectrum. Only low-frequency signals are capable of 'labeling' the neural response at any point along the tonotopic axis in terms of modulating (phase-locking) the fiber discharge pattern. In the absence of phase-locking it would be difficult, under many conditions, to identify the signal frequency driving a unit's response. AN fiber discharge rate typically saturates 20–30 dB above threshold. Beyond this level there are few, if any, cues to distinguish excitation driven by frequencies close to the unit CF from those more distant. The AN population profile in response to an intense low-frequency tone would, under these conditions, be virtually indistinguishable from the pattern evoked by a wideband noise. The rate-place patterns would be very similar. For this reason it is likely that the broadening of filter characteristics towards the low-frequency portion of the spectrum is associated with the capability of AN fibers to synchronize to frequencies below 4 kHz.

In the mammalian auditory nerve there is a tend-

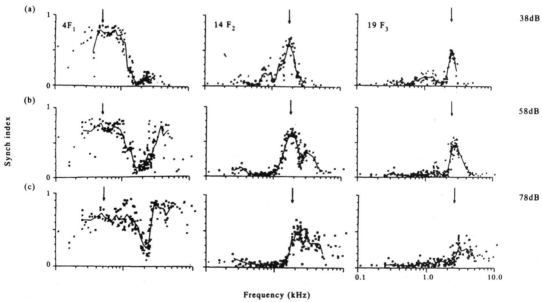

Figure 9. Synchrony-distributed representation of the vowel /ɛ/ in the auditory nerve for three intensity levels. The synchronization to F_1, F_2 and F_3 are shown as a function of the tonotopic affiliation of AN fibers. The arrows indicate the tonotopic location appropriate for each formant peak. (Adapted from Young and Sachs 1979.)

ency for broad frequency selectivity to be associated with the presence of phase-locking and for very sharp tuning to be correlated with discharge-rate information. The tuning of AN fibers is relatively broad (as measured by the unit's Q_{10dB}, defined as: the fiber CF divided by BW_{10}—the bandwidth of the response function 10 dB above threshold) for low-CF (<2 kHz) units (Q_{10}s between 1 and 2) and rather sharp for fibers with CFS greater than 4 kHz (Q_{10}s between 4 and 20). Thus, at low intensities, where rate-place cues would be expected to play a dominant role in the coding of spectral information, the tuning of high-CF fibers is very sharp. And this high degree of selectivity is maintained up to approximately 50–60 dB SPL. Such sharp tuning may be the natural consequence of a reliance on rate-place cues for the encoding of spectral information beyond the range of phase-locking (i.e., above 4 kHz).

There are at least two principal consequences of distributing temporal information pertaining to the lower formants over a large number of AN fibers. First, such distributed coding emphasizes spectral peaks at the expense of other components of the acoustic waveform. Lower amplitude components, particularly those located in the spectral trough between widely separated formant peaks (e.g., F_1 and F_2 for high and mid front vowels, F_2 and F_3 for back vowels) will not be represented clearly, if at all, in such neural activity patterns. In this sense, a distributed representation reduces the amount of data encoded in the peripheral neural activity pattern. It is similar to the 'dominant frequency' model first proposed by Carlson et al. (1975), and elaborated upon by Geisler et al. (1985), and Ghitza (1988). These models assume that only a small portion of the spectrum is behaviorally significant, and that the remainder is essentially 'window dressing' with respect to biologically relevant information. A behavioral study by Kakusho et al. (1971) is consistent with this interpretation. In their experiment, listeners were asked to discriminate between synthetic vocalic stimuli of variable spectral complexity. Reduced spectra were hardly distinguishable from full spectrum vowels, as long as the former contained the three lowest formants (each formant needed to contain at least three harmonics). Remez et al. (1981) have demonstrated that intelligibility is even preserved when each formant is represented by only a single frequency component ('sinewave speech').

A second consequence of distributed coding is the protection of the remaining information from the potentially deleterious effects of background noise and acoustic interference. Distribution of key, information-laden components ('info-elements') of the acoustic signal across a broad tonotopic range reduces the probability that extraneous signals will severely compromise their representation. Since most interference is of a transient or narrow-band nature, the neural activity evoked by the info-elements will be preserved across much of the tonotopic axis, or will be interfered with only momentarily. It would be considerably more difficult to encode info-elements against sustained, broadband interference. Under these conditions other strategies, based on common modulation patterns and binaural correlation may be required (Bilsen 1977; Bregman 1990).

6.2 Synchrony-distributed Information in the Posteroventral Cochlear Nucleus

Essential to the dominant frequency model is the means by which common synchronous activity, distributed across the tonotopic axis, is recognized and integrated at the level of the cochlear nucleus and beyond. Most cells in the CN receive direct excitatory input from a relatively narrow tonotopic range of AN fibers (an 'isofrequency' projection). For this reason their ability to monitor the spread of common synchronous activity over a broad tonotopic range is limited. Such cells, however, may serve to transmit synchronous neural activity to higher centers possessing the required integrative machinery.

One class of neuron in the cochlear nucleus does appear to possess specific response properties required for the analysis of distributed temporal information. The O_Cs of the posteroventral division (Sect. 4.2) behave in a manner consistent with the dominant frequency model. In response to low-frequency sinusoidal or amplitude-modulated input the average rate of these cells grows with intensity over a broad dynamic range, in tandem with the presumed tonotopic breadth of the active AN projections. Thus, discharge rate in these units appears to reflect both the tonotopic extent of coherent temporal activity, as well as the intensity of the driving component.

The O_C's ability to integrate coherent synchronous activity relies, in all probability, on two different properties. One concerns the broad frequency selectivity that reflects the wide tonotopic extent of the AN fiber projection (Sect. 4.2). The other involves some form of 'coincidence detection.' The latter refers to a situation in which a cell is sensitive to the relative arrival time of two or more nerve impulses from afferent inputs. Such neurons generally fire only if a certain minimum number of inputs discharge within a very small time window (on the order of tens or hundreds of microseconds). O_Cs behave like coincidence detectors in that the variance of their initial spike latency, as well as the variance of their phase-locked response to low-frequency modulations, is exceedingly small, far less variable than the analogous discharge measures for their AN fiber projections. In this sense, onset units may act as correlators of afferent temporal activity, similar in function to that proposed for the cross-channel correlation model of Deng et al. (1988) discussed in Sect. 5.2.

Coincidence detection is a potentially very powerful

means of protecting info-elements from the destructive effects of noise. Because noise, by definition, implies the absence of sustained correlation, neural elements particularly responsive to correlated inputs are capable, in principle, of withstanding appreciable levels of acoustic interference, as long as the background is itself not highly correlated with the foreground signal. Under such circumstances the temporal pattern of neural activity will remain relatively unaffected at all but the lowest signal-to-noise ratios. Rhode and Greenberg (1991) have examined the ability of various cell types in the CN to encode amplitude modulation in noise. Although all response classes exhibit impressive AM coding in noise, O_C units are among the least sensitive to background interference.

In response to vocalic stimuli, synchrony to both F_1 and f_0 will be dispersed across a broad tonotopic range of ANF inputs. At low SPLs the phase-locked response to f_0 will be more broadly distributed than F_1-synchronized activity. Fibers with CFs below F_1, between F_1 and F_2, and above F_3 will exhibit appreciable phase-locking to the fundamental frequency. This common synchrony to a low-modulation frequency could serve to encode important vocalic information in several different ways. In the presence of competing speech or other background sounds, the common f_0-synchronized activity serves as a means to identify tonotopically disjoint regions of the neural excitation pattern as originating from the same sound source. In noisy conditions the ability to track such common modulation patterns may act as a powerful cue for segregation and grouping of acoustic information into coherent 'event streams' (Bregman 1990). Moreover, the phase-locked manner of the 'common source' coding would minimize the potentially disruptive effects of background noise. Even in the absence of acoustic interference, f_0 synchrony may serve to 'bind' disparate portions of the tonotopic activity pattern together, to form a single sound source.

At higher sound pressure levels the dispersion of f_0 synchrony decreases in the auditory nerve, while phase-locking to F_1 expands appreciably. The tonotopic distribution of synchrony to F_0 is generally complementary to that of F_1. Rarely are fibers in a CF region highly synchronized to both. Most fibers will be predominantly synchronized to either f_0 or F_1, with the exception of the relatively small proportion phase-locked to F_2 and F_3. In consequence, the distribution of phase-locking to f_0 can serve as a 'negative' image of the tonotopic dispersion of F_1 synchrony, and vice versa. This complementary pattern has potentially significant consequences for coding vocalic stimuli in the upper reaches of the auditory pathway, as discussed in Sect. 7.

At the level of the cochlear nucleus virtually all cell types are capable of synchronizing to amplitude modulation within the frequency range of the speech fundamental (80–400 Hz). O_C units exhibit the greatest precision of phase-locking to low-frequency amplitude modulation, followed by pauser/buildup, chopper, O_L, and primary-like units. Thus, low-frequency modulation is a potentially powerful cue for informational encoding, source segregation and signal extraction in noise.

Coherent, low-frequency modulation of neural activity may also serve to provide a form of 'pitch-synchronous' analysis (PSA). A major drawback of conventional Fourier analysis is its reliance on a fixed time window of arbitrary length. In the analysis of acoustic signals of variable or unknown periodicity such fixed-interval analyses may provide erroneous estimates of the spectrum. Synchronizing the analysis to the pitch period provides one means of circumventing this problem. Scott (1976) has suggested that F_1 is estimated by the auditory system completely in the time domain by a form of PSA. In Scott's model each glottal pulse triggers the beginning of a new analysis frame, over which interval the number of major oscillations is counted. Category boundaries separating vowels are based not on the absolute frequencies of $F_1, F_2 \ldots F_n$, but rather on the number of modulations per pitch period. A related form of periodicity analysis has recently been proposed by Langner (1988, 1991), and by Patterson and Holdsworth (1991). In Langner's model, onset units act as pitch-synchronous triggers, and choppers serve as 'intrinsic oscillators' upon which the analysis of the signal's temporal fine structure is ultimately made. Activity from these two neural populations is presumably correlated in a more central auditory region, such as the inferior colliculus.

7. Central Auditory Mechanisms

At the higher reaches of the auditory pathway, the ability of neurons to phase-lock diminishes appreciably. At the level of the inferior colliculus, in the upper brainstem, units rarely synchronize to frequencies above 1 kHz (Yin and Kuwada 1984), and the upper limit of phase-locking for units in the thalamic and cortical regions is only 200–300 Hz (Ribaupierre et al. 1972).

The question naturally arises as to how information encoded in terms of synchrony in the auditory nerve and cochlear nucleus is converted into some form 'understood' by the higher levels of the auditory pathway. The basic issues are the nature of this transformed temporal information, and the type of mechanisms responsible for the conversion.

In 1948, Lloyd Jeffress proposed a model for binaural analysis of sound based on coincidence detection and neural delay lines. Jeffress' model was concerned exclusively with 'time-intensity' trading for localization of sound sources. Licklider (1951) extended this model into the domain of pitch analysis for complex sounds, using a mathematical technique known as 'autocorrelation.' Autocorrelation is used to estimate the periodicity of an arbitrary waveform. In Licklider's model an exact copy of the original waveform (as filtered and neurally transduced in the auditory periphery) is 'correlated' (multiplied) with the reference signal after a variable time delay. This delay is a consequence of neural circuitry which preserves the fine temporal details of the waveform, but sends the signal down a longer path. This 'high road' has, at various points along its route, connections (taps) to the more direct, 'low road.' Each successive tap represents an incremental delay. At each tap a correlational operation is performed. At most taps, the original and delayed version will not be highly correlated since they are out of phase with one another. However, for periodic or quasi-periodic signals, such as voiced speech, there will be some delay interval over which the correlation between the two waveforms is high relative to that of other taps. This interval of maximum correlation provides an estimate of the signal periodicity. Because each tap has a well-defined location, the neural autocorrelation effectively converts a temporal measure of periodicity into a spatial representation, which in Licklider's model, runs orthogonal to the primary, iso-frequency representation of afferent activity and encodes the waveform periodicity (fundamental frequency). Patterson's (1986) 'pulse-ribbon' model of periodicity pitch follows Licklider's model closely, except that the tonotopic frequency axis is spatially organized as a spiral, rather than as a linear array. The spiral organization has a built-in delay that functions in a manner similar to an autocorrelation.

To date, anatomical and physiological support for a delay-line and autocorrelational analysis is equivocal. In the barn owl, Carr and Konishi (1987) have published preliminary evidence for a delay line in nucleus laminaris, the avian homologue of the medial superior olive, but without any direct support for neural correlation. Yin and colleagues (e.g., Yin and Kuwada 1984) have adduced strong evidence in the cat inferior colliculus for some form of correlational operation pertaining to binaural analysis and have recently presented some rather preliminary evidence consistent with a delay line in the medial superior olive.

The most interesting results, in this regard, come from a study by Langner and Schreiner (1988; Schreiner and Langner 1988). They find in the inferior colliculus of the cat a topographic representation of waveform periodicity based on a rate measure of best modulation frequency. This best modulation frequency (BMF) representation spans a range between 50–500 Hz, and its spatial organization appears to cut across the tonotopic frequency axis. However, the anatomical and physiological basis of this BMF map remains obscure. It is not entirely clear whether such a coarse topographic representation would be

adequate to account for the precision of pitch discrimination among human listeners (ca. 1 Hz at 1 kHz or 0.1 percent).

A related issue is whether such a correlational analysis pertains to the processing of formant-related information. Lyon (1984) has used an autocorrelational model to provide 'front-end' spectral information for a speech-recognition system. The psychophysical constraints for spatial autocorrelation of speech is less stringent than for periodicity pitch as a consequence of discrimination performance being one to two orders of magnitude less fine than for pitch (Flanagan 1955; Mermelstein 1978).

In the upper brainstem nuclei, and especially in the auditory cortex, the discharge rate of neurons is appreciably lower than observed among cells in the cochlear nucleus and auditory nerve. This decrease in excitability may reflect, in part, the behavioral state of the animal, which is usually under anesthesia. However, there is reason to believe that even in the awake, behaving animal, cortical and thalamic neurons are less excitable than units in the periphery. Abeles (1982) has suggested that this lesser degree of responsiveness reflects the prevalence of encoding information through coincidence detection, rather than via energy integration. Most of the spectral analysis and preliminary acoustic feature extraction is performed, according to Abeles's logic, in the caudal stations of the auditory pathway. What remains to be done at higher levels is a synthesis of primitive elements into a unified, coherent picture of the acoustic stream. In essence the role of the cortical regions of the auditory system may be to process auditory 'events,' whose features change much more slowly than the acoustic spectrum, thus alleviating the need to update the neural stream more frequently than several times a second.

Steinschneider et al. (1982) have demonstrated that neurons in the thalamic radiations and auditory cortex of awake monkeys are capable of synchronizing highly to the fundamental frequency of synthetic speech sounds, suggesting that the temporal capability of at least some central auditory neurons is sufficient to encode f_0. At this level of auditory processing such temporal information may be able to encode other properties of the speech signal, including the lower formants, duration and intensity (see Sect. 6.2).

8. Clinical Implications

Individuals with moderate-to-severe hearing loss often experience little, if any, difficulty understanding speech in quiet, nonreverberant environments, but have major problems in noisy, real-life conditions. For this reason the deleterious effects of a sensorineural hearing loss are often evident only under acoustically adverse circumstances. To date, the basis of this paradox remains unresolved. There are, however, some indications that this situation reflects, in part, the distributed nature of the peripheral representation of the information-laden, low-frequency elements of the speech signal.

Severe hearing impairment is usually a consequence of damage to the sensory hair cells in the cochlea. The frequency range over which sensitivity (as measured by hearing threshold) most suffers lies above 3–4 kHz. Sensitivity to frequencies below 2–3 kHz is usually not very much poorer than in normal listeners, except in those rare instances of profound, nearly total deafness or Ménière's disease.

In quiet, the low-frequency region of the cochlea appears capable of providing a representation of speech sufficient to maintain nearly perfect intelligibility, and is a probably a consequence of the fact that virtually all information contained in the speech signal lies below 3.5 kHz (Miller 1951). Consequently, attention focuses on why the integrity of the basal cochlea, most sensitive to high-frequency signals, should have such a dramatic effect on speech intelligibility in noise.

It would appear that, for normal-hearing listeners, the basal segment of the cochlea provides a set of redundant frequency channels with which to encode low-frequency, informationally important components of the signal. In the presence of intense, low-frequency background noise, it can be inferred that much of the apical, low-frequency portion of the cochlea is responding to the noise as well as to the speech signal, thus interfering with the neural representation of the lower formants. Under such circumstances it is possible that the high-frequency channels provide a more robust representation of the low-frequency spectrum, particularly F_1 and f_0, because the background sounds are not sufficiently intense to capture the synchrony behavior of high-CF neurons.

Consistent with this interpretation is the fact that audiometric predictors of speech intelligibility are not the same under quiet and noisy conditions. In quiet, performance is most highly correlated with the pure-tone threshold at 0.5–1 kHz, while in noise the listener's sensitivity at 2–4 kHz most accurately predicts the magnitude of speech reception impairment (Smoorenburg 1990a). It is interesting to note that attempts to predict intelligibility based on other measures of hearing function, such as frequency resolution, have failed to observe statistically significant correlations (Smoorenburg 1990b).

A distributed representation of speech would also account for the failure of hearing aids to restore normal speech intelligibility. Hearing-aid users often complain that these devices are of limited help, particularly in noisy conditions. Because these aids rely principally on amplification they merely serve to boost the gain of that portion of the spectrum over which the listener is least sensitive. In essence, hearing-aid design is predicated on a place model of frequency coding. Unfortunately, amplification of the high-frequency portion of the spectrum provides little benefit to many hearing impaired because most of the information contained in the speech signal lies in their region of normal sensitivity, below 3 kHz.

It is likely that many of the problems hearing-impaired listeners experience with understanding speech are a consequence of damage to the redundant frequency channels in the auditory periphery. If this hypothesis is sustained, effective remediation of hearing deficits should focus on restoring representational redundancy through some form of frequency compression hearing aid.

9. Implications for Models of Speech Recognition

Background noise is the principal demon of computer-based, speech-recognition systems. Many systems achieve a high recognition score (95–98 percent) under ideal, quiet conditions (e.g., Klatt 1989 for a review), but few can withstand the presence of moderate-to-intense low-frequency noise.

This noise-induced impairment of automatic recognition performance may be a consequence of the 'front-end' design, which operates very much along the lines of a bank of linear, bandpass filters. Under such conditions, background noise has the potential for masking the informationally significant portions of the input spectrum without the possibility of recovering the information from other, unmasked frequency channels. In this sense, current automatic recognition systems operate in manner analogous to a sensorineural hearing loss.

Significant improvement in recognition performance in noise may require a redesign of the front-end component to withstand acoustic interference. One of the most successful recognition systems in noise focuses on the temporal aspects of peripheral coding, and integrates the activity of such synchrony information across frequency channels (Ghitza 1988). Such cross-channel summation emphasizes the output of those channels with the highest signal-to-noise ratio, and minimizes the masking effect of noise, which is usually severe over a restricted range of frequency channels. This strategy may be analogous to the way in which O_C units continue to encode signals in the presence of intense background noise.

Certain researchers are exploring the ability of neural networks to perform automatic speech recognition. These computational systems mimic certain gross properties of the auditory pathway, consisting of an initial input layer (analogous to the auditory nerve), one or more 'hidden' layers (corresponding perhaps to the auditory brainstem nuclei), and an output layer. The interesting processes occur in the hidden layers, which are capable of adjusting the strength ('weights') of neuronal interconnections to optimize the accuracy of phoneme recognition. This adjustment of weights has been likened to neural 'learning.' Waibel (1988) uses 'time delays,' not unlike autocorrelation to enhance the recognition performance, while Kohonen (1988, 1989) attempts to extract relevant acoustic features through constructing appropriate topological space pattern. One of the principal advantages of using neural networks for speech recognition is that they generally encode the acoustic waveform in a redundant fashion, particularly in the hidden layers, and in so doing, make the information less vulnerable to interfering noise. It is likely that further improvements in noisy-speech recognition can be gained through a better understanding of the noise-reduction circuitry of the auditory periphery.

10. Implications for General Models of Speech Perception

General models of speech perception are concerned with several principles of information coding of relevance to issues discussed in the present article. Of particular concern is the nature of the underlying representation of speech sounds; whether these perceptual units are continuous or discrete (Delgutte 1986) and are based on auditory or articulatory templates.

One well-known model argues that the speech stream is perceived in terms of articulatory gestures, rather than through the auditory analysis of the acoustic waveform (Liberman et al. 1967). The basic premise of this 'motor' theory is that speech invokes a unique mode of analysis, distinguished from general auditory processing in its specialization for speech-like features. At some very early stage this information is routed to linguistic-specific processors which convert the speech stream into its underlying articulatory form. The motor theory originated as a response to the enormous amount of acoustic variability inherent in speech. A search for some level of invariance, akin to perceptual experience, suggested that the underlying representation is in the set of motor gestures producing the acoustic waveform. Unfortunately for the motor theory, there is also considerable variability at the articulatory level (Holmes 1986) as well. Nor is there firm evidence, as yet, for speech-specific acoustic analysis (Kleunder and Greenberg 1989).

An alternative approach is to seek the invariant cues in the acoustic waveform itself. For example, Blumstein and Stevens (1980) have observed that each of the three place-of-articulation categories of American English stop consonants is associated with a distinctive spectral template that varies little as a function of phonetic context. In their view, other phonetic categories also possess an intrinsic acoustic essence that remains immutable across context, speaker, and production rate. Nonetheless, Kewly-Port et al. (1983) suggest that the variable, spectrally dynamic properties of the speech signal convey the lion's share of acoustic information.

A principal motivation for the design of auditory front-ends in speech analysis and recognition is the expectation that some set of properties of the auditory periphery will provide an invariant representation of the speech waveform lacking in conventional spectral analyses. In other words, much of the acoustic variability observed in the speech signal may be eliminated as a consequence of an auditory-smoothing operation that discards most of the acoustic details. Alternatively, the invariance of phonetic categories may be a function of higher-level, more cognitive operations following the auditory stage of analysis. Although the resolution of such issues must await future research, there is some evidence to suggest that much of the invariance is a consequence of more central, probably cortical, mechanisms that extract acoustic features and properties from peripheral analysis in accordance with semantic and syntactic expectation (Marslen-Wilson 1989). In this view, there is considerable advantage in postponing the final decision on phonetic identification until the last possible moment, to allay premature categorization inconsistent with the semantic intention of the speaker. On the other hand, it is certainly desirable to reduce the amount of information transmitted through the auditory pathway to the barest essentials required for accurate decoding of the speech stream for reasons of reliability (see Sect. 6). It is likely that spectral features conveying little phonetic and prosodic information, are discarded in the peripheral transduction of the speech signal.

At issue, then, is the nature of the representational code in the auditory pathway for phonetic features and categories. Delgutte and Kiang (1984) and Miller and Sachs (1983) have shown that certain properties of the auditory- nerve population response profile are generally associated with such phonetic features as voicing, frication, plosives, etc. And voice-onset time, an important cue for voiced-voiceless distinctions, may also have some correlates in the auditory nerve response (Sinex and MacDonald 1989). Despite these studies, it is still unclear whether phonetic categorization is based primarily on such peripheral representations (unlikely), or rather requires additional processing at higher levels of the auditory pathway.

11. Implications for the Sound Patterns of Language

The spectrotemporal properties of speech are generally thought to primarily reflect constraints imposed primarily by the vocal apparatus, with little significance attributed to the ear's role in shaping the acoustics of speech (e.g., Ladefoged 1982). From what is currently known about the auditory processing of complex sounds, this traditional view must be called into question.

The ear is phylogenetically far older than the human vocal apparatus. Although the latter shares certain features in common with its primate and mammalian relatives, the human speech production system is highly specialized, reflecting the rather unique properties of spoken language. The human auditory periphery and brainstem, by contrast, do not differ very much from those of most other mammals. For this reason it is likely that the auditory system has imposed far more constraints on the evolutionary design of the human vocal apparatus than the other way around.

It is likely that reliability and redundancy serve as major factors in shaping the evolution of both human and animal communication systems. For example, among certain species of monkeys in central Africa the spectrotemporal characteristics of many vocalizations appear to be optimized for reliable transmission in their specific acoustic environment (Brown 1986). Similar ecological factors may have shaped the evolutionary course of linguistic sound patterns. The similarity of sound features across the world's languages probably reflect constraints imposed as much by the acoustic ecology of reliable sound transmission as those stemming from articulatory and auditory (Lindblom 1986) factors. Indeed, many of the design features of both the articulatory and auditory systems may be principally motivated by reliable transmission and encoding in unpredictable, potentially noisy conditions.

Several acoustic properties of speech appear to be especially well adapted for ensuring reliable transmission of information. Each is considered below in turn.

11.1 Energy Distribution

Although humans are capable of producing high-frequency energy (e.g., the sibilants f and s), virtually all of the speech energy lies below 3.5 kHz. This low-frequency bias in the spectrum is usually attributed to a greater sensitivity for these frequencies among listeners. However, humans are generally more sensitive at 4 kHz than they are to signals below 1 kHz, where most of the energy in speech lies. The upper limit of neural phase locking in the auditory nerve is approximately 4 kHz (Rose et al. 1967, Johnson 1980), and this limit may well account for the predominance of low-frequency energy in the speech signal. There are obvious advantages for encoding information in terms of synchrony (see Sect. 6), the most important of which is reliability in the presence of noise. It is of significance that peripheral AN fibers of all vertebrate hearing systems, without exception, possess the ability to phase-lock their discharge to low-frequency signals, and that the energy distribution of most vertebrate vocalizations lies below 4 kHz. Thus, a low-frequency bias in vocalizations is likely to be a phylogenetically ancient adaptation, one that may have originated as a way of increasing the reliability of information coding.

11.2 Prevalence of Spectral Maxima (Formants)

Much of the speech stream is marked by formant peaks in the spectrum, thought to encode much of the phonetic information contained within the signal. It

is not known yet why, for example, the phonetic inventory of the world's languages is dominated by vowels, semivowels, glides, liquids, and formant transitions, rather than by bursts, frication, and sibilence. Nor is it clear which properties of these formant peaks make them better suited for information coding than other spectral features.

As discussed in Sect. 6, the encoding of spectral maxima is more robust in the face of acoustic interference and noise. This robustness is a consequence of two properties of the auditory periphery–neural phase-locking and low-pass filtering, which at moderate-to-high sound pressure levels distributes the formant-relevant information across a wide range of frequency channels. In this sense, the auditory periphery possesses the capability of enhancing the representation of spectral maxima relative to lower-intensity components or noise.

11.3 Prevalence of Voicing

All vowels (in English and most other languages), semi-vowels, liquids as well as many consonants are produced with the glottis in vibration. Although voicing is not necessary for continuous communication (as attested by whispered speech), people rarely speak in a voiceless manner unless compelled by pathology or secretiveness. Voicing creates a common pattern of amplitude modulation across frequency, potentially useful for binding disparate portions of the spectrum together in conditions of acoustic interference and competition (e.g., Bregman 1990, Assmann and Summerfield 1989, Scheffers 1983). It also ensures that high-frequency energy is more resistant to noise than would otherwise occur, by virtue of synchronizing the discharge of neural elements to the fundamental frequency. In addition, it takes advantage of the ability of higher auditory neurons to phase-lock to low modulation frequencies.

11.4 Alternation of Long and Short Elements

Much of the phonetic information contained within the signal resides in the consonantal segments (e.g., Miller 1951). It would be possible, then, to speak in a stream of consonants, rather than alternating them with vocalic segments, but humans do not. Consonants are generally briefer than vowels, and thus would provide a much higher rate of information transfer if vowels were excluded from the phonetic inventory. And yet there is no language which excludes vowels. Consonants may optimize the rate of information flow, but spoken devoid of vocalic context, may also be more vulnerable to the masking effects of extraneous noise.

Vocalic segments are more robustly encoded than consonants in the presence of noise, but their longer duration necessarily retards the rate of information flow, which in turn may preclude the integration of such phonetic information into higher-level syntactic and semantic units due to constraints imposed by short- and intermediate-term memory.

The alternating pattern of consonants and vowels may thus reflect a compromise between speed of information transfer and robust encoding in the presence of noise.

11.5 High Intensity of Speech

The sound pressure level of speech generally exceeds 70 dB at the receiver (Miller 1951), yet most verbal communication occurs over relatively short distances. Although it is physiologically feasible to speak at a lower intensity, this is rarely done except for whispering. This may be a consequence of the spectral peaks in the signal being more robustly encoded at higher sound pressure levels, due to the low-pass-like filtering invoked at those intensities which, in turn, distributes the information-laden elements of the speech waveform across many channels.

12. Conclusions and Future Directions

The human auditory system has a long evolutionary history reaching back into the cretaceous period more than 65 million years ago. Acoustic transduction, particularly in the periphery, is remarkably similar across mammalian species, and certain basic properties of auditory function such as phase-locking, and tonotopic organization extend in evolutionary time back to the Paleozoic era (225 million years ago). The conservatism of the auditory system suggests that this uniformity of nature's design is the result of developing effective solutions to common problems of acoustic transduction and encoding.

One of the most pervasive obstacles to effective communication is the occurrence of background interference. Because this interference is so variable, and therefore largely unpredictable, elaborate mechanisms have evolved to filter this background out, and enhance the encoding of the target signal. Within this context it is highly unlikely that the auditory mechanisms underlying the processing of speech are of evolutionary recent design. Rather, it would appear that much, if not all, of the acoustic properties of speech are the product of an evolutionary process in which the vocal apparatus (which is indisputably of recent origin) has developed to produce sounds readily detected and robustly encoded by the ear.

Future research will undoubtedly shed more light upon the evolutionary history of speech and will, in all likelihood, demonstrate that the vocal communication systems of other mammals and vertebrates share many acoustic traits in common with human speech. At present a detailed knowledge of nonhuman vocal communication systems is lacking for all but a few species; and the theoretical insights are lacking to understand precisely why speech and other communication systems sound precisely the way they do. In order to gain greater insight into the neural mechanisms underlying the processing of communication sounds it will be necessary to understand the acoustic ecology in which they evolved. And this, in turn, will require intensive study of vocal communication systems, both in the laboratory and under natural field conditions.

Another promising approach is to use models of the human auditory system and higher cortical centers to simulate the ontogenetic and phylogenetic conditions shaping the evolution of specific linguistic sound patterns (e.g., Lindblom 1986). Insights from these models will hopefully assist physiologists and psychoacousticians in their search for the neural underpinnings of speech processing.

Bibliography

Abeles M 1982 Role of the cortical neuron: Integrator or coincidence detector? *Israel Journal of Medical Sciences* **18**: 83–92

Adams J C 1991 Connections of the cochlear nucleus. In: Ainsworth et al. 1991

Ainsworth W A, Hackney C, Evans E F (eds.) 1991 *Cochlear Nucleus: Structure and Function in Relation to Modelling.* JAI Press, London

Anderson D J, Rose J E, Brugge J F 1971 Temporal position of discharges in single auditory nerve fibers within the cycle of a sine-wave stimulus: Frequency and intensity effects. *Journal of the Acoustical Society of America* **49**: 1131–39

Assmann P F, Summerfield Q 1989 Modelling the perception of concurrent vowels: Vowels with the same fundamental frequencies. *Journal of the Acoustical Society of America* **85**: 327–38

Bilsen F A 1977 Pitch of noise signals: Evidence for a central spectrum. *Journal of the Acoustical Society of America* **61**: 150–61

Blackburn C C, Sachs M B 1990 The representation of the steady-state vowel sound [ɛ] in the discharge patterns of cat anteroventral cochlear nucleus neurons. *Journal of Neurophysiology* **63**: 1191–212

Blumstein S E, Stevens K N 1980 Perceptual invariance and onset spectra for stop consonants in different vowel environments. *Journal of the Acoustical Society of America* **67**: 648–62

Bregman A S 1990 *Auditory Scene Analysis.* MIT Press, Cambridge, MA

Brown C 1986 The perception of vocal signals by blue monkeys and grey-cheeked mangabeys. *Experimental Biology* **45**: 145–65

Carlson R, Fant G, Granström B 1975 Two formant models, pitch and vowel perception. In: Fant G, Tatham M (eds.) *Analysis and Perception of Speech.* Academic Press, London

Carr C E, Konishi M 1987 Axonal delay lines create maps of interaural phase differences in the owl's brainstem. *Proceedings of the National Academy of Science* **85**: 8311–15

Delgutte B 1986 Analysis of French stop consonants using a model of the peripheral auditory system. In: Perkell J, Klatt D H (eds.) *Invariance and Variability in Speech Processes.* Erlbaum, Hillsdale, NJ

Delgutte B, Kiang N Y S 1984 Speech coding in the auditory nerve. Vol. IV: Sounds with consonant-like dynamic characteristics. *Journal of the Acoustical Society of America* **75**: 897–907

Deng L, Geisler C D, Greenberg S 1988 A composite model of the auditory periphery for the processing of speech. *J. Phon.* **16**: 93–108

Erulkar S D 1972 Comparative aspects of spatial localization of sound. *Physiological Reviews* **52**: 237–360

Evans E F, Nelson P G 1973a The responses of single neurons in the cochlear nucleus of the cat as a function of their location and anesthetic state. *Experimental Brain Research* **17**: 402–27

Evans E F, Nelson P G 1973b On the functional relationship between the dorsal and ventral divisions of the cochlear nucleus of the cat. *Experimental Brain Research* **17**: 428–42

Fekete D M, Rouiller E M, Liberman M C, Ryugo D K 1982 The central projections of intracellularly labeled auditory nerve fibers in cats. *Journal of Comparative Neurology* **229**: 432–50

Flanagan J L 1955 A difference limen for vowel formant frequency. *Journal of the Acoustical Society of America* **27**: 613–17

Flanagan J L 1972 *Speech Analysis Synthesis and Perception.* Springer Verlag, New York

Geisler C D, Deng L, Greenberg S 1985 Thresholds for primary auditory fibers using statistically defined criteria. *Journal of the Acoustical Society of America* **77**: 1102–09

Ghitza O 1988 Temporal non-place information in the auditory-nerve firing patterns as a front-end for speech recognition in a noisy environment. *J. Phon.* **16**: 109–24

Goldstein J L, Srulovicz P 1977 Auditory nerve spike intervals as an adequate basis for aural spectrum analysis. In: Evans E F, Wilson J P (eds.) *Psychophysics and Physiology of Hearing.* Academic Press, London

Greenberg S 1986 Possible role of low and medium spontaneous rate cochlear nerve fibers in the encoding of waveform periodicity. In: Moore B C J, Patterson R D (eds.) *Auditory Frequency Selectivity.* Plenum, New York

Greenberg S 1988 Acoustic transduction in the auditory periphery. *J. Phon.* **16**: 3–17

Greenberg S, Geisler C D, Deng L 1986 Frequency selectivity of single cochlear-nerve fibers based on the temporal response pattern to two-tone signals. *Journal of the Acoustical Society of America* **79**: 1010–19

Greenberg S, Rhode W S 1987 Periodicity coding in cochlear nerve and ventral cochlear nucleus. In: Yost W A, Watson C S (eds.) *Auditory Processing of Complex Sounds.* Lawrence Erlbaum, Hillsdale, NJ

Handel S 1989 *Listening.* MIT Press, Cambridge, MA

Holmes J 1986 Normalization in vowel perception. In: Perkell J S, Klatt D H (eds.) *Invariance and Variability in Speech Processes.* Erlbaum, Hillsdale, NJ

Huggins W H 1952 A phase principle for complex-frequency analysis and its implications in auditory theory. *Journal of the Acoustical Society of America* **24**: 582–89

Jeffress L A 1948 A place theory of sound localization. *Journal of Comparative & Physiological Psychology* **41**: 35–39

Jenison R, Greenberg S, Kluender K 1991 A composite model of the auditory periphery for the processing of speech based on the filter response functions of single auditory nerve fibers. *Journal of the Acoustical Society of America* **90**: 773

Johnson D 1980 The relationship between spike rate and synchrony in responses of auditory-nerve fibers to single tones. *Journal of the Acoustical Society of America* **68**: 1115–22

Kakusho O, Hirato H, Kato K, Kobayashi T 1971 Some experiments of vowel perception by harmonic synthesizer. *Acustica* **24**: 179–90

Kewly-Port D, Pisoni D B, Studdert-Kennedy M 1983 Perception of static and dynamic cues to place of articulation in initial stop consonants. *Journal of the Acoustical Society of America* **73**: 1179–93

Kitzes L M, Gibson M M, Rose J E, Hind J E 1978 Initial discharge latency and threshold considerations for some neurons in cochlear nucleus complex of the cat. *Journal of Neurophysiology* **41**: 1165–82

Klatt D H 1989 Review of selected models of speech perception. In: Marslen-Wilson W (ed.) *Lexical Representation and Process.* MIT Press, Cambridge, MA

Kluender K, Greenberg S 1989 A specialization for speech perception? *Science* **244**: 1530

Kohonen T 1988 The neural phonetic typewriter. *Computer* **21 (3)**: 11–22

Kohonen T 1989 Speech recognition based on topology-preserving neural maps. In: Aleksander I (ed.) *Neural Computing Architectures.* MIT Press, Cambridge, MA

Ladefoged P 1982 *A Course in Phonetics*, 2nd edn. Harcourt, Brace and Jovanovich, New York

Langner G 1988 Physiological properties of units in the cochlear nucleus are adequate for a model of periodicity analysis in the auditory midbrain. In: Syka J, Masterton R B (eds.) *Auditory Pathway: Structure and Function.* Plenum, New York

Langner G 1991 A model for periodicity analysis in line with physiological properties and anatomical connections of neurons in cochlear nucleus and inferior colliculus. In: Ainsworth et al. 1991

Langner G, Schreiner C 1988 Periodicity coding in the inferior colliculus of the cat. Vol. I: Neuronal mechanisms. *Journal of Neurophysiology* **60**: 1799–822

Liberman A M, Cooper F S, Shankweiler D P, Studdert-Kennedy M 1967 Perception of the speech code. *Psychological Review* **74**: 431–61

Liberman M C 1978 Auditory-nerve response from cats raised in a low-noise chamber. *Journal of the Acoustical Society of America* **63**: 442–45

Liberman M C 1980 Morphological differences among radial fibers in the cat cochlea: An electron-microscopic study of serial sections. *Hearing Research* **3**: 45–63

Liberman M C, Oliver M E 1984 Morphometry of intracellularly labeled neurons of the auditory nerve: Correlations with functional properties. *Journal of Comparative Neurology* **223**: 163–76

Licklider J C R 1951 A duplex theory of pitch perception. *Experientia* **7**: 129–33

Lindblom B E F 1986 Phonetic universals in vowel systems. In: Yaeger J J (ed.) *Experimental Phonology.* Academic Press, Orlando, FL

Lyon R F 1984 Computational models of neural auditory processing. *Proceedings of the IEEE International Conference on Acoustics, Speech and Signal Processing* 3611–14

Marslen-Wilson W 1989 Access and integration: Projecting sound onto meaning. In: Marslen-Wilson W (ed.) *Lexical Representation and Process.* MIT Press, Cambridge, MA

Mermelstein P 1978 Difference limens for formant frequencies of steady-state and consonant-bound vowels. *Journal of the Acoustical Society of America* **63**: 572–80

Miller G A 1951 *Language and Communication.* McGraw-Hill, New York

Miller M I, Sachs M B 1983 Representation of stop consonants in the discharge patterns of auditory-nerve fibers. *Journal of the Acoustical Society of America* **74**: 502–17

Miller M I, Sachs M B 1984 Representation of voice pitch in discharge patterns of auditory-nerve fibers. *Hearing Research* **14**: 257–79

Moore J K 1991 Dorsal cochlear nucleus organization. In: Ainsworth et al. 1991

Mugnaini E 1991 The granule cell-cartwheel neuron system in the cochlear nucleus complex. In: Ainsworth et al. 1991

Patterson R D 1986 Spiral detection of periodicity and the spiral form of musical scales. *Psychology of Music* **14**: 44–61

Patterson R D, Holdsworth J 1991 A computational model of auditory image construction. In: Ainsworth et al. 1991

Pisoni D B 1982 Speech perception: The human listener as cognitive interface. *Speech Technology* **1(2)**: 10–23

Remez R E, Rubin P E, Pisoni D B, Carrell T D 1981 Speech perception without traditional speech cues. *Science* **212**: 947–50

Rhode W S, Greenberg S R 1991 Coding of noise-embedded spectro-temporal information in the cochlear nucleus. In: Ainsworth et al. 1991

Rhode W S, Kettner R E 1987 Physiological study of neurons in the dorsal and posteroventral cochlear nucleus of the unanesthetized cat. *Journal of Neurophysiology* **57**: 414–42

Rhode W S, Smith P H 1985 Characteristics of tone-pip response patterns in relationship to spontaneous rate in cat auditory nerve fibers. *Hearing Research* **12**: 159–68

Rhode W S, Smith P H 1986 Encoding time and intensity in the ventral cochlear nucleus of the cat. *Journal of Neurophysiology* **56**: 262–86

Rhode W S, Smith P H, Oertel D 1983 Physiological response properties of cells labeled intracellularly with horseradish peroxidase in cat dorsal cochlear nucleus. *Journal of Comparative Neurology* **213**: 426–47

Ribaupierre F de, Goldstein M H Jr, Yeni-Komshian G 1972 Cortical coding of repetitive acoustic pulses. *Brain Research* **48**: 205–25

Robles L, Ruggero M A, Rich N 1986 Basilar membrane mechanics at the base of the chinchilla cochlea. Vol. I: Input-output functions, tuning curves, and response phases. *Journal of the Acoustical Society of America* **80**: 1364–74

Rose J E, Brugge J F, Anderson D J, Hind J E 1967 Phase-locked response to low-frequency tones in single auditory nerve fibers of the squirrel monkey. *Journal of Neurophysiology* **30**: 769–93

Rouiller E M, Ryugo D K 1984 Intracellular marking of physiologically characterized cells in the ventral cochlear nucleus of the cat. *Journal of Comparative Neurology* **225**: 167–86

Rouiller E M, Cronin-Schreiber R, Fekete D M, Ryugo D K 1986 The central projections of intracellularly labeled auditory nerve fibers in cats: An analysis of terminal morphology. *Journal of Comparative Neurology* **249**: 261–78

Ryan A F, Dallos P 1984 Physiology of the cochlea. In: Northern J L (ed.) *Hearing Disorders*. Little Brown, Boston, MA

Sachs M B 1984 Neural coding of complex sounds: Speech. *Annual Review of Physiology* **46**: 261–73

Sachs M B, Blackburn C C, Banks M I 1991 Inhibitory interactions in the ventral cochlear nucleus: Data and model. In: Ainsworth et al. 1991

Sachs M B, Kiang N Y S 1968 Two-tone inhibition in auditory nerve fibers. *Journal of the Acoustical Society of America* **43**: 1120–28

Sachs M B, Voigt H F, Young E D 1983 Auditory nerve representation of vowels in background noise. *Journal of Neurophysiology* **50**: 27–45

Sachs M B, Young E D 1979 Encoding of steady-state vowels in the auditory nerve: Representation in terms of discharge rate. *Journal of the Acoustical Society of America* **66**: 470–79

Sachs M B, Young E D 1980 Effects of nonlinearities on speech encoding in the auditory nerve. *Journal of the Acoustical Society of America* **68**: 858–75

Sachs M B, Young E D, Miller M I 1982 Encoding of speech features in the auditory nerve. In: Carlson R, Granström B (eds.) *Representation of Speech in the Peripheral Auditory System*. Elsevier, Amsterdam

Schalk T B, Sachs M B 1980 Nonlinearities in auditory-nerve responses to bandlimited noise. *Journal of the Acoustical Society of America* **67**: 903–13

Scheffers M T M 1983 Sifting vowels: Auditory pitch analysis and sound segregation (Doctoral thesis, University of Groningen)

Schreiner C, Langner G 1988 Periodicity coding in the inferior colliculus of the cat. Vol. II: Topographical organization. *Journal of Neurophysiology* **60**: 1823–40

Scott B 1976 Temporal factors in vowel perception. *Journal of the Acoustical Society of America* **60**: 1354–60

Sellick P M, Russell I J 1978 Intracellular studies of hair cells: Filling the gap between basilar membrane mechanics and neural excitation. In: Naunton R F, Fernandez C (eds.) *Evoked Electrical Activity in the Auditory Nervous System*. Academic Press, New York

Shamma S A 1985 Speech processing in the auditory system. Vol. II: Lateral inhibition and the central processing of speech evoked activity in the auditory nerve. *Journal of the Acoustical Society of America* **8**: 1622–32

Sinex D, MacDonald L P 1989 Synchronized discharge rate representation of voice onset time in the chinchilla auditory nerve. *Journal of the Acoustical Society of America* **85**: 1995–2004

Smoorenburg G F 1990a On the limited transfer of information with noise-induced hearing loss. *Acta Otolaryngologica* **469**: 38–46

Smoorenburg G F (ed.) 1990b Hearing impairment and signal-processing hearing aids. *Acta Otolaryngolica*, Supplement: 469

Sokolowski B H A, Sachs M B, Goldstein J L 1989 Auditory nerve rate-level functions for two-tone stimuli: Possible relation to basilar membrane nonlinearity. *Hearing Research* **41**: 115–24

Srulovicz P, Goldstein J L 1983 A central spectrum model: A synthesis of auditory-nerve timing and place cues in monaural communication of frequency spectrum. *Journal of the Acoustical Society of America* **73**: 1266–75

Steinschneider M, Arezzo J, Vaughan H Jr 1982 Speech evoked activity in the auditory radiations and the cortex of the awake monkey. *Brain Research* **252**: 353–65

Waibel A 1988 Consonant recognition by modular construction of large phonemic time delay neural networks. In: *Neural Information Processing Systems*. Morgan Kaufman, San Mateo, CA

Winslow R L, Barta P E, Sachs M B 1987 Rate coding in the auditory nerve. In: Yost W A, Watson C S (eds.) *Auditory Processing of Complex Sounds*. Erlbaum, Hillsdale, NJ

Yin T C T, Kuwada S 1984 Neuronal mechanisms of binaural interaction. In: Edelman G M, Gall W E, Cowan W M (eds.) *Dynamic Aspects of Neocortical Function*. Wiley, New York

Young E D, Brownell W E 1976 Response to tones and noise of single cells in dorsal cochlear nucleus of unanesthetized cats. *Journal of Neurophysiology* **39**: 282–300

Young E D, Sachs M B 1979 Representation of steady-state vowels in the temporal aspects of the discharge patterns of auditory-nerve fibers. *Journal of the Acoustical Society of America* **66**: 1381–403

Young E D, Sachs M B 1981 Processing of speech in the peripheral auditory system. In: Myers T, Laver J, Anderson J (eds.) *The Cognitive Representation of Speech*. North-Holland, Amsterdam

Young E D, Spirou G A, Voigt H F, Rice J J 1991 Dorsal cochlear nucleus: Internal organization of inhibitory connections and responses to complex stimuli. In: Ainsworth et al. 1991

Speech Perception

D. W. Massaro

This chapter gives a functional account of speech perception—how people discriminate and categorize the objects of spoken language. This functional account also includes the dynamics or time course of the processes taking the perceiver from spoken language to its understanding. Beginning with the issue of the functional units in speech perception, the chapter turns to a detailed discussion of categorical speech perception: a classic study to illustrate how speech perception is studied, with what appeared to be surprising results. These results motivated a theory that remained dominant for several decades. The chapter then gives a functional account of the results and develops a new theoretical framework, assesses theories of word recognition within a common framework, presents the state of the art in research and theory, and closes with some remarks about what remains to be learned about speech perception in the new millenium.

Speech perception is one of the most impressive demonstrations of auditory information processing. It can be described as a pattern-recognition problem. Given some speech input, the perceiver must determine which message best describes the input. An auditory stimulus is transformed by the auditory receptor system and sets up a neurological code, called a preperceptual auditory storage. This storage holds the information in a preperceptual form for roughly 250 msec, during which time the recognition process must take place. The recognition process transforms the preperceptual image into a perceptual experience, called a synthesized percept. One issue given this framework is, what are the patterns that are functional in the recognition of speech? These sound patterns are referred to as perceptual units.

1. Perceptual Units in Speech

One reasonable assumption is that every perceptual unit in speech has a representation in long-term memory, which is called a prototype. The prototype contains a list of acoustic features that define the properties of the sound pattern as they would be represented in preperceptual auditory storage. As each sound pattern is presented, its corresponding acoustic features are held in preperceptual auditory storage. The recognition process operates to find the prototype in long-term memory which best matches the acoustic features in preperceptual auditory storage. The outcome of the recognition process is the transformation of the preperceptual auditory image of the sound stimulus into a synthesized percept held in synthesized auditory memory. Fig. 1 presents a schematic diagram of the recognition process.

According to this model, preperceptual auditory storage can hold only one sound pattern at a time for a short temporal period. Recognition masking studies have shown that a second sound pattern can interfere with the recognition of an earlier pattern if the second is presented before the first is recognized. Each perceptual unit in speech must occur within the temporal span of preperceptual auditory storage and must be recognized before the following one occurs for accurate speech processing to take place. Therefore, the sequence of perceptual units in speech must be recognized one after the other in a successive and linear fashion. Finally, each perceptual unit must have a relatively invariant acoustic signal so that it can be recognized reliably. If the sound pattern corresponding to a perceptual unit changes significantly within different speech contexts, recognition could not be reliable, since one set of acoustic features would

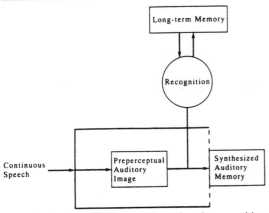

Figure 1. A schematic diagram illustrating the recognition process in speech transforming a preperceptual auditory image into synthesized auditory memory.

not be sufficient to characterize that perceptual unit. Perceptual units in speech as small as the phoneme or as large as the phrase have been proposed.

1.1 Phonemes

The first candidate considered for the perceptual unit is the phoneme. Phonemes represent the smallest functional difference between the meaning of two speech sounds. Given the word *ten*, its meaning can be changed merely by changing the consonant /t/ to /d/. The two sounds form two different words when they are combined with *-en*; they are therefore different phonemes. On the other hand, sounds are said to be within the same phoneme class if substitution of one for the other does not change the meaning of the sound pattern. One example is the word *did*. The two *d*'s in the word are not the same acoustically and, if their sound patterns were extracted and interchanged with each other, the word would not sound the same. Yet they are not functionally different since interchanging them should still give the word *did*. In this case, they are called different allophones of the same phoneme. Thus, if the substitution of one minimal sound for another changes the meaning of the larger unit, then the two sounds are phonemes. If such substitution does not change the meaning of the larger unit, then the different sounds are allophones of the same phoneme class.

Consider the acoustic properties of vowel phonemes. Unlike some consonant phonemes, whose acoustic properties change over time, the wave shape of the vowel is considered to be steady-state or tone-like. The wave shape of the vowel repeats itself anywhere from 75 to 200 times per second. In normal speech, vowels last between 100 and 300 msec, and during this time the vowels maintain a fairly regular and unique pattern. It follows that, by the above

criteria, vowels could function as perceptual units in speech.

Now consider consonant phonemes. Consonant sounds are more complicated than vowels and some of them do not seem to qualify as perceptual units. It has been noted that a perceptual unit must have a relatively invariant sound pattern in different contexts. However, some consonant phonemes appear to have different sound patterns in different speech contexts. Fig. 2 shows that the stop consonant phoneme /d/ has different acoustic representations in different vowel contexts. Since the steady-state portion corresponds to the vowel sounds, the first part, called the transition, must be responsible for the perception of the consonant /d/. As can be seen in the figure, the acoustic pattern corresponding to the /d/ sound differs significantly in the syllables. Hence, one set of acoustic features would not be sufficient to recognize the consonant /d/ in the different vowel contexts. Therefore, linguists must either modify their definition of a perceptual unit or eliminate the stop consonant phoneme as a candidate.

1.2 CV Syllables

There is another reason why the consonant phoneme /d/ cannot qualify as a perceptual unit. According to the model perceptual units are recognized in a linear fashion. Research has shown, however, that the consonant /d/ cannot be recognized before the vowel is also recognized. If the consonant were recognized before the vowel, then it should be possible to decrease the duration of the vowel portion of the syllable so that only the consonant would be recognized. Experimentally, the duration of the vowel in the consonant-vowel syllable (CV) is gradually decreased and the subject is asked when she hears the stop consonant sound alone. The CV syllable is perceived as a complete syllable until the vowel is eliminated almost entirely (Liberman et al. 1967). At that point, however, instead of the perception changing to the consonant /d/, a nonspeech whistle is heard. Liberman et al. show that the stop consonant /d/ cannot be perceived independently of perceiving a CV syllable. Therefore, it seems unlikely that the /d/ sound would be perceived before the vowel sound; it appears, rather, that the CV syllable is perceived as an indivisible whole or gestalt.

These arguments lead to the idea that syllables function as perceptual units rather than containing two perceptual units each. One way to test this hypothesis is to employ the CV syllables in a recognition-masking task. Liberman et al. found that subjects could identify shortened versions of the CV syllables when most of the vowel portion is eliminated. Analogous to interpretation of vowel perception, recognition of these shortened CV syllables also should take time. Therefore, a second syllable, if it follows the first soon enough, should interfere with perception of the first.

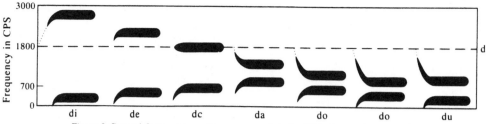

Figure 2. Second-formant transitions appropriate for /d/ before various vowels.

Consider the three CV syllables /ba/, /da/, and /ga/ (/a/ pronounced as in *father*), which differ from each other only with respect to the consonant phoneme. Backward recognition masking, if found with these sounds, would demonstrate that the consonant sound is not recognized before the vowel occurs and also that the CV syllable requires time to be perceived.

1.3 Recognition Masking

Newman and Spitzer (1987) conducted such an experiment, employing as test items three synthetic CV syllables /ba/, /da/, /ga/, each 40 msec long with 20 msec of that duration comprising the transition and the remainder the steady-state vowel. The masking stimulus was a 40 msec steady-state vowel /a/.

Figure 3 shows the percentage of correct recognitions for eight observers as a function of the silent interval between the test and masking CVs. The results show that recognition of the consonant is not complete at the end of the CV transition, nor even at the end of the short vowel presentation. Rather, correct identification of the CV syllable requires perceptual processing after the stimulus presentation. These results support the hypothesis that the CV syllable must have functioned as a perceptual unit, because the syllable must have been stored in preperceptual

auditory storage, and recognition involved a transformation of this preperceptual storage into a synthesized percept of a CV unit. The acoustic features necessary for recognition must, therefore, define the complete CV unit. An analogous argument can be made for VC syllables also functioning as perceptual units.

It is also necessary to ask whether perceptual units could be larger than vowels, CV, or VC syllables. George Miller argued that the phrase of two or three words might function as a perceptual unit. According to the above criteria for a perceptual unit, it must correspond to a prototype in long-term memory which has a list of features describing the acoustic features in the preperceptual auditory image of that perceptual unit. Accordingly, preperceptual auditory storage must last on the order of one or two seconds to hold perceptual units of the size of a phrase. But the recognition-masking studies usually estimate the effective duration of preperceptual storage to be about 250 msec. Therefore, perceptual units must occur within this period, eliminating the phrase as the perceptual unit.

The recognition-masking paradigm developed to study the recognition of auditory sounds has provided a useful tool for determining the perceptual units in speech. If preperceptual auditory storage is limited to 250 msec, the perceptual units must occur within this short period. This time period agrees nicely with the durations of syllables in normal speech (see Massaro 1996b and Massaro and Loftus 1996 for a review of the most recent research and theory).

2. Categorical Perception

One persistent and popular belief is that speech is perceived categorically. In fact, the study of speech perception has almost been synonymous with the study of how it is perceived categorically. Perception is said to be categorical if the subject can only make judgments about the name of a stimulus, not its particular sound quality. For example, the same speaker may repeat the same syllable a number of times. The acoustic patterns representing this syllable would differ from each other since a speaker cannot repeat the same sound exactly. A listener who perceives the sounds categorically would not be able to discriminate

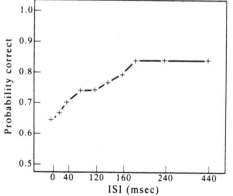

Figure 3. Probability of correct recognitions of the test CV syllables as a function of the duration of the silent inter-syllable interval (SII) in a backward recognition-masking task (results of Newman and Spitzer 1987).

any difference in the particular sound quality of each repetition of the syllable. The same listener, on the other hand, would be able to recognize a difference between any of these sounds and another syllable spoken by the same speaker. In categorical perception, the listener can recognize differences when the syllables have different names but not when they have the same name.

Subjects are certainly not limited in this way in the processing of nonspeech. They are able to discriminate two tones as different even though they can not differentially label them. This is true for all sound dimensions: subjects can discriminate many more differences than they can identify successfully. This phenomenon, in fact, was one of the observations that convinced George Miller that, although subjects can make many discriminations along a unidimensional stimulus continuum, they can identify accurately about 7 ± 2 of these stimuli. In this case, discrimination is not limited by identification, since subjects can discriminate differences along a stimulus continuum which they cannot identify absolutely.

2.1 A Seminal Study

A seminal study established the experimental paradigm for the study of categorical speech perception. Liberman et al. (1957) used synthetic speech to generate a series of 14 CV syllables as in Fig. 4, that is, where the second formant (F2) onset was varied in 120 Hz steps and the steady-state vowel was /e/. Consistent with prior studies, listeners identified these stimuli as /be/, /de/, or /ge/ as shown in Fig. 4a, which gives the results for one subject. They then tested listeners' ability to discriminate pairs of these stimuli using the ABX method, i.e., where three stimuli were presented in the order ABX: A and B differ and X was identical to either A or B; listeners had to indicate whether X was identical to A or B. This judgment was supposedly one of auditory discrimination since the subjects were instructed to use 'any cues' they could hear. The results of the same subject's discrimination of stimuli pairs immediately adjacent on the stimulus continuum ('one-step'), as well as those that were two steps and three steps apart are shown in Figs. 4b–d. The authors also compared such discrimination scores with those predicted on the basis of the identification functions. The authors concluded that discrimination was fairly well predicted by identification and thus that speech was perceived categorically. This view is still widely held today.

But with the advantage of hindsight, this conclusion can be criticized on at least two points. First, the ABX paradigm may encourage the verbal encoding of the stimuli A and B since it would be very difficult to remember their sound quality. Therefore, subjects might simply be performing the ABX discrimination task as if it were an identification task and thus it should not come as a surprise if subjects show poor

discrimination of different syllables that have the same label. Second, quantitative measures of the 'goodness-of-fit' of the predicted and obtained discrimination functions are not very impressive; in fact discrimination was generally better than that predicted and this is evident in the data presented in Fig. 4.

2.2 Negative Evidence

Subsequently experimental evidence has been obtained to show that listeners can discriminate auditory differences between stop consonants that are given the same label in identification.

Using a F2-onset stimulus continuum similar to that in Fig. 4, but with the V = /æ/, Barclay (1972) first obtained listeners' identification of the initial consonants as /b/, /d/, or /g/, and got results similar to that in Fig. 4a. He then later asked the same subjects to listen to the same continuum but reduced the eligible responses to /b/ and /g/. These subjects were successful in differentiating stimuli they had earlier assigned to the /d/ category, that is, now assigning either to the /b/ or the /g/ category.

Pisoni and Lazarus (1974) also demonstrated that subjects could discriminate between stimuli that they would give the same name to by first providing subjects more extensive training on the items in the stimuli continuum and second by employing a discrimination method that did not tax auditory memory as much. They present two pairs of stimuli, one pair always being the same and the other different; subjects simply had to indicate which pair had different stimuli. Their results show that discriminating between sounds that are usually given different names was not significantly better than that between sounds usually given the same name.

There have been many demonstrations of continuous perception of speech since these initial studies. Without a doubt, the task of the speech perceiver is to categorize. The child must decide whether the adult said, *Get the ball* or *Get the doll*. However, the decision appears to be based on continuous information provided by the speech signal. As in other domains of categorization, speech recognition involves the evaluation and integration of continuous, not categorical, features. It is particularly important that the information is maintained in a noncategorical form because it can then be supplemented with other types of information. If the child had insufficient acoustic information to distinguish between *ball* and *doll*, a nod or hand gesture by the speaker toward one of the objects could help disambiguate the instruction.

2.3 Categorical Partition

It is still a common mistake to interpret categorization behavior as evidence for categorical perception. It is only natural that continuous perception should lead to sharp category boundaries along a stimulus continuum. Given a stimulus continuum from *A* to

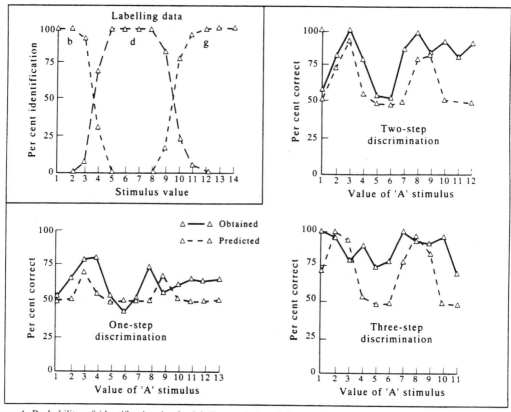

Figure 4. Probability of identification in the labeling task (top left panel) and observed and predicted probability of discrimination in the ABX task (after Liberman et al. 1957).

not A that is perceived continuously, GOODNESS(A) is an index of the degree to which the information represents the category *A*. The left panel of Fig. 5 shows GOODNESS(A) as a linear function of Variable *A*.

An optimal decision rule in a discrete judgment task would set the criterion value at 0.5 and classify the pattern as *A* for any value greater than this value. Otherwise, the pattern is classified as *not A*. Given this decision rule, the probability of an *A* response would take the step-function form shown in the right panel of Fig. 5. That is, with a fixed criterion value and no variability, the decision operation changes the continuous linear function given by the perceptual operation into a step function. Although based on continuous perception, this function is identical to the idealized form of categorical perception in a speech identification task. It follows that a step function for identification is *not* evidence for categorical perception because it can occur given continuous information.

If there is noise in the mapping from stimulus to identification, a given level of Variable *A* cannot be expected to produce the same identification judgment on each presentation. It is reasonable to assume that

a given level of Variable A produces a normally distributed range of GOODNESS(A) values with a mean directly related to the level of Variable *A* and a variance equal across all levels of Variable *A*. If this is the case, noise will influence the identification judgment for the levels of Variable *A* near the criterion value more than it will influence the levels away from the criterion value. Figure 6 illustrates the expected outcome for identification if there is normally distributed noise with the same criterion value assumed in Fig. 5.

If the noise is normal and has the same mean and variance across the continuum, a stimulus whose mean goodness is at the criterion value will produce random classifications. The goodness value will be above the criterion on half of the trials and below the criterion on the other half. As the goodness value moves away from the criterion value, the noise will have a diminishing effect on the identification judgments. Noise has a larger influence on identification in the middle of the range of goodness values than at the extremes because variability goes in both directions in the middle and only inward at the extremes.

This example shows that categorical decisions made on the basis of continuous information produce

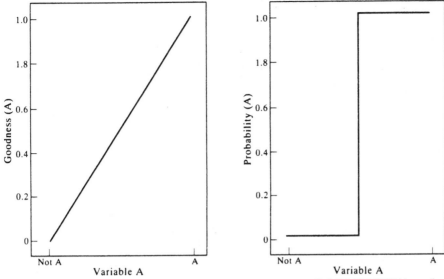

Figure 5. Left Panel: The degree to which a stimulus represents the category *A*, called GOODNESS(A) as a function of the level along a stimulus continuum between *not A* and *A*. Right Panel: The probability of an *A* response, Probability(*A*), as a function of the stimulus continuum if the subject maintains a decision criterion at a particular value of GOODNESS(A) and responds *A* if and only if the GOODNESS(A) exceeds the decision criterion.

identification functions with sharp boundaries, previously taken to represent categorical perception. Strictly speaking, of course, categorical perception was considered present only if discrimination behavior did not exceed that predicted from categorization. However, one should not have been impressed with

Normal

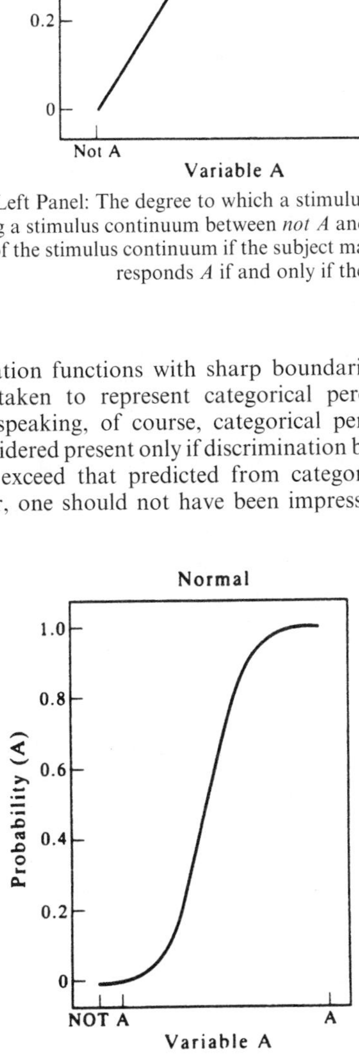

Figure 6. Probability(*A*) as a function of Variable *A* given the linear relationship between GOODNESS(A) and Variable *A* and the decision criterion represented in Fig. 5, but with normally distributed noise added to the mapping of Variable *A* to GOODNESS(A).

the failure of discrimination to exceed that predicted by categorization if the discrimination task resembled something more akin to categorization than discrimination.

Drawing upon a broad range of methodological, theoretical, and experimental issues, an attempt has been made to present the evidence against the theory of categorical perception. At the methodological level, it has been shown that the relation between identification and discrimination provides no support for categorical perception. First, the categorical model usually provides an inadequate description of the results, and it has not been shown to provide a better description than alternative models. Second, even if the results were to provide unequivocal support for the categorical model, other explanations than categorical perception would be possible.

At the theoretical level, it is necessary to distinguish between sensory and decision processes in the categorization task. What is central is that decision processes can transform continuous sensory information into results usually taken to reflect categorical perception. Finding relatively categorical partitioning of a set of stimuli in no way implies that these stimuli were perceived categorically. Tapping into the process in other ways than simply measuring the identification response reveals the continuous nature of speech perception. Perceivers can rate the degree to which a speech event represents a category and they can easily discriminate among different exemplars of the same speech category. In addition, *RT*s of identification

47

judgments illustrate that members within a speech category vary in ambiguity or the degree to which they represent the category.

Although speech perception is continuous, there may be a few speech contrasts that qualify for a weak form of categorical perception. This weak form of categorical perception would be reflected in somewhat better discrimination between instances from different categories than between instances within the same category. As an example, consider an auditory /ba/ to /da/ continuum similar to one used in the experiments described above. The F2 and F3 transitions were varied in linear steps between the two endpoints of the continuum. The syllable /ba/ is characterized by rising transitions and /da/ by falling transitions. Subjects might discriminate a rising from a falling transition more easily than discriminate two rising or two falling transitions even though the frequency difference is identical in the two cases. Direction of pitch change is more discriminable than the exact magnitude of change. This weak form of categorical perception would be due to a fundamental characteristic of auditory processing and would not be a result of having speech categories. Thus similar results would be found in humans, chinchillas, and monkeys and for nonspeech analogs. However, it is important to note that discrimination between instances within a category is still possible. Although a weak form of categorical perception might exist for a few distinctions, most distinctions do not appear to have this property, and the linguist is left with explaining continuous rather than categorical speech perception.

The research and theory in speech perception has traditionally operated on the premise that speech is primarily auditory. Recent developments, however, have stimulated a dramatic change in many researchers' conceptualization of this remarkable skill (Massaro 1998). Research from several domains now serves to substantiate the view of the multimodal nature of speech perception and the important influence of linguistic and situational constraints in speech processing. This broader view of spoken language processing offers a valuable framework for the discussion of theories of word recognition.

3. Theories of Word Recognition

Although there are several theories of spoken-word recognition, they can be classified and described fairly easily. All theories begin with the acoustic signal and usually end with access to a word or phrase in the mental lexicon. Seven models of word recognition will be discussed to highlight some important issues in understanding how words are recognized. Several important characteristics of the models will be reviewed to contrast and compare the models. Figure 7 gives a graphical presentation of these characteristics.

One important question is whether word recognition is mediated or nonmediated. A second question is whether the perceiver has access only to categorical information in the word recognition process, or whether continuous information is available. A third consideration is whether information from the continuously varying signal is used on-line at the lexical stage of processing, or whether there is some delay in initiating processing of the signal at the lexical stage. A fourth characteristic involves parallel versus serial access to the lexical representations in memory. The final characteristic to consider is whether the word recognition process functions autonomously, or whether it is context dependent (see Massaro 1996a).

3.1 Logogen Model

The logogen model described by Morton (1964) has had an important influence on how the field has described word recognition. Morton proposed that each word that an individual knows has a representation in long-term memory. To describe this representation, Morton used the term logogen— logos, meaning 'word,' and genus, meaning 'birth.' Each logogen has a resting level of activity, and this level of activity can be increased by stimulus events. Each logogen has a threshold—when the level of activation exceeds the threshold, the logogen fires. The threshold is a function of word frequency; more frequent words have lower thresholds and require less activation for firing. The firing of a logogen makes the corresponding word available as a response. Figure 8 gives a schematic diagram of the logogen model.

Morton's logogen model can be evaluated with respect to the five characteristics shown in Fig. 7. The model is nonmediated because there is supposedly a direct mapping between the input and the logogen. That is, no provision has been made for smaller segments, such as phonemes or syllables, to mediate word recognition. The perceiver of language appears to have continuous information, given that the logogen can be activated to various degrees. On the other hand, one might interpret the theory as categorical because of the assumption of a threshold below which the logogen does not fire. Processing is on-line rather than delayed. With respect to the fourth issue, words are activated in parallel rather than serially. Finally, as can be seen in Fig. 8, the logogen allows for the contribution of contextual information in word recognition. Contextual information activates logogens in the same way that information from the stimulus word itself activates logogens. The main limitation in the logogen model is its nonmediated nature. Thus, the model has difficulty explaining intermediate recognition of sublexical units (e.g., CV syllables) and how nonwords are recognized.

3.2 Cohort Model

An influential model of word recognition is the 'cohort' model (Marslen-Wilson 1984). According to

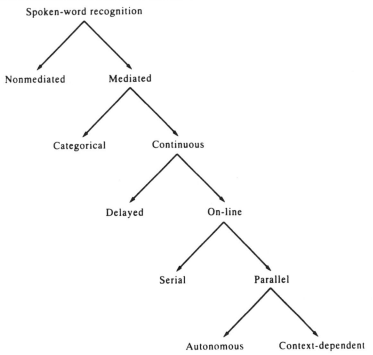

Figure 7. Tree of wisdom illustrating binary oppositions central to the differences among theories of spoken-word recognition.

this model, word recognition proceeds in a left-to-right fashion on-line with the sequential presentation of the information in a spoken word. The acoustic signal is recognized phoneme by phoneme from left to right during the word presentation. Each phoneme is recognized categorically. Word recognition occurs by way of the elimination of alternative word candidates (cohorts). Recognition of the first phoneme in the word eliminates all words that do not have that phoneme in initial position. Recognition of the second phoneme eliminates all of the remaining cohorts that do not have the second phoneme in second position. Recognition of phonemes and the elimination of alternative words continues in this fashion until only one word remains. It is at this point that the word is recognized. Figure 9 gives an example illustrating how the cohort model recognizes the word 'elephant.'

The cohort model is easy to describe with respect to the five characteristics in Fig. 7. The model is mediated, categorical, on-line, parallel, and contextually dependent to some extent. Word recognition is mediated by phoneme recognition, phonemes are recognized on-line categorically, words are accessed in parallel, and the word alternative finally recognized can be influenced by context. The primary evidence against the cohort model is that phonemes are not perceptual units and that speech perception is not categorical.

3.3 TRACE Model

The TRACE model of speech perception (McClelland and Elman 1986) is one of a class of models in which information processing occurs through excitatory and inhibitory interactions among a large number of simple processing units. These units are meant to represent the functional properties of neurons or neural networks. Three levels or sizes of units are used in TRACE: feature, phoneme, and word. Features activate phonemes which activate words, and activation of some units at a particular level inhibits other units at the same level. In addition, an important assumption of interactive–activation models is that activation of higher-order units activates their lower-order units; for example, activation of the /b/ phoneme would activate the features that are consistent with that phoneme.

With respect to the characteristics in Fig. 7, the TRACE model is mediated, on-line, somewhat categorical, parallel, and context-dependent. Word recognition is mediated by feature and phoneme recognition. The input is processed on-line in TRACE, all words are activated by the input in parallel, and their activation is context-dependent. In principle, TRACE is continuous, but its assumption about interactive activation leads to categorical-like behavior at the sensory (featural) level. According to the TRACE model, a stimulus pattern is presented

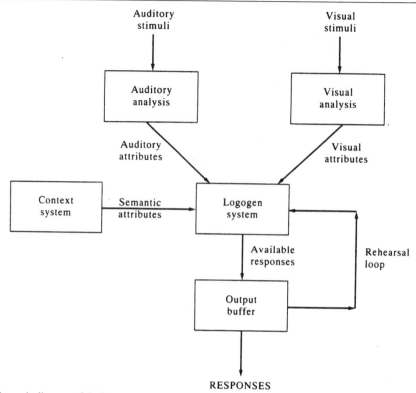

Figure 8. A schematic diagram of the logogen model. Recognition occurs when the activation in a logogen exceeds a critical level and the corresponding word becomes available as a response.

and activation of the corresponding features sends more excitation to some phoneme units than others. Given the assumption of feedback from the phoneme to the feature level, the activation of a particular phoneme feeds down and activates the features corresponding to that phoneme (McClelland and Elman 1986: 47). This effect of feedback produces enhanced sensitivity around a category boundary, exactly as predicted by categorical perception. Evidence against phonemes as perceptual units and against categorical perception is, therefore, evidence against the TRACE model.

3.4 Autonomous-search Model

A fourth model of word recognition is an autonomous-search model of word recognition. The model involves two stages—an initial access stage and a serial-search stage. This model was developed for the recognition of written words rather than for recognizing spoken words. However, advocates of the model have begun to apply its basic assumptions to spoken-word recognition (Bradley and Forster 1987). For ease of presentation, the model will be presented in terms of recognizing a written word.

The first stage in processing a written stimulus is in terms of recognizing the letters that make up a word. The abstract representation of this information serves as an access code to select some subset of the lexicon. The distinctive feature of this model is that words within this subset must be processed serially. The serial order of processing is determined by the frequency of occurrence of the words in the language. After making a match in the search stage of processing, a verification or postsearch check is carried out against the full orthographic properties of the word. If a match is obtained at this stage, the relevant contents of the lexical entry are made available.

The autonomous-search model can be described with respect to the five characteristics in Fig. 7. The model is mediated, categorical, on-line, serial, and contextually independent. Written word recognition is mediated by letter recognition, letters are recognized on-line categorically, and final recognition of a word requires a serial search. All of this processing goes on without any influence from the context at other levels, such as the sentence level. The autonomous-search model appears to fail on at least two counts: categorical perception and contextually independent processing. Evidence for continuous perception has been reviewed and there is convincing evidence for

/ɛ/	/ɛl/	/ɛlə/	/ɛləf/	/ɛləfə/
aesthetic	elbow	elegiac	elephant	elephant
any	elder	elegy	elephantine	
.	eldest	element		(1)
.	eleemosynary	elemental	(2)	
ebony	elegance	elementary		
ebullition	elegiac	elephant		
echelon	elegy	elephantine		
.	element	elevate		
.	elemental	elevation		
economic	elementary	elevator		
ecstasy	elephant	elocution		
.	elephantine	eloquent		
.	elevate			
element	elevation	(12)		
elephant	.			
elevate	.			
.				
.	(28)			
entropy				
entry				
.				
extraneous				
.				
(324)				

Figure 9. Illustration of how the word 'elephant' is recognized, according to the cohort model (Marslen-Wilson 1984). Phonemes are recognized categorically and on-line in a left-to-right fashion as they are spoken. All words inconsistent with the phoneme string are eliminated from the cohort. The number below each column represents the number of words remaining in the cohort set at that point in processing the spoken word. Note that the example is for British pronunciation in which the third vowel of 'elephantine' is pronounced /æ/.

the influence of context in word recognition (see Sect. 4).

3.5 Lexical Access from Spectra Model

Klatt (1979) developed a lexical access from spectra (LAFS) model that bypasses features and segments as intermediate to word recognition. The expected spectral patterns for words and for cross-word boundaries are represented in a large decoding network of expected sequences of spectra. Figure 10 illustrates how each word is first represented phonemically, then all possible pronunciations are determined by phonetic recording rules specifying alternative pronunciations within and across word boundaries, and these phonetic representations are converted to sequences of spectral templates like those shown in Fig. 11. Figure 10 shows a sequence of five static critical-band spectra corresponding to the middle of [t] to the middle of [a].

Central to the LAFS model is the assumption that running spectra fully represent speech and that the differences among spectra can differentiate among the meaningful differences in real speech. With respect to the five characteristics in Fig. 7, the model is mediated,

continuous, on-line, parallel, and contextually independent. A goodness-of-match is determined for each word path based on the running spectra of the speech stimulus. The goodness-of-match provides continuous and not just categorical information. Multiple alternatives can be evaluated in parallel and on-line as the speech signal arrives. Finally, the contextual dependencies built into the representation are phonologically based and, therefore, there is no provision for semantic and syntactic constraints. That is, the contribution of linguistic context is limited to its effects on articulation and, therefore, properties of the speech signal. Constraints over and above this influence are not accounted for in the model. Thus, the model could not easily account for the contribution of linguistic context.

3.6 LAFF Model

Kenneth Stevens has articulated a model describing lexical access via acoustic correlates of linguistic binary phonetic features. These features are language universal and binary (present or absent). Table 1 gives a featural representation of the word 'pawn.'

This model is driven by parsimony in that the features are assumed to be binary and robust. Binary features allow the integration process to by short-circuited in that multiple ambiguous sources of information do not have to be combined. With respect to the five characteristics in Fig. 7, the model is mediated, categorical, delayed, parallel, and contextually independent. A goodness-of-match is determined for each word path based on the distinctive features assembled from the speech input. The goodness-of-match provides just categorical information with respect to each feature. Continuous information could be derived from the number of features that match each word in memory. Multiple alternatives can be evaluated in parallel but the matching process cannot perform reliably until the complete word has been presented. Finally, the contextual dependencies built into the represention are phonologically-based and, therefore, there is no prescribed provision for linguistic constraints.

3.7 Fuzzy Logical Model of Perception

According to the fuzzy logical model of perception (FLMP), well-learned patterns are recognized in accordance with a general algorithm, regardless of the modality or particular nature of the patterns (Massaro 1987). The model has received support in a wide variety of domains and consists of three operations in perceptual (primary) recognition: feature evaluation, feature integration, and decision. Continuously valued features are evaluated, integrated, and matched against prototype descriptions in memory, and an identification decision is made on the basis of the relative goodness of match of the stimulus information with the relevant prototype descriptions.

51

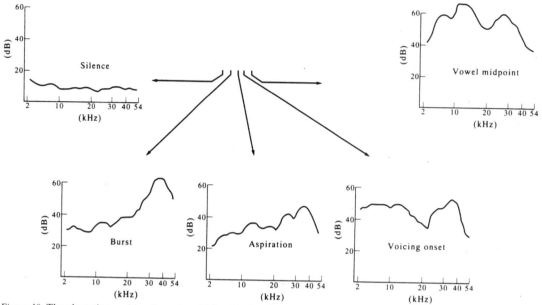

Figure 10. The phonetic transition from the middle of [ta] to the middle of [a] has been approximated by a sequence of five static critical-band spectra (after Klatt 1979).

Step1: Lexical Tree (Phonemic)

Step2: Lexical Network (Phonetic)

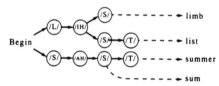

Step3: Lexical access from spectra (Spectral templates)

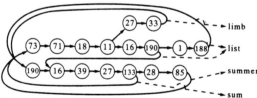

Figure 11. The lexical tree, lexical network, and lexical access from spectra of the LAFS model (after Klatt 1979).

Central to the FLMP are summary description of the perceptual units of the language. These summary descriptions are called prototypes and they contain a conjunction of various properties called features. A prototype is a category and the features of the prototype correspond to the ideal values that an exemplar should have if it is a member of that category. The exact form of the representation of these properties is not known. However, the memory representation must be compatible with the sensory representation resulting from the transduction of the speech. Compatibility is necessary because the two representations must be related to one another. To recognize the syllable /ba/, the perceiver must be able to relate the information provided by the syllable itself to some memory of the category /ba/.

Prototypes are generated for the task at hand. In speech perception, for example, the linguist might envision activation of all prototypes corresponding to the perception units of the language being spoken. For ease of exposition, consider a speech signal representing a single perceptual unit, such as the syllable /ba/. The sensory systems transduce the physical event and make available various sources of information called features. During the first operation in the model, the features are evaluated in terms of the prototypes in memory. For each feature and for each prototype, featural evaluation provides information about the degree to which the feature in the speech signal matches the featural value of the prototype.

Table 1. A conventional lexical representation for the English word 'pawn,' shown at the top, has been modified below to reflect expectations as to the temporal locations within the syllable of acoustic information important to the detection of feature values. In addition, features not specified by a plus or minus are deemed not critical to the lexical decision. (Klatt 1989).

Conventional lexical representation

	p	ɔ	n
high	−	−	−
low	−	+	−
back	−	+	−
nasal	−	−	+
spread glottis	+	−	−
sonorant	−	+	+
voiced	−	+	+
strident	−	−	+
consonantal	+	−	+
coronal	−	−	+
anterior	+	−	+
continuant	−	+	−

Modified lexical representation

	p	ɔ	n
high		−	
low		+	
back		+	
nasal			+
spread glottis		+	
sonorant	−		
voiced	−		
strident			
consonantal	+		+
coronal	−		+
anterior	+		+
continuant	−		−

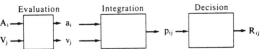

Figure 12. Schematic representation of the three operations involved in perceptual recognition. The three processes are shown in sequence, left to right, to illustrate their necessarily successive, but overlapping, procedures. These processes make use of prototypes stored in long-term memory. The sources of information are represented by uppercase letters. Auditory information is represented by A_i and visual information by V_j. The evaluation process transforms these sources of information into psychological values (indicated by lowercase letters a_i and v_j). These sources are then integrated to give an overall degree of support p_{ij}, for each speech alternative. The decision operation maps the outputs of integration into some response alternative, R_{ij}. The response can take the form of a discrete decision or a rating of the degree to which the alternative is likely.

Given the necessarily large variety of features, it is necessary to have a common metric representing the degree of match of each feature. The syllable /ba/, for example, might have visible featural information related to the closing of the lips and audible information corresponding to the second and third formant transitions. These two features must share a common metric if they eventually are going to be related to one another. To serve this purpose, fuzzy truth values are used because they provide a natural representation of the degree of match. Fuzzy truth values lie between zero and one, corresponding to a proposition being completely false and completely true. The value 0.5 corresponds to a completely ambiguous situation whereas 0.7 would be more true than false and so on. Fuzzy truth values, therefore, not only can represent continuous rather than just categorical information, they also can represent different kinds of information. Another advantage of fuzzy truth values is that they couch information in mathematical terms (or at least in a quantitative form). This allows the natural development of a quantitative description of the phenomenon of interest.

Feature evaluation provides the degree to which each feature in the syllable matches the corresponding feature in each prototype in memory. The goal, of course, is to determine the overall goodness of match of each prototype with the syllable. All of the features are capable of contributing to this process and the second operation of the model is called feature integration. That is, the features (actually the degrees of matches) corresponding to each prototype are combined (or conjoined in logical terms). The outcome of feature integration consists of the degree to which each prototype matches the syllable. In the model, all features contribute to the final value, but with the property that the least ambiguous features have the most impact on the outcome.

The third operation during recognition processing is decision. During this stage, the merit of each relevant prototype is evaluated relative to the sum of the merits of the other relevant prototypes. This relative goodness-of-match gives the proportion of times the syllable is identified as an instance of the prototype. The relative goodness-of-match could also be determined from a rating judgment indicating the degree to which the syllable matches the category. An important prediction of the model is that one feature has its greatest effect when a second feature is at its most ambiguous level. Thus, the most informative feature has the greatest impact on the judgment. Figure 12 illustrates the three stages involved in pattern recognition.

Different sources of information are represented by uppercase letters. The evaluation process transforms these into psychological values (indicated by lowercase letters) that are then integrated to give an overall value. The decision operation maps this value into some response, such as discrete decision or a rating. The model confronts several important issues in describing speech perception. One fundamental claim is that multiple sources of information are evaluated in speech perception. The sources of information are both bottom-up and top-down. Two other assumptions have to do with the evaluation of the multiple sources of information. Continuous information is available from each source and the output of evaluation of one source is not contaminated by the other source. The output of the integration process is also assumed to provide continuous information. With respect to the contrasts in Fig. 7, spoken-word recognition is mediated, continuous, on-line, serial, and parallel, and both autonomous and context-dependent.

The theoretical framework of the FLMP has proven valuable for the study of speech perception. Experiments designed in this framework have provided important information concerning the sources of information in speech perception, and how these sources of information are processed to support speech perception; they have studied a broad range of information sources, including bottom-up sources such as audible and visible characteristics of speech and top-down sources, including phonological, lexical, syntactic, and semantic constraints (Massaro 1987).

Seven models of speech perception and word recognition have been reviewed. All such models have trouble dealing with aspects of speech that are apparently easily dealt with by humans. In short, it is difficult to accommodate the extreme contextual variation in speech. The same acoustic feature is sometimes associated with one phoneme, sometimes another, for example, the voice onset time (VOT) for the voiced stop in the syllable /gi/ is roughly equivalent to the VOT of the voiceless stop in /pa/. On the other hand, the same phoneme has many different acoustic characteristics depending on its context, for example, the formant values for the high front lax vowel /I/ change dramatically when followed by the lateral /l/. Conceivably, human listeners solve this by storing a much larger inventory of phonological units than has previously been entertained, that is, separate prototypes for each V, CV, and VC sequence.

4. Linguistic Context

There is considerable debate concerning how informative the acoustic signal actually is. Even if the acoustic signal is sufficient for speech recognition under ideal conditions, few researchers would believe that the listener relies on only the acoustic signal. It is generally agreed that the listener normally achieves good recognition by supplementing the information from the acoustic signal with information generated through the utilization of linguistic context. A good deal of research has been directed at showing a positive contribution of linguistic context.

4.1 Detecting Mispronunciations

Abstracting meaning is a joint function of the independent contributions of the available perceptual and contextual information. In one experiment, Cole (1973) asked subjects to push a button every time they heard a mispronunciation in a spoken rendering of Lewis Carroll's *Through the Looking Glass*. A mispronunciation involved changing a phoneme by 1, 2, or 4 distinctive features (e.g., 'confusion' mispronounced as *gunfusion, bunfusion,* and *sunfusion,* respectively). The probability of recognizing a mispronunciation increased from 30 to 75 percent with increases in the number of feature changes, which reflects the contribution of the perceptual information passed on by the primary recognition process. The contribution of contextual information should work against the recognition of a mispronunciation since context would support a correct rendering of the mispronounced word. In support of this idea, all mispronunciations were correctly recognized when the syllables were isolated and removed from the passage.

The detection of mispronunciation technique was also used to demonstrate that additional higher-order contextual redundancy is also used in perception, e.g. more accurate detection of mispronunciation in the word 'killer' if a prior sentence included the word 'murder.'

Marslen-Wilson (1973) asked subjects to shadow (repeat back) prose as quickly as they heard it. Some individuals were able to shadow the speech at extremely close delays with lags of 250 msec, about the duration of a syllable or so. One might argue that the shadowing response was simply a sound-to-sound mapping without any higher order semantic–syntactic analyses. When subjects make errors in shadowing, however, the errors are syntactically and semantically appropriate given the preceding context. For example, given the sentence, 'He had heard at the Brigade,' some subjects repeated, 'He had heard that the Brigade.' The nature of the errors did not vary with their latency; the shadowing errors were always well-formed given the preceding context.

The field of speech perception is an area of research rich in both theories and methodologies, and developments in these two domains feed each other. This happens for several reasons: what is valued more than one experimental methodology that yields reliable results relevant to a given theoretical issue is two or more methodologies whose results show convergence. Furthermore, as new methods emerge and yield results new questions arise which often lead to new theories. It is not possible in the space of this chapter to cover all the issues and methods that occupy researchers in this area (see Massaro 1996a). However, a brief case study of the interaction of one particular methodology and certain points of theory may be illustrative.

4.2 Limitations of Results

Perceivers have been shown to be efficient exploiters of different types of context to aid in speech perception. The autonomous-search, the LAFS, and the

LAFF models have difficulty in accounting for the contribution of context because it assumes that speech perception goes on without any help of context. Even these models are not necessarily falsified by the context effects, however, because it can be claimed that the context effects that were observed occurred after speech perception. It might be argued, for example, that the rapid shadowing errors observed by Marslen-Wilson (1973) occurred at the stage of speech production rather than speech perception. Analogous to research in other domains, it is essential to locate the stage of processing responsible for experimental findings. A new task helped address this issue and, more importantly, the results can be used to reveal how stimulus information and context jointly contribute to word recognition.

4.3 Gating Task

In the gating task, portions of the spoken message are eliminated or gated out. In a typical task with single words, only the first 50 msec or so of the word is presented. Successive presentations involve longer and longer portions of the word by increasing the duration of each successive presentation by 20 msec. Subjects attempt to name the word after each presentation. Warren and Marslen-Wilson (1987), for example, presented words such as 'school' or 'scoop.' Figure 13 shows that the probability of correct recognition of a test word increases as additional word information is presented in the gating task.

The gating task appears to have promise for the investigation of speech perception and spoken language understanding. Investigators have worried about two features of the gating task that may limit its external validity. The first potentially controversial feature of the task is that subjects hear multiple presentations of the test word on a given trial. The standard procedure is to present increasingly larger

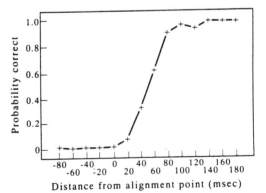

Figure 13. Probability of correct recognition of the test word as a function of the distance from the alignment point in the test word. The alignment point corresponds to a point near the onset of the final consonant of the word (results adapted from Warren and Marslen-Wilson 1987).

fragments of the same word on a given trial. The subject responds after each presentation of the fragment. The repeated presentations of the fragment may enhance recognition of the test word relative to the case in which the subject obtains only a single presentation of an item. In visual form perception, for example, it has been shown that repeated tachistoscopic presentations of a test form lead to correct recognition, even though the duration is not increased as it is in the gating task. The same short presentation of a test form that does not produce correct recognition on its initial presentation can give correct recognition if it is repeated three or four times in the task. This improvement in performance occurs even though the duration of the test stimulus was not increased. These repeated looks at the stimulus can lead to improved performance relative to just a single look. Information from successive presentations can be utilized to improve performance and therefore multiple presentations lead to better performance than just a single presentation. Based on this result, performance in the gating task might reflect repeated presentations of the test word, in addition to the fact that the successive presentations increased in duration.

The standard multiple presentation format has been compared with the format in which subjects heard only a single fragment from each word in the task. Similar results were found in both conditions. A similar study found that the average duration of the test word needed for correct identification was only 5 msec less in the task with multiple presentations on a trial than for a single presentation of the test word. Thus, using successive presentations in the gating task appears to be a valid method to increase the duration of the test word to assess its influence on recognition.

A second question concerning gating tasks has to do with how quickly subjects are required to respond in the task. It could be the case that subjects, given unlimited time to respond in the task, will perform differently from their performance in the on-line recognition of continuous speech. That is, the gating task might be treated as a conscious problem-solving task in which subjects are very deliberate in making their decision about what word was presented. This deliberation would not be possible in a typical situation involving continuous speech and, therefore, the results might be misleading. To assess performance under more realistic conditions, Tyler and Wessels employed a naming response in the gating task. Subjects were required to name the test word as quickly as possible on each trial. In addition, a given word was presented only once to a given subject. The results from this task were very similar to the standard gating test. The durations of the test words needed for correct recognition were roughly the same as that found in the standard gating task. Thus, the experiments exploring the external validity of the gating task have been very encouraging. The results appear to be generalizable to the on-line recognition of continuous speech.

4.4 Integrating Sentential Context

Tyler and Wessels (1983) used the gating paradigm to assess the contribution of various forms of sentential context to word recognition. Subjects heard a sentence followed by the beginning of the test word (with the rest of the word gated out). The word was increased in duration by adding small segments of the word until correct recognition was achieved. The sentence contexts varied in syntactic and semantic constraints. Some sentence contexts had minimal semantic constraints in that the target word was not predictable in a test given the sentence context and the first 100 msec of the target word. Performance in this condition can be compared to a control condition in which no sentential constraints were present. The experimental question is whether context contributes to recognition of the test word.

Figure 14 gives the probability of correct word recognition as a function of the number of segments in the test word and the context condition. Both variables had a significant influence on performance. In addition, the interaction between the two variables reveals how word information and context jointly influence word recognition. Context influences performance most at intermediate levels of word information. The contribution of context is most apparent when there is some but not complete information about the test word. The lines in Fig. 14 give the predictions of the FLMP which describes word recognition in terms of the evaluation and integration of word information and sentential context followed by a decision based on the outcome. As can be seen in the figure, the model captures the exact form of the integration of the two sources of information.

A positive effect of sentence context in this situation is very impressive because it illustrates a true integration of word and context information. The probability of correct recognition is zero when context is given with minimum word information. Similarly, the probability of correct recognition is zero with three segments of the test word presented without context. That is, neither the context alone nor the limited word information permits word recognition; however, when presented jointly, word recognition is very good. Thus, the strong effect of minimum semantic context illustrated in Fig. 14 can be considered to reflect true integration of word and contextual sources of information.

The form of the interaction of stimulus information and context is relevant to the prediction of the cohort model, which assumes that some minimum cohort set must be established on the basis of stimulus information before context can have an influence. In terms of FLMP description, this assumption implies that the evaluation of context should change across different

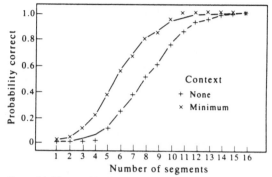

Figure 14. Observed (points) and predicted (lines) probability of identifying the test word correctly as a function of the sentential context and the number of segments of the test word. The minimum context refers to minimum semantic and weak syntactic constraints. The none context refers to no semantic and weak syntactic constraints (after Tyler and Wessels 1983).

levels of gating. To test this hypothesis, another model was fit to the results. In this model, context was assumed to have an influence only after some minimum gating interval. Because it is not known what this minimum interval should be, an additional free parameter was estimated to converge on the interval that gave the best description of the observed results. This model did not improve the description of the results, weakening the claim that context has its influence only after some minimum stimulus information has been processed. This result is another instance of the general finding that there are no discrete points in psychological processing. The system does not seem to work one way at one point in time (i.e., no effect of context), and another way in another point in time (i.e., an effect of context).

The functional account of speech perception should continue to be the goal for speech research in the new millenium. It has been seen how perceivers have continuous rather than categorical information from the speech signal in speech perception. There is also good evidence that both the speech signal and the linguistic and contextual context influence speech perception. Given these multiple influences, speech perception necessarily involves the evaluation and integration of a variety of somewhat ambiguous information sources. A decision process is also required to use the outcome of these processes in an optimal fashion. The nature and dynamics of these processes offer an immediate challenge to researchers and students.

Bibliography

Barclay J R 1972 Non-categorical perception of a voiced stop: A replication. *Perception and Psychophysics* **11**: 269–73

Bradley D C, Forster K I 1987 In: Frauenfelder U H, Tyler

L K (eds.) *Spoken Word Recognition*. MIT Press, Cambridge, MA

Cole R A 1973 Listening for mispronunciations: A measure of what we hear during speech. *Perception and Psychophysics* 13: 153–56

Klatt D H 1979 Speech perception: A model of acoustic–phonetic analysis and lexical access. *Journal of Phonetics* 7: 279–312

Klatt D H 1989 Review of selected models of speech perception. In: Marslen-Wilson W D (ed.) *Lexical Representation and Process*. MIT Press, Cambridge, MA

Liberman A L, Harris K S, Hoffman H S, Griffith B C 1957 The discrimination of speech sounds within and across phoneme boundaries. *Journal of Experimental Psychology* 54: 358–68

Marslen-Wilson W D 1973 Linguistic structure and speech shadowing at very short latencies. *Nature* 244: 522–23

Marslen-Wilson W D 1984 Function and process in spoken word-recognition. In: Bouma H, Bouwhuis D G (eds.) *Attention and Performance. Vol. X: Control of Language Processes*. Lawrence Erlbaum, Hillsdale, NJ

Marslen-Wilson W D 1987 Functional parallelism in spoken word recognition. In: Frauenfelder U H, Tyler L K (eds.) *Spoken Word Recognition*. MIT Press, Cambridge, MA

Massaro D (ed.) 1975 *Understanding Language. An Information-processing Analysis of Speech Perception, Reading, and Psycholinguistics*. Academic Press, New York

Massaro D W 1987 *Speech Perception by Ear and Eye: A Paradigm for Psychological Inquiry*. Lawrence Erlbaum, Hillsdale, NJ

Massaro D W 1996 Modelling multiple influences in speech perception. In: Dijkstra T, De Smedt K (eds.) *Computational Psycholinguistics*. Taylor and Francis Ltd, London

Massaro D W 1996a Integration of multiple sources of information in language processing. In: Inui T, McClelland J L (eds.) *Attention and Performance XVI: Information Integration in Perception and Communication*. MIT Press, Cambridge, MA

Massaro D W 1998 *Perceiving Talking Faces: From Speech Perception to a Behavioral Principle*. MIT Press, Cambridge, MA

Massaro D W, Loftus F 1996b Sensory and perceptual storage: Data and theory. In: Bjork E L, Bjork R A (eds.) *Memory, Vol. 10: Handbook of Perception and Cognition*. Academic Press, San Diego

McClelland J L, Elman J L 1986 The TRACE model of speech perception. *Cognitive Psychology* 18: 1–86

Morton J A 1964 A preliminary functional model for language behavior. *International Audiology* 3: 216–25

Newman C W, Spitzer J B 1987 Monotic and dichotic presentation of phonemic elements in a backward recognition-masking paradigm. *Psychological Research* 49: 31–36

Pisoni D B, Lazarus J H 1974 Categorical and noncategorical modes of speech perception along the voicing continuum. *Journal of the Acoustical Society of America* 55: 328–33

Tyler L K, Wessels J 1983 Quantifying contextual contributions to word-recognition processes. *Perception and Psychophysics* 34: 409–20

Warren P, Marslen-Wilson W D 1987 Continuous uptake of acoustic cues in spoken word recognition. *Perception and Psychophysics* 41: 262–75

Functional and Clinical Anatomy of the Speech Mechanism

J. C. Kahane

The speech mechanism is not a single entity, and not located in a circumscribed area of the body. It is composed of several organs in the head and neck and a diversity of tissues which are integrated with the body's major systems. Amazingly, none of these organs is specifically designed for sound or speech production. Rather, they have very well-defined functions serving primary biological and life-sustaining functions.

The speech mechanism is driven by aerodynamic forces developed in the respiratory system. This raw energy is modified, modulated, and routed within the upper airways by passive displacements of tissues and by active occlusions and shaping of the muscular walls and cavities of the upper airway and oral cavity (i.e., the vocal tract). Resultant speech movements are planned and controlled by the nervous system and provide the vehicle for actualizing thought processes and creative expressions.

Control centers in the cerebral cortex and the brain stem program speech movements and voicing instructions. These are carried to other integration centers in the cerebral hemispheres and brain stem by motor tracts whose messages may be acted on by other components of the central nervous system responsible for coordinating motor activities or integrating sensory feedback from the organs being used in speech.

These instructions ultimately reach the organs of the speech mechanism by nerves which originate in the brain stem (cranial nerves) or the spinal cord (spinal nerves). This neural processing and integration results in coordinated movements whose force and timing are appropriate for the predetermined speech and voice tasks. All the structures in the peripheral speech mechanism located in the head and neck region are supplied by cranial nerves. The muscles of the respiratory system are supplied by thoracic nerves from the spinal cord. The specific innervation to structures in the peripheral speech mechanism is described in this chapter, which reviews the anatomy and physiology of the speech mechanism in an attempt to describe the salient functional relationships underlying voice and speech production.

1. General Plan of the Peripheral Speech Mechanism

Fig. 1 illustrates the major components of the peripheral speech mechanism. Speech is the product of the interaction of the respiratory, laryngeal, and supralaryngeal areas. The airways above the vocal folds extending to the lips make up the vocal tract. The respiratory system serves as the power source which activates the larynx. The larynx serves as a tone generator and produces raw energy used in speech production. The energy produced by the vocal folds is transmitted upward into the air-filled cavities of the pharynx, oral cavity, and in some cases the nasal cavity. It is modified by the resonatory properties of these supralaryngeal cavities, whose size and shape is modified through movements of the articulators (tongue, velopharyngeal mechanism, lips, mandible, and teeth). Active movements and passive displacements of the articulators create constrictions and obstructions to airflow, essential to producing distinctive acoustic features of many classes of sounds.

Detailed descriptions of the structures of the peripheral speech mechanism follow. They are presented in the order in which they participate in the production of the aerodynamic events in speech and voice production.

2. The Respiratory System

2.1 Function

Functionally, the respiratory system serves as an air reservoir and bellows during speech production. It captures air and then pushes it through the lower airways and the larynx, in the process setting the vocal folds into vibration if they are appropriately configured. This action in turn imparts acoustic energy to the air in the vocal tract and drives the expiratory airflow into the upper airways of the tract. The vegetative function of the respiratory system, of course, is the exchange of oxygen and carbon dioxide.

2.2 Morphology

Anatomically, the respiratory system is conventionally divided into an upper and lower respiratory tract. The upper respiratory tract consists of the nasal cavities, oral cavity, pharynx, and larynx. The lower respiratory tract consists of the trachea, all the airways within the lungs, and the lungs themselves (see Fig. 2). Upon entering the chest, the trachea divides into two branches, the 'bronchi' (singular bronchus), which enter each lung. There, it undergoes repeated bifurcations, forming progressively greater numbers of smaller-diameter tubules called 'bronchi-

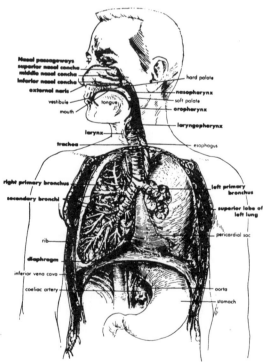

Figure 2. The upper and lower respiratory tracts with the lungs partially dissected to illustrate the branching of the bronchi and bronchioles. (From J. Crouch 1985 *Functional Human Anatomy*, 4th edn. Lea and Febiger, Philadelphia)

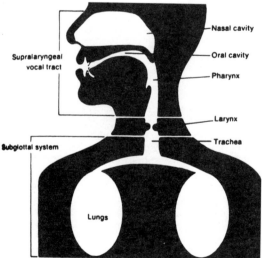

Figure 1. Schematic of the peripheral speech mechanism. (From P. Lieberman 1977 *Speech Physiology and Acoustic Phonetics: An Introduction.* Macmillan, New York)

oles,' which end in hundreds of thousands of clusters of thin-walled, grapelike structures called 'alveoli,' where oxygen and carbon dioxide exchange occurs.

2.2.1 The lungs

The lungs are two distensible, cone-shaped structures which are located in the chest cavity or thorax. They nearly fill the entire cavity and are surrounded by the ribcage anterolaterally, the vertebral column posteriorly, and by the diaphragm inferiorly. The lungs are interconnected with the inner surface of the ribcage and the diaphragm by fibroelastic membranes (pleural membranes) which place both the lungs and the bony thoracic skeleton into a state of dynamic equilibrium. In this condition, the lungs are slightly stretched and the ribcage is slightly compressed. This is called 'pleural linkage,' and it provides (a) an important nonmuscular restorative (recoil) force used in breathing and (b) a mechanical means to insure that the chest wall (muscles and ribs of the thorax) and the lungs function as a single unit. Thus, as the thoracic cavity is enlarged, the lungs become stretched, and vice versa.

2.2.2 Ribcage and muscles

The lungs are housed within a bony thorax composed of 12 pairs of ribs which are joined anteriorly by cartilagenous attachment to the sternum and posteriorly to the vertebrae of the spinal column. Small muscles between the ribs (internal and external intercostals) help to maintain the space between them and are also important in helping to raise and lower the ribs during breathing. Owing to their curved shape, movements of the ribs result in changes in the anteroposterior and transverse dimensions of the thorax. These muscles are assisted by others which attach to the ribcage (Fig. 3). The 'respiratory muscles' are functionally divided into inspiratory and expiratory groups. They are innervated by thoracic nerves from the spinal cord. The 'inspiratory muscles' work to expand the thorax and thus facilitate the development of more negative intrathoracic pressure which favors the inward flow of air into the lungs. The primary inspiratory muscle is the diaphragm, followed by the external intercostals. Expiratory muscles (internal intercostals and the abdominal rectus, internal and external abdominal oblique, and the transverse abdominal muscle) work to decrease the size of the thorax by lowering the ribs, which increases intrathoracic pressure and causes an outward flow of air from the lungs into the trachea and ultimately the upper airways. This airflow is referred to as the 'expiratory drive,' which is the activating force in the speech mechanism.

2.3 Respiratory Function during Speech

Although the lungs are filled with air before speech is initiated, they are usually inflated to only about 65

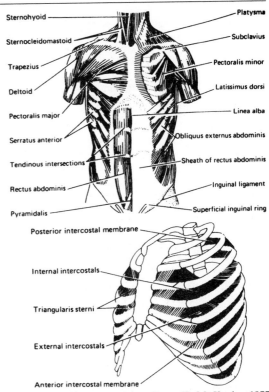

Figure 3. Respiratory muscles. (From H. M. Kaplan 1977 *Anatomy and Physiology of Speech*, 2nd edn. Macmillan, New York)

percent of their capacity. Speech is produced in the range of 30–65 percent of the individual's total capacity of the lung. This is highly efficient for most conversational speech, because at this level of lung inflation only small amounts of muscular force have to be added to the available recoil force in order to generate an adequate level of subglottic pressure (5 cm/H_2O pressure) needed to produce speech. Using a louder voice requires the use of higher lung volumes, greater control of recoil forces, and the development of greater subglottic pressure.

2.4 Differences between Nonspeech and Speech Breathing

The purpose of respiration for speech is different from breathing for life-sustaining purposes. For life, the objective is to move oxygen-saturated air into the lungs and to take carbon dioxide out of them. In speech, the need for the respiratory system is to provide adequate and controlled airflow under constant pressure to activate the speech mechanism. Other differences include the following. In quiet breathing, the duration of inspiration is nearly equal to expiration (4:6 ratio), while in speech, inspiration is very short relative to expiration (1:9 ratio), so as to minimize interruption in speech and to allow for the maximal use of expiratory volume on which to speak. In quiet breathing, small volumes of air are used, whereas in speech, significantly larger volumes are used. In quiet breathing, there is no need to control subglottic pressure, while in speech breathing, steady levels of subglottic pressure are needed to provide controlled drive to the larynx and the rest of the speech mechanism.

In summary, the respiratory system provides several essential functions during speech production which include supplying adequate subglottic pressure to activate the vocal folds and to drive the speech mechanism; providing a mechanism capable of rapid replenishment of air during speech; and providing sufficient means to increase subglottic pressure for necessary adjustments in loudness and possibly for some other prosodic features of speech.

2.5 Clinical Implications

Pathology of the lungs and thoracic cavity, particularly the mediastinum, can also affect vocal functioning by compression and damage to the recurrent laryngeal nerve. In addition, swallowing dysfunction may occur because of laryngeal deficits and compromise to the esophagus.

Respiratory dysfunction is likely to have negative consequences on speech and voice as well as breathing. Several sources for these problems include: (a) spinal cord injuries which may result in weakness of chest wall muscles and the diaphragm; (b) congenital malformations of the rib cage and vertebral column; and (c) diseases of the airway such as asthma, chronic obstructive pulmonary disease, and emphysema. These conditions affect the ability of the individual to obtain maximal vital capacity, exert control of expiratory drive, and or develop adequate amounts of subglottal pressure needed during sustained speech and voice production.

3. The Larynx

The larynx serves as the principal sound generator in the speech mechanism. It provides raw energy which is acted upon by the resonatory cavities in the vocal tract and by the articulators, whose movements modify the size of the vocal tract and modulate or pattern the pressures and air-flow used to create the acoustic properties of the speech output.

3.1 Morphology

The larynx is composed of a cartilagenous skeleton protecting a membraneously lined cavity which is a continuation of the respiratory tract. Small muscles attach to the laryngeal cartilages and move them, resulting in changes in airway resistance and vocal-fold dynamics during voice production. These anatomical features and the ways in which they contribute to vocal functioning are discussed below.

3.2 Laryngeal Skeleton

The larynx is a prominent structure in the anterior aspect of the neck, particularly in the male, where its larger size and more acutely angled thyroid cartilage make it noticeable. The larynx is situated in the lowest portion of the pharynx, with the hyoid bone above and the trachea below it (Fig. 2). The location of the larynx places it at the junction of the upper and lower respiratory tracts and thus makes it a conduit for airflow into and out of the lungs. Protection of this airway during swallowing is essential and is facilitated by the attachment of the larynx to the hyoid bone. This U-shaped bone, located between the base of the tongue and the larynx, is acted upon by the tongue and the muscles of the jaw and neck. Such actions passively move the larynx into an elevated and protected position, beneath the base of the tongue during swallowing.

The larynx is composed of a cartilagenous skeleton, a membraneous internal cavity, and intrinsic musculature. The laryngeal skeleton is composed of five cartilages which encircle the laryngeal airway (laryngeal cavity) and provide attachment for the vocal folds and the muscles which influence them. These cartilages are the 'thyroid,' 'cricoid,' 'paired arytenoids,' and the 'epiglottis' (Fig. 4). The epiglottis is the most flexible of the cartilages, and closes over the entrance to the laryngeal cavity. This is thought to provide partial protection against penetration of food and liquid into the laryngeal airway. (The principal means of keeping food and drink from the lower respiratory tract is a sphincteric closing of the laryngeal opening and the moving of the larynx up and forward in the throat.) The laryngeal cartilages are able to move as a result of action occurring at synovial joints.

The cricoid and thyroid cartilages are joined at the 'cricothyroid joint,' which allows the cricoid cartilage to rotate with respect to the thyroid. Since the vocal cords are attached anteriorly to the inside face of the thyroid cartilage and posteriorly to the arytenoid cartilages, which in turn are attached to the upper posterior rim of the cricoid, this rotation can effect lengthening or shortening of the vocal cords, with concomitant changes in tension. Such changes in tension are the principal method of changing the rate of vibration of the vocal cords. Rocking motions of the arytenoid cartilages on the upper rim of the cricoid cartilages allow the arytenoids and the attached vocal folds to move inward or outward and thus to control the airflow, including that required for voicing.

3.3 Laryngeal Muscles

Both extrinsic and intrinsic muscles act on the larynx, and are illustrated in Figs. 5 and 8. The extrinsic and intrinsic muscles are innervated from different sources. The extrinsic laryngeal muscles are innervated from cervical nerves of the spinal cord, while the intrinsic laryngeal muscles are supplied by the vagus

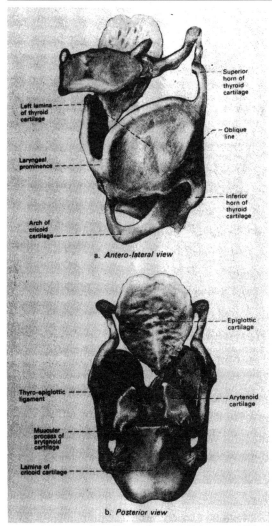

Figure 4. Laryngeal cartilages. (From S. Zukerman 1981 *A New System of Anatomy: A Dissector's Guide*, 2nd edn. Oxford University Press, New York)

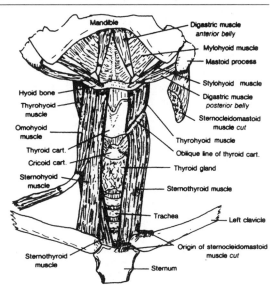

Figure 5. Extrinsic muscles of the larynx. (From H. Bateman, R. Mason 1984 *Applied Anatomy and Physiology of the Speech and Hearing Mechanism*. Charles C. Thomas, Springfield, IL)

nerve (cranial nerve 10). The extrinsic muscles (e.g., sternothyroid and thyrohyoid) are principally involved with the vertical positioning and transport of the larynx in the neck. The sternothyroid and thyrohyoid muscles have been found to be most involved in the vertical positioning of the larynx in the neck during pitch changes. In contrast, intrinsic laryngeal muscles (cricothyroid, lateral cricoarytenoid, thyroarytenoid, interarytenoid, posterior cricoarytenoid) perform discrete functions within the larynx (Fig. 8). These include movements of the cartilages, drawing the vocal folds toward (adduction) and away from (abduction) the midline, transiently changing the length, tension, and mass/unit area of the vocal folds,

and regulating the degree of glottal resistance and thereby the airflow and air pressure through the larynx and vocal tract. These roles are important for respiration, sphincteric closure, and voice functioning. The intrinsic laryngeal muscles are functionally divided into three groups: 'abductors' (posterior cricoarytenoid), 'adductors' (lateral cricoarytenoid, interarytenoid), 'tensors' (cricothyroid and thyroarytenoid vocalis fibers).

Innervation of the larynx is unique in that it comes from two branches (each paired) of the vagus nerve (cranial nerve 10), each of which is located distantly from each other. The upper branch—superior laryngeal nerve—is given off high in the neck, while the lower branch—recurrent or inferior laryngeal nerve—is given off in the root of the neck on the right side and in the mediastinum of the chest, on the left. The superior laryngeal nerve supplies the upper half of the larynx with sensory input and innervates the cricothyroid muscle. The recurrent laryngeal nerve, reaches the larynx through a groove between the trachea and the esophagus (tracheo-esophageal groove) and supplies the lower half with sensory input and all of the intrinsic laryngeal muscles except cricothyroid.

3.4 The Vocal Folds

The vocal folds are not simply longitudinally coursing elastic or muscular bands. Rather, they are multilayered structures composed of a thin epithelium which covers three layers of connective tissue (lamina propria), which in turn covers the muscular portion of the vocal folds formed by the vocalis muscle (a portion of the thyroarytenoid muscle). The epithelium and immediately adjacent connective tissue layer are functionally called the 'cover,' which is the most mobile portion of the vocal folds. The intermediate and deep layers of the lamina propria form the vocal ligament or transition, which provides longitudinal stability to the vocal folds during vibration. The vocalis muscle forms the 'body' of the vocal folds and is responsible for making fine adjustments in the longitudinal tension of the vocal folds and changes in the cover. These have differential effects on the rate of vibration of the vocal folds and therefore on pitch.

3.5 Function during Voicing

Muscular adjustments affecting the vocal folds influence the critically important movement of the cover of the vocal folds. This movement, initiated by expiratory flow, is called the 'mucosal wave.' Its dynamism is essential for imparting acoustic energy to the airstream as it passes between the vocal folds during voice production.

Vocal fold vibration occurs in a quasi-periodic fashion, thus possessing some variability and irregularity between successive glottal cycles. This cycle-to-cycle variability in fo is called frequency perturbation (or vocal jitter) and is closely associated with roughness in voice quality. Cycle-to-cycle variability in amplitude is called amplitude perturbation (or vocal shimmer) and is believed to reflect the regularity of glottal airway dynamics. Excessive vocal shimmer seems to be tied to a 'noisy' quality in voice, but the roughness or hoarseness may differ from those associated with elevated levels of jitter.

The average range of the human voice is three octaves. However, this range has been described in terms of distinct, nearly nonoverlapping ranges of consecutive frequencies, that can be produced with perceptually distinct vocal quality. These are known as *vocal registers*. Each register differs from the other on the basis of laryngeal mechanics, vibratory pattern, and mean phonatory airflow. From lowest to highest, the three vocal registers are pulse (fry), modal (chest), and loft (falsetto).

The laryngeal muscles contribute to voice production in several ways. First, the lateral cricoarytenoid and interarytenoid approach the vocal folds closely enough for the aeromechanical forces, notably the Bernouilli force, to come into play and set them into vibration. Second, the cricothyroid, sometimes aided by the vocalis muscle, can change the fundamental frequency of the vocal folds' vibration by altering their length and thus their tension and mass/unit area. Third, the adductory muscles (lateral cricoarytenoid and approximate) approach the vocal folds and thus influence the loudness of voice by increasing the resistance to airflow, thus increasing the subglottic pressure. This increase in the pressure drop across the glottis causes the vocal folds to vibrate

with greater force and amplitude. Fourth, various laryngeal muscles (lateral cricoarytenoid, interarytenoid, cricothyroid, and the vocalis fibers of the thyroarytenoid) work differentially during speech to produce voiced/voiceless distinctions (including voiceless aspiration), different voice qualities, for example, breathy voice and tense voice, and the complete glottal closure which figures in the production of glottal stop ? and ejectives.

3.6 Clinical Considerations

The larynx, though essential for phonation, is principally a respiratory organ. As such, dysphonias are frequently accompanied by decompensation of laryngeal function such as ineffective protection of the airway (aspiration) or compromise of the glottis causing breathing difficulties (dyspnea).

Dysphonia may result from misuse, abuse, or abnormal amounts of muscle tension within the larynx or because of lesions on the vocal folds. Most of these involve the cover, particularly the superficial layer of the lamina propria (Reinke's space). Though trauma to the vagus nerve is the principal source of vocal fold and intrinsic laryngeal muscle deficiencies, dysphonia may also be caused by an autoimmune disease called myasthenia gravis. In this disorder, laryngeal muscle weakness results from the inability of the muscles to utilize the transmitter substance, acetylcholine. The nerve and the muscle are otherwise normal. Tumors affecting the vagus nerve can create dysfunction in voicing, usually accompanied by hoarseness or breathiness. Tumors in the mediastinum, esophagus, and thyroid gland can cause dysphonia because of their encroachment on the recurrent laryngeal nerve along its course towards the larynx.

4. The Pharynx

The pharynx connects the oral and nasal cavities with the esophagus. It is important in breathing, swallowing, and speaking.

4.1 Functional Morphology

The pharynx is a muscular walled cavity which extends from the base of the skull to the esophagus (Fig. 9). It has an inverted cone shape which is divided into upper, middle, and lower portions. The upper portion, or nasopharynx, communicates with the nasal cavities and is primarily involved with respiratory function. The rest of the pharynx serves both respiratory and swallowing functions. The middle portion, or oropharynx, communicates with the oral cavity. The lower portion, the laryngopharynx or hypopharynx, communicates with the larynx and the esophagus.

The naso and oropharynx contain a discontinuous ring of lymphatic tissues, called Waldeyer's ring, composed of the pharyngeal tonsils (adenoids), palatine tonsils, and lingual tonsils. These lymphatic tissues provide significant immunologic benefit.

Of particular importance in the nasopharynx is the torus tubarius, a C-shaped cartilage which surrounds the opening (nasopharyngeal orifice) of the Eustachian tube. The latter connects the nasopharynx with the middle ear cavity, and serves as a mechanism for equalization of ambient pressures, drainage, and aeration of the middle ear space.

The pharynx is primarily composed of three U-shaped muscles called the 'pharyngeal constrictors.' These are innervated by the pharyngeal plexus (cranial nerves 9–10), whose neurons are carried through the vagus nerve (cranial nerve 10).

The pharyngeal cavities also form the *vocal tract*, a series of cavities through which the glottal source spectrum is modified by selective amplification, via a process called the *transfer function*. Acoustic regions of energy enhancement are called *formant regions*, which are significant for vowel productions. These are supplemented by oblique or vertically coursing muscles which arise from several areas of the base of the skull and also the soft palate. The principal functions of the pharyngeal muscles are to maintain the patency of the upper airway and to provide a muscular driving force, called pharyngeal 'peristalsis,' to transport food through the pharynx into the esophagus.

4.2 Functions during Speech

The activity of the pharyngeal muscles in speech is not as well studied as other muscle groups. However, the muscles of the upper pharynx may be involved in regulating the velopharyngeal port (see Sect. 7), and those of the middle and lower pharynx may play a role in making the pharyngeal constrictions which are part of pharyngeal and pharyngealized consonants, such as Arabic $\mathcal{S}$ and ħ, and vowels which have a marked pharyngeal constriction, such as ɒ and ɔ. Pharyngeal expansion has been observed during the production of voiced stops; this reduces to some extent the build-up of oral pressure and thus facilitates the continuance of the glottal airflow needed to maintain voicing. The absence of this expansion during voiceless stops, presumably to exploit the oral pressure build-up and ensure voicelessness, may be supported by contraction of the pharyngeal muscles.

4.3 Clinical Considerations

Impairments of the pharyngeal musculature, because of skull base tumors or malignancies of the neck, may impair swallowing, create airway obstruction, and adversely affect speech quality. Thus, an early presenting symptom of a nonlaryngeal malignancy may be dysphonia, because of the intimate relationship that the larynx shares with the pharyngeal cavity.

5. Nasal Cavity

The nasal cavity is a passageway which interconnects the ambient environment with the nasopharynx. It serves as a principal route for air exchange and conditioning (warming, moisturing, humidification, and cleaning) of the inspiratory airflow, due to its unique morphology.

5.1 Morphology

The nasal cavity is a triangular-shaped area between the roof of the mouth (hard palate) and the base of the skull (Fig. 6). It is divided into two passageways by the nasal septum, which is composed of two bones and a plate of cartilage. Three pairs of curled bones (turbinates or conchae) intrude into each nasal chamber. The turbinates are lined with respiratory epithelium which is well vascularized and which warms the inspired air. This epithelium contains mucous-secreting cells which create a mucous blanket to entrap particulate matter, and with the aid of hair-like projections called cilia, move the entrapped material out of the nasal cavity into the pharynx. In addition to this filtering function, the epithelium also moisturizes and humidifies airflow, which aids in oxygen transport across the alveolar cell membrane in the lung. The orientation of the turbinates in the nasal cavity facilitates the direction of airflow into and out of the nasal cavity. This flow pattern facilitates the sense of smell and the aforementioned air-conditioning processes.

The size of the nasopharynx is unmodifiable, although its communication with the rest of the vocal tract is regulated by the valving actions of the velopharyngeal mechanism.

5.2 Functions during Speech

The nasal cavity is important in speech because of its contribution to resonance during nasal consonant production. A significant amount of the acoustic energy that passes into the nasal cavity is absorbed by the mucosally thickened surfaces and walls of the cavity. Unlike the other articulators, the nasal cavity does not actively modify pressure and flow during speech. However, deficiencies in velopharyngeal valving, such as cleft palate, couple the nasal cavity with the rest of the vocal tract and result in acoustic distortions of vowels (hypernasality) and diminution of the pressure and flow characteristics of many consonants.

5.3 Clinical Considerations

Abnormalities of the internal nose can have a negative effect on speech production and quality. For example, a deviated nasal septum or nasal obstruction may narrow the nasal passageway and increase nasal resistance which may reduce normal nasal resonance causing hyponasality. In addition, nasal obstruction can influence oral structure and tongue posturing by forcing a person to become a mouth breather. Such individuals have a tendency to carry the tongue forward, have drying of the oral mucosa, difficulties in managing salivary secretions, and may develop reduced

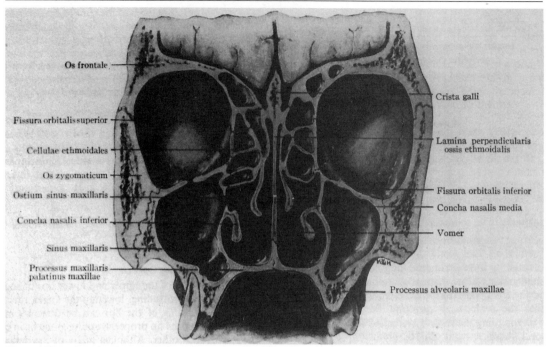

Figure 6. Frontal section through the head illustrating the anatomy of the orbits, paranasal sinuses, and nasal cavities. (From C. L. Callander 1939 *Surgical Anatomy*, 2nd edn. W. B. Saunders, Philadelphia)

tonus in the circumoral musculature. Speech may be adversely affected by interdentalization of fricatives which may lead to lisping and to dentalization of lingua-alveolars.

6. Oral Cavity

The oral cavity is involved in a number of important biological activities, one of which is preparing food to be swallowed (chewing and forming food into a bolus). The oral cavity is also important for respiration, oral resonance during speech, and providing the environment for articulation of the sounds of speech.

6.1 General Morphology

The oral cavity proper is the area enclosed by the dental arches (Fig. 7). The anterior boundary is the lips, the lateral boundary is the cheeks, the superior boundary is the hard and soft palates, the inferior boundary is the floor of the mouth, and the posterior boundary is the glossopalatine arch (anterior faucial pillar). The tongue, although not a part of the oral cavity proper, is its most prominent structure. The oral cavity is lined by several types of epithelia which protect against the abrasive forces encountered during chewing and preparation of food for swallowing. The oral cavity mucosa is kept moistened by secretions from the salivary glands (parotid, submandibular, and sublingual) which are delivered into the oral cavity. Saliva protects the mucosal surfaces against wear and

tear and enables the tongue to move freely across mucosal surfaces during speech, mastication, and swallowing. The epithelia of the oral cavity are richly innervated by the trigeminal nerve (cranial nerve 5).

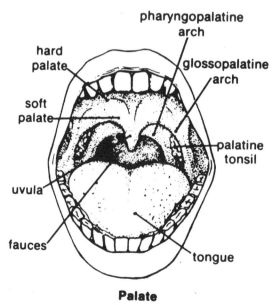

Figure 7. Schematic of oral cavity.

The teeth are housed in the alveolar processes of the upper (maxilla) and lower (mandible) jaws. The alveolar ridge, an important landmark for many speech articulations, is a C-shaped ridge that extends along the front and both sides of the hard palate. Functionally, it is a portion of the maxilla that has been thickened and reinforced so that it can support the upper teeth and the strong shearing forces to which they are subjected. The size of the oral cavity is changed by movements of the lower jaw. These changes are important for articulation and modification of vocal-tract resonance.

6.2 Functions during Speech

The mouth is the most movable and adjustable part of the vocal tract. The movements of the mandible are particularly important for the modifications of the shape and size of the oral cavity during speech production. The role of the movements of the mandible in speech is discussed further in Sect. 9.

6.3 Clinical Considerations

Significant clinical problems affecting the oral cavity proper may involve occlusion (the alignment of the upper and lower dental arches), dentition, and the architecture of the hard palate. Malocclusions or deviations in alignment of the dental arches can result from several sources. These include: heredity, congenital defects, abnormal sucking, thumb and finger sucking, tongue thrusting, abnormal swallowing habits, and from abnormal respiratory patterns (mouth breathing) and resultant compensatory positioning of the tongue caused by enlarged adenoids or palatine tonsils.

The position of individual teeth may be affected by tongue pressures and muscle forces from the lips and cheeks.

Congenital abnormalities, such as cleft palate and submucous clefts, will affect the architecture of the oral cavity, dental arches, and allow for abnormal communication with the nasal cavity. Because the oral and nasal cavities are in direct communication in a person with cleft palate, food may enter the nasal cavity creating bacterial infection. This may spread to the sinus cavities and middle ear, by way of the Eustachian tube, resulting in the development of chronic ear infection (otitis media). In addition, speech is likely to be adversely affected by loss of airflow, abnormal resonance, and maladaptive tongue posturing.

7. Velopharyngeal Mechanism

The velopharyngeal mechanism is important in helping to build up intraoral pressures for speech, blowing, and sucking. It also serves the important functions of not allowing food and liquids to enter (reflux) the nasal cavity, and is an articulator during speech.

7.1 Functional Morphology

The oropharynx and nasopharynx are interconnected by a narrow passageway bounded by the soft palate anteriorly, and the pharyngeal walls laterally and posteriorly. This passageway is called the 'nasopharyngeal portal.' It is valved by the coordinated movements of the soft palate ('velum') and the walls of the nasopharynx. This mechanism is referred to as the velopharyngeal mechanism, and the action of closing off the oral cavity from the nasal cavity is called 'velopharyngeal closure' or 'palatopharyngeal closure.' It is achieved most frequently by posterior–superior movement of the velum and medial movements of the lateral pharyngeal walls (Fig. 10, top). Several different closure patterns have been identified in normal functioning. They differ from each other based on the extent of velar and pharyngeal wall contributions.

These various valving patterns have been identified from examinations of multiview videofluoroscopic films and fiberoptic endoscopy of the velopharyngeal portal during speech. They are illustrated in Fig. 10 and are subsequently described in the order of their frequency of occurrence:

(a) Coronal Closure occurs in approximately 46% of speakers in which the majority of valving is done by the velum contacting the posterior pharyngeal wall (PPW). The lateral pharyngeal walls (LPW) move medially to abut the lateral margins of the velum. There is no PPW movement.

(b) Sagittal Closure occurs in approximately 15% of speakers and is done in the main by LPW which approximate at midline. The velum does not make contact with the PPW, but contacts the approximating LPW to complete closure.

(c) Circular Closure occurs in approximately 21% of speakers in which there are essentially equal contributions from the velum and the LPW. The dorsal surface of the M. Uvulae contacts the PPW with the LPW squeezing around it. The PPW does not move.

(d) Circular Closure with Passavant's Ridge occurs in approximately 18% of speakers in which the circular closure pattern is augmented by anterior displacement of the PPW.

The anterior displacement of the posterior pharyngeal wall during speech is referred to as Passavant's ridge or pad. It is thought to result from contraction of the pterygopharyngeal fibers of the superior pharyngeal constrictor muscle. Long thought to be a compensatory mechanism, it is now known to be seen in a small percentage of normals with intact velopharyngeal mechanisms. Its role as a significant contributor to normal mechanisms is questionable given its variable shape and size and its low position on the posterior pharyngeal wall, where it occurs below the primary site of velar contact.

7.2 Muscles

The velum, or soft palate, is a muscular structure which forms the posterior aspect of the roof of the

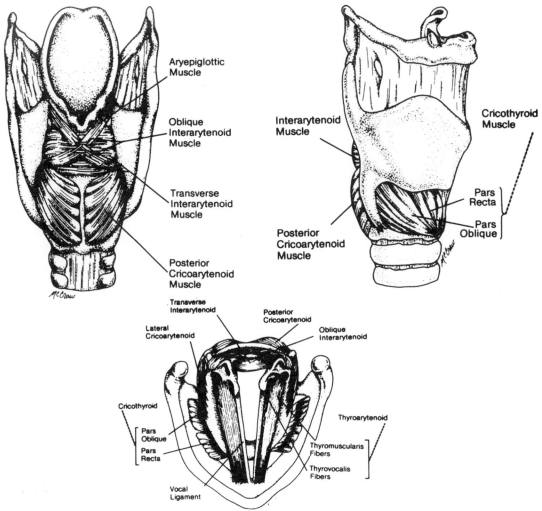

Figure 8. Intrinsic muscles of the larynx. (From N. J. Lass, L. V. McReynolds, J. L. Northern, D. E. Yoder (eds.) 1988 *Handbook of Speech–Language Pathology and Audiology.* B. C. Decker, Toronto)

oral cavity. Anteriorly, it blends imperceptively with the hard palate. However, posteriorly, it narrows slightly and terminates in a grapelike, pendulous structure called the uvula.

The muscles of the velum are sandwiched between sheets of epithelium and glandular tissue. Fig. 11 illustrates the relationship among the five pairs of muscles forming the soft palate. These include: tensor veli palatini, levator veli palatini, musculus uvulae, palatoglossus, and palatopharyngeus. Except for tensor veli palatini, which is innervated by the trigeminal nerve (cranial nerve 5), all the other velar muscles are innervated by the vagus nerve (cranial nerve 10). Interestingly, tensor veli palatini does not contribute muscle fibers directly to the soft palate. Rather, it

provides a broad, flat, tendinous sheath—palatal aponeurosis—which attaches the palatal musculature to the hard palate. Tensor is responsible for dilating the Eustachian tube, which connects the middle ear cavity and the nasopharynx. The other muscles of the soft palate elevate and draw the soft palate posteriorly (levator veli palatini), add shape to the velum and bulk to the area making contact with the posterior pharyngeal wall (musculus uvulae), and lower the velum (palatoglossus, palatopharyngeus). The principal muscle of the velum is levator veli palatini, because its action draws the velum upward and backward, occluding most of the nasopharyngeal portal. The remainder of this airway is closed by pharyngeal wall activity.

66

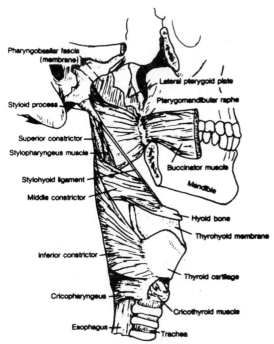

Figure 9. Muscles of the pharynx. (From H. Bateman, R. Mason, *Applied Anatomy and Physiology of the Speech and Hearing Mechanism.* Charles C. Thomas, Springfield, IL)

7.3 Functions during Speech

During speech, the velopharyngeal mechanism closes the nasopharyngeal portal to facilitate the build-up of intraoral air pressures and transoral airflows needed for oral obstruent production, as well as to prevent nasal resonances which would distort oral sonorants. It opens the nasopharyngeal portal for the production of nasal consonants and nasal vowels.

The velum has been shown to exhibit some systematic behaviors during speech. These include:

(a) velar height is higher for high vowels than low vowels;
(b) consonants require greater intraoral pressure than vowels and have greater velar height and tighter degree of closure;
(c) velar height is greater for plosives than liquids;
(d) velar height is greater for voiceless than voiced plosives;
(e) velar movements decrease with increases in rate of speech.

7.4 Clinical Considerations

Defective velopharyngeal functioning can result in significant loss in speech intelligibility and articulation. Additionally, it may cause abnormal vocal tract resonance by permanently coupling the nasal cavity (as a side branch) to the otherwise closed vocal tract. This has many adverse consequences for speech, including:

(a) hypernasal resonance distortions of vowels; (b) nasal air escape (emission) during production of consonants (plosives, fricatives, and affricatives); (c) weakening of consonants resulting from deficient intra-oral pressures and transoral airflow; and (d) development of compensatory articulatory gestures, such as glottal stops and pharyngeal fricatives.

Classification of velopharyngeal dysfunction may be clarified by distinguishing it according to etiological basis. Thus, the generic term velopharyngeal inadequacy may be caused by *velopharyngeal insufficiency* resulting from congenital and acquired structural abnormalities; *velopharyngeal incompetency,* caused by neurogenic etiologies arising from loss of muscular or neuromuscular competency or motor programming abilities; and *velopharyngeal mislearning,* which may be phonologic (i.e., phone specific) in nature or due to deafness or hearing impairment.

8. The Tongue

The tongue is the largest and most mobile structure in the oral cavity, and the most active and important of the speech articulators. It is a wedge-shaped muscular organ (Fig. 12), most of which is located in the oral cavity. Only the posterior third is located in the pharynx, and it is relatively immobile.

8.1 Functional Morphology

The tongue is covered by epithelia which provide taste, general sensation, tactile/proprioceptive feedback, and protection from the abrading forces of food during chewing and swallowing. The sensory supply to the surface of the tongue comes from the trigeminal (cranial nerve 5), facial (cranial nerve 7), and glossopharyngeal nerves (cranial nerve 9). The dorsal surface of the tongue lies under the hard and soft palates, while the undersurface of the tongue is closely associated with the floor of the mouth, and attached to it by a thin band of tissue called the 'lingual frenulum.' The tongue surface may be divided into functional subdivisions as follows. The 'apex' or 'tip' is the area lying closest to the lingual surface of the teeth; the 'blade' is the anteriormost portion of the dorsum, located just below the alveolar ridge (in the midline); the 'front' is the portion of the tongue below the hard palate and in front of the faucial pillars; and the 'back' is the area of the tongue behind the faucial pillars in the oropharynx.

8.2 Tongue Musculature

The tongue is a powerful muscular organ composed of several muscles which are arranged in interlacing arrays (Fig. 12). These muscles are functionally divided into the extrinsic group, which move and position the tongue within the oral cavity, and the intrinsic group, which change its shape. Both the extrinsic and intrinsic tongue muscles are innervated by the hypoglossal nerve (cranial nerve 12). The extrinsic muscles

67

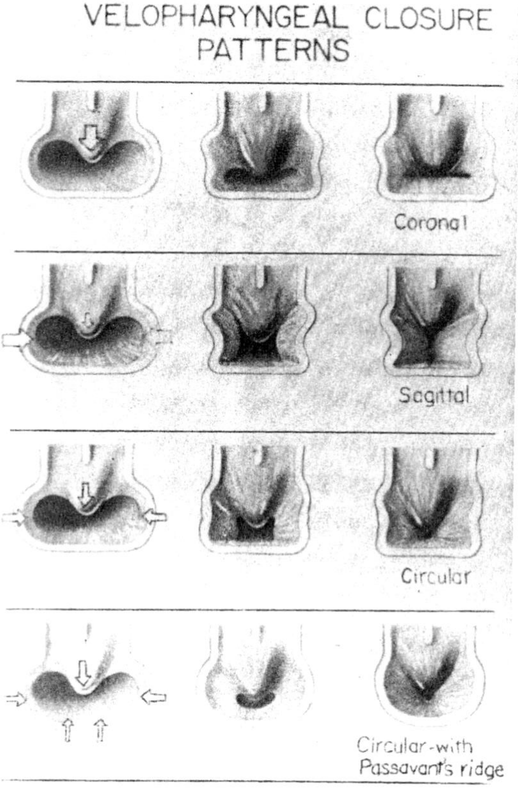

VELOPHARYNGEAL CLOSURE PATTERNS

Coronal

Sagittal

Circular

Circular-with Passavant's ridge

Figure 10. Drawings of four major types of velopharyngeal closing patterns as revealed through nasopharyngeal endoscopy. (From Siegel-Sadewitz V and Shprintzen R J: Nasopharyngoscopy of the normal velopharyngeal sphincter: An experiment of biofeedback. From *Cleft Palate Journal* **19**(3): 194–200).

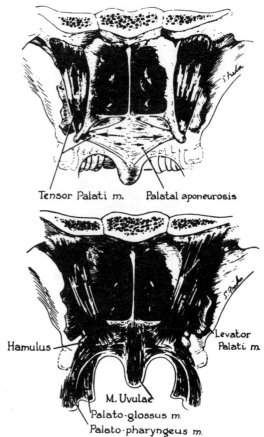

Tensor Palati *m.*   Palatal aponeurosis

Hamulus

Levator Palati *m.*

M. Uvulae
Palato-glossus *m.*
Palato-pharyngeus *m.*

Figure 11. Muscles of the soft palate. (From S. L. Silverman 1961 *Oral Physiology*. C. V. Mosby, St Louis)

(styloglossus, hyoglossus, palatoglossus, and genioglossus) protract, retract, lower, and raise the tongue. These movements are important for giving shape to the tongue during vowel production and for creating impedances to airflow such as is used for plosive consonants. Channels for the passage of airflow used in production of continuant consonants such as fricatives also result from extrinsic muscle activity. The intrinsic muscles of the tongue (superior longitudinal, inferior longitudinal, transverse, and vertical) modify the shape and topography of the tongue, which is important for refined posturings used in articulation.

8.3 Functions during Speech

The tongue is crucial to speech because it forms a movable wall for both the oral and pharyngeal cavity and alters the shape of the vocal tract when it moves. Without the tongue, all sounds other than the bilabials, labials, labiodentals, and pharyngeals would be either missing or severely distorted. The tongue is

capable of very wide ranges in shape, position, and movements, and is capable of forming one or more simultaneous constrictions anywhere in the vocal tract. The tongue basically works as a two-degrees-of-freedom system producing movements along the front-to-back and up-to-down dimensions.

8.4 Clinical Considerations

Aside from neurological damage affecting innervation of tongue musculature, the tongue is relatively free of structural abnormalities that restrict its movement. However, one condition, *ankyloglossia*, resulting from a short lingual frenulum, can physically restrict tongue movements. Commonly called 'tongue tie,' this condition can adversely affect speech by restricting or limiting the elevation of the tongue tip. This condition may impair articulation of /t/, /n/, /s/, /r/, and /l/.

9. Craniomandibular Muscles and the Temporomandibular Joint

Mandibular movements are essential for chewing and swallowing and are integral to articulatory move-

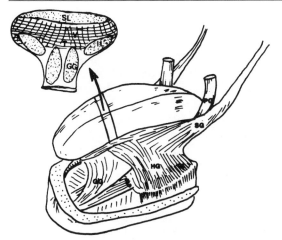

Figure 12. Tongue muscles. Intrinsic muscles (coronal section through the tongue as indicated in figure): SL = superior longitudinal, IL = inferior longitudinal, V = vertical linguae muscles, T = transverse linguae muscle. Extrinsic muscles: PG = palatoglossus, SG = styloglossus, HG = hyoglossus, GG = genioglossus.

ments in speech. These movements are made possible through the action of five pairs of muscles which attach to the mandible. These muscles are sometimes called the muscles of mastication, but are more accurately called the craniomandibular muscles. They act on the mandible to open, close, lateralize, protrude, and retrude it, and thus control changes in the size of the oral cavity and the approximation of the occlusal surfaces of the teeth.

9.1 Functional Morphology

The biomechanical system just described is illustrated in Fig. 13, where the relationship of the muscles to the temporomandibular joint (TMJ) is clearly shown. All the craniomandibular muscles are innervated by the trigeminal nerve (cranial nerve 5). The TMJ is a movable joint whose action is dependent on the coordinated functioning of both right and left joints. It is composed of the condyle of the mandible, which articulates with the glenoid fossa of the temporal bone. Inserted between these bony surfaces is an articular disc which functionally divides the joint cavity into upper and lower compartments, which function differentially. The upper compartment allows for gliding action, while the lower compartment facilitates rotary or hinge movements. Most movements of the mandible utilize combinations of both gliding and rotary displacements.

9.2 Functions during Speech

The mandible (and its TMJ) is an important articulator in speech, even though it does not directly modify the airflow by creating obstructions, as is charac-

teristic of other articulators. Aside from influencing the oral resonance properties, movements of the mandible are important in speech for several reasons. They influence the intraoral environment in which the tongue works during speech, impacting on the distance and the rate at which the tongue has to move during articulation. Also, the position of the mandible directly influences movements of the lips as well as the tongue. This is clearly seen in the rate and force of lip movement and in the degree of openness of the mandible during vowel production (e.g., the mandible also moves in a systematic fashion in the production of speech sounds). It is open slightly for 'closed' sounds (i, ɪ, u, ʊ, s, z, ʃ, ʒ), open moderately for 'mid' sounds (k, g, r, ɛ, θ), and open furthest for 'open' sounds (æ, a, ɔ, ʌ). As the mandible lowers, the front of the vocal tract widens. This offers less impedance to airflow and transmission of acoustic energy. Thus, a vowel produced with elevated mandibular position will be less intense by approximately 4–5 dB than when the mandible is in the lowered position.

9.3 Clinical Considerations

Disorders of the TMJ can result from faulty occlusion, trauma, infection, and congenital (craniofacial) abnormalities. Asymmetries of the jaw as well as restrictions in jaw movement should raise questions about the intactness of the TMJs. Because *both* TMJs are involved in all movements of the mandible, unilateral dysfunction still requires examination of both TMJs.

10. Facial Muscles

The facial muscles give expression to the face, help to shape the craniofacial skeleton, maintain occlusal relationships of the dental arches, keep food over the cutting edges of the teeth, and contribute to speech production. The muscles surrounding the opening into the oral cavity enable the upper and lower lips to move differentially during speech.

10.1 General Morphology

The facial muscles are attached to different bones of the facial skeleton. They course varying distances and directly attach to the overlying skin, thus exerting refined control over the movements in the face. All of the facial muscles are innervated by the facial nerve (cranial nerve 7). Facial muscles are arranged into distinct groups in the face—they surround the eyes, the external nose, and the external ear, insert into the scalp, and surround the mouth. Those muscles surrounding the mouth are called the 'perioral' or 'circumoral muscles,' and are of great importance for speech in that they form the upper and lower lips (Fig. 14). The upper and lower lips are composed largely of separate muscles and thus can move independently. The lower lip is more mobile than the upper one;

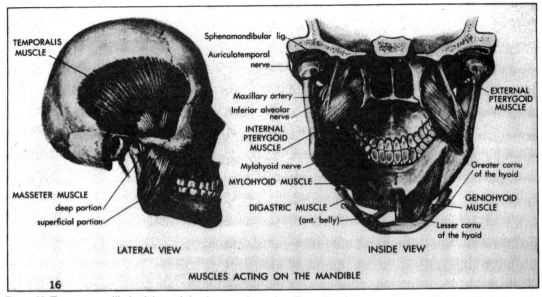

Figure 13. Temporomandibular joint and the circumoral muscles. (From *Head Anatomy*. Wernet Division, Black Drug Co, Jersey City, NJ)

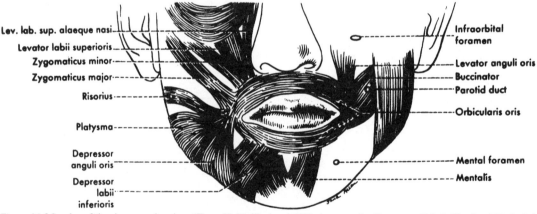

Figure 14. Muscles of the circumoral region. (From H. Hollinshead 1982 *Anatomy for Surgeons. Vol. 1: Head and Neck*, 3rd edn. Hoeber Medical Division, Harper and Row, New York)

however, this is undoubtedly related to its anatomically close association with the mandible.

10.2 The Lips

The lips are not composed of a single muscle which encircles the opening to the mouth. Although the musculature of the lips is usually referred to as the 'orbicularis oris,' the lips are composed of numerous facial muscles, whose fibers insert into the circumoral area in two layers. This is illustrated in Fig. 14. The deepest layer is formed by the principal muscle of the lips, the 'buccinator.' This is the same muscle which forms the cheek. The superficial layer is formed by all

the other muscles. Muscles of the upper and lower lips do not form a continuous ring around the oral opening, but rather encircle it through the interweaving of fibers from those muscles which insert into the area. Most of these muscles converge at the corners of the mouth into a tendinous or nodular region called the 'modiolus' before inserting into the mucous membrane or skin overlying the orbicularis oris. Specifically, muscle fibers passing through the modiolus which originate from muscles above the oral opening pass into the lower lip. Muscles passing through the modiolus from attachments below the oral opening pass into the upper lip. Muscles which do not pass through the modiolus insert into the lips as follows: those with origins above the oral opening insert into the upper lip, while those with origins below the oral opening insert into the lower lip. This arrangement allows for purse-string effects which draw the upper and lower lips together in a compressive or sphincteric pattern as is needed for closure during swallowing or other forms of intraoral sealing, such as bilabial approximations in speech.

10.3 Functions during Speech

Differential action of the upper and lower lips in such gestures as raising, protruding, lowering the angle, raising the angle, and rounding of the lips can be done by muscles which insert into the lip proper, working alone or in combination with each other. Although many of the delicate lip movements serve primary expressive functions, many postures and configurations are important for speech articulation. For example, the bilateral approximation of the lips is important for the production of consonants (/m/, /p/, /b/), labiodental approximations for /f/, /v/, and lip rounding and spreading for /w/ and /j/. Lip rounding (by the orbicularis oris) and lip spreading (by the risorius buccinator and zygomaticus major) are also important features for vowel production. As noted previously, movements of the lips are highly related to movements of the lower jaw.

10.4 Clinical Considerations

Facial expression is an important human attribute mediated by the action of the facial muscles. Though most clearly identified with facial movements, the muscles of the face are also important in protecting the eye from physical injury and dryness (orbicularis oculi), and in facilitating chewing and swallowing and controlling salivary secretions (orbicularis oris), by creating an effective anterior seal to the oral cavity. The muscles of the lips, cheeks, and the superior pharyngeal constrictors are functionally interconnected, so as to form an encircling band around the dental arches which is anchored at the base of the occiput. This unit has been called the 'buccinator mechanism.' Important function of this arrangement are to exert a molding force on the teeth and dental arches to provide balancing (or antagonistic) forces to those of the tongue.

Damage to the facial nerve causes unilateral paresis or paralysis to the facial muscles resulting in inability to close the eye (which appears droopy), flat expressionless faces, and loss of function of the lip on the affected side. Facial nerve dysfunction can result from a virus causing Bell's Palsy (which is transient), congenital aplasia of the facial nerve nucleus in Mobius Syndrome, or tumors of the parotid gland.

11. Postnatal and Aging Changes in the Speech Mechanism

The structures of the peripheral speech mechanism develop postnatally to reach maturity and then, beginning in middle age, undergo regressive or involutional changes, which result in altered or diminished capacity in speech. Changes have been reported in all structures of the speech mechanism, but their effects on speech are usually small. The most dramatic changes appear to occur in the larynx and the vocal tract, and are discussed in the following subsections.

11.1 Postnatal Changes in the Larynx

The infant's larynx is not simply a miniature of the adult's: it differs from its adult counterpart in size, consistency of tissues, position in the neck, and shape. The cartilages are smaller, but the subcutaneous and mucous membranes are more pliable than in the adult. In the infant, the hyoid bone and thyroid cartilage are close together, and the glottal aperture is small. In infancy and childhood, the membranous portion of the vocal folds is short and thickened, and the vocal processes assume a proportionally larger portion of the length of the glottis than in the adult.

As a result, the vocal folds in infants and young children are stabilized more posteriorly than in older children and adults, and the length of their vibrating mass is reduced. As a consequence of vertical growth of the pharynx and in the cervical region of the vertebral column, the larynx, over time, becomes positioned at lower levels in the neck. In infancy, the larynx is located at a level between the first and second cervical vertebrae. It descends during childhood and, after puberty, assumes its adult position, with the cricoid cartilage at the level of the sixth cervical vertebra.

Laryngeal cartilages and the vocal folds increase in size postnatally. During the first three years of life, the larynx undergoes rapid and significant growth, after which there is a period of slow, steady growth until puberty, when development once again accelerates. There are no significant morphological differences between prepubertal male and prepubertal female larynges. That is, there is 'morphological congruence' (Fig. 15c). However, the prepubertal female larynx is closer to its mature size and shape than that of the prepubertal male (Fig. 15a and b). During puberty 'sexual dimorphism' becomes established. In the pubertal male, the laryngeal cartilages and the vocal folds are significantly larger than pubertal female counterparts (Fig. 15d), and, in addition, the male undergoes significantly more growth than the female larynx from prepuberty to puberty. During this time, the male vocal folds undergo twice the growth of the female vocal folds, and both reach adult length by puberty (approximately 17 mm in the male and 13 mm in the female). As the vocal folds increase in length and thickness, the connective tissues (lamina propria) also mature, forming themselves into definitive layers which contain specific proportions of fibrous connective tissues. Perhaps the most recognizable change in the postpubertal larynx is the devel-

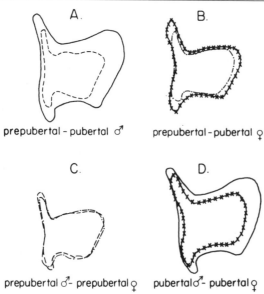

A. prepubertal - pubertal ♂

B. prepubertal - pubertal ♀

C. prepubertal ♂ - prepubertal ♀

D. pubertal ♂ - pubertal ♀

Figure 15. Typical morphology of the prepubertal and pubertal larynx based on composite photographic reconstructions. (From J. C. Kahane 1978 A morphological study of the human prepubertal and pubertal larynx. *American Journal of Anatomy* **151**: 11.)

opment in the male of an anterior prominence (the thyroid eminence), or 'Adam's apple,' as it is commonly called. In the female, the anterior aspect of the thyroid cartilage is rounded and thus not prominent in the neck. Research has negated the long-held notion that the angle of the thyroid laminae is 90 degrees in the male and 120 degrees in the female. There are no significant sex differences in the angulation of the thyroid laminae; however, the thyroid prominence, that is, the point where the two thyroid laminae are fused anteriorly, is acute in the male and obtuse in the female. Thus, the male thyroid cartilage is indeed more prominent in the male neck than in the female.

Growth of the larynx does not occur independently of growth of the entire body. Laryngeal growth has been shown to be related to growth in body height during infancy throughout childhood into puberty. The growth of the larynx is not laryngeal-specific, but appears to be under similar influences to those controlling general somatic growth.

The adult larynx is not immune to change. In fact, the adult larynx undergoes significant changes that result in a decrease in vocal efficiency. These may be referred to as 'involutionary' changes. They are greater in the male than in the female, and occur earlier in the male than in the female. The major involutional changes in the larynx include stiffening of the laryngeal cartilages, changes in connective tissues which affect their resiliency and recoil, atrophy of vocal fold musculature muscles which may cause them to become

slightly bowed, causing incomplete closure when they are brought to the midline, and reduced vibratory characteristics. This condition may contribute to the weaker and sometimes breathier voice heard in older speakers.

11.2 Postnatal Changes in the Voice

The principal characteristic of voice which closely mirrors maturation of the larynx is fundamental frequency (FO). This is perceived as the pitch of the voice. The differences in FO appreciated in adults evolves slowly over nearly the first two decades of life. The most rapid change in FO occurs during three periods of life: the first four months of life; from 1–3 years; and from 13–17 years. Fundamental frequency is indistinguishable in the prepubertal male and female, but at puberty a difference appears which continues for several years. During the resultant 'adolescent voice change,' the male voice has dropped one octave compared to half an octave (two to three notes) in the female. The pubescent voice is frequently hoarse and accompanied, at times, by pitch breaks or 'cracking.' The latter occurs because of the inability of the muscles in the larynx and vocal folds to maintain control during this period of rapid growth. By the end of puberty, both the male and female voice reach mature levels (approximately 120 Hz in the male and 225 Hz in the female).

In addition to changes in the absolute levels of FO, the child develops increasingly greater control of voicing during the first decade of life. By the age of 10–12 years, minimal levels of FO variability are reached and approximate those found in healthy adults.

The voice remains relatively unchanged during early and much of mid-adulthood. After that time, the male voice undergoes greater changes than the female. By the sixth decade in the male, FO is noted to rise, and female fundamental frequency has been observed to become slightly lowered. This appears to result for different reasons. In the male, the elastic and collagenous fibers in the vocal fold become stiffer and the vocal fold musculature tends to atrophy, making the folds thinner. In the female, these changes do not appear to be as pronounced, and the vocal folds become edematous due to hormonal changes associated with the menopause. The vocal range also becomes reduced in both sexes. In males, the mechanical stability of the vocal folds during vibration, that is, its control, appears to decrease with age. This has been reported to contribute to some roughness in the voice. Empirical studies have not supported the anecdotal reports that the aged voice is usually tremulous, although this characteristic certainly does appear in some individuals.

11.3 Postnatal Changes in the Vocal Tract

Postnatal changes in the pharynx result in changes to the formation of the vocal tract. The associated changes in the supralaryngeal airways are related to the growth of the tongue and larynx and to the establishment of the unique spatial relationships for the development of the vocal tract. Postnatal changes in the shape of the supralaryngeal airways (vocal tract) result from changes in the shape of the base of the skull relative to the vertebral column, to vertical growth of the pharynx, and to growth and descent of the posterior third of the tongue. The major changes occur between birth and the age of five. After this time, mature spatial relationships have been established, although the absolute size of the pharynx continues to increase.

From birth through nearly the first two years of life, the tongue at rest lies entirely within the oral cavity. The larynx is positioned high in the neck so that the tip of the epiglottis and the soft palate contact. Such an arrangement allows for efficient respiration because there is a single, relatively linear path from the nose into the lower airway. This path is highly efficient in that there is little airway resistance, since it is of fairly uniform diameter and not tortuous. Consequently, there is virtually no supralaryngeal airway or vocal tract. This anatomic arrangement is a special adaptation during infancy to allow the child to be nourished without interfering with breathing. This is accomplished by the interlocking of the nasopharynx and larynx (Fig. 16a), such that food is able to pass through the oral fauces into the pharynx and esophagus while air passes directly into the larynx.

Between 18 and 24 months, the posterior third of the tongue begins its descent into the pharyngeal cavity. It is no longer consistently positioned within the oral cavity. At this time, the larynx begins to assume a lower position in the neck as a result of growth of the pharynx and the cervical region. The upper airway begins to become more angulated (Fig. 16b), and is modified from a single tube to a double-tubed system which serves separate functions during respiration and swallowing. Interlocking of the soft palate with the epiglottis occurs less frequently, but most often during swallowing and never during vocalization or crying.

By the age of four the posterior third of the tongue has permanently descended into the pharynx, and the larynx has descended more caudally into the pharynx, making it impossible for interlocking to occur. A two-tubed system (serving respiratory and swallowing functions) has been established, as has a vocal tract that the child uses effectively as a resonator in speech.

After the age of five (Fig. 16b), the mature configuration of the upper airway has become established. This results in a greatly expanded pharynx and a more caudally positioned base of the tongue and larynx. This arrangement decreases respiratory efficiency somewhat, because of the more tortuous path that air has to take into the lower airway. However, the increased and modified shape of the supralaryngeal

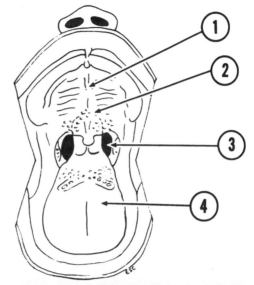

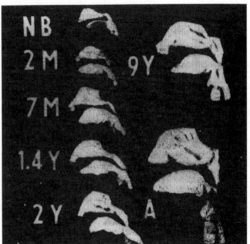

Figure 16. A. Intraoral view of newborn illustrating a possible mechanism for interlocking of the larynx and nasopharynx. 1. hard palate; 2. epiglottis (broken line) behind soft palate; 3. passageway through which milk can pass simultaneously during respiration; 4. tongue. B. Silicone rubber casts of human airways illustrating the changing morphology in the newborn (NB), at 2 months (2M), 7 months (7M), 1.4 years (1.4Y), 2 years (2Y), 9 years (9Y), and adult (A). 1, nasal airway; 2, pharynx; 3, larynx; 4, oral cavity. (From J. Laitman, E. S. Crelin 1976 Postnatal development of the basicranium and the vocal-tract region in man. In: J. F. Bosma (ed.) *Symposium on Development of the Basicranium.* Department of Health, Education, and Welfare, Washington, DC)

airway allows for enlargement of the tongue and development of the flexibility needed for speech production and manipulation and swallowing of large boluses of food, and also the development of a larger supralaryngeal airway that is important for resonance during speech.

Before puberty, there are no significant differences in the length of the pharynx. The length of the nasal opening of the pharyngeal cavity is significantly larger in the male than in the female at all ages. Growth in both sexes is continuous up to the age of 16, although it is greater in the male than in the female.

Little is known about the aging of the vocal tract. There is some evidence that the pharyngeal musculature becomes weakened, perhaps somewhat dilating the pharynx. Some muscles in the aging soft palate have been reported to atrophy.

11.4 Postnatal Changes in Speech

Little is known about the postnatal changes in the vocal tract. More research has been done concerning the childhood years than any other period. From these efforts, it has been learned that formant frequencies decrease with increases in the size of the vocal tract. However, the precise relationship of these changes is not well understood. Appreciable evidence suggests that decreases in formant frequency are not linearly related to growth of the vocal tract.

Aging effects on the vocal tract have not been studied directly. However, changes in the pharyngeal muscles may reduce the ability of the speaker to change the dimensions of the pharyngeal cavity. The effects of this, which may result from intrinsic changes in the pharyngeal muscles or their innervation, is a lessening of the ability to maintain vocal-fold vibration throughout the closure interval during stop-closure production. Another possible effect of aging, based on limited research, suggests that changes in the rigidity and possibly shape and size of the pharynx, and possibly some muscles of the soft palate, may account for the lowering of the frequency of the first formant and, to a lesser extent, the second formant. Considerably more research is needed to understand how the myriad anatomical changes in the upper vocal tract contribute to changes in speech and voice transmission.

Bibliography

Kahane J C 1979 Pathophysiological effects of Mobius syndrome on speech and hearing. *Archives of Otolaryngology* **105**: 29–34

Kahane J C 1982 Growth of the human prepubertal and pubertal larynx. *Journal of Speech and Hearing Research* **25**: 446–55

Kahane J C 1986 *Anatomy and Physiology of the Speech Mechanism*. ProEd Publishers, Austin, TX

Kahane J C 1990 Age-related changes in the peripheral speech mechanism: Structural and physiological changes. In: Cherow E *Proceedings of the Research Symposium on Communication Sciences and Disorders and Aging*, ASHA Reports 19. American Speech–Language and Hearing Association, Rockville, MD

Kahane J C 1996 Life span changes in the larynx. An anatomical perspective. In Brown W S, Vinson B P, Crary M A (eds.) *Organic Voice Disorders*. Singular Publishing, San Diego, CA

Kent R D 1976 Anatomical and neuromuscular maturation of the speech mechanism: Evidence from acoustic studies. *Journal of Speech and Hearing Research* **19(3)**: 421–47

Laitman J, Crelin E S 1976 Postnatal development of the basicranium and vocal-tract region in man. In: Bosma J F (ed.) *Symposium on Development of the Basicranium*. Department of Health, Education, and Welfare, Washington, DC

Netter F H 1988 *Respiratory System*. Ciba Collections of Medical Illustrations, Vol. 7. Ciba, West Caldwell, NY

Orlikoff R F, Kahane J C 1996 Structure and function of the Larynx. In Lass N J (ed.) *Principles of Experimental Phonetics*. Mosby, St. Louis, MI

Peterson-Falzone 1988 Speech disorders related to craniofacial structural defects. Part 1. In: Lass N J, McReynolds L D, Northern J, Yoder D E (eds.) *Handbook of Speech-Language Pathology and Audiology*. BC Decker, Toronto

Peterson-Falzone 1988 Speech disorders related to craniofacial structural defects. Part 2. In: Lass N J, McReynolds L D, Northern J, Yoder D E (eds.) *Handbook of Speech-Language Pathology and Audiology*. BC Decker, Toronto

Siegel-Sadawitz V L, Shprintzen R J 1982 Nasopharyngoscopy of the normal velopharyngeal mechanism. An experiment of biofeedback. *Cleft Palate Journal* **19(3)**: 194–200

Trost-Cardamone J 1986 Effects of velopharyngeal competency on speech. *Journal of Childhood Communication Disorders* **10(1)**: 31–49

Trost-Cardamone J 1989 Coming to terms with VPI: A response to Loney and Bloem. *Cleft Palate Journal* **26**: 68–70

Neuromuscular Aspects of Speech

H. Hirose

Physiologically, speech is a product of neural control by the central nervous system. It is generally believed that there is a rich and direct outflow of nerve impulses from the cerebral cortex of the brain in a moment-by-moment control of the articulatory organs during speech production. At the level of the peripheral articulatory organs, these impulses elicit pertinent muscle contractions necessary for speech movement.

Several experimental techniques in physiology can be used to assess speech movement in phonetic research. Among them, electromyography (EMG) has been used to obtain the most direct information on muscle activity responsible for articulatory gestures. This article describes the use of EMG in phonetic research.

1. Electromyography

Electromyography is a technique for providing graphic information about the time-course of the electrical activity of the muscle fibers that accompanies muscle contraction and subsequent effects, including the development of tension and movement.

Each muscle contains numerous muscle fibers. Groups of muscle fibers within the muscle are connected to a single motor nerve. The combination of a motor nerve and all the individual muscle fibers innervated by that nerve is known as a motor unit. Thus, all muscles consist of a number of motor units.

All the individual muscle fibers in a motor unit contract almost simultaneously when the unit receives an impulse via the motor nerve. When a nerve impulse reaches the neuromuscular junction, the region of connection between nerve and muscle, a chemical reaction is initiated and an electrical discharge or firing is elicited as an action potential, and the fiber contracts.

If an appropriate probe (electrode) is placed close to the muscle fiber, momentary differences in the electrical potential at the probe can be picked up when the muscle contracts. This is the basic process involved in EMG.

As the force of contraction increases, the firing rate of a given motor unit increases and, at the same time, many additional electrical potentials are released from other motor units in the same muscle. Thus, in a normal situation, the EMG display represents a signal from many individual unit spike potentials which are random in phase.

In speech physiology, it can be assumed that relative EMG signal amplitudes, firing rates of single motor units, and difference in timing and general pattern are related to different phonetic events.

2. Brief History of EMG Research in Speech Science

EMG research on the speech organs was virtually an unexplored frontier until the late 1950s, although Stetson did pioneering work in a much earlier period. One of Stetson's notions was that every syllable is accompanied by a 'ballistic chest pulse' produced by the action of the internal intercostal muscle. However, his EMG recordings appeared to be technically inadequate, and his conclusions were mostly defeated later.

Post-1950 EMG studies on respiratory muscle activities during speech production were extensively reported by Draper and his colleagues, who explored activity of the diaphragm and intercostal muscles (Ladefoged 1964).

Slightly later, laryngeal muscle activity during phonation was studied by Faaborg-Andersen. The palatal and pharyngeal EMG activities related to speech production were examined by Fritzel and others. EMG activity of the tongue during speech was examined by MacNeilage and his associates, while facial muscle activities for labial articulation were studied by Harris and her group and by Fromkin. These studies opened a new era in speech research (Harris 1970).

After the early era of EMG investigation in speech research, extensive use of EMG in the field of experimental phonetics led to a new dimension in research on the nature of laryngeal and supralaryngeal control in human speech production. In this type of research, different types of electrodes are in use and multichannel recordings are employed. Also, the computer processing of recorded signals has become available for obtaining averaged measures of muscle activity correlated with pertinent speech gestures.

3. General Techniques in EMG

3.1 Electrodes

In order to obtain a precise placement of electrodes in a target muscle, needle electrodes are generally used, particularly for clinical purposes. In speech research, however, three other types are commonly employed: paint-on, surface, and intramuscular hooked-wire. In addition, a grounding electrode is attached to the ear lobe or some other distant part of the body. Among the three types of pick-up electrodes, paint-on and surface types are usually attached to the skin of the face to obtain facial muscle activity, particularly from the labial muscles, since these muscles are situated immediately underneath the skin. 'Paint-on electrode' refers to a liquid suspension of metal powder. When it is painted on to the skin and dried with a tip of lead wire embedded in the painted spot, it can pick up EMG potentials through the skin. Hooked-wire electrodes can be inserted directly into muscles using a hypodermic needle to implant the wires.

3.2 Recording and Processing of EMG Signals

EMG signals are amplified and recorded on a data recorder for off-line processing or directly fed into a signal processor. The general purpose of EMG processing is to obtain the average measures of muscle activity related to a given phonetic event.

As mentioned earlier, the EMG signal is the sum of the action potentials of many motor units. Since there may be some variabilities in the pattern of muscle activity even for repetitions of the same token, and since electrodes can only pick up a limited sample of firing units for each articulatory gesture, averaging the raw signals after full-wave rectification and integration is highly advisable. For limited cases where noiseless, clean EMG signals are obtained in original recordings, a simple rectification–integration procedure may give a representative pattern for a given single token.

After appropriate processing, a graphic representation of the EMG signal is obtained in which the temporal pattern of activity of a pertinent muscle as a whole is displayed with reference to corresponding speech events.

4. Significance of EMG: What EMG Can Tell

4.1 Physiological Aspects of EMG in Normal Subjects

In speech research, EMG can verify whether a given muscle participates in a particular articulatory act, assuming that an ideal placement of the electrode is made into the target muscle. Furthermore, EMG study enables one to establish the exact function of muscular action in the execution of a particular articulatory behavior. For example, EMG can clarify whether a pair of opposing movements are both muscularly controlled or whether one of the pair is merely passive.

In general, EMG has proved to be useful for the research of kinesiological aspects of human behavior, including speech production. It is assumed that recorded EMG reflects the amount of activity of that muscle, indicating the strength of contraction or degree of movement.

Physiologically, it has been revealed that there is a direct relationship between the mechanical tension and the integrated EMG. The integrated EMG provides a composite picture of the number and frequency of active muscle fibers.

It must be mentioned that any voluntary movement requires the coordinated activity of many different muscles to achieve smooth execution of action. This type of coordination is controlled spacio–temporally by the central nervous system, with the possible help of different types of feedback mechanisms. Thus, EMG kinesiology is concerned with the biomechanical analysis of various movements or gestures, reflecting the motor command from the central nervous system.

4.2 Some Representative Results of EMG Studies

4.2.1 Laryngeal EMG

The intrinsic laryngeal muscles consist of the thyroarytenoid (TA or VOC), the lateral cricoarytenoid (LCA), the interarytenoid (INT or IA), the posterior cricoarytenoid (PCA), and the cricothyroid (CT), where the TA, LCA, and INT are known as the adductors, the PCA as the abductor, and the CT as the tensor of the vocal folds.

Prime examples of the value of laryngeal EMG data in phonetic research come from studies elucidating the CT's contribution to pitch control and the adductor–abductor activity for voicing control.

CT activation increases longitudinal tension of the vocal folds during phonation and thus elevates pitch

(fundamental frequency: F0) of voice. EMG studies have shown that this mechanism underlies the regulation of F0 for accent, stress, and intonation, where previously it had been suggested that the respiratory system (pressure of air from the lungs) was the principal means of controlling F0.

A number of studies on different languages have revealed that the abduction and adduction of the vocal folds for control of voicing distinction in speech are clearly accomplished by the action of the PCA and INT in a reciprocal fashion, in that the glottal opening gesture is obtained by activation of the PCA with suppression of INT (Sawashima and Hirose 1983).

Figure 1 compares computer-averaged EMG patterns of the five intrinsic laryngeal muscles for the production of a pair of Japanese test words, /keNri/ versus /geNri/, embedded in a frame sentence

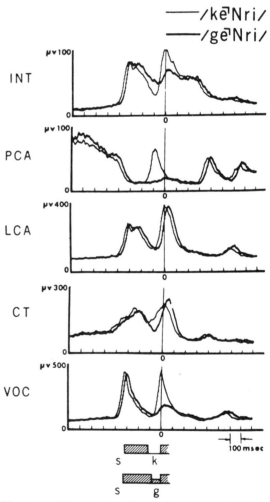

Figure 1. Activity patterns of five intrinsic laryngeal muscles for the production of a pair of Japanese test words.

sorewa...desu (*that is...*), where the production of voiceless [k] and its voiced cognate [g] were compared in a ceteris paribus condition. The 0 point on the abscissa (time axis) indicates the stop release used as the line-up point during the averaging process. The reciprocal or mirror-image relationship between the PCA and the INT is clearly seen in this figure. That is, PCA activity starts to increase about 100 msec before the [k] gesture, where INT-suppression begins correspondingly.

For the LCA and VOC, these two muscle activities increase at the initiation of each utterance, namely for the carrier portion preceding the test word, and decrease for word-initial consonant production, where the degree of suppression is similar regardless of the voicing distinction in the paired consonants, although reactivation in the VOC is more dominant after the voiceless [k].

For most voiced–voiceless pairs, the general pattern of CT activity is similar and characterized by two peaks separated apparently by suppression for the initial consonant of the test words. It should be noted, however, that the degree of suppression is different depending upon whether the initial consonant is voiced or voiceless, in that the suppression is more marked for the voiceless cognate than for the voiced. The difference is also related to the degree of reactivation after the suppression, and it is apparently more marked for the voiced cognate. The CT may contribute to an increase in the tension of the vocal fold which might serve to eliminate voicing.

4.2.2 EMG of Supralaryngeal Articulators

There are many speech muscles accessible by EMG techniques in the supralaryngeal regions. Among them, the facial muscles around the lip opening are relatively easy to access. The orbicularis oris is, for example, known to be active for lip closure, protrusion, and rounding. The levator veli palatini, which is responsible for velum elevation for the production of non-nasal sounds, can be reached through either the nose or the oral cavity.

Despite its central role in speech, EMG data from the tongue have been very scarce. By a combination of through-the-mouth and through-the-underside-of-the-chin insertions, Baer and his colleagues found a quantal difference in the neuromuscular orchestration of American English front vowels /i e æ/ versus back vowels /a o u/. Front vowels showed high activity in the anterior genioglossus and suppressed activity in the hyoglossus and styloglossus, and back vowels the reverse. The activity of the posterior genioglossus correlated with vowel height, showing its greatest level for the high vowels /i u/.

EMG can also reveal some of the mechanisms controlling pharyngeal cavity volume during voicing distinctions. For pharyngeal expansion during voiced stop production, active expansion was created by gre-

ater activity in the levator palatini elevating the velum and in the sternohyoid lowering the larynx, while passive expansion occurred due to suppression of the muscle of the pharyngeal wall (Bell-Berti 1975).

4.3 Diagnostic Approach in Pathological Cases

EMG was developed initially in the field of neurology and physical medicine because of requirements for improved diagnostic and prognostic methods. In particular, a major application of EMG examination has been in differentiating between two causes of muscular weakness: neurogenic (deficiency in the nerves) and myogenic (deficiency in the muscle).

When complete relaxation is obtained in healthy muscle, no activity is recorded during an EMG examination. With muscle contraction, the motor unit activity is recorded as action potentials as described in Sect. 3. Amplitude and duration of single action potentials of normal muscles in head and neck regions are generally smaller than those reported for the limb muscles.

As the strength of muscle contraction increases, the number of motor units firing increases to form the so-called interference pattern. If there is neurogenic paralysis due to complete denervation, no volitional activity is obtained, but some involuntary small potentials known as fibrillation voltage are often recorded. EMG evidence of complete denervation generally suggests a poor prognosis for recovery from paralysis. If the denervation is incomplete, volitional activity is partially preserved, and different types of abnormal firing patterns such as polyphasic (complex) voltage or high-amplitude voltage are often seen. These patterns of denervation are indicative of neurogenic paralysis.

On the other hand, if there is myogenic paralysis, the number of firing motor units is well preserved, while the amplitude of each unit is much smaller than normal. This type of pathological pattern is known as low voltage.

In the field of speech pathology, for example, the clinical use of EMG is aimed at the differential diagnosis of immobile vocal folds, prognostic evaluation of laryngeal paralysis, the diagnosis of laryngeal and supralaryngeal muscle involvement in motor neuron diseases, and the examination of abnormal speech kinesiology. In particular, laryngeal EMG has been widely accepted as a routine procedure for the assessment of laryngeal pathology, with special reference to the status of immobile vocal folds.

In clinical EMG, a percutaneous approach using a bipolar concentric needle electrode is generally used.

5. Limitations of EMG

It can be said that the limitations of EMG assessment in speech physiology lie partly in the technical difficulty of its application. For example, although electrode insertion techniques are well documented in the existing literature, the proper placement of electrodes in each case is not always easy, and a certain amount of practice is needed in addition to a good knowledge of the pertinent topographic anatomy and physiology of the speech musculatures. Also, certain muscles such as diaphragm are difficult to access even by a needle electrode.

In addition, unlike most other techniques used in phonetic research, needle insertion for EMG assessment generally requires a licensed medical doctor.

From a physiological viewpoint, it can be argued that the sampling size of active motor units is often too small to represent a given muscle, and there may be random fluctuations in the firing pattern even for the same volitional action. Computer processing has been introduced to overcome these problems by obtaining the averaged indication of muscle activity through repetitive recordings of the same utterance type. Another problem is that the relationship between measured EMG activity and its mechanical effect is not necessarily linear, and purely quantitative descriptions of the results obtained are sometimes difficult to interpret.

If these limitations are taken into consideration, the use of EMG can provide valuable information for speech communication research as well as clinical practice.

Bibliography

Baer T, Alfonso P J, Honda K 1988 Electromyography of the tongue muscles during vowels in /pVp/ environment. *ANN Bull Research Institute of Logopedics and Phoniatrics (University of Tokyo)* **22**: 7–19

Bell-Berti F 1975 Control of pharyngeal cavity size for English voiced and voiceless stops. *Journal of the Acoustical Society of America* **57**: 456–61

Harris K S 1970 Physiological measures of speech movements: EMG and fiberoptic studies. In: *Speech and the Dentofacial Complex: The State of the Art*. American Speech and Hearing Association Report 5, Washington, DC

Ladefoged P 1964 *Three Areas of Experimental Phonetics*. Oxford University Press, London

Sawashima M, Hirose H 1983 Laryngeal gestures in speech production. In: MacNeilage P F (ed.) *The Production of Speech*. Springer-Verlag, New York

The Neurophysiology of Speech

V. L. Gracco and K. G. Munhall

1. Introduction

Speaking is at the center of human social and intellectual behavior. It is one of the universal human activities and people appear to talk with little effort from a very young age. Yet, to say even single words the human nervous system overcomes a remarkable information-processing load. To produce each utterance the speech motor system is constantly receiving, integrating, and exchanging a vast array of information through a variety of sensory-motor channels. The present chapter outlines what we know about the neurophysiological basis of this skilled behavior. A fundamental premise of this chapter is that in order to understand the neurophysiology of speech it is essential to understand the vocal tract itself, at the level of the sound generating apparatus, at the level of the basic neural architecture, and at the level of the sensorimotor processes operating during articulation.

A current view in the psycholinguistic literature is that two broad processes underlie language formulation (Levelt 1989, 1992; Garrett 1991). The first process is grammatical encoding, or the creation of lexical items within a syntactic frame, and the second is phonological encoding, including the specification of prosodic structure. These two broad processes cre-

ate the phonetic plan which is supposed to interface seamlessly with speech motor processes that generate the sequence of sounds specified in the plan. This general scheme has two major areas that lack specific details: the interface between the phonetic plan and the speech motor system, and the neurophysiology of the speech motor system itself. The present chapter addresses the latter concern. While there is a volume of literature on the psychological constructs for language and their potential neural correlates, there is almost no programmatic approach to delineating the fundamental neuroanatomical and neurophysiological substrate for speech motor output. Without such an understanding of the basic neurophysiological processes associated with speech one can easily generate overspecified models and unnecessarily detailed theories to explain all aspects of cognitive and language function. In this chapter, basic neuroanatomic and neurophysiological processes for speech will be outlined to provide the framework for interpreting higher-level cortical functions.

2. Physical Structure

In order to understand the neural structure for speech it is necessary to identify the physical components of the controlled system. The human vocal tract, stretching from the lungs to the lips, can be thought of as an 'acoustic tube' whose behavior is determined by a number of independent articulators including the lungs, larynx, pharynx, tongue, lips, jaw, and velum. Generally speaking, movements of the vocal tract can be classified into two major categories; those which produce and release constrictions (valving) and those which modulate the shape or geometry of the vocal tract. The valving and shaping actions are generally associated with the production of consonant and vowel sounds, respectively (Öhman 1966; Perkell 1969). Anatomically the vocal tract structures display muscular architecture, connections, and orientation that reflect their role in producing these classes of sounds. For example, the orientation of the muscles of the pharynx, primarily the pharyngeal constrictors, is arranged to generate a sphincteric action on the long axis of the vocal tract producing a change in the cross-sectional area and the tension or compliance of the pharyngeal tissues. The muscles of the velum are oriented primarily to raise and lower the soft palate separating the oral and nasal cavities. Perioral muscles are arranged such that various synergistic muscle actions result in a number of characteristic movements such as opening and closing of the oral cavity and protruding and retracting the lips. Some of the components, such as the tongue and larynx, can be subdivided into extrinsic and intrinsic portions each of which appear to be involved in different functional actions. Intrinsic tongue muscle fibers are oriented to allow fine grooving of the longitudinal axis of the tongue and tongue tip and make lateral adjustments characteristic of liquid and continuant sounds. Extrinsic tongue muscles are arranged predominantly to allow shaping of the tongue mass as well as elevation, depression, and retraction of portions of the tongue. Intrinsic laryngeal muscles are arranged to reciprocally open and close the glottis and adjust the tension of the vibrating vocal folds, while extrinsic laryngeal muscles are oriented to displace the entire laryngeal complex (thyroid cartilage and associated intrinsic muscles and ligaments).

Individual articulatory actions such as those described above, however, never have isolated effects in real speech. Considering the structural arrangement of the vocal tract and the vast interconnection of muscles, cartilages, and ligaments it is clear that complex biomechanical interactions are the rule. Passive or reactive changes in the vocal tract due to inherent mechanical coupling are a consequence of almost any vocal tract action. A single articulatory action almost always generates primary as well as secondary effects throughout the vocal tract.

The biomechanical environment for speech is complicated further by the different viscoelastic and other biomechanical properties of vocal tract structures. The dynamic nature of the tissue load against which the different vocal tract muscles contract is extremely heterogeneous. For some structures such as the lips and vocal folds, inertial considerations are minimal, while for the jaw and respiratory structures inertia is a significant consideration. The tongue and lips are soft tissue structures that undergo substantial viscoelastic deformation during speech while the jaw and perhaps the lips display a degree of anisotropic tension. Even seemingly homogeneous structures, like the upper and lower lips, display different stiffness properties (Ho et al. 1982) possibly contributing to their differential movement patterns (Gracco and Abbs 1986; Gracco 1988).

This complexity in the speech apparatus leads to two conclusions: (a) the control mechanism must account for or represent the peripheral motor system in order to control it. Such neural representations of the motor periphery and its dynamics have recently come to be known as 'internal models.' (see below); (b) the understanding of speech motor control will require that researchers build computer models of the speech articulators. Only through detailed biophysical models of the vocal tract and considerations of potential biomechanical interactions can the neural control principles for speech be separated from structural or cognitive/linguistic influences. A number of recent advances in physiological modeling of the vocal tract have been made and this work will provide a valuable tool for future research (e.g., Wilhelms-Tricarico 1995; Sanguineti et al. 1997; Sanguineti et al. 1998; Lucero and Munall 1998).

3. Sensory-motor Control

We have hinted that speech is not just a motor act but rather should be considered a sensory-motor process. By this we mean that sensory feedback plays a major role in the control process for speech movement. The issue of sensory feedback has generated considerable controversy and dichotomous theoretical positions in both speech production and motor control in general. Perhaps the most prevalent position is one in which voluntary movement is viewed as built from explicit sensory-mediated consequences. Once acquired the role of sensory information is no longer necessary. In the field of speech, such a position seems to have originated from the apparent resistance of various methods of sensory reduction to significantly degrade speech motor performance in adults. For example, following experimental reduction in oral kinesthesia, global measures of speech production have been found to be minimally disrupted (Gammon et al. 1971; Scott and Ringel 1971). Additionally, reduced or distorted auditory information has resulted in only mildly distorted or essentially normal speech motor output (Kelso et al. 1984; Lane and Tranel 1971). Other considerations such as neural transport delays involving afferent-to-efferent loops and the apparent ballistic nature and short duration of many speech movements have led to the position that speech movements are exclusively preprogrammed with sensory information only used in long-term adaptation of speech skill acquisition (Borden 1979). From this perspective, speech movements would be generated from pre-set motor patterns and executed independent of any afferent-dependent actions. Similar results and resulting theoretical positions have been postulated based, in part, on limb studies in which functionally deafferented animals (Polit and Bizzi 1979; Taub and Berman 1968) and man (Rothwell et al. 1982) are capable of executing learned and novel motor tasks. These results indicate that motor tasks can be carried out with reduced or absent afferent input, apparently relying on some stored motor commands. However, it is also true that motor acts executed in the absence of afferent information are often only grossly normal, often lacking their normal precision.

An alternative perspective can be suggested from considerations of the numerous studies demonstrating movement changes following dynamic mechanical perturbation to a moving articulator. It has been observed that loads applied to the lips or jaw result in changes in articulatory movement. Perturbation of a moving articulator results in compensation from other articulators to achieve a goal at the task level. For example, disruptions to the lips result in compensatory changes in the lips and jaw (Abbs and Gracco 1984; Gracco and Abbs 1985, 1988) and the larynx (Löfqvist and Gracco 1991; Munhall et al. 1994); jaw loads result in compensatory changes in the tongue (Kelso et al. 1984), lips (Folkins and Abbs 1975; Shaiman 1989), and velum (Kollia et al. 1992). Task specific responses are observed when an articulator is actively involved in the sound segment being produced but not when an articulator is not involved (Kelso et al. 1984; Shaiman 1989). The results of these studies, the density of sensory receptors found within the vocal tract and the discrimination possible with such articulators as the tongue and lips (see Kent et al. 1990 for review), all suggest that speech is always sensory-motor in nature. This proposal has been detailed in various forms in a number of related publications (cf. Abbs et al. 1984; Gracco 1987, 1988, 1990, 1991, 1994; Gracco and Abbs 1987, 1989; Gracco and Löfqvist 1994). Auditory feedback also plays a role in speech motor control. Experimental interference with the hearing of one's own speech using distorted auditory feedback (masking) results in changes in a number of speech output variables including fundamental frequency, vocal intensity, and to a lesser extent, speech movements (Siegel and Pick 1974; Lane and Tranel 1971; Forrest et al. 1986). Delayed auditory feedback results in a slowing of speaking rate which can result in a breakdown in fluency (Lee 1950; Fairbanks 1955; Howell et al. 1987) while low pass filtering results in changes in nasal resonance (Garber and Moller 1979) and both

increases and decreases in lip, jaw, and tongue movement (Forrest et al. 1986). Recently, a number of investigations have used perturbations of the frequency content of the auditory feedback signal to examine changes in fundamental frequency and intonation (Elman 1981; Kawahara 1993).

From an engineering perspective, the speech motor control system can be characterized as one of a set of classic control models. Theoreticians focusing on the sensory-dependent, sensory-independent issue have also focused, in parallel, on the issue of whether speech motor action is regulated by a closed loop or an open loop system. In this context the term closed loop is often used synonymously with feedback and the term open loop is often used synonymously with no feedback. This simplistic dichotomy has a long and unproductive history and is based on the inaccurate assumption that open loop implies the lack of sensory influence (see discussion by Abbs and Cole 1982). In reality, the distinction is determined by the control action to the motor system. For example, an open loop control system is one in which the control action (the input) is independent of the output; a closed loop control system is one in which the control action is somehow dependent on the output. More recently, modeling in motor control has focused on so-called internal models of articulators. These control systems represent the biomechanical and dynamic characteristics of the articulators and thus allow feedforward or predictive planning and control. In doing so, they combine features of both open and closed loop systems. For example, Wolpert et al. (1995) have used a Kalman filter model to sensory-motor integration in arm movements. In this model, the position of the hand is estimated by using the control action, the sensory feedback and a model of the limb motor system. This type of model allows increased accuracy in motor planning and it can overcome some of the problems posed by sensory feedback delays.

4. Serial Timing

Speech is dynamic in nature and normal speech production involves the sequencing of vocal tract configurations adjusted for context. An important theoretical issue is to determine how the nervous system integrates speech production units into coherent packages for information transfer. As pointed out by Lashley (1951), serial actions such as those for speech, locomotion, typing, and the playing of musical instruments cannot be explained in terms of successions of external reflexes. Rather the apparent rhythmicity found in all but the simplest motor activities suggests that some sort of temporal patterning may form the foundation for motor as well as perceptual activities. A number of observations are consistent with the presence of some kind of rhythm generating mechanism as the basis for sequential speech motor adjustments. For example, compensatory adjustments for lower lip perturbations during an oral closing movement demonstrate changes in interarticulator timing consistent with the operation of an underlying oscillatory or rhythm generating mechanism (Gracco and Abbs 1988, 1989; Saltzman et al. 1995; Saltzman et al. 1992). Other results such as minimal movement duration changes from static (Lindblom et al. 1987) and dynamic perturbation (Gracco and Abbs 1988) and durational consistencies across experimental sessions (Kozhevnikov and Chistovich 1965) are consistent with an underlying mechanism in which sequential timing is maintained. However, a strictly isochronous mechanism is not plausible given the different duration requirements for consonants and vowels.

An important consequence of incorporating a central rhythm generator into the speech production process is the ability to explain rate, stress, and final lengthening changes with manipulation of a single mechanism: global (over the course of an utterance) and local (phone and syllable level) changes in rhythmic frequency. Moreover, the rhythmic nature of the output is potentially available to facilitate speech perception by making signal stream segmentation more predictable (Cutler and Mehler 1993; Lashley 1951; Martin 1972). The rhythmic modulation of speech production would provide the perceptual system with a predictable framework for sampling and parsing the output. The breakdown in speaking rhythm associated with a number of different speech motor disorders (Kent and Rosenbek 1982) and the pervasive rhythmicity found throughout the nervous system (Llinás 1986, 1991) strongly suggest that the underlying rhythm is a network property rather than the property of a specific neuroanatomical location. However, to date no studies have been undertaken to investigate differences in neural activity associated with rhythmic and nonrhythmic speech and nonspeech actions.

5. Neural Substrate

The picture painted by this brief survey of speech behavior is a complex one. It appears that even simple articulation involves a range of specialized motor and cognitive processes and that the neural mechanisms may reflect this complexity. It has been known for over 100 years that multiple regions of the brain are involved in some manner in producing speech and language (Broca 1861, 1960; Wernicke 1874). While the content of the spoken message represents, in a broad sense, the cognitive and linguistic character of human communication, the final common filter is the speech production process. Alterations in the pragmatic, semantic, and syntactic content of a message will alter the articulatory (kinematic) character of the motor output. Similarly, nervous system damage will effect articulation, either directly if damage is confined to specific sensory-motor centers, or indirectly, by affecting the communicative aspects of the message.

The neural substrate for speech has been identified from a variety of sources including human mapping studies using electrical stimulation (Penfield and Roberts 1959; Ojemann 1983; Mateer 1983) and neuroanatomical studies of nonhuman primates (Muakassa and Strick 1979; Woolsey et al. 1952). A number of cortical and subcortical regions have been identified in which a representation of the vocal tract can be found (see Gracco and Abbs 1987 for review). Cortical regions with vocal tract representations include the primary motor and sensory areas (MI and SI, respectively), the so-called nonprimary motor areas including supplementary motor area (SMA) and pre-motor area (PM; lateral precentral cortex), and a posterior parietal region. The general PM area and posterior parietal regions (including portions of the temporal region in man) comprise the areas associated with Broca's and Wernicke's area, respectively (Penfield and Roberts 1959). Extensive subcortical representations can also be found in the cerebellar cortex, deep cerebellar nuclei, and regions of the basal ganglia. In addition, electrical stimulation of cortical face areas causes contralateral, bilateral, and ipsilateral sensations (Penfield and Jasper 1954). Recently, cerebral magnetic fields following unilateral electric stimulation of the tongue revealed bilateral representation in somatic sensory cortex (SI and SII; Karhu et al. 1991). Additional evidence on bilateral cortical representation has come from spatial distribution of somatosensory evoked potentials to taps applied to the tongue (Ishiko et al. 1980) and to electrical stimulation of the lips (Findler and Feinsod 1982).

An interesting aspect of orofacial representations is their extrinsic (and generally reciprocal) connections. For example, the different cortical areas are connected to different subcortical structures and contain projections from or project to distinct and (relatively) non-overlapping regions of the thalamus. The PM area receives input from the deep cerebellar nuclei via the thalamus and projects to the MI as well as contributing direct descending projections to brain stem nuclei. Similar segregated extrinsic connections are found for regions of the basal ganglia and SMA. In addition, there are rather dense projections from parietal areas to the motor and premotor as well as temporal regions and descending projections to brain stem nuclei (Gracco and Abbs 1987). A number of neuroanatomical studies suggest that large regions of the cortex and subcortex are interconnected and maintain relatively segregated modules that ultimately converge at the output. These diverse neural areas represent large regions of the nervous system. They display an extrinsic organization consistent with the concept of neural modules hypothesized by Mountcastle suggesting distributed processing functions (Mountcastle 1978). It should be noted that these large scale networks all have access to peripheral sensory information from somatic receptors as well as the visual and auditory receptors and therefore display 're-entrant' characteristics with changes in one system allowing changes or readjustment in all convergent systems (Edelman 1987).

6. Speech Motor Disorders

A source of information on the nervous system organization for speech comes from neurological disorders. From a synthesis of various observations some general conclusions can be drawn. A surprising characteristic of almost all lesions involving the central nervous system is the incidence of motor impairments accompanying cognitive or linguistic impairments and the converse. It appears as suggested by Jackson (1875) that the so-called higher centers of the nervous system may be extensions of the lower nervous centers representing impressions and movements. Consistent with the neuroanatomical substrate outlined above, damage of the cerebellum and PM area often results in sensory-motor impairments of some similarity at least to acoustic and perceptual examination (Kent and Rosenbeck 1982). Damage to either of these regions often produces a breakdown in speech that can be characterized by a disruption of the smooth timing of sequential speech movements. Cerebellar patients often show a decomposition of movement as though the various parts of a complex movement had to be thought out one by one. Dysmetria is also a characteristic of cerebellar damage suggesting that the ability to integrate somatic and visual information to produce appropriately calibrated actions has been affected. These symptoms are generally consistent with those associated with Broca's aphasia (due to anterior premotor lesions). For example, electrical stimulation of the PM area, which receives output from the deep cerebellar nuclei via the thalamus causes speech arrest (Penfield and Roberts 1959) and an inability to sequence multiple speech movements (Mateer 1983). Because of the limited data available it is not clear just how similar the damage to these regions is but it can be suggested that there may be considerable overlap. A similar suggestion can be made regarding the impairments associated with basal ganglia and SMA damage. Basal ganglia damage, characterized by Parkinson's disease, often results in speech characterized by imprecise consonant production, mono-pitch and loudness, and articulator movements that are reduced in amplitude and speed. SMA damage results in speech impairments ranging from total speech arrest to imprecise articulation. Finally, damage to the posterior portion of the brain (Wernicke's area) produces speech and language impairments consistent with a role in the complex processing of multimodal input and the contribution of that processing to the final motor output. Patients with damage to posterior portions of the brain display output impairments that have been suggested to reflect

inappropriate phonological selection compared to the more phonetic errors exhibited by anterior (Broca's) aphasics (Blumstein 1981). Thus there appears to be some general functions associated with the hypothetical distributed processing modules known to represent vocal tract sensory-motor structures.

Based on changes in the readiness potential (Bereitschaftspotential—BP) overlying the frontal cortex during sequential motor tasks it has been suggested that SMA may be involved in the triggering or timing of serial elements (Deecke et al. 1985). The BP changes precede the slow potential changes overlying other areas of cortex and are temporally related to the onset of the serial action. These observations are consistent with regional cerebral blood flow studies indicating parallel SMA changes for both 'internal programming' and execution of a sequence of finger movements (Roland et al. 1980). Recent work (Cappell et al. 1995) reported neuromagnetic activity in regions presumed to overly SMA when subjects were speaking covertly. It has been suggested that SMA is involved in motor preparation in a variety of studies. From blood flow (Roland et al. 1980) and fMRI (Rao et al. 1993) studies, the SMA, but not the motor cortex, has been shown to increase activation in response to instructions to imagine, but not execute, complex movements of the finger. From EEG recordings, prior to movement activation, there is widespread activation over large areas of cortex that seems to be largest over the vertex possibly reflecting SMA participation (Deecke et al. 1969; Deecke and Kornhuber 1978). To date, however, it has not been determined whether the SMA activity is precisely related to the initiation of any movement-related (or imagined) action as opposed to the production of movement sequences.

More recently, neuroimaging studies employing positron emission tomography (PET) have been used to investigate brain regions involved in speech and language production. For the most part the results of these studies are consistent with both lesion and neuroanatomical data. For volitional breathing tasks involving both inspiration and expiration, bilateral increases in rCBF have been noted in primary motor cortex dorsally just lateral to the vertex, in SMA, and in the right lateral pre-motor cortex and left ventrolateral thalamus (Ramsay et al. 1993). The differences between the active inspiration and expiration conditions included more extensive blood flow and rCBF changes in the cerebellum during active expiration. For most speech production studies, the results have found activations in all areas that contain orofacial representations including sensorimotor cortex, pre-motor areas including Broca's area and SMA, and to a lesser extent the anterior cingulate and regions of the basal ganglia and the cerebellum (Friston et al. 1991; Murphy et al. 1997; Hirano et al. 1996; Larsen et al. 1978; Peterson et al. 1989; Roland 1985). While a number of studies employing both rCBF and, more recently, functional magnetic resonance imaging (fMRI) have demonstrated neural activations related to speech and language function, to date there have been no studies that have clearly defined the functional role of any of the classic speech production areas. In part this is a result of a limited focus on speech as a sensorimotor function. Most of the more recent work using improved neural imaging techniques and equipment has focused on the memory and/or language characteristics of speech with little emphasis on the articulatory components of the spoken message. It still remains to be determined whether the different cortical and subcortical neural systems involved in speech can be separated along functional lines. One interesting hypothesis is that offered by Kimura (1993). The difference in the anterior and posterior speech regions (Broca's area versus Wernicke's area, respectively) is hypothesized to reflect the level of linguistic/articulatory control with the anterior speech region primarily involved in mediating speech production at a phonemic/syllabic level while the posterior region is primarily involved in mediating speech production at a multi-syllabic level.

7. Summary

Speaking is a communicative act in which the output represents a synthesis of potentially independent processes. The processes overlap in time and each stage of the output reflects, to some extent, the influence of all contributing levels. A primary component of the speech production process is preparation for speaking. That is, excitability levels associated with sensory and motor regions are increased in a general sense and specific regions involved with communication are tuned for the upcoming motor commands. The overall levels of excitability are dependent on certain pragmatic requirements (emotional content, speaking rate, noisy environment, etc.) that determine the overall effort level. Patterned neural commands specify the coordination within and across articulators and are conditioned by ascending projections from somatic sensory receptors found throughout the vocal tract. The speech motor system receives input in the form of a phonological code specifying unique vocal tract configurations for each phone of the language. At the level of the phonological encoding process the unit of organization appears to be larger than individual phonetic gestures. A level of organization, on the order of a syllable, which may contain one or more phonetic gestures, is hypothesized. This syllable-level temporal organization may form the rhythmic basis for all higher level (suprasegmental) temporal phenomena. It is further hypothesized that the rhythmic organization reflects a system property rather than a manifestation of a single rhythmic or oscillatory source. Moreover, these hypothetical processes appear to be consistent with known (or inferred) nervous system functions. The motor preparation process involves the SMA/basal ganglia network in which cortical and subcortical sensory and motor areas are activated in preparation for action and tuning the sensory-motor centers in ways that reflect a time scale involving utterance-level and possibly suprasegmental adjustments. It should be noted that while this process may be thought of as motor, it is dependent on the communicative requirements of the situation and involves setting up sensory as well as motor consequences. Hence, all functional speech processes are sensory-motor and communicative and reflect a synthesis of all available levels or organization. The phonological encoding process involves structures that impart meaning, perhaps lexical items, that are parsed into multi-syllabic phonetic codes that are executed on a syllable-by-syllable basis. In concert with Broca's area, the cerebellar nuclei adjust the spatiotemporal characteristics of the motor commands for sequencing within a syllable and adjust the overall rhythmicity of the system based on phonetic context. The cerebellum has extensive connections onto almost all regions of the nervous system to allow it to play an executive role in sensory-motor integration and motor command adjustment. In contrast to the general setting of sensory-motor excitability levels associated with the SMA/basal ganglia system, the cerebellar/PM system appears to be involved in more specific changes associated with contextual adjustments of motor commands.

References

Abbs J H, Cole K J 1982 Consideration of bulbar and suprabulbar afferent influences upon speech motor coordination. In: Grillner S, Lindblom B, Lubker J, Persson A (eds.) *Speech motor control.* Pergamon, New York: 159–88

Abbs J H, Gracco W L 1984 Control of complex motor gestures: Orofacial muscle responses to load perturbations of the lip during speech. *Journal of Neurophysiology* 51(4): 705–23

Abbs J H, Gracco V L, Cole K J 1984 Control of multimovement coordination: Sensorimotor mechanisms in speech motor programming. *Journal of Motor Behavior* 16: 195–232

Blumstein S E 1981 Neurolinguistic disorders: Language-brain relationships. In: Filskov S B, Boll T J (eds.) *Handbook of Clinical Neuropsychology.* Wiley, New York

Border G J 1979 An interpretation of research on feedback interruption. *Brain and Language* 7: 307–19

Broca P 1960 Remarks on the seat of the faculty of articulate language, followed by an observation of aphemia. In: *The Cerebral Cortex* (von Bonin G ed. and trans.). Charles C. Thomas, Springfield, NJ 49–72

Cappell J, Zonenshayn M, Koppell B, Llinás R 1995 Neuromagnetic activity during covert speech. *Human Brain Mapping* S1: 243

Cutler A, Mehler J 1993 The periodicity bias. *Journal of Phonetics* 21: 103–8

Deecke L, Kornhuber H H 1978 An electrical sign of participation of the mesial 'supplementary' motor cortex in human voluntary finger movement. *Brain Research* **159**: 473–76

Deecke L, Kornhuber H H, Lang W, Land M, Schreiber H 1985 Timing functions of the frontal cortex in sequential motor and learning tasks. *Human Neurobiology* **4**: 143–54

Deecke L, Scheid P, Kornhuber H H 1969 Distribution of readiness potential, pre-motion positivity, and motor potential of the human cerebral cortex preceding voluntary finger movements. *Experimental Brain Research* **7**: 158–68

Edelman G M 1987 *Neural Darwinism*. Basic Books, New York

Elman J 1981 Effects of frequency-shifted feedback on the pitch of vocal productions. *Journal of the Acoustical Society of America* **70**: 45–50

Fairbanks G 1955 Selective vocal effects of delayed auditory feedback. *Journal of Speech and Hearing Disorders* **20**: 333–46

Findler G, Feinsod M 1982 Sensory evoked response to electrical stimulation of the trigeminal nerve in humans. *Journal of Neurosurgery* **56**: 545–49

Folkins J W, Abbs J H 1975 Lip and jaw motor control during speech: Responses to resistive loading of the jaw. *Journal of Speech and Hearing Research* **18**: 207–20

Forrest K, Abbas P J, Zimmermann G N 1986 Effects of white noise masking and low pass filtering on speech kinematics. *Journal of Speech and Hearing Research* **29**: 549–62

Friston K J, Firth C D, Liddle P F, Frackowiak R S J 1991 Investigating a network model of word generation with positron emission tomography. *Proceedings of the Royal Society of London* **244**: 101–6

Gammon S A, Smith P J, Daniloff R G, Kim C W 1971 Articulation and stress/juncture production under oral anesthetization and masking. *Journal of Speech and Hearing Research* **14**: 271–82

Garber S R, Moller K T 1979 The effect of feedback filtering on nasalization in normal and hypernasal speakers. *Journal of Speech and Hearing Research* **22**: 321–33

Garrett M 1991 Disorders of lexical selection. In: Levelt W J M (ed.) *Lexical Access in Speech Production*. Blackwell, Cambridge, MA: 143–80

Gracco W L 1987 A multilevel control model for speech motor activity. In: Peters H, Hulstijn W (eds.) *Speech Motor Dynamics in Stuttering*. Springer-Verlag, Berlin: 57–76

Gracco V L 1988 Timing factors in the coordination of speech movements. *Journal of Neuroscience* **8**: 4628–34

Gracco V L 1990 Characteristics of speech as a motor control system. In: Hammond G (ed.) *Cerebral Control of Speech and Limb Movements* Elsevier, Holland 3–28

Gracco V L 1991 Sensorimotor mechanisms in speech motor control. In: Peters H, Hultsijn W, Starkweather C W (eds.) *Speech Motor Control and Stuttering*. Elsevier, Holland: 53–78

Gracco V L 1994 Some organizational characteristics of speech movement control. *Journal of Speech and Hearing Research* **37**: 4–27

Gracco V L, Abbs J H 1985 Dynamic control of perioral system during speech: Kinematic analyses of autogenic and nonautogenic sensorimotor processes. *Journal of Neuroscience* **54**: 418–32

Gracco V L Abbs J H 1986 Variant and invariant characteristics of speech movements. *Experimental Brain Research* **65**: 156–66

Gracco V L, Abbs J H 1987 Programming and execution processes of speech movement control: Potential neural correlates. In: Keller E, Gopnik M (eds.) *Symposium on Motor and Sensory Language Processes*. Erlbaum, Hillsdale, NJ: 163–201

Gracco V L, Abbs J H 1988 Central patterning of speech movements. *Experimental Brain Research* **71**: 515–26

Gracco V L, Abbs J H 1989 Sensorimotor characteristics of speech motor sequences. *Experimental Brain Research* **75**: 586–98

Gracco V L, Löfqvist A 1994 Speech motor coordination and control: Evidence from lip, jaw and laryngeal movements. *Journal of Neuroscience* **14**: 6585–97

Hirano S, Kojima H, Naito Y, Honjo I, Kamoto Y, Okazawa H, Ishizu K, Yonekura Y, Nagahama Y, Fukuyama H, Konishi J 1996 Cortical speech processing mechanisms while vocalizing visually presented language. *NeuroReport* **8**: 363–67

Ho T P, Azar K, Weinstein S, Dowley W W 1982 Physical properties of human lips: Experimental and theoretical analysis. *Journal of Biomechanics* **15**: 859–66

Howell P, El-Yaniv N, Powell D J 1987 Factors affecting fluency in stutterers. In: Peters H F M, Hulstijn W (eds.) *Speech Motor Dynamics in Stuttering*. Springer-Verlag, New York: 361–69

Ishiko N, Hanamori T, Murayama N 1980 Spatial distribution of somatosensory responses evoked by tapping the tongue and finger in man. *Electroencephalography and Clinical Neurophysiology* **50**: 1–10

Jackson J H 1875 *Clinical and Physiological Researches on the Nervous System*. Churchill, London

Karhu J, Hari R, Lu S -T, Paetau R, Rif J 1991 Cerebral magnetic fields to lingual stimulation. *Electroencephalography and Clinical Neurophysiology* **80**: 459–68

Kawahara H 1993 Transformed auditory feedback: Effects of fundamental frequency perturbation. *Advanced Telecommunications Research Institute International Technical Report, TR-H-040*

Kelso J A S, Tuller B, V.-Bateson E, Fowler C A 1984 Functionally specific articulatory cooperation following jaw perturbations during speech: Evidence for coordinative structures. *Journal of Experimental Psychology: Human Perception and Performance* **10**: 812–32

Kent R D, Martin R E, Sufit R L 1990 Oral sensation: A review and clinical prospective. In: Winitz H (ed.) *Human Communication and its Disorders*. Ablex, Norwood, NJ: 135–91

Kent R D, Rosenbek J C 1982 Prosodic disturbance and neurologic lesion. *Brain and Language* **15**: 259–91

Kimura D 1993 *Neuromotor Mechanisms in Human Communication*. Oxford University Press, New York

Kollia H B, Gracco V L, Harris K S 1992 Functional organization of velar movements following jaw perturbation. *Journal of the Acoustical Society of America* **91**: 2474

Kozhevnikov V, Chistovich L 1965 Speech: Articulation and Perception. *Joint Publications Research Service* **30**: 453

Lashley K S 1951 The problem of serial order in behavior. In: Jeffress L A (ed.) *Cerebral Mechanisms in Behavior: The Hixon Symposium*. Wiley, New York

Lane H L, Tranel B 1971 The Lombard sign and the role of hearing in speech. *Journal of Speech and Hearing Research* **14**: 677–709

Larsen B, Skinhoj E, Lassen N A 1978 Variations in regional cortical blood flow in the right and left hemispheres during automatic speech. *Brain* **101**: 193–209

Lee B S 1950 Effects of delayed speech feedback. *Journal of the Acoustical Society of America* **22**: 824–26

Levelt W J M 1989 *Speaking: From Intention to Articulation.* MIT Press, Cambridge, MA

Levelt W J M 1992 Accessing words in speech production: Stages, processes and representations. *Cognition* **42**: 1–22

Lindblom B, Lubker J, Gay T, Lyberg P, Branderal P, Holgren K 1987 The concept of target and speech timing. In: Channon R, Shockery L (eds.) *In Honor of Ilse Lehiste.* Foris Publications, Dordrecht, The Netherlands: 161–81

Llinás R R 1986 Neuronal oscillators in mammalian brain. In: Cohen M J, Strumwasser F (eds.) *Comparative Neurobiology: Modes of Communication in the Nervous System.* Wiley, New York: 279–90

Llinás R R 1991 The noncontinuous nature of movement execution. In: Humphrey D R, Freund H-J (eds.) *Motor Control: Concepts and Issues.* Wiley, New York: 223–42

Löfqvist A, Gracco V L 1991 Discrete and continuous modes in speech motor control. *Perilus* **14**: 27–34

Lucero J C, Munhall K G 1998 A model of facial biomechanics for speech production. Manuscript submitted to the *Journal of the Acoustical Society of America*

Martin J G 1972 Rhythmic (hierarchical) versus serial structure in speech and other behavior. *Psychological Review* **79**: 487–509

Mateer C A 1983 Motor and perceptual functions of the left hemisphere and their interactions. In: Segalowitz S J (ed.) *Language Function and Brain Organization.* Academic Press, New York: 145–70

Mountcastle V B 1978 An organizing principle for cerebral function: The unit module and the distributed system. In: Edelman G M, Mountcastle V B (eds.) *The Mindful Brain: Cortical Organization and the Group-Selective Theory of Higher Brain Function.* MIT Press, Cambridge, MA: 7–50

Muakassa K F, Strick P L 1979 Frontal lobe inputs to primate motor cortex: Evidence for four somatotopically organized 'premotor' areas. *Brain Research* **177**: 176–82

Munhall K, Löfqvist A, Kelso J A S 1994 Lip-larynx coordination in speech: Effects of mechanical perturbations to the lower lip. *Journal of the Acoustical Society of America* **96**: 3605–16

Murphy K, Corfield D R, Guz A, Fink G R, Wise R J S, Harrison J, Adams L 1997 Cerebral areas associated with motor control of speech in humans. *Journal of Applied Physiology* **83(5)**: 1438–47

Öhman S E G 1966 Coarticulation in VCV utterances: Spectrographic measurements. *Journal of the Acoustical Society of America* **39**: 151–68

Ojemann G A 1983 Brain organization for language from the perspective of electrical stimulation mapping. *The Behavioral and Brain Sciences* **6**: 189–230

Penfield W, Jasper H 1954 Epilepsy and the functional anatomy of the human brain. Little, Brown, Boston, MA

Penfield W, Roberts L 1959 *Speech and Brain Mechanisms.* Princeton University Press, Princeton, NJ

Perkell J S 1969 Physiology of speech production: Results and implications of a quantitative cineradiographic study (Research Monograph No. 53). MIT Press, Cambridge, MA

Petersen S E, Fox P T, Posner M I, Mintun M, Raichle M E 1989 Positron emission tomographic studies of the processing of single words. *Journal of Cognitive Neuroscience* **1**: 153–70

Polit A, Bizzi E 1978 Processes controlling arm movement in monkeys. *Science* **201**: 1235–37

Ramsay S C, Adams L, Murphy K, Corfield D R, Grootoonk S, Bailey D L, Frackowiak R S, Guz A 1993 Regional cerebral blood flow during volitional expiration in man: A comparison with volitional inspiration. *Journal of Physiology (London)* **461**: 85–101

Rao S M, Binder J R, Bandettini P A, Hammeke T A, Yetkin Y Z, Jesmanowicz A, Lisk L M, Morris G M, Mueller W M, Estkowski L D, Wong E C, Haughton V M, Hyde J S 1993 Functional magnetic resonance imaging of complex human movements. *Neurology* **43**: 2311–18

Roland P E 1985 Cortical organization of voluntary behavior in man. *Human Neurobiology* **4**: 155–67

Roland P E, Skinhoj E, Lassen N A, Larsen B 1980 Different cortical areas in man in organization of voluntary movements in extrapersonal space. *Journal of Neurophysiology* **43**: 137–50

Rothwell J C, Traub M M, Day B L, Obeso J A, Thomas P K, Mardsen C D 1982 Manual motor performance in a deafferented man. *Brain* **105**: 515–42

Saltzman E, Löfqvist A, Kinsella-Shaw J, Kay B, Rubin P 1995 On the dynamics of temporal patterning in speech. In: Bell-Berti F, Raphael L (eds.) *Producing Speech: Contemporary Issues for Katherine Safford Harris.* American Institute of Physics, Woodbury, NY: 469–88

Saltzman E, Löfqvist A, Kinsella-Shaw J, Rubin P E, Kay B 1992 A perturbation study of lip-larynx coordination. In: *Proceedings of the 1992 International Conference of Spoken Language Processing (ICSLP '92): Addendum, Banff, Alberta, Canada.* Priority Printing, Edmonton, Canada

Sanguineti V, Laboissière R, Ostry D J 1998 An integrated model of the biomechanics and neural control of the tongue, jaw, hyoid and larynx system. *Journal of the Acoustical Society of America* **103**: 1615–27

Sanguineti V, Laboissière R, Payan Y 1997 A control model of human tongue movements in speech. *Biological Cybernetics* **77**: 11–22

Scott C M, Ringel R L 1971 Articulation without oral sensory control. *Journal of Speech and Hearing Research* **14**: 804–18

Shaiman S 1989 Kinematic and electromyographic responses to perturbation of the jaw. *Journal of the Acoustical Society of America* **86**: 78–87

Siegel G M, Pick H L 1974 Auditor feedback in the regulation of the voice. *Journal of the Acoustical Society of America* **56**: 1618–24

Taub E, Ellman S J, Berman A J 1966 Deafferentation in monkeys: Effects on conditioned grasp responses. *Science* **151**: 593–94

Wernicke C 1874 *Der Aphasische Symptomcomplex.* Cohen and Weigert, Breslau

Wilhelms-Tricarico R 1995 Physiological modeling of speech production: Methods for modeling of soft-tissue articulators. *Journal of the Acoustical Society of America* **97**: 3085–98

Wolpert D M, Ghabramani Z, Jordan M 1995 An internal model for sensorimotor integration. *Science* **269**: 1880–82

Woolsey C N, Settlage P H, Meyer D R, Spencer W, Pinto Hamuy T, Travis A M 1952 Patterns of localization in precentral and 'supplementary' motor areas and their relation to the concept of a premotor area. *Association for Research in Nervous and Mental Disease* **30**: 238–64

Psycholinguistics
M. A. Garman

Psycholinguistics is concerned with language abilities in the individual, and is formed around questions such as: How does a listener recover a message from speech signal and/or written text? and How does a speaker express ideas in terms of articulatory and/or graphological sequences? The nature of such abilities may be approached through the concept of 'microgenesis,' of which the first element contrasts with 'ontogenesis' and with 'phylogenesis' (the development of language in the species). The second element '-genesis' reminds us that language abilities are fundamentally creative. This is obviously so in the case of language production, but equally true also of language comprehension, where the listener/reader does not so much 'recover' a message from the language signal, but rather uses cues in the language signal to guide the creation of a message, which may only partially overlap that of the speaker/writer. As well as the cues in the language signal, the listener/reader of course also makes use of a body of relatively stable, long-term knowledge of the language system, and nonlinguistic information as well (e.g., perception of the situation of utterance). So also for the speaker/writer, who does not so much encode a message in the form of a signal, but rather selects signal properties in the light of linguistic and nonlinguistic knowledge of what the listener/reader needs to work with. Psycholinguistics, in these terms, is about the interaction between 'knowing that' (e.g., meaning-form relations), and 'knowing how' to implement this knowledge under real-time pressures. Two particularly important parameters of such performance are time and accuracy, and these turn up as dependent variables in a large range of experimental studies (see further below). The chronological dimensions that are relevant to this field of study may be further refined by reference to the terms 'micro-/macro-chronic' (Catford 1977) of which the first concerns the timescale of psycholinguistic 'processes' (e.g., the mapping of ideas into linguistic forms, and of these forms into signal properties), and the second deals with the timescale of the 'product.' Processes are typically measured on a timescale marked off in milliseconds, while the product may occupy seconds, or, especially in the case of written language, much longer units of time.

Given the wide range of human abilities involved in all aspects of language use, psycholinguists come from a variety of disciplinary backgrounds, of which the following may be mentioned here: cognitive-semantics, language philosophy, psychology, linguistics, and speech science (phonetics). In a sense, phoneticians have historically been closest to what is now called the psycholinguistic approach, since their discussion of, for example, articulatory elements such as consonants and vowels has traditionally been in terms of the processes involved in the product: 'bilabial voiceless stop' defines a product in terms of the processes that are involved in its production. In such an interdisciplinary field, relations between disciplines have not always been clear (e.g., speech science and cognitive-semantics), or fruitful (though they have usually been instructive). The situation has not always been helped by partial representations of certain disciplines to others. Much of the recent tradition of psycholinguistics has been inspired by the work of Chomsky in linguistics, which has accordingly been largely represented within the field as Chomsky's model of the ideal speaker/hearer (as this has developed over the years since the early 1960s). Some methodological debate has arisen as the result of the notion that psycholinguists were somehow to take the (current) Chomsky model and show that it had 'psychological reality.' An appreciation of the issue may be gained by considering the following view:

> the task of psycholinguistics is not to confirm Chomsky's account of linguistic competence by undertaking experiments... [it] *is to my mind very much more difficult and interesting. It is, by doing experiments, to find out what are the mechanisms that underlie linguistic competence.*
>
> (Sutherland 1966: 161–62)

There is much to be said for this view, although the notion of 'doing experiments' is one that needs particular attention. The familiar problem of the observer paradox has been particularly noticeable in studies that have sought to quantify linguistic performance of various kinds: once you start measuring how people produce or understand language in specific situations, they notice, and this affects what is measured. The type of situation, and the means of measurement, may introduce certain behavioral properties that are not found in more naturalistic settings (see further below).

The following may be considered in looking for the cornerstones of psycholinguistics: the interface between thought and language; the nature of the language signals which are transmitted and received (see further Sect. 1 below); the biological foundations of language in the sense of the observable anatomical structures and physiological processes that serve as the substrate of human language abilities (see Sect. 2; see also *Neurolinguistics*; *Language and the Brain*); and the nature of the evidence for the operations of the abstract language system, that is, that part of language abilities which mediates between input and output, and which may function even when decoupled from the overt language signal (see Sect. 3).

1. Characteristics of the Language Signal

It is usual in speech science to refer to the 'speech chain' model whereby one (talking) head communicates with another (listening) head via a communication chain that centres on the speech signal (Denes and Pinson 1963). In psycholinguistics, it is convenient to think of just one (talking and listening) head at the center of the picture, and to bring in at least the written language modalities (writing and reading) as well (ideally other forms of signal such as signed language should be considered; also the visible aspects of speech as exploited in lip-reading). Such a configuration might be referred to as the language 'switchboard,' perhaps, or possibly a better term would be the language 'central processing unit (CPU).' One of the characteristics of this CPU is that it can operate a variety of mediating functions between categories of input and output.

Some of these input–output relations have ready labels in everyday language, while others are not so well-defined. Thus, 'reading' is ambiguous between 'visual input—cognitive output' ('silent reading') and 'visual input—cognitive + speech outputs' ('reading aloud'); 'writing' is usually thought of as 'cognitive input—writing output,' while 'dictation' is available for the situation 'speech input—writing output.' 'Naming' refers to 'visual input—speech output'; though notice that the visual input may be 'verbal' (i.e., consisting of the letter sequence of a word) or pictorial, or it may be the visual presence of an object itself, for which the term 'confrontation naming' is sometimes used. On the other hand, if the letter sequence in the input is not a word, then the term used is 'pronunciation' (you can pronounce *mav* but you cannot name it).

In many of these input–output relations, the issue of 'cognitive' involvement is like the wild card in the pack; it is regarded as part of the game, but it obeys its own laws. In discussions of language processing, 'cognition' conveniently refers to those aspects that are adjacent to strictly language phenomena, but the boundary line is far from clear. We have already seen that there may be visual input that is not 'verbal' (i.e., linguistic), so that presenting a picture of a hammer (instead of an object hammer) for naming may be represented as *visual input—cognitive system—speech output*. But we may ask how far cognition may be involved in the case where the word *hammer* is the visual input; and so too we may ask, for example, how far is cognition involved in dictation? To the extent that we do understand what we are being asked to dictate, is the cognitive level serving as output (from the speech input) or as input (to the writing output), or both? To some extent, answers to these questions are forthcoming from close observation of behavior; for instance, if a dictation sequence contains the input ... /ri:d/ ..., then the corresponding graphological sequence might be either 'reed' or 'read,'

and the choice between the two will be more or less determined by context, the processing of which must reflect cognitive involvement.

Other input–output relations may be more complex. Consider one speaker spelling out a word for the benefit of another, so as to exclude from earshot some third party such as a child who is deemed not to be able to decode what is being transmitted. This device is not infallible; common experience suggests that either the child is familiar enough with certain key terms (such as 'ice-cream') to make a fair guess at the message; or, embarrassingly, the receiving adult proves not to be very adept at catching the spelled sound sequence. This is not too surprising, since it demands a rather unnatural task of the CPU; after /si:/ has been recognized in context as the letter *c* rather than either of the words 'see' or 'sea,' it and the other letters thus perceived must be held in memory long enough to assemble a visual code, which can then be used to enter the mental lexicon.

1.1 The Speech Signal

Articulatory factors: the speech signal is produced through a multichannel vocal tract, whose channels are in simultaneous activity (e.g., lips, tongue, velum, vocal cords). This leads to great difficulties of 'segmentation,' since what is a segment boundary for one channel may not be in another. It also leads to 'articulatory variance' (the 'same' sound may be differently produced on different occasions), reflecting articulatory context/timing; this is describable in terms of 'coarticulation' effects.

A standard view has been that this multichannel system is under some unitary control, i.e., that there is some high-level executive component that provides input, which may be specified separately for syllabic framework and the segments that fill places within this framework. The segments may be conceived as being linguistic entities (i.e., abstract phonological elements) or psychophonetic (target articulations). In either case, coarticulations arise through the 'smearing' of ideal, discrete segment boundaries (Perkell 1980). There are alternatives, though, including the view that coarticulations arise through the operation of 'collectives' of motor-command centres at the executive end of the speech production process: the results of electromyographic studies point to the existence of surprisingly constant relationships across muscle groups (in the face of variation of individual muscles within these groups), e.g., controlling lips, tongue, and jaw in speech (Scott-Kelso et al. 1983). In terms of this approach, the question is not how coarticulations arise, but rather how do segments get established in the stream of speech (see *The Neurophysiology of Speech*)?

Acoustic properties: air is the crucial medium for the transmission of speech. The dynamics of this transmission are organized in terms of 'amplitude,' the displacement of air particles from their position of rest; 'frequency,' the number of times that the pattern of displacement occurs per unit time; and 'intensity,' manifest in the frequency value for a given amplitude level, or vice versa. In physical terms, speech sounds are complex, involving either wave patterns that can be analyzed into combinations of constituent simple waves ('periodic' sounds) and 'harmonics,' or fundamentally unwavelike amplitudes across the frequency spectrum ('aperiodic' sounds).

Auditory factors: air particles, set in motion by the articulators, ultimately transmit their displacement patterns to the ear via the middle and inner ear systems, where a mechanical-to-electrical transduction takes place. The auditory system functions as a multichannel device, accepting a large number of simultaneous frequency and amplitude data points (complex sounds have amplitudes at various frequencies), through a 'gliding time-window' of about 250 msec, as defined by the poststimulus recovery period of the auditory system, which generates a series of neural pulses in response. Thus it acts in reverse, and complementary, fashion to the articulatory system. It may be that the auditory system disentangles coarticulations as overlapping boundaries between linguistic segments, and conveys these segments to higher levels for further processing. According to a standard view, this is what happens: the percepts of the auditory system are the analogues of the target articulations of the articulatory system. This implies some stage of 'phoneme-assembly' (both for articulation and perception of linguistic units such as 'words'). But an alternative view sees the forms of words as specified in terms of complex neuromotor and neurosensory patterns, which can be mapped (coarticulations and all) onto the complex speech signal via encoding and decoding processes that make no reference to individual sound segments (phonemes) at all (see *Speech Perception*).

The main point to make, in summary, is that the articulatory and auditory systems are fundamentally compatible with each other, in spite of considerable differences in anatomical and physiological detail. This is all the more remarkable in view of the fact that each to some extent is recruited to the service of language from other biologically primary functions. There is also a fundamental continuity of transmission between articulatory activity, resulting air-particle dynamics, and auditory stimulation.

1.2 Writing Systems

If the discussion of the written language signal was organized in the same terms as for speech, a transmission chain might consist of: manual factors—graphic properties—visual factors. But unlike their counterparts in the speech system, these form a fundamentally indirect transmission chain. There is nothing corresponding to the transmitting substance

of air: hand movements in writing/typing manipulate physical substances which produce marks on paper, but the nature of these substances is immaterial to the processes of visual perception. As a result of this radical discontinuity, writing systems are not so physically constrained by input/output demands, although they are constrained by practical requirements such as two-dimensional representation, and relative permanence. They also strikingly rely on preexisting language knowledge. Psycholinguistically speaking, the organization of written language appears to be fundamentally different from that of speech, and written language abilities appear to be less integrated into the general linguistic capacities of humans.

Possible writing systems are conventionally arranged on a continuum from pictographic/ideographic, through logographic, to phonographic systems that are lexically based (e.g., the semitic triconsonantal roots), or syllabic (e.g., the syllabaries of the Indian subcontinent), or alphabetic. In addition, feature-based aspects may be brought into the account: parts of Korean (Han'gŭl) characters represent articulatory features.

A fundamental question is whether different principles of representing language in written form call forth distinct styles of processing. If so, it is worth focusing on 'logographic' versus 'phonographic' systems, since they seem to offer a contrast between two distinct states of affairs: direct 'visual form → meaning' mappings versus indirect 'visual form → sound → meaning' mappings. On closer examination, however, it seems that the issue is nowhere near as clear-cut as this in the way that actual orthographies work. If the Chinese system is taken as a type of logographic script, it is clear that it violates the pure 'one symbol for one meaning' implied by the term logograph. Indeed, the idea that Chinese characters are wholly noncompositional is hard to square with the native observation that, encountering a character for the first time, an experienced reader generally has a number of strategies for uncovering the meaning; and to some extent this even extends to clues to sound also.

At the other extreme, if English is taken as a type of alphabetic script, then it is clear that it violates the strict 'one symbol for one sound' principle. More than this, it shows a number of logographic-looking symbols, in £, $, %, &, @, and a range of more or less specialized letter forms, such as *etc*, *cm* and the like. So it is probably unrealistic to expect that comparing English and Chinese subjects reading their native scripts will straightforwardly involve a comparison of markedly distinct processing strategies.

If these are cases where the difference of script type is less than might be imagined, there are other examples where considerable differences may be found within a single type. In the case of syllabaries, for example, the Japanese kana system shows markedly less compositionality than the Kannada system (of southern India), which clearly allows for the isolation of constituent consonant and vowel components in a way that borders on the alphabetic.

In conclusion, it is suggested that the traditional typology of writing systems gives few clues to the psycholinguist who is seeking straightforward mappings between orthographic type and processing style. It may be suspected that this is not entirely the fault of the typology; generally, writing systems work not because they offer a strict code on the sound system or the vocabulary of a language, but because they offer a range of clues to the language-knowing reader concerning what language forms are being referred to on the page. Readers are constantly and naturally picking up phonographic and other cues together, from constituent parts of the graphic array and from larger symbol forms and sequences. Japanese is a striking example, with its historically distinct kanji and kana systems in interplay; but English may not be so very different from this, after all. Whatever the script being processed, the reader's knowledge of his language is assumed, and this will include knowledge of the way words sound, their morphological structure, where relevant, as well as their grammatical class and their meaning.

2. Biological Foundations

This area provides only indirect and general evidence for the nature of human language abilities. Nevertheless it is important to gain an appreciation of what constitutes a biological level of description, in order to gain an awareness of how it differs from the linguistic and psychological levels. Eventually, it may be possible to understand how to relate them to each other. For the moment, it is worth some effort to understand how *not* to relate them: it is *not* the case that biological structures and processes directly constitute the mechanisms that psycholinguists search for as underlying language abilities. Nevertheless, they may hold indirect clues as to how those processes might operate, and interact. The available literature is large; the following sketch may be supplemented initially by reference to Eccles (1977) on general characteristics, and Perkins and Kent (1986) for language and speech.

2.1 Main Properties of the Human Nervous System

The human nervous system is made up of two subsystems, the peripheral, being the system connecting the muscles and sensory organs with the central, which is that part of the nervous system that is contained within the skull (the brain), and the spinal vertebrae (the spinal cord). It is noteworthy that this fundamental division does not have a straightforward correspondence with anything discussed above, since language signals (Sect. 1) are processed by both peripheral and central nervous systems. Furthermore,

there are indications that even the abstract language system may not be subserved by the central nervous system alone, since, for example, phenomena such as the perception of speech rhythms and rhymes in silent reading may be affected by occupying the peripheral speech systems with irrelevant activity.

Brain-body connections through the central/peripheral interface may be of three types: 'bilateral' (e.g., left and right sides of the brain jointly control muscles on both sides of the face); 'contralateral' (left brain areas connect with right side of body, and vice versa); and 'ipsilateral' (usually subsidiary types, where the same side of brain and body are involved). In these terms, production of the speech signal is more bilaterally controlled than is speech perception or the production and perception of written language. It remains to be seen, however, how far such hardware-partitioning may be understood in the light of the processing characteristics of these different channels.

2.2 The Brain

This may be thought of as divided into twin hemispheres, each of which comprises cortical versus subcortical structures, comprising the cerebrum. These structures surround the brain stem, which is to be thought of as a highly specialized continuation of the upper spinal cord. Fairly independently of each of these components, the cerebellum lies at the rear of the junction between brain stem and cerebrum. Functional analyses indicate that these anatomically distinct structures cooperate in complex and highly integrative fashion, for language as well as for other high-level behavior.

The cortex appears as a thin layer consisting of dense populations of specialized cells (neurons), presenting a greyish appearance (hence 'grey matter'), forming the outer part of the cerebral hemispheres (left and right), and convoluted into ridges and depressions (resulting in increased surface area). Structurally, it can be mapped (the topographical approach) into areas between major fissures (the frontal, parietal, and temporal lobes), and other regions and landmarks (including the posterior, occipital lobe, which is much less well-defined in such terms); it can also be cross-sectioned (the histological approach), in terms of which, overall, there are about 6 layers of cells, of varying types, depths, and organization, about $\frac{1}{5}$th inch thick; in detail, regions have been mapped and numbered (referred to as 'Brodmann's areas,' after the originator, at the beginning of the twentieth century).

Functionally, the two cerebral hemispheres show massive parallelism, but also some striking asymmetries, particularly with regard to speech, but also for handedness and other functions. The most usual situation is left hemisphere dominance (which results, through contralateral connections, in right-body control). Within each hemisphere, some gross function/loci correlations can be noted: in the frontal lobe, descriptors include those factors which together make up the behavioral complex referred to as 'personality'; in the parietal lobe, body-surface senses and spatial orientation, used, for instance, in putting on clothes; in the temporal lobe, hearing, and the awareness of time relations; in the occipital lobe, vision; and, on the borders of these lobes, some precise mapping is possible of motor and sensory cortex. For speech, the phenomenon of cerebral dominance (usually the left hemisphere) is marked by the lower motor area (Brodmann's 44 and 45) identified by Paul Broca as crucial for speech output; and by the upper temporal area (Brodmann's 41 and 22) identified by Carl Wernicke as crucial for speech understanding.

Subcortical systems involve two different types of neural substrate: pathways and cell nuclei. Pathways, made up of the connecting fibers of cortical cells, present a whiteish appearance (sheathed in a white fatty substance, myelin, for insulation—hence 'white matter'); electrical activity along these nerve fibers reaches interconnections called synapses, where chemical changes take place, and stimulate further cells into electrical activity. Such electrochemical pathways establish two sorts of connection: (a) cortical-cortical (e.g., the corpus callosum, the main connecting pathway between the cerebral hemispheres), and intra-hemispheric connections (as in the bundle of fibers known as the arcuate fasciculus, connecting Wernicke's and Broca's areas); and (b) cortical-to-lower cell nuclei (see below).

Subcortical cell nuclei (thalamus, basal ganglia, limbic system) are involved in varying degrees with integrating and programming different areas of cortical activity, and seem to be particularly linked with short-term memory and motor patterns. Their specific role in language is controversial (see *Subcortical Aphasia*).

Within the brain stem, there are ascending and descending connections between specialized populations of cell nuclei, serving the speech production and perception systems, and that for written language production. The counterpart of these stages of processing for written language perception is found in the layering of cells in the retina of the eyes. In each case, functional analyses reveal that considerable signal processing takes place at these levels of representation: i.e., they are not to be thought of as simply 'relay stations' between more important loci of origin and destination. Thus, the anatomical levels do not neatly coincide with determinable stages in signal processing, and the functional picture is one that has largely to be unravelled. A particular case in point is found in the operation of the cochlea and the auditory nerve in speech perception. It is here that mechanical-to-electrical transduction takes place, from the propagation of waves along the basilar membrane in the cochlea to the transmission of neural impulses along the 30 000 fibers of the auditory nerve, in the per-

ipheral nervous system. Even at the level of basilar membrane responses it is not possible to say, neatly, that frequency is represented in terms of position along the membrane (although this is a first approximation), and that amplitude is purely the distance of the maximally displaced portion of the membrane from its resting position (though this also is true in a general sense): complex interactions have already taken place, and the resulting patterns of neural fiber discharge will not yield to simple 'frequency-encoding' (inter-pulse intervals) or 'place-encoding' (certain fibers versus others) theories. A different type of example is found in retinal signal processing, since the retina is strictly not part of the peripheral nervous system at all in spite of the fact that it directly receives the light that is focused into the eye by the sensory structures of the cornea and the lens. This is not to deny that specific functional properties cannot be determined: again the visual system provides a marked example of how very precise cortical mapping (of the occipital lobe cortex) reveals a high degree of cell structuring (in columnar arrangement, at right angles to the surface of the cortex) with a striking degree of functional specialization between cells in adjacent columns. But the relation between these properties and the nature of writing systems remains fundamentally obscure.

2.3 Language in the Left and Right Hemispheres

To some significant extent, the discovery of relations between brain and language functions is dependent on the nature of the methods of investigation. These include:

(a) The Wada test: developed for use prior to surgery in language-relevant areas of the brain, this involves injecting sodium amytal into the carotid artery in the neck on one side. In the left side, it will paralyze the left hemisphere of a conscious patient for a few minutes, allowing for determination of left-dominance for language.

(b) Direct mapping by electrical stimulation: on a locally anesthetized but fully conscious patient. Originally carried out for more precise determination of language-relevant areas of cortex prior to surgical procedures, for example, in otherwise untreatable epileptic conditions, this procedure was important in early investigations, revealing the existence of a number of specific areas for sensory perception, and motor control, including speech.

(c) Indirect instrumental analyses 'electroencephalographic' (EEG) and 'regional cerebral blood flow' (rCBF) investigations. These involve the taking of readings simultaneously from various points on the scalp, while the subject performs some language-related task. EEG traces represent areas of increased electrical activity during such tasks, ('average evoked responses' or AERs, and 'event-related potentials' or ERPs); RCBF methods display those areas receiving increased blood-flow during task performance. The technique of *computerised [axial] tomography* (C[A]T) has significantly advanced the scanning of the brain for asymmetries in its internal dimensions, as well as for the presence of small lesions. More recently, *positron emission tomography* (PET) and *magnetic resonance imaging* (MRI) methods have become available in certain centres, and have further advanced the understanding of brain-function relations in normal and pathological states. PET monitors for the metabolic activity in the brain involving glucose, oxygen, and neurotransmitter substances which can be radioactively labelled and their observed uptake related to the type of function the brain is called upon to perform. Different parts of the brain are involved in single-word processing, such as listening to a word vs. reading it aloud and repeating it. Sentence processing has also been investigated by these means, but it is very difficult, given the current state of the technology, to relate aspects of brain response patterns to particular aspects of multiword sequences, and it is likely that as the techniques improve, the picture will become more, rather than less, complex and difficult to interpret. This is not to deny the potential usefulness of such information, particularly in language disorders: it appears that subcortical lesions, which show up on older types of investigation, may regularly be accompanied by smaller cortical lesions, which show up on PET scans, raising the issue as to how far an observed language processing impairment may be attributable to cortical as opposed to subcortical dysfunction in such cases (Caplan 1987).

(d) Linguistic-behavioral methods: these include 'dichotic' listening, and 'dichoptic' visual perception, in which competing or complementary stimuli are presented in a controlled way to left and right ears, or left and right visual fields, and the effects on perception are observed. The main results can be summarized under the following two headings. *Right ear advantage* (REA) for speech sounds: this appears to derive from differential treatment of certain auditory stimuli via the contralateral pathways from the bilaterally represented auditory nerve origins in the middle ear structures, through the bilaterally represented cell nuclei of the brain stem, and up to the bilaterally represented strips of auditory cortex on the upper surfaces of the temporal lobes. The differential processing preference ensures that certain sounds being processed through the right ear/left auditory

cortex system are perceived more efficiently than they are through the complementary system on the other side. This effect is observed only weakly for liquids, and definitely for stop consonants, particularly in linguistic-contrastive contexts. It has been claimed that this argues for a specialized speech processor in the dominant hemisphere, but the evidence so far seems consistent also with a lateralised specialized 'dynamic sound' processor.

So-called '*split-brain*' studies: these include a range of investigations arising from the existence of a small population of subjects who have received radical surgery for epilepsy, by severance of the corpus callosum, or cerebral commissure (the bundle of cortical-cortical fibers that serve as the main connecting trunk between the left and right hemispheres). It has been observed that objects presented to the right hemisphere (e.g., by left-visual field brief display, or by left-hand manipulation out of sight) cannot be named, though they can be matched by left hand responses. This argues for a special role in speech production by the left hemisphere. In spite of such evidence, it has increasingly been maintained that the non-dominant hemisphere is a participant in many aspects of linguistic processing. It can comprehend visually presented words, especially concrete nouns, match objects to auditory or visual naming or description, spell auditorily presented words, process kanji better than kana symbols (see Sect. 1.2 above), develop considerable vocabulary skills, and process intonation patterns. It also seems to be involved in making inferences, and quite generally in the coding and decoding of pragmatic aspects of communication. Whether there is just one processing style that is characteristic of right vs. left hemisphere functions is not yet clear: it is perhaps more likely that the right hemisphere performs a number of different, if related, subordinate roles in the comprehension of language (Beeman and Chiarello 1998) and in the planning of message structure in language production.

3. The Abstract Language System

Because the abstract language system is difficult to observe directly, the discussion here will concentrate on the search for appropriate indirect sources of evidence concerning its operations. The models and processes will be considered in more detail in later sections.

3.1 Methodology

Empirical work in the modern era got under way in the 1960s, in experimental psychology laboratories, where experiments were run to probe aspects of language comprehension processing, driven by hypotheses drawn from Chomsky's work in formal properties of phrase structure grammar and transformational grammar. Two sorts of linguistic concept were under investigation: the linguistic structures that were manipulated by grammatical rules, and the rules themselves, particularly those that formed part of the transformational component. Within a few years, intensive work had demonstrated the effectiveness of a number of experimental methods for addressing these issues. These included:

(a) Click location studies: a brief, wide-spectrum burst of noise was systematically introduced into the tape-recorded versions of linguistic structures. Perceived as a click, this noise was located at predetermined points and subjects were required to report, after each presentation, where the click had occurred in relation to the associated linguistic structure. Results suggested that, independently of intonation structuring, linguistic units such as syllables, words, syntactic phrases, and clauses were 'psychologically real' in the sense that they formed good units in perception of utterances, and accordingly resisted interruption by extraneous sounds such as clicks.

(b) Probe-latency tasks: in these, subjects were presented with a sentence stimulus, after which a word from the sentence was re-presented on its own, to which the subject had to respond with the next word in the sentence. It thus probed the strength of word-word associative links in the memory representation of the stimulus. The hypothesis was that these would vary in strength as predicted by the configurations of PSG. Results suggested that this was the case, with larger response latencies being observed where the word-word relations fell across, as opposed to within, syntactic boundaries.

(c) Word-relatedness judgments: in this type of study, sentences were presented to subjects who were then asked to rate each word-pair in successive sequences for degree of interrelatedness in the sentence. The judgments were entered into a type of confusion matrix, which was then subjected to hierarchical cluster analysis. Results revealed structures very like those proposed in PSG configurations for the sentences concerned, with the added dimension that a metric of degree of relatedness (of individual words, and of phrasal groupings) was provided by the measure.

(d) Sentence-matching: in this type of study, subjects were presented with lists of sentences and had to match the occurrence of one sentence type with another. Base list search time was established, and mean search times were then

compared with this, for various differences of sentence type, such as active-passive, affirmative-negative, and declarative-interrogative. Early results suggested that related to the structures that the latter types within each such pairing took longer to process, in conformity with the view that they were transformationally more complex; further, that in combinations of such types (e.g., negative-passives), the increase in latencies was cumulative.

(e) Semantic judgment tasks: in these, linguistic materials were presented for judgments in terms of categories such as 'true/false,' in relation to some predetermined norm or pictured event. Syntactic form of linguistic stimulus was manipulated, and where this involved transformational relations among sentences, results showed that transformational rule operations correlated with increased processing load, suggesting that mental operations like transformational rules were involved in the processing of syntactic form for meaning.

This list is not exhaustive, but is indicative of early experimental approaches: Levelt (1978) provides a review.

The following trends have emerged from the earlier tradition:

(a) *Naturalistic vs. experimental studies*: there has been an historical trend (from the 1960s) away from the possibly artefactual findings deriving from highly structured experimental designs, and a corresponding emphasis on the importance of balancing such findings against the results of more naturalistic evidence. The discovery of 'task effects' in the sorts of finding outlined above was influential in this regard. It was found, for example, that passives were more complex than negatives in a sentence-matching task, but that their relative ordering was exactly reversed in a true/false judgment task. This was interpretable as deriving from a difference of 'setting,' whereby subjects were more ready to process form (including the formal markers of passive versus active) in the matching task, but were readied to pay more attention to meaning (presence versus absence of *not*) in the latter task. It was also found that passives were not more difficult to process than actives in nonreversible sentences such as *The biscuit was eaten by the dog*, that is, where plausible lexical-semantic constraints are operative (compare the reversible *the cat was chased by the rat*, where the meanings of the words alone is not sufficient to arrive at a plausible interpretation). In similar vein, negatives were shown to be more easily processed in 'contexts of plausible denial.' However, the shift away from a reliance on purely experimental procedures is not unproblematic. 'Naturalistic' language use covers a wide range of types, and the data is often messy, containing much that the investigator may not be interested in (at the time) and not much of what is immediately at issue; in practice, investigators have made concessions to the concept of naturalism, while constraining the elicitation procedure as far as possible. Analyzing naturalistic data also raises problems; it may contain false starts, hesitations, errors, and a wide variety of 'target' linguistic phenomena which, although they occur together, have tended to be analyzed as special, discrete categories of evidence, in rather different research traditions (as will be seen below). The linguistic properties of such data are often complex and problematic, and have not generally been given the attention within psycholinguistic research that they deserve.

(b) *Production vs. comprehension studies*: likewise, there has been a tendency to focus more on the previously neglected area of language production. Earlier 'verbal stimulus → nonverbal response' studies have been increasingly supplemented by those in which linguistic analysis of the verbal product is used to enquire into underlying processes. This trend, while logically distinct from the shift to naturalistic data, has historically helped to serve it.

In the assessment of language disorders a variety of psycholinguistic methods have been employed, reflecting the methodological concerns of the mainstream field at the time. Typically used are the analysis of spontaneous speech (which has been of particular and growing importance in recent approaches), comprehension, especially of grammatical structures as well as of words, repetition, naming, sentence completion, and the ability to make grammaticality judgments, and provides higher-order labels for groups of related objects or activities. Differential assessment is particularly strong in the area of the mental lexicon, where dissociations may be found between word forms vs. meanings, input vs. output, and spoken vs. written modalities.

3.2 Competence and Performance

As formulated by Chomsky, this distinction disambiguated the Saussurean concept of *langue* versus *parole*, in favor of the interpretation that saw the langue/competence construct as a mental capacity for language (rather than an aggregate of all individual acts of parole/performance by speakers in the language community). The early (1960s) psycholinguists' view was that competence, as displayed through linguists' intuitions supplemented by formal

linguistic-analytical procedures, was a 'given': measures of psycholinguistic performance, in the experimental investigations of the time, were thought to be glimpses of this underlying concept. The experimental findings quickly disconfirmed the possibility that there was any direct manifestation of competence in performance; and psycholinguists increasingly accepted that their glimpses of language competence were 'through a glass darkly.' At the same time, the concept of competence itself was undergoing revision; first, a distinction had to be made between strictly grammatical competence ('knowing the rules') and a more general language competence ('knowing about the rules,' including the constraints on their application). Some commentators (e.g., Sutherland 1966) saw further ambiguities, for example, between 'competence' and 'mechanism': by analogy with relatively simple (compared to humans) devices such as computers, one could ask whether competence was comparable to some high-level executive program which defines the function of a machine (to perform task A rather than task B); or whether it was more like the capacities of the mechanisms that carry out the tasks: a software versus hardware distinction. At the same time also, driven by their increasing awareness of task-effects, researchers were beginning to wonder whether the concept of performance too should not be subcategorized: with different categories not perhaps all deriving from the same underlying competence (however this was to be understood). It was suggested that competence was only knowable through potentially disturbing processes of observation. Thus, using linguistic intuitions and subjecting them to formal analytical procedures results in a linguistic grammar (LG) that is actually a performance construct which was, by virtue of its linguistic idealization (abstracting away from human factors such as attention and memory), fundamentally unlike the underlying entity in language performance, the mental grammar (MG). From this point of view, difficulties in glimpsing the LG-version of 'competence' in any type of psycholinguistic performance might derive in part from the fact that each is the result of rather different operations of the mental grammar (MG). If these are taken to include speaking, reading, listening,..., or taking part in a psycholinguistic experiment,... or even having linguistic intuitions and subjecting them to formal analytical procedures, then the distinction between competence and performance itself is called into question (Bever 1970). Valian (1979) argues for a distinction nevertheless, on the grounds that no empirical evidence can falsify the fundamental distinction between knowledge and its implementation.

3.3 Naturally Displayed Evidence (Production)

The naturalistic data used as a source of psycholinguistic evidence (the term 'naturally displayed evidence' comes from Garrett 1982), has produced a number of categories of productions. Two main traditions of psycholinguistic research have looked, respectively, at nonfluencies, and at errors. These are to be considered as 'marked' sources of evidence; nonfluencies are marked with respect to the fluent signal, and errors are marked with respect to their targets. It is important to look at them together, if only because they tend to occur together in naturalistic speech samples; however, for convenience the traditional route is followed here and they are considered separately.

3.3.1 Nonfluencies

These include a range of phenomena such as breaks in the signal, pause fillers, repetitions, reformulations, and constructional switches. They may be analyzed for their contexts, for their variability, and for their assumed functions.

(a) Contexts: within the clause, there may be evidence from the relative incidence at various determined positions in clause structure for (i) planning, (ii) structural assembly, and (iii) lexical search activities; beyond the clause, there may be evidence, from cumulative incidence graphs, for cycles of longer 'fluent phases' alternating with short 'hesitation phases,' indicative of very long-range planning (Beattie 1983). Also, grammatical factors appear to play a role in pause location and duration: more likely to occur between clauses than within them, and to be longer for unrelated clauses versus coordinated versus subordinate versus relative (German data).

(b) Variation: there are some cross-linguistic differences (French speakers pause less often but for longer durations than English), and possibly some idiosyncratic individual differences also; but task-related variation is an important factor—reading aloud (least nonfluency) versus rehearsed speech versus spontaneous speech (most nonfluency) suggests that much nonfluency drives from the demands of planning and producing speech at the same time.

(c) Functions: it is usual (Goldman-Eisler 1972) to identify three main functions, (i) for breathing, (ii) for planning, and (iii) for communicative demarcation. (i) Breathing: breathing for speech is a nontrivial modification of normal 'tidal' breathing. Typically, inspiration for speech occurs in pauses of 400–1200 + msec, in between grammatical and/or prosodic groups. The relation between duration and location of such pauses may be understood as resulting from the fact that speakers take such opportunities for breathing, and this results in longer durations of pause. (ii) Planning: speakers may pause in order to plan, on occasion; but they may also pause because they have run out of

plan; (iii) Communicative demarcation: there is some evidence that nonbreath pauses within grammatical and/or prosodic (80–400msec) may show reliable duration/linguistic structure correlation, particularly in oral reading.

3.3.2 Errors

Normal, habitual errors may be indicative of some important properties of the processing systems involved. They may be conveniently discussed under four main headings, slips of the tongue, of the pen, of the ear, and of the eye. In addition, there are some other types which are considered separately:

(a) Slips of the tongue: in a typical sample of spontaneously occurring speech errors, collected by the usual diary method, over half are articulatory substitutions, and one-fifth of these are exchange errors; two-thirds of these are intractably ambiguous (e.g., *cat fat* might involve exchange of phoneme, syllable, or word elements). Of the rest, there is evidence for consonants, in word-initial positions, in stressed syllables, being particularly prone to exchange; and for the view that it is syllabic constituents, for example, 'onsets,' that are involved (e.g., *show snovelling*, in which onset /d/-interchanges with onset /sn/-, in spite of their internal differences of structure). In other cases, individual phonemes within syllabic constituents are available for movement. There is apparently very little evidence for features (as in 'ti*k* of the tu*m*' for 'tip of the tongue').

Berg (1991) presents evidence that, while the onset effect, and the stressed-syllable effect, hold for English and other languages such as German (and possibly also Swedish and Dutch), Spanish shows no evidence for either, a crosslinguistic finding that challenges any account of these effects in terms of simple properties of psycholinguistic processes.

Dell (1990) considers the relative invulnerability of 'function' words to phonological speech errors from the point of view of (i) their status (function versus content words), and (ii) their frequency (function words are heavily represented in the higher frequency range of vocabulary). He concludes that there is no evidence for the differential status hypothesis, and that it is their higher frequency that protects certain words (function and content alike) from phonological errors.

Grammatical errors are also found, and relate to two distinct levels: first, 'functional' (linearly distal, similar word class, semantic relation evident, e.g., 'as you *reap*, Roger, so shall you *sow*'), and second, 'positional' (proximal, different form class, no semantic relation, e.g., 'have you got something *to better* do?').

Occasionally, both types may be evident: 'it makes the *warm breather to air.*'

(b) Slips of the ear: there is a distinction between those slips involving misperception of sounds and those resulting from wrong matching of sounds to words. For misperceptions, there are very few cases of misperceiving prosodic features such as stress; of the segmental phonemic misperceptions, it appears that they decrease with later position in the word; they tend to be unidirectional (e.g., $/\theta/ \rightarrow /f$, but not $/f/ \rightarrow /\theta/$); a high proportion of them result in real words of the language. These characteristics have been identified as typical of a hypothesis-testing process, in contradistinction to speech production (where, for instance, sound substitutions tend to be bidirectional). For lexical mismatches, polysyllabic words show fewest distortions at their beginnings and ends, which ties in with some other findings regarding the relative salience of these portions of stored forms of the language (see tip of the tongue errors, below; see also Browman 1980; Garnes and Bond 1980).

(c) Slips of the pen: around 20 percent are based on phonographic values (e.g., *there/their*), but hardly any are based on visual confusions (as would be the case in, for example, *there/theme*). Units involved may be letter features (as in the closed curvature/vertical line arrangement of both *cl* and *d*), letters (as in the deletion of *i* in *inhibtions*), morphemes (e.g., the anticipatory substitution in *slowing catching up*), and words (as in the double occurrence of *the* either side of a line break in *saw the the movement*; see Hotopf 1983).

(d) Slips of the eye: these appear to show little or no effect of phonographic values; contributing items may be parts of words, from different lines of text, even upside down. In some cases, vertical proximity is crucial:

   ... the be*st* beer
in the *world*...   (1)

where the elements that are underlined here contributed to an impression of having seen 'worst.' In some cases, the linear order may be interrupted:

   ... the co*ntract*
Gerald *Sey*mour...   (2)

yielding an impression of having seen 'Sentry.' It appears that information can be collected, in parallel, from a wide range within the visual angle, as elements within a sort of visual mosaic, and assembled in such a way as to result in real-words perception. The effect of the existence of stored forms of words (as

sequences of letters) appears to be quite strong in the choice of which elements in the mosaic are consciously perceived (see Cowie 1985).

(e) Others: environmental contaminants: non-speech input interacting with speech production; Garrett (1980) provides the example (3) of a speaker, addressing a dog (looking woebegone), and simultaneously noticing a book with the blurb 'a novel of intrigue and menace' on its cover: the speaker says:

are you trying to send me a *menace*, dog?
(target: ... message ...).   (3)

(f) Tip-of-the-tongue (TOT) states: speakers occasionally experience problems in retrieving the form of a word which they feel they know well; they know what it means, they can even say, typically, that it begins with such-and-such a sound, and/or how it ends; they may also feel they know how many syllables it has, whether the stress falls on the first syllable, and so on. The distinction between various types of particular knowledge, and between knowledge of particular and global characteristics of the sought-after word, provides insights into the fractionation of word retrieval processes. It is usually the case that least information is available regarding the middles of words (see Brown and McNeill 1966).

The errors observed in both child and adult language disorders reflect the same levels of processing, so that, for example, the traditional adult aphasiological terms *phonemic* and *verbal paraphasia* can be interpreted in terms of normal psycholinguistic processing models, and certain terms, for example, *perseveration* are found in both approaches. But the traditional terminology underdetermines the range of possible errors that are subject to current analyses, with, for example, phonemic paraphasias differing between fluent and nonfluent types of aphasia. Moreover, pathological errors are of higher incidence overall, show fewer structural constraints, and tend to be more complex, and variable, in their characteristics, especially in certain types of disorder, for example, *jargon aphasia*; see Buckingham (1985).

3.3.3 Unmarked evidence

However revealing such marked sources of evidence are, it is clearly important to be able to tap the vast proportion of naturalistic data that is neither nonfluent nor errorful. If it is the case that linguistic grammars based on intuitions plus hypothesis-testing procedures are limited by *sui generis* properties of that type of performance, then one cannot expect such grammars to provide information about various categories of on-line speech behavior produced in naturalistic situations. Such data will have properties that go well beyond human intuitions (e.g., regarding the relative incidence of different types of grammatical forms in running text), and which will not yield either to hypothesis-testing, unless this is based on the analysis of empirical evidence in the form of naturalistic texts.

4. Conclusion

Much of current psycholinguistic research involves a balance of naturalistic/experimental methods, production/comprehension channels, and written/spoken language modalities. The primary foci concern the processing of speech for the identification/production of lexical elements, the establishment of grammatical relations between these elements, and the determination of discourse representations. Serial processing accounts (in which stages of processing are autonomous, and one stage is completed before the next stage begins) appear to have given ground in the face of empirical evidence that favors more complex models in which processing takes place simultaneously at more than one level, with interactions between levels (parallel-interactive models). As a result, one thrust of research is into the computer modeling of parallel systems (Rumelhart and McClelland 1986), and another concern is the empirical documentation of exactly which levels may interact: it is possible effects may spill over from the highest to the lowest levels (as in cascade arrangements). Alternatively, it may be that only adjacent levels interact. There may be, as Fodor (1983) suggests, a language module, which is impenetrable by external influences such as those deriving from pragmatic/discoursal representations or alternatively, an interactive system of levels of representation that shade imperceptibly from linguistic to nonlinguistic modes of knowledge.

For example, the way in which anaphoric expressions are processed may depend on linguistic factors such as their type (pronominal, proverbal, etc.), their distance from the antecedent phrase, the length of the antecedent, etc. Tanenhaus and Carlson (1990) take the distinction proposed by Sag and Hankamer (1984), between 'deep' anaphors such as:

Someone had to put the cat out, so I did it   (4)

and 'surface' anaphors:

Someone had to put the cat out, so I did.   (5)

The point is that *it* in the deep version refers to an abstract representation of the preceding sentence, whereas *did* in the surface type relates specifically to the syntactic constituent *put the cat out*. The prediction from this observation is that syntactic nonparallelism of antecedent/anaphor will disrupt the processing of the surface type, as in (6):

*the cat had to be put out, so I did   (6)

but that this will not affect the deep version:

the cat had to be put out, so I did it.   (7)

Perhaps the most interesting aspect of Tanenhaus and Carlson's experimental results was in the distinction they found between categorial and latency data (see the distinction noted earlier in Sect. 1 between accuracy and timing of language behavior). Their subjects' categorial responses were in terms of whether the anaphors made sense in context, or not: nonparallel contexts depressed the 'makes sense' ratings for surface anaphors, but not for deep anaphors (as predicted). But the latency data (how long it took for subjects to make their judgments) showed increased processing times for both surface and deep types of anaphor. This suggests a problematic relationship between levels of representation in processing, in this case syntax and whatever discourse structures are tapped into by deep anaphors. It is in such unexpected findings as these that further glimpses can be had of the object of psycholinguistic investigation.

Bibliography

Aitcheson J 1983 *The Articulate Mammal*, 2nd edn. Hutchinson, London

Aitcheson J 1987 *Words in the Mind*. Blackwell, Oxford

Beattie G W 1983 *Talk: An Analysis of Speech and Nonverbal Behavior in Conversation*. Open University, Milton Keynes

Beeman M, Chiarello C (eds.) 1998 *Right Hemisphere Language Comprehension: Perspectives from Cognitive Neuroscience*. Erlbaum, Hillside, NJ

Berg T 1991 Phonological processing in a syllable-timed language with pre-final stress: Evidence from Spanish speech error data. *Language and Cognitive Processes* 6: 265–301

Bever T G 1970 The cognitive basis for linguistic structures. In: Hayes J R (ed.) *Cognition and the Development of Language*. Wiley, New York

Browman C P 1980 Perceptual processing: Evidence from slips of the ear. In: Fromkin V A (ed.) *Errors in Linguistic Performance: Slips of the Tongue, Ear, Pen and Hand*. Academic Press, New York

Brown R, McNeill D 1966 The 'tip of the tongue' phenomenon. *Journal of Verbal Learning and Verbal Behavior* 5: 325–37

Buckingham H W 1985 Perseveration in aphasia. In: Newman S, Epstein R (eds.) *Current Perspectives in Dysphasia*. Churchill Livingstone, Edinburgh

Butterworth B 1980 Evidence from pauses in speech. In: Butterworth B (ed.) *Language Production. Vol. 1: Speech and Talk*. Academic Press, London

Caplan D 1987 *Neurolinguistics and Linguistic Aphasiology: An Introduction*. Cambridge University Press, Cambridge

Catford J C 1977 *Fundamental Problems in Phonetics*. Edinburgh University Press, Edinburgh

Cowie R 1985 Reading errors as clues to the nature of reading. In: Ellis A W (ed.) *Progress in the Psychology of Language*, vol. 1. Erlbaum, London

Dell G S 1990 Effects of frequency and vocabulary type

on phonological speech errors. *Language and Cognitive Processes* **5**: 313–49

Denes P B, Pinson E N 1963 *The Speech Chain*. Bell Telephone Laboratories, Baltimore, MD

Eccles J C 1977 *The Understanding of the Brain*, 2nd edn. McGraw-Hill, New York

Fodor J A 1983 *The Modularity of Mind: An Essay on Faculty Psychology*. Bradford, Cambridge, MA

Garman M 1990 *Psycholinguistics*. Cambridge University Press, Cambridge

Garnes S, Bond Z S 1980 A slip of the ear: A snip of the ear? a slip of the year? In: Fromkin V A (ed.) *Errors in Linguistic Performance: Slips of the Tongue, Ear, Pen and Hand*. Academic Press, New York

Garnham A 1989 *Psycholinguistics*. Routledge, London

Garnsey S M (ed.) 1993 *Event-related Potentials in the Study of Language*. Special Issue, *Brain and Language* **8**: 337–640

Garrett M F 1980 Levels of processing in sentence production. In: Butterworth B (ed.) 1980

Garrett M F 1982 Production of speech: Observations from normal and pathological language use. In: Ellis A W (ed.) *Normality and Pathology in Cognitive Functions*. Academic Press, London

Gernsbacher M A (ed.) 1994 *Handbook of Psycholinguistics*. Academic Press, San Diego, CA

Goldman-Eisler F 1972 Pauses, clauses and sentences. *L&S* **15**: 103–13

Harley T A 1995 *The Psychology of Language: From Data to Theory*. Psychology Press, Hove

Hotopf W N 1983 Lexical slips of the pen and tongue: What they tell us about language production. In: Butterworth B (ed.) 1980

Johnson-Laird P N 1983 *Mental Models*. Cambridge University Press, Cambridge

Lesser R, Milroy L 1993 *Linguistics and Aphasia: Psycholinguistic and Pragmatic Aspects of Intervention*. Longman, London

Levelt W J M 1978 A survey of studies in sentence perception: 1970–76. In: Levelt W J M, Flores D'Arcais G B (eds.) *Studies in the Perception of Language*. Wiley, Chichester

Levelt W J M 1989 *Speaking: From Intention to Articulation*. MIT Press, Cambridge, MA

Paradis M 1987 *The Assessment of Bilingual Aphasia*. Erlbaum, Hillsdale, NJ

Perkell J S 1980 Phonetic features and the physiology of speech production. In: Butterworth B (ed.) 1980

Perkins W H, Kent R D 1986 *Textbook of Functional Anatomy of Speech, Language and Hearing*. Taylor and Francis, London

Rumelhart D E, McClelland J L 1986 *Parallel Distributed Processing: Explorations in the Microstructure of Cognition, vol. 1: Foundations*. MIT Press, Cambridge, MA

Sag I, Hankamer J 1984 Toward a theory of anaphoric processing. *Linguistics and Philosophy* **7**: 325–45

Scott-Kelso J A, Tuller B, Harris K S 1983 A 'dynamic pattern' perspective in the control and coordination of movement. In: MacNeilage P F (ed.) *The Production of Speech*. Springer, New York

Sutherland N S 1966 Comments on the Fodor and Garrett paper. In: Lyons J, Wales R J (eds.) *Psycholinguistics Papers*. Edinburgh University Press, Edinburgh

Tanenhaus M K, Carlson G N 1990 Comprehension of deep and surface verbphrase anaphors. *Language and Cognitive Processes* **5**: 257–80

Valian V 1979 The wherefores and therefores of the competence-performance distinction. In: Cooper W E, Walker E C T (eds.) *Sentence Processing: Psycholinguistic Studies Presented to Merrill Garrett*. Erlbaum, Hillsdale, NJ

Van Lancker D (ed.) 1997 *Current Studies of Right Hemisphere Function*. Special Issue, *Brain and Language* **57**: 1–178

Viviani P, Terzuolo C 1983 The organization of movement in handwriting and typing. In: Butterworth B (ed.) 1980

Language Production

H. L. Petrie

Although it is simple to ask how people turn ideas into words, it has been extremely difficult to specify what processes take place between the genesis of a thought and its articulation in words. *A priori*, it is clear that two broad classes of processes must be involved. The first class is conceptualization processes, that is, deciding what to say. This may range from very high-level, conscious decisions, such as 'shall I tell my shaggy dog story or have they heard that before?' to detailed, nonconscious decisions such as whether to refer to an object with a fully specified noun phrase (*the red ball*) or a reduced one (*the red one*, appropriate if there are perhaps only one red and

one green ball under discussion). The second class is formulation processes; these are all the linguistic decisions about how to say something. Again, these are usually nonconscious, except in unusual circumstances such as when one has a word on 'the tip of one's tongue' but cannot remember what it is (Paradis 1994).

Psycholinguists have used a number of research techniques to explore what processes are involved in language production. Natural phenomena such as pauses, hesitations, and speech errors which occur during speech have been analyzed for clues as to underlying processes. Experimental techniques have also been used to study language production; these usually involve having people describe simple visual displays, in order to limit some of the formulation processes required so that others are highlighted. Although these techniques have yielded much useful information about the processes of language production, this constitutes only a skeleton of what goes on between thought and speech.

1. The Study of Language Production

Research into the processes involved in language production is not as well developed as research in the complementary area of language comprehension. One reason for this has been the far greater reliance, in studying language production, on the analysis of naturally occurring phenomena such as pauses, hesitations, and speech errors which occur during spontaneous speech, rather than on the use of experimental manipulations which have been used so successfully in the study of language comprehension. Clearly, there are difficulties in attempting to manipulate the production of speech. Osgood (1971) made an interesting early attempt when he conducted an experiment involving demonstrations of simple objects. For example, he placed an orange ring in the middle of a table; he then removed the orange ring and took a black ball and held it shoulder high. Participants in the experiment were asked to describe the demonstration in a single sentence so that someone who had not seen it would understand what had happened.

Although he did not put it in these terms at the time, Osgood was trying to manipulate the conceptualization processes involved in language production, that is, the decisions that the speaker must make about what to say. Osgood's research did not lead to any fruitful line of investigation about language production, partly because he had, and there still exists, no vocabulary for describing in what terms conceptualization processes take place, that is, what the language of thought might be. Researchers have since attempted to manipulate the formulation processes in language production, that is, all the linguistic decisions that the speaker must make about how to say something. However, some of the experimental tasks which have been successfully used (see, for example, Kempen and Huijbers 1983) are descended from Osgood's, in that they involve the description of simple visual displays, now usually presented on a computer screen. The names of the objects involved or the syntactic structure to be used can be specified, so that the experimenter can concentrate on how the participants formulate their descriptions of the display in different circumstances (examples of this research are discussed in Sect. 4).

2. Early Research on Language Production

Much of the early research on language production analyzed the occurrence of pauses and hesitations in spontaneous speech. A number of questions were addressed with these analyses. For example, Goldman-Eisler (1968) found that pauses were more likely to occur before unpredictable words in speech, and Maclay and Osgood (1959) found that pauses were more likely to occur before content words than before function words. Both these results suggest that pauses represent points of lexical selection in producing speech. Goldman-Eisler (1968) also found that the overall pause rate (ratio of pause time to total speaking time) was higher during a semantically difficult task (interpreting cartoons) than a simple task (describing cartoons), which suggests that pauses also represent time taken to plan the overall semantic structure of speech. These and other observations led Goldman-Eisler to propose that language production processes proceed in a cyclic pattern, with periods of high pause and hesitation activity alternating with periods of low pause and hesitation activity. They argued that the first type of period occurs at the beginning of the articulation of ideas, when both overall semantic planning and local lexical selection processes contribute greatly to pause and hesitation rates; the second type of period occurs towards the ends of ideas, when only lexical selection time is required and hence pause and hesitation rates are low. However, the details of this proposal have remained controversial.

Questions concerning the planning of syntactic structure in speech were also investigated using analyses of pauses and hesitations. For example, considerable research effort has been expended on the question of the fundamental units of syntactic planning in language production. The first researcher to pursue this question was Boomer (1965), who found that pauses and filled pauses (FPS) were most likely to occur at the beginnings of phonemic clauses, which are phonologically-defined units usually corresponding to a surface clause. Boomer therefore proposed that speech is planned before articulating each phonemic clause. However, not all pauses (or FPS) fall at clause boundaries, and more importantly not all clauses are preceded by a pause (or FP). Brotherton (1979) found that only about 40 percent of clauses were preceded by pauses; in fact, she found that 12 percent of all clauses were in fluent runs of three or more clauses produced without any pauses. So the argument that clauses are planned in preceding pauses is a weak one.

Ford and Holmes (1978) investigated the question of syntactic planning units using a technique long exploited in experimental psychology, the dual task (DT) situation. A person is asked to do two tasks simultaneously, in this case speak spontaneously and press a key whenever they hear a tone. The reaction times (RTS) in response to tones are noted, as well as the points in speech at which they occur. It is assumed that the RTS will be longer at points when the processing required for language production is higher, as there will be less mental capacity left to respond to the tone. An everyday example of the DT effect is when an experienced driver who is conducting a conversation with a passenger in normal traffic conditions then breaks off if the traffic becomes problematic: there is no longer enough mental capacity to talk and drive simultaneously.

Ford and Holmes used this DT technique to investigate, first, whether planning is done in terms of sentences or constituent clauses, and second, whether it is done at surface-structure level, as suggested by the early pause studies, or at the deep-structure level posited by transformational grammars. Looking at RTS during clauses which were both surface and deep clauses (see Table 1, panel A), they found that RTs at the end of the first clause of a sentence were significantly longer than RTs at the beginning of either the first or second clause. On the basis of this result, they argued that planning occurs within sentences, clause by clause, and that planning for a clause occurs towards the end of the previous clause. To support

their argument that planning does not span sentences, they looked at final clauses in sentences and found that RTs were not longer at the ends of these clauses (Table 1, panel B), suggesting that planning was not taking place for a sentence at the end of the previous one. To differentiate between the surface and deep clauses as potential planning units, Ford and Holmes analyzed surface clauses which correspond to two or more deep clauses (Table 1, panels C and D). Using similar arguments to those discussed above, they concluded that it is the deep clause which is the important planning unit. This is a most interesting model of syntactic planning, but further research has not yet been conducted to provide further evidence for it. Undoubtedly, this is partly due to the controversy over the status of transformational grammars.

3. The Two-stage Theory of Language Production

The most influential theory of language production has been the two-stage theory proposed by Garrett

Table 1. Mean reaction times (milliseconds) to tones during first and second halves of surface and deep clauses (data from Ford and Holmes 1978).

A: Clauses which are both surface and deep clauses
e.g., 'If capital punishment were brought in'

	First clause		Second clause	
	// __ First half __ / __ Second half __ //		__ First half __ / __ Second half __ //	
Mean RT	431	470	399	—

B: Final clauses in sentences
(i) Clauses which are both deep and surface clauses

	// __ First half __ / __ Second half __ //	
Mean RT	426	429

(ii) Deep clauses which do not correspond to surface clauses

	// __ First half __ / __ Second half __ //	
Mean RT	385	401

C: Surface clauses which contain more than one deep clause
e.g., 'I began working a lot harder'

C.1: Analysis of deep clauses
(i) first or only surface clause in sentence

	First deep clause		Second deep clause	
	// __ First half __ / __ Second half __ //		__ First half __ / __ Second half __ //	
Mean RT	423	448	384	—

(ii) subsequent surface clause in sentence

	First deep clause		Second deep clause	
	// __ First half __ / __ Second half __ //		__ First half __ / __ Second half __ //	
Mean RT	406	477	417	—

C.2: Analysis of surface clauses

	First surface clause		Second surface clause	
	// __ First half __ / __ Second half __ //		__ First half __ / __ Second half __ //	
Mean RT	430	429	413	—

(e.g., 1976). Using evidence from his own corpus of 3400 speech errors and other published corpora of errors, Garrett proposed that the two principal planning stages during language production are independent and serially ordered. The first of these stages he called the *functional stage*; this consists of abstract representations of words, as yet without any information about their phonology (Kempen and Huijbers 1983 called such representations 'lemmas'), and a framework describing the syntactic relations between these words. Two processes are critical in producing the functional stage: the selection of lexical items and the insertion of these items into the syntactic framework. Garrett proposed that, at the functional stage, several surface clauses of eventual speech are being planned simultaneously and that at this stage the temporal ordering of items to be spoken has not yet been specified. The second stage of representation Garrett called the *positional stage*; this consists of the phonologically specified morphemes (called 'lexemes' by Kempen and Huijbers) for the utterance, which are now stored in the order in which they are going to be spoken. This stage of planning covers only one surface clause at a time.

Garrett used a number of arguments about the nature and distribution of speech errors to support his two-stage theory of production. For example, he argued that one of the processes of lexical selection is the matching of a specification of the required semantic features with those of items in a mental lexicon in order to select an appropriate lexeme. Errors in this process can lead to word-substitution errors, as in this example from Garrett (1976):

> one of them was rejected without any revision at all   (1)
> (for 'accepted').

Garrett argued that such errors occur at the functional stage, as there is semantic similarity but no phonological similarity between the selected word and the intended word. Most importantly, he noted a number of differences between errors (particularly exchange errors) involving whole words and lexical/stem morphemes on the one hand and those involving single sounds and grammatical morphemes on the other. Word errors show the following characteristics: the two elements involved are of the same syntactic class; the elements are not necessarily phonologically similar; elements can be moved across a number of words, and often across syntactic boundaries, such as clauses; and accommodation (syntactic and/or phonological) to the new environment takes place. An example of syntactic accommodation is where the appropriate verb form is used although the verb occurs in the wrong position in the utterance:

> 'I'd hear one if I knew it' for 'I'd know one if I
>   heard it'   (2)
> (Garrett 1976).

In this error, the first verb *(hear)* occurred in the

present tense and the second *(know)* occurred in the past tense, the intended sequence of tenses, even though the order of the verbs themselves was reversed. Garrett reasoned that these word-exchange errors occur during the process of lexical insertion at the functional stage, when lemmas are slotted into the wrong part of the syntactic framework. Because the exchanged items have no tendency to be phonologically similar, this stage must occur before phonological information about words is available. However, accommodation of word forms does occur, which suggests that the functional stage does have access to a lexicon involving word forms.

Sound and grammatical morpheme errors, on the other hand, show the following characteristics: elements are from different syntactic categories; elements are phonologically similar; elements move over only short ranges, usually within a phrase; and accommodation does not occur to the new environment where the element appears. For example, in

> 'I haven't satten down and writ the letter yet' for   (3)
> 'I haven't sat down and written the letter yet'
> (Garrett 1976).

the grammatical morpheme for the past participle *(-en)* has moved forward to the verb *sit,* but this does not result in the correct form of the verb; compare this with example (2), where the stems of the verbs *hear* and *know* are exchanged but appear in their correct final forms.

A number of criticisms have been made of the two-stage theory, based on further analyses of speech errors. For example, Dell and Reich (1981), in an analysis of over 4000 errors, found that in substitution errors there was a significant tendency for the word substituted to be phonologically related to the target, particularly on the first sound. Yet, according to the two-stage theory, such errors occur at the functional stage, when no information about phonology is available. They also found that in sound errors there was a significant tendency for the elements created to show a lexical bias, that is, to be real English words; see also work by Baars et al. (1975) on lexical bias in artificially induced speech errors. Yet, according to the two-stage theory, such errors occur at the positional stage, which has no information about word forms.

Meara and Ellis (1982) also conducted a fascinating analysis of Welsh speech errors which suggests that phonological information is available from the earliest stages of speech formulation, a situation not compatible with the two-stage theory. Stemberger (1985) collected more than 7200 errors and found five errors which involved movement of grammatical morphemes but also accommodation of the new environment in which they occurred, as in:

> 'they're just clouds that are been diverting' for   (4)
> 'they're just clouds that are being diverted'
> (example from Stemberger 1985).

According to the two-stage theory, such errors occur at the positional stage and should not show any accommodation.

4. Developments Since the Two-stage Theory

A number of developments and alternatives to the two-stage theory were proposed in the 1980s. The one which builds most on the two-stage theory has been developed by Bock (1987). Like Garrett, Bock proposed that there are two stages of processing in language production, but she is less convinced of their independence. First, she elaborated on Garrett's functional stage, referring to it as 'functional integration.' To Garrett's proposal that lemmas are slotted into syntactic frameworks during this stage, she added the notion of 'conceptual accessibility.' This proposed that the assignment of lexical items to syntactic functions will be affected by the ease of retrieving the lexical items from the mental lexicon. For example, in attempting to describe an event in which a woman pats a cat, *woman* may either be the subject of an active verb (*The woman pats the cat*) or the object of a passive verb (*The cat is patted by the woman*). Numerous studies have shown that the grammatical form of a sentence can be varied between active and passive by making different participants in such events more accessible. Bock found this effect by using word imageability as the measure of conceptual accessibility. Using three different syntactic sentence structures, she found that subjects tended to assign the more imageable noun to an earlier syntactic function within the sentence. However, within a syntactic function such as a noun phrase, imageability had no effect on the ordering of nouns. This suggests that conceptual accessibility has no effect on the fine-grained serial order of the final utterance, which is planned at the following stage, Garrett's positional stage. However, as Levelt (1989) noted, Bock's results are based on the written reproduction of sentences given to the experimental participants, not on spontaneous speech, and so need to be regarded cautiously.

Bock elaborated on Garrett's positional stage in a similar manner and referred to it as 'constituent integration.' She postulated that the serial order of lexical items is affected by 'phonological accessibility,' meaning the ease of access of the phonological forms. This type of accessibility, Bock postulated, can be measured by the frequency of words in the language. She cited evidence from conventional phrases (*salt and pepper, bread and butter*) and from spontaneous speech that word order in phrasal conjuncts is affected by word frequency and hence by phonological accessibility. This is in contrast to her finding mentioned above that, in such constructions, order is not affected by imageability and hence not by conceptual accessibility.

However, unlike Garrett, Bock argued that the two stages of planning are not completely independent of each other. She cited evidence that syntactic structures (i.e., the functional integration) can be altered to allow phonologically accessible words to appear earlier in a sentence. This suggests that there must be interaction between the two stages. She proposed that there are two ways in which this might occur: either there is feedback from the latter stage to the earlier stage, or there is a parallel race between different possible functional representations of a sentence where the first to be translated into a fully specified constituent representation is the one which is articulated. There is evidence suggestive of both these kinds of processes. For example, Bock found that phonological-priming words (which sounded like a word in a sentence to be recalled) affected the syntactic structure of sentences. So phonological activation appears to be affecting functional integration decisions. However, evidence from speech errors gives clear evidence that two syntactic formulations for a sentence can be available and, if the speaker is not careful, can be erroneously blended:

'this is getting very difficult to cut this' (a possible (5)
blend of 'this is getting very difficult to cut' and 'it
is getting very difficult to cut this').

Example (5) might have been caused by a simple perseveration error, but the following is more difficult to account for by any simple mechanism:

'we've got our hands cut out for us' (a possible (6)
blend of 'we've got our work cut out for us' and
'we've got our hands full').

Kempen and Hoenkamp (1987) have broken more profoundly with the serial notion of the two-stage theory of language production. A fundamental problem with positing that the functional stage of planning prepares a frame outlining several clauses and then passes this frame to a positional stage for detailed specification is that one would expect substantial breaks in speech flow between these frames. As Kempen and Hoenkamp noted, this does not characterize spontaneous speech which has frequent short breaks. They proposed instead that language-production processes must function largely in parallel and in an incremental fashion, so that as soon as a meaningful fragment is output from one level of processing it is passed to the next level for further transformation. To explore which planning processes might proceed in parallel, Kempen and Huijbers (1983) conducted a study in which participants were asked to describe simple visual displays (see Sect. 1 above). They suggested that selection of lemmas for an utterance may occur in parallel, but that selection of lexemes can only occur serially. This proposal leads to predictions about the relative times (latencies) to initiate utterances of different forms. These predictions are shown schematically in Table 2. For example, if one asks speakers simply to name the actor

Table 2. Alignment of lexical selection processes for different sentence types as hypothesized by Kempen and Huijbers (1983).

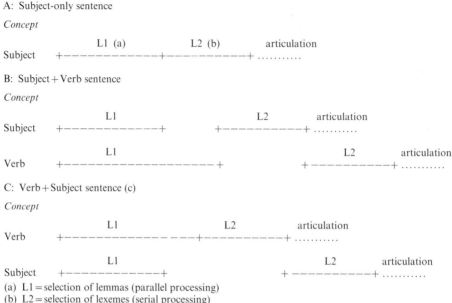

A: Subject-only sentence

Concept

             L1 (a)   L2 (b)   articulation
Subject   +——————————+—————————+ ....

B: Subject + Verb sentence

Concept

             L1   L2   articulation
Subject   +—————————+   +—————————+ ....

             L1   L2   articulation
Verb   +———————————+   +—————————+ ....

C: Verb + Subject sentence (c)

Concept

             L1   L2   articulation
Verb   +—————————————+—————————+ ....

             L1   L2   articulation
Subject   +—————————+   +—————————+ ....

(a) L1 = selection of lemmas (parallel processing)
(b) L2 = selection of lexemes (serial processing)
(c) The experiment was conducted in Dutch, for which a verb+subject sentence is meaningful

in a display, the latencies will give an indication of the time required to retrieve the lemma and then the lexeme for that actor (see Table 2, panel A). If one asks speakers to produce an actor–action sequence, then retrieval of the lexemes can only start after an interval corresponding to the longer retrieval time for the two lemmas involved (see Table 2, panel B). Finally, if one asks speakers to produce an action–actor sequence (a meaningful sentence in Dutch, the language in which the study was conducted), the latency will correspond only to the retrieval time for the lemma and lexeme for the action, but there may then be a break before articulation of the actor, if retrieval of its lexeme takes longer than articulation of the action (see Table 2, panel C). The pattern of latencies supported Kempen and Huijbers's view that selection of lemmas can proceed in parallel but selection of lexemes must proceed serially.

Other researchers have departed even more radically from the two-stage serial theory by proposing spreading activation theories of language production which involve completely parallel processing. Such parallel distributed processing (PDP) or connectionist theories have caused a revolution in the way in which researchers conceptualize cognitive processes, and language production is no exception. They propose that knowledge is encoded as a network of connected nodes between which activation can spread. Dell (e.g., 1988) has produced a detailed connectionist account

of one aspect of the language production process, the retrieval of lexemes for lemmas.

Many questions remain to be answered in the study of language production. There is not even agreement as to what type of theory needs to be built to account for the processes involved, and whether it should be highly parallel, partly parallel or not at all parallel in its processing, or whether it should have feedback between different representations. However, work in the 1980s, particularly by Levelt and his colleagues (see Levelt 1989), has provided a vocabulary to facilitate discussion of the problems and a theoretical framework within which to situate this discussion. In addition, the successful use of experimental techniques has provided a new set of tools with which to study the processes. All these factors can be expected to lead to important developments in the understanding of language production processes.

Bibliography

Baars B J, Motley M T, MacKay D 1975 Output editing for lexical status from artificially elicited slips of the tongue. *Journal of Verbal Learning and Verbal Behaviour* **14**: 382–91

Bock J K 1987 Co-ordinating words and syntax in speech plans. In: Ellis A W (ed.) *Progress in the Psychology of Language,* vol. 3. Erlbaum, London

Boomer D S 1965 Hesitation and grammatical encoding. *Language and Speech* **8**: 148–58

Brotherton P L 1979 Speaking and not speaking. In: Siegman

A W, Feldstein S (eds.) *Of Speech and Time: Temporal Speech Patterns in Interpersonal Contexts*. Erlbaum, Hillsdale, NJ

Butterworth B L 1980 *Language Production. Vol. 1: Speech and Talk*. Academic Press, London

Dell G S 1988 The retrieval of phonological forms in production: Tests of predictions from a connectionist model. *Journal of Memory and Language* 27: 124–42

Dell G S, Reich P A 1981 Stages in sentence production: An analysis of speech error data. *Journal of Verbal Learning and Verbal Behaviour* 29: 611–29

Ford M, Holmes V M 1978 Planning units and syntax in sentence production. *Cognition* 6: 35–53

Garrett M F 1976 Syntactic processing in sentence production. In: Wales R J, Walker E (eds.) *New Approaches to Language Mechanisms*. North-Holland, Amsterdam

Garrett M F 1990 Sentence processing. In: Osherson D N, Lasnik H (eds.) *An Invitation to Cognitive Science. Vol. 1: Language*. MIT Press, Cambridge, MA

Goldman-Eisler F 1968 *Psycholinguistics: Experiments in Spontaneous Speech*. Academic Press, London

Kempen G, Hoenkamp E 1987 An incremental procedural grammar for sentence formulation. *Cognitive Science* 11: 201–58

Kempen G, Huijbers P 1983 The lexicalization process in sentence production and naming: Indirect election of words. *Cognition* 14: 185–209

Levelt W J M 1989 *Speaking: From Intention to Articulation*. MIT Press, Cambridge, MA

Maclay H, Osgood C E 1959 Hesitation phenomena in spontaneous English speech. *Word* 15: 19–44

Meara P, Ellis A W 1982 The psychological reality of deep and surface phonological representations: Evidence from speech errors in Welsh. *Linguistics* 19: 798–804

Osgood C E 1971 Where do sentences come from? In: Steinberg D D, Jakobovits L A (eds.) *Semantics: An Interdisciplinary Reader in Philosophy, Linguistics and Psychology*. Cambridge University Press, Cambridge

Paradis M 1994 Neurolinguistic aspects of implicit and explicit memory implications for bilingualism and SLA. In: Ellis N (ed.) *Implicit and Explicit Language Learning*. Academic Press, London

Petrie H L 1987 The psycholinguistics of speaking. In: Coates R, Deuchar M, Gazdar G, Lyons J (eds.) *New Horizons in Linguistics*, vol. 2. Penguin, Harmondsworth

Stemberger J P 1985 An interactive action model of language production. In: Ellis A W (ed.) *Progress in the Psychology of Language*, vol. 1. Erlbaum, Hillsdale, NJ

Development of Language Perception in Infants

P. W. Jusczyk

Breakthroughs in the methods used to study the perceptual capacities of infants since the late 1960s have enabled speech researchers to investigate language perception at a point well before infants begin to produce speech. Many of the methods rely on presenting infants with one type of speech sound repeatedly (e.g., a syllable such as [ba]) and observing how they respond to various changes in the speech sounds (e.g., changing the syllable to another one such as [pa], or changing the intonation contour of the syllable). The use of such methods has enabled investigators to learn much about the basic abilities that infants from any culture bring to the language learning situation. The knowledge gained about the initial state of infants' perceptual capacities has led to studies of how these capacities influence, and are influenced by, the acquisition of a native language.

1. Delineating the Basic Capacities

Research in this field began in earnest with the demonstration by Eimas et al. (1971) that infants, as young as 1 month old, are able to discriminate syllables, such as [ba] and [pa], differing by a single phonetic feature. Subsequent research addressed both the nature and

extent of the underlying speech perception capacities. Some of the early studies suggested that the underlying perceptual mechanisms were innate and specialized for speech processing. However, demonstrations of parallels in the way in which infants perceive certain nonspeech sounds, as well as studies of the speech perception capacities of nonhuman mammals, suggest that the earliest stages of speech perception are based on general auditory processing mechanisms.

Many studies have explored the extent of infants' capacities for perceiving speech (Aslin et al. 1983). Studies were undertaken examining infants' abilities to distinguish contrasts between speech sounds that differed along a single phonetic feature dimension such as voicing, place of articulation, manner of articulation, etc. These studies revealed that, during the first few months of life, infants can detect virtually all the kinds of phonetic differences between speech sounds in the language spoken in their native environment. Moreover, prior to 6 months, infants do not appear to require a period of prior exposure to such contrasts. Thus, infants successfully discriminate foreign language contrasts that do not occur in their native language (Werker 1991). Furthermore, infants' capacities for speech perception are not limited to discriminating differences between sounds. They are also able to cope with the kind of acoustic variability in the speech signal that is introduced when different talkers utter the same word. This latter ability is an important prerequisite to learning the vocabulary of the native language. At the same time, there is also evidence that, shortly after birth, infants do recognize differences in talkers' voices (Mehler 1985).

2. Sensitivity to Properties of the Native Language

A growing body of evidence indicates that, during the second half of the first year of life, speech perception capacities undergo some reorganization whereby they become more closely attuned to the sound properties characteristic of the native language (Jusczyk 1992; Werker 1991). This perceptual reorganization, which parallels changes occurring in speech production, is manifested in several ways. For instance, between 6 and 12 months of age, infants begin to show a loss of sensitivity to nonnative language phonetic contrasts. Thus, infants from English-speaking homes who can discriminate phonetic contrasts from English, Hindi, and Inslekampx (an Interior Salish Northwest Native American language) at 6 months of age, show no evidence of discriminating the non-English contrasts by 12 months of age (Werker 1991). Just how widespread this decline in sensitivity to nonnative contrasts is, and which factors determine whether or when a decline actually occurs, are not yet clear.

During the same period, there are indications that infants are becoming more attuned to the sound structure of their native language. By 6 months, infants' vowel categories appear to be organized around prototypical instances characteristic of vowel categories of adult speakers of the language. Thus,

infants are better able to generalize from prototypical instances to new instances of the adult category. Additionally, there are indications that infants are learning about the characteristic sound patterns of words in their native language (Jusczyk 1992). For example, by 6 months of age, American infants prefer to listen to words that follow the prosodic patterns of English as opposed to ones which follow those of a foreign language like Norwegian. Furthermore, by 9 months of age, both American and Dutch infants display sensitivity to the kinds of ordering constraints that hold among phonetic segments within a word. Thus, they listen longer to lists of words that follow the native language constraints than they do to ones which violate the constraints (Jusczyk 1997).

Bibliography

Aslin R N, Pisoni D B, Jusczyk P W 1983 Auditory development and speech perception in infancy. In: Haith M, Campos J (eds.) *Handbook of Child Psychology. Vol. 2: Infancy and Developmental Psychobiology*. Wiley, New York

Eimas P D, Siqueland E R, Jusczyk P W, Vigorito J 1971 Speech perception in infants. *Science* 171: 303–06

Jusczyk P M 1997 *The Discovery of Spoken Language*. MIT Press, Cambridge, MA

Jusczyk P W 1992 Developing phonological categories from the speech signal. In: Ferguson C A, Stoel-Gammon C, Menn L (eds.) *Phonological Development: Models, Research, Implications*. York, Timonium, MD

Mehler J 1985 Language related dispositions in early infancy. In: Mehler J, Fox R (eds.) *Neonate Cognition*. Erlbaum, Hillsdale, NJ

Werker J F 1991 The ontogeny of speech perception. In: Mattingly I G, Studdert-Kennedy M (eds.) *Modularity and the Motor Theory of Speech Perception*. Erlbaum, Hillsdale, NJ

Babbling in Hearing and Deaf Infants

C. Stoel-Gammon

Infants produce various kinds of vocalizations in the first year of life, ranging from cries, coughs, and burps shortly after birth to long strings of syllables with varying intonation patterns at 12–15 months. Even after they begin to talk, children continue to produce nonmeaningful utterances, often mixing meaningful and nonmeaningful forms in the same utterance. Researchers who study prelinguistic development have adopted the general term 'vocalization' to refer to infants' nondistress, nonmeaningful vocal productions; the term 'babbling' is usually reserved for

describing speechlike syllables produced in the second half of the first year.

1. Normal Development of Prelinguistic Vocalizations

Normally developing infants, regardless of the linguistic community in which they are being raised, pass through the same general stages of vocal development from birth to the appearance of the first recognizable words. The onset of a new stage is marked by the appearance of a type of vocalization which did not occur in the preceding stage; however, vocal behaviors characteristic of earlier stages continue to be present. Thus, each stage contains a wider variety of vocalizations than the one before it. The description of stages presented below, with approximate ages for each stage, is based primarily on the work of Oller (1980) and Locke (1983).

Stage 1 (0–2 months): This stage is characterized by a majority of 'reflexive' vocalizations such as cries, wheezes, coughs, and burps. These vocal types are labeled reflexive because they involve automatic, involuntary motor patterns. In addition, some non-reflexive vowel-like sounds occur.

Stage 2 (2–4 months): Typically called the 'cooing' stage, this period is characterized by the appearance of comfort-state vocalizations which sound like vowels and consonants produced at the back of the mouth. Due to differences between the vocal tracts of the infant and the adult, infant productions in this period have a marked nasal quality.

Stage 3 (4–6 months): This is the stage of 'vocal play' during which infants seem to be exploring the capabilities of their vocal apparatus. Their productions are characterized by a wide range of intensity (loudness) and fundamental frequency (pitch) differences, resulting in the productions of yells, whispers, squeals, and growls. Infants may also produce various types of trills, sustained vowels, and some rudimentary consonant-vowel syllables.

Stage 4 (6–9 months): During this period, infants enter the 'canonical' stage characterized by the appearance of consonant–vowel (CV) syllables. The most striking characteristic of the stage is the production of repeated syllables such as [mama] or [dada] which sometimes resemble words of the ambient language. Upon hearing such utterances, parents often report that their baby has begun to call them by name. In most cases, however, there is no evidence of a sound–meaning correspondence in the infants' productions and thus no basis for calling these babbled forms 'words.'

Research has shown that the great majority of consonantal sounds in this period are characterized by a limited set of articulatory features. In terms of manner of articulation, consonants are generally stops, (e.g., [b, d, g]), nasals (e.g., [m, n]), or glides (e.g., [w]); fricatives, affricates, and liquids occur infrequently (Locke 1983). In terms of place of articulation, consonants produced at the front of the mouth (e.g., [b, d, m, n]) are far more frequent than back ones (e.g., [k, g]). Glottal consonants [ʔ, h] are present in previous stages and continue to occur in the canonical stage. Interestingly, the consonantal types which predominate in the canonical period are the same as those which appear in children's early words. The most frequent vowel sounds are the lax front and central vowels [ɪ, ɛ, æ, ə]; unlike the pattern observed for consonants, these vowels are not the most frequent in early word productions.

Stage 5 (9–15 months): This period, referred to as the 'variegated' stage, is characterized by productions of CV syllables in which a variety of consonants and vowels can cooccur; instead of the repeated sequence [mamama], the baby may utter something like [dibagu]. The repertoire of sound types increases substantially at this age as different kinds of consonants and vowels are produced. A second characteristic of this stage is the presence of long utterances with distinctive intonation patterns. These types of utterances, often called 'jargon babbling,' sound as though babies are making statements and asking questions, using words from 'their own' language.

Research (Mitchell and Kent 1990; Smith et al. 1990) raises doubts about the view that Stages 4 and 5 are sequential. Rather, it appears that some, perhaps most, infants begin to produce both repeated and variegated babbles at about the same time. Thus, it may be preferable to consider these as a single stage.

2. Prelinguistic Vocal Development: Deaf Infants

It is well-documented that a severe hearing loss has grave consequences for speech and language development. Deaf individuals are unable to hear either their own speech or the speech of others, and typically have difficulties acquiring spoken language. Research on the vocal development of deaf and hearing-impaired infants is particularly important because it provides information about the role of audition in the prelinguistic period. Until recently, little was known about the effects of deafness in infancy because it was difficult to identify a hearing loss in the first year (Stoel-Gammon and Kehoe 1994). In many cases, an infant's inability to hear was not discovered until 12–15 months old, or even later, when the parents voiced concerns that their baby was not saying words. Advances in hearing assessment now allow for the detection of a hearing loss at younger ages and allow researchers to determine the similarities and differences in the vocal development of hearing and hearing-impaired infants.

Like their hearing peers, deaf infants vocalize at birth and then proceed through the first three stages outlined in Sect. 1. Thus, for the first 6 months, their vocal development is indistinguishable from other infants. Around 6 months, however, differences between the two groups appear. First, hearing-impaired infants fail to enter the 'canonical' stage on schedule, continuing to produce precanonical vocalizations for many months. Some begin to produce CV syllables characteristic of the canonical stage at the end of the first year (i.e., around 12 months); others do not reach this stage until the end of the second year (Oller and Eilers 1988). The second difference between the two populations centers around the range of sound types which is produced after 6 months. In normally hearing infants, the variety of consonantal sounds increases with age as their sound repertoires expand in terms of place and manner of articulation. In contrast, the consonantal inventories of hearing-impaired subjects remain constant or decrease as they grow older (Stoel-Gammon and Otomo 1986). Stoel-Gammon (1988) reported that the inventories of hearing-impaired infants were composed primarily of labial and glottal consonants; in contrast, the inventories of hearing infants contained a variety of lingual sounds (e.g., alveolars and velars) as well as labials and glottals. It has been hypothesized that labial consonants like [p, b, m] are favored in the vocalizations of the hearing-impaired because the lip movements associated with their production are highly visible, whereas the lingual movements needed to articulate alveolar and velar sounds cannot be seen.

There is some evidence that deaf infants exposed to sign language engage in 'manual babbling' prior to acquiring a referential system of signing. Pettito and Marentette (1991) analyzed the 'manual activities' of three hearing and three deaf/hearing-impaired infants, classifying these activities as gestures (e.g., holding a cup to lips as if to drink) or manual babbling (hand movements that were not standard signs but contained phonetic and syllabic organization characteristic of signed languages). The groups did not differ in the types and quantities of gestures used; however, the deaf/hearing-impaired infants produced significantly more manual babbling that their hearing peers. If replicated, these findings suggest parallels between manual babbling of deaf infants and vocal babbling of infants with normal hearing.

Bibliography

Locke J 1983 *Phonological Acquisition and Change.* Academic Press, New York

Mitchell P R, Kent R D 1990 Phonetic variation in multisyllabic babbling. *J. Ch. L.* **17**: 247–65

Oller D K 1980 The emergence of speech sounds in infancy. In: Yeni-Komshian G, Kavanagh J F, Ferguson C A (eds.) *Child Phonology*. Academic Press, New York

Oller D K, Eilers R E 1988 The role of audition in infant babbling. *Child Development* **59**: 441–49

Petitto L A, Marentette P F 1991 Babbling in the manual mode: Evidence for the ontogeny of language. *Science* **251**: 1493–96

Smith B L, Brown-Sweeney S, Stoel-Gammon C 1989 A quantitative analysis of reduplicated and variegated babbling. *First Language* **9**: 175–89

Stoel-Gammon C 1988 Prelinguistic vocalizations of hearing-impaired and normally hearing subjects: A comparison of consonantal inventories. *Journal of Speech and Hearing Disorders* **53**: 302–15

Stoel-Gammon C, Kehoe M M 1994 Hearing impairment in infants and toddlers: Identification, vocal development, intervention. In: Bernthal J E, Bankson N W (eds.) *Child Phonology: Characteristics, Assessment, and Intervention with Special Populations*. Thieme Medical Publishers, New York

Stoel-Gammon C, Otomo K 1986 Babbling development of hearing-impaired and normally hearing subjects. *Journal of Speech and Hearing Disorders* **51**: 33–41

Acquisition of Phonemes

C. Stoel-Gammon and L. Menn

A standard question in child phonology is: 'In what order do children acquire the phonemes of their native language?' Speech pathologists would like to determine a normal order of acquisition so that they can recognize abnormality and perhaps target remedial intervention towards the earlier phonemes first. Other investigators, including many linguists, wish to test the predictions of various phonological theories against data from child phonology.

However, there are problems with this question as it is formulated. First, it is assumed that there is a typical or perhaps universal order of acquisition for children learning a given language. Second, some investigators address the question of when children master appropriate pronunciations of the phonemes of a language, while others address the very different question of when children give evidence of acquiring the phonemic contrasts of the language. Third, investigators who address the 'appropriate pronunciations' issue appear to consider that 'acquisition' has

occurred when a child produces an acceptable allophone of a consonant phoneme in singleton initial, intervocalic, and final positions; but other variables in test stimuli are often overlooked. (One phonotactic problem is the frequent use of *yellow* as the test item for initial /j/ because children may assimilate /j/ to the following /l/, yielding /lɛlo/. This error is unlikely to occur in words like *yes* or *you*.) Fourth, criteria for acquisition of vowels are rarely set out at all, and many articulation tests do not contain target words with the full set of English vowels. Fifth, different studies use different methodologies for collecting the samples (e.g., single-word tests, spontaneous running speech) and different criteria for determining 'acquisition' or 'mastery' of phonemes. Sixth, dialect differences—such as the acceptability of alveolar flap for medial /t/, and other types of variation—have generally been ignored.

Despite these problems, there has been considerable effort in the field of speech-language pathology to develop a set of norms that can be used for identification of children with atypical phonological development. The standard references for acquisition of American English are large-group studies utilizing elicited productions, such as the study by Wellman et al. (1931) of 204 children aged 2–6 years, and Templin's investigation (1957) of 480 children, aged 3–8 years. Data from these two studies reanalyzed by Sander (1972) to determine the ages at which 50 percent and 90 percent of the children tested produced 'acceptable' allophones of American English consonants in word-initial, word-medial, and word-final positions. The 50 percent mark was reached before age 2 for labials /p/, /b/, /m/, and /w/, and also for /h/ and /n/. Except for /b/, these reached 90 percent by age 3. The velars /k/, /g/, /ŋ/, and the alveolar stops /t/ and /d/ reached 50 percent correct production on their test materials at age 2; /b/, /k/, /g/, and /d/ reached 90 percent by age 4, but /t/ and /ŋ/ did not do so until age 6. The greatest lag between the 50 percent and the 90 percent criteria was shown by /s/: this reached 50 percent at age 3, but did not reach 90 percent until age 8. Thus, even with these simplified and averaged data, 'order of acquisition' is not well defined. Furthermore, longitudinal studies of pronunciation have found considerable individual differences in the order of acquisition of stops (Macken 1980) and fricatives (Edwards 1996). Stoel-Gammon and Herrington (1990) have found that the American English vowel system is generally completed before the consonantal system is complete, and that the vowels acquired early are /i/, /u/, /a/, /o/, and /ʌ/; again, no finer-grained generalization can be maintained.

A study of 997 children by Smit et al. (1990) differs from previous large-group ones by presenting separate norms for boys and girls. Although general patterns are similar to those reported by Sander (1972), mastery—defined as the age at which 90 percent of the age group produced the phoneme correctly in word-initial and word-final position—occurred earlier for girls than boys for nearly all phonemes that exhibited gender-based differences. For example, /ʃ/ and /tʃ/ were mastered by girls by the age of 6, and by boys at the age of 7; but /θ/ was mastered at 6 by girls, and not until 8 by boys. This finding is important for the identification of children with delayed articulatory

development. Given the differences in age of mastery, use of a single set of norms for all children means that boys will be overidentified as having a delay, whereas girls will be underidentified.

General statements for English can at best be sustained at the level of phoneme classes: in general, stops precede fricatives and affricates, while glides precede liquids. The same patterns have been documented for children with phonological delays (Dinnsen 1992). But individual differences, particularly in the early stages of phonological acquisition, make these statements probabilistic rather than universal; there is considerable individual variation across normally developing and phonology disordered children. As yet, no theory is able to account both for the degree of observed variation and the degree of observed commonality of acquisition of phones and of phonemic contrasts across children or across languages.

Bibliography

Dinnsen D 1992 Variation in developing and fully developed phonetic inventories. In: Ferguson C A, Menn L, Stoel-Gammon C (eds.) *Phonological Development: Models, Research, Implications.* York Press, Timonium, MD

Edwards M L 1996 Word position effects in the pronunciation of fricatives. In: Bernhardt B, Gilbert J, Ingram D (eds.) *Proceedings of the UBC International Conference on Phonological Acquisition.* Cascadilla Press, Somerville, MA

Macken M A 1980 Aspects of the acquisition of stop systems: A cross-linguistic perspective. In: Yeni-Komshian G, Kavanagh J F, Ferguson C A (eds.) *Child Phonology,* vol. 1. Academic Press, New York

Sander E 1972 When are speech sounds learned? *Journal of Speech and Hearing Disorders* 37: 55–63

Smit A B, Hand L, Freilinger J J, Bernthal J E, Bird A 1990 The Iowa Articulation Norms Project and its Nebraska replication. *Journal of Speech and Hearing Disdorders* 55: 779–98

Stoel-Gammon C, Herrington P B 1990 Vowel systems of normally developing and phonologically disordered children. *Clinical Linguistics and Phonetics* 4: 145–60

Templin M C 1957 *Certain Language Skills in Children: Their Development and Interrelationships.* Institute of Child Welfare Monographs, 26. University of Minnesota Press, Minneapolis, MN

Wellman B L, Case I M, Mengert I B, Bradbury D E 1931 Speech sounds of young children. *University of Iowa Studies in Child Welfare* 2: 5

Acquisition of Vocabulary

M. D. Barrett

Children usually acquire their first word at about one year of age; it has been estimated that the vocabulary of an educated 20-year old contains between 50 000 and 250 000 words. Taking the mid-figure of 150 000 words, this means that children must be capable of acquiring words at an overall average rate of more than 20 words per day. These words which children acquire are of many different kinds, including words for referring to people, objects, actions, attributes, relationships, places, mental states, mental processes, abstract concepts, etc.; words which are used to fulfil specific pragmatic functions within the context of particular interactional exchanges (such as *thanks*, *please*, and *hello*); and words which are used to fulfil particular syntactic functions (such as *and*, *the*, and *to*). It can be seen from these basic facts that vocabulary development is an extraordinary process, entailing the acquisition of a vast number of words from a large variety of different categories.

1. Early Vocabulary Development

Studies documenting the rate of vocabulary growth through the second year of life have typically relied upon counts of the number of different words which young children spontaneously produce. These studies suggest that the first word is usually acquired somewhere between 8 and 16 months of age, and that in the months immediately following, vocabulary development proceeds at a very slow rate, with only one or two new words being acquired each week. But as children approach the 50-word level, there is often a sudden spurt in the rate at which new words appear in the child's productive vocabulary, and within 2–3 weeks, this rate may increase to eight or more new words per week.

However, studies relying upon children's spontaneous production of words probably underestimate the rate of early vocabulary growth. If measures are made of young children's word comprehension rather than production, it is found that, on average, children are able to comprehend 50 words before they can produce 10 words, and the rate of acquisition between the 10-word and 50-word level in comprehension is twice as fast as the rate which is revealed by the use of production measures.

The words which are acquired during the second year of life are of many different kinds. Some early words are used as direct expressions of the child's internal affect states; these words are often non-conventional and idiosyncratic (e.g., [ae::] as an expression of pleasure, [ubiba] as an expression of frustration). Other early words are entirely context-bound; that is, they are produced by the child only in very limited and specific situations or contexts in which particular actions or events occur (e.g., a child might use the word *choo-choo* only while pushing a toy train along the floor, or *bye* only when another person leaves the room). However, some words are used in a variety of different behavioral contexts right from the outset, either as the names of objects (e.g., *teddy*, *ball*, *doggy*), as proper names for individual people or animals (e.g., *mummy*, *Adam*, *Spot*), or to refer to actions (e.g., *wash*, *kick*, *tickle*). In addition, children usually acquire some words during the

second year of life for referring to the properties or qualities of objects or events, such as the disappearance of objects (e.g., *gone*), the recurrence of objects and actions (e.g., *more*), the spatial location of objects (e.g., *in*, *on*, *up*, *down*), and the attributes and states of objects or people (e.g., *big*, *dirty*, *nice*). And finally, social–pragmatic words are also often acquired during this period (e.g., *no* to oppose the actions of agents, *please* to request objects from other people, *look* to direct the attention of people).

It seems likely that these various types of words are acquired during this early period of vocabulary development because these are the words which are the most pertinent to the child's current cognitive activities. For example, it is precisely at this time of life that children are building up an extensive knowledge of object categories, and consolidating their understanding that objects occupy specific locations in space, and can disappear and recur. It is also during this early period that they are consolidating their understanding that people are agents who can perform actions on objects, and building up a knowledge of recurrent interpersonal routines and activities. It is therefore not surprising to find that the words which are acquired during the second year of life are precisely those which serve to encode notions concerning objects, spatial locations, disappearance, recurrence, the actions of agents, and interpersonal transactions.

Once acquired, early words are not always used by young children in an unchanging manner through the second year of life; instead, words can exhibit some marked developmental changes during this period. For example, after their initial acquisition, context-bound words often exhibit decontextualization; that is, their production becomes dissociated from the single context within which they were initially used, and they begin to be used much more widely in a variety of different behavioral contexts (e.g., *choo-choo* might eventually come to be used as a nominal for referring to trains in a variety of different situations, and *bye* might eventually become a more flexible social–pragmatic word which is used in a variety of situations involving departure).

Some of the most interesting changes in word use which occur during this early period of development are those which are commonly exhibited by object names. When object names are first acquired, they are often underextended; that is, they are often used to name only a subset of the full range of objects which are properly labeled with those words in the adult language (e.g., *duck* may be used to refer only to toy ducks, and not to refer to real ducks). The extension of an underextended word usually broadens at a subsequent point in time (e.g., *duck* would normally come to be used to refer to real ducks as well). Occasionally such words become overextended at this stage (e.g., *duck* may eventually be used to refer not only to ducks but also to swans and geese). These overextensions are subsequently rescinded. The process of rescission may occur in conjunction with the acquisition of a new word which takes over the labeling of the over-extended referents (e.g., the child may stop using *duck* to refer to swans in conjunction with the acquisition of the word *swan*); sometimes, there is a short transitional period during which the overextended referents are variably referred to by means of either word before the overextension is fully rescinded (i.e., for a short period of time, swans may be referred to by means of either *swan* or *duck* before the overextension of *duck* is finally rescinded).

These changes in word use have been interpreted by researchers in this field as evidence for the progressive modification and reorganization of the information which is stored in the vocabulary entry for an object name (see, for example, the articles in Seiler and Wannenmacher 1983; Kuczaj and Barrett 1986). For example, it has been argued that the child acquires the meaning of an object name in the following way (see Barrett 1995). The child begins by acquiring a mental representation of a prototypical referential exemplar for the object name, by observing the type of object in connection with which other people most commonly use the word. This prototypical referent then functions for the child as a specification of the type of object which can be labeled with that word; at this point, the child only uses the word to refer to objects which closely resemble the prototype (i.e., the word is underextended). Subsequently, the child identifies some of the more salient features of the prototype, and begins to extend the word to other objects which display just some of the same features (i.e., the word's extension is broadened, and the word may become overextended, but only to objects which have features in common with the prototypical referent). Finally, if another competing name for a particular object is acquired, the prototypical referents of the two competing names are compared with one another, and the contrasting features which differentiate these prototypical referents from one another are eventually identified and used to determine a boundary between the extensions of the two words (i.e., the overextension is rescinded). Thus, the changes which occur in young children's uses of object names have been interpreted by some researchers as indicating that, by about 2 years of age, children's vocabulary entries for object names must contain information about prototypical referents, prototypical features, and contrasting features which differentiate prototypical referents from one another.

There has also been considerable discussion among researchers of the notion that, midway through the second year of life, there is a sharp discontinuity in children's vocabulary development, and that this discontinuity is responsible for the sudden spurt in the rate of acquisition of new words which typically occurs as children approach the 50-word level. It has

been argued that, prior to the vocabulary spurt, the child does not yet understand that words can be used referentially as the names of particular objects; as a consequence, the child acquires mainly context-bound and social-pragmatic words during this initial stage. But midway through the second year, it is suggested, children suddenly acquire a fundamental insight into the symbolic properties of words: that words can be used in order to name particular objects. And as a consequence of this realization, many existing context-bound words are decontextualized into object names and many new object names are suddenly acquired; hence the occurrence of the vocabulary spurt. This view draws support primarily from the fact that the spurt itself consists of a sudden upturn in the rate of acquisition of object names (rather than of any other type of word).

However, there are certain other facts which serve to cast some doubt upon this explanation of the vocabulary spurt. For example, it has become clear from certain studies that, although some children do indeed show this classic pattern of an initial slow acquisition of context-bound and social-pragmatic words followed by the sudden and rapid acquisition of large numbers of object names, there are other children who instead acquire object names among their very first words, well before their vocabulary spurt has occurred. This implies that these particular children have already acquired the naming insight, right at the outset of their vocabulary development. In addition, it has been found that not all children exhibit a sudden spurt in the rate of their early vocabulary growth; as many as a quarter of all children do not exhibit this phenomenon. This substantial minority of children instead acquire words at a much steadier rate throughout the second year of life, and this rate is only occasionally punctuated by small upward and downward fluctuations and plateaus. Furthermore, these children give no evidence of acquiring a sudden naming insight, and object names never come to predominate over other types of words in their early vocabularies.

Consequently, it is now appreciated to a much greater extent than previously that there are considerable individual differences between children in their early vocabulary development, and that theoretical interpretations of the phenomena which characterize vocabulary development during the second year of life need to pay much closer attention to these differences than they have hitherto.

2. Later Vocabulary Development

Estimates of the rate of vocabulary growth after about two-and-a-half years of age vary considerably, with the vocabulary size of a 6 year old having been estimated to be anywhere between 2500 to 13 000 words. Despite the uncertainty which surrounds all such estimates of later vocabulary sizes, it can nevertheless be seen from the magnitude of these figures that children must be highly efficient word learners.

One reason for this efficiency is that children are able to acquire a new word on the basis of just a single exposure to that word, as long as the situation in which that exposure occurs contains a suitably clear referent for that word. Such a single exposure can be quite sufficient for the child to acquire an initial prototypical referential exemplar for the word, and to assign the word to the appropriate lexical field. However, this initial fast mapping is then usually followed by a more extended period of learning in which the precise details of the word's meaning in relationship to the meanings of the other words in the same lexical field are only slowly worked out. This pattern of fast mapping followed by a more extended period of semantic fine-tuning has been observed for both object names (e.g., animal names) and attribute names (e.g., color terms and shape terms) in children aged over 2 years old.

A second reason for children's efficiency at word learning is that they become very adept at picking up information about the meaning of a word simply from the verbal context in which the word is produced by another person (this applies even in the absence of any clear referent for the word in the immediate situation). This ability increases through childhood. With an object name or an action name, for example, 4- and 5-year-old children are able to extract some information from the verbal context of the word about the properties of the object or action to which the word refers (even though these children cannot then formulate explicit definitions of such a word at this age). By 11 years of age, not only can children begin to acquire the meaning of an abstract word (such as *courage*, *justice*, etc.) from just a single presentation of that word in a verbal context; from four or five such presentations, they are able to derive the full meaning of such a word, for which they can then offer an explicit definition. Furthermore, children are able to deploy this ability both on unknown words produced by interlocuters, and on unknown words encountered during reading (see McKeown and Curtis 1987).

However, despite children's undoubted efficiency at word learning, the meanings of some particular types of words still seem to give them considerable difficulty in acquisition. Words which refer to mental states and processes are an interesting example. Words such as *know*, *guess*, and *think* usually begin to appear in children's speech at about 2 years of age. However, at this early stage, these words are used as pragmatic-conversational devices rather than to refer to mental states and processes; for example, *you know* might be used as a pause-filler, *I guess* as a reluctant version of *yes*, *I think* to weaken an assertion (as in *I think it's gone*), etc. Use of these words to refer to mental states and processes only seems to emerge in the second half of the third year of life. However, although 3 year olds

use words like *remember*, *know*, and *guess* appropriately in distinctive situations, even 4 and some 5 year olds still confuse the meanings of these three words when their knowledge is tested under controlled conditions, revealing that the meanings of these three words are not yet properly differentiated from one another. Indeed, it is typically not until children are 6 years old that they finally begin to use these three words in ways which indicate that the definitive distinctions between the meanings of the words have been properly mastered.

Perhaps rather surprisingly, however, young children do not seem to have very great difficulty acquiring personal pronouns such as *I, you, he, she, we*, etc. This is curious, because these words differ from many other types of word in that their referents shift depending upon who is doing the speaking. For example, *I* refers to the self when it is the self who is speaking, but refers to the other person when it is the other person who is speaking; thus, the reference of *I* differs in production and in comprehension (referring to myself in production but referring to the other person in comprehension).

However, these complexities appear to be mastered by young children with comparative ease. They usually begin (before 2 years of age) by understanding *you* and *your* when these words are spoken to them by other people, and by producing *I* and *my* themselves; that is, both first and second person pronouns are first mastered in relationship to themselves as the referent. The inanimate third person singular pronoun *it* also usually begins to appear in children's speech at this early stage, although this word usually appears only in the postverbal position in the child's sentences at this stage. Shortly thereafter, children begin to comprehend *I* when it is spoken to them by another person, and to produce *you* to refer to the addressee. The remaining personal pronouns (e.g., *he, she, his, her, we, our*, etc.) are subsequently acquired, and the full set of pronouns is often mastered by the age of 3 years 3 months; these remaining pronouns are not acquired in any clear-cut or consistent order. Despite the complexities concerning the shifting referents of pronouns, children rarely confuse the different pronouns, and make comparatively few errors in their use of these words (see Chiat 1986).

Relational words have received a great deal of attention from researchers into children's vocabulary development. These are words which serve to express relationships between two or more objects or events. They often occur in antonymous pairs: for example, *big/little, tall/short, thick/thin, more/less, before/after*, etc. One reason why these words have attracted so much attention from researchers is because the dimensional adjectives (*big/little, tall/short*, and *thick/thin*) are often acquired in the same consistent order by different children. *Big* and *little* are usually the first pair to be acquired, and even children as old as 4 and

5 years still tend to use these two terms irrespective of whether they are referring to the overall size, to the height, or to the width of an object. Children subsequently acquire *tall* and *short* for referring to the dimension of height, and they finally acquire *thick* and *thin* for referring to the dimension of width. It has been argued that this order of acquisition occurs because *big* and *little* are the most general of all these terms in that they serve to specify extent in any or all of the three dimensions, and so they are the simplest of these various word pairs for children to learn. Height is then argued to be the most perceptually salient dimension of an object, and so *tall* and *short* are learnt next. Finally, width or thickness is the least salient dimension, and so *thick* and *thin* are the last of these three word pairs to be learnt by children.

In addition, it has been claimed by some researchers that, within many pairs of relational words, one of the two words is normally acquired before the other word: *tall* before *short*, *thick* before *thin*, *more* before *less*, and *before* before *after*. This claim has been made most strongly in connection with the words *more* and *less* (the evidence concerning the other word pairs is much more equivocal). The word *more* is often acquired initially in the second year of life, although it is normally only used at this early stage to comment upon, or to demand, a recurrence of an object or action that has gone before (as in *more biscuit, more cuddle*, etc.); it is usually not for another year or two that *more* starts to be used in its relational or comparative sense (as in *you've got more than me, there's more here than there*, etc.). However, it has been found that, up until the age of about 5 years, children tend not to use the word *less* in their spontaneous speech at all. Furthermore, when children aged under 5 are tested for their understanding of the word *less*, they often respond as if *less* meant the same as *more* (e.g., if they are shown two toy apple trees which have different numbers of apples on them, and they are asked to indicate which tree has less apples on it, they typically choose the tree which has more apples on it). However, this response seems to occur, not because young children actually believe that *less* means the same as *more* (they do differentiate between the two words under certain tightly controlled conditions), but because they seem to have a nonlinguistic response bias towards choosing the larger of two sets in forced-choice tasks of this nature which usually overrides their lexical knowledge (see Clark 1990).

Finally, it should be noted here that researchers into children's later vocabulary development have become increasingly aware of the extent to which children rely upon learning strategies to aid their lexical acquisitions. For example, when hearing a new word with which they are unfamiliar, young children often rely upon a strategy of simply mapping the unfamiliar word onto an unfamiliar referent. Consequently, if they are exposed to an unfamiliar color word, say, in a situation which contains several objects of familiar colors and one object of a novel color, then they typically assume that the unfamiliar word refers to the novel color (the same finding has also been obtained with object names and shape terms). This strategy often assists the correct fast mapping of new words on to the appropriate concepts, although it can also lead the child into making mapping errors under certain circumstances (e.g., if the novel word referred not to the unfamiliar color but to a particular shade of one of the known colors).

Another strategy upon which children often rely when making lexical acquisitions is to assume that the meaning of a new word must contrast in some way with the meanings of other known words. Consequently, when children acquire a second word (e.g., *toy*) for referring to an object for which they already have a name (e.g., *doll*), they typically search for differences in the meanings between the two words; this strategy usually leads them to infer that the new word designates either a subkind, a superordinate, or a part of that object, and to avoid the conclusion that the new word has the same meaning as the old word.

Thus, the overall picture which emerges from studies of children's later vocabulary development is one in which the child is viewed as an extremely efficient word learner, able to map words to meanings very rapidly and with minimal exposure by relying upon important facilitative learning strategies, but with certain lexical domains (e.g., words referring to mental states and processes) presenting the child with particular difficulties in acquisition.

3. Norms of Vocabulary Development

As noted earlier, there are widespread individual differences in vocabulary development. These individual differences have been documented in a major norming study of 1803 children aged between 8 and 30 months of age (Fenson et al. 1993). This study utilised the MacArthur Communicative Development Inventories, an assessment tool which contains two parental report instruments, the CDI: Infants (for children aged 8–16 months) and the CDI: Toddlers (for children aged 16–30 months). These two instruments contain vocabulary checklists, and parents are asked to indicate which of the words in these lists the child either uses or understands. Because of the large sample size involved, this study arguably provides the most authoritative vocabulary development norms which are currently available.

This study found that, at 8 months of age, the children produced one or two words on average (with 80% of the children producing between zero and three words at this age). At 12 months, the mean productive vocabulary size was four words (with 80% of the 12 month olds producing between one and 19 words); at 16 months of age, the mean was 25 words (with 80% of the 16 month olds producing between four and 118 words); while at 20 months of age, the mean was 150 words (with 80% of the 20 month olds producing between 45 and 360 words). At 2 years of age, the mean vocabulary size was 320 words (with 80% of the two year olds producing between 95 and 540 words), and at 30 months, the mean vocabulary size was 565 words (with 80% of 30 month olds producing between 305 and 650 words). It should be noted that the figures for 30 month olds are probably underestimates, as by this point in their development, children almost certainly know more words that those that are included in the CDI: Toddlers checklist.

The figures for vocabulary comprehension (which is only assessed by the CDI: Infants, not by the CDI: Toddlers), were as follows. At 8 months of age, the children could comprehend about 14 words on average (with 80% of the children understanding between five and 57 words); at 12 months of age, the mean number of words understood was 55 words (with 80% of the children understanding between 20 and 170 words); and at 16 months of age, the mean number of words understood was 165 words (with 80% of the children understanding between 70 and 290 words). However, it is possible that these figures for word comprehension are overestimates, as parents using the CDI: Infants word comprehension checklist might be rather liberal in their attributions of word comprehension to their children; studies in the laboratory, where gestural and contextual cues to the meanings of words can be more tightly controlled, suggest that parents tend to overattribute word comprehension to their children in naturalistic settings.

The above norms represent total vocabulary sizes in production and in comprehension as estimated by the CDI. For more detailed information on the proportions of particular types of words (including common nouns, verbs, and adjectives) in children's vocabularies at different ages as estimated by the CDI, the interested reader should consult the CDI User's Guide (Fenson et al. 1993).

From a clinical perspective, it should be noted that children who fall outside the 80% range for their age on the CDI are either developmentally advanced or developmentally delayed compared to the majority of their peer group. For children falling into the latter category, further investigation and intervention may be advisable.

Bibliography

Barrett M D 1995 Early lexical development. In: Fletcher P, MacWhinney B (eds.) *The Handbook of Child Language*. Blackwell Publishers, Oxford

Chiat S 1986 Personal pronouns. In: Fletcher P, Garman M (eds.) *Language Acquisition*, 2nd edn. Cambridge University Press, Cambridge

Clark E V 1990 Children's language. In: Grieve R, Hughes M (eds.) *Understanding Children*. Blackwell Publishers, Oxford

Fenson L, Dale P S, Reznick J S, Thal D, Bates E, Hartung J, Pethick S, Reilly J 1993 *The MacArthur Communicative Development Inventories: User's Guide and Technical Manual*. Singular Publishing Group, San Diego, CA

Kuczaj S A, Barrett M D (eds.) 1986 *The Development of Word Meaning*. Springer-Verlag, New York

McKeown M G, Curtis M E (eds.) 1987 *The Nature of Vocabulary Acquisition*. Lawrence Erlbaum, Hillsdale, NJ

Seiler T B, Wannenmacher W (eds.) 1983 *Concept Development and the Development of Word Meaning*. Springer-Verlag, Berlin

Acquisition of Grammar

H. Tager-Flusberg

Within a few months of acquiring an initial vocabulary of about 50–100 words (see *Acquisition of Vocabulary*) young children, usually in the latter half of the second year, begin combining words together to form their first sentences. This new stage in language acquisition marks an important milestone because even the simplest two-word utterances show evidence of early grammatical development. Research on children's grammatical development began with descriptive studies in the 1930s; however, it was not until the publication of Chomsky's seminal work that theoretically focused research began in earnest, with an emphasis on studies of the acquisition of English, but also including since the 1980s some important cross-linguistic studies.

The child's task in acquiring the grammar of their native language is complex: they must be able to segment the stream of language they hear into basic units such as words, morphemes, and phrases; they must discover the major parts of speech of noun, verb, article, etc. and map the appropriate lexical items into them; they must acquire the major phrase structure rules for organizing basic phrasal units like noun phrase and verb phrase, as well as for organizing basic sentence structures for declaratives, questions, and negation; and finally they must figure out the syntactic rules for complex sentences involving the coordination and imbedding of multiple clauses. Research has indicated that children use a variety of clues to facilitate the process of grammatical development. Prosodic cues may help the child break into the linguistic stream to help identify word and phrase boundaries, and later on children make use of semantic and pragmatic as well as syntactic and morphological information in developing the underlying grammatical knowledge that allows them to produce and understand the full range of unlimited and novel sentences in their native language.

1. Measuring Grammatical Development

1.1 Mean Length of Utterance (MLU)

One of the most obvious ways in which children's sentences change over time is that they gradually grow longer. This fact is the basis of one of the most widely used measures of grammatical development: the MLU or mean length of utterance, which is the average length of a child's utterances as measured in morphemes, based on a sample of 100 utterances (Brown 1973). Thus, it is a measure of production rather than comprehension. The basic assumption of this measure is that each newly acquired element of grammatical knowledge adds length to the child's utterances. Longitudinal studies of language acquisition have confirmed that children's MLU increases gradually over time, though at different rates for different children, and norms for MLU between the ages of 2 and 5 have been developed. Despite its widespread use in research and clinical studies, MLU has received some criticism; it is quite limited in use and only valid up to an average sentence length of 4.0 morphemes.

To overcome some of these problems, other measures of grammatical development have been introduced which analyze more directly the grammatical content of a child's productive language.

1.2 Language Assessment, Remediation, and Screening Procedure (LARSP)

The LARSP profile analysis, introduced by David Crystal and his colleagues, provides a comprehensive measure of a child's phrases and clauses (Crystal et al. 1976). On the basis of this analysis, the child is assigned to one of seven developmental stages: (a) one-word utterances; (b) two-word utterances; (c) three-word utterances; (d) four-word utterances; (e) complex sentence formation defined in terms of coordination or subordination; (f) consolidation of grammatical systems, including complex complementation and fewer error patterns; and (g) remaining structures such as connectivity between sentences, emphatic expression, etc. This sequence of stages reflects the order of emergence of these structural patterns identified in the general literature on language acquisition. This measure is widely used in clinical settings with

diverse populations of children; it is useful both because of its hierarchical organization and because it allows one to identify specific problems at either the phrasal or clausal level.

1.3 Assigning Structural Stage (ASS)

Another measure that assigns a child's productive language to a structural stage is the ASS (Miller 1981). The child's utterances are analyzed in five main categories: (a) noun phrase elaboration; (b) verb phrase elaboration; (c) negatives; (d) questions; and (e) complex sentences. On the basis of this categorization a child's language is assigned to a stage that is parallel to MLU ranges. The limitation of this approach is that the product of this measure is simply a stage assignment, and details about the structures used or those that are omitted are not taken into consideration.

1.4 Index of Productive Syntax (IPSyn)

More recently, the ASS has been modified and adapted into a new measure, the IPSyn, which consists of 56 items divided into four subscales: (a) noun phrase; (b) verb phrase; (c) question/negation; and (d) sentence structure (Scarborough 1990). Within each subscale the items are sequenced developmentally based on current knowledge about patterns of language acquisition. A child is credited with a point system for the use of one or two different examples of each item; scores are summed within and across subscales to yield a total IPSyn score (maximum 120), but there is no stage assignment. This is a reliable measure that correlates with MLU but is useful beyond an MLU of 4.0. Thus far, it has been used mainly in research studies with a variety of populations.

1.5 Tests of Comprehension

Comprehension of grammatical structures is much more difficult to measure than production. Although in naturalistic contexts young children give the impression they understand more than they produce, this may reflect the child's use of nonlinguistic context rather than grammatical structure to figure out the underlying meaning relations of sentences. Methods to assess comprehension typically include: (a) the use of diary studies, which document the conditions and contexts in which a child does or does not understand a particular structure; (b) act-out procedures, in which the experimenter asks the child to act out a sentence or phrase using toys; (c) direction tasks, in which the child is asked to carry out a direction; (d) picture-choice tasks, in which the child is asked to select from a set, the picture that best represents the linguistic form presented; and (e) preferential-looking paradigm, in which the child is placed equidistant between two video-monitors on which different scenes are simultaneously presented. A linguistic message, which corresponds to one of the scenes, is played in synchrony with them and the amount of time the child spends watching each scene is recorded. If the child spends significantly longer watching the correct scene, then they are credited with understanding the linguistic form of the message. This paradigm is complex and lengthy but it avoids some of the limitations of other methods and can be used with infants as young as 9 months old (Golinkoff et al. 1987).

2. Two-word Utterance Stage

2.1 Semantic Relations

When children begin to combine words to form the simplest sentences most are limited in length to two words, although a few may be as long as three or four words. These early sentences are often unique and creative composed primarily of nouns, verbs, and adjectives. In English, function words and grammatical morphemes are usually omitted, making the child's productive speech sound 'telegraphic'; however, this is less true for children learning other languages that are rich in inflectional morphology.

Crosslinguistic studies of children at this stage have shown that there is a universal small set of meanings or semantic relations that are expressed (Brown 1973). Table 1 lists the eight most prevalent semantic relations together with examples of each. These examples illustrate that children talk a lot about objects by naming them, and by discussing their locations or attributes, who owns them, and who is doing things to them. They also talk about people, their actions, their locations, their actions on objects, and so forth. Objects, people, actions, and their interrelationships preoccupy the young child universally. These are precisely the concepts that the child has differentiated during the infancy period according to the developmental psychologist, Jean Piaget.

2.2 Limited Scope Formulae

Initial studies of utterances produced in the two-word stage found that children used highly consistent word order. Indeed, the semantic relations approach assumed that the child uses a productive word order rule which operates on broad semantic rather than syntactic categories. This research was limited by

Table 1: Set of prevalent semantic relations expressed in two-word stage.

Semantic relation	Examples
Agent + Action	*Mommy come. Daddy sit.*
Action + Object	*Push car. Eat cookie.*
Agent + Object	*Mommy sock. Dog book.*
Action + Location	*Go out. Sit floor.*
Entity + Location	*Cup table. Truck box.*
Possessor + Possession	*My bottle. Mommy shirt.*
Entity + Attribute	*Big book. Box shiny.*
Demonstrative + Entity	*Dat milk. Dis paper.*

focussing primarily on languages that make extensive use of order to mark basic relations in sentences, and on a small number of subjects. It is now acknowledged that there is considerable individual variation among children learning different languages, and even for children learning English. Nevertheless, word order rules are used at this early stage of grammatical development, but they are more limited and more narrowly defined in semantic scope than is suggested by the semantic relations approach and therefore have been called 'limited scope formulae' (Braine 1976). For some children ordered combinations of words may even be based on specific lexical items rather than on semantic categories. Over time, these more limited rules expand to encompass broader semantic and later syntactic categories, and begin to resemble the adult grammar.

2.3 Null Subjects

One characteristic of children's two-word sentences is that they often omit the subject. This has been interpreted from the perspective of current linguistic theory, which proposes a parameter-setting approach. Hyams (1986) argues that all children begin with the subject parameter set in the null position (which holds for languages like Italian or Spanish) so that children learning English must eventually switch the parameter setting to the position marked for required subjects.

Although this proposal is attractive because it connects early grammar to linguistic theory, there are several criticisms of this approach. While English-speaking children do omit subjects, in fact they include them significantly more often than Italian-speaking children, which suggests that they know that subjects need to be expressed. Subjects are probably omitted because young children have limited processing capacity, and for pragmatic reasons, subjects are more readily omitted than objects as they are often provided by the context.

2.4 Comprehension of Word Order

Studies of children's comprehension of grammar at this stage of development has focused on their ability to use word order to interpret the basic relations in a simple sentence. Studies using a variety of methods, including act-out and picture-choice tasks, have led to conflicting findings: some suggest that children can use word order in their productive speech before they can in comprehension, while others suggest the opposite. In a study using the preferential-looking paradigm, which makes less extraneous processing demands on the child, it was found that children aged 18 months, who were not yet producing two-word utterances, looked reliably longer at the correct scene corresponding to sentences like *Cookie Monster is tickling Big Bird*. Thus, it appears that comprehension of word order does precede its production.

3. Development of Grammatical Morphology

3.1 Brown's 14-morpheme Study

As children progress beyond the two-word stage, they gradually begin to fill in the inflectional morphology and function words that are omitted in their early language. The process of acquiring the major grammatical morphemes in English is gradual and lengthy and some are still not fully controlled until the child enters school, that is, at around 5 years. The most comprehensive study of morphological development was conducted by Roger Brown (1973), using the longitudinal data collected from three children.

Brown selected for his study a set of 14 English morphemes that are among the most frequently used. These included two prepositions (*in*, *on*), articles (*a*, *the*), noun inflections marking possessive (*'s*), and plural (*-s*), verb inflection marking third person singular present tense for regular (*-s*), and irregular verbs (e.g., *does*), past tense for regular (*-ed*) and irregular verbs (e.g., *went*), and the verb *to be* used as auxiliary and main verb (copula) in both contractible and uncontractible forms. Brown coded for each transcript the percentage of each morpheme supplied in its obligatory contexts, counting 90 percent as the point marking full acquisition. The most significant finding was that the order in which these morphemes was acquired was strikingly similar across the three children, and this has been confirmed in later studies including larger samples of children. The order of acquisition is not accounted for by frequency of use by the child or mother; instead it is related to measures of linguistic complexity—both semantic and syntactic.

3.2 Overgeneralization and Rule Productivity

One striking error that children make in the process of acquiring grammatical morphemes is the overgeneralization of regular forms to irregular examples. For example, the plural *-s* is frequently added to nouns that take an irregular plural, such as *mans* instead of *men*, or *mouses* instead of *mice*; and the regular past tense ending *-ed* is sometimes used on verbs that are marked with an irregular form, such as *falled*, *goed*, or *teached*. These errors may not be frequent, but they can persist well into the school years and are quite resistant to feedback or correction. They are taken as evidence that the child is indeed acquiring a rule-governed system, rather than learning these inflections on a word-by-word basis.

Other evidence for the productive use of morphological rules comes from an elicited production task introduced by Jean Berko (1958), called the 'Wug test.' The child is shown drawings depicting novel creatures, objects, and actions and asked to supply the appropriate description which would require the inclusion of noun or verb inflections. For example, a creature was labeled a wug, and then the child had to fill in the blank for *there are two* ____ . Preschool-aged children performed well on this task demonstrating their internalized knowledge of English morphological rules that can be applied productively.

3.3 Crosslinguistic Data

There is a growing literature on the acquisition of morphology in other languages. Overgeneralization errors have been recorded in children learning many different languages suggesting this is a universal pattern for this aspect of grammatical development. However, the slow and gradual development of English morphology does not hold for languages that have richer morphological systems. For example, children acquiring Turkish include case-marking suffixes on nouns at even the earliest stages of language development, and children learning Italian acquire verb inflections marking person, tense, and number very rapidly and in a less piecemeal fashion than has been found for English morphology. These crosslinguistic variations seem to reflect differences among languages in the amount of inflectional morphology within a language and the degree to which inflections are optional. For example, English marks verbs only for the past tense or third person singular present tense or progressive aspect, while Italian verbs are always marked in various ways. Children appear to be highly sensitive to these differences from the beginning stages of acquiring grammar (Slobin 1985).

4. Sentence Modalities

4.1 Simple Declaratives

As children progress beyond the two-word stage, they begin combining words into three-, and then four-word sentences. In doing so, they link together two or more basic semantic relations that were prevalent early on. For example, *agent+action* and *action +object* may be linked to form *agent+action+object*. These simple declarative sentences include all the basic elements of adult sentences. Gradually these may get enriched with the addition of prepositional phrases, more complex noun phrases that include a variety of modifiers, and more complex verb phrases including auxiliary and modal verbs. All these additions add length to the declarative sentences of young children.

4.2 Negation

Although children do express negation even at the one-word stage, for example, using the word *no!*, the acquisition of sentential negation is not fully acquired until much later. Ursula Bellugi (Klima and Bellugi 1966) identified three stages in the acquisition of negation in English:

(a) the negative marker is placed outside the sentence, usually preceding it (e.g., *not go movies*; *no Mommy do it*);

(b) the negative marker is sentence internal, placed adjacent to the main verb but without productive use of the auxiliary system (e.g., *I no like it*; *don't go*);

(c) different auxiliaries are used productively and the child's negations approximate the adult forms (e.g., *you can't have it*; *I'm not happy*).

Although the existence of the first stage has been questioned by some researchers, there does appear to be crosslinguistic support for an initial period when negative markers are placed outside the main sentence.

Negation is used by children to express a variety of meanings. These emerge in the following order, according to studies of children learning a wide range of languages: 'nonexistence'—to note the absence of something or someone (e.g., *no cookie*); 'rejection'—used to oppose something (e.g., *no bath*); and finally, 'denial'—to refute the truth of a statement (e.g., *that not mine*). Some children show consistent patterns of form–meaning relations in their negative sentences. For example, one child used external negation to express rejection, while at the same stage reserved sentence internal negation forms to express denial. These patterns may have had their source in the adult input.

Studies of children's comprehension of negative sentences find that they are influenced by the pragmatic context in which the sentence is presented. Thus, sentences expressing denial are more easily understood in plausible rather than implausible nonlinguistic contexts. Together, these studies suggest that the development of negation is influenced by grammatical and semantic, as well as pragmatic factors.

4.3 Questions

There are several different forms used to ask questions. These include rising intonation on a declarative sentence; *yes–no* questions, which involve subject–auxiliary verb inversion; *wh*-questions, which involve *wh*-movement and inversion; and tags, which are appended to declaratives and may be marked lexically (e.g., *we'll go shopping, okay?*) or syntactically (*we'll go shopping, won't we?*). Children begin at the one- or two-word stage by using rising intonation and one or two fixed *wh*-forms, such as *what that?* Gradually, over the next couple of years syntactic forms of questions develop with inversion rules acquired simultaneously for both *yes–no* and *wh*-questions. Some data suggested that for *wh*-questions, inversion rules are learned sequentially for individual *wh*-words such as *what*, *where*, *who*, *why*, and may be closely linked in time to the appearance of those words used as *wh*-complements. Thus syntactic rules for question formation may be *wh*-word specific in early child language.

Several studies of English and other languages have investigated the order in which children acquire various *wh*-questions and the findings have been consistent. Children generally begin asking and understanding *what* and *where* questions, followed by *who*,

then *how*, and finally *when* and *why*. One explanation for this developmental sequence is that it reflects the semantic and cognitive complexity of the concepts encoded in these different types of questions. Thus, questions about objects, locations, and people (i.e., *what*, *where*, *who*) involve less abstract concepts that those of manner, time, and causality (i.e., *how*, *when*, *why*). The early emerging *wh*- questions are also syntactically less complex in that they involve simple noun phrase replacement, whereas the later developing questions involve prepositional phrases or full sentence complements.

Children use questions to express a range of functions. Most questions asked by 2- and 3-year-olds seek information or facilitate the conversation by asking for clarification or expressing agreement. Older children begin asking questions more to direct the behavior of others, especially to gain attention. Typically there are strong form-function relationships, that may reflect the input directed to children: *wh*-questions are used to seek information, while yes–no forms are used for conversational and directive functions. Thus, as for negation, the development of questions is determined not only by linguistic complexity, but also by semantic and pragmatic factors that interact with the acquisition of the requisite syntactic rules.

4.4 Passives

Despite the rarity of the passive construction in everyday conversations in English, a good deal of attention has been paid to how children use and understand passive sentences. Because the order of the agent and patient is reversed, this particular construction can reveal a great deal about how children acquire word order rules that play a major role in English syntax.

Elicited production tasks have been used to study how children construct passive sentences, typically using sets of pictures that shift the focus to the patient. Younger children tend to produce primarily truncated passives (e.g., *the window was broken*) in which no agent is specified. These truncated passives generally have inanimate subjects, while full passives are produced by children when animate subjects are involved, suggesting that full and truncated passives may develop separately and be unrelated for the younger child. It has been suggested that truncated passives are really adjectival whereas the later appearing full forms are complete verbal passives.

Numerous studies have used an act-out procedure to investigate children's comprehension of passive voice sentences. Typically these studies compare children's comprehension of passive sentences to active sentences that are either reversible—in which either noun could plausibly be the agent (e.g., *the boy kisses the girl*; *the boy is kissed by the girl*), or semantically biased—in which one noun is more plausibly the agent than the other (e.g., *the girl feeds the baby*; *the girl is fed by the baby*). Studies find that children correctly interpret the plausible passive sentences before they do the reversible sentences. Preschoolers acquiring English tend to make errors systematically on the reversible passive sentences, suggesting the use of a processing strategy, called the word-order strategy, whereby noun–verb–noun sequences are interpreted as agent–action–object. Children learning languages other than English may develop different processing strategies that closely reflect the canonical ways of organizing the basic relations in a sentence in their native language. For example, Japanese is a verb-final language that marks the agent with a suffix *-ga*, rather than with a fixed word order, although there is a preference for an agent–object–verb order. Preschool-aged Japanese children tend to use a strategy that takes the first noun marked with *-ga* as the agent of the sentence. Thus, children's processing strategies are tailored to the kind of language they are acquiring and show that preschoolers have already worked out the primary ways their language marks the basic grammatical relations.

Studies of the acquisition of other languages such as Sesotho, in which the passive construction is very frequent because subjects always mark sentence topic, find that children acquire the passive much earlier and use it much more productively than do English-speaking children. Again, this suggests that children are sensitive to the typology of their language and that these factors influence the timing of development for the passive.

The semantic characteristics of the verb also influence the child's comprehension of passive sentences. While 5-year olds do correctly understand passive sentences which have action verbs, they find it more difficult to interpret passive sentences with nonaction verbs (e.g., *Donald was liked by Goofy*). Thus, the acquisition of passive voice continues into the school years as the child's knowledge becomes less constrained by semantic aspects of the verb.

5. Complex Sentence Structures

5.1 Coordinations

As early as 30 months of age, children begin combining sentences to express compound propositions. The simplest and most frequent method children use to combine sentences is to conjoin two propositions with *and*. One question that has been investigated in numerous studies is the order in which different forms of coordination develop. Both sentential (e.g., *Mary went to school and Peter went to school*) and phrasal coordinations (e.g., *Mary and Peter went to school*) tend to emerge at the same time in development suggesting that these forms develop independently and are not, for young children, derived from one another. Children form phrasal coordinations by directly conjoining phrases, not via deletion rules.

From the beginning children are sensitive to the different contexts in which phrasal and sentential forms of coordination are used appropriately in both production and comprehension. Children use sentential forms to describe events that are separated in time or space or involve different referents, while phrasal forms are used when events occur at the same time, in the same place, or involve the same referents. Semantic factors also influence the course of development of coordination. Children use coordinations first to express additive meaning, where there is no dependency relation between conjoined clauses (e.g., *maybe you can carry this and I can carry that*). Later temporal relations (e.g., *Joey is going home and take her sweater off*) and then causal relations (e.g., *she put a bandaid on her shoe and it maked it feel better*) are expressed, suggesting that children begin demonstrating greater semantic flexibility even while limiting themselves to the use of a single connective *and*.

5.2 Relative Clauses

Sometime after children begin using coordination, relative clauses emerge in their spontaneous speech. Initially they are used to specify information exclusively about the object of a sentence (e.g., *let's eat the cake what I baked*), and often the relative pronoun is omitted or incorrect. The use of relative clauses in the spontaneous speech of young children is quite rare, perhaps because children avoid these syntactically complex constructions, or because they lack the occasion to use them when the context is shared by the speaker and listener.

Elicited production techniques have been used successfully with preschoolers. These studies have also found that children find it easiest to add relative clauses to the ends of sentences rather than to embed them within the matrix clause. This suggests that some processing constraints operate on young children's productive capacities. Studies of children's comprehension of relative clause constructions, which typically involve act-out procedures, confirm that object relatives are easier to process than subject relatives (which are usually embedded), though different theoretical interpretations have been offered for these findings. Some suggest this is related to processing limitations and the use of comprehension strategies, while others offer interpretations from linguistic theory. There is also evidence to suggest that children are sensitive to semantic and prosodic factors in tasks that require children to interpret sentences with various types of relative clauses.

5.3 Anaphoric Reference

Children's knowledge of grammar continues to develop beyond the preschool years. One area that has received a good deal of attention from researchers is their knowledge of coreference relations within sentences; especially how anaphoric pronouns and reflexives link up with referents. This research has been conducted primarily within a Government-Binding theoretical framework, investigating children's knowledge of the main binding principles. Spontaneous productions of pronominal forms suggest that quite young children use them correctly in their productive speech; however, the limits of their knowledge cannot be accurately assessed in naturalistic contexts.

More controlled studies have utilized a variety of methods including comprehension, picture-matching, and judgment tasks. Generally, children appear to develop knowledge of the main principles in the following order. By the age of 6 children know 'principle A,' which states that reflexives are bound to referents within the same clause (e.g., *John watched Bill wash himself*; *himself* must refer to Bill, not John). Sometime later, knowledge of 'principle B' emerges, which states that anaphoric pronouns cannot be bound to referents within the same clause (e.g., *John asked Bill to hit him*; *him* must refer to John in the *ask*-clause, not Bill in the *hit*-clause). The last principle to emerge sometime during middle childhood, is 'principle C,' which states that backward coreference is only allowed if the pronoun is in a subordinate clause to the main referent (e.g., *when he came home, John made dinner*). Some researchers have argued that the grammatical knowledge of these principles is acquired much earlier than the research would suggest but that children's performance on tasks that tap this knowledge is limited by processing factors, pragmatic knowledge, or lexical knowledge. This debate continues in the developmental psycholinguistic literature.

6. Basic Theoretical Approaches

6.1 Semantic Bootstrapping

Current theories in language acquisition attempt to address the central question of how the young child achieves the learnability task in acquiring the abstract and formal syntactic system of their language. In the 1970s and 1980s one idea that gained prominence in the literature was that children may use semantics or meaning to help them break into the grammar of their language. This approach was taken up by analyses of two-word utterances in the semantic relations approach, outlined in Sect. 2.1. Steven Pinker (1984) has been the main proponent to argue that children may use semantics as a bootstrap into syntax, particularly to acquire the major syntactic categories on which grammatical rules operate. Thus, children can use the correspondence that exists between names and things to map on to the syntactic category of noun, and physical attributes or changes of state to map on to the category of verb. At the initial stages of development all sentence subjects tend to be semantic agents, and so children use this syntactic-semantic correspondence to begin figuring out the abstract relations for more complex sentences that require the category of subject.

6.2 Functionalism

A very different theoretical approach has been taken up by those who view the central task of the child as gaining communicative competence. Much of the research conducted within this framework has focused on the acquisition of pragmatic aspects of language, including the functions of utterances and their use in discourse and other communicative contexts. Within research on grammatical development the functional approach does not take formal syntactic theory as its primary model. Instead the structure of language is viewed from a functional, or processing perspective. One example is the competition model of language acquisition proposed by Elizabeth Bates and Brian MacWhinney (MacWhinney 1987). On this model, the child begins by establishing the basic functional categories: topic-comment and agent. Different surface representations of these functional categories then compete for expression and initially the child may use a simple one form–one function mapping. Eventually children move toward the adult system of form-function mappings.

6.3 Distributional Learning

At some point all theories of acquisition need to consider how the child learns the major syntactic categories, even if they begin with a simple lexically specific, functional, or semantic approach. One important approach to this learning problem is the distributional learning view, proposed by Maratsos and Chalkley (1980). According to this view children not only use semantic mappings to acquire a category like verb, they also use distributional factors, such as it takes an -*ed* ending to express pastness, or an -*ing* or -*s* in present tense contexts, it occurs with auxiliary verbs and so forth. Gleitman (1990) has also suggested that children must use syntactic information to learn something about the meanings of terms, such as using the argument structure of a verb to learn something about its meaning. Other kinds of distributional learning, using morpho-phonological patterns, may be central in acquiring aspects of morphology such as noun gender in languages other than English. This kind of approach argues that children are sensitive to all kinds of distributional patterns in the linguistic input to which they are exposed and some of the research summarized in previous sections supports this view.

6.4 Parameter-setting Models

Linguists working within a Government-Binding framework who have taken an interest in the question of how children acquire the grammar of their language claim that the central task of acquisition is to set the parameters of universal grammar in the direction appropriate for the language that is being acquired. Some argue that the parameters start off set in one position, which may then have to be switched. One example of this is Hyams' proposal about the null subject parameter, presented in Sect. 2.3. An alternative view would hold that parameters start off neutrally, that is, they are not set in any position. As the child is exposed to their native language they use linguistic evidence present in the environment to set the parameters accordingly. This kind of approach to child language is still relatively new and awaits further refinements from linguistic theory.

6.5 Reorganizational Processes

Numerous approaches have been proposed to explain how the child acquires the complex and abstract grammatical system of language. Children may indeed begin with functional or semantic categories, which may serve their needs during the early stages of acquisition, but these approaches are limited for the child. Eventually the child must come to employ abstract syntactic categories though these may still have correlates in meaning and function. Some theorists, taking a developmental approach, argue that the child must undergo some radical reorganization of their grammar at certain stages in development, rather than simply generalizing the categories they start off with. For example, the child may begin with categories that are defined semantically (e.g., agent, experiencer) that later become reorganized and restructured into syntactic categories (e.g., subject).

These kinds of reorganizational processes are seen as central not only to grammatical development but also to the acquisition of lexical and phonological knowledge. In this way children piece together and reformulate through a series of stages using the same fundamental developmental processes an integrated foundation of knowledge of the language they are acquiring.

7. Constraints and Individual Variation in Language Development

7.1 Critical Period Constraints

One striking feature of language development is the uniform timetable that is followed by children the world over. With the exception of certain extreme cases, children tend to master their first language by the time they are aged five or six. Indeed, children who do not acquire language by middle childhood, or who are learning a second language after this time appear to have great difficulty and never quite reach the same level of linguistic competence, especially in grammatical knowledge. These findings have led to the idea that there may be a *critical period* for acquiring language, which may be linked to the plasticity of the brain. Initially Eric Lenneberg proposed puberty as the end point of language acquisition, however recent studies by Elissa Newport and her colleagues, suggest that by the age of six, the capacity for acquiring language, either a first or second language, begins to decline, but only very gradually. The critical period

does not appear to be so fixed as had been thought by Lenneberg; in fact adolescents and adults can continue to acquire both syntax and morphology of new languages, though they might never become as proficient as native speakers.

7.2 Language Environments

One of the most important kinds of variation that can be identified is the language environment to which children are exposed. Do variations in environments and in language input lead to individual differences in language acquisition? At one extreme, there is a small number of children who were raised in almost complete isolation in severely deprived conditions. The best studied case was Genie, who after she received extensive therapy beginning at the age of 13 did acquire some syntax, but never learning the grammatical morphology of English. Other studies also document that severe deprivation and abuse lead to extreme delays in language development, yet once the children are placed in a better environment they are able to make substantial recovery.

Bibliography

Berko J 1958 The child's learning of English morphology. *Word* **14**: 150–77
Braine M D S 1976 Children's first word combinations. *Monographs of the Society for Research in Child Development*, 41. University of Chicago Press, Chicago, IL
Brown R 1973 *A First Language.* George Allen & Unwin, London
Crystal D, Fletcher P, Garman M 1976 *The Grammatical Analysis of Language Disability: A Procedure for Assessment and Remediation.* Elsevier-North Holland, New York
Gleitman L 1990 The structural sources of verb meanings. *Language Acquisition* **1**: 3–56
Golinkoff R, Hirsh-Pasek K, Cauley K M, Gordon L 1987 The eyes have it: Lexical and syntactic comprehension in a new paradigm. *J. Ch. L.* **14**: 23–45
Hyams N 1986 *Language Acquisition and the Theory of Parameters.* Reidel, Dordrecht
Klima E, Bellugi U 1966 Syntactic regularities in the speech of children. In: Lyons J, Wales R (eds.) *Psycholinguistic Papers.* Edinburgh University Press, Edinburgh
MacWhinney B (ed.) 1987 *Mechanisms of Language Acquisition.* Erlbaum, Hillsdale, NJ
Maratsos M P, Chalkley M A 1980 The internal language of children's syntax: The ontogenesis and representation of syntactic categories In: Nelson K E (ed.) *Children's Language*, vol. 2. Gardner Press, New York
Miller J F 1981 *Assessing Language Production in Children.* University Park Press, Baltimore, MD
Pinker S 1984 *Language Learnability and Language Development.* Harvard University Press, Cambridge, MA
Scarborough H 1990 The index of productive syntax. *AP* **11**: 1–22
Slobin D I (ed.) 1985 *A Cross-Linguistic Study of Language Acquisition.* Erlbaum, Hillsdale, NJ

Acquisition of Reading

J. Oakhill

When people think about children acquiring reading skills, they usually think of learning to read words—'cracking the code.' However, the real purpose of reading is finding out the meaning of the text, and this aspect of reading acquisition will be reviewed later in this chapter. There is a very large body of research into how children learn to read, and the best method of teaching them, and this chapter is necessarily very selective. Almost all of the research has been on reading words, and the balance of this chapter reflects this bias.

The first section outlines a variety of reading-related skills that children acquire in the early years of school, and considers which, if any, of these skills are prerequisites for learning to read. The second section surveys some current methods of teaching children to read, and the third gives an account of some important aspects of the development of reading skill. In the final section, comprehension is considered: both its normal development, and the causes of comprehension difficulties.

1. Reading-related Skills

Children who are learning to read already possess a wide variety of relevant skills and will acquire many others. Many of these skills are either prerequisites for reading or are related to it in other, less direct ways.

However, many children who cannot yet read have vague or even wholly misguided conceptions about it. Even those who do not will find much of the terminology used in reading lessons new. They may not be familiar with the idea of talking about language. They may lack the necessary knowledge about words, syllables, and phonemes that are prerequisites for an analytic approach to reading. To master the art of reading they will have to learn to pay attention to features of language that they have previously ignored. Although children beginning school have a good command of spoken language, which they can produce and comprehend effectively, they lack the ability to analyze and reflect on the form of language, independent of its meaning. The ability to think and talk about language is sometimes described as a 'meta-linguistic' skill, one level up from the basic linguistic skills required for using language to talk about the world.

Before discussing the development of specific reading-related skills, it is necessary to make one methodological point. Many of the findings about how the development of these skills relates to progress in reading are only correlational—they show that the age at which a child acquires a certain skill reflects the age at which that child develops a particular reading ability. However, it is a truism that correlations are not necessarily indicators of causal relations. Furthermore, even when there is a causal relation, a correlation cannot show which direction it runs in. The skills considered could, therefore, be related to reading in various ways. Ehri (1979) identifies four types of relation. First, skills may be 'prerequisites': skills upon which reading builds, and which must be acquired before reading can be learned. Second, they may have the role of 'facilitators': skills which may speed progress in beginning reading, but which are not essential. Third, they may be consequences of learning to read: skills that develop through practice at reading rather than vice versa. Finally, there may be no direct link between a skill and reading ability at all—they may be incidentally correlated, perhaps because each is related to some other factor, such as intelligence. Because a variety of explanations are possible for a correlation between a particular skill and reading ability, it is not always clear that training in that skill will improve reading. Training can only be useful if a skill is either a prerequisite for or a facilitator of reading development.

One method by which causal relations can be tested uses a mixture of longitudinal and training studies. Longitudinal studies establish which of two abilities develop first in the individual child. Since abilities that develop later cannot cause the development of abilities that develop earlier, longitudinal studies rule out whole sets of causal hypotheses. But abilities that develop earlier do not necessarily cause the development of abilities that develop later, even if the two are strongly correlated. The development of both may be caused by a third factor—a general facility with language, for example. However, if training the ability that develops early has a specific effect on the ability that develops later, and if more general training does not have the same effect, then a causal relation is indicated.

However, combined longitudinal and training studies are difficult and time-consuming to carry out, and their importance has only recently been recognized. There is, therefore, some uncertainty about which skills are necessary for reading to begin. It follows that the concept of 'reading readiness' must be questioned. Readiness tests are intended to assess whether a child is ready to begin formal reading instruction. They assess the perceptual, cognitive, and linguistic skills assumed to be used in reading (e.g., visual and auditory matching, letter-sound relations), so that appropriate prereading instruction can be given, if necessary. But reading-readiness skills will only be helpful if the skills taught are prerequisites for beginning reading. As will become clear from the evidence below, learning to read may foster some 'readiness skills,' rather than vice versa.

1.1 Understanding of Printed Language Concepts

Between the ages of 3 and 5 years children's ideas about reading change dramatically, as do their ideas about the components of written language. For instance, 3 year olds are more likely than older children to misassess their reading ability, thinking that they can read when they cannot. By 5 years, most children know if they are unable to read, and know about the importance of words. Preschool children may not know about the directional constraints in reading, and also typically have some difficulty in understanding reading and writing terminology—they often cannot distinguish between letters, words, and sentences or between letters and numerals. Thus, it cannot be assumed that children start school with any clear concept of reading. They probably know that they will learn to read, but may not know what this means. Children's early knowledge of the language and terminology of reading has been shown to correlate with their later reading skill. However, an explicit understanding of reading-related concepts may not be a prerequisite for reading. Reading instruction may encourage children to develop a more analytic approach and to learn more about the terminology, rather than vice versa, though without some basic concepts, such as an understanding of the left-to-right rule in English, reading will not progress very far.

1.2 Letter Recognition

Children's knowledge of letter names when they start school is a good predictor of reading progress during the first year, but is not related to later success in reading. However, teaching children letter names does not improve their reading, and children can learn to read without being able to name any letters. It is likely that, rather than letter knowledge having a causal role in reading acquisition, some common variable, such as an interest in written materials, underlies both letter naming and reading.

Children often have difficulty discriminating between letters that are mirror images of one another. This difficulty has nothing to do with visual discrimination, but is probably related to the need to pay attention to orientation, which will not have been important to the child previously. Although many objects have a canonical orientation, they do not assume a different identity when their orientation changes.

1.3 Word Consciousness

'Word consciousness' or 'lexical awareness' is the ability to recognize that both writing and speech are made up of distinct entities called words. Although the concept of a word is one that literate adults take for granted, it is not necessarily an obvious one to young children. Some 5 year olds still find it difficult to recognize words as distinct units. (An excellent review of research on word consciousness is given by Linnea Ehri (1979), who also addresses some of the broader issues about the relation between word consciousness and reading.)

Performance on some tasks that measure word awareness skills is correlated with early reading ability. For example, in beginning readers, reading skill correlates with ability to judge whether a sound is made up of one word or two words or whether it is a word at all. Reading ability is also related to the ability to pick out the word or words that differ between two sentences. More surprisingly, first-grade children have difficulty detecting word boundaries in printed materials, despite the fact that there are clear visual cues to where one word ends and the next begins. The ability to pick out printed words develops with increased reading proficiency.

It has not been clearly established whether teaching word consciousness skills enhances reading. Some children are aware of words before they begin to read, so word consciousness is not simply a consequence of learning to read. However, there is no evidence that it is essential for reading to begin.

1.4 Phonemic and Linguistic Awareness

Children may begin to read by learning to recognize whole words as visual patterns, more or less as 'logographs.' But learning an adequate reading vocabulary in this way would place an enormous, and unnecessary, burden on memory. Children learning an alphabetic writing system can capitalize on the fact that the written symbols are (to a greater or lesser extent) associated with phonemes. Once children have grasped this principle, which is regarded by many as the key to learning to read, they will be able to gain independence in reading, and be able to recognize for themselves words that they have never before seen written.

In particular, children must learn the rules that relate written letters or groups of letters to sounds. However, in English, these rules are complex as there is often no one-to-one correspondence between letters and sounds. Such rules are called 'grapheme-phoneme correspondence' rules (GPC rules) because they state the relation between small units of written language (graphemes) and small units of spoken language (phonemes). To apply grapheme-phoneme correspondence rules, children have to be able to break written words into parts, and put the parts back together once the corresponding sounds have been determined (these skills are called 'segmentation' and 'blending'). The use of these rules demands at least an implicit mastery of the phonemic system of the language. The phonemes or sound segments produced by application of the rules must then be blended to produce a pronunciation for the word as a whole.

However, before they can apply an analytic strategy to word decoding, children must become aware of the phonemic segments into which words can be divided. Without such awareness, decoding using grapheme-phoneme correspondence rules and blending are impossible. But experiments with young children (4 to 5 year olds) have shown that they find segmentation of words into phonemes almost impossible. Children are much better at dividing words into syllables and putting syllables together to form words. Such data clearly show that the younger children have difficulty making explicit the phonemic distinctions needed for many approaches to reading, although they are perfectly able to perceive differences at the phonemic level (e.g., they know that two words that differ in one phoneme are not the same). Prereading success on the phoneme segmentation task predicts reading success in the second grade. Young children's difficulty in this area is probably related to the fact that phonemes, unlike syllables, do not have acoustic boundaries separating them in speech. Furthermore, phonemes overlap in speech, largely because of a phenomenon known as 'coarticulation.' The way the parts of the mouth move means that, for example, the articulation of /b/ will depend on the following vowel. The first part of *bat* is pronounced differently from that of *but*. The very first bit of the word contains information about the vowel as well as about the /b/. Thus, when a word is broken into its constituent sounds, and these are said individually—for example, *cat* into /k/, /a/, and /t/—only approximations to the underlying phonemes can be derived. Therefore, no matter how fast the consecutive phonemes are spoken, they will not blend together to form *cat* unless they are distorted.

More general phonemic awareness skills have also been shown to be related to early reading. Even very obvious features of words, such as their spoken or written length, may be difficult for children to perceive. For example, pre-reading children perform at chance level when shown two cards and asked to say which shows the word *mow* and which *motorcycle*. They do not understand even this highly-salient feature of writing—that the word that looks longer has the longer pronunciation.

Young (kindergarten) children experience even greater difficulty in tasks that require them to be aware of more subtle phonemic differences between words, such as deciding whether two words begin with the same sound, or whether two words rhyme. The lack of phonemic awareness in young children is also indicated by their performance on sound deletion tasks. For instance, when asked to say what remained when a particular sound was removed from a word (e.g., /h/ removed from *hill*), children with a mental age below 7 are unable to perform the task at all, and for more

advanced children middle sounds (e.g., /s/ in *nest*) are harder than initial or final ones. Performance on this phoneme deletion task has been shown to correlate with reading skill in the first and second grades.

In an important and influential study, Bradley and Bryant (1978) addressed the question of whether there is a causal link between phonemic analysis skills and reading. They compared backward readers (10 year olds) not only with normal readers of the same age, but with normal children (6 year olds) who had the same reading age as the backward readers. They asked children to detect the odd-one-out in sequences of four spoken words (either on the basis of alliteration, or of rhyme), and to produce words that rhymed with other words that they read out. The older normal readers showed the best performance, but the important finding was that the backward readers were poorer on such tasks than the younger normal readers, even though they had, presumably, had much more experience of written language. Bradley and Bryant argue that phonemic analysis skills do not simply develop through exposure to print, but that they are causally related to reading—phonemic awareness helps children learn to read. In a later longitudinal study, they provided further evidence for this idea. They showed that performance on the odd-one-out task at 4 or 5 years was a good predictor of reading achievement, but not of mathematical ability, three years later. They also found that training in categorizing picture names by their sounds improved reading and spelling skills in nonreaders who were lagging behind in phonemic awareness, but only when it was supplemented by teaching with plastic letters that demonstrated to the children how words that have sounds in common often have common spelling patterns. The improvement in reading was long-lasting—when the children were retested at 13, those given phonological training were still ahead of the control groups (who were either given no training, or training in an unrelated skill) in reading and spelling, but the children trained in the connection between sounds and letters were still ahead of all other groups. In this study, as in the previous one, there were no differences between the groups in arithmetic—the training effect was restricted to reading and spelling. These studies by Bradley and Bryant have shown that training to rectify a deficiency in the skill of sound categorization can improve reading generally. But it is also possible that learning to read improves phonemic awareness.

Ellis and Large (1988) have suggested that the causal relation between reading and phonemic skills (they used syllable- and phoneme-segmentation, and rhyming and blending tasks) changes over the first few years of schooling. In a longitudinal study, they showed that the phonemic skills of those children who were nonreaders at age 5 predicted their reading ability at 6. However, once reading ability begins to develop, it causes the development of reading-related skills. For those children who had begun to read, reading skill at 5, and again at 6, predicted phonemic skills one year later. Ellis has suggested that the ability to read 'makes sense of' sound skills and fosters their development. Work with adults also suggests that learning to read using an alphabetic system allows phonemic awareness to develop. Chinese adults (who were fluent only in a logographic script) did poorly on phonemic segmentation tasks by comparison with those who could read an alphabetic script. Similar results have also been found when Portuguese illiterates and ex-illiterates are compared on segmental analysis tasks. The poor performance of illiterate adults on such tasks suggests that learning to read has a causal role in the development of phonemic awareness. However, whatever the precise relation between such skills and reading, young children should find an analytic approach to reading difficult.

1.5 Orthographic Awareness

The orthography, or writing system, of a language such as English comprises more than just an alphabet. There are also rules about which sequences of letters are admissible. For example, the orthographic rules of English would be violated by a word beginning *zn-*. Furthermore, some letters appear more often in certain positions in words, and some of the permissible sequences of letters are more common than others. Just as words within sentences are to some degree predictable—for example, one expects articles to be followed by nouns—so are letters within words. To the extent that a letter is highly predictable it is said to be 'redundant.'

In one type of experiment to investigate orthographic awareness, children are asked to make explicit judgments, for instance, saying which of two nonwords they think are more 'word like.' Their ability to perform this task increases with age and with reading fluency. However, studies that have investigated how orthographic structure affects speed of word identification or naming have found no improvement with age beyond the initial stages of learning to read. But, in a task that more closely approximates reading— lexical decision (deciding whether a string of letters is or is not a word)—younger children are more influenced by the orthographic features of letter strings than older children. The nonwords are either similar or dissimilar, orthographically, to real words. In this sort of task, younger children take longer to reject the wordlike nonwords.

2. Approaches to Teaching Reading

The two main methods currently in use to teach children to read are the 'whole word' (or look-and-say) approach, and the 'phonics' (or code-based) approach, though a method gaining in popularity is the 'real books' or 'apprenticeship' approach.

The contribution of the skills discussed in Sect. 1 to children's reading development may depend on how they are taught to read. Letter orientation, order, and attention to salient features of words will be important for approaches that emphasize sight recognition of words, with little attention to letter-to-sound rules. Differentiation of letters, the association between sounds and letters and blending of sounds will be more important for phonics approaches.

2.1 Whole Word (Look-and-Say)

As has already been seen, it is difficult for young children to segment and analyze words into their component features. In this approach the overall shape and gross visual features of the word are stressed, and not its component letters, so analytic skills are not necessary. The assumption behind this method is that children should be taught to read the way skilled readers do, by recognizing words 'directly' without having to analyze them into their component letters. Children are taught to recognize a small set of words from cards. These first words are those that occur very frequently in print, and ones which will be in their first reading books. Once children have built up a basic sight vocabulary they progress to the first reading book in the scheme, in which almost all the words are taken from the flashcards. The method also circumvents the problem that, in English, there are numerous exceptions to any simple set of grapheme-phoneme correspondence rules.

An approach that is related to the whole-word approach which has been widely used is the language experience approach. This approach combines learning to read with learning to write, and relates reading to the child's own experiences and spoken language. The correspondence between spoken and written language is stressed. From the start, children are encouraged to make up written sentences about things that are of interest to them. For instance, they might write their own captions for pictures, and then put together a series of such captioned pictures to make a 'story' booklet, which then becomes a text for learning to read. In one such scheme, children have their own word file or dictionary. The file contains basic words from reading books, each on a small card, together with the child's individual words, which are written on blank cards by the teacher. The philosophy of this approach is that learning to read should be related to functions of language with which children are already familiar, in particular its communicative function. The first words taught are based on children's own experiences. By using these words to compose written sentences about events that are meaningful to them, children learn both about reading and about its connection with writing. One advantage of the language experience approach is that the real function of written words—that they convey meanings—is emphasized from the outset. A second advantage is that this approach can be tailored to individual children's language capabilities and vocabulary, as well as relating reading to topics that are of interest to them.

The whole-word method has numerous disadvantages and limitations. The argument that children should be taught to identify words the way that skilled readers do is contentious. Skilled readers may access word meanings directly (without phonological recoding), but beginning readers may, nevertheless, benefit from training in decoding. Indeed, there are occasions when skilled readers need to recode phonologically, for example to identify words that are in their spoken vocabulary, but which they have not met before in written form. Equipped with only the ability to recognize words as visual patterns, beginning readers will have no tools for deciphering new and untaught words. They need to learn the alphabetic principle.

2.2 Phonics

Phonics approaches to the teaching of reading stress the importance of GPC rules. Children taught this way learn the sounds that the letters of the alphabet usually make, so that they can pronounce unfamiliar printed words. They may have to attain a certain level of proficiency in producing the appropriate letter-to-sound correspondences before they are exposed to words. This approach provides children with a more general reading skill. In principle, they should be able to 'sound out' any new word they come across. In practice, however, things are not so straightforward. Grapheme-phoneme correspondences in most of the languages that use an alphabetic writing system are irregular to a greater or lesser extent, and a letter may be associated with several different sounds. Furthermore, as discussed in the previous section, a letter's sound often depends on the surrounding letters. A more serious problem for phonics methods arises from the difficulty that young readers have in dividing words into their parts. Most 5 year olds find it impossible to perform the word segmentation and blending that are fundamental to the phonics approach.

2.3 The 'Psycholinguistic' Method

Finally, an approach to reading instruction based on Goodman's 'psycholinguistic guessing game' account of reading requires consideration (see, for example, 1967). This account assumes that readers begin with numerous expectations about the meaning and purpose of the text, and use the print only to confirm or disconfirm these predictions. Smith, another proponent of this approach, argues that, since adults can access word meanings directly without first deriving a phonological representation, there is no reason to teach children to read by this 'unnatural' method. He further argues that the reading speed of skilled readers

proves that they cannot be attending to every letter. Fluent readers make use of all kinds of information—syntactic, semantic, and pragmatic—in recognizing words, and Smith's view is that beginners should be taught to read in the same way. He argues that decoding is not only an unnatural and difficult method of learning to read, but that it can be positively harmful. He proposes that in 'making sense' of the text, children will learn whatever rules they need to. In other words, children should 'learn to read by reading'—by deriving hypotheses from the context and from prior knowledge of what the text is about (for a summary of these ideas see Smith 1973).

However, Smith is not explicit about how children should be taught. He simply suggests that children should be immersed in interesting, meaningful materials. Nevertheless, his ideas have been very influential in educational circles, and a method that has recently been popular—the real books or apprenticeship approach—was motivated by the ideas of Smith and Goodman. In this approach, the similarities between learning to read and learning to speak are stressed, and the emphasis is on books with motivating content and an interesting story line. There is little attempt at formal teaching in the initial stages, which are similar to the sorts of initiation into reading that the child might experience at home. First, children simply listen to an adult reading to them, while following the story in a book, then they attempt to read along with the adult until they feel able to 'read' some or all of the text themselves.

However, apart from Smith's failure to explain exactly how children should be taught, there are a number of flaws in his arguments. For example, there is no good evidence that skilled readers rely heavily on context to help them identify clearly printed words in normal reading. Such guesswork may sometimes be useful in identifying a visually unfamiliar word or even for working out the meaning of a wholly new word. But, in general, contextual information is usually available too late to aid word identification in skilled readers. Smith's theory predicts that skilled readers make greater use of context in word identification but, as will be seen below, the evidence suggests the reverse.

Finally, there is no reason to believe that the best way to teach reading is to train young children in the skills used by adults. Reading cannot simply be a guessing game. There must be some decoding of the printed text so that the guesses can be confirmed or disconfirmed. Furthermore, decoding usually needs to be taught. It cannot be expected to materialize as a by-product of intelligent guesswork, though some children are undoubtedly able to work out the rules for themselves, with little formal instruction. Interesting accounts of the characteristics of children who learn to read before they go to school can be found in Clark (1976).

2.4 Assessment of Teaching Methods

It is difficult to make an objective assessment of methods of teaching reading, because there are so many factors that cannot be controlled. Indeed, it has been suggested that children's progress in learning to read is much more closely related to the quality of their teacher than to the program used. Some children seem to learn by any method, and some fail by any method. However, presumably some methods produce better results on average than others.

Chall (1979) surveyed research on the relation between teaching method and reading achievement. Her conclusion was that an early emphasis on phonics led to better reading by the time the children had reached the fourth grade than did a whole-word approach, at least as far as reading new words and reading aloud were concerned. However, teaching method had little effect on comprehension, or on interest and involvement in reading. A more recent review of this research (Johnson and Baumann 1984) also confirms that early intensive instruction in phonics produces readers who are more proficient at pronouncing words than are those taught by a whole-word approach.

3. The Development of Reading

3.1 Stage Models of Reading

There are various models that attempt to give an account of the stages that children go through as they learn to read (for an example of such a model see *Disorders of Reading and Writing*). In general, such models propose that the child progresses from learning words as unanalyzed wholes to a more analytic approach in which grapheme-phoneme and orthographic rules are used. For instance, two such models are similar in proposing three stages:

(a) a logographic stage in which familiar words are recognized as visual patterns, using salient visual features, and new words cannot be identified at all;

(b) an alphabetic phase, in which the child learns and uses GPC rules and can tackle novel words and decode nonwords;

(c) an orthographic phase where the child learns the conventions of the English orthography, and identifies words by making use of orthographic units, without the need for phonological conversion.

A detailed comparison and critique of these two models, and a related one, can be found in Stuart and Coltheart (1988), who argue that the way in which children approach initial reading is not invariant, but depends on what skills they have available to them: for instance, children who already have some phonological skills may not enter the logographic phase at all.

3.2 Meaning Access: Direct or Mediated

The conversion of a written word into its spoken form may be a useful way of recognizing that word, even in skilled readers. The ability to carry out this so-called phonological recoding may be an important part of the development of reading. Phonological recoding in word recognition requires the use of spelling-to-sound rules, such as the GPC rules discussed earlier.

Since the sight vocabularies of beginning readers are relatively underdeveloped in comparison with their aural vocabularies, phonological coding is important for these readers in retrieving the meanings of words that they have heard but never before encountered in print. However, even beginning readers can recognize some words directly, from their visual appearance. Although the research in this area has produced somewhat inconsistent results, most evidence suggests that phonological recoding skills are relatively late in developing. Children progress from accessing the lexicon without the use of phonology to the use of both phonology and direct (visual) access. However, some studies have shown the reverse pattern: that young children rely more on phonological information in word recognition than older children. These discrepant results may have arisen because of the sorts of stimuli used in the experiments: high frequency, concrete words might invite direct access, whereas less frequent, abstract words may require phonological mediation. Of course, the relative use of different strategies in word recognition may depend not only on age, reading ability, and type of word, but also on the method used to teach reading.

Words could also be converted to a phonological form after they are recognized, by simply looking up the pronunciation in the mental dictionary. So, even if children can access the meanings of words directly, phonological recoding may play some part in their reading strategies, and those of skilled readers, because it provides a more durable medium than visual coding for storing early parts of a sentence so that they can be combined with what comes later. There is good evidence that children use postlexical phonology to aid comprehension. Indeed, older children and adults find it hard to suppress phonological coding even when it is disadvantageous (e.g., in remembering lists of phonologically-confusable picture names). Even Japanese subjects reading Kanji, a logographic script, store the symbols in a phonological rather than a visual or semantic form. In these cases, a phonological code cannot be produced from the pictures or logographs by using GPC rules. The word must be accessed from the visual pattern and its phonological form retrieved and used as a memory code.

3.3 Use of Context in Reading

A number of experimental studies have investigated changes in children's use of context as their reading skill develops. However, a distinction must be made between the use of context to correct or prevent errors, and the use of context to speed word recognition. In general, older readers are better at using context to make predictions (e.g., guessing what the next word might be) or to check them, but they do not use context as much as younger readers to identify words in the normal course of reading. The use of context in reading has played an important role in some theories of reading acquisition. Certain theorists (notably, Frank Smith) have based their ideas for teaching reading on the premise that good readers are better at using contextual information to help them decipher words. However, there is no evidence to support this hypothesis at the level of word recognition and, in any case, most content words are not very predictable, so that use of context will not compensate for inadequate word decoding. In fact, all the experimental evidence on the effects of context on word recognition points to the opposite conclusion—the use of context decreases as reading skill increases (for a review, see Stanovich 1982). There is no doubt that contextual and perceptual information work together in word recognition—they interact. However, the primary use of context in poorer readers is to compensate for the fact that they cannot recognize words from their perceptual properties alone.

4. Reading Comprehension

4.1 The Development of Comprehension Skills

One might assume that, once children have learnt to decode the words in text reasonably efficiently, comprehension will follow automatically. Since children learning to read have, for some years, been understanding spoken language, one would expect the skills they have learnt to transfer to understanding language in written form. However, this does not always seem to be the case. Reading comprehension is highly correlated with listening comprehension but, in fact, children's listening comprehension may not be as highly developed as one would expect from their level of language development—many children who have reading comprehension problems also have listening comprehension problems. However, there are also a number of reasons why beginning readers might have problems that are specific to reading. Both of these possibilities will be discussed here in relation to the development of comprehension skills.

Writing is not simply 'speech written down.' The language of books is a particular language register that children may not be familiar with unless they have had many books read to them before and as they learn to read. In addition, written language does not have all the supporting cues (stress, intonation, gestural, and facial expression) that accompany everyday oral interactions. If children are to read with understanding, they need to be initiated into this 'language of books.'

A second problem is that young children may be so engrossed in the word-decoding aspect of reading that they do not have the cognitive capacity to simultaneously carry out comprehension processes. In addition, the rapid loss of information from short-term memory makes it difficult for very slow readers to 'hold' information from early in a sentence so that they can integrate it with what comes later. If word recognition is slow and labored, much of the prior context may have been forgotten by the time the current word has been recognized. Decoding skills will obviously improve with practice so, as children get older, they can devote more attention to comprehension. Indeed, it has been shown that in the later primary school years, comprehension skills replace decoding skills as the most important predictors of overall reading ability. A related problem is that beginning readers may think that 'getting the words right' is the point of reading, and may not connect this activity with having stories read to them. It may not be until children's word recognition skills become relatively fast and automatic, that they are able to give their full attention to comprehending the content of the text.

In the remainder of this section, consideration is given to comprehension skills where there is likely to be some overlap between written and spoken language understanding. However, it should be borne in mind that some of the processes may be more difficult to carry out in the case of written text, for the reasons given above.

Understanding a text results in a mental representation of the state of affairs the text describes—a mental model of the text. Even after the individual words have been identified and grouped into phrases, clauses, and sentences, a number of other skills will also be necessary to construct such models. The meanings of individual sentences and paragraphs must be integrated, and the main ideas of the text identified. In many cases, inferential skills will be needed to go beyond what is explicitly stated, since authors necessarily leave some of the links between parts of the text implicit. The development of children's ability to make inferences from text is considered later, and also a number of more specific skills that are necessary for comprehension. For story understanding, these include: identifying the main characters and their motives, following the plot, and deriving the main theme. In the case of expository texts, the skills include identifying the topic, differentiating between important and trivial information, following the argument, and extracting the gist meaning of the passage.

The development of children's ability to monitor their own comprehension—to be aware of whether they have adequately understood a text—is also reviewed. As reading progresses beyond the beginning stages, such 'metacognitive' skills become increasingly important. Although beginning readers also need to make use of metalevel knowledge (the technical vocabulary of reading), comprehension processes are much more dependent than word recognition and decoding on metacognitive abilities. Children need to be aware that they have not adequately understood a piece of text, and to know what to do to remedy their lack of understanding.

4.1.1 Understanding the Structure of the Text

Many recent theories of comprehension have drawn attention to the fact that information in a text is hierarchically structured. This structure arises because each text is focused round one or more main ideas, with subsidiary ideas and trivial details subordinated to the main ones. Proper understanding of a text depends on an understanding of the main point, and on sensitivity to the relative importance of the other ideas.

During the primary school years there is a marked increase in children's ability to pick out the main idea of a text, and to judge the relative importance of different aspects of a text. Even at 12, most children are only able to distinguish explicitly between the very important and very unimportant information (and not between intermediate levels). In contrast, children's recall of text is very sensitive to level of importance (as determined by adults): even 5 year olds are more likely to recall the main events in a text than the trivial details. This discrepancy between awareness of levels of importance and the effect of importance on recall may be related to children's developing metacognitive skills (see below)—children may pay more attention to the more important ideas in a text, even though they cannot explicitly identify which those ideas are.

Another important element in comprehension is understanding how the ideas in a text are related, and one way to assess children's understanding of the logical structure of texts is to ask them to tell stories themselves. Research has shown that children gradually develop the ability to tell coherent narratives and that, like adults, they expect certain types of information to be present in stories. When expected information is missing, it is often added in retelling, so that the story corresponds to what was expected. Similarly, when a story relates events out of order, the normal order is often restored in retelling and, as children get older, they are more likely to reproduce an ill-structured story in a well-structured form (for a review, see Baker and Stein 1981). The ability to understand how ideas are interconnected in a story probably develops even before children learn to read.

4.1.2 Making Inferences from Text

Inference has many roles in comprehension (for a review, see Oakhill and Garnham 1988: ch. 2). In particular, inferences are crucial to the process of connecting up the ideas in a text, since many things are left implicit. The emerging mental model of the text will indicate where such gaps arise and, therefore, which of the multitude of possible inferences need to be made. There have been numerous studies of the development of children's inferencing skills. In general, these studies support the idea that young children can make the same inferences as older ones, although they do not do so spontaneously, and only do so when prompted or explicitly questioned.

A related important question is whether inferences are drawn as a text is understood, or only later. It is quite feasible that neither younger nor older children make optional (i.e., elaborative) inferences during comprehension, but that older children are superior at answering inferential questions because they are able to recall a greater proportion of the explicit information in the text, from which they can make inferences retrospectively. The available data are compatible with this explanation of developmental trends.

4.1.3 Comprehension Monitoring

Comprehension monitoring is necessary as a means of assessing whether one's understanding is adequate, so that appropriate action can be taken to overcome any comprehension difficulties. This is one of the metalinguistic skills that children acquire as their linguistic skills develop. All readers monitor their comprehension to some extent but, in general, younger children are less likely to realize that they do not understand, or to know what to do about it if they do realize (for a review, see Garner 1987). They are, for example, unable to detect that crucial information is missing from a text, or to spot even gross inconsistencies. However, there is no good evidence that metalinguistic awareness is causally related to comprehension skill. It may be that the process of learning to read increases the child's language awareness, rather than the other way round.

Children's ideas about reading, which can be elicited in interviews, also provide some indication of their metacognitive awareness. A typical finding is that younger children generally have fewer resources to help them deal with comprehension failures.

4.2 Theories of Poor Comprehension

The problems of poor comprehenders—children who have adequate word recognition skills, but who do not understand what they read as well as might be expected, will now be considered (for a review of this area, see Yuill and Oakhill 1991). Three main types of theory have been advanced to account for children's comprehension difficulties. The first is that children have problems at the level of single words. One obvious possibility is that poor comprehenders have inadequate vocabularies—they may be able to decode many words whose meanings they do not know. In general, vocabulary size is a good indicator of reading comprehension skill perhaps, in part, because both depend on general linguistic experience. However, procedures that are effective in increasing vocabulary do not necessarily improve comprehension. Furthermore, it is possible to identify groups of children who are matched on vocabulary who nevertheless differ markedly in comprehension skill. Another potential problem at the level of words is that poor comprehenders' word recognition, though accurate, is not automatic. Some authors (notably, Perfetti, see for example, 1985) have shown that good comprehenders recognize words more rapidly than poor comprehenders and they argue that this lack of automaticity creates a 'bottleneck' in working memory. On this view, poor comprehenders have less capacity available for comprehension processes—not because they have smaller working memories, but because they make less efficient use of them. However, although there are several sources of evidence that poor comprehension and slow decoding go together, there is probably no direct causal link between the two. It may be precisely because decoding is such a basic part of reading that children who read more decode faster. Furthermore, speed and automaticity often go hand in hand with a large vocabulary and accurate decoding. When these two factors are taken into account, fast decoding is not such a reliable indicator of good comprehension.

Some work has suggested that good comprehenders, like older children, make greater use of context in reading. In general, good comprehenders are better at using context as a check on their decoding, but they do not make so much use of context as poor comprehenders to speed word recognition.

A second view is that comprehension problems arise at a higher level of text processing. One hypothesis is that poor comprehenders fail to make use of the syntactic constraints in text. Work to explore this idea has shown that poor comprehenders tend to read word-by-word, and do not spontaneously group text into meaningful phrases. Other studies that have investigated sensitivity to syntactic structure more directly have shown that, rather than using the syntactic and semantic cues in a text to integrate the meanings of the individual words, poor comprehenders seem to treat each word separately. These processing characteristics might, at least in part, be related to differences in working memory between good and poor comprehenders.

The third view is that poor comprehenders' problems arise beyond the sentence level—at the level of text integration and inference. Many studies indicate that good and poor comprehenders differ in the extent to which they integrate the information in a text, and in their use of inferences. Such studies show that the making of inferences not only helps the skilled comprehenders to understand the text, but also to remember it. If poor comprehenders make fewer inferences than good ones, one must always ask whether it is because they have poorer inferential skills, or whether they cannot remember the information on which the inferences are based. This question is particularly important because many measures of text comprehension impose demands on memory. However, the evidence suggests that the poor comprehenders's inferior inference skills cannot be explained in terms of poor memory for the text, but that poor comprehenders are less good at working memory tasks than their skilled counterparts. Since working memory is important in making inferences and in the construction of a meaning representation of the text, it is not surprising that poor comprehenders are deficient in these text-comprehension skills.

Other text-level skills differentiate between good and poor comprehenders. In Sect. 4.1.3 it was seen that young children are often poor at monitoring their comprehension, and fail to realize that they have not understood a text. Good comprehenders, like older children, seem to have a better awareness of what comprehension is and when it has been successful. There is evidence that poor comprehenders' problems arise, at least in part, because they fail to monitor their comprehension, or make less use of monitoring strategies (see Garner 1987, for a review). Again, working memory may play a part in such processing—readers with deficient working memories will have little scope for the sorts of processes required to monitor comprehension.

Of course, each of the possible explanations of poor comprehension may be right—each may characterize the difficulties of a distinct group of poor comprehenders, or may partly explain an individual child's problem. In general, though, it seems that children with a specific comprehension deficit have particular difficulties in making inferences from and integrating the ideas in text. Poorer readers also have metacognitive deficits. They often have inadequate conceptions of reading, and may not realize that the primary purpose is to make sense of the text, focusing on reading as a decoding, rather than a meaning-getting, process. Fortunately, a variety of procedures designed to help such children have proved quite successful (for a review, see Yuill and Oakhill 1991: ch. 8).

In general, children who are poor at understanding text are also poor at understanding spoken language. Many studies have found differences between good and poor text comprehenders even in listening tasks. Such findings again support the idea that decoding speed and automaticity can only be part of the poor comprehenders' problem. The skills on which good and poor comprehenders differ also suggest that they will experience difficulty with listening too. Problems with syntax, memory, and metacognitive monitoring would certainly be expected to be general comprehension problems, and not restricted to reading. This does not, of course, mean that reading is no more than decoding plus oral comprehension skills. There are many important differences between oral and written language, but children who have trouble understanding written language often have trouble with spoken language too. So, although slow decoding might contribute to reading comprehension problems, particularly in the initial stages of learning to read, it is unlikely to be their only cause.

Bibliography

Baker L, Stein N L 1981 The development of prose comprehension skills. In: Santa C, Hayes B (eds.) *Children's Prose Comprehension: Research and Practice*. International Reading Association, Newark, DE

Bradley L, Bryant P E 1978 Difficulties in auditory organisation as a possible cause of reading backwardness. *Nature* **271**: 746–47

Chall J S 1979 The great debate: Ten years later, with a modest proposal for reading stages. In: Resnick L B, Weaver P A (eds.) *Theory and Practice in Early Reading*, vol. 1. Lawrence Erlbaum, Hillsdale, NJ

Clark M M 1976 *Young Fluent Readers*. Heinemann Educational, London

Ehri L C 1979 Linguistic insight: Threshold of reading acquisition. In: Waller T G, MacKinnon G E (eds.) *Reading Research: Advances in Theory and Practice*, vol. 1. Academic Press, New York

Ellis N, Large B 1988 The early stages of reading: A longitudinal study. *Applied Cognitive Psychology* **2**: 47–76

Garner R 1987 *Metacognition and Reading Comprehension*. Ablex, Norwood, NJ

Goodman K S 1967 Reading: A psycholinguistic guessing game. *Journal of the Reading Specialist* **6**: 126–35

Johnson D D, Baumann J F 1984 Word identification. In: Pearson P D (ed.) *Handbook of Reading Research*. Longman, London

Oakhill J, Garnham A 1988 *Becoming a Skilled Reader*. Blackwell, Oxford

Perfetti C A 1985 *Reading Ability*. Oxford University Press, Oxford

Smith F 1973 *Psycholinguistics and Reading*. Holt, Rinehart and Winston, New York

Stanovich K E 1982 Individual differences in the cognitive processes of reading. Vol. II: Text-level processes. *Journal of Learning Disabilities* **15**: 549–54

Stuart M, Coltheart M 1988 Does reading develop in a series of stages? *Cognition* **30**: 139–81

Yuill N M, Oakhill J V 1991 *Children's Problems in Text Comprehension: An Experimental Investigation*. Cambridge University Press, Cambridge

Language Development and Brain Development
J. L. Locke

The title of this chapter implies that language and brain development are related. This may be obvious, but the nature of the association is less so. Are developments in the two areas synchronized—paced by some third factor—or do advancements in one area promote progress in the other? What is the role of genetics and environmental stimulation? How do we begin to answer questions such as these?

One approach would be to identify portions of the brain that appear to be responsible for language in the adult brain and then watch these areas develop in the infant and young child. (A more detailed explanation of many of the views expressed here, along with supporting literature, is contained elsewhere. See Locke 1993 and 1997.) This approach has been tried, but it misses an important fact—the human capacity for linguistic communication involves an entire suite of social, vocal, and cognitive capabilities. In all three of these areas, there are some elementary operations that function at birth and other processes that emerge only gradually. Fully grammatical language appears at the end of several years of development—like the rich sound of a fully instrumented orchestra after all the individual sections have sporadically chimed in during the preceding warm-up period.

For these and other reasons, the approach to brain and language development that makes the most ontogenetic sense is to explore the neurology of the development growth path that leads from the infant's first use of voice to express emotion to the child's use of grammatical language to convey thought.

1. Helplessness

There is a larger biological context for infant development that favors learning of social behavior, including speech and language. In all probability, our species would not have anything like the linguistic capability of modern humans were it not for one simple fact: our young are born helpless. The linguistic relevance of this derives from two related facts about the human infant. One is that it cannot escape from adults, hence the sight and sound of people who are usually talking. The other is that this constant exposure to talking comes at a time when the infant's brain is being designed to accommodate ongoing experience.

The helplessness of the human infant is related to its gestational period, which was truncated by specific events in evolution. Skeletal evidence suggests that when early hominids began to stand erect and walk, pressures on the hip and pelvis gradually reduced the distance between sacroiliac and hip joints, permanently narrowing the female birth canal. This narrowing produced an obstetrical dilemma: if infants were to be born at all, their birth had to be moved up, to earlier in the gestational period when their head and brain were still small enough to pass through the birth canal. Earlier delivery thus reduced maturity at birth, much as premature delivery does today. Over countless generations, neonates became increasingly helpless, requiring round the clock care. As a result, the human infant's brain does most of its forming during a protracted interval of frequent handling and other forms of social stimulation. It is hard to think of a developmental circumstance that would more favorably affect acquisition of a complex set of behaviors such as language.

Helplessness benefits social learning in other ways, too. The infant's parents, as all other mature humans, are evolutionarily adapted to feed and protect their progeny. But several hundred millenia of evolution do not guarantee uniformly high quality of care. There is room for individual variation, and a factor in this variation is the infant's own behavior. The infant who fails to respond preferentially to primary caregivers, lacks facial expression, or cries inconsolably may receive less care than other infants, and may even be abandoned or abused. Infants are thus set up by nature to engage in social interactions from the start. That they can do so is an indication that in the first few months of life, long before they are able to crawl, some measure of control develops over systems of social signaling and response. Eye movements and head turnings make it possible for infants to express interest in ongoing activity; vocal and facial expressions enable displays of emotion.

Deeply mired in vegetative need, infants engage and respond to others for nonlinguistic reasons (Locke 1996), but in doing so they increase their exposure to the sights and sounds given off by talking people. They also develop interactive routines, and experience feedback from their own vocal and gestural behavior. These experiences contribute to infants' knowledge of vocal communication and speech and, while doing so, prepare their brain to analyze and interpret spoken language.

2. The Infant as Neural Architect

This scenario differs from classical conceptions of brain and behavior development. Until recently, the brain was considered an enabling mechanism. As the brain matured, the infant was able to do more things, and to do things more proficiently. According to this view of development, the neural systems that produce behavior are largely preformed. To become a language user, the infant need (and could) only await the expression of its genetic plan while in perceptual contact with a linguistic environment. According to this passive scheme, genes are solely responsible for the

neural systems that language requires and the environment provides the material to be learned. The infant need not *do* anything.

It is now clear that in behavior development there is a bidirectional or reciprocal relationship between structure and function. The brain affects behavior, and behavior affects the brain. This is because neural systems develop in response to stimulation that is provided, in part, by the infant itself. The brain probably could not develop in any other fashion because there are too few genes to specify all the neuronal interconnections that exist in the mature mammalian nervous system. A more nearly correct sequence than the unidirectional one is:

$$[\text{Genes} \rightarrow \text{Structure} \leftrightarrow \text{Function} \leftrightarrow \text{Behavior}]$$

When early experience is less than nature intended, the brain responds to this, too. Helen Neville and her colleagues (Neville et al. 1983) found that in congenitally deaf subjects, visual stimulation evoked responses in cortical areas normally associated with auditory processing in hearing subjects. In other words, vision took over parts of the brain not needed by audition.

Excessive stimulation also causes cerebral reorganization. Elbert and his colleagues (Elbert et al. 1995) imaged both cerebral hemispheres of left-handed string players (violinists, cellists, guitar) while an experimenter touched the thumb and little finger of their left or right hand. The musicians were found to have a differently organized left-hand processing system than other (nonmusical) left-handers but not, as expected, a differently organized system for processing right-hand stimulation. There also was an effect of experience within the group of musicians—the earlier they began to play, the more different the manual areas of the relevant (right) hemisphere.

The effects observed by Neville and Elbert and their colleagues were initiated in childhood, but cerebral reorganization also occurs in fully mature primates. When stimulation from the arms is surgically discontinued in adult monkeys, the responsible brain region is colonized by the chin, a neighboring function (Pons et al. 1991). Likewise, in our own species the well-known phantom limb sensation has been induced in adults by lightly touching the chin area of limb amputees (Yang et al. 1994). These findings indicate that the brain reorganizes experience throughout the life of the individual. But this is not to say that there are no early or critical periods in which the brain is unusually responsive to stimulation and activity.

In a variety of mammals, early experience is essential to the development of neural structures that will interpret that experience. In cats, for example, there is a critical period for the development of vision. If the kitten receives no exposure to patterned light within a narrowly circumscribed period in early life, the cat is functionally blind.

3. A Critical Period for Language

In 1967, Eric Lenneberg excited scholars in a variety of disciplines by proposing that linguistic capability, somewhat analogously to vision, develops within a circumscribed period in early life. Now, more than 30 years later, there are four types of evidence for a critical or sensitive period for language. First, there are case studies of individuals who were socially and linguistically deprived in their infancy. These cases are rare and notoriously difficult to interpret, but have produced evidence that is consistent with a critical period hypothesis. The second kind of evidence involves nurturantly reared children who lived for a period with undiagnosed hearing loss and, as a result, had reduced exposure to both spoken and signed language. Research of this type suggests that there are degrees of sensitivity, with the first few years being the most sensitive.

The third type of evidence involves children with damage to putative language regions of the left cerebral hemisphere. These studies reveal that many children experiencing such damage—even the entire removal of the left hemisphere—go on to acquire a normal or nearly normal command of spoken language, regardless of when, precisely, the damage occurred in childhood. This research demonstrates the plasticity of the developing brain, for comparable damage in adulthood usually produces lasting linguistic deficits.

A fourth type of evidence, not considered until recently, involves children with unexplained lexical delays. Some of these children go on to develop normal language while others experience lingering problems in adulthood. The difference seems to relate to the absolute level and rate of word learning. If lexically delayed children do not acquire some minimum store of words—perhaps as many as 2000 by the age of 4 years—there is a substantial probability of continuing grammatical deficits (Locke 1997).

4. The Social and Emotional Path to Spoken Language

It was suggested earlier that there is at least one wrong way to achieve a developmental neurolinguistic account—identifying language regions in the adult brain and watching them grow in the infant. The reason this is wrong, it was said, is that there is a path to spoken language, a path that does not begin with the child's first efforts to learn material that is linguistic. Rather, the path begins with processes that orient the infant to the behavior of talking people, and bias the infant to attend and respond to certain aspects of such behavior (Locke 1996). This is an intensely social and emotional experience from the beginning, and it involves social and emotional systems in the brain.

The infant's responsiveness to facial and vocal activity is presumed to be heavily influenced by genetic factors as well as early experience, and is supported by specific neural preadaptations. Nonhuman primates have brain cell assemblies that fire primarily to faces or to facial activity and to voices or vocal activity; clinical and electrophysical research reveals that humans have mechanisms that are similarly dedicated to processing of faces and facial activity, and to voices and vocal activity.

This set of neural and cognitive mechanisms constitutes a specialization in social cognition (Brothers 1997). These mechanisms are extremely useful in early life, because they enable the infant to extract messages from the face and voice that are vitally important to the infant's survival. Some of these messages are indexical, that is, relevant to the identity of the people who are around the infant. Other messages carry information about the emotional states and intentions of these people. It is difficult to think of information that would be more important to an individual who is critically dependent on others. But voices that are speaking also contain all the information about linguistic structure that exists, so the socially cognitive mechanisms that keep infants locked in to the sounds of speech also enable them to learn spoken language (Locke 1995).

5. Phases in the Development of Linguistic Capacity

The first phase in the development of linguistic capacity is *vocal learning*. In this phase, infants learn and respond to properties of the human voice and speech. During the final trimester of gestation the fetus may perceive and react to the resonance and prosody of the mother's voice. Intrauterine exposure to maternal prosody appears to explain a documented postnatal listening preference for the mother's speech as well as the language she spoke during pregnancy. In the first few months of postnatal life, infants respond differentially to variations in vocal emotion. In their own utterances, infants may occasionally imitate the intonation contours of others.

In the second 6 months of life, infants reveal an ability to use prosodic cues to locate linguistic units in larger streams of speech. During this period, listening experience reinforces some adult-like perceptual categories that are evident in the first few weeks of life and weakens others. Infants' utterances may reveal some learning of ambient sound patterns. During the vocal learning phase, then, infants become acquainted with vocal cues that identify people, regulate social behavior, and superficially characterize the expression of their native language.

Longitudinal research now indicates that infants who proceed most directly into vocal and word learning, all other factors being equal, are those who:

(a) take vocal turns with a partner;
(b) attend to and mimic prosodic variations;
(c) gesture communicatively;
(d) store and reproduce ambient phonetic patterns;
(e) act in accord with the inferred mental activity of others.

These behaviors precede and may facilitate language.

A neurodevelopmental account is needed for all these precursive behaviors, just as we need a similar account for the vocal learning of the fetus and neonate. An obvious strategy is to look for parallel discontinuities in brain and behavior development as infants proceed through the various precursive behaviors to fully fledged grammatical language. Many of the nuances are undoubtedly hard to detect, but there are several larger shifts that may be easier to trace. Since phonetic and grammatical operations are performed primarily in the left cerebral hemisphere in the linguistically competent, one could look for a functional shift in hemispheric priorities, and possibly a structural asymmetry, as infants progress from purveyors of vocal behavior and emotion to generators of linguistic content.

In the phonetic domain, we need to consider babbling. Babbling involves the raising and lowering of the mandible during phonation, thereby producing rhythmic sequences of consonant–vowel syllables (e.g., dada). Observational studies indicate that babbling typically begins abruptly, usually at about 6 to 7 months. At this same age, a sharp increase in rhythmic hand movements and right-handed reaching has been observed.

Does babbling mark the onset of left hemisphere control of speech-like activity? An experiment conducted in my laboratory seems to suggest that it does (Locke et al. 1995). In that experiment, we observed normally developing 4 to 5 month olds who had not yet begun to babble; 6 month olds, who had just recently begun to babble; and 7 to 9 month olds, who had been babbling for 1 or more months. We began by placing a rattle in the right or left hand of each infant according to a predetermined schedule, then we counted the number of shakes per second. As expected, we obtained a significant increase in shakes per second from the prebabbling to the babbling period. Right-handed shaking significantly exceeded left-handed shaking overall. There also was a significant interaction, due primarily to the greater amount of right- than left-hand shaking in the infants who had most recently begun to babble.

These behavioral findings suggest that early in the second 6 months of postnatal development the left hemisphere typically assumes control of both right-handed and speech-like activity. What, then, is revealed by studies of the brain itself? Is there any evidence that manual and vocal control areas in the left hemisphere of the brain developmentally pass up homologous areas of the right hemisphere at the age when babbling normally begins?

Simonds and Scheibel (1989) counted the length of dendrites in the left and right speech-motor and motor areas in 17 children who died between 3 and 72 months of age. Dendrite location was categorized, along the dendritic spine, as proximal (the three dendrites clos-est to the soma) and distal (the three dendrites beyond the proximal ones). The investigators found that at 3 months there were no differences in the number of left or right dendrites in speech-motor and motor areas. However, at 5 to 6 months there were more distal dendrites in the left hemisphere in both speech-motor and motor areas. There is, thus, some correspondence between the hemisphericity of vocal-motor control systems and the hemisphericity of vocal-motor behavior.

As infants take in information about vocal characteristics of the ambient language, they also store utterances. This *storage phase* may begin as early as 5 months, when infants may selectively respond to their name. By 8 months, infants may comprehend as many as 36 words (Bates et al. 1994). Whether for perceptual, motoric, or other reasons, infants typically do not produce stored utterances much before 11 months. The first recognizable infant speech is usually a single word. First words are often hard to differentiate from babbled syllables, which do not stop the moment speech begins. The first utterance may also be a formulaic phrase—a rote or nearly rote copy of word sequences that have been heard frequently in the speech of others, for example, 'shoes and socks' or 'time to go to bed.' The length, stress pattern, and intonation contour of these sequences may be fairly well preserved, even if the individual sounds are imprecise.

I assume that utterance storage reflects the action of neural mechanisms that support a range of socially cognitive operations, not merely linguistic ones. For one thing, in adults, the right, so-called 'nonlinguistic' hemisphere appears to be unusually active in the processing and storage of idiomatic material (Van Lancker 1987). For another thing, of the children who incur unilateral damage in infancy or early childhood, subjects with *right* hemisphere lesions perform significantly worse on lexical comprehension, relative to healthy controls, than do left hemisphere-damaged patients (Aram and Eisele 1994; Thal et al. 1991). These findings suggest that there may be several quasi-linguistic areas or regions that are lexical but not grammatical (Neville et al. 1991), and may not even be exclusively lexical (Markson and Bloom 1997).

If utterances continue to accumulate as rotely learned prosodies, it is assumed that the storage system will overload. The reason is that all spoken languages are phonological—dependent on the user's implicit discovery that words are composed of a finite set of recombinable units. Most languages have no more than 40 or 50 individual units, or phonemes, from which all words are constructed. Therefore, to approach each item, whether a word or phrase, as a wholly unique pattern is to miss the point of spoken languages, and to underutilize a storage system that evolution has provided for this kind of material.

Utterance storage limitations may be forced into

the open by the so-called 'lexical spurt,' a marked quickening of the pace at which new words are comprehended and/or produced. These spurts usually occur at about 18 to 20 months, when the number of words acquired per week may quadruple (Bates et al. 1988; Goldfield and Reznick 1990). At this point in development, there may be as many as five words comprehended to every word produced. I have hypothesized that this burgeoning store of words triggers or reinforces the activation of analytical mechanisms—the onset of the *analytical and computational phase* in the development of linguistic capacity (Locke 1997).

The structure analysis system locates recurring elements within and across utterances, and thereby enables the learning of rules by which utterances are synthesized and parsed. In effect, it presents the child with the units needed for morphology, phonology, syntax, and the lexicon—thereby endowing children with the capacity to compute linguistic forms, allowing them to make infinite sentential use of finite phonemic means.

Normally, this process works smoothly, but if the infant has no stored utterances there will be nothing for its analytical mechanisms to work on, and no stored forms to modify by application of computational rules. It is presumed, in such a circumstance, that the infant's brain would develop the potential to deal with all other species-typical capabilities that were being environmentally challenged at the moment, but not grammatical behavior, which requires a certain amount of prior success. Where the storage phase is affected by external factors, including the availability of appropriate stimulation, the functions established in the analytical and computational phase are affected primarily by internal factors—the pressures provided by utterances requiring additional analysis and organization.

In English-learning children, the presently most convincing evidence that analysis and computation are underway comes from their regularization of verb tenses and noun plurals. When this occurs, irregular verbs like 'went' may be temporarily and inconsistently expressed as 'goed,' and nouns like 'foot' may be expressed as 'foots.' Since children are usually not exposed to such forms in the speech of others, they are assumed not to be reproduced, but *computed.*

As we have seen, the task of associating neural and linguistic developments is facilitated by discontinuities in both of these areas. Since children typically begin to regularize irregular forms between 20 and 37 months of age (Marcus et al. 1992; Marcus 1995), we can ask if there are any suspicious brain developments in this age range. And, indeed, between 2 and 4 years of age there is massive development of the brain in general, and the left hemisphere in particular (Thatcher et al. 1987). Moreover, if damage occurs to the left hemisphere during the analytical and com-

putational phases, it now impairs performance on lexical comprehension and expression tasks—and various syntactic measures—more than damage to the right hemisphere (Aram et al. 1985; Aram et al. 1987; Dennis and Kohn 1975).

The developmental neurolinguistic story is not over at this point, of course. At 6 years, language regions of the left hemisphere continue to differentiate, and to distance themselves from corresponding areas in the right hemisphere (Scheibel 1993). On the behavioral side, lexical learning continues, and a range of linguistic operations become increasingly automatic. But much of what makes us grammatical is in place by the age of four.

In the future, one anticipates a more precise statement about the relationship between language development and brain development than is now possible. Optimism is appropriate because the developmental neurosciences are in their ascendancy. We have just recently begun to image brain structure and function in living children, and new behavioral techniques are being used in human infants. With advances in relevant knowledge occurring on a yearly basis, it should soon be possible to achieve a more comprehensive neural account of the child's path to spoken language.

References

Aram D M, Eisele J A 1994 Limits to a left hemisphere explanation for specific language impairment. *Journal of Speech and Hearing Research* **37:** 824–30

Aram D M, Ekelman B L, Rose D, Whitaker H A 1985 Verbal and cognitive sequelae following unilateral lesions acquired in early childhood. *Journal of Clinical and Experimental Neuropsychology* **3:** 55–78

Aram D M, Ekelman B L, Whitaker H A 1987 Spoken syntax in children with acquired unilateral hemisphere lesions *Brain and Language* **31:** 61–87

Bates E, Bretherton I, Snyder L 1988 *From First Words to Grammar: Individual Differences and Dissociable Mechanisms.* Cambridge University Press, Cambridge

Bates E, Marchman V, Thal D, Fenson L, Dale P, Reznick J S, Reilly J, Hartung J 1994 Developmental and stylistic variation in the composition of early vocabulary. *Journal of Child Language* **21:** 85–123

Brothers L 1997 *Friday's Footprint: How Society Shapes the Human Mind.* Oxford University Press, Oxford

Dennis M, Kohn B 1975 Comprehension of syntax in infantile hemiplegics after cerebral hemidecortication: Left-hemisphere superiority. *Brain and Language* **2:** 472–82

Elbert T, Pantev C, Wienbruch C, Rockstroh B, Taub E 1995 Increased cortical representation of the fingers of the left hand in string players. *Science* **270:** 305–7

Goldfield B A, Reznick J S 1990 Early lexical acquisition: Rate, content, and the vocabulary spurt. *Journal of Child Language* **17:** 171–83

Lenneberg E H 1967 *Biological Foundations of Language.* John Wiley, New York

Locke J L 1993 *The Child's Path to Spoken Language.* Harvard University Press, Cambridge, MA

Locke J L 1995 Development of the capacity for spoken language. In: Fletcher P, MacWhinney B (eds.) *Handbook of Child Language.* Blackwell Publishers, Oxford

Locke J L 1996 Why do infants begin to talk? Language as an unintended consequence. *Journal of Child Language* **23**: 251–68

Locke J L 1997 A theory of neurolinguistic development. *Brain and Language* **58**: 265–326

Locke J L, Bekken K E, McMinn-Larson L, Wein D 1995 Emergent control of manual and vocal-motor activity in relation to the development of speech. *Brain and Language* **51**: 498–508

Marcus G F 1995 Children's overregularization of English plurals: A quantitative analysis. *Journal of Child Language* **22**: 447–59

Marcus G F, Pinker S, Ullman M, Hollander M, Rosen T J, Xu F 1992 Overregularization in language acquisition. *Monograph of the Society for Research in Child Development* **57** (Serial No. 228)

Markson L, Bloom P 1997 Evidence against a dedicated system for word learning in children. *Nature* **385**: 813–15

Neville H J, Nicol J I, Barss A, Forster K I, Garett M F 1991 Syntactically based sentence processing classes: Evidence from event-related brain potentials. *Journal of Cognitive Neuroscience* **3**: 151–65

Neville H J, Schmidt A, Kutas M 1983 Altered visual-evoked potentials in congenitally deaf adults. *Brain Research* **266**: 127–32

Pons T P, Garraghty P E, Ommaya A K, Kaas J H, Taub E, Mishkin M 1991 Massive cortical reorganization after sensory deafferentation in adult macaques. *Science* **252**: 1857–60

Scheibel A B 1993 Dendritic structure and language development. In: de Boysson-Bardies B, de Schonen S, Jusczyk P, MacNeilage P, Morton J (eds.) *Developmental Neurocognition: Speech and Face Processing in the First Year of Life*. Kluwer, Boston, MA

Simonds R J, Scheibel A B 1989 The postnatal development of the motor speech area: A preliminary study. *Brain and Language* **37**: 42–58

Thal D J, Marchman V, Stiles J, Aram D, Trauner D, Naas R, Bates E 1991 Early lexical development in children with focal brain injury. *Brain and Language* **40**: 491–527

Thatcher R W, Walker R A, Giudice S 1987 Human cerebral hemispheres develop at different rates and ages. *Science* **236**: 1110–13

Van Lancker D 1987 Nonpropositional speech: Neurolinguistic studies. In: Ellis A (ed.) *Progress in the Psychology of Language, Vol. 3*. Erlbaum, Hillsdale, NJ

Yang T T, Gallen C, Schwartz B, Bloom F E, Ramachandran V S, Cobb S 1994 Sensory maps in the human brain. *Nature* **368**: 592–3

Biological Bases of Speech

B. Lindblom

This chapter reviews evidence for the claim that speech is biologically unique. In part, its uniqueness derives from the fact that speech presupposes language, and that language is unique. In part, the production and perception mechanisms of speech exhibit their own unique features.

1. Spoken Language and Animal Communication

In the wild, humans' closest relatives, the apes, make various vocal noises (Goodall 1986). Gorillas, for instance, produce aggressive calls, alarm calls, 'wraaghs,' cries, 'pig grunts,' 'belch' vocalizations, 'question' barks, chuckles, and hoots (Fossey 1983). To be sure, these animals invoke vocalizations as an important part of their communicative behavior; but they do not speak.

Nor can they be taught to speak (Pierce 1985). A well-known case is Viki. In the 1940s, this chimpanzee was adopted by two psychologists who raised her with their own child and who tried to teach her to speak English. Despite five years of intensive training and clear signs of intelligence, Viki never used more than three words vaguely resembling 'mama,' 'papa,' and 'cup' (Hayes and Hayes 1951). There are several

causes why nonhuman primates fail to develop even an approximation of speech. One factor may be their alleged inability to control vocal behavior voluntarily, a claim which is, however, subject to some dispute (Aitken 1981; Sutton 1979).

It is true that the vocal signals of other species sometimes exhibit speechlike properties. When a dog barks, it moves its jaw up and down during each bark. Similar open–close movements characterize the communicatively significant 'lip-smacks' of macaques (Rosenblum 1975), which, resembling human articulatory movements, have been identified as precursors of spoken syllables (cf. the frame–content model of MacNeilage and Davis 1990).

Birdsong shares with speech certain neurobiological features. Vocal learning is restricted to humans, birds, and marine mammals. White-crowned sparrows deprived of hearing other birds until after 7 weeks of age will not learn to sing normally. If, during that time, they hear the songs of other species, their behavior will not be normal either. The song has to be that of its conspecifics, which indicates that this species is born with a readiness to recognize its own characteristic song (Marler 1984).

Experiments in nature have provided analogous

information on language and speech. One example is Genie. Imprisoned by her psychopath father, this girl was not exposed to spoken language until in her teens. She learned to use speech, but her language never reached normal grammatical complexity (Curtiss 1977).

Birds produce sound by means of the syrinx, a mechanism connected to the brain via bilateral nerve paths. An adult male chaffinch whose right syrinx–brain connection has been cut is capable of normal song behavior, but disrupting the left branch will destroy the song and make the bird unable to learn it again. However, if the disruption takes place in a young bird, normal behavior will develop irrespective of the side of the lesion (Nottebohm 1971, 1972).

This plasticity is reminiscent of the human brain. Most people have language mechanisms in the left hemisphere. If a lesion interferes with development, the opposite hemisphere is able to take over—provided that it occurs well before the age of 10, when lateralization of language functions has been permanently established. This resilience of brain tissue indicates that, like song acquisition, speech development must occur during a critical time window (Lenneberg 1967, Newport 1988, Johnson and Newport 1989).

Apes are much more successful at using sign language than speech. Experiments in teaching them American Sign Language (ASL) have demonstrated that, while they are unable to learn syntax in any serious way (Terrace 1979), they are nevertheless able to acquire vocabularies of a few hundred words. Vervet monkeys use three distinct alarm calls: short tonal chirps indicate the presence of a leopard; a high-pitched chatter signals a python; and a martial eagle evokes a low-pitched staccato grunt (Seyfarth et al. 1980). In a sense, these signals link sound to meaning in a primitive, wordlike way. Appropriate responses to spoken words have also been elicited from parrots, dolphins (Herman et al. 1984), sea lions, and dogs (Warden and Warner 1928).

Accordingly, animals can both learn and use human words. However, there is an enormous quantitative difference between their lexical abilities and those of *Homo sapiens*. That difference is one of the keys to the uniqueness of speech. Estimates of vocabulary size indicate that, on average, a 6 year old child knows around 13 000 words and an 8 year old has close to 30 000, which implies an average rate of vocabulary growth of over 20 new words per day (Miller 1977). The rate stays high: the average college student's recognition vocabulary is estimated at 150 000 items. While apes learning ASL acquire a few hundred words only after explicit training, children learn much more, and do so spontaneously (Miller 1977, 1991).

The size of animal vocabularies appears to be uniformly small: birds use up to around 12 distinct signal types, while monkeys and apes have somewhat larger inventories. There appear to be few, if any, animal communication systems in excess of 40 elements (Wilson 1975).

Why there should be these discrepancies is not well understood, but a relevant fact is that human words contain discrete vowel and consonant phonemes, whereas animals communicate by means of indivisible sound modulations like the three vervet calls mentioned above (Studdert-Kennedy 1983).

A hypothetical code that uses n different symbols to form word sequences k symbols long is capable of representing $i \Sigma n^{k(i)}$ words. If $n = 25$ and $k = 1$ through 5, over 10^6 words can be generated. Those numbers give a sense of the power of combinatorial phonemic coding. Lacking that principle, animals are reduced to very limited message sets. Although human languages do not exploit its full combinatorial possibilities, it is nevertheless that principle that accounts for the impressive human lexical capacity.

Another factor making speech unique is syntax, a mechanism with expressive combinatorial power that, mathematically, is even greater than that of the lexicon. It has become clear that the ASL acquired by chimpanzees lacks several of the key properties of human syntax. Ape language tends to be shallow in structure, confined to lexical items, with grammatical morphemes, so crucial to human sentence structure, typically missing (Bickerton 1990).

2. Vocal Tracts and the Human Brain

Phonemic coding and syntax, two attributes of language, make speech different from animal communication. However, the uniqueness of speech derives not only from its dependence on language; speech itself exhibits special characteristics.

First, human vocal tracts differ from those of non-human primates. In apes, the position of the larynx is high, which gives them long mouths and short pharynges. In human males, the larynx is lower and the mouth and pharynx cavities are more comparable in length. The proportions of the vocal tracts of human infants resemble those of chimpanzees. During normal development, relative pharynx length increases. The larynx descends, more so in male than in female speakers.

Whether those differences came about because of speech is controversial. One view (Ohala 1984) says that, since larynx position in humans is primarily a male feature that appears only at puberty along with an elongation of the vocal cords, which is common also in other species, it should be seen not as an adaptation for speech but as an instance of sexual dimorphism. Others (e.g., Miller 1991, Lieberman 1991) argue that it was speech criteria that drove this phylogenetic reshaping of vocal-tract morphology, and that this innovation brought tangible benefits in the form of a larger range of more distinctive phonetic possibilities.

Second, human brains differ from those of non-human primates. One aspect is sheer size. The weight of an animal's brain tends to bear a law-governed relation to its body weight (Jerison 1980). If brain weight grows in proportion to body surface (cm^2), and body weight increases in proportion to body volume (cm^3), then the brain ought to be scaled to the $\frac{2}{3}$ power of body weight (Gould 1979). For mammals, that expectation is borne out. Observations of species from mice to elephants are adequately summarized by $E = k \times W^{2/3}$ (E = brain weight, W = body weight, k = constant). Apes, hominids, and humans have larger brains than predicted by that rule (Tobias 1987). Plotting the difference between the actual weight of a primate's brain and E, the equation-based estimate, versus evolutionary time, produces a curve moderately increasing from *Australopithecus afarensis* and *A. africanus* to *Homo habilis*. From *H. habilis* to *H. erectus*, it becomes steeper, reaching its maximum rate of change between *H. erectus* and *H. sapiens*. Anthropological evidence (Isaac 1978) suggests that these transitions in brain development coincide with changes in technology and lifestyles of our ancestors (Fig. 1). These may also have been associated with the beginnings of spoken language (Aiello and Wheeler 1995).

Spoken language and handedness are both in the left hemisphere, suggesting the possibility that the brain mechanisms for speech evolved from those for manual movements (Kimura 1979). However, deciding whether the manual system is a true 'preadaptation' for speech or simply a parallel development is not unproblematic, since many complex systems, including neuromotor systems, appear to be hierarchically organized (Simon 1969, Pinker and Bloom 1990).

One account of the hemispheric lateralization of human language and handedness (MacNeilage 1991) suggests that the reasons why they are both in the left hemisphere go back a very long time, about 60 000 000 years. It assumes that early primates (prosimians) developed the use of their right hand for holding on to trees and maintaining body position and the left hand for reaching out and catching insects and food. This behavior—still found in bush babies—created a division of labor for the two hemispheres: food-grabbing, a visuo–spatial task, was handled by the right hemisphere, and posture and balance by the left. During primate evolution, body movements acquired communicative significance. These gestural signals were thus elaborations of the basic postural mechanisms controlled by the left hemisphere. Accordingly, a point of departure for primate evolution was a link between the control of posture and communicative behavior. Gradually, as primate species evolved that were mainly terrestrial, and therefore did most of their food-gathering on the ground, the right limb was freed from the demands of postural control and was specialized for fine motor-control tasks such as manipulating food items in coordination with a mostly supportive left hand. According to this theory, both human language and handedness were constrained to evolve from phylogenetically old behaviors controlled by the left hemisphere. Other consequences of this account include the expectations that not only humans but also nonhuman primates should show consistent hand preferences given the appropriate visuo–spatial and manipulatory tasks, and that, in individual subjects, footedness (an aspect of postural control) should correlate strongly with the cerebral localization of language. There appears to be substantial evidence for both predictions (MacNeilage et al. 1987, 1988, 1993).

The brains of apes and humans differ with respect to the relative proportions of corresponding regions. The prefrontal cortex, which is involved in learning and cognitive tasks, is especially enlarged in humans (Deacon 1988). Electrical stimulation studies have demonstrated subcortical control of vocalization in monkeys. In humans, language use is heavily, but not exclusively, cortical.

Accordingly, human brains have structures with no equivalents in other animals. One such region is the premotor area of Broca in the left hemisphere and close to the primary motor area that directly controls speech musculature. Damage to this area and its associated systems produces the syndrome of Broca's aphasia (see *Aphasia*), which is characterized by a lack of spontaneous speech and by short, dysfluent, and articulatorily and syntactically deviant utterances in which grammatical morphemes are conspicuously rare. Another complex of symptoms is Wernicke's aphasia (see *Aphasia*). Sufferers have posterior lesions, show reduced comprehension, and have difficulties finding the correct words. Their utterances tend to be fluent but devoid of content.

Sign language is visual–gestural, speech is vocal–auditory. Nonetheless, aphasia in deaf native signers parallels aphasia in hearing subjects both with respect to how language is affected and where the lesions are localized. The terms Broca's and Wernicke's aphasia have been applied to both modalities. To some, such parallels reflect the brain's organization into separate modules and provide support for an autonomous, modality-independent representation in the brain (Poizner et al. 1987). But Broca's area is far from a neatly delimited module. It makes rich connections with subcortical and prefrontal circuits. Therefore, the full syndrome of Broca's aphasia is likely to involve not only the cortical area of Broca *per se*, but also its more diffuse connections.

3. The Production and Perception of Speech

Human subjects have great difficulty in identifying auditory or visual stimuli presented at speeds faster than about seven events per second. By contrast,

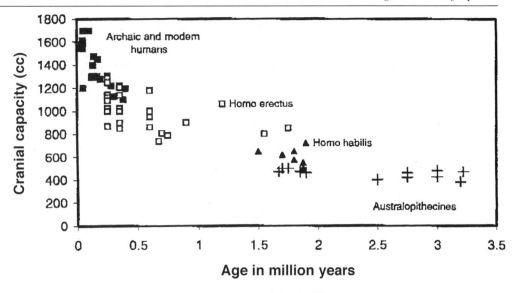

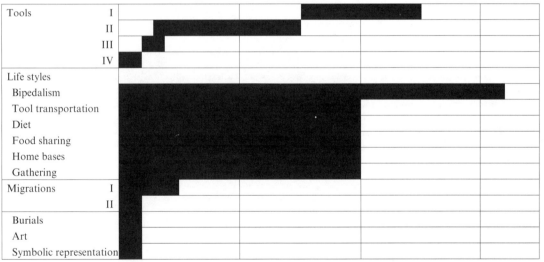

Figure 1

speech often exceeds rates of 15 phonemes per second without loss of intelligibility. When judging the order of a series of sounds, human listeners need longer sound durations if the sequence is made up of non-verbal hisses, tones, and buzzes, but significantly shorter durations if the series is phonemes in words. To some experimenters, those findings imply that the order of phonemes is not perceived directly, but is derived from a larger linguistic unit (Warren 1982). Others, including proponents of the 'motor theory of speech perception,' maintain that the high transmission rate of speech is the product of biologically specialized mechanisms for both producing ('en-coding') and perceiving ('decoding') speech (Liberman and Mattingly 1985).

The acoustic correlates of phonemes are not like beads on a necklace. According to one frequently used metaphor, they are more like fresh eggs having passed through the rollers of a wringer on to a moving belt. Phonemes are coarticulated ('encoded'): the articulatory movements for one phoneme are initiated before those of the previous phoneme are over. Their phonetic manifestations overlap in time and give rise to 'coarticulation.'

Speech sounds never occur in phonetically 'pure form.' They are inevitably colored by the preceding

137

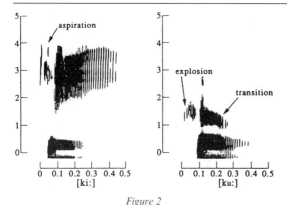

Figure 2

and following sounds. The pronunciation of *a* followed by the pronunciation of *b* will not be equal to the pronunciation of *ab*, as illustrated by the spectrograms of the words *key* and *coo* in Fig. 2.

Although humans intuitively analyze these words as consonant–vowel sequences, there is no nonarbitrary time-point where the consonant ends and the vowel begins. Furthermore, one would say that the two words begin with the 'same' consonant but have different vowels. While it is easy to see the spectrographic differences between the vowels, it is more difficult to say what the psychological constancy of the /k/ phoneme corresponds to acoustically. Both of these difficulties exemplify two general problems that phoneticians have battled with at least since the advent of sound spectrography in the 1940s: the segmentation and invariance problems.

While coarticulation makes it possible to produce a large number of phonemes per unit time, there seems to be a price for invoking such a strategy: phonetically, the discreteness and invariance of linguistic units are lost and replaced by continuity and context-dependence.

As mentioned, one way of resolving those issues has been proposed by motor theorists who hypothesize a specialized decoding mechanism capable of recovering the units of the underlying message. In support of this position, physically identical components of speech and nonspeech stimuli have been used to provide evidence for phonetic and nonphonetic modes of perceptual processing, known as the paradigm of 'duplex perception' (Liberman and Mattingly 1989). Other approaches look more closely at the signal itself and/or at clues from how perception works in general.

Evidence from several experiments on speech perception by animals suggests that special processing need *not* be involved. In one such study (Kluender et al. 1987), Japanese quail were trained to peck in response to syllables containing /d/, but to avoid pecking when hearing the corresponding /bV/ or /gV/ sequences. After successfully mastering this task for a

given vowel set, the quail were presented with new stimuli containing the same consonants but different vowels. The birds were able to generalize their responses to the new stimuli. Since quail do not have a special speech processor, the syllables were apparently sufficiently rich acoustically to support correct categorization. Consequently, at least for isolated, clearly spoken syllables, phonetic categories appear to be definable acoustically.

Another approach observes that, for perception in general, input signals never activate an empty system (Lashley 1951). They always 'resonate with' internalized schemata (Bregman 1990; Shepard 1984). Speech perception is supported by rich knowledge schemata, namely those of language. Language is redundant: at all levels of structure, it codes the information in multiple and overspecified ways. For example, many words or letters could be removed from this text without preventing the reader from understanding it. A receiving system in possession of such a redundant code is protected against signal degradation. It is set up to cope with partial information.

There are many speech experiments demonstrating signal–knowledge interaction in compelling ways. A case in point is the phenomenon of 'perceptual filling-in,' the effect of hearing something not physically present (Shepard 1984). If someone says *less'n six*, a hearer is likely to assume that the speaker said *less than* if the phrase occurs after *How many people came?*, but *lesson* if it follows *What is your homework?* In either case, the hearer will normally be unaware of the ambiguity of the homophonous *less'n*. Linguistic knowledge supplements the signal and strongly contributes to shaping the percept. Perceptual filling-in of this type implies a signal from which something is missing, but which is otherwise sufficiently rich to support the restoration.

The mechanisms of production produce stimuli that can be either rich or poor in physical information. Like other movements, speech gestures are under output-oriented control. That is, the brain recruits and styles muscle activity according to externally defined goals. Clearly, humans are capable of adjusting their performance to the needs of the situation, using a greater vocal effort against noise, and speaking more clearly when talking to a foreigner or to someone who is hard of hearing. Speaking with a pipe between the teeth requires modifying articulations in order to remain intelligible. Humans are good at making such compensations, presumably because motor control in general has evolved to be intrinsically output-oriented and compensatory.

Articulatory behavior resembles other motor processes also in that, whenever attaining a given goal becomes less crucial, simplifying 'short-cuts' will be invoked. In speech, the effects of this process are apparent when demands for information are reduced. When speaking informally and casually, speakers pro-

138

Clear speech

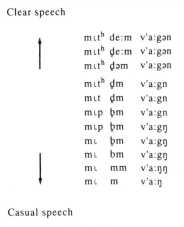

Casual speech

Figure 3

duce signals that are poorer in physical cues and that show more coarticulation and far-reaching reductions of the linguistic elements of the utterance.

Thus, speech production is characterized by both plasticity and economy. This malleability is illustrated with some German data in Fig. 3. The variants of the phrase *mit dem Wagen* go from carefully articulated, clear speech to more casual, reduced pronunciations (Kohler 1990).

Supported by everyday observation as well as experimentation, the above account suggests that speaking and listening are unique to humans but build on general biological processes. Speech production is adaptive. Communicating successfully, speakers can, and typically do, adapt their speech to the short-term needs of the listener. It has been suggested that the difficulty of identifying phonetic invariants is a direct consequence of this adaptive organization of speaker–listener interactions (Lindblom 1990).

4. Speech Development

It has been seen that the speech signal is highly encoded and often received under less-than-ideal conditions. Its perception by the adult listener appears remarkably error-free. People have often wondered how children cope with all the complexities of speech, and answers to questions about speech development have been sought both in innate mechanisms and environmental factors.

Infants begin to communicate as early as the second month of life, engaging in face-to-face 'protoconversations' (Trevarthen and Marwick 1986). Imitation of facial gestures has been reported for children as young as 12–21 days (Meltzoff 1986). The character of this 'intersubjectivity' changes during mother–infant interaction, but its origin is no doubt innate.

A special sensitivity to speech is present very early (Studdert-Kennedy 1986). The brain of a 3 month old

processes speech differently from music. From that age on, speech appears to activate the left hemisphere more than music, which engages a right-hemisphere mechanism.

Several research groups have found that, during the first six months, infants are extremely good at discriminating a wide range of phonetic contrasts, including nonnative speech sounds. Such findings have suggested that the categories manifested in infant speech discrimination are precursors of the categories to be fully established later, and that children gradually lose their initial ability to discriminate nonnative speech sounds. However, under suitable testing conditions, somewhat older children can recover this ability, suggesting that perceptual acuity is not lost, but that language experience induces a reorganization of the child's speech perception system (Werker and Pegg 1992).

Normal-hearing children are exposed to speech before birth. Newborn babies prefer their mother's voice to that of an unknown speaker. Acoustically, the mother's body is likely to act as a filter, passing low but attenuating high frequencies. Accordingly, *in utero* speech emphasizes rhythm and intonation cues, sounding much like 'hummed' speech (Fifer and Moon 1989).

Baby-talk is the style of speech used in communicating with infants. It has been described as a 'simplified register,' since its characteristics are adapted to match the child's stage of linguistic development (Ferguson 1977). For several languages, it has been shown that pitch contours tend to show much wider excursions in baby-talk than in adult-to-adult conversations. This exaggerated prosody presumably serves to catch the child's attention so that important affective and pragmatic information can be conveyed (Fernald 1984).

From the 1960s on, the study of early vocal development was strongly influenced by the writings of Roman Jakobson. He saw this process as governed by principles unique to language (Jakobson 1941). The step from nonlinguistic babbling to phonological speech was assumed to be abrupt. His views long remained unchallenged, but have been replaced by accounts emphasizing the continuous nature of phonetic development (Oller 1980, Vihman et al. 1985). During the first year, children vocalize in similar ways, presenting the same sequence of achievements cross-linguistically. A prominent landmark at about six months is the sudden onset of 'canonical babbling,' sequences of reduplicated syllablelike elements, such as [baba], [dada], etc. (Roug et al. 1989). Such 'protosyllables' may reflect not only the constraints imposed by anatomical and neural development, but also the child's first attempts to sound like other people. These utterances apparently also supply the phonetic raw materials for the child's first words, an observation that has thrown doubt on Jakobson's claim that the transition from babbling to speech is discontinuous (Vihman 1990).

Further evidence comes from observations of communicatively disabled children. Deaf children do not produce canonical babbling during the first year. When they do vocalize, they show a much higher proportion of labial articulations (Oller et al. 1985, Stoel-Gammon 1988). Significantly more labial consonants also seem to be used by sighted than by blind children (Mulford 1988).

These facts show that speech development is not governed by principles special to language. Like many other behaviors, it unfolds as an interplay between 'prewired' mechanisms and experience.

5. Phonology: The 'Fossils' of Speech

Examining the sounds of the world's languages, one finds a remarkable degree of regularity. Vowels and consonants are not drawn arbitrarily from all humanly possible vocalizations. Some patterns contain sounds that are 'easy to make'; others seem to serve listener needs, presenting sound differences that are 'easy to hear' (Ladefoged 1993).

The interaction of those forces is seen in the structure of phonetic inventories. Small systems lack segmentswith extreme articulations: for example, Hawaiian has /p k ʔ h m n l w/. Such series resemble the inventories of babbling and early speech. They appear 'elementary' compared with many of the consonants that are found only in very large systems. !Xũ, for instance, has close to 100 distinctive consonants, half of which are clicks, and nearly 50 vowels and diphthongs.

Vowels pattern similarly. A five-vowel system is likely to use /i e a o u/. Often, such a 'plain' series is matched by one or several additional systems that add an 'elaboration' in the form of a secondary articulation or a phonation type, for example, nasalization or breathy voice. It is significant that small systems recruit only 'elementary' or plain vowels. They never substitute secondary for plain articulations, or show a mixture of plain, elaborated, and complex segments (Lindblom et al. 1992).

How such patterns enter the language is not well understood. According to one theory, the seeds of historical sound change are sown by listener errors (Ohala 1981). Failure to take contextual factors into account often leads to a misidentification of the intended utterance. If, when becoming the speaker, the listener adopts the misidentified form, this initiates a sound change that may spread through the speech community. In this scenario, sound change is like a mutation arising from an imperfect copying of genetic information.

There is a curious parallel between the phonetic variations of speech and the 'fossils' that they leave in phonological systems. Both seem to reflect the tug-of-war staged by the listener's need for clarity, on the one hand, and the speaker's continual propensity to simplify, on the other. Perhaps the law-governed relationships mentioned above between system size and phonetic content imply that sound systems are molded by the same factors that determine the ebb and flow of signal information in speaker–listener interactions: both must meet the criterion of 'sufficient discriminability' (Lindblom 1990).

6. Speech and Natural Selection

A biological perspective on speech is a natural one for many reasons. Several aspects of speech share, and build on, mechanisms that evolved before spoken language emerged, for example, those of motor control and perception. There are similarities between speech development and birdsong acquisition.

Nevertheless, the search for precursors in animal communication does not help much in bridging the enormous gap that separates language and speech from nonhuman behaviors. Accordingly, the main conclusion that must be drawn is that speech is special, partly because of its dependence on the unique phenomenon of language, and partly because of its own properties.

That conclusion raises an overarching question for the study of speech in a biological context: namely how, if it is unique, it could have evolved according to the principle of gradual cumulative selection which has been so firmly established in other domains of biology by the Neo-Darwinian theory of evolution (Dawkins 1983, 1986).

This is an issue surrounded by a great deal of controversy. Influential linguists (Chomsky 1986) and psychologists have argued that language is too complex to have evolved by natural selection, and that language is in fact an embarrassment for evolutionary theory (Premack 1986). Others dismiss such views as based on an 'argument from personal incredulity' and charge their opponents with failing to grasp the enormous complexity-generating power of the variation-selection mechanism at the heart of the Neo-Darwinian framework.

Whatever the final outcome of such debates, they are likely to have a lasting and profound influence on the crossdisciplinary endeavor of understanding a behavior that more than anything else determines humankind's place in nature.

Bibliography

Aiello L, Wheeler P 1995 The expensive-tissue hypothesis. *Current Anthropology* **36(2)**

Aitken P G 1981 Cortical control of conditioned and spontaneous vocal behavior in rhesus monkeys. *Brain and Language* **13**: 171–84

Bickerton D 1990 *Language and Species*. Chicago University Press, Chicago, IL

Bregman A 1990 *Auditory Scene Analysis*. MIT Press, Cambridge, MA

Chomsky N 1986 *Knowledge of Language: Its Nature, Origin and Use.* Praeger, Westport, CT

Curtiss S 1977 *Genie: A Psycholinguistic Study of a Modern-day 'Wild Child.'* Academic Press, New York

Dawkins R 1983 Universal Darwinism. In: Bendall D S (ed.) *Evolution from Molecules to Men.* Cambridge University Press, Cambridge

Dawkins R 1986 *The Blind Watchmaker.* Norton, New York and London

Deacon T W 1988 Human brain evolution. Vol. II: Embryology and allometry. In: Jerison H J, Jerison I (eds.) *Intelligence and Evolutionary Biology.* Springer Verlag, Berlin

Ferguson C A 1977 Baby talk as a simplified register. In: Snow C E, Ferguson C A (eds.) *Talking to Children: Language Input and Acquisition.* Cambridge University Press, Cambridge

Fernald A 1984 The perceptual and affective salience of mothers' speech to infants. In: Feagans L, Garvey C, Golinkoff R (eds.) *The Origins and Growth of Communication.* Ablex, New Brunswick, NJ

Fifer W, Moon C 1989 Early voice discrimination. In: von Euler C, Forssberg H, Lagercrantz H *Neurobiology of Early Infant Behavior.* Stockton Press, New York

Fossey D 1983 *Gorillas in the Mist.* Houghton Mifflin, Boston

Goodall J 1986 *The Chimpanzees of Gombe.* Harvard University Press, Cambridge, MA

Gould S J 1979 Sizing up human intelligence. In: *Ever Since Darwin.* Norton, New York

Hayes K J, Hayes C 1951 The intellectual development of a home-raised chimpanzee. *Proceedings of the American Philosophical Society* **95**: 105–09

Herman L M, Richards D G, Wolz J P 1984 Comprehension of sentences by bottle-nosed dolphins. *Cognition* **16**: 129–219

Isaac G 1978 The food-sharing behavior of protohuman hominids. *Scientific American*: 90–108

Jakobson R 1941 *Child Language, Aphasia and Phonological Universals.* Mouton, The Hague

Jerison H J 1980 The evolution of intelligence. *Interciencia* **5(5)**: 273–80

Johnson J S, Newport E L 1989 Critical period effects in second language learning: The influence of maturational state on the acquisition of English as a second language. *Cognitive Psychology* **21**: 60–99

Kimura D 1979 Neuromotor mechanisms in the evolution of human communication. In: Steklis H D, Raleigh M J (eds.) *Neurobiology of Social Communication in Primates.* Academic Press, New York

Kluender K R, Diehl R, Killeen P 1987 Japanese quail can learn phonetic categories. *Science* **237**: 1195–97

Kohler K 1990 Segmental reduction in connected speech: Phonological facts and phonetic explanations. In: Hardcastle W J, Marchal A (eds.) *Speech Production and Speech Modeling.* Kluwer, Dordrecht

Ladefoged P 1993 *A Course in Phonetics.* Harcourt Brace and Jovanovich, Orlando, FL

Lashley K S 1951 The problem of serial order in behavior. In: Jeffress L A (ed.) *Cerebral Mechanisms in Behavior.* Wiley, New York

Lenneberg E 1967 *Biological Foundations of Language.* Wiley, New York

Liberman A M, Mattingly I 1985 The motor theory of speech perception revised. *Cognition* **21**: 1–36

Liberman A M, Mattingly I 1989 A specialization for speech perception. *Science* **243**: 489–94

Lieberman P 1991 *Uniquely Human.* Harvard University Press, Cambridge, MA

Lindblom B 1990 Explaining phonetic variation: A sketch of the H&H Theory. In: Hardcastle W J, Marchal A (eds.) *Speech Production and Speech Modeling.* Kluwer, Dordrecht

Lindblom B, Krull D, Stark J 1992 Phonetic systems and phonological development. In: de Boysson-Bardies B, de Schonen S, Jusczyk P, MacNeilage P, Morton J (eds.) *Developmental Neurocognition: Speech and Face Processing in the First Year of Life.* Kluwer, Holland

MacNeilage P F 1991 The 'ostural origins' theory of primate neurobiological asymmetries. In: Krasnegor N, Rumbaugh D, Studdert-Kennedy M, Schiefelbusch R (eds.) *Biobehavioral Foundations of Language Development.* LEA, Hillsdale, NJ

MacNeilage P F, Davis B L 1990 Acquisition of speech production: The achievement of segmental independence In: Hardcastle W J, Marchal A (eds.) *Speech Production and Speech Modeling.* Kluwer, Dordrecht

MacNeilage P F, Studdert-Kennedy M, Lindblom B 1987 Primate handedness reconsidered. *Behavioral and Brain Sciences* **10**: 247–303

MacNeilage P F, Studdert-Kennedy M, Lindblom B 1988 Primate handedness: A foot in the door. *Behavioral and Brain Sciences* **11**: 737–44

MacNeilage P F, Studdert-Kennedy M, Lindblom B 1993 Hand signals: Right side, left brain and the origin of language. *The Sciences* **Jan/Feb**: 32–37

Marler P 1984 Song learning: Innate species differences in the learning process. In: Marler P, Terrace H S (eds.) *The Biology of Learning.* Springer Verlag, New York

Meltzoff A N 1986 Imitation, intermodal representation and the origins of mind. In: Lindblom B, Zetterström R (eds.) *Precursors of Early Speech.* Stockton Press, New York

Miller G A 1977 *Spontaneous Apprentices.* Seabury Press, New York

Miller G A 1991 *The Science of Words.* Freeman, New York

Mulford R 1988 First words of the blind child. In: Smith M D, Locke J L (eds.) *The Emergent Lexicon.* Academic Press, New York

Newport E L 1988 Constraints on learning and their role in language acquisition: Studies of the acquisition of American Sign Language. *Language Sciences* **10**: 147–72

Nottebohm F 1971 Neural lateralization of vocal control in a passerine bird. Vol. I: Song. *Journal of Experimental Zoology* **177**: 229–61

Nottebohm F 1972 Neural lateralization of vocal control in a passerine bird. Vol. II: Subsong, calls and a theory of vocal learning. *Journal of Experimental Zoology* **179**: 35–49

Ohala J J 1981 The listener as a source of sound change. *Papers from the Parasession on Language and Behavior.* Chicago Linguistic Society, Chicago,

Ohala J J 1984 An ethological perspective on common cross-language utilization of F0 of voice. *Phonetica* **41**: 1–16

Oller D K 1980 The emergence of the sounds of speech in infancy. In: Yeni-Komshian G H, Kavanagh J F, Ferguson C A (eds.) *Child Phonology. Vol. 1: Production.* Academic Press, New York

Oller D K, Eilers R E, Bull D H, Carney A E 1985 Prespeech vocalizations of a deaf infant: A comparison with normal metaphonological development. *Journal of Speech and Hearing Research* **28**: 47–63

Pierce J D 1985 A review of attempts to condition operantly Alloprimate vocalizations. *Primates* **26**: 202–13

Pinker S, Bloom P 1990 Natural language and natural selection. *Behavioral and Brain Sciences* **13**: 707–84

Poizner H, Klima E S, Bellugi U 1987 *What the Hands Reveal About the Brain.* MIT Press, Cambridge, MA

Premack D 1986 *Gavagai!* MIT Press, Cambridge, MA

Rosenblum L A (ed.) 1975 *Primate Behavior. Developments in Field and Laboratory Research,* vol. 4. Academic Press, New York

Roug L, Landberg I, Lundberg L-J 1989 Phonetic development in early infancy: A study of four Swedish children during the first eighteen months of life. *Journal of Child Language* **16**: 19–40

Seyfarth R M, Cheney D L, Marler P 1980 Monkey responses to three different alarm calls: Evidence for semantic communication and predator classification. *Science* **210**: 801–03

Shepard R 1984 Ecological constraints on internal representation: Resonant kinematics of perceiving, imagining, thinking and dreaming. *Psychological Review* **91(4)**: 417–47

Simon H A 1969 The architecture of complexity. In: Simon H A (ed.) *The Sciences of The Artificial.* MIT Press, Cambridge, MA

Stoel-Gammon C 1988 Prelinguistic vocalizations of hearing-impaired and normally hearing subjects: A comparison of consonantal inventories. *Journal of Speech and Hearing Disorders* **53(3)**: 302–15

Studdert-Kennedy M 1983 On learning to speak. *Human Neurobiology* **2**: 191–95

Studdert-Kennedy M 1986 Sources of variability in early speech development. In: Perkell J S, Klatt D H (eds.) *Invariance and Variability of Speech Processes.* LEA, Hillsdale, NJ

Sutton D 1979 Mechanisms underlying vocal control in non-human primates. In: Steklis H D, Raleigh M J (eds.) *Neurobiology of Social Communication in Primates.* Academic Press, New York

Terrace H S 1979 *Nim.* Knopf, New York

Tobias P V 1987 The brain of *homo habilis*: A new level of organization in cerebral evolution. *Journal of Human Evolution* **16**: 741–61

Trevarthen C, Marwick H 1986 Signs of motivation for speech in infants, and the nature of a mother's support for development of language In: Lindblom B, Zetterström R (eds.) *Precursors of Early Speech.* Stockton Press, New York

Vihman M M 1990 The ontogeny of phonetic gestures: Speech production. In: Mattingly I, Studdert-Kennedy M (eds.) *Modularity and the Motor Theory of Speech Perception.* LEA, Hillsdale, NJ

Vihman M M, Macken M A, Miller R, Simmons H, Miller J 1985 From babbling to speech: A reassessment of the continuity issue *Lg* **61(3)**: 395–443

Warden C J, Warner L H 1928 The sensory capacities and intelligence of dogs, with a report on the ability of the noted dog 'Fellow' to respond to verbal stimuli. *Quarterly Review of Biology* **3**: 1–28

Warren 1982 *Auditory Perception.* Pergamon, New York

Werker J F, Pegg J E 1992 Infant speech perception and phonological acquisition. In: Ferguson C A, Menn L, Stoel-Gammon C (eds.) *Phonological Development.* York Press, Parkton, MD

Wilson E O 1975 *Sociobiology.* Belknap Press, Cambridge, MA

Aging and Language

J. Maxim

There is evidence that normal aging is accompanied by changes in the ability to process, understand, and use language. These changes have been shown to affect the ability to listen, speak, read, and write. There is also great variation in performance among elderly people under experimental conditions. A distinction has to be made between normal or 'senescent' changes and abnormal or 'senile' changes. This may seem a somewhat artificial approach but it is necessary to distinguish language changes which might normally happen with increasing age from those which result from disease processes commonly associated with aging (see *Acquired Causes*).

A second crucial aspect of language change with age concerns the systems involved in these changes. Because the ability to process and use language for communication involves both language and cognition, it is essential to disentangle the strands of these mental processes in order to establish why language may change with increasing age. While research has not yet explained why language-processing changes, some of the processes which may change have been identified. However, it is likely to be some time before the necessary synthesis of neuro-imaging, cognitive neuropsychology, and psycholinguistics provides possible explanations.

1. Language Changes in the Elderly Population

The predominant view of language has traditionally been that it is a skill that shows little change in adult life. Research in the 1950s on the IQ (intelligence quotient) of cross-sections of the population suggested that verbal IQ changed very little with increasing age until a person reached their seventies, when there was some decline on complex tasks. Such aspects of language as vocabulary were shown to change hardly at all. While some longitudinal studies have shown that healthy elderly people remained remarkably stable on verbal tests, ill health has been linked to IQ decline.

In IQ testing, language has been used to investigate various cognitive skills. One aspect of language which did show a steady decline with age was psychomotor speed, i.e., the ability to coordinate mental and physical action. Later research suggested that language comprehension changed with age, particularly the ability to understand text and the ability to understand certain types of complex sentence structures. Research into spoken language has produced far more equivocal results, but this area is hampered by methodological problems of comparing age cohorts significantly different in terms of health, education, and social conditions (see Maxim and Bryan 1994).

1.1 Aging and Language Processing

Language can be viewed as a set of processes which function together but can be tested separately. This enables specific questions to be asked about language change with age, particularly whether it is the storage facilities or the processes linking them that change with age.

Using this approach to look at vocabulary skills, research suggests that elderly people may continue to expand their vocabulary store as long as they remain healthy and active. Their ability both to recognize words as part of their vocabulary and to recognize the meaning of these words does not change with age, but they may find difficulty in actively retrieving a particular word when they need it. Generative naming tasks, for example, naming as many animals or cities as possible in a given time, show an age deficit, although the elderly can achieve better scores if the time element is waived. The storage facilities remain, but retrieval is less efficient. The term 'benign senescent forgetfulness' has been used to describe this irritating facet of aging.

Studies of single-word processing have concluded that the normal, healthy, elderly person has retained memory stores for vocabulary and the networks needed for semantic association between words, but that word retrieval is slower and more difficult when the task involves retrieving single words in isolation. There is some evidence that the elderly benefit more than younger people when asked to retrieve a single word for a particular context. Far less is known about the ability to process sentences and larger units of text, but, in sentence repetition and correction tasks, the elderly perform less well on lengthy or complex sentences (see Sect. 1.2, and Kemper 1992).

Language processing in the elderly has also been investigated to establish whether there is a difference between language competence and language performance. The evidence heavily favors an intact language competence and minimally impaired language performance, both in understanding and language production.

1.2 Aging and Understanding Language

Deterioration in the ability to hear is common in old age, but not inevitable, and obviously affects the individual's everyday ability to understand. Experiments have also shown that elderly people have greater difficulty understanding sentences that are complex either in grammatical form or in terms of the semantic structure, or indeed in both. This does not mean that the elderly cannot understand these particular sentence types, but rather that they fail to understand a percentage of the sentences presented to them: their overall performance is worse than that of younger people on the same task. Sentence length does not appear to be an important factor in the ability of the elderly to understand language, but both increased sentence complexity and speed of delivery have been shown to impair the ability of older people to understand (Jaccoby and Hay 1998).

The sentence types which cause particular difficulty in understanding for the elderly are also sentences on which younger people do not perform at ceiling level. Most of these sentence types place a particular load on working memory to help processing. The sentence is constructed in such a way that a parsing mechanism cannot perform at a first attempt and requires a second pass before the process is complete, for example, sentences in which the action does not take place in the same order as the clauses within the sentence, sentences containing a left-branching subordinate clause, and ambiguous sentences.

There is further evidence that, when listening to a passage, the elderly do not pick up the same information as efficiently as younger people. Listening to and understanding text is a more complex process than sentence comprehension, and a number of different factors appear to affect the performance of older people, who do not necessarily use the same strategies as younger people to remember, and who are worse at remembering texts which are not logically ordered. If the topic of the text is well known to them, older people perform as well as or better than younger people (Light 1992).

The contextual information in a passage and the way that it is manipulated have also been studied. Both older and younger people seem able to make similar use of context to aid their processing of a passage, but, if there is intervening information or if inferences to be understood, older people perform less well than younger people. There is also some evidence to suggest that older people, while remembering specific facts or actions in a passage, have greater difficulty than younger people in processing grammatically encoded information about the relationships between the events (Kemper 1992, Hamm and Hasher 1992).

1.3 Aging and Spoken Language

Although the production of fine, rapid movements of the lips and tongue does slow with age, the ability to produce intelligible speech changes very little unless dentition is compromised. However, studies show that the age of a speaker can be guessed with considerable accuracy, even when only a prolonged vowel sound is heard, reflecting age changes in vocal quality, vocal stability, and voice pitch. The fundamental frequency of male voices decreases over adult life until about 60 years of age, when it begins to rise again. In adult women, fundamental frequency remains stable until early old age, when it decreases. However, there is also some evidence of ethnic and cultural variation in voice changes with age.

Phonological and grammatical systems within the clause appear to be almost impervious to aging. Indeed, these systems even seem resistant to change in diseases causing dementia, such as Alzheimer's disease. Some studies suggest that the healthy elderly make more errors in grammatical form than younger people. There is also some evidence that the elderly may have greater difficulty in monitoring their own output, in making language repairs when necessary and in producing left-branching grammatical structures (sentence-initial subordinate clauses). However, the small number of studies and the different methods of analysis used in them mean the evidence is equivocal.

Studies of connected discourse produced by elderly people suggest that there may be errors of reference and fewer propositions than in the language of younger people, but there is little evidence to suggest a sentence-length difference among young, middle-aged, and older adults. There may be a reduction in types of clause structure and verb phrases. The difficulty with these studies is that they have mostly not been replicated, often use widely differing parameters, and do not all control adequately for cognitive function, education, and sociolinguistic variables (see Brownell and Joanette 1993).

Studies which allow the elderly to tell their own stories usually report less difference in language use between elderly and young people than studies which require the subjects to retell a story provided for them.

All these studies suggest some diminution in language performance, but the elderly are still able to communicate adequately. Indeed, some studies of storytelling suggest that well-rehearsed older people are more fluent and better at this skill than younger people (Kemper 1992).

1.4 Aging, Language, and Modality Differences

Performance in tasks requiring reading and writing skills is not directly comparable to performance in tasks requiring understanding of spoken language or spoken-language output. Studies using material in a written and spoken form generally show that older people do better on the written material, as do younger people; but, on delayed recall, the elderly perform worse with written material. The writing and speaking styles of older adults are more divergent than those of younger people. There is therefore some evidence that the elderly perform more variably across modalities of input than do younger people (Kemper 1992).

1.5 Aging and Communication

Studies have investigated whether the elderly change their communicative strategies to compensate for deficits in peripheral senses or changes in language processing. Apart from unsubstantiated suggestions that the elderly withdraw from active communication within the community in which they are living, there is no evidence of change, nor is there evidence that elderly people in their own homes communicate any differently from those in sheltered accommodation.

2. Aging, Cognition, and Language

Aging, cognition, and language have complex interactions, but it is clear that some cognitive functions which support and interact with language also change with age. In particular, aspects of memory, attention, and certain cognitive skills such as problem-solving, are known to change with age and will impinge on the older person's ability to process language (see Brownwell and Joanette 1993).

2.1 Aging, Memory, and Language

A dominant theme in gerontology research is the role of memory in language changes with age. Memory is needed for encoding into memory stores, for retaining language in short- or long-term stores, and for retrieving from stores. There are several types of memory which show differential change in normal aging, but almost all aspects of memory are important for language in some way. While experimental evidence suggests that several types of memory are compromised in the elderly population, these losses rarely do more than inconvenience the individual in everyday life (Craik and Jennings 1992, Jaccoby and Hay 1998, Schacter 1996). Because such losses can cause anxiety, it is important to emphasize that some studies show that the elderly can perform as well as younger people if they are given techniques to improve memory, if the task contains information familiar to them, or if they are given time to practice the task (Meyer et al. 1998).

This raises the issue of the roles of different types of memory in language processing, considered an online or automatic process in normal circumstances. When language processing is compromised and requires more effort, the role of different types of memory may be adapted so that language can be stored and processed slowly. Episodic memory, which is memory for time-related or autobiographical events, and working memory do show an age decrement while semantic memory, concerned with language and knowledge, is more resistant to aging.

The semantic memory store is well preserved in relation to what is contained in the memory, and healthy elderly people continue to take in new words to the store, although semantic memory processing becomes more variable with age. Retrieval becomes more difficult, but the ability to recognize words in the memory and to use networks of associations between the words is well maintained. Again, these changes usually do not affect normal communication, although the elderly frequently complain of difficulty in retrieving items from semantic memory.

2.2 Aging and Attention

Attention is central to linguistic or cognitive processing. The ability to process language may therefore be limited by the attentional capacity available to the individual. Sustained attention (vigilance), which requires the person to focus on one task, does not change with age, but selective attention, the ability to ignore irrelevant information, may do so. Research in this field has consistently shown that the elderly have more difficulty than younger people in allocating attention to the target task.

There is some evidence for modality differences in attention. Early results on tasks which require use of the visual modality suggested that the elderly had greater difficulty than younger people in ignoring irrelevant information, but later research has shown that they can perform equally well, though they are penalized by visual perceptual problems which the younger groups do not have. Studies using dichotic listening tasks show that the elderly can perform well on sustained attention tasks but show decrements on some selective attention tasks which require more effortful processing or speed of response. These listening tasks may be compromised by 'presbyacusis' (age-related hearing loss); some experiments have therefore used 'young elderly' people who have no hearing loss; but there are similar patterns of performance even in this group (Hartley 1992).

2.3 Aging, Problem-solving, and Classification Skills

One common image of aging is that of increased rigidity or difficulty in changing set. Cross-sectional studies on age differences in problem-solving ability have often used tasks that require language mediation. These studies have consistently shown that, in novel situations, elderly people find it difficult to generate the concepts necessary to solve a problem. In comprehending ambiguous sentences, the elderly are less likely than younger people to interpret both meanings. They also find it difficult to find strategies or to change to new strategies. However, when given a strategy such as category classification, to help with, say,

remembering word lists, the performance of the elderly improves, although not usually to the level of the younger group. Some studies have found no differences in these skills between groups of highly educated older and younger people and have concluded that these skills do not show an age decrement if they are in everyday use. The very few longitudinal studies of problem-solving abilities also suggest that the age decrement is very small (Salthouse 1992).

3. Normal and Abnormal Language Changes

It is not always easy to differentiate between language change during normal aging and those language changes due to age-related diseases. In the early stages of Alzheimer's disease, for example, which causes dementia, language testing can aid diagnosis but cannot yet confirm it. This area requires further research into what is retained in normal aging in order to establish a baseline for investigating what degenerates in abnormal aging. There is, however, a considerable overlap in performance on language tests and in communicative competence between the normal, healthy elderly and those suffering from a range of conditions such as depression, aphasia (a language disorder most commonly caused by stroke), and states of confusion caused by ill health (see Maxim and Bryan 1994).

4. Summary

Research into language change with age is complicated by the different methodologies and theories used and by the small number of replicated studies in this area; but there are a few leads. Language does change with increasing age, but, unless illness intervenes, the changes do not affect everyday communication. What can make communication harder for the elderly person are the changes in the peripheral senses, particularly hearing and sight. In addition, language processing is slower in older adults and, under stressful or multi-input conditions, some difficulty may be noticed.

Under experimental conditions, the healthy elderly perform less well on language tasks than younger people, but there is no evidence to suggest that the underlying competence of the language system itself is compromised. While the language system works more slowly in older people, other cognitive parameters of language such as attentional resources and certain aspects of memory may also show small changes which add to the language-processing load.

Bibliography

Brownell H H, Joanette Y 1993 *Narrative Discourse in Neurologically Impaired and Normal Aging Adults*. Singular, San Diego, CA

Hamm V P, Hasher L 1992 Age and the availability of inferences. *Psychology and Ageing* 56–64

Hartley A A 1992 Attention. In: Craik F I M, Salthouse T A (eds.) *The Handbook of Aging and Cognition*. Erlbaum, Hillsdale, NJ

Jaccoby L L, Hay J F 1998 Age-related Deficits in Memory: Theory and Application. In: Conway M A, Gathercole S E, Cornoldi C (eds.) *Theories of Memory*, vol. 2 Psychology Press, Hove, East Sussex

Kemper S 1992 Language and Aging. In: Craik F I M, Salthouse T A (eds.) *The Handbook of Aging and Cognition*. Erlbaum, Hillsdale, NJ

Light L L 1992 The Organization of Memory in Old Age. In: Craik F I M, Salthouse T A (eds.) *The Handbook of Aging and Cognition*. Erlbaum, Hillsdale, NJ

Maxim J, Bryan K 1994 *Language of the Elderly*. Whurr, London

Meyer B J F, Young C J, Bartlett B J 1988 *Memory Improved: Reading and Memory Enhancement across the Life Span through Strategic Text Structures*. Erlbaum, Hillsdale, NJ

Salthouse T A 1992 Reasoning and Spatial Abilities. In: Craik F I M, Salthouse T A (eds.) *The Handbook of Aging and Cognition*. Erlbaum, Hillsdale, NJ

Schacter D L 1996 *Searching for Memory*. Basic Books, New York

Pragmatic Principles in Verbal Communication

O. Togeby

A communicational event is not a brute fact, but a social act made possible by shared principles and rules among the participants in the event. Communication is both controlled by pragmatic principles, and, as far as verbal behavior is concerned, governed by conventional grammatical rules.

1. Principles and Rules

In grammatical description, it is normal to talk about rules; if constitutive grammatical rules are broken, the sentence will not be acceptable, resulting in no meaning and no communication; if conventional regulative (strategic) grammatical rules are broken, the meaning will normally get across, but it will result in social friction. A constitutive rule (Searle 1969) is a *sine qua non* for the type of event in question, while regulative rules only regulate existing types of action. In chess, for example, the constitutive rules define how to move the pieces and how the game is won, while the strategic rules establish how to make a good opening.

As opposed to conventional rules, principles are motivated and negotiable (Leech 1983). There are four types of pragmatic principles in the literature:

(a) metapragmatic axioms, that is, transcendental statements, which define cooperation between communication partners, and which do not need to be proved;

(b) communicational ideals, that is, philosophically *a priori*, but normally counterfactive presumptions, made by the communication partners about the rules and goals of the interaction;

(c) maxims, that is, general guidelines for the communication of information by the utterance of a sentence, principles which cannot be broken, but which, if they are not fulfilled, will result in some extra meaning effect; and

(d) motivated super-rules and norms for politeness

and processibility, according to which so-called 'indirect speech acts' are performed and interpreted.

2. Metapragmatic Principles

Watzlawick et al. (1968) have formulated the following set of metapragmatic principles, or axioms, for communication:

(a) One cannot not communicate. All behavior is interpreted as a communication by the other persons in the situation.

(b) Every communication has a content and a relationship aspect such that the latter classifies the former, and is therefore a meta-communication. Every utterance will at the same time communicate: 'This is how I see It' and 'This is how I see You and Me.' In later speech act theories, the two aspects are called 'propositional content' and 'illocutionary force,' respectively.

(c) The nature of a relationship is contingent upon the punctuation of the communicational sequences between the communicants. An utterance does not, in isolation, count as a type of speech act, but the interpretation of the utterance is always dependent on the context, especially on whether the utterance is taken to be the initial act of an interaction or a reaction to the other's act.

(d) Human beings communicate both digitally and analogically. Digital (verbal) language has a highly complex and powerful logical syntax, but lacks adequate semantics in the field of interpersonal relationship, while analogic language (style, body language) possesses the semantics but has no adequate syntax for unambiguous definition of the nature of relationships. Translation between digital and analogical communication is very difficult.

(e) All communicational interchanges are either symmetrical or complementary, depending on whether they are based on equality or difference. Competition in a debate is symmetrical, and interaction between mother and child, teacher and pupil is typically complementary.

Searle's Principle of Expressibility (Searle 1969) has the same status as metapragmatic axioms: Anything that can be meant can be said. This means that if explicit verbal communication is analyzed and explained, all other types of communication are explained too. This principle of expressibility is obviously in contradiction with the problems of translation between digital and analogical language, and with the principle of relevance in actual communication.

3. The Ideal Speech Situation

The communication process is explained (Habermas 1970, 1971, 1976) as being constituted by the anticipated ideal speech situation, according to which the speech acts form a system which finally enables us to identify three basic differentiations of intersubjectivity.

(a) People discriminate between *being* and *appearance* by expressions which refer to the truth-value of the utterance (to claim, to dispute), between *being* and *essence* by expressions which refer to the self-representation of persons (to reveal, to hide), and between *being* and *ought to be* by expressions which refer to the normative status of rules (to prescribe, to follow).

(b) Pure intersubjectivity is determined by a symmetrical relation between I and You, and between We and They.

(c) The ideal speech situation exists only where there is complete symmetry in the distribution of assertion and disputation, revelation and hiding, prescription and following among the communication partners.

Insofar as we have mastered the means of constructing an ideal speech situation, we can conceive the ideas of truth, freedom, and justice—only as ideas, since on the strength of communicative competence we cannot produce the ideal speech situation independent of the empirical structures of the social system to which we belong; we can only anticipate it.

The communicator undertakes to communicate only free, true, and just information to the audience, and the audience is only able to interpret the text if it has confidence in the communicator's implicit guarantee of truth, freedom, and justice. The audience may often have been disappointed or even deceived, yet it must always already have presumed the ideals of truth, freedom, and justice of the utterance if it wants to participate in the communication of it. The audience will only be able to add the necessary context for interpretation of the text if it acknowledges one true, free, and just intention behind all the words and structures in the utterance.

4. The Cooperation Principle

Best known among pragmatic principles is Grice's Cooperative Principle (Grice 1975): make your contribution as is required, at the stage at which it occurs, by the accepted purpose or direction of the talk exchange in which you are engaged! The other four Grician maxims are derived from this supermaxim: The Maxim of Quality: try to make your contribution one that is true, or more specifically: (a) do not say what you believe to be false, and (b) do not say that for which you lack adequate evidence! The Maxim of Quantity: (a) make your contribution as informative as the current purpose of the exchange requires, (b) do not make your contribution more informative than is required! The Maxim of Relevance: make your contributions relevant! The Maxim of Manner: be perspicuous, and, specifically: (a) avoid obscurity, (b) avoid ambiguity, (c) be brief, (d) be orderly!

The Grician maxims are of another epistemological status than the metapragmatic axioms and the communicational ideals. They are not transcendental conditions of communication, but general pragmatic guidelines presumed by the partners of communication. In spite of their syntactic form as imperatives, the four maxims and the supermaxim are not, on the other hand, normative rules. The maxims are psychologically active principles which cannot be broken, but only violated by a clash between two maxims, or exploited. But even when they are violated or exploited (in the form of irony, metaphor, or meiosis) it will only result in a specific conversational implicature, that is, some extra communicated meaning. *You are the cream in my coffee* gets its meaning from the obvious categorial falsity. A 'person' cannot be 'cream,' but in virtue of the cooperation principle it must mean something relevant to the hearer, presumably something like: 'You are my pride and joy.'

5. The Relevance Principle

Since Grice's original formulation of the maxims in 1967, many authors have discussed the epistemological status of the maxims and their internal ranking. Sperber and Wilson (1986) have suggested that all the mental processes of communication can be explained by the principle of relevance alone if it is reformulated as follows:

(a) An act of physically expressing something carries a guarantee of relevance, and this fact—which is called the 'Principle of Relevance'—makes manifest the intention behind the utterance.

(b) Contextual information is needed to resolve what should be seen as the semantic incompleteness and vagueness of all linguistically coded messages. At every stage of the inferential interpretation process, that is, in disambiguation, reference assignment and semantic enrichment, the hearer will, because of the guarantee of relevance, choose the context involving the most relevance and least processing effort.

(c) An utterance is chosen in accordance with the Principle of Optimal Relevance if the information which the communicator intends to convey to the addressee is relevant enough to make it worth the addressee's while to process the physical stimulus, and if the stimulus is the most relevant one the communicator could have used to communicate the assumptions. Every act of physical communication communicates the presumption of its own optimal relevance.

(d) A speaker aiming at optimal relevance will leave implicit as an implicature of the utterance everything the hearer can be trusted to supply from the context and from encyclopedic knowledge using less effort than would be needed to process an explicit prompt. The more information the communicator leaves implicit as implicatures, the greater the degree of mutual understanding presupposed to exist between the communicants.

6. Principles of Politeness and Processibility

Pragmatic principles can be taken to be mere strategic problem-solving super-rules. It is taken for granted that all communication participants have a face, that is, they have two particular needs—roughly, the need to be unimpeded (negative face) and the need to be approved of in certain respects (positive face), and they are rational agents, that is, they choose the means which will satisfy their ends.

Given that face consists of a set of needs which are only satisfiable by the actions of others, it will generally be in the mutual interest of both partners of communication to maintain each other's face. So the speaker will want to maintain the hearer's face, unless he or she can get the hearer to maintain the speaker's face without recompense, by coercion, trickery, etc. (Brown and Levinson 1987).

Because regulative speech acts, that is, speech acts which regulate the future acts of one of the communication partners—impositives and commissives—intrinsically threaten the negative face of the other (the need of unimpediment), the speaker will want to minimize the face threat of these speech acts by tact and generosity: he or she will want to minimize cost to other; minimize benefit to self.

Because expressives and assertions potentially threaten the other's positive face (needs of approval) the speaker will want to minimize the face threat of these

speech acts by approbation, modesty, agreement, and sympathy: he or she will want to minimize dispraise to other; minimize praise to self; minimize disagreement between self and other; minimize antipathy between self and other.

The aim of these politeness maxims is to avoid communication conflicts in situations where speaker and hearer have conflicting interests and desires. The speaker has to minimize the expression of his or her own wants and interests in order to save the other's face, and to get the intentions of the speech act across without conflict. Instead of saying: *Take me home!* the speaker may say: *Are you able to take me home?* The imperative will put the other in a situation where a refutation would be face-threatening, while the interrogative form makes a refutation without conflict possible: *No, I am not able* does not threaten the face of the one who asked (Leech 1983).

One example of the rationally motivated problem-solving super-rules is the Processibility Principle:

(a) Messages must be comprehensible, clear, brief, orderly, easy to process. The end-focus principle derived from this super-principle states the iconicity of information structure.

(b) In the process of information, the speaker refers to what is already known to the hearer at the beginning of the utterance, and predicates the new, relevant, and focused information at the end (Leech 1983).

Bibliography

Beaugrande R-A de, Dressler W U 1981 *Introduction to Text Linguistics*. Longman, London

Brown G, Yule G 1983 *Discourse Analysis*. Cambridge University Press, Cambridge

Brown P, Levinson S C 1987 *Politeness: Some Universals in Language Usage*. Cambridge University Press, Cambridge

Grice H P (1967) 1975 Logic and conversation. In: Cole P, Morgan J L (eds.) *Syntax and Semantics 3: Speech Acts*. Academic Press, New York

Habermas J 1970 Toward a theory of communicative competence. In: Dreitzel H P (ed.) *Recent Sociology 2*. Macmillan, New York

Habermas J 1971 Vorbereitende Bemerkungen zu einer Theorie der kommunikativen Kompetenz. In: Habermas J, Luhmann N (eds.) *Theorie der Gesellschaft oder Sozialtechnologie*. Suhrkamp Verlag, Frankfurt

Habermas J 1976 Was heisst Universalpragmatik? In: Apel K-O (ed.) *Sprachpragmatik und Philosophie*. Suhrkamp Verlag, Frankfurt

Leech G N 1983 *Principles of Pragmatics*. Longman, London

Levinson S C 1983 *Pragmatics*. Cambridge University Press, Cambridge

Searle J R 1969 *Speech Acts*. Cambridge University Press, London

Sperber D, Wilson D 1986 *Relevance: Communication and Cognition*. Blackwell, Oxford

Watzlawick P, Beavin J H, Jackson D D 1968 *Pragmatics of Human Communication*. Faber and Faber, London

Sociolinguistics and Language Pathology
W. Li and H. Zhu

1. Introduction

Sociolinguistics is a discipline which studies the situated language behaviors of individuals in their social groups. Sociolinguists argue that language is best studied in the context of its use. For example, the following utterances perform a similar speech act, that is, asking the hearer to close the door, but they tend to be used in very different situations, to different addresses, and for different purposes:

(a) Would you be kind enough as to close the door?
(b) Do you mind closing the door?
(c) Close the door please.
(d) Door!
(e) Were you born in a barn?

In the meantime, sociolinguists suggest that language should be studied in relation to the speaker, especially to his or her social identity. No two speakers speak in exactly the same way at all times. People often use language to signal their membership of particular groups. Social status, sex, age, ethnicity, and the kinds of social networks people belong to turn out to be important dimensions of identity. In this chapter, we shall outline the key concepts and methods of sociolinguistics and discuss its relevance to language pathology. (In writing this chapter, we have benefited from discussions with colleagues in the Department of Speech, University of Newcastle upon Tyne. Brigid O'Connor read and commented carefully on an early draft of the chapter.)

2. The 'Standard' Language and Language Standard

A person's speech and language is considered to be disordered when it deviates sufficiently from a norm to interfere with communication. The norm is usually defined as the phonological, lexical, syntactic, and discourse features of the standard language. The concept of a 'standard' in any language is an out-growth of a number of social, political, economic, and educational factors. Usually, the language varieties spoken by the socially, politically, economically, and educationally privileged and powerful groups come to gain sufficient prestige to become the standard variety of the language. In Britain and the USA, for example, the so-called standard English is the variety of language usually associated with white, middle to upper class, well-educated, English-as-first-language speakers. Such standard forms become tantamount to official versions of the language that hold currency in education, even when no official language has been designated by the national government.

A moment's reflection, however, tells us that most people grow up speaking the non-standard varieties of language first, and only acquire the 'standard' at a later age, if ever. Language acquisition takes place in a social context, and this social context is first and foremost the family and community where the interaction is mostly informal and spontaneous. Nevertheless, young children are capable of style-shifting before they reach adolescence. The following two extracts are taken from an interview by Romaine (1975: 204–5) with a six-year-old girl in Edinburgh:

(a) I fall out (au-1) the bed. She falls out (au-1) the bed and we pull off the covers. I fell out (au-1) the bed so D. says, 'Where are you J?' I says, 'I'm down (au-1) here'. She says, 'Come up. Babies *dinnae* do that. They should be in their cot' (gs-1). So she gets out (au-1) the bed. She falls out (au-1) cause she bumps her head on the wall and she says, 'Oh, this is a hard bed too.' So she says, 'Oh, I'm on the *floor*' (e).
(b) It's a house (au-0), my house (au-0) that I live in now (au-0), cause I flitted (I-2) (gs-1). The house (au-0) is still in a mess anyway. It's still got plaster and I've no fireplace now (au-0), all blocked up. Working (ing-1) men plastered where they used to be, there and there, and they did (I-1) the same to (gs-0) the fireplace. They just knocked it all out (au-0) (gs-1).

We can see that (a) is much closer to the Scots end of this girl's repertoire than (b). All of the variables Romaine studied have non-standard realizations in (a), e.g., (au-1) indicates a pronunciation with /u/ instead of (au) in words like *down*; (gs-1) indicates the use of a glottal stop; (ing-1) indicates the use of [n]. There are also other marked Scots forms in the first extract such as the pronunciation /fler/ for 'floor' and the use of the Scots negative form *dinnae* instead of English *don't*. Extract (b) is by comparison much closer to standard Scottish English.

Style-shifting is an important sociolinguistic concept. The ability to move from one speech style to another, according to context, is an integral part of a speaker's communicative competence. In the meantime, sociolinguists suggest that stylistic variations in the speech of individual speakers often echo the variations which exist between speakers of different social background and characteristics. Sociolinguists argue that linguistic features that are commonly found in less formal contexts also tend to be more common in the speech of lower social class speakers generally. Reid (1978) studied the speech of 11-year-old boys in three different schools in Edinburgh, representing three social classes (middle middle class, upper working class, and middle working class). The children's speech was recorded in four situations: reading a text, interview with an adult, peer-group discussion, and

Table 1. Percentage of non-standard variations in the speech of Edinburgh schoolboys in four styles.

	Reading	Interview	Peer group	Playground
(ing)	14	45	54	59
(gs)	25	71	84	79

playground interaction. Table 1 shows the results of two phonological variables (ing) and (gs).

As we can see, apart from the deviation in the playground situation for the variable (gs), that is the use of glottal stops, there is a progressive increase in the frequency of use of non-standard variants of both variables from reading style to playground interaction. The slope is somewhat steeper for (gs) than (ing), which perhaps indicates the greater social significance of this variable. The greatest shift occurs between the reading style and the other three spontaneous speaking styles.

Table 2 shows the effect of social grouping, in this case three different schools (1–3) representing three social classes (1 = middle working class; 2 = upper working class; 3 = middle middle class), in relation to three styles (the playground style has been excluded, because the percentages are the same as those for peer-group interaction).

These figures suggest that children of 11 years old are not only capable of adapting their speech style to different contexts (e.g., they use the non-standard variants considerably more in peer-group interaction than in one-to-one interviews and even more than in reading a text), but they are also aware of the 'norm' of the social group to which they belong (e.g., children from School 3, representing middle-middle class, use the non-standard variants much less, especially in reading style, than those from the other two schools). Social class differences in speech style already exist among young children. In fact, the patterns of social and stylistic variation in the speech of these Edinburgh boys are strikingly adultlike. Reid (1978: 169) observes that 'It is as true of the eleven year old Edinburgh boys as of older informants investigated previously in

a similar way in the United States and in Britain that there are features of their speech which relate in a systematic way to their social status and to the social context in which their speech is produced.'

Studies such as Romaine's and Reid's give rise to two important sociolinguistic principles worthy of speech-language pathologists' attention:

(a) The principle of style-shifting. There are no 'single-style' speakers of a language. Each individual controls and uses a variety of linguistic styles appropriate to the situation.
(b) The principle of non-conformity. Although speakers of similar social background and characteristics (e.g., age, sex, social class, social network, ethnicity) tend to share certain linguistic features, no two speakers speak in exactly the same way in all circumstances.

Speakers, young and old, are generally aware of the language standard of the situation in which they find themselves as well as that of the social group to which they belong, and this 'standard' has nothing to do with the so-called 'standard' language, but is defined by the context of use and the user of the language.

3. Language Standard in Bilingual and Multilingual Populations

The issue of language standard is by no means confined to monolingual speakers of major world languages such as English. Over half of the world's population is born and brought up in bilingual, or even multilingual, families and communities. Many people learn a second or third language at school and some use it regularly at work. Nevertheless, we know relatively little of the normal language development

Table 2. Percentage of non-standard variants (ing) and (gs) in relation to school attended and style.

			Reading	Interview	Group
(ing)	School	3	0	5	0
		2	7	21	45
		1	30	96	100
(gs)	School	3	20	37	58
		2	22	68	85
		1	31	98	100

Table 3. Language choice by British-born Chinese children[1].

Age	Addressee types											
	Family members						Non-family members					
	1	2	3	4	5	6	7	8	9	10	11	12
16	CE	C	CE	CE	—	CE	CE	C	CE	CE	E	E
15+	—	C	CE	CE	CE	—	CE	C	CE	CE	E	E
14	—	C	CE	CE	—	CE	CE	CE	CE	CE	E	E
12+	CE	C	CE	CE	CE	CE	CE	C	CE	CE	CE	CE
12	—	—	CE	CE	CE	—	CE	C	CE	CE	CE	CE
11+	—	C	CE	CE	CE	CE	CE	CE	CE	CE	E	E
10+	—	C	CE	CE	CE	—	CE	CE	CE	CE	E	E
10	C	C	CE	CE	—	CE	CE	C	CE	CE	E	E
9+	—	C	CE	CE	CE	CE	CE	C	CE	CE	E	E

[1] + = girls; C = Chinese; E = English;
Addressee types:
1 = grandparent, male; 2 = grandparent, female; 3 = parent, male; 4 = parent, female; 5 = brother; 6 = sister; 7 = grandparent generation, male; 8 = grandparent generation, female; 9 = parent generation, male; 10 = parent generation, female; 11 = child generation, male; 12 = child generation, female.

and behavior of bilingual and multilingual speakers. Table 3 is taken from a study of language choice patterns of British-born Chinese children in Britain (Li 1994: 94–95). As we can see, there is a wide range of variation both in terms of the addressee types and of speakers of different ages and sexes.

As in style-shifting of monolingual speakers, bilingual and multilingual speakers can switch from one language to another according to whom they are talking to, the social context of the talk, the function, and topic of the discussion. Bilingual and multilingual children learn the rules of code-switching from the community of adults and other children, and are capable of assessing the appropriate language choice of the situation, the topic, and the language preference of the listener.

It is important to remember that bilingual and multilingual speakers develop domains of competence in each language, and equal knowledge of all the languages in a bilingual or multilingual speaker's repertoire is rare. For example, a child may learn to speak Spanish as a home language with his or her parents and siblings, and later on enters an English-as-the-language-of-instruction school and interacts with English-speaking children on a daily basis. He or she may have acquired a fairly large 'domestic' vocabulary, while the 'academic' vocabulary is mostly English. The rate of language development, in terms of vocabulary and grammar, of both languages of such a child may not be equal to that seen in a monolingual child speaking only Spanish or English. Research has shown that bilingual children at different stages of development often show signs of dominance in one of their languages, and even for the so-called 'simultaneous bilinguals,' that is, children who are exposed to two languages from birth, one language often develops faster than the other, crossing all the thresholds (e.g., words and phases, simple sentences, complex sentences) first.

Moreover, normally developing bilingual speakers sometimes show speech patterns which may be considered atypical or even disordered in monolingual speakers. In a study of phonological development of 16 British-born Cantonese-English bilingual children between the age of 25 and 51 months, Dodd et al. (1996) report that the children's phonological error patterns were very different for their two emerging languages, and that these error patterns reflected delay or were atypical of monolingual children's developmental errors (see Table 4).

While delayed phonological acquisition may not be surprising—given the need to master two phonological systems in the preschool years and perhaps proportionately less exposure to each language compared with monolingual children—the observation of so many atypical error patterns was unexpected. Many of these errors are usually associated with phonological disorder in English and Cantonese respectively. However, it seems unlikely that all of the children in the sample were phonologically disordered, given an incidence rate for phonological disorder of about 3–5% for English-speaking children. Rather, it seems plausible that bilingual children have their special language learning strategies and the bilingual environment results in the development of rather unique speech patterns. The language standard for bilingual and multilingual speakers, therefore, cannot be defined without careful consideration of all the social, psychological, developmental, and linguistic factors affecting language learning.

Table 4. Expected, delayed, and atypical error patterns in Cantonese and English (number of children evidencing the error pattern).

Cantonese	English
Expected	
Final consonant deletion (2)	Final consonant deletion (1)
Stopping (3)	Stopping (1)
Fronting (4)	Fronting (1)
Affrication/Frication (1)	Cluster reduction (2)
Deaspiration (1)	Weak syllable deletion (2)
Deaffrication (1)	Gliding (3)
	Voicing (1)
	Consonant harmony (2)
Delayed	
Final consonant deletion (9)	Final consonant deletion (7)
Fronting (4)	Fronting (3)
Affrication/Frication (4)	Cluster reduction (10)
Deaffrication (5)	Consonant harmony (1)
Consonant harmony (3)	Weak syllable deletion (1)
	Voicing (2)
Atypical	
Initial consonant deletion (3)	Initial consonant deletion (1)
Voicing (8)	Voicing (2)
Backing (7)	Deaffrication (2)
Aspiration (4)	Affrication (2)
Addition (7)	Addition (2)
Gliding (4)	Nasalization (1)
	Transposition (1)

4. Sociolinguistic Methodology

The concern for systematic study of language in relation to the context of use and its user has led to the development of sociolinguistic methods of collecting and analysing language data. Sociolinguists argue that any conclusions we come to about speakers' language behavior must be solidly based on evidence, but random observations about how a few people we happen to observe use language would not enable us to make any useful generalizations about behavior, either linguistic or social. While sociolinguists draw their data from a variety of sources, including censuses, documents, surveys, and interviews, most sociolinguistic studies typically involve the investigator observing 'naturally occurring' linguistic events, for example, conversations. However, given our own sociolinguistic background, hence our perception of language standard, how can we obtain objective language data from the real world without injecting our own perspective into the data and thereby confounding the results before we even begin? How can we be sure that the data we have collected are uncontaminated by the process of investigation itself? This is a basic scientific quandary, particularly observable in the social sciences where, in almost every possible situation, there is one variable that cannot be controlled in every possible way, namely, the observer-/investigator/analyst/theorist him or herself. Sociolinguists call it the 'observer's paradox', that is, if language varies as much as it does, the presence of an observer will have some effect on that variation. How can we minimize this effect?

One possible resolution of the observer's paradox is to make use of the familiarity between the investigator and the target speakers. Some sociolinguists would use only established members of groups as fieldworkers. While this may be ideal, the nonlinguists may not be as effective in directing activities on to the focus of the investigation, and there is no assurance at all that the temporary investigator status of a group member would not itself produce odd effects in the respondent performances. In addition, the unnaturalness of the respondent's telling a familiar, in-group fieldworker what he or she already knows is an obvious drawback. Milroy et al. (1995) discuss an example from their work in the Chinese community in Tyneside in the north-east of England. In this case, while the fieldworker's relationship provided him with smooth access to the family setting which was usually closed to outsiders, it constrained in an interesting way his own linguistic behavior as well as that of the people he was observing.

In the following extract, the attempts by the fieldworker (himself Chinese) with a Chinese adult in English received little cooperation—first no response, then a minimal negative response followed by a change of addressee to exclude him temporarily from the conversation, before the informant (a woman in her early forties) turned back to address him in Chinese:

Fieldworker:
  Haven't seen Robert Ng for a long time.
Informant:
  (2.0)
Fieldworker:
  Have you seen him recently?
Informant:
  No.
Fieldworker:
  Have you seen Ah Ching?
Informant:
  ...(2.0) (To daughter)   Ning ngaw doei haai lai.
                       (Bring my shoes.)
  (To fieldworker)   Koei hoei bindou a?
                       (Where was she going?)

As Milroy et al. explain, while intergenerational communication between adults and children in the Tyneside Chinese community is normally in both English and Chinese, most adults prefer to speak and to be spoken to in Chinese. Intragenerational conversation, however, at least among adults, is most often exclusively in Chinese. Since the fieldworker in the present case was accepted by most families as a friend of the parent generation, his use of English was confined to conversation with the British-born children. It was therefore particularly difficult for him to initiate and sustain an exchange in English with a Chinese adult. Examples such as this give us further insight into the effect of the field relationships between the researcher and the people in the field on the kind of linguistic data obtained and ultimately analyzed.

A better resolution of the observer's paradox, which in principle can never be entirely resolved, is to consider the collection of speech and language samples, in whatever form it may be, as a communicative event and account for all the factors that are involved in the event. Such an approach is provided in the Ethnography of Communication model proposed by Hymes (1974). For convenience, Hymes uses the word SPEAKING as an acronym for the various factors he deems to be relevant in understanding a particular communicative event. The *Setting* and *Scene* (S) of speech are important. Setting refers to the concrete physical circumstances in which speech takes place, for example, time and place. Scene refers to the abstract psychological setting, or the cultural definition of the occasion. Within a particular setting, participants are free to change scenes, as they change the level of formality (e.g., from joyful to serious) or as they change the kind of activity in which they are involved (e.g., begin to drink or to recite poetry). The *Participants* (P) include various combinations of speaker–listener, addressor–addressee, or sender–

receiver. They generally fill certain socially defined roles. *Ends* (E) refer to the conventionally recognized and expected outcomes of an exchange as well as to the personal goals that participants seek to accomplish on particular occasions. A medical consultation has a conventionally recognizable end in view, but the various participants have different personal goals. *Act sequence* (A) refers to the way the message is delivered: the precise words used, how they are used, and the relationship of what is said to the actual topic at hand. *Key* (K) refers to the tone, manner, or spirit in which a particular message is conveyed: light-hearted, serious, sarcastic, and so forth. *Instrumentalities* (I) refers to the choice of channel, for example, oral, written, or electronic, and to the actual forms of speech employed, such as language, dialect, code, or register that is chosen. *Norms of interaction and interpretation* (N) refers to the specific behaviors and properties that attach to speaking and also to how these may be viewed by someone who does not share them, for example, loudness, silence, gaze, and so on. *Genre* (G) refers to clearly and conventionally defined types of discourse, such as sermons, lectures, editorials, poems, and riddles. The SPEAKING model offers us a necessary reminder that talk is a piece of highly skilled work in the sense that, if it is to be successful, the speaker must demonstrate a sensitivity to and awareness of each of the eight factors outlined in it. Changes of any of the factors may lead to noticeable changes in the way people communicate. Consequently, students of naturally occurring language behavior must take into consideration these factors so that their findings and conclusions can be properly interpreted.

5. Sociolinguistics and Language Pathology

Sociolinguistic data and methods have wide-ranging implications for language pathology. The most important one has to do with attitudes towards language variation. Speech and language pathologists must see language variation as a normal phenomenon and not as an indicator of communication disorder. Awareness of the range of 'language standard' in different communities is a necessary, and indeed critical, first step for developing speech and language programs compatible with the types of language likely to be heard in various communities.

Another important implication of sociolinguistic research concerns the definition of pathological speech. Traditional definitions of speech disorder have typically categorized speech as being pathologic if it deviates sufficiently from a rather rigid, unicultural, middle-class set of linguistic norms. Recent sociolinguistic studies provide a theoretical orientation and database for defining pathology from the perspective of language norms generated by various speech communities. Where existing data are inadequate to permit a cultural orientation to defining and diagnosing communication disorder, clinicians and researchers can utilize the procedures developed by sociolinguists in collecting and analyzing language samples.

This brings us to the issue of assessment in speech and language clinics. English-speaking speech and language pathologists are fortunate to have both standardized tests and 'normative' data on monolingual children's language development, on which they rely heavily. However, most standardized tests are based on linguistic presuppositions consistent with 'standard' English and do not take into account regional and social variations. For this reason many of these tests, when administered and scored according to prescribed norms, yield data that unfairly penalize speakers of non-standard dialects and give the inaccurate impression of a communication disorder when in fact no disorder exists. Consider only phonological disorder for a moment: it is fairly easy to envisage a situation where aspects of social class or regional variation in speech can complicate a clinicial assessment (we have taken the examples from Ball 1992). Assuming a client presents with a fricative simplification process, whereby target labio-dentals and interdentals are realized as labio-dentals and target alveolars and palato-alveolars as alveolars, we might feel we have a relatively common and uncomplicated simplification of contrasts to deal with. However, if this client originates from a region, such as London, where the merger of interdentals with labio-dentals is common and is from a social group likely to use this feature, then this analysis must be challenged. It may well be that what we have there is simply a process affecting the alveolar versus palato-alveolar contrast, with the loss of interdentals simply reflecting community norms. Other speaker variables such as age and sex should also be considered in clinical assessment. Certain variants of specific linguistic variables may reflect older community speech norms, or may be markers of sex differences.

Stylistic variations in speech must also be considered in clinical assessment, if only because so much of the data speech-language pathologists rely on is obtained in ways which are unusual to say the least in comparison with normal, casual conversations. It must be remembered that a client's normal context of interaction is with family, friends, and colleagues, not with speech-language clinicians. If all we can gain on occasions is a speech style radically different from that used by the speaker with their friends and family, then we are in great danger of making a false analysis of the linguistic repertoire and abilities normally open to the patient. It would be necessary, therefore, to consider a speech therapy session as a particular communicative event and take into account all the factors involved therein in analyzing and interpreting the language data. In this regard, the SPEAKING model described above may be a useful analytic framework.

Apart from issues of assessment, the planning of remediation programs must be reconsidered. In the case noted above, serious consideration must be given as to whether training in the production of the contrast between interdental and labio-dental fricatives should be given, when such a contrast may not exist, or exist only peripherally in the client's speech community.

6. Language Pathology in Multicultural Contexts

The difficulty of defining what is normal language behavior becomes more acute when bilingual and multilingual communities are concerned. Recent sociolinguistic studies have highlighted the significance of language choice, code-switching, and code-mixing amongst bilingual and multilingual speakers. Nevertheless some people, including professionals in the social, educational, and health services who routinely work with the bilingual and multilingual population, still regard a normal speaker as having perfect knowledge of both or all the languages and rarely, if ever, mixing them in conversations. The notion of *semi-lingualism*, developed by educational psychologists, is sometimes used to describe a condition where bilingual children are said to know neither of their two languages well enough, according to monolingual criteria, to sustain the advanced cognitive processes which enable them to benefit from mainstream education. As Martin-Jones and Romaine (1985) point out, this line of reasoning is suspiciously like a new version of language deficit theory and cannot easily be sustained in the face of sociolinguistic evidence.

An additional difficulty in assessing bilingual and multilingual speakers, especially children, is that, at present, it is hard to specify what is developmentally normal, since very little is known about bilingual language acquisition and developmental patterns. As the study of Cantonese/English-speaking children cited above suggests, bilingual speakers may acquire language patterns in a different way from their monolingual counterparts. Speech-language pathologists therefore cannot simply follow their usual practice of assessing the language abilities of bilingual and multilingual speakers using standardized tests and normative data. Taylor et al. (1987) recommend speech-language pathologists working with bilingual and multilingual speakers to engage themselves in a number of assessment activities that involve cultural considerations. At the pre-assessment level, these activities include:

(a) Familiarization with cultural, social, and cognitive norms of the individual's community.
(b) Familiarization with linguistic and communicative norms of the individual's speech community.
(c) The selection of appropriate, unbiased, standardized, and criterion-referenced tests.
(d) Preparation of culturally appropriate natural elicitation procedure.

At the assessment level, culturally valid procedures

must be employed to obtain a sample of the client's communicative behavior. Three essential elements of this process involve:

(a) The administration of unbiased evaluation procedure.
(b) The collection of idiosyncratic sociocultural and communicative behaviors.
(c) The elicitation and observation of spontaneous communicative behavior in a variety of settings.

Following the collection of data from formal tests and natural language samples, the speech-language pathologist must then engage in several post-assessment, culturally based activities. They are:

(a) scoring and error analysis of data from structured and spontaneous elicitations
(b) consideration of peer and/or community definition of communication pathology
(c) peer and/or community corroboration of test and natural data.

7. Summary and Further Reading

In this chapter we have suggested that sociolinguistics is concerned with language *in situ* and *in vivo*, alive in its geographical, social, situational setting, and space. According to sociolinguists, language is better understood in terms of *community* norms rather than some idealized form produced by some perfect speaker. They have developed methods which enable us to observe and analyze language in its naturally occurring contexts. The focus of sociolinguistic studies is on the *communicative competence* of the speaker, the ability to select, from the totality of the linguistic resources available to him or her, forms which appropriately reflect the social forms governing behavior in specific encounters. Sociolinguistic data and methods have important implications for speech-language pathology. They not only help raise the awareness of different language standards in various communities, but also provide analytic frameworks and models for studying language behavior.

A comprehensive introduction to sociolinguists is provided in Wardhaugh (1998). A more detailed, critical account of sociolinguistic method can be seen in Milroy (1987), which also discusses some practical applications of sociolinguistics. Labov (1972a, 1972b) and Gumperz and Hymes (1972) are classics in sociolinguistics. Romaine (1995) offers an advanced introduction to bilingualism. Discussion of the implications of sociolinguistics for speech-language pathology can be found in Taylor (1988) and Ball (1992).

Bibliography

Ball M J 1992 *The Clinician's Guide to Linguistic Profiling of Language Impairment*. Far Communications, Kibworth

Dodd B, So L, Li Wei 1996 Symptoms of disorder without impairment. In: Dodd B, Campbell R, Worrall L (eds.) *Evaluating Theories of Language*. Whurr Publishers, London

Gumperz J J, Hymes D (eds.) 1992 *Directions in Sociolinguistics*. Holt, Rinehart and Winston, New York, PA

Hymes D 1974 *Foundations in Sociolinguistics*. Pennsylvania University Press, Philadelphia, PA

Kayer H (ed.) 1995 *Bilingual Speech-Language Pathology: An Hispanic Focus*. Singular Publishing, San Diego, LA

Labov W 1972a *Sociolinguistic Patterns*. Pennsylvania University Press, Philadelphia, PA

Labov W 1972b *Language in the Inner City*. Pennsylvania University Press, Philadelphia, PA

Li W 1994 *Three Generations, Two Languages, One Family*. Multilingual Matters, Philadelphia, PA

Martin-Jones M, Romaine S 1985 Semilingualism: A half-baked theory of communicative competence. *Applied Linguistics* **6**: 105–17

Mattes L J, Omark D R 1991 *Speech and Language Assessment for the Bilingual Handicapped*, 2nd end. Academic Communication Associates, Oceanside, CA

Milroy L 1987 *Observing and Analysing Natural Language*. Blackwell Publishers, Oxford

Milroy L, Li Wei, Moffatt S 1995 Discourse patterns and fieldwork strategies in urban settings. In: Ivan W (ed.) *Verbale Kommunikation in der Stadt*. Gunter Narr, Tubingen

Omark D R, Watson D L 1983 *Assessing Bilingual Exceptional Children: In-service Manual*. Los Amigos Research Associates, San Diego, CA

Reid E 1978 Social and stylistic variation in the speech of children. In: Trudgill P (ed.) *Sociolinguistic Patterns in British English*. Edward Arnold, London

Romaine S 1975 *Linguistic Variability in the Speech of some Edinburgh School Children*. Unpublished MLitt thesis, University of Edinburgh

Romaine S 1995 *Bilingualism*, 2nd edn. Blackwell Publishers, Oxford

Taylor O L 1988 Speech and language differences and disorders of multicultural populations. In: Lass N J, McReynolds L V, Northern J L, Yoder D E (eds.) *Handbook of Speech-Language Pathology and Audiology*. B. C. Decker Inc, Toronto

Taylor O L, Payne K, Anderson, N 1987 Distinguishing between communication disorders and communication differences. *Seminar in Speech and Language* **8.4**: 415–28

Wardhaugh R 1998 *An Introduction of Sociolinguistics*, 3rd edn. Blackwell Publishers, Oxford

General Aspects of Speech and Language Pathologies

Overview

J. M. Cooper

In a comprehensive work on language and linguistics it is important to consider how language may fail to develop, or, having developed, later break down— what effects this may have, and what might be done to help restore this function. This overview is intended to familiarize the reader with the scope of the pathology of language.

1. Defining Language Pathology

The term 'language pathology' is a complex concept that requires definition. As used in this encyclopedia, it covers all the disorders of linguistic communication, including those of speech, hearing, reading, writing, and signing. It refers not only to the breakdown of the 'symbolic' aspects of communication, involving problems in syntax, semantics, and pragmatics, but also to the breakdown of the 'nonsymbolic' aspects, that is, problems of voice, fluency, and articulation.

Historically, the terms 'speech' and 'language' have often been confused (see *Historical Perspective*). In much of the literature the term 'language disorders' is frequently used in a restricted way, referring only to the symbolic aspects of disorders of communication, that is, those concerned with the formulation and structure of meaning. The term 'speech disorders' is used in reference to the nonsymbolic disorders, that is, those concerned with the motor act of uttering speech sounds. To separate language and speech in this way, however, causes problems when considering, for example, phonological disorders (see *Phonological Disorders of Language*). The term 'speech' is also ambiguous as it is often used in a broad sense, referring to any aspect of oral communication that is spoken language which must include syntax, semantics, and pragmatics.

'Communication disorder' is now an accepted term used to refer to a number of clinical entities and includes all the disorders that arise, either in the encoding of messages to stimulate meaning in the mind of another and/or the decoding of the intended meaning received from others. It thus embraces any dis-turbance (i.e., disorder) in the exchange of ideas and intentions between communicating parties.

Language pathology can therefore be defined as the field of study concerned with disorders of communication. It is an interdisciplinary study embracing knowledge from the behavioral, biological, linguistic, and physical sciences.

There are several ways in which such disorders can be explored and it is helpful to consider various theoretical models or approaches to the subject which have developed from the fields of medicine, psychology, and linguistics (see *Models*). Communication disorders have been characterized more by divisiveness than by synthesis. Difficulties in defining the conditions, discovering their causes (see *Developmental Causes*; *Acquired Causes*), establishing accurate techniques of evaluation, and arriving at universally acceptable and successful patterns of management account in part for the wide variation in prevalence estimates. The continuing difficulty in gathering accurate epidemiological data (see *Incidence and Prevalence*) must be stressed, and that which is available in the 1990s should be viewed with caution when used in planning service needs for these disorders.

2. The Effects of Communication Disorders

Communication disorders must be viewed within the context of expected behavior and not just as etiological categories. If the ability to listen, speak, read, write, or sign has not developed to a level where it can be meaningfully used, or has developed but then became impaired, then the individual can be said to be communicatively disordered. This may in turn affect educational achievement, interpersonal relationships, social adjustment, employment success, indeed, most human endeavors and the quality of life.

However, it is important to recognize genuine difficulties and not to confuse them with perceived difficulties which can arise from cultural prejudice or intolerance. For example, regional accents in some circumstances are considered socially unacceptable, and a very weak voice or hesitant response may irritate. These do not come within the province of language pathology but rather of elocution which aims to foster the art of clear speaking, the development of the aesthetic quality of the voice, and of rhetorical excellence.

3. Terminology and Classification of Communication Disorders

Although since the 1970s there has been a considerable growth of knowledge in the field of language pathology, terminological difficulties still beset this area of study. The increase in knowledge has been stimulated by many different disciplines and this has generated many terms, some of which are interchangeable. Some terms hold different meanings for different people and for different cultures, and some are now rarely used or are obsolete, for example, 'dyslalia,' 'logorrhea,' 'idioglossia,' 'rhinolalia,' etc. There are other terms which are gaining popularity and still others which have shifted in meaning. An example of the latter category is the term 'palilalia,' which was originally used to refer to involuntary repetition of words and phrases. In the 1990s it is gaining popularity as a term to describe more specifically a condition of neurological deterioration characterized by acceleration of speech rate and disruption of rhythm, viz., neurogenic stuttering (see *Disorders of Fluency*).

Some inconsistencies in regard to the terminology are unavoidable in the articles on language pathology contained in this book, but this is due to the state of knowledge in the 1990s. For the same reason no definitive lists of 'cause and cure' will be found—language pathology is a field with vast areas still to be explored, and answers that are popular today may be outmoded by tomorrow. A terminological compromise has therefore been adopted and the chapters referring to language pathology have been selected to provide information based upon the long-established categories of voice, articulation, language, and fluency in relation to spoken language, and reading and writing disorders in relation to written language.

Descriptions of specific clinical entities such as, for example, deafness, cleft palate, or mental retardation have for the most part been rejected in favor of viewing communication disorders within the context of their language characteristics and not as etiological labels. Little relevant information is conveyed by such labels because those sharing the same label often exhibit very different communicative abilities and difficulties. This does not, however, deny the extreme importance of exploring etiology (see *Developmental Causes*; *Acquired Causes*).

4. Language Pathology as a Clinically Applied Science

Language pathology is responsible not only for obtaining knowledge about communication disorders, but also for the management of them, that is, the prevention, identification, evaluation, and intervention of such disorders.

It must be acknowledged that the prevention of disorders of communication is still in the early stages. An expansion of knowledge is needed about conditions which cause these disorders and with which they are associated. Although professional practice has focused on identification, evaluation, and intervention, obviously prevention should be the prime objective.

The early identification of a communication disorder in children and adults is very important and will affect the outcome of any intervention measures that may follow. Identification includes routine developmental screening procedures and/or systematic observation in young children and examination of 'at risk' indicators in both children and adults. The 'at risk' indicators are biological, genetic, and perinatal events as well as adventitious disease, degeneration, or trauma affecting the nervous system and severe emotional or environmental deprivation. In the selection, use, and interpretation of screening tests their reliability and validity must be carefully considered.

If evidence of language pathology is identified, referral for a full and comprehensive evaluation of the communication disorder should follow. This may involve a variety of professional personnel and a wide range of assessment procedures. This detailed evaluation of the problem forms the database from which decisions about future management and intervention strategies can be formulated. For the intervention process to take place satisfactorily the knowledge obtained must be useful and it must be accurate. The problems must be analyzed to determine important variables, relationships between them described, and crucial questions asked so that definitive answers can be arrived at. However, it will be appreciated that analyzing any form of human behavior is necessarily problematic; the possibility always remains that an unknown condition may come between suspected cause and observable effect.

The ultimate objective of language intervention is effective communication and any intervention can only be justified if it is reasonably calculated to achieve this objective. It cannot always remove the problem but it should enable the person to communicate more efficiently. The strategies employed in achieving this will vary. Intervention is experimental because of the complex interaction of numerous variables and it therefore has to be approached tentatively. The nature of the undertaking and the emphasis upon results cannot always be approached in the same manner as a laboratory experiment and no single theoretical system can be applied. It is essential that the practitioner should have freedom to design, observe, implement, and then to interpret the results in order to adapt and modify the intervention process to suit the individual patient.

The knowledge gained from clinical management research leads in turn to additional perspectives and insights on theories of language acquisition and use.

It can be seen that the management aspect of language pathology calls for attempts to change or modify language function and thus the dynamic features of this work enter the domain of clinical practice and education.

5. Language Pathology as a Clinical Profession

The professionals who undertake the investigative and therapeutic tasks are variously named throughout the world—speech pathologists, speech and language pathologists, speech therapists, speech and language therapists, logopedists, orthophonists, phoniatrists, etc. This profusion of titles continues to be the subject of much discussion, particularly in the USA and UK. The issues that are raised in selecting an appropriate label are not trivial, as they are about professional status and rewards, academic orientation, and financial remuneration. There would be merit in achieving consistency of terminology, not only of the professional label but of classification (see Sect. 3). Certainly within the European Union, such harmony of the nomenclature would be advantageous. However, it is not just these terminological disparities but the variation of more fundamental issues which needs to be understood and addressed. The range of professional skills and the depth of study undertaken in preparation to carry out this work also varies from country to country (see *International Perspective*). In some countries there are limitations on the range of communication disorders studied and treated; in others the work with communication disorders in children may be separated from those of adults. In some countries where the study of language pathology has developed to a high degree of academic endeavor this has resulted in specialism and this is reflected in the use of such terms, for example, as 'voice therapist' and 'aphasiologist.'

For the purpose of the chapters contained in this book the terms 'language pathologist,' 'speech and language pathologist,' 'clinician,' and 'therapist' have usually been adopted and used interchangeably. The term 'voice therapist' has also been used with specific reference to clinical management of disorders of voice (see *Disorders of Voice*).

The study of language pathology and the preparation of the professional personnel is usually conducted in universities or institutions of higher education which can provide the necessary exposure to relevant teaching, research, and clinical experience.

The emphasis of the education and preparation of these professional personnel has shifted in recent years from lists of subjects studied, the number of hours of study undertaken, and the number of hours of clinical practice that have been completed, to what knowledge the potential professional should possess and what skills should have been mastered. These must include an understanding of the following:

(a) the anatomical, physiological, acoustic, psychological, linguistic, and phonetic bases of communication disorders;
(b) the etiological bases of communication disorders;
(c) the nature of research methodology relevant to the study of communication disorders;
(d) the wide variety of handicapping conditions in which a communication disorder is a concomitant condition;
(e) the diversity of social and cultural patterns that affect language;
(f) the nature of prevention of communication disorders.

Professional training must also include the ability to:

(a) identify children and adults with communication disorders by the use of appropriate screening and assessment procedures;
(b) assess the nature and severity of the communication disorders by the use of diagnostic procedures which assumes competence in behavioral assessment techniques, both formal and informal;
(c) plan and conduct programs of intervention for adults and children with communication disorders including the interpretation of diagnostic data, case selection and prioritization, therapeutic approaches, data recording, and consultation with other professionals and with relatives;
(d) critically evaluate intervention strategies and modify accordingly;
(e) apply the assessment and intervention procedures to a variety of appropriate settings including, for example, hospitals, community clinics, schools, homes, and private offices;
(f) participate in planning and conducting programs directed towards prevention of communication disorders.

6. Transferring Knowledge and Clinical Skills

In the second half of the twentieth century, considerable academic and professional advances have been made in the field of language pathology. Techniques of evaluation and intervention have become extremely sophisticated in certain parts of the world. The countries in which extensive advances have occurred have a considerable influence on practice in the less developed nations. Where specific management techniques have proved to be effective, then it may be justifiable to consider transferring them to countries which are just starting to develop services for children and adults with communication disorders but this should not preclude the careful examination of alternative methods which might be more suitable to the social and cultural patterns of those countries. The relativity and universality of conditions and procedures must continue to be explored.

7. Interprofessional Practice

The language pathologist is not alone in caring for those with communication disorders. There are many elements in the management of them which will involve a number of other professionals and, most importantly, parents and relatives. It is important therefore that language pathology is recognized not only as a field of interdisciplinary study but that its clinical application is recognized as an area of interprofessional practice. However, it is normally the language pathologist who assumes the primary responsibility for the management of communication disorders in both children and adults and for coordinating the interprofessional input so that it focuses on the whole person rather than on separate aspects of the communication disorder. The language pathologist will synthesise information and, in consultation with the relevant health, education, and social services, plan for and expedite appropriate service provision for the communication disordered population and, equally importantly, take an active

role in planning programs of prevention of these diseases.

8. Future Study and Application

Language pathology is made up of different types of knowledge, it is an epistemological hybrid and therefore any future advance of knowledge in this field must continue to be through the development and investigation of a variety of theoretical concepts and methods involving many different disciplines. This approach must apply to the future study and application of knowledge about epidemiology, etiology, classification, and management of communication disorders. A discipline and its professional exponents continue to develop over time and are influenced from many sources and by the environmental and economic climate of the time. The rapid development of technology, for example, is having, and will continue to have, a profound effect. In the future, in addition to the disciplines already contributing information, more can be anticipated from the computer sciences, the neurosciences, and the biochemical sciences and this input will in turn be reflected at best in the prevention, but certainly in the alleviation of communication disorders.

Historical Perspective

J. M. Cooper

As long as people have spoken they have wondered about those who are unable to do so. Descriptions of speechlessness or disturbances of speech abound in the medical, and particularly the surgical, literature, and speculation about the cause of such conditions also appears in the works of philosophers, theologians, poets, and prophets from earliest times. Probably the first reference appears in the Egyptian surgical text—the Edwin Smith Surgical Papyrus (c. 2500 BC); this treatise shows remarkably advanced clinical knowledge as, for example, it suggests that injury to the head is connected with inability to speak. Disturbances of speech are mentioned in the Bible. In China the terms for 'speech disorder' and 'voice disorder' are recorded on tortoise shells going back to 1300 BC, and in the medical literature of the Song dynasty (970–1279 AD) there is reference to an artificial larynx.

In the works of Homer two terms are used to denote speechlessness, 'aphasia' and 'anaudos.' A third term, 'aphonos,' meaning literally 'the privation of voice,' which is frequently translated as 'mutism' (see

Mutism), is used by Sophocles and Herodotus. Indeed, there are many references to descriptions of speechlessness and speech impediments throughout Classical literature. In the fifth century BC a community of physicians was founded in the Aegis Islands, led by Hippocrates of Kos, who compiled their writings into a corpus which bears his name. These writings include a collection of clinical observations of speechlessness and speech disorder with various theories regarding causes and cures. These physicians were hampered by an inadequate knowledge of anatomy and physiology, and believed that any pathological condition was caused by an imbalance of the 'humors,' that is, heat, cold, moisture, and dryness. Speechlessness was attributed to the result of excess humidity in the brain. The Hippocratic Corpus affirmed the thesis that the organs of speech, voice, and articulation are in the head, as first mentioned in the Smith papyrus about 2000 years before, and that injury to the head can destroy the ability to speak.

Two other Greek scholars, Aristotle and Demosthenes, born in the same year, 384 BC, also made valuable contributions to the study of speech disorders and their treatment—apparently both had personal speech problems. The first true claim that the distinctive characteristic of humans is their ability to speak, appears in Aristotle's writings and, as elaborated by the Stoic philosophers, exerted a great influence on medical thought. Aristotle also compiled a classification of disorders of speech and voice, and though many of his theories may now be regarded as wildly inaccurate they were to influence thinking for many years. However, the alliance of medicine and philosophy began to divide during the Hellenic age. The concept of the soul as a separate entity from the body took shape and philosophers believed that speech was the reflection of the light of the soul, thus rejecting the idea that speech disorder resulted from corporal injury.

In the early Christian era, Claudius Galen of Greece was to have a profound influence upon medicine and surgery. He, like Aristotle, accepted that speech was the distinguishing human characteristic but gave prominence to the notion that the tongue was the main organ of speech and therefore lingual disability was the cause of most speech disorders. He was the first physician to recognize that the muscles are controlled by the brain. However, the dichotomy of thinking which Galen had attempted to merge continued to polarize, and for many years physicians concerned themselves only with the physical components of speech, that is, vocalization and articulation, while any study about the nature of that faculty was considered to be the province of the philosopher and the theologian.

During the Middle Ages in Europe there was little advance in medical knowledge. However, the Arabs collected numerous Greek manuscripts on science and added useful comments. An Arabian physician, Avicenna, compiled a *Canon of Medicine* which was used as a text for medical students in European universities up until the seventeenth century. In this he commented on the part the nervous system played in speech, but he also overemphasized the effect of lingual deficiency.

With the questioning spirit of the Renaissance, the breach between the philosophers and medical practitioners began very slowly to close. Several prominent names in the history of speech disorders emerged. In 1541, Ambrosia Paré, a master barber–surgeon, published the first description of an obturator as an aid to improve voice in patients with a cleft palate. Also in the sixteenth century Mercuriales, an eminent physician, made important investigations into the nature and treatment of stuttering, and introduced both a psychological as well as a neurological factor as a cause for speech disorder. He believed that congenital deafness was a major cause of speechlessness in children.

An important development in the eighteenth century was the science of pathology and the key figure in this new science was Giovanni Morgagni (1682–1771). He carried out a series of postmortem examinations which enabled him to account for the relationship between changes in the body and certain diseases. In the history of speech pathology he is noted for attributing the cause of stuttering to deviations in the hyoid bone. In the same century a group of philosopher–psychologists, known as Associationists, in their study of normal development of language in children, demonstrated an interest in disturbances of language, attributing them to psychological rather than generic causes. The term 'Associationists' came from their use of expressions such as 'association of ideas' or 'power of association.'

The nineteenth century brought many advances in the surgical and prosthetic treatment of cleft palate and removal of the larynx. Aphasia and disorders of reading and writing were to receive much attention in this period although rehabilitation for these conditions was not often attempted until the twentieth century. The names Broca, Bastian, Jackson, Kussmaul, Wernicke, and others were to contribute extensively to the literature in these areas. 'Connectionist' models of language were developed during the nineteenth century which suggested that specialized language centers localized in different regions of the brain were interconnected by bundles of nerve fibers. Depending on the site of the lesion, different 'syndromes' would arise (see *Historical Perspective of Aphasia*). Some of the most influential early work on the acquired dyslexias was that of Dejerine (1892) who used postmortem findings to confirm that 'pure alexia' and 'alexia with agraphia' arose as the result of the 'disconnection' of different language centers. Later, however, opponents of the connectionist models argued that language was a unitary function and that different aspects could not be selectively impaired by brain damage.

It was also in Victorian Britain that the Elocutionists, who were mainly concerned with raising standards in the use of the English language, began to show interest in those with defects of speech. John Thelwall was probably the most prominent figure in this movement.

The beginning of the twentieth century saw the development and growth of more organized treatment of communication disorders in many countries in Europe, later spreading to the USA and then gradually to many other countries around the world.

Studies in the physics of sound and the physiology of human speech organs, which had advanced so considerably during the nineteenth century, continued to develop. The application of psychology became popular and the educational theories of, for example, Piaget, Montessori, and Froebel influenced much of the treatment. The period between the two World

Wars saw important developments in linguistics, including the work of Sapir and Bloomfield in the USA and the Prague school in Europe. After World War II the work of Luria in the Soviet Union became very influential and the interaction between linguistics and psychology introduced a further dimension at this time.

During the last quarter of the twentieth century specialists have replaced general physicians and philosophers in the study of speech disorders. As well as language pathologists, experts from the fields of the neurosciences, psychology, and linguistics are all participating in the investigation of these ancient and persisting problems.

Bibliography

Eldridge M 1968 *A History of the Treatment of Speech Disorders*. E & S Livingstone, Edinburgh

Fabbro F 1994 Left and right in the Bible from a neuropsychological perspective. *Brain and Cognition*, **24**: 161–83

O'Neill Y N 1980 *Speech and Speech Disorders in Western Thought Before 1600*. Greenwood Press, Westport, CT

Rieber R W, Bruker R S 1966 *Speech Pathology*. North-Holland, Amsterdam

Rockey D 1980 *Speech Disorder in Nineteenth-century Britain*. Croom Helm, London

Whitaker H A 1998 Neurolinguistics from the middle ages to the pre-modern era: Historical vignettes. In: Stemmer B, Whitaker H A (eds.) *Handbook of Neurolinguistics*. Academic Press, San Diego, CA

Models

D. Crystal

With a subject as complex and multifaceted as language pathology, it is unlikely that any single approach could be devised which would provide a coherent and comprehensive account. This is always so when a range of professions contribute to the study of a subject, and especially so when these professions reach across the boundary between arts and sciences (as in the case of language pathology, where the contributing disciplines include medical science, linguistics, psychology, and education). In such circumstances, different models of inquiry evolve, each of which illuminates our understanding of the subject from a different point of view.

1. The Notion of Model

'The purpose of scientific thought is to postulate a conceptual model of nature from which the observable behavior of nature may be predicted accurately' (Walker 1963: 5). A model is an attempt to visualize a complex set of abstract or physical relationships, so that they become more intelligible. Models are inevitably simplifications of reality, in which certain features are emphasized at the expense of others. By formulating a model in a certain way, hypotheses can be generated about the nature of the reality the model purports to represent, and these can be subjected to experimental test. A fruitful model will provide many such hypotheses, as well as a range of fresh insights into the nature of a field. At the same time, models tend to make their users think in a certain way, so that it becomes difficult to step back and see that there are other ways of conceptualizing the field, and that

other models may also be a source of insight. Often, models from different research traditions are used simultaneously in relation to different aspects of the field.

Several models have come to be used in language pathology, largely arising out of the subject's multidisciplinary background. Some have been developed to impose order on the field as a whole; others relate to the study of an individual disorder or group of disorders. These models can be grouped according to various principles. One principle reflects the contributing disciplines: medical science, on the one hand; and behavioral science, on the other. Another principle relies on the distinction which in linguistics was formulated in terms of diachronic and synchronic dimensions of language study (Saussure 1959): language pathologies are thereby investigated from a developmental or nondevelopmental point of view.

2. The Medical Model

The earliest models providing accounts of abnormal linguistic behavior were derived from philosophy and theology (O'Neill 1980); in medieval times, for example, speech was seen as a psychic rather than a physical reflex, and aberrations were, as a result, often viewed in relation to notions of spiritual or mental well-being (see *Historical Perspective*). A scientific model was not forthcoming until the nineteenth century, when the work of European neurologists introduced a medical mode of inquiry into the subject. The essential features of the medical model are an emphasis on cause and effect: the signs and symptoms of disease are explained by postulating a causative agent (a disease or trauma), and intervention is focused on identifying that agent (diagnosis) and eliminating it, thus providing a cure. In the case of language pathology, it quickly became plain that quite a large number of abnormal spoken language symptoms could be explained with reference to a physical (or organic) cause. Such causes included deafness, brain damage (both in children and adults), orofacial abnormalities, and pathologies of the vocal tract. In some cases, detailed studies of an anatomical, physiological, or neurological kind indicated the possibility of fundamental classifications of abnormal linguistic behavior, notably the early division of aphasia into Broca's and Wernicke's types (see *Historical Perspective of Aphasia*; *Syndromes of Aphasia*).

The medical model has become an essential primary step in the investigation of any postulated language pathology. It is standard practice to determine whether there is any physical factor present in an individual, before proceeding to examine other factors. Thus, typically a hearing test will be carried out, and often there will be investigations by ear, nose, and throat, neurological, pediatric, orthodontic, or other specialists. The strengths of the medical model are plain, and are those associated with orthodox medical practice in other areas of life. At the same time, the limitations of this model, with respect to language pathology, have also become increasingly apparent. In particular, as the range of conditions widened, it became clear that several pathologies of language did not seem to have any organic cause capable of being elucidated in medical terms. Examples included most kinds of stuttering, certain voice problems, various categories of reading difficulty, and the many types of child language delay. Indeed, informal estimates indicated that perhaps in as many as 60 percent of all cases the linguistic symptoms could not be assigned a straightforward medical cause. Often, there was nothing physically wrong with the person (as far as tests could tell), or the nature of the physical abnormality did not seem correlatable with the range of linguistic symptoms manifested. Alternative models were therefore devised.

3. The Behavioral Model

A further difficulty with the medical model was its limited ability to provide guidelines for treatment or teaching. Whereas a physical problem could be remediated using physical techniques (e.g., medicines, surgery), only a few linguistic handicaps could benefit in this way (e.g., from hearing aids, vocal fold surgery). In most cases, there was no way of relating a medical diagnosis to a specific linguistic treatment regime. Moreover, there seemed to be no neat correlation between the type and severity of a condition and the range of linguistic symptoms encountered. For example, a group of identically deaf children of a given age could display a wide range of language abilities. In order to devise appropriate teaching programs for

these people, as well as for those who had no medical symptoms at all, a behavioral model of investigation was introduced.

There are as many potential behavioral models, in fact, as there are relevant behavioral sciences. In language pathology, the two approaches usually encountered stem from psychology and linguistics. The psychological approach has traditionally operated with a wide range of test procedures, investigating such factors as memory, attention, personality, intelligence, and perception, and characterized by the use of experimental and statistical techniques. The linguistic approach has focused on the description of language behavior as captured in samples of speech or writing. An analysis is made of an aspect of the language used, and the results are displayed in the form of tables, charts, or other descriptive devices which enable patterns of abnormality to be seen and paths of intervention proposed. The diagnoses which emerge from this approach use the terms of psychological or linguistic analysis: language pathologies are defined with reference to disturbances in underlying cognitive skills, such as memory or attention, or at the linguistic levels of phonetics, phonology, graphology, grammar, semantics, or pragmatics.

Attempts made to correlate the findings of the behavioral and medical models have so far achieved only limited success. For example, there are many important individual differences, described in linguistic terms, between patients who have lesions in Broca's area. However, there are clear cases where the explanation for a condition requires reference to both medical and behavioral models. Examples here would include those voice disorders where only a combination of physical and psychological factors seem able to explain the development of a laryngeal pathology (Greene and Mathieson 1989). Yet, when such cases as the latter are examined, the need for a further explanatory model becomes apparent.

4. The Developmental Model

Developmental factors are by no means ignored in medicine (e.g., in pediatrics, and in the universal notion of the 'course' of a disease), psychology (notably in developmental psychology), and linguistics (notably in child language acquisition). In a developmental model, however, physical or behavioral changes over time become the primary focus of attention. This is, so far, a poorly investigated approach to language pathology. The concept of development is occasionally recognized, such as in the diagnosis of language 'delay,' and in the recognition that some pathologies are 'resistant to therapy.' Hints at the normal developmental course of a pathology are also found in aphasiology, where experienced clinicians are prepared to give an indication of the time it normally takes for the restoration of certain functions. But for the most part, detailed information is lacking about the way language handicaps spontaneously develop, and about the rate at which they resolve (or fail to resolve) during therapy. Many longitudinal case studies of individual pathologies are required before the field can build up a bank of prognostic data comparable to that routinely available in medical science in the 1990s.

It is essential to aim for a developmental perspective because this model provides valuable information for all main areas of clinical study. Time is part of the task of assessment, in that any evaluation needs to consider just how much progress has been made in a given period of time. Time is part of the task of intervention, in that the value of any remedial program needs to be judged in terms of how long it takes to be implemented, and whether enough time is available in order to implement it. Time is part of the task of diagnosis, in that ultimately one would expect different types of pathology to be defined partly in terms of the time scale involved (in much the same way as part of the definition of a disease is the time it takes to run its course).

5. The Interactive Model

A further approach, which also has received little study to date, focuses on the social interaction between the linguistically handicapped person and others. Language pathologies are unlike most other forms of handicap in that they do not become apparent until communication is attempted—and communication is a two-way process. A popular way of modeling language handicap, within the general framework of the medical approach, is a model derived from information theory which identifies stages in a 'chain' of communication. A message is conceived as being sent through a sequence of neurological, physiological, and anatomical stages of expression and being received through an analogous sequence of anatomical, physiological, and neurological stages. In terms of this model, deafness would be an 'input' pathology, stuttering would be an 'output' pathology, and aphasia would be a 'central' pathology. This model is a useful way of identifying the main physical locus involved in a condition, but it only goes a small way toward an explanation of the handicap as a whole, for it takes no account of the various kinds of social interaction which relate speaker and listener (or reader and writer) while they are engaged in the task of communication. Nor does it allow us to focus on the patient as a whole—an emphasis which has inspired 'holistic' models of treatment in the 1990s (Crystal and Varley, 1998).

As with the developmental model, the importance of interaction emerges in relation to each of the main clinical tasks. In relation to diagnosis, a difficulty in coping with normal interaction is central to the definition of pragmatic speech disorders, such as failure to follow the normal rules of conversation, or failure to speak at all (mutism) (see *Mutism*). In terms of assessment, it is a commonplace that the results of tests and other procedures depend very largely on the nature of the interaction between tester and testee. In terms of teaching, it is only common sense that success here will depend on the ability of the therapist to match language stimuli to the level of attainment reached by the patient—something which is not always easy to achieve. Certain aspects of language, moreover, seem to be more affected by interaction than others. In phonology and vocabulary, for example, the role of imitation is important; but in grammar, more attention needs to be paid to the way patients demonstrate an emerging awareness of linguistic rules, independent of the input.

6. Integration

Each of these approaches provides insight into the nature of language pathology. Occasionally they come into conflict—such as when the medical and the behavioral approaches lead to incompatible recommendations about intervention (as in the treatment of a voice pathology, where surgery and voice rest might be alternative ways of proceeding. But for the most part, these models happily coexist within the field, each providing a fruitful source of research hypotheses. Most case studies routinely incorporate information of a medical, behavioral, developmental, and social kind (though emphases vary), and the importance of integrating these different perspectives is stressed in the training of language pathologists. Within each heading, moreover, there are further possibilities, depending on the theoretical approaches used. Within the behavioral approach, for example, there are several ways of dealing with grammatical disability, using any of the grammatical theories available in linguistics. Within the developmental approach, there are several ways of modeling the order of emergence of phonological abilities. The pages of any research journal illustrate the range of models which exist in the domain of language pathology. If there is a problem, in the 1990s, it is not a shortage of models but a shortage of model users, and a shortage of time for the modelers to take further the approaches they have devised.

Bibliography

Crystal D, Varley R 1998 *Introduction to Language Pathology*, 4th edn. Whurr, London
Greene M, Mathieson L 1989 *The Voice and its Disorders*, 5th edn. Whurr, London
O'Neill Y V 1980 *Speech and Speech Disorders in Western Thought before 1600*. Greenwood Press, Westport, CT
Saussure F de 1959 *Course in General Linguistics*. Philosophical Library, New York
Walker M 1963 *The Nature of Scientific Thought*. Prentice-Hall, Englewood Cliffs, NJ

Acquired Causes

B. M. Ansel and R. L. Ringel

Throughout the duration of an individual's lifetime, there are many factors that may influence the development and course of the communication process. These factors may exert their effects on the organism prior to birth (prenatal), during the birth process (natal), at some time soon after birth (postnatal), and at any time during the lifespan. Some diseases or injuries may exert their consequences on the developmental aspects of speech and language function, while others are acquired after a course of normal speech and language development. Both acquired and developmental disorders may affect speech and language performance by interfering with central and/or peripheral nervous-system function, or by a failure to develop or maintain speech structure integrity. Of special interest are those pathologies which will have their effect on speech and language performance by causing already developed patterns of speech and language behavior to be disrupted. It is helpful to remember that some illnesses which are considered to be acquired may actually have their genesis at a prenatal stage, though the manifestation of the disease does not become apparent until some years later.

Even within the category of individuals who have developed and then subsequently lost speech or language functions, there are further important distinctions to be made. These distinctions are based on such factors as the extent to which the processes which are essential for communication are involved, the age of the patient at the onset of the disease or injury, and the course of the disease.

1. Disruption of the Communication Process

When the mechanisms which are responsible for the motor aspect of speech production are damaged, it may be expected that the system will fail in its accuracy, speed, range of motion, endurance, coordination, and strength. These failures are the consequence of such structural changes in neural and muscle tissue as atrophy, edema, dystonia, and demylinization. The output manifestation of such failures may be seen in disturbances of the respiratory, phonatory, articulatory, resonance, and prosodic aspects of speech production.

Most language disorders stem from neurological defects or abnormalities. The damage usually originates in brain centers and pathways, often from injuries due to cerebral vascular accident, trauma, or degenerative brain disease. These disorders may disrupt the reception, processing, perception, and recall of language, as well as language formulation and

expression. Language disturbances may be manifest in both the receptive and productive aspects of speech. Such disorders may be characterized by semantic, syntactic, morphological, phonological, and pragmatic confusions. Language formulation and processing may be disrupted in modalities other than oral communication (e.g., reading, writing, and other symbolic skills).

In addition to the role played by the central and peripheral nervous system in regulating the communication process, the autonomic nervous system, through its sympathetic and parasympathetic components, also exerts an important control function by governing the activity of the cardiovascular, smooth muscle, and glandular structures. Although much of the effect of the autonomic nervous system on speech and language performance is indirect, nonetheless, the effects of disease or accident on this portion of the nervous system may be seen in the speech, voice, and language changes associated with certain endocrine imbalances and with cranial nerve dysfunctions emanating from parasympathetic nerve failure. The critical balance of secretions from the endocrine system may also be disturbed, with subsequent voice changes, when masculinizing or feminizing hormones are used in the treatment of certain types of diseases.

2. Distinguishing Acquired from Developmental Disorders

Acquired disorders of communication are those in which it is assumed that normal speech and language proficiency has been attained and subsequently disturbed or lost due to illness, accident, abusive lifestyle, or as an unavoidable consequence of medical or surgical treatment (i.e., iatrogenic). An appreciation of the speaker's prior experience and ability to integrate and coordinate the speech and language systems is an essential factor in understanding acquired communication disabilities. In contrast, the young, developmentally impaired speaker cannot be expected to have already developed language experience and sophistication, world knowledge, phonological rule mastery, fluency, or articulation skills at a level comparable to that of a more mature speaker. In the child, the immature speech and language system is in a developmental stage, patterns of learning are not yet well-established, and language knowledge is not yet stored or retrieved in the manner believed to be characteristic of the experienced speaker.

Age of onset is thought to be a more important variable influencing recovery from acquired neurological insult than is extent or site of the lesion. In younger children, greater plasticity of the central nervous system may favor the reacquisition or recovery of language. As plasticity is reduced, so is the potential of the nervous system to undergo reorganization subsequent to injury. In neurological impairment, age at onset appears to be correlated with etiology, type, and severity of aphasia. Some authorities report that, if damage is confined to a single hemisphere of the brain and occurs before the age of 9 years, the child may regain the lost ability and will continue to develop normally thereafter (Dennis 1980; Leonard 1986). A more conservative view of language acquisition in the presence of brain injury suggests that if the damage occurs somewhat earlier, for example between the ages of 5 to 6 years of age, then language function may be expected to remain largely unaffected (Varga-Khadem et al. 1991). However, increasing evidence suggest that the traditional, plasticity-oriented view that 'the earlier the onset, the greater the recovery' is at best a gross oversimplification. Recent studies of focal brain damage in very young children have revealed persisting effects on linguistic development and skills (Aram et al. 1986; Bates et al. 1994; Thal et al. 1991; see *Language Development and Brain Development*). With respect to Traumatic Brain Injury (TBI), there is considerable recent evidence that both mortality rates and long-term functional outcomes are significantly poorer in children who sustain severe TBI during the first 4 years of life than in children injured during the elementary school years (Bagnato and Feldman 1989; Berger et al. 1985; Frankowski 1985; Luerssen et al. 1988). Although the child who suffers injury before 3 years of age may proceed through the major stages of language development seen in children acquiring language for the first time, in children suffering injury after the age of 3 the recovery is slower, and residual problems are likely to persist. Children are particularly vulnerable in acquired disorders because at any age during development, brain injury may preferentially disrupt new learning. Young children may be disproportionately affected by cerebral insult since learning is necessary for their acquisition of new skills. The importance of understanding the process of neural organizations in language acquisition is not limited to the study of disorders of communication, for there is evidence that plasticity and reorganization may be a natural property of the developing nervous system and not restricted to compensatory changes in damaged brains (Nobre and Plunkett 1997).

Not only are the critical issues those associated with the potential of the nervous system to recover function but, within the acquired disability group, the ease and accuracy with which a diagnosis of the communication disorders may be made must be considered. This is especially true in differential diagnosis of elderly individuals, because only limited normative data is available for this population. The language changes which may accompany normal aging are also poorly documented. When normal aging influences are better understood, it may become possible to differentiate more effectively between the language variants of some forms of aphasia, Alzheimer's disease, Huntington's disease, and dementia in the elderly. Also, the importance of considering indices of a patient's age other than years lived (chronological age) enters into the diagnostic picture. It has been reported that speech performance is a correlate of physiological health as well as chronological age (Ringel and Chodzko-Zajko 1988). To the extent that physiological age is influenced by life-style, such factors as substance abuse (tobacco products, drugs, alcohol) or exposure to environmental toxins become an important consideration in understanding acquired communication disorders.

3. Course of the Communication Disorders

Within the category of acquired disorders of communication there are those which occur in a sudden or precipitate way (acute), and others which are the result of a long-standing disease process (chronic). Further, some diseases are progressive in their course, while others are characterized by a rather stable symptom complex. The speed of a disease's onset and its course or progression are distinctly different aspects of the disease process. There are some diseases which are relatively slow in onset but continue in a ravaging course (e.g., Parkinson's disease and multiple sclerosis), while others are sudden in appearance but do not present a pattern of continuing degeneration (e.g., ablative surgery, acquired neurogenic stuttering, conversion aphonia, cerebral vascular accidents). Some diseases which may affect the communication process are slow in onset and nonprogressive once the structural or psychogenic factors reach their plateau (e.g., vocal nodules and adult stuttering), whereas still others (e.g., cerebral or endocrine system tumors, and laryngeal cancer) are likely to continue in their degenerative action until intervention is undertaken.

For the speech and language pathologist, knowledge of how quickly the speech and language symptoms have appeared, and whether they are likely to remain stable or continue to worsen, is essential in diagnostic and management decisions. Degenerative diseases may be expected to cause an organism to become progressively less and less functional. As a disease runs its course, many different organs and systems are likely to become involved and, consequently, the symptomatology typically evolves into a more severe and complex pattern. In patients with amyotrophic lateral sclerosis (ALS), Huntington's chorea, Parkinson's disease, or multiple sclerosis, there is continuous degeneration of speech and language performance, and the symptoms progressively worsen and seldom stabilize. In contrast, some illnesses (e.g., cerebral vascular accident, laryngectomy or glossectomy, traumatic brain injury, or acute infection) have a sudden onset and are often followed by a period of neurological recovery and later stabilization. In such cases, the level of disability incurred as a result of neurological insult or ablative actions remains relatively stable throughout the patient's life span.

4. Therapeutic Implications

The patient with an acquired disorder of communication brings to the therapeutic encounter different abilities and needs than those characteristic of the developmentally disabled. Netsell (1984) notes that a young school-age child with a head injury who has progressed normally would require a different treatment program than a youngster with a developmental disability. When the causative events occur early in the developmental sequence, the resultant speech-and language-symptom complex will appear quite different from those seen in a mature speaker. Netsell also observes that an adult with a developmental dysarthria (e.g., cerebral palsy) (see *Developmental Dysarthrias*) will show different disabilities, and has different needs in terms of speech motor learning, than an adult of the same age who was neurologically normal prior to incurring insult.

Again, it must be stressed that the difference is essentially that patients with acquired disorder at one time had normal speech and language function, while the developmentally impaired have never experienced such success. This very different history is likely to influence the patient's acceptance and adjustment to the communicative disorder, the ability to draw upon compensatory strategies, and the expectations held about achieving some level of acceptable communication performance. It is with such a perspective that the speech and language pathologist may assist the patient in dealing with his or her acceptance of the communication disability, and in the setting of realistic goals and expectations about recovery. A great influence in all such considerations is the understandable fear of the recurrence or progression of the disease in a patient who has experienced either a sudden or gradual change in their health. Also, factors such as the loss of social and economic status because of the acquired inability to communicate further complicate many aspects of the diagnostic and therapeutic programs.

One final thought on the developmental–acquired issue relates to the ability with which causative factors of disorders of communication may be identified.

Speech and language assessment, like any field of clinical or scientific endeavor, is limited by the knowledge base and technology of the time. As brain imaging, electrophysiological procedures, and metabolic evaluation techniques advance, so will understanding of the etiology of many of the diseases that affect communication ability. Refinement of speech and language age norms and assessment measures may also allow the earlier identification of subtle speech and language abnormalities, and lead to earlier and more efficient methods of intervention. What must be stressed is that the categorization of the disorders is a dynamic process, changing as a function of the current knowledge and technology.

Bibliography

Aram D M, Elkelman B L, Whitaker H A 1986 Spoken syntax in children with acquired unilateral hemisphere lesions. *Brain and Language* **27**: 75–100

Bagnato S F, Feldman H 1989 Closed head injury in infants and preschool children: Research and practice issues. *Infants and Young Children* **2**: 1–13

Bates E, Thal D, Aram D, Eisele J, Nass R, Trauner D 1994 From first words to grammar in children with focal brain injury. In Thal D, Reilly J (eds.) *Special Issue on Origins of Communication Disorders, Development Neuropsychology*

Berger M S, Pitts L H, Lovely M 1985 Outcome from severe head injury in children and adolescents. *Journal of Neurosurgery* **62**: 194–99

Dennis M 1980 Language acquisition in a single hemisphere: Semantic organisation. In: Caplan D (ed.) *Biological Studies of Mental Processes*. MIT Press, Cambridge, MA

Frankowski R F 1985 Head injury mortality in urban populations and its relation to the injured child. In Brooks B F (ed.) *The Injured Child*. University of Texas Press, Austin, TX, 20–29

Leonard L 1986 Early language development and language disorders. In: Shames G H, Wiig E H (eds.) *Human Communication Disorders*. Charles E Merrill, Columbus, OH

Leurssen T G, Klauber M R, Marshall L F 1988 Outcome from head injury related to patient's age: A longitudinal prospective study of adult and pediatric head injury. *Journal of Neurosurgery* **68**: 409–16

Netsell R 1984 A neurobiologic view of the dysarthrias. In: McNeil M R, Rosenbeck J C, Aronson A E (eds.) *The Dysarthrias: Physiology, Acoustics, Perception, Management*. College-Hill Press, San Diego, CA

Nobre A C, Plunkett K 1997 The neural system of language and development. *Current Opinion in Neurobiology* 7: 262–68

Ringel R L, Chodzko-Zajko W J 1988 Age, health and the speech process. *Seminars in Speech and Language: Aging and Communication* **9(2)**: 95–107

Thal D J, Marchman V, Stiles J, Aram D, Trauner D, Nass R, Bates E 1991 Early lexical development in children with focal brain injury. *Brain and Language* **40**: 491–527

Varga-Khadem F, Isaacs H, Papaleloodi C E, Wilson J 1991 Development of language in six hemispherectomized patients. *Brain* **114**: 473–95

Developmental Causes

S. O. Richardson

Children with developmental language pathology constitute a population with highly specific problems in development and in learning. Disorders of communication are characteristic of individuals with developmental disabilities. Children with developmental language pathology are a heterogeneous group and the range of severity of the problem between mild and severe is quite broad. There are probably multiple etiologies for any underlying deficits of the developmental language disorders. However, etiology in its usual sense is often difficult to specify (see *Incidence and Prevalence*). Identification of causal factors is confounded by the diversity of communicative disorders that are related to a single category, and by the number of diagnostic categories associated with a single communicative problem. Classification by etiology does not yield homogeneous language performance groups.

There is evidence of structural or morphologic differences in the brain of individuals with written language disorder, dyslexia. Similar studies are presently being carried out on individuals with other developmental deficiencies. However, there is much evidence implicating the familial nature of many of the disorders of communication.

Etiological considerations include neurological disorders or dysfunction; hearing loss; mental retardation; autism; craniofacial anomalies or other structural or functional problems; and psychosocial or emotional factors.

1. Neurological Causes of Developmental Language Pathology

The developmental language pathology due to disorders of the central nervous system includes dysarthria, dyspraxia, dysphasia, and dyslexia.

1.1 Malformed or Malfunctioning Focal Areas in the Brain

Focal alterations are only inferred in the case of children with developmental language disorders. Children who incur left-hemisphere damage in the early preschool years usually make a satisfactory language recovery, because of the plasticity of the brain and the fact that other areas can take over for the damaged one (see *Language Development and Brain Development*). If the damage occurs to one side of the brain during intra-uterine life, there may be a reduction in the capacities of the damaged hemisphere but this may lead to superior function of the undamaged side. Thus, some children with left-hemisphere associated developmental language disorders may be superior in spatial, artistic, or musical abilities, functions which are characteristic of the right hemisphere.

Children with cerebral palsy due to brain injury are quite heterogeneous and demonstrate various problems in articulation (dysarthria), phonation (dysphonia), fluency, and in the comprehension and use of language (dysphasia).

1.2 Impaired Cerebral Dominance

In a study of 100 adult brains, Geschwind and Levitsky demonstrated asymmetries in the surface area of the planum temporale, a language-pertinent site. The planum was larger on the left side in 65 percent of brains, indicating left dominance for language, approximately equal on the two sides in 24 percent, and larger on the right side in 11 percent (Geschwind and Levitsky 1968). Subsequent studies confirm that such asymmetry can be detected as early as 31 weeks of gestation, which supports the notion of an innate biological characteristic of language functions that is not secondary to environmental factors.

Impaired or delayed cerebral dominance is considered to be of etiological importance in developmental language pathology. It is hypothesized that the usual course of language development begins with bilateral language representation in the two brain hemispheres. This later becomes lateralized to the left hemisphere which is usually dominant for language. It is conjectured that such lateralization is defective in the individual with spoken or written language disorder.

In 1979, Galaburda and Kemper described the pathology found in the first microscopic examination of the architectural structure of the cells in the central nervous system of a dyslexic person. The patient was left-handed, had a positive family history of reading underachievement, had been delayed in the development of speech, and had documented difficulties with reading and spelling. At autopsy, the planum temporale on the left was approximately equal in size to that on the right, and cortical dysplasias and ectopias were observed in the limbic, primary, and association cortices of the left hemisphere. Similar findings have resulted from the postmortem examinations of nine other dyslexic brains. These observations clearly demonstrate the possibility of a causal relationship of brain structure to specific developmental dyslexia (Bigler et al. 1998).

1.3 Delayed Cerebral Maturation

Some authors propose the possibility of a neurological lag in the maturation of specific cortical association areas related to language. This lag presumably is due to delayed rate of nerve myelinization, synaptic growth, or to neurohumoral transmitter concentration delay. Although the theory of delay in brain maturation may reinforce the notion that communication skills will eventually improve, it must not be assumed that problems will correct themselves simply with the passage of time. Even with remediation, many youngsters with developmental language disorder continue to perform poorly in language functions as they grow into adult life.

2. Hearing Loss

Communicative disorders associated with hearing loss are related to the degree and type of hearing loss and to the time of onset of the loss. The child with a profound bilateral hearing loss present at birth has more difficulty in acquiring language than a child who sustains a hearing impairment after some speech and language have been acquired. A hearing loss may also cause difficulty with articulation and voice quality, which would interfere with speech intelligibility. In general, children with sensorineural hearing loss have the most severe speech and language problems (see *Deafness and Sign Language*).

2.1 Chronic Otitis Media During the First Three Years of Life

Chronic or recurrent otitis media with effusion can result in a conductive hearing loss which may interfere with a child's hearing during the critical period of language development. Children normally abstract and identify the phonemes of their native language early in their preschool years. Children with mild to moderate hearing loss, even if intermittent, may not receive enough acoustic information to deal with all of the speech sounds. Such a lag during the early years can also affect the development of auditory perception for speech and can interfere seriously with the development of the phonological and syntactic systems, which can have an adverse affect on semantics and understanding language.

2.2 Hearing Loss and Mental Retardation

When hearing loss is combined with mental retardation, the communication problems become magnified (see Sect. 3). Audiometric testing becomes extremely difficult. The individual is deprived of some or all auditory stimulation, and also functions in general as a much younger person chronologically. Among the syndromes that are associated with mental retardation and/or hearing loss are the following: Cockayne, Down, Goldenhar, Herrmann, Hurler–Hunter, Klippel–Feil, Mobius, Pierre Robin, Richards–Rundle, Treacher Collins, Waardenburg, and Wildervank.

2.3 Congenital Viral Infections

Congenital viral infections such as cytomegalovirus and rubella usually cause moderate to severe sensorineural hearing impairment, among other symptoms.

3. Mental Retardation

One of the primary characteristics of mental retardation is language pathology. The nature of the disorder may affect articulation, intelligibility, and the comprehension and use of spoken and written language, and may include difficulty in the pragmatics of language.

Etiological factors are difficult to identify. Prenatal and perinatal causes account for the majority of the identified cases of severe handicap. Chromosomal abnormalities constitute about a third of the known prenatal causes. Structural abnormalities of the central nervous system, fetal infection, abnormalities arising from drug or alcohol addiction, biochemical, and degenerative disorders are other identifiable causes.

The etiology of the language disorder will be related to the cognitive deficit present in the mentally retarded individual, but other causal factors may also be involved.

4. Autism

One of the major symptoms of autism (see *Autism*) is the absence of, or marked delay in, the acquisition of language. When language does develop it is usually quite different from that of a normal child. Autistic children who are also mentally retarded have added restrictions on their cognitive development so that they may not be able to achieve any functional language.

Autism is classified by the American Psychiatric Association as a pervasive developmental disorder (PDD). Although the condition originally was considered to be due to deviant interaction with parents, the majority of investigators currently accept the notion that neurological impairment of subcortical neural structures with secondary impairment of cortical development produce the autistic syndrome.

The presence of the Fragile X chromosome in the autistic population also appears to constitute a significant subgroup, ranging from 0 to 17 percent of samples at different centers, indicating the possibility of a genetic cause in some cases of autism.

5. Structural Anomalies of the Speech Mechanism

Gross structural anomalies of the larynx, pharynx, nasopharynx, velum, tongue, hard palate, jaw, teeth, or lips can create obstacles to the development of normal articulation. Advances in surgical, orthodontic, and prosthetic correction of both congenital and acquired laryngeal, oral, and facial abnormalities have greatly reduced the number and severity of articulation and voice disorders in this category.

The most common of the craniofacial anomalies which cause disorders of voice (dysphonia) and disorders of articulation (dysarthria) are cleft lip and/or cleft palate. The hypernasality characteristic of cleft-palate speech, even after corrective surgery in many cases, may also be heard in a child with velopharyngeal insufficiency due to a soft palate which is too short, or in an individual with a submucous cleft palate. Children with cleft palate often have hearing loss, which may compound their communication disorder, as in the Pierre Robin syndrome.

Few deviations from normal structure, other than the above, are sufficient causes of articulation disorders although they may interact with other factors, thereby serving as contributing causes in the development of an articulation disorder. Many persons still believe that a child with an articulation problem is 'tongue-tied.' While a very short lingual frenulum can sometimes interfere with the formation of consonants, true tongue-tie rarely occurs. In true tongue-tie the lingual frenulum is bound down to the lower central incisors.

6. Psychosocial or Emotional Factors

Psychological, social, and environmental factors clearly demonstrate a relationship with speech, hearing, and language performance. Communication disorders occur with some frequency in a large variety of psychiatric and mental disorders; in the presence of parent–child, family, and psychosocial stress; and in movement disorders, such as Gilles de la Tourette syndrome.

Children from lower socioeconomic levels or whose parents have less education generally perform more poorly on speech and language measures than those from a higher socioeconomic level with more education. It is unclear whether this is a result of fewer opportunities for experiences, less language stimulation, cultural traditions involved with child rearing, or bias in measurement. Regardless of the reason, these factors should be considered in evaluating children's performance and in determining cause.

One of the language disorders most difficult to classify by etiology is stuttering. No single cause is known although the literature on stuttering contains over 1000 years of accumulated theories. However, although etiology is unclear, there is some agreement that predisposing factors include: impaired cerebral dominance (see Sect. 1.2); instability of the neuromuscular mechanism for speech in early life; stressful environmental conditions; and a family history of stuttering and/or other language pathology.

Bibliography

Bigler E D, Lajiness-O'Neill R, Howes N L 1998 Technology in the assessment of learning disability. *Journal of Learning Disability* **31**: 67–82

Galaburda A M, Kemper T L 1979 Cytoarchitectonic abnormalities in developmental dyslexia: A case study. *Annals of Neurology* **6**: 94–100

Geschwind N, Levitsky W 1968 Human brain: Left–right asymmetries in temporal speech region. *Science* **161**: 186–87

Richardson S O 1989 Developmental language disorder. In: Kaplan H I, Sadock B J (eds.) *Comprehensive Textbook of Psychiatry*, vol. 2, 5th edn. Williams & Wilkens, Baltimore, MD

Volkmar F R, Cohen D J 1988 Diagnosis of pervasive developmental disorder. In: Lahey B, Kazdin A (eds.) *Advances in Clinical Child Psychology*, vol 11. Plenum, New York

Incidence and Prevalence
P. M. Enderby

Epidemiology is traditionally described as the study of disease in relation to populations. More recently it has been realized that this science can be broadened to investigate not just disease, but also disability and handicap. It is frequently used to identify the etiological factors in the pathogenesis of disease: to provide the data essential for management and to assist with prevention, control, and treatment of disorders.

The epidemiology of a disease is an integral part of its basic description, in the same way as the clinical findings and pathology of that disease or disorder are assumed to be essential. The subject has its special techniques of data collection and interpretation, and its necessary jargon for technical terms. The terms particularly relevant for this chapter are 'incidence' and 'prevalence.'

For a conventional incidence rate, only the first occurrence of the disorder would qualify, that is, when the person is first demonstrated to have a known condition or disability. Each new case (incidence) then enters the prevalence pool and remains there until the person either recovers or dies. Thus, 'incidence' is the number of new cases of a disorder occurring in a given population during a specified time, and 'prevalence' is the number of people with that disorder at any one time in a given population. If recovery and death rates are low then 'chronicity' is high, and even a low incidence rate will produce a high prevalence rate. Therefore, prevalence rates cannot be taken as simple reflections of incidence rates because they depend on outcome and the availability of effective treatment.

The difficulty with the precision of these terms has led to problems with epidemiological studies of well-defined and easily identified diseases. It is not surprising, therefore, that it is even more difficult to estimate the size and needs of speech- and language-impaired populations. The difficulty of studying these populations is exacerbated as the terminology for the different conditions is not uniform. Many studies of speech and language population have used the terms 'impairment,' 'disability,' and 'handicap' indiscriminately and it is sometimes difficult to elucidate from the studies how the populations described are disadvantaged.

A further difficulty which compounds the problems of gaining reliable and accurate data regarding the incidence and prevalence of speech and language pathology is the fact that these disorders form a heterogenous group as they are often secondary to a variety of underlying medical and surgical problems, or part of a general or specific developmental disorder (see *Developmental Causes*; *Acquired Causes*). There is little detailed information on the size of the speech and language symptoms associated with these problems. Nevertheless, reliable estimates of the size of the speech- and language-disabled population are needed for service planning and, while the existing literature cannot provide any definitive statement until more comprehensive data becomes available from well-planned studies, a review of it can be used to assist with the identification of service planning needs.

The likely incidence, prevalence, and number of persons with speech and language disorders associated with underlying diseases referred to here have been estimated, and also must be read, taking into account the above reservations.

1. Population Data

Enderby and Philipp (1986) reviewed the available literature and attempted to estimate the number of people in the UK with speech and language disorders associated with a range of developmental problems and medical conditions. These authors acknowledged that such estimates were sometimes difficult to derive because definitions in the literature were not uniform, and available information was sparse and was often based on specific populations rather than community-based studies. However, on the basis of the 1983 estimated population of the UK (56 377 000 persons—Office of Population Census and Surveys 1984)—Enderby and Philipp suggested that 800 000 people had a severe communication disorder (i.e., had difficulty making themselves understood by anyone other than their immediate family). In addition, a further 1.5 million had a moderate communication disorder (i.e., a speech and language defect which is noticeable to the lay person though the speaker may remain intelligible). This makes a total of 2.3 million people in the UK having some speech or language disorder. This figure does not, however, include data for autism, mutism, stuttering, psychological speech loss, familial dystonias, and psychiatric speech disturbances.

2. The Number with Speech and Language Disorders

2.1 Developmental Speech and Language Impairments

Ingram (1972) cautions readers that 'before estimates of the prevalence of disorders of speech in childhood are accepted the criteria of what constitutes a speech defect and the methods of selection should be reviewed with care.' A review of the studies by Morley (1972), Butler et al. (1973), and Peckham (1973) shows a reasonable consensus, and the average of the estimates cited suggests that 12.1 percent of early school-age children have speech or language problems which may be a consequence of pathology or delay.

A review conducted by Law et al. (1998) concerning children aged up to 7 years suggests that the number of potential cases of primary speech and language delay, that is, those delays which cannot be attributed to other conditions such as hearing loss, developmental disabilities etc, is high. When determined by a cut off on a standardised test the median is 5.95 percent but the range was found to be wide.

2.2 Learning Difficulties: Children

There is no sharp dividing line between intellectual 'normality' and 'subnormality' (Ingram 1972). An operational rule often applied by education authorities suggests that children with an intelligence quotient (IQ) of between 50 and 70 are designated moderately learning disabled, whereas children with an IQ of less than 50 are designated severely learning disabled. Estimates of the numbers of children who have an intellectual impairment (i.e., IQ less than 70) vary in different studies. However, it is generally agreed that approximately 50 percent of these children show a severe speech or language difficulty. An examination of the figures in these studies suggests that there are in the region of 300 children with speech and language disorders per 100 000 population (Fraser and Green 1991).

2.3 Learning Difficulties: Adults

The epidemiology of speech disorders for mentally handicapped adults is even less developed than that for mentally handicapped children. Abell (1988) has estimated that in the total UK population (all ages), one person in 2000 will be 'profoundly' mentally handicapped (i.e., IQ less than 20); one person in 300 will be 'severely' or 'moderately' mentally handicapped (i.e., IQ between 20 and 50); and one person in 70 will be mildly mentally handicapped (i.e., IQ between 50 and 70). These estimates are equivalent to 50, 333, and 1429 per 100 000 population respectively and amount to 1812 mentally handicapped people per 100 000 population.

2.4 Stuttering

Bloodstein (1981) refers to seven studies of populations over the age of 12 years, all of which were on selected populations, for example, school and university students, or army recruits. The same author (Bloodstein 1987) reviewing 38 studies of schoolchildren from three continents estimated an incidence of between five and 15 percent and prevalence rate of 1 percent. Andrews (1987) also reports the generally held consensus that just under 5 percent of all children will experience a period of stuttering that lasts 3 months or more, but because of late onset and early remission the prevalence rate seldom rises above one percent, and in many of these the persistent dysfluency will be mild and will not cause educational or vocational disadvantage. Four out of five children who experience a period of stuttering will no longer be stuttering by the age of 16. Nevertheless a common consensus of opinion among clinicians is that three in 1000 children may well be seriously affected. Three times as many boys as girls will stutter and the sex ratio increases with age as the girls recover more quickly than boys (see *Disorders of Fluency*).

2.5 Stroke

Some 220 persons per 100 000 population (UK) have a first or recurrent stroke each year. Allowing for the death rate and spontaneous recovery, Bonita and Anderson (1983) suggest that 30 percent of sufferers will have speech and language problems at 1 month poststroke, that is, 66 per 100 000. However they, along with other authors, caution readers regarding the timing and intensity of speech therapy treatment, as 22 percent of patients who had speech and language problems at 1 month either died or recovered without therapy by 6 months. A prevalence rate of stroke and persisting speech and language disorders of between 30–50 per 100 000 has been described by a number of authorities.

2.6 Progressive Illnesses

Many of the progressive neurological diseases may lead to speech, language, or swallowing disorders.

2.6.1 Parkinson's Disease

This disease has an incidence rate of 20 cases per 100 000 population and a prevalence of 160 per 100 000. The proportion of Parkinson's disease patients with speech disorders has been reported in a number of studies, and an average of the estimates in these studies indicates that 63 patients per 100 000 population have a speech disorder. In addition, 10 percent of Parkinson's disease patients (i.e., 16 per 100 000 population) have problems with swallowing. More recent studies would suggest this is an underestimate.

2.6.2 Multiple Sclerosis

Given the uncertain onset of multiple sclerosis, incidence rates of this disease are difficult to determine but suggested to be 10 per 250 000 (Langton Hewer 1993). The prevalence of multiple sclerosis is 80 per 100 000 population. Approximately one-half of multiple sclerosis patients have some degree of speech and language disorder, and one-third of these have great difficulty with communication. This suggests that approximately 40 multiple sclerosis patients per 100 000 population have some speech or language disorder.

2.6.3 Motor Neurone Disease

Motor neurone disease has an incidence of 1.6 per 100 000 population and a prevalence rate of 6 per 100 000. In 25 percent of cases, dysarthria and dysphagia are the first symptoms of motor neurone disease. However, all motor neurone disease patients will eventually have some degree of difficulty with speaking and swallowing as the disease progresses.

2.6.4 Other Progressive Diseases

Patients with Friedrich's ataxia, muscular dystrophy, myasthenia gravis, and Huntington's disease may also have quite severe communication problems. It is estimated that approximately 11 patients per 100 000 population will have speech or language disorders associated with these conditions. Altogether Enderby and Davies (1989) estimated that approximately 136 patients per 100 000 population may have speech, language, or swallowing problems associated with these progressive diseases.

2.7 Head Injuries

The most common communication problems following head injury are dysarthria and voice disorders. Using prevalence data cited by Field (1976) it can be calculated that there are approximately 16 000 people with speech and language pathology following head injuries in the UK. This is equivalent to 28 cases per 100 000 population. Recent studies have identified a high prevalence of pragmatic and non-verbal communication disorders in patients with right hemisphere damage which are suggested to being as disabling as the more obvious dysarthrias and dysphasias.

2.8 Voice Disorders

This section considers those voice disorders related to polyps, nodules, edema of the vocal chords, dysphonia associated with functional disorders, and laryngectomy.

The incidence rates reported are very variable and it is possible that the different estimates are a result of many patients with dysphonia not viewing the disorder as disabling or abnormal. However, it is estimated that the annual incidence of dysphonia is 28 per 100 000 population. Lundman et al. (1978) extrapolating from Swedish data, give a UK prevalence population of some 3000 laryngectomy patients and estimates that 250 operations are performed each year. In a review carried out by Philipp (cited in Enderby and Philipp's 1986 paper) it is suggested that the possible prevalence of this impairment is three per 100 000 population.

2.9 Care of the Elderly

Some 14 percent of the UK population is aged 65 years and over. Many of the elderly who have speech and language problems will already have been considered in previous sections of this paper (e.g., strokes, progressive illnesses, etc.). However, problems of communication may also arise among the elderly from conditions of unknown or uncertain diagnosis, general deterioration, and the aging process.

The Frenchay HSTMS data (Enderby and Davies 1989), on the experience of data from one health district in the UK, suggests that up to 46 new referrals per 100 000 population who have not been accounted for in previous sections covered by this article might be expected to reveal speech and language problems.

3. Conclusion

This chapter has not considered all types of speech and language impairments or their causes, for example, deafness has been omitted. Despite this, the numbers with communication impairment are much larger than previously recognized. In the 1990s health provision is being increasingly based upon the perceived needs of the population. It is therefore important to develop accurate ways of improving knowledge of the epidemiology of those with speech and language problems. There are many gaps in the information that is available (in 1999). Not only is it difficult to judge the

numbers of people who have certain disorders, it is also extremely difficult to know the proportions of patients who would benefit from the remediation of these disorders, and the impact of treatment on the prevalence rate of any disorder in the population. A great deal more still needs to be known about the natural course of speech and language disorders. Evaluations of different procedures on those disorders or health prevention techniques are difficult to judge with regard to the cost effectiveness and impact on the adequacy of communication of the population.

Bibliography

Abell S 1988 The mentally handicapped. In: Rose N (ed.) *Essential Psychiatry*. Blackwell Scientific, Oxford

Andrews G 1987 A tutorial on stuttering. In: Rustin L, Purser H, Rowley D (eds.) *Progress in the Treatment of Fluency Disorders*. Taylor and Francis, London

Bloodstein O 1981 *Handbook on Stuttering*. National Easter Seal Society, Chicago, IL

Bloodstein O 1987 *A Handbook of Stuttering*. National Easter Seal Society, Chicago, IL

Bonita R, Anderson A 1983 Speech and language disorders after stroke: An epidemiological study. *New Zealand Speech and Language Therapy Journal* **38**: 2–9

Butler N R, Peckham C, Sheridan M 1973 Speech defects in children aged 7 years. *British Medical Journal* **3**: 253–57

Enderby P M, Davies P 1989 Communication disorders: Planning a service to meet the needs. *British Journal of Disorders of Communication* **24**: 301–31

Enderby P M, Philipp R 1986 Speech and language handicap: Towards knowing the size of the problem. *British Journal of Disorders of Communication* **21**: 151–65

Field J H 1976 *Epidemiology of Head Injuries in England and Wales*. HMSO, Leicester

Fraser B, Green M 1991 Changing perspectives on mental handicap. In: Fraser W I, MacGillvray R C, Green A M (eds.) *Caring for People with Mental Handicaps*. Butterworth Heinemann, Oxford

Ingram T 1972 Classification of speech and language disorders in young children. In: Rutter M, Martin J A M (eds.) *The Child with Delayed Speech*. Heinemann Medical for Spastics International Medical Publication, London

Langton Hewer 1993 The Epidemiology of disabling neurological disease. In: Greenwood R, Barnes M, McMillan T, Ward C (eds.) *Neurological Rehabilitation*. Churchill Livingstone, Edinburgh

Law J, Boyle J, Harris F, Harkness A 1998 Screening for Speech and Language Delay: A systematic review of the literature. *Report to D.O.H.* London

Lundman M, Teneholtz, Galyas F 1978 *Technical Aids for the Speech Impaired. Proposal for Research and Development Activities*. ICTA, Stockholm

Morley M E 1972 *The Development and Disorders of Speech in Childhood*, 3rd edn. Churchill Livingstone, Edinburgh

Office of Population Census and Surveys, England and Wales 1984. *Population Trends* **30, 37**

Peckham C S 1973 Speech defects in a national sample of children aged seven years. *British Journal of Disorders of Communication* **8**: 2–8

International Perspective
K. G. Butler

The treatment of language disorders is primarily provided by language pathologists (also known as 'speech therapists,' 'speech and language therapists,' 'logopeds,' etc.; see *Overview*). These professionals function in both the educational and health systems, depending upon the development of the profession within the particular country or region of the world. Just as there are significant differences in the education of language pathologists around the world, there are varying approaches to the assessment and treatment of language pathology across countries, and it should be noted that even the concept of language disorders and a definition thereof also varies.

Most practitioners in an education, health, or social welfare system identify and remain within the system that fosters their traditions. Language pathologists differ from other human services professionals in that they may be involved across work settings, such as schools, hospitals, community or government agencies, or individual or group practice. Evaluation and intervention with language-disordered children may largely be based upon developmental and educational principles of instruction, and so language pathologists may work in an education system with other educationalists. Those working within the health system may well adopt a more medical approach which emphasizes diagnosis and treatment within a hospital or rehabilitation setting. In either case, it should be recognized that in many places around the globe, language pathology includes speech disorders within its definition and within both educational and health settings.

Language pathology changes over time, and, in the last decade of the twentieth century, new areas of concern are surfacing in certain parts of the world. For example, dysphagia (swallowing disorders) which may occur following damage to the oral and laryngeal structures is a disorder increasingly addressed by language pathologists, as are cognitive–communicative disorders following acute brain trauma, or very early prelinguistic intervention with premature infants in intensive care units in pediatric hospital settings. As services become more widespread and more sophisticated, additional new service aspects will undoubtedly emerge.

1. Entering the Twenty-first Century: The Status of Language Pathology Worldwide

Among the industrialized nations of the world where medical and educational systems are readily available to the citizens, services to the language and hearing handicapped are normally provided. However, in many countries, identification and treatment of communication disorders is severely limited. Countries where only basic educational needs have been met have begun to develop special services and to establish training programs within their own countries. In countries where literacy is high, language and hearing services may also be found; in countries where literacy is low, and in those where nutritional and health needs have yet to be met, institutions of higher education, where they exist, have still to develop programs to train language pathologists.

In those countries that have developed educational standards for the professional working with the language impaired such standards may vary from a few weeks of instruction to several years. Obviously, the level of skill required depends upon the tasks to be performed and the role to be assumed within the broader society. Instruction in such settings also varies. Some experts utilize a linguistic approach, others a behavioral approach, still others a psychological approach to both assessment and treatment. Some will view the comprehension and production of spoken language as the province of language pathology; others view the entire realm of speaking, reading, and writing as within the proper scope of practice in speech therapy.

While there are many differences, as noted above, there are also commonalities that can be identified internationally. The discipline identified as communication disorders is reflected throughout the world by its pioneers and their descendants. For example, in the USA, those who founded training programs in universities and colleges in the 1920s and 1930s were influenced by physicians in the UK and much of Europe in terms of identification and treatment, particularly in the areas of voice and stuttering. There has long been crossfertilization of research and practice through the professional literature and through international conferences and congresses, such as those provided by the International Association of Logopedics and Phoniatrics.

In general, the assessment and treatment of language disorders in a particular country in the 1990s and beyond will reflect: (a) the emergence of high-quality training programs in communication sciences and in disorders; (b) the financial resources provided through the educational and health systems to support (re)habilitation; (c) the existence of a multidisciplinary or team approach and its codification in governmental regulations; and (d) the importance of language and hearing disorders as viewed by those who establish national priorities for the handicapped and/or the disabled. Around the world, service provision and the training of professionals is developing and changing and the following subsections will simply serve to illustrate the status in some countries in the light of the comments above.

1.1 The USA and Canada

Language pathologists in the USA are now required to have completed a two-year master's program, as well as an undergraduate degree in the discipline. This is followed by an internship year and by a national examination. Canada is moving to a similar requirement of an undergraduate degree followed by a master's degree for qualification to practice. Both countries have passed national legislation requiring the identification and treatment of language- and hearing-disordered children. In the US educational system, under laws passed in 1975 and again in 1988, services are now provided to children from birth through to age 21.

In Canada, services were first provided in hospital and health settings, consonant with the development of the profession in Britain, although children's communication disorders are also provided for in school settings.

There are many similarities in training and delivery of services in North America. Both governments have developed national laws and regulations, and have provided funding for expanded services which have grown rapidly since the 1970s. In many parts of North America, states require a professional license (such as those earned by physicians, lawyers, and other professional groups). Language-hearing services are also provided to adults through the health systems in both countries.

Unlike the early years, the most commonly treated disorder in the 1990s is not fluency or articulation/phonology, but rather language disorders either as a primary diagnosis, or language disorders secondary to mental retardation, deafness, emotional and behavioral disorders, or disorders which are physiological or neurological in nature. Between 60 to 80 percent of the typical language pathologist's time is spent in providing intervention services to children and adults with language disorders.

In summary, the 200 or more training programs in the USA and the 6 training programs in Canada add an additional several thousand language pathologists each year to the almost 65 000 professionals holding advanced degrees in the discipline. These professionals provide services to the more than 35 million hearing handicapped and the estimated 10 percent of the population with language handicaps in both countries.

1.2 Australasia

In Australia, as in the UK (see Sect. 1.3), the education of speech therapists is at first degree level but post-graduate education is becoming increasingly available. Clinicians work in many settings, with a good number serving in government departments of education, and many in remote and rural areas.

In New Zealand the program in communication disorders was originally educationally oriented but is now beginning to develop a clinical model as well as the basis for its undergraduate program. Services are provided for all ages of the population.

1.3 Western Europe and the European Union

Over the past few decades language pathology has developed extensively throughout the Western European countries. In some countries the work has, to a certain extent, been dominated by the medical profession; in others, for example, the UK, the profession has developed its own autonomy. Among these countries, there is considerable variation in the range of language pathologies that are treated, the age of the population that is referred, and the setting of the service provided.

The development of programs in communication disorders began early in the twentieth century. There are now 15 undergraduate courses which the professional body, the College of Speech and Language Therapists, recognizes as leading to a certificate to practice, and postgraduate education is increasingly available. British publications in the area of communication disorders are widely read around the world. Most speech and language therapists work under the umbrella of the National Health Service (NHS) although much of the work takes place in educational or social service settings, and there is a small but growing private practice sector. Services are provided from birth and throughout all ages. There are about 4000 practicing professionals and the average availability of language pathologists within the NHS is 5.9 per 100 000 population, a gross shortfall when seen against the estimated need of 26.2 per 100,000 population (see Enderby and Davies 1989).

Members of the College of Speech and Language Therapists have been influential in the establishing of education programs, particularly in Australia, New Zealand, Canada, Hong Kong, and South Africa.

The development of the political entity of the European Union (EU) is likely to provoke far-reaching modifications in professional training and practice in the member countries. (In 1998 the member states are Austria, Belgium, Denmark, Finland, France, Germany, Greece, Ireland, Italy, Luxembourg, The Netherlands, Portugal, Spain, Sweden, and the United Kingdom.)

As of January 1991, an EC Directive came into force formalizing the arrangements by which certain EC migrants holding relevant professional qualifications may have these recognized by another member state. However, where there are substantial differences in professional training, a professional wishing to move from one member state to another may be required to choose between taking an aptitude test or a period of supervised practice. A professional wishing to work in another member state can apply to a 'designated authority' in the 'host' country for a ruling on whether their qualification can be accepted as equivalent or what steps they need to take to obtain recognition.

Since there is considerable variation in the education of speech and language pathologists, there will undoubtedly be a need to establish a more formal recognition and identification of skills and abilities required by the profession across all countries. This collaboration should enhance the body of knowledge in the field of language pathology, and the harmonization of standards of clinical practice should help to achieve the highest standards of care for the communication handicapped.

1.4 Scandinavia

Logopeds in Sweden and Denmark are trained primarily in medical settings, and serve in clinics and at times in school settings. In Norway the initial training is in education but with a strong clinical emphasis. Research and clinical practice are well established.

1.5 Central and Eastern Europe

During the early part of the twentieth century, centers of learning were being established in Russia, Poland, Hungary, Czech Republic, and Slovakia with training for logopeds already being well established. Prior to World War II, there was much sharing of research and practice between Western and Eastern Europe. Following the war, research in Eastern Europe suffered due to lack of advanced technology and instrumentation, difficulty of obtaining journals and books, and the lack of opportunity to share information with colleagues outside the Eastern bloc. However, the massive political changes between 1989 and 1992 reunited professionals working in the field of language pathology with their Western European colleagues and the exchange of information has been reinstated.

1.6 Africa and Israel

In South Africa the universities of Pretoria and Witwatersrand have long had excellent programs which train language pathologists of both dominant and minority cultures, but other universities have developed programs, notably in Cape Town and Durban.

In North Africa, programs in Egypt have been established and others are evolving, as is the case in Israel. In western and eastern African countries, however, the work with the communicatively handicapped is dependent on a number of voluntary agencies and some medically funded research programs, tending to represent isolated attempts to meet the most basic and severe needs of the language and hearing handicapped.

1.7 Asia

The leading country in Asia in terms of language pathology is Japan, with well-established research centers in Tokyo and Kyoto. Phono-surgery is a topic of significant interest to medical specialists. Language pathologists, on the other hand, have only begun to serve in school settings, and to deal with language disorders in educational and rehabilitation settings since the 1980s. Work in aphasia has been underway for some time; child-language services are currently being expanded. Research in reading disabilities is probably more prevalent than in oral language disorders. The nonalphabetic characteristics of the Japanese and Chinese languages are a barrier to the use of research conducted in regard to child language with speakers of alphabetic systems.

Taiwan, in the late 1970s, undertook a national effort to provide services to handicapped individuals, and has developed training programs in medical centers, particularly Taipei. A national association has been formed and, in the 1990s, language pathology is emerging as a profession in this country.

In contrast, China has yet to establish such programs. Teachers of the deaf are receiving training from American colleagues through a funded project from a private philanthropic source.

1.8 Hong Kong

In Hong Kong, for many years, a few selected professionals from the health and education services (e.g., nurses and teachers) were sent to the UK and Australia to undertake training as language pathologists. Since 1988 a course has been set up at Hong Kong University but services for the language impaired will remain understaffed for some time to come.

1.9 Southeastern Pacific Countries

Most southeastern countries have yet to develop programs, either of training or for the provision of services. The islands of the Pacific, with the exception of Hawaii, have been unable to provide language services. Some attempts have been made to establish the incidence of hearing loss in Samoa, Papua New Guinea, Guam, and elsewhere. Micronesia is composed of tiny islands scattered over eight million square kilometers of ocean in the South Pacific, with nine recognized major languages and many district dialects. There are high prevalence rates of otitis media, but there is no ear, nose, and throat physician within the eight million square kilometers and no audiological or language pathology services were being provided in the 1990s (Stewart et al. 1989).

1.10 India

The development of the profession in India began in the 1960s and was influenced greatly by both the UK and the USA. Educational courses commenced at an early stage and have produced relatively small numbers of well-qualified graduates. The University of Mysore has shown particular strength in the postgraduate field, especially in the area of speech science. It has been estimated that there are over seven million individuals with cerebral palsy and even more with hearing loss. The demand for services is overwhelming and the Indian government has set up a number of scientific institutes to assess needs and develop strategies to meet them.

1.11 South America

A few programs of training exist in the South American countries but the status of language pathology as a profession is only slowly evolving, and like other Third World countries the needs of the communicatively handicapped have a low priority.

2. Implications for the Future

Language pathology services vary dramatically around the world, ranging from extensive services for the general population of a country, to little or no services in Third World countries. In most countries, the development of educational programs to train specialists in language pathology goes hand in hand with public education and its attempts to assist individuals with disabilities of all kinds. Thus, those countries in which legislation has been passed to provide national support for educational, social, and health services are those which also have the strongest university programs in speech therapy.

Demographics also vary country by country. For example, in the USA there is an aging of the general population, but also a massive immigration which swells the ranks of young children with limited English proficiency. Both of these events have given rise to the need for increasing language assessment and intervention. Health costs, however, have risen very rapidly, and resources, particularly in the health system, are becoming more difficult to access. Language pathologists working in the educational system may find themselves in large school districts where anywhere from 59 to almost 100 different languages are spoken. Ascertaining speech and language disorders in multilingual settings is a problem, since most assessment instruments have been normed on the dominant language of the country, if normed at all.

While we have not yet reached the status of the 'global village' that some futurists predict, language pathologists now comprise a group of professionals which is estimated to be at least 125 000 worldwide. While only a few are multilingual, the proportion of those who are skilled in serving multicultural populations will increase over time. The advent of advanced technology to serve nonspeaking populations continues to expand rapidly. The research which underpins the practice of language pathology, and which is published in journals which reach across the globe, bodes well for the profession and for the consumer of language pathology services.

Bibliography

Butler K G 1986 *Language Disorders in Children*. Pro-Ed, Austin, TX

Butler K G 1986 Language research and practice: A major contribution to special education. In: Morris R J, Blatt B (eds.) *Special Education Research and Trends*. Pergamon, Oxford

Enderby P, Davies P 1989 Communication disorders: Planning a service to meet the needs. *British Journal of Disorders of Communication* 24: 301–31

Gerber S E, Mencher G T (eds.) 1988 *International Perspectives on Communication Disorders*. Gallaudet University Press, Washington, DC

Moll K L 1983 Training programs in logopedics. *Folia Phoniatrica* 35: 198–219

Stewart J L, Anae A P, Gipe P N 1989 Pacific Islander children: Prevalence of hearing loss and middle ear diesease. *Topics in Language Disorders* 9: 76–83

Developmental Speech and Language Pathologies

Deafness and Sign Language

E. Pizzuto and V. Volterra

The acquisition, development, and use of spoken language crucially depend on hearing. Any hearing loss thus interferes with the use of speech, especially when it is present at birth or acquired during the first years of life, before the development of spoken language. Hearing impairments occurring later in life also affect language comprehension and production, but have a less significant impact, because spoken language development has already taken place. This chapter is concerned only with early childhood deafness and its consequences on the communication and language patterns of deaf children and adults. It focuses on the linguistic abilities deaf individuals can express, not only in spoken languages (with their subsidiary written codes), but also in the visual-gestural or sign languages used as primary means of communication within the different deaf communities existing in the world.

1. Early Childhood Deafness

Deafness is a complex sensory impairment, including a wide range of types and degrees of hearing losses. Along with the age of onset of deafness, the different typologies of hearing impairment are one of the key elements that can lead to very different outcomes concerning the child's communicative and linguistic development.

A hearing loss may affect one ear (unilateral), or both ears (bilateral). The main classification of auditory impairments is based on the physiological structures of the auditory pathway being damaged, thus distinguishing between conductive, sensorineural, mixed, and central deafness. In the conductive type, a damage to structures of the middle ear (caused by illnesses such as otitis media or traumatic events) impinges upon the transmission of sound to the inner ear. In many cases, the damage is transitory and hearing may be partially or entirely recovered with or even without medical treatment. Sensorineural deafness is determined by lesions within the inner ear, or along the auditory nerve to the brain. The damage is generally permanent and more severe than in conductive deafness. Mixed types of deafness are transitory forms in which, for example, middle ear inflammations determine temporary conductive deafness in a child with sensorineural deafness. Central or cortical deafness, more rare and still poorly understood, involves a damage of the auditory nerve in the brain stem or in the hearing centers of the cortex.

The degree of hearing loss is commonly measured by means of pure tone audiometric tests. A special machine generates pure tones at different frequencies and intensities, covering the range of speech sounds, and the subject's responses are recorded. The hearing loss is evaluated by measuring in decibels (dB) the loss of pure tone receptivity in the better ear. Based on the degree of hearing loss, the following forms of deafness are distinguished: *mild* (26 to 40 dB loss), *moderate* (41 to 55 dB), *moderately severe* (56 to 70 dB), *severe* (71 to 90 dB), and *profound* (more than 91 dB). Pure tone audiometric tests require the subject's active collaboration, and may be difficult or impossible to use at an early age. Before 1 year of age, other techniques can be used such as automated auditory brainstem response, which can detect the subject's response to external auditory stimuli by analyzing variations in the electric activity of the brain.

The causes of deafness vary widely, and may remain unknown. According to studies conducted in the United States, genetic-hereditary deafness (which can have dominant or recessive traits) accounts for 50% of all cases of childhood deafness of known origins (Vernon and Andrews 1990). Other frequent causes include maternal rubella, childhood illnesses (measles, mumps, and meningitis), and birth- or pregnancy-related complications (prematurity, trauma, anoxia, Rh incompatibility, toxic medications).

Data concerning Western developed countries indicate that about 1 in 1000/1500 children suffer from sensory-neural deafness (usually severe to profound) which is present at birth or acquired shortly after. A much larger number of children suffer from milder middle-ear conductive deafness acquired during preschool or school years. Although in these forms hearing may improve, in many cases the hearing loss becomes permanent and may also have serious consequences for the development and use of spoken language. Data on the incidence of childhood deafness outside Western countries are very limited, though they suggest that in many developing countries in Africa, Central Asia, and South America the number of deaf children may be significantly larger (Schein 1987).

1.2 Individual Variability

In addition to the various types and forms of hearing loss, and the age of onset of deafness, several factors contribute to generate marked individual differences among deaf children and adults. From a medical point of view, one important variable is the presence or absence of other impairments besides deafness. Hereditary deafness usually does not carry along any other impairment, but damage to other sensory systems is possible when deafness is caused by maternal or childhood illnesses. The family and sociocultural background, quality, and type of language intervention received, and the educational program attended also significantly influence deaf children's developmental patterns (see Sect. 4).

With regard to family background, a crucial source of individual differences is linked to whether a deaf child is born within a hearing family or within a family where one or both parents are deaf themselves. The largest majority of deaf children (90–95%) have hearing parents who communicate with their child primarily in spoken language. In these families, due to the difficulties the child encounters in naturally acquiring spoken language, child–parents communication is often severely restricted, and both the child and the parents go through a difficult and complex process of psychological adjustment to each other's communicative needs (Gregory 1995). A small minority of deaf children (5–10%) have deaf parents who communicate with their child in their native sign language. In these families, unlike in those with hearing parents, the child acquires naturally the visual-gestural language to which he/she is exposed (see Sect. 2 and 4), and the patterns of parents–child communication are comparable to those proper of hearing parents and hearing children.

2. Sign Language and Deaf Communities

It has been known since antiquity that deaf people used among themselves visual-gestural signs, noted for example in ancient Greece by Plato (*Cratilus*, xxxiv). However, the beginning of the modern study of sign language can be dated to 1960, when William Stokoe published the first structural analysis of American Sign Language (ASL), the language used by deaf people in the United States and parts of Canada and

Mexico, soon followed by the first ASL dictionary (Stokoe et al. 1965), and by more detailed studies of the structure, processing, and neurological organization of the language (Klima and Bellugi 1979).

ASL remains the most extensively investigated sign language, but since the 1970s research has been extended to several other sign languages used in the world, including many European ones, replicating the major finding of earlier research on ASL: although perceived and produced in the visual-gestural medium, all sign languages examined possess the distinctive structural properties of natural human languages (see Sect. 2.1).

Studies conducted in recent years in several countries have shown that adult deaf people constitute specific minority communities, with their own organizations, social structures, attitudes, values, cultural history, visual arts, and, above all, their sign languages (Erting et al. 1994). Sign languages are used as the prevailing means of communication among most deaf adults even though the number of native deaf signers is very small. As noted, only a small minority of deaf children, namely those born within deaf families receive a sign language as their native linguistic input. The large majority of deaf individuals have hearing parents, and learn their national sign language at widely different ages, from the school years through adulthood, whenever they happen to find themselves in settings where there are other signers.

Sign languages have been in the past disregarded or even overtly opposed within the surrounding hearing societies: they were considered primitive communicative systems which could hinder the acquisition of spoken languages by deaf children. Only since the 1980s have some national or international organizations such as the American Commission on Education of the Deaf, and the European Parliament, recognized sign languages as full-fledged native minority languages. Nonetheless, recent surveys indicate that in most countries of the world the needs of the deaf populations continue to be largely ignored (Lane et al. 1996).

2.1 Sign Language Structure

A traditional misconception about sign languages was that signs were akin to spontaneous gestures that may accompany speech in hearing people. Since gestures are often supposed to be understood across different cultures, it was believed that there was just one universal sign language. Contrary to this view, it has been shown that, unlike coverbal gestures, all sign languages are autonomous systems, with lexical, morphological, and morphosyntactic structures which are functionally analogous to those found in spoken languages. There are structural similarities across sign languages, like across spoken languages, but there are as many different sign languages as there are national or local communities of deaf signers.

Each sign language has developed its own lexicon and its grammar independently of other sign as well as spoken languages. Thus, for example, ASL is different from, and historically unrelated to British Sign Language (BSL), even though the American and English hearing populations use two varieties of the same spoken language. Interlinguistic differences are most evident at the lexical level. Figure 1 illustrate the signs meaning MOTHER in BSL, ASL, Danish, and Italian sign languages. Following a common convention, and due to the lack of a standardized orthographic system for writing sign languages, signs are rendered in this text in capitalized English glosses, as in MOTHER.

Signs have an underlying structure which is functionally analogous to the phonological structure proper of spoken languages. In any given sign language, a restricted number of contrastive units combine to produce all the signs of the language. These units have been described as formational parameters and comprise four classes of elements: the *places of articulation*, *hand configurations* (or *handshapes*), *movement*, and *palm orientation* with which each sign is produced. Each sign language uses a specific set of locations, handshapes, movements, and orientations, combined according to language-specific rules.

All sign languages investigated so far have revealed a rich morphological and morphosyntactic structure organized in space as well as in time. Systematic alterations of the signs' formational parameters, especially of the movement and place of articulation, are used to signal morphological distinctions between different classes of signs (e.g., between nouns and verbs), and several grammatical categories (e.g., singular versus plural in nouns and verbs, person, aspect, and subject-object relations in verbs). A crucial feature of sign languages' grammar is the use of marked locations in the signing space for specifying grammatical relations. This is illustrated in Figure 2 by a sequence of signs composing a simple declarative sentence of Italian Sign Language (LIS) meaning 'the cat chases the dog.'

In producing the sentence, the signer first articulates with his/her left hand the noun DOG (Fig. 2a), followed by a particular type of sign categorized as a classifier because it refers to a class of referents. This sign, which means 'single entity,' is associated with the noun DOG and remains positioned at a marked location (Fig. 2b), while the signer produces with their right hand the noun CAT (Fig. 2c), followed by another 'single entity' classifier (Fig. 2d). In the actual flow of signing, this second classifier then becomes the

a

b

c

d

Figure 1. Four different signs meaning 'mother' in: British Sign Language (a), American Sign Language (b), Danish Sign Language (c), and Italian Sign Language (d).

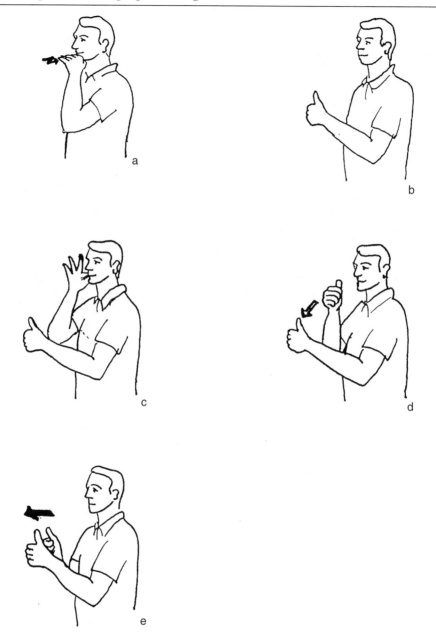

Figure 2. A sentence from Italian Sign Language meaning 'the cat chases the dog'. The signs illustrated are: DOG (a), SINGLE-ENTITY (b), CAT + SINGLE-ENTITY (c), SINGLE-ENTITY + CHASE (d), CHASE (e).

first segment of the verb CHASE, which is produced with a directional movement starting at the point marked earlier by the classifier for CAT (Fig. 2d), and ending at the point marked by the classifier for DOG (Fig. 2e). The grammatical relation between subject and object is thus marked in LIS (and other sign languages) by verb spatial inflections, and by the spatial arrangement of the signs, rather than by a sequential ordering of the sentence elements, as is used in several spoken languages such as English.

182

The primarily spatial features of sign languages' grammar have led researchers to explore possible differences in the neurological organization of sign as compared to speech. Most of the studies have been conducted on ASL, and show that in signers, as in speakers, there is a pattern of left-hemisphere specialization for language processing, and a complementary right-hemisphere specialization for visuospatial functioning (see Poizner et al. 1987).

3. Auxiliary Manual Codes

While sign languages are natural languages with their own lexicon and grammar, there are other manual codes that are not autonomous languages, but auxiliary systems devised to teach spoken and written language to deaf children. One such system is fingerspelling, used since the seventeenth century in several language communities with an alphabetic writing system. Specific handshapes represent the letters of the alphabet, and spoken or written words can be articulated as handshapes sequences. Fingerspelling can be incorporated in sign languages to represent proper names, or words for which there are no corresponding signs, and may obey particular formational constraints in sign languages in which it is used frequently, as in ASL.

All the manual codes employed within educational, speech training, or family contexts are forms of bimodal communication: different combinations of signs taken from the national sign languages, fingerspelling, and artificially created manual signals are used simultaneously with speech. The systems used vary widely depending upon the detail with which they represent the structure of speech and the number of artificial signs or fingerspelled sequences they include. All forms of manually coded speech follow the word order pattern proper of the spoken language being coded, and the visual-spatial devices of sign languages' grammar are not used. In the simplest forms of manually coded speech, the content words occurring in sentences (nouns, verbs, adjectives, adverbs) are combined with the corresponding signs borrowed from the national sign languages, and few invented signs or fingerspelled sequences represent the most common function words, or grammatical morphemes, such as articles or prepositions for which no corresponding natural signs exist. In more complex forms of sign-supported speech, there are more invented signs or fingerspelled sequences for spoken grammatical morphemes. For example, in a system known as Signing Exact English, the manual letters L-Y are added to adjective signs to signal the morpheme proper of English adverbs. There are also systems that aim at facilitating lip-reading, such as cued speech, in which specific hand configurations and positions represent vocalic and consonantal sounds that deaf children find particularly difficult to discriminate.

4. Language Learning and Use in Deaf Children and Adults

There are remarkable differences in the communicative and language abilities that deaf children and adults can display in sign as compared to spoken languages. Beyond individual variability, the language skills that deaf individuals can achieve when they acquire a sign language as their native language are comparable to those found in native speakers of spoken languages. But learning and using spoken language is a very difficult task for all deaf children, many of whom never attain an appropriate competence.

Since the 1970s the acquisition of sign languages by deaf children of deaf parents has been explored with the same methodologies used in research on spoken languages. The most detailed information concerns the development of ASL (Newport and Mayer 1985), but the major findings have been replicated in other sign languages including BSL, LIS, Dutch, and Danish Sign Languages. These findings show that the timing and pace of sign language acquisition correspond fairly closely to those observed in spoken language acquisition. Signing children produce their first signs around 1 year of age, when hearing children begin to produce their first words. For several months the repertoire of signs remains limited, and children's utterances consist of only one element. There have been reports of an earlier appearance of signs as compared to words, but additional evidence suggests that many putative early signs are comparable to communicative gestures observed in hearing children acquiring spoken languages, and that lexical development in sign is not more precocious than in speech (Volterra and Erting 1994). The errors children make in their early signs involve substitutions of the signs' formational parameters, and are comparable to phonological simplifications observed in hearing children's early word production. Around 18–24 months, the first two- and multi-sign utterances are noted, the repertoire of signs increases significantly, and the acquisition of grammatical and morphological structures begins. The acquisition of sign language visual-spatial grammar is a slow process which begins around 30 months, with the acquisition of spatial inflections of verbs, but continues to well over 3 years of age, and several manual and non-manual markers that signal grammatical agreement are mastered at only around 6 years. These patterns are similar to those identified in hearing children who acquire morphologically complex spoken languages.

While a sign language can be acquired in a natural way, under the appropriate input conditions, spoken language does not develop spontaneously in deaf children with severe to profound hearing losses. In all cases, several years of intensive instruction are required. The level of spoken language comprehension and production a deaf child will attain is not easily predictable, and the timing and pace at which different children develop their spoken and, subsequently, written language skills can vary widely, in relation to all those factors generating individual variability within the deaf population (see Sect. 1.2). An early diagnosis of deafness (within 1 or at most 2 years of age), along with the provision of effective hearing aids and language intervention programs (see below), are additional important variables that can favour the development of spoken language. However, the evidence available shows that on the average, even with instruction, the acquisition of spoken language is markedly delayed: first words may not appear until 2 or 3 years of age, vocabulary grows at a very slow rate, two- and multi-word utterances may only begin around age 4 or 5 years, and the acquisition of morphology and grammar is likewise delayed and may remain incomplete. For example, studies conducted on school-age deaf children and adolescents acquiring spoken English show that, compared to their hearing peers, deaf children produce shorter and syntactically simpler utterances, made primarily of nouns and verbs, with few or no function words. The performance of deaf children on spoken language production and comprehension tasks also improves fairly slowly as a function of age.

The difficulties deaf children encounter in using spoken language are most frequently carried over in the development of reading and writing skills, and persist in adulthood. Studies on American and English deaf readers show that, on average, their reading comprehension skills are considerably lower than those of hearing children. Data on the development of written English indicate that deaf subjects produce shorter sentences and simpler syntactic structures than hearing controls, display poor vocabulary and lexical rigidity, encounter problems with relative, subordinate, and passive sentences, and have particular difficulties with several function words and grammatical morphemes (articles, prepositions, conjunctions, pronouns, verbal auxiliaries). Similar difficulties have been documented for written Italian in deaf children and adults.

In recent years, researchers have begun to investigate the development of sign, speech, and literacy in deaf children and adults as a function of the input received within the family or school context. Concerning the development of sign, studies of preschool age deaf children of hearing parents with no sign input have shown that these children spontaneously develop a gestural communication system that possesses some of the properties of early sign language. Studies of school-age children of hearing parents exposed to bimodal communication, with different forms of sign-supported speech, also indicate that these children can go beyond the input they receive: they spontaneously produce some of the linguistic devices proper of the visual-spatial grammar of sign languages, which are

not provided in the manually coded speech they receive. These data have been interpreted as evidence that some language abilities can develop even in the absence of appropriate input, and may thus be innate. However, other investigations on older deaf individuals have found that there are marked differences between the abilities attained by non-native signers and those of native signers: non-native signers are significantly less fluent, especially in the use of the complex spatial morphology of sign languages. The relevance of appropriate sign language input for the development of adult language skills thus cannot be underestimated.

Several investigations have begun to assess the effectiveness of the use of signs in promoting the development of spoken language and literacy in school-age deaf children of both deaf and hearing parents. It has been reported that the use of sign-supported speech facilitates child–parents and child–teachers communication, but apparently does not enhance spoken and written language abilities to the extent expected by the proponents of these methodologies. There are data showing that American deaf children of both deaf and hearing parents, educated by using ASL as the primary language of communication and instruction, attain a significantly higher level of proficiency in spoken English and literacy (Strong and Prinz 1997). These results have led to several countries adopting bilingual-bicultural programs in which deaf children, of both deaf and hearing parents, are taught in the national sign language as the primary language of communication and instruction, and English or other spoken languages, with their related written forms, are taught as second languages.

Together with the data on adult sign languages, those on the role of the input in the development of sign, spoken, and written language abilities contribute to clarify an issue that has been hotly debated since the eighteenth century: whether deaf children should be taught only to use oral language, because their knowledge of sign could hinder the development of spoken language, or whether, on the contrary, signing should have a primary role in the education of deaf children. These opposing views are known as the 'oralist' and 'manualist' positions. The information available indicates that a sign language allows deaf individuals to express language abilities comparable to those of hearing individuals, albeit in the visual rather than the vocal modality. There are no data showing that sign language negatively interferes with spoken language learning, while there is evidence that it can favor the development of both spoken language and literacy. However, as noted, the spoken language abilities of deaf children and adults may remain more limited compared to their sign abilities, due to the different processing demands of the two language modalities. A sign language relies on the unimpaired visual-gestural modality, and thus can be perceived and produced effortlessly by deaf individuals, whereas spoken language crucially relies on the impaired sense of hearing, and its use always requires considerable effort. The educational and technical tools currently in use are still insufficient to overcome the problems that deafness creates for spoken and written language use, and need to be improved.

4.1 Technological Advancements and Medical Intervention

Hearing aids are the major type of technological device for helping deaf individuals to perceive speech sounds. The largest majority of children who are born deaf have some residual hearing, and hearing aid devices have shown remarkable improvement in the last decades. However, hearing aids amplify all sounds in the environment, and special training is necessary for learning to discriminate speech sounds against background noise. The effectiveness of hearing aids depends on the degree, type, and form of deafness, but auditory gains can vary considerably even among children with the same kind of deafness.

In recent years, a new type of medical surgery known as cochlear implant has been proposed as an effective treatment for restoring the sense of hearing, and allowing deaf children to communicate orally. In cochlear implants, an electronic device is permanently installed into the inner ear and connected with a processor placed outside, in order to allow the perception of sounds by direct stimulation of the auditory nerve. This major surgical operation is preceded and followed by intensive language training. Originally proposed for individuals with acquired deafness and, subsequently, only for children who could not benefit from traditional hearing aids, cochlear implants have been recently made on a growing number of children with early profound deafness. There is still a hot debate on the effectiveness of cochlear implants: several medical professionals strongly advocate the advantages of this surgery, while many international and national deaf associations have raised strong reservations on the effectiveness of implants, and the ethical problems connected with the use of invasive surgery with children (see Lane et al. 1996). The scientific research conducted on children with cochlear implants is still extremely limited, and it has methodological restraints that do not allow an appropriate evaluation of the results achieved (e.g., reports are limited to small and heterogeneous groups of subjects and/or language tasks). More objective research data are necessary to assess the efficacy of this medical treatment.

5. Present and Future Trends

The study of sign languages has opened new perspectives for a deeper understanding not only of deafness, but also of human language. It has been clarified that, despite a sensory deprivation which hampers the development of spoken language, deaf individuals can express their language capacities via the visual-gestural modality, creating natural sign languages which are structurally and functionally comparable to spoken languages. Comparative explorations of sign and spoken languages, and of their processing demands, have led to more accurate descriptions of the defining features, and of the neurological organization underlying human language. Yet, much remains to be understood concerning the communicative and linguistic needs of deaf individuals, and the problems that most of them face in developing appropriate spoken and written language abilities that have not been overcome. Recent findings on the positive role that sign language knowledge can have for improving literacy skills are encouraging, but these research lines need to be substantially expanded. Extensive research also needs to be conducted on the employment of today's visual and multimedia technologies (including speech sound displays, video captioning, electronic communication, multimedia applications with sign and written language) as a major means for helping deaf individuals to overcome the limitations imposed by their hearing loss.

Bibliography

Erting C J, Johnson R C, Smith D L, Snider B D 1994 *The Deaf Way—Perspectives from the International Conference on Deaf Culture*. Gallaudet University Press, Washington, DC

Gregory S 1995 *Deaf Children and their Families*. Cambridge University Press, Cambridge

Klima E S, Bellugi U 1979 *The Signs of Language*. Harvard University Press, Cambridge, MA

Lane H, Hoffmeister R J, Bahan B 1996 *A Journey into the Deaf World*. DawnSignPress, San Diego, CA

Newport E L, Mayer R P 1985 The acquisition of American Sign Language. In: Slobin D I (ed.) *The Crosslinguistic Study of Language Acquisition*, 2 Vols. Erlbaum, Hillsdale, NJ: 881–938

Poizner H, Klima E S, Bellugi U 1987 *What the Hands Reveal about the Brain*. MIT Press, Cambridge, MA

Schein J D 1987 The demography of deafness. In: Higgins P C Nash J E (eds.) *Understanding Deafness Socially*. Charles C Thomas Publisher, Springfield, IL: 3–27

Stokoe W C, Casterline D, Croneberg C 1965 *A Dictionary of American Sign Language on Linguistic Principles*. Gallaudet College Press, Washington, D.C.(2nd ed. 1975 Linstok Press)

Strong M, Prinz P M 1997 A study of the relationship between American Sign Language and English literacy. *Journal of Deaf Studies and Deaf Education* **2(2)**: 37–46

Vernon M, Andrews J F 1990 *The Psychology of Deafness*. Longman, New York

Volterra V, Erting J C 1994 *From Gesture to Language in Hearing and Deaf Children*. Gallaudet University Press, Washington, DC

Developmental Dysarthrias

E. Davies

1. Introduction

The term 'developmental dysarthria' encompasses a range of sensori-motor speech disorders which arise as a result of pre-, peri, or post-natal neurological damage (i.e., conditions which occur *prior to* or *contiguous with* the child's acquisition of motor speech control. Damage to the neural mechanisms which regulate the synchronous control of *respiration, phonation, resonance, prosody*, and *articulation* can result in *anarthria* (complete absence of articulate speech), or, more commonly, *dysarthria* (disordered speech). Dysarthrias are dynamic, varying across the range from minimal dysfunction to complete absence of intelligible speech, dependent upon the degree of severity of the underlying neuropathology. In any one child or adult with developmental dysarthria intelligibility may vary according to a multiplicity of interacting factors, for example, affective state, situational context, time of day, fatigue, or drug therapy.

Although developmental dysarthrias are primarily the outcome of neurological impairment and may be classified according to a medical model, they may not exist in isolation. It is impossible to separate the development of motor speech skills from the development of other related skills for example, sensory, perceptual, and cognitive. If, as Peterson and Shoup (1966, cited in Netsell 1986: 7) state 'there is considerable reason to believe that the phonologic aspects of speech are primarily organized in terms of the possibilities and constraints of the motor mechanism with which speech is produced' then the child with developmental dysarthria is more likely to experience difficulties with the internal representation of speech sounds, and with phonological processing in general. There is a significant difference, however, between the all-pervasive problems of motor *control* experienced by those with developmental dysarthria and the specific problems of motor *programming* demonstrated by those with speech dyspraxia, in whom the automatic functions of chewing, sucking, and swallowing are preserved. The consistency of errors in those with dysarthria is in marked contrast to those exhibited by children and adults with developmental dsypraxia where variability is a key diagnostic factor. The picture may be further complicated in those instances where dysarthria and dyspraxia co-exist.

In addition to phonetic and phonological disorders, language acquisition may be disordered as a consequence of brain damage where the processes of comprehension and/or production of language may be impaired. In many cases language acquisition may be delayed as a result of the child's inability to learn through exploration and play.

Social interaction may also be constrained by physical disability, limited intelligibility, reduced number of communicative partners, and their feedback to the dysarthric speaker. Pragmatic aspects of communication are often affected as the dysarthric speaker is unable to participate as an equal partner in the communication act.

As speech and feeding share the same embryonic origins and much of the same musculature, developmental dysarthria may be compounded by difficulties with chewing, sucking, and swallowing.

The dysarthrias associated with cerebral palsy may be further complicated by the existence of persisting primitive reflexes (e.g., sucking) and/or pathological reflexes (e.g., 'snap' reflex) which distort attempts to target articulatory placement.

2. Differential Diagnosis

Differential diagnosis may be made on the basis of the presence, or absence, of distinctive speech errors which are consistent with particular categories of dysarthria.

The distinctive speech errors, or clusters of symptoms, are usually classified according to the scheme proposed by researchers at the Mayo Clinic in the late 1960s and early 1970s (Darley et al. 1975). The Mayo Clinic classification identified five distinct categories of dysarthria—'flaccid', 'spastic', 'ataxic', 'hypokinetic,' and 'hyperkinetic' (slow and fast), plus a sixth 'mixed' form. Each type is described and traced to the assumed location of neuropathology and underlying neurological condition. There appears to have been a wholesale adoption of the Mayo model by clinicians working with both acquired and developmental dysarthrias. Whilst there are obvious diagnostic advantages and therapeutic implications in using such a model, there are inherent problems in applying the classification too rigidly to developmental dysarthrias where the categories (described in Sect. 2) may be somewhat blurred because of diffuse congenital brain damage.

3. Classification

The following characteristics are identified in the specific categories of dysarthria:

3.1 Flaccid dysarthria

Flaccid dysarthria results from specific muscular or lower motor neuron lesions (e.g., muscular dystrophies, bulbur palsies, bulbar poliomyelitis, Moebius syndrome). The muscular weakness and reduced tone (hypotonia) gives rise to the following speech charac-

teristics, in addition to drooling and/or feeding difficulties, mimicking those of pseudobulbar palsy:

Respiration: weak and unsustained
Phonation: breathy with audible inspiration
Resonance: hypernasal because of palato-pharyngeal incompetence. Nasal air emission. Occasional reflux of food/liquid
through nose
Articulation: weak and imprecise
Prosody: distorted by lack of synchronous coordination of all of the above

3.2 Spastic dysarthria

This results from lesions(s) of the upper motor neurons (e.g., pseudobulbar palsy). The increased tone
(hypertonicity) may be so severe that oral and articulatory movements are impossible. The child may be
anarthric (speechless) and have significant problems
with feeding. Drooling is frequently a major problem
because of the constant open-mouthed posture and
limited tongue movement to initiate swallowing.
Speech characteristics are as follows:

Respiration: reduced control of airflow
Phonation: phonatory stenosis, hyperaddution of
vocal folds, creating harsh, strangled
voice quality
Resonance: palato-pharyngeal incompetence leading to variable hypernasality
Articulation absent or slow and imprecise; poor
coarticulation reducing rate and accuracy
Prosody: inappropriate breaks affecting rate,
rhythm, stress, and intonation

3.3 Ataxic dysarthria

Ataxic dysarthria arises from the cerebellar damage
of cerebral palsy. Muscle tone is reduced, affecting
control for speech and feeding:

Respiration: reduced control of airflow
Phonation: delayed voice onset—excessive volume
on initiation, fading rapidly. Prolonged
intervals in phonation
Articulation: mistargetted, slurred; some phoneme
prolongation
Prosody: grossly distorted—rather 'drunken'
quality of excess and equal stress, and
dysrhythmia

3.4 Hyperkinetic (slow) dysarthria

This results from lesions of the extrapyramidal system—athetoid, dyskinetic, and dystonic forms of cerebral palsy. Fluctuations in muscle tone produce
distorted movements and postures. Fine motor control is severely impaired, for both speech and feeding:

Respiration: shallow, irregular
Phonation: problems in initiating and sustaining
voice. Excessive loudness with
increased tone, fading to a whisper with
sudden decrease in tone. Inappropriate
phoneme voicing
Articulation: mistargetted, reduced intelligibility
Prosody: grossly distorted

3.5 Mixed dysarthria

The mixed dysarthrias described by the Mayo clinic
classification relate to the progressive problems exhibited by those with progressive neurological diseases
such as motor neuron disease or multiple sclerosis.
Specific features become evident as the disease progresses, whereas in those with developmental dysarthria characteristics of multiple forms of dysarthria
may be present from the outset.

4. Identifying The Problems

Respiration is essential for life support. Although the
neuroanatomic structures for breathing are shared for
speech this functional adaptation is phylogenetically
much more recent. Breathing and speech are controlled by independent neural functional systems and
breathing will take precedence over speech because of
its survival value. It may be difficult, if not impossible,
to sustain and maintain the tidal airflow at the appropriate pressure for the appropriate length of time
necessary for speech. Respiration may be shallow and
irregular—'gulp' or 'belly' breathing—close to the
limits for life—and incapable of adaptation for higher
cortical functions (Davies and Gordon 1986).

Even if breath control is adequate for *phonation*
there may be insufficient muscle tone to bring the
vocal folds together to initiate voice (as in flaccid
dysarthria). Conversely the vocal cords may be held
in hyperaddution because of increased tone in the
spastic form of dysarthria. Voice onset time is delayed
and, on release of closure, there is rapid, wasteful
expulsion of air. The fluctuations of muscle tone
observed in the dyskinetic forms of cerebral palsy
will have features of both hypo- and hypertonic voice
quality.

Resonance, because of the problems of insufficient,
increased, or fluctuating muscle tone, will vary from
normal to grossly abnormal and/or hypernasal.

The problems of *articulation* were once the primary
focus of dysarthria therapy. If sucking, chewing, and
swallowing, which share the same neuroanatomic
structures are impaired, then what are the implications
for the phonetic abilities which constitute motor
speech skills?

If there is a 'learned cognitive element to *phonetic
development* as well as phonological development'
(Hewlett 1990: 16), the child with developmental dysarthria becomes locked in to a sensorimotor loop of

mistargetted approximations, substitutions, or omissions, determined by his/her physiological limitations. Milloy and Morgan-Barry (1990: 114) identify the following phonetic errors which may occur as a result of problems of motor control: fronting; backing; gliding; lateral realization of lingual fricatives; vocalization of 'l' and 'r' hypernasalization.

They also identify the *phonetic* and *phonological* processes related to temporal co-ordination; voicing difficulties, including devoicing of initial consonants, or voicing of unvoiced phonemes, prevocalizations; consonant cluster reduction; one or both elements reduced; final consonant deletions; stopping of fricative or frication of stops; prolongation of phonemes; within-word pauses; weak syllable deletion.

Unlike the adult with acquired dysarthria who may have intact phonological representation in order to self-monitor and self-correct, the child with developmental dysarthria is doubly disadvantaged. With problems at *both phonological* and *phonetic levels* there may be little self-awareness of the dysarthric speech output, nor any attempt at repair, other than repetition of the same unintelligible utterance.

Prosody is inevitably affected if spatiotemporal organization is disordered. Timing, pacing, intonation, stress, and rhythm contribute significantly to listener intelligibility. Equally, abnormal prosody may be as disruptive to intelligibility as phonetic mistargetting.

Nonverbal communication may also be limited in the child with developmental dysarthria because of damage to the neural mechanisms supplying the face, head, neck, and upper limbs. Eye gaze and fixation may be reduced because the child cannot sustain his/her head upright and in the mid line. Facial expression can be distorted by grimacing, or by the open-mouthed posture of the child with suprabulbar or pseudobulbar palsy. Gesture may also be limited because of increased, decreased, or fluctuating tone in the upper limbs.

The implications for the *pragmatic aspects* of communication are evident. The child with developmental dysarthria may have difficulties in initiating, or sustaining, interaction in which he/she is an unequal partner. Repair strategies like repetition or rephrasing or spelling which help the listener to understand may also be limited for a multiplicity of reasons related to neurophysiological and neuropsychological factors.

Psychologically, an oversupportive environment where the child's needs are anticipated, can be as restrictive as one which provides too little stimulation. The expectations of parents/care-givers can influence significantly the child's interactive skills. In each extreme the child may become the passive listener rather than an active participant in communication interaction. A happy medium is often difficult to attain.

4.1 Feeding difficulties

Feeding disorders may be the first indicators for the child 'at risk' of developmental dysarthria. While speech and feeding share the same neuroanatomic structures the neural functional systems develop independently. Sucking, chewing, and swallowing functions are regulated by pacemaker neurons in the brain stem and are established *in utero*, whereas speech control matures in the cortex as a continuous, nonlinear process throughout critical sensitive periods in the first two years of life, and this development continues until puberty.

Pathological or persisting primitive feeding reflexes interfere with the child's oral and articulatory control, and may continue their disruptive influence throughout life.

4.2 Assessment

Although significant advances have been made in acoustic and physiological measurements since the Mayo Clinic's original perceptual classification of the dysarthrias, these techniques appear to have had a slow uptake amongst clinicians working with children/adults with developmental dysarthria. This may reflect the limited access to cineradiography, videofluoroscopy, electromyography (EMG—the technique for recording muscle action potential), and strain gauge transducers which measure muscle strength and resistance. It may also stem from a reluctance to expose children to procedures whose clinical implications are, as yet, unknown or unproven. The majority of clinicians are, therefore, still dependent upon auditory and visual analysis of dysarthric speech patterns, using profiles which have been developed, primarily, for those with acquired dysarthria. These may be supplemented by analyses of feeding behaviors (e.g., Evans-Morris 1985) and communication interaction checklists. These procedures should provide the basis for remediation.

4.3 Intervention

The primary aim of therapy is to establish the maximum degree of intelligibility possible within the physiological constraints imposed by neurological impairment. For those individuals for whom intelligibility is an unrealistic goal then the focus of therapy is broadened to establish effective communication by whatever means possible.

Intervention may involve a variety of therapeutic approaches:

Didactic
Teaching strategies to improve motor co-ordination and control.
Use of techniques such as proprioceptive neuromuscular facilitation to develop muscle control, strength, and sensitivity.
Reduction of maladaptive behaviors assumed by the dysarthric speakers.

Prosthetics

Use of such devices as palatal prosthesis to improve oro-pharyngeal closure and to reduce hypernasality and nasal emission.

Other prostheses to support sitting, balance, and head position are important aspects of total management.

Augmentative and Alternative Modes of Communication (AAC)

Unaided modes of communication, for example, facial expression, gesture, sign may be available to supplement speech. These approaches may be temporary as a mode of support until communication skills improve or may be used to supplement communication throughout life.

Aided means of communication, that is, those which require some display, for example, picture boards, photographs, symbol systems, or traditional orthography may be provided as a temporary or permanent means of communication for the individual with anarthria or severe dysarthria.

These displays may be used to provide an interface to technological aids which provide a visual display or spoken output. This aspect of provision has seen the most dramatic growth in the last decade.

Maintenance

Management of the client with developmental dysarthria is long-term and often life-long. Therapy may be offered at intervals in order to maintain communication competence.

Counseling

Counseling should be an integral part of therapy to provide support for the client and care-givers and to ensure that therapeutic gains are maintained.

Medical support may be necessary for the prescription of muscle relaxants (e.g., Baclofen), atropine derivatives (for control of drooling), or anti-convulsants.

Surgical intervention may be necessary to target specific problems, for example, pharyngoplasty to reduce hyponasality or resection of salivary ducts to control excessive drooling.

Dysarthria therapy is essentially a team approach to ensure maximum communicative competence.

Bibliography

Darley F L, Aronson A E, Brown J R 1975 *Motor Speech Disorders*. W. B. Saunders, Philadelphia, PA

Davies E, Gordon N 1986 Children with delayed development of speech and language. In: *Neurologically Handicapped Children: Treatment and Management*. Blackwell Scientific, London

Enderby P 1983 *Frenchay Dysarthria Profile*. College Hill Press, San Diego, CA

Evans-Morris S 1985 Developmental implications for the management of feeding problems in neurologically impaired infants. *Seminars in Speech and Language* **6**: 293–315

Hewlett N 1990 Process of development and production. In: Grunwell P (ed.) *Developmental Speech Disorders*. Churchill Livingstone, Edinburgh

Kraat A 1987 *Communication Interaction Between Aided and Natural Speakers: A State of the Art Report*. Trace Research and Development Center, Madison, WI

Milloy N, Morgan-Barry R 1990 Developmental neurological disorders. In: Grunwell P (ed.) *Developmental Speech Disorders*. Churchill Livingstone, Edinburgh

Netsell R 1986 The acquisition of speech motor control: A perspective with directions for research. In: *Neurobiologic View of Speech Production and the Dysarthrias*. College Hill Press, San Diego, CA

Robertson S 1982 *Dysarthria Profile*. (Personal publication)

Disorders of Fluency

H. H. Gregory and C. B. Gregory

As language develops and as articulatory proficiency is acquired, there are at the same time changes in the way in which sounds, syllables, and words flow together in children's speech. Optimal speech flow is referred to as fluent, and disruption in this flow as disfluent. Studies show that children become more fluent with age. There are fluctuations in the fluency of individual children from time to time and considerable variability among children. Likewise, there are broad differences in the fluency of acceptable adult speech. Although this variability exists, certain deviations in fluency are identified as problems, either by the speaker or listeners. This article will focus on defining and describing the two most common fluency problems, stuttering and cluttering, both beginning in childhood. Acquired neurogenic and psychogenic stuttering in adults will also be considered (see Sect. 3).

1. Stuttering

1.1 The Problem of Definition

The definition of stuttering must consider both overt (auditory and visual characteristics) and covert features (feelings and thoughts). Looking first at overt features, to define the beginning of a stuttering problem in a child is far from a matter of saying definitely that the child either is or is not a stutterer. The diagnosis is one of degree taking into consideration the quantity and quality of disfluency. Certain disfluencies, word and phrase repetition and most of the non repetitious disfluencies (such as pauses, interjections, and revisions) occur frequently in the speech of most preschool children. Within-word breaks in fluency (sound and syllable repetitions and prolongations of sounds) are much less frequent. Clinicians are more concerned about increases in these latter types of disfluencies in a child's speech as indicating the beginning of a stuttering problem. In addition, there is more concern about one-syllable word and part-word repetition (sound or syllable) if there is a higher frequency of repetition per instance (two or more) and more so if increased tension manifests itself in an irregular tempo. Most clinicians and researchers agree that a key aspect of disfluency that defines stuttering is increased tension. There is more concern about the speech of a child if there is a disruption of airflow or phonation between the units of a repetition. Of course, other signs of tension in the lips, jaw, larynx, or chest are more obvious characteristics. A complete blockage of voice or airflow is the most apparent sign of stuttering. Recent research has emphasized the gathering of better data comparing the disfluency of nonstuttering and stuttering children, resulting in improved qualitative and quantitative diagnostic criteria.

If the progression of development continues and awareness of difficulty with speaking increases, the older child or the adult will begin to struggle with tense interruptions and acquire patterns such as word substitutions, starters ('uh, uh, uh, uh,—well uh, well uh'), hand gestures, or sudden gasps of air. Depending on the circumstances that exist, a vicious cycle may develop, including increased expectation of difficulty, more fear, more tension, and more stuttering.

Stuttering can vary from very mild (hard glottal initiations and slightly tense repetitions) to severe (blocking and struggle). The speech of some stutterers is characterized by a degree of cluttering in which speech is more rapid, slurred, jerky, and contains articulation errors (cluttering is discussed in Sect. 2).

Covert aspects of stuttering include the fear associated with the expectation of difficulty and the frustration that coincides with feelings of communicative failure. Clinical observations and parents' reports indicate that as the overt features of stuttering increase, these covert characteristics grow stronger. The desire to inhibit or avoid stuttering can be described by older children and adults and is sometimes mentioned by preschool children ('Can you help me to talk better?'). As stuttering persists, the person's self-concept is influenced by communicative difficulty and maladaptive attitudes.

In summary, the reference for defining stuttering is a continuum of disfluency from that which is more typical of most children, to quantities and qualities of disfluency that are very unusual. Likewise, the covert features vary in degree from no apparent awareness to a strong desire to avoid and inhibit stuttering complicated by handicapping attitudes that pervade the person's life.

1.2 The Prevalence and Incidence of Stuttering

Stuttering is present in about 1 percent of the school-age population. Although the highest incidence is between ages 2 and 5, many cases are of short duration and new cases appear regularly during this period. Thus, the prevalence at these preschool ages remains fairly stable at about 1.5 percent. The lifetime expectancy of ever stuttering, even for a short period, is approximately 5 percent (see *Incidence And Prevalence*). It seems appropriate to conclude that developmental, or what is sometimes referred to as idiopathic stuttering, begins in childhood and that the incidence is particularly high at the time that relational language is developing.

The male–female ratio among stutterers, as revealed by surveys, has varied from 2.2:1 to 5.3:1. There is evidence that the sex ratio increases with age. Either more boys begin to stutter later or girls tend to recover more readily. The generally accepted ratio is three or four males to each female (see *Incidence And Prevalence*).

There are some variations in incidence and prevalence among cultures, differences that have been hypothesized to be related to societal pressures to achieve and conform. So far as is known at present, stuttering occurs all over the world. The very low incidence of stuttering acquired in adulthood will be discussed later.

1.3 The Development of Stuttering

Stuttering begins in childhood between the ages of 18 months and 9 years. It may develop rather suddenly, but in most instances it develops over a period of weeks. During the early stages, the cyclic nature of the problem is often observed for the first time. Many parents report that stuttering in their children was present for a few days, then there was what they describe as a period of normal speech, followed by stuttering again. Clinical experience indicates that the longer the cycles of fluency, the better the prognosis. In most cases, initial stuttering is characterized by repetitions of sounds and syllables (parts of words or one-syllable words) and perhaps some prolongations of sounds. A few children, however, show obvious tension and blocking as the earliest signs. Onset tends to be more sudden in this latter group. The reader should recall at this point what was said earlier about defining stuttering in terms of the quantity and quality of disruption in the flow of speech.

The following developmental progression reflects

and summarizes the way in which the growth of the problem of stuttering is often described in the literature: speech is a forward moving, ballistic process. The normal speech of adults is often characterized by some tension and some fragmentation (word repetition, interjections, rephrasing, etc.). All speech in the process of development is likewise characterized by some tension, to a greater or lesser degree, and some fragmentation. Repetition of a word (usually the first word in a phrase and usually a function word or a pronoun) is a fairly frequent occurrence in children. After a certain point in development, a syllable repetition and then a sound repetition reflects even greater tension and more disruption. A sound prolongation reflects still greater tension and fragmentation. Tense repetitions may end in prolongations. Finally, a tense labial, lingual, or laryngeal posture obviously reflects more tension and serious fragmentation. With even greater tension, there may be tremors of the lips, jaw, or vocal mechanism.

Speech pathologists prefer to describe a stuttering child's speech behavior and attitudes about speaking on an individual basis and not to try, as was done earlier, to place them into a certain stage of the development of stuttering, such as primary, transitional, or secondary.

1.4 Spontaneous Recovery from Stuttering

Some children have transient episodes of stuttering. Based on retrospective research, clinical observations, and parent reports, a conservative estimate is that about two-thirds of children who show a noticeable degree of stuttering at some time, regain normal fluency. In discussing prevalence, it was observed that between 2 years 6 months and 5 years of age, some children are recovering from stuttering at the same time that new cases are appearing. Females have a higher rate of recovery, another female advantage as far as not developing stuttering is concerned. There is evidence that those who are more severe and who have a family history of stuttering have a lower probability of recovering. Based on self-reports, speaking more slowly, relaxing, and going ahead and talking despite some insecurity are factors believed to be associated with recovery.

Of course, there are problems with studies of spontaneous recovery such as how stuttering and recovery are defined and the accuracy of memory of those reporting in retrospective investigations. These difficulties must be considered in evaluating studies of spontaneous recovery. However, clinical experience does support the research that has been done.

1.5 The Causes of Stuttering

For years there was hope of finding the one cause of the problem and the best way of treating it. Today with reference to research knowledge and clinical experience, it is recognized that stuttering is a complex problem with many factors contributing to its development in children and its maintenance in children and adults. Therefore, research has been directed toward a better understanding of these factors. Clinical evaluation is seen as a process of determining if there is concern about a child's disfluency, and if so, what factors appear to be contributing to the condition. In older children and adults where the diagnosis of stuttering is more obvious, the clinician describes the speech characteristics and begins the process of understanding the person's attitudes. Based on these observations, treatment programs are formulated manipulating the variables studied in the evaluation. Clinical experience revealing that there is improvement when this is done, provides a rationale for this strategy.

The following is an analysis of the major areas of contemporary research and clinical study related to stuttering. As implied above, research results and clinical observations must be viewed in terms of the degree of confidence one has in the importance of particular factors in stuttering. It appears that no variable is indisputably related to stuttering. Thus, needs for further research will be noted. Even though there is no certainty about the causes of stuttering, there will be brief references to the implications of present knowledge for prevention and intervention.

1.5.1 Family History of Stuttering

The development of more precise genetic models and increased precision in the conduct of family history studies has led Kidd (1984) to believe strongly in the possibility that a genetic factor functions to make some children more susceptible to stuttering. It is assumed that environmental factors interact with this predisposition. According to present thought, a genetic susceptibility is possibly necessary, but certainly is not sufficient to produce stuttering. In addition, females are more resistant to an inherited predisposition to stutter than are males. The offspring of a female stutterer is more likely to stutter. However, if either parent stuttered, the familial risk is higher. Kidd states:

> A lower overall incidence among females in conjunction with a higher incidence of affected relatives of female stuttering probands suggests that more factors promoting stuttering are required for a female to stutter and that families of female probands have more of those factors since they have more affected members.
>
> (Kidd 1984: 160)

There is no specific information about the genetic material that may be involved in stuttering. Rapid progress is being made in the study of chromosomal differences, and looking to the future, this is an area of study that offers promise.

Children who stutter tend to have a higher than

expected incidence of articulation and language problems. It has been speculated that stuttering, late talking, and articulation difficulties are different manifestations of what in all probability is an inherited condition. Thus, family history may alert us to the possibility of developmental language problems (see *Specific Language Impairment: Subtypes and Assessment*). It is also possible that family history influences the parents' evaluation of a child's speech.

In terms of primary prevention, that is, dealing with the process that leads to a disorder, a profile of high risk would have stuttering in the family at the base. If there is stuttering in the family and/or delay of language development, the family should be counseled about language development and the relationship between communicative and other environmental stress and fluency. Increasing attention is being given to the prevention of stuttering and much progress is being made.

1.5.2 Linguistic Processes in Stuttering

Since the incidence of stuttering is highest during the years of the greatest development of language (ages 2 to 5), there has been considerable interest in the relationship between the two. There is a great deal of agreement, with reference to studies, surveys, and clinical experience, that there is a higher prevalence of problems of articulation and language in children who stutter. Researchers have looked for more specific relationships between the characteristics of the communicative message (idea, word selection, and syntax) and fluency. Most studies of either nonstuttering or stuttering children, ages 2 to 4, have revealed a greater than expected number of disfluencies on function words and pronouns at the beginning of syntactic units. It is hypothesized that younger children respond to these syntactic units as the basic units of speech formulation and speech motor production. In both nonstuttering and stuttering children, there is a transition during ages 4 to 8, to more disfluency on content words. In explaining this, it is frequently speculated that preschool children do not have an awareness of words, and that this awareness is acquired during this transition period. Learning to read probably contributes to this, since word recognition and recall become important at this time. Thus, words become more prominent as units of expressive speech.

Investigations have provided convincing evidence that there is a relationship between syntactic complexity and disfluency or stuttering. However, it is difficult to relate the loci of disfluency precisely to a linguistic factor. One must keep in mind that more complex syntactic structures are usually longer and probably spoken at a faster rate, two other factors that affect fluency. Several prominent discussants of speech fluency and language have concluded that disfluency and stuttering occur at a point in the utterance where there is a combination of stresses. Different

children come to the speaking situation with different capacities and experiences and thus respond in unique ways. In experimental designs, it is difficult to deal with all of the variables related to stuttering in a way that allows systematic observation of the influence of separate language factors (syntactic, semantic, pragmatic, etc.).

Perhaps one of the most recent research approaches producing interesting findings has been the measurement of alpha-wave suppression using electroencephalography (EEG). Adult stutterers, compared to nonstutterers, show more suppression of alpha (increased activity) over the right hemisphere immediately preceding an overt language task or when listening to speech. Nonstuttering subjects show more suppression during these tasks over the left hemisphere, as expected in terms of cerebral dominance for language. The usual left hemisphere dominance is explained in terms of the left hemisphere ordinarily being more of a segmental–temporal processor, whereas the right hemisphere is more of a time-independent, holistic processor. Apparently, stutterers process language differently. A very provocative finding (see Moore and Boberg 1987) is that this brain functioning, as reflected in the EEG, changed following therapy in two studies that have been reported. Therapy emphasized the temporal–segmental aspects of speech, and it is speculated that EEG change mirrored the improvement in speech. However, it is also hypothesized that the right hemisphere subserves higher emotional and mood functions. It is, therefore, also possible that therapy reduced emotional reactivity and right hemisphere excitability.

Although much research will be done in this area, the field already appears to be in a strong position to look at language factors clinically. If necessary in therapy, specific articulation and language problems can be treated in a way that does not increase speech stress, for example, by gradually incorporating changes into the hierarchy of therapy activities. This hierarchy, often adhered to in helping the child speak in a more relaxed way, follows a language developmental progression going from shorter to longer utterances and from less to more meaningful content.

1.5.3 Speech Motor Processes

There has been a long history of interest in the malcoordination of the speech mechanism as an etiological factor in stuttering. Since about 1970, there has been a renewal of this interest. At the same time, it has been noted that care must be taken not to fragment various components of speech and language production, for example, linguistic and motor functions. Nevertheless, although findings are somewhat mixed, the motor speech reaction time differences in which stutterers show slower voice initiation times imply the possibility of a slower reacting speech motor system in stutterers. Positive evidence of a difference is stronger in adults than in children. Of course, motor speech behaviors are quite variable in children. Small differences with considerable variability make it difficult to reveal these differences, that may be present, in a significant way. The differences, if actual, are minimal, and there is still debate about the influence of emotional conditioning in the small differences found.

In speech pathology, measures of diadochokinetic rates of the speech structures and the sequential chaining of syllables are used routinely in evaluations. In terms of therapy, procedures that approach the modification of speech fluency by increasing the duration of speech segments with smoother blending would seem to be appropriate when a minimal motor deficit is either found or assumed to exist. When modeling changes in speech, a strategy to enhance both language facility and motor coordination can be used by proceeding from shorter, less complex utterances to longer and more syntactically complex ones. Propositionality is regulated at the same time by going from less to more meaningful topics.

1.5.4 Auditory Processes

Since the discovery that delaying one's auditory feedback (DAF) has an effect of increasing disfluency and stuttering-like behavior, there has been much study of the auditory system of stutterers. Studies of the central neural auditory system in stutterers have been inconclusive. The most positive findings have been the results of dichotic listening tasks using meaningful words. Stutterers show more reversals of the usual better right ear scores and smaller between-ear difference scores. Since individual test scores are not sufficiently reliable, clinical use of dichotic listening is not suggested. Some clinicians include tests of auditory processing such as memory span, and when deficits are found, procedures for improving these functions are included in therapy. It is presumed that improving this ability will improve auditory–motor functioning and the capacity for fluency.

1.5.5 Psychological Factors

The consideration of these factors in stuttering is almost as complex as the subject of stuttering itself. Just as it is difficult to separate out the precise way in which linguistic and motor factors contribute to stuttering, it is impossible to say that a factor is not related to the psychology of stuttering. In terms of the development of the problem, some theorists view the environment as primary and others believe that environmental influences interact with physiological predispositions (perhaps genetically based). Reports of parents and the clinical observation of children, indicate that unless abated by correct management (either naturally in the environment or through clinical intervention), learning enters into the acquisition of increased tension and fragmentation of fluency

(more stuttering). Awareness (expectation of difficulty) is accompanied by the development of negative emotion related to speaking. Eventually, the person's self-concept is influenced by the difficulty of communicating.

Research has focused on parent–child interaction studies showing that parents of stuttering children respond more negatively to their children and tend to apply more communicative stress, for example, speak more rapidly, ask more questions, and allow inadequate opportunities for their children to respond to questions. Such studies support clinical observations and provide support for counseling parents about the modification of communicative and interpersonal stress, either in the prevention of stuttering or in early intervention.

Social–psychological conditions such as increased propositionality of speech, increased time pressure, and increased audience size increase stuttering. Observations that stutterers have little or no difficulty when speaking alone has been confirmed by many studies. The more authority the listener is perceived to have, the more the speaker stutters. These observations support the use of a desensitization approach in therapy, going from less propositional (involving less meaning and communicative responsibility) to more propositional utterances, and finally, from easier to more difficult speaking situations. These dimensions can be integrated with procedures referred to earlier as related to linguistic and motor processes.

Personality dynamics as related to stuttering and stuttering therapy has received less attention in recent years. This appears to result from the negative findings of studies comparing groups of stutterers and non-stutterers using various psychological test procedures (e.g., questionnaires, projectives). In making decisions about treatment, the trend in the 1990s has been to explore in more depth the personal adjustment of the individual child or adult, or in the case of children, the family interaction. More multidisciplinary cooperation with clinical psychologists and psychiatrists is another trend aimed toward dealing effectively with psychological factors related to stuttering.

1.5.6 Differential Evaluation—Differential Therapy

Research aimed toward defining subgroups of stutterers has not been conclusive. However, descriptions of evaluation and treatment are based on the conceptualization of stutterers as a heterogeneous group. Most clinicians believe that the evaluation of a child or adult stutterer should be broad including a thorough case history and testing or observation of the subject's speech and other variables as discussed above. There are commonalities in therapy, but the process is individualized for each subject.

For children, in addition to an analysis of fluency, other characteristics of the child's development (language, articulation, and motor control), environmental variables such as communicative stress (the way people talk to the child), and interpersonal stress (the way people interact in the family) are examined. With school-age children, the characteristics of the speech behavior, environmental factors, and the child's attitudes are considered, but language and articulation problems may also be involved.

In terms of treatment approaches, there is more controversy existing about the methods for working with upper school-age subjects and adults than for the younger age groups. Gregory and Gregory (1991) have described this controversy in terms of the 'stutter more fluently' and the 'speak more fluently' models. The 'stutter more fluently' approach emphasizes monitoring, analyzing, and gradually modifying stuttering. Supposedly, the reduction of the desire to avoid brought about by these procedures, results in increased fluency. The 'speak more fluently' approach stresses the use of various procedures to increase fluency with minimal or no attention to the person's stuttering. In this case, negative emotion is said to be reduced by the person's increased confidence in the ability to speak without stuttering. Many clinicians have resolved this controversy by utilizing a combination of the two models. Identification, monitoring and gradual modification of stuttering and associated unadaptive speaking characteristics (rapid rate, erratic prosody, etc.) are combined with fluency-building skills such as easier initiation, blending, and variation in rate, loudness, effort, and inflection. There is a paradox here that stutterers should understand. 'Acceptance and modification of stuttering' as a part of therapy contradicts 'building fluency' and vice versa. It is very difficult, through research, to prove that one model is more effective than the other. Many variables enter into the outcome of therapy and it is difficult to assess the influence of all of them.

Most authorities agree that if and when work is more direct in modifying the speech of younger preschool and school-age children, more easy relaxed speech is modeled for them, and attention is given to the stuttering that persists only to the extent necessary. Thus, this represents more emphasis on the 'speak more fluently' model (see *Disorders of Fluency: Intervention*).

1.5.7 Transfer and Follow-up

Although generalization of changes will occur in therapy, that is, modified speech learned in one situation will generalize to another similar situation, it is essential for the clinician and the client to plan for the acquisition of changes in situations other than where the previous learning took place. Actually, this process of situational transfer is a continuation of procedures earlier in therapy in which changes are made first in shorter then longer utterances, and first in less meaningful and then in more meaningful contexts. A commonly used approach is for the client and the

clinician to generate a hierarchy of speaking situations from the easier to the more difficult, and then to practice gradual changes in speech and other behaviors following this hierarchy.

Since stuttering is known to be cyclic before, during, and to a lesser extent following therapy, and as there is a tendency for regression to occur following a core period of therapy, it is important that a therapy program provides follow-up. Activities aimed toward the maintenance and extension of change over time include a home program of practice and scheduled visits to the clinic for review. As the parents of children, the children themselves, or adult clients encounter new experiences in life, the attitudinal aspects of therapy, as well as the speech modification aspects, need continuing attention.

Persons who stutter commonly report having had therapy that was only partially successful. It is widely believed that this occurrence can be reduced if therapy programs provide, and clients are helped to accept, follow-up programs. Therapy failure is often related to ineffective follow-up programs or a client's lack of motivation to participate in such a program.

2. Cluttering

2.1 The Problem of Definition

Cluttered speech is excessively rapid in rate, contains stuttering-type repetitions of sounds, one-syllable words, parts of words, and phrases. Articulation is slurred and indistinct. Often, there is a burst of speed within a phrase, and the same melodic pattern is repeated in almost every phrase. It has been called 'disorganized speech' because that is how it sounds. The recognition of cluttering may be hampered by the condition being mild or by its being combined with stuttering. Rapidity with impaired intelligibility are the first two distinguishing characteristics of speech that should bring cluttering to a listener's attention. In children with this problem, speech is not clear from the beginning of connected speech production. Weiss (1964), one of the most prolific contributors of information about cluttering, postulates that stuttering develops as an attempt on the part of a child to avoid or inhibit cluttering. Other writers about fluency problems agree that this does occur, but they indicate that stuttering arises in other ways most of the time. The literature on cluttering contains much conjecture based on clinical observation. Very little research has focused on the etiology, description, and development of the disorder.

To further differentiate cluttering from stuttering, covert characteristics of expectation, fear, tension, and struggle do not develop in children who clutter. Thus, there is not a progression of development in the breakdown of fluency like that described for stuttering. Adult clutterers are usually not particularly aware of their less intelligible speech. Possibly, compared to stutterers, clutterers are less sensitive. They often come to our attention as young people who are having trouble being understood in a speech class or at work. Actually, cluttering has come to the author's attention only infrequently when it was not a factor in a stuttering problem. Most clinicians who see children in the early stages of developing a stuttering problem, report observing children in whom there is a cluttering component. Likewise, adult stutterers seen in therapy may have a combined stuttering–cluttering problem.

2.2 The Prevalence and Incidence of Cluttering

Prevalence and incidence data like that given for stuttering are just not available for cluttering. Although Europeans interested in speech and language disorders have been the major contributors of information about cluttering, they have not while in Europe, or in many cases after moving to the USA, gathered this kind of data. American and British authorities on fluency problems have focused mainly on stuttering and have taken only passing notice of cluttering. Based on clinical reports, one would say that the prevalence is much lower than that of stuttering. It also appears to occur more frequently in males.

In addition to the lack of interest, perhaps the difficulty of sorting out cluttering from other speech and language problems has contributed to the sparsity of demographic studies. This paucity of detailed research about cluttering points to the need for more basic information concerning all of the disorders of speech and language.

2.3 Associated Language Problems

The description of cluttering involves characteristics of fluency and articulation. Most observers have reported that clutterers also have specific problems of expressive language (semantic and syntactic) and deficiencies in reading, spelling, writing, and formulation. When reading aloud, clutterers may skip entire lines, repeat sections, and insert nonexisting words or phrases. They may have poor recall and ability to tell a story. Illegible handwriting is a counterpart of inarticulate speech. When there is a rapid rate, jerky rhythm, and slurred speech, some specialists see associated language problems as the confirming sign that the problem is cluttering. Clinical writers speak of cluttering as a complex of language and learning disorders.

2.4 Motor Coordination

Reports dating back many years have described clutterers as having poor overall coordination. Developmental histories reveal delays in sitting, standing, and walking. As described previously, there has been a long history of interest in the relationship between the coordination of the speech structures and stuttering. However, research of this type has not been done focusing on such variables as voice reaction time,

general reaction time (e.g., finger tapping), voice onset time, and the physiology of cluttering. This is hard to understand since one would think that there would be more interest in the specific underlying abilities of subjects with this complex problem. Again, the dearth of research may relate to the low prevalence of the problem, the difficulty defining the problem, and the possibility that those with the problem in its mild or moderately severe form do not seek help.

2.5 Intelligence and Personality

Like stuttering, cluttering may occur in a person anywhere along the range of intellectual ability. Cluttering is seen often in the mentally retarded and at least one observer states the belief that many of the mentally retarded stutterers are actually clutterers (Daly 1986). Historical reports state that clutterers are impaired in their expressive language abilities and have problems of concentration and attention span. Along with short attention span, clutterers are generally seen as hyperactive, impulsive, restless, and irritable. Their personalities are probably influenced greatly by their perceptual capacities, short attention span, etc.

However, clutterers are said to have high mathematical–quantitative intelligence. As one might expect, rhythmical and musical abilities are poor. It must be concluded, as the reader no doubt discerns, that more objective observations of these and other characteristics of clutterers are needed.

2.6 The Cause of Cluttering

Although the problem of cluttering has not been researched as extensively as stuttering, those who have worked with clutterers clinically express great certainty that the disorder runs in families and is associated with an organically based central language imbalance. Clutterers have been observed, as noted above, to be more poorly coordinated. However, neurological examination does not reveal significant neurologic signs. Until now, detailed and extensive family history studies (like those done in stuttering) to clarify the possibility of genetic factors have not been carried out.

Those who write about cluttering report that it is seen in patients where there is known brain damage and other obvious symptoms. These cases are sometimes described as incapacitated, in contrast to those in which there are no neurological signs, who are designated as underendowed.

Electroencephalographic (EEG) studies of clutterers and stutterers in textbooks on fluency disorders dating back to 1951 purport to show that abnormal brain wave activity was found three to four times as often in clutterers as in stutterers (Daly 1986). This was cited as evidence for a pathogenetic etiology of cluttering. More recently, considering that the behavior can be modified with effort, and that in stutterers the EEG pattern changes as the behavior changes, there is increased thought that EEG findings in clutterers may reflect a functional difference.

As professionals are more accepting of the observation that some stutterers have reduced capacity for speech and language production, there is an even stronger impression that clutterers as a group have a reduced capacity. More research is needed. Studies should focus on diagnostic refinements and more careful comparisons of subjects showing certain disfluency characteristics, on measures of language, brain functioning, and response to treatment. Family history studies should be considered, but they are likely to be difficult because retrospective reports will be unreliable due to the unawareness of, and difficulty in, identifying cluttering among family members. Indeed, it is possible that family history studies of stuttering have included reports of family members being stutterers when they were actually clutterers.

2.7 The Treatment of Cluttering

There has not been as much interest in cluttering as in stuttering and there has not been as much controversy about therapy. When clutterers are able to decrease their speech rate, there is an immediate improvement. However, it is very difficult for them to maintain this change and therapy requires considerable concentration and effort. This trouble is related to their previous inattention to their speech and unawareness of the nature of their problem. A person who stutters will often show great improvement in therapy immediately and display what may be called a flight into fluency. In stutterers this immediate fluency is of a short duration, but the person experiences great freedom from the problem while it lasts. This does not occur in clutterers. In addition, clutterers do not experience cyclic variation before, during, and after therapy, as do stutterers.

Useful techniques for improving the speech rate of clutterers include 'syl–lab–i–fi–ca–tion' drill, first on words and then phrases, choral reading, and the use of DAF. When using DAF at 180 milliseconds delay, the person is instructed to speak in a slow drawl to counteract the disruptive effect of the delay. Then, as the delay is decreased, rate can be increased to normal. The clinician models this increase in rate, and at the same time may model better inflection. Sound discrimination techniques and the imitation of correct production can be used to improve articulation. The syllabification procedure also contributes to better speech sound production. The improvement of grammar, syntax, formulation, and composition can follow activities used in language therapy.

Clutterers, like stutterers, profit from learning to speak in phrases, realizing that speech involves pausing, at which time normal inhalation for the support of speech occurs. It is also emphasized in therapy that listeners can comprehend phrased speech better. As

might be expected, clutterers and stutterers report that phrasing enhances their thought and expressive language processes. Clutterers find speech change more difficult to achieve and stutterers find speech change easier to attain but more difficult to accept. Both find it difficult to maintain (see *Disorders of Fluency: Intervention*).

3. Acquired Stuttering in Adulthood

3.1 The Problem of Definition

Although there has been some debate about the nature of the dysfluent behaviors that characterize adult onset stuttering and whether the condition is neurogenic or psychogenic, there is not as much difficulty defining this problem clinically compared to developmental stuttering and cluttering. (There is disagreement about the spelling of the word *dis*fluent (*dys*fluent) or *dis*fluency (*dys*fluency). Earlier in this chapter, *dis*fluent has been used in terms of the Latin word root *dis*- meaning 'apart, separated from, not.' This is used commonly in connection with developmental stuttering. The Greek word root *dys*- is used in adult acquired stuttering because this refers to 'ill' or 'bad.'

Neurogenic stuttering is observed to occur as a result of stroke, head trauma, progressive diseases such as Parkinson's, brain tumor, dialysis, dementia, and the use of drugs. Psychogenic stuttering, first described as a form of conversion reaction by Breuer and Freud in 1936, has been reported to be the result of acute anxiety, adverse combat experience, depression, and to be associated with multiple somatic complaints.

Dysfluencies most frequently observed in both neurogenic and psychogenic stutterers are sound, syllable, and word repetitions. Some earlier observers implied that the loci of dysfluency in neurogenic stutterers was as likely to be on the final syllable of multisyllable words as on the initial or medial. More careful studies have revealed very little repetition in the final syllable position. Psychogenic stutterers are more dysfluent on initial and medial syllables. The reader may recall that developmental stutterers are most often disfluent on initial syllables, followed by some disfluency on medial syllables, and practically no disfluency on final syllables. There is debate about the occurrence of struggle behaviors in neurogenic stutterers, but some recent reports describe the development of accessory features such as grimacing, implying some reaction to the stuttering. Psychogenic stutterers are reported to show signs of excessive tension and struggle quite frequently. However, a mark of psychogenic stuttering is considerable variation, somewhat like developmental stuttering.

3.2 Differential Evaluation

The following are statements that relate to the differential evaluation of acquired stuttering.

(a) If the problem is considered to be acquired, there is no childhood history of stuttering.

(b) If psychogenic, neurogenic disorder has been eliminated by neurological examination.

(c) If neurogenic, it has been established by medical examination that the person presents a neurological problem such as stroke, trauma, tumor, or disease.

(d) Psychogenic stuttering may coexist with physiological complaints such as headache, weakness, numbness, and tingling.

(e) As compared to the neurogenic group, psychogenic stutterers are much less likely to show associated speech and language problems.

(f) Just as a neurogenic stutterer is expected to have a diagnosed neurological problem, the onset of stuttering in psychogenic cases is almost always accompanied by a psychological disturbance surrounding the onset of stuttering.

(g) Psychogenic stuttering is characterized by a sudden onset that is often related to an emotionally stressful life event. Stuttering due to stroke usually has an abrupt onset, and aphasia is often, but not always present. The onset in closed head injury, brain tumor, progressive disease, and the use of drugs is, as expected, more gradual.

(h) Neurogenic stuttering may be persistent or transient. Both types are associated with more than a single brain lesion. The persistent type tends to be associated with multiple lesions of both brain hemispheres. Transient stuttering lasting only a few days or months is usually related to multiple lesions of one cerebral hemisphere.

(i) Rapid improvement with therapy is an almost certain confirmation of psychogenic stuttering.

3.3 The Treatment of Adult Onset Stuttering.

More systematic observation of neurogenic and psychogenic stuttering is a development of the late 1980s. There is very little comment in the literature on therapy.

Concerning neurogenic stuttering, case reports indicate that those who have progressive diseases, as expected, profit little from speech therapy. Those who have suffered stroke or closed head injury may profit more, but there is little information relating treatment to recovery. Helm-Estabrooks (1986) has described the best available protocol for the evaluation and management of neurogenic stuttering. In evaluation, speech dysfluencies and concomitant speech and language skills are assessed. Medical records are always available, usually including site of lesion tests.

For those predicted to be in the transient category, Helm-Estabrooks advises that they be reassured that their fluency will improve. Relaxation using biofeed-back to the speech musculature, and training to control rate using pacing techniques and DAF have been beneficial. A pacing board has six multicolored squares and raised wooden dividers. Subjects tap their fingers from square to square when speaking in a syllable-by-syllable or word-by-word manner. One may think that this procedure is providing inhibition of speech in somewhat the same way as it is done with a clutterer. DAF inhibits rate, but has not been as effective with neurogenic cases as the pacing board.

Roth, Aronson, and Davis (1989), reporting on their work at the Mayo Clinic in the USA, are the most definitive source of information on the treatment of psychogenic stuttering. Adult psychogenic stutterers respond well to some of the same procedures used to help adult stuttering that begins in childhood. They can be shown how to ease the severity of their stuttering and then by more relaxed approaches and smooth movements increase fluency. The therapy program should include counseling that helps clients understand their problem and that enables the clinician to evaluate the need for psychotherapy to resolve emotional conflicts that may interfere with recovery.

Bibliography

Bloodstein O 1995 *A Handbook on Stuttering*. Easter Seal Society, Chicago, IL

Conture E 1990 *Stuttering*, 2nd edn. Prentice-Hall, Englewood Cliffs, NJ

Curlee R, Siegel G (eds.) 1997 *Nature and Treatment of Stuttering: New Directions*. Allyn and Bacon, New York

Dalton P, Hardcastle W J 1977 *Disorders of Fluency*. Edward Arnold, London

Daly D 1986 The clutterer. In: St Louis K O (ed.) *The Atypical Stutterer*. Academic Press, London

Gregory H (ed.) 1999 *Stuttering Therapy: Principles and Procedures*. Singular, San Diego, CA

Gregory H H, Gregory C B 1991 Therapy for adolescents: Speech and attitude change. In: Rustin L (ed.) *Parents, Families, and the Stuttering Child*. Far Communications Ltd, Kibworth

Helm-Estabrooks 1986 Diagnosis and management of neurogenic stuttering in adults. In: St Louis K O (ed.) *The Atypical Stutterer*. Academic Press, London

Kidd K K 1984 Stuttering as a genetic disorder. In: Curlee R F, Perkins W H (eds.) *Nature and Treatment of Stuttering: New Directions*. College-Hill Press, San Diego, CA

Moore W H, Boberg E 1987 Hemisphere processing and stuttering. In: Rustin L, Purser H, Rowley D (eds.) *Progress in the Treatment of Fluency Disorders*. Taylor and Francis, London

Roth C R, Aronson A E, Davis L J 1989 Clinical studies in psychogenic stuttering of adult onset. *Journal of Speech and Hearing Disorders* **54(4)**: 637–46

Starkweather C W 1987 *Fluency and Stuttering*. Prentice-Hall, Englewood Cliffs, NJ

Van Riper C 1982 *The Nature of Stuttering*. Prentice-Hall, Englewood Cliffs, NJ

Weiss D A 1964 *Cluttering*. Prentice-Hall, Englewood Cliffs, NJ

Disorders of Fluency: Intervention

L. Rustin and F. Cook

Theories concerning the aetiology of stuttering have been debated, researched, and documented through countless conferences and publications by academics and clinicians throughout the nineteenth and twentieth centuries. While controversy persists, the current consensus supports the view that there is no single cause of stuttering and no simple cure. As Gregory and Gregory (see *Disorders of Fluency*) explain, stuttering is likely to be the result of an interaction between a number of factors for each individual including a physiological predisposition, developmental linguistic abilities, and psychosocial influences.

The treatment of stuttering has a similar history of argument and discussion. Each decade sees new methods proclaimed which, when examined, are often extensions of established techniques. However, the very fact that many authorities are acknowledging the complexity and heterogeneity of the problem suggests that we are closer to being able to offer a range of solutions to this perplexing communication disorder.

1. The Interactionist Framework

This chapter will present a range of therapeutic approaches for stuttering: (a) in early childhood (2–7 years), (b) in older children (8–14 years), and (c) for the chronic problem in adolescents and adults. The importance of assessment will be stressed for each phase of the problem, as well as the need to involve parents, carers, and significant others in the therapy process. The authors will refer to their own protocols for assessment and the therapy programs which arise from a specific interactionist framework. Other treatment approaches which demonstrate the range of alternatives available will also be presented.

Generally speaking for the younger child, while there is continuing debate on the use and the timing of direct intervention, there is overall agreement that parents should be an integral part of therapy. For the older child, with a more persistent problem, most writers recommend some form of direct speech modification or speech control techniques but also that environmental stressors and emotional aspects should be addressed within therapy, again with parental or carer involvement. And finally, for the chronic stuttering problem of adolescence and adulthood, the most effective therapy programs denote stuttering as a multidimensional problem by addressing the psychosocial aspects as well as motor speech control skills.

A number of authors have developed constructive models for illustrating the multifactorial nature of

stuttering and many of these have been influential in the framework (see Fig. 1) developed by Rustin et al. (1996) described below. There are many other major contributors in this field such as Gregory and Hill (1984), Starkweather (1987), Conture (1990), Smith and Kelly (1997), and Guitar (1998).

Figure 1 illustrates the factors which these authors believe interact and contribute to the development and maintenance of stuttering. It can be used effectively to inform an assessment protocol for each individual who presents for stuttering therapy.

2. Assessment Protocols

This section will consider the assessment of stuttering in childhood generally, and then discuss intervention approaches for early and more persistent stuttering, initially from the authors' perspective, followed by an overview of other programs.

2.1 The Protocol

(a) formal and informal measures of speech, language, fluency, and the communication skills of the child;
(b) an interview to gauge the level of the child's concern and his or her understanding of the problem;
(c) a parent-child interaction video to observe the communication styles within the family;
(d) a detailed parental interview to explore the history and development of the problem, and pertinent issues within family relationships and lifestyle.

From this detailed assessment, a profile of the child's strengths and needs can be conceptualized covering the cognitive, linguistic, social, emotional, and neurophysiological components of the child's stuttering. On the basis of this unique profile, it is possible to formulate treatment recommendations tailored to the individual and to the family.

3. Treatment Approaches—Early Stuttering (2–7 years)

The following options may be recommended for the young child who stutters:

3.1 Advice only

This would be offered to parents who are not anxious about their child's speech, where the episodes of disruptions in speech are brief with no evidence of struggle or effort, and where there is no significant family history or concurrent speech and language problems or other areas of concern. Advice and guidance covering the following topics would normally be offered:

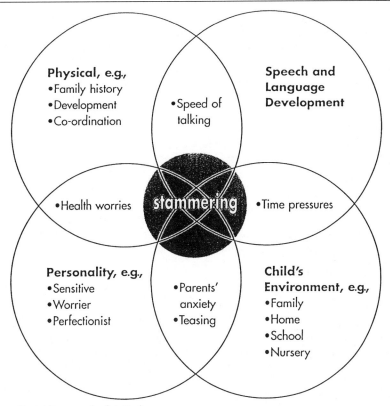

Figure 1. The interactionist framework of stuttering.

(a) information regarding the development of stuttering;
(b) the importance of family interaction styles including the influence of speech rates, rapid questioning, and the value of good turn taking, listening, and opportunities for individual 'quality time' for the child and the parents;
(c) consistency within the household—that is, the influence of appropriate routines and sensible boundaries for behavior.

Review sessions should be offered at 1 month, 3 months, and 6 months as necessary.

3.2 Parent Child Interaction Therapy (Rustin et al. 1996)

This would be recommended for parents who are concerned about their child's speech, and while the stuttering may still be cyclical there may be more evidence of the difficulty with perhaps signs of tension and frustration. There could also be a family history and/or associated speech and language factors, other psychosocial concerns, and relevant demands within the interaction styles of the family.

Parent child interaction therapy is brief and effective and involves both parents (unless a one-parent family). The goals of interaction therapy are to enable the parents, through videotape feedback, to identify aspects of their interactions which aid fluency and those which may be imposing demands on the child's ability to be fluent. Emphasis is placed on encouraging the parent's ability to recognize and implement targets for change. The most commonly observed *less helpful* parental styles would include excessive questioning, speaking at a faster rate than the child, the use of complex language models, overly directive play, or reduced listening and attention.

Therapy consists of 6 weekly sessions of 1 hour's duration followed by a 6 week consolidation period and a further review session. During the first phase, targets for change are identified and practiced in the clinic and at home. These are consolidated during the second phase with regular contact being maintained by post and telephone. Where fluency gains are noted in the review session, the parents continue to carry out their targets, monitoring change, and returning homework sheets. Review appointments are made at 3-monthly intervals for up to 1 year. The majority of families with children at some risk of stuttering have not needed further intervention.

3.3 Other Management

Clinicians may need to include some additional management strategies to address issues such as late or

199

erratic bedtimes or eating problems, any of which may be unsettling within the family lifestyle generally. It may also be useful to consider the interaction styles of the whole family in order to incorporate better listening and turn taking rules, as well as helping the parents to learn ways to increase their child's confidence and self-esteem.

3.4 Parent Child Interaction and Direct Therapy

This is recommended for families where, following the parent child interaction sessions, the stuttering is persisting. These children may be older, with a longer history of stuttering, and have other factors that put them at continued risk. The dysfluencies will have reduced in severity (i.e., the blocking), but the frequency may persist.

It is always recommended that direct fluency therapy is undertaken with the parents observing and participating in the activities, in order to assist in transferring the new skills into the home environment. Rustin and colleagues recommend a cognitive behavioral approach for direct therapy. The cognitive aspect is aimed at helping the child to understand concepts about stuttering and talking, while the behavioral aspect uses modeling, imitation, and positive reinforcement to help the child gain greater control over the speech.

There are three main concepts:

(a) rate of speech, for example, 'slow' versus 'fast' talking;
(b) disrupted speech, for example, 'bumpy' versus 'smooth' talking;
(c) tension and struggle, for example, 'hard' versus 'easy' talking.

Most children respond to rate reduction with an immediate increase in fluency; however, other aspects of speech production may need to be changed if there is associated struggle or blocking. These concepts need to be taught in concrete terms and therapy begins with a series of activities which introduce the ideas, for example, 'slow' versus 'fast' being taught through play using *slow* and *fast* trains or cars. The parents participate throughout and learn to use the same methods which are practiced in the clinic and then at home.

3.5 Other Treatment Programs

3.5.1 Fluency development system for young children (Meyers and Woodford 1992).

This program teaches cognitively based fluency exercises with a key goal being to '*use slow speech to talk more efficiently.*' Play characters are introduced which demonstrate fast and slow speaking rates: a 'turtle' for slowness and a 'racehorse' for rapidity. A story is used, based on the Aesop's fable of the tortoise and the hare, where ultimately the slower, more careful character wins the race by dint of taking his time and not rushing! The theme is developed using picture material and toys. The child learns to identify when the clinician or parent is using 'turtle talking' or 'racehorse talking.' As the program develops, it encourages the child to try both styles and the adults identify which one the child is using. The concepts of 'bumpy versus smooth,' 'hard versus easy' are also taught using the same cognitive and behavioral techniques with activities and games to ensure transfer into the home environment.

3.5.2 The Lidcombe program (Onslow et al. 1994)

This program, based on behavior modification principles, is a structured approach involving a high level of parental participation. Parents are taught to reinforce fluency and punish stuttering, initially in the clinic and then in the child's environment. The phases in the therapy program are: (a) parent training; (b) treatment during sessions; (c) treatment on-line; and (d) maintenance sessions.

4. Summary

The importance of a structured assessment protocol based on a theoretical framework has been discussed and illustrated. Treatment approaches which are known to increase a child's fluency have been described, including indirect and direct methods as well as the role of parents.

5. Treatment Approaches for Persistent Stuttering (8–14 years)

By this stage, a child is likely to have been stuttering for a number of years. The level of awareness that a child has about his or her dysfluency is perhaps being influenced by the reactions of peers and others within his or her social environment with consequent effect on self-esteem. The child may be developing self-help strategies to overcome, mask, or hide the problem. The assessment protocol described above will help clinicians identify those particular aspects which must be taken into account for an individual child.

5.1 Intensive Group Treatment with Active Parental Involvement

Intensive group programs offer clients and their families the time to focus clearly on a range of skills which need to be acquired to improve communication and to understand the nature of stuttering. The group setting provides parents and children with support and a shared social context for acquiring new skills. While each individual family presents in a unique way, a child and his or her parents will gain from contact with others who are experiencing similar difficulties. Shared knowledge is a powerful medium for change.

The following intensive group treatment program comprises 2 full weeks of daily therapy with a children's and a parents' group. The groups have both parallel and integrated sessions. The goals of intervention are:

(a) for both the children and their parents to gain an understanding of the nature of stuttering;
(b) to identify the positive changes that can be made by both the children and their parents;
(c) to practice changes in patterns of communication within a secure framework.

Regular follow-up and maintenance schedules follow the intensive course for a minimum of 1 year.

5.1.1 The children's group

There are two principal components: (a) social skills and relaxation training, and (b) a fluency control program.

The *social skills* aspect of the program follows the hierarchy developed by Rustin (1987) and includes the foundation skills of observation, listening, turn taking, praise and reinforcement, problem solving, and negotiation. The approach focuses on specific social situations that cause particular problems for a child or for the group as a whole. The problem-oriented approach to skills training captures the children's imagination and, coupled with the use of role play and problem-solving exercises, provides opportunities to practice and explore alternative strategies. Relaxation is taught through games and exercises and gradually transferred into speaking activities (Rustin and Kuhr 1989).

Fluency control techniques are taught using a cognitive behavioral approach. The children are encouraged to identify the characteristics of stuttered speech and to contrast these with normal speech. Emphasis is placed on exploring the factors that facilitate *more* fluent speech rather than following a rigid technique. A structured individual program is introduced to practice the controlled speech in graded steps, then in group activities, and finally in situations in everyday life.

5.1.2 The parents' group program

The parents experience the games and exercises that are taught to the children including direct instruction in fluency control, relaxation, and social skills. Problem-solving and negotiation skills are introduced at a later stage. Each day pertinent homework tasks are set and discussed the following day. The parents' group is thus encouraged to generate a variety of viewpoints about stuttering and its management within everyday life. This opportunity to brainstorm ideas and use problem-solving strategies enables each family to initiate productive changes for itself. Family sessions are used to practice problem-solving and to negotiate real issues for each family member. These family sessions have a powerful influence on the ways in which the family manages the stuttering and other important aspects of family life.

The implicit aim of this method of working is to shift the responsibility for treatment from the clinician to the family unit.

5.2 Individual Family Communications Skills Training

This program also has its core in the social skills hierarchy developed by Rustin (1987) but with a particular emphasis on negotiation. Clinical observation suggests that where conflict is managed successfully through sensitive negotiations within the family, the child is more likely to implement speech control techniques. Successful negotiation provides the child who stutters with experience in influencing decision making within the family, which enhances self-esteem and self-confidence.

Therapy consists of six weekly sessions of 1 hour's duration, with each session targeting an aspect of communication skills, for example, listening or turn taking. The importance of homework is emphasized from the outset. An activity associated with the specific communication skill is completed by the family at least once a week, and a 5 minute play or conversation time is established for the child and each parent in turn, during which each attempts to meet their chosen targets. The use of video feedback allows the therapist to adopt a facilitative role which encourages self-evaluation on the part of the family. The goal is to increase competence in all aspects of communication. Fluency control training, following the strategies in Rustin's (1987) treatment manual, is scheduled once the initial stage of the program has been completed.

5.3 Other Treatment Programs

5.3.1 Personalized fluency control therapy (Cooper and Cooper 1985)

This was one of the first fully integrated published programs. It has a clear assessment component and uses extensive worksheets and materials to help children identify personal stuttering characteristics, learn strategies for understanding and coping with the problem, and for fluency training. There are four stages: (a) identification and structuring; (b) examination and confrontation; (c) cognition and behavior orientation; and (d) fluency control. The authors suggest that the materials and worksheets can be adapted for children of all ages, both on an individual basis and within a group setting.

5.3.2 The stuttering intervention program (Pindzola 1987)

This structured program, which includes an assessment procedure, works directly on the child's speech production but incorporates parents, teachers, and other significant carers within the child's environment through counseling activities. The direct fluency-shaping program includes gradual increase in complexity of spoken language tasks with individual targets and plans. There are handouts for parents and teachers.

5.3.3 *The fluency development system for young children (Meyers and Woodford 1992)*

This published program was referred to in the previous section but is also recommended for children up to 9 years of age. In addition to the cognitive, fluency-shaping approach, it includes components for dealing with time pressures and difficult speaking situations. The authors suggest that it may be used on an individual basis or in a group setting.

5.3.4 *Easy does it—2 (Heinze and Johnson 1985)*

This approach combines stuttering modification and fluency shaping for children from 7–13 years. The cognitive aspects are dealt with through strategies to distinguish fluency from stuttering and desensitizing a child to fluency disrupters such as time pressures. There are also transfer and maintenance components in the program.

5.3.5 *The Monterey fluency program (Ryan and Van Kirk 1978)*

This is a highly behavioral, fluency-shaping model based on the theory that stuttering is a learned behavior. There are two particular management components: the GILCU (Gradual Increase in Length and Complexity of Utterance) for milder stuttering and DAF (Delayed Auditory Feedback), which requires specialized equipment. The authors target the production of fluent speech during three phases of the program: (a) establishment; (b) transfer; and (c) maintenance. Schedules of reinforcement and step-by-step instructions are prominent in this approach. There is no focus on attitudes or emotions, the implicit philosophy being that teaching a child to control his/her speech will help him/her deal with negative feelings.

5.3.6 *Extended length of utterance (Costello 1983)*

This is a similar fluency-shaping program based on operant learning principles and controlled linguistic complexity. It is again highly structured and its authors suggest that it can be used with all age groups but particularly with children. More recently parents have been included in the therapy sessions; however, transfer and maintenance components are not specifically addressed.

6. Summary

The longer the child has been stuttering, the more it impacts on the daily lifestyle of the individual and his or her confidence and self-esteem. Assessment and intervention must take into account the psychosocial factors and the role of learning in the child's development of coping strategies. A range of therapeutic programs were discussed, most using a combination of direct fluency-control techniques and addressing the emotional aspects of stuttering.

7. Chronic Stuttering in Adolescents and Adults

Stuttering in adolescents and adults is a complex, multidimensional problem which may now be termed chronic. During adolescence, clients begin to develop strategies and avoidances to their stuttering in an attempt to control, camouflage, or obviate any appearance of abnormality. The self-concept of 'being a stutterer' with an intricate web of negative associations may begin to dominate a person's life. By adulthood, the stutter may be the central issue in the person's life affecting work, family, and social dimensions.

A confusing array of treatment approaches have been described and published since the 1970s. Gregory (1979), in order to make sense of the controversies, proposed a dichotomy which divided therapies into the *speak-more-fluently* versus the *stutter-more-fluently* schools of thought. Followers of the speak-more-fluently approach advocated that therapy should aim to replace stuttered speech with fluent speech. This usually involved teaching a fluency technique with explicitly described features in a highly structured behavioral style. Commonly these features include controlling the speech rate, using an easier onset to words, and flowing the speech. While for advocates of the stutter-more-fluently approach, total fluency was not the major goal of therapy which was more concerned with helping the client to understand the stuttering behaviors, to confront fears and feelings, to reduce avoidances, and then to modify the struggle and tension to achieve an easier, more relaxed pattern of speaking.

Extremists on both sides are now rare and it is much more common to offer a *combined* approach to therapy, where some form of speech control is taught in parallel with helping clients to gain a better understanding of their negative perceptions and beliefs about the stuttering which will have played an important role in the development of this longer-term chronic problem.

7.1 Assessment

The importance of a detailed assessment procedure has been emphasized throughout this paper. With adolescents and adults the origins of the problem are not so significant, the focus is more on the factors which are interacting to maintain the current level of difficulty. Thus the protocol should include formal evaluations of the fluency, language, and social skills of the client as well as, through a detailed interview, his or her perception of the problem, its consequent effect on lifestyle, self-image, and educational or career progress (Rustin et al. 1995).

In addition, for the adolescent client, an interview with the parents (where applicable) will offer clinicians further insight into the physiological and developmental aspects of the stuttering and psychosocial information regarding relationships with peers, family, or other groups which may be key factors in intensifying negative beliefs and assumptions (Rustin et al. 1996).

There are a number of questionnaires and checklists available to clinicians which offer more formal evaluations of clients' perceptions and attitudes towards their stuttering, their avoidances, and their ability to take responsibility for therapy (see Guitar 1998 for a full description and discussion).

7.2 Approaches to Intervention

Therapy approaches are selected by clinicians based on the results of the assessments and the needs of the individual client. The treatment that is provided is often determined in large measure by the setting. The choices could include individual, intensive, or non-intensive sessions, or group, intensive, or nonintensive, sessions. Some clients will benefit from a combination of both. Individual sessions offer scope for a more 'tailor made' package which addresses particular problems, while group therapy offers broader insights into the stuttering, as well as opportunities for sharing ideas and practicing new skills in a safe environment.

Intervention with adolescents will be discussed first. However, apart from the approach developed by the authors at the Michael Palin Centre, there are few published programs developed particularly for this age group.

7.3 Adolescents (15–18 years)

Van Riper (1982) maintained that 'adolescents are often the clinician's toughest cases. They cannot bear to confront their stuttering deviancy long enough to do anything about it. They resist being singled out. They want the security of peer group affiliation with an intensity which is almost overwhelming' (207).

The Communication Skills Approach (Rustin et al. 1995) has been developed to take account of the complexities of working with this age group. These authors recommend intervention on a group therapy basis because, they suggest, one of the difficulties in engaging these clients in therapy is their changing role in relation to 'authority' figures. Peers become a powerful influence and a well-organized, facilitative group setting reinforces self-help strategies and commonalities in developing problem-solving skills. However, all aspects of the Communication Skills Approach are adaptable to individual, nonintensive settings.

The goals for intervention with this age group are:

(a) to increase understanding of the nature of stuttering and its development;
(b) to increase awareness of the antecedents and consequences of stuttering and develop alternative and more effective strategies;

(c) to improve social competence through communication skills training.

There are five interdependent components: fluency control, relaxation, social skills, problem solving, and negotiation. While these topics are similar to those used for the younger age group they are adapted to meet the more sophisticated needs of the adolescent who stutters.

7.3.1 Fluency control component

The objective here is for each client to develop a fluency control technique which feels as close to normal, spontaneous speech as possible, while offering a sense of being in control. Clinical experience has shown consistently that while this client group seeks 'total fluency,' any technique which feels or sounds 'contrived' will be rejected. The individual fluency control may include any or all of *easy onset* to words, *flowing the words together, and slower rate.*

Once each client has established his or her personal fluency factors, a program of graded steps is followed as part of the daily schedule of activities. Initially this will be on an individual basis, then within group activities through to assignments outside the clinic. The client is encouraged from the beginning to self-monitor and self-reinforce, with the clinician deliberately taking an increasingly less-active role.

7.3.2 Social competence

An implicit aim for all components of the program involves the clients gaining a full understanding of the underlying rationale and designing their own individual targets for change. Social skills, relaxation, problem solving, and negotiation are all taught using guided discovery, thus there are activities designed to elicit, identify, and explore the relevance of each topic to stuttering and communication.

The client is encouraged to take personal responsibility for his or her progress by actively construing alternative strategies, by developing hypotheses about the outcomes of these strategies, and by being given the opportunity of testing these out in role play and in real-life settings.

7.4 Adults

Therapy for adults, whichever approach is chosen, should be a collaborative effort between client and clinician. This means that, throughout therapy, an adult client is actively engaged in gaining a clear understanding of his or her stuttering, in developing a joint plan for the therapy, and for setting aims and objectives. Some of the following approaches to intervention may be used with both adolescents and adults and will suit both individual and group therapy.

7.4.1 Cognitive behavior therapy

This approach combines speech modification or speech control with strategies for exploring the cognitive and affective aspects of this communication problem. Thus, as well as fluency training the client will use explicit methods to explore the underlying beliefs and assumptions which exacerbate the anxiety and fear associated with speaking. The goal is to help the client to identify the negative thoughts and biased perceptions which strengthen and maintain the problem. The client learns to identify unhelpful beliefs and to challenge negative thinking through the use of behavioral experiments.

7.4.2 Fluent or easy stuttering (Van Riper 1982)

Van Riper was a leading proponent of stuttering modification therapy. The approach includes teaching the stutterer to modify hard, tense moments of stuttering to slow, easy effortless ones. The client works his or her way slowly through each sound of the stuttered word with a gradual transition from sound to sound with light articulatory contacts. The goal for therapy is controlled fluency or acceptable stuttering. Van Riper developed a number of phases to achieve this aim including *identification*, *desensitisation*, *modification*, and *stabilisation*. Throughout the program the client learns to confront the problem and to take responsibility for change.

7.4.3 Approach avoidance conflict (Sheehan 1975)

This therapy has twin goals, to increase a stutterer's approach tendencies and decrease his avoidances. Sheehan presents five phases of therapy: (a) the self-acceptance; (b) the monitoring; (c) the initiative; (d) the modification of pattern; and (e) the safety margin. The sessions are loosely structured and counseling in nature with little emphasis on data collection.

7.4.4 Intensive fluency training (Boberg and Kully 1994)

These clinicians have delivered intensive group therapy courses for adults using fluency-shaping techniques. The program is divided into seven phases: (a) baseline; (b) identification; (c) early modification; (d) prolongation; (e) rate increase and cancellation; (f) self-monitoring and transfer training; and (g) transfer. Throughout this therapy program, objective speech measurement and use of criterion levels are used to plot progress. The fluency skills include prolongation, easy onset of phrases, soft contact on consonants, and continuous airflow. Normal-sounding speech is transferred from the clinic to a variety of non-clinical situation using a series of standard and personal assignments.

7.4.5 Precision fluency shaping program (Webster 1980)

The goal of this therapy is to teach clients fluency-generating target behaviors that, when used correctly, will result in fluency. The target behaviors include increasing syllable durations and using gentle voice onset. The program begins by teaching the client to prolong syllables, using a stopwatch to measure their duration. The client is then taught to coordinate diaphragmatic breathing with these prolonged syllables. Gentle voice onsets are then taught with a specially designed voice–onset computer to monitor progress.

7.4.6 Summary

By adulthood, stuttering has become a chronic problem which has played a major role in the way a person perceives him or herself in respect of his ability to communicate effectively. A detailed assessment is an essential first step in understanding the depth and breadth of the problem for each individual. There is a wide range of approaches to choose from and the experienced clinician will ensure that the therapy offered reflects the goals of the client. The main focus may be on speech motor skills through fluency-shaping or modification strategies, or it may be that the client would gain greater benefit through exploring the role of cognitions and beliefs. In many cases, both aspects need to be addressed.

8. Outcome Measures

This is a controversial topic in the field of stuttering. For many years researchers have attempted to define stuttering behaviors in order to use these as outcome measures to indicate efficacy in therapy. There is ongoing debate as to the best ways of counting stuttering reliably and whether this type of data collection truly reflects the severity of a problem notorious for its variability. Measuring treatment efficacy can not be judged simply on presence of overt stuttering, but must also gauge how confident the person is in his or her communication abilities. Attitudes to communication, anxiety scales as well as personal report of improvement must therefore be included in efficacy studies.

9. Discussion

Intervention in stuttering is a complex problem. The disorder usually starts in early childhood, is resolved quickly for many, but can develop into a problem that causes great distress and anxiety affecting every part of an individual's life. Throughout history 'cures' have been hailed with enthusiasm, and quickly discredited.

Therapy involves hard work and dedication by both client and clinician over a long period of time. It must include regular follow-up sessions over many months and for some, even years. There is, at present, no cure for stuttering. It is more a question of finding the right combination of solutions.

Bibliography

Boburg E, Kully D 1994 Long term results of an intensive treatment program for adults and adolescents who stutter. *Journal of Speech and Hearing Research* **37**: 1050–9

Conture E G 1990 *Stuttering* 2nd ed. Prentice-Hall, Englewood Cliffs, NJ

Cooper E B, Cooper C S 1985 *Cooper Personalized Fluency Control Therapy—revised*. DLM, Allen, TX

Costello J M 1983 Current behavioral treatment of children. In: Prins D, Ingham RJ (eds.) *Treatment of Stuttering in Early Childhood: Methods and Issues*. College-Hill Press, San Diego, CA

Gregory H H, Hill D 1984 Stuttering therapy for children. In: Perkins WH (ed.) 1993 *Current Therapy of Communication Disorders: Stuttering Disorders*. Thieme-Stratton, New York

Gregory H H 1979 *Controversies about Stuttering Therapy*. University Park Press, Baltimore, MD

Guitar B 1998 *Stuttering: An Integrated Approach to Its Nature and Treatment*. Williams and Wilkins, Baltimore, MD

Heinze B A, Johnson K L 1985 *Easy Does it—2: Fluency activities for School-aged Stutterers*. LinguiSystems, East Moline, IL

Meyers S C, Woodford L L 1992 *The Fluency Development System for Young Children*. United Educational Services Inc, Buffalo, NY

Onslow M, Andrews C, Lincoln M 1994 A control/experimental trial of an operant treatment for early stuttering. *Journal of Speech and Hearing Research* **37**: 1244–59

Pindzola R 1987 *Stuttering Intervention Programme*. Pro-Ed, Austin, TX

Rustin L 1987 *Assessment and Therapy Programme for Dysfluent Children*. NFER-NELSON, Windsor

Rustin L, Botterill W, Kelman E 1996 *Assessment and Therapy for Young Dysfluent Children*. Whurr, London

Rustin L, Cook F, Spence R 1995 *The Management of Stuttering in Adolescence*. Whurr, London

Rustin L, Kuhr A 1989 *Social Skills and the Speech Impaired*. London: Whurr and Charles C Thomas, Springfield, IL

Ryan B, Van Kirk B 1978 *Monterey Fluency Programme*. Monterey Learning Systems, Palo Alto, CA

Sheehan J 1970 *Stuttering: Research and Therapy*. Harper and Row, New York

Sheehan J 1975 Conflict theory and avoidance-reduction therapy. In: Eisenson J (ed.) *Stuttering, a Second Symposium*. Harper and Row, New York

Smith A, Kelly E 1997 Stuttering: a dynamic, multifactorial model. In: Curlee Richard F and Siegel Gerald M (eds.) *Nature and Treatment of Stuttering: New Directions* 2nd ed. Allyn and Bacon, Boston, MA

Starkweather C W 1987 *Fluency and Stuttering*. Prentice-Hall, Englewood Cliffs, NJ

Van Riper C 1982 *The Nature of Stuttering* 2nd ed. Prentice-Hall, Englewood Cliffs, NJ

Webster R L 1980 Evolution of a target-based behavioral therapy for stuttering. *Journal of Fluency Disorders* **5**: 303–20

Recommended Reading

Bloodstein O 1995 *A Handbook of Stuttering* 5th ed. Singular Publishing Group, San Diego, CA

Curlee R F, Siegel G M 1997 *Nature and Treatment of Stuttering: New Directions* 2nd ed. Allyn and Bacon, Boston, MA

Guitar B 1998 *Stuttering: An Integrated Approach to Its Nature and Treatment*. Williams and Wilkins, Baltimore, MD

Learning Disabilities

A. Van Hout

1. Introduction

Like other specific developmental disabilities, 'learning disabilities' are usually defined by two criteria, a negative one which excludes any evident causal mechanism (see Rudel 1981) and a positive criterion that focuses on symptoms analysis and on their classification. The occurrence of learning problems in children with normal intelligence and sociocultural background, not suffering from any sensorial or psychological disturbances, suggests a causative intrinsic brain dysfunction. Learning disabilities are disorders affecting lately acquired skills, and mainly become apparent at school age: they include difficulty at reading, spelling, calculation, and writing. Learning disabilities greatly depend on the degree of human civilization and on the tasks required by it, so they would not be noticed in cultures living on hunting or fishing in the same way as, in our still predominantly literary society, we don't speak of 'developmental dysmusias' or of a 'developmental software usage inability!'

There is now a consensus for a nosologic separation between the so-called 'learning disabilities' and the developmental disorders present from the start. In early occurring disorders, such as developmental dysphasia, agnosia, and dyspraxia, while it is true that the corresponding tasks imply learning at least some basic components, the major role is nonetheless played by nature rather than nurture.

Learning difficulties are by no means uncommon in these early occurring conditions, but, as these difficulties are often seen as a direct consequence of the primary basal disorders, they are labelled as 'learning retardation' rather than as 'specific learning disabilities.' It is therefore assumed that alleviation of the primary disorders will reduce the learning difficulties too. So the treatment of such 'secondary' conditions is different from that used to tackle 'specific learning disabilities,' which by definition have no evident causal mechanism, and which require a custom-made treatment according to the specific deficit profile.

Implementation of those learned skills has been a subject of discussion. Some authors, for instance Marshall (1980), have suggested the existence of preformed neuronal networks for lately developing functions, for example, for the two reading pathways in developmental dyslexias. This stance is supported by brain imaging and neuroanatomical findings, which for some subtypes of learning disorders show abnormalities of specific areas. The anatomic substrates do not appear randomly distributed but rather confined to well-defined brain sectors. In opposition to this 'inborn conception,' other authors, such as Ellis (1985), suggest that the elaborate skills of reading or calculation build up progressively from subsets of other abilities, and these are a prerequisite for subsequent acquisition. This conception opens the way to early detection and remediation strategies. It does not stand in direct opposition with the above-mentioned view; synaptic connections of a higher order might develop from those early areas and explain an extended topography of the dysfunctional brain structures.

This chapter will concentrate on learning difficulties occurring in dysphasias, dyspraxias, developmental agnosias, and attention deficit disorders. As dyslexia is treated elsewhere (see *Reading Difficulties; Classification of Developmental Dyslexia and Intervention*), for specific learning disabilities the chapter will particularly focus on developmental dysgraphias and dyscalculias.

2. Learning Disorders and Hyperkinesia with Attentional Deficits

From a conceptual point of view, these learning disorders have been mainly described in the context of behavioral problems and secondarily as deficits of attentional mechanisms. This conception is still prevalent in the *Diagnostic and Statistical Manual of Mental Disorders, Fourth Edition* (*DSM-IV*), which provides definitions and operational classifications accordingly. Historically, in 1947, Strauss and Lehtinen emphasized similarities between the behavioral features encountered in some brain-damaged children and those found in children with no apparent lesion but with learning difficulties at school. This unexpected parallel led to the concept of 'minimal brain damage' in children with learning disorders, ultimately called 'minimal brain dysfunction,' as it was clear that the alleged brain 'damage' was hypothetical.

This rather fragile concept, whose validity became more and more controversial, grouped all symptoms together, not only those related to learning and memory but also neurological problems related to motor and gnosic aspects or to the control of emotions and social behavior. Among the behavioral problems, hyperkinesia or 'hyperkinetic reaction of childhood' was initially considered a major problem, but it was soon discovered that the core symptom was an attentional disorder, which could be accompanied by hyperkinesia or not, and that the concurrence of hyperkinesia and learning disorders was not mandatory, as hyperkinesia affected only some 75 percent of the children with learning disabilities.

Hyperkinesia is difficult to define and partly based on subjective criteria, as showed by the diversity of estimates on prevalence according to country and study (Rutter 1981, Zentail 1984). Positive diagnosis relies on behavioral scales filled out by parents and teachers. Actometers have been used to measure the frequency of movements per day, but their degree of correlation to learning disorders is not very high, the overall amount of movement being less relevant than their aimless, pointless nature, which is unrelated to action. Progressively, the patent behavioral elements of the syndrome gave way to a more cognitive approach based on how information is grasped and retained. Wender (1971) spoke of a 'primary dysfunctional area' encompassing an alteration of perception and of attentional abilities. Attentional problems soon appeared to be at the very heart of many learning pathologies of the child, as a multitude of cognitive processes rely on the attentional mechanism. Hyperkinesia and perceptual deficits were seen as associated symptoms of this core problem, at least in children whose learning difficulties were not 'pure,' affecting one kind of learning only. Progressively, the concept of attention deficiency took over that of hyperkinesia (e.g., *Attention-Deficit Hyperactivity Disorder*, ADHD, defined for instance in the *DSM-III* and *DSM-IV*).

Attention is a very complex function organized both at conscious and subconscious level. The concept of cortical arousal represents a general level of awakening of the brain. To execute a given task, selective attention mechanisms must be at work, extracting the relevant stimuli for task execution. To permit action or problem solving, these mechanisms need be maintained long enough by means of sustained attention. For attention to be effective, however, some kind of attention to the environmental world also has to be maintained (in the jungle, the hunter has to focus on its pray but also on its own potential hunter) so that complex interaction mechanisms are at work, from a state of diffuse alertness to a more specific focal concentration. In humans, attention seems distributed unequally between both hemispheres of the brain, verbal stimuli being treated mainly by the left hemisphere and global attention being rather under the control of the right hemisphere.

Kinsbourne and Kaplan (1979) were among the first to develop models of attentional deficits based on cortical hyperexcitability: they thought that ADHD children treated neutral stimuli in the same way as the specific stimuli for a given task. Selectivity of attention was believed to be the most defective element, the child paying equal attention to flying moths as to the blackboard. The lack of selectivity of attention can be diagnosed by 'continuous performance tasks,' whereby the child has to choose a target stimulus between repetitive stimuli presented in succession. Omission errors occur (the child neglects stimuli) but 'commission errors' may also develop, indicating that owing to the high level of cortical activation, an impulsive motor answer precedes a full analysis of the stimulus, and the child treats with equal importance both neutral and target stimuli. However, the first hypothesis of Kinsbourne and Kaplan has now been dismissed in favor of a nearly opposite notion of 'cortical hypoactivity,' as it was discovered that, during continuous performance tasks, children with attention deficits do not deteriorate their performance in the face of distractors. For some children the presence of distractors even improves performance, as if additional sensorial afferents were needed in order to reach a sufficient level of brain activation. In this context, hyperkinesia is regarded as a means for the child to reach sufficient sensory stimulation, and the positive action of psychostimulant drugs is thought to depend on an increase in cortical arousal. A frontal origin underlying these problems is proposed (Hynd et al. 1990), as MRI studies disclose the absence of the normal right-left asymmetry at this level.

However, not all ADHD children develop learning disorders; for instance, the *DSM-IV* distinguishes between ADHD with or without associated learning disorders. If attentional disorders are the cause of some learning problems, the administration of drugs such as methylphenidate should reduce both attention deficits and the associated learning problems (see Stahl 1996). However, some 80 percent of children with ADHD suffer from learning disorders which are not due to attentional problems only, but also to associated disorders in information coding or retrieval. These specific cognitive disorders have been generally analyzed in an overall comparative setting in relation to neuropsychological investigations on acquired brain lesions in adults.

These findings on adults were often regarded as comparative models giving hints on the brain dysfunctions that could determine them. This 'analogical reasoning' was adopted not only in the neurological approach by Rapin and Allen (1988), but also in more recent approaches based on cognitive neuropsychology (see Temple 1991), for the purpose of comparing acquired and developmental dyslexias and dyscalculias. According to Marshall (1980), this procedure holds true and can be followed as long as

no clear divergence emerges between acquired and developmental problems. The more specific the difficulty, for instance only learning to read or only learning to calculate, the less attentional problems appear to be a direct cause, although entities were defined where the two did coexist, such as for instance in 'dyslexia plus' according to Denckla (1978).

3. Learning Disorders in Developmental Dysphasias

Learning difficulties in reading, spelling, or calculation are commonly found in developmental dysphasias, although paradoxically some children, particularly those with severe semantic comprehension problems, are sometimes able to develop written language better than verbal skills. Among the school subjects in which these children are poor, the most studied is reading. Two main questions have been addressed regarding the relationship between dysphasia and reading retardation: Is there a relationship between this dysphasia subtype and a particular form of learning disorder? Is there a relationship between linguistic parameters and a particular form of learning disorder?

Among the studies examining the linguistic parameters related to reading deficiency in children with developmental language disorders, one finds longitudinal data focusing on the relationship between language disorders and learning disabilities. For instance, Silva (1980) carried out a prospective study of children diagnosed as 'language retarded' at about 3 years of age and found a prevalence of reading disorders of 80 percent when they were 8 years old. However, this group of 'language retarded children' encompassed a wide range of disorders: beside dysphasias, there were children with lately maturing normal language, globally retarded children, and children with a 'simple language retardation.' In their longitudinal study, Bishop and Adams (1990) chose not to consider children with global retardation, and concluded that those who recovered a normal language by the age of five were less likely to develop reading retardation.

Most authors dealing with the relationships between linguistic parameters in language disturbed children and their reading abilities (Haynes and Naïdoo 1991; Korkman and Häkkinen-Rihu 1994) find that there are links between phonemic discrimination and short-term memory disturbances on one hand and phonological errors in reading words on the other. The relationships with textual reading measured for comprehension show a different pattern of prediction. For instance in Bishop and Adams' (1990) longitudinal study, receptive and expressive disorders of syntax were better predictors than phonological deficits of the late ability of children to read and comprehend texts.

The Haynes and Naïdoo (1991) study focuses on children who had been institutionalized owing to the severity of their language disorder. Early reading acquisition in those children disclosed the strongest correlation with the syntactic aspects of language. Although the children received remedial reading teaching, their reading skills became, if anything, relatively worse with increasing age, with only 23 percent of them mastering the basic reading and decoding skills at the end of their stay. The retardation of reading involved both decoding and comprehension, and the level of decoding skills was positively correlated with that of short-term verbal memory. The role of 'working memory' is important to maintain information when reading with a phonological strategy. In the study of Korkman and Häkkinen-Rihu (1994) which used a large neuropsychological battery (NEPSY), the degree of dysphasia was severe enough for the patients to have to attend special schools (see *Specific Language Impairment: Subtypes and Assessment*). The more significant variables related to reading achievement were: a subtest of metaphonological skills, a subtest of naming, and a subtest of syntactic comprehension. Expressive phonological skills and dyspraxia showed correlations with reading only if matched by receptive phonological treatment defects. Therefore, at least for reading, the correlation between learning retardation and dysphasia is stronger for specific linguistic parameters than for a given dysphasia subtype *per se*.

Another way to address the language reading relationship was the searching for associated verbal skills defects among children with specific difficulties. For instance, Duffy et al. (1988) developed the procedure of 'brain evoked potential mapping' for different stimuli in children defined as 'dyslexic' without attentional deficit problems. On the basis of their verbal performance in standardized tests, three groups were identified: (a) one with specific difficulties in phoneme decoding (phonemes differing by one articulatory feature only were presented within syllabic pairs, the child having to give 'same/different' answer); these children mainly made phonological errors in reading (like the dysphonetic form of Boder 1973); (b) a second group had mostly naming difficulties (they resembled the dyseidetic form of Boder 1973); (c) the third group scored in the lower range for all language skills, particularly listening comprehension. In other words, even by looking at the issue from the opposite angle, the same correlation appears in children combining oral and written language problems, that is, a predominance of receptive phonological or verbal difficulties or of naming disorders in reading difficulties.

The issue has been raised of the expressive or/and receptive value of phonological skills as reading predictors. Stackhouse (1982) has shown that children with purely expressive phonological difficulties, as observed for instance in labio-palatal fissures, do not show phonological disorders in reading, except for their oral mispronunciations. However, children with

apraxic dysphasia did show marked phonological errors in reading, only if they also had phonemic discrimination problems. Stackhouse and Snowling (1994) made a follow-up study on apraxic children and found that with increasing age they were progressively able to pronounce short words correctly but their respective phonological abilities allowed them to segment words into syllables only and not into phonemes. Their reading comprehension of whole texts was better than their understanding of words presented in isolation. As for spelling, an autocorrective tendency with defective subvocalization and reduced short-term memory gave rise to errors of perseveration with frequent transcription of a recurrent neutral vowel.

In conclusion, there seems to be a consensus on the existence of correlations between receptive phonological problems and short-term memory problems on the one hand and written word decoding skills on the other. There are, however, examples indicating the opposite, as described by Jeeves and Temple (1987) in subjects with callosal agenesis who had reached a reading level close to normal, in spite of severely defective metaphonological skills and short-term memory span. This could be the exception that confirms the rule, or it may be that the variables that appeared positively correlated were only the expression of a common more basic disability, yet to be confirmed.

4. Learning Disorders in Developmental Dyspraxia

Developmental dyspraxia is often confused with the so-called 'clumsy child' (Gubbay 1975) and refers to long lasting motor coordination disorders, involving either gross motor skills (balance, jumping) or fine ones (shoe lacing, button fastening), although no manifest neurological disorders are found on standard clinical examination. According to the American Psychiatric Association (*DSM-III*), it affects about 10 percent of school-age children. Some authors, such as Ayres (1972), stress that dyspraxia is frequently observed in children with learning disorders, hinting at a possible cause-effect relationship between the two. They have gone so far as suggesting specific motor training to help improve school performance. According to this author, the basic deficit consisted in a sensory-motor integration defect, thus the inability to plan motor skills was secondary to sensory disorders. This relates to training programmes such as those of Laszlo and Bairstow (1983) who insisted that kinesthetic problems are at the origin of lack of motor coordination.

Dewey (1995) claimed that the 'gesture disorder' is at the basis of this problem and proposed a taxonomy based on adult acquired apraxias classifications: (a) some children, who also suffer from a marked visual-perceptual deficit, present general motor skills problems. They are similar to the 'planning problems secondary to distorted sensory information' in adults;

(b) other children present problems of balance, coordination, and performing transitive gestures (involving the transfer of movement onto an object, for instance nail hammering as against waving goodbye), that resemble the executive or ideomotor apraxia in the adults; (c) a third group has no such difficulties in individual gestures but is impaired in sequences of movement, being thus similar to the ideational apraxic primary planning defect in adults.

4.1 Relationship of Developmental Apraxia and Language Disorders

From a developmental point of view it has been suggested that language and gestural communication evolve in parallel and are positively correlated to verbal comprehension disorders in children under 12 months of age (Bates et al. 1979). Dewey (1995) showed that children with severe developmental dyspraxia also achieved the worst scores on a verbal comprehension test. According to Korkman and Häkkinen-Rihu (1994), some verbal dyspraxic children disclose deficits not only in oro-facial sequential movements but also in limb gestures. The same is reported by Dewey (1995), who also found a close parallelism of error types (for action and movement) between oro-facial and limb sequences of gestures. However, there are also subtypes of verbal dyspraxic children, defined by both linguistic and nonverbal abilities, and as they may or may not go along with receptive phonemic discrimination problems, the sequential abilities may or may not be associated; so, the concurrence of both disorders is more a matter of symptom distribution rather than indicative of a common underlying cause.

5. Learning Disorders in Developmental Perceptuospatial Disorders

Difficulties of visuo-spatial perception are often hard to distinguish from praxic or gestural disorders and are sometimes considered as their cause (see Sect. 4). These difficulties may also be accompanied by learning disabilities, usually affecting calculation (see Sect. 7). When reading retardation occurs as well, it is frequently noticed that this is affected to a lesser degree than spelling (see Sect. 6). In the past, visuo-spatial perceptual disorders were thought to be the cause of dyslexia, but this has been largely dismissed (see Van Hout and Estienne 1994), although, at subcortical level, deficits in the treatment of low contrast visual material due to thalamic magnocellular impoverishment can be experimentally shown.

5.1 Developmental Prosopagnosia

This disorder has been described in children and adults (Campbell 1992) but the subjects did not show specific learning disorders. One of them—referred to as 'doctor S'—even had a medical degree and achieved unusually high verbal scores. However, two genetic syndromes with prominent visuo-spatial defects and specific calculation disorders have been studied in depth: the Turner syndrome and the Williams syndrome.

5.2 Turner Syndrome

The cognitive profile of girls deprived genetically of one sexual chromosome has been described by Rourke (1985) as a form of 'right hemisphere dysfunctional syndrome.' Money (1973) demonstrated a normal distribution of IQ in these girls, once considered mentally retarded, but with a wide gap between verbal and performance skills, verbal being superior. Factorial analysis showed superiority of the 'comprehension' factor as against the 'spatial one' (mostly block designs and object's assembly) and the 'freedom from distractibility' (including the subtests of arithmetic, digit span, and code). Although reading abilities are always normal or even above average, arithmetic difficulties give rise to problems at school and appear in the context of visuo-spatial difficulties (both on the praxic and gnosic side) and lateral orientation problems. Some frontal executive functions are defective (mainly the Stroop test and self-ordered pointing tasks). Abnormalities in the asymmetric pattern of the frontal and parieto-occipital areas found on MRI are consistent with these findings. These deficits are long lasting and persist in adult age.

On the behavioral side, these girls are usually described as sociable and talkative. They show little concern about the bad prognosis that their syndrome casts over their social future (they are very short and are bound to be sterile), and this 'indifference' has been attributed to anosognosia, a symptom of the right hemisphere syndrome. Calculation disorders mainly consist in the inability to carry out operations, often with misalignment of digits. Knowledge of tables and arithmetic facts is usually average, but the Piagetian notions of inclusion or conservation are disturbed even in the long term. Netley (1977) suggested an explanation for this particular phenotype based on genetic behavior relationship. According to her theory, the Y chromosome of males determines a visuo-spatial, right hemisphere mediated maturation which, although slower, ultimately develops a function superior to the one observed in females. In the normal female, the acquisition of visuo-spatial abilities depends on the activation of some loci of the X chromosome which are similar to parts of the Y chromosome. In Turner syndrome, these loci possibly remain inhibited in the same way as the second X chromosome of normal girls, thus preventing the normal expression of visuo-spatial abilities.

5.3 Williams Syndrome

Williams syndrome, or 'infantile hypercalcemia,' is due to a homozygotic deletion including the elastine gene on chromosome 7 (7q, 11.23). Although those children have a psychomotor delay, particularly for language, with first sentences acquisition only by the age of five, once language starts to develop it appears well constructed and out of proportion in respect of a general mental deficiency. Vocabulary grows rapidly too, but pragmatic aspects of language are defective. The most prominent difficulty is a marked defect for visuo-constructive skills, the child being unable to draw the simplest things either in copy or spontaneously (Meyerson and Frank 1987). What appears to be absolutely impossible for them is drawing a whole structure, whereas if they are given details and verbal clues they can obtain some kind of copy of a whole drawing by using a piecemeal approach (Bellugi et al. 1988). Those findings suggest a developmental right hemisphere syndrome. Praxias and gnosias are grossly altered, although the ability to recognize faces is preserved. Tridimensional praxias are defective too, and the children fail the simplest items on the subtest of cubes on the Wechsler Intelligence Scale for Children (WISC).

These children usually suffer from general learning difficulties with reading limited to simple words and severe arithmetic difficulties: the simplest operations, involving two digits only, appear impossible, although their preserved verbal memory allows them to master the tables. Piagetian abilities do not reach the 'operative' stage even after puberty. From a behavioral point of view, these children are hyperkinetic and anxious, but their social relationships are good, even 'too good,' as the children lack social inhibition. MRI studies have shown a bilateral reduction of the postero-parietal, posterior temporal, and occipital areas. A cyto-architectonic study of one case made by Galaburda et al. in 1994 shows cellular anomalies indicating an abnormal cellular migration with an increase in subcortical neurons and anomalous layering of the cortex. Moreover, a poor vascular development was found, probably due to impaired elastin (which is part of the capillary walls), as well as a rarefaction of myelin indicating disturbances of brain development between the second and third quarter of fetal life.

6. Developmental Dysgraphia

Although writing is a specific task heavily relying on cognitive mechanisms, its acquisition also depends on general motor skills. While it is true that developmental dysgraphia can occur independently of motor problems, a general lack of coordination or clumsiness has a negative impact on the development of writing skills. Learning to write implies elaborate movements of the hand and fingers for specific drawings of letters and their bindings. This task has been shown to be directly linked to motor coordination of fingers, as measured by fingers-thumb coordination tasks. Pencil grip allows smoothness of movements but is not directly related to letter writing perform-

ance. Functional pencil grip, that is, using the thumb in opposition to the first two fingers, is acquired between 4 and 6 years of age, but later the whole arm may be at work, especially the shoulder, which regulates the letter strokes by means of elevation movements.

The acquisition of regular penmanship is a multiple-stage process: at first, the child must integrate motor schemes with spelling, then verbal memory must be at work in order to create or even just copy long lengths of text. Writing speed increases with age and is related to acquired automaticity. Writing impairments severe enough to interfere with legibility occur in about 5 to 10 percent of children. There are at least three recognized subtypes of developmental dysgraphia: spelling dysgraphia, motoric and dyspraxic dysgraphia, and visuo-spatial dysgraphic.

6.1. Spelling Dysgraphia

In this form of developmental dysgraphia, spelling too is disturbed like reading, but the reading disorder is closer to 'dyslexia plus' (specific reading retardation with attention deficit disorder) than to 'pure dyslexia.' The children are aware of their spelling difficulties, which they try to correct by multiple autocorrections, so that their final word attempt is difficult to decode because of the many juxtapositions. It is not uncommon that these children are unable to reread their own writing, and their oral spelling is slightly better than written spelling. The degree of their reading retardation is less severe than that of the spelling disorder. This spelling problem is often of a dyseidetic kind (difficulties in remembering word form), with an increase in the number of errors for irregular words. Verbal intelligence versus performance intelligence shows a discrepancy which is in favor of verbal IQ and there are also accompanying symptoms, such as 'soft' neurological signs and defects of visuo-spatial abilities, including constructional drawing skills. A concurrent 'spatial dyscalculia' where digits are wrongly aligned occurs frequently. Critchley (1970) has used the eponymic specification of '*developmental Gerstmann syndrome*' to describe a similar developmental syndrome, distinct from dyslexia, where visuo-spatial problems, constructional apraxia, and associated soft signs are prominent and where spelling errors affect letter sequences. The acquired form of this syndrome, whose validity has been discussed, consists in a concurrence of four symptoms: difficulties in right-left orientation; difficulties to recognize fingers (finger's agnosia); difficulties with arithmetic (mainly a spatial dyscalculia); difficulties with spelling (the errors involving letter sequence disturbances). For some authors, however, (see Van Hout and Estienne 1994), this eponym should be reserved to a small group of children with a very elevated IQ, but who present a marked dysgraphia together with spelling disorders.

6.2. *Motoric or Dyspraxic Dysgraphia*

This is the most severe form of dysgraphia and sometimes alternative means of writing such as typing have to be offered. It may occur either in isolation or in the context of global motor difficulties, in the so-called 'clumsy' children. The latter experience difficulties with either fine motor skills (shoe lacing, drawing, and building), or with gross coordination (dressing, sport's practice). Writing problems consist of either apraxia or lack of coordination. In the latter case, hand writing is irregular, as if the tuning of direction, strength, and speed was disturbed. The movements are jerky, either hypo- or hyperkinetic, and cause defective letter angulations and bindings. In dyspraxia, individual movements are usually preserved but their smooth succession is impaired, so that the letters are better written in isolation than within words; the sequencing of letters is disturbed often showing static disorientation (mirror writing). The children are often much better at oral spelling and tend to correct their own productions, giving rise to superposed writings that only add to their difficulty to read their own written productions.

There are cases, such as 'ideomotor apraxic agraphia' in adults, that show no associated problems, either motor or visual-constructional, and where spelling and writing are in the normal ranges. For these lesions, a defect in the graphemic buffer which maintains the graphic motor pattern during the writing execution has been identified. In children with a similar profile the same causative mechanism could be at work.

6.3. *Visuo-spatial Dysgraphia*

Here, the difficulty to produce and reproduce letters appears along with other marked difficulties, affecting not only visuo-motor integration but also perceptual problems, drawing is disturbed and alignment of script is abnormal, with slopes and misplaced spaces. In this form of dysgraphia copying appears to be the most difficult among the various writing tasks.

7. Developmental Dyscalculias

These are usually defined as a specific deficit of arithmetical abilities in children of normal intelligence, measured by means of the same negative definition criteria normally used for the other specific learning disorders (O'Hare et al. 1991). They affect about 6 percent of school-age children and are therefore slightly more common than isolated dyslexia and slightly less common than dyslexia plus ADHD (respectively affecting 2 and 10 percent of children). However, compared to dyslexia, development dyscalculias are less often isolated and are usually found in connection with reading retardation (often of the 'dyslexia plus' type). As is often the case in studies on learning disabilities, two main approaches have been adopted for the analysis of developmental dyscalculias. The first one consists of submitting large neuropsychological batteries of subtests to large groups of children. The second is more focused on cognitive neuropsychology and relies on single case studies, drawing parallels with the defects of architectural cognition as observed in acquired adult dyscalculias.

Calculation depends on the ability not only to compute and remember the arithmetic procedures, but also to treat numbers as linguistic entities. Digits have their oral counterpart in natural language and their correct manipulation relies on two codes that have to coincide in order to read or write figures. The rational character of the numeric symbols is often in contrast with irregularities for their verbal counterpart. Translation of the written form of numbers into their oral form depends on rules that are rooted into the history of the spoken language itself and that vary from language to language, for instance, in French 80 is read 'four twenties' and 70 is read 'sixty ten.' Moreover, the rule of reading the teens plus the name of units does not apply to the numbers from 11 to 16. This peculiarity appears to be enough to delay learning to count for French speaking children as against, for example, Chinese children (Van Hout 1995).

Language difficulties, can, therefore, be at the origin of deficits in treating the written form of numbers. In such cases, according to subclassifications, one speaks of 'dyslexia and dysgraphia for numbers,' of 'numbers dysphasia,' or of 'verbal dyscalculia.' Within this latter category, a subgroup of 'syntactical dyscalculia' has been isolated to refer to special problems in transcoding figures with more than one digit. In some cases a specific verbal memory, that of 'arithmetic facts,' is defective, while in others, the procedural steps of arithmetic operations are too quickly forgotten: this condition is called 'anarithmetia' by Badian (1983) and 'operational dyscalculia' by Kosc (1974); it entails either an overall forgetfulness for all kinds of procedures, or difficulties to shift from one kind of procedure to another, or specific difficulties with a given kind of procedure.

However, beside linguistic and memory aspects, computing often implies a spatial component, for instance in order to evaluate quantities, in writing the digits to compute, or in the direction used to carry out computations. The latter component varies according to the type of computation (from left to right to read digits and for the algorithms of addition, subtraction, and multiplication; but from right to left to estimate the size of the written number and for the calculation of the partial remains of division). Difficulties with this aspect of arithmetic are called 'spatial dyscalculia' by Badian (1983) and 'practognosic dyscalculia' by Kosc (1974).

A fourth subgroup is defined by Kosc (1974) as ideognosic dyscalculia, namely the inability to understand the concrete signification of computations and numbers relationships. In these children the so-called Piagetian notions (for instance, sequencing, matching, and comparison of quantities) are particularly defective (Piaget and Szemiska 1972). This difficulty is greater in the so-called 'idiots-savants' where some calculation abilities are overdeveloped in a mechanical way, relying on purely mnesic mechanisms with ultra-rapid specifications.

Cognitive neuropsychological research studies have drawn parallels between developmental dyscalculias and acquired acalculias in adults. They usually take the form of single case studies (Temple 1989, 1991). Dissociations of abilities have been described with specific defects fitting the McCloskey et al. (1984) model, respectively for: (a) number processing (including lexical and syntactic processing of numbers, Arabic number treatment being separated from Roman number treatment); (b) knowledge of numerical facts (memorized results for simple operations; knowledge of tables); (c) procedural knowledge or ability to carry out the algorithms for the different operations. The in-depth analysis of selected single cases made by Temple (1977) shows similarities with the data obtained from studies on adults. It has been underlined by this author that double dissociations of skill can be demonstrated for those three abilities, indicating a modularity in the developmental organization of the arithmetical architecture. This conclusion from selected single case studies clashes with the findings of large neuropsychological batteries submitted to large groups of dyscalculic patients: here, the types of errors appear equally distributed among the children (Shalev et al. 1988). However, the testing of calculation abilities in these patients does not go as far as neurocognitive analysis.

7.1. Developmental Dyscalculias and Right Hemisphere Dysfunction

In adult acalculias, the lesion is usually located in the left hemisphere. Right hemisphere lesions only give rise to calculation disturbances 'secondary' to spatial problems. In developmental dyscalculias, to reach an algorithmic abstraction the child first has to master the conceptual notions of sequencing, inclusion, and cardinalization that build up mathematical reasoning; in other words, he/she has to rely on mechanisms controlled by the right hemisphere.

Strang and Rourke (1985) described a predominantly 'right hemisphere deficiency' in children suffering from specific dyscalculia. They broke down the children with calculation difficulties into three subgroups: (a) group 1: globally and severely retarded in all skills; (b) group 2: better at arithmetic than at reading and spelling; (c) group 3: normal reading and spelling levels, but arithmetic scores lower by at least two standard deviations than average. This is the group with specific arithmetic disabilities, and the

authors have shown that with increasing age the arithmetic deficit becomes more severe compared to other skills.

The administration of extended neuropsychological batteries showed the following: (a) group 1: a global alteration in all performances; (b) group 2: normal visuo-spatial abilities but verbal abilities sometimes low, with motor abilities of the right hand lower than those of the left hand; (c) group 3: an opposite profile, with an alteration in visuo-spatial abilities, particularly in memory and categories (when there is a need for complex spatial analysis), preservation of verbal skills and alteration in motor performances (labyrinths, pegboard) as well as in sensory scores (graphiesthesia, stereognosia) of the left hand. The profile of this last group with a specific deficiency in arithmetic is thus compatible with a right hemisphere deficiency. This syndrome may even extend to specific behavioral components: (a) language used in excess, even with logorrhea and with a defective pragmatic value; (b) social integration difficulties, mostly due to problems in comprehending the non-verbal behavior of other people; (c) a general clumsiness.

Strang and Rourke (1985) have drawn similarities between this profile and the 'developmental learning disabilities of the right hemisphere' described by Weintraub and Mesulam (1984) in adults with persisting behavioral problems and severe calculation disorders. They also reported its high frequency in various developmental neurological pathologies (in hydrocephalia and in the late sequel of brain irradiation for leukemia or tumors), thus introducing the notion of 'nonverbal learning disabilities' where the main learning problem affects calculation. The same 'nonverbal disability syndrome' has been described in the context of two developmental syndromes due to chromosomal abnormalities: Turner syndrome and Williams syndrome, thus leading to suspect a genetic origin of this disorder (see Sect. 5).

Bibliography

American Psychiatric Association 1980 *Diagnostic and statistical manual of mental disorders*, (third edition). Washington, DC

American Psychiatric Association 1995 *Diagnostic and statistical manual of mental disorders*, (fourth edition). Washington, DC

Ayres A 1972 Type of sensory integration dysfunction among disabled learners. *American Journal of Occupational Therapy* **26**: 13–18

Badian N 1983 Arithmetic and non verbal learning. In: Myklebust H (ed.) *Progress in Learning Disabilities*. Grune & Statton, New York

Bates E, Benigni L, Bretherton I, Camaioni L, Volterra V 1979 *The Emergence of Cognition and Communication in Infancy*. Academic Press, New York

Bellugi U, Sabo V, Vaid J 1988 Spatial deficit in children

with Williams syndrome. In: Stiles-Davis J, Kritchevsky M, Bellugi U (eds.) *Spatial Cognition*. Erlbaum, Hillsdale, NJ

Bishop D, Adams C 1990 A prospective study of the relationship between specific language impairment, phonological disorders and reading retardation. *Journal of Child Psychology and Psychiatry* 31: 1027–50

Boder E 1973 Developmental dyslexia: a diagnostic approach based on three atypical reading-spelling patterns. *Developmental Medicine and Child Neurology* 15: 663–87

Campbell R 1992 *Mental lives: Case Studies in Cognition*. Blackwell, Oxford

Critchley M 1970 *The Dyslexic Child*. Thomas, Springfield, NJ

Denckla M 1978 Anomalies of motor development in hyperactive boys. *Annals of Neurology* 3: 231–3

Dewey D 1995 What is developmental dyspraxia. *Brain and Cognition* 29: 254–74

Duffy F, Denckla M, McAnulty G, Holmes G 1988 Neurophysiological studies in dyslexia. In: Plum F (ed.) *Language Communication and the Brain*. Raven Press, New York

Ellis A 1985 The cognitive neuropsychology of developmental and acquired dyslexia: A critical survey. *Cognitive Neuropsychology* 2: 169–205

Galaburda A, Wang P, Bellugi U, Rossen M 1994 Cytoarchitectonic anomalies in a genetically based disorder: Williams syndrome. *Neuroreport* 3: 735–57

Gubbay S 1975 *The Clumsy Child*. Sanders, New York

Haynes C, Naïdoo S 1991 *Children with Speech and Language Impairment*. MacKeith Press, London

Hynd G, Semrud-Clikeman M, Lorys A, Novey E, Epiopulos R 1990 Brain morphology in developmental dyslexia and attention deficit disorder-hyperactivity. *Archives of Neurology* 47: 919–26

Jeeves M, Temple C 1987 A further study of language function in callosal agenesis. *Brain and Language* 32: 325–35

Kinsbourne M, Kaplan P 1979 *Children's Learning and Attention Problems*. Little Brown, Boston, MA

Korkman M, Häkkinen-Rihu P 1994 A new classification of developmental language disorders. *Brain and Language* 47: 96–116

Kosc J 1974 Developmental dyscalculia. *Journal of Learning Disabilities* 7: 46–59

Laszlo J, Bairstow P 1983 Kinaesthesis: its measurement, training and relationship with motor control. *Quarterly Journal of Experimental Psychology* 35: 411–21

Marshall J 1980 On the biology of language acquisition. In: Kaplan D (ed.) *Biological Studies of Mental Processes*. MIT Press, Boston, MA

McCloskey J, Caramazza A, Basili A 1984 Cognitive mechanisms in number processing and calculation: Evidence from dyscalculia. *Brain and Cognition* 4: 71–196

Meyerson M, Frank R 1987 Language, speech and hearing in Williams syndrome: intervention approaches and research needs. *Developmental Medicine and Child Neurology* 29: 258–70

Money J 1973 Turner's syndrome and parietal lobe functions. *Cortex* 9: 387–93

Netley C 1977 Dichotic listening of callosal agenesis and Turner syndrome patients. In: Segalowitz S, Gruber F (eds.) *Language Development and Neurological Theory*. Academic Press, New York

O'Hare A, Brown J, Aitken K 1991 Dyscalculia in Childhood. *Developmental Medicine and Child Neurology* 33: 361–67

Piaget J, Szemiska A 1972 La *genèse du nombre*. Delachaux et Niestlé, Genève

Rapin I, Allen D 1988 Syndromes in developmental dysphasias and adult aphasia. In: Plum F (ed.) *Language Communication and the Brain*. Raven Press, New York

Rourke B (ed.) 1985 *Neuropsychology of Learning Disabilities: Essentials of Subtype Analysis*. Guilford Press, New York

Rudel R 1980 Learning disability—diagnosis by exclusion and discrepancy. *Journal of the American Academy of Child Psychology* 19: 567–39

Rutter M 1981 Syndromes attributed to 'minimal brain dysfunction' in childhood. *American Journal of Psychiatry* 139: 21–3

Shalev R, Wertman R, Amir N 1988 Developmental dyscalculia. *Cortex* 24: 555–61

Silva P 1980 The prevalence, stability, and significance of developmental delay in preschool children. *Developmental Medicine and Child Neurology* 22: 768–77

Stackhouse J 1982 An investigation of reading and spelling performances in speech-disordered children. *British Journal of Communication* 17: 52–9

Stackhouse J Snowling M 1994 Barriers to literacy development in two cases of developmental verbal dyspraxia. *Cognitive Neuropsychology* 9: 273–99

Stahl S M 1996 *Essential Psychopharmacology*. Cambridge University Press, New York

Strang J, Rourke B 1985 Arithmetic disability subtypes: the neuropsychological significance of specific impairment in childhood. In: Rourke B (ed.) *Neuropsychology of Learning Disabilities: Essentials of Subtype Analysis*. Guilford Press, New York

Strauss A, Lehtinen L 1947 *Psychopathology and Education of the Brain Injured Child*. Grune and Stratton, New York

Temple C 1989 Digit dyslexia: a category-specific disorder in developmental dyscalculia. *Cognitive Neuropsychology* 6: 93–116

Temple C 1991 Procedural dyscalculia and number fact dyscalculia: double dissociation in developmental dyscalculia. *Cognitive Neuropsychology* 8: 155–76

Temple C 1997 *Developmental Cognitive Neuropsychology*. Psychology Press, Hove

Van Hout A 1992 *Acquired aphasias in children*. In: Boller F, Grafman J (eds.) *Handbook of Neuropsychology*. Vol. 7. Elsevier, Amsterdam

Van Hout A 1995 Apprentissage du calcul et dyscalculies. *Approche Neuropsychologique des Apprentissages de l'Enfant* 4–6: 4–74

Van Hout A, Estienne F 1994 *Les dyslexies: décrire, évaluer, expliquer, traiter*. Masson, Paris

Weintraub S, Mesulam M 1983 Developmental learning disabilities of the right hemisphere. Emotional, interpersonal, and cognitive components. *Archives of Neurology* 40: 463–69

Wender P 1971 *Minimal Brain Dysfunction in Children*. John Wiley, New York

Zentail S 1984 Context effects in the behavioral ratings of hyperactivity. *Journal of Abnormal Child Psychology* 12: 345–52

General Aspects of Developmental Language Disorders
S. L. James

Most children learn to talk and to understand language with no apparent difficulty. Around 12 months of age, they begin producing their first words. By the time they begin school at 5 or 6 years of age, they have large vocabularies, understand and produce a wide variety of sentences, and are able to participate in extended conversations.

For some children, however, the process of language development is difficult and does not follow the normal developmental pattern. These children have a developmental language disorder. In general, a child can be considered language disordered when their use or understanding of language is below that expected for their chronological age and level of functioning. Although this is a very broad definition, it suggests that at least three pieces of information are required in order to make an initial diagnosis of language disorder: (a) information about the child's language production (use), (b) information about the child's language comprehension (understanding), and (c) information about language production and comprehension in normally developing children.

The following exploration of the population of children with language disorders will move beyond this general definition to look at more specific behaviors and aspects of development: the potential impact of language disorders on some other aspects of development or performance; the patterns of development found in language disordered children; the components of language that may be disordered; and some groups of children who are at high risk for language disorders.

1. Language Disorders and Performance in Other Areas

A child who has difficulty understanding or producing language is likely to have problems in other areas of performance in which language plays an important role. Two areas frequently affected are social interactions and academic performance.

1.1 Language Disorders and Social Interactions

Language is a social tool that allows interaction among people. Even before they have any words, infants use sounds and gestures to initiate and maintain interactions with the adults in their environment. A language/communication disorder can adversely affect the parent–child interaction from infancy on. It is suggested that infants who are at high risk for language disorders, such as those who are mentally retarded, hearing impaired, or brain damaged, use communication behaviors that are less predictable and more difficult to interpret than do normally developing infants. As a result, these infants' parents have more difficulty deciding what the child wants or needs. The infant may feel helpless because they are ineffective in influencing the environment and getting their wants or needs met. The parent may feel frustrated because they are unable to figure out what an appropriate response might be to the child's communicative attempts. Communicative interactions are not rewarding for either the child or the parent, and the motivation to communicate declines.

It has been reported that language-disordered children and their parents engage in significantly fewer interactions than do normally developing children and their parents. In those interactions that do occur, parents of children with language disorders tend to be more directive and controlling. The parent initiates almost all interactions, constantly tries to elicit a response from the child, and uses a large number of commands or directives. Although parents of normally developing children also use a large number of directives when their children are very young, the directiveness of their language decreases as the children develop the ability to use language for self-regulation. Language-disordered children may not develop the ability to use language for self-regulation because of their language problems, and their parents may continue to use directive or controlling language in interacting with the children. Because of the overall reduction in interactions and the one-sided nature of the communicative interactions between language-disordered children and their parents, language-disordered children have less opportunity to use their language as a tool to initiate and maintain social interactions.

The difficulty in using language as a social tool appears to have adverse affects on language-disordered children's interactions with their peers. Studies of language/learning disabled adolescents have revealed that they have trouble making friends and interacting with classmates. Van Kleeck and Richardson (1988) suggest that youngsters with language disorders lack many of the communication abilities that affect children hitting it off with each other in the first steps of friendship building. These include the ability to communicate clearly, to exchange information successfully, to explore interpersonal similarities and differences, to establish joint play activities, to resolve conflicts, and to share private thoughts and information. Consequently, language-disordered children may grow even more socially isolated as they grow older.

1.2 Language Disorders and Academic Performance

Just as language plays a crucial role in social development, it also plays a crucial role in learning and academic performance. Much of academic success depends on learning to read and write. Oral language skills are the basis for reading and writing skills, and a problem in oral language development is likely to have a negative impact on the child's reading and writing development. Because language is the primary medium for teaching and learning, deficits in oral and written language skills can have a profound effect not only on performance in the language arts but also in other content areas such as mathematics, natural sciences, and social sciences. Thus, academic success depends to a large extent on oral and written language skills, and children with language disorders are at high risk for academic difficulties.

Children who are identified as language disordered in the preschool years often have language problems that persist into the school years. From about 30 to 75 percent of the children with preschool language disorders continue to exhibit problems in oral language in later childhood and adolescence and between 50 and 95 percent demonstrate significant reading disorders during the school years and beyond (Scarborough and Dobrich 1990). Even when their receptive and expressive language skills reach normal or nearly normal levels in the late preschool years, these children may continue to have reading problems or to demonstrate other learning problems (see *Disorders of Reading and Writing*; *Learning Disabilities*).

It should not be surprising that children with developmental language disorders have academic problems when the linguistic demands inherent in the classroom situation are considered. As Wallach (1989) points out, the language faced by children in school is quite different from the language faced by children at home and in other casual language situations. In casual conversations, there usually are a number of cues from the nonverbal context that facilitate understanding of the linguistic message. For example, when a child is faced with a command such as *Please throw the banana peel in the garbage*, the child's ability to understand and respond appropriately is helped by the fact that they are holding a banana peel and that something needs to be done with it. In addition, the person giving the command may accompany the command with a gesture such as pointing toward the garbage can. In contrast, the language in instruction has been described as decontextualized, suggesting that less of the meaning or content can be obtained from the nonverbal context. Wallach suggests that reading is a perfect example of decontextualized language because the meaning is entirely encoded in words and sentence structures on the page.

In the very early grades, the language used in the classroom more closely resembles the casual language used at home in its reliance on nonverbal context to facilitate understanding. As children move through the grades, however, they must rely more and more on their linguistic knowledge to obtain the relevant information. The increased emphasis on decontextualized language in the later grades would help explain why children with language disorders exhibit more frequent and more severe academic problems as they move through the grades. In addition, the language used by teachers increases in grammatical complexity in the later grades. Nelson (1984) points out that Grade 6 teachers speak more rapidly and use longer and more complex sentences than do teachers in Grades 1, 2, and 3.

Furthermore, most of the content to be learned is presented in print by Grade 4. All of these factors—greater use of decontextualized language, greater grammatical complexity of the teacher's language, and increased use of written materials—place greater linguistic demands on children in the classroom. Children with normal language abilities can handle these increased demands. However, children with developmental language disorders are likely to have increasing difficulty as they progress through school and their academic performance is likely to suffer.

2. Patterns of Development in Language-disordered Children

One way of describing children with developmental language disorders is by the way that their language differs from the pattern demonstrated by normally developing children. Generally, these differences can be characterized by the rate at which language forms and structures are acquired or by the sequence of development for certain forms and structures. Differences in the rate of development are more common than differences in the sequence of development. Below is a description of some of the patterns found among language-disordered children.

2.1 Disorders of Rate

Some language-disordered children have been found to exhibit an overall delay in the development of various language forms and structures. A child exhibiting this pattern follows the normal sequence of development, but at a slower rate of acquisition. In addition, the rate of development tends to be very similar across all forms/structures. Depending on the severity of the delay, children exhibiting this pattern of development may eventually 'catch up' with their normal peers. For example, a child who is one year behind in language production at age 3 years may produce age-appropriate forms/structures by the time they enter school. Other children who exhibit delays in the rate of language development will never reach the level of children with normal language development. These children reach a plateau in their development of language and they continue to show a delay, which becomes more severe over time as their normal peers continue to acquire increasingly sophisticated language abilities. This pattern of language development is often associated with mental retardation.

Another, more common, pattern of disordered rate is one in which the delay is not equal across all forms and structures. The child with this pattern exhibits the same sequence of development with a slow rate of development; however, some forms or structures are only slightly delayed, while others are considerably delayed. Thus, this pattern is characterized by a slow, but uneven rate of development for different language forms and structures. The majority of the children identified as having a developmental language disorder show this pattern. Like some children with a general overall delay across all language forms/structures, children showing this pattern may exhibit near normal oral language skills by the time they enter school.

2.2 Disorders of Sequence

Disordered patterns of language development that are characterized by deviations from the normal sequence of development are not common. However, there are instances where a child acquires later developing forms or structures before they learn some of the earlier developing ones. This pattern is sometimes seen in children who have suffered from a serious illness for a number of months. Due to the illness, the child's language learning may have been interrupted and they may have failed to acquire some forms or structures that would have been learned during the period of illness. Those forms/structures may then develop after the child has acquired other forms that typically develop later.

2.3 Other Disordered Patterns

Leonard (1986, 1998) describes two other less common patterns of development that may be found in the population of children with developmental language disorders. These two patterns cannot be categorized as disorders in either rate or sequence *per se*. In one pattern, the child uses a language form or structure that appears in the language of normally developing children; however, the frequency with which they use that form or structure is deviant. For example, normally developing children have been observed to produce sentences that are best described as 'topic–comment' in which the topic of the sentence is named and a comment about it follows (e.g., '*Cookies, I like them*'). The writer knows of one case of a language-disordered child whose predominant sentence structure was 'topic–comment.' Although rare, the extreme overuse of a normal form/structure may charac-

terize the language of some language-disordered children.

The second pattern is one in which a language-disordered child uses a form or structure that has never been reported for normally developing children. Leonard cites the case of an English-speaking child who substituted a non-English consonant for the fricatives /s/, /f/, and /z/.

3. Components of Language that may be Disordered

Another way of describing the language development of children with language disorders focuses on the particular components of their language that are disordered. Impairments can and do occur in all five components of language: phonology, morphology, syntax, semantics, and pragmatics. The kind of disorders that may be found in each of these components will be explored briefly.

3.1 Disorders of Phonology

Although part of phonological acquisition involves learning the motor speech movements necessary to produce the phonemes of one's native language, it also involves learning linguistic units and rules. Children with developmental language disorders can have difficulty in any or all of these aspects. For example, they may have difficulty learning the phonemes that make up their native language. They also may have problems in learning the rules for combining phonemes into acceptable sequences of sounds. Finally, they may exhibit impairments in the use and understanding of the suprasegmental features of the language, including intonation, stress, and rhythm.

3.2 Disorders of Morphology

The morphological component of the language consists of rules for combining morphemes (meaningful units). The acquisition of knowledge about grammatical morphemes, including noun plurals and possessives, auxiliary verbs, verb tense markers, and a number of other prefixes and suffixes, is part of morphological development. Morphological forms allow speakers to provide much greater specificity in their use of language. For example, through the addition of verb tense markers, a speaker is able to tell a listener whether an event occurred in the past, present, or future. Morphological markers are used to indicate whether the speaker is talking about one or more than one object (noun plurals), to indicate ownership (noun possessive), to provide information about case, gender, and number (personal pronouns), and to make a comparison (comparative and superlative markers).

The grammatical morphemes that have received the most attention in studies of language development are those originally studied by Brown (1973). These include the present progressive (go*ing*), the prepositions *in* and *on*, noun plurals (dog*s*), noun possessives (mommy*'s*), articles (*a, the*), irregular past tense (*threw, ran*), regular past tense (open*ed*), uncontractible copula (This *is* big), contractible copula (It*'s* big), regular third person singular (It run*s*), irregular third person singular (He *has* it), uncontractible auxiliary (*Is* she coming?), and contractible auxiliary (She*'s* going). Most language-disordered children have some difficulty acquiring these 14 morphemes. Although they are likely to acquire them in the same sequence as normally developing children, their rate of development typically is much slower. Like younger normally developing children, they frequently omit the morphemes in sentences. For example, a language-disordered child may omit the noun plural and produce the following sentence '*I want two cookie—*,' or might leave off the verb tense marker and say '*Yesterday, she walk—home.*'

In addition to the morphemes studied by Brown, language-disordered children may have difficulty with a number of other morphological forms, including various prepositions (e.g., *to, from, beside, behind, over*), modal verbs (e.g., *can, will, could, should*), and comparative and superlative suffixes (e.g., small*er*, small*est*).

Children with developmental language disorders may have trouble understanding as well as producing morphological forms. For example, a language-disordered child who is asked to point to the picture of '*cars*' may point to the picture showing only one car rather than the one showing several cars. Problems in comprehending grammatical morphemes can result in considerable confusion and misunderstanding on the part of the child.

Recent studies suggest that some types of specific language impairment, characterized by disorders of morphology in particular, are genetically determined (Gopnik 1997).

3.3 Disorders of Syntax

Children with language disorders often have problems in acquiring various aspects of syntax. These problems are reflected in a significantly reduced mean–length–of–utterance (MLU) compared to peers of the same age. Part of this reduced MLU is due to their tendency to omit grammatical morphemes. However, they also may have trouble acquiring rules for grammatically complete simple sentences containing a subject, verb, and object (S–V–O). For example, a 3 year old child with a language disorder produced the following utterance to describe a picture of a boy riding a horse: '*Boy a horse.*' Although he included the subject (*boy*) and the object (*horse*) and even expanded the object noun phrase by using the article *a* (a later developing grammatical morpheme), he failed to include a main verb. Most normal children in an early stage of language development would be likely to say '*Boy ride*,' '*Ride horse*,' or '*Boy ride horse*.'

Another area of syntactic development that is problematic for many language-disordered children is learning rules for different sentence types, such as negative sentences and questions. They may produce primitive forms of these sentences, such as those used by younger normally developing children. For example, the negative sentence 'I don't want to do that' may be produced as '*I not wanna do that.*' In this case, the failure to produce the negative contraction *don't* is not due to the absence of *do* from the child's repertoire. Rather, the child seems to lack the syntactic rule for forming the negative. Yes/no questions may consist of a statement produced with a rising intonation pattern, for example, '*That my book?*' WH questions will begin with the WH word, but like yes/no questions will have the copula or auxiliary verb omitted: '*Where my book?*'

The acquisition of later developing structures such as passive and complex sentences is likely to be very delayed among children with developmental language disorders. They especially seem to have problems with sentence forms in which the agent–action–object relationship is reversed or interrupted. This is true in passive sentences and in some complex sentences. For example, in the passive sentence '*The girl was chased by the boy*,' the agent of the action is in the object rather than the subject position of the sentence. In the sentence '*The dress that I tore was new*,' the relative clause '*that I tore*' interrupts the subject–verb relationship. Even older adolescents with language disorders rarely use these kinds of sentences in their spoken or written language. They also are likely to have difficulty comprehending them in either spoken or written form (Bishop 1997).

3.4 Disorders of Semantics

Most children with developmental language disorders are delayed in vocabulary development. They are likely to be slow in acquiring their first words and the rate at which they add new words to their vocabulary is slower than normal. This delay is present in both production and comprehension. Children diagnosed as language disordered in the preschool years may continue to exhibit deficits in vocabulary comprehension into the school years, even when their other oral language skills have reached near normal levels.

The performance of older language-disordered youngsters on certain kinds of vocabulary comprehension tests may be misleading. They often score within the normal range on vocabulary tests, such as the *Peabody Picture Vocabulary Test* (Dunn and Dunn 1981), which requires choosing a single meaning for each word. However, when faced with a word with more than one meaning, they are likely to have problems selecting alternate meanings. For example, they might be unable to provide two interpretations for a sentence such as '*The glasses were very dirty.*'

Children with developmental language disorders also tend to have difficulty with more abstract words, such as relational terms used to talk about time, space, and size dimensions. These kinds of words require an understanding of the relationship among entities or events. For example, understanding words like 'before' and 'after' requires an understanding of the temporal relationship between two or more events. In order to comprehend prepositions such as 'under' and 'over,' a child must have some knowledge of the spatial relationship between two objects. Comprehension of dimensional adjectives such as 'tall' and 'short' involves comparing an object to some standard.

Another area of semantics that may be disordered is the use and understanding of figurative language. Figurative language includes forms such as idioms ('She broke the news'), metaphors ('He's as happy as a lark'), proverbs ('Don't count your chickens before they're hatched'), and jokes and riddles. The ability to handle these figurative forms requires the individual to disregard the literal meaning of the words or sentence and recognize the generalized, more abstract meaning. Figurative language is especially difficult, even for older language-disordered adolescents.

In addition to the difficulties in acquiring word and sentence meaning, a number of language-disordered children have word-finding problems. They are unable to produce a presumably known word when it is needed. Although this inability to retrieve words does not seem to reflect a deficit in vocabulary knowledge *per se*, it affects the child's ability to express meaning clearly and effectively. Children who have word-finding problems may use circumlocutions in which they 'talk around' the desired word. For example, they may describe the object for which they cannot recall the name, such as referring to an *elephant* as 'a big animal with a trunk.' They also may substitute a word that is similar in meaning or sound to the target word. For example, one language-disordered child called a *bus* 'a truck,' while another referred to a *television* as a 'telephone.'

3.5 Disorders of Pragmatics

Pragmatic knowledge encompasses such diverse aspects as the use of language for different communicative intents or functions, rules governing conversational and narrative discourse, and rules for the use of different speech styles in different communicative situations. Children with developmental language disorders may exhibit deficits in any or all of these aspects.

Language-disordered children may express fewer communicative intents than normal children at the same age. Even in the preschool years, normally developing children use their language for a variety of intents, including to request, to respond, to describe,

to express attitudes and feelings, to regulate conversations, and to tease and joke. Preschool language-disordered children may use only a few of these communicative intents. They also may be limited in the diversity of the syntactic structures or forms used to express different communicative intents. However, it should be noted that language-disordered children's use of communicative intents has been reported to be very similar to normal children at the same MLU level. In other words, their ability to use communicative intents seems to be commensurate with their morphological and syntactic abilities.

Another aspect of pragmatics that may be disordered is the ability to engage in conversational discourse. Deficits may be seen in the ability to initiate or end conversations, to take turns talking, and to maintain the topic. Generally, studies of language-disordered children's conversational abilities have suggested that they are able to engage in conversational interactions, but that they tend to be somewhat passive. They take turns and maintain the topic, but they rarely initiate conversations or contribute new information to the topic under discussion. However, when the conversational behaviors required are limited primarily to single-word responses and do not demand syntactic skills, language-disordered children have been found to demonstrate conversational skills as good or better than normal children at the same language level.

In addition to problems in conversational discourse, language-disordered children may also show deficits in their narrative discourse abilities. The ability to produce narratives, such as stories, shows significant development during the school-age years. Results of studies suggest that school-age children with language disorders have difficulty producing organized, cohesive narratives. In addition, their comprehension of narratives may be deficient in comparison to their normal peers.

Finally, children with language disorders may have difficulty making appropriate speech style adjustments for different listeners and different communicative situations. Speech style adjustments may include changes in length and complexity of utterances, the amount of information provided, and politeness. Available evidence suggests that language-disordered children are aware of the need to change their speech style for different listeners and situations and do make a number of adjustments in their speech to different listeners. For example, they have been found to use more self-repetitions when speaking to younger versus older children. However, the limited syntactic abilities of language-disordered children may interfere with their ability to make certain kinds of adjustments. For example, they are less likely than peers of the same age to adjust the length of utterances addressed to younger versus older listeners.

3.6 Metalinguistic Abilities in Language-disordered Children

Another area of language knowledge that may be problematic for children with developmental language disorders is metalinguistics. Metalinguistic abilities involve conscious awareness of the units and rules of the native language system. They differ from linguistic abilities, in that they require additional optional processing. Linguistic abilities—knowledge of phonology, syntax, semantics, and pragmatics—allow the production and understanding of language in an almost automatic way, without thinking about the units and rules being used.

In contrast to linguistic abilities, individuals' metalinguistic abilities involve conscious thought; use of them is optional, and generally invoked only when needed. If presented with a sentence such as '*The clothes that he chose was expensive*' and asked if it was acceptable, the hearer would call on their knowledge of syntax to make a judgment. They would consciously think about the syntactic rule that is violated in the sentence, would recognize that the subject 'clothes' is plural and the verb 'was' is singular and, therefore, that the problem is in the lack of agreement between the subject and the verb. Although they might not describe the rule violation in exactly that way, conscious awareness of syntax would allow it to be identified. In addition, the hearer would be able to correct the sentence so that it was grammatically acceptable. Clearly, this kind of additional conscious processing goes far beyond what people do when they produce and understand language in normal conversational interactions.

Metalinguistic abilities are dependent on linguistic knowledge; however, it is possible to have normal linguistic skills and lack metalinguistic abilities. This is the case with young children who are able to produce and understand utterances, but do not seem to be able to reflect consciously on the units and rules underlying their comprehension and production. Metalinguistic abilities do not show significant development until the early school years, and they continue to develop throughout adolescence. They appear to be related to reading development.

Because metalinguistic development is dependent on linguistic development, children with developmental language disorders might be expected to show metalinguistic deficits. This assumption is supported by the results of studies indicating that language-disordered children perform poorly on tasks requiring phonological, morphological, syntactic, and pragmatic awareness.

4. Language Disorders in Specific Populations

Normal language development is related to development in a number of other areas, including intellectual, emotional, auditory (hearing), and neurological development. Children with deficits in these areas are at risk for language disorders. For example, children who have noticeable deficits in intellectual development (i.e., mentally retarded children) generally show significant delays in all components of language. Children who exhibit emotional disorders are likely to have some problems in language, especially in the pragmatic component. Because children learn language by hearing other people use it, a child who has a hearing impairment will have considerable difficulty developing language normally. Blind children also might be expected to exhibit developmental language disorders because of their difficulty in making the connection between language and the objects and events represented by the language. Finally, children who demonstrate problems in learning also tend to exhibit language deficits. Learning-disabled children are likely to have difficulty producing and understanding both oral and written language.

There is another group of children who seem to exhibit normal intellectual, emotional, auditory, and visual development during the early years, but whose language development is impaired. They may have disorders in one or more of the components of language, and their language problems may persist into adulthood. Because these children seem to demonstrate problems only in the language area, they have been referred to as 'specifically language impaired.'

In the following sections, the language development of children in the various populations mentioned above will be explored.

4.1 Mentally Retarded Children

Mental retardation is defined by the American Association on Mental Deficiency as 'significantly subaverage general intellectual functioning existing concurrently with deficits in adaptive behavior and manifested during the developmental period' (Grossman 1983: 1). Significant subaverage intellectual functioning generally refers to an IQ two or more standard deviations below the mean on a standardized test of intelligence. Deficits in adaptive behavior refer to limitations in self-help skills, speech and language development, social development, and, in older children, in academic and reasoning skills. Thus, language abilities are one of the adaptive behaviors that are assessed in diagnosing a child as mentally retarded.

Studies of retarded children's language production and comprehension have revealed that they are likely to exhibit difficulties in all of the language components. Their phonological development is delayed, and they tend to use the same phonological rules or processes as those used by younger normally developing children. Their morphological and syntactic development tends to follow the same sequence as that found in normal children, but the rate of development is slower. For example, grammatical morphemes and different sentence types are acquired in the same developmental order as in normal children, but at a much later age. Retarded children's morphological and syntactic development is delayed in relation to their mental age also. They do not use the same level of morphological and syntactic structures used by normal children at the same mental age. For example, their sentences are shorter and less complex and contain fewer later developing morphemes.

The vocabularies of retarded children contain more concrete words than the vocabularies of their normal peers. They tend to talk about observable objects, people, and events. They have difficulty understanding and using prepositions, time words, and dimensional adjectives. Words with multiple meanings are difficult for them, and they rarely comprehend or use figurative language. However, their vocabulary development appears to be less delayed in comparison to mental-age matched peers than their morphological and syntactic development.

The pragmatic development of retarded children is similar in sequence, but slower in rate, in some aspects. For example, they express the same communicative intentions as those used by younger normal peers. However, their conversational development does not seem to follow the normal sequence. As they get older, normally developing children become more competent conversational partners who are able not only to maintain topic, but to take control of the conversation. Even as adults, retarded individuals rarely assume conversational control, even when their conversational partner is a younger child.

It should be noted that the language deficits observed in retarded children do not seem to be explained simply by the mental retardation. If their language development were simply a function of their intellectual development, their level of language development would be expected to be consistent with their mental age. As noted previously, however, the morphological and syntactic development of some retarded children seems to be delayed in relation to their cognitive abilities or mental age. The presence of a language delay that is greater than would be predicted on the basis of mental age alone is especially prevalent in the Downs Syndrome population. It has been suggested that these delays may be due to deficits in adaptive and motivational behaviors rather than linguistic or cognitive deficits.

Regardless of the relationship between mental age and language abilities, children with mental retardation are likely to exhibit deficits in some of the components of language. In general, retarded children acquire language forms and structures in the same sequence as the normally developing child, but at a slower rate. Thus, the differences in retarded children's language development tend to be quantitative rather than qualitative.

4.2 Emotionally Disturbed Children

Children who exhibit emotional problems frequently demonstrate disorders in language production and/or comprehension as well. Although autism is the emotional disorder that has received the most attention in the years up to the 1990s, it is not the only one that affects children's language development (see *Autism*). Almost any disturbance in emotional development may have a language problem associated with it.

In very severe cases of emotional disturbance, a child may not talk at all. Although these children are capable of speaking, they do not do so. They may make sounds, such as screeching, but they produce no intelligible speech (see *Language Disorders in Psychoses*). Other emotionally disturbed children imitate or repeat almost everything that is said to them. The exact repetition of another's speech is referred to as 'echolalia,' and is a behavior that is rare among normally developing children. If one were to say to an echolalic child, 'Would you like a drink of water?,' the child would be likely to repeat the question word for word. Echolalia is especially common among children with autism, but may be found in other emotional disorders also.

Children with emotional disorders may exhibit deficits in any or all of the components of language. However, the component that is most likely to be impaired is pragmatics. Because pragmatics involves the use of language in context to communicate with others, it is not surprising that emotionally disturbed children have problems in this aspect. There is some evidence that children with severe emotional disturbances use their language for different communicative intentions, but that they may not use the full range of intentions expressed by normally developing children. For example, one 4 year old child, who was observed over a number of months at a school for emotionally disturbed children, used his gestures and vocalizations to call the listener's attention to objects or events; however, he never used these communication acts to get something that he wanted (e.g., an out-of-reach toy or food item). He would cry until an adult figured out what he wanted and gave it to him, but he would not point to the desired object. In contrast, normally developing preverbal children use their gestures to request objects.

Emotionally disturbed children generally have considerable difficulty carrying on conversations. This difficulty is especially evident in the area of topic maintenance. They often produce utterances that seem to be completely unrelated to the previous speaker's utterance. Examples (1) and (2) from a couple of older children observed at a school for emotionally disturbed children will help demonstrate these problems:

John and his teacher were looking at a picture (1)
of a barn and animals that he had painted.
The teacher said, 'This is a really good picture

of a farm, John. Would you like to share it with the rest of the class?' John responded, 'The next batter stepped up to the plate and hit a home run.'

As Jenny walked into the room, her speech-language pathologist said, 'Hi, Jenny. How are you today?' Jenny looked around the room and said, 'Chair, chair, chair. Lots of chairs.' The therapist said, 'Yes, there do seem to be a lot of chairs in here today. Shall we sit on chairs or shall we sit on the floor?' Jenny said, 'I forgot to eat my lunch.' (2)

These examples were not isolated instances in which the child was momentarily distracted and, therefore, gave an inappropriate response. They illustrate a rather consistent failure to maintain the topic. The children's utterances simply are unrelated to the content of the other speaker's preceding utterance.

Another aspect of pragmatics that is especially problematic for many emotionally disturbed children is in using the appropriate forms in conversational interactions. One 12 year old, upon seeing the author appear in his classroom for the first time, came over and asked in rapid succession: 'What are you doing here?' 'How old are you?' 'Do you have a husband?' Although the questions might have been appropriate under other circumstances, they were not appropriate questions to address to a strange adult. He also did not follow up on any of the responses, but simply asked the next question as soon as the previous one had been answered. He was attempting to initiate and maintain a conversation, but he did not use the appropriate forms to do so.

Some children seem to have a stereotyped form that they use in certain situations. For example, one 9 year old's usual greeting upon seeing someone was 'Welcome to our school. Let me kiss your hand.'

As these examples suggest, some emotionally disturbed children exhibit relatively normal morphological, syntactic, and vocabulary production, but have difficulty using their language to communicate effectively with others. Other children with emotional disorders demonstrate noticeable delays in their development of morphology, syntax, and semantics.

4.3 Hearing-impaired Children

In this section, the focus will be on children whose hearing impairment is sensorineural as opposed to conductive. A sensorineural hearing loss is one that results from damage to the cochlea (sensory organ in the inner ear) or the auditory nerve, and generally is irreversible. Conductive losses occur from a condition in the outer or middle ear and usually can be reversed or improved through medical treatment. Although the development of cochlear implants holds great promise for treatment of sensorineural hearing loss, the resulting hearing is far from normal and not all hearing impaired persons are candidates for this treatment.

The language development of children with impaired hearing depends on a number of factors. Among the most important are:

(a) the degree of the hearing loss,
(b) the age at which the child acquired the loss,
(c) the age at which the hearing loss was identified, and
(d) the amount and type of habilitation.

Usually one thinks of hearing impaired children as having a severe to profound sensorineural hearing loss—the so-called 'deaf child.' Certainly, those children will have great difficulty acquiring oral language and may be taught language through manual communication. However, there is some evidence suggesting that children with mild and moderate sensorineural hearing losses may demonstrate significant delays in language development.

A child whose hearing loss is present at birth or occurs sometime before speech and language is acquired will have a much more difficult time acquiring oral language than a child whose onset of loss occurs later. Many experts refer to the child whose hearing loss occurs anytime prior to 3 years of age as prelingually hearing impaired. If the onset is after age 3 years, the child is considered postlingually hearing impaired. It should be recognized, however, that the child who has even one or two years of exposure to spoken language has a base on which to build and may have an easier time acquiring oral language than the child who was born with a hearing loss.

The importance of the age at which the hearing loss is identified is related to early treatment. The earlier the loss is identified, the sooner the child can be provided with amplification and placed in an appropriate language and communication program. There is considerable evidence that children who receive early intervention develop better language skills.

There has been considerable controversy over the mode in which hearing impaired children should receive language input. Some experts argue for the oral–aural method in which input is received through speechreading and amplification of residual hearing. Manual communication, such as sign language, is prohibited because the oral–aural proponents argue that the auditory modality is the most important for speech and language development. Other experts believe that some form of manual communication should be part of the child's language input. Manual communication includes both fingerspelling and various sign language systems, such as American Sign Language, Seeing Essential English, Signing Exact English, and Signed English (see *Deafness and Sign Language*). An approach that is used in many schools for the deaf is Total Communication, which includes sign language, fingerspelling, speech, and speechreading. No one approach is appropriate for all hearing impaired children. Some children do well with an oral–aural approach, while others do better in a program incorporating manual communication.

Children with severe to profound hearing losses are likely to exhibit significant delays in acquiring the morphological, syntactic, and semantic components of the language system. However, the sequence in which they acquire forms and structures is similar to that followed by hearing children. Their pragmatic development, at least in the area of communicative intentions, has been found to be similar in both rate and sequence to that of hearing children in the early preschool years.

While it is recognized that even a mild to moderate sensorineural hearing loss may result in a language delay, less attention has been given to the impact of a fluctuating conductive impairment on children's language development. Studies of infants and young children with recurrent middle ear infections (otitis media) suggest that these children are likely to exhibit language disorders beginning in the preschool years, even as early as 1 year of age. Clearly, hearing loss in any form and of any degree can interfere with a child's speech and language development.

4.4 Blind Children

Vision would seem to play an important role in language acquisition, because children rely so much on context in the early stages of language development. They seem to learn to relate words to objects and events by seeing the objects and actions that are being labeled or described. Their early comprehension of language is very dependent on contextual cues. Furthermore, a crucial part of the early adult–child communicative interaction involves eye contact and looking at the same objects. Therefore, it would seem that a child who was born without sight or who lost sight at a very early age would have difficulty acquiring language.

Few studies have focused on the language development of blind children. The few investigations that have been done suggest that there is little difference between the language development of blind children and their sighted peers. For example, blind children have been reported to reach early language milestones, such as producing two-word sentences, at about the same time as sighted children and to use language to talk about things in the same way as sighted children at the same linguistic level. The one area in which blind children have been found to have difficulty is in the acquisition of pronouns, especially of the *I–you* distinction.

A more recent longitudinal study of three blind children and one sighted child suggests that there may be some other important differences between blind and sighted children's semantic and pragmatic development (Anderson et al. 1984). The blind children's acquisition and use of early words differed in subtle ways from that of the sighted child. For example, the blind children in this study used action words only to refer to self-actions in contrast to the sighted child

who used them to refer to actions of others as well as his own actions. The blind children overextended very few of their early words to other referents (8 to 13 percent), while the sighted child overextended 41 percent of his words which is a similar percentage to that reported in other studies of sighted children.

The blind children's conversations also seemed to reflect difficulty in establishing the appropriate perspective. This was especially evident in their use of pronouns. They used third person pronouns (e.g., *she* and *her*) to refer to themselves, and they frequently used the second person *you* when *I* or *me* would have been correct. However, this problem in perspective-taking also showed up in other ways. In one example, the child opened a conversation by saying 'Did you go see Nicole?' As the conversation progressed, it was clear that what the child wanted to communicate was that he saw Nicole. A temporary misunderstanding resulted because the child not only used the inappropriate pronoun (*you* for *I*), but he also introduced the topic by asking a question when a statement would have been more appropriate.

Although blind children acquire language at about the same rate and in the same sequence as sighted children, it appears that they may differ in subtle aspects of semantic and pragmatic development and use. Future studies may reveal other kinds of subtle differences in blind children's language development.

4.5 Learning-disabled Children

The most commonly accepted definition of learning disability was developed by the USA National Joint Committee on Learning Disabilities:

> Learning disability is a generic term that refers to a heterogeneous group of disorders manifested by significant difficulties in the acquisition and use of listening, speaking, reading, writing, reasoning, or mathematical abilities. These disorders are intrinsic to the individual and are presumed to be due to central nervous system dysfunction. Even though a learning disability may occur concomitantly with other handicapping conditions (e.g., sensory impairment, mental retardation, social and emotional disturbance) or environmental influences (e.g., cultural differences, insufficient/inappropriate instruction, psychogenic factors), it is not the direct result of those conditions or influences.
>
> (Hammill et al. 1981: 337)

This definition suggests that children with learning disabilities will exhibit problems in the acquisition of oral language and of reading and writing skills. The label of learning disability usually is applied when a child exhibits significant learning problems that cannot be explained through other causes such as emotional disturbance, mental retardation, hearing loss, or environmental or cultural disadvantage.

A learning disability is not usually diagnosed until the school years. However, many learning-disabled children have a history of speech and language difficulties in the preschool years. This is not to suggest that all children with preschool language deficits are learning disabled; however, a preschool language disorder may be an early signal of learning disability.

Learning-disabled children are likely to exhibit comprehension and production problems in all components of the language system. They typically acquire language forms and structures in the same order as their normally developing peers, but their rate of development may be delayed.

Their phonological production is likely to be inconsistent. They may produce sounds correctly in syntactically simple sentences and incorrectly when the sentence increases in complexity. They exhibit difficulties in both morphological and syntactic development. They have problems using and comprehending grammatical morphemes, such as noun plurals and possessives, articles, verb tense markers, and auxiliary verbs. Their acquisition of the rules for forming different sentence types, such as questions, negatives, passives, and complex sentences, will be delayed. Even adolescent and adult learning-disabled individuals have problems in producing and comprehending complex sentences.

Semantic deficits include difficulties in understanding words and sentences that have more than one meaning. For example, a learning-disabled child would have trouble interpreting the two possible meanings of the sentence *'The duck is ready to eat'* (i.e., 'the duck is ready to eat some food' or 'the duck is prepared for consumption by others'). Most of these children are delayed in producing and understanding terms that express relationships in time (soon, later, before, after), space (above, beside, behind), and quantity (more, less, none, all). Their use and understanding of figurative language is relatively delayed. Many children with learning disabilities have word-finding difficulties.

The pragmatic deficits of learning-disabled children include difficulty in initiating and maintaining conversations, providing cohesive narratives, and making appropriate adjustments in speech style for different listeners. These pragmatic problems are likely to interfere with social interactions with peers.

In addition to linguistic deficits, most learning-disabled children exhibit deficiencies in metalinguistic abilities. They have considerable difficulty with tasks that require the ability to reflect consciously on and manipulate the units and rules of the language system. It has been suggested that these metalinguistic problems may be related to the difficulty in reading and writing development demonstrated by many learning-disabled youngsters.

4.6 Specifically Language-impaired Children

As mentioned earlier in this section, some children have trouble acquiring the language system even though their early development in other areas appears to be normal. They have no identifiable intellectual, emotional, or hearing impairments. Their problems seem to be limited to the development of language and may involve production and comprehension of all components of the language system. They are likely to exhibit delays in phonological, morphological, syntactic, semantic, and pragmatic development. Although their rate of language development is slower, they appear to acquire language forms and structures in the same sequence as normally developing children. Some of these children may later be diagnosed as learning disabled.

A number of labels have been used to refer to these children, including 'childhood aphasic' and 'developmentally aphasic.' These terms suggest that the language difficulties are a result of brain dysfunction. In contrast to children with 'acquired aphasia,' however, there is little evidence to support the existence of neurological problems in children with specific language impairment. Acquired aphasia in both adults and children results from identifiable injury to the brain, usually as a result of serious illness or trauma to the head (see *Aphasia*). The language development of children with acquired aphasia differs from that of children with specific language impairment in at least two ways. First, the language development of children with acquired aphasia is normal up until the time of the brain injury. Children with specific language impairment typically demonstrate delays and deficits in very early childhood. Second, aphasic children who suffer brain injury at a young age are likely to exhibit few residual language problems in later childhood and adolescence. In contrast, specifically language-impaired children often demonstrate language deficits that continue well into the school years.

Studies in the 1980s and early 1990s have focused on some cognitive abilities of children with specific language impairment. The results of the studies suggest that language-disordered children have subtle conceptual and processing deficits that appear when the demands on the child's ability to process and use information are high. For example, language-disordered children have more difficulty with problems that require size judgments than those that require color judgments due to the greater conceptual complexity of size relations.

Children with specific language impairments also have been reported to differ from their normal peers in their performance on tasks based on Piaget's theory of cognitive development. In particular, they differ in their symbolic play behaviors. In comparison to age-matched normal peers, they have been found to engage in more concrete, less complex play behaviors with objects.

These findings suggest that in addition to difficulties in language development, children with specific language impairments also exhibit less obvious impairments in some cognitive abilities. Additional research is needed to determine how children's language impairments and specific cognitive delays or deficits are related.

There is evidence that the families of children with specific language impairments have a significantly higher incidence of developmental language disorders than families of normally developing children (Tallal et al. 1989). There is a higher rate of language disorders among mothers, fathers, and siblings of language-disordered children. These results suggest that one of the factors contributing to developmental language disorders is the family unit. Whether this relationship is due to genetic or environmental influences has yet to be determined.

5. Conclusions

Language-disordered children may have difficulty in producing and comprehending any or all of the components of the language system, including phonology, morphology, syntax, semantics, or pragmatics. They also may have problems in acquiring the ability to think consciously about and reflect on language units and rules (metalinguistic abilities). Most language-disordered children will exhibit varying degrees of delay in the acquisition of different forms or structures. Their language development typically is slower in rate, but is similar in sequence to that found in normally developing children.

The language problems found among language-disordered children are likely to impact on their development and/or performance in other areas. In particular, they tend to exhibit problems in social interactions and in academic performance. Their early communicative and social interactions with parents may be impaired. When they enter school, they may have difficulty interacting with peers, resulting in increasing social isolation. Their academic performance is likely to suffer because of their deficits in oral and written language. Their academic difficulties may become more severe as they progress through the grades because of the increasing linguistic demands inherent in the classroom situation.

Developmental language disorders are prevalent among children who have intellectual, emotional, auditory, visual, and learning deficits. These populations are likely to exhibit delays in some or all components of the language system. In addition, there is a group of children who appear to develop normally in all aspects except language. They are not mentally retarded, emotionally disturbed, or hearing or visually impaired. Although learning problems may show up in some of these children during the school years, they are not all learning disabled. These children are referred to as specifically language-impaired. Results

of studies suggest that these children not only demonstrate problems in language, but that they also may have subtle deficits in some cognitive abilities. In addition, there is evidence supporting familial aggregation of developmental language disorders. Future research should focus on the specific nature of the relationship among developmental language disorders and cognitive deficits and the role that genetics and environment may play in language disorders.

Bibliography

Anderson E, Dunlea A, Kekelis L 1984 Blind children's language: Resolving some differences. *Journal of Child Language* 11: 645–64

Bernstein D, Tiegerman E 1989 *Language and Communication Disorders in Children*, 2nd edn. Merrill, Columbus, OH

Bishop D V M 1997 *Uncommon Understanding*. Psychology Press, Hove

Brown R 1973 *A First Language: The Early Stages*. Harvard University Press, Cambridge, MA

Davis J, Elfenbein J, Schum R, Bentler R 1986 Effects of mild and moderate hearing impairments on language, educational, and psychosocial behavior of children. *Journal of Speech and Hearing Disorders* 51: 53–62

Dunn L, Dunn L 1981 *Peabody Picture Vocabulary Test—Revised*. American Guidance Service, Circle Pines, MN

Gopnik M 1997 *The Inheritance and Innateness of Grammar*. Oxford University Press, New York

Grossman H 1983 *Classification in Mental Retardation*. America Association on Mental Deficiency, Washington, DC

Hammill D, Leiger J, McNutt G, Larsen T 1981 A new definition of learning disabilities. *Learning Disabilities Quarterly* 4: 336–42

James S 1988 The development of oral language and reading. In: Hedley C, Hicks J (eds.) *Reading and the Special Learner*. Ablex Publishing Corporation, Norwood, NJ

Kleeck A van, Richardson A 1988 Language delay in children. In: Lass N, McReynolds L, Northern J, Yoder D (eds.) *Handbook of Speech-Language Pathology and Audiology*. B. C. Decker, Toronto

Leonard L 1986 Early language development and language disorders. In: Shames G, Wiig E (eds.) *Human Communication Disorders*, 2nd edn. Merrill, Columbus, OH

Leonard L 1998 *Children with Specific Language Impairment*. MIT Press, Cambridge, MA

Nelson N 1984 Beyond information processing: The language of teachers and textbooks. In: Wallach G, Butler K (eds.) *Language Learning Disabilities in School-Age Children*. Williams and Wilkins

Scarborough H, Dobrich W 1990 Development of children with early language delay. *Journal of Speech and Hearing Research* 33: 70–83

Tallal P, Ross R, Curtiss S 1989 Familial aggregation in specific language impairment. *Journal of Speech and Hearing Disorders* 54: 167–73

Wallach G 1989 Current research as a map for language intervention in the school years. *Seminars in Speech and Language* 10: 205–71

Specific Language Impairment: Subtypes and Assessment
M. Korkman

The term specific language impairment (SLI) refers to impairments of language that become manifest during early childhood when linguistic skills fail to develop as expected. SLI is to be distinguished from acquired language disorders, in which a brain disease or insult, occurring later than infancy, cause an arrest or a deterioration of language skills that were previously acquired normally. A diagnosis of SLI also excludes children in which a language impairment accompanies a more general condition, such as mental retardation, a hearing impairment, cerebral palsy, fetal alcohol exposure, etc. These children may have a language impairment but it is not specific and is therefore not called SLI.

SLI is often used synonymously with developmental language disorder (DLD) and developmental dysphasia. Most children with disordered language development also have verbal learning problems at school, especially dyslexia. The term language learning impairment (LLI) has therefore also been employed to denote children with SLI and/or dyslexia. Of these terms DLD and SLI are the ones most commonly used.

Children with SLI are thus children, who, for no apparent reason, in the absence of general retardation, brain damage, or other obvious causes, show a selective incapacitating impairment of language. Neuropsychological research has attempted to find explanations for SLI through studies comparing children diagnosed as SLI or DLD to normal children on a wide variety of tasks. Differences have been demonstrated in all aspects of language and also in many nonlanguage domains of development, such as motor, attention, memory, and nonverbal perception. Unsolved problems in this research area are how the observed deficits relate to language development, and how to integrate the diverse findings.

In the attempts to integrate the findings, one approach is to search for underlying primary deficits that may explain many of the overt signs. Another approach is to classify SLI children and look for different patterns of SLI. The approaches may be combined to specify subtypes of SLI that may be characterized by different underlying mechanisms. In the previous chapter the manifestations and effects of developmental language disorders in general were described. The focus of the present chapter is on mechanisms possibly underlying subtypes of SLI, as well as methods of neuropsychological assessment and intervention.

1. Prevalence and Etiology

The prevalence of SLI is high. Most estimates have concluded that around 3 percent of all children aged between 3 and 7 suffer from SLI. Some estimates even suggest the rate is between 6 and 7 percent or even higher (see Rapin et al. 1992). The diagnosis is age-dependent, as many children with SLI eventually acquire normal speech. Boys are more often affected than girls. Language learning problems remain through school age in the majority of children, most commonly in the form of dyslexia. Many children may thus move from the diagnostic category of SLI to that of dyslexia. However, not all dyslexic children have suffered from SLI as young children.

SLI is often genetically determined. Familial aggregation of SLI has been demonstrated in many studies (e.g., Gopnik and Crago 1991). In a review of genetic studies of SLI, Palmour (1997) concluded that between 20 and 40 percent of the first-degree relatives of persons with SLI have a history of speech delay, as compared to between 3 and 19 percent of the relatives of control subjects. Precisely what is inherited is not known. Not all SLI children have a familial background to the SLI. A positive family history (affected first-degree relatives) occurs in only around 35 to 55 percent of all children with SLI (Palmour 1997).

SLI is not typically a consequence of anatomical brain abnormality, but subtle signs of abnormality or atypical brain organization have been associated with SLI. Brain imaging techniques have revealed an absence of asymmetry in certain (perisylvian) areas of the cerebral cortex in children with SLI. These regions are usually asymmetric so that the left, which is known to be important for language, has a larger cortical surface. One study, employing magnetic resonance imaging (MRI), demonstrated an inverse asymmetry in eight boys with SLI, the right perisylvian region being larger than the left (Plante et al. 1991). The researchers postulated a disturbance of neural development in this region. However, absence of, or inverse symmetry in, the perisylvian regions may occur in normal individuals as well, so the relationship of atypical asymmetry and SLI is complex. Another related finding has been obtained from autopsy studies of individuals with childhood language impairment and dyslexia. It consisted of minor multifocal neural abnormalities, predominantly in the left hemisphere, also suggestive of deranged neural development (see Rapin et al. 1992). Further support for a possible left-hemisphere dysfunction in SLI children has been obtained from a study assessing the metabolic activity of the brain of children with SLI. These children had low activity in the left hemisphere (fronto-temporal) regions, which also are important for language (Lou et al. 1990). The numbers of cases in the autopsy studies and the metabolic studies are, however, too small to be conclusive.

2. Mechanisms Proposed to Underlie SLI

Language involves many separate subprocesses or components. Reception and comprehension of language involves: auditory analysis of the sound composition of speech (phonological decoding); identifying the 'phonological gestalt' or pattern of a string of speech sounds and matching it with the appropriate word in the word store; and processing a sequence of words that are organized and modified according to syntactic and morphological rules. In addition, short-term-memory processes allow keeping the sequence in mind long enough to be processed as a whole. Expression involves a preverbal concept of the message to be communicated, activating the word store in long-term memory and selecting the appropriate words, combining and conjugating the words according to rules of syntax and morphology, programming a complex pattern of articulatory movements, which, in turn, also involves mechanisms of tactile and kinesthetic feedback from oral movements as well as auditory feedback by matching the produced speech with a concept of the target phonemes and auditory gestalts. If any of these components are defective, language breaks down or does not develop appropriately. Not surprisingly, many separate deficits have been proposed as underlying and explaining language disorders.

One proposed mechanism is a deficit in the ability to process rapidly changing input of any kind. The phonological elements of speech (speech sounds) may have a duration of only a few tens of milliseconds, and may be particularly hard to identify and process (Tallal et al. 1996). Examples of sounds that are difficult to clearly perceive are stop consonants in the beginning of words (e.g., 'p' in 'point'), and consonant clusters (e.g., the 's-p-r-' sequence in 'spring'). According to this view, a general rate problem may then disproportionately affect speech, resulting in problems with the auditory phonological decoding and comprehension of speech.

A comparable, yet different, mechanism has been proposed to underlie dyslexia. Since many of the children with SLI also suffer from dyslexia, this hypothesis is relevant also for children with SLI. Many separate research groups (e.g., Bradley and Bryant 1985; Scarborough 1990; Torgesen et al. 1994) have found learning to read and spell to be related to the capacity of children to isolate the phonological elements of speech on nontimed tasks. It is therefore possible that dyslexic children do not have a generalized rate problem, as proposed above, but that they are specifically impaired in the capacity to decode language phonologically. In severe cases this leads to

difficulties in processing, understanding, and expressing language, that is, to SLI.

Gopnik and Crago (1990) closely analyzed a family in which 16 of the 22 studied family members suffered from SLI. They found that the affected members had specific problems with syntax and morphology (the grammatical aspects of language), and with phonology (the production of speech sounds). According to the authors, the root of the SLI in these individuals was an inability to construct general linguistic rules from individual exemplars. Consequently, they were not able to infer and generalize rules for expressing past tense, plurals, etc., and, more speculatively, speech sounds, from one word to another.

Another subprocess of language proposed to be decisive for normal language is verbal short-term or phonological working memory (Gathercole and Baddeley 1990; see also Bishop 1992, for review). Working memory refers to keeping verbal sequences in mind while processing them (as when looking up a phone number and then dialling it from memory). The short-term-memory span, or working-memory capacity, is often below normal in children with SLI. This may affect their ability to process, comprehend, and learn language efficiently. An alternative explanation could, however, be that impaired phonological working memory may follow from impaired phonological decoding and perception, and be a consequence rather than a cause of SLI.

One plausible primary deficit in SLI is a difficulty to organize speech production and articulation. All children with SLI have some speech output difficulty, the most frequent form being one of impaired phonology of speech, evident as poor articulation. The problem is likely to be an inability to transform the intended message into the appropriate, complex phonological motor patterns, rather than a purely motor disability, a condition which would be called dysarthria. In mild or compensated disorders the child may have problems only with articulation, whereas, in severe cases, the motor programming deficit may render the child's speech unintelligible or reduce it to effortful one-word utterances (see Bishop 1992).

Some SLI children also perform poorly on naming tasks. This problem is not simply one of reduced vocabulary. Rather, these children demonstrate a poor ability to retrieve the words that actually are included in their working vocabulary; they may know a word but have difficulties accessing it smoothly. Such word finding difficulties are also called dysnomia or problems of lexical or semantic retrieval. Also learning new words and names may be impaired. The root of the problem may lie in generally slow processing. A general rate problem is thus thought to affect this aspect of language as well (see Wolf 1991). Alternatively, the problem may be a specifically language-related deficit in the ability to search from the word store.

3. Classifications

Children with SLI form a heterogeneous group. Whereas some children are unable to express or comprehend hardly any language, other DLD children may communicate efficiently, evidencing only misarticulations, or problems comprehending more complex verbal instructions or passages. Both the level and the pattern or type of SLI may differ. The different mechanisms proposed above may be related to different types of SLI.

Subtypes of SLI are included in a number of proposed classifications. Some of the classifications are theoretical constructions based on clinical experience (American Psychiatric Association 1994; Rapin and Allen 1988) or linguistic theories (Bishop and Rosenbloom 1987); others are developed by means of statistical subgrouping techniques of patient data (e.g., Aram and Nation 1975), or combinations (Korkman and Häkkinen-Rihu 1994; Wilson and Risucci 1986). Three of these classifications are reviewed in the following paragraphs.

3.1. The DSM-IV Classification

The most widely used classification of SLI is probably that proposed in the *Diagnostic and Statistical Manual of Mental Disorders*, of which the fourth edition is now in use (*DSM-IV*; American Psychiatric Association 1994). This classification is developed by a board of acknowledged experts in the field and is thus based on clinical experience. *DSM-IV* proposes a classification of communication disorders that includes also stuttering. The specifically language-related subtypes are:

(a) *Expressive Language Disorder.* Characteristics of this subtype are limited speech and vocabulary, word-finding errors, shortened and simplified sentences, with better comprehension skills.
(b) *Mixed Receptive-Expressive Language Disorder.* Characteristics of this subtype are the same as above with additional difficulty in understanding words and sentences.
(c) *Phonological Disorder.* Characteristic of this disorder is a failure to produce or sequence speech sounds in a way that is appropriate for the child's age and dialect. The disorder includes both a primarily motor variant, in which the articulation is deficient, and a more perceptual condition, in which the linguistic categorization of speech sounds is deficient.

3.2. Rapin and Allen's Classification

Widely used is also the classification by Rapin and Allen (1988). These authors subdivide language impairments, including acquired impairments, into four main categories, some of which are further divided into subtypes:

(a) *Disorder of phonological decoding.* This category includes only one type of language impairment, that of acquired verbal auditory agnosia, in which a previously speaking child loses the ability to decode and comprehend and, consequently, to produce speech.
(b) *Disorders of phonological encoding (speech sound production).* This category includes two subtypes: verbal dyspraxia, in which the child has a severe oromotor programming deficit and extremely dysfluent speech, and a phonological programming deficit syndrome in which only articulation is severely affected but speech is otherwise adequate and fluent.
(c) *Disorder of morphological and syntactic decoding and encoding.* One subtype is mentioned: the phonological syntactic deficit syndrome, in which speech is dysfluent, poorly articulated, and lacks the function words.
(d) *Disorders of higher-level processing.* Two subtypes are included: a semantic-pragmatic deficit syndrome, in which speech is fluent but its content is not appropriate to the context and often echolalic (the child repeats, echoes, what he/she hears), and a lexical-syntactic deficit syndrome, characterized by word-finding difficulties while speech is otherwise fluent.

3.3. Korkman's Classification

This classification is based on an empirical study of 80 children with SLI. It was first drafted with the aid of a statistical subgrouping technique, then modified to suit clinical classification purposes, and, finally, validated empirically (Korkman and Häkkinen-Rihu 1994). It includes three types of specific disorders, which may overlap:

(a) *The Specific Verbal Dyspraxia Subtype.* Children in this subtype are characterized by a deficit in the capacity to organize the phonological motor patterns involved in speech production (verbal dyspraxia). The children have poor results on tasks requiring repetition of complex words and nonsense words as well as on tasks requiring the production of oromotor sequences (such as 'puh-tuh-kuh puh-tuh-kuh'). If the deficit does not overlap with other types of language impairment, performance on other language tasks is normal.
(b) *The Specific Comprehension Subtype.* This subtype is somewhat heterogeneous, but common characteristics are problems in the domain of comprehension. Tests show that children have difficulties in comprehending verbal instructions and concepts. In addition, they may or may not have difficulties in auditory phonological discrimination and processing (e.g., sound blending and deletion tasks). They may

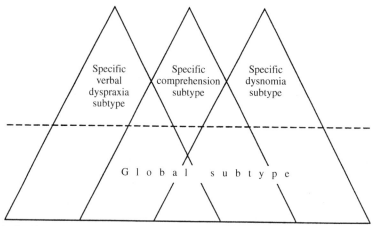

Figure 1. Korkman's classification of specific language impairment in children. The classification includes three subtypes of impairment, those of verbal dyspraxia, comprehension, and dysnomia. The types of impairment may overlap. When all types of impairment are present, the child has a global language impairment. (Source: Korkman, Häkkinen-Rihu 1994. Reproduced with permission.)

be secondarily impaired in naming tasks and in speech production and articulation.

(c) *The Specific Dysnomia Subtype.* This subtype is characterized by dysnomic problems, observed as impaired performance on naming tasks, such as speeded naming and name learning. If specific affected children do not have articulation or comprehension problems. Their SLI may not be detected until the problem is manifested as dyslexia.

(d) *The Global Subtype.* Children in this category are characterized by global and severe language disorders affecting all domains of language: comprehension; naming; expression; and articulation.

Korkman's classification is summarized in Fig. 1 illustrating the dimensions that may be affected in SLI: verbal praxis; receptive functions; and naming. When the separate disorders are severe the risk of overlap of impairments is greater.

4. Neuropsychological Assessment of SLI

4.1. Diagnostic Branching

Cantwell and Baker (1987) proposed a scheme for diagnosing language disorders as a step-by-step process, progressing from general to more precise distinctions. A modified version of their diagnostic scheme is proposed below.

The first diagnostic distinction is to ascertain that the SLI is not caused by a hearing impairment. Even a moderate hearing impairment, causing no obvious difficulties in hearing environmental sounds may, if uncorrected, significantly delay language devel-

opment. It is therefore imperative that all children with language impairment undergo an audiological examination.

The second distinction is whether the child suffers from a more generalized communication disorder in the autistic spectrum. Children with Autistic Disorders are characterized by abnormal development in social interaction and communication, affecting also language, as well as markedly restricted interests and stereotyped activities (see American Psychiatric Association 1994). In contrast, children with SLI do not differ from the normal variation with respect to interest in social contact and interaction.

The next diagnostic question is whether the child suffers from mental retardation. When the child's verbal and nonverbal capacities, as measured by a standardized test of intelligence or development, are below the normal range, he/she may be diagnosed as retarded.

When assessing children with language impairment it is important to take into account the possibility that they may suffer from an acquired language impairment, even when no trauma, acute infection, or brain injury has been stated. Such cases are rare but may occur in epileptic disorders, specifically in the Landau-Kleffner syndrome and a related condition connected with a characteristic finding on the EEG (continuous spikes and waves during slow sleep). In these disorders varying and often selective patterns of deterioration of language or other skills may occur (see Beaumanoir et al. 1995).

When a child does not receive any of the above diagnoses, but demonstrates clear evidence of delay in language development and impaired results on language tests, SLI may be diagnosed. However, a primary diagnosis of retardation, hearing loss, communication disorder, or epilepsy does not exclude the possibility of language problems which require assessment and intervention. The mechanisms of the language disorder in these children may differ from those characteristic of SLI.

When a diagnosis of SLI has been established, the subsequent question is what type of SLI the child suffers from. The clinician may apply one of the classifications proposed above or elsewhere, and select the category that makes the most appropriate fit to the child's signs and findings. If none of the categories of the selected classification applies, the results may be expressed descriptively, by specifying the strengths and weaknesses in the child's linguistic ability profile.

One final step in the diagnostic process is to specify the mechanisms underlying the child's SLI. The mechanisms and classifications presented above may provide sources for such interpretations. For example, the Specific Verbal Dyspraxia subtype in Korkman's classification is thought to be related to impaired phonological-motor programming (verbal praxis). Other types of theory-based inferences may be derived from other theories postulating mechanisms of SLI (see above). The inferences drawn from clinical data concerning the primary deficits underlying a child's SLI may vary considerably between clinicians, depending on which theoretical frame of reference the clinician adopts. A consensus is yet to be achieved.

4.2. Assessment

In clinical practice, assessment of children with SLI is performed by collecting many types of data concerning the child. The data is often gathered by a multidisciplinary team. Prenatal, birth and developmental history, and family history may be compiled by a physician, who also sends the child to audiological examinations when needed. A neuropediatric status examination and EEG recording are indicated especially in severe cases and if the course of the disorder is atypical (e.g., when there are signs of deterioration of skills). Psychological assessments are called for to evaluate the child's general cognitive capacity

and social skills. More precise linguistic assessments are performed by the speech pathologist. Special education teachers, occupational therapists, physiotherapists, and social workers may also be involved in the assessments and treatment. In addition, a neuropsychological assessment is recommended to assess the child's neurocognitive functions comprehensively. This is called for since many SLI children have problems affecting other domains of development, such as attention, motor functions, or visuo-spatial perception. In addition, a neuropsychological in-depth analysis of language functions may contribute to specifying the mechanisms underlying the child's SLI.

A neuropsychological assessment that may be administered to children with SLI is proposed in the Table. The assessment consists of subtests from the NEPSY (acronym formed from NE in neuro- and PSY in psychological; Korkman et al. 1998). The NEPSY is available in many countries and languages. Tests with corresponding content may be derived also from other sources. The NEPSY conforms to Korkman's classification of SLI—the characteristic test findings of the subtypes may be identified using the NEPSY language subtests. Brief assessments are proposed for other domains of development. The selection of subtests for children younger than 5 years is slightly different.

5. Intervention

The most important treatment of SLI is speech and language therapy. As soon as suspicions of delayed language development are raised, the need for therapy should be evaluated by a speech and language therapist or pathologist. Speech and language therapy should be based on assessments and follow-up, guiding its timing, content, and complementary intervention.

Cognitive and neuropsychological research has also provided intervention methods that may be applied in addition to speech therapy. One such method was developed by Tallal and her collaborators (e.g., Tallal

Table 1. NEPSY subtests proposed for neuropsychological assessment of children with SLI.

In-depth assessment of language	Brief assessment of other domains
Phonological processing	Tower (a test involving planning)
Speeded naming	Auditory attention
Comprehension of instructions	Visual attention
Repetition of nonsense words	Fingertip tapping (a motor subtest)
Verbal fluency	Imitating hand positions
Oromotor sequences	Visuomotor precision
Memory for names	Design copying
Narrative memory (for story)	Memory for faces
Sentence repetition (memory span)	

et al. 1996). This method is based on the assumption, described above, that SLI children suffer from a primary deficit in perceiving the most rapid phonological segments of speech. SLI children were trained with modified audiotaped speech and computer programs, in which phonological segments were prolonged and presented in a higher volume. Based on individual performance on tasks of discrimination, the rate of presentation of the auditory stimuli was successively increased. The children who underwent this training caught up with normal children on tests of language perception and comprehension after a training period of only 4 weeks.

Another approach is the training of phonological awareness in young children. This training is based on the solid evidence of the importance of phonological analysis as a prerequisite for acquiring reading and spelling (see above). Training of phonological awareness through sound categorization games, such as detecting rhymes and alliterations, has been found to enhance reading and spelling acquisitions in normal preschool children with poor performance on tests of phonological awareness. Most effective was training that also included teaching sound-letter associations by using plastic letters (Bradley and Bryant 1985).

This type of training should, logically, also apply to children with SLI. A 1-year training program for preschool children with SLI was, indeed, shown to be helpful in reducing the risk of dyslexia (Korkman and Peltomaa 1993). Children with SLI were divided into an experimental group and a control group that were similar with respect to results on test of intelligence, language, attention, and other neuropsychological performance. The experimental group participated in a training program the year before they started school for a 1 hour session each week. The program included listening exercises consisting of rhyming, alliteration, sound blending, and word segmentation games, and teaching preliminary sound-letter combinations by using block letters corresponding to the letters of the children's own names. The control group received alternative, traditional intervention, including placement and treatment in special kindergarten groups for language disordered children. The children were then followed up and tests of reading and spelling were administered at the end of the first school year. The results on these tests were significantly better in the experimental group than in the control group.

Bibliography

American Psychiatric Association 1994 *Diagnostic and Statistical Manual of Mental Disorders*, 4th edn. Washington, DC

Aram D N, Nation J E 1975 Patterns of language behavior in children with developmental language disorders. *Journal of Speech and Hearing Research* **18**: 229–41

Beaumanoir A, Bureau M, Deonna T, Mira L, Tassinari C A (eds.) 1995 *Continuous Spikes and Waves During Slow Sleep.* John Libbey

Bishop D V M 1992 The underlying nature of specific language impairment. *Journal of Child Psychology and Psychiatry* **33**: 3–66

Bishop D V M, Rosenbloom L 1987 Classification of childhood language disorders. *Clinics in Developmental Medicine* **101–2**: 16–41

Bradley L, Bryant P E 1985 Rhyme and reason in reading and spelling. *International Academy for Research in Learning Disabilities Series.* University of Michigan Press, Ann Arbor, MI

Cantwell D P, Baker L 1987 *Developmental Speech and Language Disorders.* Guilford Press, New York

Gathercole S E, Baddeley A D 1990 Phonological memory deficits in language disordered children: Is there a causal connection? *Journal of Memory and Language* **29**: 336–60

Gopnik M, Crago M B 1991 Familial aggregation of a developmental language disorder. *Cognition* **39**: 1–50

Korkman M, Häkkinen-Rihu P 1994 A new classification of developmental language disorders (DLD). *Brain and Language* **47**: 96–116

Korkman M, Kirk U, Kemp S L 1998 *NEPSY—A Developmental Neuropsychological Assessment.* The Psychological Corporation, San Antonio, TX

Korkman M, Peltomaa K A 1993 Preventive treatment of dyslexia by a preschool training program for children with language impairments. *Journal of Clinical Child Psychology* **22**: 277–87

Lou H C, Henriksen L, Bruhn P 1990 Focal cerebral dysfunction in developmental learning disabilities. *The Lancet* **Jan. 6**: 8–11

Palmour R M 1997 Genetic studies of specific language impairment. *Journal of Neurolinguistics* **10**: 215–30

Plante E, Swisher L, Vance R 1991 MRI findings in boys with specific language impairment. *Brain and Language* **41**: 52–66

Rapin I, Allen D A 1988 Syndromes in developmental dysphasia and adult aphasia. In: Plum F (ed.) *Research publications: Association for research in nervous and mental disease: Vol. 66. Language, communication, and the brain.* Raven Press, New York 57–75

Rapin I, Allen D A, Dunn M A 1992 Developmental language disorders. In: Segalowitz S J, Rapin I (vol. eds.), Boller F, Grafman J (series eds.) *Handbook of Neuropsychology* Vol. 7. Elsevier, Amsterdam, 111–37

Scarborough H S 1990 Very early language deficits in dyslexic children. *Child Development* **61**: 1728–43

Tallal P, Miller S L, Bedi G, Byrna G, Wang X, Nagarajan S S, Schreiner C, Jenkins W M, Merzenich M M 1996 Language comprehension in language-learning impaired children improved with acoustically modified speech. *Science* **271**: 81–84

Torgensen J K, Wagner R K, Rashotte C A 1994 Longitudinal studies of phonological processing and reading. *Journal of Learning Disabilities* **27**: 276–86

Wilson B C, Risucci D A 1986 A model for clinical-quantitative classification. Generation 1: Application to language-disordered preschool children. *Brain and Language* **27**: 281–309

Wolf M 1991 Naming speed and reading: The contribution of the cognitive neurosciences. *Reading Research Quarterly* **26**: 123–40

Developmental Disorders of Language: Evaluation of the Effectiveness of Intervention

G. C. Bedi and E. Dorsett

The term developmental language impairment refers to children who have at least average intelligence but do not acquire communication skills with the same facility as other children of the same age. Their communication deficit(s) can be specific or global, ranging from a primary deficit in expressive functions to a combination of deficits in both receptive and expressive functions. Affected functions can include understanding and/or production of sounds (phonology), words and/or sentences (syntax). Developmental language impairment is distinguished from acquired language impairment in that these difficulties cannot be attributed to neurological disorder or injury, hearing impairment, nor can they be attributed to behavioral or emotional disorders. The prevalence of language impairment in children is 7% (Leonard 1996).

The efficacy of speech and language therapy or its role in promoting improvement in language functioning has often been debated. Results of a meta-analysis of 43 treatment studies indicated that children with language impairment who received speech and language therapy performed significantly better than the majority of children with language impairment who did not receive therapy (Nye et al. 1987). In contrast, following a scholarly rather than a statistical review of speech and language treatment studies, Leonard (1981) suggested that the possibility that improvement in language skills was the result of maturation rather than direct therapy should be considered.

There are several ways in which efficacy of treatment can be assessed. First, and most predominantly employed, are pre- and post-test studies in which improvement is measured by comparing abilities prior to training to abilities immediately following a therapeutic course. Less frequently, follow-up studies are used to determine if the effects of treatment are maintained after that treatment has been concluded for some period of time. Finally, efficacy can be measured as generalization or the child's ability to use what was mastered in therapy in other environments or as his/her ability to produce new language structures that were not specifically trained.

As can be gleaned from the above discussion, changes that occur during the course of the child's development can complicate the interpretation of results from studies that examine response to intervention. Specifically, if the effect of general development is not controlled, researchers have no way of knowing whether the intervention promoted the change or if the child would have achieved the same gains simply as a result of maturation. This experimental control can be accomplished by designing studies to include one or more of the following techniques:

(a) use of a comparison group that receives similar but different therapy;
(b) delay training for a portion of the subjects so that their pre-test performance can be compared to the post-test performance of the trained group;
(c) train one language structure while leaving another form untrained;
(d) train pseudo-language forms for which improvement in understanding or in producing could only be the result of the treatment;
(e) employ statistical analyses that control extraneous variables.

1. Efficacy of Training Aimed at Improving Receptive Functions

Few studies have examined the efficacy of therapy aimed at improving perception of sounds, understanding of words, or understanding of sentences (Leonard 1981:96). Dollaghan and Kaston (1986) reported four case studies in which receptive functions were improved following a training program in which children were trained to detect and request clarification of commands that they did not understand. Improvement in receptive language, measured as the child's increased ability to ask for clarification, was noted. Three of these children retained this skill when reassessed 3–6 weeks following the conclusion of the training.

The ability to perceive and process speech sounds has been more extensively studied than receptive language (Brady et al. 1994; Korkman and Peltomaa 1993; Lundberg et al. 1988; Warrick et al. 1993). However, recognizing that a significant proportion of children with language impairment have difficulty acquiring reading skills (Catts 1993), most of these studies have been designed to assess the efficacy of training phonological awareness or, the ability to perceive and manipulate sounds in words, in preventing or mitigating later difficulty acquiring reading rather than assessing the effect of treatment upon oral language. One study that did examine the effect of phonological training upon receptive language found no significant improvement following training (Lundberg et al. 1988).

2. Auditory Rate Processing Deficit Affects Receptive Language

A considerable body of research has shown that children with language impairment have difficulty perceiving speech sounds that incorporate very rapidly changing or rapidly sequenced acoustic cues. This finding was determined using the following operant task. Children were first trained to press a particular panel after hearing a particular tone (Press panel 1 after hearing tone 1 and panel 2 after tone 2). Then the tones were presented in various sequences (1-1, 2-1, 1-2, 2-2). A discrimination task required the children to make same/different judgements about pairs of tones. A sequencing task required the children to reproduce the sequence by pressing the correct panels, in the correct order. For example, if the child heard tone 1–tone 1 he/she would press panel 1 twice. If the child heard tone 2–tone 1 he/she would press panel 2 and then panel 1. On both the auditory discrimination test and the sequencing task, the duration of time between the two tones systematically varied from 4062 msec to 8 msec. The children with language impairment were impaired on both tasks, relative to unimpaired children, but only when the duration between the two tones was brief (Tallal and Piercy 1973:74).

There are sounds in English that incorporate rapidly changing acoustic cues. For example, during the production of stop consonants (b, d, g, p, t, k) a rapid rise and/or fall in frequency occurs in approximately 40 msec. When stop consonant-vowel syllables were used in the discrimination and sequencing tasks (ba-ba, da-da, ba-da, da-ba), children with language impairment were unable to discriminate or sequence stop consonant-vowel syllables while unimpaired children could perform this task successfully (Tallal and Piercy, 1974). However, if the duration of the frequency shift during the stop consonant was synthetically extended to twice the duration during which it naturally would occur (80 msec), children with language impairment were just as accurate as unimpaired children in discriminating stop consonant-vowel syllables (Tallal and Piercy, 1975).

In summary, children with language impairment had difficulty perceiving very rapidly sequenced sounds and speech sounds that had rapidly changing acoustic components. However, they showed accurate perception if the duration of the rapidly changing acoustic components of speech was extended. Based on these research findings, some training programs have focused upon improving receptive language functions by improving auditory rate processing.

3. Training Receptive Functions by Improving Auditory Rate Processing

Tallal et al. (1996) and Merzenich et al. (1996) developed and implemented a receptive language and speech discrimination training program that was based upon remediation of auditory rate processing deficits. This intensive and structured training involved two simultaneously occurring components:

(a) language and phonology training using ongoing, natural speech that was acoustically modified, via a computer algorithm, to extend in duration and increase in amplitude (20 dB) the rapidly changing acoustic components of speech;

(b) individually adaptive, computer-based training aimed at improving the children's auditory rate processing (Tallal et al. 1996; Merzenich et al. 1996).

Thus, children received language and phonology training using acoustically modified speech, which they could more accurately perceive, simultaneously with training aimed at improving their auditory rate processing. Training was conducted 3 hours per day, 5 days a week for 4 consecutive weeks.

Results of two independent training studies of school-aged children with language impairment that employed this training indicated that auditory rate processing, speech discrimination, and receptive language were significantly improved. In the second of these studies, it was demonstrated that this specialized treatment was significantly more effective than language and phonology training that was conducted in natural speech and was paired with computer training which was not aimed at improving auditory rate processing. Children who received this specialized training made significantly more growth in their receptive language and auditory processing skills than did children who received similar training presented in natural speech paired with computer games which were not aimed at improving auditory processing rate. Results of a follow-up study indicated that at both 6 weeks and 6 months after training the children who received the specialized training continued to perform significantly better than the children who did not receive the specialized training (Bedi et al. submitted).

Alexander and Frost (1982) assessed the efficacy of auditory rate processing training in improving the speech perception of children with language impairment. The results of their study indicated that while auditory rate processing improved, the training did not have a significant effect upon speech discrimination. The actual training program was not precisely described; however, it was clear that the course of training was very brief. Children received a total of three, hour-long training sessions, once a week, on alternate weeks. Thus, failure to find an effect of the auditory rate processing training upon speech discrimination could have been the result of a lack of intensity in the training program rather than a failure of the method itself.

Another study, while not directly training auditory rate processing, implemented a training program that took into consideration the slow auditory processing rate of children with language impairment. Acquisition of receptive and expressive vocabulary was examined when new words were trained under slow, normal, or fast rate of speech (Ellis Weismer and Hesketh 1993). Results of this well-controlled study demonstrated that acquisition of vocabulary was facilitated by the presentation of unknown words at a speech rate that was slower than normal. Children with language impairment and unimpaired children did not significantly differ in their ability to benefit from slower speech rates. However, a trend was noted which suggested that the performance of children with language impairment was more strongly facilitated by slow speech rate.

While the body of research examining training of receptive functions in children with language impairment is small, the majority of that research has focused upon improving receptive functions by remediating perceptual deficits theorized to underlie the disorder. Some researchers believe the core perceptual impairment is in phonological awareness while others believe that the core deficit is impaired auditory rate processing. Training aimed at improving receptive language by improving phonological awareness skills has not been shown to be effective. However, other studies have demonstrated that auditory rate processing training results in improved receptive vocabulary, receptive language, and speech discrimination.

4. Efficacy of Training Aimed at Improving Expressive Functions

Most treatment studies for the development of expressive functions have examined imitation-based and modeling-based training. A newer approach, conversational recasting, has also been studied. These interventions predominantly vary in terms of how new language forms are taught. The difference between imitation-based training and modeling-based training primarily relates to the amount of structure in the instructional sequence and the degree to which the therapist employs operant training techniques. Conversational recasting attempts to create a more natural language-learning environment.

4.1 Imitation

Therapists using imitation-based training produce an example of a language form and then prompt the child to repeat the example. Correct reproductions are reinforced and reinforcement is faded as the child becomes more proficient. A hallmark of this approach is that a high number of responses are obtained from the child. Instructional objectives proceed systematically from easy to difficult. Pictures or role playing with toys may be presented along with the structures to be imitated.

Hegde (1980) used imitation to train production of auxiliary 'is' in the form of noun + is + verb-ing (i.e., 'The boy is dancing') or the copula "is" in the form of noun + is + adjective (i.e., 'The girl is happy'). Two language-impaired boys participated in the study. To determine if training one form would generalize to production of the other form, each boy was trained to produce only one of these constructions. After each training session, production of novel sentences of the same form as had been specifically trained and production of the untrained construction were assessed. The percentage of correct responses of the trained form increased as training progressed. More importantly, this pattern also applied to the untrained forms. Further, assessment of conversation across settings and people showed an increase in use of both trained and untrained forms. These combined results indicate that imitation-based training was effective and that it generalized to untrained forms as well as settings other than the therapy room.

Generalization of training to other settings was also studied by Mulac and Tomilson (1977). Two groups of three children with language impairment were trained to produce 'is' questions (i.e., 'Is it a dog?'). Upon completion of the language training program, both groups participated in an investigator-designed but parent-implemented, carry-over program for 2 weeks. At this stage of the training both groups showed consistent production of the target. The two groups were then differentiated from each other. One of the groups received an additional 2 weeks of training from instructors in settings other than the therapy room while the other group did not receive any additional training. To assess generalization, target production was measured during six different language tasks that ranged from direct imitation to spontaneous conversation. These language tasks were presented in both the home and in settings other than the therapy room. The group that received additional training demonstrated a higher frequency of target production across all six tasks, indicating that target production and generalization across settings was promoted by extended training.

Efficacy of imitation in promoting generalization to untrained structures has been further studied (Connell 1986). Four children received imitation-based training of nominative case (i.e., *Him*, he is walking) and auxiliary 'be' (i.e., He *is* walking). After each training session, ability to produce these same structures in response to novel pictures was assessed. In addition, use of the trained forms (auxiliary 'be' and nominative case) as well as of untrained forms (copula, third person and question inversion) in conversation was measured. Each child showed increased production of the targets that was coincident with the onset of training, providing evidence that the training was effective. Further, all children showed mastery of two of the three untrained forms, providing evidence of limited generalization of imitation-based training to untrained forms.

These studies suggest that imitation-based training is effective for training production of specific targets within the therapy session. Further, the efficacy of imitation-based training with regard to generalization to other language environments as well as to untrained forms has been demonstrated. Generalization to new settings appears to be facilitated by providing thera-

233

pist-directed instruction in extra-clinical settings. Further, generalization to untrained forms appears limited to structures of similar communicative function.

4.2 Modeling

Modeling is similar to imitation in that the child is presented with examples of the target structure. However, he/she is not expected to immediately produce the target response following the presentation of the models (Courtright and Courtright 1979). In another form of modeling the child is presented with several examples of the target structure and then intermittent opportunities for production are provided (Ellis Wiesmer and Murray-Branch 1989). As with imitation-based training, pictures or role playing with toys may accompany the models. In all versions of modeling instructional objectives are individually selected for each child and reinforcement is not heavily used to elicit, increase, or shape a child's verbalizations.

Leonard (1975) conducted a carefully controlled study to investigate modeling-based training of auxiliary 'is' and the negative modal 'don't.' Children with language impairment were trained to produce successive approximations of the target forms. These successive approximations were based upon a developmental sequence ('Daddy sleep' then 'Daddy sleeping' and finally, 'Daddy is sleeping') or upon an additive sequence of increasing length ('is' then 'is sleeping' and finally, 'Daddy is sleeping'). Children who received the training produced the target structures significantly more frequently than did children for whom training was delayed. Further, production of targets was attained significantly faster when a developmental rather than an additive sequence was employed.

Generalization of modeling-based training to untrained forms has been assessed (Leonard 1974). Children with language impairment were trained to produce sentences that contained the auxiliary 'is' and the negative modal 'don't.' Production of these targets was assessed immediately after training. Also, the following untrained forms were assessed: auxiliary 'is' question inversion ('Is the girl smiling?'), the copula 'is' ('The cat is white'), the copula 'is' question inversion ('Is Daddy old?'), the auxiliary 'are' ('The kids are running') and the negative modal 'can't' ('They can't see'). To control for changes related to maturation the performance of children who were immediately trained was compared to that of children for whom training had been delayed. Children who received training used the trained structures significantly more often than did children who did not receive training. Further, training of auxiliary 'is' resulted in a significant increase in the use of auxiliary 'is' question inversions, copula 'is' and copula 'is' question inversions. However, there was no significant increase in the use of the auxiliary 'are' and training

of the negative modal 'don't' did not lead to an increase in the use of the negative modal 'can't.' These results suggested that generalization was limited to language forms that had similar communicative function.

Wilcox and Leonard (1978) also demonstrated that generalization following modeling-based training was limited to structures that were similar in communicative function to the target structures. Children with language impairment were trained to produce questions in the form of wh word (who, what, or where) + auxiliary (is or does) + noun + verb. Six groups of four children received training for only one of these structures. At the conclusion of training the childrens' ability to produce their particular target question in response to novel picture cues was assessed. In addition, their ability to produce untrained wh questions was assessed. Once again, results indicated that trained children produced significantly more target questions than did untrained children. In addition, the trained children produced more questions that employed untrained wh words with the trained auxiliary than they did untrained wh words with the untrained auxiliary. Specifically, if the child was trained to produce 'who is' questions, he/she produced more when or where + is questions than he/she produced when or where + does questions. These results replicated the findings of Leonard (1974).

In another version of modeling, sometimes referred to as focused stimulation, models of the form the child needs to acquire are extensively incorporated into a story that is read to the child, role playing or other activities. The therapist then attempts to get the child to produce the targets in response to specific questions (Friedman and Friedman 1980).

Culatta and Horn (1982) assessed the efficacy of focused stimulation in training four children with language impairment to produce targets selected according to each child's language abilities. The percentage of correct productions of targets during unstructured conversations was assessed. Immediately after training, production of the target increased to 90–100% accuracy for all the children. Follow-up data collected during at least seven sessions following conclusion of the training showed that production of the target was maintained at approximately 90% accuracy. These results suggest that this variation of modeling-based therapy was effective.

In summary, results obtained from efficacy studies of modeling-based training are similar to those obtained from efficacy studies of imitation-based training. Specifically, modeling-based training has also been demonstrated to be effective for training production of specific targets within the therapy session. Further, this training generalizes to other language environments. Again, generalization to untrained forms appeared to be limited to those forms that are of similar communicative function as the target form.

4.3 Conversational Recasting

Conversational recasting-based therapy is modeled upon mother-child interactions in which the mother immediately rephrases the child's utterances into a more grammatically correct form. Specifically, recasting is defined as the following of a child's utterances with a reply that retains the child's basic meaning, but incorporates predetermined linguistic targets (Nelson et al. 1996).

The efficacy of conversational recasting in improving expressive functions was assessed for eight children who were primarily producing single word utterances (Schwartz et al. 1985). After training, the child's formations during spontaneous conversation with his/her mother as well as in response to novel picture cues was assessed. Children who received the training showed significantly more multiword productions than did children who did not receive training. These results suggest that conversational recasting-based therapy is also an effective method for improving expressive functions.

4.4 Comparing Techniques for Improving Expressive Functions

Results of studies that attempted to determine whether imitation-based training or modeling-based training was more effective are equivocal. Two studies by Courtright and Courtright (1976:79) provide evidence for the superiority of modeling-based training. Children with language impairment were trained to use 'they' or to produce a novel language form, 'boy means to running' using modeling- or imitation-based training. One week after training had concluded production of the target structure in response to novel pictures was assessed. Children trained using modeling-based training produced significantly more target structures than did children trained using imitation. In contrast, when imitation was compared to modeling for efficacy in training the use of an invented morpheme, imitation was found to be more effective than modeling for children with language impairment. However, modeling was more effective than imitation for unimpaired children (Connell 1987). These findings were replicated (Connell and Stone 1992).

As noted above, a key feature that distinguishes imitation from modeling is that during imitation-based training a high number of responses are obtained from the child. Leonard (1996) has postulated that the differing results of Courtright and Courtright (1976:79) and Connell (1987) and Connell and Stone (1992) may be related to differences in experimental design. Specifically, that the two studies by Connell did not include opportunities for production during the modeling-based therapy while such

opportunities were provided during imitation-based training. However, the findings of Ellis Weismer and Murray-Branch (1989) that simply obtaining elicited productions does not enhance the efficacy of modeling-based therapy, do not support Leonard's interpretation.

Treatment outcome as a function of varying opportunity for production during training has been further assessed (Friedman and Friedman 1980). Eight structures, such as personal pronouns and conjunctions, were taught using both imitation and focused stimulation. A comparison of the pre- and post-training expressive language showed that both treatments were equally effective. However, those children with more impaired expressive language prior to training appeared to improve the most when given imitation-based training. These results suggest that imitation-based training, which incorporates a high frequency of child productions during therapy, may be more effective for children with more severe language impairment and provide collateral support for the findings of Connell (1987) and Connell and Stone (1992).

Using both imitation-based training and conversational recasting-based training Camarata et al. (1994) taught various structures to children with language impairment. Target structures were individually selected for each child and within each training session the child received both types of training. Elicited and spontaneous productions of the target structures were measured throughout training. Not surprisingly, during imitation-based training children produced more elicited targets and produced elicited targets after fewer sessions than during conversational recasting-based training. However, conversational recasting-based training resulted in more spontaneous production of targets. Further, spontaneous production of targets was obtained after fewer sessions of conversational recasting training than imitation-based training.

These results were replicated in a well-controlled study that compared children with language impairment to that of younger unimpaired children who were matched to the children with language impairment for verbal abilities (Nelson et al. 1996). Each child was trained to produce novel language forms. The novel targets were randomly assigned to a no training condition, an imitation-based training condition or a conversational recast-based training condition. Again, elicited and spontaneous productions of the target structures were measured. Those targets that were trained, regardless of the method employed, were more likely to be spontaneously produced than were untrained targets. For both groups of children conversational recasting-based training resulted in greater production of the target during spontaneous speech. Overall, these results indicated that conversational recasting was more effective than imitation-based treatment. That both groups of children showed greater improvement following conversational recast training, suggests that this treatment may have been more effective because it more closely resembles the natural environment for learning language.

5. Conclusions

Treatment studies for receptive functions are distinguished from treatment studies for expressive functions in that they attempt to remediate deficits in phonological awareness or auditory rate processing that are theorized to preclude the development of receptive skills. In contrast, treatment studies for expressive functions focus upon determining the best method for teaching production. Are structures learned best when they are grouped according to communicative function, when production of the target is elicited from the child, or when the therapy session closely approximates language learning as it occurs for unimpaired children?

Clearly, training aimed at improving receptive or expressive language functions has been successful in teaching children with language impairment to understand or produce targets in the therapeutic setting. However, measuring how well language targets are produced in a clinical setting may not be the most appropriate determination of efficacy. It is vital to ascertain how well training generalizes to untrained language forms and/or to other language environments. Further, it is important to establish that learning is retained after training has been concluded for some period of time. Several studies have documented that training generalizes to untrained forms or to settings other than the therapy room. Significantly fewer have determined that treatment effects are retained after therapy has concluded.

Future treatment studies should attempt to remediate deficits theorized to underlie language impairment and should determine the efficacy of this training as the continued ability to demonstrate new learning after training has been concluded. It is important to note that the majority of studies reviewed in this chapter measured treatment outcome as increased understanding or production of target structures. Considerably fewer studies obtained global measures of language change following training. Therefore, future training studies should document outcome using standardized assessments of language in addition to frequency counts for targeted forms.

Duration of training may be a significant variable affecting treatment outcome. Most studies reviewed in this chapter assessed outcome following a fairly brief course of treatment during which therapy sessions were the same approximate duration and frequency as speech and language therapy when delivered in the community or school. Yet, simply providing additional training without increasing the duration or frequency of sessions can enhance efficacy

of training aimed at improving expressive functions (Mulac and Tomlinson 1977). Further, the dramatic difference in efficacy of training aimed at improving receptive functions as studied by Tallal et al. (1996) and Alexander and Frost (1982) strongly suggests that more intensive training results in stronger treatment effects. Treatment outcome as a function of treatment intensity needs to be more specifically studied especially in consideration of the manner in which most speech and language therapy is currently delivered.

Bibliography

Alexander D W, Frost B P 1982 Decelerated synthesized speech as a means of shaping speed of auditory processing of children with delayed language. *Perceptual and Motor Skills* **55**: 783–92

Bedi G C, Miller S, Byma G, Merzenich M, Jenkins W M, Tallal P (Submitted) Efficacy of neuroscience-based training for receptive language and auditory discrimination deficits in children with language-learning impairment: A follow-up study

Brady S, Fowler A, Stone B, Winbury N 1994 Training phonological awareness: A study with inner-city kindergarten children *Annals of Dyslexia* **44**: 26–59

Camarata S M, Nelson K E, Camarata, M N 1994 Comparison of conversational-recasting and imitative procedures for training grammatical structures in children with specific language impairment. *Journal of Speech and Hearing Research* **37**:1414–23

Catts, H W 1993 The relationship between speech-language impairment and reading disabilities. *Journal of Speech and Hearing Research* **36**: 948–58

Connell P J 1986 Teaching subjecthood to language-disordered children. *Journal of Speech and Hearing Research* **29**: 481–92

Connell P J 1987 An effect of modeling and imitation teaching procedures on children with and without specific learning impairment. *Journal of Speech and Hearing Research* **30**: 105–13

Connell P J, Stone C A 1992 Morpheme learning of children with specific language impairment under controlled instructional conditions. *Journal of Speech and Hearing Research* **35**: 844–52

Courtright J A, Courtright I C 1976 Imitative modeling as a theoretical base for instructing language-disordered children. *Journal of Speech and Hearing Research* **19**: 655–63

Courtright J A, Courtright I C 1979 Imitative modeling as a language intervention strategy: The effects of two mediating variables. *Journal of Speech and Hearing Research* **22**: 389–402

Culatta B, Horn B 1982 A program for achieving generalization of grammatical rules to spontaneous discourse. *Journal of Speech and Hearing Disorders* **47**: 174–80

Dollaghan C, Kaston N 1986 A comprehension monitoring program for language impaired children. *Journal of Speech and Hearing Disorders* **51**: 264–71

Ellis Weismer S, Hesketh L J 1993 The influence of prosodic and gestural cues on novel word acquisition by children with specific language impairment. *Journal of Speech and Hearing Research* **36**: 1013–25

Ellis Weismer S, Murray-Branch J 1989 Modeling versus modeling plus evoked production training: A comparison of two language intervention methods. *Journal of Speech and Hearing Disorders* **54**: 269–81

Friedman P, Friedman K A 1980 Accounting for individual differences when comparing the effectiveness of remedial language teaching methods. *Applied Psycholinguistics* **1**: 151–70

Hegde M N 1980 An experimental-clinical analysis of grammatical and behavioral distinctions between verbal auxiliary and copula. *Journal of Speech and Hearing Research* **23**: 864–77

Korkman M, Peltomaa A K 1993 Preventive treatment of dyslexia by a preschool training program for children with language impairments. *Journal of Clinical Child Psychology* **22(2)**: 277–87

Leonard L B 1974 A preliminary view of generalization in language training. *Journal of Speech and Hearing Research* **39(4)**: 429–36

Leonard L B 1975 Developmental considerations in the management of language disabled children. *Journal of Learning Disabilities* **8(4)**: 232–7

Leonard L B 1981 Facilitating linguistic skills in children with specific language impairment. *Applied Psycholinguistics* **2**: 89–118

Leonard L B 1996 *Children with Specific Language Impairment*. The MIT Press, Cambridge, MA

Lundberg I, Frost J, Petersen O 1988 Effects of an extensive program for stimulating phonological awareness in preschool children. *Reading Research Quarterly* **23(3)**: 263–84

Merzenich M M, Jenkins W M, Johnston P, Schreiner C, Miller S L, Tallal P 1996 Temporal processing deficits of language-learning impaired children ameliorated by training. *Science* **271**: 77–81

Mulac A, Tomlinson C N 1977 Generalization of an operant remediation program for syntax with language delayed children. *Journal of Communications Disorders* **10**: 231–43

Nelson K E, Camarata S M, Welsh J, Butkovsky L, Camarata M 1996 Effects of imitative and conversational recasting treatment on the acquisition of grammar in children with specific language impairment and younger language-normal children. *Journal of Speech and Hearing Research* **39**: 850–9

Nye C, Foster S H, Seaman D 1987 Effectiveness of language intervention with the language/learning disabled. *Journal of Speech and Hearing Disorders* **52**: 348–57

Schwartz R G, Chapman K, Terrell B Y, Prelock P, Rowan L 1985 Facilitating word combination in language-impaired children through discourse structure. *Journal of Speech and Hearing Disorders* **50**: 31–9

Tallal P, Miller S L, Bedi G, Byma G, Wang X, Nagarajan S, Schreiner C, Jenkins W M 1996 Language comprehension in language-learning impaired children improved with acoustically modified speech. *Science* **271**: 81–4

Tallal P, Piercy M 1973 Defects of non-verbal auditory perception in children with developmental aphasia. *Nature* **241**: 468–9

Tallal P, Piercy M 1974 Developmental aphasia: Rate of auditory processing and selective impairment of consonant perception. *Neuropsychologia* **12**: 83–93

Tallal P, Piercy M 1975 Developmental aphasia: The perception of brief vowels and extended stop consonants. *Neuropsychologia* **13**: 69–75

Warrick N, Rubin H, Rowe-Walsh S 1993 Phoneme awareness in language-delayed children: Comparative studies and intervention. *Annals of Dyslexia* **43**: 153–73

Wilcox M J, Leonard L B 1978 Experimental acquisition of wh- questions in language-disordered children. *Journal of Speech and Hearing Research* **21**: 220–39

Reading Difficulties

M. J. Snowling

For most children, learning to read involves the integration of a system for processing written language with one which already exists for processing spoken language. When learning to read in an alphabetic script such as English, the child has to learn that printed words convey meanings, that the printed letters (graphemes) in written words map on to the individual speech segments (phonemes) of spoken words and that there are irregularities in these mappings. In addition, when reading continuous text, the child has to integrate the meanings of words in phrases and sentences, using knowledge of syntax and text integration. The attentional resources which these various processes require are considerable and place limitations on the extent to which the novice can be expected to read well. This is especially true if the child has basic language deficiencies.

Children experience difficulties learning to read for two main reasons. They may be generally slow in all curriculum areas, perhaps because of a global language difficulty. These children are usually described as 'backward' or simply, poor readers. On the other hand, they may have a specific reading difficulty (or 'dyslexia'). Arguably, these children have more specific language problems than generally backward readers (Hulme and Snowling 1988). From a linguistic perspective, they have specific difficulties with one or more of the component subskills which contribute to fluent reading.

1. Phonological Difficulties

It is widely held that phonological awareness is one of the best predictors of reading achievement, even when the substantial effects of IQ are partialled out

(Goswami and Bryant 1990). Moreover, phonological deficits, including difficulties with phoneme segmentation and nonword repetition, are characteristic of dyslexic children, who also have difficulty using phonological short-term memory codes (Olofsson and Strömqvist 1997). It is therefore not surprising that the primary problem which they have with reading is in the use of phonological strategies. This can be seen most directly in their approach to reading nonsense words (words which are new to them). There have been many studies showing that dyslexics have non-word reading deficits which are out of proportion to the problems that they have in reading words. Moreover, case-study evidence concerning such individuals (described as developmental phonological dyslexics) has shown that the striking discrepancy between word and nonword reading skill is not transient; it may persist throughout development, imposing a constraint upon reading unfamiliar materials, such as technical or foreign words.

2. Morphological Problems

The development of alphabetic competence (the appreciation that there are mappings between sounds and letters), must be accompanied by increasing proficiency with orthographic processing (Frith 1985). Words in English orthography vary in the directness of mapping sound on to spelling. Some words (e.g., *cat*) have a simple pattern where each phoneme is represented by a single letter; in other cases more complex (e.g., *head*) or obscure relationships (e.g., *yacht*) exist. Many are nevertheless rule-governed, and dictated by morphological factors (e.g., sign-signature). These 'opaque' orthographic conventions, violating the simple application of letter-sound rules, are gradually learned. However, some dyslexic children are unable to make this advance; their reading remains alphabetic, proceeding on the basis of sound. Thus, they have more difficulty in reading irregular words than regular or nonsense words. These children have been described as developmental surface dyslexics. Their reading development is 'arrested' at a later stage than that of phonological dyslexics (see *Developmental Disorders of Language: Evaluation of the Effectiveness of Intervention*).

3. Syntactic Deficits

A number of studies have suggested that dyslexic readers have difficulties with syntactic processing, for example, problems with judgments of grammatical well-formedness, and a delay in the acquisition of certain syntactic structures (Shankweiler and Crain 1986). A problem with these studies, is that certain syntactic structures—for example, some types of relative clause—may only be encountered with any frequency in written language. It follows that poor

readers will have had less exposure to these than good readers and, hence, will have difficulty in dealing with them. Thus, it remains equivocal whether syntactic processing problems actually affect the *reading* process.

4. Semantic Deficits

The reading difficulties which characterize dyslexic children are specific difficulties with decoding processes. However, there are also children who can decode well but who have comprehension difficulties. Indeed, a syndrome of 'hyperlexia' in which decoding skills are precocious has been posited. These children are proficient in the use of phonics. Detailed examination of their reading comprehension shows that it is generally in line with (poor) vocabulary development. Thus, the existence of 'hyperlexia' indicates that the development of single-word reading skills can advance without the support of comprehension. This pattern of performance can also be observed in children learning to read in a second language.

5. Knowledge of the World

Reading for meaning involves the integration of information gleaned from a text with the reader's existing knowledge of the world. Oakhill and Garnham (1988) review studies showing that young readers and poor comprehenders have difficulties in making inferences from, and integrating the ideas in, texts. It has also been shown that readers of low verbal ability have more difficulty in choosing story-appropriate completions for sentences during reading, regardless of grammatical category, than children of higher verbal ability but similar decoding skill. Moreover, when subsequently asked to answer questions about texts they read, they can answer those requiring memory for facts as well as controls can, but they have difficulty with those on which they have to bring general knowledge of the world to bear.

6. Conclusions

It is clear that there are numerous *specific* difficulties which children can encounter when learning to read. Collectively, these difficulties extend beyond single-word processing and may affect reading comprehension. The capacity of individual children to overcome such difficulties will depend upon the interaction of their cognitive strengths and weaknesses with the teaching they receive (Snowling 1987).

Bibliography

Frith U 1985 Beneath the surface of developmental dyslexia. In: Patterson K E, Marshall J C, Coltheart M (eds.) *Surface Dyslexia*. Routledge and Kegan Paul, London

Goswami U, Bryant P 1990 *Phonological skills and learning to read.* Erlbaum, Hove

Hulme C, Snowling M 1988 The classification of children's reading difficulties. *Developmental Medicine and Child Neurology* **37**: 167–69

Oakhill J, Garnham A 1988 *Becoming a skilled reader.* Blackwell, Oxford

Olofsson Å, Strömqvist S 1997 *Cross-linguistics studies of dyslexia and early language development.* European Communities, Luxembourg

Shankweiler D, Crain S 1986 Language mechanisms and reading disorder: A modular approach. *Cognition* **24**: 139–68

Snowling M 1987 *Dyslexia: A Cognitive Developmental Perspective.* Blackwell, Oxford

Classification of Developmental Dyslexia and Intervention

J. Robertson and D. J. Bakker

1. Introduction

Historically, writing in the field of disturbed reading can be found initially in the work of Kussmaul (1877), who used the term 'alexia' for this disorder. The studies of Dejerine (1871) revealed specific lesions in the posterior temporal region, thus demonstrating its neurological basis. Alexia or acquired dyslexia refers to those subjects who had previously obtained literacy in a normal developmental sequence and subsequently lost the ability by brain trauma. These studies provided the basis for the later study of Hinshelwood (1900) who discussed other cases with apparently similar difficulties but who had not experienced brain trauma. Berlin (1887) had already coined the term (developmental) dyslexia for this phenomenon. Though reading and spelling difficulties are central in developmental dyslexia, other difficulties may involve poor short and long term memory, orientation, and in certain subjects problems of time management and general organization. Identification traditionally has been made on the basis of discrepancy between general ability and ability in reading and spelling. The discrepancy definition, though problematic, (Stanovich 1991) is still widely used. It has been demonstrated that a hereditary factor is involved in the development of dyslexia (Pennington 1994, Fisher et al. 1998).

2. The Existence of Sub-types of Dyslexia

A concept central to the study of dyslexia is that of the sub-types. Some experts argue that the differences between dyslexic subjects are quantitative, that the observed differences found in varying degrees between dyslexic pupils are also found between those experiencing more general reading problems. According to them dyslexic pupils do not represent a distinct, qualitatively different group (Bryant and Goswami 1990, Snowling 1995, Stanovich et al. 1997). Others, however, argue that the differences are qualitative and that these qualitative differences can usefully be linked

to differential intervention (Boder 1973, Gjessing and Karlsen 1989, Hooper 1996, Ridder et al. 1997).

Practitioners especially recognize that while individual differences between dyslexic pupils exist, subtype theory can be useful in informing teaching decisions. Within an educational context teachers generally teach through the strongest modality while aiming to strengthen the weaker modality. Decisions may be based on analysis of pupil reading and spelling behavior. This approach was formalized in the work of Boder (1973), which contributed to both theory and practice in the field. Her work emerged as a result of the analysis of both reading and spelling errors of dyslexic subjects and the diagnostic assessment led to theory postulating the existence of three groups, these being Dysphonetic, Dyseidetic, and Alexic. Dysphonetic (the largest group) pupils are found to have a limited sight vocabulary, to read by the direct route (visual analysis directly to meaning without phonemic conversion), and to encounter problems with unknown words. They are unable to blend words or syllables and attempt unknown words by minimal clues, for example, by first and last letter only. When spelling they spell by sight and cannot spell words they cannot read and are incapable of using graphophonic conversion to access unknown words for either reading or spelling. This group experience difficulty in the auditory modality. The Dyseidetic group exhibit poor reading with poor visual memory for words and visual gestalts. Spelling, though poor, is not bizarre and shows evidence of spelling by ear and by attempting unknown words by simplistic graphophonic conversion, such as 'laf' for 'laugh.' The main difficulty lies in the visual modality. The Alexic (and smallest) group comprises complete nonreaders, who show both visual confusion coupled with inability to relate sound to symbol. There is evidence of difficulties in both the visual and auditory modalities. Though the work of Boder was subsequently criticized as being based on too few and carefully selected examples (Thomson 1984) there was an attempt to highlight the observed differences in performance, which can exist between subjects identified under the global term of dyslexia. It was thought that consideration of these differences could be utilized to provide differential intervention.

Our own work (Bakker 1979, 1990, 1994, 1998, Robertson 1996) derived from a neuropsychological framework, which also devised differentiated intervention based on differences in reading behavior. A central concept here is the Balance Model of Reading and Dyslexia.

3. The Balance Model of Reading

Theory here suggests bihemispheric involvement in the reading process. The beginning reader needs to be aware of the unique perceptual features of an alphabetic system, wherein the orientation of the symbols is crucial to accuracy. Certain letters are mirror images of others, for example, b and d, or differ only slightly, such as p and q. Others are inversions of each other, such as n and u or m and w. Moreover, the beginning reader must be aware of the fact that lower cases and capitals represent the same letters and that the meaning of a word largely depends on the left to right arrangement of the letters (e.g., name, mean, mane, amen). These small differences of orientation and other perceptual features are essential in enabling the child to gain accurate grapho-phonic representations for each array of letters and sound values. The right hemisphere is well-suited to this purpose with the emphasis on the perception and direction of visual stimuli. Experimental evidence has shown that the right hemisphere is specialized in extracting relevant visual and directional features from complex visuo-spatial information (Bentin 1981), including text (de Graaff 1995).

In initial reading, the main emphasis is on the pupil acquiring a letter-by-letter and ultimately word-by-word knowledge of the symbols, which comprise the alphabetic system. Reading cannot remain at this micro focus level as ultimately the reader needs to move from the perceptual reading mediated by the right hemisphere to the advanced and fluent reading mediated by the left hemisphere. As the reader increases in skill, attention is no longer focused on the perceptual features of the words but now centers on the linguistic or communicative intent of the writing. The symbols now have less importance than the meaning of the words or the grammar of the structure. The latter processes involve primarily the left hemisphere, which in the majority of right-handed people is specialized for language (Daniele et al. 1994, Paulesu et al. 1996).

In the Balance Model there is a clear need for the involvement of both hemispheres in the reading process. The reading of the novice reader focuses on the perception of letter forms, which are ordered in our culture in a left to right direction. This perceptual load alludes to the right hemisphere and subsequently transfers to the left hemisphere when the symbols have lost their novelty. Theory here would be supported by the Novelty Model of Goldberg and Costa (1981) who presented evidence that novel stimuli are processed by the right hemisphere and familiar information by the left. Experimental evidence on the involvement of both hemispheres in the reading process is well documented in the literature and includes the Positron Emission Tomography (PET) studies (Gross-Glenn et al. (1986) and the study of cerebral blood flow (CBF), (Hynd et al. 1987). Further work by Huettner et al. (1989) suggested that the subcortical structures and right hemisphere are functionally and anatomically linked to the dominant left hemisphere language centre. According to the Balance Model, initial reading involves mainly the right hemisphere and the balance of activity transfers to the left hemisphere as reading skill develops. Experimental ERP studies (event related potentials) have shown that the hemispheric shift in the primary mediation of reading takes place at about 7 or 8 years of age and is a feature of normal reading development (Licht et al. 1988).

4. The Balance Model of Dyslexia

According to the theory of the Balance Model, two sub-types of Dyslexia can result if the pattern of normal development does not take place. The resultant sub-types are the P-type (perceptual) and the L-type (linguistic). The P-type pupil has begun to read using predominantly right hemisphere strategies but has failed to transfer the primary control of reading to the left hemisphere. Reading therefore shows a reliance on the visuo-spatial strategies generated by the right hemisphere and is oversensitive to the perceptual features of the text. Reading behavior is slow with an abundance of 'spelling-like' reading. Text is accessed via the indirect route whereby words are analyzed visually, then decoded according to grapho-phonic features before the meaning is accessed. In contrast, the L-type pupil has neglected the initial primary involvement with the perceptual features of the text and has begun to read inappropriately by using linguistic strategies, generated by the left hemisphere. Reading here is fast, perceptually careless, and reveals many inaccurate responses to text. Text access is by the direct route (visual analysis to meaning) and shows that many surface features are unheeded. The L-type reader may omit letters, words, or even lines of text in an attempt to read globally. Within psycho-neurological approaches one of us (Bakker 1990) has devised both a diagnostic procedure and empirically tested intervention procedures. Sub-type identification is made partly on the basis of observed reading behavior and it is estimated (Bakker 1998) that 60%

of dyslexic subjects can reliably be classified according to this model.

Identification procedures are based on analysis of the pupils' reading style, reading-time, and pattern of errors. Errors are divided into two types: substantive and fragmentation errors. Substantive errors are omission or additions of words or letters, word substitutions or reversals of letters in words or words within a sentence. Fragmentation errors are hesitations, overt grapho-phonic conversion, and repetition of words or sentences. Substantive errors impact on reading accuracy whereas fragmentation errors impact more on speed and fluency of reading. The L-type pupil makes above average number of substantive errors and below average number of fragmentation errors. The P-type pupil shows the reverse profile with analysis revealing below average substantive errors and above average fragmentation (or time-consuming) errors.

It is these differences in approach to text which are the basis of the neuropsychological intervention techniques (Bakker 1990). These rest on the basis that, while neuropsychological stimulation clearly cannot change the macro aspects of the brain, it can change its fine 'tuning' and response to written text. Two intervention techniques were devised, which can both provide differential intervention for the P-type and L-type pupils (Bakker et al. 1990, Bakker et al. 1995, Grace 1990, Kappers 1997, Kappers and Hamburger 1994, Robertson 1996, 1998, Dryer 1997). These are Hemisphere Specific Stimulation (HSS) and Hemisphere Alluding Stimulation (HAS), respectively.

5. Hemisphere Specific Stimulation (HSS)

HSS can be delivered either via the tactile receptors of the hands or by visual perception using a computer. The aim of HSS tactile is to stimulate the contralateral hemisphere by touch and not by sight. To this end a training box was devised and letters and words are presented via the fingers of the left and right hand for L- and P-types, respectively. The aim for the L-type is to stimulate the under-used right hemisphere by presenting text to the left hand and by emphasizing the perceptual aspects of that reading material, in addition to using as far as possible concrete and imageable words. Conversely the P-type pupils are provided with textual material, presented to the right hand, in order to stimulate the underused left hemisphere and to encourage involvement with the semantic and linguistic features of the text. In the case of nonreaders a developmental sequence is proposed whereby the pupil receives initial stimulation of the right hemisphere with subsequent stimulation of the left (Kappers 1997). In both cases words and sentences are presented using raised letters, which the pupil feels and subsequently names. The level of reading is obviously tailored to the child's independent reading level and the emphasis of the additional tasks provides for

the differential needs of the L- and the P-types. Thus, the L-type pupil is presented with a variety of additional tasks, which include decisions on whether word pairs are identical as well as picture and word matching. The initial responses of L-type dyslexics demonstrate an immediate differential response to the reading task, which is plainly visible to the teacher. The L-type pupil clearly responds to a limited amount of information, for example, they may feel a downstroke of a letter and name it from one stroke while not considering alternatives, as from one downstroke a letter could be either b, d, h, l, k. The pupil thus makes an inappropriate and hurried response. The additional tasks here are designed to encourage the pupil to investigate all aspects of the letters and words presented, before making decisions as to which letters or words are the correct ones. Guessing is therefore discouraged and the teacher encourages decision-making only after all the perceptual features of the stimuli have been explored. The pupil is instructed explicitly to use this strategy.

In contrast, the P-type, while receiving text in his or her right hand, is encouraged to take risks in making word decisions and to interact with the meaning of the text as opposed to the individual letters within the words. Reading behavior for this sub-type may include feeling the letter continuously before being able to name it. The approach to the task is therefore demonstrably different from that of the L-type pupil. Additional tasks here may include reading words or sentences with letters or words deleted and questioning on the serial position of words within the sentence. Such tasks presumably provoke left-hemisphere activity. Another element of the training is that of rhyming, a phonological skill, which has also been found to have greater involvement with the left hemisphere (Ogden 1996). The aim here is to encourage reading fluency and the pupil may be encouraged to guess in order to decrease the over-reliance on the alphabetic symbols.

HSS visual is delivered via the visual half-fields and involves the use of a fixation point and words flashed in the right or left of the periphery. The fixation point is an important element in ensuring access to the visual half-fields. In HSS visual there is a crossed relationship between field and hemisphere as the words flashed in the right visual field activate the left hemisphere. Intervention can again be provided to provoke greater involvement by either the right or the left hemisphere. In both cases flashing times are less than 300 msec to prevent lateral eye movements during presentation. The HEMSTIM computer program has been devised to deliver HSS training via the visual half-fields (revised version Bakker and Vonk 1998) and allows the duration of the flashed stimulus to become increasingly shorter depending on the performance of the subject. Vocabulary is again tailored to the independent reading level of the pupil and words are flashed in the left visual half-field for the L-types and in the right visual half-field for the P-types, to stimulate the underused hemispheres. Word properties are adjusted differentially, as concrete words are used for the L-types and abstract words for the P-types.

6. Hemisphere Alluding Stimulation (HAS)

During the process of reading, words are projected to both hemispheres but this process can be adapted so that a stronger appeal can be made to one hemisphere over the other. The HAS process adapts the medium of text and effectively alters the reading process so that appeal can be made more to the underused right hemisphere (for L-types) and to the underused left hemisphere (for P-types).

The L-types require stimulation of the right hemisphere, which is specialized for the perception of form and direction and so text is adapted to make it perceptually complex. Relevant illustrations are included and the text may be presented, for example, by material being presented in a mix of fonts and lower and upper case letters. Similar to HSS tactile this procedure has the additional effect of slowing down the reading considerably. Following the reading of adapted text, exercises are given which may include finding lower case and upper case words within one word string, for example, MhOoTuHsEeR. Other tasks include placing a row of geometric shapes in various sizes into size order to reveal a word or matching visually similar shapes (with words written in them being an additional feature). These tasks are all designed to activate the right hemisphere by forcing the pupil to pay attention to the perceptual differences between letters and words; consequently reading speed will slow down. Reading behavior is being deliberately altered so that the recognition of the importance of the perceptual differences between letters and words can be acknowledged.

HAS for the P-type is designed to encourage interaction with the left hemisphere and to stimulate the use of linguistic strategies. Text for this group is presented in a simple font and illustrations are avoided. Text is modified by deleting words within sentences, with the aim of encouraging the pupil to engage in decision-making based on semantics and syntax rather than the micro aspects of the individual letters. In doing so the left hemisphere becomes more involved in the reading process. Exercises for this group include reading sentences where words are in the wrong order or sentences, which contain a superfluous word, which interferes with the meaning of the text.

Both intervention methods involve a designated number of sessions and these vary between studies, in the range of 12 and 24. Bakker (1990) suggested that following 10 sessions there appeared to be a levelling off of improvement and currently within the reading clinics, where the techniques are used, they may incor-

porate two booster sessions after the intervention has ceased.

7. Results of the Intervention

Experimental and clinical studies validate both the classification and the intervention methods. All studies to date showed the benefits of right hemisphere stimulation in L-type dyslexic subjects (Grace 1987, Robertson 1996, Kappers 1997). The current state of the knowledge cannot state with certainty whether treatment via the tactile or the visual half-field (via the HEMSTIM computer program) is most effective. Results between studies vary but a general finding is that stimulation of the right hemisphere in L-types by direct (HSS) stimulation results in a decrease in the number of substantive errors and an increase in the number of fragmentation errors. This could indicate an increased ability to attend to the micro aspects of the alphabetic symbols, in addition to the macro aspects of the text meaning. Other studies show that reading speed has decreased and that pupils ostensibly demonstrate the ability to access the indirect route for reading by the use of explicit grapheme-phoneme conversion when appropriate. It could be hypothesized that the reading process had become more perceptually careful for these subjects. Findings in these studies would be consistent with the Novelty Theory of Goldberg and Costa (1981) stating that the right hemisphere is more effective in processing novel stimuli. It also shows consistency with the theories of hemisphere specific activation and reciprocal balance (Kinsbourne 1989). The right hemisphere is primed by the nature of the tasks, for the processing of text to take place.

In contrast, P-type pupils, given direct stimulation of the left hemisphere, showed a decrease in the number of fragmentation errors and an increase in reading speed and fluency. Research evidence (Bakker et al. 1990) for P-type dyslexic children would suggest benefit from using the tactile receptors of the right hand rather than the right visual half-field.

In certain studies, which have also measured reading comprehension, there have been gains for both groups. This could occur due to a decrease in the substantive errors for the L-types and a decrease in the perceptual attention taken by explicit phoneme–grapheme conversion in the P-types. Both elements would impact overall on the derivation of meaning from the text.

Research evidence supports the use of HSS particularly for the L-type pupils and though speculative, a possible reason for this could relate to ongoing studies into the speed of information processing. HSS tactile slows the reading process by the requirement to palpate the letters while the medium of modified text of HAS also slows down access to text. This reduction of speed necessary for accurate perception of the letters could increase the potential for perceptual attention, which would be desirable for L-type pupils. Current research suggests dyslexic subjects are weak in processing either visual or auditory stimuli rapidly (Rennie 1991, Galaburda and Livingstone 1993, Holmes 1994, Nicholson and Fawcett 1994, Tallal 1997, Stein and Walsh 1997).

Studies using HAS for both the L- and P-type pupils also support the theoretical basis, as again reading accuracy was improved in the L-types and reading fluency in the P-types. An interesting finding of some studies is that the approach, encouraged with the modified materials, transfers to normal text reading and that the pupils themselves are aware of this and may comment on this overt change of reading behavior. Another interesting finding is that there are some factors which Kappers (1997) terms as 'beyond the method,' and an important one is that the reading gains may continue as a significant rate after the direct intervention has ceased. This is encouraging, as both transfer of learning and retention in the long term are central problems within the dyslexia field.

Within the neuropsychological literature the results of studies vary. This has been noted by other workers and Bakker (1994) noted that in addition to differences in sub-type and hemisphere, effects may be investigation-specific, as L-types may benefit in one study and P-types in another. Some experimental results have also been skill-specific, as certain studies have found improved comprehension, which was not found in others. Results within studies also vary as certain pupils show very little gain whereas other students with entrenched reading difficulties may be almost 'cured' by the approach. Work thus far does suggest that there are some merits in pursuing a method of intervention, which can harness observation of reading behavior and link it to differential intervention.

Other workers have used different measures with the same aim; the work in the field of peripheral vision being a pertinent example.

8. Differential Intervention and Peripheral Vision

Other workers, from a different theoretical point of view, have also derived intervention according to theoretical principles of peripheral vision (Geiger and Lettvin 1987, Geiger et al. 1991, Geiger and Lettvin 1998). Their work found that dyslexic subjects and normal readers differ in relation to foveal and peripheral vision. Theory here relates to the Aubert-Foerster Law (1857) and the phenomenon of lateral masking. Their experiments showed that in persons at risk of reading failure, there is an interaction between foveal and peripheral vision that degrades the ability to read in the foveal field. Normal reading seems to involve a learned strategy for suppressing or masking information away from the fovea. The form-resolving field (FRF) of the normal reader is narrow and symmetrical, with the best letter recognition in and around

the center of gaze. Recognition of individual letters degrades as the angular distance from the gaze decreases. In contrast the FRF of dyslexic subjects is wider in the direction of the reading, that is to say, it is wider in the right hemifield for native English speakers and wider in the left hemifield for native Hebrew speakers. Subsequent work (Geiger et al. 1993) showed that the FRF is a good measure of the distribution of lateral masking over the visual field and can effectively provide a discriminate measure between dyslexic and nondyslexic subjects. Subsequently it became apparent that lateral masking is modifiable and that intervention can be provided to alter distribution over the visual field to the more customary pattern. Following intervention, reading skill improved and simultaneously the FRF narrowed to resemble that of a normal reader.

Intervention is provided in two parts. One part involves spending 1 hour a day performing novel, small scale hand-eye coordination activities like painting, drawing, or clay-modeling. This is to encourage the subject to attempt new visual strategies to optimize performance. It is considered important that the tasks are self-selected and are perceived as enjoyable to preserve motivation. Their main purpose however is to narrow the distribution of lateral masking and to form a new operationally defined visual strategy, unlike other methods in the past, which have emphasized motor-skill training only (Frostig and Horn 1964). The second element is to read words in isolation, using a specially designed mask sheet for reading. In experiments with older subjects (Geiger and Lettvin 1987) the mask sheet was blank whereas for children it was made of a colored transparent sheet. The mask provided differential intervention by altering the position of the marked fixation point. If the subject had lateral masking in or near the center (as revealed by their FRFs) a fixation point was marked to the left of the window while other subjects used a centrally located window. The distance of the fixation point was determined individually and was revealed by measuring the FRF for best recognition. The masking was important as it allowed identification of the arrangement of observed letters to be associated with spoken words. The isolation of the words by a window in the sheet reinforced the grapheme-phoneme correspondences within the words. This, in combination with the hand-eye coordination tasks reinforced the knowledge of what to look for with central vision and thus altered the FRF to resemble that of a normal reader. The intervention was found to be successful with children and adults; both improved in reading ability. This outcome was subsequently confirmed by further studies (Fahle and Luberichs 1995). An interesting finding with three of the four adult subjects was the discovery of other changes of a more general nature. In all cases the subjects lost their ability to perceive simultaneous spatial arrangements but enhanced their ability to perceive sequential aspects. All three subjects reported they could no longer attend to simultaneous stimuli and despite improvements in reading, stopped practicing the regime. After a few months, their reading ability, their FRFs, and their ability to perceive complex gestalts had all returned to the pre-intervention state. Again results may demonstrate the impact of slowing down presentation of words and text but results with both children and adults thus far have been promising.

9. Conclusion

Further research is clearly needed so that both methods can benefit from independent validation. In the neuropsychological intervention a central problem is classification as the error analysis is open to subjective interpretation, particularly in regard to the fragmentation errors. This is a crucial starting point to the allocation of subject to sub-type and ultimately to differential intervention. So if consistency is not possible, then the idea of differential intervention would not be possible. Currently it cannot be guaranteed that an L-type in one study would be an L-type in another study. There is therefore a need for some standardization of classification criteria. Some workers also argue for the existence of a mixed sub-type, whose reading shows characteristics of both types and whose reading shows qualitatively different patterns of reading from the other two groups (Masutto et al. 1994, Robertson 1996). The existence of a mixed sub-type grouping would not only increase coverage within the population of dyslexic subjects from the current figure of 60 percent but could also provide a means of refining differential intervention even more. Further study is ongoing on the Geiger and Lettvin intervention.

Yet, despite these considerations, the impact of neuropsychological and peripheral vision interventions within the field of dyslexia make a significant contribution to writing and demonstrate the central importance of intervention research within this area. This may be one way in which dyslexic subjects themselves can benefit from the amount of research currently generated in this field.

Bibliography

Aubert H, Foerster J 1857 Beitraege zur Kenntniss des indirecten Sehens. *Graefes Archiv. Ophthalmol.* 3: 1–47

Bakker D J 1979 Hemisphere differences and reading strategies: two dyslexias? *Bulletin of the Orton Society* 29: 84–100

Bakker D J 1990 *Neuropsychological Treatment of Dyslexia.* Oxford University Press, New York

Bakker D J 1994 Dyslexia and the Ecological Brain. *Journal of Clinical and Experimental Psychology* 25: 734–43

Bakker D J 1998 *Iron will be Sharpened by Iron: The Balance Model Explained* Memorial Lecture. Free University of Amsterdam

Bakker D J, Bouma A, Gardien C J 1990 Hemisphere-specific

treatment of dyslexic sub-types: A field experiment. *Journal of Learning Disabilities* 23: 433–38

Bakker D J, Licht R, Kappers E J 1995 Hemispheric stimulation techniques in children with dyslexia. In: Tramontana M G, Hooper S R (eds.) *Advances in Child Neuropsychology (Vol. 3).* Springer Verlag, New York, 144–77

Bakker M G, Vonk M I 1998 *HEMSTIM for windows.* Spin Software B.V., The Hague

Barr W B 1997 Examining the right temporal lobe's role in nonverbal memory. *Brain and Cognition* 35: 26–41

Bentin S 1981 On the representation of a second language in the cerebral hemispheres of right-handed people. *Neuropsychologia* 19: 599–603

Berlin R 1887 *Eine besondere Art der Wordblindheit (Dyslexia).* J F Bergmann, Weisbaden

Boder E 1973 Developmental dyslexia: A diagnostic approach based on three atypical reading patterns. *Developmental Medicine and Child Neurology* 25: 664–87

Bryant P E, Goswami U 1990 Comparisons between backward and normal readers: A risky business. *Journal of the Education Section of the British Psychology Society* 14: 3–28

Daniele A, Giustolisi L, Caterina Silver M, Colosimo C, Gainotti G 1994 Evidence for a possible neuroanatomical basis for lexical processing of nouns and verbs. *Neuropsychologia* 32: 1325–41

De Graaf MB 1995 *Hemispheric Engagement during Letter and Word Identification in Beginning Readers.* Doctoral dissertation, Free University, Amsterdam

Dejerine J 1871 Sur un cas de eccite verbale avec agraphis, suivi d'autopsia. *Mem. Social Biology* 3: 197–201

Dryer R 1997 The balance model of dyslexia and remedial training: an evaluative study. In press to *Journal of Learning Disabilities*

Fahle M, Luberichs J 1995 Extension of a recent therapy for dyslexia. *German Journal of Opthalmologie* 4: 350–54

Fisher S, Marlowe A, Lamb J, Maestrini E, Williams D, Richardson A, Weeks D, Stein J F, Monaco A, 1998 *A genome-wide search strategy for identifying quantitative trait loci involved in reading disability with detailed analysis of chromosome 6p.* Paper presented a the International Conference on Genetics and Reading and Spelling Disability. Marburg

Frostig M, Horne D 1964 *The Frostig Program for the Development of Visual Perception* Follett Publishing, Chicago

Galaburda A M, Livingstone M 1993 Evidence for a magnocellular defect in developmental dyslexia. In: Tallal P, Galaburda A M, Llinas R R, von Euler C (eds.) *Temporal Information Processing in the Nervous System.* The New York Academy of Sciences, New York

Geiger G, Lettvin J Y 1987 Peripheral vision in persons with dyslexia. *New England Journal of Medicine* 316: 1238–43

Geiger G, Lettvin J Y 1998 How dyslexics see and learn to read well: to appear In: Everatt J (ed.) *Vision and Attentional Processes in Reading and Dyslexia.* Routledge, London

Geiger G, Lettvin J Y, Zegarra-Moran O 1992 Task determined strategies of visual process. *Cognitive Brain Research* 1: 39–51

Geiger G, Lettvin J Y Fahle M 1993 Dyslexic children learn a new visual strategy for reading: A controlled experiment *Vision Research* 9: 1223–33

Gjessing H J, Karlsen B 1989 *A Longitudinal Study of Dyslexia.* Springer Verlag, New York

Goldberg E, Costa L D 1981 Hemisphere differences in the acquisition and use of descriptive systems. *Brain and Language* **14**: 144–73

Grace G M 1990 *Effects of Hemisphere-specific Stimulation on Academic Performance and Event-related Potentials in Dyslexic Children* Unpublished doctoral dissertation, Victoria University. Victoria, Canada

Gross-Glenn K, Duari R, Roshii F, Barker W W, Chang J Y, Apicella A, Boothe T, Lubs H A 1986 Pet scan studies during reading in dyslexic and non-dyslexic adults. *Neuroscience Abstracts*

Hinshelwood J 1990 Congenital Word Blindness. *The Lancet* **1**, 1506–08

Holmes B 1994 Fast words speed past dyslexics. *New Scientist* 27 August, 10

Hooper S R 1996 Sub-typing specific reading disabilities: classification approaches, recent advances and current status. *Mental Retardation and Developmental Disabilities Research Reviews* **2**: 14–20

Huettner M, Rosenthal B L, Hynd G W 1989 Regional cerebral blood flow (rCBF) in normal readers: bilateral activation with narrative text. *Archives of Clinical Neurology* **4**: 71–8

Hynd G W, Hynd C R, Sullivan H G, Kingsbury T Jr. 1987 Regional cerebral blood flow (rCBF) in developmental dyslexia: activation during reading in a surface and deep dyslexic. *Journal of Learning Disabilities* **20**: 294–300

Kappers E 1997 Outpatient treatment of dyslexia through stimulation of the cerebral hemispheres. *Journal of Learning Disabilities* **30**: 100–25

Kappers E J, Hamburger H B 1994 Neuropsychological treatment of dyslexia in outpatients. In: Licht R, Spyer G (eds.) *The Balance Model of Dyslexia: Theoretical and Clinical Progress*. Van Gorcum, Assen

Kinsbourne M 1989 Neuroanatomy of Dyslexia. In: Bakker D J, van der Vlugt H (eds.) *Learning Disabilities Vol. 1: Neuropsychological Correlates and Treatment*. Lisse, Swets and Zeitlinger, Amsterdam

Kussmaul A 1877 Disturbances of speech. *Cyclopedia of the Practice of Medicine* **14**: 575–81

Licht R, Bakker D J, Kok A, Bouma A 1988 The development of lateral event-related potentials (ERPs) related to word naming: a four year longitudinal study. *Neuropsychologia* **26**: 327–40

Masutto C, Bravar L, Fabbro F 1994 Neurolingusitic differ-entiation of children with subtypes of dyslexia. *Journal of Learning Disabilities* **27**: 520–26

Milner B, Johnsrude I, Crane J 1997 Right temporal-lobe contribution to object-location memory. *Biological Science* **352**: 1469–74

Nicholson R I, Fawcett A J 1994 Reaction time and dyslexia. *Quarterly Journal of Experimental Psychology* **47A**: 29–48

Ogden J A 1996 Phonological dyslexia and phonological dysgraphia following left and right hemispherectomy. *Neurpsychologia* **34**: 905–18

Paulesu E, Frith U, Snowling M J, Gallagher A, Morton J, Frackoviak R S J, Frith C D, 1996 Is developmental dyslexia a disconnection syndrome? Evidence from PET scanning. *Brain* **119**: 142–57

Pennington B F 1995 Genetics of Learning Disabilities. *Journal of Child Neurology* **10**: 69–77

Rennie J 1991 Dyslexia: A problem of timing. *Scientific American* November, 14

Ridder W H III, Borsting E, Cooper M, McNeel B, Huang E 1997 Not all dyslexics are created equal. *Optometrist vision Science* **74**: 99–104

Robertson J 1996 *Specific Learning Difficulties (for example Dyslexia): Differential diagnosis and intervention*. Doctoral thesis, Victoria University. Manchester, England

Robertson J 1998 Neuropsychological intervention in dyslexia: Two studies on British pupils. In press to *Journal of Learning Disabilities*

Snowling M J 1995 Phonological Processing and Developmental Dyslexia. *Journal of Research in Reading* **18**: 132–38

Stanovich K E 1991 Discrepancy definitions of reading disability: has intelligence led us astray? *Reading Research Quarterly* **26**: 7–29

Stanovich K E, Siegel L S, Gottardo A 1997 Progress in the Search for Dyslexia Sub-types. In: Hulme C, Snowling M J *Dyslexia: Biology, Cognition and Intervention*. Whurr, London

Stein J, Walsh V 1997 To see but not to read; the magnocellular theory of dyslexia. *Trends in Neuroscience* **20**: 147–52

Tallal P 1997 *Language Learning Impairments: Integrating Basic Science, Technology and Remediation*. Keynote lecture at the 25th Anniversary Conference of the British Dyslexia Association. York, England

Thomson M 1984 *Developmental Dyslexia* Whurr, London

SECTION IV
Acquired Speech Pathologies

Disorders of Voice
L. Mathieson

A voice disorder exists when any acoustic aspect of the voice differs from the norm. The broadest interpretation of the term also includes abnormality of sensation associated with voice production. The severity of voice disorder ranges from complete absence of voice (aphonia), through varying degrees of vocal impairment (dysphonia), to intermittent or episodic dysphonia or aphonia interspersed with normal voice. These conditions can be congenital or acquired, organic or nonorganic, and can occur in children and adults of all ages. Everyone has the potential for acquiring a voice disorder, even if it is only the dysphonia associated with the common cold. A voice disorder is a symptom which indicates that there is an underlying organic or behavioral disorder. Not only can the voice abnormality be the first indication of otherwise unrecognized illness, but its resolution depends on the accurate diagnosis and treatment of the underlying factors in conjunction with appropriate symptomatic treatment.

Although severe voice disorders are easily recognized, the borderline between normal and abnormal voice is poorly defined. To the singer, actor, or public speaker, any reduction in vocal efficiency, however slight, will cause justifiable concern. Other speakers might only regard severe dysphonia or aphonia as a problem. The changing nature of the voice also tends to obscure the division between normal and abnormal. As a result of age-related changes in the vocal tract, the mechanisms of phonation are subtly altering throughout the lifespan. The point at which age-related vocal change is regarded as a voice disorder (presbyphonia) will depend on the rate and extent of physiological aging as well as the demands that individuals make on their voices. In females, vocal changes can occur premenstrually, during pregnancy, and following the menopause as the result of hormonal effects on the vocal tract while mood changes are reflected universally in altered vocal quality. The criteria by which a voice is rated as abnormal finally depend on social, cultural, and occupational norms and requirements as well as objective evaluation.

1. The Effect of Voice Disorder on the Individual

All voice disorders reduce the speaker's communicative effectiveness in various ways. Although language and articulation remain intact and potentially intelligible unless there are associated speech problems, impaired phonation affects audibility. The speaker has great difficulty in being heard against background noise socially and in the workplace and as a result either uses greater effort to talk more loudly or withdraws. This aspect of disordered voice frequently creates genuine fatigue, and patients regularly complain that it is too much effort to maintain conversation. The effect of this can be to create further difficulties with family and colleagues. Physical effects include a sore, aching, dry vocal tract that frequently leads some patients to worry that they have cancer even when this possibility has been excluded by thorough examination.

The paralinguistic features of voice are inevitably compromised so that the verbal message does not accurately convey the intention of the speaker. This is particularly distressing when the voice quality arising from the dysphonia leads the listener to make erroneous inferences about the speaker. Similarly, the linguistic contribution of the voice is impaired so that it might not be possible, for example, to raise the intonation at the end of a question or to stress segments satisfactorily.

Voice disorders affect the linguistic message as a whole, and as a result many patients are concerned by the altered way in which they are perceived and treated by others. People speak to them less, and they are talked over or shouted at as if to compensate for the deficit. As the voice is also important as an element of self-image and the way in which individuals present themselves to others, voice disorders frequently affect speakers' confidence and ability to interact in situations which they regard as difficult.

In practical terms, the patient's employment can be at risk, particularly in the case of a professional voice user.

2. Aspects of Disordered Voice

Impairment of any one or all of the vocal parameters gives rise to abnormal voice, and rarely is one affected without other aspects of voice being involved.

2.1 Abnormal Vocal Quality

Abnormality of the fundamental note produced by the vocal folds gives rise to descriptions such as husky, breathy, harsh, and other subjective terms. This terminology is inevitably unsatisfactory; one person's 'breathy' is another's 'husky.' Speech and language pathologists and others have attempted to correlate the perceptual terms used to describe abnormal voice with acoustic characteristics but the problem is far from being resolved. Voice quality is regarded as abnormal if there is a significant noise component of the vocal note, perceived as breathiness or roughness. Aesthetic judgment can also rate certain vocal qualities as abnormal although they would be considered to be within normal limits in another cultural setting. It is diagnostically significant whether the abnormal vocal quality is variable, intermittent, or consistent.

2.2 Pitch Abnormalities

Vocal pitch is disordered if it is too high or too low for the speaker's age or gender and if it has risen or fallen from the individual's usual speaking fundamental frequency. Instability of pitch can be manifested in pitch breaks or in the inability to maintain a note of consistent pitch.

2.3 Abnormal Loudness

In most cases of voice disorder, there is a reduction in vocal intensity eventually as inefficient vocal fold adduction develops. Where excessive loudness has been a cause of the developing problem, the resulting vocal fold damage finally reduces volume. More rarely, excessive loudness is due to underlying neurological or psychological factors. Variability in loudness is also a feature of voice disorders. Loudness deteriorates in one speaker by the end of the day, but in another the voice is much quieter in the morning. Others will have adequate volume as they begin to speak which gradually deteriorates. Some speakers experience loudness decay towards the end of each phrase or sentence while others never have adequate volume.

2.4 Reduced Range and Flexibility

Limited pitch range is a feature of many voice disorders. Not only are the highest and lowest notes unavailable, but flexibility of vocal note pitch change within the remaining range is reduced. Similar problems can occur with vocal loudness where the speaker is unable to control volume. The reduction of pitch and loudness range and flexibility impairs the subtle vocal changes which are essential components of the linguistic and paralinguistic features of voice.

2.5 Disordered Resonance

Excessive and insufficient nasal resonance (hyper- and hyponasality) occurs in certain voice disorders (see Sects. 3.3, 7.1.2, 7.1.3).

3. The Anatomy of Voice Disorder

All disorders of voice are the result of abnormal structure or function of one or more parts of the vocal tract (Fig. 1). In many instances, abnormality in one part results in other abnormalities as the speaker attempts to compensate for the original problem. For the purposes of anatomical classification of voice disorders, the vocal tract can be divided into three sections in relation to the space bounded by the vocal folds known as the glottis: subglottic, glottic, and supraglottic.

3.1 Subglottic Vocal Tract

Abnormalities of the subglottic vocal tract include deficiencies of capacity and control of breathing for speech. This results in the inability to sustain normal phonation for the required length of time, so that in severe cases the speaker might need to inspire for each word.

Alterations in expiratory airflow and muscle tone (tonicity) of the approximated vocal folds, or incoordination of the two systems, gives rise to changes in subglottic air pressure. These changes have an immediate effect on vocal loudness. Reduced subglottic air pressure causes the vocal note to become quieter, and the speaker will be unable to shout or raise the voice. Depending on the severity of the problem, the voice might not be loud enough to be heard against background noise or even in quiet conversation. In

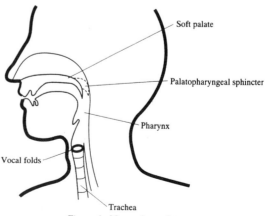

Figure 1. Normal vocal tract.

very severe cases, either the contrastive loudness required for stressed syllables cannot be produced or the voice becomes a whisper. In contrast, when rapid, forceful exhalation cannot be controlled, and particularly when this occurs in conjunction with strong adduction of the vocal folds, phonation will be abnormally loud because of the raised subglottic air pressure.

3.2 The Glottis

The quality of the vocal note is affected adversely by abnormalities of closure of the vocal folds (Fig. 2), which can be hyper- or hypoadducted. Severe hyperadduction gives rise to a strained, strangled quality, as if the speaker is attempting to phonate while lifting a heavy object. Varying degrees of hyperadduction result in the voice being harsh, overloud, and effortful. If this method of phonation is regularly used, producing voice can cause discomfort, and vocal fold damage can occur. Alternatively, hypoadduction of the vocal folds results in a breathy voice with reduced volume. Inadequate approximation occurs when the movements of either one or both vocal folds are weakened or paralyzed. Inappropriate tonicity of the vocal folds will also be reflected in the vocal pitch.

Vocal-fold mucosa abnormalities affect the mass of the vocal fold. Consequently, when vocal-fold mass is increased, the speaker's habitual pitch is lowered because of the reduced frequency of vocal-fold vibration. In addition, vocal-fold mucosa abnormalities affect the vibratory characteristics of the wave of mucosal movement, which plays an important role in normal phonation. Inhibition of the amplitude and pattern of this wave adversely affects vocal quality.

In some conditions, a double note is produced by the larynx (diplophonia) because there are two vibrating sources. This can arise from the vocal folds themselves if they are asymmetrical in tone or mass, or as a result of vigorous ventricular band movement occurring simultaneously with vocal-fold vibration.

3.3 The Supraglottic Tract

Abnormalities of the supraglottic tract also affect the quality of the voice, not at its point of generation but in the resonance of the fundamental laryngeal note. For example, if the nasal airway is blocked, an imbalance of resonance occurs which results in a 'cold-in-the-nose' quality known as hyponasality. In contrast, if the soft palate, or velum, does not close off the nasal airway competently, the resulting resonance is hypernasal as in cases of cleft palate. Vocal resonance is also affected more subtly by variations in tension of the muscles of the pharynx and the oral cavity. Tension in these structures tends to reduce their dimensions and increase the rigidity of their walls. As a result, a degree of hypernasality is perceived by the listener although there is a competent palato-pharyngeal sphincter.

4. The Diagnosis of Voice Disorders

Examination of the larynx and vocal tract is essential in any case of voice disorder which lasts for more than three weeks. Its primary purpose is to identify or exclude malignant disease. In all cases of dysphonia, diagnosis of its cause and observation of the structure and function of the larynx is fundamental to formulating the treatment program.

Laryngeal examination (laryngoscopy) (Fig. 3) is carried out by laryngologists routinely as an out-patient procedure, although in some cases it is necessary to examine the patient using direct laryngoscopy under general anesthetic. In indirect laryngoscopy, a laryngoscopic mirror is held at the back of the patient's mouth to reflect the image of the vocal folds below. The patient is asked to produce a vowel sound so that the vocal fold movement can be observed. The larynx is similarly observed during rhino-laryngoscopy, in which a flexible tube containing fibreoptic bundles is inserted into the patient's nose until it is suspended just above the larynx. Rhino-laryngoscopy and rigid endoscopy, which involves placing a rigid endoscope on the patient's tongue in order to obtain an image of the larynx, can be used with videorecording equipment and stroboscopy. The stroboscope allows the vocal-fold mucosal wave to

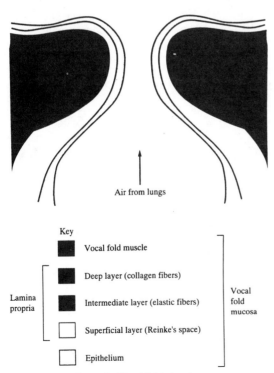

Figure 2. Vocal fold structure.

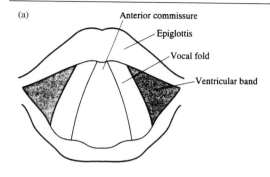

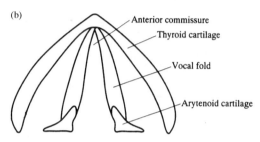

Figure 3. The vocal folds: (a) laryngoscopic view of the vocal folds (b) vocal fold attachments.

be viewed as if in slow motion and provides unique diagnostic information.

The diagnostic process also includes instrumental acoustic evaluation of the vocal parameters. Vocal-fold function is analyzed by electroglottography and air flow and pressure are measured.

5. The Classification of Voice Disorders

The classification of voice disorders is not clear-cut. Behavioral voice disorders which are the result of vocal abuse or misuse can give rise to organic changes of the vocal folds. Conversely, organic dysphonias are frequently compounded by changed phonatory behavior as the speaker attempts to compensate for the primary difficulty. In both instances, it is possible that psychological elements will contribute to the voice disorder either as cause or effect. Even in cases where the underlying cause of the voice disorder is largely psychogenic, abnormal function and, possibly, structure of the vocal folds can be observed as a result. Classification is somewhat arbitrary, therefore, but the disorders fall logically into two large groups, behavioral and organic voice disorders. Each group consists of a number of subcategories.

6. Behavioral Voice Disorders

This category includes the dysphonias which occur either as a result of the way in which the vocal tract is used during phonation or where the cause is psycho-

logical. It excludes all those disorders where there is a primary organic cause. Organic changes can occur in this group, however, as the result of vocal-fold misuse or abuse.

6.1 Muscular Tension Dysphonia (without mucosal changes)—Vocal Strain

Muscular tension dysphonia is also known as hyperkinetic, habitual, or mechanical dysphonia. It is characterized by excessive tension in the muscles involved in phonation, particularly the intrinsic laryngeal muscles.

The initial symptoms experienced by the speaker, often before voice changes are noted, are varying degrees of discomfort within the vocal tract. These sensations might be as mild as a tingling or awareness of the throat, but can be as severe as soreness and aching. There is frequently heightened sensitivity of the larynx, which results in coughing in response to minor irritations. As vocal misuse continues, the voice becomes hoarse and breathy. In the early stages, dysphonia might be apparent only after long periods of talking or at the end of the day. Gradually, the dysphonia increases in severity and is in evidence whenever phonation is attempted. The original pattern of misuse is frequently compounded at this stage as the speaker endeavors to compensate for the inadequate voice. Effort on phonation is increased still further in an attempt to achieve a clearer vocal note and greater loudness. The use of a hard glottal attack at the onset of words with an initial vowel is a common feature, as is frequent throat clearing in an attempt to remove mucus produced by the irritated larynx.

The effect of excessive tension on the vocal-fold movements is to cause strong overadduction in the anterior section. This tends to be accompanied by a posterior glottic chink as the vocal folds fail to meet in the region of the arytenoid cartilages (Fig. 3(b)). In cases where laryngeal tension is even greater, the false vocal cords (ventricular bands) can also be forced towards the midline. This is known as 'ventricular band voice,' although it is the forceful use of the vocal folds themselves which gives rise to the harsh, creaky phonation.

As a result of strong adduction, the vocal folds can become pink following prolonged periods of misuse, but frequently their appearance is unremarkable. Some individuals maintain a low level of vocal misuse for many years which is only troublesome when they have to speak for a long time or in a large or noisy environment. Symptoms are exacerbated by smoking and dusty, dry, or polluted atmospheres. Some women are particularly vulnerable to such vocal problems premenstrually (see Sect. 8.2). The progress from misuse to vocal abuse can be rapid, however, so that damage to the vocal-fold mucosa is incurred within days or weeks.

6.2 Muscular Tension Dysphonia (with mucosal changes)—Vocal Abuse

In cases of established vocal abuse, tissue changes of the vocal folds occur and take several forms. These changes are exacerbated by smoking, excessive alcohol, prolonged exposure to dry, polluted atmospheres, and the inhalation of substances such as cocaine. Some chronic asthma sufferers have edematous vocal folds following the use of aerosol corticosteroids over a long period.

6.2.1 Chronic Laryngitis

As the result of prolonged traumatization, the vocal-fold mucosa becomes edematous and inflamed. Consequently, the habitual speaking pitch is lowered and the vocal note is breathy. A common history is that the chronic laryngitis follows an acute infective laryngitis in which phonation becomes severely dysphonic and is accompanied by a sore throat. Subsequently the chronic noninfective laryngitis becomes established as the speaker uses effort to phonate in the early stages of the infection. Semipermanent changes take place in the larynx as a result of this vocal abuse. These changes become long-term if the faulty voice patterns remain and exposure to laryngeal irritants continues.

6.2.2 Polypoidal Degeneration (Reinke's edema)

In this condition, vocal abuse results in the superficial layer of the lamina propria, or Reinke's space (see Fig. 2), filling with fluid. As a result, the vocal folds increase in mass, causing the voice to deepen dramatically. The edema also results in stiffness of the vocal-fold mucosa, so reducing the mucosal wave on phonation and therefore affecting vocal quality further. There is considerable evidence that this particular symptom occurs most frequently in smokers over 40 years old. Opinions vary as to the relative contributions of smoking and vocal abuse, but it is generally accepted that prolonged smoking is the primary cause.

6.2.3 Vocal-fold Polyps

Excessively vigorous approximation of the vocal folds causes a submucosal hemorrhage which with connective tissue forms a polyp. In most cases these are single, but in some instances they are numerous.

6.2.4 Vocal Nodules (screamer's or singer's nodes)

Prolonged vocal abuse is similarly required to produce the changes in vocal-fold epithelium which constitute vocal nodules. These structures are bilateral and occur at the junction of the anterior third and posterior two-thirds of each vocal fold. The site of the prospective nodules is inflamed in the early stages, and on laryngeal examination mucus can be seen pooling here during phonation. As the vocal abuse continues to cause damage to the mucosa, soft swellings appear which subsequently develop into white, fibrosed, conical nodules. These hardened structures obstruct the approximation of the vocal folds and impair the movement of the mucosal wave during phonation. In severe cases, the nodules are surrounded by edema, and submucosal hemorrhages might also be apparent. The voice is breathy and the upper range is impaired in direct relationship to the size of the nodules.

In children, there is a much higher incidence of vocal nodules in boys than in girls. The picture changes, however, in adults, when the condition is seen most frequently in young to middle-aged females.

Although it is possible during one exceptionally vigorous episode of vocal abuse to cause temporary damage to the vocal-fold epithelium, these semipermanent changes generally represent consistent damage over a substantial period. Any successful treatment should be preceded by identification of the reasons for the individual's damaging vocal behavior.

6.2.5 Contact Ulcers

The mucosal changes which constitute contact ulcers occur bilaterally on the posterior part of the vocal folds which overlay the arytenoid cartilages (Fig. 3(b)). Initially there is edema in the area, which will eventually develop crater-like thickening of the epithelium on one fold which, in the advanced stages, is matched by raised tissue on the other fold. The abuse arises from the speaker using an excessively low speaking fundamental frequency in which the arytenoid cartilages strike each other in a strong 'hammer and anvil' movement. As the condition progresses, the voice becomes hoarse and even deeper, with pain occurring as phonation is attempted.

There is a much higher incidence of contact ulcers among American males than in men in the UK. This appears to be the result of different cultural patterns, as men in the USA generally use a lower speaking fundamental frequency. There may be variations in other cultures. In the comparatively rare cases of contact ulcers in British males, the speaker is frequently found to perceive a low habitual pitch as indicating desired authority or gravitas.

This condition is aggravated and maintained by gastric reflux in patients who regularly suffer from indigestion. Stomach acid rises in the esophagus and overspills into the posterior part of the larynx, causing inflammation and ulceration. This is particularly likely to occur when the patient is lying down, unless pillows are used to raise the head.

6.3 Prognosis in Vocal Abuse Dysphonia

Voice disorders arising from abuse cannot remain constant. The voice will either continue to deteriorate because the damaging phonatory behavior persists, or it should improve as the result of suitable intervention. In the majority of cases, voice therapy undertaken by an appropriately qualified speech and language therapist will reverse the mucosal changes. Advice is given concerning voice conservation and vocal hygiene, in addition to a program of vocal re-education. Advanced changes require microsurgery, but these cases must also receive voice therapy if recurrence is to be avoided. The patient's cooperation and motivation are significant factors in the rate and permanence of improvement.

6.4 Psychogenic Dysphonias

Voice disorders whose cause is primarily psychological comprise this category. This diagnosis can only be made when all other possibilities have been excluded; it is particularly important to keep a diagnosis of psychogenic dysphonia under review to ensure that misdiagnosis of an early organic condition has not occurred.

6.4.1 Anxiety State Dysphonia

The excessively anxious individual can produce voice problems which arise from the constantly tense state of the vocal-tract musculature. A range of vocal symptoms of varying severity is produced, with normal voice frequently apparent between episodes of dysphonia. These patients will sometimes complain of a feeling of a lump in the throat known as 'globus.' While this sensation is frequently due to extreme tension of the pharyngeal muscles, careful examination must be carried out to exclude organic causes.

6.4.2 Conversion Symptom Aphonia

This condition can occur dramatically, with sudden total voice loss without organic cause. In other cases, the conversion aphonia is triggered by acute laryngitis, the voice failing to return as the infection subsides. On laryngeal examination, structure is normal but the vocal folds are bowed and fail to meet in the midline on attempts at phonation. There is no laryngeal discomfort in most cases. These individuals are not malingering, although there are usually identifiable gains arising from the lack of voice. The psychological mechanism involves repression of anxieties which are then converted into a physical symptom, aphonia being only one. The inability to communicate easily is frequently the primary gain, for it relieves the individual of the burdens of arguments or discussions which are painful or which produce conflict. The increased attention and sympathy of others is frequently a welcome secondary gain. An important diagnostic feature of the condition is the lack of concern exhibited by the sufferer, who frequently appears to relish the interest created by the symptom. In other cases, however, there is genuine dismay upon the realization that the symptom is not organically based, but psychogenic.

This condition should be identified and treated as soon as possible in order to avoid prolonged reinforcement of the symptom. Prognosis will depend on the patient's general psychological state. Voice therapy should restore the voice in the first or second treatment session, but longer-term counseling and support is frequently necessary to ensure that the aphonia, or another conversion symptom, does not recur.

6.4.3 Delayed Pubertal Voice Change (puberphonia, mutational falsetto)

The retention of the boy's voice in a male of 18 years or older can result from a hormonal failure to produce the normal primary and secondary sexual characteristics at the age of puberty. Medical treatment is required to rectify the hormonal deficiency (see Sect. 8.1).

More commonly, although normal pubertal changes have taken place and the vocal folds and larynx have enlarged appropriately, the mature male voice has not been established. Although physically capable of producing the deeper note and distressed by the pitch of the habitual voice, the speaker is unable to produce the required sound. In many of these cases, the deeper voice is heard on laughing and coughing, and in some cases pitch breaks occur during spontaneous speech. These occasional revelations of normal vocal-fold function are diagnostically significant and indicate the possibility of resolving the condition. The suggested reasons for mutational falsetto include a particularly overprotective mother and a remote father; the desire to retain a beautiful treble singing voice or very early breaking of the voice which the boy rejects but subsequently cannot retrieve. There is scant evidence that the condition is related to homosexuality.

The typical patient is in his late teens or early twenties and has finally realized that his voice is not going to change spontaneously. Frequently, he will have endured endless teasing from his peers and he has decided that he must seek a normal voice for social and career reasons. Prognosis is good in the self-motivated individual, with a high possibility of normal voice being achieved in the first or second session of voice therapy. The transition from the clinically controlled setting to general use of the new voice will take further time as the speaker overcomes his self-consciousness. The outcome is less optimistic for the man who has been persuaded to seek help reluctantly.

6.4.4 The Transsexual Voice

A transsexual is an individual who has the conviction that he or she has been born with a body of the wrong gender. A feeling of being a woman trapped in a man's body, or vice versa, is described, and this awareness frequently appears to have been present since childhood. Transsexuals want to acquire the physical features of the desired body and will pursue hormonal treatment and surgery to this end while living their lives as a person of the opposite sex.

Consequently, the voice is normal but inappropriate. This is the only condition the voice therapist treats where structure and function of the larynx are normal but abnormal function is required. In the female-to-male transsexual, the voice is deepened as a result of the male hormones which are administered and have the effect of thickening the vocal folds. Voice therapy is therefore usually unnecessary. The female hormones taken by the male-to-female transsexual do not have a feminizing effect on the vocal folds, and therefore therapy is necessary. This will consist of a program directed at all aspects of verbal and nonverbal communication, including the voice. In some cases, particularly those where the larynx is large and the vocal folds are long so that a female voice is extremely difficult to achieve, laryngeal surgery is performed.

6.5 Hearing Loss and Voice Disorders

Abnormalities of pitch, resonance, and loudness occur in individuals with severe hearing loss or total deafness because of the impaired ability to monitor the voice. Pitch is typically raised, and pitch changes are exaggerated. Excessive loudness is a common feature, and there are fluctuations between hyper- and hyponasality, with excessive nasal resonance tending to prevail. Increased laryngeal and pharyngeal tension is a feature of phonation in the individual with hearing loss. There are indications that as a result there is a predisposition to vocal misuse and abuse. The congenitally deaf speaker who has never heard normal voices will have more severely disordered vocal parameters than the individual with an acquired hearing loss.

Vocal changes also occur in the elderly as hearing loss becomes increasingly severe. Usually, excessive vocal loudness occurs as speakers attempt to hear their own voices. In contrast, some elderly individuals talk too quietly while trying to avoid inappropriately loud phonation.

7. Organic Voice Disorders

Organic voice disorders arise from congenital and acquired abnormalities of the vocal tract and other systems relating to phonation. They fall into two categories, either structural or neurological.

7.1 Structural Disorders

These refer to abnormalities of formation and dimension of the vocal tract.

7.1.1 Congenital Laryngeal Web

A web of mucous membrane across the anterior commissure (Fig. 3) is present at birth in some babies. It does not completely obstruct the airway but when the web is large there is stridor, or crowing, on inspiration. The voice is usually hoarse but if the web is small, breathing is unaffected and dysphonia does not occur. In these cases the web might not be discovered until a boy's voice does not break at puberty or a girl's voice remains childish due to the reduced vibrating length of the vocal folds. In severe cases, surgery is necessary, but intervention is avoided when the effects of the web are slight.

7.1.2 Cleft Palate

This is a congenital condition arising from the failure of the palatal muscles and the palatal plates, that is, the bones which form the hard palate, to fuse in the midline during the first three months of pregnancy. There are varying degrees of severity ranging from a total cleft of the hard and soft palate to a submucous cleft in which the normal mucosal cover conceals a cleft of the palatal muscles. Surgery aims not only to close the cleft but also to restore movement of the soft palate which is essential for normal speech. When elevated, the normal soft palate makes contact with the posterior wall of the pharynx, forming what is known as the palatopharyngeal sphincter. Impaired function of this sphincter allows fluids to be regurgitated through the nose during swallowing and also affects articulation (see *Acquired Disorders of Articulation: Classification and Intervention*) and vocal resonance. Audible nasal escape, in which turbulent air is emitted from the nose during the production of consonants, is also associated with incompetency of the palatopharyngeal sphincter.

The hypernasality is due largely to the abnormal linking of the nasal and oral structures. In addition, the speaker frequently elevates the posterior part of the tongue and tenses the jaw and pharynx in an attempt to reduce nasal escape. This pharyngeal constriction enhances the impression of hypernasality. There is also evidence that an incompetent palatopharyngeal sphincter results in abnormal production of the laryngeal note. Forceful adduction of the vocal folds used as a compensatory valving activity, in an attempt to create sufficient intraoral air pressure for the articulation of consonants, results in vocal misuse or vocal nodules. Alternatively, the voice can be quiet and breathy as the speaker attempts to conceal the abnormal vocal resonance.

There is also inadequate closure of the palatopharyngeal sphincter, with similar effects on vocal resonance in abnormalities of vocal tract dimensions. A congenital short palate or an excessively deep and wide pharynx will prevent efficient valving. These conditions can remain concealed by enlarged adenoids as the soft palate approximates to the enlarged adenoidal pad rather than the posterior wall of the pharynx. Following adenoidectomy, the resulting hypernasality indicates the inadequacies of the sphincter. In some cases of potentially normal closure, however, there is a period of hypernasality postadenoidectomy as the palatal movements adjust to the new dimensions. Careful monitoring and investigation of the situation by the surgeon and therapist are necessary.

Congenital and acquired palatal paralysis also give rise to hypernasality. In rare cases, hypernasality is a psychogenic condition.

7.1.3 Nasal Obstruction

Insufficient nasal resonance, or hyponasality, is the result of nasal airway obstruction, which can be congenital or acquired. A deflected septum associated with cleft palate or a broken nose can cause varying degrees of nasal obstruction. Nasal tumors and polyps are removed in order to facilitate nasal breathing and improve vocal resonance. Frequently, children are hyponasal and mouth-breathers as the result of enlarged adenoids. In cases of allergic rhinitis, which can be perennial or seasonal, the nasal mucosa becomes edematous and there is a marked increase in mucus secretion leading to further obstruction of the nasal airway. These individuals are also particularly prone to produce nasal polyps.

All cases of nasal obstruction and hyponasality should be investigated by an ear, nose, and throat surgeon to establish the etiology of the condition. Voice therapy cannot be effective until the appropriate medical and surgical treatment has been undertaken.

7.1.4 Laryngeal Trauma

Compression injuries, such as those caused by attempted strangulation or a blow to the larynx, and penetration injuries which can be caused by gunshot and stabbing wounds, are the two main categories of direct laryngeal trauma. The primary damage is frequently compounded by swelling and infection, which further compromise the airway and phonation. Laryngeal fractures, such as those occurring in road traffic accidents, can be accompanied by torn vocal folds and dislocated arytenoid cartilages. The voice quality, following the necessary surgery, healing, and recovery, will depend on the eventual structure and function of the vocal folds. It is often many months before the situation is stable, and the voice can be further affected by the depression and anxiety associated with the long period of recovery. In some cases, the litigation for damages in relation to the accident prolongs the dysphonia and other symptoms arising from the trauma.

The larynx can also be damaged by the ingestion of caustic substances, while inhalation of certain fumes and scorching smoke will burn the mucosal lining. Until it resolves, the resulting edema causes the voice to be deep and hoarse. Voice rest is essential at this stage, and further advice on voice conservation and vocal hygiene will be helpful to the patient until recovery is complete. A psychogenic component to the dysphonia, as a result of the psychological trauma of such accidents, should also be considered.

Some cases of laryngeal damage arise from the intubation procedures which are necessary in administering general anesthetics and during intensive care.

Rough insertion of an endotracheal tube or the use of an excessively large tube can cause edema and inflammation in addition to dislocating the arytenoid cartilages. In some cases, superficial abrasions result in intubation granuloma on the posterior part of the vocal folds in the area of the arytenoids. The patient should be seen by a voice therapist if the resulting dysphonia does not resolve spontaneously, although removal of the granuloma by laser might be considered in some cases.

7.2 Neurological Dysphonia

Neurological dysphonia can arise from central and peripheral lesions of the nervous system. In all instances, it is the movement and muscle tone of the vocal folds which are primarily affected. Although the structure of the vocal-fold mucosa remains normal, its vibratory characteristics are altered by the changed tonicity of the underlying muscle.

7.2.1 Vocal Fold Paralysis

Varying degrees of paralysis of the vocal folds can occur unilaterally or bilaterally when one or both of the recurrent laryngeal nerves supplying the larynx are damaged. The dysphonia is caused by the inefficient approximation of the vocal folds in combination with loss of stiffness and mass of the paralyzed fold and reduced resistance to the expired air. As a result, the voice is breathy and lacks volume. The speaker needs more frequent intake of breath than normal because of the inefficient valving of the larynx during phonation. The voice disorder is frequently compounded by compensatory strategies, such as raising vocal pitch or increasing laryngeal effort, which are used in an attempt to increase audibility.

The prognosis for recovery of vocal-fold movement depends on the extent and permanence of the damage to the laryngeal nerve supply. For example, when one vocal fold has been paralyzed as the result of a viral infection affecting the recurrent laryngeal nerve, function frequently returns spontaneously over a period of months. The paralysis will be permanent, however, if it is the result of the nerve being severed during surgery or as the result of other trauma.

Management of vocal-cord palsy dysphonia is by voice therapy or a combination of voice therapy and surgery. Depending on the etiology of the palsy, therapy is directed at either accelerating the recovery of the paralyzed fold or encouraging the healthy fold to move across the midline to approximate with the immobile fold. Surgery is not considered until at least six months from onset of the condition and probably not under a year. This allows time for spontaneous recovery and for the effects of therapy to be established.

Surgical procedures for unilateral vocal fold paralysis aim to move the immobile vocal fold towards the mid-line (medialization procedure) in order to facilitate vocal fold approximation on phonation. In some cases, an injection of a substance (e.g., collagen, Teflon) which will increase the mass of the vocal fold and so extend its free edge to the mid-line, is preferred. In cases of bilateral abductor paralysis, where the vocal folds are paralyzed in the mid-line, laryngeal surgery is directed at improving the airway while attempting to retain functionally useful voice.

7.2.2 Spasmodic Dysphonia

This condition is also known as spastic dysphonia, but the term 'spasmodic' more accurately indicates the laryngeal spasm which occurs on phonation. It is also important that spasmodic dysphonia is not confused with the voice disorder resulting from spastic muscles in certain types of dysarthria (see Sect. 7.2.3).

Spasmodic dysphonia is typified by the distinctive strained, strangled vocal quality which sounds as if the speaker is trying to phonate with tightly closed vocal folds. The underlying cause of the condition has been disputed for many years, but there is now agreement that the majority of cases exhibit a focal dystonia. Dystonias are disorders of movement which affect the whole body or specific groups of muscles, causing involuntary movements of the affected muscles, particularly when voluntary movement is attempted. The combination of these bizarre movements combined with freedom from the symptoms during some involuntary behaviors, such as laughing, had led many authorities to favor a psychogenic etiology. The issue is complicated by the fact that not only do a number of patients who suffer such symptoms develop psychological symptoms as a result of the primary disorder, but clinical experience suggests that some cases of spasmodic dysphonia do have a psychogenic basis. This latter group appears to be presenting with a form of conversion symptom aphonia which can be resolved by the appropriate therapy in a way which is not possible with neurogenic spasmodic dysphonia.

An early symptom of the disorder is a slight 'catch' in the voice which gradually becomes a more noticeable obstruction to phonation. As speaking becomes increasingly effortful, the primary symptoms are accompanied by concomitant movements. The sufferer might overbreathe in an attempt to create sufficient air pressure to overcome the laryngospasm or grimace as additional effort is used to force the voice.

The preferred treatment is unilateral or bilateral botulinum toxin injection into the vocal fold adductor muscles. This procedure causes chemical denervation and thus considerably reduces the laryngeal spasm. It has the advantage of being performed while the patient is conscious but has to be repeated at intervals ranging from 4 to 9 months. Voice therapy, and in some cases psychotherapy, can be helpful adjuncts to

treatment before and after the injection but are usually unsatisfactory as sole methods of treatment.

7.2.3 Dysphonia as a Feature of Dysarthria

'Dysarthrias' are disorders of articulation resulting from neurological lesions which cause weakness and paralysis of the muscles of articulation and swallowing. They are developmental or acquired (see *Acquired Dysarthrias*; *Developmental Dysarthrias*). Dysphonia which presents as part of this neurological picture is sometimes called 'dysarthrophonia' and will vary considerably according to the type and site of the lesions involved. Conditions such as strokes (cerebrovascular accidents) can damage nerve pathways so that the articulatory muscles become either spastic or flaccid. The resulting dysphonias are correspondingly effortful and strained-strangled because of the hyperadducted vocal folds, or breathy and weak as a result of the failure of the floppy vocal folds to adduct efficiently. Cerebral tumors and trauma, cerebral palsy, multiple sclerosis, viral infections, poliomyelitis, myasthenia gravis, and other conditions can all cause dysarthria in which the alteration in muscle tone is the chief factor giving rise to the associated dysphonia.

Voice disorders also occur when the dysarthria is due to disorders of movement. In Parkinsonism, the voice is monotonous and lacks volume because of the weak, rigid movements of the vocal folds. In severe cases, the accelerated speech rate in conjunction with impaired articulation and almost inaudible voice renders speech unintelligible. The rapid, jerky movements which characterize chorea, as seen in the hereditary Huntington's chorea, cause irregularities in respiratory and laryngeal movements with subsequent involuntary pitch and volume changes. In a number of disorders in which tremor is a feature, laryngeal tremor will be apparent on phonation with disturbance of the vocal note. Where there are multiple lesions throughout the system in conditions such as motor neurone disease (amyotrophic lateral sclerosis), multiple sclerosis, and Wilson's disease, the voice will reflect the predominant features of the resulting dysarthria.

Evaluation of neurological dysphonias is inevitably complex, as there can be a multiplicity of factors giving rise to dysphonia in these patients. For example, a young adult who has contracted Guillaun-Barré syndrome which results in widespread paralysis and weakness of muscles can be dysphonic as a result of the vocal-fold weakness. In addition, it is possible that there are granulomatous changes to the vocal folds as a result of prolonged intubation in intensive care. Finally, these physical constraints on phonation can be exacerbated by the problems of psychological adjustment during the recovery period.

8. Dysphonia and Endocrinological Changes

Abnormalities and variations in the hormones secreted by the endocrinological system can have significant effects on the voice because of the way in which they affect the mass of the vocal folds. Vocal pitch in males and females will be temporarily or permanently altered, mildly or dramatically, according to the cause and the extent of the hormonal imbalance.

8.1 Male Endocrine Dysphonias

The larynx and vocal folds do not undergo the expected dramatic increase in size at puberty if the normal secretion of male hormones fails to occur. In these individuals, the lack of secondary sexual characteristics such as facial and pubic hair as well as the absence of rapid general growth which usually occurs at puberty indicate the lack of appropriate levels of male hormones. The voice retains the high pitch of the prepubertal boy's voice because the vocal folds have not doubled in length and increased in mass in the usual way at puberty.

Damage to the testicles prior to puberty can prevent development of male secondary sexual characteristics including the adult male voice. The castration of prepubertal males was therefore carried out in the past to ensure the valued castrati singing voice.

8.2 Female Endocrine Dysphonias

Mild vocal changes occur in some females in relation to the menstrual cycle as a result of the vocal folds becoming edematous premenstrually, reflecting the tendency to fluid retention throughout the body. Increased breathiness and slightly lowered pitch can also be present during pregnancy. Although these vocal changes are usually subtle and pass unnoticed by most women, the professional singer or actor is particularly at risk of damaging the vocal folds during this time. Inflammation and submucosal hemorrhage of the vocal folds are possible if particularly demanding roles are undertaken during the premenstrual and menstrual period.

More obvious dysphonic changes are apparent in some females at the time of the menopause. The decrease in secretion of estrogens (female hormones) and relative increase in androgens (male hormones) result in an increase of vocal-fold mass and deepening of the voice. In cases of dysphonia related to the menstrual cycle and menopause, the symptoms usually resolve spontaneously without intervention. When they give rise to particular concern, general advice concerning voice conservation and vocal hygiene is important to ensure maximum vocal efficiency and to prevent vocal abuse. In more severe cases of menopausal vocal deterioration, or where the retention of the quality of the voice is vitally necessary, as in the case of professional singers, hormonal treatment should be considered.

Virilization of the female voice, 'androphonia,' can occur following the administration of androgens in cases of carcinoma and when anabolic steroids are prescribed. Initially the voice is unstable and exhibits

pitch breaks, but, as the vocal change stabilizes, the firm, clear note of a male voice becomes established. Other male characteristics, such as excessive hair growth, resulting from the administration of these virilizing agents, are gradually reversed by withdrawal of these substances. The voice changes, however, are irreversible, although in some instances voice quality might be improved by voice therapy.

Deepening of the voice will also be particularly noticeable in women when there is underactivity of the thyroid gland, a condition known as myxedema. The skin becomes rough and dry, while movements and intellectual processes are slowed. The vocal folds gradually increase in mass as part of this process, and the voice becomes deep and hoarse. When myxedematous changes occur in males, the deepened voice is less noticeable. Congenital underactivity of the thyroid gland results in the baby's cry being abnormally low-pitched and with restricted pitch range, in addition to intellectual impairment and distinctive physical appearance. Similar vocal changes gradually occur in juvenile myxedema as a result of thyroid dysfunction. The administration of thyroxine is required to compensate for the underactivity of the thyroid gland.

9. Dysphonia due to Laryngeal Disease

Diseases of the larynx can be benign, premalignant, or malignant. In order to make a conclusive diagnosis, thorough examination of the larynx and vocal tract is necessary. In some cases this will be carried out under general anesthetic and, where appropriate, a tissue sample will be taken and analyzed.

9.1 Benign Laryngeal Neoplasm
9.1.1 Papilloma

These benign growths arising from the mucous membrane of the respiratory tract occur chiefly on the vocal folds but can also be present in the trachea.

Multiple or single papillomata appear in children and adults, although single papilloma are more usually found in adults. A virus appears to be responsible, but there are indications that there is also a hormonal influence. Vocal change is one of the earliest symptoms of the condition. Subsequently, the primary hoarseness is compounded by the pattern of vocal abuse which becomes established as the speaker attempts to overcome the dysphonia.

In children, the primary aim of treatment is to preserve the airway by removing or limiting the obstruction created by the papillomatosis. A number of techniques are used with the aims of removing the papillomata successfully and reducing the rate of recurrence, a particular problem with this condition. There is a tendency for laser surgery to be used with adults, while excision might be preferable for children. Interferon therapy, which interferes with virus infection, is an encouraging development. Following removal of the papillomatosis, appropriate voice therapy consisting of advice and, if relevant, a vocal re-education program is necessary if vocal abuse is to be eliminated or avoided.

9.1.2 Laryngeal Cysts

Cysts can develop in various parts of the larynx, usually as the ductal system of the mucous gland network degenerates in individuals over 50 or 60 years old. They are particularly common on the ventricular bands, where they affect vocal efficiency in some speakers. When a cyst occurs less commonly on the vocal fold, the voice is significantly impaired as a result of reduced vocal-fold movement. With enlargement of the cyst, the mucus membrane stiffens and the mucosal wave is reduced or disappears. The voice subsequently becomes breathy, lacks volume, and will be restored only when the cyst is drained. Voice therapy, postoperatively, helps vocal rehabilitation.

9.2 Malignant Laryngeal Neoplasm (laryngeal carcinoma)

The possibility of laryngeal carcinoma is the major reason that any individual who develops a voice problem lasting for three weeks or more should be examined by a laryngologist. Although this condition occurs most frequently in middle-aged or elderly men who smoke, it can develop in males and females of all ages, and the possibility of this etiology in cases of dysphonia must always be considered. Early diagnosis and treatment by radiotherapy results in a permanent cure rate of 80–90 percent. Advanced cases and those in which radiotherapy has been unsuccessful undergo partial or total surgical removal of the larynx (laryngectomy).

Tumors can develop at any site in the larynx, with those on the vocal folds being the most common, signaling their presence at an early stage by hoarseness. Those arising above and below the vocal folds produce dysphonia at a later stage in their development as the tumor extends to involve the glottis. Radiotherapy and, where necessary, surgery are primarily life-saving procedures with the secondary objective of providing the patient with suitable phonation postoperatively.

Even in cases successfully treated by radiotherapy, in some patients the voice can be adversely affected. Permanent changes to the vocal-fold mucosa impair the normal movements of the mucosal wave and the regularity of the free edge of the vocal fold. Post-radiotherapy dysphonia can also be partly or entirely psychogenic as a result of anxiety. Where appropriate, voice therapy enables the patient to develop maximum vocal recovery.

Partial laryngectomy (Fig. 4) is designed to remove the laryngeal tumor while preserving some vocal function, although dysphonic. This procedure is frequently regarded unfavorably as being insufficiently radical

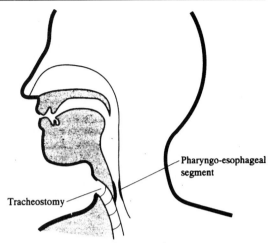

Figure 4. Vocal tract post laryngectomy.

to ensure removal of all the diseased tissue. Total laryngectomy results in aphonia. The diseased larynx and vocal folds are excised and the severed trachea is turned forwards to a permanent opening in the neck (tracheostomy) to allow the patient to breathe. As a result, the airway and esophagus are then separate. At this stage the laryngectomee is able to articulate speech silently and, if observed carefully, can be understood. Pseudovoice is achieved by using air to cause vibration of the sphincter at the upper end of the esophagus (the pharyngo–esophageal (P–E) segment). Traditionally, the laryngectomee was taught how to inject air into the esophagus from the mouth by compressing the oral muscles. As the air returns spontaneously, it vibrates the P–E segment, making a sound which is gradually developed into pseudovoice. When successful, this esophageal voice is fluent and has the quality of a moderately husky voice produced by vocal folds. It is quieter than laryngeal voice, however, and speech rate is reduced in order to accommodate air injection and return.

A considerable number of patients, however, are unable to achieve pseudovoice in this way. Tracheo–esophageal prostheses have been developed, therefore, in order to make the acquisition of pseudovoice available to a larger number of laryngectomees and to improve the efficiency of alaryngeal speech. Air from the lungs is directed from the trachea via the prosthesis into the esophagus so that the P–E segment is vibrated during speech. The patient is able to produce pseudovoice sooner after surgery and with a more normal speech rate. Prostheses are not suitable for all laryngectomees, and the procedure is not always successful in producing satisfactory voice.

Many patients benefit from being introduced to augmentative and alternative communication aids in the early stages following laryngectomy, even if these are eventually unnecessary. An electronic larynx held to the neck provides a sound source which makes the laryngectomee's speech audible prior to the acquisition of pseudovoice or when pseudovoice cannot be achieved. Excessively quiet pseudovoice is more easily heard when a small amplifier is used.

9.3 Inflammatory Laryngeal Conditions

Laryngeal inflammation results in dysphonia because of the increased mass and altered vibratory characteristics of the vocal folds. Rare causes include conditions such as tuberculosis, fungal infections, and advanced syphilis.

9.3.1 Acute Laryngitis

Viral infections affecting the upper respiratory tract and causing acute inflammation of the laryngeal mucosa can result in a hoarse voice or aphonia. As the infection subsides, the voice usually improves after two or three days, although voice problems sometimes persist for up to two weeks. The dysphonia is more persistent if the voice is not rested during the acute stage of the infection, and in some cases the dysphonic episode acts as a trigger for psychogenic dysphonia.

9.3.2 Chronic Laryngitis

See Sect. 6.2.1 for a discussion of chronic laryngitis.

9.3.3 Chronic Hyperplastic Laryngitis

This condition is premalignant. There is extensive inflammation throughout the laryngeal mucosa and marked thickening of the vocal-fold epithelium characterized by raised white patches called leukoplakia. Unlike acute and chronic laryngitis, there is no improvement through reduction of irritants and vocal abuse. The thickened vocal-fold epithelium requires surgical stripping, and voice therapy is necessary in some cases.

9.3.4 Laryngeal Rheumatoid Arthritis

Local inflammation of the laryngeal joints in the early stages of the condition causes acute pain on phonation. Difficulty in moving the vocal folds to the midline results in marked dysphonia. In some cases,

the laryngeal joints fuse so that the vocal folds are immobilized and surgery might be necessary.

10. Future Developments in the Diagnosis and Treatment of Dysphonia

The sophistication of the instrumentation used in laryngeal imaging, analysis of function, and in biofeedback for the patient continues to develop. It is the expertise of the clinicians employing such equipment and integrating it with their therapeutic skills which is fundamental to the successful treatment of dysphonic patients. The increasing establishment of voice clinics facilitates the delivery of specialized diagnostic and therapeutic services. These clinics are held by a professional team consisting of at least a laryngologist, a voice therapist, and a nurse, but can also include a psychiatrist, social worker, technician, and others. By using state-of-the-art instrumentation, detailed diagnosis and analysis of the disordered larynx and its behavior enables the team to make highly informed decisions concerning the management program for each patient. In the future, it is probable that more patients will have access to voice clinics, particularly if routine examination and treatment are not successful.

See also: Incidence And Prevalence; Developmental Causes; Acquired Causes; Mutism.

Bibliography

Aronson A 1990 *Clinical Voice Disorders*, 3rd edn. Thieme, New York
Baken R J 1987 *Clinical Measurement of Speech and Voice*. Taylor and Francis, London
Colton R H, Casper J K 1990 *Understanding Voice Problems*. Williams and Wilkins, Baltimore, MD
Doyle P C 1994 *Foundations of Voice and Speech Rehabilitation following Laryngeal Cancer*. Singular Publishing, San Diego, CA
Greene M C L, Mathieson L 1989 *The Voice and Its Disorders*, 5th edn. Whurr Publishers, London
Hirano M, Bless D M 1992 *Videostroboscopic Evaluation of the Larynx*. Singular Publishing, San Diego, CA
Morrison M, Rammage L 1994 *The Management of Voice Disorder*. Chapman and Hall, London
Rubin J, Sataloff R, Korovin G, Gould W 1995 *Diagnosis and Treatment of Voice Disorders*. Igaku-shoi, New York
Wilson D K 1987 *Voice Problems of Children*. Williams and Wilkins, Baltimore, MD

Acquired Dysarthrias

H. Hirose

The term dysarthria has traditionally been defined as 'disorders of oral speech resulting from lesions within the nervous system' (Arnold 1965). Recently, the concept of dysarthria has become more comprehensive and refined. For example, Darley et al. (1975) state that dysarthria comprises a group of speech disorders resulting from disturbances in muscular control due to impairment of any of the basic motor processes involved in the execution of speech. In other words, the term is restricted to neurogenic speech dysfunctions, those resulting from impairment of the central or peripheral nervous system. Based upon the above concept, the term 'motor speech disorders' has been used synonymously with dysarthria. By definition, then, dysarthria must be distinguished from language disorders or more broadly based cognitive disorders. Also, the definition of dysarthria does not cover speech disorders of an organic (structural) or psychological origin.

1. Classification of Dysarthria

Several attempts of classification were reported. From their comprehensive analysis of deviant speech, Darley et al. (1969) suggested five representative types of dysarthria of neurological origin. They were: flaccid dysarthria (in bulbar palsy); spastic dysarthria (in pseudobulbar palsy); ataxic dysarthria (in cerebellar disorders); hypokinetic dysarthria (in parkinsonism); and hyperkinetic dysarthria (in dystonia and chorea). In addition, mixed dysarthrias were described that result from disorders of multiple motor systems and are associated with such conditions as amyotrophic lateral sclerosis, Wilson's disease, and multiple sclerosis (see *Acquired Causes*). In this chapter, dysarthria secondary to cerebral palsy is excluded (see *Developmental Dysarthrias*).

2. Diagnosis and Evaluation of Dysarthria

The diagnosis of dysarthria is usually straightforward, if the presence or absence of speech problems is the sole concern in each clinical case. However, a more precise description of dysarthric symptoms is often quite difficult, since they include a variety of signs as diverse as those reported in literature on speech pathology and neurology, which have been based essentially on simple acoustic impressions.

In recent years, there have been several attempts to provide a more precise documentation of dysarthric symptoms. They include perceptual evaluation, acoustic analysis, and physiological assessment of abnormal articulatory movements.

2.1 Perceptual Evaluation

Darley and his colleagues (1969) studied recorded speech samples obtained from different types of neurological patient groups. Based on the perceptual judgment, they rated each of the samples on each one of 38 dimensions of speech and voice using a seven-point scale of severity. These dimensions pertain to pitch, loudness, voice quality, respiration, prosody, and articulation. As a result, they found that the speech pattern mirrored a different kind of abnormality of motor functioning related to each type of neurological disorders. They argued that a single

dimension was unique in a given neurological disease and the distinctive co-occurence of several dimensions aids in the identification of neurological disorders. Further, through correlation studies of scale values for different sets of dimensions in each representative disorder type, eight clusters of three or more deviant speech dimensions emerged. These clusters are: articulatory inaccuracy, prosodic excess, prosodic insufficiency, articulatory–resonatory incompetence, phonatory stenosis, phonatory incompetence, resonatory incompetence, and phonatory–prosodic insufficiency. Thus, Darley et al. concluded that each of different types of neurological disorder is characterized by its unique set of clusters obtained from perceptual evaluation. According to the above concept, the characteristics of each type of dysarthric speech were provided.

Although it is apparent from these studies that perceptual judgment by well-trained human ears is reliable and clinically useful for the diagnosis of dysarthric speech, it has often been claimed that strict criteria are not available for training others to use such scales reliably and, therefore, the acoustic analysis of speech sounds would be more appropriate for the objective assessment of dysarthric abnormality, particularly for the evaluation of the severity of symptoms.

2.2 Acoustic Analysis

Several attempts have been reported to assess speech production impairments associated with neurological disorders using acoustic analysis.

Among those, Ludlow et al. (1985) developed a set of experimental speech production tasks and recorded patients' speech. The recorded materials were then analyzed using spectrographic techniques. They included as speech tasks: maximum phonation length, rate of sentence production, rate of syllable repetition, latency of speech initiation, imitation of pitch glide, imitation of pitch contours in sentences, imitation of loudness levels, and imitation of stress contrasts. By comparing the results with normative data, Ludlow et al. concluded that the assessment system had been validated for the objective assessment of the patterns and degree of pathology and changes in pathology with different treatment regimen.

Similar attempts using spectrographic analysis have been reported by different authors and more precise descriptions of speech characteristics revealed by perceptual judgments were made. As for temporal aspects of speech, for example, so-called bladylalia (slow speech) can be identified when the segmental duration exceeds 140 percent of the normal mean. Also, the vowel/consonant duration ratio is significantly lower than the normal in those cases who are judged to have a slow speaking rate.

The technique of signal processing has been adopted for the evaluation of dysarthric speech. For example, Ziegler and von Cramon (1986) calculated sound pressure level (SPL) contours for each test utterance sample containing plosives obtained from spastic dysarthric subjects, in order to assess the quality of consonant production. In their method, the maximal rate of SPL change at the closure and release of the plosives in the test words was derived as the relative SPL differences immediately neighboring the target vowel. It was noted that reduction of SPL differences in plosive–vowel and vowel–plosive transitions occurred in most of their dysarthric cases. Thus, the parameter of 'SPL difference' came to be regarded as a quantitative indication of abnormal plosive production in spastic dysarthrias. This is one of the objective methods to describe the degree of imprecise consonants in dysarthric speech.

Another method is to obtain several acoustic parameters which are characteristic for dysarthric speech using acoustic analyses such as 'linear predictive coefficients' (LPC) analysis. In this case, speech samples are analyzed using a computer and the rate of change in the power and spectral fluctuations on the time is obtained. The results of analyses have indicated that the rate of the spectral change appears to correspond well to the degree of severity of spastic dysarthria.

2.3 Physiological Assessment of Abnormal Articulatory Movements

Dysarthric speech is the end product of the pathological dynamics of the articulators, so its perceptual and acoustic characteristics must depend on the motor characteristics of the articulators. Therefore, the analysis of the motor patterns of the articulators in dysarthric subjects seems to be a more direct approach to disclose the nature of dysarthric speech. In this sense, objective analysis of the motor patterns of the pathological dynamics in dysarthric speech has received a great deal of attention.

Since speech is a complex voluntary movement specific to human beings, execution of speech is thoroughly under the control of the central nervous system. At the level of the execution of voluntary movement, a flow of nerve impulses comes down the pyramidal pathway in accordance with the motor plans and programs to achieve a final goal of movement. During this process, elaborate contributions of the subsystems of the central nervous systems are required. The pathophysiological manifestations of the dysarthric subjects can be interpreted as examples of disturbances in the process of skilled movements.

In recent years, various kinds of observation techniques have been developed for the assessment and analysis of the dynamic patterns of human speech movements. They include: cineradiography and X-ray microbeam analysis; fiberoptic observation and photoglottography; palatographic recording; ultrasonic technique; position–sensitive detector and electromyography. By means of these methods, characteristics of motor patterns of each type of dysarthrias are fairly well described (Hirose 1986).

The articulatory patterns of cerebellar ataxic subjects are characterized by inconsistency in both range and velocity of movement, while the maximum velocity is not much less than that of the normal subject. The abnormal patterns of articulatory movement in cerebellar disorders must be explained as impairments of the programming and updating function of the cerebellum.

Abnormal articulatory patterns in subjects with Parkinson's disease are evidenced by a disturbance in rhythmic performance in the repetitive production of syllables as well as reduction in the range of movements. These hypokinetic patterns can be related to a deterioration in the reciprocal adjustment of the antagonistic muscles for speech articulation. In other words, the physiological mechanism of hypokinesia or rigidity in these subjects can be generally considered to be based on the abnormal muscle contraction in a persistent fashion.

Dysarthric manifestation associated with pathologies along the pyramidal pathway is generally classified as spastic and flaccid dysarthria. When the primary motoneuron is exclusively involved (as in pseudobulbar palsy), spastic dysarthria is manifested, while flaccid dysarthria occurs when the secondary motoneurons are affected (as in bulbar palsy). In both cases, speech is perceived as slow, hypernasal, and breathy, with monotone and reduced loudness. In motor terms, these abnormal speech patterns can be explained by reduced range of articulatory movement and slowing down in the rate of the speech. These two pathological groups can be distinguished on a neurological basis and on other clinical features such as voice characteristics.

3. Treatment of Dysarthria

Dysarthria treatment could be focused according to cause (e.g., myasthenia gravis, Parkinson's disease); the type of dysarthria (spastic, flaccid, ataxic, and so on); or the primary function involved (e.g., respiration, phonation, articulation).

It should be the first step of treatment to attempt to restore function. In this step, medical approaches including medication, surgical intervention, and prosthetic aids are to be considered. The effect of medication is limited to certain disorders such as myasthenia gravis in which anticholinesterases and steroids are known to be effective. Also, L-dopamin is generally effective for Parkinson's disease and penicillamin is used for Wilson's disease. Recently, thyrotropin-releasing hormone (TRH) has been used for ataxic cases, but its effect is still questionable.

As for surgical treatment, a pharyngeal flap operation is often indicated to restore velopharyngeal closure function in those cases with velopharyngeal insufficiency due to muscle weakness in pseudobulbar palsy or oculopharyngeal dystrophy. In general, however, surgical intervention is not indicated for progressive diseases.

Prosthetic aids to help articulatory movements include a palatal lift prosthesis to restore velopharyngeal function as mentioned above. Also, a chin-cap can be applied to those cases with dropping chin due to flaccid paralysis of jaw muscles. Further, a wrap or a girdle is used to help abdominal muscles to restore the function of breath support during speech.

The second step is to encourage the patient to use their residual function to maximal extent to compensate for the dysfunction or even restore function (see *Acquired Disorders of Articulation: Classification and Intervention*). Speech therapy in general is strongly indicated in this step to improve the respiratory, phonatory, and articulatory abilities of the patient.

The third step of treatment may be the application of an alternative mode of communication and/or augmentative communication often supported by instrumental aids.

It must be mentioned that any of the methods or approaches referred to above are bound to overlap and interact with each other.

Bibliography

Arnold G E 1965 Central nervous disorders of speaking: Dysarthria. In: Luchsinger R, Arnold G E (eds.) *Voice, Speech, Language*. Wadsworth, Belmont

Darley F L, Aronson A E, Brown J R 1969 Clusters of deviant speech dimensions in dysarthrias. *Journal of Speech and Hearing Research* **12**: 462–96

Darley F L, Aronson A E, Brown J R 1975 *Motor Speech Disorders*. Saunders, Philadelphia, PA

Hirose H 1986 Pathophysiology of motor speech disorders (dysarthria). *Folia phoniatrica* **38**: 61–88

Ludlow C L, Bassich C, Connor N P 1985 An objective system for assessment and analysis of dysarthric speech. In: *Speech and Language Evaluation in Neurology: Adult Disorders*. Grune and Stratton, New York

Wertz R T 1978 Neuropathologies of speech and language: An introduction to patient management. In: Johns D F (ed.) *Clinical Management of Neurogenic Communicative Disorders*. Little Brown, Boston, MA

Ziegler W, von Cramon D 1986 Spastic dysarthria after acquired brain injury: An acoustic study. *British Journal of Disorders in Communication* **21**: 173–87

Acquired Disorders of Articulation: Classification and Intervention

H. Ackermann

Besides inborn structural anomalies of the vocal tract, for example, cleft palate or deterioration of language acquisition such as developmental apraxia of speech (see *Developmental Dysarthrias*), a variety of acquired medical conditions, affecting either the peripheral speech apparatus (e.g., injuries, surgical resection, polymyositis, muscular dystrophy, myasthenia gravis), the cranial nerves (e.g., polyneuritis), or the central nervous system (CNS) (e.g., closed head trauma, cerebrovascular disorders, degenerative diseases of the lower or upper motor neuron, the basal ganglia, or the cerebellum), may disrupt articulation.

1. Classification of Acquired Disorders of Articulation

Apart from a few exceptions, for example, implosives, the speech sounds of the various human languages are produced by laryngeal and supralaryngeal modulation of the expiratory air flow (Kent 1997a). Therefore, the perceived sound features depend upon the activity of the vocal folds, the position of the velum, and the configuration of the oral cavity. The peripheral speech apparatus, thus, comprises three functional components, that is, respiration, phonation, and articulation. In consideration of this model, compromised articulation seems to reflect a disorder at the level of the supralaryngeal vocal tract. However, reduced respiratory support, severe laryngeal tremor or hearing deficits may disrupt articulatory performance as well. In a broader sense, thus, disorders of articulation encompass all instances of an impaired distinctiveness of the produced speech sounds.

Broca (1861) reported a case of sudden 'speechlessness'—the patient's utterances were restricted to repetitions of the syllable 'tan'—due to an extensive perisylvian lesion of the left hemisphere as disclosed at post-mortem examination. Explicitly, Broca considered this disorder an inability 'to execute coordinated articulatory movements' rather than a disruption of language faculty. It is now well established that damage to the anterior perisylvian area, including, presumably, the anterior insula, may give rise to a fairly consistent syndrome of speech deficits such as slowed tempo, articulatory impreciseness, and altered prosodic features which sometimes evolves from an initial period of mutism (Alexander et al. 1989; Dronkers 1996). Several labels have been offered for this type of communication disorder, for example, *phonetic disintegration*, *apraxic dysarthria*, *apraxia of speech*, *cortical dysarthria*, or in line with Broca *aphemia* (see Schiff et al. 1983 for references). Modern concepts of apraxia of speech often assume disrupted 'programming' of articulatory gestures, that is, impaired higher level aspects of speech motor control, to be the underlying deficit (see *Verbal Apraxia*).

Besides the anterior perisylvanian language zone, several further cortical and subcortical structures of the CNS are engaged in the control of the up to about 100 muscles participating in speech production: the motor cortex, the basal ganglia, and the cerebellum shape the neural signals driving via brainstem nuclei and cranial nerves the respiratory, laryngeal, and orofacial muscles. At least the basal ganglia might be, in addition, relevant for speech monitoring. Principally, dysfunctions at any of these levels may impede respiratory, laryngeal, and/or orofacial activities. Depending on the nature, the site and the severity of the respective lesions, the disorders will be restricted to a single structure of the vocal tract, for example, hypernasality due to velopharyngeal incompetence following damage to the pharyngeal nerves, or extend to all functional components of the speech apparatus, that is, respiration, phonation, and articulation, as, for example, in the case of degenerative CNS diseases or systemic affections of the cranial nerves or the respective musculature.

With the exception of apraxia of speech, Darley et al. (1975) applied the notion *dysarthria* to all speech disorders arising from disrupted neuromotor control of the muscles engaged in respiration, phonation, and articulation, including even abnormalities of speech production following isolated injury to a cranial nerve such as *velopharyngeal incompetency*. In consideration of the variety of speech deficits of a neuromuscular origin, 'it is more appropriate to pluralize the problem and refer to the dysarthrias rather than to dysarthria' (Wertz 1985). It must be noted that the definition provided by Darley and co-workers even extends to abnormalities such as voice tremor and spasmodic dysphonia which, most presumably, both reflect a disorder of the central motor system (see *Disorders of Voice*). Because of a pathomechanism restricted to the laryngeal level, the latter syndromes often are, however, referred to as *dysphonias*.

Besides disordered neuromotor control, acquired structural anomalies of the vocal tract due to, for example, injury or surgical intervention, such as glossectomy, may disrupt articulatory performance. Per definition, these impairments are not labelled as dysarthrias.

Disorders of articulation may be classified along a variety of dimensions such as age of onset, medical diagnosis, involved neuroanatomic structures, and perceptual characteristics (Wertz 1985). Prerequisite to (eventual) medical or surgical therapy, the underlying disease process, for example, multiple sclerosis,

must be determined. As concerns the planning of speech therapy, delineation of the profile of functional deficits is of predominant importance. In spite of concerns about its reliability, the Mayo Clinic classification of dysarthrias as proposed by Darley et al. (1975) represents the most widely adopted system in this regard. The neuromotor speech disorders are grouped according to pathophysiological concepts, that is, flaccid, spastic, hypokinetic, hyperkinetic and ataxic dysarthrias, each characterized by a rather distinct profile of speech and voice abnormalities (Table 1).

2. Symptomatology and Pathophysiology of the Dysarthrias

2.1 (Neuro-)Muscular Diseases

Besides other muscle groups, myasthenia gravis, that is, a disorder characterized by disrupted synaptic transmission at the level of the neuromuscular junction, may involve the speech apparatus, giving rise to abnormalities of articulation and/or phonation. Rarely, dysphonia or velopharyngeal incompetency even emerge as the initial sign of myasthenia gravis (for example, Neiman et al. 1975). Furthermore, muscular dystrophies, for example, the facioscapulohumeral and oculopharyngeal variants, or polymyositis have been noted to impair orofacial, laryngeal, and/or respiratory functions (Adams and Victor 1989). Neuromuscular diseases extending across all the structures of the speech apparatus must be expected to result into the syndrome of flaccid dysarthria, characterized, among others, by articulatory impreciseness (Table 1). However, as a rule, dysphonia and dysphagia prevail above impaired articulation.

2.2 Disorders of the Peripheral Nervous System

Dependent upon the site of lesion, disorders restricted to a single cranial nerve yield dysphonia, velopharyngeal incompetency, or impaired tongue motility. Disease processes either within or outside the brainstem may extend to several or all cranial nerves supplying the vocal tract, for example, nasopharyngeal tumors, Chiari malformation, polyneuritis, encephalitis, or progressive bulbar palsy, that is, a form of degenerative motor system disease (Adams and Victor 1989). In these instances, flaccid dysarthria must be expected. Furthermore, amyotrophic lateral sclerosis may present with this syndrome prior to its development into a mixed flaccid-spastic constellation.

2.3 Syndromes of the Upper Motor Neuron

Imaging data revealed functional lateralization of speech motor control toward the left hemisphere at the level of the precentral gyrus (Wildgruber et al. 1996). Because of bilateral innervation of (most of)

Table 1. The Mayo Clinic classification of dysarthrias (syndromes restricted to a single component of the central motor system).

Dysarthria type	Site of lesion	Motor deficits (limbs)	Most salient speech characteristics
Flaccid	speech musculature, lower motor neuron	weakness, reduced muscle tone, muscle atrophy	hypernasality, imprecise consonants, breathy voice, monopitch
Spastic	upper motor neuron	weakness, increased muscle tone, hyperreflexia	imprecise consonants, monopitch, reduced stress, harsh voice
Ataxic	cerebellum, cerebellar afferents	incoordination (dysmetria); stance/gait ataxia	imprecise consonants, excess and equal stress, irregular articulatory breakdown, vowels distorted
Hypokinetic	substantia nigra	akinesia, bradykinesia, muscle rigidity, rest tremor	monopitch and loudness, reduced stress, imprecise consonants
Hyperkinetic (quick movements)	striatum	involuntary choreic movements	imprecise consonants, intervals prolonged, variable rate, monopitch
Hyperkinetic (slow movements)	extrapyramidal system	dystonia, athetotic movements	imprecise consonants, vowels distorted, harsh voice, irregular articulatory breakdown

(Adapted from Darley et al. 1975)

the cranial nerve nuclei, compensation via the contralateral motor cortex can be expected in unilateral upper motor neuron dysfunctions, giving rise to, if anything, slight and transient dysarthria. Nevertheless, however, a subgroup of patients with unilateral upper motor neuron syndrome may show persistent dysarthria (Duffy and Folger 1996). Spastic dysarthria associated with bilateral dysfunctions of the precentral gyrus and/or corticobulbar tracts has been reported to exhibit slowed articulatory gestures of reduced amplitude, hypernasality due to insufficient velar elevation, tongue retraction, increased constriction of the pharynx, and hyperadduction of the shortened vocal folds (Ziegler and von Cramon 1986). In its extreme, anarthria and aphonia emerge. Patients with rather complete speechlessness may, nevertheless, show unimpaired spontaneous emotional expressions within the vocal domain such as laughter or crying ('automatic-voluntary movement dissociation'; Mao et al. 1989). These observations indicate that two separate neural systems subserving orofacial and laryngeal control converge onto the lower motor neurons.

2.4 Basal Ganglia Disorders

Parkinson's disease may give rise to the syndrome of hypokinetic dysarthria including reduced vocal intensity, monopitch, breathy and harsh voice quality, and articulatory impreciseness. In addition, voice tremor, speech freezing and hastening, acquired stuttering, and palilalia, that is, compulsive repetition of mostly utterance-final words or phrases, have been observed. In contrast to striatal and cerebellar lesions, Parkinsonian dysarthrics, as a rule, exhibit normal or even accelerated speech rate as well as uncompromised articulatory movement velocity. As concerns Huntington's chorea, acoustic analyses of speech utterances point to similar motor deficits within the speech apparatus as those reported for arm movements (Ackermann et al. 1997; Konczak et al. 1997; for further references see Ackermann and Wiles 1996).

In more advanced stages of the disease, *spasmodic dysphonia* and *essential voice tremor* may compromise the production of distinct speech sounds. The former syndrome, characterized by strained and harsh voice quality, low volume and pitch, vocal tremor, and irregularly distributed stoppages as well as catches of the voice, is now widely recognized as a variant of focal dystonia (see *Disorders of Voice*). Tentatively, therefore, this disorder must be attributed to an impairment of basal ganglia circuitries. The same suggestion applies to voice tremor, being either a component of the syndrome of essential tremor or an isolated sign (essential voice tremor).

2.5 Dysfunctions of the Cerebellum and/or the Afferent Cerebellar Tracts

Speech abnormalities have been noted in a variety of cerebellar disorders such as hereditary or sporadic atrophy of this organ, inflammatory diseases, or intoxication, for example, due to lithium medication. At the perceptual level, cerebellar dysarthria is characterized by slowed speech tempo, 'scanning' rhythm, and articulatory impreciseness. Kinematic analyses revealed slowed articulatory movements, that is, bradykinesia. Finally, fluctuations of loudness as well as pitch, including voice tremor at a frequency of about 3 Hz, have been observed. Most likely, cerebellar dysarthria results from damage to the superior paramedian regions of the cerebellar hemispheres (Ackermann et al. 1997; for further references see Ackermann and Wiles 1996).

Friedreich's ataxia, a hereditary degenerative disorder, compromises, among others, the somatosensory cerebellar afferent input sparing, as a rule, the cerebellum itself. During follow-up of the disease, presumably, all patients will develop dysarthria. Among others, the speech and voice abnormalities include irregular fluctuations of pitch and loudness as well as slowed speech tempo (Ackermann and Hertrich 1993; Hertrich and Ackermann 1993). Besides the trigeminal nuclei, the frontal lobes project via internal capsule and potine nuclei to the cerebellum. Conceivably, the dysarthria-clumsy hand syndrome reflects rather circumscript damage to these pathways either at the level of the internal capsule or the basis pontis (Sohn et al. 1990; Kim et al. 1995).

2.6 Diseases Affecting Several Components of the Central Motor System

A variety of CNS disorders such as multiple sclerosis, progressive supranuclear palsy, or amyotrophic lateral sclerosis may compromise several cerebral structures contributing to speech motor control. For example, multiple system atrophy involves both the basal ganglia and the cerebellum. Consequently, a constellation of mixed dysarthria develops comprising Parkinsonian as well as ataxic features (Kluin et al. 1996).

3. Perceptual and Instrumental Assessment

Neurological diagnoses do not provide a sufficient basis for the selection and ordering of intervention procedures. Rather, treatment must be tailored to each patient according to the profile of deficits across the various subsystems of the speech apparatus. In order to focus therapy for articulatory disorders, the clinician has to document the patients' deficits and their hierarchical relationship, to establish the speech diagnosis, that is, the type of dysarthria, to determine the severity of the dysfunctions, and to assess probability for improvement (Wertz 1985).

At the physiologic level, the speaking mechanism can be considered a series of functional components (valves) interrupting or releasing expiratory air stream (Netsell and Rosenbek 1985). Dysarthria emerges when neuromuscular disorders compromise speed,

range, or co-ordination of the respective muscles. As a framework for the functional evaluation of speech disorders, Rosenbek and LaPointe (1985) proposed to combine a system of point-places (respiration system, larynx, velopharyngeal port, tongue blade, tongue tip, lips, jaw) with a process model (articulation, resonance, phonation, respiration, prosody). The basic components of (non-instrumental) speech examination include client history, inspection of the structures of the speech apparatus, assessment of orosensory functions as well as performance of non-speech, speech-like, and citation tasks (Kent 1997b). Besides detailed sensory-motor and auditory-perceptual evaluation, a variety of instrumental techniques are available including acoustic analyses, aerodynamic tests, fiberoptic videotaping as well as kinematic measurements and electromyographic recordings of respiratory, laryngeal, and orofacial muscle activities. These data allow for a 'physiological approach' to treatment, that is, to estimate the severity of each functional component's involvement and to generate hypotheses about the respective mechanism (Netsell and Rosenbek 1985).

In addition to severity and type of the speech and voice deficits, the therapeutic approach must take into account subjects' medical status, including motor disabilities outside the speech domain and concomitant cognitive disorders, the intellectual capabilities and the personal motivation of the patients, their need to communicate as well as the expected course of the underlying disease. Since effective therapy may entail, for example, in the Parkinsonian patients, intensive treatment lasting several hours daily, the ability of the patient to cope with these demands merits consideration.

4. Principles of Management

Four approaches to dysarthria therapy are available: behavioral treatment techniques (drill, exercises), instrumental aids including prosthetic and augmentative devices, medication, and surgical procedures. In the absence of medical or surgical intervention acting upon the underlying disease, 'compensated intelligibility' rather than 'normal speech' must be considered the goal of dysarthria therapy (Rosenbek and LaPointe 1985).

4.1 Behavioral Techniques

The concept of drill is fundamental to behavioral treatment of dysarthrias. Traditional approaches within this domain aim at the formation of response contingencies to stimulus presentation in order to establish new skills, compensation strategies, or adjustments (Kearns and Simmons 1990). Drill activities require multiple productions of the target by the client in response to stimulus presentation (Roth and Worthington 1996). Since speech production depends upon complex motor behavior, procedures of cognitive learning such as explanation or modeling seem to be less effective than intense repetitive practice.

In severe dysarthria behavioral treatment begins with exercises on individual components of the speech apparatus or even with nonspeech movements (Rosenbek and LaPointe 1985; Netsell and Rosenbek 1985; Roth and Worthington 1996). As concerns respiration, inefficient use of the breath stream for speech rather than reduced total air volume in the lungs represents the main problem of dysarthrics. The goal of therapy, thus, is to establish controlled expiration. Postural adjustments such as lying supine and/or monitoring the amount of air inhaled as well as the evenness of exhalation may improve respiratory support to speech. The phonatory abnormalities observed in dysarthria may be classified into three patterns of deviant vocal fold movements: hyper- and hypoadduction as well as incoordination. In contrast to hypoadduction of the vocal folds, hyperadduction and incoordination show only limited impact on speech intelligibility and, therefore, as a rule, do not represent primary targets for intervention. As concerns hypoadduction, therapy focuses on efficient laryngeal closure during speech. Training aims, for example, at the improvement of voluntary control of vocal fold abduction/adduction through physical maneuvers that elicit glottal closure such as lifting and pushing. Speaking more slowly and with greater effort, for example, in terms of increased jaw opening, can ameliorate velopharyngeal insufficiency. Nonspeech exercises such as blowing and sucking are not effective in restoring velopharyngeal functions. Articulation drill relies on individualized word lists which improve existing and facilitate lacking motor capabilities. Encouraging the patient to exaggerate intended orofacial gestures can be helpful. Once a patient is able to combine several differentiated sounds, training proceeds to the level of utterances. In order to improve intelligibility, establishment of an optimum speech rate may be necessary ('allowing more time for articulation'). At later stages of treatment or in less impaired individuals, exercises aim at the simultaneous coordinated activity of all functional components, for example, learning to change stress and rhythm.

Besides systematic drill, based on phonetic principles, and rate control, movements of the speech apparatus can be supported by proprioceptive neuromuscular facilitation (Robertson and Thomson 1987). This procedure aims at increasing neuronal excitability by stimulation, for example, icing or brushing, and manipulation, such as pressure, stretch, or resistance.

Ramig and co-workers introduced a therapy program for Parkinson's disease that focuses on vocal loudness (The Lee Silverman Voice Treatment; Ramig et al. 1994, 1995): patients are trained to increase vocal fold adduction in maximum effort tasks and to generalize the effects on louder speech. As a rule,

subjects receive treatment four times a week for 16 individual sessions a month. Besides significant increases of speech intensity and fundamental frequency variability, this approach also achieves sustained improvement of disordered articulation or speech tempo during further follow-up (Dromey et al. 1995).

Recently, the behavioral techniques for the therapy of articulatory disorders have been extended by so-called pragmatic approaches. Rather than articulatory impairment, treatment focuses on the efficacy of verbal communication in various contexts (Kearns and Simmons 1988). Thus, the patient and his relatives are instructed, for example, to alter the communication environment, to modify the length of utterances, to enhance self-monitoring, and to ensure the orientation of a listener to the topic at hand in order to improve communication.

Yorkston and co-workers (1993) proposed an intervention plan for dysarthria in amyotrophic lateral sclerosis which introduces the various therapy procedures dependent upon the stage of the disease. This schedule also provides a general framework for the approach to articulation disorders. At stage 1, characterized by still unimpaired speech production, treatment is, of course, not necessary. A major role of the clinician is, when requested by the patient, to provide information on the disease and its eventual impact on verbal communication. In the case of detectable speech disturbances, which at the cost of more or less effort still allow the intended message to be conveyed (stage 2), facilitating of communication in natural settings may be helpful, for example, minimizing environmental adversity or maximizing the hearing of frequent partners (pragmatic approach). Reduced speech intelligibility (stage 3) requires the use of behavioral modification techniques. For example, patients are encouraged to maintain a slowed speaking rate, to exaggerate articulatory movements, and/or to rely on energy-conserving techniques during verbal communication. Furthermore, instrumental aides or prostheses such as palatal lifts may be beneficial. Individuals suffering from mainly unintelligible natural speech output (stage 4) or from loss of useful speech (stage 5) have to rely on augmentative communication systems such as alphabet supplementation, portable writing devices, computer-based instrumentation, or eye-pointing indication procedures.

Several studies indicate that drugs such as amphetamine, bromocriptine, or piracetam enhance the effects of behavioral therapy in aphasic patients (Huber et al. 1997). It is unsettled so far whether this approach supports the shaping of articulatory skills as well.

4.2 Instrumental Aids and Prostheses

Besides behavioral techniques, a variety of instrumental aids and prostheses are available to the clinician in order to improve intelligibility (see, e.g., the respective chapters in Berry 1983). Biofeedback has been shown to support behavioral exercises. This instrumentation transforms covert physiologic processes of speech production into precisely tuned auditory, visual, or tactile signals (Nemec and Cohen 1984). On these grounds, the patients are enabled to focus on key elements of their speech difficulty by means of continuous comparison of actual performance with a given target (Netsell and Daniel 1979).

Besides biofeedback procedures, a variety of other instrumental aids as well as specific prostheses have been proven valuable for dysarthria therapy. Accelerated speech tempo as observed, for example, in Parkinson's disease can impair the intelligibility of speech utterances. Boards segmented into several sections by raised dividers (*pacing boards*) may help patients to better control their speech rate (Lang and Fishbein 1983). The patient moves a finger along the board and produces one syllable per segment. As a less inconvenient alternative, *delayed auditory feedback* can be used to reduce speech tempo. A microphone positioned near the patient's mouth receives the emitted speech signals and delivers them with a selected delay to his or her ears (Adams 1997).

Lowered voice volume represents a significant problem especially in Parkinsonian patients. In most healthy individuals masking noise produces a consistent increase in loudness during speech (*Lombard effect*). Patients with Parkinson's disease show marked improvement of vocal intensity under these conditions as well (Adams and Lang 1992). As an alternative, *voice amplifiers* have been proposed (Darley et al. 1975).

Velopharyngeal incompetency, that is, reduced or missing elevation of the velum giving rise to inadequate nasal emission, may significantly impair intelligibility of speech utterances due to, for example, decreased intraoral pressure. Dental prostheses such as *palatal lifts* may improve this condition (Johns 1985). Patients with velopharyngeal insufficiency due to lesions of the upper as well as the lower motor neuron or even myasthenia gravis have been reported to benefit from application of these devices.

Involuntary movements of orofacial structures may interfere with speech production. Immobilization of the mandible by means of an *occlusal splint* or *bite raiser* can be helpful for these patients (Netsell 1985).

Nonverbal systems of communication have to be considered in patients with persistent anarthria or unintelligible speech if improvement of articulatory or phonatory functions cannot be expected. Patients with sufficient motor capabilities of at least one hand may use a typewriter. In cases of insufficient manual control, presentation of pictures, words, or letters by means of boards or electronic devices represents an alternative. Dependent upon residual motor functions

an adequate 'indicating mode' has to be selected (Silverman 1983). Patients able to point with a finger or a headstick or to activate a series of switches can indicate by themselves message components displayed on a board or screen ('direct-selection strategy'). More disabled patients transmit information by signaling 'yes' or 'no' in response to pictural or verbal material presented by another person ('scanning strategy').

4.3 Medication

Some medical conditions giving rise to articulatory disorders are susceptible to pharmacological intervention, for example, myasthenia gravis and multiple sclerosis. Under these conditions, therapy may allow to reinstate 'normal speech.' As concerns Parkinsonian dysarthria, the therapeutic efficacy of dopaminergic drugs has been questioned (Clough 1991). Conceivably, L-DOPA and dopamine agonists exert a differential influence on the various speech and voice deficits in this disease. Moreover, essential voice tremor seems to be less susceptible to drug therapy than essential tremor of the hands (Koller et al. 1985).

Injection of botulinum toxin into the laryngeal muscles has been shown to significantly reduce the symptoms of spasmodic dysphonia. This procedure either aims at unilateral paralysis of the vocal folds or slight bilateral paresis (see Ackermann and Wiles 1996 for references; see *Disorders of Voice*). Application of botulinum toxin, thus, must be restricted to spasmodic dysphonia with hyperadduction of the folds.

4.4 Surgery

Rarely, for example in the case of nasopharyngeal tumors, does surgical intervention target the underlying disease process of disorders of articulation. Unilateral section of the recurrent laryngeal nerve represents an alternative to botulinum toxin injection in patients with spasmodic dysphonia (Dedo and Behlau 1991). The reported numbers of successfully treated patients in terms of effective conversational voices extend from about 30 to 80 percent. Recurring spasticity can be corrected by laser thinning of the paralyzed vocal fold via direct laryngoscopy (see Ackermann and Wiles 1996 for references; see *Disorders of Voice*).

Pharyngeal flaps connect tissue from the posterior pharyngeal wall with the soft palate in order to improve velopharyngeal closure during speech. This surgical procedure is recommended for patients with velopharyngeal incompetence in case of unsuccessful behavioral therapy or palatal lift prostheses, given that the lateral pharyngeal wall shows an adequate degree of motility. Injection of teflon or similar materials into the posterior pharyngeal walls, producing an anteriorly projecting bulge, provides an alternative in this regard (Darley et al. 1975). Usually, these interventions do not allow the restoration of 'normal speech.'

5. Evaluation of Treatment Efficacy (Behavioral Techniques, Instrumental Aids)

So far, the effectiveness of dysarthria therapy most widely has been evaluated in Parkinson patients (Enderby and Emerson 1995). The first investigations during the 1960s and 1970s failed to document carryover or maintenance of treatment-related changes during follow-up once intervention had been discontinued. Therefore, transfer to daily life is considered a significant problem of behavioral treatment in this disease (Comella et al. 1994). As concerns the domain of speech and voice functions, recent studies, however, documented treatment effects lasting for up to 1 year, the longest period of follow-up so far, in mild to moderate Parkinson patients receiving intensive daily therapy for 2 to 4 weeks (Robertson and Thomson 1987; Ramig 1998).

A number of single- and multiple-case studies demonstrated improved intelligibility and enhanced speech motor functions following adjustment of instrumental aids such as a palatal lift or delayed auditory feedback (see, e.g., the respective chapters in Berry 1983). Since these procedures may pose considerable demands on compliance and co-operation, patients must be carefully selected in order to achieve long-term treatment effects.

At least during the first months after brain damage of sudden onset, spontaneous recovery of neurological impairments can be expected to some extent. It is difficult, therefore, to estimate the contribution of eventual therapy on any observed improvement during this period. However, various case studies documented beneficial effects of speech exercises concomitant with instrumental aids even long after the recognized period of spontaneous recovery in subjects with cerebrovascular accident (e.g., Simpson et al. 1988) or closed head injury (e.g., Workinger and Netsell 1992). It must be, thus, recognized that behavioral treatment supported by instrumental aids enables dysarthric patients to speak more intelligibly.

Bibliography

Ackermann H, Hertrich I 1993 Dysarthria in Friedreich's ataxia: Timing of speech segments. *Clinical Linguistics and Phonetics* 7: 75–91.

Ackermann H, Wiles C M 1996 Dysarthria and dysphonia. In: Brandt T, Caplan L R, Dichgans J, Diener H C, Kennard C (eds.) *Neurological Disorders: Course and Treatment*. Academic Press, San Diego, CA: 193–6

Ackermann H, Hertrich I, Daum I, Scharf G, Spieker S 1997 Kinematic analysis of articulatory movements in central motor disorders. *Movement Disorders* 12: 1019–27

Adams R D, Victor M 1989 *Principles of Neurology, 4th ed.* McGraw-Hill, New York

Adams S G 1997 Hypokinetic dysarthria in Parkinson's disease. In: McNeil M R (ed.) *Clinical Management of Sensorimotor Speech Disorders*. Thieme, New York: 261–85

Adams S G, Lang A E 1992 Can the Lombard effect be used to improve low voice intensity in Parkinson's disease? *European Journal of Disorders of Communication* 27: 121–7

Alexander M P, Benson D F, Stuss D T 1989 Frontal lobes and language. *Brain and Language* 37: 656–91

Berry W R (ed.) 1983 *Clinical Dysarthria*. College-Hill, San Diego, CA

Broca P 1861 Remarques sur le siège de la faculté du langage articulé, suivies d'une observation d'aphémie (perte de la parole). *Bulletins de la Société Anatomique de Paris* 36: 330–57

Clough C G 1991 Parkinson's disease: Management. *Lancet* 337: 1324–27

Comella C L, Stebbins G T, Brown-Toms N, Goetz C G 1994 Physical therapy and Parkinson's disease: A controlled clinical trial. *Neurology* 44: 376–8

Darley F L, Aronson A E, Brown J R 1975 *Motor Speech Disorders*. Saunders, Philadelphia, PA

Dedo H H, Behlau M S 1991 Recurrent laryngeal nerve section for spastic dysphonia: 5- to 14-year preliminary results in the first 300 patients. *Annals of Otology, Rhinology and Laryngology* 100: 274–79

Dromey C, Ramig L O, Johnson A B 1995 Phonatory and articulatory changes associated with increased vocal intensity in Parkinson disease: A case study. *Journal of Speech and Hearing Research* 38: 751–64

Dronkers N F 1996 A new brain region for coordinating speech articulation. *Nature* 384: 159–61

Duffy J R, Folger W N 1996 Dysarthria associated with unilateral central nervous system lesions: A retrospective study. *Journal of Medical Speech-Language Pathology* 4: 57–70

Enderby P, Emerson J 1995 *Does Speech and Language Therapy Work: A Review of the Literature*. Whurr, London

Hertrich I, Ackermann H 1993 Dysarthria in Friedreich's ataxia: Syllable intensity and fundamental frequency patterns. *Clinical Linguistics and Phonetics* 7: 177–90

Huber W, Willmes K, Poeck K, Van Vleymen B, Deberdt W 1997 Piracetam as an adjuvant to langauge therapy for aphasia: A randomized double-blind placebo-controlled pilot study. *Archives of Physical Medicine and Rehabilitation* 78: 245–50

Johns D F 1985 Surgical and prosthetic management of neurogenic velopharyngeal incompetency in dysarthria. In: Johns D F (ed.) *Clinical Management of Neurogenic Communicative Disorders*, 2nd ed. Little, Brown & Co, Boston, MA: 153–77

Kearns K P, Simmons N N 1988 Motor speech disorders: The dysarthrias and apraxia of speech. In: Lass N J, McReynolds I V, Northern J L, Yoder D E (eds.) *Handbook of Speech-Language Pathology and Audiology*. Decker, Toronto, 592–621

Kearns K P, Simmons N N 1990 The efficacy of speech-language pathology intervention: Motor speech disorders. *Seminars in Speech and Language* 11: 273–95

Kent R D 1997a *The Speech Sciences*. Singular Press, San Diego, CA

Kent R D 1997b The perceptual sensorimotor examination for motor speech disorders. In: McNeil M R (ed.) *Clinical Management of Sensorimotor Speech Disorders*. Thieme, New York: 27–47

Kim J S, Lee J H, Im J H, Lee M C 1995 Syndromes of pontine base infarction: A clinical-radiological correlation study. *Stroke* 26: 950–5

Kluin K J, Gilman S, Lohman M, Junck L 1996 Characteristics of the dysarthria of multiple system atrophy. *Archives of Neurology* **53**: 545–8

Koller W, Graner D, MlCoch A 1985 Essential voice tremor: Treatment with propranolol. *Neurology* **35**: 106–8

Konczak J, Ackerman H, Hertrich I, Spieker S, Dichgans J 1997 Control of repetitive lip and finger movements in Parkinson's disease: Influence of external timing signals and simultaneous execution on motor performance. *Movement Disorders* **12**: 665–76

Lang A E, Fishbein B 1983 The 'pacing board' in selected speech disorders of Parkinson's disease. *Journal of Neurology, Neurosurgery & Psychiatry* **46**: 789–91

Mao C C, Coull B M, Golper L A C, Rau M T 1989 Anterior operculum syndrome. *Neurology* **39**: 1169–72

Neiman R F, Mountjoy J R, Allen E L 1975 Myasthenia gravis focal to the larynx: Report of a case. *Archives of Otolaryngology* **101**: 569–70

Nemec R E, Cohen K 1984 EMG biofeedback in the modification of hypertonia in spastic dysarthria: Case report. *Archives of Physical Medicine and Rehabilitation* **65**: 103–4

Netsell R 1985 Construction and use of a bite-block for the evaluation and treatment of speech disorders. *Journal of Speech and Hearing Disorders* **50**: 103–6

Netsell R, Daniel B 1979 Dysarthria in adults: Physiologic approach to rehabilitation. *Archives of Physical Medicine and Rehabilitation* **60**: 502–8

Netsell R, Rosenbek J C 1985 Treating the dysarthrias. In: Darby J K (ed.) *Speech and Language Evaluation in Neurology: Adult Disorders*. Grune & Stratton, Orlando, FL: 363–92

Ramig L O 1998 Voice treatment for individuals with Parkinson disease. Paper presented at the 7. Rhein-Ruhr-Meeting, Bochum, Germany, June 5–6, 1998

Ramig L O, Bonitati C M, Lemke J H, Horii Y 1994 Voice treatment for patients with Parkinson disease: Development of an approach and preliminary efficacy data. *Journal of Medical Speech-Language Pathology* **2**: 191–209

Ramig L O, Countryman S, Thompson L L, Horii Y 1995 Comparison of two forms of intensive speech treatment for Parkinson disease. *Journal of Speech and Hearing Research* **38**: 1232–51

Robertson S J, Thomson F 1987 *Working with Dysarthric Clients: A Practical Guide to Therapy for Dysarthria*. Communication Skill Builders, Tucson, AZ

Rosenbek J C, LaPointe L L 1985 The dysarthrias: Description, diagnosis, and treatment. In: Johns D F (ed.) *Clinical Management of Neurogenic Communicative Disorders*, 2nd ed. Little, Brown & Co, Boston, MA: 97–152

Roth F P, Worthington C K 1996 *Treatment Resource Manual for Speech-Language Pathology*. Singular Press, San Diego, CA

Schiff H B, Alexander M P, Naeser M A, Galaburda A M 1983 Aphemia: Clinical-anatomic correlations. *Archives of Neurology* **40**: 720–27

Silverman F H 1983 Dysarthria: Communication-augmentation systems for adults without speech. In: Perkins W H (ed.) *Dysarthria and Apraxia*. Thieme, New York: 115–21 (Current Therapy of Communication Disorders)

Simpson M B, Till J A, Goff A M 1988 Long-term treatment of severe dysarthria: A case study. *Journal of Speech and Hearing Disorders* **53**: 433–40

Sohn Y H, Lee B I, Sunwoo I N, Kim K W, Suh J H 1990 Effect of capsular infarct size on clinical presentation of stroke. *Stroke* **21**: 1258–61

Wertz R T 1985 Neuropathologies of speech and language: An introduction to patient management. In: Johns D F (ed.) *Clinical Management of Neurogenic Communicative Disorders*, 2nd ed. Little, Brown & Co, Boston, MA: 1–96

Wildgruber D, Ackermann H, Klose U, Kardatzki B, Grodd W 1996 Functional lateralization of speech production at primary motor cortex: A fMRI study. *NeuroReport* **7**: 2791–95

Workinger M S, Netsell R 1992 Restoration of intelligible speech 13 years post-head injury. *Brain Injury* **6**: 183–7

Yorkston K M, Strand E, Miller R, Hillel A, Smith K 1993 Speech deterioration in amyotrophic lateral sclerosis: Implications for the timing of intervention. *Journal of Medical Speech-Language Pathology* **1**: 35–46

Ziegler W, von Cramon D 1986 Spastic dysarthria after acquired brain injury: An acoustic study. *British Journal of Disorders of Communication* **21**: 173–87

Verbal Apraxia

J. C. Rosenbek

Verbal apraxia is a speech disorder resulting from brain damage. The person with verbal apraxia has difficulty producing the sounds of a language clearly, with normal rate, and in the proper order. This problem exists despite the person knowing exactly what he or she wants to say. The condition goes by a variety of other names including apraxia of speech (AOS), aphemia, and speech apraxia. Verbal apraxia's history is colorful involving as it does more than 150 years of observation, research, rivalry among different study centers, and harsh words between researchers, including linguists, neurologists, phoneticians, and speech-language pathologists. This history has been elegantly portrayed by Square and Martin (1994) and Lebrun (1989).

Most of this chapter will be spent on modern issues, most of which are being studied and discussed with far less mordancy than in the past. These are: verbal apraxia's evolving definition, the possibility of subtypes, characteristics of the disorder and how these characteristics are to be explained, localization of the brain lesions causing verbal apraxia, and description of current approaches to evaluation and treatment.

1. Verbal Apraxia Defined

Darley's (1969) definition:

> An articulatory disorder resulting from impairment, as a result of brain damage, of the capacity to program the positioning of speech musculature and the sequencing of muscle movements for the volitional production of phonemes. No significant weakness, slowness, or inco-ordination in reflex and automatic acts. Prosodic alterations may be associated with the articulatory problem, perhaps in compensation for it ...

continues with refinements to be the modern definition despite its having appeared originally in an unpublished paper. Three refinements are especially noteworthy. First, verbal apraxia is now considered a speech, rather than merely an articulatory, disorder. Second, sensory has been added to make it a sensory-motor disorder (Wertz et al. 1991). Third, a portion of the prosodic alterations such as slowness, because of their ubiquity in the speech of apraxic speakers, are now considered primary (although see Marquardt et al. 1995) rather than compensatory signs making verbal apraxia a sensory-motor speech and prosodic disorder. Also undergoing refinement is Darley's notion of programming as an explanation for apraxic errors, a topic to which we will return in the section on pathophysiology. Resistent to refinement is Darley's success in differentiating verbal apraxia from aphasia—a language disorder—and dysarthria—a different kind of motor speech disorder resulting primarily from abnormal strength or tone.

2. Types of Verbal Apraxia

In the early days when the term itself was a lightening rod, few were the researchers or clinicians who dared to suggest the possibility of types of verbal apraxia. In these less stormy times it is common to hypothesize that types exist. Of course safety is not the reason so much as is the appearance of new data supporting the notion of types. The bases for at least two cortical and one subcortical type have been established (Square et al. 1982; Kertesz 1984), albeit tenuously. Specifically, distinct patterns of verbal apraxia may result from both frontal and parietal lobe lesions and from involvement of the basal ganglia.

The reality of such types remains controversial, however. It can be posited that some differences among 'types' of verbal apraxia may merely reflect the co-occurrence of apraxia and some other condition such as dysarthria (Square and Martin 1994). Sound distortions as well as substitutions, for example, are identified as kernel features of verbal apraxia resulting from frontal lobe and basal ganglia lesions. Dis-

tortions are also a cardinal feature of dysarthria leading some researchers to speculate that the apraxic person who produces distorted sounds is also dysarthric. It is recognized that similar speech errors such as distortions can occur for different reasons—verbal apraxia and dysarthria being two of these. However, those who believe in parsimony seek a single explanation. For those persons dysarthria as an explanation for sound distortion is the only acceptable answer. Defining a term on the basis of perceptual phenomena such as sound distortion makes such conflicts over interpretation inevitable.

For the reality of apraxic subtypes to be established three conditions will need to be met. The first is identification of distinctly different error patterns in large groups of subjects. The second is to establish a different site of lesion or damage for each group, and the third is to establish different pathophysiologic explanations for the different types. These conditions have been met for the dysarthrias and time will tell if it is possible for verbal apraxia.

2.1 Oral and Limb Apraxia

The relationship of verbal apraxia to oral, nonverbal apraxia (ONVA) or to limb apraxia (LA) is now seldom debated at least among speech scientists in the Americas. The inability to move facial, lingual, and laryngeal structures on command as in sticking out the tongue or puckering the lips which improves but remains abnormal upon demonstration is one popular definition of ONVA. The same differences between requested and imitative movements of the limbs as in saluting or waving serve to define LA. Either condition, and especially ONVA, may co-exist with verbal apraxia but can be seen separately and may be present in a variety of aphasic syndromes from which verbal apraxia is absent. These dissociations support the hypothesis that speech and nonverbal oral and limb movements are organized differently in the nervous system. Clinically, the presence of an ONVA may contribute to more confident speech diagnosis but its presence does not guarantee the co-occurrence of verbal apraxia nor its absence the absence of verbal apraxia. As a result, the study of both ONVA and LA is often specialized and independent of speech research. See Square-Storer and Roy (1989) for a thorough discussion.

3. Signs of Verbal Apraxia

Signs of verbal apraxia were originally identified primarily by auditory perceptual analysis, usually in the form of broad phonetic transcription in which the main features of the speech signal are identified after careful listening and coded with a standard system of written symbols. An even earlier approach was merely to report impressions about the errors without worrying about their exact transcription. Just listening was the way Darley did it, and his earliest descriptions were a distillation of his having evaluated innumerable patients. As a summary of what he had heard, he highlighted 'phonemic' sound substitutions, variability, and trial and error groping. These characteristics supplemented by others were what Darley and the legion following in his wake listened for and when they heard this pattern they said a person was verbally apraxic. And then the trouble began. Phonemic substitutions did not seem to differentiate the apraxic speaker from the aphasic one, and a group primarily of linguists, argued that verbal apraxia was not a distinct entity but was instead merely a form of aphasia in which phonemic errors rather than semantic or syntactic ones predominated. A generation of researchers spent most of their time collecting data to defend one or the other position—verbal apraxia was a nonaphasic syndrome or it wasn't.

Narrow phonetic transcription in which errors of both speech sounds and prosodic features are more discriminatingly specified appeared in the 1980s and helped to resolve the issue. Broad phonetic transcription identified substitutions as the most frequent error type. Narrow phonetic transcription suggests distortions are the most frequent error type. The findings of two studies can be cited as typical. Square et al. (1982) analyzed the phonetic and initiation/transitionalization errors made by four apraxic speakers and reported that distortions of both consonants and vowels are more frequent than substitutions. Odell et al. (1990) completed narrow phonetic transcriptions of four 'pure' apraxic speakers. Distortions were the most frequent error type (25 percent), followed by omissions, substitutions, distorted substitutions, and additions. Abnormal prolongations accounted for 66 percent of the distortion errors. Odell and her colleagues concluded that distortions should be included among the core features of AOS.

Narrow phonetic transcription has further enriched the portrait of AOS by revealing some of the prosodic abnormalities as well. Odell et al. (1991) identified three prosodic abnormalities in those same four apraxic talkers. These were: syllabic stress errors as when the stress is misplaced in a multi-syllable word, difficulties in making the transition from one sound to another, and difficulty in initiating speech. Especially the last two of these features have been informally confirmed by generations of clinicians charged with treating apraxic speakers. Apraxic speakers are slow and give the appearance of having to move cautiously and with great effort from one sound to another. They also have difficulty moving from silence to speech, giving rise to Darley's original characterization of their trial and error groping. In addition, they seem to recognize this difficulty, and to be confident—even when there is scant objective reason for the confidence—that they can speak correctly if they just continue trying.

The final feature that fleshes out the portrait of

verbal apraxia and one confirmed in research and clinical practice is variability. Unless they are very severe or very mild, apraxic speakers do not necessarily do the same thing each time they try to produce an utterance. They may produce an utterance correctly one time and then make a different set of errors on each subsequent attempt at the same utterance. They are more variable than dysarthric speakers with the possible exception of those with ataxia to whom they bear at least a superficial resemblance and they are more variable than patients with conduction aphasia (Seddoh et al. 1996) with whom they are sometimes confused.

4. Localization of Verbal Apraxia

Verbal apraxia in its pure form results from infarction to areas served by small or branch vessels. A lesion in the distribution of the opercular branch of the superior division of the middle cerebral artery may produce an isolated verbal apraxia as may a small lesion in the parietal lobe (Square-Storer and Apeldoorn 1991), perhaps in the mid parietal lobe or even the operculum. In addition Square-Storer and Apeldoorn (1991) are among those to identify verbal apraxia after basal ganglia lesions, perhaps principally involving the putamen and caudate, lesions which also result from what is called small vessel disease. The interested reader should study Square and Martin's excellent chapter (1994) on motor control for further information. More recently, the precentral gyrus of the insula has been identified by Dronkers (1996) as a site whose injury may result in verbal apraxia.

The matter of localization is not settled but the possibility of multiple sites important to skilled speech movements and hence that verbal apraxia can result from different lesion locations is predicted from modern theories positing that widely distribution regions of nervous system are integrated for the performance of a variety of motor, linguistic, and cognitive functions. Indeed, Square and Martin (1994) end their summary of neural control of motor performance with the observation that 'motor subsystems are functionally heterogeneous (distinct) and organized in parallel' (p. 481). If true, it is conceivable that different lesions sites will produce one or more apraxic syndromes. Much work remains to be done if this hypothesis is to be confirmed.

5. Pathophysiology

Speech praxis is normal speech movement and is the responsibility of what might be called a psychomotor level of motor control (Darley et al. 1975). In a hierarchical organization of the processes critical to normal verbal expression, the psychomotor level resides between the executive and language processing levels. For Darley et al. (1975) what happens at the psychomotor level is what they call the programming of speech movements. Programming, in turn, can be defined as the selection and ordering of movement sequences necessary to normal speech. Damage to the neural substrates critical to programming of speech movements leads to the perceptual signs previously described. Before and after Darley et al. (1975), other explanations for verbal apraxia have been posited. Buckingham (1979) reviewed several of these earlier notions including one that hypothesizes faculties, for example, the 'faculty of articulate language' that reside in certain centers of the nervous system such as area 44 in the frontal lobes. Damage to the faculty of articulate language would produce verbal apraxia. More recent explanations for the condition are based in modern theories of motor control, most of which emphasize the interaction of cognitive, linguistic, sensory, and motoric processes (see McNeil and Kent 1990, for a review).

Whether such theories provide more explicit explanations of the pathophysiology of verbal apraxia than did the original idea of 'programming' warrants continued debate. That they have spurred nearly two generations of instrumental assessments and physiologic (primarily) explanations for the perceptual symptomatology, however, is sure. McNeil and Adams (1991), for example, employed a kinematic measurement approach in comparing lip and jaw movements in groups of normal geriatric, ataxic dysarthric, conduction aphasic, and apraxic speakers. Findings for the apraxic speakers including longer segmental (sound) durations were interpreted as supporting the hypothesis of 'motor control deficits' (p. 290) for the apraxic speakers. Acoustic analysis is the most frequent instrumental approach to understanding verbal apraxia and the consistent and inconsistent findings from a substantial body of work have been summarized by Wambaugh et al. (1996a). Typical of acoustic research is that of Rogers (1997) into the relative durations of vowels preceding voiceless and voiced stop consonants as produced by apraxic speakers. His findings are interpreted as ruling out attempted compensation, co-existing language impairment, or secondary effect of slowed speaking rate as explanations for the errors. Instead, Rogers interprets the data as contributing to the general notion that apraxic speakers have difficulty with relational timing among articulators or in realizing contrastive rules as in the relative duration of vowels preceding voiced and voiceless final—position stop-plosives. Impaired relational timing across the articulators is an apt explanation for the movement abnormalities identified by Ziegler and von Cramon (1986) and by Itoh et al. (1980).

Impaired relational timing or dysco-ordination, slowness, and variability are the trenchant movement abnormalities that define verbal apraxia at the physiologic level. Most researchers agree such abnormalities are more comfortably explained as motoric than linguistic. Whether these terms are more useful

than Darley's programming is probably mostly a matter of taste. Weismer and Liss (1991) may have the right idea. They argue that attributing errors to language dysfunction, motor impairment, or something else is less important than identifying the influences on apraxic performance. That brings this chapter to treatment after a brief discussion of evaluation.

6. Evaluation

Verbal apraxia is unlike high blood pressure or diabetes in that no measurement establishes its presence. Instead the examiner must elicit and interpret a variety of speech-language responses from each speaker. That interpretation, of course, cannot be idiosyncratic and instead is based on the data specifying how apraxic speakers perform. Because the profile of verbal apraxia continues to evolve and to be debated, the savvy practitioner is careful to see evaluation as the process of creating hypotheses about the presence of the condition and of assigning relative levels of confidence to each hypothesis in turn.

6.1 Language Testing

Verbal apraxia is not aphasia but can co-exist with this condition and is to be separated from it for reasons of localization and management. Therefore a critical component of any evaluation is language testing to rule out the presence of an aphasia that might explain the verbal expressive abnormalities of a brain-damaged person. The goal is to establish the speaker's language competence and performance in auditory and reading comprehension, writing, and naming. To the degree that a person's verbal expressive deficit is accompanied by normal or near normal comprehension, writing, and naming the hypothesis of a motor speech problem—either an apraxia or a dysarthria—is supported.

The complication comes when language performance is not normal. In that condition the diagnostician is left to make judgments about the relative amount of deficit across all language modalities as compared to the speaker's verbal expressive problems. Because evaluation is a process of hypothesis creation and testing, the dilemma of a person with impairments across all aspects of speech-language performance—auditory comprehension, reading, writing, and speaking—is not insurmountable. To the degree that auditory comprehension is less impaired than verbal expression, it is to that degree that the hypothesis a person has a motor speech disorder is supported. To add confidence and specificity to the hypothesis the evaluator must test nonverbal and verbal performance more exhaustively.

6.2 Oral Motor, including Speech Performance

A variety of nonspeech and speech tasks will aid the diagnostician in separating verbal apraxia from dysarthria and aphasia. In general apraxic speakers do not have range and strength deficits although some apraxic speakers may have a very mild degree of both unilateral face and tongue weakness. Dysarthric speakers are likely to have a significant amount of both. A speaker with moderate weakness may cause a diagnostic dilemma. The diagnostician must decide if the weakness is sufficient to explain speech differences. That can be a tough call made easier by listening to the error types. Even severe tongue and face weakness does not produce sound substitutions and distorted substitutions. These are apraxic errors. The distribution and type of involvement in the other so-called functional components of the speech mechanism—velopharynx, larynx, and respiratory structures—also aid in the decision making. Apraxic speakers do not have resonance imbalance such as hypernasality unless it existed premorbidly from another—usually developmental—cause although they do have articulatory errors resulting from the mistiming or other inappropriate movement of the velopharynx. Apraxic speakers do not have a dysphonia unless they have a structural abnormality such as a cancer or tissue changes resulting from misuse, tobacco, inhaler use, or gastroesophageal reflux disease. They do make articulatory errors with the larynx, however, as when a voiceless cognate is substituted for a voiced sound in the syllable final position. They do not have inadequate respiratory drive unless they have lung disease from smoking, allergy, or infection. A person with articulatory errors and resonance imbalance, dysphonia, or reduced loudness and loudness control is likely to be dysarthric rather than apraxic, although the two conditions can co-occur.

Imitative productions of words and sentences will help the diagnostician differentiate verbal apraxia from some forms of aphasia and from other influences on connected speech such as cognition, culture, and education. Apraxic speakers have approximately equal difficulty with utterances produced spontaneously and imitatively, although they may do somewhat better in imitation if the clinician does it therapeutically which is to say with maximum cueing. Many aphasic persons have much more difficulty with imitation; this is especially true for those with conduction aphasia, the aphasic syndrome with which verbal apraxia is most often confused. Persons with other explanations for abnormal verbal expression such as dementia often do much better even with simple nontherapeutic imitation.

The hypothesis that a person has verbal apraxia alone (a very rare condition) or as the most prominent part of a mixed disorder such as apraxia plus aphasia, then is strengthened by two outcomes of careful evaluation: (a) the relative amount of difficulty across the various modalities of communication performance; and (b) the type of difficulty. Apraxic speakers have inordinate difficulty with verbal expression that may

improve upon imitation but does not disappear. The difficulty they have is in the form of a mix of substitution, distortion, distorted substitution, omission, and addition errors. Absolute confidence about the diagnosis is seldom possible, especially for those persons with a mix of conditions. To increase one's confidence in the diagnosis, nothing is so powerful as treatment.

7. Treatment for Verbal Apraxia

Treating verbal apraxia is easy to the degree that the apraxia is pure. A co-existing aphasia complicates treatment because the clinician must determine which condition is the greatest barrier to functional verbal expression. If aphasia is, then it must be treated first because at least some language (and cognitive) competence is critical to successful apraxia treatment. Muscles move in response to meanings and not the other way around. Not only is treatment easy with those having a major apraxic component in their verbal expressive deficit, it is also highly likely to be successful. Indeed, the prognosis for improvement is good both with and without treatment. So good is the chance of spontaneous improvement that many purely apraxic patients recover before being identified. There are exceptions, of course. Speakers can remain apraxic for a lifetime even in the absence of aphasia. Most of these, however, are functional talkers.

A chapter's length makes a full discussion of treatment impossible. The approach in this section will be to emphasize treatment principles and demonstrate them with brief examples.

7.1 Principle One

The first principle of treatment is that the speaker must accept a new approach to speaking because the usual (normal) approach will not work or will not work as effectively as something new. The new approach begins with silence during which the utterance to be produced is visualized, rehearsed, or in some other way *planned* before it is uttered. Once initiated the utterance is produced with what might be called closed-loop control which is to say with caution and careful monitoring. This is not to say that the apraxic talker is taught to speak like an automaton; slow, plodding, equal and even stress is unnatural and its intelligibility may be degraded. It is to say that the verbal apraxic cannot talk, at least about anything beyond the highly automatic and social, without concentrating.

7.2 Principle Two

The second principle of treatment is that talking is the best treatment. In other words, the apraxic person needs to practice speaking. Nonverbal movements such as protruding the tongue and puckering the lips are of no use unless the person is absolutely unable to produce any speech sounds or combinations. Only then is work with nonverbal responses justified and even then only those movements that are part of sounds are appropriate for practice. In other words, such activities as trying to move the tongue tip to the nose are inappropriate. Additionally, nonverbal movements must be integrated into speech movements as quickly as possible. If they cannot be—and often they cannot because the brain seems to treat speech and nonspeech gestures differently—the prognosis is not bright.

7.3 Principle Three

The third principle is that merely talking is not therapeutic. If apraxic speakers got better by talking most would not appear in therapy, because talking is something apraxic speakers struggle with as soon as they become aware of the world after the acute stage of the illness causing their brain damage. It is this principle that motivates clinicians to employ the best that is in their art and phonetic and skill-learning sciences on the patient's behalf. Apraxic speakers appear to need structured practice of responses selected according to phonetic and linguistic principles, 'appear' because no clinical trial has yet been completed with them to demonstrate treatment efficacy. Acting on appearances is no shame and the best that can be done in the present environment.

Structured approaches to AOS abound (Square-Storer 1989) and they will not be reviewed here although a brief review of one, the minimal contrast treatment refined by Wambaugh et al. (1996b), can serve as an example for all the others. In this approach the apraxic speaker's errors are analyzed and then pairs of words (sounds and phrases would work as well for more or less severe patients) are practiced first with the patient imitating the clinician. A series of backup cueing steps is also included involving another chance at imitation of the clinician, written cues, integral stimulation, modeling of the utterance with a pause after a prolonged production of the target sound within the word, work on the sound in isolation, and other permutations to help the speaker produce the utterance with a minimum of failure. All the elements of successful cueing are in this package as they are in so many others. In addition, practice materials are drawn from the patient's own pattern of errors and careful attention is given to measuring acquisition and generalization. Linguistic variables such as word frequency and function are not recognized in this program but are by the clinicians who assembled it. To return to the principle: apraxic speakers improve speech performance by systematically practicing logically organized movement sequences under the tutelage of a professional speech-language pathologist.

7.4 Principle Four

Treatment must achieve functional effects. Functional speech is speech that communicates the speaker's intent. Most of what happens between the clinician and apraxic speaker is not functional although some portion of every session is, of course, devoted to talking (or at least communicating) about something in addition to the practice materials and responses. However, the assumption has always been that improved performance on treated stimuli in the clinic makes communication with other persons outside the clinic more likely. Data in support of that assumption are in short supply. An essay on skill learning by Schmidt and Bjork (1996) contains notions that, if true for relearning by apraxic speakers, make it unlikely that such data will ever appear. Schmidt and Bjork argue among other things that quick performance change during treatment may not predict stable performance later and in other environments. Less frequent feedback, systematic response disruptions during treatment, and greater response variability during training are among the suggestions they make for increasing the possibility that a skill will generalize. Interestingly the recent emphasis on high correct response rates in treatment with apraxic speakers and on structuring their treatment according to the guidelines of single case design with the emphasis on frequent measurement of acquisition may mitigate against functional performance of treated responses.

Perhaps it is time for a series of shifts in apraxia treatment. One shift would be toward less success with each motor performance and more success with managing the inevitable disruptions that threaten their speech outside the clinic. Another would be far more emphasis on functional activities conducted outside the clinic suite. Another would be to emphasize the measurement of functional performance first rather than as a consequence of acquisition in the clinic.

8. Summary

Verbal apraxia has had a tumultuous history. It was not easily accommodated by early schemes of central nervous system organization. Its future is secure, however, because modern models of nervous system functioning reserve a place for it atop the sensory motor system. This is fortunate for researchers and clinicians alike. Researchers profit because the condition provides a laboratory for testing theories about the interaction of cognitive, linguistic, and motor systems. Clinicians profit because they have a category for a small, unique group of patients who deserve unique treatment approaches.

Bibliography

Buckingham H W 1979 Explanations in apraxia with consequences for the concept of apraxia of speech. *Brain and Language* **8**: 202–26

Darley F L 1969 unpublished Input and output disturbances in speech and language processing. Paper presented to the American Speech and Hearing Association. Chicago, IL

Darley F L, Aronson A E, Brown J R 1975 Motor Speech Disorders. W B Saunders, Philadelphia, PA

Dronkers N F 1996 A new brain region for coordinating speech articulation. *Nature* **384**: 159–61

Itoh M, Sasanuma S, Hirose H, Yoshika H, Ushijima T 1980 Abnormal articulatory dynamics in a patient with apraxia of speech: X-ray microbeam observation. *Brain and Language* **11**: 66–75

Kertesz A 1984 Subcortical lesions and verbal apraxia: In: Rosenbek J C, McNeil M R, Aronson A E (eds.) *Apraxia of Speech: Physiology-Acoustics-Linguistics-Management.* College-Hill Press, San Diego, CA: 73–90

Lebrun Y 1989 Apraxia of speech: The history of a concept. In: Square-Storer P (ed.) *Acquired Apraxia of Speech in Aphasic Adults.* Taylor & Francis, London, 3–19

Marquardt T P, Duffy G, Cannito M P 1995 Acoustic analysis of accurate word stress patterning in patients with apraxia of speech and Broca's aphasia. *American Journal of Speech-Language Pathology* **4**: 180–85

McNeil M R, Adams S 1991 A comparison of speech kinematics among apraxic, conduction aphasic, ataxic dysarthric, and normal geriatric speakers. In: Prescott T E (ed.) *Clinical Aphasiology, vol 19.* pro-ed, Austin, TX

McNeil M R, Kent R 1990 Motoric characteristics of adult aphasic and apraxic speakers. In: Hammond G R (ed.) *Advances in Psychology: Cerebral Control of Speech and Limb Movements.* Elsevier, New York: 349–86

Odell K, McNeil M R, Rosenbek J C, Hunter L 1990 Perceptual characteristics of consonant productions by apraxic speakers. *Journal of Speech and Hearing Disorders* **55**: 345–59

Odell K, McNeil M R, Rosenbek J C, Hunter L 1991 A perceptual comparison of prosodic features in apraxia of speech and conduction aphasia. In: Prescott T E (ed.) *Clinical Aphasiology, Vol 19.* pro-ed, Austin, TX: 295–306

Rogers M A 1997 The vowel lengthening exaggeration effect in speakers with apraxia of speech: compensation, artifact, or primary deficit? *Aphasiology* **11**: 433–45

Schmidt R A, Bjork R A 1996 New conceptualizations of practice: Common principles in three paradigms suggest new concepts for training. In: Robin D A, Yorkston K M, Beukelman D R (eds.) *Disorders of Motor Speech:* *Assessment, Treatment and Clinical Characterization.* Paul H. Brookes, Baltimore, MD: 3–23

Seddoh S A K, Robin D A, Sim H-S, Hageman C, Moon J B, Folkins J W 1996 Speech timing in apraxia of speech versus conduction aphasia. *Journal of Speech and Hearing Research* **39**: 590–603

Square P A, Darley F L, Sommers R K 1982 An analysis of the productive errors made by pure apraxic speakers with differing loci of lesions. In: Brookshire R H (ed.) *Clinical Aphasiology: Conference Proceedings, 1982.* BRK Publishers, Minneapolis, MN: 245–50

Square P A, Martin R E 1994 The nature and treatment of neuromotor speech disorders in aphasia. In: Chapey R (ed.) *Language Intervention Strategies in Adult Aphasia, 3rd ed.* Williams and Wilkins, Baltimore, MD: 467–499

Square-Storer P 1989 *Acquired Apraxia of Speech in Aphasic Adults.* Taylor & Francis, Philadelphia, PA

Square-Storer P, Apeldoorn S 1991 An acoustic study of apraxia of speech in patients with different lesion loci. In: Moore C, Yorkston K, Beukelman D (eds.) *Dysarthria and Apraxia of Speech: Perspectives on Management.* Paul H. Brookes, Baltimore, MD: 271–88

Square-Storer P, Roy E A 1989 The apraxias: Commonalities and distinctions. In: Square-Storer P (ed.) *Acquired Apraxia of Speech in Aphasic Adults.* Taylor & Francis, Philadelphia, PA: 20–63

Wambaugh J L, Doyle P J, Kalinyak M M, West J E 1996a A critical review of acoustic analyses of aphasic and/or apraxic speech. *Clinical Aphasiology* **24**: 35–63

Wambaugh J L, Doyle P J, Kalinyak M M, West J E 1996b A minimal contrast treatment for apraxia of speech. *Clinical Aphasiology* **24**: 97–108

Weismer G, Liss J M 1991 Acoustic/perceptual taxonomies of speech production deficit in motor speech disorders. In: Moore C A, Yorkston K M, Beukelman D R (eds.) *Dysarthria and Apraxia of Speech: Perspectives on Management.* Paul H. Brookes, Baltimore, MD: 245–70

Wertz R T, LaPointe L L, Rosenbek J C 1991 *Apraxia of Speech in Adults.* Singular Publishing Group, Inc, San Diego, CA

Ziegler W, von Cramon D 1986 Timing deficits in apraxia of speech. *European Archives of Psychiatry and Neurological Sciences* **236**: 44–49

Acquired Language Pathologies

Historical Perspectives of Aphasia

Yvan Lebrun

Brief accounts of speech loss presumably due to damage suffered by the central nervous system can be traced back to the Renaissance, the Middle Ages, and even to antiquity. Yet, it was not until the second half of the nineteenth century that language disorders due to brain injury started to be studied systematically and a specific terminology began to emerge.

1. Aphasia

At a meeting of the French Anthropological Society in April 1861 Paul Broca (1824–80), one of the founding members of the Society and a noted surgeon and scholar, demonstrated the brain of a man who had been unable to speak for the last 21 years of his life. Whatever this man wanted to say, only the syllable *tan*, generally repeated twice in succession, would come from his lips. It was only when he was very angry that he would produce a swearword instead of the meaningless syllable *tan*. At autopsy, Broca found an extensive lesion affecting primarily the anterior part of the left cerebral hemisphere.

At a meeting of the French Anatomical Society a few months later Broca gave a detailed account of the case, and proposed to call *aphemia* the speech loss which the cerebral lesion had caused. He had coined the word using two Greek lexical elements: *a*, which means 'without' or 'deprived of,' and the root of the verb *phemein*, which means 'to speak.'

In a lecture delivered in 1864 at the Parisian hospital *Hôtel-Dieu* where he worked and taught, Armand Trousseau (1801–67), who apparently was somewhat jealous of Broca's growing popularity, took exception to the term *aphemia*, claiming that in Greek the word actually meant 'infamy.' He proposed that speech loss following brain damage should be called *aphasia* instead. The lecture was published in the *Gazette des Hôpitaux Civils et Militaires* (1864) and 1 year later included in Trousseau's *Clinique Médicale de l'Hôtel-Dieu de Paris*, a volume of lectures which went through several editions.

In a witty and well-documented response, also published in the *Gazette des Hôpitaux Civils et Militaires* (1864), Broca defended his coinage, but in vain: *aphasia* soon supplanted *aphemia*, and it was adopted by all Western European languages. With the passing of time, *aphasia* came to be applied not only to speech loss but also to other language impairments following damage suffered by the central nervous system. The word is used nowadays as a generic term to refer to diminished verbal competence consequent upon cerebral injury.

The word *aphemia* has not completely disappeared, though. It is still used to denote a selective loss or disturbance of speech production after brain injury: the patient can no longer utter words (adequately), but has retained all other verbal skills.

As a matter of fact, Broca believed that his patient, whom everybody in the hospital called Tan (his real name was Leborgne), had presented with a selective loss of the ability to produce speech. He considered that Tan's comprehension of spoken language was unimpaired and that, had he not been illiterate, he could have expressed himself in writing. We now know that patients, whose speech production has been reduced to a recurrent utterance, usually have comprehension difficulties and can no longer use written language. Actually, the language impairment which Tan suffered from is a severe form of aphasia. This is why it is often called *la grande aphasie de Broca* in French. In English it is generally referred to as *aphasia with recurrent* (or *recurring*) *utterance*. Another name is *monophasia*.

2. Motor or Broca's Aphasia

In his lectures on aphasia in 1864 at the *Hôtel-Dieu*, Trousseau insisted that speech loss rarely occurred in isolation: usually it was accompanied by agraphia, that is, the loss of writing skills, and there could be alexia, that is, an impairment of reading.

In various papers published between 1861 and 1865, Broca associated speech loss (with or without concomitant agraphia) with anterior cerebral damage, particularly with the posterior part of the third frontal convolution on the left. This brain region is now often referred to as *Broca's area*.

As the frontal lobes were considered to primarily

fulfil motor functions, speech loss consequent upon brain damage came to be called *motor aphasia. Broca's aphasia* was used as a synonym. At present, *motor aphasia* is used to denote a variety of aphasia in which verbal expression, spoken as well as written, is arduous and limited, whilst comprehension of (simple) verbal messages is relatively preserved. *Broca's aphasia* nowadays is used interchangeably with *motor aphasia*, or else refers to a specific form of motor aphasia characterized by sparse and labored oral expression, writing and reading difficulties, and relatively preserved auditory comprehension.

In the nineteenth century, motor aphasia was ascribed to an impairment of the memory of words or to an impairment of the memory of the movements necessary to produce speech. The latter impairment, which was regarded as a selective disorder leaving inner speech, verbal comprehension, and writing unaffected, was often called *pure motor aphasia*. It corresponded to *aphemia* as Broca had originally conceived it.

3. Sensory or Wernicke's Aphasia

In 1874 Max Cohn and Weigert, publishers in Breslau, Germany, brought out a short monograph by Carl Wernicke (1848–1905) entitled *Der aphasische Symptomencomplex*. In this monograph Wernicke, who was at the time assistant physician in the psychiatric department of the city hospital, described a particular type of aphasia which was characterized by a severe disorder of speech comprehension and an inappropriate use of words in conversational as well as in repetitive speech. The comprehension impairment was due neither to deafness nor to dementia, and the patient was not aware of his deviant speech production.

Wernicke ascribed the condition to damage to the superior temporal gyrus, where images of spoken words were supposed to be stored. Because these images were impaired, the patient could no longer decode speech nor choose his or her words appropriately. The use of written language was also disturbed, as reading and writing skills were acquired on the basis of one's command of spoken language. Because images of spoken words resulted from auditory sensations received by the brain, Wernicke called the condition *sensory aphasia*.

Wernicke's description of sensory aphasia was not the first account of the aphasic syndrome. Several physicians had mentioned this type of aphasia prior to the publication of Wernicke's monograph in 1874. Indeed, in 1843, Jacques Lordat (1773–1870), who was professor of medicine at the university of Montpellier, France, had reported on the derangement of language which he had experienced and which was in fact sensory aphasia. And in 1865, in a paper read at the French Academy of Medicine, Jules Baillarger (1806–91) had mentioned a form of aphasia in which speech was not abolished but wrong words were used. Wernicke's is nevertheless the first attempt to delineate the aphasic syndrome and to establish clinical-anatomical correlations. This is why sensory aphasia is often called *Wernicke's aphasia*, and the posterior upper part of the temporal lobe, *Wernicke's area*.

4. Conduction Aphasia

In his 1874 monograph Wernicke contrasted sensory aphasia with a form of aphasia in which inappropriate word choice occurred in the absence of comprehension difficulties. The patient, therefore, was aware of his or her lexical mistakes and attempted to correct them. In this case the patient was *agraphic*, but not *alexic*. Wernicke ascribed this type of aphasia to damage to the insula of Reil, which was assumed to contain the fibres connecting the temporal with the frontal lobe. Because the condition was due to a severance of communication between two language centres, Wernicke spoke of *conduction aphasia*. The name is still used to refer to a particular type of aphasia, but it is considered that the pathophysiology of conduction aphasia is more complicated than Wernicke had presumed.

5. Transcortical Aphasia

In 1885, elaborating on a theoretical typology of aphasia proposed by Ludwig Lichtheim (1845–1928), professor of medicine at the University of Bern, Switzerland, Wernicke introduced the notion of *transcortical aphasia*. According to Wernicke there were two forms of transcortical aphasia. One form resulted from the interruption of the communication between the sensory language centre in the temporal lobe and the centre where concepts were stored. Because both centres were located in the cortex, Wernicke proposed to call this type of aphasia *transcortical sensory aphasia*. The second form of transcortical aphasia was due to a disconnection between the centre of concepts and the motor language centre in the frontal lobe. It could therefore be called *transcortical motor aphasia*.

Nowadays, *transcortical sensory aphasia* applies to a severe form of sensory aphasia: the patient has major comprehension difficulties and the verbal output is often so deviant that it becomes unintelligible. However, oral repetition, and in some cases also oral reading (without comprehension, however), are preserved to a large extent. *Transcortical motor aphasia*, however, refers to a form of aphasia in which oral expression is hampered by a strong tendency to involuntarily repeat one's own words (perseverations) or the speech partner's words (echolalias). Comprehension of (simple) language is preserved, and so is the ability to slavishly repeat words or sentences produced by the examiner. Thus, the feature common to the two forms of trancortical aphasia is the relative intactness of repetitive speech.

6. Crossed Aphasia

In 1836 at a medical congress in Montpellier, France, Marc Dax (1770–1837), a general practitioner in Sommières, a small town in the south-eastern part of France, read a paper to the effect that speech loss resulted from a left-sided cerebral lesion far more frequently than from a right-sided lesion. In 1863, his son Gustave Dax (1815–93), who had succeeded him as a general practitioner in Sommières, sent the French Academy of Medicine a memoir which comprised his father's paper of 1836 as well as cases collected by himself, all of which tended to show that speech loss resulted from left-sided cerebral lesions. From this Gustave Dax concluded that spoken language had its seat in the left half of the brain.

In 1865, Paul Broca, on the basis of cases he had examined or which had been reported by others, came to the same conclusion.

In the last quarter of the nineteenth century it was found that sensory aphasia, agraphia, and alexia were generally due to left-sided lesions, at least in right-handed patients.

From these various observations the notion evolved that the left cerebral hemisphere was *dominant for language* in right-handed people, that is to say, that it played a much more important part in verbal activities than the right hemisphere. Indeed, the latter was deemed 'uneducated in words.' In left-handed people, the opposite was true: the right hemisphere was dominant for language. Thus, language was said to be 'represented' in the left half of the brain in right-handers, and in the right half of the brain in left-handers.

However, in *The Lancet* (1899) Byrom Bramwell (1847–1931), physician to the Royal Infirmary in Edinburgh, Scotland, reported the case of a left-hander who had had aphasia with right-sided hemiplegia. Bramwell reasoned that the patient's motor deficit testified to the presence of left-sided brain damage. This damage must be the cause not only of the paralysis, but also of the language impairment. Presumably the patient's left hemisphere was dominant for language, while obviously his right hemisphere was dominant for manual agility. Bramwell proposed to speak of *crossed aphasia*, when, as a consequence of such physiological decussation, aphasia occurred in a left-hander after exclusive left-sided brain damage.

With the passing of time it was realized that aphasia due to damage confined to the left side of the brain was the rule rather than the exception in left-handers: about 65 percent of all left-handed patients with aphasia following unilateral brain damage proved to have injuries on the left. However, in the group of right-handers with aphasia consequent upon unilateral brain lesions, less than 3 percent had injuries confined to the right hemisphere. Nowadays, the phrase, *crossed aphasia* is used exclusively to refer to the rare cases of aphasia resulting from right-sided cerebral damage in right-handed people.

7. Anarthria

In 1906 Pierre Marie (1853–1940), a French neurologist, published in *La Semaine Médicale* a series of three papers which created a commotion. In these papers, Marie opposed Broca's view that the third frontal convolution played an important part in the production of speech. He further denied that there existed in the brain auditory or motor images of words. He also claimed that there was only one aphasic syndrome, namely Wernicke's aphasia. Broca's aphasia was simply a combination of Wernicke's aphasia with anarthria. However, Marie never succeeded in clearly specifying the nature of anarthria. Nowadays, the word *anarthria* is still occasionally used either as a synonym of *aphemia* or as a synonym of *speech apraxia*. The latter denotes a particular disorder of motor speech. The patient with apraxia of speech finds it difficult to produce speech in an easy, fluent, and correct way. Delivery is slow, protracted, and disorderly. The patient often cannot utter the constituent phonemes adequately or in the proper sequence.

8. Agrammatism and Paragrammatism

A few years after the publication of Wernicke's monograph *Der aphasische Symptomencomplex*, Adolf Kussmaul (1822–1902) in a book entitled *Die Störungen der Sprache* (1877) pointed out that the verbal output of aphasics, in addition to containing wrong words, may infringe grammatical rules. This grammatical disorder was called *agrammatism*. In 1913 Arnold Pick (1851–1924), who was professor of neuropsychiatry at the German University in Prague, distinguished two forms of agrammatism, one characterized by the absence of function words and the paratactic use of uninflected content words, and the other by grammatical and syntactical errors. A little later, Karl Kleist (1879–1960) proposed to call the former *agrammatism* and the latter *paragrammatism*. Agrammatism was observed primarily in patients with Broca's aphasia, whilst paragrammatism was typical of Wernicke's aphasia. Due to the absence of function words and inflectional marks, the verbal output of Broca's aphasics was said to resemble telegraphic style.

Later on, a distinction was made between *expressive* and *receptive* agrammatism. The former name refers to the absence of grammatical morphemes and syntactical structures, while the latter denotes an impairment of comprehension of grammatical and syntactical cues. The pathophysiology of expressive and receptive agrammatism is still a matter of controversy.

Bibliography

Code C, Wallesh C, Joanette Y, Lecours A (eds.) 1996 *Classic Cases in Neuropsychology*. Psychology Press, Hove

Eggert G 1977 *Wernicke's Works on Aphasia*. Mouton, The Hague

Eling P (ed.) 1994 *Reader in the History of Aphasia*. Benjamins, Amsterdam

Hécaen H, Dubois J 1969 *La naissance de la neuropsychologie du langage*. Flammarion, Paris

Neurolinguistics

J. C. Marshall and J. M. Gurd

The expression 'neurolinguistics' has come to be used in connection with almost any study that refers to the involvement of the central or peripheral nervous system in language capacity or skill. Since all cognition is dependent upon the material substrate of the brain and its attendant sense organs, this vapid employment has little to recommend it.

A more reasonable usage accordingly restricts the term to studies in which language disorders (the aphasias; see *Developmental Causes*; *Acquired Causes*), either acquired or developmental, are described from the standpoint of a more or less explicit theory of linguistic form (Caplan 1987). Linguists may well find it inconceivable that one could avoid linguistics in any discussion of language disorder, but the history (and often the current practice) of aphasiology shows, sadly, that they are wrong. Paradis (1983) is an important sourcebook of early attempts to explain the patterns of aphasia in bilingual and polyglot patients. Even in these cases the level of linguistic knowledge deployed in their analysis is not high.

Nonetheless, linguistic inquiry has always exerted some influence. The German grammatical tradition that began with von Humboldt and culminated in ferocious clashes between Paul, Wundt, and Marty (Blumenthal 1970) sensitized neurologists to differing ways of describing disorders of phonology, morphology, and syntax after brain damage. The principal source of influence was Steinthal, von Humboldt's sole student, whose work is frequently cited in Kussmaul's seminal book on language disorder (Kussmaul 1885).

Under the label '*Akataphasia*,' Steinthal (1871) gave the first account of one form of what was later to be called 'agrammatism' (Pick 1913). One of the original group of neogrammarians, Delbruck (1886) distinguished different varieties of paraphasia (semantic and phonological substitutions) in a paper that was crucial to the development of Freud's early work on language disorders. In his monograph on aphasia (1891), Freud also drew attention to similarities between normal 'tips of the slung' and aphasic speech

errors, a topic that continues to intrigue linguists (Talo 1980). The best review of the German aphasiological tradition is De Bleser (1987).

Apart from occasional references to Saussure, French aphasiology paid little attention to linguistics until the 1970s. One striking exception is Alajouanine et al. (1939), the first serious monograph to document the phonetics and phonology of aphasic speech prior to Blumstein (1973). Later the work of Martinet (1967) greatly influenced the vocabulary of neurolinguistics in French-speaking countries (Tissot et al. 1973, Lecours et al. 1979).

The structuralism of the Prague school (founded by Baudouin de Courtenay and Trubetzkoy) played a vital role in the inception of Soviet neurolinguistics. The influence was mediated primarily by the friendship between Jakobson and Luria, who first met in Berlin in 1925. Jakobson's firm emphasis upon 'aphasia as a linguistic problem' ensured that Soviet studies (Luria 1970) were informed by a degree of phonological (Jakobson 1968) and syntactic (Jakobson 1956) sophistication that did not always obtain in the West. Even Stalin's status as a linguistic expert did not (quite) suffice to destroy Soviet expertise in aphasiology (Stalin 1950).

Modern neurolinguistics is largely dominated by concepts drawn from generative grammar (Chomsky 1965, Kean 1978). Although the initial links made between the two domains were somewhat loose (Marshall and Newcombe 1966, Weigl and Bierwisch 1970, Whitaker 1971), advances in government and binding theory (Chomsky 1981) have proved a fertile source of specific hypotheses about the nature of syntactic comprehension disorders in aphasia (Caplan and Hildebrandt 1988, Grodzinsky 1990, Druks and Marshall 1991). Investigations of sign language aphasias illustrate well how discoveries about the normal structure of a linguistic system and its inherent patterns of breakdown can proceed hand-in-hand (Poizner 1987).

The study of developmental language disorders is likewise better informed by explicit linguistic characterizations that make precise reference to the ontogeny of normal language growth (Clahsen 1991, Leonard 1998, Gopnik 1997). The artificial barriers between linguistics, psychology, and the biological sciences, so long derided by Chomsky (1978), are at last starting to come down.

Bibliography

Alajouanine T, Ombredane A, Durand M 1939 *Le Syndrome de Désintégration Phonétique dans l'Aphasie*. Masson, Paris

Blumenthal A 1970 *Language and Psychology: Historical Aspects of Psycholinguistics*. Wiley, New York

Blumstein S 1973 *A Phonological Investigation of Aphasic Speech*. Mouton, The Hague

Caplan D 1987 *Neurolinguistics and Linguistic Aphasiology: An Introduction*. Cambridge University Press, Cambridge

Caplan D, Hildebrandt N 1988 *Disorders of Syntactic Comprehension*. MIT Press, Cambridge, MA

Chomsky N 1965 *Aspects of the Theory of Syntax*. MIT Press, Cambridge, MA

Chomsky N 1978 On the biological basis of language capacities. In: Miller G A, Lenneberg E (eds.) *Psychology and Biology of Language and Thought*. Academic Press, New York

Chomsky N 1981 *Lectures on Government and Binding*. Foris, Dordrecht

Clahsen H 1991 (transl. Richman K) *Child Language and Developmental Dysphasia*. Benjamins, Amsterdam

De Bleser R 1987 From agrammatism to paragrammatism: German aphasio-logical traditions and grammatical disturbances. *Cognitive Neuropsychology* **4**: 187–256

Delbruck B 1886 Amnestische Aphasie. *Jenaische Zeitschrift für Naturwissenschaft* **20**: 91–8

Druks J, Marshall J C 1991 Agrammatism: An analysis and critique, with new evidence from four Hebrew speaking aphasic patients. *Cognitive Neuropsychology* **8**: 415–33

Freud S 1953 *On Aphasia*. International Universities Press, New York

Gopnik M 1997 *The Inheritance and Innateness of Grammar*. Oxford University Press, New York

Grodzinsky Y 1990 *Theoretical Perspectives on Language Deficits*. MIT Press, Cambridge, MA

Jakobson R 1956 Two aspects of language and two types of aphasic disturbance. In: Jakobson R, Halle M *Fundamentals of Language*. Mouton, The Hague

Jakobson R 1968 *Child Language, Aphasia and Phonological Universals*. Mouton, The Hague

Kean M-L 1978 The linguistic interpretation of aphasic syndromes. In: Walker E (ed.) *Explorations in the Biology of Language*. MIT Press, Cambridge, MA

Kussmaul A 1885 *Die Störungen der Sprache*. Vogel, Leipzig

Lecours A R, Lhermitte F, Bryans B 1979 *Aphasiology*. Baillière Tindall, London

Leonard L 1998 *Children with Specific Language Impairment*. MIT Press, Cambridge, MA

Luria A 1970 *Traumatic Aphasia*. Mouton, The Hague

Marshall J C, Newcombe F 1966 Syntactic and semantic error in paralexia. *Neuropsychologia* **4**: 169–76

Martinet A 1967 *Eléments de linguistique générale*. Colin, Paris

Paradis M (ed.) 1983 *Readings on Aphasia in Bilinguals and Polyglots*. Didier, Montreal

Pick A 1913 *Die agrammatischen Sprachstörungen*. Springer, Berlin

Poizner H, Klima E S, Bellugi U 1987 *What the Hands Reveal about the Brain*. MIT Press, Cambridge, MA

Stalin J 1950 *Marxism and Problems of Linguistics*. Foreign Languages Publishing House, Moscow

Steinthal C 1871 *Einleitung in die Psychologie und Sprachwissenschaft*. Dummler, Berlin

Talo E S 1980 Slips of the tongue in normal and pathological speech. In: Fromkin V A (ed.) *Errors in Linguistic Performance: Slips of the Tongue, Ear, Pen, and Hand*. Academic Press, New York

Tissot R, Mounin G, Lhermitte F 1973 *L'Agrammatisme*. Dessart, Brussels

Weigl E, Bierwisch M 1970 Neuropsychology and linguistics: Topics of common research. *Foundations of Language* **6**: 1–18

Whitaker H A 1971 *On the Representation of Language in the Human Brain*. Linguistic Research, Edmonton

Language and the Brain

J. M. Gurd and J. C. Marshall

Although the study of language and the brain has a long 'prehistory,' modern concern with the topic is usually held to begin with Paul Broca's observation that there is a reliable association between (relatively) focal damage to left frontal cortex and severe dysfluency in spontaneous and repetitive speech (Broca 1865). He accordingly argued that, in adults, one aspect of the language faculty was typically 'localized' in the third frontal convolution of the left hemisphere of the brain. Broca coined the motto 'One speaks with the left hemisphere,' and he held that the clinico–anatomical correlation he observed enabled one to localize 'The memory of the procedure that is employed to articulate language.' The phrasing is important in that Broca sought thereby to distinguish a purely motoric impairment of the speech organs (dysarthria) from more 'central' disorder of language *per se* (aphasia).

1. Brain–Language Relationships and the Aphasias

The early (modern) history of brain/language relationships is accordingly the study of how different types of language impairment (the 'aphasias'; see *Aphasia*; *Syndromes of Aphasia*) are correlated with injury to different loci within the brain. Until the advent of *in vivo* neuroradiology (such as Computerized Axial Tomography (CT) or Magnetic Resonance Imaging (MRI)), the demonstration of the locus of pathology was dependent upon histology at autopsy.

'Aphasia' refers then to the loss or impairment of language skills consequent upon acquired brain damage. Since the loss is rarely if ever total, British and European (but not North American) writers often employ the term 'dysphasia.' Nothing of consequence follows, although users of computerized search-facilities should be aware that 'dysphasia' in the USA may refer to a congenital or developmental impairment of language. Without further qualification, 'aphasia' is a diagnostic label applied to adult patients whose linguistic development and mature skill was within normal limits prior to the brain lesion (or lesions) that provoked the language disorder. Such brain injury can, of course, be sustained at any age, but the interpretation of postnatal damage to a *developing* system is fraught with difficulties that make the acquired aphasias of childhood a topic unto itself (see *Acquired Childhood Aphasia*). Nonetheless, the term 'aphasia' carries no intrinsic reference to the *nature* of the brain damage that is its proximate cause. Relatively isolated disorder of language can be provoked by such distinct pathologies as cerebro-vascular accident (stroke), space-occupying lesion (neoplasm), penetrating missile injury, and closed-head injury. Language impairment can also be seen (although usually in conjunction with other disorders of cognitive functioning) after central nervous system infections (*herpes simplex encephalitis*, for example), in multiple sclerosis, in Parkinson's disease, and in such degenerative 'dementing' illnesses as Alzheimer's disease and Pick's disease.

Similarly, the term 'aphasia' carries no intrinsic reference to the *locus* of the responsible brain damage. Nonetheless, in the vast majority of right-handed individuals (and a clear majority of left-handers), the left hemisphere is the neuronal substrate for core language skills. The most compelling evidence for this claim continues to come from the differential incidence of acquired aphasias consequent upon unilateral lesions of the left and the right cerebral hemispheres in adults. So called 'crossed aphasias,' where a right-hemisphere lesion provokes frank disorder of language in right-handed patients can be seen in clinical practice, but are extremely rare (Coppens and Hungerford 1998). Within the left hemisphere, it is lesions of the perisylvian region that are most typically associated with aphasic symptomatology, lesions, that is, centered upon the frontal convolutions (Broca's aphasia), upon the superior temporal gyrus (Wernicke's aphasia), and the arcuate fasciculus (Conduction aphasia); lesions within restricted temporal, parietal, and frontal borderzones of the perisylvian region may be associated with transcortical sensory and transcortical motor aphasias. Language disorders have also been reported consequent upon damage to the left supplementary motor area (Jonas, 1981) and a number of subcortical structures, including the left thalamus and putamen, and the left basal ganglia and internal capsule. The extent to which subcortical structures are *directly* implicated in language processing remains controversial; while it is possible that lesions to these areas exert remote effects upon language-committed cortex (Nadeau and Crosson, 1997; Wallesch 1997), there is little doubt that such subcortical regions participate in the cortical circuits essential to language. The linguistic impairments that follow brain damage to these varied left hemisphere sites include peturbation of segmental phonology, morphology, syntax, semantics and lexical structure or functions.

The study of patients with lesions to the *right* hemisphere has shown that this hemisphere is involved in the processing of the pragmatic aspects of verbal communication (see Paradis 1998). There is also converging evidence from many sources that lexical semantics is at least partially represented in the right hemisphere, although the left hemisphere lexicon contains a more detailed representation of word-meanings (Code 1987).

In short, the traditional enterprise of seeking correlations between aphasic syndromes and their responsible gross lesion sites has proved remarkably successful, although there are admittedly many anomalies and mysteries when one considers a finer grain of analysis and even worse problems when one moves from symptom localization to function localization (Caplan 1981).

2. Neuronal Architecture

In terms of discovering a specialized neuronal architecture that subserves the language faculty, it is encouraging to find that the architectonic structure of the human cortex appears to map reasonably well on to many of the classical speech and language areas postulated in clinical neurology. The microscopic neuronal structure of cortex differs considerably from area to area, from layer to layer, and in terms of the pattern of connectivity between different regions. Thus Braak (1980) reports that lesion studies of Broca's aphasia 'are in concert with the location and expansion of the inferofrontal region'; likewise, the histologically distinct superofrontal magnopyramidal region contains the supplementary motor area, which lesion studies implicate in the control of speech; and the temporal magnopyramidal region, uniquely endowed 'with specialized pyramids which elsewhere do not occur in the temporal lobe' forms a crucial part of Wernicke's area (Braak 1980).

Furthermore, there are strong lateral asymmetries in the size of both the temporal speech region and the anterior speech region in the majority of normal, right-handed individuals; there is some *prima facie* evidence that these anatomic asymmetries, favoring the left hemisphere, are correlated with cerebral dominance for speech and language functions (Gurd and Marshall 1992); similar asymmetries are found in language-related regions of the human thalamus. Differences in the distribution of grey and white matter (the ratio of grey to white is greater in the left hemisphere) have likewise been discovered. It is also known that there are significant differences in the concentration of various chemical neurotransmitter substances in both cortical and subcortical regions of the human brain.

A number of the anatomic asymmetries that characterize the adult brain are present at birth, and can even be observed as early as 31 weeks of gestation. It is likely that individual differences in brain asymmetry may be associated with differential rate (and extent) of recovery from aphasia and with predispositions to developmental language disorder in children (Plante et al. 1991).

Although we are far from understanding *how* these anatomical and chemical asymmetries are responsible for functional differences between and within the cerebral hemispheres, there seems little doubt that the language faculty does inhabit a biologically distinct architecture. In the discussion so far, however, the aphasiological evidence considered has been drawn solely from studies of *spoken* language. It is logically possible that the underlying lateral specialization of the brain is concerned with auditory versus visuo–spatial processing. If this were so, one might expect that written or signed languages would find their neuronal locus in the right hemisphere.

3. Written Language Skills

With respect to written language skills, the evidence from pathology unambiguously shows that this is not so. With the exception of reading disability consequent upon left visuo–spatial neglect, the acquired dyslexias are strongly associated with left hemisphere lesions in all orthographic systems (Patterson 1990). A substantial majority of aphasic subjects experience associated reading and writing difficulties (Webb and Love 1983), and it is typically, but not invariably, the case that the qualitative form of the aphasia is mirrored by the disorder of reading and writing (Langmore and Canter 1983; Marshall 1987) (see also *Disorders of Reading and Writing*).

It might be argued that the correlation follows from claims that written language is 'parasitic' upon spoken language. Orthographies typically map (more or less regularly) on to a level (or levels) of representation (phonological, syllabic, or morphological) of their respective spoken forms; reading and writing skills are typically acquired after spoken language and using the latter as a means of instruction. Nineteenth-century neurologists accordingly formulated models of reading in which the visual stimulus was mapped on to an abstract phonological representation of the spoken language and all subsequent processing was common to reading and the comprehension of speech (Lichtheim 1885); similarly, it was claimed that spontaneous writing drew upon the processing machinery of spoken language up to *phonological* encoding of the message which constituted the access code for the retrieval of graphic form (Wernicke 1874). These theories predict that *dissociated* disorders of spoken and written language will only be found when the qualitative form of the disorder can be interpreted as an impairment of relatively peripheral mechanisms of input analysis (auditory or visual) or output execution (the vocal tract or the 'graphic tract').

It is now known that these predictions are false. For example: both global aphasia and severe Wernicke's aphasia can co-exist with relatively well-preserved reading. In some cases of Wernicke's aphasia (with total destruction of Wernicke's area), the qualitative form of relatively preserved oral reading and reading comprehension suggests that the patients can access phonological form directly from print, thus casting doubt upon a right-hemisphere interpretation of their reading performance (Sevush et al. 1983). Similarly, there are cases of 'auditory analogue to deep dyslexia' (in which the patient makes semantic substitutions in single-word oral repetition) in which fairly good written language skills (expression and comprehension) co-exist with massive deficits for both the expression and comprehension of spoken language (Michel and Andreewsky 1983). It is likely that the operation of a right-hemisphere lexicon, which has a distinctive nonphonological mode of speech processing, is implicated in these pathologies.

Contrariwise, deep dyslexia (Marshall and Newcombe 1973), in which patients make numerous semantic paralexias on single word-reading (*ill*—'sick'), can be seen in the context of well-preserved spontaneous speech (Low 1931); high-level modality-specific word comprehension deficits are likewise seen in deep dyslexia (Shallice and Coughlan 1980). Deep agraphia (with copious semantic substitutions in writing words to dictation) can be found in the context of fully intact repetition and reading aloud of single words. In yet other cases, the qualitative form of equally severe disorders may differ across modalities of language use. Thus Assal et al. (1981) have reported a patient whose disorder of written language was most akin to Wernicke's aphasia but with a disorder of oral language that resembled Broca's aphasia. The conclusion from these patterns of impaired and preserved performance is that the left hemisphere is indeed specialized for language *per se*, rather than for language as physically expressed in any particular sensory–motor mode. Nonetheless, it would seem that the existence of dissociated disorders of written and spoken language implies that the *detailed* neuronal representation of language in different modalities may be distinct even for relatively 'central' aspects of syntactic and semantic form.

4. Signed Languages

Are these conclusions also true for what is known of the biological instantiation of signed languages? (see also *Deafness and Sign Language*). Although early case reports of sign language aphasias tend to be inadequately reported with respect to neurological status and, especially, the nature of disordered signing, there is no doubt that the vast majority of the patients have left hemisphere pathology. In the first report of sign aphasia consequent upon a right hemisphere cerebro–vascular accident, the patient was left-handed. Reports, in which neurological and linguistic data are better documented, concur in finding frank sign aphasias after left-hemisphere damage. By contrast, Kimura et al. (1982) have described a native signer who, consequent upon right-hemisphere stroke, showed no disturbance of sign language or finger-spelling. In a similar case of right-hemisphere pathology, mild disturbance of sign expression and comprehension had a purely visuo–spatial interpretation and there was no aphasic involvement; by contrast, 16 cases of deaf signers with left-hemisphere pathology showed fairly severe aphasic symptomatology which appeared to parallel (in a typologically quite distinct language) the form of Broca's, Wernicke's, and anomic aphasias seen in hearing patients (Corina 1998).

5. Motor Skills

It is known that, in hearing subjects, the left hemisphere is specialized for the formulation, control, and execution of skilled motor acts. Various types of praxic impairment involving non-repetitive movement (including ideational and ideomotor apraxia) are thus consequent upon left-hemisphere damage (in right-handed subjects). The expression and comprehension of conventional gestures and pantomime are frequently observed to be impaired in (hearing) aphasic patients and there is a strong correlation between aphasic and apraxic disorder in hearing subjects (see Marshall 1980, for review). These associations have led Kimura (1981) to conjecture that 'a common system in the left perisylvian area of the brain' is the neuronal locus for language and, more generally, for skilled motor control. For Kimura, then, the aphasias are simply a subset of apraxic disorders of complex motor sequencing.

It would seem, however, that this hypothesis is false.

Although there is a statistical association between aphasia and apraxia, the correlation between the severity of the two impairments is not particularly high. Furthermore, there are many single-case reports of striking dissociation between the two functions. Thus Selnes et al. (1982) have reported transient aphasia with persistent apraxia after left-hemisphere stroke; Assal (1973) has described a light-music pianist who presented with Wernicke's aphasia and word deafness consequent upon left-hemisphere embolism. When first examined, there was severe aphasia across all sensory modalities but no apraxic disorder, either bucco–lingual, ideomotor, ideational, or constructional. Three months later the aphasia had regressed only slightly, but the patient's musical abilities were (with the exception of writing melodies to dictation, reading scores aloud, and naming melodies) totally intact. Musical perception showed no impairment. Not only could he play melodies without difficulty but he could compose them at the piano and write them down accurately. This is rather obviously not a picture of generalized movement disorder, and it would appear that the association of aphasic and apraxic disorder is rather due to the contiguity of the anatomical substrates that underlie language and praxis.

By virtue of this contiguity one would expect some statistical association between aphasia and apraxia in large groups of deaf signers with left-hemisphere pathology. Available case reports, however, show that, as in hearing patients, the two functions are dissociable. Furthermore, the nature of the error patterns of aphasic signers are clearly related to the linguistic structure of the language and not to any general motor disorder.

6. Specialization for Language

The sign aphasias thus provide further evidence that the underlying specialization of the left hemisphere is indeed for language irrespective of the sensory–motor modality that instantiates the physical expression of a language. Whether 'central' linguistic aspects of sign language draw upon a neuronal substrate that is strictly identical to the substrate that represents spoken language is unknown. It would be reasonable to expect subtle differences. Nonetheless, it is no longer in doubt that the basic specialization of the left hemisphere is for linguistic structure *per se*; there now seems little point in attempting to 'reduce' language capacity and skill to the interaction of more 'basic' cognitive functions. For human beings, language *is* a basic cognitive ability.

7. Conclusion

It is, however, worth stressing how little is known about human neuroanatomy (Crick and Jones 1993); the structure of the brain of the macaque monkey is known in some detail, but this information about a species that is conspicuously lacking any language faculty is of dubious relevance to the current topic. Likewise, the lesion studies (in humans) that have provided the basic information about the biology of language have often seemed to rely upon dubious inferences from pathological symptoms to normal functions; it is, after all, the remaining (relatively) intact areas of the brain that mediate aphasic output, not the tissue brain damage has destroyed.

Advances in nuclear medicine and functional neuroanatomy (functional Magnetic Resonance) do, however, now allow the mapping of those areas of the brain that are differentially active when normal people are engaged in different cognitive tasks. The precision of current techniques is still poor (in terms of spatial, and especially temporal resolution) but is rapidly improving (Posner and Carr 1992). In essence, such techniques as positron-emission tomography (PET scanning) measure (on-line) the metabolic rate of different brain areas by imaging differential regional cerebral blood flow (rCBF). The assumption is that, in the normal brain, the areas engaged in the performance of particular tasks will show an increased metabolic rate, indicative of the 'work-load' imposed upon those regions when the task is carried out. Although many investigations are somewhat crude, it is encouraging that, on the whole, the results of such studies provide good converging evidence for the localization of speech and language centers and circuits derived from lesion studies (Démonet 1998).

It is reasonable to hope that the next decade will see significant advances in the understanding of how the human brain represents language.

Bibliography

Assal G 1973 Aphasie de Wernicke sans amusie chez un pianiste. *Revue Neurologique* **129**: 251–55

Assal G, Buttet J, Jolivet R 1981 Dissociations in aphasia: A case report. *Brain and Language* **13**: 223–40

Braak H 1980 *Architectonics of the Human Telencephalic Cortex.* Springer-Verlag, Berlin

Broca P 1865 Sur le siège de la faculté du langage articulé. *Bulletin de la Societé d'Anthropologie* **6**: 377–93

Caplan D 1981 On the cerebral localization of linguistic functions: Logical and empirical issues surrounding deficit analysis and functional localization. *Brain and Language* **14**: 120–37

Code C 1987 *Language, Aphasia and the Right Hemisphere.* Wiley, New York

Coppens P, Hungerford S 1998 Crossed aphasia. In: Coppens P et al. (eds.) *Aphasia in Atypical Populations.* Erlbaum, Mahwah, NJ

Corina D 1998 Aphasia in users of signed languages. In: Coppens P et al. (eds.) *Aphasia in Atypical Populations.* Erlbaum, Mahwah, NJ

Crick F, Jones E 1993 Backwardness of human neuroanatomy. *Nature.* **361**: 109–10

Démonet J F 1998 Tomographic brain imaging of language functions. In: Stemmer B, Whitaker H A (eds.) *Handbook of Neurolinguistics.* Academic Press, San Diego, CA

Gurd J M, Marshall J C 1992 A gene for language? *Current Biology* **2**: 447–49

Jonas S 1981 The supplementary motor region and speech emission. *Journal of Communication Disorders* **14**: 349–73

Kimura D 1981 Neural mechanisms in manual signing. *Sign Language Studies* **33**: 291–312

Kimura D, Davidson W, McCormick W 1982 No impairment in sign language after right-hemisphere stroke. *Brain and Language* **17**: 359–62

Langmore S E, Canter G J 1983 Written spelling deficit of Broca's aphasics. *Brain and Language* **18**: 293–314

Lichtheim L 1885 On aphasia. *Brain* **7**: 433–84

Low A A 1931 A case of agrammatism in the English language. *Archives of Neurology and Psychiatry* **25**: 556–97

Marshall J C 1980 Clues from neurological deficits. In: Bellugi U, Studdert-Kennedy M (eds.) *Signed and Spoken Language: Biological Constraints on Linguistic Form.* Verlag Chemie, Weinheim

Marshall J C 1987 Routes and representations in the processing of written language. In: Keller E, Gopnik M (eds.) *Motor and Sensory Processes of Language.* Erlbaum, London

Marshall J C, Newcombe F 1973 Patterns of paralexia: A psycho-linguistic approach. *Journal of Psycholinguistic Research* **2**: 175–99

Michel F, Andreewsky E 1983 Deep dysphasia: An analogue of deep dyslexia in the auditory modality. *Brain and Language* **18**: 212–23

Nadeau S E, Crosson B 1997 Subcortical aphasia. *Brain and Language* **58**: 355–402

Paradis M 1998 *Pragmatics in Neurogenic Communication Disorders.* Pergamon, Oxford

Patterson K E 1990 Basic processes of reading: Do they differ in Japanese and English? *Japanese Journal of Neuropsychology* **6**: 4–14

Peterson L N, Kirshner H S 1981 Gestural impairment and gestural ability in aphasia: A review. *Brain and Language* **14**: 333–48

Plante E, Swisher L, Vance R, Rapcsak S 1991 MRI findings in boys with specific language impairment. *Brain and Language* **41**: 52–66

Poizner H, Battison R 1980 Cerebral asymmetry for sign language: Clinical and experimental evidence. In: Lane H, Grosjean F (eds.) *Recent Perspectives on American Sign Language.* Erlbaum, Hillsdale, NJ

Poizner H, Bellugi U, Iraqui V 1984 Apraxia and aphasia in a visuo-gestural language. *American Journal of Physiology* **246**: 868–83

Poizner H, Klima E S, Bellugi U 1987 *What the Hands Reveal about the Brain.* MIT Press, Cambridge, MA

Posner M I, Carr T H 1992 Lexical access and the brain: Anatomical constraints on cognitive models of word recognition. *American Journal of Psychology* **105**: 1–26

Ratcliff G, Dila C, Taylor L, Milner B 1980 The morphological asymmetry of the hemispheres and cerebral dominance for speech: A possible relationship. *Brain and Language* **11**: 87–98

Ryding E, Bradvic B, Ingvar D H 1987 Changes in regional cerebral blood flow measured simultaneously in the right and left hemisphere during automatic speech and humming. *Brain* **110**: 1345–58

Selnes O A, Rubens A B, Risse G L, Levy R S 1982 Transient

aphasia with persistent apraxia: Uncommon sequelae of massive left-hemisphere stroke. *Archives of Neurology* **39**: 122–6

Sevush S, Roeltgen D P, Campanella D J, Heilman K M 1983 Preserved oral reading in Wernicke's aphasia. *Neurology* **33**: 916–20

Shallice T, Coughlin A K 1980 Modality specific word comprehension deficits in deep dyslexia. *Journal of Neurology, Neurosurgery, and Psychiatry* **43**: 866–72

Teszner D, Tzavaras A, Gruner J, Hécaen H 1972 L'asym-

metrie droite-gauche du *planum temporale*: A propos de l'étude anatomique de 100 cerveaux. *Revue Neurologique* **126**: 444–49

Wallesch C-W 1997 Symptomatology of subcortical aphasia. *Journal of Neurolinguistics* **10**: 267–76

Webb W G, Love R J 1983 Reading problems in chronic aphasia. *Journal of Speech and Hearing Disorders* **48**: 164–71

Wernicke C 1874 *Der aphasische Symptomenkomplex*. Cohn and Weigart, Breslau

Neurolinguistic Assessment of Aphasia

C. Luzzatti

1. Introduction

Aphasia is a language impairment affecting the production and comprehension of verbal communication in individuals with a normal language acquisition history. Typically, this acquired disorder results from a left-hemisphere brain lesion and generally involves the different linguistic units and modalities. The lesion results in general phonological, lexical-semantic, and morpho-syntactic damage, both of the spoken and written modality. However, even a lay person who has had the opportunity to interact verbally with aphasic subjects will report considerable variability amongst the observed language disorders. This diversity is mostly due to the differing degrees of impairment affecting, in each patient, the linguistic units and modalities to a variable extent. Other factors, however, must be taken into account as well. First, the use of partially spared abilities in a communicative interaction may differ considerably between individuals, irrespective of the degree of impairment of each single unit or modality. Second, the units of classical descriptive linguistics have been shown to be insufficient to describe the phenomena of normal and pathological language processing, thus introducing the need for a further level of description, namely that of psycholinguistic processing (see *Psycholinguistics* for a detailed description of current models of language processing). In the light of these considerations, it should be clear that the description of an aphasic patient, whether for clinical, experimental, or rehabilitative purposes, requires an extensive assessment of the underlying level(s) of impairment.

The aim of this chapter is to review the principles underlying the assessment of language disorders. The first section of the chapter will discuss the historical background of language assessment in aphasia, as well as the origin of the classical terminology first developed by Wernicke and still largely used in clinical and experimental aphasiology. In the second section the general principles, as used by contemporary authors for a clinical description of aphasic language disorders, are analyzed. The last section of the chapter describes the major tests used for the assessment of aphasic language disorders.

2. Historical Background

2.1 The Rationale of Neurolinguistic Assessment

Since the early descriptions of cognitive disorders by neuropsychologists in the nineteenth century, a multitude of factors have contributed to the determination of the rationale underlying a detailed assessment of cognitive impairments. These factors are intimately connected with the multiple aspects of neuropsychology. The first aim of neuropsychology was to identify the separate cortical sites of the different cognitive abilities. Localization of function in different cerebral areas was principally based on functional-anatomical correlative studies on patients with cerebral brain lesions. A functional analysis required a detailed assessment of both the impaired and the spared cognitive abilities. Once different cognitive abilities were localized in different areas of the brain, a second goal of neuropsychology emerged: in the absence of neuro-imaging techniques, neuropsychological assessment was the major, if not the only, instrument for the localization of brain lesions. Moreover, an accurate assessment of cognitive and neurolinguistic impairment is crucial for theoretical and experimental neuropsychological and neurolinguistic studies, because the isolated impairment of cognitive abilities is a proof of their functional independence. A clear example of this approach is Wernicke's model of language processing, which continues to exert its influence until today.

2.2 The Wernicke-Lichtheim Model and the Expression–Reception Dichotomy

The description of a language disorder is still often based on the comprehension-production dichotomy that contrasts 'expressive' and 'receptive' aphasia, or 'motor' and 'sensory' aphasia. This dichotomy originates from the language processing model proposed by Wernicke (1874), which was further modified by Lichtheim (1885) and by Wernicke himself (1886).

According to this model (see Fig. 1a), the left hemisphere contains two distinct centers, **A** and **M**, that store the *auditory* and *motor word representations*, respectively. The two centers are localized in the auditory and motor associative areas and connected through the functional and anatomical pathway **AM**. The sensory and motor representations of words are elementary units of processing in which the input and output *word images* (*Wortbegriff* = the lexeme without semantic representation, akin to the present-day concept of phonological input and output lexica) are stored. Word images are matched to word meanings (*Objektbegriff*). Wernicke explicitly described the latter as a network of knowledge distributed on a large part of the cerebral cortex, whereas Lichtheim schematized it in the center **B**, connected to the input and output centers **A** and **M** via the pathways **BA** and **BM**. The model is completed by a center *a* for the auditory analysis and a center *m* for the articulatory motor control, thus determining the paths *aAB* and *BMm* which account for the auditory comprehension and oral production of a word, respectively.

The model predicts functional sites of lesions, each of which may result in specific verbal disorders. A lesion of the centers **A** and **M** would produce a *comprehension* and a *production* disorder (*cortical sensory aphasia* and *cortical motor aphasia*, respectively, more commonly referred to as Wernicke's and Broca's aphasia). A lesion of the path **AM** would result in repetition disorders with spared comprehension (*conduction aphasia*), while a lesion of the path **AB** would produce comprehension disorders with spared repetition (*transcortical sensory aphasia*). Finally, a lesion of **BM** would result in disorders of spontaneous speech output with spared comprehension and repetition (*transcortical motor aphasia*). A more extensive version of the model also describes the processing of written language and the effect of brain lesions on reading and writing (see Fig. 1b).

During the following decades, these simple schemata were further detailed by specifying different aspects of the language deficits. The most important modifications came from contemporary linguistics and psychological theory. A first enrichment resulted from the introduction of syntax as a further variable to be considered in the evaluation of an aphasic impairment (an aspect that had been almost completely neglected by Wernicke). The inclusion of syntax gave rise to the concept of *agrammatism* (Pick, 1913; Isserlin, 1922). In the psychological framework of a *Gestalt* theory of language, Goldstein (1924, 1948) introduced the concept of *anomic aphasia* (*amnestische Aphasie*). A further example is the analysis of language disorders carried out by Jakobson (1964), in the framework of a structural linguistic approach.

The independent development of the different European (Kleist in Germany, Head in the UK, Ala-

1a)   1b)

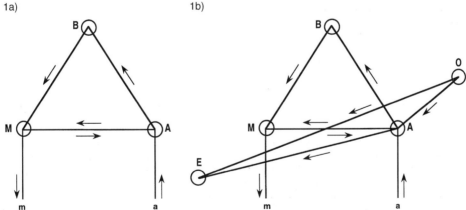

Figure 1. The Wernicke-Lichtheim language model and the related disorders for spoken (Fig. 1a) and written language (Fig. 1b).

Centers: **A** = center for auditory word representations (Wortbegriff); **M** = center for motor word representations; **B** = center for object concepts (Objektbegriff); **a** = auditory speech input; **m** = motor speech output; **O** = center for reading words; **E** = center for writing words

Disorders of spoken language by lesions in: **M** = cortical motor aphasia; **A** = cortical sensory aphasia; **AM** = conduction aphasia; **BM** = transcortical motor aphasia; **Mm** = subcortical motor aphasia [= pure anarthria]; **AB** = transcortical sensory aphasia; **aA** = subcortical sensory aphasia [= pure word deafness]; **O** = cortical alexia; **E** = cortical agraphia

jouanine in France, and Luria in the Soviet Union) and American aphasiological schools between the First and Second World Wars inevitably produced a large heterogeneity in the assessment of aphasic disorders. By the end of the 1960s, however, a terminological reunification took place with the renaissance of neurolinguistics within and around the Boston research groups directed by Norman Geschwind and Harold Goodglass. The classical Wernicke-Lichtheim taxonomy of language disorders was there enriched with more recent neurolinguistic concepts (e.g., anomic aphasia, global aphasia, agrammatism) and psychometric principles.

The major shortcoming of the Wernicke-Lichtheim model, limiting its strict application, lies in the fact that the centers **A** and **M** are specified as being auditory and motor associative areas, both in a philogenetic and an ontogenetic perspective. However, these modality-specific aspects are largely lost during their functional development. Accordingly, the two centers essentially become supramodal language areas, damage to which results in phonological and lexical disorders, usually observed in both production and comprehension. The fact that posterior lesions (**A**) also produce output disorders, while anterior lesions (**M**) also result in input disorders, already had been pointed out by Wernicke himself. This pattern of disorder was explained as arising from a close interaction between the two centers, such that anatomical damage to only one center also causes a functional impairment of the other. It is for this reason that the large majority of aphasic patients do not show exclusively motor or sensory deficits, but rather a general language impairment with a variable degree of severity, involving both the input and the output modality of both spoken and written language.

Dissociated patterns of impairments are indeed possible, but instead of damage to one single modality, they usually reflect damage to an isolated language component, such as phonology, lexicon, lexical semantics, or morpho-syntax. Within this framework, *conduction aphasia* can be reconsidered (and described) as a mainly phonological disorder with spared lexical-semantic and morpho-syntactic abilities, *anomic aphasia* as the result of a selective damage to lexical retrieval functions and *transcortical sensory aphasia* as a lexical-semantic damage with preservation of the phonological and morpho-syntactic components; finally *agrammatism* would arise from a selective morpho-syntactic damage sparing phonological and lexical-semantic abilities.

3. The Variables of Neurolinguistic Assessment

3.1 Spontaneous Speech

Traditionally, the evaluation of aphasic language disorders starts with the analysis of spontaneous speech in a communicative interactive context. This may be done by asking patients to describe the onset of their disease, their family, job, and hobbies. The patient's output is analyzed according to different parameters of the linguistic performance.

General communicative ability: The first step in the assessment process is to evaluate the patients' residual ability to interact in a communicative set. This includes: (a) the overall informative content patients are still able to transmit, irrespective of the type and severity of the language disorder; (b) the use of pragmatic rules in an interactive context, such as turn-taking, the appropriate reference to shared knowledge, and the use of indirect speech acts.

The patients' utterances are then analyzed and the abnormal features of each single linguistic component are described.

Articulation: Following a cerebral lesion a patient may suffer from an articulatory disorder. This disturbance may follow a paresis of the cranial nerves or, alternatively, may be related to the damage of a center that specifically accounts for speech-motor control. In the first case, the disorders usually follow bilateral hemispheric brain lesions, or lesions of the brain stem. Speech is usually hypoarticulated and slurred. A paresis of the velum causes uncontrolled air flow through the nose, resulting in a hypernasal speech output, while a paresis of the back of the tongue produces reduced differentiation of the vowels which blend into a central hypoarticulated vocalization [ə]. Due to its paretic origin the impairment is usually associated with other symptoms, such as drooling and swallowing disorders. There is a further disorder of articulation which is caused by unilateral left-hemisphere lesions and which does not follow a paresis of the speech organs underlying articulation. This deficit—which can occur in isolation or in association with a more extensive language disorder—has been called *anarthria* (Marie 1906) or *phonetic disintegration syndrome* (Lecours and Lhermitte 1976). Patients articulate slowly and with difficulty, giving the impression of having to struggle in order to attain the target articulatory positions. Typical features of this disorder are *devoicing of voiced sounds* (/b/, /g/, /d/, /v/ become /p/, /k/, /t/, /f/) because of a delayed voice onset, and *substitution of a fricative with the corresponding affricate* or *plosive sound*, because of an excessive contraction causing occlusion—instead of narrowing—of the air flow. In some cases altered articulation sounds like a *foreign accent*. A disorder of articulatory programming is referred to by some authors with the term *apraxia of speech* (Rosenbeck et al. 1984; Buckingham 1991) to designate this disorder (see *Verbal Apraxia*).

Phonology: Damage at the phonological level may result in *substitutions, deletions, additions,* or *transpositions* of sounds. Repeated repair attempts go under the label of *conduite d'approche*. In some cases, multiple phonemic errors may no longer allow interlocutors to identify the target word (*phonemic neologism*). In a few cases a phonemic error may result in an existing word (e.g., *cable* vs. *table*), thus resembling a lexical substitution (*formal paraphasia*).

Lexical semantics: The most frequent disorder is *anomia*, a difficulty in retrieving words. In a few cases the naming impairment may only involve a single class of words (e.g., nouns or verbs) or a particular subset of nouns (e.g., proper names only). When the disorder is less severe, the retrieval of a target word may be merely delayed (anomic latency) or a nonretrieved word may be substituted by a *circumlocution*.

Lexical-semantic damage may also give rise to substitutions of the target lexeme with a semantically related word (*semantic paraphasia*; e.g., *glass* instead of *bottle*). Finally, there are impairments that are more strictly semantic than lexical, namely those which are not caused by a retrieval disorder of lexical information, but rather by a primary *damage to the underlying semantic knowledge*. As a consequence, a patient is no longer able to discriminate between elements of semantically related categories (e.g., *cats* vs. *dogs*) or identify the distinctive features of elements within the same category (e.g., the difference between a *cup* and a *mug*).

Syntax and syntactic implementation of lexical morphology: A syntactic disorder may result in an impoverishment of the sentence structure and in the omission of function words (articles, pronouns, prepositions, conjunctions, and auxiliary verbs) and of inflections. In languages like Italian or Hebrew, where the omission of inflections would give rise to a nonword, inflections are substituted with less marked endings. Accordingly, the patients' utterances assume the aspect of a telegraphic message, a phenomenon that is usually called *agrammatism*. In contrast, some patients produce sentences that are long and complex, but contain morphological and syntactic errors both in the realization of inflectional agreement and in the appropriate choice of function words. This disorder is usually called *paragrammatism*.

Automatised utterances: An aphasic language disorder manifests itself not only as an impairment in the production of phonemes and lexical elements that are appropriate for a certain linguistic act, but also as the failure to inhibit the uncontrolled production of automatised elements. *Automatisms* are idiosyncratic lexical elements or short phases that patients may recurrently produce across communicative situations or testing sessions. In some severe cases, spontaneous speech may be limited to a few stereotyped elements only, as is the case for consonant-vowel syllabic *recurring utterances* in global aphasia (e.g., *ta-ta*). *Perseveration* is another uncontrolled phenomenon by which lexical elements that are appropriate in a certain context are thereafter automatically reproduced over a certain period of time. *Echolalia* is the disinhibited repetition (much like an echo) of what has just been heard by the patients in their immediate environment.

3.2 Specific Verbal Tasks for Different Units and Modalities

Once a patient's spontaneous speech output has been assessed, the residual verbal abilities may be further tested by means of specific tasks addressing the different linguistic units and modalities.

Naming: The ability to retrieve individual words is typically tested using naming in response to the visual presentation of objects or pictures (*confrontation naming*). Abnormal naming responses include *anomia* (with or without *circumlocutions*), *semantic paraphasias* and *perseveration*. In general, a word that cannot be retrieved in a certain condition is not necessarily lost from a patient's lexicon: while a lexical item may not be accessible at that very moment and to that particular task, it may well emerge on a repeated presentation of the stimulus later in the session, or it may be cued through automatized series (e.g., the word 'Wednesday' may be cued listing the days of the week starting from Monday) or may be facilitated by a semantic cue (e.g., the word 'newspaper' may be cued by the sentence: 'Every morning I read the . . .').

Comprehension of spoken language: Comprehension may be tested both for single words and sentences. The examiner may ask a patient to point to objects among different alternatives placed in front of him. The same objects may also be used to test the comprehension of sentences with variable degrees of complexity (e.g., 'Put the pencil into the mug,' 'Before handing me the fork, put the glasses under the napkin,' etc.). A sentence-to-picture matching task can be used to test specific syntactic aspects, such as the agent-theme relation in reversible active and passive sentences (e.g., 'In which of these two pictures is the lion being chased by the tiger?').

Repetition: As may be evinced from the historical introduction, a test of the ability to repeat verbal stimuli was crucial for the evaluation of Wernicke's model. An impaired or flawless performance of the repetition task allowed him to discriminate among aphasic subtypes and, in particular, to delineate the conduction and transcortical aphasia profiles. An impaired ability to repeat words and sentences usually reflects a primary disorder of phonological processing, characterized by a high incidence of phonemic errors and of recursive phonemic repairs (*conduites d'approche*). In some cases, however, impaired repetition may be caused by a verbal short-term-memory disorder, thus resulting in a reduced verbal span in the absence of phonemic paraphasia. A complete evaluation of spared repetition abilities starts with single, short, simple words, and continues with progressively longer and more complex words and sentences. Verbal short-term-memory span may be tested with simple words (usually nouns) or digits.

Reading and writing: Reading tasks usually include word naming and the comprehension of written material. Writing tasks include tracing of single letters, spelling of words as dictated by the examiner, and written naming of objects and pictures.

4. The Taxonomy of Aphasic Language Disorders

Until recently, following Wernicke's model of language processing, the description (and classification) of language disorders was based on different degrees of impairment across modalities, with the underlying assumption that input and output language disorders were at opposite ends of the continuum: *expressive—* or *motor*—aphasias were thus set against *receptive—* or *sensory*—ones.

A classification of aphasic disorders by language modalities is often inadequate for the description of the impairments. Current descriptions (and classifications) are still based on the *anterior/posterior* dichotomy, the emphasis no longer being on a dissociation along the comprehension/expression dimension but rather on the qualitative aspects of spontaneous speech along the *fluency/nonfluency* dimension (Benson 1967, 1993; Kerschensteiner et al. 1972; Kertesz 1979; Goodglass and Kaplan 1983; Basso 1990). The variables used for fluency judgments are fairly heterogeneous, ranging from impairments of the articulatory motor control (*articulatory agility*) to verbal inertia (*rate of speech*) and primary damage to the syntactic realization of sentences (*phrase length* and *grammatical complexity*). Nonfluent language disorders include *Broca's*, *global*, and *transcortical motor aphasia*; fluent language disorders include *Wernicke's*, *anomic*, *conduction*, and *transcortical sensory aphasia*.

4.1 Fluent Language Disorders

Fluent aphasic output is abundant; articulation, prosody, and phrase length are normal; sentences have a complex syntactic structure, but do contain many interruptions, agreement errors, and substitutions of function words. The lexical component is impaired as evidenced by the presence of word finding difficulties and lexical substitutions, and phonology is affected, resulting in phonemic substitutions and phonemic neologisms. In severe fluent language disorders the rate of phonemic and lexical substitutions may be so high that the patient's output results in a sequence of nonwords (*neologistic jargon*) or in a sequence of existing words that are combined into meaningless sentences (*semantic jargon*). Patients afflicted with severe fluent aphasia are often unaware of their output deficit (*anosognosia*).

Wernicke's aphasia is the prototypical fluent language disorder: patients show an almost homogeneous impairment of the phonemic, syntactic, and lexical-semantic components. In contrast, phonological impairment (and therefore repetition deficits) predominate in *conduction* aphasia, lexical access disorders typify *anomic* aphasia, and semantic deficits (or deficits of the lexical-semantic interface) characterize *transcortical sensory* aphasia. Comprehension impairments vary according to the severity of language disorders: they are minimal or mild in *conduction* and *anomic* aphasia, and severe in *transcortical sensory* aphasia.

4.2 Nonfluent Language Disorders

Nonfluent speech output is sparse (< 50 words per minute), phrases are short, words are produced with effort and little prosody, or are poorly articulated; sentence structure is simplified and lacks subordinate clauses; function words are often omitted.

Broca's aphasia is the prototypical nonfluent language disorder. Nonfluency is caused either by the impairment of syntactic structure (*agrammatism*), or by an articulation deficit (*apraxia of speech*). *Global aphasia* is the most severe type of nonfluent language disorder. Speech is usually reduced to a few stereotyped utterances and there is almost always a severe disorder of articulation. Auditory comprehension and repetition are also severely impaired, and reading and writing abilities are often nonexistent. Finally, the salient aspect of *transcortical motor aphasia* is the extreme paucity of spontaneous spoken and written output, in spite of an almost intact ability to name objects, repeat, read aloud, or write from dictation.

4.3 Disturbances of Single Language Modalities

In some rare cases language modalities may be affected in isolation.

Pure anarthria (or *aphemia*) is a disorder of articulatory motor control and is not caused by paresis of the organs underlying speech articulation. Auditory and written comprehension are intact, whereas spontaneous speech, confrontation naming, repetition, reading aloud, and so on, are impaired. The disorder has already been described in Sect. 3.1.

Pure word deafness is a pure auditory disorder reflecting a deficit in understanding spoken language and repetition. This deficit is not caused by hearing loss and consists of an impaired phonological analysis of verbal strings. Verbal output, reading, and writing are usually intact.

Alexia and agraphia: Acquired impairments of reading and writing will be described in more detail in a different chapter (see *Disorders of Reading and Writing*). In this section we will only mention some rare cases where written language may be impaired in the absence of any disorder of spoken language, thus involving only the input (*pure alexia*) or output processing (*pure agraphia*) or reflecting a more general disorder of orthographic representations (*alexia with agraphia*).

4.4 Information-processing Models

The principle underlying the grouping of aphasic language disorders along the classical taxonomy has been a matter of fierce discussion since the 1980s (Caramazza 1986; Poeck 1986; Marshall 1986; Caplan

1995). In particular, it has been claimed that aphasic syndromes do not represent a unitary or theoretically sound set of symptoms and that the patients classified under a certain aphasic label are afflicted with a cluster of symptoms that may or may not be associated because of anatomical, functional, or neuropathological reasons. Only a more detailed description of normal and impaired language processing would allow researchers and clinicians to set up a taxonomy of language impairments. In fact, since the 1970s, cognitive psychologists have developed different models which describe in detail single levels of linguistic processing within an information-processing framework. The models describe different processing routines and different subcomponents for each of these (see *Psycholinguistics*). At least as far as phonological and lexical abilities are concerned, an aphasic language disorder could be accounted for by the impairment of one or more units of the model (see *Neurolinguistics*). The use of information-processing models provided a far more accurate description of language impairments and accounts for the wide range of variability among patients. However, a cognitive neuropsychological diagnostic procedure requires an extensive set of tasks for each different route of processing and underlying subcomponent. Compared to tests aimed at a classical clinical assessment, the goal of a complete cognitively sound diagnostic procedure is extremely ambitious, and has been attempted by only a few research groups. Other tasks have been devised to test single performances, as for reading and writing. Finally, the use of cognitively sound testing procedures may lead to the development of rehabilitation programs focused on the treatment of the specific impaired subcomponents, as well as on the evaluation of the efficacy of a given treatment.

5. Review of the Major Tests for the Assessment of Language Disorders

5.1 Standard Aphasia Batteries

The first aim of standard aphasia assessments is to evaluate the presence, type, and severity of a language disability. A further aim of language assessment is to measure the evolution of a patient's impairment and in particular to evaluate the efficacy of rehabilitation programs. Tests usually consist of a set of tasks designed to examine production and comprehension in the oral and written modality. It should be noted that the tests differ in terminology, internal organisation, and type of abilities under focus, depending upon the underlying theoretical principles. For instance, some tests describe a language disorder by focusing in particular on the degree of impairment of each single linguistic unit, whereas others are more concerned with the pragmatical use of language and the general communicative disability that may arise following a given brain lesion. Clearly, the dis-

criminative capacity of a test is a function of the underlying constructive principles and of the psychometric properties of the tasks. As a general rule, the diagnostic validity of an aphasia battery depends upon the number of variables being considered, and the number of items for each variable (therefore, but not always, on the length of the test battery). The validity of a battery also depends on its psychometric properties (e.g., independence of variables, reliability of tasks, etc.). Furthermore, the development of comparable aphasia examinations across different languages is crucial for the comparison of patients in cross-linguistic studies.

A reliable measure of the different aspects of a language impairment is also an obvious requirement for cognitive neuropsychological studies. A few tests have been devised with the aim to describe and measure language impairments at the different psycholinguistic processing levels and routines of spoken and written language (PALPA: Kay et al. 1992; LeMo: De Bleser et al. 1998; BADA: Miceli et al. 1986; PAL: Caplan in preparation). Due to the complexity of these test batteries and the large number of subtests they contain, their experimental use for the detection of dissociated impairments requires extensive normative studies and the evaluation of the tests' constructive and diagnostic validity, as well as the identification of clear principles for the discrimination between spared and impaired levels of processing.

Table 1 summarizes the principal aspects of the major European and North American test batteries used for diagnostic and rehabilitative purposes. A detailed description of the major aphasia tests available for English-speaking patients may be found in Lezak's (1995) handbook on neuropsychological assessment.

5.2 Tests of Single Language Abilities

Studies of aphasic patients have used a multitude of tasks to assess the impairment of single language components (such as phonology, lexicon, morphology, lexical semantics, syntax, reading, writing, and phonological short-term memory). Their full listing and description is beyond the limits of the present review. Therefore, only those tasks that are used most widely and for which normative data were obtained, thus allowing their application on aphasic samples or in single case studies, will be considered. For an extensive description of all tasks available for the English-speaking population, the interested reader is referred to Lezak (1995).

5.2.1 Lexical abilities

Naming from visual input is the easiest and most common condition for testing lexical abilities in aphasic patients. The obvious limitation of a visual confrontation task is that the items to be named can only be concrete objects or actions. It has been shown that,

Table 1. Major aphasia examinations developed since the 1970s.

Test	Authors	Theoretical frame
Aachen Aphasia Test (AAT)	Huber et al. 1983; Huber et al. 1984	Neurolinguistics
Amsterdam-Nijmegen Everyday Language Test (ANELT)	Blomert et al. 1994	Pragmatics
Aphasia Language Performance Scale (ALPS)	Keenan and Brassell 1975	Pragmatics
Batteria per l'Analisi dei Deficit Afasici (BADA)	Miceli et al. 1996	Psycholinguistics
Bilingual Aphasia Test (BAT)	Paradis 1987	Neurolinguistics
Boston Diagnostic Language Examination (BDAE)	Goodglass and Kaplan 1983	Neurolinguistics
Communication Abilities in Daily Living (CADL)	Holland 1980	Pragmatics
Esame del Linguaggio (2nd ed.)	Ciurli et al. 1996	Neurolinguistics
Functional Communication Profile (FCP)	Sarno 1969	Pragmatics
Minnesota Test for Differential Diagnosis of Aphasia	Schuell 1973	Speech pathology
Montreal-Toulouse Language Examination (MT-beta)	Béland et al. 1990–93	Neurolinguistics
Multilingual Aphasia Examination (MAE)	Benton and Hamsher 1989	Neurolinguistics
Neurolinguistic Evaluation of Lexical Morphology (LeMo)	DeBleser et al. 1994	Psycholinguistics
Neurosensory Center Comprehension Examination for Aphasia (NCCEA)	Spreen and Benton 1977; Spreen and Strauss 1991	Neurolinguistics
Porch Index of Communicative Ability (PICA)	Porch 1983	Speech pathology
Profile of Communicative Appropriateness	Penn 1985	Pragmatics
Psycholinguistic Assessment of Language Processing in Aphasia (PALPA)	Kay et al. 1992	Neurolinguistics
Psycholinguistic Assessment of Language (PAL)	Caplan in preparation	Psycholinguistics
Western Aphasia Battery (WAB)	Kertesz 1979, 1982	Neurolinguistics

Language: A = Arabic, D = Dutch, E = English, F = French, G = German, I = Italian, P = Portuguese, S = Spanish

Language	Length	Norms	Statistical background	Comments
G, D, I	3 h	+	ALLOC, PSCA	Qualitative and quantitative assessment of spontaneous speech + 5 subtests. Psychometric single case analysis allows decisions for dissociations between tasks and for modifications after retest; ALLOC allows discrimination between standard aphasic subtypes
D, E, G	15–30′	+		
E	30′	—	—	No discrimination between aphasic subtypes
I	8 h	—	—	
65 languages	2 h	+	—	65 languages + 160 bilingual contrastive pairs. Tasks for different levels and modalities. Translation abilities of bilingual subjects are also tested
E, F, I, S, P	2 h	+	factor analysis, discriminant analysis	Aphasia rating scale + Subtest profile; classifies patient into aphasic subtypes
E, I	1 h	+	—	Language is examined in a practical and natural communicative context; discriminates aphasic subtypes
I	2–3 h	—	—	
E	30′	—	—	Clinical functional evaluation
E	30′–3 h	—	—	Systematic description of the patient's disability
F, S, A	2–3 h	+	+	
E, F, G, I, S	2 h	+	+	Derived from NCCEA; also norms for children
G	6–12 h	+	+	Evaluates lexical impairments of spoken and written language along the different processing routines
E	2 h	+	+	Identifies aphasic patients and discriminates between aphasic subtypes; no assessment of spontaneous speech
E	30′	+	+	Same 10 items across modalities; no assessment of spontaneous speech
E	1–2 h	—	—	Pragmatic profile which provides a checklist of behaviors which are judged in a communicative context on a five-point rating scale
E	1–6 h	—	+	Information processing assessment (60 tasks) of auditory processing, reading and spelling, lexical semantics, and sentence processing. No assessment of spontaneous speech
E, S	2–5 h	+	+	Information processing assessment of different linguistic units and processing routes
E, P	1–2 h	+	+	

after a cerebral lesion, lexical-semantic abilities may be selectively impaired such as to reveal a dissociation between verbs and nouns and within nouns, a dissociation between natural items (animals, fruit, vegetables), and artifact items (tools, pieces of furniture, modes of transportation, etc.). A naming task should, therefore, contain different types of items. Furthermore, the patient's performance to pictorial stimuli varies as a function of the quality and complexity of the drawing, its prototypicality for the target word, the individual's familiarity with that object, and the word frequency of the corresponding lexical label. Snodgrass and Vanderwart (1980) tested name agreement, image agreement, familiarity, and visual complexity of a set of 260 drawings that are generally used in visual confrontation naming tasks.

The *Boston Naming Test* (BNT: Kaplan et al. 1983) is the best-known confrontation naming task. It consists of 60 drawings of natural and artifact objects ordered according to familiarity and word frequency from more common to less familiar items.

The active lexicon of an individual may also be tested by means of *fluency tests*. In this type of tasks, patients are asked to name *items within a certain category* (e.g., animals, vegetables, items that can be found in a supermarket) or *words beginning with a certain letter*. In the latter condition the productivity associated with each letter of the alphabet is influenced by numerosity (the number of words in a language beginning with that letter) and word frequency of each single item. Letter productivity has been tested for the English vocabulary (Borkowsky et al. 1967) and it obviously varies across languages. Performance of fluency tests (either by category or by letter of the alphabet) is highly sensitive to age and educational level (e.g., Novelli et al. 1986; Spreen and Strauss 1991).

Age of acquisition is another important variable that has been shown to influence the lexical performance of aphasic patients. The *Peabody Picture Vocabulary Test* (PPVT: Dunn 1981) matches the lexical knowledge of a patient with that of normal individuals (aged from $2\frac{1}{2}$ to 18). The task consists of 175 picture sets, each set consisting of four pictures. For each set a stimulus word is spoken aloud and the individual is asked to point to the corresponding picture among the four alternatives. The picture sets are ordered by increasing difficulty (age of acquisition). The score obtained by an individual gives the number of correct responses and may be transformed to percentile rank and age equivalent score. English norms are based on a sample of 4200 subjects.

5.2.2 Reading and spelling

Since the 1980s cognitive neurolinguists have developed a large number of tasks to evaluate the impairment of reading and writing abilities. According to contemporary information-processing models, reading tests should include words with regular pronunciation, words with irregular pronunciation, and nonwords. Irregular words can be read only via the lexicon, nonwords via the grapheme-to-phoneme conversion route, while regular words can be read using both routes. The lists of words used in reading tasks should vary also according to grammatical class, word length, and word frequency. Analogous to reading tasks, writing tasks should contain words with regular spelling, words with irregular spelling, and nonwords. Cognitive neuropsychologists studying reading and writing disabilities have usually devised their own lists of items, designed specifically for the processing unit under study. For most of the tasks no normative data on normal subjects are available.

The *National Adult Reading Test* (NART: Nelson 1982) assesses the ability to read words with irregular pronunciation. It has been standardized on a large sample of English-speaking normal adult individuals. As expected, the scores attained on the test correlate significantly with the educational level of tested individuals.

Spelling abilities may be assessed in English-speaking patients by means of the *John Hopkins University Dysgraphia Battery* (Goodman and Caramazza 1985). The test includes tasks for the writing and spelling of both regular and irregular words of different grammatical classes and variable length and frequency, the writing and spelling of nonwords, and the written naming of object drawings.

5.2.3 The Token Test

A simple, yet remarkably sensitive task for the assessment of comprehension deficits in aphasic patients is the *Token Test* (De Renzi and Vignolo 1962; De Renzi and Faglioni 1978). It consists of a series of verbal commands, of increasing complexity, to be performed on 20 tokens differing in colour (black, white, red, yellow, and green) shape (squares and circles), and size (large and small). The *Token Test* is usually listed among the auditory comprehension tasks. However, it has been shown that failure on this task can reflect the impairment of many different abilities related to comprehension, ranging from *lexical discrimination* to *syntactic analysis* and *phonological short-term memory*, and that it provides a good index of the overall severity of an aphasic language disorder.

Bibliography

Basso A 1990 Valutazione, recupero e terapia dell'afasia. In: Denes G F, Pizzamiglio L (eds.) *Manuale di Neuropsicologia*. Zanichelli, Bologna: 271–97

Béland R, Nespoulous J-L, Lecours A R 1990 MT-86 Beta Aphasia Battery: a subset of normative data in relation to age and level of education. *Aphasiology* **4**: 439–62; **7**: 359–82

Benson D F 1967 Fluency in aphasia: correlation with radioactive scan localization. *Cortex* **3**: 373–92

Benson D F 1993 Aphasia. In: Heilman K M, Valenstein E

(eds.) *Clinical Neuropsychology* (3rd ed.) Oxford University Press, New York, 17–36

Benton A L, Hamsher K de S 1989 *Multilingual Aphasia Examination*. A J A Associates, Iowa City, IA

Blomert L, Kean M L, Koster C, Schokker J 1994 Amsterdam-Nijmegen Everyday Language Test: Construction, reliability and validity. *Aphasiology* **8:** 381–407

Borkowsky J G, Benton A L, Spreen O 1967 Word fluency and brain damage. *Neuropsychologia* **5:** 130–40

Buckingham H W 1991 Explanations of the concept of apraxia of speech. In: Sarno M T (ed.) *Acquired Aphasia* (2nd ed). Academic Press, San Diego, CA

Caplan D 1995 Language disorders. In: Mapou R L, Spector J (eds.) *Clinical Neuropsychological Assessment: A Cognitive Approach*. Plenum Press, New York

Caramazza A 1986 On drawing inferences about the structure of normal cognitive systems from the analysis of impaired performance: The case for single patient studies. *Brain and Cognition* **5:** 45–66

Ciurli P, Marangolo P, Basso A 1996 *Esame del Linguaggio* (2nd ed.). Organizzazioni Speciali, Firenze

De Bleser R, Stadie N, Cholewa J, Tabatabaie S 1998 *LeMo-Lexicon: modellorientierte Einzelfalldiagnostik bei Aphasie, Dyslexie and Dysgraphie*. Hogrefe, Göttingen

De Renzi E, Faglioni P 1978 Normative data and screening power of a shortened version of the Token Test. *Cortex* **14:** 41–49

De Renzi E, Vignolo L A 1962 The Token Test: a sensitive test to detect receptive disturbances in aphasia. *Brain* **85:** 665–78

Dunn L M 1981 *Peabody Picture Vocabulary Test* (Revised). American Guidance Service, Circle Pines, MN

Goldstein K 1924 Das Wesen der amnestischen Aphasie *Schweizer Archiv für Neurologie und Psychiatrie* **15:** 163–75

Goldstein K 1948 *Language and Language Disturbances*. Grune and Stratton, New York

Goodglass H, Kaplan E 1983 *Boston Diagnostic Aphasia Examination (BDAE)* (2nd ed.) Lea and Febiger, Philadelphia, PA

Goodman R A, Caramazza A 1985 *The John Hopkins University Dysgraphia Battery*. John Hopkins University, Baltimore, MD

Holland A L 1980 *Communicative Abilities in Daily Living: A Test of Functional Communication for Aphasic Adults*. Pro-Ed, Austin, TX

Huber W, Poeck K, Weniger D, Willmes K 1983 *Der Aachener Aphasie Test (AAT)*. Hogrefe, Göttingen

Huber W, Poeck K, Willmes K 1984 The Aachen Aphasia Test (AAT). *Advances in Neurology* **42:** 291–303

Isserlin M 1922 Über Agrammatismus. *Zeitschrift für die gesamte Neurologie und Psychiatrie* **75:** 322–410

Jakobson R 1964 Toward a linguistic typology of aphasic impairments. In: De Reuck A V S, O'Connor M (eds.) *Disorders of Language*. Churchill, London

Kaplan E F, Goodglass H, Weintraub S 1983 *The Boston Naming Test* (2nd ed.) Lea and Febiger, Philadelphia, PA

Kay J, Lesser R, Coltheart M 1992 *PALPA: Psycholinguistic assessment of language processing in aphasia*. Lawrence Erlbaum, Hove

Keenan J S, Brassell E G 1975 *Aphasia Language Performance Scales (ALPS)* Pinnacle Press, Murfreesboro, TN

Kerschensteiner M, Poeck K, Brunner E 1972 The fluency-nonfluency dimension in the classification of aphasic speech. *Cortex* **8:** 233–47

Kertesz A 1979 *Aphasia and Associated Disorders: Taxonomy, Localization and Recovery*. Grune and Stratton, New York

Kertesz A 1982 *Western Aphasia Battery*. The Psychological Corporation, San Antonio, TX

Lecours A R, Lhermitte F 1976 The 'pure form' of the phonetic disintegration syndrome (pure anarthria); anatomo-clinical report of a historical case. *Brain and Language* **3:** 88–113

Lezak M D 1995 *Neuropsychological Assessment* (3rd ed.) Oxford University Press, New York

Lichtheim L 1885 On Aphasia, *Brain* **7:** 433–84

Luzzatti C, Laiacona M, Allamano N, De Tanti A, Inzaghi M G 1998 Writing disorders in Italian aphasic patients: a multiple single-case study of dysgraphia in language with shallow orthography. *Brain* (in press)

Marie P 1906 Révision de la question de l'aphasie: la troisième circonvolution frontale gauche ne joue aucun rôle spécial dans la fonction du language. *Semaine Médicale* **26:** 241–47

Marshall J C 1986 The description and interpretation of aphasic language disorders. *Neuropsicologia* **24:** 5–24

Miceli G, Laudanna A, Burani C, Capasso R 1996 *Batteria per l'Analisi dei Deficit Afasici*. IRCCS Santa Lucia, Rome

Nelson H E 1982 *The National Adult Reading Test (NART): Test manual*. NFER-Nelson, Windsor

Novelli G, Papagno C, Capitani C, Laiacona M, Vallar G, Cappa S 1996 Tre test clinici di ricerca e produzione lessicale: taratura su soggetti normali. *Archivio di Psicologia, Neurologia e Psichiatria* **47:** 477–506

Paradis M 1987 *Bilingual Aphasia Test*. LEA, Hove

Penn C 1985 The profile of communicative appropriateness: a clinical tool for the assessment of pragmatics. *South African Journal of Communication Disorders* **32:** 18–23

Pick A 1913 *Die agrammatischen Sprachstörungen*. Springer Verlag, Berlin

Poeck K 1986 What do we mean by 'Aphasic Syndromes'? A neurologist's view. *Brain and Language* **20:** 79–89

Porch B E 1983 *Porch Index of Communicative Ability. Manual*. Consulting Psychologists Press, Palo Alto, CA

Rosenbeck J C, Kent R D, LaPointe L L 1984 *Apraxia of Speech: Physiology, Acoustics, Linguistics, Management*. College-Hill Press, San Diego, CA

Sarno M T 1969 *The Functional Communication Profile: Manual of directions*. Institute of Rehabilitation Medicine, NY University Medical Center, New York

Schuell H 1973 *The Minnesota Test for Differential Diagnosis of Aphasia* (2nd ed.). University of Minnesota Press, Minneapolis, MN

Snodgrass J G, Vanderwart M 1980 A standardised set of 260 pictures: norms for name agreement, image agreement, familiarity and visual complexity. *Journal of Experimental Psychology: Human Learning and Memory* **6:** 174–215

Spreen O, Benton A L 1977 *Neurosensory Center Comprehensive Examination for Aphasia*. University of Victoria Neuropsychology Laboratory, Victoria, BC

Spreen O, Strauss E 1991 *A Compendium of Neuropsychological Tests*. Oxford University Press, New York

Wernicke C 1874 *Der aphasische Symptomenkomplex*. Cohn and Weigert, Breslau

Wernicke C 1886 Die neueren Arbeiten über Aphasie. *Fortschritte der Medicin* **4:** 371–77, 463–82

Aphasia

R. Lesser

The study of acquired aphasia has changed dramatically since the 1970s. Advances in cognitive neuropsychology (a discipline which did not materialize in that form until the 1980s), in the application of specialist aspects of linguistics, and in neurology (in particular, in neuroradiology and neurobiology) have combined to produce new insights into the nature of aphasia. The purpose of this chapter is to review some of these changes and to describe the understanding in the 1990s of what aphasia is. It should be mentioned here that it is international practice for the terms 'dysphasia' and 'aphasia' to be used interchangeably.

About the surface phenomena of acquired aphasia there is little controversy. After injury of some kind to the brain (from a stroke, a head injury, surgery to remove a tumor, a toxic event which has affected the brain's supply of oxygen, etc.) many individuals experience difficulty in the use of their own language. The difficulty does not concern, or is not restricted to, the articulation of speech, but concerns the higher cognitive functions of language. There are often other consequences of the brain damage, and therefore other higher cognitive functions (memory, perception, and the organization of action) may also be impaired. As language is such an important part of human behavior, however, aphasia tends to be the dominant feature where this is present. It must not be forgotten, nevertheless, that individuals diagnosed as aphasic may suffer from other disorders which their difficulties in talking mask.

It is also widely agreed that aphasic individuals differ, and that they differ not only in the obvious dimension of degree of severity, but also in the quality and type of aphasia. Here controversy blossoms. There is disagreement as to whether the cases of individuals differ only due to the coincidental presence in varying degrees of complementary disorders (such as the ones referred to above), or as to whether they can be satisfactorily categorized into sets of syndromes on the basis of dysfunctions within aphasia itself, or as to whether the heterogeneity is such that each individual should be 'profiled' in detail, because each case is as unique as a fingerprint or DNA.

Such opinions are often influenced by the needs of different disciplines, and the study of aphasia is indeed a study where diverse disciplines interact, notably language pathology/therapeutics, neurology, psychology, and linguistics in their relevant subspecialisms. This has its impact not only on discussions about whether and how to classify people who have already been clinically diagnosed as having aphasia but also about whom to diagnose as aphasic. The problem is illustrated by two examples. First, there

has been controversy as to whether the progressively acquired language disorder which accompanies dementia of the Alzheimer type should be included within the aphasias. Neurologists frequently describe such patients as having aphasia among their symptoms. In contrast, many aphasia therapists would resist such a use of the term, in the belief that the patients they typically work with have disorders which are confined to the language system but which leave other aspects of cognitive functioning intact (see *Language Dysfunction in Dementia*).

A second example is in the labeling of brain-damaged patients who have right cerebral damage. Most individuals seem to have those aspects of language which are involved in the production of the grammatical, morphological, and phonological facets of language predominantly lateralized to the left cerebral hemisphere, and therefore can suffer impairment of these systems after left brain damage. Other aspects of language seem, however, to involve also (or only) the right cerebral hemisphere; these are lexical semantics, prosody, and aspects of pragmatics such as inferencing and interpreting speaker intent rather than literal meaning. Many people with right brain damage, therefore, experience a disorder of these aspects of language, although this is unlikely to be recognized in the limited interview situation of a neurological clinic. Neurologists consequently have resisted describing these patients as aphasic, while linguists and language therapists have been happy to include them among subjects for investigation and remediation, as examples of people with acquired disorders of language, that is, aphasia. For present purposes an operational definition of aphasia as comprising those acquired disorders of language which are conventionally so labeled in clinics will be accepted, thereby avoiding these controversies by excluding both the language of dementia patients and that of the right brain damaged. But before further discussion of the influences on the study of aphasia of the many disciplines involved, a look at some descriptions of individuals who have been labeled as aphasic will illustrate the heterogeneity of this condition, even when this narrow operational definition is taken.

1. Case Studies

1.1 Case Study: Jim

Jim was a manager for a nationalized industry, responsible for deploying 128 employees. A heart attack did not prevent him from sometimes staying on duty in emergencies for 48 hours at a time. On retirement he took a climbing holiday with his wife in

Scotland, during which he caught what seemed to be a summer cold. Still ill on returning home he called the doctor; two days later he was barely conscious and was admitted to hospital. Jim remembers coming to in the hospital, hearing a remote voice telling him he had had a stroke.

He was paralyzed down his right side, blind, and unable to speak. His feeling of disturbed hearing during the first week focused on his left ear: voices sounded far away but not indistinct. His vision returned slowly, but reading remained difficult because the printed characters ran together and seemed to slope downwards; the edges of the pavement and stairs also seemed to slope away, a difficulty Jim surmounted by going down steps backwards. Color vision took a year to come back. Watching rapid movement (as when traffic is passing in a public street) still causes transient attacks of breathlessness and tingling sensations.

Later Jim described his experiences as speech came back. At first he was aware that he was speaking in single words: it was not till 4 months later that his wife commented that he had at last produced a full sentence. As soon as Jim appreciated what had happened to him with the stroke, he set himself to recover his lost speech. He kept a tally of what day of the week it was from his wife, found initially that he could count up to six and extended it the following day to 12; he set himself to remember, and later to pronounce, the names of his family and the 128 employees at his work. His technique of recovering oral speech was to practice subvocally, and to speak with normal loudness when he had prepared a group of words. Three years after the stroke he describes himself, when lost for a word, as working it out by using a gesture to act it out and then usually getting the word. His wife's understanding of his difficulties and her intuitive awareness of when to offer help and when to hold back have been invaluable to him.

1.2 Case Study: Edward

Edward, a graduate in mechanical engineering with his own business, at the age of 45 began to experience episodes of dizziness during which he heard voice-like noises and had some disturbances of speech. A left temporo-parietal space-occupying lesion was diagnosed, thought to be an infiltrating gliomatous tumor, and surgery was not advised. Two years later, since the expected rapid expansion of the tumor had not occurred, the diagnosis was changed to benign meningioma. Since his speech and reading ability deteriorated over the next 6 years to such an extent that his ability to continue his work was in question, it was decided to remove the slow-growing meningioma surgically.

Thirteen years later he still has major word-finding difficulties in conversation, which formal naming tasks throw into sharp focus. His speech is also marked by repetitive attempts to produce a word by attempting its pronunciation (a form of phonemic paraphasia). He frequently seems to have a better visual than phonological representation of a word he is trying to find, and can often specify how many letters it contains. Discharged from speech therapy several years ago, he continues his naming exercises and is an avid subject for students and researchers who continue to test his naming ability and to analyze his disorder. His reading ability has improved, although he still makes occasional errors when reading aloud words which are irregularly spelled, such as reading 'break' as /brik/. His pronunciation of words he is reading aloud often shows the reading analogy of phonemic paraphasias, phonemic paralexias. Like Jim his understanding of his situation is excellent, and so, on the surface, is his comprehension of language; yet when asked to define printed words he has been asked to read he can make fundamental errors such as describing 'heir' as a four-legged animal (hare) and 'soul' as 'on my shoes' (sole).

1.3 Case Study: Jane

Jane had a stroke which left her with a right hemiplegia at the age of 59. The owner of a beauty parlor, who had always prided herself in her appearance, she became depressed at this transformation of her life and, since a severe aphasia left her with no means of expressing her frustrations in words, attempted suicide. The tensions of this time caused a break with one of her married children. Unlike Jim and Edward, her difficulties in understanding language were obvious; she had difficulty in understanding verbal (but not nonverbal) instructions and in answering simple yes/no questions, and was uncertain in locating parts of her body by name such as her wrists and shoulders. She was equally at a loss whether verbal materials were given to her in a written or auditory form. Her spontaneous spoken output was restricted to 'yes' and 'no,' and her ability to repeat even monosyllabic words or speech sounds was extremely limited with a distorted production (verbal apraxia).

In the three years following the stroke, with periods of speech therapy and intensive practice from a tape recorder at home, she recovered the ability to use some functional phrases spontaneously, for example, in advising a fellow aphasic stroke patient to 'fight all (the) time' and in offering visitors refreshment. Her ability to discriminate between words which are closely semantically associated, however, remains impaired; for example, she has difficulty in choosing between a picture of a stamp and a picture of an envelope when she reads or hears the word 'stamp.'

1.4 Case Study: Mary

Mary, a widowed housewife, at 76 was older than Jane when a stroke two days after an operation for gallstone removal left her aphasic. She is not hemiplegic, but has a right visual field defect following the accident. This makes for difficulties when she goes out since she tends to bump into objects on the right and can miss seeing turnings. Her 'small talk' is unaffected, and her speech in such a context is fluent and articulated clearly. She is very concerned, however, by the change in her ability to speak. Any formal language task stresses her, and she tries to avoid, by reverting to discussing her troubles, any tasks such as picture description or comprehension tests which the therapist attempts with her. Her speech often includes 'jargon' words which are unintelligible strings of sounds which she does not attempt to correct. Although she scores low on formal tests of verbal comprehension, she manages to live satisfactorily on her own and to do her own shopping in the nearby supermarket using a list the therapist has worked out with her. Her ability to read (silently) such functional material is superior to her ability to discriminate between phonemically similar words in hearing, although a test of pure-tone hearing does not show any greater impairment than would be expected for her age.

2. Interpreting Aphasia before the 1980s

As the above brief examples show, clinical observations of people diagnosed as being aphasic draw attention both to their variability and to certain similarities, as well as to the frequent presence of other consequences of brain damage. This section will review how such clinical observations were developed into the current interpretations of the nature of aphasia (see Fig. 1). A superficial examination of the cases described above would suggest that aphasic people can be distinguished as to whether their disorder is primarily one of the expression of speech or its

comprehension. This medical shorthand persists in the 1990s, despite its inadequacy in any other setting than an acute medical ward where rapid decisions about the status of cognitive functions have to be made. Jim and Edward appear to have 'expressive' disorders, Jane and Mary 'comprehension' ones. In fact, even with the skimpy information given in the case descriptions above, it is clear that all the patients have disorders which affect the expression of speech, and that three (Edward as well as Jane and Mary) have specific disorders of verbal comprehension. Edward's appears to be limited to reading on the above description, but he also makes some errors when asked to choose appropriate pictures on hearing 'reversible' sentences (e.g., *The man's following the horse/The horse's following the man*). Detailed testing of Jim was not undertaken, but his self-report suggests some initial difficulty with understanding spoken language, and patients with the 'agrammatic' speech he demonstrated have sometimes been reported to have similar difficulties in understanding speech (the controversial issues relating to this will be discussed below). Even a cursory examination, therefore, shows the unsatisfactory nature of a dichotomous interpretation of aphasia as binary in nature, affecting expression *or* comprehension.

The primary influences in refining interpretations of aphasia up to the 1980s were from psychometrics and neurology. Linguistic and computational influences have increased since then, and will be outlined later. Several texts have surveyed the historical development of aphasiology since the 1860s (and indeed much earlier, dating back to 2800 BC). Here will be discussed only briefly those texts which have had a

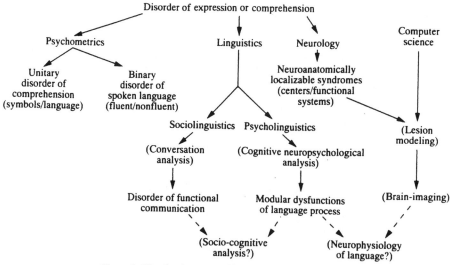

Figure 1. The development of interpretations of aphasia.

material consequence for the modern analysis of aphasia and which still have currency in some quarters.

3. Psychometrics

The psychometric approach to aphasia arose from dissatisfaction with the subjective nature of clinical observations at a time when behavioral psychology was a dominant paradigm in the 1960s. Although behaviorism soon lost its attractiveness, some of its influences on aphasiology can still be traced. One tenet was that the critical dimension through which aphasia should be analyzed was spoken language, the overt behavior through which aphasia could be examined. Unlike comprehension, spoken language can be tape-recorded, and measured objectively through word counts, type–token ratio, phrase length, noun–pronoun ratio, word frequency, etc. When this was applied to aphasia, an objective dichotomization of aphasic patients was reported between fluent speakers and nonfluent speakers and duly mapped on to sites of brain lesion. Although the limitation of this approach for understanding the nature of aphasia soon became apparent, the terms 'fluent' and 'nonfluent' still have currency in the 1990s as a shorthand summary of a first examination of a patient. The emphasis on examination of spoken language has its modern form in the application by linguists of the techniques of discourse and conversation analysis to aphasia.

Another by-product of the behaviorist era was the development of psychometric tests specifically for aphasia. The prime example of this, the Porch Index of Communicative Ability, was designed to meet psychologists' standards for reliability, standardization, and validity. It too quantifies aphasia through the overt behavior of the patients during the test. For example, tests which require the patient to read a card and place it according to the written instruction are classed, not as tests of reading comprehension, but as tests of gesture. Although the test battery meets its criteria for reliability and standardization, its face validity as a measure of communicative ability is questionable. Nevertheless it continues in clinical use, particularly as a measure of change after intervention. Porch's factor analysis of results from his standardization data led him to propose a classification which distinguishes types of behavior only through their accompanying behaviors, that is, *aphasia without complications*, *aphasia with verbal formulation problems*, and *aphasia with illiteracy*.

Other investigators came to similar conclusions, though from a different orientation, that is, one which focuses on comprehension rather than the production of spoken language. This unitary nature of aphasia as essentially a disorder of comprehension has been seen by some as extending to the use of concepts and symbols in general, though some of the evidence on which this interpretation is based (e.g., the inability to match percepts or to make clay models of animals) could be reinterpreted as gnosic or praxic disorders co-occurring with aphasia. Examinations of whether aphasia is an 'asymbolia' have assessed aphasic patients' understanding and use of signs and symbols in nonverbal communication or in reading, and on the whole support the view that language and nonverbal communication to a large extent draw on different systems.

Yet others have concluded that the comprehension disorder in aphasia is specifically restricted to language, with other aspects of cognition spared. Prominent amongst these investigators was the language therapist, Schuell (Schuell et al. 1964). A test of auditory comprehension using tokens was developed in the 1960s (De Renzi and Vignolo 1962), the application of which showed impairment in the great majority of aphasic patients, including those where previous clinical examination had failed to suggest any. The nature of the deficit in verbal comprehension has been the subject of much debate, much of it focusing on the question of whether it is due to a central loss of language ability (perhaps selective to one domain of language such as grammar) or to limitations of processing capacity. Some of this debate will be described in the later discussion of the cognitive neuropsychological approach to aphasiology. Meanwhile the current view of those who interpret aphasia as a unitary disorder (*aphasia without adjectives*) is summarized by Darley (1982: 447) as follows: 'Patients with aphasia emerge from varying analyses displaying marked commonalities, which leads us to believe they share a common impairment. This disorder is unitary and involves impairment of all aspects of language processing.'

4. Neurological Syndromes

This view of aphasia as unitary, developed by language pathologists and applied in stimulation therapy, was of little interest to neurologists concerned with localization of site of damage from patterns of behavioral symptoms. Such potential for localizing brain damage was useful to neurologists and neurosurgeons, particularly in the days before brain-imaging was able to give information on anatomical sites of damage and impaired utilization of glucose. Two neurologically based interpretations of aphasia which correlated types of aphasia with lesion sites became influential. One was developed in Russia by Luria (1966) drawing much of his localization evidence from studies of young soldiers with head wounds. His observations led him to conclude that different types of aphasia resulted from injury in different locations, and he drew up a sixfold classification of the principle syndromes (*efferent motor, afferent motor, dynamic, sensory, acoustic–amnesic,* and *semantic*)—later extended to include a seventh, *nominal*. Each location affected different language behaviors through its interruptions of mental functions such as kinetic organization or appreciation of logical relations. Although damage in different areas had these different results, Luria recognized that the sites thus identified could not be considered as the location of the functions, but envisaged the functions rather as drawing on extensive brain systems which could be interrupted by local damage.

Luria's model of aphasia has not been as influential outside Eastern Europe as another neurological model emanating from the USA, though based on earlier work in Western Europe. This is the Boston classification of aphasia (Goodglass and Kaplan 1983), which still provides the dominant neurological paradigm for aphasia, although its validity has been much questioned by adherents of the cognitive neuropsychological approach to aphasia. This classification uses the behaviors of fluent speech, auditory verbal comprehension, repetition, and naming to distinguish six types of aphasia. In *Broca's aphasia* the impairment is essentially in the production of fluent, well-articulated, and grammatically complex speech. In *Wernicke's aphasia* the key impairment is in comprehension. Disturbance of repetition is the identifying feature of *conduction aphasia*, and disturbance of naming in *anomia*; while repetition is preserved in the absence of comprehension in *transcortical sensory aphasia*, and in the absence of fluent self-initiated speech in *transcortical motor aphasia* (see *Syndromes of Aphasia*).

These observations are explained within a model in which heard language is considered to be processed within a posterior zone in the left temporal lobe (Wernicke's area), and passed during repetition of heard speech along the arcuate fasciculus (a bundle of nerve fibers which links the temporal, parietal, and frontal lobes) to a lower part of the frontal lobe (Broca's area). In this zone it is processed for the grammatical production and articulation of speech. The parietal lobe is involved in naming, since it functions as an association area in which all the experiences which contribute to word meaning are combined. There is thus a central language zone, according to this model, which corresponds closely to the main territory of the middle cerebral artery of the left hemisphere. The two transcortical aphasias follow damage which has left the greater part of this central language zone intact (thus preserving repetition) but has interrupted its connections with word meaning (*transcortical sensory aphasia*) or speech initiation (*transcortical motor aphasia*). This set of six syndromes in the Boston classification has been further elaborated to cope with the number of patients whose language behavior is difficult to classify, for example, by adding *global aphasia* for patients with difficulties in all functions, *mixed aphasia* for Broca's aphasics with poor comprehension and various types of *subcortical aphasias*. This model has been criticized on two grounds, first its

grossly oversimplistic conceptualization of 'language' and second (in common with other syndrome-based models) for its dependence on assumptions of homogeneity within syndromes which are essentially polythetic in nature.

5. Psycholinguistic Modeling of Aphasia

An alternative to the syndrome-based analysis of aphasia has been developed in cognitive neuropsychology, in which the complexes of symptoms which occur in aphasia are interpreted through psycholinguistic models derived from studies of normal language processing in laboratory experiments. So far this has been best developed for the processing of single words, although some attempts have been made to apply linguistic proposals about sentence processing to aphasia. Before looking at these in a little more detail, the assumptions on which these models are based need to be admitted.

The first assumption is that mental processes are modular in nature, that is, that they consist of inherently independent, although interacting, operational modules, such that any one of them can malfunction selectively and to a much greater degree than others with which it has links. The notion of modularity, which derives particularly from the development of computing, has been productively applied in fields as varied as Chomskyan linguistics and the physiology of visual perception. The modules of language envisaged in this scheme are more elaborate than the crude divisions of language behaviors used in the Boston analysis, although they are still grossly underspecified. They comprise analyzers, lexicons, buffers, conversion procedures, and a semantic system, as will be described below. A second assumption is that extrapolations can be made from abnormal mental functioning (as in aphasia) to normal functioning and that the behavior does reveal the performance of the normal system minus the impaired module or modules, rather than a new system developed through the patient's coping strategies. This psycholinguistic modeling uses a more abstract level of analysis than neurological models and is essentially independent of any mapping on to brain locations, although its claims are being tested against the evidence of functional localization through brain imaging.

5.1 Disorders of Auditory Comprehension

A lexical psycholinguistic model which has been used for the analysis of aphasia is presented in Fig. 2. It includes the processing of words through reading and writing. These will not be discussed here as they form the subject of a separate chapter (see *Disorders of Reading and Writing*), although it is important to remember that aphasia includes disorders to these systems as well as to the primary systems of producing and comprehending spoken language.

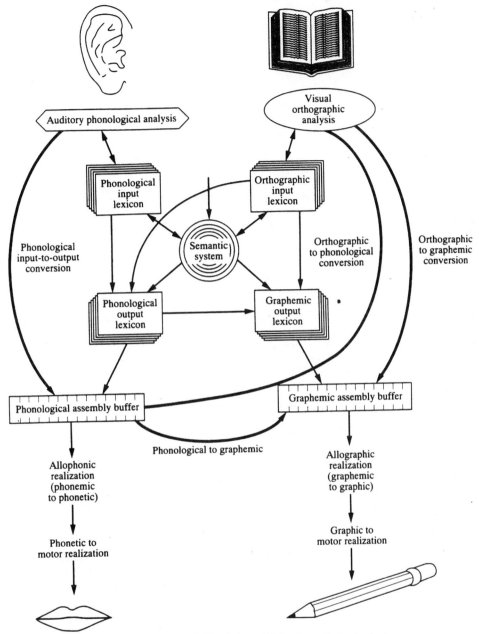

Figure 2. A lexical psycholinguistic model for the analysis of aphasia.

The model proposes that hearing words must have as a preliminary stage some analysis of the string of speech sounds. In cognitive neuropsychological modeling this is only one aspect in which a presumed module is grossly underspecified. The confusion results in different terminology for this module, describing it as acoustic, or auditory, or phonological. It is suggested that the function of the analysis system is to extract individual speech sounds from the speech wave. This already implies a degree of abstraction in speech perception, beyond variations of speaker characteristics and allophones. The cohort theory of word perception proposed by Marslen-Wilson and Tyler (1980) supports this claim of the sequential processing of speech sounds, with each possible word beginning with such sounds being alerted and the possible cohort becoming reduced as the analysis progresses. An impairment in this analyzer would result in a behavior described as 'word-sound deafness.' In its pure form auditory comprehension is affected, but not reading comprehension or other uses of language. The patient may be helped by lip-read and contextual cues. Although speech is unaffected, the task of repeating words will be impossible if the impairment is severe, but a slow rate of presentation may assist a partially damaged analyzer to cope. Ellis and Young (1988) suggest that the acoustic analysis system of the right hemisphere may be called into play in such circumstances.

The phonological input lexicon (or speech input lexicon, or auditory input lexicon) is a notion developed from Morton's (1981) logogen system. Its independence from both the semantic system and a visual input lexicon, used in reading, was first established by cognitive psychologists in laboratory work with normal subjects, who showed no effect of cross-priming from one lexicon to the other. This proposal has been amply supported by evidence from the selective nature of brain-damage in affecting either auditory or visual verbal processing. (The term *lexicon* suggests a store of words. This may be misleading: it is more likely to be a process whereby distributed word fragments shared by a number of words are actively computed.) This lexicon recognizes spoken words as having been heard before, though the model proposes that understanding of their meaning does not occur at this stage. The usual way to test the relative intactness of this lexicon in a patient is to give a spoken 'lexical decision' task, that is, to ask the listener to distinguish between words and nonwords from a heard list. Patients with damage to the lexicon will make errors on this, with particular uncertainty about low-frequency words. Such patients are described as having 'word-form deafness.' Unlike the patient with word-sound deafness, the word-form deaf patient will still be able to repeat words and nonwords which are heard, since this can be achieved without use of a lexicon. Without any contextual information the patient will not be able to say what the words mean, although able to say when words sound different from each other. It is characteristic of some normal older speakers to have difficulty with repetition of nonwords and to tend to repeat them as words, as if use of the lexical route for repetition is dominant.

There are other patients who perform well on auditory lexical decision tasks but fail to understand spoken word meaning. If they understand written words, and their speech is unimpaired, this cannot be a difficulty with the semantic system itself. The model interprets it as an access problem specific to access to the semantic system from the auditory input lexicon, and describes these patients as having 'word-meaning deafness.' The fluctuating periods of non-comprehension in some aphasic patients may be due to transient access failure of this kind, although it

could also be explained by a temporary overloading of the phonological analyzer. The phenomenon of semantic satiation which occurs in normal subjects on hearing the same word repeated several times suggests that an interpretation as an access problem is the more plausible, since such subjects can continue to repeat the words while having lost access to their meaning; an analyzer problem would also be expected to result in accumulating errors in repeating the same word since feedback would be impaired.

The ultimate module needed for lexical comprehension is the semantic system. Since the semantic system is defined (inadequately) as the component which deals with meaning, this is a tautology. A substantial literature has speculated on the nature of this semantic system. Data from brain-damaged patients suggests that a verbal semantic system may be separable from a visual semantic system (Morton 1981), and that broken links between the two systems may be the source of the problem in *optic aphasia*. Category-specific impairments have also been reported, with the most frequent dissociation being between abstract and concrete words. Most commonly words of high imageability are understood better than those with low imageability. Impairment of the verbal semantic system, according to the model, will affect all forms of verbal comprehension (auditory, reading, and signing), and the production of speech, sign, and writing. Semantic paraphasias and paragraphias (production of a word related in meaning, such as 'brother' for 'sister') may be expected to occur with a semantic disorder, though as these also occur in normal subjects occasionally, they are more likely to be due to a slippage in the output system rather than inherently in the semantic system itself. A more reliable indicator of a semantic system disorder may be acceptance of a heard semantic associate for a word as the target word itself, for example, as when a patient seeking the word 'sister' accepts 'brother' as correct.

In all the above forms of aphasia it is rare to find a patient with a disorder which can be attributed exclusively to one malfunctioning process, and also rare to find a patient in whom the process seems to be completely unavailable at all times. It is more common to find patients with relatively impaired processes and fluctuating behaviors, which suggest that overloading of the system under some conditions exposes its weaknesses. This same observation applies to the other phenomena of the aphasias, including difficulties in the production of spoken words (see Sect. 5.2 below).

5.2 Disorders in Speaking Words

Though the different types of auditory comprehension difficulties outlined above are hard to identify in the clinical examination of aphasic people, the differential analysis of disorders in word production has for a longer time been easier due to the observable phenomena of speech. These include circumlocutions during word-finding difficulties, semantic paraphasias, phonemic paraphasias (misproductions phonologically related to the target word), neologisms (uninterpretable strings of speech sounds, which form 'new words'), and phonetic distortions of words. Lesser (1989) has attempted to interpret these phenomena in terms of the model presented in Fig. 2, and to relate them to clinical classifications and implications for therapy.

A central *semantic disorder* (in which comprehension would also be implicated) could result in the production of semantic paraphasias, as in globally aphasic patients provided that their output difficulties are not so great as to make all speech difficult. In some other cases it can result in what has been described as 'semantic jargon.' This consists of fluent speech, well-articulated and structured, using recognizable words, but speech which does not make sense as a coherent whole, and which seems tangential to the context in which it is uttered. In such cases damage to the right cerebral hemisphere, as well as the left, may be implicated.

Neologisms have been explained as productions of phonemic strings which fill gaps where the listener would have expected content words. This is because they frequently can be analyzed as carrying inflections and showing the stress pattern typical of nouns. It has been hypothesized that a free-running phonological processor fills these gaps with strings of phonemes (which conform to the language's phonotactic rules) so as to maintain the sentence-like form of an utterance. Whether the underlying disorder is semantic in nature is debatable; in support of this interpretation is the observation that patients with a marked degree of neologistic speech also have comprehension disorders, and appear to be unaware of the bizarre nature of their speech. However, neologisms may be due to a difficulty in activating lexical units in the phonological output lexicon, with a consequent difficulty in activating later stages, including selection of phonemes.

In other cases, where the dominant behavior is circumlocutions, as in some types of *anomic aphasia,* the essential difficulty can be interpreted as being in the access from the semantic system to the phonological output lexicon. Such patients can clearly show in their circumlocutions that they have knowledge of many aspects of the word's meaning, but they are unable to access the form of the word in their lexicon. In normal subjects, this is the tip-of-the-tongue feeling sometimes occurring when they try to recall low-frequency words. In aphasic patients, although word frequency is influential too, this difficulty can occur with high frequency and high imageability words, and is typically examined through picture naming tests. It is not uncommon for patients with this *lexical access word-finding disorder* to produce exploratory phonemic paraphasias when seeking to retrieve a word, as if

attempting a production which includes the same sound or syllable as the target might assist retrieval. This implies that fragmentary information about the item in the lexicon is available, as well as its semantic specification. When given the target word, such patients generally immediately recognize it as the one they were seeking; the word is therefore represented in their lexicon, but was not accessible reliably at will. A degree of variability seems characteristic of such patients, that is, although they may make a similar number of errors when given the same list for naming several times, the items on which they make the errors may differ. Patients with such a disorder of access to the phonological output lexicon have no difficulty in repeating words they hear, and their phonemic paraphasias are therefore of a different nature from those which occur from an output process from the phonological output lexicon, the assembly of the word structure in the output buffer.

This more peripheral disorder results in phonemic paraphasias which are more prominent on longer words than shorter, and which occur even when the target word has been modeled for the patient to echo, as in a repetition task. This kind of behavior has been labeled *'conduction aphasia'* in the neurologically based classification. The essential difficulty seems to be in organizing the selection of phonemes and syllables and in assembling them in the correct order for realization in speech. In this *lexical assembly disorder* similarity of phonemes and syllables within the word seems to increase the difficulty for the patient, but there seems to be little carry-over in the phonemic paraphasias from word to word, other than those which can be attributed to perseveration of segments from one planning phrase to another. This has been attributed to an inability to clear the phonological output buffer. The fact that phonemic paraphasias occur predominantly within rather than across words incidentally provides some justification for examining this phenomenon within a lexical rather than a sentence model.

Phonemic paraphasias occur also with another type of difficulty, one which affects the allophonic realization of the phonemes themselves. These phonetic distortions in an *allophonic realization disorder* can be such as to shift the realization from one phoneme category to another in the listener's ear, as when an early onset of voicing of a bilabial stop results in /b/ rather than /p/. This can occur in apraxia of speech, interpreted as a disorder in the programming of the speech sounds, and is considered to be one of the features of *Broca's aphasia* in the neurological classification. It is typically described as variable in nature, with overlearned phrases and emotionally salient phrases being well-articulated. In this it differs from the even more peripheral disorder of speech production, dysarthria, in which the phonetic distortions occur whatever the nature of the utterances (see *Acquired Dysarthrias*).

This psycholinguistic model of lexical processing therefore gives some coherence to the interpretation of some aphasic disorders, and is particularly helpful in providing a rationale for therapy (see *Acquired Disorders of Language (Aphasia): Evaluation of the Effectiveness of Intervention*). Its assumptions of serial processing and of isolable modules have been criticized, however. Some theorists incorporate forward cascading and/or reverse feedback in the model, with activation from a later stage flowing back to an earlier stage. As with the difficulty which the neurological classifications present for categorizing an individual, it is rare to find a patient whose disorder can be interpreted exactly within this model without resort to a multiplicity of presumed malfunctions; a prime example of this is in Howard and Franklin's (1988) analysis of an individual's disorder as having eight components. Lexical analyses of this kind are, of course, also inherently limited in that they take no cognizance of longer stretches of utterance.

5.3 Disorders of Understanding and Speaking Sentences

When it was revealed through the Token Test (De Renzi and Vignolo 1962) that patients previously categorized as having good comprehension did make errors in comprehending sentences, it first seemed that such comprehension difficulties did not differ among types of aphasia. It was then proposed that patients with *Wernicke's aphasia* failed on such tests because of their 'lexical' disorder (not further specified in terms of a psycholinguistic model) while patients with a *Broca's aphasia* failed because of a 'syntactic' disorder. This led to much scrutiny of the comprehension of patients with the agrammatic speech associated with *Broca's aphasia*. In such speech, content words predominate and syntax is restricted to simple structures. In some patients function words and inflections are omitted. Berndt (1987) has commented that nonfluency is not necessarily accompanied by such omission of grammatical markers, nor indeed by gross structural simplifications, and also that structural abnormalities can occur despite retention of grammatical markers. Moreover omission of grammatical markers is not necessarily accompanied by poor performance on tests of 'syntactic' comprehension where the patient has to choose a correct picture to match a plausibly reversible sentence (such as *The rock hits the car*).

It is clear that there are different possibilities for dysfunctions in sentence production, and that the behavior of 'agrammatism' may be due to different origins. Schwartz (1987) has applied Garrett's (1980) model of sentence production by normal speakers to the analysis of aphasic utterances. Schwartz's adaptation of Garrett's model describes the transition from the stage at which the message to be conveyed is established as comprising both abstract lexical selection and abstract formulation of a functional argument structure—the thematic roles of who-does-what-to-whom. When this functional level of representation has been generated, a syntactic planning frame is developed in parallel with retrieval of lexical form from the phonological output lexicon. The lexical items are, it is suggested, inserted phoneme by phoneme into the planning frame at a positional level of representation in which the final order of items has been established and grammatical morphemes are added.

Such a model can account for the dissociation of retrieval of content words and grammatical morphemes in agrammatism. Parisi (1987: 216) also notes that: 'To be able to produce function words is not the same thing as to be able to put content words in syntactic constructions. These seem to be two distinct components of the sentence production capacity.' He also concludes that there is no clear distinction between agrammatic speech and the 'paragrammatic' speech classically associated with *Wernicke's aphasia,* in which errors on function words predominate. There seems, rather, to be a continuum of difficulty in sentence production in aphasia, in which, despite the theoretically procedural independence of content word and function word production, disruption of one tends to be accompanied by disruption of the other.

It is not inherent in these sentence production models that patients who have difficulty in producing sentences should necessarily have difficulty in comprehending them. (Indeed, in the lexical model described above, there is an inherent theoretical dissociation between the ability to comprehend and to produce.) Although cases have been described of agrammatic speakers who perform well on comprehension tasks there is a substantial body of literature which suggests that most aphasic people experience difficulties in sentence comprehension. This has been shown both in metalinguistic judgment tasks, in picture-choice tasks, and in object manipulation tasks. Given that comprehension requires an initial parsing of the sentence, and that grammatical morphemes are thought to play an important role in this parsing, Bradley and her colleagues (Bradley et al. 1980) linked the comprehension and production difficulties of agrammatic patients through their impairment of the parsing and grammatical uses of these morphemes (although they agreed that their semantic representations were retained in the lexicon in which content words are also stored). Bradley's inferences were shown to be questionable on experimental grounds, but nevertheless this discussion reinforced the possibility of making a distinction between inherent knowledge of syntax and its availability for use in speech or comprehension—a distinction similar to that in lexical models between degradation of semantic knowledge and access from it in word retrieval difficulties.

Testing such a distinction, Linebarger et al. (1983) gave patients, who had failed on sentence–picture choice tasks of comprehension, sets of other sentences to judge for their grammaticality. They reported success on the latter task in judging violations of transformational operations, verb subcategorization and, to some extent, the appropriate usage of grammatical words. This underlines the importance of examining how the particular methodology used influences the results on comprehension tasks. It has been suggested that a judgment task of this kind allows the patients to focus on the critical aspect of the deviant sentence, without requiring them to construct the sentence themselves either for speech or in the process of comprehension. Thus, this type of judgment task allows for a trade-off between semantics and syntactic operations, rather than making demands on both. There is support for a 'mapping hypothesis' to account for such results, that is, that agrammatic patients have difficulty in coordinating sentence meaning with sentence form (i.e., mapping syntax on to semantics), and that this is bidirectional in nature, affecting both the production and the comprehension of sentences.

It has also been pointed out that sentence–picture matching tasks draw on nonlinguistic operations as well as linguistic and that there are verb-specific effects in such comprehension tasks, which can be related to expectancies about the grammatical position of thematic roles. Current constraint-based models in linguistic theory also give more weight to the role of lexical-level information in sentence comprehension than syntax (MacDonald 1997). This goes counter to the claims of appliers of the Chomskyan Government–Binding theory that picture-choice and object-manipulation tests do examine syntactic comprehension rather than semantic comprehension. Object-manipulation tasks have similar limitations to picture-choice tasks. They also impose the additional load of formulation of a complex action plan and errors on such a task have been shown to correlate with degree of limb apraxia.

An alternative tack which has been used to examine this question of the extent to which impairment in sentence production in speech reflects impaired comprehension is through the use of on-line comprehension tasks. One form of examination of on-line processing uses a technique of measuring the time it takes to react to a target word or 'probe' which occurs during a heard sentence. The delay in responding is used as an indication of the amount of processing occurring at that point, and the position of the probe can be varied to assess this. The type of sentences used can also be varied, for example, scrambled strings which have neither syntactic nor semantic structure, semantically anomalous sentences which nevertheless retain syntactic structure, and sentences which conflict with pragmatic expectations created by a context. This technique has been used to examine the effects of semantic, pragmatic, and syntactic violations on sentence processing by aphasic speakers. Results suggest that some patients with agrammatic speech can construct a syntactic representation of sentences, while others can only construct local syntactic groupings. This raises the question of how much sentence comprehension is influenced by the limitations of working memory, and whether the inability to construct a broad syntactic framework is due to a central syntactic disorder or to a constricted syntactic processing buffer. The buffer does not seem to be the one used for processing word lists, since digit span scores do not correlate significantly with sentence comprehension scores, and this would argue for a specific buffer for syntactic operations. The conclusion that a syntactic deficit in production is not necessarily accompanied by a deficit in comprehension also supports a model in which a syntactic buffer is specific to comprehension.

A similar on-line technique has also been used by Shankweiler et al. (1989) to examine specifically the processing of grammatical words by agrammatic speakers. In this case the task was to judge the grammaticality of sentences in which there were misselections of grammatical words, some of them within-category, others crossing categories, as between prepositions and determiners. The position of the aberrant word was varied, as was its proximity to the 'licensing' word which dictated its grammaticality or not. The aphasic patients performed essentially in the same way as controls, although consistently slower and less accurate, and less sensitive to within–category substitutions. Shankweiler and his colleagues conclude that this is evidence that the agrammatic speakers retained basic syntactic knowledge, and were capable of using this during on-line processing, despite the failure of some of them on picture-choice tests of sentence comprehension. They therefore note that 'a unitary account of agrammatism that cuts across both production and perception of language remains elusive' (Shankweiler et al. 1989: 28), and they also prefer an account of aphasic disorders in terms of processing difficulties rather than a reduction of grammatical knowledge.

Aphasia is thus proving to be a rich area for testing and modifying psycholinguistic models. In parallel their application has revolutionized the assessment of language disorders in clinical practice, and lead to a new rationale for devising and evaluating therapy targeted at an individual's specific dysfunctions.

5.4 Disorders of Discourse, Pragmatics, and Functional Communication

It will have been clear from the discussion in the preceding section that there are many unanswered questions about the nature of aphasic disorders at the sentence level. Similar controversies are arising at the level of discourse, with its closer relationship to pragmatics and functional communication. Studies in the

1970s had suggested that aphasic patients retained discourse abilities in that they adhered to the rules for the well-formedness of texts in both procedural and narrative discourse, and that the pragmatic level of language use was generally spared in aphasia. In this they were contrasted with demented and schizophrenic speakers and, in some cases, with people with right-brain damage who showed a limitation in the ability to draw inferences in language and to use non-literal meaning.

The more detailed examination of the discourse produced by aphasic speakers, however, is revealing ways in which they differ from normal subjects also at this level. Studies of connected speech in aphasia have used four types of discourse: expository, that is, discussion of a topic or picture description, common in many formal test batteries of aphasia; procedural, in which the patient is asked to report on the ordered steps or procedures that are required for an everyday activity (such as changing a light bulb); narrative, or the telling of a story, perhaps prompted by a sequence of pictures; and conversational, that is, dyadic exchanges between listener and hearer, often in a spontaneous natural context.

Ulatowska and Bond (1983) have primarily reported on their studies of procedural and narrative discourse in aphasia. They have come to the conclusion that the essential structures of discourse are maintained in mild and moderate aphasia, for example, in narrative—the production of a setting, a complicating action, and a resolution—but that optional structures may often be omitted, for example, an abstract, a coda, and an evaluation. Similar observations have been made of procedural discourse obtained through role-play by means of the Everyday Language Test (Blomert et al. 1987). Discourse grammar therefore appears to be less disrupted than sentence grammar. Disruptions at the sentence level, however, do have consequences for discourse, characterized by Ulatowska and Bond (1983) as accounting for the fact that discourse, while maintaining comprehensibility, may lack clarity. The particular aspects in which sentence-level disorders affect discourse are analyzed by Ulatowska as being in the use of connectors to express cohesion, in poor control over tenses, and, most importantly, in reference. Aphasic patients may not supply the appropriate referent for the listener when they use pronouns instead of nouns, or fail to renominalize later to maintain a clear referent. Similarly on introducing an object they may use a definite article instead of an indefinite article. The listener therefore carries an undue load in attempting to interpret the aphasic speaker's meaning at a discourse level. These aspects which affect clarity of discourse, Ulatowska points out, can be observed in normal speakers; it is only the degree of difficulty which is different in aphasia. In this respect discourse analyses give different results from sentence and

phonological analyses in which aphasic language can differ qualitatively from normal language in respect of the production of neologisms and speech restricted to content words.

A burgeoning area of examination of aphasic language is through conversation analysis. This draws particularly on natural language samples, often between the aphasic person and carer at home, and thus addresses more closely the functional communication abilities of the patient than formal clinical tasks. Preliminary analyses at this level suggest that, while turn-taking abilities are preserved, repair sequences are often abnormal in being other-elicited and prolonged, while word-finding episodes in which both partners have cooperated may have elaborate closing sequences such as occur at the end of telephone conversations where speakers cannot see each other. Lesser and Milroy (1993) review the potential of conversational analysis for examining aphasia and its relevance to remediation.

6. Conclusion

The above discussion has only briefly described some of the main areas in which the study of aphasia has developed since the 1970s. The main ones which have been described are those which owe most to cognitive neuropsychology and to linguistics. The sociolinguistic examination of aphasia, with its emphasis on natural conversation, has been developing independently of the cognitive neuropsychological. A rapprochement between the two is looked for, in which cognitive neuropsychology begins to deal with naturalistic data and examines language above the levels of word and sentence, while the analysis of aphasic conversations begins to offer processing explanations as well as descriptions.

However, aphasiology is an interdisciplinary study, and developments are also occurring on other fronts. These include the attempt to map language (normal and disordered) on to brain function through functional Magnetic Resonance Imaging (f MRI), Positron Emission Tomography (PET) scan and other brain-imaging studies. Others include examination of the response of aphasic patients to pharmacological intervention based on a physiological interpretation of the disorder. Yet others include the computer modeling of language learning and language breakdown, a study which has been accelerated by the advent of connection is parallel processing and 'neural networks' in which computers reproduce some of the characteristics of the representation of knowledge in the brain.

As Fig. 1 envisages, a continuing advancement of knowledge about the relationships between language behavior and its neural substrate can be anticipated, as well as a greater understanding of the nature of the complex disorders in such case studies as those described at the beginning of this chapter. By 2020 notions of aphasia in the 1990s may seem as ingenuous as do now some of the interpretations which appeared definitive in the 1970s.

Acknowledgment

One of the case studies has been taken from an unpublished report written in cooperation with Mrs Marion Watt.

Bibliography

Berndt R S 1987 Symptom co-occurrence and dissociation in the interpretation of agrammatism. In: Coltheart M, Sartori G, Job R (eds.) *The Cognitive Neuropsychology of Language*. Erlbaum, London

Blomert L, Koster C, van Mier H, Kean M L 1987 Verbal communication abilities of aphasic patients: The everyday language test. *Aphasiology* **1(6)**: 463–74

Bradley D, Garrett M, Zurif E 1980 Syntactic deficits in Broca's aphasia. In: Caplan D (ed.) *Biological Studies of Mental Processes*. MIT Press, Cambridge, MA

Caplan D 1987 *Neurolinguistics and Linguistic Aphasiology*. Cambridge University Press, Cambridge

Coltheart M, Sartori G, Job R 1987 *The Cognitive Neuropsychology of Language*. Erlbaum, London

Darley F L 1982 *Aphasia*. W B Saunders, Philadelphia, PA

Davis G A 1983 *A Survey of Adult Aphasia*. Prentice Hall, Englewood Cliffs, NJ

De Renzi E, Vignolo L 1962 The token test: A sensitive test to detect receptive disturbances in aphasia. *Brain* **85**: 665–78

Ellis A W, Young A W 1988 *Human Cognitive Neuropsychology*. Erlbaum, Hove

Garrett M F 1980 Levels of processing in sentence production. In: Butterworth B (ed.) *Language Production*, Vol. 1. Academic Press, New York, NY

Goodglass H, Kaplan E 1983 *The Assessment of Aphasia and Related Disorders*. Lea & Febiger, Philadelphia, PA

Howard D, Franklin S 1988 *Missing the Meaning? A Cognitive Neuropsychological Study of the Processing of Words by an Aphasic Patient*. MIT Press, Cambridge, MA

Howard D, Hatfield F M 1987 *Aphasia Therapy: Historical and Contemporary Issues*. Erlbaum, Hove

Lesser R 1989 *Linguistic Investigations of Aphasia*, 2nd edn. Whurr, London

Lesser R, Milroy L 1993 *Linguistics and Aphasia: Psycholinguistic and Pragmatic Aspects of Intervention*. Longman, London

Linebarger M C, Schwartz M F, Saffran E M 1983 Sensitivity to grammatical structure in so-called agrammatic aphasics. *Cognition* **13**: 361–92

Luria A R 1966 *Higher Cortical Functions in Man*. Basic Books, New York

MacDonald M C 1997 Lexical representations and sentence processing: An introduction. *Language and Cognitive Processes* **12**: 121–36

Marslen-Wilson W D, Tyler L K 1980 The temporal structure of spoken language understanding. *Cognition* **8**: 1–71

Morton J 1981 The status of information processing models of language. *Philosophical Transactions of the Royal Society of London Biological Sciences* **295**: 387–96

Parisí D 1987 Grammatical disturbances of speech production. In: Coltheart M, Sartori G, Job R (eds.) *The Cognitive Neuropsychology of Language*. Erlbaum, London

Pizzamiglio L, Parisí D 1970 Studies on verbal comprehension in aphasia. In: Flores D'Arcais G B, Levelt W J M (eds.) *Advances in Psycholinguistics*. North Holland, Amsterdam

Schuell H, Jenkins J, Jiminez-Pabon E 1964 *Aphasia in Adults: Diagnosis, Prognosis and Treatment*. Hoeber, New York

Schwartz M F 1987 Patterns of speech production deficit within and across aphasia syndromes: Application of a psycholinguistic model. In: Coltheart M, Sartori G, Job R (eds.) *The Cognitive Neuropsychology of Language*. Erlbaum, London

Shankweiler D, Crain S, Gorrell P, Tuller B 1989 Reception of language in Broca's aphasia. *Language and Cognitive Processes* **4**: 1–33

Ulatowska H K, Bond S A 1983 Aphasia: Discourse considerations. *Topics in Language Disorders* **3(4)**: 21–34

Syndromes of Aphasia

D. Tranel and S. W. Anderson

1. Introduction

The study of language and its disorders (aphasia) is one of the most extensively developed areas of research and clinical application in neuropsychology. A good deal has been learned about neural systems related to capacities such as speed production, aural comprehension, lexical retrieval, and reading and writing (Benson 1993; Damasio and Damasio 1992). Understanding of brain-language relationships has been facilitated by multi-disciplinary approaches to the study of language, and scientists from fields such as cognitive psychology and linguistics, together with neuropsychologists and neurologists, have made important contributions to the investigation of speech and language (Fromkin and Rodman 1998; Garrett 1995; Goodglass 1993; Rosch et al. 1976; Zurif et al. 1993).

1.1 What are Syndromes Good for?

Before elaborating each of the major syndromes of aphasia, we would like to discuss for a moment the concept of *syndrome*, as it applies to disorders of speech and language.

We will focus primarily on the "classical" aphasia taxonomy, which may be defined roughly as those sets of language impairments, and their neuroanatomical correlates, which have occurred with sufficient regularity to have earned labels of common usage among clinicians (see Benson 1988; Goodglass 1993; Goodglass and Kaplan 1972; Whitaker 1984). The discovery of systematic relationships between specific regions of damage in the left hemisphere and particular patterns of aphasia provided some of the first compelling evidence that human cognitive operations could be linked to specific structural correlates. Certain of the aphasic syndromes which were described over a century ago on the basis of autopsy studies have stood the test of time well, with many confirmatory findings coming from modern neuropsychology and neuro-imaging (Benton and Anderson 1998; see *Historical Perspectives of Aphasia*).

With increasingly sophisticated linguistic probes and neuro-imaging techniques, there also has been growing appreciation for the variability inherent in aphasia, both with regard to functional differences between subjects with similar lesions, and in differences in the sites of anatomical damage in subjects with similar speech and language profiles. It is clear that the traditional aphasia diagnostic categories map only loosely on to behavioural and anatomical templates. Nonetheless, the classical taxonomy has survived because of its utility as shorthand for summarizing and transmitting information about certain general consistencies across individuals with aphasia. It should be obvious, but perhaps worth stating, that the use of this system in no way obviates the need for attention to the unique features of each patient's linguistic profile for aphasia clinical work and research.

The system is not static; it has undergone considerable revision and will continue to do so. A significant limitation at the present time is that many patients do not readily fit into a single diagnostic category. Also, the limited number of discrete categories does not accommodate easily the change which often characterizes aphasia, particularly during the acute recovery period. A patient with an aphasia which is best characterized as "global" today may become a Broca's aphasic by next week; a patient with Wernicke's aphasia may eventually be better classified as an anomic aphasia. Even in these situations, however, the classical aphasia taxonomy may be useful. For example, considerable information is conveyed among experienced clinicians with a statement such as, 'Following the sudden onset of global aphasia two weeks ago, Ms. X has shown gradual recovery into a severe Broca's aphasia.'

For aphasia, but by no means unique to this topic, there are many possible classification systems, and the traditional diagnostic categories are not well suited for all purposes. For example, it is often problematic to use the traditional diagnostic categories as the basis for forming groups in neurolinguistic research (for discussion, see Caramazza 1984; Schwartz 1984). A major difficulty in this context is the *polytypic* nature of the diagnostic categories, in that members of a category need not share any single attribute, and any one attribute may be represented in multiple categories (for discussion, see Schwartz 1984). For example, several patients may have been diagnosed with transcortical motor aphasia based on a profile of relative strengths and weaknesses in certain abilities (i.e., relatively preserved aural comprehension and verbatim repetition, in the context of effortful, dysfluent speech, etc.), but may differ significantly in overall severity of aphasia and other details of their linguistic profile, so that no scores on standardized test batteries would be identical across subjects. However, behaviors such as the production of phonemic paraphasic errors occur in virtually all of the major aphasia diagnostic categories.

Furthermore, the traditional aphasia diagnoses are based on broad and multifaceted constructs. For example, 'aural comprehension' may involve several dissociable components, and a 'naming impairment' may differentially involve various categories of entities, such as persons, animals, or artifacts, or may be restricted to certain grammatical classes (e.g., nouns vs. verbs) (see section on Anomic Aphasia below).

It also has become evident that the relationships between various signs in aphasic syndromes do not necessarily reflect principles of language organization. Certain signs may tend to co-occur simply due to damage in independent functional systems in neighboring structures. To illustrate, take the example of how anomia due to olfactory nerve damage is probabilistically associated with higher-order executive function deficits from orbital frontal lobe damage—here the inability to smell has nothing to do with judgment, decision-making, or social conduct. In a similar manner, the co-occurrence of pure alexia and right hemiachromatopsia likely reflects an accident of neuroanatomical contiguity, rather than an important functional relationship. As pointed out by Poeck (1983) and others, it is possible that even the two pillars of aphasia diagnosis, Broca's and Wernicke's aphasias, would be unknown if the vascularization of the brain were different. Obviously, all of the associations in aphasia profiles are not simply artifacts, but the meaning of the aphasic syndromes, and their associated validity and clinical utility, have changed. The classical aphasic syndromes once were intimately linked to theoretical accounts of the brain basis of language, but as neurolinguistic theories have evolved, the syndromes have come to serve a more utilitarian and atheoretical function. Although it can be argued that certain aspects of the classical aphasia taxonomy in use today reflect accidents of history, this system has persisted, at least in part, due to its utility in representing the natural categories imposed by damage to language-related brain regions.

2. Syndromes of Aphasia

We define aphasia as *an acquired disturbance of the comprehension and formulation of verbal messages*. It is caused by dysfunction in language-related cortical and subcortical structures in the left hemisphere. (In the case of language more so than any other domain of cognition, it is absolutely essential to keep in mind that typical brain-behavior relationships assume left hemisphere dominance for speech. This is true of virtually all, about 98%, dextrals, and most, about 70%, sinistrals.) Aphasia can be further specified as a defect in the two-way translation mechanism between thought processes and language, that is, between the nonverbal mental representations whose organized manipulation constitutes thought, and the verbal symbols and grammatical rules whose organized processing constitutes sentences. Aphasia can compromise either the *formulation* or *comprehension* of language, or both, and it can affect *syntax* (the grammatical structure of sentences), the *lexicon* (the dictionary of words that denote meanings), or *word morphology* (the combination of phonemes that results in word structure).

As alluded to earlier, deficits in various aspects of language occur with different severity and in different patterns, producing a number of distinctive syndromes of aphasia. Each syndrome has a defining set of neuropsychological manifestations (Table 1),

associated with a typical site of neural dysfunction (Table 2). Cerebrovascular disease is the most common cause of aphasia, with head injury and tumors being less frequent etiologies. Aphasia can also occur in the setting of progressive degenerative diseases, particularly Pick's disease and sometimes Alzheimer's disease, resulting in so-called "progressive aphasia" (see *Language Dysfunction in Dementia*). Below, we review the major aphasia syndromes, providing for each a description of prototypical neuropsychological manifestations and the characteristic neuro-anatomical features.

It is worth noting that some aphasia syndromes are considerably more common than others. The Broca, Wernicke, and global subtypes are most frequent. Focal damage to neural sectors in the territory of the left middle cerebral artery is relatively common, and these aphasia syndromes, all related to dysfunction of various sectors in the vicinity of the Sylvian fissure, occur with regularity in neurological patients with focal left hemisphere lesions.

There are well-developed treatment programs which can have a major beneficial effect on recovery from aphasia (e.g., Sarno 1991). In general, patients whose aphasia is caused by head injury fare better than patients whose aphasia is due to vascular causes, and younger age and higher premorbid intelligence are also related to better recovery. Most studies have found that the more severe the initial aphasia, the poorer the recovery, and global aphasics typically show the least recovery, compared to other subtypes (Basso 1989; Holland 1989). Finally, the issue of potential gender differences in aphasia and its recovery has received considerable attention (e.g., Hier et

Table 1. Aphasic syndromes: neuropsychological correlates.

Syndrome	Speech and language capacities			
	Speech	Comprehension	Repetition	Naming
Broca's aphasia	Nonfluent; effortful	Intact or largely preserved	Impaired	Impaired
Wernicke's aphasia	Fluent; well articulated	Impaired	Impaired	Impaired
Global aphasia	Extremely sparse; nonfluent	Impaired	Impaired	Impaired
Conduction aphasia	Fluent or relatively fluent	Intact or largely preserved	Impaired	Impaired
Transcortical aphasia				
Motor version	Nonfluent; effortful	Intact or largely preserved	Intact	Somewhat impaired
Sensory version	Fluent; well articulated	Impaired	Intact	Somewhat impaired
Anomic aphasia	Fluent	Intact	Intact	Severely impaired
Crossed aphasia	Variable; somewhat nonfluent	Somewhat impaired	Somewhat impaired	Impaired
Subcortical aphasia	Severely dysarthric but often fluent	Impaired or somewhat impaired	May be normal or impaired	Normal or impaired

Table 2. Aphasic syndromes: neuroanatomical correlates.

Syndrome	Examples of neural correlates
Broca's aphasia	Left frontal operculum (Broca's area)
Wernicke's aphasia	Left posterior superior temporal gyrus (Wernicke's area)
Global aphasia	Entire perisylvian region on left, including frontal operculum, parietal operculum, and posterior temporal region
Conduction aphasia	Parietal operculum, supramarginal gyrus, insula
Transcortical aphasias	
Motor version	Left prefrontal (in front of or above Broca's area)
Sensory version	Left posterior temporal (behind and below Wernicke's area)
Anomic aphasia	Left inferotemporal; temporal pole
Crossed aphasia	Right perisylvian (frontal, parietal, temporal)
Subcortical aphasia	Left basal ganglia; thalamus

al. 1994; Kimura 1983; McGlone 1977; Sarno et al. 1985), but careful neuroanatomical and neuro-psychological studies of this question have shown that lesion location, and not gender, is far and away the most important determinant of the nature and severity of speech and language deficits (Damasio et al. 1989).

2.1 Broca's Aphasia

In 1861, Paul Broca presented a preliminary report on 'loss of speech' as a result of unilateral left frontal lobe damage. He followed this two years later with a description of autopsy findings from several nonfluent aphasic patients, noting that virtually all had damage in the posterior portion of the left frontal lobe (Broca 1863). This condition, which Broca termed 'aphemia,' provided the first evidence of left hemisphere language specialization, and also was interpreted as consistent with the proposals of Gall and Bouillaud that the 'organs' of speech and language were located in the frontal lobes. (It appears likely that Marc Dax discovered the relationship between left hemisphere damage and language impairment some 25 years before Broca, but this discovery was not made known to the medical or scientific community until his son, Gustav Dax, published his father's manuscript in 1865 [see Benton 1984; Critchley 1965].) Broca did not claim that damage to this area accounted for all language impairments, but rather described 'aphemia' as just one syndrome which could be distinguished from other (e.g., 'amnestic') language impairments.

The hallmark of Broca's aphasia is *nonfluent* speech output, which means that speech production is effortful, sparse, and agrammatic. Paraphasias (word substitutions) are common, usually involving omission of phonemes or substitution of incorrect phonemes (e.g., 'lockter' for 'doctor'; 'predisent' for 'president'). Verbatim repetition, confrontation naming, and writing are all impaired. However, Broca's aphasics have relatively good comprehension of language, in both its aural and written forms; this capacity may even be entirely spared. Interestingly, most patients with Broca's aphasia can sing, even when they are severely

nonfluent with propositional speech, indicating that the production of singing is mediated by alternate brain regions (perhaps by homologous right hemisphere structures).

When damage is limited to Broca's area (cortex of the inferior frontal gyrus in areas 44 and 45), the most common outcome is mild and transient speech problems. The syndrome of Broca's aphasia typically results when there is additional damage to the left frontal operculum, underlying white matter, and the anterior insula (Alexander et al. 1990; Damasio 1989; Mohr et al. 1978; Naeser and Hayward 1978).

Figure 1 shows a three-dimensional MR reconstruction of a 76-year-old, right-handed man who developed Broca's aphasia after a left frontal infarct. The lesion includes the precentral gyrus and "Broca's area", that is, pars opercularis and triangularis of the inferior frontal gyrus, formed by areas 44 and 45. In addition to aphasia, the patient had a right hemiparesis, with the face and arm being affected most severely, and this sign is typical of Broca's aphasics. No visual field impairment was present.

2.2 Wernicke's Aphasia

The second major aphasic syndrome was described in 1874 by Carl Wernicke, a 26-year-old German neuropsychiatrist. Wernicke's 'sensory aphasia' was characterized by fluent but disordered speech, defective aural comprehension, and impairments of reading and writing. He associated this linguistic profile with damage in the posterior portion of the left superior temporal gyrus, a localization which has been supported by multiple modern neuro-imaging studies.

Wernicke's aphasia is often considered a sort of flip side to Broca's aphasia. The affected patient, in contrast to a Broca's aphasic, produces fluent, well-articulated speech. Effort is normal, and the patient may even be hyperfluent, producing elaborate, rambling responses to simple questions. Phrase length, most aspects of grammatical structure, and articulation and prosody are normal. However, Wernicke's aphasics produce speech which is highly contaminated

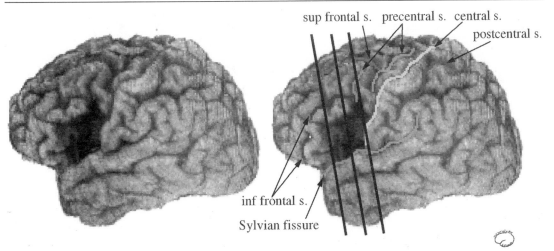

sup frontal s.   precentral s.   central s.

postcentral s.

inf frontal s.

Sylvian fissure

Figure 1. Example of a patient with Broca's aphasia, with a lesion in the left frontal operculum (Broca's area).

with paraphasic errors, including *semantic* (e.g., 'milk' for 'cow'), *phonemic* (e.g., 'peepas' for 'people'), and *neologistic* (e.g., 'encomfer'). The speech is remarkably devoid of specific nouns, and instead, comprises primarily pronouns, prepositions, and functors. Also, Wernicke's aphasia is marked by a major impairment of comprehension, for both aural and written forms of language. The comprehension impairment, together with the fluent nature of the speech production, sets this aphasia apart from Broca's aphasia. Verbatim repetition and naming are also defective in Wernicke's aphasia. Wernicke's aphasia is related to damage in the left posterior superior temporal gyrus (Wernicke's area) and nearby regions in the temporal and lower parietal cortices (Kertesz et al. 1993; Naeser and Hayward 1978).

The development of Wernicke's aphasia may be accompanied by a right-sided visual field defect (homonymous hemianopia) due to interruption of the optic radiations, but other neurological manifestations, such as motor or sensory changes, are often absent. In fact, there may be no other neurological signs, outside of the aphasia. As noted by Wernicke, a patient may present with an isolated and rather striking disturbance of speech and comprehension, which can easily lead to misdiagnosis, particularly as psychiatric disease. Consideration of the content of the disordered speech, together with the age and history of the patient, will help steer the diagnosis in the correct direction, and neuro-imaging (MR or CT) will confirm the neurological basis for the presentation.

Patients with Wernicke's aphasia tend to recover considerably, especially with speech therapy. Lesion size is a factor, and smaller lesions can be expected to result in better recovery. Involvement of neighboring regions in addition to the posterior superior temporal gyrus, including the supramarginal and angular gyri

and the middle temporal gyrus, is associated with poorer outcome (Kertesz et al. 1993). After relatively small lesions, patients may be left with only mild word finding defects and mild impairments in confrontation naming. Functional imaging has suggested that increased activation of left frontal and right posterior temporal regions may be involved in recovery from Wernicke's aphasia (Weiller et al. 1995).

Figure 2 shows a three-dimensional MR reconstruction of a 56-year-old, right-handed man who developed Wernicke's aphasia after a small left posterior temporal infarct. The lesion involves the posterior third of the superior temporal gyrus, in the heart of what is known as 'Wernicke's area.' The lesion shown here is quite circumscribed; commonly, lesions producing Wernicke's aphasia will also involve nearby structures in the inferior parietal lobule (supramarginal gyrus) and temporal lobe (angular gyrus).

2.3 Global Aphasia

The idea that a severe 'total' or global aphasia could result from dysfunction of both 'expressive' and 'receptive' language capacities was recognized by early aphasiologists, including Pick, Wernicke, and Lichtheim (see Benson 1988). 'Expressive-receptive' was one of only four categories of aphasia identified in the early standardized survey of Weisenburg and McBride (1935). Neuroanatomical factors in global aphasia were not given much consideration in early accounts, other than recognition of the large size of the lesions. As summarized by Russell Brain (1961; 103): 'Massive lesions so disorganize both the receptive and expressive aspects of speech as to cause total or global aphasia.'

Global aphasia involves severe impairment in nearly all speech and linguistic capacities. Comprehension and production of speech are both affec-

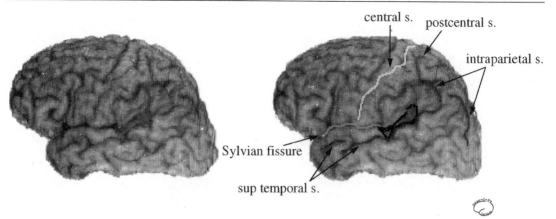

Figure 2. Example of a patient with Wernicke's aphasia, with a lesion in the left posterior superior temporal gyrus (part of Wernicke's area).

ted. The patient cannot speak, and also cannot understand spoken and written language. Verbatim repetition, naming, reading, and writing are all severely impaired. The patient may, however, retain the capacity for singing, and it is worth testing for this, as the production of fluent singing can be highly encouraging in a patient who is otherwise virtually mute.

Global aphasia is related to extensive destruction of the left perisylvian region, including Broca's area, the inferior parietal cortices, Wernicke's area, and underlying white matter and subcortical structures. Another rare pattern is two noncontiguous lesions, one involving Broca's area and the other involving Wernicke's area. In this presentation, the patient will *not* have a right hemiparesis, due to the sparing of motor cortex between the two lesions, and the prognosis for recovery of some linguistic abilities is considerably better (Legatt et al. 1987; Tranel et al. 1987). Although in most cases, global aphasia has a grimmer prognosis than any of the other aphasia syndromes, there also is evidence that the recovery period for global aphasia may be delayed or extended relative to other aphasias, with significant recovery occurring up to several months, or even years, after onset (Sarno and Levita 1971).

Figure 3 shows the three-dimensional MR reconstruction of two patients with global aphasia. The top image depicts a 74-year-old, right-handed man who suffered a large infarct in the territory of the left middle cerebral artery, which damaged virtually all of the language-related regions in the perisylvian sector, including Broca's area, Wernicke's area, and the parietal opercular region in between. The other case, a 68-year-old, right-handed man, had a similar presentation; virtually all of the regions in the immediate vicinity of the Sylvian fissure are damaged, although there is some sparing of the more posterior aspects of the region. Both lesions are shown in lateral (left side

of figure) and coronal (right side of figure) orientations. As is typical of global aphasics, the patients had a right hemiplegia affecting face, arm, and leg, a right hemisensory impairment, and a right homonymous hemianopia.

2.4 Conduction Aphasia

Among his other contributions, Carl Wernicke postulated the existence of a distinct aphasic syndrome which would arise from a lesion interrupting communication between anterior and posterior language-related areas, and he termed this condition *conduction aphasia*. Lichtheim (1885) agreed with Wernicke's conceptualization, and added the key observation that the lesion which caused conduction aphasia should impair the ability to repeat spoken sentences. The behavioral syndrome described by these early investigators can be readily identified, although modern neuro-imaging has not supported the notion that isolated interruption of white matter pathways between Broca's and Wernicke's areas can account fully for the disorder.

Behaviorally, conduction aphasia is hallmarked by a severe defect in verbatim repetition. Other aspects of language, including fluency and comprehension, are relatively less affected. Phonemic paraphasic errors are common, and naming is usually impaired. Patients often manifest hesitation in speech production marked by frequent phonemic corrections in an effort to home in on the target sound (so-called *conduit d'approche*). The patients cannot write to dictation (a defect akin to the repetition impairment), but they usually write much better when copying another script or when producing spontaneous compositions.

Conduction aphasia is related to damage to either the supramarginal gyrus (area 40) in the lower parietal region, or to the primary auditory cortices with extension into the insular cortex and underlying white mat-

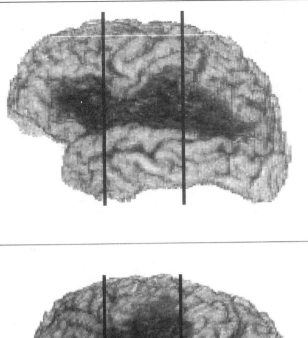

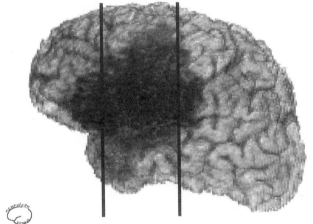

Figure 3. Two examples of patients with global aphasia, with large left perisylvian lesions.

ter (Benson et al. 1973; Damasio and Damasio 1980; Hyman and Tranel 1989). The auditory association cortices in posterior area 22 are spared, allowing the preservation of comprehension. Neurologic signs vary considerably; many patients manifest some degree of motor or sensory impairment (including visual field defects) in the acute phase, but neurologic abnormalities may recover quickly and completely, leaving a relatively isolated disturbance of language. Conduction aphasia tends to show a good response to speech therapy.

Figure 4 shows a three-dimensional MR reconstruction of a 35-year-old, right-handed woman who developed conduction aphasia after a left middle cerebral artery territory infarct. The lesion is in the left supramarginal gyrus (area 40), the parietal operculum, and the posterior insula (arrows). The lesion spares the primary auditory cortex and the main part

of Wernicke's area (posterior area 22), and it also spares entirely the frontal operculum (Broca's area).

2.5 The Transcortical Aphasias

Lichtheim's (1885) elaboration of Wernicke's model included a 'conceptual center' which housed the meanings attached to auditory word images believed to be stored in Wernicke's area. According to this model, disruption of the pathways to or from the conceptual center would result in aphasia but not affect repetition. Spared verbatim repetition distinguished the *transcortical* aphasia (named by Wernicke) from the four aphasia subtypes described above. Specifically, Broca's, Wernicke's, global, and conduction aphasias share the feature that verbatim repetition is impaired, and all are associated with damage to the perisylvian region on the left. In fact, impaired repetition is a reliable sign pointing to dysfunction of cortices in and

311

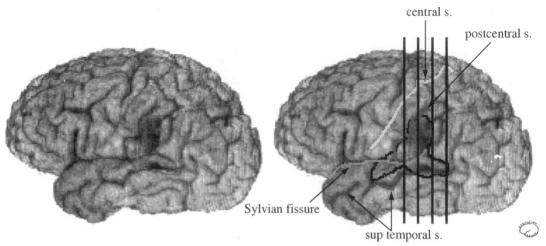

Figure 4. Example of a patient with conduction aphasia, with a lesion in the left supramarginal gyrus, parietal operculum, and posterior insula.

around the Sylvian fissure. When the lesion is situated either more anteriorly (in front of or above Broca's area) or more posteriorly (behind and below Wernicke's area), the aphasia that develops, known as *transcortical aphasia*, lacks the feature of impaired repetition (see Rapcsak and Rubens 1994, for review). We describe below the two most common subtypes of transcortical aphasia.

2.5.1 Transcortical motor aphasia

The profile of transcortical motor aphasia resembles Broca's aphasia, except that the patient can repeat verbatim (Rubens 1976). Speech is nonfluent, effortful, and sparse; comprehension is relatively preserved; reading and writing are usually disturbed. Con-

frontation naming may be at least partially spared; in particular, naming of specific objects (noun retrieval) may be normal, whereas naming of actions (verb retrieval) is more likely to be impaired (Damasio and Tranel 1993). Transcortical motor aphasia has a good prognosis if the lesion is fairly circumscribed, but when substantial white matter involvement is present, recovery is poorer.

Figure 5 shows a three-dimensional MR reconstruction in lateral view. The patient is a 49-year-old, right-handed man who sustained a lesion in the left premotor region. The damage is in the left frontal operculum just anterior to the precentral sulcus, but most of Broca's area is spared. The man had transcortical motor aphasia.

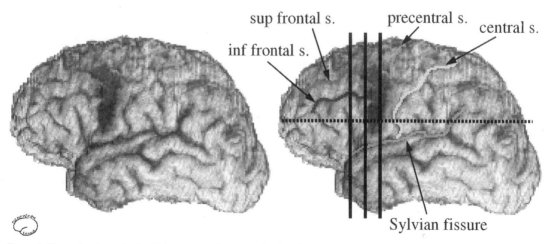

Figure 5. Example of a patient with transcortical motor aphasia, with a lesion in the left premotor region (mostly anterior to Broca's area).

2.5.2 Transcortical sensory aphasia

The profile of transcortical sensory aphasia resembles Wernicke's aphasia, except that verbatim repetition is spared. This syndrome is related to damage in the left inferotemporal region, situated primarily in the angular gyrus; this region can be designated as the temporal-occipital-parietal junction (Alexander et al. 1989). Speech is fluent, with normal grammar, articulation, and prosody; comprehension is usually at least mildly impaired. There is some degree of confrontation naming impairment, and naming defects may be more severe for certain categories of items (e.g., tools/utensils) than for others (e.g., animals). Transcortical sensory aphasia is fairly uncommon, although many patients who present acutely with Wernicke's aphasia gradually resolve into a transcortical sensory profile (Alexander 1997).

Figure 6 shows a typical patient with transcortical sensory aphasia, with a lesion in the left inferotemporal region, situated primarily in the angular gyrus. The top part of Fig. 6 shows a three-dimensional MR reconstruction of a standard brain (left lateral and ventral views), onto which has been plotted the left occipitotemporal infarct sustained by a 43-year-old, right-handed woman. The bottom part of Fig. 6 depicts T_1 weighted MR images of the patient's brain in transverse (middle row) and coronal (bottom row) sections.

2.6 Anomic Aphasia

As noted above, naming defects are common in virtually all of the classic aphasia subtypes (Goodglass 1993; Goodglass and Wingfield 1997; Semenza and Zettin 1989). Such defects can also occur in relative isolation. A severe impairment of confrontation naming (anomia), unaccompanied by other speech or language impairments, is designated 'anomic aphasia.' The Wernicke-Lichtheim model did not account for such a syndrome, but other aphasiologists of the time, such as Pitres (1898), clearly distinguished an anomic (or what was sometimes termed 'amnesic') aphasia marked by pure word finding impairment. Early accounts did not provide specific anatomical correlates of anomic aphasia, but later studies have indicated an association with lesions in left inferotemporal or anterior temporal regions, mostly outside the classic language areas of the left hemisphere.

Different profiles of naming impairment have been associated with different patterns of brain damage (Damasio et al. 1996; Ferreira et al. 1997; Goodglass et al. 1986; Hart et al. 1985; Hillis and Caramazza 1991; Tranel et al. 1997a, 1997b; Warrington and McCarthy 1983). First, as alluded to earlier, there is a distinction between retrieval of nouns and retrieval of verbs. Noun retrieval is associated with the left inferior and anterolateral temporal regions; verb retrieval is associated with the left premotor/prefrontal region (Damasio and Tranel 1993;

Daniele et al. 1994; Hillis and Caramazza 1995; Miozzo et al. 1994). Second, there are distinctions between different categories of nouns. Proper noun retrieval is associated with the left temporal polar region (area 38), while common noun retrieval is associated with the inferotemporal region, including areas 20/21 and the anterior part of area 37. Finally, there are distinctions between different categories of common nouns. For example, retrieval of names for animals has been associated with the anterior part of the inferotemporal region, while retrieval of names for tools has been associated with the occipital-temporal-parietal junction (Damasio et al. 1996; Tranel et al. 1997). These patterns have been supported by electrophysiological (Nobre et al. 1994; Ojemann 1991) and functional imaging studies (Mazoyer et al. 1993; Petersen et al. 1988).

Figure 7 shows the three-dimensional MR reconstruction of a 25-year-old, right-handed man who suffered a hemorrhage and surgical intervention in the region of the left anterior-inferior temporal lobe. The lesion involves the temporal lobe at the pole (arrows), with extension posteriorly and ventrally into the anterior part of the inferotemporal region. The patient had a severe impairment of confrontation naming (anomia), but no other speech or language impairment.

2.7 Crossed Aphasia

As noted above, aphasia is associated almost exclusively with lesions in the left hemisphere, owing to the fact that most individuals have left hemisphere dominance for speech. However, it was observed by early aphasiologists that some sinistrals developed aphasia following right hemisphere lesions. In fact, by the end of the nineteenth century, it was generally believed that the right hemisphere was specialized for language in left-handed persons. In this context, Byrom Bramwell (1899) published a paper on a case of 'crossed' aphasia, in which a left-handed patient developed aphasia following a left hemisphere lesion. Although based on an erroneous assumption about lateralization of language in sinistrals, Bramwell's paper led to an ongoing series of studies of patients with seemingly anomalous brain organization for language.

Today, the term "crossed aphasia" refers to the relatively rare instances whereby aphasia develops in a fully right-handed person following a *right* hemisphere lesion (Joanette 1989). The speech and language deficits associated with crossed aphasia are quite variable, but it has been suggested that they fall into two broad categories (Alexander 1997). One includes those patients whose aphasia-lesion patterns more or less resemble the standard types found with left hemisphere lesions, for example, Broca-type aphasia with Broca area lesions, Wernicke-type aphasia with Wernicke area lesions, and so on. The

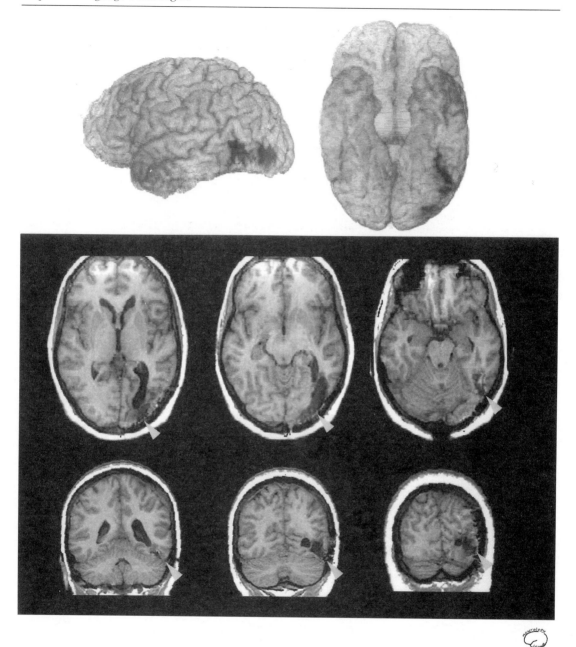

Figure 6. Example of a patient with transcortical sensory aphasia, with a lesion in the left inferotemporal region, primarily in the angular gyrus.

other comprises patients who manifest major anomalies in the aphasia-lesion relationship, for example, a large perisylvian lesion that produces only minimal aphasia, or an anterior lesion that produces a fluent aphasia (Alexander et al. 1989). Finally, significant

defects in nonverbal, spatial capacities, including visuoperceptual discrimination, visuoconstruction, and nonverbal memory, are not uncommon in patients with crossed aphasia, suggesting that the neural organization in such patients does not involve a mere

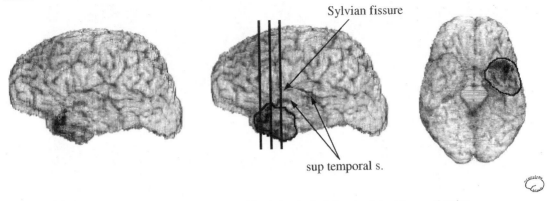

Sylvian fissure

sup temporal s.

Figure 7. Example of a patient with anomic aphasia, with a lesion in the left anterolateral temporal region.

reversal of hemispheric dominance, but rather, the addition of language mediation to right hemisphere structures that are also subserving many spatial functions (Brandt et al. 1989).

Figure 8 shows the lesion in a 73-year-old, fully *right-handed* man who developed severe aphasia following an infarct in the *right* perisylvian region. The lesion is shown on a lateral view of a three-dimensional brain reconstruction (bottom), and on axial T_1 weighted MR cuts of this reconstruction (middle row). The area of abnormal signal on the MR cuts is shown in the T_2 weighted axial MR cuts in the top row.

2.8 Sign Language Aphasia

Deaf individuals who normally communicate with a sign language can become aphasic in sign language as a result of focal brain injury (e.g., Poizner et al. 1987). Interestingly, the lesions that produce 'sign language aphasia' are located in the *left* hemisphere, in the same perisylvian regions as those associated with traditional aphasic syndromes in hearing individuals. This suggests that even a visually-based language such as American Sign Language is mediated by structures in left hemisphere. Recent evidence has even demonstrated dissociations in naming profiles in sign language which resemble those found in hearing persons (Emmorey and Corina 1993; Hickok et al. 1996).

2.9 Subcortical Aphasia

One of the more important advances resulting from application of computerized tomographic (CT) scanning to the study of aphasia in the mid-1970s was improved understanding of the 'atypical' aphasias resulting from subcortical damage (see also *Subcortical Aphasia*). It is now evident that aphasia can result from lesions to the left basal ganglia, especially the caudate nucleus. This so-called 'subcortical' or 'basal ganglia' aphasia is marked by severe dysarthria (Alexander 1989; Cappa et al. 1983; Damasio et al. 1982; Naeser et al. 1982). Linguistic impairments are

variable. Patients with subcortical aphasia usually manifest relatively fluent, paraphasic, and highly dysarthric speech. Typically, auditory comprehension is impaired to some extent, and not infrequently, there is a repetition impairment. This profile does not conform to any of the typical cortical-related aphasia subtypes, and accordingly, it has been termed 'atypical' aphasia by some authors. Right hemiparesis and/or hemisensory impairment is a frequent accompanying neurological sign. Subcortical aphasia has a good prognosis for recovery, especially when caused by hemorrhagic lesions.

Disorders of speech and language may also follow lesions to the left thalamus, especially when damage involves the ventrolateral and anteroventral nuclei (Graff-Radford and Damasio 1984; Graff-Radford et al. 1984; Mohr et al. 1975; Raymer et al. 1997). The aphasia associated with left anterior thalamic lesions shares several of the characteristics of the transcortical aphasias.

2.10 Progressive Aphasia

Progressive aphasia (see also *Language Dysfunction in Dementia*) is defined as a progressive deterioration in speech and language, with an insidious onset and in the relative absence of decline in other aspects of cognition (Mesulam 1982; Weintraub et al. 1990). Several neuropathological substrates have been associated with this condition, including (roughly in decreasing order of frequency) Pick's disease (lobar atrophy), focal spongiform degeneration, and rarely, Alzheimer's disease. The exclusivity of the language impairment was emphasized in initial descriptions of the disorder, but this 'purity' is probably not typical of the majority of progressive aphasics, in whom careful testing will usually reveal cognitive impairments in domains outside of language. Nonetheless, affected patients do manifest a disturbance in speech and language that is out of proportion to other cognitive defects, and that remains a predominant sign well

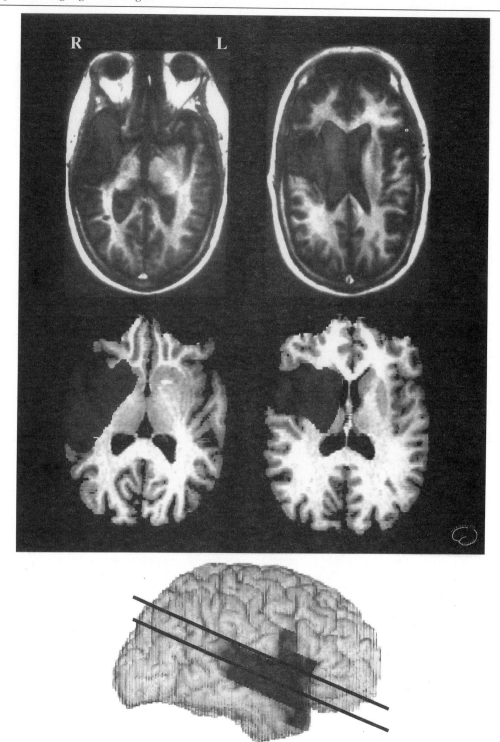

Figure 8. Example of a patient with crossed aphasia, with a lesion in the right perisylvian region.

into the disease course. Progressive aphasia has been associated primarily with dysfunction of the dominant (left) temporal lobe (Graff-Radford et al. 1990; Kertesz et al. 1994).

3. Conclusion

The development of the classical aphasia diagnostic system provides a rich entry in the history of the study of brain-behavior relationships. Despite its imperfections, the system has persisted from beginnings in the era of phrenology into the current context of neurolinguistics and sophisticated neuroimaging. The ongoing application of this classificatory system in hospitals and clinics around the world attests to its utility, even as the role of syndromes in aphasiology has diminished as a framework for theories and models. The future relevance of the diagnostic system will depend on continued research to find meaningful relationships between aphasia profiles, neuroanatomical factors, and outcome variables.

Acknowledgments

We thank Thomas Grabowski for his generous and careful preparation of the figures, and Antonio and Hanna Damasio for their collaboration in some of the research reported in this chapter. Supported by NINDS Grant P01 NS19632.

Bibliography

Alexander M P 1989 Clinical-anatomical correlations of aphasia following predominantly subcortical lesions. In: Boller F, Grafman J (eds.) *Handbook of Neuropsychology*, Vol.2. Elsevier, Amsterdam: 47–66

Alexander M P 1997 Aphasia: Clinical and anatomic aspects. In: Feinberg T E, Farah M J (eds.) *Behavioral Neurology and Neuropsychology*. McGraw Hill, New York: 133–49

Alexander M P, Fischette M R, Fischer R S 1989 Crossed aphasia can be mirror image or anomalous. *Brain* **112**: 953–73

Alexander M P, Hiltbronner B, Fischer R 1989 The distributed anatomy of transcortical sensory aphasia. *Archives of Neurology* **46**: 885–92

Alexander M P, Naeser M A, Palumbo C 1990 Broca's area aphasia. *Neurology* **40**: 353–62

Basso A 1989 Therapy of aphasia. In: Boller F, Grafman J (eds.) *Handbook of Neuropsychology*, Vol. 2. Elsevier, Amsterdam: 67–82

Benson D F 1988 Classical syndromes of aphasia. In: Boller F, Grafman J (eds.) *Handbook of Neuropsychology*, Vol. 1. Elsevier, New York

Benson D F 1993 Aphasia. In: Heilman K M, Valenstein E (eds.) *Clinical Neuropsychology*, 3rd ed. Oxford University Press, New York: 17–36

Benson D F, Sheremata W A, Bouchard R, Segarra J M, Price D, Geschwind N 1973 Conduction aphasia: A clinicopathological study. *Archives of Neurology* **28**: 339–46

Benton A 1984 Hemispheric dominance before Broca. *Neuropsychologia* **22**: 807–11

Benton A, Anderson S W 1998 Aphasia: Historical perspectives. In: Sarno M T (ed.) *Acquired Aphasia*, 3rd ed. Academic Press, New York: 1–24

Brain R 1961 *Speech Disorders*. Butterworth, Washington, DC

Bramwell B 1899 On 'crossed' aphasia and the factors which go to determine whether the 'leading' or 'driving' speech-centres shall be located in the left or in the right hemisphere of the brain. *Lancet* **1**: 1473–79

Brandt J P, Tranel D, Damasio H, Tranel A P, Jones R D 1989 Evidence for atypical neural architectures in neuropsychologically normal adults. *Society for Neuroscience* **15**: 302

Broca P 1861 Perte de la parole. Ramollissement chronique et destruction partielle du lobe antérieur gauche du cerveau. *Bulletins de la Société d'Anthropologie* **2**: 235

Broca P 1863 Localisation des fonctions cérébrales: Siège du langage articulé. *Bulletins de la Société d'Anthropologie* **4**: 200–3

Cappa S F, Cavalotti G, Guidotti M, Papagno C, Vignolo L A 1983 Subcortical aphasia: Two clinical-CT scan correlation studies. *Cortex* **19**: 227–41

Caramazza A 1984 The logic of neuropsychological research and the problem of patient classification in aphasia. *Brain and Language* **21**: 9–20

Critchley M 1965 Dax's law. *International Journal of Neurology* **4**: 199–206

Damasio A R, Damasio H 1992 Brain and language. *Scientific American* **267**: 88–95

Damasio A R, Damasio H, Rizzo M, Varney N, Gersh F 1982 Aphasia with lesions in the basal ganglia and internal capsule. *Archives of Neurology* **39**: 15–20

Damasio A R, Tranel D 1993 Nouns and verbs are retrieved with differently distributed neural systems. *The Proceedings of the National Academy of Sciences* **90**: 4957–60

Damasio H 1989 Neuroimaging contributions to the understanding of aphasia. In: Boller F, Grafman J (eds.) *Handbook of Neuropsychology* Vol. 2. Elsevier, Amsterdam: 3–46

Damasio H, Damasio A R 1980 The anatomical basis of conduction aphasia. *Brain* **103**: 337–50

Damasio H, Grabowski T J, Tranel D, Hichwa R D, Damasio A R 1996 A neural basis for lexical retrieval. *Nature* **380**: 499–505

Damasio H, Tranel D, Spradling J, Alliger R 1989 Aphasia in men and women. In: Galaburda A (ed.) *From Neurons to Reading*. MIT, Cambridge, MA: 307–30

Daniele A, Giustolisi L, Silveri M C, Colosimo C, Gainotti G 1994 Evidence for a possible neuroanatomical basis for lexical processing of nouns and verbs. *Neuropsychologia* **32**: 1325–41

Emmorey K, Corina D 1993 Hemispheric specialization for ASL signs and English words: Differences between imageable and abstract forms. *Neuropsychologia* **31**: 645–54

Ferreira C T, Giusiano B, Poncet M 1997 Category-specific anomia: implication of different neural networks in naming. *NeuroReport* **8**: 1595–1602

Fromkin V, Rodman R 1998 *An introduction to language*, 6th ed. Harcourt Brace, New York

Garrett M 1995 The structure of language processing: Neuropsychological evidence. In: Gazzaniga M (ed.) *The Cognitive Neurosciences*. MIT, Cambridge, MA: 881–99

Goodglass H 1993 *Understanding aphasia*. Academic Press, New York

Goodglass H, Kaplan E 1972 *The Assessment of Aphasia and Related Disorders*. Lea and Febiger, Philadelphia, PA

Goodglass H, Wingfield A (eds.) 1997 *Anomia: Neuro-*

anatomical and Cognitive Correlates. Academic Press, New York

Goodglass H, Wingfield A, Hyde M R, Theurkauf J C 1986 Category specific dissociations in naming and recognition by aphasic patients. *Cortex* 22: 87–102

Graff-Radford N R, Damasio A R, Hyman B T, Hart M N, Tranel D, Damasio H, Van Hoesen G W, Rezai K 1990 Progressive aphasia in a patient with Pick's disease. *Neurology* 40: 620–26

Graff-Radford N R, Damasio H 1984 Disturbances of speech and language associated with thalamic dysfunction. *Seminars in Neurology* 4: 162–68

Graff-Radford N R, Eslinger P J, Damasio A R, Yamada T 1984 Nonhemorrhagic infarction of the thalamus: Behavioral, anatomic, and physiologic correlates. *Neurology* 34: 14–23

Hart J, Berndt R S, Caramazza A 1985 Category-specific naming deficit following cerebral infarction. *Nature* 316: 439–40

Hickok G, Bellugi U, Klima E S 1996 The neurobiology of signed language and its implications for the neural organisation of language. *Nature* 381: 699–702

Hier D B, Yoon W B, Mohr J P, Price T R, Wolf P A 1994 Gender and aphasia in the Stroke Data Bank. *Brain and Language* 47: 155–67

Hillis A E, Caramazza A 1991 Category-specific naming and comprehension impairment: A double dissociation. *Brain* 114: 2081–94

Hillis A E, Caramazza A 1995 Representations of grammatical categories of words in the brain. *Journal of Cognitive Neuroscience* 7: 396–407

Holland A L 1989 Recovery in aphasia. In: Boller F, Grafman J (eds.) *Handbook of Neuropsychology*, Vol. 2. Elsevier, Amsterdam: 83–90

Hyman B T, Tranel D 1989 Hemianesthesia and aphasia: An anatomical and behavioral study. *Archives of Neurology* 46: 816–19

Joanette Y 1989 Aphasia in left-handers and crossed aphasia. In: Boller F, Grafman J (eds.) *Handbook of Neuropsychology*, Vol. 2. Elsevier, Amsterdam: 173–83

Kertesz A, Hudson L, MacKenzie I R A, Munoz D G 1994 The pathology and nosology of primary progressive aphasia. *Neurology* 44: 2065–72

Kertesz A, Lau W K, Polk M 1993 The structural determinants of recovery in Wernicke's aphasia. *Brain and Language* 44: 153–64

Kimura D 1983 Sex differences in cerebral organization for speech and praxic functions. *Canadian Journal of Psychology* 37: 19–35

Legatt A D, Rubin A J, Kaplan L R et al. 1987 Global aphasia without hemiparesis. *Neurology* 37: 201–5

Lichtheim L 1885 On aphasia. *Brain* 7: 433–85

Mazoyer B M, Tzourio N, Frak V, Syrota A, Murayama N, Levrier O, Salamon G, Dehaene S, Cohen L, Mehler J 1993 The cortical representation of speech. *Journal of Cognitive Neuroscience* 5: 467–79

McGlone J 1977 Sex differences in the cerebral organization of verbal functions in patients with unilateral lesions. *Brain* 100: 775–93

Mesulam M M 1982 Slowly progressive aphasia without generalized dementia. *Annals of Neurology* 11: 592–98

Miozzo A, Soardi S, Cappa S F 1994 Pure anomia with spared action naming due to a left temporal lesion. *Neuropsychologia* 32: 1101–9

Mohr J P, Pessin M S, Finkelstein S, Funkenstein H H, Duncan G W, Davis K R 1978 Broca aphasia: Pathologic and clinical aspects. *Neurology* 28: 311–24

Mohr J P, Watters W C, Duncan G W 1975 Thalamic hemorrhage and aphasia. *Brain and Language* 2: 3–17

Naeser M A, Alexander M P, Helm-Estabrooks N, Levine H L, Laughlin S A, Geschwind N 1982 Aphasia with predominantly subcortical lesion sites. *Archives of Neurology* 39: 2–14

Naeser M A, Hayward R W 1978 Lesion location in aphasia with cranial computed tomography and the Boston Diagnostic Aphasia Exam. *Neurology* 28: 545–51

Nobre A C, Allison T, McCarthy G 1994 Word recognition in the human inferior temporal lobe. *Nature* 372: 260–63

Ojemann G 1991 Cortical organization of language. *Journal of Neuroscience* 11: 2281–87

Petersen S E, Fox P T, Posner M I, Mintun M, Raichle M E 1988 Positron emission tomographic studies of the cortical anatomy of single-word processing. *Nature* 331: 585–89

Pitres A 1898 L'aphasie amnesique et ses varietes cliniques. *Progres Medical* 28: 17–23

Poeck K 1983 What do we mean by 'aphasic syndromes'? A neurologist's view. *Brain and Language* 20: 79–89

Poizner H, Klima E S, Bellugi U 1987 *What the hands reveal about the brain.* Harvard University Press, Cambridge, MA

Rapcsak S Z, Rubens A B 1994 Localization of lesions in transcortical aphasia. In: Kertesz A (ed.) *Localization and Neuroimaging in Neuropsychology.* Academic Press, New York: 297–329

Raymer A M, Moberg P, Crosson B, Nadeau S, Gonzalez Rothi L J 1997 Lexical-semantic deficits in two patients with dominant thalamic infarction. *Neuropsychologia* 35: 211–19

Rosch E, Mervis C B, Gray W D, Johnson D M, Boyes-Bream P 1976 Basic objects in natural categories. *Cognitive Psychology* 8: 382–439

Rubens A B 1976 Transcortical motor aphasia. In: Whitaker H, Whitaker H A (eds.) *Studies in Neurolinguistics*, Vol. 1. Academic Press, New York: 293–303

Sarno M T 1991 Recovery and rehabilitation in aphasia. In: Sarno M T (ed.) *Acquired Aphasia* 2nd ed. Academic Press, New York: 521–82

Sarno M T, Buonaguro A, Levita E 1985 Gender and recovery from aphasia after stroke. *Journal of Nervous and Mental Disorders* 173: 605–9

Sarno M T, Levita E, 1971 Natural courses of recovery in severe aphasia. *Archives of Physical Medicine and Rehabilitation* 52: 175–78

Schwartz M F 1984 What the classical aphasia categories can't do for us, and why. *Brain and Language* 21: 3–8

Semenza C, Zettin M 1989 Evidence from aphasia for the role of proper names as pure referring expressions. *Nature* 342: 678–79

Tranel D, Biller J, Damasio H, Adams H P, Cornell S 1987 Global aphasia without hemiparesis. *Archives of Neurology* 44: 304–8

Tranel D, Damasio H, Damasio A R 1997a A neural basis for the retrieval of conceptual knowledge. *Neuropsychologia* 35: 1319–27

Tranel D, Damasio H, Damasio A R 1997b On the neurology of naming. In: Goodglass H, Wingfield A (eds.) *Anomia: Neuroanatomical and Cognitive Correlates.* Academic Press, New York: 65–90

Warrington E K, McCarthy R A 1983 Category-specific access dysphasia. *Brain* **106**: 859–78

Weiller C, Isensee C, Rjntjes M, Huber W, Muller S, Bier D, Dutschka K, Woods R P, Noth J, Diener H C 1995 Recovery from Wernicke's aphasia: A positron emission tomographic study. *Annals of Neurology* **37**: 723–32

Weintraub S, Rubin N P, Mesulam M M 1990 Primary progressive aphasia: Longitudinal course, neuropsychological profile, and language features. *Archives of Neurology* **47**: 1329–35

Weisenburg T, McBride K E 1935 *Aphasia*. Commonwealth Fund, New York

Wernicke C 1874. *Der aphasische Symptomenkomplex*. Cohn und Weigert, Breslau

Whitaker H A 1984 Two views on aphasia classification. *Brain and Language* **21**: 1–2

Zurif E, Swinney D, Prather P, Solomon J, Brushells C 1993 An on-line analysis of syntactic processing in Broca's and Wernicke's aphasia. *Brain and Language* **45**: 448–64

Subcortical Aphasia

S. F. Cappa and J. Abutalebi

The concept of subcortical aphasia is still controversial in aphasiology. In particular, the role in language processing of subcortical structures, such as the basal ganglia and the thalamus of the dominant hemisphere, is still a matter of debate. The present chapter starts with a brief anatomo-physiological review, followed by a selective summary of the clinical literature, which indicates that aphasia can be observed after lesions confirmed to the subcortical structures of the brain. We will then discuss whether this evidence necessarily implies a participation of the subcortical nuclei in the neural substrate of linguistic function, and present some models of this participation. Finally, recent advances in cognitive neuroscience, in particular functional brain imaging results, will be considered from the point of view of their contributions to our current understanding of subcortical aphasia and its implications for neural models of language organization.

1. Subcortical Structures

Subcortical aphasias are acquired languages disorders due to damage to the subcortical area of the language-dominant hemisphere. Since a working knowledge of the neuroanatomy of this region is a prerequisite for understanding the discussion on its participation in cognitive functions, an elementary summary of anatomical and physiological aspects will be provided. Readers interested in a more complete overview are referred to specialized sources (e.g., Nolte and Angevine 1995; Carpenter and Sutin 1983).

In the aphasia field it is customary to include under the general heading of subcortical structures both the grey nuclei and the white matter located deep within the cerebral hemispheres: that is, the basal ganglia, the thalamus, and the white matter surrounding these nuclei (for instance, the periventricular white matter,

PVWM). The basal ganglia comprise (see Fig. 1): the striatum (which includes two contiguous nuclei, the caudate nucleus, and the putamen), the globus pallidus, the subthalamic nucleus, and the substantial nigra. These nuclei are primarily involved in motor control and, in ways that are less well understood, in cognitive functions. While there is no evidence for a participation in language processing of the two latter nuclei, the former two structures (striatum and globus pallidus) are the usual candidates for a linguistic role (Alexander et al. 1987; Nadeau and Crosson 1997). The other subcortical grey matter structure, the thalamus, consists of a collection of both association and relay nuclei, which, among other functions, provides a gateway for all the main inputs to the cerebral cortex. Several thalamic nuclei have been suggested to be involved in language: in particular, the ventral anterior nucleus (VA), which is directly linked to the premotor cortex, and the pulvinar (in connection with the temporo-parietal cortex). Other possible candidates are the reticular nucleus (RN), the centromedian nucleus (CM), the anterior nuclei, and ventral lateral nucleus (VL) (Ojemann 1975; Wallesch and Papagno 1988; Crosson 1992; Cappa and Vallar 1992).

The basal ganglia and the thalamus are linked in multiple connections to the cortex, in particular through the cortico-thalamo-cortical loop and the cortico-striato-pallido-thalamo-cortical loop. These circuits, in addition to their well-known participation in sensory and motor processes, may play a specific or a nonspecific (i.e., activation) role in language processing (Cappa and Vallar 1992). One widely accepted model of the basal ganglia-thalamo-cortical circuits (Alexander and Crutcher 1990) identifies four separate circuits (motor, oculomotor, limbic, and 'prefrontal'). It is the latter, which projects to the dorsolateral and

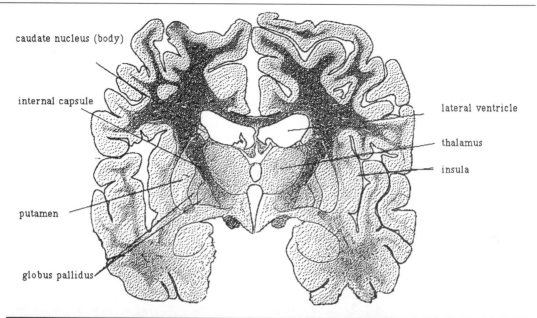

caudate nucleus (body)

internal capsule

lateral ventricle

thalamus

insula

putamen

globus pallidus

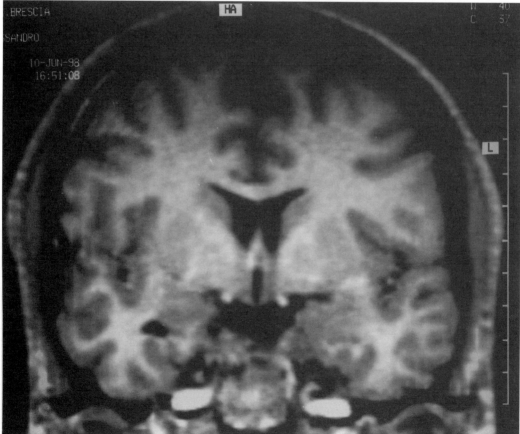

Figure 1. Coronal brain slice (a) and corresponding magnetic resonance imaging section (b) showing the main subcortical structures (courtesy of the Institute of Radiology, University of Brescia).

lateral orbitofrontal cortex, that has been associated with cognitive processes.

2. Can Aphasia follow from purely Subcortical Lesions?

2.1 Historical Aspects

The first studies suggesting an involvement of subcortical structures in language can be dated back to the nineteenth century. Broadbent (1872, cited in Wallesch and Papagno 1988) proposed that words were generated as motor acts in the basal ganglia. Conversely, Kussmaul (1877) did not assign any language function to the basal ganglia, but suggested that they may contribute to speech articulation. Wernicke (1874) and Lichtheim (1885), whose names are linked to the standard 'associationist' anatomo-functional model of language organization, located linguistic representations in discrete cortical areas. Operations on these representations were performed via the fibre tract connections among the committed cortical areas. According to this view, all aphasic disorders result, in an orderly fashion, from lesions to cortical areas or to their connections. In the latter cases the lesion can be limited to the white matter: it is only in this sense that the term 'subcortical aphasia' can be found in the classic aphasiological literature based on the Wernicke-Lichtheim model. The characteristics of these 'subcortical' language disorders are predicted by the model: for example, 'conduction aphasia' results from lesions interrupting the arcuate fasciculus (i.e., the fibre tract connecting Wernicke's area to Broca's area). The point of view of the 'holistic' school was of course different. Moutier (1908), who described three cases of subcortical aphasia with a nonfluent output, and his teacher Pierre Marie (1906, 1926) suggested that lesions within the 'quadrilatère,' which included the basal ganglia and surrounding white matter, were responsible for central articulatory impairment (anarthria). In general, it must be underlined that case studies of subcortical aphasia were not plentiful in the anatomo-clinical literature, and often lacked a detailed description of the clinical picture (Henschen 1922; Nielsen 1946). It is noteworthy that on the basis of this rather meager evidence, Nielsen (1946) explicitly denied any involvement of subcortical grey nuclei in mental activities, and considered aphasia as an epiphenomenon of white matter damage.

Hypotheses about the involvement of subcortical nuclei in cognitive activities, and especially about their participation in language function flourished again after the introduction of noninvasive brain imaging techniques (CT-scan and MRI). Series of patients with aphasia associated with *in vivo* evidence of lesions limited to subcortical structures started to appear in the neurological literature in the late 1970s. These reports, in a period still dominated by 'aphasia classi-

fication,' initiated the quest for a typical 'subcortical aphasic syndrome.'

Extensive reviews of *in vivo* correlation studies can be found in Alexander (1989) and in Cappa and Vallar (1992), to which the reader is referred. The following selective review separately considers aphasia after lesions of the basal ganglia region, and aphasia due to thalamic damage. This division reflects the different functional roles assigned to these structures in motor, sensory, and cognitive processes, which makes it likely that their contribution to language processing, if any, should be distinct. Another crucial difference between these structures pertains to their pattern of blood supply. Basal ganglia receive their arterial input primarily from branches of the middle cerebral artery, while the arteries supplying the thalamus originate mostly from the posterior cerebral artery. This different pattern of vascularization obviously plays a crucial role in determining the localization of vascular lesions in the brain and, therefore, in generating different 'aphasic syndromes.'

2.2 Aphasia Profiles after Lesions to the Basal Ganglia Region

Several investigations from the 1960s and 1970s, reporting series of patients who had undergone 'functional' neurosurgical procedures for the treatment of movement disorders, suggested a potential role of basal ganglia in language. In particular, stereotactic operations (essentially pallidectomies carried out to improve motor symptoms in Parkinson's disease) and electrical stimulation of the basal ganglia provided some interesting insights. For instance, Svennilson et al. (1960) reported naming deficits and paraphasia in about a quarter of patients who had undergone a pallidectomy of the dominant hemisphere. Furthermore, it was observed that perioperative electrical stimulation of the head of the dominant caudate nucleus produced a language output, consisting of irrelevant short sentences (Van Buren 1963; Van Buren et al. 1966).

However, the major contributions to research on subcortical language functions came from clinical aphasiology: the 1970s opened a new era in this field, due to the introduction of *in vivo* high resolution imaging of brain lesions with computerized tomography (CT). Several studies reported correlations between subcortical lesions as shown by CT-scan, clinical findings, and language behaviors (Cambier et al. 1979; Mazzocchi and Vignolo 1979; Alexander and Lo Verme 1980; Damasio et al. 1982; Naeser et al. 1982; Cappa et al. 1983; Wallesch et al. 1983; Perani et al. 1987). These investigations have documented beyond reasonable doubt that aphasia can indeed be observed after lesions confined to the basal ganglia region of the language-dominant hemisphere. One of the major limitations of these clinico-radiological studies was the fact of combining cases with a different vascular aetiology (hemorrhages and infarctions) in the same investigation. Indeed, the mass effect of intracerebral hemorrhages can produce extensive clinical deficits unrelated to the primary area of damage, due to the associated intracranial hypertension. It would therefore seem to be preferable to consider language deficits caused by hemorrhages and by infarctions separately. Another factor which may interfere with the interpretation of these group studies is related to the timing of language evaluation with respect to lesion onset. In the acute stage, structures surrounding the damaged areas may be dysfunctional because of oedema and other factors, so that the language evaluation must be postponed for at least a few days. However, the later the evaluation is conducted, the more likely that the language disturbances have changed because of spontaneous recovery or compensation. In more recent studies these factors have been taken into consideration (Weiller et al. 1993; Mega and Alexander 1994; D'Esposito and Alexander 1995).

Most of these investigations have used some form of standardized aphasia testing for language evaluation. While it is sometimes difficult to compare the findings among different studies, a relatively coherent pattern appears to emerge. Clinico-radiological correlation studies have demonstrated that subcortical aphasia following damage to the basal ganglia region is often characterized by expressive and lexico-semantic impairment, generally consisting in nonfluent output with semantic and verbal paraphasias. However, it must be underlined that fluent aphasia, perseverations, and echolalia have been reported, although less frequently. Comprehension and repetition are often normal or only mildly impaired. Word-finding difficulties and written language deficits are the rule (Cappa et al. 1983; Basso et al. 1987). Speech disorders such as hypophonia, dysarthria, and 'foreign accent syndrome' have also been reported (in particular, the latter disorder has been associated with putaminal damage by Blumstein et al. 1987).

What has really proven to be difficult is the attempt to correlate the symptoms described above with precise lesion sites within the basal ganglia region. Some investigators have tried to propose fine-grained correlation patterns. For example, by reviewing the above mentioned reports and analyzing a new series of patients, Alexander and coworkers (1987) tried to define the precise characteristics of aphasia associated with damage to the basal ganglia region. They suggested that small lesions mainly limited to the striatum and/or the lateral part of the anterior limb of the internal capsule would not cause aphasia, or at least only mild word-finding difficulties. Similarly, an additional, limited superior extension of the lesion into the PVWM resulted in no language disturbances, but only in speech disorders such as dysprosody. When the lesions involved the anterior superior PVWM, a severe reduction in language production

(hesitation and difficulties to initiate language) could be observed. This was attributed to a disconnection of the supplementary motor area from Broca's area, resulting in a form of transcortical motor aphasia. Extensive lesions including the striatum, the medial part of the anterior limb of the internal capsule, and the anterior superior PVWM yielded word-finding difficulties, mild disturbances in comprehension, and occasional phonemic paraphasia. It has been suggested that putaminal damages with posterior extension to the temporal isthmus resulted in fluent aphasia with impaired comprehension and neologisms. If the putamen was damaged more extensively, hypophonia was observed. Lesions located laterally to the putamen (i.e., below the insular cortex) were associated to a clinical picture of conduction aphasia. It must be underlined that this attempt to summarize the results of clinico-radiological correlation studies resulted in a revival of the Wernicke-Lichtheim hypothesis. Damage to white matter pathways was considered to be responsible for the language disorders observed in subcortical aphasia, insofar, as the authors argued, there was little evidence of the involvement of striatal structures themselves. While the present chapter represents an effort to put some order into a remarkably complex situation, it must be remarked that some cases do not fit easily with this model, and that a wide variety of clinical pictures seems to be associated with apparently similar lesion sites, as shown by CT, but also, more recently, by MRI. A possible exception to this lack of strong clinico-anatomical correlation may be provided by lesions in the subcortical territory of the anterior choroidal artery (globus pallidus, posterior limb of internal capsule, and posterior part of putamen) which are often associated with transcortical motor aphasia patterns (Wallesch 1985; Decroix et al. 1986; Cappa and Sterzi 1990; Nagaratnam and Gilhotra 1998).

There is some clinical evidence that subcortical aphasia due to basal ganglia damage often recovers more rapidly than what would be expected with a clinical picture of comparable severity due to a cortical lesion (Vallar et al. 1988). Residual, mild lexical-semantic deficits can be observed with adequate testing in recovered patients. Recent reports of subcortical aphasia in bilingual subjects have been suggested to support a role of the basal ganglia in switching among mechanisms of language output in different languages (see *Aphasia in Multilinguals*; Fabbro and Paradis 1995). This interesting idea is in need of converging evidence from other investigation modalities, such as functional imaging (see Sect. 3.3 below).

In summary, the occurrence of aphasia after lesions involving the capsulo-striatal region or the surrounding white matter is well-documented. However, a 'typical' aphasic syndrome does not appear to exist, although a pattern of non-fluent aphasia with prevalent lexical dysfunction appears to be relatively frequent. Disagreements about specific lesion-behavior correlation within this region might be in part explained by methodological differences.

2.3 Aphasia Profiles after Thalamic Lesions

Also as regards the case of the thalamic area, reports on the 'side effects' of surgical ablation and electrical stimulation suggested a possible participation in language function of several thalamic nuclei, namely the VA, VL, and the anterior nuclei (Schaltenbrand 1965; Ojemann 1975).

The evidence that dominant thalamic lesions may produce cognitive and language deficits was considerably strengthened by clinico-radiological studies. Unlike the case of the basal ganglia, it has been widely accepted that a typical 'thalamic aphasia' syndrome can be characterized on clinical grounds. The term 'thalamic aphasia' defines a clinical picture which shares some features with both transcortical sensory and transcortical motor aphasia (Cappa and Vignolo 1979; Puel et al. 1986). A relatively fluent output, with semantic paraphasias and word-finding deficits, intact repetition abilities, and spared auditory comprehension are the main features of thalamic aphasia. Although the output is relatively fluent, some aspontaneity with prolonged latencies in oral production can be observed (Démonet et al. 1992). Lesions of the dominant anterolateral thalamus (including VA, VL, and the anterior nuclei) have been more consistently associated to persistent aphasia, while patients with lesions in the posterior parts are less frequently aphasic (Cappa et al. 1986). When aphasia is associated to damage confined to the pulvinar, the language output may be more fluent.

It is interesting to observe that recent reports of category-specific naming deficits after thalamic lesions are available. For example, Lucchelli and de Renzi (1992) and Moreaud et al. (1995) have reported cases of proper name anomia caused by lesions to the ventral part of left thalamus. Crosson and Nadeau (1998) have reported a case of selective anomia for medical terms after a left pulvinar lesion. These observations could support the hypothesis of an important role of the thalamus in lexical retrieval.

3. The Role of Subcortical Nuclei in Language Function

3.1 The Pathophysiology of Subcortical Aphasia

There is still considerable controversy about the pathophysiology of subcortical aphasia, in particular for the nonthalamic cases. The main question is whether aphasia after subcortical lesions is directly related to the lesion of the subcortical structures, or if it is rather the consequence of a concomitant involvement of the overlying cortex. For example, aphasia after nonthalamic subcortical damage has been attributed to different mechanisms: (a) lesion of the basal ganglia, which are directly involved in language processing (Crosson 1985; Wallesch and Papagno 1988); (b) disruption of fibre tracts connecting cortical language areas (Alexander et al. 1987; Alexander 1992); (c) diaschisis, that is physiological deactivation of cortical structures remote from the primary site of lesion (Perani et al. 1987; Vallar et al. 1988); (d) involvement of the cerebral cortex caused by hypoperfusion, producing a selective neuronal loss with preservation of macroscopic integrity of the cerebral cortex on CT-scan (ischemic penumbra—Olsen et al. 1986; Godefroy et al. 1994). The *in vivo* measurement of regional cerebral blood flow (rCBF) and metabolism with positron emission tomography (PET) and single photon emission tomography (SPECT) has provided some evidence for a dysfunction of the ipsilateral cerebral cortex, remote from the primary subcortical lesion, in patients with subcortical aphasia (Perani et al. 1987; Weiller et al. 1993; Okuda et al. 1994). This dysfunction could be due to diaschisis, or to ischemic penumbra, and be actually responsible for the aphasic symptoms. These findings have led some investigators to deny any major role of the dominant basal ganglia in language (Nadeau and Crosson 1997; Crosson and Nadeau 1998). It must be underlined, however, that these findings are also compatible with the view that the subcortical structures are linked with cortical areas in language-related functional networks, so that localized damage results in distant effects (hypometabolism, associated with hypoperfusion) in connected regions not directly affected by the lesion. The hypothesis is reinforced by PET studies that have shown reverse distant effects (i.e., functional metabolic depression) in subcortical regions in patients with aphasia associated to localized cortical damage (Cappa et al.1997). More direct evidence for the possible three dimensional (cortico-subcortical) nature of language-related cerebral networks is provided by the results of cognitive activation studies (see Sect. 3.3 below).

3.2 Neural Models of Language

In this section two models of subcortical participation in language function will be briefly reviewed. The first is the 'Lexical Decision-Making Model' developed by Wallesch and co-workers (Wallesch 1985; Wallesch and Papagno 1988). In this model, subcortical structures are assigned an information-processing function. The basic assumption is that multiple lexical alternatives (for instance, the response alternatives in a naming task) are formulated and released in the posterior perisylvian cortex, then carried to the anterior perisylvian cortex and the striatum in parallel modules. The role of the striatum is to monitor the lexical alternatives and to select the most appropriate one. The main reason to postulate this kind of function for the basal ganglia lies in their key position within the system, due essentially to their multiple afferents from the cortex, including the limbic cortex. The striatum is thus considered to be responsible for the integration of various situational, emotional, and motivational inputs in order to drive the selection of the appropriate lexical item among multiple alternatives. The function assigned to the thalamus within this model is essentially that of gating the efferent linguistic operations. The ventral thalamic nuclei are thought to verify the release of the adequate lexical alternative from the anterior language cortex. Because of the failure of this gating function, a lesion to the ventral part of thalamus may thus result in semantic paraphasia.

In summary, once the best-fitting lexical alternative is chosen, the production process is controlled by a cortico-striato-pallido-thalamo-cortical loop.

Crosson (1985, 1992) proposed a model in which the subcortical nuclei are potentially involved in preverbal semantic monitoring, that is, a function that the posterior language cortex is assumed to operate upon the anterior areas. In Crosson's model semantic monitoring is due to the reciprocal connections, involving thalamic nuclei (ventral nuclei and pulvinar), between the frontal and temporo-parietal areas. Temporo-parietal areas are assumed to inhibit the caudate nucleus, which has an inhibitory activity on the globus pallidus, which in turn inhibits the ventral thalamus. The latter structure has an excitatory action on the frontal language cortex. After the verification of the semantic content of the message that has to be generated, the caudate is released from cortical inhibitory activity. This leads to the activation of frontal language areas with the production of semantically (and phonologically) monitored speech. According to this model, subcortical lesions in different sites within this complex loop are expected to primarily produce language deficits confined to the lexical-semantic level.

A substantial revision of the model, which emphasizes the role of thalamic nuclei in 'selective engagement' of cortical language mechanisms, has been recently presented by Nadeau and Crosson (1997) and Crosson and Nadeau (1998). The authors suggest that an extensive neural network, including the frontal lobes, the inferior thalamic peduncle, the reticular nucleus, and the centromedian nucleus of the thalamus, is responsible for the lexical selection process. Disruption in several locations within this network may hinder this gating function and produce thalamic aphasia. No specific linguistic role is assigned to the basal ganglia in this modification of the model.

Irrespective of substantial differences, the models described above converge on ascribing a crucial role to subcortical nuclei at the lexical level of language organization, in particular for the processes involved in lexical retrieval. It is however clear that these models can be criticized on several grounds. In the first place, all the models fail to account for the variability

in the clinical pictures of aphasia associated with subcortical damage. This variability is then attributed to the extension of damage to neighboring structures (in particular white matter pathways), which results in additional symptoms. While this explanation is plausible, it is unfortunately unconstrained and difficult to falsify. A related problem is that the models propose such extensive and widely distributed systems subserving lexical processing that any specific prediction appears to be inherently difficult to disprove on the basis of pathological evidence (Cappa 1997). Nevertheless, it must be acknowledged that these efforts to build neurologically plausible models of language organization in the brain represent serious attempts to move beyond the simple 'correlational' approach which has until recently characterized aphasiological research. From this point of view, it is important to consider the potential contribution of the increasingly sophisticated imaging techniques, such as PET and functional magnetic resonance imaging (fMRI).

3.3 Evidence from Functional Brain Imaging in Normals

Functional brain imaging allows the *in vivo* investigation of the cerebral correlates of linguistic processing in normal subjects as well as in aphasic patients. PET and fMRI data can be collected while the subjects are engaged in language production tasks (for instance, generating nouns or verbs, naming pictures, etc.) or during language comprehension (i.e., listening stories, etc.). These findings provide a detailed topography of the brain structures involved in a language task, with a spatial resolution in the order of a few millimeters. Functional imaging can thus be expected to shed some light on the debated role of subcortical structures in linguistic processing. An analysis of the now extensive literature on PET language studies indicates that the activation of subcortical structures during language tasks has been reported only in the most recent investigations. In particular, most brain activation studies, published before 1994, do not document a well-defined activation pattern of subcortical structures during linguistic processing (Peterson et al. 1988; Démonet et al. 1992; Howard et al. 1992). This may be due to the fact that most of the studies performed in that period used less sensitive methods for data acquisition and data analysis. A further, theoretically interesting source of variability is related to the characteristics of the language activation paradigm. It has already been underlined that empirical evidence from clinical studies supports a role of the subcortical structures in the lexical level of language organization, and that this relative selectivity has inspired the models of subcortical linguistic functions reviewed above. It is thus particularly interesting to distinguish between the tasks which emphasize the requirements for phonological processing and those involving lexical-semantic analysis. This is of course a very broad distinction, which does not take into account the many subtle differences among tasks possibly accounting for the variability in the pattern of brain activation. However, it is remarkable to observe that no significant patterns of activation involving the subcortical structures have been reported for phonological processing tasks, including those published after 1994 (Fiez et al. 1995; Frith et al. 1995; Price et al. 1996a; Herbster et al. 1997; Rumsey et al. 1997). However, consistent activation, involving both the thalamus and the basal ganglia, has been reported for several single-word processing tasks after 1994. These include studies of implicit (Price et al. 1996a) and explicit (Herbster et al. 1997) reading, noun, and verb retrieval (Warburton et al. 1996), picture naming (Price et al. 1996b; Martin et al. 1995), word repetition (Price et al. 1996c), and even word translation (Klein et al. 1995).

4. Conclusion: Is the concept still useful?

The concept of subcortical aphasia has strong links with the theoretical framework of the so-called 'neo-classical' school of aphasia investigation, with its specific emphasis on the identification of aphasic syndromes associated to well-defined lesion sites (Goodglass and Kaplan 1983). One of the basic tenets of this approach is the idea that a careful analysis of the clinical and neurolinguistic features of these different aphasic syndromes, and of their localization in the brain, may constitute a privileged avenue to investigate the organization of language in the brain. This approach can thus be considered as a continuation of the traditional clinico-anatomical correlation method in neuropsychology, and has allowed only limited theorizing about a physiological model of language organization in the brain.

It is now clear that the classical clinico-anatomical findings must be integrated with the results coming from other research fields, apart from clinical aphasiology. In the first place, the knowledge about language structures has increased enormously in the last decade (Jackendoff 1994), and the application of psycholinguistic methods to aphasia investigation has considerably enlarged our understanding of aphasic impairments as dysfunctions of normal language processing (Caplan 1992). Secondly, methods are now available for the *in vivo* investigation of the location and time course of cerebral activity during linguistic tasks in normal subjects (Posner & Raichle 1994). The integration of the precise anatomical localization of linguistic processes allowed by PET and fMRI studies, with the temporal resolution afforded by neurophysiological methods, such as electrical and magnetic evoked responses, is starting to increase our understanding of language organization in the brain. Future developments include the possibility to apply methods assessing neurotransmitter function *in vivo*

to the investigation of language tasks. The integration of these multiple research approaches is the mission of cognitive neuroscience; in the case of language, the goal is the development of explicit neurological models of language implementation in the brain. Specific hypotheses about the linguistic role of subcortical structures need to be formulated within this complex framework.

Bibliography

Alexander G E, Crutcher M D 1990 Functional architecture of basal ganglia circuits: neural substrates of parallel processing. *Trends in Neuroscience* **13:** 266–71

Alexander M P 1989 Clinical-anatomical correlations of aphasia following predominantly subcortical lesions. In: Boller F, Grafman J (eds.) *Handbook of Neuropsychology*, Vol. 2. Elsevier, Amsterdam

Alexander M P 1992 Speech and language deficits after subcortical lesions of the left hemisphere: a clinical, CT, and PET study. In: Vallar G, Gappa S F, Wallesch C W (eds.) *Neuropsychological Disorders Associated with Subcortical Lesions*. Oxford University Press, New York

Alexander M P, Lo Verme S R 1980 Aphasia after left hemispheric hemorrhage. *Neurology* **30:** 1193–202

Alexander M P, Naeser M A, Palumbo C L 1987 Correlation of subcortical CT lesion sites and aphasia profiles. *Brain* **110:** 961–91

Basso A, Della Sala S, Farabola M 1987 Aphasia arising from purely deep lesions. *Cortex* **29:** 29–44

Blumstein S E, Alexander M P, Ryalls J H, Katz W, Dworetzky B 1987 On the nature of the foreign accent syndrome: a case study. *Brain and Language* **31:** 215–44

Broadbent G 1872 *On the Cerebral Mechanism of Speech and Thought*. London. (Cited by Wallesch C W, Papagno C 1988)

Cambier J, Elghozi D, Strube E 1979 Hémorragie de la tete du noyau caudé gauche. *Revue Neurologique* **135:** 763–74

Caplan D 1992 *Language, Structure, Processing and Disorders*. MIT Press, Cambridge, MA

Cappa S F 1997 Subcortical Aphasia: Still a Useful Concept? *Brain and Language* **58:** 424–26

Cappa S F, Cavallotti G, Guidotti M, Papagno C, Vignolo L A 1983 Subcortical aphasia: Two clinical-CT scan correlation studies. *Cortex* **19:** 227–41

Cappa S F, Papagno C, Vallar G, Vignolo L A 1986 Aphasia does not always follow left thalamic hemorrhage: A study of five negative cases. *Cortex* **22:** 639–47

Cappa S F, Perani D, Grassi F, Bressi S, Alberoni M, Franceschini M, Bettinardi V, Todde S, Fazio F 1997 A PET follow-up study after stroke in acute aphasics. *Brain and Language* **56:** 55–67

Cappa S F, Sterzi R 1990 Infarctions in the territory of the anterior choroidal artery: A cause of transcortical motor aphasic. *Aphasiology* **4:** 213–17

Cappa S F, Vallar G 1992 Neuropsychological disorders after subcortical lesions: implications for neural models of language and spatial attention. In: Valler G, Cappa S F, Wallesch C W (eds.) *Neuropsychological Disorders associated with Subcortical Lesions*. Oxford University Press, New York

Cappa S F, Vignolo L A 1979 Transcortical features of aphasia following left thalmic hemorrhage. *Cortex* **15:** 121–30

Carpenter M B, Sutin J 1983 *Human Neuroanatomy* (8th ed.) Williams & Wilkins, Baltimore, MD

Crosson B 1985 Subcortical functions in language: a working model. *Brain and Language* **25:** 257–92

Crosson B 1992 *Subcortical Functions in Language and Memory.* Guilford Press, New York

Crosson B, Nadeau S E 1998 The role of subcortical structures in linguistic process. In: Stemmer B, Whitaker H A (eds.) *Handbook of Neurolinguistics.* Academic Press, New York

D'Esposito M, Alexander M P 1995 Subcortical aphasia: Distinct profiles following left putaminal hemorrhage. *Neurology* **45:** 38–41

Damasio A R, Damasio H, Rizzo M, Varney N, Gersh F 1982 Aphasia with nonhemorrhagic lesion in basal ganglia and internal capsule. *Archives of Neurology* **39:** 15–20

Decroix J P, Graveleau P, Masson M, Cambier J 1986 Infarctions in the territory of the anterior choroidal artery: A clinical and computed tomographic study of 16 cases. *Brain* **109:** 1071–85

Démonet J F, Chollet F, Ramsay S, Cardebat D, Nespoulous J L, Wise R, Rascol A, Frackowiak R S J 1992 The anatomy of phonological and semantic processing in normal subjects. *Brain* **115:** 1753–68

Fabbro F, Paradis M 1995 Differential impairments in four multilingual patients with subcortical lesions. In Paradia M (ed.) *Aspects of Bilingual Aphasia.* Pergamon Press, New York

Fiez J A, Raichle M E, Miezin F M, Petersen S E I 1995 PET Studies of auditory and phonological processing: effects of stimulus characteristics and task demands. *Journal of Cognitive Neuroscience* **7:** 357–75

Frith C D, Kapur N, Friston K J, Liddle P F, Frackowiak R S J 1995 Regional cerebral activity associated with incidental processing of pseudo-words. *Human Brain Mapping* **3:** 153–60

Godefroy O, Rousseaux M, Pruvo J P, Cabaret M, Leys D 1994 Neuropsychological changes related to unilateral lenticulostriate infarcts. *Journal of Neurology, Neurosurgery and Psychiatry* **57:** 480–85

Goodglass H, Kaplan E 1983 *The Assessment of Aphasia and Related Disorders.* Lea and Febiger, Philadelphia, PA

Henschen D E 1922 *Klinische und anatomische Beitraege zur Pathologie des Gehirnes.* Nordiska Bokhandlen, Stockholm

Herbster A N, Mintun M A, Nebes R D, Becker J T 1997 Regional blood flow during word and nonword reading. *Human Brain Mapping* **5:** 84–92

Howard D, Patterson K, Wise R, Douglas Brown W, Friston K, Weiller C, Frackowiak R 1992 The cortical localization of the lexicons. *Brain* **115:** 1769–82

Jackendoff R 1994 *Pattern in the Mind.* MIT Press, Cambridge, MA

Klein D, Milner B, Zatorre R J, Meyer E, Evans A C 1995 The neural substrates underlying word generation: A bilingual functional-image study. *Proc. Natl. Acad. Sci. USA* **92:** 2899–903

Kussmaul A 1877 *Die Stoerungen der Sprache.* Vogel, Leipzig

Lichtheim L 1885 On aphasia. *Brain* **7:** 433–84

Lucchelli F, De Renzi E 1992 Proper name anomia. *Cortex* **28:** 221–30

Marie P 1906 Revision de la question de l'aphasie. III. L'aphasie de 1861 à 1866: Essai de critique historique sur la genèse de la doctrine de Broca. *Sem. Méd.* (Paris) **26:** 565–71

Marie P 1926 *Travaux et mèmoires.* Masson, Paris

Martin A, Haxby J V, Lalonde F M, Wiggs C L, Ungerleider L G 1995 Discrete cortical regions associated with knowledge of color and knowledge of action. *Science* **270:** 102–5

Mazzocchi F, Vignolo L A 1979 Localization of lesion in aphasia: Clinical-CT correlation in stroke patients. *Cortex* **15:** 627–54

Mega M S, Alexander M P 1994 Subcortical aphasia: the core profile of capsulostriatal infarction. *Neurology* **44:** 1824–29

Moreaud O, Pellat J, Charnallet A, Carbonnel S, Brennen T 1995 Déficit de la production et de l'apprentissage des nomes propres après lésion tubéro-thalamique gauche. *Revue Neurologique* **151:** 93–9

Moutier F 1907 *L'aphasie de Broca.* Steinheil, Paris

Nadeau S E, Crosson B 1997 Subcortical aphasia. *Brain and Language* **58:** 355–402

Naeser M A, Alexander M P, Helm-Estabrooks N, Levine H L, Laughlin S A, Geschwind N 1982 Aphasia with predominately subcortical lesion sites: Description of three capsular/putaminal aphasia syndromes. *Archives of Neurology* **39:** 2–14

Nagaratnam N, Gilhotra J S 1998 Acute mixed transcortical aphasia following an infarction in the left putamen. *Aphasiology* **12:** 489–93

Nielsen J 1946 *Agnosia, Apraxia, Aphasia.* Hoeber, New York

Nolte J, Angevine J B 1995 *The Human Brain.* Mosby, St. Louis, MO

Ojemann G A 1975 Language and the thalamus: object naming and recall during and after thalamic stimulation. *Brain and Language* **2:** 101–20

Okuda B, Tanaka H, Tachibana H, Kawabata K, Sugita M 1994 Cerebral blood flow in subcortical global aphasia. Perisylvian cortical hypoperfusion as a crucial role. *Stroke* **25:** 1495–99

Olsen T S, Bruhn P, Oberg R G E 1986 Cortical Hypoperfusion as a possible cause of 'subcortical aphasia.' *Brain* **109:** 393–410

Perani D, Vallar G, Cappa S F, Messa C, Fazio F 1987 Aphasia and neglect after subcortical stroke. A clinical/cerebral perfusion correlation study. *Brain* **110:** 1211–29

Petersen S E, Fox P T, Posner M I, Mintun M, Raichle M E 1988 PET studies of the cortical anatomy of single-word processing. *Nature* **331:** 585–89

Posner M I, Raichle M E 1994 *Images of Mind.* Scientific American Library, New York

Price C J, Moore C, Humphreys G W, Frackowiak R S J, Friston K J 1996b The neural regions sustaining object recognition and naming. *Proc. R. Soc. Lond. B* **263:** 1501–07

Price C J, Wise R S J, Frackowiak R S J 1996a Demonstrating the implicit processing of visually presented words and pseudowords. *Cereb. Cortex* **6:** 62–70

Price C J, Wise R J, Warburton E A, Moore C J, Howard D, Patterson K, Frackowiak R S, Friston K J 1996c Hearing and saying. The functional neuro-anatomy of auditory word processing. *Brain* **119:** 919–31

Puel M, Cardebat D, Démonet J F, Elghozi D, Cambier J, Guiraud-Chaumeil B, Rascol A 1986 Le role du thalamus dans les aphasies sous-corticales. *Revue Neurologique* **142:** 431–40

Rumsey J M, Horwitz B, Donohue B C, Nace K, Maisog J M, Andreason P 1997 Phonological and orthographic components of word recognition. *Brain* **120**: 739–59

Schaltenbrand G 1965 The effects of stereotactic electrical stimulation in depth of the brain. *Brain* **88**: 835–40

Svennilson E, Torvik A, Lowe R, Leksell L 1960 Treatment of parkinsonism by stereotactic thermolesions in the pallidal region. *Acta Psychiatrica et Neurologica Scandinavia* **35**: 358–77

Vallar G, Perani D, Capa S F, Messa C, Lenzi G L, Fazio F 1988 Recovery from aphasia and neglect after subcortical stroke: Neuropsychological and cerebral perfusion study. *Journal of Neurology, Neurosurgery, and Psychiatry* **51**: 1269–76

Van Buren J M 1963 Confusion and disturbance of speech from stimulation in vicinity of the head of the caudate nucleus. *Journal of Neurosurgery* **20**: 148–57

Van Buren J M, Li C L, Ojemann G A 1966 The fronto-striatal arrest response in man. *Electroencephalography and Clinical Neurophysiology* **21**: 114–30

Wallesch C W 1985 Two syndromes of aphasia occurring with ischemic lesions involving the left basal ganglia. *Brain and Language* **25**: 357–61

Wallesch C W, Kornhuber H H, Brunner R J, Kunz T, Hollerbach B, Suger G 1983 Lesion of basal ganglia, thalamus and deep white matter: Differential effects on language functions. *Brain and Language* **20**: 286–304

Wallesch C W, Papagno C 1988 Subcortical aphasia. In: Rose F C, Whurr R, Wyke M A (eds.) *Aphasia*. Whurr, London

Warburton E, Wise R J S, Price C, Weiller C, Hadar U, Ramsay S, Frackowiak R S J 1996 Noun and verb retrieval by normal subjects: studies with PET. *Brain* **119**: 159–79

Weiller C, Willmes K, Reiche W, Thron A, Isensee C, Buell U, Ringelstein E B 1993 The case of aphasia or neglect after striatocapsular infarction. *Brain* **116**: 1509–25

Wernicke C 1874 *Der Aphasische Symptomencomplex*. Cohn und Weigert, Breslau

Acquired Childhood Aphasia

B. E. Murdoch

The term *acquired childhood aphasia* refers to disturbances in language function resulting from some form of cerebral insult incurred after language acquisition has already commenced (Ozanne and Murdoch 1990). Typically the affected child has commenced learning language normally and has been acquiring developmental milestones at an appropriate rate prior to their injury. Generally, the classical descriptions of acquired childhood aphasia (Alajouanine and Lhermitte 1965; Gloning and Hift 1970; Guttman 1942) suggest that its symptomatology is rather stereotyped and, with only some rare exceptions, the acquired aphasia in children does not appear to fall into clear-cut syndromes evocative of the well-documented aphasia types described in adults.

1. Acquired Childhood Aphasia; Clinical Features and Relationship to Adult Aphasia

Although variations exist between reports in the literature, the symptoms most commonly cited in the classical studies to be characteristic of acquired childhood aphasia include: initial mutism (suppression of spontaneous speech); followed by a period of reduced speech initiative; a nonfluent speech output; simplified syntax (telegraphic expressions); impaired auditory comprehension abilities (particularly in the early stages post-onset); an impairment in naming; dysarthria; and disturbances in reading and writing (primarily in the acute stage post-onset). Many investigators have noted that features of fluent aphasia and receptive disorders of oral speech such as literal and verbal paraphasias, logorrhea, and jargon are rare in children with acquired aphasia, or in the majority of cases, absent (Alajouanine and Lhermitte 1965; Hécaen 1976). Until the 1980s it was generally thought that the clinical features of acquired childhood aphasia were manifestly different to those of adult aphasia, with two major differences indicated. First, the recovery process was often described as being more rapid and complete in children. Lenneberg, in his seminal book *Biological Foundations of Language* (1967) stated that when a focal brain lesion is sustained between 3 and 4 years of age, aphasic symptoms last only a few weeks, while lesions occurring between 4 and 10 years of age are associated with complete recovery, although the recovery may be spread over several years. Second, it has been widely stated that acquired childhood aphasia is predominantly nonfluent (expressive) in nature, its major features being mutism and lack of spontaneity of speech, with fluent paraphasic speech being rarely observed (Alajouanine and Lhermitte 1965; Hécaen 1976; Satz and Bullard-Bates 1981).

Since the mid 1980s, however, with the introduction of new techniques of brain imaging and the development of more sensitive and discriminating linguistic and neuropsychological tests, the classical notions of acquired childhood aphasia have been challenged. The often described complete or near-complete recovery of language function following brain injury in childhood has been questioned, with the findings of several studies reported in the literature suggesting recovery is not as complete as often stated. Persistent language problems have been reported in children subsequent to closed head injuries (Jordan and Murdoch 1990; Jordan et al. 1988) and in children treated for posterior cranial fossa tumors (Hudson and Murdoch 1992; Murdoch and Hudson-Tennent 1994). Even as far back as the 1960s, Alajouranine and Lhermitte (1965) noted that recovery of language in children with acquired aphasia is not tantamount to full recovery. Although 75 percent of their children with acquired aphasia recovered normal or near-normal language within 1 year post-onset, none demonstrated normal academic progression at school because of disorders of written language and difficulty acquiring new knowledge. Satz and Bullard-Bates (1981) reviewed the literature relating to the prognosis of acquired childhood aphasia and concluded that, although spontaneous recovery occurs in the majority of children, 20 to 50 percent of cases still present with aphasia 1 year post-onset. In addition, despite apparent recovery from aphasia, intellectual, cognitive, or school achievement may still be impaired (Chadwick 1985; Satz and Bullard-Bates 1981; Watamori et al. 1990).

Factors identified by various authors that may influence the recovery of language in acquired childhood aphasia include: the site of lesion; the size and side of lesion; the etiology; the associated neurological disturbances; the age of onset; the type and severity of the aphasia; and the presence of electroencephalographic abnormalities. As yet, however, our current knowledge is inadequate for determining which of these factors assist and which factors impede recovery. In particular, the wide diversity of etiologies, severities of aphasia, and length of follow-up reported in the various studies of acquired childhood aphasia, make it difficult to work out which of the factors are most important in determining the final outcome of the aphasia.

In addition to the questions being raised with regard to recovery from acquired childhood aphasia, the findings of studies reported since the mid 1980s suggest a need to reappraise the traditional concept of the clinical features of acquired aphasia in children. Although in past years acquired childhood aphasia has generally been regarded as being of a nonfluent type, a number of publications in more recent years have documented the occurrence of an initial fluent aphasia in children with acquired brain lesions (van Dongen et al. 1985; van Hout et al. 1985; van Hout and Lyon 1986; Visch-Brink and van de Sandt-Koenderman 1984). Fluent aphasias reported in association with acquired brain lesions in children include Wer-

nicke's aphasia (van Hout and Lyon 1986), transcortical sensory and anomic aphasia (Martins et al. 1987; Cranberg et al. 1987), and conduction aphasia (Martins and Ferro 1987; Tanabe et al. 1989). In addition, although the absence or rarity of receptive speech disorders such as pharaphasias, logorrhea, and perseveration, especially in children under 10 years of age, was stressed in the classical descriptions of acquired childhood aphasia, more recent studies have documented the occurrence of these features in the spontaneous speech and test responses of children with acquired aphasia (van Dongen et al. 1985; van Hout and Lyon 1986; van Hout et al. 1985).

In summary, although a nonfluent aphasia pattern is the predominant form encountered in acquired childhood aphasia, according to some authors accounting for in excess of 85 percent of total aphasias in children (Satz 1991), fluent aphasia does occur in some cases. According to van Hout (1992) essentially all of the aphasic syndromes documented in adults may also be exhibited in children with acquired brain lesions, although the frequencies with which each occurs differs somewhat between adults and children. Moreover, although the anatomic-clinical correlations of acquired childhood aphasia is not as clearly understood as in adults, studies based on brain imaging have shown that correlations between type of aphasia and lesion localization in general parallel those in adults (Cranberg et al. 1987; Martins and Ferro 1993; Tanabe et al. 1989). Anterior cortical lesions with or without subcortical involvement are associated with non-fluent aphasias (Cranberg et al. 1987; Martins and Ferro 1993) while fluent aphasias usually occur in association with lesions involving the temporo-parietal cortex, including Wernicke's area (van Dongen et al. 1985; Klien et al. 1992; Martins and Ferro 1991; Paquier and van Dongen 1991).

2. Acquired Childhood Aphasia of Different Etiologies

The cerebral insult causing acquired childhood aphasia can result from a variety of etiologies, including traumatic brain injury, brain tumors, cerebrovascular accidents, infections, and convulsive disorder. The classical descriptions of the clinical features of acquired childhood aphasia are largely based on the findings of studies which have included aphasic children with a variety of underlying etiologies. Evidence is available, however, that suggests that etiology may influence factors such as the type of aphasia experienced as well as the prognosis. For instance, children with acquired aphasia resulting from traumatic brain injury are reported to characteristically exhibit expressive language deficits and have a better prognosis for recovery than children who have suffered cerebrovascular accidents (Ewing-Cobbs et al. 1985). In contrast, brain lesions caused by infectious disorders (e.g., herpes simplex encephalitis) have been linked to severe childhood aphasias and more persistent language problems (van Hout et al. 1985). Acquired childhood aphasia associated with convulsive disorder has been reported to have the poorest prognosis for recovery of all acquired childhood aphasias (Miller et al. 1984). Consequently, there is a need to examine the clinical features of the acquired childhood aphasia associated with each etiology separately.

Although caused by essentially the same range of disorders of the nervous system as adult aphasia, the relative importance of each of the different etiologies of acquired childhood aphasia to the occurrence of language disturbance in children differs from the situation seen in adults. Whereas in peacetime cerebrovascular accidents are the most common cause of aphasia in adults, traumatic brain injury is the most common cause of acquired childhood aphasia.

2.1 Acquired Childhood Aphasia following Traumatic Brain Injury

Traumatic brain injury is the primary cause of all childhood admissions to hospital in most Western countries and consequently is a common cause of acquired childhood aphasia. Although head injuries can be classified as either open (penetrating) or closed (nonpenetrating) head injuries, by far the majority of cases of acquired childhood aphasia associated with this etiology reported in the literature have resulted from closed head injuries. In general, closed head injuries cause diffuse rather than focal brain lesions. According to the traditional view, the prognosis for recovery from closed head injury in childhood is extremely good, the recovery often being described as rapid and complete. In particular, the recovery shown by children who have suffered mild head injuries has been reported to be excellent (Bijur et al. 1990) while recovery from severe head injuries, although less certain, has been reported to be far better for children than adults (Craft 1972). This difference may result from two factors. First, it may be due to the different nature of the impacts causing head injury in children versus adults (childhood head injuries are generally associated with lower speed impacts). Second, it may be related to differences in the basic mechanisms of brain damage following head injury in the two groups, which in turn are related to differences in the physical characteristics of children's heads and adult's heads.

Although the rate of spontaneous recovery in children following head injury, particularly those with mild head injury, is often described as excellent, persistent and long-term language disorders have been reported in children following severe traumatic brain injury (Gaidolf and Vignolo 1980; Hécaen 1976; Jordan and Murdoch 1990; Jordan et al. 1988; Satz and Bullard-Bates 1981). The language features of 26 cases of acquired childhood aphasia were studied by Hécaen (1976). Although the etiology of the group was heterogeneous, 10 cases of head trauma were included.

Hécaen described the associated aphasia as being characterized by a period of mutism followed by the recovery of language, marked by decreased initiation of speech, naming disorders, dyscalculia, and dysgraphia. Receptive disorders were less frequent, occurring in one-third of his children with acquired aphasia.

Jordan et al. (1988) assessed the language abilities of a group of 20 closed head injured children, between 8 and 16 years of age, at least 12 months post-injury, and found them to be mildly language impaired when compared to the language abilities of a group of age and sex matched controls. In particular, these workers identified a specific deficit in naming. The linguistic impairment exhibited by the closed head injury subjects studied by Jordan et al. (1988), however, did not conform to any recognized developmental language disorder. Rather, it was noted by these workers that the observed language disturbance was similar to that reported to occur following closed head injury in adults in that their closed head injured children also presented with a 'sub-clinical aphasia' characterized by dysnomia. Jordan et al. (1988) concluded that, in contrast to the traditional view that the immature brain makes a rapid and full recovery following traumatic injury, closed head injury in children can produce long-term and persistent language deficits. In a follow-up study of the same group of head injured children 12 months later, Jordan and Murdoch (1990) observed that the naming deficit had persisted. At the same time, verbal fluency abilities had deteriorated. A more detailed examination of the naming errors produced by the closed head injured indicated that, although the head injured children produced more errors on a test of naming than nonneurologically impaired controls matched for age and gender, the error pattern was the same (Jordan et al. 1990).

Ewing-Cobbs et al. (1985) examined the language abilities of a group of children and adolescents with closed head injury using an aphasia test battery. Their findings showed that during the early stages of recovery (less than 6 months post-trauma) a significant proportion of their subjects demonstrated linguistic impairments. In particular, naming disorders, dysgraphia, and reduced verbal productivity were prominent. These authors concluded that the language disorder identified was evidence of a 'subcortical aphasia' rather than a frank aphasia disturbance. Further, comparison of recovery related to the severity of injury indicated that children with moderate-severe closed head injury were more likely to demonstrate poorer performance on the naming and graphic subtests when compared to their mildly head-injured counterparts. In a further study of 23 children and 33 adolescents with traumatic brain injury, Ewing-Cobbs et al. (1987) identified 'clinically significant language impairment' in a large proportion of their subjects, with expressive and graphic functions most affected.

In summary, contrary to the traditional view that

children make a rapid and full recovery from traumatic brain injury, a number of studies reported since the mid 1980s have documented the existence of persistent language deficits subsequent to severe closed head injury in children. The language impairment subsequent to closed head injury is characterized initially by reduced verbal output or, in its most severe form, mutism, which is followed in the longer-term by subtle high-level language deficits. Subclinical language disturbance, as reflected in impoverished verbal fluency, dysnomia, and decreased word-finding ability is consistently reported in the literature. Frank aphasia, however, occurs in only a very small proportion of children suffering from closed head injury, if at all. The pattern of language impairment reported subsequent to childhood closed head injury is, therefore, similar to that reported in the literature on adult closed head injury.

2.2 Acquired Childhood Aphasia following Treatment for Brain Tumor

Acquired language disorders are a recognized sequelae of treatment for brain tumors in childhood (Hudson and Murdoch 1992; Hudson et al. 1989; Murdoch and Hudson-Tennent 1994). Tumors located in the posterior cranial fossa (i.e., infratentorial tumors involving the cerebellum, fourth ventricle and/or brainstem) occur more commonly in childhood than supratentorial tumors, accounting for up to 70 percent of all pediatric intercranial neoplasms. Given the high prevalence of posterior fossa tumors in childhood, those studies that have demonstrated the occurrence of language deficits subsequent to treatment for childhood brain tumors have been based on examination of children with tumors involving the cerebellum, fourth ventricle, and/or brainstem.

The most common posterior fossa tumors are medulloblastomas, astrocytomas, and ependymomas. Although the anatomical location of these tumors in the posterior cranial fossa does not in itself lead to the prediction of an associated language deficit, there are several factors occurring secondary to their presence and removal than can conceivably lead to disturbances in language function. For example, compression of the cerebral cortex due to dilation of the ventricular system associated with hydrocephalus could conceivably impair the language abilities of children with these tumors. In that they emerge from or invade the fourth ventricle, thereby obstructing the flow of cerebrospinal fluid, posterior fossa tumors are frequently accompanied by hydrocephalus. The mass effect of the tumor itself may also impede the flow of cerebrospinal fluid as well as contribute to tissue destruction and cortical compression. The invasion and compression of cerebral tissue may also result in vascular changes which could be related to the dysfunction in the central speech and language centers. In addition, radiotherapy, often administered

after surgical removal of certain types of posterior fossa tumors in order to prevent tumor spread or recurrence, may induce changes in brain structure and function. It is noteworthy, however, that any language deficits associated with radiotherapy may only appear in the long-term, as the negative effects of radiotherapy have been reported to appear as delayed reactions.

The most detailed studies of the language abilities of children treated for posterior fossa tumors to date are those reported by Hudson, Murdoch and colleagues (Hudson and Murdoch 1992; Hudson et al. 1989; Murdoch and Hudson-Tennent 1994). Hudson et al. (1989) were the first authors to systematically examine the language abilities of children treated for posterior fossa tumors using a battery of specific language tests. They examined six children who had undergone surgery for removal of a posterior fossa tumor at least 12 months prior to language assessment. The language abilities of the six subjects were reported to range from normal to severely impaired, with four of the six children exhibiting a language deficit. The linguistic deficits identified by Hudson et al. (1989) included deficits in the areas of expressive vocabulary and word finding, receptive syntax, expressive syntax, and reading.

As a follow-up to their earlier study, Hudson and Murdoch (1992) examined the language abilities of 20 children treated for posterior fossa tumors. The results of the standardized language assessments administered by these workers indicated that, as a group, the children treated for posterior fossa tumor performed significantly below their nonneurologically impaired peers on both receptive and expressive language tasks. Hudson and Murdoch (1992) noted, however, that the mean overall language quotient obtained by their group of tumor cases was within the normal range. Consequently, they suggested that the children treated for tumor evidenced a mild language disturbance which the authors described as 'subclinical' in nature. In particular, impairments were noted in the areas of auditory comprehension, oral expression, and high-level language abilities. Unexpectedly, the confrontation naming, rapid naming, and word fluency abilities of the tumor subjects were reported by Hudson and Murdoch (1992) to not differ significantly from those of the control subjects.

Murdoch and Hudson-Tennent (1994) examined the language abilities of the 20 tumor cases reported by Hudson and Murdoch (1992) on an individual basis and showed that the nature and severity of language impairment following treatment for posterior fossa tumor in childhood varies widely from case to case. Only three of the children treated for tumor exhibited a global language deficit as indicated by a uniform reduction across all receptive and expressive language skills. Five subjects demonstrated a competent standard of language usage. The remaining 12 subjects were shown to have strengths and weaknesses across the various language abilities that were assessed. Particular difficulties with expressive semantic and/or syntactic language tasks were exhibited by six of the children treated for tumor, with five cases demonstrating language deficits that were predominantly receptive in nature. Although when considered as a group the naming abilities of the 20 children treated for posterior fossa tumors were not significantly below those of a control group, when examined individually, seven of the tumor subjects were reported to perform poorly on naming tasks.

The performance of each of the children treated for posterior fossa tumor on the language tests administered by Hudson and Murdoch (1992) may have been influenced by a number of variables relating to their medical condition and treatment. Factors considered by Murdoch and Hudson-Tennent (1994) to be possibly important in this regard included: the inclusion of radiotherapy in the treatment protocols; the age of the subjects at diagnosis; the type of tumor experienced; the occurrence of associated hydrocephalus; and the duration of presurgical symptoms.

In summary, although language impairment is not the inevitable outcome of surgery to remove posterior fossa tumors in children, in some cases language deficits do occur. Further, it appears that all aspects of language may be compromised in this population and hence there is a need to monitor both the receptive and expressive language abilities of children treated for posterior fossa tumors. Finally, given that neurological deterioration can occur many months to years after radiotherapy, clinicians need to be aware of the possible development of language problems in children treated for brain tumors long after treatment is completed.

2.3 Acquired Childhood Aphasia following Cerebrovascular Disorders

Although cerebrovascular disorders constitute a far smaller proportion of the neurological disease of childhood than of adulthood, they do occur more frequently than is generally thought and are a significant cause of morbidity and mortality in the child population. The causes of vascular diseases of the brain in children, however, differ from those in adults. Although some vascular diseases of the brain such as embolism arising from subacute or acute bacterial endocardial valvular disease occur at all ages, others, such as cerebrovascular disorders associated with congenital heart disease, are peculiar to childhood.

Whereas aneurysms are the most frequent cause of hemorrhagic strokes in adults, vascular anomalies are the most common cause of primary central nervous system hemorrhage in infants and children. The most important of these are angiomas. Rather than being vascular neoplasms, angiomas represent developmental malformations and can be classified as arteriovenous (AV), venous, cavernous, or capillary. AV malformations are the most common and result from the embryonic failure of capillary development between artery and vein, causing enlargement of vessels and abnormal shunting of blood.

Arterial occlusion in childhood usually results from congenital dysplasia of the vessels, cerebral arteritis, trauma, or thromboembolic disease, the latter condition usually occurring in infants or children with congenital heart disease. In particular, cerebral embolism in childhood is usually associated with cardiac disease, specifically cyanotic congenital heart disease, bacterial endocarditis, or rheumatic valvular disease. In fact, congenital or acquired heart disease is cited as the most common cause of ischemic strokes in children.

Very few studies have specifically examined acquired childhood aphasia with cerebrovascular disorders. A number of the studies that have been published, however, indicate that the pattern of language symptoms is similar to that seen in cases of adult aphasia of vascular origin (Aram et al. 1983; Cranberg et al. 1987; Dennis 1980). In the majority of studies reported in the literature, children with acquired aphasia subsequent to cerebrovascular accidents are included in groups of aphasic children of mixed etiologies. The findings reported in various case studies suggest that, in the acute stages, the language impairments exhibited by these children include comprehension deficits, neologisms, paraphasias, mutism, nonfluent telegraphic style, difficulties on repetition tasks, reading and writing impairments, naming difficulties, dysarthria, oral dyspraxia, poor metalinguistic judgments of grammatical and agrammatical sentences, and simplified story grammar (Aram et al. 1983; Cranberg et al. 1987; Cooper and Flowers 1987; Dennis 1980; Ferro et al. 1982; van Hout et al. 1985). In the majority of cases reported, the clinical signs of aphasia usually resolved within 10 months of the lesion (Aram et al. 1983; Cranberg et al. 1987; Ferro et al. 1982). Where long-term language problems remained, these included word-retrieval problems (Aram et al. 1987; Cranberg et al. 1987), difficulty with comprehension of complex syntactic relationships (Cooper and Flowers 1987; Cranberg et al. 1987) and difficulty producing complex grammatical constructions (Aram et al. 1986; Cranberg et al. 1987). In addition, most children who had suffered a cerebrovascular disorder, examined long-term, presented with academic difficulties (Aram and Ekelman 1988; Cooper and Flowers 1987; Cranberg et al. 1987).

The most comprehensive series of studies to specifically investigate the linguistic impairments in children who have suffered cerebrovascular disorders are those conducted by Aram and colleagues (Aram et al. 1985, 1986, 1987). These workers reported that, when compared to a nonlesioned control group, children with cerebrovascular disorders have longer latency times and make more errors on lexical retrieval tasks (Aram et al. 1987), more errors on most measures of syntactical abilities, both receptively and expressively (Aram et al. 1985, 1986) and more errors on the Revised Token Test (Aram et al. 1987). Despite these poorer performances compared to controls, however, Aram and colleagues stressed the good performance of their subjects with unilateral cerebrovascular disorders on most linguistic tasks. This good prognosis, however, does not appear to hold if the lesion is bilateral or if the child has ongoing seizures.

In summary, it would appear that children with unilateral vascular lesions in the left hemisphere usually recover adequate language skills, however, long-term linguistic deficits may persist in some cases. These deficits include difficulties with lexical retrieval, syntax, and comprehension. Despite recovery of most language skills, a large percentage of children with left unilateral vascular lesions demonstrate long-term academic difficulties.

2.4 Acquired Childhood Aphasia following Infectious Disorders

Infectious disorders of the central nervous system are a well-documented cause of acquired aphasia in children. Van Hout et al. (1985) reported that 38 percent of their child cases with acquired aphasia had an infectious disorder. Similarly, 15 percent of the children with acquired aphasia seen by van Dongen et al. (1985) in their clinic over a 4-year period also had an infectious disease. The infectious disorders involved can include those caused by bacterial, spirochetal, viral, and other less common micro-organisms. The major infectious disorders that have been documented to cause acquired childhood aphasia include encephalitis, meningitis, and cerebral abscess.

Although a number of authors have noted the presence of language impairments among the sequelae of infections of the central nervous system (Feldman et al. 1982; Jadavji et al. 1986), to date no study has systematically investigated the effects of conditions such as meningitis or encephalitis on language abilities. Children with these conditions, however, have often been included in studies of acquired childhood aphasia of mixed etiology (Cooper and Flowers 1985; van Hout et al. 1985). Unfortunately, in these studies the specific language outcomes attributable to the infectious disorder are usually lost in the group results. When combined with the few individual case reports in the literature, however, the case descriptions included within group data do provide some insight into the nature of the language impairment caused by infections of the central nervous system.

Cooper and Flowers (1987) described two cases of children with infectious disorders both of whom initially presented as mute. One case with meningoencephalitis exhibited global aphasia following the period of mutism, while the other with suspected encephalitis demonstrated poor receptive language skills, paragrammaticism, and naming difficulties in the acute stage. Other language symptoms described in the acute stage following an episode of encephalitis include paraphasias, poor repetition skills, stereotypes, and perseveration (Cooper and Flowers 1987; van Hout et al. 1985).

A case of acquired childhood aphasia subsequent to an infection of the unknown type was described by van Hout et al. (1985) as exhibiting the features of a conduction aphasia. The child's comprehension abilities remained relatively intact in the presence of marked naming problems. Slight paragrammaticism and phonemic paraphasias were noted to be present in the child's spontaneous speech output but were reportedly more prominent on repetition tasks. In a later study, a case of Wernicke's aphasia in a 10-year-old boy subsequent to herpes simplex encephalitis was reported by van Hout and Lyon (1986). Their subject exhibited a number of features which, at the time, were considered atypical of the usual descriptions of acquired childhood aphasia in that he displayed symptoms such as a severe comprehension deficit, neologistic jargon, logorrhea, and anosognosia, the latter few features in particular usually described as absent in children with acquired aphasia. Van Hout and Lyon (1986) attributed the severe language disorder evidenced by their subject to the destructive bilateral damage to the temporal lobes caused by herpes simplex encephalitis. The potential involvement of both cerebral hemispheres in lesions caused by infectious disorders may at least partly explain the reported poor prognosis for language recovery in these conditions (Cooper and Flowers 1987).

Although earlier studies of acquired childhood aphasia often included children with language impairments caused by brain abscess (Guttman 1942; Collignon et al. 1968), cerebral abscess has only rarely been the cause of the acquired aphasia exhibited by children included in more recent studies. As the cerebral abscess cases included in earlier studies were primarily the result of complications of severe otitis media and mastoiditis, the absence of such cases in more recent studies is likely a consequence of the use of antibiotics to treat otitis media.

2.5 Acquired Childhood Aphasia Associated with Convulsive Disorder

The first cases of acquired childhood aphasia with convulsive disorder were reported by Landau and Kleffner (1957). Since then, in excess of 160 cases have been reported. Known since then as Landau-Kleffner syndrome or, alternatively, as acquired epileptic aphasia or acquired verbal agnosia, the syndrome appears to incorporate a heterogeneous group of conditions with variable etiologies (Deonna et al. 1977). Most authors agree that males are affected twice as often as females (Cooper and Ferry 1978; Msall et al. 1986).

Acquired epileptic aphasia is characterized by an initial deterioration of language comprehension followed by disruption of the child's expressive abilities. Onset has been reported to occur between the ages of 2 and 13 years with the majority of children experiencing their first loss of language function somewhere between 3 and 7 years of age. In some cases the onset of language deterioration is abrupt while in others the language disturbance develops gradually. Comprehension may be totally lost or reduced to understanding only short phrases and simple instructions (Worster-Drought 1971). Often due to the reduced comprehension ability the presence of hearing loss is suspected in the early stages of the disorder and many of the subjects are initially thought to be deaf. In the majority of cases, however, their audiogram is within normal limits (Cooper and Ferry 1978; van Harskamp et al. 1978; van de Sandt-Koenderman et al. 1984). In association with the reduction in comprehension, the spontaneous speech of the child also changes. Expressively the child may become 'mute, use jargon or produce odd sounds, exhibit misarticulations, inappropriate substitution of words and anomia, or resort to gestures and grunts' (Cooper and Ferry 1978: 117).

Preceding, co-occurring with, or following the language deterioration there may be a series of convulsive seizures (van de Sandt-Koenderman et al. 1984). Although seizures do occur often, they are not the defining feature of the syndrome. Miller et al. (1984) reported that of those cases that exhibit seizures, 43 percent experience the seizures before the language regression, 16 percent display co-occurrence of seizures and language regression and 41 percent experience seizures sometime after the language regression. Regardless of whether or not there are clinically observable seizures, however, all patients with the syndrome exhibit epileptiform discharges in their electroencephalograms (Deonna et al. 1982). The electroencephalographic abnormalities usually take the form of bilateral synchronous disturbances, frequently with a temporal predominance (Deonna et al. 1982; Gascon et al. 1973). Other clinical measures, such as X-ray, arteriography, computerized tomography, and cerebrospinal fluid examination usually yield complete normal results.

A number of other associated problems may also occur in acquired epileptic aphasia in addition to the language impairment. Emotional problems have been reported in a number of cases (Miller et al. 1984) and behavioral problems such as aggressiveness, temper outbursts, refusing to respond, inattention, withdrawal, and hyperactivity occur frequently (Campbell and Heaton 1978; Deonna et al. 1977; Gascon et al. 1973). One surprising feature of this syndrome is that the child's nonverbal intelligence usually remains unimpaired (Miller et al. 1984).

The cause of acquired epileptic aphasia is unknown. Miller et al. (1984) pointed out that speculation regarding the neurological basis of this syndrome is likely to continue until a noninvasive assessment of cortical structure and function is better developed. Despite this, however, several hypotheses as to the pathogenesis of aphasia with convulsive disorder have been proposed. Landau and Kleffner (1957) postulated that the speech and language regression may be the result of functional ablation of the primary cortical language areas by persistent electrical discharges. Gascon et al. (1973), however, suggested that the electrical discharges by these children occur secondary to a lower level of subcortical de-afferenting process and that the discharges are not directly responsible for the aphasia.

As for the actual cause of the convulsive disorder, the data on which several hypotheses are based were obtained from patho-anatomical studies (Miller et al. 1984). One hypothesis proposes that there exists a pathogenetic mechanism related in an unknown way to the convulsive disorder (Gascon et al. 1973). For instance, there may be an unusual genetic pattern of cerebral organizations that makes a child particularly sensitive to brain damage or seizure activity as far as language is concerned (Deonna et al. 1977). Another hypothesis suggests that the convulsive disorder and language loss is caused by an active low-grade selective encephalitis that affects the temporal lobes (McKinney and McGreal 1974; Worster-Drought 1971). It has also been suggested that acquired epileptic aphasia may be caused by vascular disorders. A diminished vascular supply in the territory of the left middle cerebral artery was found in one subject with this disorder examined by Rapin et al. (1977).

The prognosis of aphasia with convulsive disorder is unclear. van de Sandt-Koenderman et al. (1984) caution that many reports concentrate on the medical aspects of the syndrome, whilst the aphasia is poorly described. Consequently the many contradictory statements about the prognosis may be due to the variation in the particular aspect of the disorder being described as recovering. A medical examination of a child may declare him/her 'completely recovered' when there may be still demonstrable aphasic characteristics evidenced if sufficiently sensitive testing is carried out. Often the language recovery in acquired epileptic aphasia is very limited. Miller et al. (1984) stated that over 80 percent of cases reported in the literature have receptive and expressive deficits that persist for longer than six months. According to Paquier et al. (1992), the long-term outcome of the aphasia is unpredictable despite the fact that epilepsy and electroencephalographic abnormalities usually regress with time. In general, it appears that the prognosis for recovery is poor if there has been no progress within 1 year post-onset. Some children with this disorder go through periods of exacerbations and remissions.

Mantovani and Landau (1980) found that children who exhibit this latter type of course have a relatively good prognosis.

In addition to speech/language therapy, children with acquired epileptic aphasia are usually treated with anticonvulsant drugs. Although the epileptic seizures usually respond to conventional anticonvulsant treatment, the reduction in seizure activity may not be accompanied by normalization of EEG findings (Appleton et al. 1993). In addition, anticonvulsants often fail to alleviate the language deficit (Paquier et al. 1992).

Bibliography

Alajouanine T, Lhermitte F 1965 Acquired aphasia in children. *Brain* **88:** 653–62

Appleton R, Hughes A, Beirne M, Acomb B 1993 Vigabatrim in the Landau-Kleffner syndrome. *Developmental Medicine and Child Neurology* **35:** 456–59

Aram D M, Ekelman B L 1988 Scholastic aptitude and achievement among children with unilateral brain lesions. *Neuropsycholgia* **26:** 903–16.

Aram D M, Ekelman B L, Rose D F, Whitaker H A 1985 Verbal and cognitive sequelae following unilateral lesions acquired in early childhood. *Journal of Clinical and Experimental Neurophyscholgy* **7:** 55–78

Aram D M, Ekelman B L, Whitaker H A 1986 Spoken syntax in children with acquired unilateral hemisphere lesions. *Brain and Language* **27:** 75–100

Aram D M, Ekelman B L, Whitaker H A 1987 Lexical retrieval in left and right brain lesioned children. *Brain and Language* **31:** 61–87

Aram D M, Rose D F, Rekate H L, Whitaker H A 1983 Acquired capsular/striatal aphasia in childhood. *Archives of Neurology* **40:** 614–17

Bijur P E, Haslum M, Gloning J 1990 Cognitive and behavioural sequelae of mild head injury in children. *Paediatrics* **86:** 337–44

Campbell T F, Heaton E M 1978 An expressive speech program for a child with acquired aphasia: A case study. *Human Communication* (Summer): 89–102

Chadwick O 1985 Psychological sequelae of head injury in children. *Developmental Medicine and Child Neurology* **27:** 72–75

Collignon R, Hécaen H, Angelergues G 1968 A propos de 12 cas d'aphasie acquise chez l'enfant. *Acta Neurologie et Psychiatrica Belgica* **68:** 245–77

Cooper J A, Ferry P C 1978 Acquired auditory verbal agnosia and seizures in childhood. *Journal of Speech and Hearing Disorders* **43:** 176–84

Cooper J A, Flowers C R 1987 Children with a history of acquired aphasia: Residual language and academic impairments. *Journal of Speech and Hearing Disorders* **52:** 251–62

Craft A W 1972 Head injury in children. In: Vinken P J, Bruyn G W (eds.) *Handbook of Clinical Neurology Vol. 23.* Elsevier, Holland

Cranberg L D, Filley C M, Hart E J, Alexander M P 1987 Acquired aphasia in children: Clinical and CT investigations. *Neurology* **37:** 1165–72

Dennis M 1980 Strokes in childhood 1: communicative intent expression and comprehension after left hemisphere arteriopathy in a right-handed nine-year-old. In: Reiber R W (ed.) *Language Development and Aphasia in Children.* Academic Press, New York

Deonna T, Beaumanoir A, Gaillard F, Assal G 1977 Acquired aphasia in childhood with seizure disorder: A heterogeneous syndrome. *Neuropadiatrie* **8:** 263–73

Deonna T, Fletcher P, Voumard C 1982 Temporary regression during language acquisition: a linguistic analysis of a two-and-a-half year old child with epileptic aphasia. *Developmental Medicine and Child Neurology* **24:** 156–63

Ewing-Cobbs L, Fletcher J M, Levin H S 1985 Neuropsychological sequelae following paediatric head injury. In: Ylvisaker M (ed.) *Head Injury Rehabilitation: Children and Adolescents.* Taylor and Francis, London

Ewing-Cobbs L, Fletcher J M, Levin H S, Eisenberg H M 1987 Language functions following closed head injury in children and adolescents. *Journal of Clinical and Experimental Neuropsychology* **19:** 495–502

Feldman W, Ginsburg C, McCracken G, Allen D, Ahmann P, Graham J, Graham L 1982 Relation of concentrations of haemophilus influenza type B in cerebrospinal fluid to late sequelae of patients with meningitis. *The Journal of Pediatrics* **100:** 209–12

Ferro J M, Martins I P, Pinto F, Castro-Caldas A 1982 Aphasia following right striato-capsular infarction in a left handed child: A clinico-radiological study. *Developmental Medicine and Child Neurology* **24:** 173–82

Gaidolfi E, Vignolo L A 1980 Closed head injuries of school aged children: Neuropsychological sequelae in early adulthood. *Italian Journal of Neurological Sciences* **1:** 65–73

Gascon G, Victor D, Lombrosco C T, Goodglass H 1973 Language disorder, convulsive disorder and electroencepholographic abnormalities. *Archives of Neurology* **28:** 156–62

Gloning K, Hift E 1970 Aphasie im Vorschulatter. *Zeitschreift für Nevenheilkunde* **28:** 20–28

Guttman E 1942 Aphasia in children. *Brain* **65:** 205–19

Hécaen H 1976 Acquired aphasia in children and the otogenesis of hemispheric functional specialization. *Brain and Language* **3:** 114–34

Hudson L J, Murdoch B E 1992 Chronic language deficits in children treated for posterior fossa tumour. *Aphasiology* **6:** 135–50

Hudson L J, Murdoch B E, Ozanne A E 1989 Posterior fossa tumours in childhood: Associated speech and language disorders post-surgery. *Aphasiology* **3:** 1–18

Jadavji T, Biggar W, Gold R 1986 Sequelae of acute bacterial meningitis in children treated for seven days. *Paediatrics* **78:** 21–28

Jordan F M, Murdoch B E 1990 Linguistic status following closed head injury in children: A follow-up study. *Brain Injury* **4:** 147–54

Jordan F M, Ozanne A E, Murdoch B E 1988 Long-term speech and language disorders subsequent to closed head injury in children. *Brain Injury* **2:** 179–85

Jordan F M, Ozanne A E, Murdoch B E 1990 Performance of closed head injury children on a naming task. *Brain Injury* **4:** 27–32

Klein S, Masur D, Farber K, Shinnar S, Rapin I 1992 Fluent aphasia in children: Definition and natural history. *Journal of Child Neurology* **7:** 50–59

Landau W M, Kleffner F R 1957 Syndrome of acquired aphasia with convulsive disorder in children. *Neurology* **10:** 915–21

Lenneberg E 1967 *Biological Foundations of Language*. Wiley, New York

Mantovani J F, Landau W M 1980 Acquired aphasia with convulsive disorder: Course and prognosis. *Neurology* **30**: 524–29

Martins I P, Ferro J M 1991 Type of aphasia and lesions' localization. In: Martins I P, Castro-Caldas A, van Dongen H R, van Hout A (eds.) *Acquired Aphasia in Children*. Kluwer, Dordrecht

Martins I P, Ferro J M 1987 Acquired conduction aphasia in a child. *Developmental Medicine and Child Neurology* **29**: 532–36

Martins I P, Ferro J M 1993 Acquired childhood aphasia: A clinicoradiological study of 11 stroke patients. *Aphasiology* **7**: 489–95

Martins I P, Ferro J M, Trindade A 1987 Crossed aphasia in a child. *Developmental Medicine and Child Neurology* **29**: 96–109

McKinney W, McGreal D A 1974 An aphasic syndrome in children. *Canadian Medical Association Journal* **110**: 637–39

Miller J F, Campbell T F, Chapman R S, Weismer S E 1984 Language behaviour in acquired aphasia. In: Holland A (ed.) *Language Disorders in Children*. College Hill Press, Baltimore, MD

Msall M, Shapiro B, Balfour P B, Niedermeyer E, Capute A J 1986 Acquired epileptic aphasia: Diagnostic aspects of progressive language loss in preschool children. *Neurology* **25**: 248–51

Murdoch B E, Hudson-Tennent L J 1994 Differential language outcomes in children following treatment for posterior fossa tumours. *Aphasiology* **8**: 507–34

Ozanne A E, Murdoch B E 1990 Acquired childhood aphasia: neuropathology, linguistic characteristics and prognosis. In: Murdoch B E (ed.) *Acquired Neurological Speech/Language Disorders in Childhood*. Taylor and Francis, London

Paquier P F, van Dongen H R 1991 Two contrasting cases of fluent aphasia in children. *Aphasiology* **5**: 235–45

Paquier P F, van Dongen H R, Loonen C B 1992 The Landau-Kleffner syndrome or acquired aphasia with convulsive disorder. *Archives of Neurology* **49**: 354–59

Rapin I, Mattis S, Rowan J A, Golden G G 1977 Verbal auditory agnosia in children. *Developmental Medicine and Child Neurology* **119**: 192–207

Satz P 1991 Symptom pattern and recovery outcome in childhood aphasia: a methodological and theoretical critique. In: Martin I P, Castro-Caldas A, van Dongen H R, van Hout A (eds.) *Acquired Aphasia in Children: Acquisition and Breakdown of Language in the Developing Brain*. Kluwer, Dordrecht

Satz P, Bullard-Bates C 1981 Acquired aphasia in children. In: Sarno M T (ed.) *Acquired Aphasia*. Academic Press, New York

Tanabe H, Ikeda M, Murasawa A, Yamadak K, Yammamoto H, Nakagawa Y, Nishimura T, Shiraishi J 1989 A case of acquired conductive aphasia in a child. *Acta Neurologica Scandinavia* **80**: 314–18

van de Sandt-Koenderman W M E, Smit I A C, van Dongen H R, van Hest J B C 1984 A case of acquired aphasia and convulsive disorder: Some linguistic aspects of recovery and breakdown. *Brain and Language* **21**: 174–83

van Dongen H R, Loonen M C B, van Dongen K J 1985 Anatomical basis of acquired fluent aphasia in children. *Annals of Neurology* **17**: 306–9

van Harskamp F, van Dongen H R, Loonen M C B 1978 Acquired aphasia with convulsive disorder in children: A case study with a seven year follow-up. *Brain and Language* **6**: 141–48

van Hout A 1992 Acquired aphasia in children. In: Segalowitz S J, Rapin I (eds.) *Section 10: Child Neuropsychology (Part 2) Vol. 7*. In: Boller F, Grafman J (eds.) *Handbook of Neuropsychology*. Elsevier, Amsterdam

van Hout A, Evrard P, Lyon G 1985 On the positive semiology of acquired aphasia in children. *Developmental Medicine and Child Neurology* **27**: 231–41

van Hout A, Lyon G 1986 Wernicke's aphasia in a 10-year-old boy. *Brain and Language* **29**: 268–85

Visch-Brink E G, van de Sandt-Koenderman M 1984 The occurrence of paraphasias in the spontaneous speech of children with an acquired aphasia. *Brain and Language* **23**: 258–71

Watamori T S, Sasanuma S, Veda S 1990 Recovery and plasticity in child-onset aphasics: Ultimate outcome at adulthood. *Aphasiology* **4**: 9–30

Worster-Drought C 1971 An unusual form of acquired aphasia in children. *Developmental Medicine and Child Neurology* **13**: 563–71

Aphasia in Multilinguals

F. Fabbro

1. Describing Multilingualism

The current approach in linguistic, psychological, and neurolinguistic domains is to consider as bilingual or multilingual (terms to be understood as synonyms for the purpose of this chapter) all those people who use two or more languages or dialects in their everyday lives (throughout this chapter, dialects are subsumed under the term 'language') (Grosjean 1994). Actually, at the linguistic level no objective criteria to distinguish between languages and dialects have been proposed so far (Pinker 1994) and at the neurolinguistic level the question whether the structural distance between two languages or two dialects or between a language and a dialect may affect their respective cerebral representation is still debated (Paradis 1995).

Several neuropsychological studies suggest that it is not correct to consider multilingual subjects as 'two monolinguals in one person' (Grosjean 1989). Indeed it is not necessary for multilinguals to have a perfect knowledge in all the languages they know, to be considered as such. The extremist view of the 'perfect' bilingual derives from a language culture which is essentially monolingual. Multilinguals acquire and use their languages for different purposes, in different domains of life and with different people. For example, a Canadian born in Quebec may acquire Quebecois as her mother tongue (L1) and use it with her family and friends, standard French as a second language (L2) being the official language of education, and English as a third (L3) language, the latter not being used everyday but, for example, to write scientific articles or give lectures at international congresses. Irrespective of the degree of knowledge this person has of these three languages, she should definitely be considered a multilingual.

On the basis of these methodological premises it was soon found that at present more than half of the world population is multilingual (Grosjean 1982, 1994). As a direct consequence, multilingual individuals suffering from developmental or acquired disorders of speech or language do not represent isolated, exceptional cases—as one might be inclined to think when reading the specialized literature—but probably rather the majority of clinical cases.

2. The Assessment of Bilingual Aphasia

A systematic assessment for all the languages known by an aphasic patient is an essential prerequisite for both clinical procedures (diagnosis, rehabilitation program, assessment of progress in recovery, etc.) and neurolinguistic research on multilingualism. For this reason Michel Paradis and associates (Paradis and Libben 1987) have developed the Bilingual Aphasia Test (BAT), which consists of three main parts: part A for the evaluation of the patient's multilingual history (50 items), part B for the systematic and comparable assessment of language disorders in each language known by the subject (472 items repeated in each known language) and part C for the assessment of translation abilities and interference detection in each couple of language (58 items each). The BAT is currently available in 65 languages (part B) and 160 bilingual pairs (part C). Parts B and C of this test have not been simply translated into different languages, but rather *adapted* across languages. For example, for the verbal auditory discrimination test the English items have not been simply translated into Friulian: when adapting this test for the Friulian version, the author and co-workers had to find for each item four Friulian words that differed from each other only by one single initial phoneme and could also be easily

represented in a picture. Thus, the English stimuli 'mat, cat, bat, hat' became '*cjoc, çoc, poc, toc*' (drunk, base of a tree, chicory, bit).

The person administering the test is not required to make any judgment: he/she simply notes the answers given by the patient, which will than be processed by means of a computerized system indicating for each part (B and C) the absolute number and the percentage of correct answers for each linguistic skill (comprehension, repetition, judgment, lexical access, propositionizing, reading, and writing) at each linguistic level (phonology, morphology, syntax, lexicon, and semantics). For some parts of the test, such as spontaneous speech, description of a short story illustrated by pictures, and spontaneous writing, a thorough neurolinguistic analysis on the basis of strict, objective criteria is required (for the post-test analysis of part B see Paradis and Libben 1987). The examination of bilingual aphasics by means of the BAT provides a quantification and classification of language disorders for each language, thus allowing a direct comparison of performances in the different languages known by the patients. Before the introduction of the BAT, the study of bilingual aphasics was mainly anecdotal (Paradis 1983). Therefore, the results of studies previous to the BAT should be seen as a starting point for a more thorough and systematic neurolinguistic analysis (Fabbro 1997).

As pointed out by Grosjean (1989, 1998), when assessing residual language in bilingual aphasics, a series of methodological precautions should be taken: each language should be assessed on a separate day and the code-switching habits of the patient before pathological onset should be thoroughly described, for example, by asking relatives, friends, etc. the relevant information. Indeed, in some bilingual communities code-switching is sociolinguistically accepted and quite common during everyday conversation (e.g., among English-French bilinguals in Montreal, Canada), whereas it hardly ever occurs in other bilingual environments (e.g., Friulian-Italian in Friuli, see Francescato and Salimbeni 1976). On the one hand, if the patient exhibits frequent pathological switching and/or mixing, the assessment of L1 ought to be done by a person not knowing the patient's L2, and vice versa for the second language, so as to avoid confusing any pathological behavior with deep-rooted habits. On the other hand, the assessment of translation abilities should be made by someone knowing all the languages at issue.

3. Clinical Aspects of Multilingual Aphasia

Several clinical studies have shown that bilingual aphasics do not necessarily manifest the same language disorders with the same degree of severity in both languages. For this reason it is no longer ethically acceptable to assess aphasic patients by only examining one language (Paradis 1995). In addition, the clinical assessment of both monolingual and multilingual aphasics should take account of three different phases in time: (a) the *acute phase*, which generally lasts 4 weeks after onset; (b) the *lesion phase*, which lasts several weeks and perhaps even up to 4–5 months post-onset; and (c) the *late phase*, beginning a few months after onset and continuing for the rest of the patient's life (Alexander 1989).

During the *acute phase* a regression of the diaschisis takes place, that is, a regression of the functional impairment effects in structurally unaffected cerebral regions of the ipsilateral and contralateral hemisphere which are functionally connected to the brain area where the damage occurred. These effects have been highlighted by tests based on the quantitative assessment of the regional glucose metabolism by means of positron emission tomography (Cappa 1998). During the acute phase of bilingual aphasics, several dynamic language disorders have been observed, such as temporary mutism in both languages with preserved comprehension (Aglioti and Fabbro 1993; Fabbro and Paradis 1995b), severe word-finding difficulties alternatively in one language with concurrent relative fluency in the other language and good comprehension in both (the so-called alternating antagonism; see Paradis et al. 1982; Nilipour and Ashayeri 1989), and severe impairment of the language acquired during childhood with complete preservation of the one learnt at school ('selective aphasia'; see Paradis and Goldblum 1989). The study of these dynamic phenomena is also useful for setting up theoretical neurofunctional models of brain functioning in multilinguals (Green 1986; Paradis 1993a), though it does not allow us to draw unequivocal conclusions on the relationship between linguistic functions and neuroanatomical structures.

The *lesion phase* is the period of greatest interest for brain-behavior relationships, because during this period language disorders can be more clearly correlated to the site and entity of the lesion. Since such disorders are also more stable, it is far more convenient to carry out a complete assessment of the patients' residual language abilities in this phase, by taking into account *all* the languages they knew before the pathological event. Aphasic disorders may or may not vary across languages in one and the same patient; they may be classified as typical of one single aphasic syndrome, though with different degrees of symptomatic severity according to the language (Fabbro and Paradis 1995b; Yiu and Worral 1996). However, the hypothesis of the existence of a clinical picture of *differential aphasia*, namely a type of aphasia in one language (e.g., Wernicke's aphasia) and another type (e.g., Broca's aphasia) in another language, still lacks sufficient corroborating data (Silverberg and Gordon 1979; Paradis 1998).

A necessary prerequisite of a consistent rehabilitation program for aphasic monolingual and bilingual patients is a systematic assessment of language disorders. As far as rehabilitation programs for multilingual aphasics are concerned, several questions have been raised, many of which still need a satisfactory answer. For example, is it better to set up a rehabilitation program for both languages or only one? In this latter case, which language should be chosen? Can rehabilitation effects on one language spontaneously transfer to the other language? (Paradis 1993b). Practical reasons and common sense suggest that it may be easier to start rehabilitation in one language only and that the choice should be based on the neurolinguistic assessment of residual abilities as well as on sociolinguistic criteria (e.g., preference will be given to the language the patient and his/her closest relatives wish be recovered first). It has been observed that the positive effects of speech and language therapy on one language generally have advantageous repercussions for the other language(s) too (Fredman 1976; Fabbro et al. 1996).

In the *late phase* different patterns of recovery can be observed in multilingual patients. Sometimes this phase may hardly differ from the previous one, since recovery or even improvement do not always occur. Language recovery phenomena are thought to be due to the 'take-over' of linguistic functions by the contralateral hemisphere or by undamaged areas within the same hemisphere (Cappa 1998). Improvement in communication skills probably may depend on the application of explicit compensatory strategies (Paradis 1994; Paradis and Gopnik 1997). Recovery, either spontaneous or following rehabilitation, may continue also during the late phase, though generally less intensively than during the lesion phase. Patients should be periodically reassessed, so as to re-examine recovery patterns and possibly revise the rehabilitation program. The most common patterns of recovery, described by Pitres (1895) in the first paper on bilingual aphasia ever published, are: (a) parallel recovery, when both languages are recovered simultaneously; (b) selective recovery, when only one language slowly comes back and the other is never recovered; (c) successive recovery, when one language improves before the other(s).

4. Neurolinguistic Research on Multilingualism

The present section deals with theoretical and experimental aspects of the representation of languages in the brain of multilingual individuals. This problem has been tackled from several different perspectives, but careful consideration of clinical cases and observation of normal multilingual subjects with electrophysiological and neuroimaging techniques in particular have contributed to broaden our knowledge about this interesting domain of neuroscience.

4.1. Recovery Patterns in Multilingual Aphasics

Several studies have tried to interpret the different recovery patterns observed in multilingual aphasics

(Paradis 1977, 1989, 1993c, 1998). The main issues at stake regard the following aspects: the reason why recovery patterns differ so much across patients, the pathophysiological mechanisms accounting for one or another recovery pattern in a given patient, and the reason why a language recovers better than the other(s). A series of well-grounded corresponding hypotheses have been put forward which, however, succeeded in explaining only some aspects of this complex problem. Further research needs to be done in order to clarify it.

A large number of neurologists in the past (Pitres, Freud, Minkowski, Pötzl) and also some contemporary scholars (Paradis) have suggested that when a language is not available, it is not because its neural substrates have been physically destroyed, but because its system has been weakened. This weakening can be explained in terms of increased inhibition, raised activation threshold, or unbalanced access resources among the various languages (Green 1986; Paradis 1998). However, in some cases dissociations in the recovery of the two languages observed in the lesion phase and in the late phase cannot be ascribed to neurofunctional impairments only, but also to the consequences of the destruction of cortical and/or subcortical neural substrates (Fabbro et al. 1997; Fabbro 1998). Actually, in the late phase dynamic phenomena have hardly ever been described, thus suggesting that after 1 or 2 years from onset, the recovery pattern remains stable since it is most probably the result of pathological phenomena that are partly due to neurofunctional impairments and partly to the loss of cerebral tissue orginally involved in the organization of linguistic functions.

Differences in age and manner of acquisition/learning seem to strongly influence the way languages are stored in the brain. When a second language is learnt formally and mainly used in school, it apparently tends to have a more restricted representation in specific subcortical structures (basal ganglia and cerebellum) than the first language, whereas if it is acquired informally the way it usually happens with the first language, it is more likely to be subserved also by subcortical structures. Two aphasic patients (B. K. and E. M.) with lesions to the left basal ganglia showed greater disruption of the grammatical components of their respective first language than of their second language and this symptomatological picture remained stable for more than 5 years after their stroke (Fabbro and Paradis 1995a; Aglioti et al. 1996). The difference in representation between an informally acquired first language and a formally learnt second language seems to be due to different appropriation strategies occurring in the process (Paradis 1994). Most probably in the two above-mentioned patients the grammatical components of the first language were more extensively organized in the procedural memory systems.

As to the role of the formal characteristics of languages in determining the pattern of recovery, researchers have concluded that the structural distance between languages do not seem to have any influence on the way a bilingual aphasic may recover his/her languages. It has not been demonstrated so far that aphasics knowing two structurally close languages (e.g., French and Italian) have a greater chance of developing a parallel recovery with respect to patients knowing two structurally distant languages (e.g., English and Japanese).

4.2. Aphasic Reactions in Multilinguals

Some patients present language disorders that seem to be typical of multilingual aphasics only. Subjects may *switch* from language to language, alternating their verbal expression between one and the other. Other subjects may *mix* linguistic elements from various languages within a single sentence. Switching and mixing are frequent in normal bilingual speakers too, but they reflect a pathological behavior when produced during conversation with an interlocutor who is unable to understand both languages. In such cases, even if repeatedly asked to use only one language, some aphasics would go on producing mixing and/or switching phenomena. It is not always possible to draw a clear distinction between mixing and switching, but it seems that pathological switching tends to be related to lesions of the frontal lobes (both left and right) and other right-hemisphere structures, whereas mixing tends to be correlated with postrolandic lesions of the left hemisphere (Fabbro 1999).

Multilingual aphasics may also present disorders of translation (Paradis 1984; Fabbro and Gran 1997). One of these phenomena is the *inability to translate*, which may affect both directions of translation, namely from L1 into L2 and vice versa from L2 into L1 (Aglioti and Fabbro 1993); another one is *spontaneous translation*, a compulsive 'need' to translate everything which is being said by the patients themselves and/or by their interlocutors (De Vreese et al. 1988); another still is *translation without comprehension* occurring when patients do not understand commands that are given to them but can nevertheless correctly translate the sentences uttered by an interlocutor to express these commands (Veyrac 1931; Fabbro and Paradis 1995b); and finally *paradoxical translation*, when a patient can translate only into the language that he/she cannot speak spontaneously (Paradis et al. 1982).

The fact that these so-called polyglot reactions (see Lebrun 1991) only occur in multilingual patients is just an impression: indeed mixing, switching, and pathological translation are simply much more evident when different languages are at stake, but they most probably occur also in monolinguals, only with different apparent features. Actually, all verbal functions that are present in a bilingual individual have their homologue in a monolingual speaker. Bilinguals switch and mix languages, monolinguals switch and mix registers; bilinguals translate from one language into another, monolinguals may paraphrase from one register to another (i.e., they can express the same concept addressing their own little child or an audience of experts). This is another reason why it is no more reasonable to postulate the existence of neural mechanisms specific to multilinguals, as maintained by several neurologists in the past (Paradis 1993c, 1998).

4.3. Lateralization of Languages

In the late seventies Albert and Obler (1978), when trying to explain a few cases of non-parallel recovery among their patients, suggested that bilinguals had a more symmetric representation of language in the two cerebral hemispheres. The hypothesis appealed to the scientific imagery of many researchers who over the past 15 years have carried out studies on the cerebral organization of language in bilinguals and multilinguals. These studies have been generally performed with the help of typical techniques of experimental neuropsychology, namely dichotic listening, tachistoscopic technique, and finger-tapping, but their results have been rather controversial (see Paradis 1990). By analyzing a large number of cases of bilingual aphasics it was shown that the incidence of aphasia following a lesion to the *right* hemisphere (crossed aphasia) is as high in bilinguals as in monolinguals (Karanth and Rangamani 1988).

However, it is known that the right hemisphere (also called the 'minor' hemisphere) is crucially involved in the processing of the pragmatic aspects of language use (Chantraine et al. 1998). During the first stages of second-language learning, both in children and adults, the right hemisphere tends to be more involved in verbal communication processes because beginners try to compensate the lack of implicit linguistic competence in L2 with pragmatic inferences. The greater involvement of the right hemisphere during verbal communication in L2, however, does not necessarily imply a greater representation of language processes (phonology, morphology, syntax, and the lexicon) in this hemisphere (see Paradis 1994, 1998).

4.4. Experimental Studies about the Multilingual Brain

While clinical neurolinguistic studies have initially focused on the elaboration of test methods for a correct, complete, and systematic assessment of language disorders and then on the description of the linguistic symptomatology in the different phases that follow a cerebral lesion, experimental studies in this field have basically tried to answer the question whether the languages known by polyglots are (completely or partially) represented in different cerebral structures.

One of the first methods developed to assess the cerebral representation of linguistic functions is electrocorticostimulation during brain surgery (Ojemann and Whitaker 1978; Rapport et al. 1989). In these studies the patients were administered naming tests in both languages while different cortical areas were stimulated in such a way as to produce a transient functional inhibition of the stimulated area, thus indicating if that area was involved in language processing. The results were interpreted as showing that specific cortical areas were shared by both languages, whereas other areas, when stimulated, selectively inhibited only one language. The results obtained by means of this technique have been criticized because these studies cannot be repeated on a population of a statistically sufficient size and because the spatial definition of such brain mapping lacks in exactness.

A series of studies carried out by Helen Neville and associates (Neville et al. 1992, 1997; Weber-Fox and Neville 1996) by means of electrophysiological techniques (event-related potential, ERPs) have shown differences in the brain organization of languages depending on the age of acquisition and the learning strategies. In early bilinguals, closed-class words of both languages tend to be represented in the frontal lobe of the left hemisphere, whereas open-class words tend to involve post-rolandic cortical structures. However, in bilinguals having learned the second language after a certain critical age (about 7 years), unlike closed-class words of L1, closed-class words of L2 seem not to be represented in left-hemisphere frontal areas.

PET studies have revealed that if L2 has been learned only formally, for example, in school, the cortical areas involved in the comprehension of stories presented in L2 were activated to a lesser extent than when the same stories were presented in L1. In addition, only while listening to stories in L1 were perisylvian language areas of the left cerebral hemisphere and of the right cerebellum activated (the cerebellum notably being involved in the organization of procedural memory in language) (Perani et al. 1995).

A recent study using functional resonance imaging (fMRI) has revealed a differentiated representation of L1 versus L2 in Broca's area in fluent bilinguals having learnt L2 after the age of 10, whereas no such difference has been found in Wernicke's area. However, in fluent bilinguals having acquired L2 in early childhood, the cortical representation of the two languages was similar in both Broca's and Wernicke's area (Kim et al. 1997). Another similar study (Dehaene et al. 1997) has shown that in moderately fluent French-English bilinguals, activation of the right hemisphere turned out to be on average greater during listening of stories in L2 than in L1. In the same subjects a greater intersubject variability in the anatomical representation of L2 has been observed. The greater right-hemisphere activation in L2 might depend on a more extensive use of pragmatic (right-hemisphere related) strategies in L2 processing.

5. Conclusions

More than 50 percent of the world population uses two or more languages/dialects in their everyday lives. Multilingual aphasias are therefore an important aspect of clinical practice and research in the field of language disorders. In order to make a correct diagnosis, choose a proper rehabilitation program and efficiently control therapeutical intervention, adequate assessment procedures have to be applied, such as those developed in the Bilingual Aphasia Test. Clinical and experimental studies conducted so far have tried to describe the way languages are represented in the brain of multilingual individuals. The cerebral organization of languages seems to be determined by the age of acquisition or learning and by the patterns of use of such languages. Further clinical research based on an appropriate methodology and future experimental studies, both at neuroanatomical and at functional levels, will hopefully lead to a more advanced understanding of the organization of the multilingual brain.

Bibliography

Aglioti S, Fabbro F 1993 Paradoxical selective recovery in a bilingual aphasic following subcortical lesions. *Neuro-Report* **4**: 1359–62

Aglioti S, Beltramello A, Girardi F, Fabbro F 1996 Neurolinguistic and follow-up study of an unusual pattern of recovery from bilingual subcortical aphasia. *Brain* **119**: 1551–64

Alexander M P 1989 Clinical-anatomical correlations of aphasia following predominantly subcortical lesions. In: Boller, F, Grafman J (eds.) *Handbook of Neuropsychology*, vol 2. Elsevier, Amsterdam: 47–66

Albert M L, Obler L K 1978 *The Bilingual Brain*. Academic Press, New York

Cappa S F 1998 Spontaneous recovery from aphasia. In: Stemmer B, Whitaker H A (eds.) *Handbook of Neurolinguistics*. Academic Press, San Diego, CA: 536–47

Chantraine Y, Joanette Y, Cardebat D 1998 Impairments of discourse-level representations and processes. In: Stemmer B, Whitaker H A (eds.) *Handbook of Neurolinguistics*. Academic Press, San Diego, CA: 262–75

Dehaene S, Dupoux E, Mehler J, Cohen L, Paulesu E, Perani D et al. 1997 Anatomical variability in the cortical representation of first and second language. *Neuroreport* **8**: 3809–15

DeVreese L P, Motta M, Toschi A 1988 Compulsive and paradoxical translation behaviour in a case of presenile dementia of the Alzheimer type. *Journal of Neurolinguistics* **3**: 233–59

Fabbro F 1997 Bilingual aphasia research is not a tabula rasa. *Aphasiology* **12**: 138–41

Fabbro F 1999 *The Neurolinguistics of Bilingualism*. Psychology Press, Hove

Fabbro F, De Luca G, Vorano L 1996 Assessment of language rehabilitation with the BAT in four multilingual aphasics. *Journal of the Israeli Speech, Hearing and Language Association* **19**: 46–53

Fabbro F, Gran L 1997 Neurolinguistic research in simultaneous interpretation. In: Gambir Y et al. (eds.) *Con-ference Interpreting: Current Trends in Research*. Benjamins, Amsterdam: 9–28

Fabbro F, Paradis M 1995a Acquired aphasia in a bilingual child. In: Paradis M (ed.) *Aspects of Bilingual Aphasia*. Pergamon Press, London: 67–83

Fabbro F, Paradis M 1995b Differential impairments in four multilingual patients with subcortical lesions. In: Paradis M (ed.) *Aspects of Bilingual Aphasia*. Pergamon Press, Oxford: 139–76

Fabbro F, Peru A, Skrap M 1997 Language disorders in bilingual patients after thalamic lesions. *Journal of Neurolinguistics* **10**: 347–67

Francescato G, Salimbeni F 1976 *Storia, lingua e società in Friuli*. Casamassima, Udine

Fredman M 1976 The effect of therapy given in Hebrew on the home language of the bilingual or polyglot adult in Isreal. *British Journal of Disorders of Communication* **10**: 61–69

Green D 1986 Control, activation, and resource: A framework and a model for the control of speech in bilinguals. *Brain and Language* **27**: 210–23

Grosjean F 1982 *Life with Two Languages. An Introduction to Bilingualism*. Harvard University Press, Cambridge, MA

Grosjean F 1989 Neurolinguists, beware! The bilingual is not two monolinguals in one person. *Brain and Language* **36**: 3–15

Grosjean F 1994 Individual Bilingualism. In: Asher R E (ed.) *The Encyclopaedia of Language and Linguistics*. Pergamon Press, Oxford: 1656–60

Grosjean F 1998 Studying bilinguals: Methodological and conceptual issues. *Bilingualism, Language and Cognition* (in press)

Lebrun Y 1991 Polyglotte Reaktionen. *Neurolinguistik* **5**: 1–9

Karanth P, Rangamani G N 1988 Crossed aphasia in multilinguals. *Brain and Language* **34**: 169–80

Kim K H S, Relkin N R, Lee K M, Hirsch J 1997 Distinct cortical areas associated with native and second languages. *Nature* **388**: 171–74

Neville H J, Mills D L, Lawson D S 1992 Fractionating language: different neural subsystems with different sensitive periods. *Cerebral Cortex* **2**: 244–58

Neville H J, Coffey S A, Lawson D S, Fischer A, Emmorey K, Bellugi U 1997 Neural systems mediating American Sign Language: Effects of sensory experiences and age of acquisition. *Brain and Language* **57**: 285–308

Nilipour R, Ashayeri H 1989 Alternating antagonism between two languages with successive recovery of a third in a trilingual aphasic patient. *Brain and Language* **36**: 23–48

Ojemann G A, Whitaker H A 1978 The bilingual brain. *Archives of Neurology* **35**: 409–12

Paradis M 1977 Bilingualism and aphasia. In: Whitaker H, Whitaker H A (eds.), *Studies in Neurolinguistics*, vol 3. Academic Press, New York: 65–121

Paradis M (ed.) 1983 *Readings on Aphasia in Bilinguals and Polyglots*. Didier, Montreal

Paradis M 1984 Aphasie et traduction. *Meta Translators' Journal* **24**: 57–67

Paradis M 1989 Bilingual and polyglot aphasia. In: Boller F, Grafman J (eds.) *Handbook of Neuropsychology*, vol 2. Elsevier, Oxford: 117–40

Paradis M 1990 Language lateralization in bilinguals: Enough already! *Brain and Language* **39**: 576–86

Paradis M 1993a Linguistic, psycholinguistic, and neuro-linguistic aspects of 'interference' in bilingual speakers: The activation threshold hypothesis. *International Journal of Psycholinguistics* 9: 133–45

Paradis M (ed.) 1993b *Foundations of Aphasia Rehabilitation*. Pergamon Press, Oxford

Paradis M 1993c Multilingualism and aphasia. In: Blanken G et al. (eds.) *Linguistics Disorders and Pathologies*. De Gruyter, Berlin: 278–88

Paradis M 1994 Neurolinguistic aspects of implicit and explicit memory: implications for bilingualism and SLA. In: Ellis N (ed.) *Implicit and Explicit Language Learning*. Academic Press, London: 393–419

Paradis M (ed.) 1995 *Aspects of Bilingual Aphasia*. Pergamon Press, Oxford

Paradis M 1998 Language and communication in multilinguals. In: Stemmer B, Whitaker H A (eds.) *Handbook of Neurolinguistics*. Academic Press, San Diego, CA: 418–31

Paradis M, Goldblum M C 1989 Selective crossed aphasia in a trilingual aphasic patient followed by reciprocal antagonism. *Brain and Language* 36: 62–75

Paradis M, Goldblum M C, Abidi R 1982 Alternate antagonism with paradoxical translation behavior in two bilingual aphasic patients. *Brain and Language* 15: 55–69

Paradis M, Gopnik M 1997 Compensatory strategies in genetic dysphasia: Declarative memory. *Journal of Neurolinguistics* 10: 173–186

Paradis M, Libben G 1987 *The Assessment of Bilingual Aphasia*. Erlbaum, Hillsdale, NJ

Perani D, Dehaene S, Grassi F, Cohen L, Cappa S F, Dupoux E, Faxio F, Mehler J 1996 Brain processing of native and foreign languages. *Neuroreport* 7: 2439–44

Pinker S 1994 *The Language Instinct*. Penguin Books, London

Pitres A 1895 Aphasia in polyglots. In: Paradis M (ed.) 1983 *Readings on Aphasia in Bilinguals and Polyglots*. Didier, Montreal: 26–49

Rapport R L, Tan C T, Whitaker H A 1983 Language function and dysfunction among Chinese- and English-speaking polyglots: Cortical stimulation, Wada testing, and clinical studies. *Brain and Language* 18: 342–66

Silverberg R, Gordon H W 1979 Differential aphasia in two bilingual individuals. *Neurology* 29: 51–5

Veyrac G J 1931 A study of aphasia in polyglot subjects. In: Paradis M (ed.) 1983 *Reading on Aphasia in Bilinguals and Polyglots*. Didier, Montreal: 320–38

Weber-Fox C M, Neville H J 1997 Maturational constraints on functional specializations for language processing: ERP and behavioral evidence in bilingual speakers. *Journal of Cognitive Neuroscience* 8: 231–56

Yiu E M, Worrall L E 1996 Sentence production ability of a bilingual Cantonese-English agrammatic speaker. *Aphasiology* 10: 505–22

Phonological Disorders of Language

A. R. Butcher

A person with a 'phonological disorder' is unable to make one or more of the phonological contrasts of the language. For example, an English speaker who makes all initial stops voiceless and unaspirated will not distinguish between words such as *pin* and *bin* or *curl* and *girl*. Someone who has a 'lisp,' on the other hand, whose only speech abnormality is a strange-sounding 's,' would be said to have a phonetic disorder, as no loss of contrast is involved. The exact definition of the term phonological disorder may differ according to whether one takes a strict linguistic approach or a more practical clinical approach. A distinction should certainly be made between a developmental disorder in children and an acquired disorder in later life.

1. The Symptoms of Phonological Disorder

As an illustration of the effects of a developmental phonological disorder, consider the following hypothetical and relatively straightforward cases. (1) represents the case of a child aged 3 years and 9 months, whose pronunciations of a small set of words are indicated by the broad phonetic transcriptions in square brackets:

back	[bak]	snail	[neɪl]	try	[taɪ]	(1)
floor	[fɔ]	sting	[tɪŋ]	black	[bak]	
pot	[pɒt]	tie	[taɪ]	scream	[kim]	
nail	[neɪl]	splash	[paʃ]	four	[fɔ]	
spot	[pɒt]	cream	[kim]	sleep	[sip]	

Clearly, as far as these words are concerned, the differences between this child's pronunciation and that of a normal adult are to be found in the initial consonant clusters. Whereas words with a single initial consonant, such as *back*, *tie*, and *nail* all appear to have an acceptable pronunciation, in words beginning with a cluster of consonants, such as *floor*, *sting*, and *splash*, only one of the consonants is pronounced. This leads to several pairs of words in this list having identical pronunciations (*back* and *black*, *pot* and *spot*, *cream* and *scream*, etc.) and, if this set of words is representative, the child's speech will exhibit a great deal of such homophony. For example, *team, steam,* and *stream* would all be pronounced [tim] and *go, grow,* and *glow* would all be pronounced [gəʊ]. While there is no mispronunciation of individual sounds, child (1) is unable to make a number of phonological contrasts and would be said to be suffering from a phonological disorder. Although many potentially problematic utterances may be disambiguated by context, there is, nonetheless, a serious impediment to communication.

Consider, on the other hand, the case of another child (2), aged 3 years and 4 months, who pronounces these same words as:

back	[bak]	snail	[ɬneɪl]	try	[tʊaɪ]	(2)
floor	[flɔ]	sting	[ɬtɪŋ]	black	[blak]	
pot	[pot]	tie	[taɪ]	scream	[ɬkʊim]	
nail	[neɪl]	splash	[ɬplaʃ]	four	[fɔ]	
spot	[ɬpot]	cream	[kʊim]	sleep	[ɬlip]	

In this case, /s/ is systematically pronounced as [ɬ], a voiceless alveolar lateral fricative, and /r/ as [ʊ], a voiced labiodental approximant. Two sounds are thus pronounced in a manner which would not be regarded as normal in adult speakers of most accents. However, if these are the only nonstandard sounds, then no phonological contrast is affected: *pot* contrasts with *spot* and *tie* with *try*. Even when two mispronunciations occur in the same word, *cream* still contrasts with *scream*. There should, then, be no more homophones than in normal adult speech, and, after an initial 'tuning in' on the part of the listener, no impairment of the child's communicative ability. Child (2) has a phonetic disorder, rather than a phonological one. Of course, in reality, it would be unusual to find a child exhibiting either type of disorder in its 'pure' form. It is unlikely that a child such as (1) would have a normal adult pronunciation of all the sounds he produces. Similarly, it is highly probable that a child such as (2) would mispronounce /ʃ/ in the same way as /s/, thereby losing a contrast between words such as *sip* and *ship*.

Finally, let us consider the case of a 63 year old stroke patient (3), who produces the forms:

pad	[pad, bad]	dart	[tɑt, dɑt]	(3)
girl	[kɜl, gɜl]	blade	[pleɪd, bleɪd]	
pin	[pɪn, bɪn]	curl	[kɜl, gɜl]	
crime	[kɹaɪm, gɹaɪm]	tart	[tɑt, dɑt]	
bin	[pɪn, bɪn]	grime	[kɹaɪm, gɹaɪm]	
		trip	[tɹɪp, dɹɪp]	
		bad	[pad, bad]	
		drip	[tɹɪp, dɹɪp]	
		played	[pleɪd, bleɪd]	
		stop	[stop, zdop]	

This speaker shows random variation in his pronunciation. Each word is produced correctly approximately 50 percent of the time. The remainder of the time, initial /bdg/ are produced as their voiceless aspi-

rated counterparts and /ptk/ are produced as voiced (or more likely voiceless unaspirated) [bdg]. As with child (1), each phoneme is realized as an acceptable English sound but once again contrasts are being lost: this time not because one member of an opposition consistently stands for both but because either may stand for the other. This too, then, could be characterized as a phonological disorder.

2. A Linguistic Definition

A definition of phonological disorder which is theoretically straightforward can be formulated on the basis of one simple linguistic criterion. It can be said that such a disorder is present whenever at least one phonological contrast of the language is unable to be signaled. Such a definition would no doubt produce the desired categorization of the three hypothetical cases illustrated above. Child (1) and adult (3) would be classed as having a phonological disorder, whereas child (2) would not. However, a strict linguistic definition is liable to result in some unsatisfactory categorizations when applied to real cases.

First, it takes no account of the extent of the disorder or of the severity of the misarticulations. Thus, if child (2) does indeed produce both /s/ and /ʃ/ as [ɬ] (and, presumably, /z/ and /ʒ/ as [ɮ]), then his disorder must be categorized as phonological, even if no other contrasts are affected and even if, as one suspects, his ability to communicate is practically unhindered. At the other extreme, a speaker with multiple severe misarticulations may be unintelligible to the unfamiliar listener, even if phonological contrasts are theoretically intact. Take, for example, a child who pronounces /p/ and /b/ as bilabial fricatives [ɸ] and [β], /t/ and /d/ as ungrooved alveolar fricatives [θ] and [ð], and /k/ and /g/ as velar fricatives [x] and [ˈ]. A skilled observer, such as a speech therapist or phonetician, would be able to differentiate these sounds from any others produced by the child and would be able to establish that all phonological contrasts are being made. Thus, according to the strict linguistic criterion, the child is not suffering from a phonological disorder. People having prolonged contact with the child (such as family members) would doubtless be in a position to understand his speech. For most listeners, however, the severity of the misarticulations would prevent rapid 'tuning in' to the child's system. They would have difficulty perceiving distinctions between such sounds as [ɸ] and [f], [θ] and [s], or maybe [x] and [h]. In other words, although the phonology may be intact as far as the linguist is concerned, for the listener, a number of important contrasts would be absent.

Second, a linguistic definition says nothing about the cause of the disorder. The speech production mechanism may be disrupted by conditions which are clearly of anatomical or physiological origin, such as cleft palate or cerebral palsy (see *Acquired Disorders of Articulation: Classification and Intervention*; *Devel-*

opmental *Dysarthrias*). In cases of this sort some speakers will have a reduced system of phonological contrasts, whereas others will produce sounds which, though distorted, are still distinct from one another. At the other end of the scale, the child who pronounces both /s/ and /θ/ as [θ] would be categorized as suffering from a phonological disorder, just as the child who produces all fricatives as stops or the one who fails to pronounce any syllable-final consonants. It is likely, however, that cases of the latter type result from a specific linguistic disability of a type quite distinct from that which results in an isolated 'lisp.' The child with the interdental /s/ (=[θ]) probably has a similar kind of fine motor-control problem to the child with the lateral /s/ (=[ɬ]). The fact that a phonological contrast happens to be neutralized in one case and not in the other is, in this case, irrelevant as far as diagnosis and remediation are concerned.

3. A Clinical Definition

A categorization of pronunciation disorders based on theoretical linguistic criteria alone will be of limited value to the clinician, since it will not necessarily bear any relationship to the underlying cause of the disorders, nor be crucial for the planning of therapy. The main reason for this is that a linguistic definition is based on what is perceived to come from the speaker's mouth rather than what is happening in the speaker's brain. It is what Hewlett (1985) has called 'data-oriented' rather than 'speaker-oriented.' A clinically relevant 'neurolinguistic' definition of phonological disorder should distinguish between how the speaker represents the phonological contrasts of the language in his brain and how he realizes those contrasts as phonetically distinct sounds in his vocal tract. It can then be said that a phonological disorder is present when a speaker fails to operate with the appropriate adult system of contrasts at the level of phonological representation in the brain. Fig. 1 illustrates schematically how such a speaker (A) differs from a normal adult speaker (N) and a speaker with an articulatory disorder (B). Speaker (B) 'knows' the distinction between /s/ and /θ/ but is not able to say [s]. His inadequate control of his tongue muscles causes /s/ to sound like [θ]. Speaker (A), on the other hand, does not know the distinction between /s/ and /θ/. He has a single phoneme (perhaps it should be called '/S/' rather than /θ/, since it does not have the same status as normal adult /θ/), and this is realized as [θ]. Since the speech output from both (A) and (B) in this case sounds the same, a linguistic definition, operating at level III, could only distinguish between (N) on the one hand and (A) and (B) on the other. A neurolinguistic definition, taking level II into account, however, would distinguish between all three cases and would identify only case (A) as a true phonological disorder. Such a definition has one obvious advantage as far as the speech pathologist is

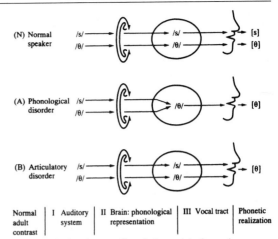

Figure 1. A simple neurolinguistic model of speech processing. A phonologically disordered speaker fails to assign two distinct sounds to different mental phonological categories. An articulatorily disordered speaker has two different mental categories but cannot make the necessary distinct sounds.

concerned, in that it would provide the criterion for a meaningful differential diagnosis of disorders. If misarticulations result from an inadequate command of the phonological system, they would need to be treated in a different way from misarticulations which result from an inadequate control of the vocal tract muscles. There does appear, however, to be one significant disadvantage: a neurolinguistic definition presupposes access to the phonological system as it is represented in the speaker's brain. Quite obviously there is no direct access to the speaker's brain. The definition relies on evidence from the speech output, but it does not have to be based on the perception of the speech output nor does it have to rely on the speech output alone. The following guidelines could be applied in deciding whether or not abnormal pronunciation results from a disorder of phonological organization in the brain:

(a) The speaker fails to distinguish in pronunciation between two or more sounds or combinations of sounds which are contrastive in the normal adult language. The use of acoustic measurement and other instrumental phonetic procedures should confirm that the distinction is entirely lacking as opposed to merely inaudible.

(b) There is no evidence of any organic cause of the misarticulations, such as structural abnormality (e.g., cleft palate) or neurological disorder (e.g., dysarthria).

(c) A number of contrasts are affected—that is, the problem is not confined to a small area of the phonology and indeed may be accompanied by disorder in other areas of language, par-

343

ticularly syntax and perhaps in other modalities (see *Disorders of Reading and Writing*).

(d) The speaker is able to make many, if not all, of the distinctive sounds in isolated syllables when directly imitating another speaker (as shown below, this criterion is not relevant in some acquired disorders, such as conduction aphasia and verbal apraxia).

(e) There is no evidence of hearing impairment. The speaker may in fact be able to distinguish perceptually all or many of the contrasts which he has problems in producing (although his ability to do so may be difficult to test in certain acquired disorders).

(f) There is no evidence of general intellectual disability. It would probably be more helpful, however, to include such groups as the hearing impaired, the intellectually disabled, and others as special categories of phonological disorder, rather than exclude them altogether.

These criteria appear neither as simple nor as rigorous as in the case of the pure linguistic definition but the resultant classification is a clinically more meaningful one. After reviewing the linguistic description and characterization of the main types of disorder, the necessity for refining the definition still further will be considered.

4. The Linguistic Description of Phonological Disorder

Most aspects of disordered phonology can usefully be described in terms of the differences between the disordered system of contrasts and structures and those of the normal adult. In many types of disorder these differences are quite systematic, in that whole classes of sounds are affected in a similar way. These systematic differences mainly involve simplifying phonological structures, facilitating the pronunciation of sequences of sounds, and reducing the system of contrasts. It is known which of these patterns occur during normal language acquisition, and in what order they are lost and at roughly what age. Developmental phonological disorder is characterized primarily by retention of such patterns beyond the age at which normal adult pronunciation of the sounds is expected. Some phonologically disordered speakers (particularly those with an acquired disorder) will also show evidence of patterns not encountered during normal acquisition. Only the most commonly found patterns of disordered phonology in English are outlined below although most of them are generally held to be valid for all languages (see e.g., Ingram 1976, 1986; Locke 1983).

4.1 Simplification of Structures

4.1.1 Syllable deletion

Probably the most drastic simplification pattern (and one of the most persistent in children) is the omission of entire syllables. It is normally those syllables which are unstressed in the normal adult form which are absent in immature and disordered speech. Such syllables are more likely to be dropped when they occur before the stress and in words of more than two syllables. It would be normal for words such as *tomato* and *remember* to persist as [mɑtəʊ] and [membə] until a comparatively late stage of acquisition, whereas pronunciations such as [bɒ] for *bottle* and [lɪ] for *listen* should disappear very quickly. Persistence of this phenomenon much beyond the end of the fourth year would be an indication of disorder.

4.1.2 Final consonant deletion

Children's earliest words consist almost entirely of single open syllables. Thus words such as *bath* and *milk* are likely to be pronounced as [bɑ] and [mɪ]. The pattern seldom persists beyond the monosyllabic word stage, although forms such as [gɒfɪ] for *goldfish* and [tefəʊ] for *telephone* may occur later. In the course of normal acquisition, this pattern should have disappeared by age three and a half. It is a common characteristic of developmental disorders but comparatively rare in acquired disorders.

4.1.3 Cluster reduction

This is something which occurs in the speech of all children for a time and is one of the most common characteristics of both developmental and acquired speech disorders (cf. the illustration of child (1) in Sect. 1 above). The pattern is usually seen as one of the reducton of two- and three-term clusters to a single consonant. Thus, words beginning with an obstruent plus a liquid or glide are pronounced with only the obstruent (e.g., *play* as [peɪ] or *frog* as [fɒg]). A developmentally more advanced phase involves pronunciation of a cluster but with an inappropriate second term, possibly assimilated to the first (e.g., *play* now becomes [pweɪ] and *frog* [fwɒg]). When the appropriate glide does appear, it may be preceded by an epenthetic vowel ([pəleɪ], [fəɹɒg]). These patterns may be observed during the third and fourth years of normal acquisition, but most children will be producing these clusters correctly by age 4 years 6 months. Initial /s/-clusters seem more difficult (and may not be mastered in normal acquisition until age 5 or older) but show much the same kind of progression, with the simplest stage being the pronunciation of a single stop or nasal. Thus, *stop* will appear as [top], *snow* as [nəʊ] and *splash* as [paʃ]. In this case, the intermediate stages may show assimilated forms of the single consonants, such as [n̥əʊ] for *snow* and [w̥ɪm] for *swim*, and again vocalic transitions may appear in such forms as [sənəʊ] and [səwɪm].

In some cases of disordered speech, clusters may be reduced so as to be represented by one of the sounds which is omitted by the child with normal developmental speech patterns. Thus, whereas stop+approximant clusters are normally reduced to a stop, some speakers may reduce them to an approx-imant. In this case, *play* might be pronounced as [leɪ] rather than [peɪ] and *train* as [weɪn] rather than [teɪn]. Similarly, /s/+nasal clusters may be reduced to a fricative (not necessarily [s]) rather than a nasal. A word such as *snow* would be pronounced [səʊ] rather than [nəʊ] and a word such as *small* might become [sɔl] or even [fɔl] rather than the more usual [mɔl].

4.1.4 Consonant addition

Some disordered speakers pronounce consonants where none would appear in the corresponding target form. This is particularly common in words which begin with a vowel and could be seen as representing an overgeneralization of the consonant–vowel (CV) structure, that is, even to the exclusion of V-only syl-lables. The most common initial adjuncts in devel-opmental disorders seem to be the bilabials [w] and [m], resulting in words such as *uncle* and *apple* being pronounced [wʌŋkʊ] and [wapʊ] or [mʌŋkʊ] and [mapʊ]. Another kind of addition involves the inser-tion of nasals after vowels or, in the case of diph-thongs, their substitution for the off-glide, so that words like *car* and *top* are pronounced [kɑn] and [tɒmp] or *boy* and *bike* become [bɔn] and [bʌŋk].

4.2 Facilitation of Sequences

4.2.1 Obstruent voicing

A common phenomenon in the early stages of normal acquisition and in many cases of phonological dis-order is the use of only voiced stops (or perhaps it would be more accurate to say unaspirated ones). Thus, *car* may be pronounced as [gɑ], *pram* as [ba], and *chair* as [dɛː]. In normal development this usually coincides (and disappears) with the open-syllable stage but if syllable-final consonants are present, they may well all be voiceless. If fricatives are used they are likely to behave in the same way, as shown in (4):

cake	[geɪk]	pretty	[bɪdi]	(4)
please	[bis]	cuddle	[gʌdʊ]	
dog	[dɒk]	nappy	[nabi]	

This is usually seen as a type of regressive assimilation of voice, whereby the consonant is voiced if the fol-lowing segment is voiced (a vowel) and voiceless if the following segment is voiceless (silence). Thus, both types of sound may be pronounced correctly, but they are not being used contrastively since their occurrence is predictable from their position in the structure. Most children will use voicing contrastively in initial position by the first half of the third year. An apparent lack of distinction in final consonants may persist for a little longer until the child has learnt to use longer vowels before voiced consonants.

4.2.2 Consonant harmony

Some children show a tendency for all consonants in a word to have the same place of articulation.

Persistence of this pattern beyond age 3 would indicate a developmental disorder, and it is also characteristic of some types of acquired disorder. It is usually inter-preted as assimilation across the intervening vowel. Prevocalic consonants are more likely to be influenced by postvocalic ones than vice versa. The most easily influenced sounds are the alveolars and the most influential ones are the velars. By far the most com-mon pattern is thus 'regressive velar harmony,' wher-eby an initial alveolar sound accommodates to the place of articulation of a following velar. The assim-ilated sounds are pronounced appropriately elsewhere and thus the contrast is only lost in certain contexts as in (5):

doggy	[gɒgi],	drink	[gɪŋk],	table	[peɪbʊ],	(5)
cut	[kʌk],	gun	[gʌŋ],	fish	[fɪf],	
but	dolly	[dɒwi]				
	hat	[hat]				

Another possibility is assimilation of manner of articulation and, in particular, of nasality. Thus, *gun* might be pronounced [ŋʌn] and *dummy* as [nʌmi].

4.2.3 Consonant–Vowel harmony

Consonants which are in contrast in normal adult speech may appear to be in allophonic variation in some cases of phonological disorder. A speaker may use one consonant exclusively before front high vow-els and another before back high vowels, for example. Thus, pronunciations such as those in (6) might result:

pea, tea	[ti]	pool, tool	[pul]	(6)
take, cake	[teɪʔ]	cook, took	[pʊʔ]	

where [t] is used before /i/, /ɪ/, and /eɪ/, and [p] before /u/, /ʊ/, and /əʊ/. Consonantal alternations before other vowels might well conform to the target pattern.

4.2.4 Metathesis

Some types of developmental disorder are char-acterized by sequencing problems which result in the switching of consonants within a word, and this is also one of the most common patterns in the speech of fluent aphasics. It seems more likely to happen, the greater the similarity between the consonants concerned, and it occurs within syllables as well as between them. Fricatives and affricates are once again the most vulnerable sounds, so that words such as *fish* and *teacher* may emerge as [ʃɪf] and [tʃitə]. A more unusual version of this process leaves the initial con-sonant in place and inserts the final consonant between it and the vowel—that is, a target CVC is pronounced as CCV—thus creating clusters rather than reducing them. This would give rise to pro-nunciations such as [dlɒ] for *doll* and [snʌ] for *sun*.

4.2.5 Dissimilation

In some cases the sequencing problem seems to revolve around the pronunciation of two successive realizations of the same consonant within a word. Thus, words such as *cake* and *paper* will cause difficulty. The second sound may be simply omitted or replaced by a glottal stop, but in some cases a kind of dissimilation seems to be operating, producing forms such as [keɪt] and [peɪkə].

4.3 Reduction of the Consonant System

4.3.1 Stopping

It is very common in the early stages of speech development, and also in many cases of phonological disorder, for fricatives and affricates to be missing. Thus, the entire class of obstruents will be represented by stops as in (7):

| foot | [pʊt] | sock | [tɒk] | shoes | [tud] | (7) |
| this | [dɪt] | van | [ban] | juice | [dut] | |

The process is often described as one of 'substitution' by a stop at the nearest place of articulation, but this hardly captures the unevenness of the resulting reduction of the system in English. Normally [p] and [b] stand for /f/ and /v/ as well as /p/ and /b/, but, whereas [k] and [g] signal the same contrast as in the target system, [t] and [d] may stand for all other obstruents—/t, θ, s, ʃ, tʃ/ and /d, ð, z, ʒ, dʒ/. In some cases nasals may also be pronounced as oral stops, thus reducing the system still further. In normal acquisition obstruent contrasts should begin to emerge by the second half of the third year, but not at all places in the structure and not for all places of articulation at once. As with other distinctions, these are usually most stable among voiceless consonants in word-initial position. Voiceless labials are usually the most easily resolved (some children distinguish /p/ from /f/ in their earliest words). The pronunciation of [d] for /ð/, on the other hand, is very widespread in disordered speech, and even in normal acquisition may continue until well after 5 years old.

4.3.2 Fronting

This is another fairly common characteristic of disordered and early normal speech. In its most noticeable form, it consists of the pronunciation of /k/, /g/, and /ŋ/ as [t], [d], and [n] respectively, so that words such as *coming* and *going* are pronounced [tʌmɪn] and [dəʊɪn]. The palato-alveolars /tʃ/, /dʒe/, /ʒj/, and /de/ may also be fronted, resulting in pronunciations such as [tsɛː] for *chair*, [dzus] for *juice*, and [sip] for *sheep*. This can only be determined, however, if no stopping is taking place, since, as noted above, stopping also leads to the merger of /tʃ/ and /ʃ/ with /t/, and /dʒ/ and /ʒ/ with /d/. Obviously, if these two quite common processes coincide then the reduction in the system of obstruent contrasts is severe, there being no manner distinction, and only a two-way place distinction of lingual versus labial. Normally both processes should have disappeared by about the end of the third year.

4.3.3 Gliding

The liquids /l/ and /r/ cause difficulties both in normal acquisition and in disordered speech. In some cases they may also be 'stopped'—that is, pronounced as [d]. This appears to be comparatively rare, however. A more frequent and more persistent phenomenon is the failure to distinguish them from the glides /w/ and /j/. Thus, both may be pronounced as [w], or /r/ is pronounced as [w], and /l/ as [j], resulting in such forms as either [jɒwi] or [wɒwi] for *lorry* and [jɒji] or [wɒwi] for *lolly*. Normally developing children should have mastered most of these distinctions by midway through the third year, but the lack of /r/ ~ /w/ contrast is notorious for persisting in some cases into adulthood, and is therefore not a very reliable indicator of phonological disorder. A rather different kind of 'gliding' pattern is the use of glides where the target form requires a fricative, for example, words such as *foot, sock,* and *shoe* may be pronounced [wʊt], [jɒk], and [ju].

4.3.4 Glottalizing

A pattern which occurs in the speech of some normally developing children involves the pronunciation of some consonants as glottal stops. Thus, *apple* may be pronounced as [aʔʊ] and *doggy* as [dɒʔi]. This phenomenon is also quite common in disordered speech. Rather less common is the occurrence of glottal approximants (e.g., *pussy* and *toffee* pronounced [pʊhi] and [tɒhi]). Yet another pattern is the inappropriate addition of glottal closure to an intervocalic consonant (e.g., *water* and *dinner* pronounced as [wɔʔtə] and [dɪʔnə]).

4.3.5 Systematic sound preference

In some types of disorder pronunciations may differ from the normal adult forms, not in a way which can be described in terms of systematic sound changes, but through the use of one particular 'preferred' sound in place of one or more members of the target system or at one particular place in the structure. Thus, one speaker might prefer to use [f] in initial position, pronouncing *car, bike,* and *lorry* as [fdg], [faɪk], and [fɒwi]. Another might substitute [l] for /s/ and /z/ in all positions, rendering *sock, seesaw,* and *toys* as [lok], [lilɔ], and [tɔɪl].

4.4 Reduction of the Vowel System

4.4.1 Vowel length neutralization

The first words of many children appear to favor long tense-sounding vowels, especially where the high vowels /i/ ~ /ɪ/ and /u/ ~ /ʊ/ are concerned. Thus, early pronunciations of *milk,* and *book* may sound like [mi] and [bu]. It is probable that the open-syllable structure contributes to this impression, but there seems little doubt that control over vowel length is lacking at first, not only as regards systemic contrasts but also as regards cueing final consonant voicing and stress. Normal children are still misarticulating up to about 20 percent of vowels at age 1 year 6 months, but should have acquired the full adult system by the age of 2. It is not clear how common this pattern is in acquired disorders.

4.4.2 Vowel quality neutralization

A phenomenon which disappears very early on from normal speech, but is common in certain types of acquired disorder is the neutralization of vowel quality distinctions. This seems to be largely a question of lack of control over the vocal tract musculature, with consequent overlapping of formant frequency values. This can result in inconsistent realizations of contrasts such as /i/ ~ /e/ ~ /eɪ/ or /u/ ~ /ɔ/ ~ /əʊ/, rather than a consistent reduction in the underlying system of contrasts. It seems possible, on the other hand, that a persisting lack of contrast between more open vowels such as /a/ ~ /dg/ ~ /ʌ/ ~ /ɜ/ may represent a neutralization of these contrasts at the level of phonological representation. Some disordered speakers may reduce their vowel system toward a corner of the 'vowel space' rather than toward its center. The front close area seems to be most commonly favored, in which case words such as *spoon* and *foot* and *glass* will have pronunciations such as [pin] and [fɪt] and [geːs].

4.5 Reduction of Prosodic Systems

Although there is a fairly clear idea of the order in which the main systemic prosodic contrasts emerge and the age range during which each is acquired (see Crystal 1986: 185–86 for a useful summary), very little is known about the nature of disordered prosody. The segmental and prosodic aspects of the earliest words are 'fused,' in the sense that the same sequence of segments is always accompanied by the same pitch contour. During the first half of the second year the separation of segmental and prosodic levels should take place, with the development of a range of contrasts, such as loudness, pitch range, and length. From around 1 year 6 months to 2 years 6 months the system of tonal contrasts is acquired. Most children seem to begin by distinguishing falling from nonfalling tones, then go on to distinguish high and low contours within these categories. Finally bidirectional (falling–rising, rising–falling) tones are distinguished from their unidirectional counterparts. During the same period, the normal child should begin to use prosody to integrate two or more words into longer utterances, and also to shift the position of the tone within the utterance to signal emphasis or focus. Intonation systems seem to remain relatively intact in most forms of acquired disorder, although in some cases, consistent but largely phonetic changes can give the impression of foreign accent.

Rhythm may appear to be 'syllable timed' up to the age of 4 or 5 years, that is, consisting of more or less equally spaced equal-length syllables, rather than of equally spaced stressed syllables with unstressed syllables in between. It seems that, having learnt not to delete unstressed syllables, it may be some time before the child learns to reduce them, rather than give them equal weight with the stressed ones. This also appears to be a feature of some types of acquired disorder, but in many cases is probably the result of problems at the segmental phonetic level rather than at the level of representation of prosodic contrasts (see also *Autism*).

5. A Linguistic Typology of Acquired Phonological Disorders

5.1 Fluent Aphasia

Aphasia involves lesions in the cortex of the brain. There may be central impairment at the phonological level (Wernicke's aphasia), in which case both speech and comprehension are affected, or, possibly, impairment of the link between perception and production (conduction aphasia), in which case only production appears to be affected. Speech is fluent, without phonetic distortions, and prosodic patterns are intact. The phonemic inventory is normally not reduced and the phonotactics of the language are preserved. There are probably two types of disorder. In the first type, lexical selection is impaired but phonological output is not. Speech production takes place without the prior selection of intended words. Since the resulting output appears to have no intended meaning, it is not possible to speak of 'targets' and 'errors.' In the second type, there appears to be a phonological disorder interfering at a stage after the selection of the intended words. In this case the intended targets can usually be identified, although there are frequent phonological errors, typically with no self-correction. Variability is extreme, and often quite complex sequences can be produced successfully. Errors are predominantly of a sequential kind (see Lecours and Roussillon 1976; Martin and Rigrodsky 1974), involving patterns such as metathesis, consonant harmony, cluster reduction, and consonant addition. There are often problems with words containing more than one occurrence of the same phoneme, giving rise to 'dissimilations.' Conduction aphasia typically shows a better capacity for self-correction but an impaired capacity for repetition (see Gandour 1998).

5.2 Nonfluent Aphasia/Verbal Apraxia

It is not clear to what extent verbal dyspraxia may occur independently of some degree of aphasia but it is the dyspraxic element of nonfluent (Broca's) aphasia which is of concern here. It appears there may be damage to the area of the left hemisphere of the brain concerned with control of the speech muscles. Right hemisphere control may be sufficient for the less precisely controlled nonspeech movements of the same muscles. Comprehension is generally unaffected. It is the motor programming of speech which is impaired, giving rise to errors which appear to be both phonetic and phonological. Speech is slow and laborious with much groping and 'experimentation.' Gross phonetic deviations from the target sounds lead to apparent reduction and disorganization of the phonemic inventory and apparent violation of the phonotactics. These errors are not totally consistent and, although many of them may be described in terms similar to those used for child phonology—cluster reduction, consonant harmony, stopping, fronting, loss of the obstruent voicing distinction, metathesis—these terms must be understood as referring to trends rather than rules. Consonants appear to be affected more than vowels, fricatives more than others, and clusters more than singletons. Complex sequences which cause problems may be broken up into CV sequences (thus, *try* may become [təɹaɪ] and *plane* [pəleɪnə]). Many errors are anticipatory (i.e., the articulation is influenced by a sound occurring later in the intended utterance); thus, there are more problems with initial sounds than with final ones (one difference from developmental patterns is that final consonant deletion is not so frequent; see *Verbal Apraxia*).

5.3 Dysarthria

Dysarthia, acquired or congenital, occurs as the result of extra pyramidal, brainstem, cerebellar, or lower motor neuron damage. This is usually the result of a neurological condition, such as cerebral palsy or Parkinson's disease, which causes a general disorder of movement, but the common factor is that there is an impairment at a level of the speech production process below that at which encoding of the intended message takes place. Comprehension remains intact. Only the actual articulation of sounds is affected. Speech errors are consistent but not phonological (see *Developmental Dysarthrias; Acquired Dysarthrias*).

6. A Linguistic Typology of Developmental Phonological Disorders

6.1 Delayed Phonological Development

Both delayed and deviant language acquisition have sometimes been labeled 'developmental aphasia.' Since the medical reasons for these disorders are unknown, there seems to be no reason to assume that they are the same as for acquired aphasia and, despite the possible linguistic parallels, the term will not be used here (see *General Aspects of Developmental Language Disorders; Specific Language Impairment: Subtypes and Assessment*).

In the course of normal phonological acquisition

the most common immature patterns are lost very approximately by the following ages and in the following order (cf, for example, Grunwell 1987: 228–31):

	Years	Months
(a) Reduplication by age	2	0
ACQUISITION OF FULL VOWEL SYSTEM	2	0
(b) Consonant harmony	2	6
(c) Velar fronting	2	6
ACQUISITION OF FULL INTONATION SYSTEM	2	6
(d) Stopping of /f/ and /s/	2	9
(e) Final consonant deletion	3	0
(f) Context sensitive voicing	3	0
(g) Reduction of stop-initial clusters and stopping of affricates	3	3
(h) Palatoalveolar fronting	3	6
(i) Reduction of /s/-initial clusters	3	6
(j) Weak syllable deletion	3	9
(k) Gliding of /r/→[w] and stopping of /ð/	4	0+

The list is necessarily very approximate because very few children will show evidence of all these patterns and all those that do occur will overlap chronologically to a greater or lesser extent. Thus, it is no surprise to find a normal child who has acquired a voicing contrast in initial and medial position but still persists in deleting final consonants. In fact almost any pattern in the above list could swap position with either of its immediate neighbors, and many could change places with patterns two places further up or down the list, without the child in question being considered to have deviant speech.

Delayed development is characterized by the use of pronunciation patterns which would be appropriate to an earlier stage of phonological acquisition than that indicated by the chronological age of the child. The delay is 'across the board,' however, immature patterns which have disappeared will have disappeared in the normal order, and thus the speech patterns of a child with delayed speech should be similar to those of a normal child of a younger age. By far the majority of cases of developmental phonological disorders come under the heading of delay. Schwartz et al. (1980), for example, compared a group of three normal speaking children (mean age 1 year 8 months) with a group of three language disordered children (mean age 3 years 1 month). These groups were matched as to their stages of linguistic development, as measured by their mean length of utterance. Schwartz et al. found no differences in the phonological patterns which occurred nor in the variability of occurrence. There were no unusual co-occurrences of patterns, no differences in the occurrence of unusual patterns nor in the absence of common patterns. The authors concluded that for the vast majority of children with disordered speech, there is parallel development of linguistic levels, with global delay.

6.2 Deviant Phonological Development

Deviant development, on the other hand, is characterized by the occurrence of unusual pronunciation patterns, the persistence of 'early' acquisitional patterns when 'later' ones have disappeared, and the variable occurrence of normal immature patterns.

6.2.1 Unusual pronunciation patterns

It is not easy to define what an 'unusual' pattern is. It seems to be the case that there is a continuous scale of frequency of occurrence with, at one end, those patterns such as cluster reduction and syllable deletion which seem to occur in the speech of every child, and at the other those patterns which are so unusual as to be unique to one particular child. Thus, in theory, the list of unusual processes is infinitely long but, of the patterns outlined above in Sect. 4, the following are the more unusual:

   (a) glottalization—the replacement of consonants by glottal stops certainly occurs in the speech of some normally developing children and should be seen as on the borderline between 'usual' and 'unusual.' Substitution by glottal approximants and addition of glottal stops to appropriately articulated consonants is much more unusual, however;

   (b) gliding of fricatives is also unusual but not unknown during normal acquisition;

   (c) cluster reduction, although an almost universal phenomenon, should be classed as unusual if the pattern involves reduction to a glide or to /s/;

   (d) consonant addition is an unusual pattern, whatever form it takes;

   (e) consonant–vowel harmony, metathesis, and dissimilation are all patterns which are not expected to occur during normal phonological acquisition;

   (f) systematic sound preference is also rarely found in normal immature speech but is quite a common feature of developmental disorder;

   (g) vowel fronting, or almost any other reduction in the vowel system, is a fairly reliable indication of deviant phonological development.

6.2.2 Inappropriate persistence of immature patterns

The list presented in Sect. 5.1 gives a rough indication of what would constitute a gross change in the order of acquisition of contrasts—what Grunwell (1987: 234) calls a 'chronological mismatch.' Thus, for example, if 'reduplication' were to persist after fricatives began to be acquired, or 'weak syllable deletion' to be lost before 'velar fronting' had ceased, this would be con-

sidered deviant rather than delayed speech. A child who had mastered the pronunciation of initial clusters, but continued to omit final consonants altogether would pronounce words such as *stamp, frock,* and *black* as [sta], [fɹo̥], and [bla]. Although the process of final consonant deletion is in itself quite normal, it is not normal for it to persist when the process of cluster reduction has been lost. In such cases there is also likely to be a mismatch between the lexical and grammatical levels on the one hand and the phonological level on the other.

6.2.3 Variable occurrence of normal patterns

It is by no means the case that normal children acquiring language show totally consistent use of a particular pattern in all their pronunciations. Nevertheless, extreme variability in the occurrence of patterns may be taken to be evidence of deviant phonology, especially when the inconsistency consists of alternating between two immature patterns, rather than between an immature pattern and the adult pattern. For example, if a child pronounces *mouse* and *grass* as [maʊ] and [ga] but *house* and *cheese* as [haʊt] and [tid], then it might be concluded that some forms show final consonant deletion, whereas others have 'stopping' of alveolar fricatives. Another child may show variation in pronunciation such that *coat* is sometimes [təʊt] and sometimes [gəʊt], *card* is [tad] or [gat], and *cake* is [teɪt] or [geɪk]. In this case there is variation between velar fronting and context-sensitive voicing. Inconsistent use of patterns is not a hard and fast indicator of phonological deviance. Some variability is present in all children's speech and is usually an indication of change in progress—that is, evidence of an immature pattern being lost, a contrast being acquired and not yet generalized throughout the lexicon. Thus, a child who showed inconsistent pronunciation of words such as *drink* and *fish,* with forms such as [gɪŋk] and [dɪŋk], and [fɪf] and [fɪʃ] would be varying between use and nonuse of consonant harmony in a developmentally normal fashion. Only if inconsistency is persistent and does not indicate development—that is, incipient acquisition of a contrast—can it be seen as deviant.

6.3 Developmental Verbal Dyspraxia

This disorder appears to bear some similarity to the acquired form of dyspraxia and seems to involve a failure to learn the motor planning skills needed for the execution of articulatory movements. Fronting- and stopping-type patterns seem to be common, as are all types of structure simplification. Most dyspraxic children have a very reduced system of contrasts and structures in speech but many are able to imitate accurately sounds in isolation (see Milloy and Summers 1989).

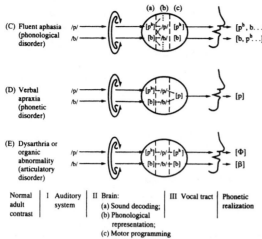

Figure 2. A slightly more refined neurolinguistic model. The phonologically disordered speaker recognizes distinct sounds in speech but fails to assign them to appropriate phonological categories. The phonetically disordered speaker categorizes the sounds correctly but lacks the 'program' to translate them into movements. The articulatorily disordered speaker has the correct phonological categories and phonetic programming but cannot execute the movements properly.

7. Refining the Definition

It seems likely, then, that developmental phonological disorders and acquired fluent aphasias represent a deficit at the level of phonological representation in the brain; whereas dysarthrias, whether acquired or congenital, represent an articulatory deficit at the same level as that caused by orofacial abnormality. Verbal apraxia, on the other hand, seems to affect a level of processing which is somewhere between these two: the level of motor programming of speech, or 'cognitive phonetics' as Tatham (1984) has called it. Thus, in order to represent the differences between these types of speech disorder diagrammatically, it is necessary to distinguish three levels of speech processing within the brain, as in Fig. 2: II(a) a sound decoding level at which incoming speech sounds are segmented and categorized; II(b) a level of phonological representation onto which the decoded sounds are mapped and from which intended target phonemes are generated; and II(c) a sound encoding or motor programming level at which selected targets are translated into vocal tract configurations. Fluent aphasias can then be seen as either a disruption between level II(a) and level II(b)—a failure to map incoming sounds on to the correct phonemes—or a failure within level II(b) to generate phonemes appropriate to the intended message. Verbal apraxia can be seen as a breakdown at level II(c), whereby appropriate programming of the phonetic realization of target phonemes cannot be carried out. Dysarthria is an impairment of the peripheral system of nerves,

muscles, or vocal tract structures which prevents correct execution of the motor programs (level III). It has been suggested (Hewlett 1985) that the term 'phonological disorder' should be reserved for disorders originating at level II(b), whereas disorders at levels II(c) and III should be termed respectively 'phonetic' and 'articulatory disorders.' However, the possibility of interaction between these levels should not be ignored, particularly in the cases of developmental disorder. In the most obvious case, profound peripheral hearing loss will prevent the development of normal function at all three postulated levels in the brain. Less obviously, impairment of the neurological or organic structures of the vocal tract may adversely affect the learning of cognitive phonetic skills involved in the control and timing of articulatory movement. Impaired phonetic skills, in turn, may impede the establishment of appropriate adult phonological categories. Developmental articulatory and phonetic disorders may thus also have long-term effects at the level of phonological representation (see *Models*).

Bibliography

Crystal D 1986 Prosodic development. In: Fletcher P, Garman M (eds.) *Language Acquisition: Studies in First Language Development*, 2nd edn. Cambridge University Press, Cambridge

Gandour J T 1998 Phonetics and phonology. In: Stemmer B, Whitaker H A (eds.) *Handbook of Neurolinguistics*. Academic Press, San Diego, CA

Grunwell P 1987 *Clinical Phonology*, 2nd edn. Croom Helm, London

Hewlett N 1985 Phonological versus phonetic disorders: Some suggested modifications to the current use of the distinction. *British Journal of Disorders of Communication* **20**: 155–64

Ingram D 1976 *Phonological Disability in Children*. Arnold, London

Ingram D 1986 Phonological development: Production. In: Fletcher P, Garman M (eds.) *Language Acquisition: Studies in First Language Development*, 2nd edn. Cambridge University Press, Cambridge

Lecours A R, Roussillon F 1976 Neurolinguistic analysis of jargon aphasia and jargon agraphia. In: Whitaker H, Whitaker H A (eds.) *Studies in Neurolinguistics*, vol. 2. Academic Press, New York

Locke J L 1983 *Phonological Acquisition and Change*. Academic Press, New York

Martin A D, Rigrodsky S 1974 An investigation of phonological impairment in aphasia, Parts I and II. *Cortex* **10**: 317–46

Milloy N, Summers L 1989 Six years on—do claims still hold? Four children reassessed on a procedure to identify developmental articulatory dyspraxia. *Child Language Teaching and Therapy* **5**: 287–303

Schwartz R G, Leonard L B, Folger M K, Wilcox M J 1980 Early phonological behaviour in normal-speaking and language disordered children: Evidence for a synergistic view of linguistic disorders. *Journal of Speech and Hearing Disorders* **45**: 357–77

Tatham M A A 1984 Towards a *cognitive* phonetics. *Journal of Phonetics* **12**: 37–47

Morphosyntactic Disorders of Language

W. D. Dressler

As early as Francis Bacon it was suggested that the study of the abnormal illuminates the understanding of what is normal. Thus, impairments of morphology and syntax in aphasia, dementia, schizophrenia, and disturbed language acquisition may also offer psycholinguistic and neurolinguistic insight into the nature of morphology and syntax. Data from language disorders, however, do not provide direct evidence for or against the claims of a linguistic model. Rather such language data must be interpreted in light of: (a) a neuropsycholinguistic theory of the respective disorder; (b) a psycholinguistic theory of normal language performance and of acquisition; (c) a linguistic theory; and (d) bridge theories combining (a)–(c) (i.e., interdisciplinary integration). This makes statements on morphological implications of language disorders particularly hypothetical. Since evidence from morphology-rich languages is most conclusive, illustrations will heavily rely on them.

1. Impairments of Morphosyntax in Aphasia

There are many more studies on morphological disturbances in aphasia than on all other language disorders put together. Most studies are restricted to inflectional morphology, but it depends on the grammatical model (and its integration) which grammatical disturbances are assigned to syntax, to morphology, or to both.

The linguistically most relevant classification of aphasics is represented by the classical (although often disputed) clinical distinction between agrammatism (nonfluent Broca-patients) that presents reduced grammar and paragrammatism (fluent Wernicke-patients) with errors in the selection of the grammatical means of expression. Thus, Wernickes (with paragrammatic disturbances) confuse inflectional affixes both in spontaneous speech and in all tests (i.e., apparently, irrespective of the syntactic construction signaled by inflectional markers) and, in a similar vein, they confuse elements of semantic paradigms (e.g., antonyms or words within a word field, actors within the cast of a text, etc.). This seems to support the old Jakobsonian idea of a disturbance of paradigmatic relations in paragrammatism (although, *pace* Jakobson, Wernickes make other grammatical errors as well, and Brocas also produce 'paradigmatic' errors). This, therefore, supports the notion of an inflectional paradigm. Moreover, such aphasics rarely substitute one word for another one outside the lexical category (e.g., word field), similarly they rarely confuse affixes which belong to different morphological classes (at least in the sense of macroclasses such as verb versus noun).

The nature of agrammatism is very much disputed, due to differences in theories (and bridge theories), cross-linguistic divergencies in data, and variability in performance between subjects and in the performance of a single subject. Agrammatics substitute one inflectional form for another; they omit grammatical words, but inflectional affixes only if the resulting form is an inflectional form itself: thus the reduction of the target *cut-s* to the incorrect output *cut* can be interpreted as a substitution of the marked nominal plural or third person singular by the respective unmarked inflectional form. This may support either a full listing hypothesis (i.e., all inflectional forms are stored and not derived by rule) or, alternatively, a word well-formedness condition of some sort. 'Illegal' inflectional forms then have to be interpreted as morphological analogies. For example, the illegal German past participle *ge-fang-t* instead of *ge-fang-en* (from the strong verb *fang-en*) is seen as analogous to *-t* participles of weak verbs. However, it is rarely the case that forms such as *ge-fang* are produced, where the obligatory participle suffix is omitted, the prefix *ge-* (omissible in another class) is preserved.

The study of aphasic patients originally speaking languages with a rich inflectional morphology (e.g., Italian, French, etc.) has shown the limits of the classification of specific syntactic errors such as agrammatisms and paragrammatisms (Menn and Obler 1990). Broca's aphasics with Italian as mother-tongue have been found to frequently omit closed class words and to make several substitutions, for instance in noun-adjective agreement as regards both gender and number (Miceli et al. 1989). At present it is therefore preferable to indicate the type and the percentage of errors of omission and substitution for each grammatical component (e.g., articles, pronouns, auxiliary verbs, etc.; see Paradis and Libben 1987).

As to word-formation in aphasia, derivational affixes are mainly substituted for each other within the same class, for example, preverbal prefixes (sometimes even inflectional prefixes) or suffixes adjectivizing nouns. In particular, Wernickes (cf. also schizophasics) often produce morphological neologisms, that is, nonexisting words formed via existing word-formation rules or by analogy: this presents a dissociation between lexical storage and word-formation rules. Jargon aphasics may produce word-like items which show no apparent morphological relation to any existing word of the language, but are nevertheless correctly inflected or subjected to correct word-formation: this presents a dissociation between lexicon and both inflection and word-formation. Aphasics have significantly more processing difficulties with semantically and/or formally opaque compounds and affixed words than with transparent ones.

Most linguists and psycholinguists in the late twentieth century assume that all derived words are stored as such (in the case of neologisms, only if these are not ad hoc formations immediately forgotten after production). There is an open debate, however, as to whether all inflectional forms of each word are stored as well (full listing hypothesis), or only the irregular or the most frequent ones, or whether all inflectional forms (or the totally regular and/or less frequent ones) are derived by rules from their respective base forms (e.g., nominative singular of nouns). Experiments with German subjects in the 1990s have shown that both paragrammatics (Wernickes) and normal controls decompose inflected open-class words (inflectional forms of nouns, verbs, adjectives) during access, whereas closed-class words (inflectional forms of pronouns, articles, auxiliary verbs) are accessed as units; agrammatics, on the other hand, decompose both classes. This confirms the concept of rule-derived inflection.

2. Morphology in Deep Dyslexia

Selective reading errors (not accompanied by errors when speaking or listening) which cannot be explained by pure visual impairments often comprise morphological errors such as substitutions of inflectional forms or of underived words for derived words (e.g., *sick* for *sickness*). This is clearly a disturbance of the interaction between reading mechanisms and morphological parsers (involved in morphological synthesis and decomposition). Note that an analogous interpretation cannot be upheld for aphasia (see above). Furthermore, in dyslexia, more concrete meanings are more easily accessible than more abstract ones, both in the lexicon and in morphological processing. Thus derivations signaling concrete and transparent meanings are least impaired.

3. Morphology in Dementia

In senile dementia, word-finding difficulties, that is, impairment of lexical retrieval, have been identified by several authors as primary disturbances (including retrieval of morphologically complex words). Lexical substitutions (comparable to verbal paraphasias) represent only secondary impairments of morphology. Probably the general atrophy of the brain involved in both syndromes affects lexical storage irrespective of morphological complexity.

4. Morphology in Developmental Dysphasia

Most types of impaired language acquisition may be conveniently lumped together under 'dysphasia,' the clinical cover term for children with retarded development of language and/or severe problems with the normal acquisition of language (see *Specific Language Impairment: Subtypes and Assessment*). Studies on German dysphasic children have established a selective (not a general) syntactic-agreement-related morphological deficit, that is, of gender, number, case exponency in pronouns and, even more, in articles (articles being the main exponents of grammatical information in German noun declension), of case in nouns, and of person and number inflection in verbs. This (and also data from Hebrew- and Italian-speaking children) may be interpreted as a selective disturbance of agreement and, more generally, of the interaction between a syntactic and a morphological module and as support for any model of grammar which assumes the existence of such autonomous modules and of specific interactions among them (see Leonard 1998).

Data from children with various types of language problems show a selective deficit of the components of language acquisition, that is, of an unbalanced development of linguistic competence, with inflectional morphology often being the most or longest disturbed component. This supports a modular approach (see Temple 1997).

5. Morphology in Mental Retardation

With Down's syndrome children, even more than with normal children, morphological abilities can be used as a diagnostic device for stage of development. Generality and regularity of both inflectional and derivational rules, along with both formal and semantic transparency, are important factors in determining level and stage of acquisition.

Bibliography

Bleser R de, Bayer J 1986 German word formation and aphasia. *Linguistic Review* **5**: 1–40

Clahsen H 1989 The grammatical characterization of developmental dysphasia. *Linguistics* **27**: 897–920

Coltheart M, Patterson K, Marshall J C (eds.) 1980 *Deep Dyslexia*. Routledge and Kegan Paul, London

Dressler W, Stark J A 1988 *Linguistic Analyses of Aphasic Language*. Springer, New York

Friederici A 1985 Levels of processing and vocabulary types. *Cognition* **19**: 133–66

Hamanaka T, Kanemoto K, Ohigashi Y, Hadano K 1985 Paraphasia and related disorders in primary degenerative dementia. *Studia Phonologica* **19**: 11–17

Leonard L B 1998 *Children with Specific Language Impairment*. MIT Press, Cambridge, MA

Menn L, Obler L K 1990 *Agrammatic Aphasia. A Cross-Language Narrative Sourcebook*. Benjamins, Amsterdam

Miceli G, Silveri M C, Romani C, Caramazza A 1989 Variation in the pattern of omissions and substitutions of grammatical morphemes in the spontaneous speech of so-called agrammatic patients. *Brain and Language* **36**: 447–92

Nespoulous J-L, Villiard P 1990 *Morphology, Phonology, and Aphasia*. Springer, New York

Paradis M, Libben G 1987 *The Assessment of Bilingual Aphasia*. Erlbaum, Hillsdale, NJ

Schaner-Wolles C, Dressler W U 1985 On the acquisition of agent/instrument nouns and comparatives by normal children and children with Down's syndrome. *Acta Ling Hung* **35**: 133–49

Seeman M V, Manuck M N 1985 *New Perspectives in Schizophrenia*. Heath, New York

Temple C 1997 *Developmental Cognitive Neuropsychology*. Psychology Press, Hove

Disorders of Reading and Writing

M. J. Snowling and A. Edmundson

In any literate society, a serious yet largely 'hidden' handicap is the inability to read and/or spell. This condition, usually referred to as 'dyslexia,' can occur in adulthood as the consequence of brain damage, for example, following stroke or other neurological insult. It can also occur in children as a developmental difficulty.

While developments in the area of acquired dyslexia have included a revival of the view that there are 'disconnection' syndromes, the trend during the late 1980s and the 1990s has been to move away from the traditional neurological syndrome classifications. Emphasis is now placed on detailed analysis of the processing disorders underlying acquired reading and writing difficulties. Moreover, psycholinguistic classification systems rooted in cognitive–psychological models have been adopted for both the acquired and the developmental dyslexias (Temple 1997).

1. The Cognitive Approach

Cognitive psychologists assume that skills such as reading and writing involve a number of processing stages, each of which is carried out by a specialized processing module. The processing components are described in terms of their function, without attempting to localize the modules in the brain. There has been extensive research on reading and writing within this framework, and detailed processing models have been developed based on converging evidence from studies of skilled performance and from case studies of patients with acquired reading and writing disorders.

1.1 Models of Reading

An influential account of skilled reading is the 'dual-route' theory which claims that there are two different processing routes for reading, a lexical–semantic route and a sublexical route. In addition, skilled readers have an internal dictionary or 'lexicon' in which knowledge about each word in their vocabulary is stored. Familiar written words are processed as units by the lexical–semantic route; in order to recognize the printed word, it has to be matched to its stored visual representation in the lexicon. The speed with which this occurs is dependent upon how frequently the particular word is encountered in its written form. The stored representations for high frequency words are accessed more rapidly than for low frequency words.

To obtain a pronunciation for a word, stored information about its meaning (or semantics) is first accessed. This in turn is used to access stored information about its pronunciation. It is important to note that the use of the lexical–semantic route involves access to stored information at each processing stage. Novel letter strings cannot be read in this way because, by definition, they are not represented in the lexicon.

The 'sublexical' route involves the use of letter–sound correspondences to convert the letters of a word into a phonological code. Following the recognition of individual letters, knowledge of letter–sound correspondences is used to work out how each letter is pronounced. Reading in this way allows the accurate pronunciation of regular words like *hat* and *brush* which have predictable relationships between their spelling and their pronunciation. It also allows pronunciations to be derived for unfamiliar letter strings, such as novel surnames or 'nonwords' like *fron*. Historically, it was widely believed that letter–sound correspondences were obligatorily used in skilled reading. However, English, like many other languages with alphabetic writing systems, does not have a simple one-to-one correspondence between letters and sounds. Reading via the sublexical route therefore leads to 'irregular' words, such as *sword* and *pint*, being mispronounced.

The idea that words can be read by two different processing routes was developed with reference to English, an alphabetic language. The dual-route theory of reading has since been shown to be applicable to other languages with rather different types of writing systems. Japanese, for example, has two writing systems. The *kana* system is a syllabic writing system. Each spoken syllable that occurs in Japanese corresponds to a written *kana* which can be read aloud sublexically using knowledge about the *kana*: syllable correspondences. The other writing system uses symbols known as *kanji*, each of which represents a Japanese word. The lexical-semantic route is used to read *kanji*, being visually recognized and matched to its stored visual representation in the lexicon.

Since the dual-route model of reading was first proposed, a third reading route has been postulated. This third route is again a lexical route. Once the stored visual representation has been accessed, a word's stored pronunciation is directly accessed. Because this route bypasses the semantic representation, it is referred to as the 'direct lexical' route.

Although this processing model has been very influential, various details about how it actually works have not been sufficiently specified. For example, while the use of letter–sound correspondences may be crucial for the acquisition of reading (see Sect. 3.2) it is not clear to what extent skilled readers rely on this somewhat error-prone route for reading. Some theorists suggest that the reader has control over which reading routes are used; others have claimed that the different reading routes operate automatically and simultaneously when a word is presented.

1.2 Models of Spelling and Writing

Normal skilled spelling has been less extensively investigated than reading. Cognitive models of spelling have therefore drawn quite heavily on evidence obtained from investigations of acquired spelling disorders. As with reading, it is suggested that a number of different processing routes are available for spelling, the distinction again being made between sublexical and lexical processing routes.

The sublexical route for spelling involves using knowledge about sound–letter correspondences to convert from the word's pronunciation to its spelling. In writing spontaneously, this requires the stored pronunciation for the word to be accessed. When writing a word to dictation, the pronunciation is provided by the speaker. As with the sublexical reading route, the sublexical writing route is error-prone. Good attempts can be made to spell unfamiliar or novel words, but spelling errors occur for words with irregular spellings.

In addition to a sublexical route for writing to dictation, two lexical routes are hypothesized. In both of these, the spoken word that has been dictated is recognized and matched to a stored auditory representation in the lexicon. The lexical–semantic route then proceeds via the word's semantic representation which is used to access stored information about its spelling. The direct lexical route bypasses the semantic system, the stored auditory representation directly accessing the stored spelling.

Lexical processing routes are also available for writing spontaneously. The word's semantic representation can be used to access its stored spelling directly. Alternatively, the stored pronunciation of the word can be obtained, and this can be used to access the stored spelling.

It will be apparent from this brief discussion that many parallels can be drawn between the processing routes involved in reading and spelling. For example, reading by a sublexical route is claimed to involve the use of letter–sound correspondences while spelling by a sublexical route involves sound–letter correspondences. One question which arises is whether the same stored knowledge is employed (in reverse directions) for reading and spelling, or whether the psychological processes involved in the two tasks are quite different. One line of evidence, that seems to favor models in which sublexical reading and spelling are considered to involve functionally separable processes, is that dissociations between letter–sound knowledge and sound–letter knowledge have been reported in patients with acquired reading and writing disorders.

Once a spelling has been obtained for a word, this information can be passed on to any one of a number of different processing modules, depending on whether the word is to be written down, or typed, or spelled out aloud.

Models of writing are not as fully specified as models of spelling. The aspect that has been most widely studied to date is the selection of the appropriate form of the letter. Each letter can be written in a variety of ways including uppercase, lowercase, and cursive script. If the word is to be written down by hand, it is suggested that information about its spelling is passed to a module which contains stored representations of the various different forms of each of the letters. The appropriate form is selected, and then the sequence of strokes required to produce the letter on the paper is specified. Eventually, processing models for writing will have to account for the fact that the size of writing and the muscle systems involved in writing can vary. Large writing on a vertical surface such as a blackboard, for example, uses arm movements as well as the finger and wrist movements involved in writing on a narrow-feint notepad.

The accounts of the processes involved in reading and writing that have been discussed assume first, that processing occurs in a series of discrete and sequential processing stages and second, that functionally distinguishable processing routes exist. A number of challenges have been made to these assumptions. The advances made in the 1980s in cognitive psychology have led to the development of new interactive models. These interactive models allow considerable exchange of information between the different levels of processing within the system, and dispense with the idea of different sublexical and lexical processing routes. However, although the theoretical emphasis in the 1990s is on the development of interactive accounts of processing, stage models are still proving to be of considerable practical use for the assessment and remediation of acquired disorders of reading and writing.

2. Acquired Disorders of Written Language

In 1973, Marshall and Newcombe introduced a new classification system for acquired dyslexia, using the dual-route model of reading to provide elegant explanations for the syndromes that they described. They hypothesized that patients with 'surface dyslexia' were reading sublexically, making use of letter–sound correspondences. 'Deep dyslexic' patients were relying on the lexical–semantic reading route. Since Marshall and Newcombe's paper, a new discipline, known as cognitive neuropsychology has burgeoned and been applied to the study of acquired disorders of reading and of other areas of cognition. Cognitive neuropsychology rejects the classical neurological syndromes on the grounds that they are not homogenous disorders, and advocates that acquired disorders of reading and writing should be considered in terms of the processing problems that underlie them. Because many different processing modules are involved in reading and writing, difficulties which superficially appear to be similar can in fact arise from disruption at different stages in the underlying processing. The symptoms of 'alexia with agraphia,' for example, may be a consequence of many different processing difficulties.

Since Marshall and Newcombe's seminal paper, patients with a variety of acquired reading and writing difficulties have been identified and quoted in the literature. A comprehensive review is given by Ellis and Young (1988) and some of the cases in that review are used to illustrate the following sections.

2.1 Acquired Reading Disorders

2.1.1 Surface Dyslexia

Marshall and Newcombe (1973) described a patient, J.C., who seemed to be using letter–sound correspondences when reading aloud. For example, he pronounced the word *island* as 'is-land' rather than 'eye-land.' In reading aloud, J.C. regularized the pronunciations of irregular words, and made phonologically plausible errors. His understanding of written words was based on his pronunciation of them. For example, he read *begin* as 'beggin' (i.e., collecting money). Marshall and Newcombe termed this syndrome 'surface dyslexia.' Generally, it is held that surface dyslexics read regular words more accurately than irregular words. Thus, the regularity effect is both a necessary and sufficient symptom for the diagnosis of surface dyslexia. Three other symptoms usually accompany the regularity effect. The errors produced when reading irregular words aloud are regularizations. Errors in reading polysyllabic words are often the result of stressing the syllables incorrectly (as in the example of J.C.'s pronunciation of *begin*). Finally, when asked to read two-letter strings silently to themselves and decide if they sound the same or not, surface dyslexic readers perform accurately with

pairs of regular words; they are also good at deciding about nonwords, but they make errors on irregular words. These four symptoms all arise as a consequence of relying on letter–sound correspondences to read aloud.

A similar dissociation between the sublexical and lexical reading routes has been reported in Japanese patients. Japanese surface dyslexic patients can read words written in the syllabic *kana* script by means of the sublexical reading route, but are poor at reading *kanji* as these are normally processed lexically.

2.1.2 Deep Dyslexia

The defining characteristic of 'deep dyslexia' (or 'phonemic dyslexia') is the occurrence of semantic errors in reading aloud. For instance, another patient, G.R., read *speak* as 'talk' and *daughter* as 'sister.' He also made visual errors, reading *perform* as 'perfume,' and errors which seemed to be a combination of both visual and semantic factors (e.g., *sympathy* was read as 'orchestra,' presumably because of the visually similar word *symphony*). A number of other symptoms usually occur in these patients. Deep dyslexic patients are unable to read nonwords. This indicates that they cannot use letter–sound correspondences for reading aloud, and their ability to read real words is affected by a number of different variables. The 'imageability' of a word is the ease with which a mental image of its meaning can be conjured up. High imageability words such as *apple* are read more accurately than low imageability words like *faith*. The part of speech is also very influential, with nouns being the easiest, and function words like *the* and *of* being the most difficult.

Deep dyslexics produce a variety of reading errors. As well as semantic errors, function words are often substituted for other function words. Visual errors, mixed visual/semantic errors, and derivational errors such as reading *wise* as 'wisdom' are also quite common.

Theoretical accounts of deep dyslexia conclude that these patients are relying on the lexical–semantic route for reading. One explanation for the frequent semantic errors could be that this route is normally error-prone. However, semantic errors occur only rarely in the reading and speech of non-brain-damaged individuals. The alternative hypothesis is that, in addition to the sublexical processing route being impaired, the processing of the lexical–semantic route is also disrupted in deep dyslexia.

Sasanuma (1980) reports a case of a Japanese deep dyslexic patient. Y.H.'s oral reading of words written in the syllabic *kana* was severely impaired. When reading *kanji*, her errors were predominantly semantic and she showed an effect of part of speech, with nouns being read most accurately, and an imageability effect.

2.1.3 Phonological Dyslexia

Like deep dyslexic patients, phonological dyslexic patients show a dissociation between their ability to read words and nonwords. However, while these patients cannot read nonwords aloud, their reading of real words is generally quite accurate. This has been interpreted to suggest that they are using the direct lexical route to read aloud. One such patient, W.B. (Funnell 1983), read only 5 percent of nonwords aloud. He failed to respond to about half of them, and for those that he attempted he usually produced the pronunciation for a visually similar real word. In contrast, he read approximately 90 percent of real words correctly irrespective of their part of speech, their imageability, or their regularity.

Phonological dyslexics might be using an intact lexical–semantic route rather than the direct lexical route. However, further evidence from W.B. seems to rule this possibility out. Assessment of W.B.'s semantic knowledge about words found that he made confusions between words of similar meaning. If W.B.'s reading involved the semantic representations he would have made semantic errors in reading aloud. This was not the case.

2.1.4 Reading in Dementia

Additional evidence that reading can proceed via a direct lexical route comes from patients with a rather different form of acquired reading difficulty. The case of a woman called W.L.P. who was suffering from presenile dementia is reported. The pattern of deterioration of W.L.P.'s language skills was charted. As is often reported in cases of dementia, W.L.P.'s reading was relatively well-preserved in relation to other aspects of her language. At the time when she had no apparent understanding of the meaning of common words, W.L.P. could read many regular and irregular words aloud. Her lack of understanding of their meaning was demonstrated by her reaction to the task. For example, when given the word *hyena* to read aloud, she said 'hyena ... hyena ... now what in the heck is that?' Because of her poor comprehension it seemed unlikely that she was using the lexical–semantic route as this involves the word's semantic representation. Reading via the sublexical route was also ruled out because she could read many of the irregular words aloud. Like the phonological dyslexic patients, W.L.P. seemed to be relying on a direct lexical route for reading (see *Language Dysfunction in Dementia*).

2.2 Problems with Classification

Cognitive neuropsychology rejected the classical neurological syndromes of acquired dyslexia because they were not homogenous and initially replaced them with new syndromes such as surface and deep dyslexia. As cognitive neuropsychology has developed, it has become apparent that the new 'syndromes' are not homogenous. For example, the term 'surface dyslexia' is used to describe all patients who rely on the sublexical reading route to read aloud. However, there may be many different reasons why letter–sound cor-

respondences have to be used in reading aloud. Some surface dyslexics use the sublexical route to read aloud because of difficulties with access to stored visual information in the lexicon. When these surface dyslexics misread a word they also miscomprehend it because they have to use the word's pronunciation to access its stored semantic representation. Other surface dyslexics can access the lexicon from the written word, but disruption at some subsequent processing stage prevents them from accessing the word's pronunciation by this route. These patients read words aloud by the sublexical route, but can comprehend even the irregular words that they mispronounce because they have access from the written form of the word to its semantic representation.

A further problem with the new cognitive–neuropsychological syndromes is that, as with the classical neurological syndromes, few patients fit neatly into the syndrome classifications. The cases in which clear-cut dissociations have been found between the different processing routes have been cited as converging evidence for the existence of functionally separable processing routes. However, many patients with acquired reading difficulties show less clear-cut dissociations. For example, a patient who makes semantic reading errors may also be found to have some residual knowledge of letter–sound correspondences and hence be able to read some nonwords.

One response to these problems of classification has been to suggest that more precise syndromes should be identified. However, given the complexity of the underlying processing system, this suggestion would seem to be impractical. Alternatively, it has been suggested that, instead of grouping patients into syndromes, each patient should be considered in terms of their specific underlying processing difficulties. This solution has proved useful for the planning of remediation programmes (see Sect. 4). Syndrome labels such as surface dyslexia have, however, been retained to some extent as they provide a useful shorthand to describe the kind of symptoms exhibited by a patient.

2.3 Acquired Disorders of Writing

Because of the neurological organization of the brain, a lesion which produces an acquired language disorder also often leads to paralysis of the preferred arm and hand. As a result, many dysphasic patients have difficulties with writing. However, acquired disorders of spelling and writing cannot all be accounted for simply by the fact that the person is now having to use their nonpreferred hand to write with.

2.3.1 Acquired Spelling Disorders

As with acquired reading disorders, the application of cognitive processing models led to the identification of new syndromes of acquired dysgraphia. The emphasis is now on the identification of each patient's particular processing difficulties.

Patients have been described who make semantic errors, such as writing *chair* as 'table,' when asked to write words to dictation. A patient, J.C., could not write nonwords to dictation and showed a response to the part of speech and imageability when writing words to dictation. Function word substitutions occurred, for example *our* being written as 'MY.' J.C.'s difficulties could not be explained in terms of problems perceiving the words and nonwords that she was asked to write because she could repeat them accurately. It is suggested that J.C. was using a lexical–semantic route for writing to dictation, hence she could be described as 'deep dysgraphic.'

Patients have also been reported who are relying on a sublexical spelling route. For example, R.G. could provide acceptable spellings for dictated nonwords. He could spell 93 percent of regular words correctly, but only 38 percent of irregular words. Spelling errors generally were in the form of nonwords which had the same pronunciation as the target word. Another patient, G.E., seemed to be using a direct lexical spelling route in writing to dictation. G.E. could write words to dictation although all other aspects of his language were severely impaired. While he could make reasonable attempts at spelling some short nonsense words to dictation, his spelling of real words was much more accurate. This led to the suggestion that he must be using lexical knowledge when writing real words to dictation. This was supported by the finding that his ability to spell words accurately was unaffected by their regularity. Neither part of speech nor image-ability influenced his spelling performance. Involvement of a lexical–semantic route in spelling was ruled out by his poor comprehension of spoken words. For example, when he was asked to select the picture that went with the spoken word from amongst a set of semantically related pictures, he chose the correct picture for only 66 percent of the words. In contrast, he correctly wrote 94 percent of the words to dictation. It was concluded that G.E.'s remarkably preserved ability to spell to dictation was supported by a direct lexical spelling route.

In some patients with both acquired reading and spelling disorders, the pattern of spelling errors can mirror the pattern of reading errors. Thus, a deep dysgraphic patient may also be deep dyslexic. This is not necessarily the case. J.C., the deep dysgraphic patient, generally read both words and nonwords accurately and did not produce semantic errors in reading. R.G., the surface dysgraphic, could write but not read nonwords, and read but not write irregular words.

2.3.2 Acquired Writing Disorders

Acquired writing disorders are now beginning to be interpreted within cognitive processing models, the development of models of writing being influenced by the dissociations observed in patients.

M.W. is described as a patient whose pattern of spelling errors differed in oral and written spelling. When asked to write single letters to dictation, M.W. occasionally wrote an incorrect letter. Such letter substitutions did not occur when he spelled words aloud orally, but were evident in tasks which involved writing. For example, they were produced in writing to dictation and spontaneous writing and in both copying and delayed copying when M.W. was asked to transcribe a stimulus written in upper case into lower case or vice versa. It is suggested that M.W. had a difficulty with accessing the appropriate stored representations for the written forms of letters.

A patient with somewhat similar difficulties is described by Black et al. (1989). Oral and typed spelling were accurate but letter substitution errors occurred in writing. It was reported that the production of letter substitutions was influenced by the frequency of occurrence of the particular letter. The letters that occur most frequently in English tended to be written correctly. Because case errors did not occur, it is suggested that the letter forms were selected appropriately, the processing impairment being problems with passing this information to the stored motor patterns for writing.

While both of the above patients were able to select the appropriate case for letters, other patients have been reported to make case errors. For example, 5 months post-stroke, one patient, D.K. (Patterson and Wing 1989), accurately copied 83 percent of words written in uppercase letters, but only 21 percent of words written in lowercase. He was also severely impaired at transcribing between upper- and lowercase and vice versa. Another (Italian) patient, despite being asked to write in script, wrote words in mixed upper- and lowercase and appeared to have no control over this 'case-mixing.'

Theoretical accounts of different types of acquired writing difficulties are still largely speculative as the processes, involved in writing are not yet fully specified. Nevertheless, the application of cognitive neuropsychology to the study of writing is currently stimulating considerable interest.

3. Developmental Disorders of Written Language

3.1 Developmental Analogues of the Acquired Dyslexias and Dysgraphias

Following the successful application of cognitive models to the analysis of acquired disorders of reading and spelling, there have been a number of attempts to describe developmental dyslexias by analogy to acquired dyslexias. In children, two main types of reading disorder have been described. Children with developmental phonological dyslexia can read words significantly better than nonwords of similar phonological structure, yet, as far as has been ascertained, their visual word recognition is normal. The first case to be described, H.M. (Temple and Marshall 1983), a 15 year old girl, was reading at the 10-year level. She made a high proportion of visual and derivational errors in her word reading, and had extreme difficulty in reading nonwords aloud. Children with developmental surface dyslexia show a contrasting pattern of deficit, making predominantly phonological or 'regularization' reading errors, and having particular difficulty reading irregular or exception words. It can be assumed from the case descriptions that these children's visual word recognition is impaired, but that their phonological reading skills are good. However, perhaps the best-known patient described in the literature is C.D. whose nonword reading was impaired, despite a marked regularity effect in her reading. This illustrates one of the problems of an approach which attempts to classify reading disorders.

There have also been less clear case studies reporting other forms of reading disorder in children, for instance children who make semantic errors in single-word reading and therefore resemble deep dyslexics. Unfortunately in these cases, the proportion of errors which could unequivocally be classified as semantic was low and, given generally poor levels of reading attainment, these are expected, even in normal development.

A disappointing feature of the early case studies of developmental dyslexia using the cognitive approach, was that they focused exclusively on the reading strategies of the affected children and tended to explore neither their spelling performance (which was always affected), nor the skills underlying reading and spelling, such as phonological and visual processing abilities. However, Campbell and Butterworth (1985) presented an informative case of developmental dyslexia, R.E., who was an undergraduate student. By this time her reading and spelling skills were within the normal range. In spite of her high level of literacy, she was found to be virtually unable to read nonwords aloud, thus resembling a phonological dyslexic. Moreover, her spelling errors were primarily dysphonetic. Campbell and Butterworth went on to examine her phonological processing skills in depth; R.E. had marked verbal short-term memory difficulties and extreme difficulty with tasks requiring phoneme awareness. It was argued that these problems were the cause of the difficulties she had experienced in learning literacy skills. Studies like these are incapable, by their very nature, of demonstrating causes. Nonetheless, they are highly suggestive of the possibility that phonological dyslexia is traceable to difficulties with phonological awareness and verbal short-term memory.

A major criticism of many case studies of developmental dyslexia collectively, is that they have failed to include comparison with appropriately matched normal readers. When studying development, it is crucial to know the extent to which patterns of per-formance are normal, in which case a delayed pattern of development might be assumed, as opposed to a different pattern. In the absence of such data, it is impossible to make the claim that there is anything atypical about the reading strategies and error patterns shown by the individuals tested. Indeed, data from normal 10 year old readers shows that patterns of reading, indistinguishable from those of developmental phonological and developmental surface dyslexics described in the literature, are quite common in normally developing readers. These data provide a definite challenge to the view that it is possible to use similar models of reading (and spelling) to classify acquired and developmental disorders.

3.2 A Framework for the Normal Development of Literacy

Developmental models focusing on the acquisition of literacy provide an important framework within which to examine the reading and spelling skills of dyslexic children. Frith (1985) views the child as passing through a series of stages or phases before becoming fully literate, each stage building on the previous one. In the initial stage, it is widely held that reading is visually based and proceeds by the use of partial cues. According to Frith, children in this early 'logographic' phase make visual reading errors because they remember words according to features like first letters, 'wish' for *water*, or word length, 'gentlemen' for *grandmother*. It is also important to note that at this stage the child has no strategies for deciphering unfamiliar printed words (other than by visual approximation to known words) and spelling is rudimentary, perhaps being restricted to a few rote words.

The next stage, the alphabetic, is one in which the child begins to be able to decode, recognizing the importance of letter–sound correspondences. It is widely held that a prerequisite for transition into this phase is the development of phonological awareness, providing insight into the alphabetic principle. Furthermore, once the child recognizes that there are relationships between sounds and letters as embodied in print, this will bring with it the ability to spell, or at least to transcode phonetically, spoken into written words.

The final stage, the orthographic, is characterized by both automaticity and flexibility. Reading and spelling proceed independently of sound at this stage and lexical analogies can be used both in reading and spelling.

There is considerable debate about whether it is appropriate to view reading development as a series of stages. However, it is suggested that the development of reading must be viewed as the acquisition of two distinct systems; a lexical–semantic system for the processing of familiar printed words and a secondary, phonological or sublexical reading system which the child can use to decipher unfamiliar words. There is ample evidence that children make use of a sight vocabulary when reading and also can resort to the use of phonological strategies when presented with unfamiliar words. Furthermore, it seems clear that awareness of the phonological structures of words will be central to the development of decoding competence since this relies upon knowledge of letter–sound correspondences.

3.3 The Cognitive-developmental Approach to Dyslexia

According to Frith, the classic developmental dyslexic who has problems with both reading and spelling, fails to make the transition to the alphabetic phase of literacy development. This hypothesis makes sense in view of the vast amount of literature pointing to phonological deficits in dyslexic children (for a review of these see Snowling 1987). Consistently, studies pursuing the causes of dyslexia have highlighted difficulties with phonological awareness, verbal short-term memory, naming, and nonword repetition. It would be premature to attribute causal status to all of these difficulties. Nonetheless, they are significantly associated with dyslexia in children and plausibly contribute to the difficulty experienced in learning to use letter–sound and sound–letter rules, all of which places heavy demands on sound-processing and memory skills. Moreover, the pattern of reading most commonly associated with dyslexia is one where reading of words outstrips nonword reading. This is exactly as would be predicted given 'arrest' at the logographic stage. Snowling and colleagues presented a series of seven individual case studies of children who fell into this pattern and, interestingly, the pattern of performance of those with higher reading age was similar to those who were still at the beginning stages. These data suggested that, in spite of phonological problems, it is possible to learn to read, presumably by using an atypical or compensatory pathway. Indeed, one of the younger dyslexics in this study, J.M., has been followed longitudinally and, some four years later, although a better reader, still could not read nonwords and still spelled phonetically. It has been argued that he has learned to read by relying heavily upon visual and semantic strategies.

Among developmental dyslexics, there are also those who appear to be arrested at the alphabetic phase. Frith referred to these as developmental dysgraphics, because their spelling problems were more marked than their reading difficulties. The classic feature of these children is that they read well in context but, in single-word reading rely heavily upon sound, thus, for example, confusing homophones like *pear–pair*, *leek–leak*. Their spelling is phonetic. An example is the case of a dyslexic undergraduate, J.A.S., described by Goulandris and Snowling (1991). On the face of it, J.A.S. was an adult reader, and she could read nonwords proficiently. However, she performed randomly on tasks requiring her to discriminate between homophones. Moreover, her spelling was almost entirely phonetic and she showed particular difficulty when required to spell irregular words. The interesting feature about J.A.S. was that, unlike the majority of dyslexics, she did not have phonological problems. Instead, her visual memory was seriously impaired, providing a plausible account of her failure to learn orthographic principles.

The last type of developmental literacy problem is that of specific dysgraphia. In this condition, spelling problems exist in the absence of reading difficulty. Thus, these individuals have moved into the orthographic phase for reading but not for spelling. Like developmental dysgraphics, their spelling is phonetically correct but frequently violates English spelling conventions. Interestingly though, when such children are studied in detail, their problems appear to be due primarily to the way in which they process words during reading. Even though they are relatively good readers, they are less good than normal readers who are also good spellers, in proof reading and in nonword reading. These results suggest that as a group, they tend to process words holistically, without detailed visual attention to their letter-by-letter structures. A problem with this interpretation is that many such poor spellers also have problems on tasks requiring explicit phoneme segmentation. It is therefore plausible that their spelling problems originate from reading difficulties in common with other dyslexics, but that they have largely resolved their earlier reading problems by the time their spelling becomes the focus of their difficulties.

Thus, there is some support for Frith's idea that developmental difficulties with literacy can be usefully grouped according to the point in time when development becomes arrested. However, there are a number of difficulties with the theory. Notably, it is difficult to make predictions about how dyslexics will develop following arrest. Frith does not rule out the possibility that teaching might provide a stimulant to development, or that it could proceed along alternative pathways. However, these options are not spelled out in the model, and nor are the specific characteristics of the various phases. Specifically, the differences between reading in the logographic phase and reading in the orthographic phase are unclear.

An alternative model of the processes required for learning to read was proposed by Seymour (1986) with a view to classifying reading difficulties. The model had three components: a visual processor, involved in the registration and parsing of printed words, a phonological processor containing both a grapheme–phoneme convertor and a phonological word store involved in the sound translation of words, and, finally, a semantic processor containing word meanings. Working within this framework, Seymour used both reaction-time and error measures to investigate the responses of individual dyslexic children and normal 11 year olds to words which differed on various dimensions such as frequency of occurrence and spelling regularity, and in their visual configuration. Seymour unveiled a constellation of processing deficits but because these were seldom pure, he concluded there was no evidence for distinct subtypes. Rather, these children could be characterized by the processing system that was most severely affected. Some dyslexics had difficulties primarily with the phonological processor. He referred to these as developmental phonological dyslexics. Others had problems in one or other mode of operation within the visual processor; he referred to these as visual processor dyslexics, and, finally, still others had impairments of the multiletter routes to phonology and/or semantics. These children were reminiscent of the surface dyslexics described by other authors. Seymour described them as 'developmental morphemic dyslexics.'

3.4 Reading Comprehension Deficits (Hyperlexia)

The focus of much work on developmental reading disorders has been on the problems of children who have decoding problems. Amongst dyslexics, it is widely held that reading comprehension is in advance of decoding skill and any comprehension difficulties experienced by dyslexic children are attributable to decoding problems at the single-word level. These views have been formalized in an interactive-compensatory model of reading, indicating that children who are poor decoders actually use context more during reading (because there is time for it to have an effect) than good decoders who do not require this resource. However, there are children who can decode well but who have comprehension difficulties.

Several papers have postulated a syndrome of 'hyperlexia' in which decoding skills are precocious, but in which children do not understand what they read. Much of this work has been carried out with children who have developmental language problems or who show autistic features. It was generally assumed that these children 'barked at print,' having learned to read in a mechanistic manner, without attention to meaning. However, detailed examination of the reading skills of so-called hyperlexic children has revealed that, while their decoding skills are advanced, their comprehension is generally not unexpectedly poor given their overall IQ and language skills. Thus, they can choose semantically appropriate completions for sentences which they read and they can detect semantic anomalies in texts to the same extent as mental age-matched controls. Moreover, the majority can answer questions based on passages they have read. For a minority of these children only, there are problems to do with integrating the meanings of single sentences, so that they have difficulties with text inte-

gration and, also, in answering questions that require inferences to be made.

3.5 Problems of Classification

A number of different problems encountered when trying to classify developmental reading and spelling disorders have emerged during this review. First, the development of literacy should, in principle, encompass the child's acquisition of reading, spelling, and writing. There is no consensus concerning whether reading difficulties should be considered separately from spelling problems; schemes which examine the processes separately may come up with different results to those which take an integrated approach. Moreover, almost nothing is known about specific writing difficulties, although the problems that 'clumsy' children have with this and other fine-motor tasks are well-known.

Second, there is the major question concerning the appropriate controls which must be included if valid comparisons are to be made between dyslexic and normal readers. The absence of these in much of the case-study literature renders the validity of many classification schemes questionable. Related to this is the issue of development itself; many classification schemes look at individuals at one point in time—a stance which is perhaps indefensible given a developmental disorder.

Finally, a major theoretical issue concerns the cause or causes of specific reading difficulties. From a biological viewpoint, there is increasingly good evidence that dyslexia is inherited (Lewis 1992). However, the mode of transmission remains unknown. In some there is thought to be autosomal dominant transmission, but there is almost certainly genetic heterogeneity. An important extension to the work on the genetics of dyslexia has found that some, but not all, of the subcomponents of reading are heritable. Specifically, phonological skills have greater heritability than orthographic skills, although, importantly, both are amenable to training. These findings fit well with the present knowledge concerning the cognitive causes of reading failure.

Surprisingly, in the light of a wealth of knowledge concerning the nature of developmental dyslexia, there have been relatively few attempts to tie the underlying cognitive and linguistic impairments of these children with the pattern of reading and spelling performance they exhibit. Equally, there have been few attempts to show how these patterns might change through time, or in relation to the teaching received. Arguably, a full understanding of developmental disorders of literacy will await the outcome of studies which investigate how individual dyslexics, with particular constellations of cognitive strengths and weakness, actually learn to read, and how they respond to different programs of intervention.

4. Implications for Treatment

4.1 Implications for the Treatment of Acquired Disorders

Over the years, a variety of therapy models have been advocated for acquired dyslexia. For example, it has been suggested that tracing the letters of the word with the finger would aid reading. While the conclusion has often been that therapy for such disorders is of only limited success, a number of single-case studies have provided cause for more optimism. These studies have shown that therapy can be very beneficial when it is designed to overcome the specific processing problems underlying the reading disorder.

De Partz (1986) reported a successful remediation program carried out with a French gentleman named S.P., who was identified as being deep dyslexic, producing many semantic errors and being unable to relate sounds to letters. De Partz derived a therapy program that aimed to use S.P.'s spare knowledge about words to overcome these difficulties. For each letter of the alphabet, S.P. was asked to identify a word beginning with that letter. He then practiced associating the letter–word pairs until on seeing the letter he could automatically say the paired word. Over a period of time, S.P. learned to read letter strings by segmenting and blending the initial phonemes from the associated words. Later stages of the therapy program involved teaching S.P. a further strategy, again based on his knowledge of words, to allow him to derive the appropriate phonology for letter combinations such as vowel digraphs (-*ou*-, -*au*-, etc.). At the end of a year of intensive therapy, S.P. was able to read slowly but accurately.

While this therapy program was shown to be effective for a patient with deep dyslexia, it would not be useful for surface dyslexic patients because they already rely heavily on letter-to-sound conversion in reading. Therapy methods that encourage surface dyslexic patients to focus on the meaning of a word rather than on the letters that form it have also been described.

Byng and Coltheart (1986), for example, demonstrated that picture cues could be used to reteach a surface dyslexic patient, E.E., to read a set of highly irregular words. E.E.'s ability to read the set of words was assessed repeatedly over a number of weeks prior to the start of the therapy. No change was seen, indicating that his reading was not spontaneously improving. Picture cues were then used for a two-week phase of therapy. E.E. was given half of the set of words and asked to practice reading them aloud with the help of the pictures. At the end of the therapy, he was then asked to read the words aloud without the help of the cues. His performance was found to have significantly improved on the treated words, with some slight improvement also being seen on the words that had not been treated. A fortnight of therapy was then carried out for the untreated words. Subsequent reassessment found that E.E. was able to read all of the words.

Cognitive neuropsychological principles have also been applied to the remediation of the writing difficulties of deep dysgraphic and surface dysgraphic patients, and the results have been similarly encouraging. However, the application of cognitive neuropsychology to the remediation of acquired disorders of language, including reading and writing, is still in its infancy. The preliminary studies produced evidence that a therapy program was of benefit to one patient with a particular processing difficulty. Now, research in this field is being extended to include replication studies in which therapy programs are being evaluated with a number of patients with the same underlying processing difficulties. Future work will include the development of a 'theory of therapy.' Different therapeutic approaches—the reorganization of processing, the relearning of information, and the facilitation of the impaired access to stored information—have all been shown to be effective. The next stage will be to evaluate systematically which therapy approach, or approaches, are more successful for a given underlying processing difficulty.

4.2 Implications for the Treatment of Developmental Reading Disorders

Despite the enormous number of published studies on developmental dyslexia, there has been scarcely any research directed at the question of how best to treat these difficulties. Although there is a good deal of anecdotal and clinical evidence concerning teaching methods, it is fair to say that their efficacy is open to empirical investigation. Broadly, there have been two approaches to the treatment of the problems. The first has focused on the improvement of skills thought to be important for literacy development, the second has directly addressed the reading and spelling problems.

One of the best studies of the first type was reported by Bradley and Bryant (1983). As part of a longitudinal study examining the relationship between phonological awareness and literacy development, they focused upon 65 children who initially were poor at sound categorization. These children were split into four groups for the purpose of a training study. The first group was trained in sound categorization, and a second, in addition to this, was taught letter–sound correspondences. There were also two control groups; one group was taught to group words according to semantic categories; the other received no training.

After training, spread over 2 years, the group that had been taught sound categorization and letter–sound correspondences was some 8 to 10 months ahead of the taught control group in reading scores. The group that had only been taught to categorize sounds was about 4 months ahead of the control group in reading but this difference was not statistically significant. Nonetheless, these results were highly suggestive; the group taught to categorize sounds and to link letters to sounds showed very impressive improvements but it is difficult to be sure of the source of their gains. They may have been entirely due to training in letter–sound correspondences which, after all, is a direct part of teaching people to read and spell. It might be that this group's success depended upon having both sound categorization and letter–sound training. Nevertheless, the study certainly highlighted the importance of training underlying phonological skills as part of a remedial program.

The predominant approach to teaching dyslexic children, once they have failed to learn in the normal way, recognizes their difficulty with sounds. The most popular teaching schemes embody highly structured phonic teaching with explicit emphasis on learning to relate spelling patterns to sound. A number of studies carried out using variants of multisensory teaching techniques have reported gains in reading performance but these studies have lacked appropriate experimental controls, limiting their validity. Thus, research on the remedial methods suitable for developmental dyslexics is just beginning. Moreover, given the knowledge of individual differences in reading skill and between developmental dyslexics, it is unrealistic to look for a panacea. Future research will have to make use of both single case-study evidence and multivariate techniques to throw light on the best ways of treating developmental reading disorders.

Bibliography

Aaron P G 1989 *Dyslexia and hyperlexia: (Diagnosis and Management of Developmental Reading Disabilities)*. Kluwer, Boston, MA

Black S E, Behrmann M, Bass K, Hacker P 1989 Selective writing impairment: Beyond the allographic code. *Aphasiology* 3(3): 265–77

Bradley L, Bryant P E 1983 Categorising sounds and learning to read: A causal connection. *Nature* 301: 419–21

Byng S, Coltheart M 1986 Aphasia therapy research: Methodological requirements and illustrative results. In: Hjelmquist E, Nilsson L G (eds.) *Communication and Handicap*. North Holland, Amsterdam

Campbell R, Butterworth B 1985 Phonological dyslexia and dysgraphia in a highly literate subject: A developmental case with associated deficits of phonemic awareness and processing. *Quarterly Journal of Experimental Psychology* 37A(3): 435–75

De Partz M-P 1986 Re-education of a deep dyslexic patient: Rationale of the method and results. *Cognitive Neuropsychology* 3(2): 149–77

Ellis A W, Young A W 1988 *Human Cognitive Neuropsychology*. Erlbaum, Hove

Frith U 1985 Beneath the surface of developmental dyslexia. In: Patterson K E, Marshall J C, Coltheart M (eds.) *Surface Dyslexia*. Routledge and Kegan Paul, London

Funnell E 1983 Phonological processes in reading: New evidence from acquired dyslexia. *British Journal of Psychology* 74(2): 159–80

Goulandris N K, Snowling M 1991 Visual memory deficits: A plausible cause of developmental dyslexia? *Cognitive Neuropsychology* 8(2): 127–54

Lewis B A 1992 Pedigree analysis of children with learning disorders. *Journal of Learning Disabilities* 25: 586–97

Marshall J C, Newcombe F 1973 Patterns of paralexia: A psycholinguistic approach. *Journal of Psycholinguistic Research* 2(3): 175–99

Patterson K E, Wing A M 1989 Processes in handwriting: A case for case. *Cognitive Neuropsychology* 6(1): 1–2

Sasanuma S 1980 Acquired dyslexia in Japanese: Clinical features and underlying mechanisms. In: Coltheart M, Patterson K E, Marshall J C (eds.) *Deep Dyslexia*. Routledge and Kegan Paul, London

Seymour P H K 1986 *Cognitive Analysis of Dyslexia*. Routledge and Kegan Paul, London

Snowling M J 1987 *Dyslexia: A Cognitive Developmental Perspective*. Blackwell, Oxford

Temple C 1997 *Developmental Cognitive Neuropsychology*. Psychology Press, Hove

Temple C M, Marshall J C 1983 A case study of developmental phonological dyslexia. *British Journal of Psychology* 74(4): 517–33

Language Dysfunction in Dementia

R. Morris

Dementia can be defined as a progressive and generalized impairment in mental functioning in an alert patient. It is caused by a wide range of diseases including the two main forms, namely Alzheimer's disease (AD) and multi-infarct dementia (MID). Disorders of language have long been associated with the different forms of dementia, over and above the generalized decline in mental functioning.

In 1906, when Alois Alzheimer first described the symptomatology of AD, he remarked on the prominence of language difficulties. More recently, the revised *Diagnostic and Statistical Manual of Mental Disorders IV* indicated that patients with dementia show specific signs of aphasia with difficulties in naming objects and in defining words and concepts. On standardized tests, patients with AD typically show

Table 1. Typical progression of language disorder in Alzheimer's disease.

Early changes
    Circumlocutory discourse
    Word-finding difficulties
    Difficulty in naming objects
Later symptoms
    Simplified syntax
    Impaired comprehension
    Verbal perseveration
    Content vague and meaningless
    Paraphasias
Final symptoms
    Meaningless repetition of words
    Repetition of nonsense sounds

fluent speech and articulation, but with impaired naming and comprehension. The syntax of speech is relatively preserved but semantic processing is impaired. In MID, the pattern of language impairment is more variable depending on the brain areas most affected by cerebrovascular disease.

1. Staging of Language Dysfunction in Dementia

As dementia progresses the pattern of language impairment changes, as illustrated in Table 1. At the early stages of AD, the errors in speech are largely associated with word-finding difficulties. Speech has a normal fluency, prosody, and articulation rate, but subtle deficits are indicated by pauses and circumlocutory speech, as the patient is unable to retrieve a particular word (see Fig. 1). Marked language deficits usually become noticeable only after a year following the onset of the illness. At this stage semantic substitution errors become apparent, with patients confusing semantically related words such as 'sister' for 'daughter,' or 'table' for 'chair.' Paraphrasic errors become more common, either of the phonetic or semantic type, and there is impaired comprehension in which the patient only understands simple comments or instructions. In the later stages of the disease, the syntax of the language becomes simplified and eventu-

F	A	S
foot	air	sun
free	alive	sea
fall	attitude	stamp
fly	attitude	sigh
fall	air	
fie	axis	

Figure 1. Word-finding difficulty in Alzheimer-type dementia illustrated by the performance of a patient on the FAS test of verbal fluency, in which the patient has to recall words beginning with F, A, or S and is given one minute for each letter. A normal person can recall approximately 14 words or more for each letter. Note the repetition of words, reflecting verbal perseveration.

ally speech may become reduced to meaningless repetition of short phrases or nonsense sounds.

2. Comparisons with Aphasia caused by Focal Brain Damage

Comparisons have been made between language functioning in dementia and in patients with focal lesions of the brain. Standardized assessment batteries have been used to determine profiles of impairment in dementia and some studies suggest that the pattern of disorder most closely resembles transcortical sensory aphasia, characterized by good fluency, good repetition, and poor comprehension. Kertesz and his colleagues (1986) used the Western Aphasia Battery with demented patients and found a variety of profiles including transcortical sensory, Wernicke's, and global aphasia. In their sample of patients, transcortical motor and Broca's aphasia were relatively rare. In general the pattern of impairment tends to resemble aphasia associated with lesions in the posterior language areas of the brain. However, none of the main patterns of aphasia accurately fit the language disturbances in dementia (see *Syndromes of Aphasia*). This observation has led Emery (1988) to coin the term 'regressive aphasia' to describe the aphasic disorder in dementia, which she characterizes as linguistic reversion to earlier, less complex linguistic forms, with the more complex, abstract, and relational forms being compromised by the illness.

3. Experimental Studies of Language Dysfunction in Dementia

More detailed investigations have been used to explore different aspects of language dysfunction at the early stages of dementia, and include the nature of the naming deficit in AD, syntactical operations, comprehension, and semantic processing.

3.1 Anomia in Dementia

The naming disorder is particularly prominent at the early stages of dementia and naming dysfunction can occur even in mild dementia where overall language function appears normal. Dementia patients tend to make naming errors that are semantically related to the target word and are more likely to make errors with words that are less frequently encountered in everyday language. One suggestion is that confrontation-naming failure in dementia results from impaired visual perception. This is supported by the finding that naming improves in demented patients if they are allowed to handle objects. Demented patients also tend to show a greater deficit when the perceptual difficulty of objects is increased. For example, the degree of impairment is greater with line-drawing representations than with photographs of objects or real objects. Another source of naming errors in dementia is an impairment in semantic processing, where the patient may perceive the item correctly but fails to access the semantic representation. There is evidence that in AD patients confrontation-naming impairment is correlated with an inability to retrieve items from specific semantic categories and that subgroups of patients who have normal perceptual discrimination still have difficulties in naming.

3.2 Grammatical Operations

Many patients with dementia are able to perform correct grammatical operations, even when they have lost the ability to engage in meaningful speech. For example, the ability to modify word endings, negate sentences, and add plural endings can be essentially normal. However, on closer examination syntactical errors are apparent, particularly beyond the early stages of the disorder. Sentences may be left unfinished, and breakdowns may occur in the use of phrase markers and grammatical agreement. Syntax appears to be less impaired when the context cues or structures the syntactic task. Formal assessment of syntactical ability in AD has been conducted by Emery (1988) using the Test for Syntactic Complexity and Chomsky's Test of Syntax. This shows that early AD patients are unable to process complex syntactic structures, for example, making passive subject–object discriminations and consistently imposing active voice constructions on passive voice constructions. They were also unable to interpret correctly sentences in which the grammatical relations that held among the words in a sentence were not expressed in the surface structure (e.g., a patient is presented with a blindfolded doll and is asked the question 'Is this doll easy to see or hard to see?'). One cause of syntactical errors stems from the fact that complex grammatical forms place a demand on the working memory of a subject, as the surface form of a phrase has to be held in memory while it is processed. A working memory deficit in AD would contribute to syntactical errors of processing. Another difficulty in interpreting the cause of these types of errors is that the complexity of syntactical processing is usually associated with the complexity of semantic processing, so semantic errors could cause deficits in the complex syntactical tasks.

3.3 Comprehension and Semantic Processing

Simple comprehension in dementia tends to be preserved, with patients able to respond to simple commands and questions. As is the case with syntactical processing, however, understanding of more complex sentences or phrases is impaired, for example, the use of inference, the understanding of causal relationships, and comparatives. The degree of impairment is illustrated on the Token Test (De Renzi and Vignolo 1962), a test of verbal comprehension, where there is an inverse relationship between semantic complexity and performance. The more subtle aspects of impaired comprehension are reflected in the pragmatic level of language. At this level patients appear to lose the sense of terms that denote awareness of the truth values of statements and there is a lack of questions and commands that imply that the speaker is using language as a vehicle for interaction with other people, for conveying or receiving information about the world (see Paradis 1998).

The breakdown of semantic knowledge has been posited as the basis for the impairment in comprehension and naming ability. Dementia patients, for example, have substantial difficulties in generating members of semantic categories and in making judgments about the physical properties and functions of objects. There is some support for the notion that patients with dementia lose the knowledge of specific semantic attributes representing knowledge about a concept. Warrington (1975) studied three patients with suspected AD and found that when presented with photographs of objects and animals, the patients were able to make judgments about the semantic category of the item (e.g., animal versus not animal) but not about specific attributes of the items (e.g., red versus yellow). Similarly, AD patients only made errors when asked specific yes/no questions about the specific attributes concerning the exemplar of a category rather than about category membership (e.g., when presented with a tool and asked 'is it used to cut things?' or 'is it used to hold things?').

Despite the problems associated with accessing specific semantic attributes, this is likely to be a feature of faulty retrieval operations rather than a breakdown in the structure of semantic knowledge. A series of studies indicates that semantic priming effects are normal, at least at the early stages of AD. Thus, AD patients show a normal facilitatory effect in the speed of naming a visually presented word if it is preceded by a semantically related word (e.g., 'doctor' followed by naming the word 'nurse'). This suggests a distinction between an impairment in tasks that require a self-directed search of semantic memory versus those in which access to semantic memory is automatic and guided by pre-existing semantic associations (see *Language and Memory Systems*).

Bibliography

American Psychiatric Association 1994 *Diagnostic and Statistical Manual of Mental Disorders IV*, rev. edn. Author publishes, Washington, DC

Appell J, Kertesz A, Fisman M 1982 A study of language functioning in Alzheimer patients. *Brain and Language* **17**: 73–91

Cummings J L, Benson F, Hill M A, Read S 1985 Aphasia in dementia of the Alzheimer's type. *Neurology* **35**: 394–96

De Renzi E, Vignolo L A 1962 The Token Test: A sensitive test to detect receptive disturbances in aphasia. *Brain* **85**: 665–78

Emery O 1988 Language and memory processing in senile dementia Alzheimer's type. In: Light L L, Burke D M (eds.) *Language, Memory, and Aging.* Cambridge University Press, New York

Huff F J, Corkin S, Growdon J H 1986 Semantic impairment and anomia in Alzheimer's disease. *Brain and Language* **28**: 235–49

Kertesz A, Appell J, Fisman M 1986 The dissolution of language in Alzheimer's disease. *Canadian Journal of Neurological Science* **13**: 415–18

Kirschner H S, Webb W G, Kelly M P 1984 The naming disorder of dementia. *Neuropsychologia* **22**: 23–30

Paradis M 1998 *Pragmatics in Neurogenic Communication Disorders.* Pergamon, Oxford

Warrington E K 1975 The selective impairment of semantic memory. *Quarterly Journal of Experimental Psychology* **27**: 635–57

The Right Hemisphere and Verbal Communication

D. Van Lancker

In discussions of the brain and communicative abilities, most commentaries have emphasized cortical regions. This focus probably derived from the earlier assumption that all 'higher' human behaviors, including language, evolved exclusively with neocortical development. However, subcortical nuclei, such as basal ganglia and thalamus, especially those in the right hemisphere, and adjacent white matter, have come into awareness as contributory to specific aspects of communicative function. Structures of the limbic system may also be relevant to communication, but the facts of their laterality are still not well understood.

It is only recently possible to operationally clarify the term 'verbal communication' utilizing advances in language science. A definition of communication includes and requires traditional linguistic categories: phonetics, phonology, morphology, syntax, and linguistic semantics. This portion of communication is highly structured and describable in terms of discrete units and rules. Communication also encompasses systematic practices of language use, or pragmatics, a new and growing field of linguistic research. The field of pragmatics of language is concerned with speakers' intended meanings (as in sarcasm), inferences made by listeners (utilizing word knowledge and context), nonliteral meanings (from idioms and metaphors), the role of topic and theme in language production and comprehension, rules of conversation, and many other features of the larger units of discourse and interaction. As a final definition, the term 'speech' refers to motor and perceptual functions, 'language' to internal, mental knowledge, while 'pragmatics' addresses the parameters of everyday language use. These three components, intimately interleaved in any instance of verbal behavior, make up verbal communication.

1. Cerebral Laterality

The idea of (cortical) cerebral lateralization of behaviors, as is well known, originated in the identification of speech and language abilities, as well as reading and writing, with left hemisphere structures. This laterality model was derived almost exclusively from observing the effects of stroke and other brain damage on adults. People with damage to the left hemisphere very frequently suffer from speech and language deficits, whereas those with right hemisphere damage almost never do. Thus it is interesting that verbal communication provided the inception of the modern theories of brain laterality, which have grown immensely from the 1860s, the time of the first descriptions of aphasia. For many years, only scattered references to the right hemisphere as having a role in communicative function appeared—mostly commentaries on Hughlings Jackson's (1874) views about right hemisphere modulation of automatic speech. Because of the functional significance of language and the strong evidence for its lateralization, for many decades the left hemisphere was considered the 'dominant' hemisphere. The right hemisphere referred to as the 'minor' hemisphere, where, eventually, relatively little studied functions such as visual-spatial abilities came to light.

2. Methods of Study

Over the years, with the advent of new analysis technologies, the lateralization of classic linguistic function to the left hemisphere continues to be confirmed strongly by focal lesion studies. It is supported to a weaker degree by clinical procedures such as the Wada, whereby a single hemisphere is anesthetized while the other is probed for language and memory function (Loring et al. 1992). There has long been a question about the cerebral site of residual aphasic speech. Czopf (1981) and Kinsbourne (1971) each tested a series of aphasic persons and reported that residual speech ceased with right sided injection, supporting the notion that the right hemisphere subserves speech in aphasia. Unexpected language recovery after massive left sided damage also implicates the right hemisphere as a site of residual or recovered language function in severe aphasia (Cummings et al. 1979). Studies using structural and functional imaging as well as dichotic listening and EEG results have documented variable amounts of right hemisphere involvement in recovery of language following stroke; most agreement is on the role of the right hemisphere in recovery of receptive language (Gainotti 1993). Callosotomy (or split-brain) studies, whereby the single hemispheres of patients who have undergone sectioning of the corpus callosum (the band of fibers connecting the two cerebral hemispheres) are probed, also supports the left hemisphere representation of classically linguistic elements (Sperry 1974). In normal subjects, dichotic listening (simultaneous presentation of two different syllables or words, one at each ear) and split-visual field visual presentation can assay questions about laterality of specific aspects of speech and written language perception; again the left hemisphere performs classically linguistic tasks more efficiently, but some contribution of the right hemisphere is seen. To study the electrical activity of the brain, auditory and visually evoked responses as well as electroencephalography have been extensively utilized. Intersurgical use of stimulating electrode grids and implants in patients undergoing diagnostic procedures can also yield information about speech, language, and communicative function. Direct cortical stimulation while administering language tasks is utilized to map language representation during surgery, usually for treatment of epilepsy or tumor. The hegemony of the left hemisphere for speech and language functions is confirmed for the most part, although some sites on the right hemisphere, when stimulated with the electrode, were associated with vocalization, speech arrest, hesitation, slurring distortion, or repetition (Penfield and Roberts 1959; 121, 131, 132). Of course, since these methods are of necessity confined to people with brain damage undergoing treatment, extrapolation to normal brain organization must be made with caution.

Surprisingly, recent functional neuro-imaging studies, such as Positron Emission Topography (PET), only weakly support the classic model of speech and language lateralization. In those studies, researchers report considerable activation, sometimes greater activation, of the right hemisphere, for most speech tasks presented (Roland 1993). From these studies it is tempting to infer much greater involvement of the right hemisphere in speech and language function than has been previously inferred from the focal lesion data. However, because of numerous methodological uncertainties in the paradigm, interpretation of brain function underlying language processing from PET results is premature. MRI studies are also in the early development state at this time, and are handicapped for use in speech research by the contaminating effects of any movement by the subject.

The model of cerebral laterality discussed here is applicable only to adults. Neurological maturation, cerebral plasticity, and reorganization at earlier ages, and other issues must be considered in discussing language laterality in children. Pre-pubescent children have less lateralized communication functions. Very young children who have undergone left or right hemispherectomy (usually due to infantile hemiplegia) can develop nearly fully normal communicative function, although subtle tests of formal linguistic structure reveal superior performance in hemispherectomized children with an intact left hemisphere (Dennis and Kohn 1975). Similarly, the role of each respective hemisphere in second language learning is much less clear than for native speakers acquiring language in the usual way. This chapter focuses on the knowledge base obtained from studies in adult native speakers of a language.

3. Nonpropositional Speech

Hughlings Jackson developed the distinction between 'propositional speech' (newly created utterances) and 'automatic speech' (1874). In the subsequent years of aphasiological literature, nearly all writers use the term 'automatic speech,' for which they variously include expletives, interjections, pause-fillers, serial speech, conventional sayings, poems, songs, nursery rhymes, and social formulas. Most observers note that these expressions are, relatively, much better articulated and intoned than the other aphasic efforts at speech production. Hughlings Jackson placed the source of automatic speech in the right hemisphere, presumably an inference based on the ubiquity of the phenomenon across all types and sites of left hemisphere damage. However, most modern writers have been curiously reticent on this point. One reason is that many residual expressions, or recurrent utterances, are 'nonsense utterances,' syllables, or pieces of whole utterances, for which it is difficult to postulate a right hemisphere involvement. It is surprising that little other than anecdotal data on residual aphasic speech was available until the work of Code (1982) on British English and Blanken and Marini (1997) on German aphasic speakers. Code's surveys revealed that the notion of 'automatic speech' needs to be expanded, because a 'Pronoun (I) + verb' form was a highly common residual utterance-type (present in 14 of 75 patients). This is likely a common occurrence which has been merely overlooked in clinical descriptions. One earlier study described an aphasic patient who also used conventional sentence stems 'I would say that'; 'I must say'; 'well gee, I'm sorry the'; 'Well the only thing I can say again is'; 'I don't think'; 'I know' (Buckingham et al. 1975). In Code's data, expletives formed the second most frequent kind of recurrent utterance (11/75). Other categories were proper nouns (5/75), yes/no (4/75), numbers (5/75), repetitions (14/75), and other (22/75). The German data corresponded closely to the British groupings, with the majority consisting of (mild) expletives, inter-jections utterances, speech formulas (thanking and greeting), proper nouns, Pronoun (I) + verb, and other (Blanken and Marini 1997).

The cerebral source of the recurrent utterances remains controversial. Some views favor a role of the right hemisphere in the real word utterances (those listed above), possibly interacting with basal ganglia and limbic structures, with a probable left hemisphere source for the 'nonsense' utterances, while others pre-fer to consider a single source for the entire array. The adult left hemispherectomized subject offers non-ambiguity regarding the source of residual aphasic speech. Such individuals are rare. However, a striking example is seen in the normally developing, right-handed, adult patient E C, whose surgery for tumor included removal of all four left cerebral lobes, limbic forebrain, left thalamus, and basal ganglia (Smith 1966). In a 6 minute interview 5 months after surgery, E C was alert but profoundly aphasic. He could not name anything, but could repeat a few words (*book, house, develop, November*) with articulatory effort, dysfluency, errors, and pausing between syllables. His spontaneous speech was sparse, featuring expletives most copiously, and including 'one,' 'three,' and 'I,' 'no place,' and pause fillers ('um,' 'boy,' 'well, yes,' 'well, no,' 'ah,' 'oh'). E C also produced instances of 'sentence stems': 'I can't'; 'that's a'; 'I don't'; 'I couldn't say in (sic) then.' The spontaneous utterances were better articulated and intoned than repeated utterances. E C produced no nonsense utterances, lending support to the two-source model of recurrent utterances.

In comparison to countless discussions of preserved automatic speech, only one study describes a selective loss of such speech (Speedie et al. 1990). Interestingly, the injury from stroke was to the right basal ganglia. A 75-year-old, right-handed man was unable, in con-trast to pre-stroke function, to recite familiar verses, prayers or blessings, to swear, or to sing familiar songs. As is well known, conversely, the basal ganglia are implicated in hyperactivation of interjections and expletives (coprolalia) in Tourette's syndrome. A study of pre- and post-onset usage of overlearned utterances in Parkinson's disease, which involves a different kind of basal ganglia dysfunction and might be expected to lead to a diminution of production of automatic speech, would be useful in addressing these questions.

4. Phonetics, Phonology, and Prosody

Phonetics, the sounds of speech, and phonology, the sound patterns of language, form flexibly mani-pulable, structured units of language, and are pri-marily represented in the left hemisphere. That is, newly created utterances, formed by phonological and syntactic rules operating on phonological and lexical units, are best, possibly exclusively, processed by the left hemisphere in the adult. Although the right hemi-sphere produces and understands some speech, the production evidence reviewed above reveals a large discrepancy between articulatory facility for holistic exemplars of automatic speech, compared to prop-ositional utterances. Speech comprehension achieved by the severely left hemisphere-damaged adult may be attributed less to phonetics or phonology than to other, more global functions. As a corollary to the notion that the right hemisphere is less capable of phonological processing, it may be the case that the right hemisphere cannot rhyme, as was first suggested from observations in split-brain subjects. In a case of a severely impaired left hemisphere but intact right hemisphere, a patient denied that written words such as 'write' and 'light' formed a rhyme, but instead endorsed a rhyming relationship between 'hospital' and 'doctor.' Thus the right hemisphere may tend to recognize semantic relationships, even distant ones, but not a phonological likeness.

Prosody, or melody of speech, made up of pitch, loudness, rate, and voice quality, has received increased attention in normal and brain-damaged sub-jects. Prosody functions to cue linguistic, attitudinal, and emotional information, but it has been most tho-roughly studied in its role of signaling emotional meanings. 'Dysprosody' was first described as a linguistic disorder following left brain damage (Mon-rad-Krohn 1947). More recent claims about the role of the right hemisphere in modulating 'affective speech' have not been well supported (Baum and Pell, in press). Instead, various other factors play an impor-tant role. Evidence suggests that right cortical audi-tory function is specialized for complex pitch perception (Sidtis 1980); pitch, of course, is a major cue in emotional and linguistic prosody. Deficient pitch processing may partially account for poor right hemisphere performance on prosodic stimuli (Van Lancker and Sidtis 1992). Deficient familiar voice rec-ognition (phonagnosia) has also been identified with focal damage to the right parietal lobe (Van Lancker et al. 1989), conforming with the notion that complex auditory patterns are a right-sided specialty; prosodic contours form auditory patterns. In production, evi-dence points to a specialized ability of the right hemi-sphere to sing. The special function of singing has spawned a speech treatment technique called Melodic Intonation Therapy (MIT) (Helm-Estabrooks 1983).

Dysprosody has been associated significantly with subcortical damage from stroke (Cancelliere and Ker-tesz 1990). Fronto-subcortical circuits in emotional processing have been implicated in other studies (Bre-itenstein et al. 1998); prosodic deficits are reported in Parkinson's and Huntington's disease. An important role of basal ganglia structures in regulating mood and motivation has recently been better understood; mood and motivational deficits impact on voice pros-ody. While some role of the right hemisphere can be posited, particularly in connection with basal ganglia structures, multiple parameters underlie the perception and production of prosodic material in speech, engaging various neurological structures.

5. Word Storage

There is a venerable body of information about lexical (word) organization in the respective hemispheres. Earlier findings indicated that the right hemisphere recognizes visually presented words better to the extent that stimuli were more frequent and less abstract. Studies in split-brain (callosal-sectioned) subjects and in normal subjects using central or split-visual field tachistoscopic presentation continue to be fertile methods of inquiry. Such studies suggest a hemispheric difference in lexical organization with right hemisphere word relations more closely simulating worldly contexts. For example, a partial split-brain patient described rich, contextual details for written words presented to the left visual field (right hemisphere); shown the target word 'knight,' he said 'two fighters in a ring...ancient...wearing uniforms and helmets on horses, trying to knock each other off...knights?' (Sidtis et al. 1981). Normal subjects identified relatedness of word pairs such as words like 'coffin' and 'ground' better than linguistically related pairs presented to the right hemisphere (Drews 1987). Some have suggested that 'deep dyslexia' (reading 'window' when presented with the written word 'door') is attributable to right hemisphere processing. Similar hemisphere differences in judging semantic relations and in generating misreadings (paralexias) give suggestion of somehow different semantic organization in the right hemisphere: relatively idiosyncratic, more diffuse, influenced by contextual more than linguistic-structural principles of organization.

Persons with right hemisphere damage have told stories with less emotive and specific content than matched normal subjects (Wechsler 1973). Aphasic patients read emotional words more correctly (presumably utilizing the intact right hemisphere) than concrete or nonemotional abstract words (Landis et al. 1982). A series of studies suggested a similar paucity in emotional words in split-brain patients (a condition called 'alexithymia'), giving as an explanation the lack of communication to the speaking left hemisphere from the allegedly more affectively laden repertory of the right (TenHouten et al. 1986). From their studies of patients with focal lesions, working with different types of emotional stimuli, Bowers et al. (1993) coined the term 'affective lexicon' to describe the specialization of the right hemisphere.

Another series of observations on patients with global aphasia suggests a presence of familiar proper nouns in the intact right hemisphere. Patients with severe difficulty matching a spoken word such as 'glass' or 'pencil' to a picture are, in contrast, well able to match spoken names to familiar persons and places

(Van Lancker and Klein 1990; McNeil et al. 1994). In production, 8 percent of the recurrent utterances from the British survey were familiar proper names with a comparable count in the German corpus. Preservation of proper noun comprehension and production in severe aphasia is particularly striking, because proper names are linguistically more complex than common nouns. However, these words typically contain a broad constellation of emotional and contextual attributes. One explanation is that the right hemisphere is specialized for information in the world that is personally relevant. Support for this notion is seen in disturbances of the personal familiarity sensation, as in Capgras syndrome and other agnosias, in right hemisphere damage (Cutting 1990). In a study of split-brain patients, Sperry et al. (1979) found a stronger response from the separated right than the left hemisphere to pictures of family members and well-known cultural icons. The authors indicate some surprise at their findings; at the time of that study, little was suspected of the rich contextual and emotive constructs of the right hemisphere.

6. Grammar or Syntax

Little of these key properties of human language can be demonstrated as a function of the right hemisphere in any studies, whether performed on normal or neurological patients. Grammatical deficits are seen in left anterior damage; grammatical processing is associated with an intact adult left hemisphere. The sentence stems (pronoun + verb) used by severely aphasic individuals might appear to be a noteworthy counterexample to this rule. However, sentence stems were classed some time ago by linguists as conventional expressions, in the same category as speech formulas. These, while appearing to have syntactic structure, are overlearned expressions, like idioms and proverbs. Linguistic research currently underway recognizes the special status of familiar nonliteral expressions, often suggesting that they are stored and processed differently from propositional or newly created speech.

7. Nonliteral Language

For speech production, as described previously, observations from severe aphasia reveal selective preservation of pause-fillers, speech formulas, and other conventional expressions. In comprehension, studies point to an important contribution of the right hemisphere in processing non-literal meanings (Winner and Gardner 1977; Van Lancker and Kempler 1987). Proverb interpretation has a long history in intelligence and mental status testing, but the procedure is often based on verbal responses to unfamiliar proverbs. These task demands obscure information about correlative brain function that might be obtained about proverb usage.

Psycholinguistic work on familiar nonliteral

expressions reveals the complexity of these types of utterances. At the simplest level, an idiom, proverb, or speech formula is made up of stereotyped form associated with a complex, conventionalized meaning. There has been a long-standing controversy about whether to view these utterances as grammatically 'frozen.' Subsequent studies indicate that many or most of these holistic utterances can be altered by changing or adding words, and that some literal meanings of constituent words in idioms influence usage. This process of taking a familiar expression 'She has him eating out of her hand' and adding words for emphasis or other impact ('She really has him eating nearly directly out of her very hand, not to mention her handbag') probably reflects the interaction of two processes as a feature of language competence, memorized and newly created; these two processes may inhere in the two respective hemispheres, which have been described as operating by differing modes (Bradshaw and Nettleton 1983; Bogen 1969).

8. Pragmatics, or the Science of Language Use

The study of pragmatics 'ascends' from the microlevels of phonetics, phonology, words, and fixed phrases, and the grammatical rules that combine them, to larger units, those of discourse and conversation, and to overarching principles of coherence. People may know the words and the grammar, but in order to engage in communication, it is necessary to perform a great variety of inferences across larger stretches of talk. Parameters such as inference and discourse focus are of operative importance in language comprehension (Marslen-Wilson et al. 1993). This is a prolific area of research at this time, with considerable application to brain and communication studies. From these studies, it is emerging that the right hemisphere has a role in performing inferences (Gardner et al. 1983), recognizing indirect requests (Weylman et al. 1989), and many other aspects of crucially important parameters of communication such as perceiving the topic, following the theme, processing real-world context, taking into account the knowledge of conversation partners, and appreciating humor (Beeman and Chiarello 1998; Brownell and Joanette 1993). Patients with right hemisphere damage are communicatively handicapped in ways that are often difficult to identify. A number of rehabilitation handbooks have appeared to meet this need (Burns et al. 1996; Tompkins 1996).

9. The Complementary Communication Hemisphere

Just as the study of lateralized brain function has shifted characterization of brain organization from one of 'dominance' to one of complementary specialization, the study of language and the brain has led to a similar change in thinking. Although many of the elements of language communication are still considered to be strongly lateralized to the left hemi-

sphere, the complementary abilities of the right hemisphere are being recognized. There is little sign of classical linguistic functions—phonological, morphological, or syntactic creativity—that is, propositional speech, emanating from the unaided right hemisphere in the production mode; the instances appearing to suggest propositional speech in the comprehension most probably proceed with some benefit from other principles. Both hemispheres carry a huge repertory of words. Such apparent comprehension in the right hemisphere of classical linguistic elements may actually heavily utilize the parameters of context, theme, and linguistic redundancy, keying on individual vocabulary items, for example. Rather than classical linguistic components, strongly represented in the right hemisphere are types of speech and language called nonpropositional, functioning both in perception and production, possibly in concert with basal ganglia structures. These include unitary, stereotyped forms, such as familiar nonliteral expressions, and conventionalized meanings that are figurative and idiosyncratic to the occasion. Superior abilities for the production and perception of pitch contribute to prosodic competence in the right hemisphere—abilities to process the intonation contours of speech. The large vocabulary probably operates according to principles of processing that differ from those in the left hemisphere. The accessing and handling of the lexical items follows more affective, real-worldly, and personal associative and symbolic networks in the right than the left hemisphere. How unique, or strongly lateralized, or universal, is this scenario of right hemisphere communicative representation is not well understood.

The evidence available for right hemisphere communicative function conforms well with now current notions of different hemispheric modes, with the left hemisphere performing more efficiently in analytic, sequential tasks, and the right hemisphere contributing broader configurations utilizing more diffuse operations of various kinds. Permutability of discrete units according to a definable set of 'rules' or generalizations is the forte of the adult, developed left hemisphere, while pattern recognition, idiosyncratic inferencing, and broad thematic management characterizes the right. Contemporary models of speech production and perception distinguish 'bottom-up' from 'top-down' directions in processing: 'bottom-up' moves from microunits, such as elemental acoustic cues, phoneme, and syllable, through the 'higher' componential levels of morpheme and word, while the 'top-down' approach utilizes units as large as the sentence or paragraph, and concepts as general as topic, context, and linguistic redundancy broadly viewed. Language processing models have shown the importance of all these elements, interactively and in concert, in communicative competence. The evidence reviewed above leads to a picture of complementary work of the cerebral hemispheres, corresponding to greater efficiency of bottom-up linguistic processing in the left hemisphere, augmented by superior right hemisphere top-down recognition of the pragmatic parameters of human communication.

Bibliography

Baum S R, Pell M D 1999 The neural bases of prosody: Insights from lesion studies and neuroimaging. *Aphasiology*, in press

Beeman M, Chiarello C (eds.) 1998 *Right Hemisphere Language Comprehension: Perspectives from Cognitive Neuroscience*. Erlbaum, Hillsdale, NJ

Blanken G, Marini V 1997 Where do lexical speech automatisms come from? *Journal of Neurolinguistics* **10**: 19–31

Bogen J E 1969 The other side of the brain: An appositional mind. *Bulletin of the Los Angeles Neurological Societies* **34**: 135–62

Bowers D, Bauer R M, Heilman K M 1993 The nonverbal affect lexicon: Theoretical perspectives from neurological studies of affect perception. *Neuropsychology* **7**: 433–44

Bradshaw J L, Nettleton N C 1983 *Human Cerebral Asymmetry*. Prentice Hall, Englewood Cliffs, NJ

Breitenstein C, Daum I, Ackermann H 1998 Emotional processing following cortical and subcortical brain damage: contribution of the fronto-striatal circuitry. *Behavioural Neurology* **11**: 29–42

Brownell H H, Joanette Y (eds.) 1993 *Narrative Discourse in Neurological Impaired and Normal Aging Adults*. Singular Publishing Company, San Diego

Buckingham H W, Avakian-Whitaker H, Whitaker H A 1975 Linguistic structures in stereotyped aphasic speech. *Linguistics* **154/155**: 5–13

Burns M, Halper A, Mogil S 1996 *Clinical Management of Right Hemisphere Dysfunction*. Rehabilitation Institute of Chicago Publication Series Aspen Publication, Rockville, CL

Cancelliere A, Kertesz A 1990 Lesion localization in acquired deficits of emotional expression and comprehension. *Brain and Cognition* **13**: 133–47

Code C 1982 Neurolinguistic analysis of recurrent utterances in aphasia. *Cortex* **18**: 141–52

Cummings J L, Benson D F, Walsh M J, Levine H L 1979 Left-to-right transfer of language dominance: A case study. *Neurology* **29**: 1547–50

Cutting J 1990 *The Right Cerebral Hemisphere and Psychiatric Disorders*. Oxford University Press, Oxford, UK

Czopf J 1981 Über die Rolle der nicht dominanten Hemisphäre in der Restitution der Sprache der Aphasischen. *Archiven Psychiatrischen Nervenkrankheiten* **216**: 162–71

Dennis M, Kohn B 1975 Comprehension of syntax in infantile hemiplegics after cerebral hemidecortication: Left hemisphere superiority. *Brain and Language* **2**: 472–82

Drews E 1987 Quantitatively different organizational structures of lexical knowledge in the left and right hemisphere. *Neuropsychologia* **25**: 419–27

Gainotti G 1993 The riddle of the right hemisphere's contribution to the recovery of language. *European Journal of Disorders of Communication* **28**: 229–46

Gardner H, Brownell H H, Wapner W, Michelow D 1983 Missing the point: The role of the right hemisphere in the processing of complex linguistic materials. In: Perecman E (ed.) *Cognitive Processing in the Right Hemisphere*. Academic Press, New York: 169–92

Helm-Estabrooks N 1983 Exploiting the right hemisphere for language rehabilitation: Melodic intonation theory. In: Perecman E (ed.) *Cognitive Processing in the Right Hemisphere*. Academic Press, New York: 229–40

Hughlings Jackson J 1874 On the nature of the duality of the brain. Reprinted in Taylor J (ed.) *Selected Writings of John Hughlings Jackson, Vol 2 1932*. Hodder and Stoughton, London: 129–45

Kinsbourne M 1971 The minor cerebral hemisphere as a source of aphasic speech. *Transactions of the American Neurological Association* **96**: 141–45

Landis T, Graves R, Goodglass H 1982 Aphasic reading and writing: Possible evidence for right hemisphere participation. *Cortex* **18**: 105–12

Loring D W, Meador K J, Lee G P, King D W 1992 *Amobarbital effects and lateralized brain function: The Wada test*. Springer Verlag, New York

McNeil J, Cipolotti L, Warrington E 1994 The accessibility of proper names. *Neuropsychologia* **32**: 193–208

Marslen-Wilson W D, Tyler L K, Koster C 1993 Integrative processes in utterance resolution. *Journal of Memory and Language* **32**: 647–66

Monrad-Krohn G H 1947 Dysprosody or altered 'melody of speech.' *Brain* **70**: 405–15

Penfield W, Roberts L 1966 *Speech and Brain-mechanisms*. Princeton University Press, Atheneum, NY

Roland P E 1993 *Brain Activation*. Wiley, New York

Sidtis J J 1980 On the nature of the cortical function underlying right hemisphere auditory perception. *Neuropsychologia* **18**: 321–30

Sidtis J, Volpe B, Holtzman J, Wilson D, Gazzaniga M 1981 Cognitive interaction after staged callosal section: Evidence for transfer of semantic activation. *Science* **212**: 344–46

Smith A 1966 Speech and other functions after left dominant hemispherectomy. *Journal of Neurology, Neurosurgery, and Psychiatry* **29**: 467–71

Speedie L J, Brake N, Folstein S, Bowers D, Heilman K 1990 Comprehension of prosody in Huntington's disease. *Journal of Neurology, Neurosurgery, and Psychiatry* **53**: 607–10

Sperry R W 1974 Lateral specialization in the surgically separated hemispheres. In: Schmitt F O, Worden F G (eds.) *Neurosciences: Third Study Program*. MIT Press, Cambridge, MA

Sperry R W, Zaidel E, Zaidel D 1979 Self-recognition and social awareness in the disconnected minor hemisphere. *Neuropyschologia* **17**: 153–66

TenHouten W D, Hoppe K D, Bogen J E, Walter D O 1986 Alexithymia: An experimental study of cerebral commissurotomy patients and normal control subjects. *American Journal of Psychiatry* **143**:312–16

Tompkins C 1996 *Right hemisphere communication disorders: Theory and management*. Singular, San Diego, CA

Van Lancker D, Kempler D 1987 Comprehension of familiar phrases by left- but not right-hemisphere damaged patients. *Brain and Language* **32**: 265–77

Van Lancker D, Kreiman J, Cummings J 1989 Voice perception deficits: neuroanatomic correlates of phonagnosia. *Journal of Clinical and Experimental Neuropsychology* **11**: 665–74

Van Lancker D, Klein K 1990 Preserved recognition of familiar personal names in global aphasia. *Brain and Language* **39**: 511–29

Van Lancker D, Sidtis J 1992 The identification of affective-prosodic stimuli by left- and right-hemisphere-damaged subjects: All errors are not created equal. *Journal of Speech and Hearing Research* **35**: 201–27

Wechsler A 1973 The effect of organic brain disease on recall of emotionally charged versus neutral narrative texts. *Neurology* **73**: 130–35

Weylman S T, Brownell H H, Roman M, Gardner H 1989 Appreciation of indirect requests by left and right brain-damaged patients: The effects of verbal context and conventionality of wording. *Brain and Language* **36**: 580–91

Winner E, Gardner H 1977 The comprehension of metaphor in brain-damaged patients. *Brain* **100**: 717–29

Language and Memory Systems

S. Aglioti

1. Relationships between Language and Memory

Several memory traces are formed through language, a cognitive function that, among other aspects, is also extensively used for expressing considerable parts of our memory. In spite of this elementary consideration, the relationship between language and memory is intricate. The case has been reported of a 100-year-old woman who 'can play (and win) Scrabble in three foreign languages' in spite of a severe memory impairment (Parkin 1993). Patients affected by amnesia, that is, a global deficit in the ability to acquire new memories regardless of sensory modality along with loss of some memories from the preamnesic period, often show a picture characterized by intact intellectual, perceptual, and linguistic capabilities. Similarly, patients affected by aphasia, that is, a deficit in producing and/or understanding language in the absence of other cognitive impairments, show preserved spatial memory, along with minor deficits in verbal memory tasks (Burgio and Basso 1997). This is surprising unless we accept that any attempt to grasp the relationships between language and memory must start from the assumption that these two functions are not unitary.

Language is the powerful function that allows a highly sophisticated exchange of information between a source and a receiver. It is based on a mental lexicon containing thousands of memorized symbols (words) and a mental grammar, that allows to combine words in an infinite number of phrases and sentences (Pinker 1994). Pragmatic information, such as provided by prosodic cues, is also relevant to effective communication. Language is acquired by means of distinct routes for linguistic and pragmatic aspects (McDonald 1997).

There is now general agreement that the learning process in general, and hence memory, is not reducible to a single common form. Different types of information (e.g., verbal vs. nonverbal items) may be handled in different ways. Moreover, there are different time scales over which the information is handled. Several lines of evidence, including lesion studies in animals and humans, and neuro-imaging and neurophysiological studies, suggest the existence of different forms of memory and, perhaps more importantly, that each form may be subserved by multiple or at least partially separate neural systems. Thus, the relationship between language and memory can hardly be understood without taking into account the fact that these two cognitive functions are subdivided into several subsystems.

This chapter reviews evidence supporting the existence of different forms and systems for memory and language. Two additional issues are addressed. The first concerns whether or not the neural substrates subserving the acquisition and storage of mental lexicon are different from those subserving the acquisition and storage of mental grammar; the second concerns whether or not learning and using specific aspects of language has to do with the known functional differences of the different memory systems.

2. Forms of Memory and Memory Systems

Major advances in the description of memory come from attempts to break down this function into separate components. It has long been known from behavioral studies on normal subjects and brain-damaged patients that learning and memorizing verbal items can occur at different rates (and even separately) from learning and memorizing nonverbal items. Moreover, while a left temporal lobectomy selectively impairs verbal recall, a right temporal lobectomy produces deficits of nonverbal recall (Taylor 1969). Recent neuro-imaging studies in neurologically healthy individuals have shown that memory for names and faces is mediated by at least partially different brain systems, centered respectively in the left and right fronto-temporal lobes (Kelley et al. 1998). The notion of multiple forms and systems of memory became explicit in the mid 1970s on the basis of evidence supporting not only the notion of short-term and long-term memory but also of two types of long-term memory, that is, semantic and episodic memory (Schacter and Tulving 1994). Recent findings in patients with amnesia resulting from selective hippocampal damage suggest that this structure may be particularly important for event-related as opposed to fact-related memory, with the surrounding cortical areas contributing to both (Mishkin et al. 1997). Thus, a further breakdown emerged. The notion of multiple memory forms has been supported by research studies on global amnesic patients with bilateral damage of the mesio-temporal lobes. These patients, although largely unable to learn new facts and probably also new events, proved able to learn, at the same rate as normal individuals, a complex set of different abilities including skill and habit learning, priming, emotional conditioning, and other simple forms of conditioning (Squire and Zola 1997).

2.1 Memory Forms in Relationship to the Time over which Information is Handled

2.1.1 Short-term memory

The classic concept of short-term (or primary) memory has recently developed into the more sophisticated version of working memory (WM), which assumes a number of subsystems rather than a unitary module (Baddeley 1998). WM has both verbal and spatial components that are typically assessed by asking subjects to retain for 2–3 sec either the names of letters or the position of series of digits. The verbal component of WM is a temporary form of storage of verbal information that plays a crucial role in learning the novel phonological forms of new words (Baddeley 1998; Baddeley et al. 1998). Recent neuro-imaging studies using PET have shown that verbal WM is mainly subserved by left-hemisphere structures and spatial WM by bilateral or right hemisphere areas (Smith et al. 1996). Subsequent imaging studies (Smith et al. 1998) suggested a further subdivision of verbal WM: a phonological component mediated by left-hemisphere frontal speech regions including the Brodman's area 44, a pure storage buffer mediated by the left parietal cortex (area 40), and an executive component mediated by the dorsolateral prefrontal cortex (areas 9 and 46). The final product of WM is usually contemplated by the individual introspectively, in conscious awareness. It is relevant here that WM cortical networks partly overlap with the language networks in the brain.

2.1.2 Long-term memory

The system for handling traces over minutes, hours, years, or even decades is referred to as long-term memory, a kind of memory for the conscious recollection of words, scenes, faces, and stories. This system comprises a memory for facts (semantic) and a memory for events (episodic) (Tulving 1972, 1987). Knowing that Rome is the capital of Italy is a test of semantic memory, while remembering what one had for dinner the day before is a test of episodic memory. Neuropsychological and neuro-imaging studies indicate that the medial temporal lobe-hippocampal (including entorhinal, perirhinal, and parahippocampal cortices) -diencephalic system is crucial for semantic memory. Episodic memory relies upon a yet unspecified prefrontal-cortical system; however, since episodic memory also depends on semantic memory (the opposite not being true), deficits in the latter may also ensue from a mediotemporal damage (Squire and Zola 1996, 1997). Learning and retrieval within the declarative memory system typically take place with more or less complete awareness of the contents of what is learned or retrieved (explicit memory).

2.2 Nondeclarative Memory

A complex set of memory abilities kept distinct from WM and long-term memory has been labeled nondeclarative knowledge: it includes learning of perceptuo-motor skills, priming, and various forms of associative learning like emotional conditioning or classical conditioning (Thompson and Kim 1996; Squire and Zola 1996). Nondeclarative memory is studied in a broad array of tasks such as classification learning, perceptuo-motor skill learning, or the learning of artificial grammars. Each of these forms of memory most probably rely on different neural substrates: skill and habit learning appear to be linked to the striatum, the motor cortex, and the cerebellum; priming phenomena are linked to the neocortex; emotional conditioning to the amygdala and hippocampus; classical conditioning involving skeletal musculature to the cerebellum and hippocampus (Thompson and Kim 1996). A distinctive feature of these types of learning and memory is that their content cannot be accessed to through conscious efforts.

2.3 Explicit (Declarative) versus Implicit (Nondeclarative) Memory

For a taxonomy of memory it is useful to observe that operations of many forms of memory can be sometimes expressed implicitly rather than explicitly. Explicit (declarative) and implicit (nondeclarative) learning and memory are descriptive concepts of how these cognitive abilities can be expressed. This distinction is based on the presence or absence of conscious introspection about the contents of a particular memory trace (Squire and Zola 1996). Explicit memory, typically assessed through free recall tests, has the main feature that what is learned can be represented and verbalized on demand. Each different type of implicit learning and memory (perceptuo-motor skills, priming, emotional conditioning) is explored by means of appropriate tests. A rotor-pursuit test, for example, is suitable to explore the learning of motor skills. Across successive trials, subjects will learn to keep a pen on a dot moving with an erratic trajectory; however, they cannot explain what is being learned. Amnesic patients with severely impaired declarative memory were found to be able to learn a rotor-pursuit test in a number of trials comparable to normal subjects; however, in spite of the improved performance in the implicit task, even after several trial sessions these subjects reported that they had never been submitted to that test before. Thus, implicit memory and learning is measured by experience-induced changes in performance by means of tests that make no direct reference to that experience. One important difference between explicit and implicit memory is that, unlike the former, implicit memory is relatively inflexible and is only available in contexts that are identical, or very similar, to the original learning situation. Finally, explicit and implicit forms of learning and memory are differentially represented across evolution, the former being phylogenetically more recent (Sherry and Schacter 1987). These different forms of memory may have evolved because they serve different and multiple incompatible functions. Skill learning, for example, may be incompatible with effective solutions to other memory problems.

2.3.1 *Implicit and explicit forms of learning and memory have different developmental windows*

The issue of whether or not explicit and implicit memory develop over different time scales has been addressed by delivering tests tapping one form of memory (e.g., free recall) or the other (e.g., perceptual or verbal priming) to children of different ages. Homberg et al. (1993), for example, tested children between the age of 5 and 10 years on explicit memory (by using a verbal story recall task and a nonverbal pictorial recall task) and on implicit memory (by using a motor mirror tracking task and a nonmotor tower-of-Hanoi puzzle). Explicit memory tasks showed a clearly developmental profile, with an increase in the number of recalled items and attainment of adult scores between 9 and 10 years of age. By contrast, no age differences for both implicit memory tasks were detected. DiGiulio et al. (1994) found a similar pattern of results by using measures of priming for implicit memory and free recall for explicit memory. Taken together, these results suggest that the ontogenetic maturation of implicit memory precedes that of explicit memory systems and that the former is already functional when the latter is still very poor (Parkin 1997). These results are in agreement with those reported in infant monkeys, where an early developing nonlimbic habit system, analogous to implicit memory, and a late developing limbic memory system, analogous to explicit memory, have been described (Bachevalier and Mishkin 1984; Bachevalier 1990).

2.3.2 *... and a different resilience to aging and age-related pathologies*

While explicit memory deteriorates dramatically with aging, implicit memory appears largely spared in the elderly (Howard 1988). From a review of the literature, Burke and Mackay (1997) concluded that memory for highly practiced skills and familiar information is comparatively preserved in the elderly; in contrast, memory performance requiring the formation of new connections, for example, recall of recent autobiographical experiences, new facts, or the source of newly acquired facts, is comparatively impaired. These results suggest that implicit abilities be largely preserved when explicit abilities deteriorate. It is important to note that 'implicit' is a descriptive term alluding to a complex set of different abilities subserved by different neural structures that may be selectively damaged. Perceptual and conceptual priming, respectively linked to stimulus form and stimulus meaning, occur in an implicit way. However, they are likely to be mediated by different neural substrates, that is, comparatively lower-order unimodal cortices for perceptual priming and polymodal association cortices for conceptual priming. Indeed, patients affected by Alzheimer's disease and lesions involving higher-order areas show a defective conceptual priming (Gabrieli 1996).

3. Neurofunctional Dissociations within the Human Language

The functional architecture of the human language is based on a dictionary of memorized symbols, the lexicon, and a set of rules for combining these symbols, the grammar. Clinical, neuro-imaging, and neurophysiological studies show that these two groups of skills rely upon different operational mechanisms and neural substrates. Aphasic patients with anterior (frontal) lesions mainly show grammatical problems, while patients with posterior (temporo-parietal) lesions present with prominent lexical deficits (Goodglass 1993). This compartmentalization of functions may be even more selective. Dysfunction of specific semantic categories supports the notion of dissociations at the lexical level. Patients have been reported with a differential impairment in retrieving abstract versus concrete words (Tranel et al. 1997), living things versus inanimate objects (Silveri et al. 1997), animals, fruits and vegetables (Hart et al. 1985), and proper names (Semenza and Zettin 1989). A recent neuro-imaging study in both neurological patients and normal controls has shown that different parts of the left temporal lobe are responsible for the retrieval of words describing different entities. In particular, the left temporo-parietal lobe was involved in the task of naming persons, the left infero-temporal lobe in the task of naming animals, the posterior part of the left infero-temporal lobe in naming tools. Thus, lexical retrieval by category partly depends on multiple regions of the left cerebral hemisphere, located not just within the classic language areas but also in higher-order association cortices (Damasio et al. 1996). Grabowski et al. (1998) have shown that also in specific parts of the left frontal lobe there are different patterns of activation evoked by the task of retrieving words for animals, tools, and single persons. Moreover, brain-damaged subjects who show modality-specific deficits restricted to verbs in oral and written production, have been described (Caramazza and Hillis 1991).

Dissociations within the syntactic system have been found in patients affected by William's syndrome (WS), a neurodevelopmental disorder of genetic origin characterized by serious nonverbal deficits and minor linguistic deficits mostly involving lexico-semantic analysis. Further analysis of the syntactic skills of these patients demonstrates the following: intact syntactic processing for those tasks where the subject had to check the presence of a target word that could or could not constitute a syntactic error; impaired syntactical processing for tasks such as a sentence-picture test, where the subject heard a spoken sentence and had to choose from a range of pictures the one corresponding to the sentence (Karmiloff-Smith et al. 1998).

Neurophysiological studies using spectral analysis of EEG signals (Preissl et al. 1995; Pulvermuller et al. 1996) have shown that nouns and verbs have distinct neuronal generators in the intact human brain. Verbs elicit activity mainly at recording sites over the motor cortices. Nouns elicit stronger responses bilaterally at sites over posterior cortical areas. Hints at the neural representation of the two major vocabulary classes, that is, content (open-class) words and function (closed-class) words in individuals with no brain damage have been obtained from the analysis of electrocortical activity evoked by these stimuli (Pulvermüller et al. 1995). It appears that potentials evoked by function words are more negative in the left hemisphere than in the right. No asymmetrical distribution was found for potentials evoked by content words. This suggests that neuronal assemblies corresponding to function words are strongly lateralized in the left hemisphere and primarily located in the perisylvian region, while assemblies related to content words correspond to neuronal assemblies equally distributed over both hemispheres.

A similar result has been obtained by means of another event-related brain potentials study, in which detection of syntactic anomalies evoked a N400-like negative wave predominantly over the anterior scalp, with a preponderance over the left hemisphere. By contrast, detection of semantic anomalies was accompanied by a much more widespread negativity, which reached a peak over the posterior temporal areas (Rosler et al. 1993).

4. Neural and Functional Interactions between Specific Aspects of Language and Memory

Both language and memory are best described by breaking them down into subsets; thus, the search for functional and neural analogies between these two functions should take into account possible preferential links between specific aspects of language and memory. The acquisition of human vocabulary, for example, seems to be related to verbal components of the working memory. In fact, the verbal working memory is deemed to be involved in language acquisition in children and in late learners of first and second languages, but only plays a secondary role in retaining sequences of familiar words (Baddeley 1998; Baddeley et al. 1998). There is no general consensus on the studies assessing the relationship between aphasia and memory. In any case, aphasia does not seem to affect all aspects of memory. Studies on aphasics report impairment of verbal components of working memory only (Caspari et al. 1998). Beeson et al. (1993) describe deficits of both short-term and long-term memory in individuals with stroke-induced aphasia as compared to demographically matched controls and also attribute short-term deficits to posterior lesions and long-term memory deficits to anterior lesions. However, studies comparing short-term and long-term memory in a large sample of aphasic and non-aphasic left-brain damaged patients have shown that aphasia was associated only to verbal short-term memory impairment (Burgio and Basso 1997).

By using functional neuro-imaging techniques, Gabrieli et al. (1998) examined the possible common role of the anterior and inferior portion of the left prefrontal gyrus in specific aspects of language and memory. It emerged that this area is particularly active in tasks of semantic generation of words and in tasks involving an efficient encoding process that ensues in superior explicit memory. By contrast, this area was less active in nonsemantic analysis and deactivated in implicit memory tests.

5. Different Memory Systems may Mediate Learning and Implementation of Different Aspects of Language

To the purpose of the present chapter, the issue of the existence of distinct neural bases for declarative and nondeclarative aspects of language is particularly relevant. This may sound counterintuitive at first because awareness of what has been learned, typically accompanying explicit, declarative knowledge, is largely, if not entirely, mediated by language. There is evidence, however, supporting the notion that the different aspects of lexicon and grammar may reflect the distinction between explicit and implicit knowledge. It is largely acknowledged that we are not aware of some aspects of language, such as those related to syntax (Pinker 1994). Developmental studies show, for example, that children are proficient in grammatical tasks in spite of their limited lexical knowledge (Parkin 1997; Levy 1997). This notion reminds us of the ontogenetic trend observed for implicit and explicit memory. Anterograde amnesic patients can learn grammatical elements of a foreign language in spite of their severe inability to explicitly learn new words even in their mother tongue. Another possible analogy between implicit memory and syntax resides in their relatively fixed nature. Open-class (content) words, which mostly convey semantic information, may have to do with explicit memory; by contrast, closed class, that is, function words, which primarily convey grammatical information, and rules are thought to be related to implicit memory. Indeed, learning and using syntactic rules in a natural context are typically impervious to conscious analysis. In a series of studies performed by means of electrophysiological techniques (Event-Related brain Potentials, ERPs), Neville and co-workers reported that morphosyntax is affected by maturational constraints on nondeclarative memory, while lexicon is not. The first study (Neville et al. 1992) evaluated electrocortical activity evoked by closed-class words, mainly conveying grammatical information, and open-class words, which mainly provide semantic information. Monolingual English-speakers and deaf bilinguals whose mother tongue was the American sign language and with English as the second language (learned later on in life and imperfectly) were tested. Brain activity related to semantic processing was distributed over the left temporo-parietal lobe and was similar in the two groups. By contrast, brain activity during grammatical processing was distributed over the anterior left hemisphere in the monolingual hearing subjects but no asymmetry was observed in the deaf, bilingual subjects. In a subsequent research (Weber-Fox and Neville 1996), Chinese (mother tongue)/English (second language) bilinguals were asked to read English sentences that included semantic anomalies or different types of syntactic errors. Subjects were grouped according to age of exposure to the second language. While grammatical processing seemed to be affected by late exposure to the second language, semantic processing was not. On the whole these results suggest that functional specialization for grammatical processing is much more sensitive to the age of exposure than semantic processing. It should be borne in mind that implicit memory systems mature much earlier than explicit memory systems. The different critical periods for grammar and lexicon may reflect developmental differences between implicit and explicit memory. Studies on first and second language acquisition also support the notion that morphosyntactic abilities may have to do with nondeclarative learning and memory (Paradis 1994).

Evidence in favor of the hypothesis that grammatical processing is linked to the left frontal areas (including Broca's area) and basal ganglia while lexi-

cal processing is linked to the left temporal and parietal lobes has been provided by Ullman et al. (1997). These authors examined patients with explicit memory impairment and lesions to the declarative memory systems (Alzheimer's disease, patients with posterior aphasia), as well as patients with implicit memory deficits and associated damage to the frontal lobe/basal ganglia system (Parkinson's disease, patients with anterior aphasia). All subjects were tested in simple linguistic tasks that investigated into grammatical and lexical processing separately. Results showed that Alzheimer patients and posterior aphasic patients showed deficits in lexical processing, while the other two groups presented with considerable grammatical problems. That the frontal lobe/basal ganglia system has to do with grammar is also suggested by the case of a patient with bilateral damage to the putamen and the caudate nucleus. This patient had problems in understanding differences in meaning conveyed by syntax in English sentences; however, he performed within normal scores in tests of lexical access and explicit memory (Pickett et al. 1998). This has been further confirmed by the case of a patient with a lesion centered in the left basal ganglia, that led to a long-lasting aphasia for the first language but spared a later-learned second language (Aglioti et al. 1996).

6. Conclusions

Memory and language are each organized in multiple systems accounting for different functions and relying upon different neural substrates. Declarative memory involves conscious memory for facts and events (explicit memory); the establishment of new declarative memories appears to be linked to the hippocampal-medial temporal lobe and diencephalic structures; these memory traces are possibly stored in domain-specific regions of the cerebral cortex. Nondeclarative forms of memory do not involve conscious recollection and are measured through changes in performance that cannot be articulated (implicit memory). These forms of memory are mainly related to anterior cerebral cortices and to the basal ganglia or other subcortical structures.

The different aspects of language rely upon separate neural systems, lexicon being mainly related to temporo-parietal areas and syntax to frontal lobes and related subcortical structures. There is some evidence supporting the notion that lexicon is at least partly subserved by declarative systems, while grammar (morphosyntax) is at least partly subserved by nondeclarative memory systems. While the implicit memory/grammar system seems to be related to the frontal lobe/subcortical structures, the explicitly memory/lexical system is possibly mainly subserved by the hippocampal-mesiotemporal-parietal system. However, given the complexity of this issue, further research is necessary. Integrating neuropsychological techniques, neuro-imaging and event-related potentials with other techniques (i.e., transcranial magnetic stimulation) may extend the analysis of the operational mechanisms and neural substrates subserving syntax and implicit memory on the one hand, and lexicon and explicit/declarative memory on the other.

Bibliography

Aglioti S, Beltramello A, Girardi F, Fabbro F 1996 Neurolinguistic and follow-up study of an unusual pattern of recovery from bilingual subcortical aphasia. *Brain* 119: 1551–64

Baddeley A 1998 Recent developments in working memory. *Current Opinion Neurobiology* 8: 234–38

Baddeley A, Gathercole S, Papagno C 1998 The phonological loop as a language learning device. *Psychological Review* 105: 158–73

Bachevalier J 1990 Ontogenetic development of holistic and memory formation in primates. *Annals New York Academy Science* 608: 456–77

Bachevalier J, Mishkin M 1984 An early and a late developing system for learning and retention in infant monkeys. *Behavioural Neuroscience* 98: 770–84

Beeson P M, Bayles K A, Rubens A B, Kaszniak A W 1993 Memory impairment and executive control in individuals with stroke-induced aphasia. *Brain and Language* 45, 253–75

Burke D M, Mackay D G 1997 Memory, language, and ageing. *Philosophical Transactions Royal Society London B Biological Sciences* 352: 1845–56

Burgio F, Basso A 1997 Memory and aphasia. *Neuropsychologia* 35: 759–66

Caramazza A, Hillis A E 1991 Lexical organization of nouns and verbs in the brain. *Nature* 349: 788–90

Caspari I, Parkinson S R, LaPointe L L, Katz R C 1998 Working memory and aphasia. *Brain and Cognition* 37: 205–23

Damasio H, Grabowski T J, Tranel D, Hichwa R D, Damasio A R 1996 A neural basis for lexical retrieval. *Nature* 380: 499–505

DiGiulio D, Seidenberg V M, O'Leary D S, Raz N 1994 Procedural and declarative memory: A developmental study. *Brain and Cognition* 25: 70–91

Gabrieli J D 1996 Memory systems analyses of mnemonic disorders in ageing and age-related diseases. *Proceedings National Academy Sciences USA* 93(24): 13534–40

Gabrieli J D, Poldrack R A, Desmond J E 1998 The role of left prefrontal cortex in language and memory. *Proceedings National Academy Sciences USA* 95(3): 906–13

Grabowski T J, Damasio H, Damasio A R 1998 Premotor and prefrontal correlates of category-related lexical retrieval. *Neuroimage* 7: 232–43

Goodglass H 1993 *Understanding Aphasia*. Academic Press, San Diego, CA

Hart J Jr., Berndt R S, Caramazza A 1985 Category-specific naming deficit following cerebral infarction. *Nature* 316: 439–40

Homberg V, Bickmann U, Muller K 1993 Ontogeny is different for explicit and implicit memory in humans. *Neuroscience Letters* 150: 187–90

Howard D V 1988 Implicit and explicit assessment of cognitive aging. In: Howe M L, Brainerd E J (eds.) *Cognitive Development in Adulthood: Progress in Cognitive Development Research*. Springer-Verlag, New York: 3–37

Karmiloff-Smith A, Tyler L K, Voice K, Sims K, Udwin O, Howlin P, Davies M 1998 Linguistic dissociations in Williams syndrome: evaluating receptive syntax in on-line and off-line tasks. *Neuropsychologia* 36: 343–51

Kelley W M, Miezin F M, McDermott K B, Buckner R L, Raichle M E, Cohen N J, Ollinger J M, Akbudak E, Conturo T E, Snyder A Z, Petersen S E 1998 Hemispheric specialization in human dorsal frontal cortex and medial temporal lobe for verbal and nonverbal memory encoding. *Neuron* 20: 927–36

Levy Y 1997 Autonomous linguistic systems in the language of young children. *Journal of Child Language* 24: 651–71

McDonald J L 1997 Language acquisition: the acquisition of linguistic structure in normal and special populations. *Annual Review Psychology* 48: 215–41

Mishkin M, Suzuki W A, Gadian D G, Vargha-Khadem F 1997 Hierarchical organization of cognitive memory. *Philosophical Transactions Royal Society London B Biological Sciences* 352: 1461–67

Neville H J, Mills D L, Lawson D S 1992 Fractionating language: Different neural subsystems with different sensitive periods. *Cerebral Cortex* 2: 244–58

Paradis M 1994 Neurolinguistic aspects of implicit and explicit memory: implications for bilingualism and SLA. In: Ellis N (ed.) *Implicit and Explicit Learning of Languages*. Academic Press, London, 393–419

Parkin A J 1993 Implicit memory across the life span. In: Graf P, Masson E J (eds.) *Implicit Memory: New Directions in Cognition, Development, and Neuropsychology*. Erlbaum, Hillsdale, NJ, 191–207

Parkin A J 1997 The development of procedural and declarative memory. In: Cowan N, Hulme C (eds.) *The Development of Memory in Childhood*. Psychology Press, Hove, 113–37

Pickett E R, Kuniholm E, Protopapas A, Friedman J, Lieberman P 1998 Selective speech motor, syntax and cognitive deficits associated with bilateral damage to the putamen and the head of the caudate nucleus: a case study. *Neuropsychologia* 36: 173–88

Pinker S 1994 *The Language Instinct*. Penguin, Hammondsworth

Preissl H, Pulvermuller F, Lutzenberger W, Birbaumer N 1995 Evoked potentials distinguish between nouns and verbs. *Neuroscience Letters* 197: 81–83

Pulvermüller F, Lutzenberger W, Birbaumer N 1995 Electrocortical distinction of vocabulary types. *Electroencephalography Clinical Neurophysiology* 94: 357–70

Pulvermüller F, Preissl H, Lutzenberger W, Birbaumer N 1996 Brain rhythms of language: Nouns versus verbs. *European Journal Neurosciences* 8: 937–41

Rosler F, Putz P, Friederici A, Hahne A 1993 Event-related brain potentials while encountering semantic and syntactic constraint violations. *Journal of Cognitive Neuroscience* 5: 345–62

Schacter D L, Tulving E 1994 What are memory systems of 1994? In: Schacter D L, Tulving E (eds.) *Memory Systems*. MIT, Cambridge 1–38

Sherry D F, Schacter D L 1987 The evolution of multiple memory systems. *Psychological Review* 94: 439–54

Semenza C, Zettin M 1989 Evidence from aphasia for the role of proper names as pure referring expressions. *Nature* 342: 678–79

Silveri M C, Gainotti G, Perani D, Cappelletti J Y, Carbone G, Fazio F 1997 Naming deficit for non-living items: Neuropsychological and PET study. *Neuropsychologia* **35:** 359–67

Smith E E, Jonides J, Koeppe R A 1996 Dissociating verbal and spatial working memory using PET. *Cerebral Cortex* **6:** 11–20

Smith E E, Joined J, Marshuetz C, Koeppe R A 1998 Components of verbal working memory: Evidence from neuroimaging. *Proceedings National Academy Sciences USA* **95(3):** 876–82

Squire L R, Zola S M 1996 Structure and function of declarative and nondeclarative memory systems. *Proceedings National Academy Sciences USA* **93(24):** 13515–22

Squire L R, Zola S M 1997 Amnesia, memory and brain systems. *Philosophical Transactions Royal Society London B Biological Sciences* **1352:** 1663–73

Taylor L B 1969 Localization of cerebral lesions by psychological testing. *Clinical Neurology* **16:** 269–87

Thompson R F, Kim J J 1996 Memory systems in the brain and localization of a memory. *Proceeding National Academy Sciences USA* **93(24):** 13438–44

Tranel D, Damasio H, Damasio A R 1997 A neural basis for the retrieval of conceptual knowledge. *Neuropsychologia* **35:** 1319–27

Tulving E 1972 Episodic and semantic memory. In: Tulving E, Donaldson W (eds.) *Organization of Memory*. Academic Press, New York

Tulving E 1987 Multiple memory systems and consciousness. *Human Neurobiology* **6:** 67–80

Ullman M T, Corkin S, Coppola M, Hickok G, Growdon J H, Koroshetz W J, Pinker S 1997 A neural dissociation within language: evidence that the mental dictionary is part of declarative memory, and that grammatical rules are processed by the procedural system. *Journal of Cognitive Neuroscience* **9:** 266–76

Weber-Fox C M, Neville H J 1996 Maturational constraints on functional specialization for language processing: ERP and behavioural evidence in bilingual speakers. *Journal of Cognitive Neuroscience* **8:** 231–56

Rehabilitation of Acquired Language Disorders

G. Demeurisse

In nonprogressive brain injury, the usefulness of acquired language disorders rehabilitation is a less and less debated point. However, during the last few decades, empiricism has prevailed regarding the methods used in order to improve communication in aphasic patients. This chapter is a review of the main methods currently used and attempts at suggesting possible answers to questions frequently asked by the patient or by relatives concerning evolution and prognosis. Lastly, the foundations of the pathophysiology of clinical improvement will be briefly recalled.

Attempts to treat patients suffering from speech or language disorders had been already made in the second half of the nineteenth century. The first approaches, influenced by the observation of language development in normal children, involved exercises (repetition, spelling of words, etc.) based on one and the same paradigm: trial, error, correction, and repetition. The development of aphasic rehabilitation seems to gain effective momentum after the Second World War. The methods proposed were influenced by the concepts of that time about aphasia and the organization of language. In a classical way, aphasic patients are usually ascribed to clinical syndromes on the basis of the analysis of their clinical picture, pointing out which language modalities (verbal expression, verbal comprehension, reading, writing) are impaired and in which way. In certain classification systems (for instance, the *Western Aphasia Battery*), there is even a forced choice, the patient being always ascribed to an aphasic syndrome on the basis of the assessment of fluency, comprehension, repetition, and naming. However, language disorders cannot always be easily classified according to classical syndromes. Nevertheless, the knowledge of the functional anatomy of language has supported the syndromic approach by showing close relationships between the main classical aphasiological syndromes and the localization of brain lesions. At present, classical neurolinguistic evaluation methods still aim at pointing out which language abilities are preserved and at describing aphasic symptoms (without really explaining them). Consequently, traditional speech and language therapies are mainly focused on specific deficits or symptoms. Unfortunately, clustering patients into syndromes does not provide information about the underlying nature of the relevant language disorder. Further developments in cognitive neuropsychology will contribute to fill this gap by showing which component is impaired in a neuropsychological model of the language.

1. Methods

Various rehabilitation methods have been used so far. Traditional methods seek to improve language recovery itself. However, language is only one part of the communication process, which includes all forms of verbal and nonverbal communication. Besides, for a given individual, the consequences of the occurrence of aphasia are not merely restricted to the linguistic field.

As a rule, any disease may give rise to several consequences which have been classified in 1980 by the World Health Organization (WHO). The WHO had invited as consultant Dr. Philip Wood of Manchester. He proposed a three-dimensional concept classification: the *International Classification of Impairments, Disabilities, and Handicaps* (ICIDH) according to which a disease might produce consequences at three different levels (Wood 1980). Impairment is any loss or abnormality of psychological, physiological, or anatomical structures or functions. This impairment may give rise to a disability, that is, a reduction in or lack of ability to perform an activity in a way which is considered normal for a human being. A given disability may give rise to a handicap, that is, a disadvantage in an individual that limits or prevents the fulfillment of a role which is considered normal for that particular individual. Regarding aphasia, impairment corresponds to the language disorder itself, whereas disability corresponds to difficulties in communication by means of oral or written language during daily activities. Handicap depends on many factors (professional, sociocultural, etc.) and concerns various situations (e.g., impossibility to work, to take part in social life, etc.). The handicaps correlated to a given disability may vary across different individuals.

The goals of language rehabilitation may be situated at different levels. Rehabilitation may attempt to obtain a restitution of the linguistic behavior at the pre-morbid state, or to develop a new functional organization likely to use structures which were not primarily concerned with language functions, or to develop non-verbal communication behavior with a more pragmatic approach. Before undertaking treatment, a neurolinguistic evaluation has to be performed. The first evaluation aims at possibly determining which linguistic abilities are preserved, while making an inventory of possible disturbing aphasiological symptoms. The evaluation also aims at establishing the linguistic profile of the patient in relation to so-called aphasiological syndromes. The assessment should include an evaluation of spontaneous speech and of the performance at specific tests (naming, repetition, evocation of semantic categories, etc.). Generally, early evaluation is incomplete, an extensive assessment being rarely feasible soon after brain injury. Subsequent assessments should be more detailed.

1.1 Traditional Treatments

Traditional treatments seek to individualize stimuli and facilitation methods best suitable to recover a 'normal' linguistic behavior. The treatment involves training with repetitive exercises. Like language, aphasia is thus considered as a whole, made of different components (auditory comprehension, verbal expression, reading, and writing). Any of these components might be usefully stimulated or facilitated in a stimulus-response paradigm. Nevertheless, given that most aphasic patients present auditory comprehension disorders, generally exercises seek to obtain first a sufficient improvement in verbal comprehension, which seems to be an obligatory step before attempting to recover other language components. These traditional treatments mainly seek to obtain a restitution of impaired linguistic behavior. Another way to approach language therapy considers possible disturbing aphasiological symptoms. The therapy will focus in this case on the most severe and blatant symptoms: stereotypies, recurring utterances, perseverations, etc. The first step is to make the patients aware of their symptoms. The next step consists in performing tasks in which they have to take voluntary decisions in order to inhibit and control the disturbing symptom. For instance, two methods related to this concept are the treatment of word-finding difficulties using self-generated cues (Berman and Peele 1967) and the treatment of perseverations developed by Helm-Estabrooks et al. (1987).

The observation of normal language development in children has lead to a more 'didactic' approach to therapy. The first stage aims at specifying which linguistic components are disturbed or preserved. The next stage involves a relearning process akin to methods used at school to learn a foreign language. A method pertaining to this concept is the *Systematic Therapy Program for Auditory Comprehension Disorders* (STAC) by Prins et al. (1987). Patients with verbal comprehension deficits undergo a relearning program involving successive stages in a hierarchic way, starting with nonverbal tasks and ending with verbal tasks at morpho-syntactic level.

Some therapists did attempt to systematize the treatment of the patients by means of structured programs. As a rule, the patient has to perform step by step successive tasks of increasing difficulty (Holland 1970). Depending on the success of the patient for a given level of difficulty, it is possible to increase or decrease the complexity of the task. These programmed instruction methods are frequently supported by audiovisual and computerized materials.

The different approaches evoked so far are individual and based upon the concept according to which it is possible to retrain and relearn impaired language components. As a rule, exercises of increasing complexity shift from concrete to abstract tasks and from automatic to voluntary performances. The rehabilitation program is built up around the surface features of the clinical picture (for a more detailed inventory of these methods, see Methé et al. 1993).

1.2 Cognitive Approaches

Recent developments in cognitive neuropsychology have contributed to clarify some underlying mechanisms involved in the cognitive functioning of the brain, leading to the elaboration of models of normal cognitive functioning. In these models, the cognitive treatment process is organized in a modular way. Cognitive psycholinguistics thus seek to detect which component of the model is preserved or affected in an individual case. For instance, naming difficulties, which frequently occur in aphasic patients, may be provoked by an impairment of different cognitive components situated at different levels (semantic system, speech output lexicon, phoneme level). The application of the cognitive approach to language rehabilitation is of great interest, since it allows to be built up personalized rehabilitation programs based on theoretical models of language organization in healthy subjects and on the assessment of the impaired or lost mechanisms accounting for a given aphasiological symptom. It is on this mechanism that the treatment has to focus, eventually looking at developing new compensatory strategies at the cognitive level. Cognitive therapies have been used first in the rehabilitation of written language disorders (for a review of the literature, see Plaut 1996).

A growing trend in the literature concerns the development of therapies centered on lexical semantic disorders which are frequently observed in aphasic patients. Semantic therapies were described by Howard et al. (1985), Marshall et al. (1990), and Nickels et al. (1996). More recently, a new method (BOX) has been proposed by Visch-Brink et al. (1997). The development of this method is based on a two-fold rationale. At first, lexical semantic impairment may provoke disorders involving expression and comprehension of oral and written language, the lexical semantic system being the central part of language processing models (Ellis and Young 1988). Second, the lexical semantic system has to be distinguished from the visual semantic system (Warrington and Shallice 1979). The lexical semantic program proposed by Visch-Brink et al. (1997) seeks to improve language production and comprehension in patients with lexical semantic disorders. The first step consists in determining which patients present an impairment at this level of language organization. In most classical neurolinguistic evaluation batteries, lexical semantic impairment is not really considered in a specific way. This gap is filled by more recent test batteries such as the *Psycholinguistic Assessment of Language Processing in Aphasia* (PALPA) (Kay et al. 1992) and the *Semantic Association Test* (SAT) (Visch-Brink and Denes 1993). As opposed to the first semantic therapies involving among others word-picture matching tasks, in BOX the stimuli are theoretically only graphemic and the tasks are centered around the judgment of semantic links not only between written

words, but also between sentences and texts. Silent reading is sufficient. Language production is not required (but not impeded), and the responses are nonverbal. The patient has to make semantic decisions in different types of exercises presenting various levels of difficulty. According to Visch-Brink et al. (1997), before starting with such a therapy, several requirements are needed: a good general physical condition, good concentration and motivation, absence of major verbal memory deficits, relatively intact or only slightly disturbed written comprehension. Lexical semantic therapy seems hardly suitable for global aphasics. According to Avent (1997), it is appropriate for moderately to mildly impaired patients. The material might be also presented to patients with more severe written comprehension disorders if the therapist reads aloud the stimuli, thus using oral and written input modalities. The first results suggest that semantic processing therapy using semantic association tasks might be more efficient than word-picture matching tasks. In addition, transfer to spontaneous speech of the observed improvement might possibly be greater than with other therapies.

Generally speaking, the cognitive approach is promising. Unfortunately, it is rather time-consuming: a detailed cognitive analysis is unlikely to be possible in each case in order to work out a personalized therapeutic program. Nevertheless, one may hope that a better knowledge of the cognitive processes in normal subjects will lead to a modification of the general therapeutic behavior, either to obtain a restitution of the impaired language ability, or to contribute to establish compensatory strategies.

1.3 Improving General Communicative Skills

Some compensatory strategies are probably subserved by the involvement of abilities pertaining to the right hemisphere: melody, rhythm, mood, etc. The *Melodic Intonation Therapy* (MIT) (Albert et al. 1973; Sparks and Holland 1976) and the *Laughter Therapy* (Potter and Goodman 1983) are based on these right-sided functional specializations. Among these methods, the first one is the most widespread and consists in 'speaking' with an accentuated prosody induced by the combination of a melodic component (output) and of a rhythmic task (tapping with the hand). By theoretically stimulating the unaffected hemisphere (which might have some latent language abilities), these methods seek to obtain an improvement in communication which had not been achieved with more classical methods. MIT proved to be an efficient method for deblocking in case of mutism or severely reduced verbal output.

The various methods evoked so far mainly aim at improving the impaired or lost language function by means of compensatory strategies. Unfortunately, there is no systematic transfer of the improved language abilities (as assessed with a classical neurolinguistic evaluation battery) to spontaneous daily life language.

However, language is not the sole means of communication between individuals. Some rehabilitation methods seek to improve communication in general, using a more pragmatic approach. Referring to the ICIDH concept, these methods attempt to reduce disability (and possibly handicap) and not impairment. Usually, speech therapists opt for such an approach in case of failure of the other methods. However, language therapy and a more global communication therapy might also be used at the same time. Among these methods, the *Functional Communication Treatment* (Aten et al. 1982) aims at improving communication effectiveness using any means of communication in situations akin to or miming daily living activities. The *Promoting Aphasic's Communicative Effectiveness* (PACE) method is more widely used (Davis and Wilcox 1981). Communication as a whole is encouraged in the course of a dialogue between patient and therapist. The three main aspects of this dialogue are exchange of information, alternance of roles, and multimodal means of communication. In this kind of rehabilitation, there is no attempt to try to relearn or retrain language skills.

The pragmatic approach of the treatment also accounts for the use of either combined individual and group therapy, or group therapy alone. A group is usually made of one speech therapist and about five aphasic patients. Group therapy mainly aims at improving general communicative skills using any means, thus reducing the severity of disability and handicap. Although not directly involved in the therapy itself, associations of aphasics might also contribute to lessen the handicap by improving social integration.

The starting point of the rehabilitation of aphasic patients is a detailed neurolinguistic examination, as well as an inquiry concerning the personal situation of the patient (years of school attendance, diplomas, professional and social contexts, knowledge of different languages, hand preference, etc.). The subsequent choice of a specific therapeutic method is often arguable since it is based either on theoretical considerations, or on *a priori* decisions. Only treatment established according to a cognitive approach seems to be based on real scientific foundations. However, some methods seem to be more suitable to peculiar clinical pictures (e.g., the use of the MIT in case of long-lasting mutism). But, more generally, for a given clinical syndrome, no method proves to be clearly superior as opposed to another. Besides, it is hard to know which patient will respond best to which method.

Several speech therapists suggest that the therapeutic approach has to take into account the time elapsed since onset (Rothi and Horner 1983). During the first weeks (following stroke or head trauma), stimulation methods might be more suitable. Sub-

sequently, the goal of rehabilitation would be to relearn the impaired linguistic abilities and/or to develop compensatory strategies. Later on, the rehabilitation should aim at a global improvement of communication. The attitude of other therapists is less unambiguous. On the basis of their experience, depending on their clinical feelings, according to the circumstances and whatever the time elapsed since onset, stimulation and relearning methods might be used straightaway, without excluding other methods if necessary (e.g., inhibition of perseverations). Preserved linguistic abilities are at best used (e.g., intensive use of relatively preserved written language in a patient with more severe oral language disorders). Afterwards, if language improvement is considered as insufficient, therapies attempting to improve functional communication as a whole will be used (e.g., PACE).

The outstanding questions concerning the choice of a given rehabilitation method might be related to fundamental unsolved issues concerning the anatomo-functional bases of the pathophysiology of clinical recovery. This point will be evoked later in this chapter. The efficiency of the various rehabilitation methods is a crucial point which will not be considered here, since it will be treated in another chapter of this volume (see *Acquired Disorders of Language (Aphasia): Evaluation of the Effectiveness of Intervention*).

1.4 Pharmacological Treatment

The idea according to which pharmacotherapy might contribute to the improvement of cognitive disorders is not recent. Growing knowledge of the biochemistry of the central nervous system has led to identification of the specific role of different neurotransmitters, consequently leading to the development of a pharmacotherapy based on a rational approach. Concerning aphasia, a critical review of different drugs which can possibly contribute to improve language performances has been published by Small (1994). In vascular cases, improvements have been observed after the administration of Propanolol, d-Amphetamine, and Bromocriptine. In further studies, Bromocriptine was found to be ineffective for the treatment of chronic nonfluent aphasia (Gupta et al. 1995; Sabe et al. 1995; Ozeren et al. 1995). In a recent study (Tanaka et al. 1997) involving only four patients with fluent aphasia and anomia, it has been suggested that Bifemelane (a cholinergic agent) might improve both naming and comprehension.

Nootropic drugs represent another category of pharmacologic agents. Aphasic patients (n = 67) have been studied using the Aachen Aphasia Test (AAT) at baseline (6 to 9 weeks after stroke), and 5 and 12 weeks post-onset. All patients underwent rehabilitation and received either Piracetam 4.8 g/day or a placebo. After a 12-week treatment with Piracetam, a significant overall improvement has been observed

(Enderby et al. 1994). In another recent study, aphasic patients (n = 50) in whom the stroke had occurred 4 weeks to 36 months previously, have been followed by means of the AAT for a period of 6 weeks. Intensive language therapy was associated with the administration of either Piracetam 4.8 g/day or a placebo. Piracetam appeared to have a positive effect (Huber et al. 1997). So far, the administration of a nootropic agent seems to be the most promising approach. However, drug therapy has to be considered as an adjunct to language therapy.

1.5 Psychological Treatment

Irrespective of the methods used in the rehabilitation program, the psychological consequences of physical disability are often insufficiently taken into account. It is a common observation that the linguistic performances of an aphasic patient are strongly influenced by nonlinguistic parameters, either related to the patient himself (anxiety, depression, etc.), or to the surroundings (context of the conversation, presence of several persons, etc.). In order to try to influence in a positive way some of these parameters, different techniques may be used. As a rule, they attempt to reduce or manage stress, anxiety, and physical tension. Different relaxation techniques including biofeedback (Balliet et al. 1986), progressive relaxation by Jacobson (Marshall et al. 1976), and more recently sophrology (Bachy 1997) have been used in aphasic patients. Positive effects on linguistic abilities have been described. Sophrology sessions may be carried out either in group or individually. Generally, group therapy is started at first and will then be followed by individual sessions tailored to situations peculiar to the patient. It is worth mentioning that such an approach cannot be applied to all aphasic patients, since it requires first a sufficient level of auditory comprehension allowing the patient to follow the orders, and second the absence of major verbal memory deficits, because successive orders need to be tested as well.

The occurrence of a severe impairment and above all of a disability has important consequences for the patient, but also on life partners, near relatives, and friends, because it disrupts relations between these individuals. The respective roles inside the family often undergo important changes. The relationships of relatives or friends may be quite different, ranging from overprotection to rejection which, albeit rare, can be dramatic. Therefore, it is desirable to involve relatives and/or other close-related persons in the rehabilitation of the patient, in order to take advantage of their help to reduce the severity of the disability and handicap. In some cases, a psychological support to the patient's relatives might be necessary.

2. Questions Related to Recovery and Prognosis

In the course of the contacts with close relatives or life partners, several questions have to be asked. Among others, early information about the prognosis, the length of the treatment, the duration of hospitalization, and even of the pathological condition will generally be asked for. These questions may lead to tracing at this stage the general pattern of the pathological evolution following nonprogressive brain lesions. The possible evolution is obviously closely related to the etiology of the overt language disorders. As a rule, patients with post-traumatic aphasia might have a better prognosis than patients suffering from a stroke. However, as strokes are the most important cause of localized brain injury in European and North American countries, it is intended to focus on the general pattern of recovery of aphasia following a stroke (without taking into account possible effects of language or drug therapy). Various factors are likely to influence recovery from aphasia. Some of them are biographic or contextual. They may have an effect on the evolution of the impairment, and also on the degree of disability and ultimate handicap. Such factors are motivation and thymic state, general clinical conditions, sociocultural level, age, appropriateness of the behavior of life-partners, and so on.

2.1 Pattern of Language Recovery

It has been generally observed that a notable recovery occurs during the first months after onset, the greatest improvement taking place during the first 3 months (Sarno and Levita 1971; Kertesz and McCabe 1977; Demeurisse et al. 1980; Lendrem and Lincoln 1985). The degree of improvement generally decreases with passing time. However, a slight degree of recovery may still be observed even 2 years after stroke. The recovery period has often been divided into at least two stages, referring to different pathophysiological mechanisms of clinical improvement in these periods. The length of the period of 'spontaneous recovery' varies, according to different authors, from the first weeks to the first months after onset. Further improvement is likely to be more specifically related to language therapy. Irrespective of that, it is believed that speech therapy should be started as soon as possible in order to take advantage of the early period after onset, during which the most important progress is usually observed, and to try to avoid the occurrence or the increase of disturbing symptoms (e.g., sterotypies). According to a meta-analysis by Whurr et al. (1997), therapy by a trained language therapist should last at least 2 months. However, experience suggests that much longer therapies are as a rule needed to bear some success. Mazzoni et al. (1995) suggest that the length of treatment is a crucial factor of its effectiveness.

2.2 Factors Influencing Prognosis

2.2.1 Severity of language disorders

Literature data concerning the prognosis are often confusing, since the term 'prognosis' may, according to different authors, refer either to the final outcome or to the recovery rate (i.e., the degree of improvement). Early assessment of the prognosis is a hazardous task. In aphasic stroke patients, the final outcome can be deduced to a certain extent from the severity of language disorders at an early assessment. Patients with severe global aphasia usually show a poor evolution and consequently have a poor outcome (Kertesz and McCabe 1977; Demeurisse et al. 1980; Mazaux et al. 1995). In anomic aphasia, language disorders are generally mild, thus restricting the potential for further recovery. In the other aphasiological syndromes, the mean degree of recovery is rather similar whatever the initial severity of aphasia might be (Demeurisse et al. 1980), and there are high correlations between early and late assessment of the severity of language disorders (Demeurisse et al. 1985; Wade et al. 1986; Capon 1996). Consequently, in these cases, the severity of the initial clinical picture has proved to provide a good estimate of the final outcome. Except for severe global aphasia and for mildly affected patients, the initial clinical assessment unfortunately does not provide useful information on the recovery rate.

2.2.2 Size and localization of lesions

The development of *in vivo* imaging techniques prompted some authors to search for a possible contribution of these methods to provide additional information regarding the prognosis (final outcome and/or recovery rate). The difficulty to confront clinical (aphasiological) and instrumental data is due to the fact that most studies concern patients presenting not only language disorders, but also other deficits (e.g., hemiplegia). Nevertheless, useful information can be drawn from the comparative analysis of clinical and technical data. Only the techniques that are currently available to most clinicians will be further considered in the following paragraphs. Computerized tomography (CT-scan) and more recently magnetic resonance imaging (MRI) have delivered precise data on the size and the localization of lesions. As a rule, after the acute stage, large lesions are correlated to severe language disorders and a poor final outcome (Kertesz et al. 1979; Demeurisse et al. 1985; Kertesz 1988; Goldenberg and Spatt 1994). However, this only applies to cortico-subcortical lesions; in deep-seated lesions not involving the cortex, such correlation have not been observed (Demeurisse et al. 1985).

As far as clinical evolution is concerned, in a population involving various aphasiological syndromes, the rate of recovery of verbal expression disorders has been inversely correlated to the size of the cortico-subcortical lesion (Demeurisse et al. 1985), suggesting that rate of recovery of verbal expression might depend on the integrity of some left hemisphere structures. In another study in which language was assessed with the *Aachen Aphasia Test*, the lesion size was also nega-

tively correlated to the degree of improvement (Goldenberg and Spatt 1994).

Regarding the location of left hemisphere lesions, damage to the superior temporal area has repeatedly been correlated to a poor outcome in patients suffering from Wernicke's aphasia (Naeser et al. 1987; Kertesz et al. 1993). Besides, in such patients and according to Kertesz et al. (1993), a poor recovery rate has been associated with the additional involvement of the supramarginal and angular gyri. More generally, in a small population involving different aphasiological syndromes, damage to basal temporal regions seemed to have a negative effect on the recovery rate (especially on improvement related to language therapy). The site of such lesions might lead to a disconnection between neocortical association areas (perisylvian language areas) and the hippocampus, with consequent deficits in learning and memory (Goldenberg and Spatt 1994). The analysis of morphological data (lesion size and localization) is thus useful in that it provides additional information regarding the final outcome and in some degree the recovery rate.

2.2.3 Functional methods

Some functional methods might also bear information concerning the prognosis. Quantitative electroencephalography (qEEG) has been used in order to look at possible relationships between the importance of qEEG abnormalities and the clinical evolution or final outcome. As a rule, the delta activity and the importance of language disorders decrease with time, but no correlation has yet been found between instrumental and clinical data. Consequently, qEEG is not a useful technique to predict the degree of clinical improvement or even the final outcome (Capon 1996).

Isotopic methods measure the cerebral blood flow (CBF) and/or brain metabolism and were expected to yield valuable information in patients with localized brain injury. Measurements were first performed with bidimensional techniques. Using the 2d. 133 xenon inhalation method, a severe and extended cortical hypoperfusion was observed in the left hemisphere of patients presenting with severe global aphasia. But, in an unselected population (comprising various aphasiological syndromes) or even in a homogeneous group of Broca's aphasics, no significant correlation was shown between, on the one hand, left mean *CBF* values and, on the other hand, the rate of clinical recovery (between 2 weeks and 3 months after onset) or the outcome at 3 months from onset. Nevertheless, in Broca's aphasics, there was a trend in favor of a more significant clinical progress when the area of cortical hypoperfusion was small (Demeurisse et al. 1984). However, more generally, 2d. CBF measurements at rest do not provide crucial additional information concerning the prognosis.

Single-photon emission computed tomography

(SPECT) provided more accurate isotopic data which, depending on the tracer used, concern CBF or metabolism. Unfortunately, in most studies clinical assessments were not focused on language disorders and involved either global neurological scales or scales assessing functional disabilities. As a rule, a poor final outcome was correlated to the presence of an extended area of decreased isotopic activity. No useful information was provided concerning the recovery rate.

All in all, the isotopic studies do not yield useful data, especially regarding the assessment of the rate of further language improvement. However, the studies evoked so far were performed on patients at rest. Now, a rather promising approach consists in measuring CBF or metabolism during the performance of verbal tasks. Unfortunately, such functional studies are time-consuming and consequently cannot be used as routine tests. In other respects, it cannot be excluded that Positron Emission Tomography (PET) might provide useful information. However, at present, this expensive technique is not available to most clinicians and therapists involved in the treatment of aphasics.

3. Pathophysiology of Clinical Improvement

Difficulties in establishing an early prognosis might be related partially to the contribution of different mechanisms to clinical recovery at the cognitive and anatomo-functional levels. Besides, in each individual case, the respective contribution of these mechanisms to the functional restoration of langauge and communications remains undetermined. Early recovery takes place in the first weeks after onset. During this period, at the anatomo-functional level, the mechanisms which might contribute to clinical improvement are the disappearance of cerebral edema and of intracranial hypertension, the reabsorption of blood and the normalization of the hemodynamic situation in ischemic penumbra areas. Besides, other mechanisms subserve clinical improvement throughout the whole recovery process. For example, a cortical functional reorganization involving structures, not primarily and directly involved in normal language functions, might also take place. This vicarious phenomenon might occur even at the early stage of clinical improvement, probably by bringing into play silent synapses (either by release of previous inhibition or by increase of synaptic efficiency). Synaptogenesis, axonal, and collateral sprouting could theoretically also play a role after the first stage of recovery. However, these phenomena are very limited in space and their contribution to clinical improvement in patients remains hypothetical. Finally, release from possible diaschisis might also play a role in the pathophysiology of clinical improvement.

Bibliography

Albert M, Sparks R, Helm N 1973 Melodic intonation therapy for aphasia. *Archives of Neurology* **29:** 130–31

Aten J L, Caligiuri M P, Holland A L 1982 The efficacy of functional communication therapy for chronic aphasic patients. *Journal of Speech and Hearing Disorders* **47:** 93–96

Avent J 1997 The merits of BOX: How does it stack up? *Aphasiology* **11:** 1078–83

Bachy S 1997 *Aphasie et relaxation: l'effet de la sophrologie sur deux patients aphasiques présentant un manque du mot.* Mémoire de licence en logopédie, Faculté des Sciences Psychologiques et de l'Education, Université libre de Bruxelles

Balliet R, Levy B, Blood K 1986 Upper extremity sensory feedback therapy in chronic cerebrovascular accident patients with impaired expressive aphasia and auditory comprehension. *Archives of Physical Medicine and Rehabilitation* **67:** 304–10

Berman M, Peele L M 1967 Self-generated cues: a method for aiding aphasic and apractic patients. *Journal of Speech and Hearing Disorders* **32:** 372–76

Capon A 1996 Quantitative EEG with brain mapping in strokes: Is it useful for prognosis? *Brain Topography* **9:** 77–82

Davis G A, Wilcox M J 1981 'Incorporating Parameters of Natural Conversation in Aphasia Treatment'. In: Chapey R (ed.) *Language Intervention Strategies in Adult Aphasia.* Williams and Wilkins, Baltimore, MD, 169–93

Demeurisse G, Capon A, Verhas M 1985 Prognostic value of computed tomography in aphasic stroke patients. *European Neurology* **24:** 134–39

Demeurisse G, Demol O, Derouck M, De Beuckelaer R, Coeckaerts M J, Capon A 1980 Quantitative study of the rate of recovery from aphasia due to ischemic stroke. *Stroke* **11:** 455–58

Demeurisse G, Verhas M, Capon A 1984 Resting CBF sequential study during recovery from aphasia due to ischemic stroke. *Neuropsychologia* **22:** 241–46

Ellis A, Young A 1988 *Human Cognitive Neuropsychology.* Erlbaum, Hove

Enderby P, Broeckx J, Hospers W, Schildermans F, Deberdt W 1994 Effect of Piracetam on recovery and rehabilitation after stroke: A double-blind, placebo-controlled study. *Clinical Neuropharmacology* **17:** 320–31

Goldenberg G, Spatt J 1994 Influence of size and site of cerebral lesions on spontaneous recovery of aphasia and on success of language therapy. *Brain and Language* **47:** 684–98

Gupta S R, Micoch A G, Scolaro C, Moritz T 1995 Bromocriptine treatment of nonfluent aphasia. *Neurology* **45:** 2170–73

Helm-Estabrooks N, Emery P, Albert M L 1987 Treatment of aphasic perseveration (TAP) program: A new approach to aphasia therapy. *Archives of Neurology* **44:** 1253–55

Huber W, Willmes K, Poeck K, Van Vleymen B, Deberdt W 1997 Piracetam as an adjuvant to language therapy for aphasia: A randomized double-blind placebo-controlled pilot study. *Archives of Physical Medicine and Rehabilitation* **78:** 245–50

Holland A 1970 Case studies in aphasia rehabilitation using programmed instruction. *Journal of Speech and Hearing Disorders* **35:** 377–90

Howard D, Patterson K E, Franklin S, Orchard-Lisle V, Morton J 1985 The treatment of word retrieval deficits in aphasia: a comparison of two therapy methods. *Brain* **108:** 817–29

Kay J, Lesser R, Coltheart M 1992 *Psycholinguistic Assessment of Language Processing in Aphasia* (PALPA). Erlbaum, Hove

Kertesz A 1988 What do we learn from recovery from aphasia? In: S G Waxman (ed.) *Advances in Neurology, vol 47: Functional Recovery in Neurological Disease.* Raven Press, New York, 227–92

Kertesz A, McCabe P 1977 Recovery patterns and prognosis in aphasia. *Brain* **100:** 1–18

Kertesz A, Harlock W, Coates R 1979 Computer tomographic localization, lesion size, and prognosis in aphasia. *Brain and Language* **8:** 34–50

Kertesz A, Lau W K, Polk M 1993 The structural determinants of recovery in Wernicke's aphasia. *Brain and Language* **44:** 153–64

Lendrem W, Lincoln N 1985 Spontaneous recovery of language in patients with aphasia between 4 and 34 weeks after stroke. *Journal of Neurology, Neurosurgery, and Psychiatry* **48:** 743–48

Marshall J, Pound C, White-Thomson M, Pring T 1990 The use of picture/word matching tasks to assist word retrieval in aphasic patients. *Aphasiology* **4:** 167–84

Marshall R, Mary T, Watts M 1976 Relaxation training: Effects on the communicative ability of aphasic adults. *Archives of Physical Medicine and Rehabilitation* **57:** 464–67

Mazaux J-M, Lion J, Barat M 1995 *Rééducation des hémiplégies vasculaires de l'adulte.* Masson, Paris

Mazzoni M, Vista M, Geri E, Avila L, Bianchi F, Moretti P 1995 Comparison of language recovery in rehabilitated and matched, non-rehabilitated aphasic patients. *Aphasiology* **9:** 553–63

Methé S, Huber W, Paradis M 1993 Inventory and classification of aphasia rehabilitation methods. In: Paradis M (ed.) *Foundations of aphasia rehabilitation.* Pergamon Press, Oxford, 3–60

Naeser M A, Helm-Estabrooks N, Haas G, Auerbach S, Srinivasan M 1987 Relationship between lesion extent in 'Wernicke's area' on computed tomographic scan and predicting recovery of comprehension in Wernicke's aphasia. *Archives of Neurology* **44:** 73–82

Nickels L, Best W 1996 Therapy for naming deficits (part I): principles, puzzles and progress. *Aphasiology* **10:** 21–47

Ozeren A, Sarica Y, Mavi H, Demirkiran M 1995 Bromocriptine is ineffective in the treatment of chronic nonfluent aphasia. *Acta neurologica belgica* **95:** 235–38

Plaut D 1996 Relearning after damage in connectionist networks: Toward a theory of rehabilitation. *Brain and Language* **52:** 25–82

Potter R, Goodman N 1988 The implementation of laughter as a therapy facilitator with adult aphasics. *Journal of Communication Disorders* **16:** 41–48

Prins R S, Schoonen R, Vermeulen J 1989 Efficacy of two different types of speech therapy for aphasic stroke patients. *Applied Psycholinguistics* **10:** 85–123

Rothi L J, Horner J 1983 Restitution and substitution: Two theories of recovery with application to neurobehavioral treatment. *Journal of Clinical Neuropsychology* **5:** 73–81

Sabe L, Salvarezza F, Garcia-Cuerva A, Leiguarda R, Starkstein S 1995 A randomized, double-blind placebo-controlled study of bromocriptine in nonfluent aphasia. *Neurology* **45:** 2272–74

Sarno M T, Levita E 1971 Natural course of recovery in severe aphasia. *Archives of Physical Medicine and Rehabilitation* **52:** 175–78, 186

Small S 1994 Pharmacotherapy of Aphasia. A Critical Review. *Stroke* **25:** 1282–89

Sparks R, Holland A 1976 Method: Melodic intonation therapy for aphasia. *Journal of Speech and Hearing Disorders* **41:** 287–97

Tanaka Y, Miyasaki M, Albert M 1997 Effects of increased cholinergic activity on naming in aphasia. Lancet **350:** 116–17

Visch-Brink E G, Denes G 1993 A European base-line test for word picture processing. In: Stachowiak F J, De Bleser R, Deloche G, Kaschell R, Kremin H, North P, Pizzamiglio L, Robertson I, Wilson B (eds.) *Developments in the Assessment and Rehabilitation of Brain-Damaged Patients.* Gunter Narr Verlag, Tübingen, 211–16

Visch-Brink E G, Bajema I M, Van de Sandt-Koenderman M E 1997 Lexical semantic therapy: BOX. *Aphasiology* **11:** 1057–115

Wade D, Langton Hewer R, David R, Enderby P 1986 Aphasia after stroke: Natural history and associated deficits. *Journal of Neurology, Neurosurgery and Psychiatry* **49:** 11–16

Warrington E, Shallice T 1979 Semantic access dyslexia. *Brain* **102:** 43–63

Whurr R, Lorch M, Nye C 1997 Efficacy of speech and language therapy for aphasia: A meta-analytic review. *Neurology Reviews International* **1:** 9–13

Wood P 1980 *International Classification of Impairments, Disabilities and Handicaps.* World Health Organization, Geneva

Acquired Disorders of Language (Aphasia): Evaluation of the Effectiveness of Intervention

R. Whurr and M. Lorch

Aphasia is one of the most devastating human experiences. It results in a disruption of communication as a consequence of brain injury. Speech and language therapists serve to ameliorate the consequences of the language disorders through a variety of techniques. This chapter describes the condition, considers its implications for the individual, and discusses the treatments that have been employed. Developments in research methodology have provided new opportunities for demonstrating the effectiveness of particular types of intervention.

1. What is Aphasia? Definition

Aphasia (or dysphasia) is defined as a communication disorder caused by brain damage and characterized by complete or partial impairment of language comprehension and language production. It excludes language disorders or language disability associated with primary sensory (hearing or vision) deficits, movement problems, general attentional, emotional, cognitive or mental difficulties, or psychiatric disorders. Both children and adults are affected. Developmental dysphasia/aphasia refers to language difficulties that appear in the course of child language acquisition. Acquired aphasia/dysphasia is the term used to distinguish language disorders in cases where language has already been acquired (Crystal 1987).

2. Classification of Aphasia

Aphasia can vary in severity from extreme impairment in all aspects of communication to mild difficulty with a single aspect. Although most clinical forms of aphasia were described before 1900, there is still no universal classification. Diverse classification systems have been used to describe aphasia focusing on different aspects of impairment and performance.

Terminological confusion persists due in part to the multidisciplinary interest in the subject (clinical, physiological, and behavioral), but also due to the diversity of philosophical theories that have been drawn upon. There has been a tendency either to overclassify, giving rise to a proliferation of subtypes of aphasia, or underclassify using, for example, binary systems to distinguish between expression and comprehension of language. Divisions such as sensory/motor, expressive/receptive, fluent/nonfluent, anterior/posterior are used. Although these dichotomies are appealing in their simplicity, they provide a restricted view of the range of linguistic behavior. Terminological confusion is compounded by appeals to anatomically-based vs. psychologically-based models, and the disparate traditions of localizationist/specialization vs. generalist/holism. Recently there have been attempts to characterize the language impairments in aphasia in terms of linguistic levels (Crystal 1982; Lesser 1978; Whurr 1987; see *Neurolinguistic Assessment of Aphasia*).

The most common classification in use is provided by the 'Boston School' (Goodglass and Geschwind 1976). This classification focuses on patterns of language impairments in multiple modalities and relative severity of each aspect. The following types of aphasia are recognized: Broca's aphasia, Wernicke's aphasia, Conduction aphasia, Anomic aphasia, Transcortical Motor aphasia, Transcortical Sensory aphasia, Global aphasia, and mixed aphasia. There can also be pure types of acquired reading (alexia/dyslexia) or writing (agraphia/dysgraphia) disorders (see *Syndromes of Aphasia*).

All the classification systems aim to cluster patients into syndrome groups based on the presenting symptomatology. This is founded on the assumption of homogeneity within syndromes. Researchers have challenged the value of syndrome-based classification and argue that there is considerable heterogeneity in aphasic behavior (Baedecker and Caramazza 1985).

3. Causes of Aphasia

Aphasia is always the consequence of injury to the brain. The most frequent cause of aphasia is a stroke or cerebrovascular accident (CVA) particularly in the aging population. Brain injury caused by tumor, trauma, or infection may also give rise to language disorders. Differences in pathological processes—focal vs. diffuse damage, acute vs. chronic, and etiology, for example, mechanical, vascular, space occupying, degenerative, neurochemical, will affect the natural history of the aphasia.

4. Incidence and Prevalence

It is estimated that speech or language disorders occur in as many as 40 percent of all stroke patients (Gresham et al. 1995). At least 500 000 people in the USA alone incur strokes each year resulting in 80 000 new cases of aphasia annually (National Institute on Neurological Disorders and Stroke 1990). One third of all severely head-injured persons also have aphasia. Other forms of injury to the brain also result in aphasia due to diseases that affect the language areas of the brain.

5. Response to Brain Injury

The main neurobiological mechanisms traditionally thought to mediate recovery are vicariation, redundancy, and diaschisis. Vicariation is the hypothesized process whereby an area of the brain not previously involved in the particular function would take over the function of the damaged area. The notion of redundancy assumes that the uninjured neurons in the damaged area function as spare systems that can compensate for those that are nonfunctional. Diaschisis is the term used to describe when brain injury to a certain area acts to inhibit connected, noninjured areas. In this case, recovery consists of the removal of this inhibition and return to normal function.

Empirical evidence for these hypothesized processes of functional responses to brain acute focal damage is mainly negative or equivocal. The mechanisms of neuroplasticity responsible for cognitive recovery after cortical damage are still controversial. However, there appears to be a strong relationship between neuroplasticity and recovery (Blomert 1998).

The amount of language recovery in aphasic sufferers is dependent on a number of factors:

(a) cause of lesion;
(b) site of lesion;
(c) extent of lesion;
(d) associated nonlanguage deficits affecting memory, attention, vision, motor control, control of emotions, etc;
(e) language and intellectual abilities prior to illness;
(f) personality, temperament, and motivation.

Spontaneous recovery will occur as the body physically recovers from the acute effects of brain damage after suffering a CVA. Cause of lesion can be a major modulating factor in the progression and management of the impairment. Medical treatment of different types of brain damage vary from surgical intervention, radiation therapy, chemotherapy, pharmacological intervention, etc. Speech and language therapy also will vary depending on the type and severity of aphasia. The point at which treatment is begun will affect the outcome.

The consequences of brain damage for the individual are widespread. Typically, there is the physical disability due to loss of sensation and movement in the right leg, arm, and right side of the face. There may also be a variety of other subtle sensory disturbances affecting vision and/or hearing and cognitive disturbances of perception, memory, spatial awareness, etc. The main deprivation, however, is the loss of the uniquely human ability to communicate through language.

6. Psychosocial Impact of Aphasia

Loss of effective communication may result in social isolation, loss of the social role in the family and community, loss of ability to pursue work and therefore loss of income, and increased dependency on others as a consequence. As aphasia affects communication, it is not only a problem for the affected individual but also for the family and community. Roles within the family change as do economic circumstances. The family may feel as isolated as the patient. The additional roles and responsibilities to be taken over by family and friends on behalf of the aphasic person may be a source of stress and social displacement.

Several well-known figures have written about the experience of aphasia. In a letter written on June 19, 1783 three days after a stroke, Samuel Johnson described how a stroke robbed him of his speech. Walter Scott kept an account of his stroke in his diary on January 5, 1826. A recent bibliography has been compiled of the large number of writers who give personal accounts of neurological impairments and aphasia (Kent 1998).

7. New Concepts of Classification

In recent years there has been increasing interest in describing the effects of acquired language disorders using the World Health Organization's (WHO) three part classification scheme. Known as the International Classification of Impairments, Disabilities, and Handicaps (ICIDH), this framework states the consequences of a disorder can be viewed at three separate but related levels or 'planes of experience,' (WHO 1980, 25–29).

In an attempt to reflect these different planes of experience underlying illness-related phenomena, WHO recognizes the following distinctions:

(a) disease;
(b) impairment;
(c) disability;
(d) handicap.

Impairment: 'any loss or abnormality of psychological, physiological, or anatomical structure or function,' that is, dysfunction resulting from pathological changes in the system.
Disability: 'Any restriction or lack (resulting from an impairment) of ability to perform an activity in the manner or within the range considered normal for a human being,' that is, the consequence of impairment in terms of functional performance.
Handicap: 'A disadvantage for a given individual, resulting from an impairment or disability, that limits or prevents the fulfillment of a role that is normal (depending on age, sex, and social and cultural factors) for that individual.'

The schema is not exhaustive. It is restricted to key social roles regarded as indicative of disadvantage—social integration, autonomy, occupation, and economic self-sufficiency. The disadvantages experienced by the individual as a result of impairment and disabilities reflects the interaction with, and the adaptation to, the individual's surroundings. According to the ICD classification, handicap is classified according to the circumstances in which disabled people are likely to find themselves. These circumstances may place such an individual at a disadvantage in relation to their peers when viewed from the norms of society (Wood 1980; WHO 1980, 1992, 1993).

8. Assessment and Intervention

A detailed discussion of the construction and standardization of aphasia language batteries can be found in Whurr (1996). Traditional aphasia batteries focussed on the assessment of impairment. The Boston Diagnostic Aphasia Exam (BDAE) (Goodglass and Kaplan 1983) is in general use and many other aphasia batteries are derived or modified forms of this (see Whurr 1988, for discussion).

The BDAE assesses sample speech and language behavior on a six-point ordinal scale. It assesses fluency, naming, word finding, repetition, serial speech, auditory comprehension, reading, and writing. Another widely used test is the Porch Index of Communicative Ability (PICA) (Porch 1981). The

PICA employs a 16-point multidimensional scale with mean scores by modality for auditory comprehension, visual comprehension, written expression, verbal expression, and pantomime. The PICA's utility is limited to sampling single words and sentences.

There are a large number of tools for the measurement of language disability, focussing on communicative functioning, pragmatic profiles, discourse, and/or conversational analysis. In contrast, the measurement of language handicap, that is, quality of life measures, is rarely directly assessed (see *Neurolinguistic Assessment of Aphasia*).

9. Goals of Treatment

The goals of treatment for aphasia are defined by the AHCPR Guidelines for Post Stroke Rehabilitation (Gresham et al. 1995) as:

(a) to reinstate or remediate the aphasic's ability to speak, comprehend, read, and write;
(b) to assist the patient in developing strategies which compensate for, or circumvent, language problems;
(c) to address associated psychological problems that compromise the patients' and their families' quality of life;
(d) to help the family and other involved individuals to communicate with the patient.

Intervention involves the active processes of treatment/therapy/reeducation and management that aim to rehabilitate, restitute, and restore function after the loss of the function. The success of these endeavors can be evaluated by measuring the results or outcome of the intervention. The value of the gains achieved by the intervention to the recipient of the intervention, is judged as the efficacy of the intervention.

10. Types of Treatment

Various approaches employed in aphasia draw on modern developments in medicine (especially neurology), psychology, linguistics, and education. Howard and Hatfield (1987) provide a comprehensive account of various theories and therapeutics of aphasia therapy from the ancient Egyptians, through the Middle Ages to the late eighteenth century. They discuss the philosophical and psychological disputes in the nineteenth century that in turn influenced the aphasia therapy conducted in the early twentieth century.

In the nineteenth century, most of the therapy was conducted by neurologists. At that time, few patients would survive a stroke or head injury for any length of time. Therefore, the population of chronic aphasic patients requiring rehabilitation was limited. Nineteenth- and early-twentieth-century treatment methods for aphasia were similar to the educational techniques employed in teaching normal children. These techniques were based on didactic speech gymnastic drills utilizing synthetic methods. The intention was to re-educate undamaged parts of the damaged

hemisphere or homologous areas of the opposite hemisphere. A turning point in aphasia therapy was the First World War, 1914–18. With improved military medical services many young men with serious head injuries survived, a large portion of whom were aphasic. The development of neuropsychological rehabilitation services for brain damaged soldiers developed first in Germany during and after the First World War, and then in the former Soviet Union and the United States after the Second World War. This laid the foundation for the widespread establishment of civilian treatment services for aphasia sufferers. A variety of treatment techniques were described (Howard and Hatfield 1987).

Since the Second World War, there has been a considerable expansion in the provision of therapy services throughout the West. The modern schools of aphasia therapy began to develop, influenced by theoretical and empirical developments taking place in the fields of linguistics, behavioral, and cognitive psychology investigating the relationship between brain, thought, and language. Attempts were made to devise therapeutic approaches driven by theoretical developments.

In a survey of contemporary approaches to treatment, Howard and Hatfield (1987) identify eight different schools. Each is based on certain assumptions about the process of therapy, and the nature of aphasia:

(a) *Didactic School*: language was re-taught on the traditional patterns of teaching children reading, writing, and grammar;
(b) *Behavior Modification School*: viewed as a relearning process. It is prescriptive and based on how things should be learned and influenced by behaviorist psychology;
(c) *Stimulation School*: the approach is based on the notion that appropriate stimulation enables access to intact language abilities. Developed in the USA by Schuell and Wepman;
(d) *Reorganization of function*: this theory was developed by the Russian neuropsychologist A. R. Luria. It focuses on the use of intact subsystem to bypass those that are impaired;
(e) *Pragmatic School*: proponents view the problems of aphasic individuals to involve all aspects of communication rather than just language. They encourage the use of unimpaired nonlinguistic abilities to compensate for the language deficits;
(f) *Neoclassical School*: based on the Wernicke-Lichtheim model. Developed by American neurologist Norman Geschwind;
(g) *Neurolinguistic School*: this school attempts to incorporate generative linguistic theory into the process of therapy;
(h) *Cognitive Neurophysiological School*: most recently, therapy approaches have been based on explicit information processing models of normal language behavior. Procedures often derived from experimental psycholinguistics. Patterns of success and fail-

ure are interpreted as revealing the functioning of specific language processes.

11. Treatment Techniques

A large number of different techniques are employed by speech and language therapists. The following interventions have been identified by the AHCPR as having been experimentally studied:

(a) modality specific treatments based on traditional stimulus response techniques;
(b) methods that focus on underlying deficits such as perseverative behavior or difficulties with symbol use;
(c) methods that offer compensatory strategies to circumvent existing deficits;
(d) use of alternative and augmentative communication systems;
(e) developmental methods which draw on cognitive neuropsychological models of normal processing;
(f) combined programmatic approaches.

12. Treatment Efficacy

The terms efficacy, effectiveness, and efficiency have often been used interchangeably. However, to an epidemiologist, there is a distinction between efficacy and effectiveness (Muir Gray 1997). The efficacy of an intervention is its impact in the best possible circumstances, whereas effectiveness is used to describe the impact of an intervention in everyday practice. The effectiveness of a healthcare professional or service is the degree to which the desired outcomes are achieved. The quality of the service or intervention is the degree to which it conforms to pre-set standards of care.

Treatment efficacy is a broad term that encompasses several related issues. Does treatment work? Does one type of treatment work better than another treatment? In what way does treatment alter behavior? How does treatment effect recovery?

The notion of treatment efficacy focuses on those improvements in an individual's communication behavior that have resulted from clinical intervention provided by a speech–language pathologist. Efficacious treatment means improvements in communication that exceed that which can be expected by spontaneous recovery following brain damage. Efficacy is typically measured in terms of gains in scores on formal language and communication measures, or changes over initial performance on particular language tasks.

The efficacy of an intervention is its impact in the best possible circumstances in everyday practice. In order to ascertain if a treatment is efficacious assessments must be carried out both before and after the treatment, and comparisons are made between the two assessments. If there is no significant difference between the two assessments, then there is no evidence that the treatment has worked. If improvement from pre-test to post-test is demonstrated, this might be because the specific treatment was efficacious. That

is not the only possible explanation of the superior performance at post-test. There are at least four possible causes of improvement between pre-test and post-test:

(a) *Spontaneous recovery*: particularly if the brain injury is recent, the physical condition of the brain itself may have improved (e.g., by reduction of edema) over the period during which treatment was carried out. In this case, the same improvement would have been seen even if there had been no treatment at all;
(b) *Practice effects on the assessment tests*: many psychometric tests show practice effects. The improved score on the post-test assessment may be due to a practice effect. If so, the same improvement would have been seen even if there had been no treatment at all;
(c) *Nonspecific effects of treatment*: clients' abilities may improve simply through attention, encouragement and support provided by the person providing treatment. Here the improvement is due to the presence of the therapist rather than the particular form of treatment or treatment materials. The assumption is that any situation which provides attention and encouragement would have produced the same results;
(d) *Specific effects of the particular treatment used*: the specific nature of the treatment program used was responsible for the improvements seen in the post-treatment assessment.

Views on the value of intervention for language disorders have fluctuated. Proponents attribute the improvements in linguistic functioning of aphasic patients directly to speech and language therapy, whilst cynics have argued that spontaneous recovery inherent in the individual is responsible for all improvements in performance (Whurr et al. 1992).

Darley (1972) issued three challenges for the successful demonstration of treatment efficacy:

(a) demonstrate and compare the magnitude of change attributable to spontaneous recovery and the magnitude of change attributable to treatment occurring within the period of spontaneous recovery;
(b) appraise the worth of treatment;
(c) compare the potencies of different forms of treatment.

There have been more than 200 published studies on aphasia therapy employing over a thousand subjects and dozens of different methods of treatment since 1946 (Butfield and Zangwill 1946). These studies have included a variety of different research designs—large and small group investigations, well-controlled single subject experimental studies, and single case studies.

There are various arguments favouring different types of research design. Some maintain that the most robust methods for evaluating the efficacy of any treatment is a controlled clinical trial. Alternatively, there are clear arguments against the controlled clinical trial in aphasia due to the heterogeneity of the patients, the treatments, and the insensitivity of the outcome measurements (Howard 1986; Wertz 1995; Holland et al. 1996). Single treatment group design, comparative treatment, treatment versus no treatment, single case designs, withdrawal or ABA design, multiple base line design, alternating treatment design, crossover design, changing criterion design, all have strengths and weaknesses. The value of different research designs for aphasia therapy is still unresolved and the focus of discussion.

13. Clinical Evidence

Clinical evidence is the best available evidence for effective health care. The Therapeutics and Technology Assessment Subcommittee of the American Academy of Neurology (AAN 1994) produced the following classification of research design to assess safety and efficacy:

(a) *Class 1*: evidence provided by one or more well-designed randomized controlled clinical trials;

(b) *Class 2*: evidence provided by one or more well-designed randomized clinical studies such as case-control, cohort studies, and so forth;

(c) *Class 3*: evidence provided by expert opinion, non-randomized historical controls, or one or more case reports.

14. Quality of Evidence

The question of aphasia therapy efficacy was brought into focus initially by a study by Wade and colleagues in 1984. The results of this (nonsystematic) review indicated that the balance of the evidence of effectiveness (as well as the limitations of the evidence) for speech therapy was similar to the other rehabilitation therapies.

Examination of the quality of aphasia therapy research has been a focus of attention in both British and American journals. *The British Journal of Disorders of Communication* presented a forum on 'Evaluating Intervention' in 1986 with views expressed by Fitz-Gibbon, Howard, and Pring. More recently the *American Journal of Speech and Hearing Research* (1996), produced a Supplement on Treatment Efficacy by Holland et al. Both reviews highlight problems in evaluating data that is based on such a variety of research designs.

According to Holland and colleagues (1996) 'if one applies the AAN criteria to the available data, it must be concluded that generally, treatment for aphasia is efficacious.' However, the AAN criteria are not based on the systematic evaluation of the quality of evidence but more on the quality of the evidence to assess safety and efficacy. The gradation of Class 1–3 evidence is assessed on the assumption that the most safe and efficacious research design is the well-designed randomized controlled clinical trial (RCT).

15. Research Methodology

An RCT is a trial in which participants are randomly assigned to two groups: the experimental group receiving the intervention that is being tested, and the comparison group or controls receiving an alternative treatment or placebo. The two groups are then followed up to see if any differences between them result. This helps people assess the relative effects of the two interventions.

Howard (1986) and Wertz (1996) conclude that the RCT experiments in aphasia therapy have failed to prove the efficacy of treatment. They argued that RCT is an unsuitable method to assess treatment efficacy in aphasia, promoting the single case method instead. In reply, Fitz-Gibbon (1986) proposed that the large body of data collected in RCT group studies could be utilized for hypothesis generation. Fitz-Gibbon recommended the use of a set procedure that would allow for a systematic summarization of a large body of literature.

16. Systematic Review and Meta-analysis

There are various methods for evaluating the quality of a corpus of published and unpublished research data. The systematic review is a review in which all the trials on a topic have been systematically identified, appraised, and summarized according to predetermined criteria. It can, but does not have to, involve meta-analysis as a statistical method of adding together and numerically summarizing the results of the trials that meet minimum quality criteria. For this reason, systematic reviews are sometimes termed meta-analysis although many systematic reviews do not involve meta-analysis. A meta-analysis is a statistical technique that summarizes the results of several studies in a single estimate. More weight is given to results of larger studies. It is regarded as a valuable retrospective research evaluation technique (Chalmers et al. 1993).

Since the 1970s RCTs have been considered the 'gold standard' in the evaluation of effectiveness and other methodologies such as the case-control study, cohort studies, and surveys have been eclipsed by the RCT. The electronic database developed by the Cochrane Collaborative Review is an example of rigorously evaluated studies based primarily on medically conducted RCTs. Unfortunately, for a variety of reasons, the RCTs conducted on aphasia therapy have failed to prove efficacy of treatment in aphasia (Howard 1986; Wertz 1996, 1998; Greener et al. 1998).

Meta-analysis is a method of systematic data summary and synthesis. It combines results from a range of different studies to calculate the magnitude of the experimental effect, or 'effect size' (ES) of the variables under consideration by different researchers. Its utility is in highlighting gaps in the literature, identifying mediating or interactional relationships that cannot have been hypothesized and tested in individual studies, and suggesting new directions for research. Furthermore, meta-analysis can address such questions as: to what degree is treatment effective? how much improvement can be expected, by whom and under what conditions?

There are two types of meta-analysis depending on the source of the data analyzed: (a) MAL meta-analysis in which the data are abstracted from published papers in the literature, that is, data on groups of patients; and (b) MAP meta-analysis in which the data have been obtained from original single patient data. Meta-analysis is a powerful tool but needs to be treated with caution as systematic reviews can vary in quality and require rigorous appraisal (Muir Gray 1997).

17. Meta-analysis of Aphasia Treatment

Several meta-analytic studies have been conducted on the aphasia therapy published data (Whurr et al. 1992; Robey 1994; Nye et al. 1997; Robey 1997; Whurr et al. 1997; Robey 1998). Although different methodologies were utilized, Whurr and Robey have been largely in concord.

Whurr et al. (1992) examined 166 studies from 1947–88 from the review of 45 papers. In the Whurr et al. (1992) study of 1336 treated subjects, the effect size (ES) of 0.592 indicated that aphasic people who received treatment moved from the 50th to 73rd percentile. This 23 percentile shift indicates that 73 percent of patients who receive treatment improved more than half a standard deviation compared to those who did not receive treatment. This review found that overall speech and language therapy for adult aphasic people yielded positive results.

Summarizing the trends reflected in Whurr et al. (1992), a profile emerged of aphasia treatment and the characteristics of patients being investigated. Eighty-eight percent of the subjects were male, with a mean age of 62 years, typically diagnosed as having mixed receptive–expressive aphasia, referred from a hospital setting. Patients would probably have been evaluated with a language test. They would typically receive individual treatment consisting of multimodality language stimulation in the first 6 months post-illness, of 1 hour per week, lasting on average for 28 weeks. The findings of Whurr et al. (1992) indicate that the greatest response to treatment would occur in the second month provided by a trained speech and language therapist.

Robey (1994) had an initial pool of 48 reports. After exclusions, 21 studies provided sufficient information for inclusion in the analysis. The findings of this study can be summarized as follows:

(a) the effect of treatment beginning in the acute stage of recovery is nearly twice as large as the effect of spontaneous recovery alone;
(b) treatment initiated after the acute period achieves considerably smaller but appreciable effect;
(c) the separation of treated and untreated populations exceeds the criterion value for a medium sized effect when treatment is begun in the acute period;

(d) the separation of treatment and untreated populations in the chronic stage of recovery corresponds to a small medium sized effect.

Robey (1998b) also concluded that the treated patients did better than untreated patients. The most benefit was obtained by at least 2 hours a week of multimodality stimulation treatment. People with severe aphasia benefited more from treatment delivered by trained speech and language therapists as opposed to service deliverers.

A review of the published RCTs in aphasia therapy (Greener et al. 1998) under the auspices of the Cochrane Collaboration was recently completed. Twelve eligible RCT trials were identified. The main conclusion drawn by Greener and colleagues (1998) was that within the context of RCT methodology for evaluating evidence, the value of SLT treatment for aphasia was inconclusive. The reason for this finding was attributed to the lack of complete reporting and poor methodology.

In his 1998b study, Robey identified 479 studies, of which 55 reports of clinical outcome satisfying the essential criteria for meta-analysis were used. Different statistical methods were used in analyzing the data in various papers by Whurr et al. and Robey. In spite of this, both conclude that problems with internal validity and statistical conclusion validity, construct validity, and external validity place limitations on the identification of the source(s) of efficacy (Nye et al. 1997). Whurr and colleagues (1992) pointed out the serious shortcomings of the quality of evidence; few studies fulfilled the basic requirements of experimental design by failing to report crucial data on dependent variables.

Most of the published studies on aphasia therapy since 1946 have failed to report important details. Future researchers are entreated to follow basic criteria when embarking on aphasia treatment research:

(a) specification of subject characteristics entered into trials;
(b) objective, detailed qualitative and quantitative measurement of the type and degree of aphasia in terms of language impairment, disability and handicap;
(c) complete specification of treatment;
(d) complete specification of measurement of outcome.

18. Evidence-based Treatment

Researchers evaluating the effectiveness of speech therapy intervention have had to make judgments based on the 'best available data.' In their evaluation of clinical effectiveness, the clinical standards advisory group (Clinical Standard Advisory Group 1998) reported on clinical effectiveness using stroke care as an example. They found that the existing evidence in this instance is not clear and does not indicate which types of therapy work best. 'Evidence based medicine is the conscientious, explicit and judicious use of current best evidence in making decisions about the care of individual patients. The practice of EBM means integrating individual clinical expertise with best available external clinical evidence from systematic research' (Sackett et al. 1998).

19. Treatment Outcomes

Decisions about what is the best intervention for aphasic patients are now being influenced by the new paradigms of disability, handicap, and impairment developed by the World Health Organization. The perspective of outcomes now encompasses a wide framework. Proposals for key questions about outcomes according to Muir Gray (1997):

(a) how many outcomes were studied?
(b) how large were the effects found?
(c) with what degree of confidence can the results of the research be applied to the whole population?
(d) does the intervention do more good than harm?
(e) how relevant are the results to the local population or service?

20. Conclusions

In the second half of the twentieth century, the measurement and intervention techniques used in the remediation of language disorders attained a certain level of sophistication. From its inception as an offspring of education, the modern field of speech and language therapy has evolved to become a scientifically driven clinical discipline. Clinical evidence has been amassed on the effect of speech and language therapy on aphasic persons. New techniques of systematic review and statistical meta-analysis provide opportunities to assess the retrospective data. New efforts are being made to design empirical studies of treatment efficacy which fulfill research methodology criteria.

Bibliography

American Academy of Neurology 1994 *The Therapeutics and Technology Assessment.* Subcommittee of the American Academy of Neurology

Baedecker W, Carammaza A 1985 On considerations of method and theory governing the use of clinical categories in neurolinguistics and neuropsychology: The case against agrammatism. *Cognition* 20: 277–82

Blomert L 1998 Recovery from Language Disorders: Interaction between Brain and Rehabilitation In: Stemmmer B, and Whitaker H A (eds.) *Handbook of Neurolinguistics.* Academic Press, New York

Butfield E, Zangwill O 1946 Re-education in aphasia; a review of 70 cases. *Journal of Neurosurgery and Psychiatry* 9: 75–79

Clinical Standards Advisory Group 1998 *Clinical Effectiveness Report on Clinical Effectiveness using Stroke Care as an Example.* HMSO, London

Chalmers I, Sandercock P, Wennberg J 1993 The Cochrane Collaboration: Preparing, maintaining, and disseminating systematic reviews of the effects of health care. *Annals of the New York Academy of Sciences* 703: 156–65

Code C, Muller D 1995 *Aphasia Therapy: from Theory to Practice.* Whurr, London

Crystal D 1982 *Profiling Linguistic Disorder.* Edward Arnold, London

Crystal D 1987 *The Cambridge Encyclopedia of Language.* Cambridge University Press, Cambridge

Darley F 1972 The efficacy of language rehabilitation in aphasia. *Journal of Speech and Hearing Research* 37: 3–21

Enderby P 1993 Speech and language therapy for aphasia. *Current Opinion in Neurology* 6: 761–64

Fitz-Gibbon C T 1986 In defence of randomised controlled trials, with suggestions about the possible use of meta-analysis. *British Journal of Disorders of Communication.* 21: 117–24

Friedman C, Demets A (eds.) 1996 *Fundamental Clinical Trials,* 3rd ed. Mosby, St Louis, IN

Goodglass H, Geschwind N 1976 Language Disorders (Aphasia). In: Carterette E C, Friedman M (eds.) *Handbook of Perception,* vol. 7. Academic Press, New York

Goodglass H, Kaplan E 1982 *The Assessment of Aphasia and Related Disorders,* 2nd ed. Lea and Febinger, Philadelphia, PA

Greener J, Enderby P, Whurr R, Grant A 1998 Treatment for aphasia following stroke: evidence for effectiveness. *International Journal of Language and Communication Disorders* 33: 158–61

Gresham G E, Duncan P W, Stason W B et al. 1995 Agency for Health Care Policy and Research *(AHCPR) Guidelines -Post Stroke Rehabilitation. Clinical Practice* Guideline No. 16. AHCPR Publication No. 95-0662 May 1995. US Department of Health and Human Services. Rockville, MD http://www.medlib.com/ahcpr/psrehab/tr001fvn.htm

Holland A, Fromm D, Deruyter F, Stein M 1996 Treatment efficacy: Aphasia. *Journal of Speech and Hearing Research* 39: 27–36

Howard D 1986 Beyond randomised controlled trials: the case for effective case studies of the effects of treatment in aphasia. *British Journal of Disorders of Communication* 21: 89–102

Howard D, Hatfield M 1987 *Aphasia Therapy: Historical and Contemporary Issues.* Erlbaum, London

Kent R 1998 Renewal and Rediscovery: Insights from Memoirs of Illness and Disability (An Annotated Bibliography). *Asha Magazine* 22: Http://www.asha.org/professionals/publications/kent.htm

Lesser R 1978 Linguistic Investigations of Aphasia. Arnold, London

Muir Gray J A 1997 *Evidence-based Healthcare. How to make Health Policy and Management Decisions.* Churchill Livingstone, New York

National Institute on Neurological Disorders and Stroke 1990 *Aphasia: Hope Through Research.* Publication 90–391. Bethesda, MD

Nye C, Lorch M P, Whurr R 1997 The utility of meta-analysis in the determination of efficacy of treatment in aphasia: A reply to Robey (1994). *Brain and Language* 57: 280–82

Porch B 1971 *Porch Index of Communicative Ability.* Consulting Psychologists Press, Palo Alto, CA

Pring T 1986 Evaluating the effects of speech therapy for aphasics and volunteers: developing the single case methodology. *British Journal of Disorders of Communication* **21**: 103–15

Robey R R 1994 The efficacy of treatment for aphasic persons: A meta-analysis. *Brain and Language* **47**: 582–608

Robey R R 1998a On Nye, Lorch, and Whurr (1997). *Brain and Language* **61**: 145–46

Robey R R 1998b A meta-analysis of clinical outcomes in the treatment of aphasia. *Journal of Speech, Language, and Hearing Research* **41**: 172–87

Rose F C, Whurr R, Wyke M (eds.) 1988 *Aphasia*. Whurr, London

Sackett D L, Scott Richardson W, Rosenberg W, Haynes R B 1998 *Evidence-based Medicine: How to Practice and Teach EBM*. Churchill Livingstone, Edinburgh

Wade D, Skilbeck C, Langton Hewer R, Wood V 1984 Therapy after Stroke: Amounts, determinants and effects. *International Rehabilitation Medicine* **6**: 105–10

Wertz R 1995 In: Code C, Muller D. *Aphasia Therapy: From Theory to Practice*. Whurr, London

Wertz R, Collins M, Weiss D et al. 1981 Veterans administration cooperative study on aphasia: A comparison of individual and group treatment. *Journal of Speech and Hearing Research* **24**: 580–94

Whurr R 1987 Towards a linguistic typology of aphasia. In Crystal D (ed.) *Linguistic Controversies*. Edward Arnold, London

Whurr R 1988 The assessment of aphasia. In: Rose C, Whurr R, Wyke M (eds.) *Aphasia*. Whurr, London

Whurr R 1996 *Aphasia Screening Test*, 2nd ed. Whurr, London

Whurr R, Lorch M, Nye C 1992 A meta-analysis of studies carried out between 1946 and 1988 concerned with the efficacy of speech and language therapy treatment for aphasic patients. *European Journal of Disorders of Communication* **27**: 1–17

Whurr R, Lorch M, Nye C 1997 Ethicacy of speech and language therapy for aphasia: A meta-analysis review. *Neurology Reviews International* **1**(3): 9–13

Wood P 1980 The Language of Disablement: a glossary relating to disease and its consequences. *International Rehabilitation Medicine* **2**: 86–92

World Health Organization 1980 *International Classification of Impairments, Disabilities, and Handicaps: A Manual of Classification, Relating to the Consequences of Disease*. World Health Organization, Geneva, 25–29

World Health Organization 1992 *International Statistical Classification of Diseases and Related Health Problems (Icd-10)*. World Health Organization, Geneva

World Health Organization 1993 *International Classification of Impairments, Disabilities, and Handicaps: A Manual of Classification, Relating to the Consequences of Disease*. World Health Organization, Geneva

Language Pathology in Neuropsychiatric Disorders

Autism

S. Baron-Cohen

Autism is often described as the most severe of all of the child psychiatric disorders. Yet, surely each disability is severe in its own way? Autism has gained this reputation because, unlike all other childhood disorders, people with autism appear to be virtually cut off from other people—'in a world of their own.' It is in this sense that autism is also categorized as a psychosis: like schizophrenia, autism appears to be qualitatively unlike anything in the normal range of experience. In contrast, neurotic disorders (such as anxiety or depression) seem closer to experiences in the normal range.

Even the other communication disorders of childhood do not leave the sufferer isolated to quite the same degree as occurs in autism. Thus, although dysphasic disorders of childhood include language comprehension or expression deficits, somehow the social contact between the sufferer and other people is not severed: children with various dysphasias still find some way of making and developing relationships with others—family, teachers, and friends (see *General Aspects of Developmental Language Disorders*). They may use sign language, impoverished speech, or even simply eye contact and gesture. Not so children with autism. For them, even understanding what communication is for seems to be missing. As will be described below, this is part of the social difficulties that lie at the core of autism.

1. What is Autism?

Autism is a psychiatric disorder which begins during the first three years of life (possibly from birth, or even before). It affects approximately four children in every 10 000, although some studies have suggested it may be as common as 15–20 per 10 000. Males are affected three times as often as females, and two-thirds of people with the condition have learning difficulties in addition to the problems specific to autism. That is, two-thirds of children with autism have an IQ (or measured intelligence) below the average range. And even those whose intelligence is in the normal range show an unusual pattern of skills, with visuospatial intelligence usually being superior to verbal abilities.

Various sets of diagnostic criteria exist, but all of these share an emphasis on three key symptoms. First, the child fails to make normal social relationships, or to develop socially in the normal way. Instead, social interests tend to be one-sided, nonreciprocal, and exist only to satisfy the child's immediate wishes. Missing are any genuinely social games (or turn-taking), any attempt to share interests through joint-attention behaviors (such as using the pointing gesture to indicate things of interest to people, or showing people things of interest), normal use of eye contact, or any friendship beyond the most superficial acquaintance. A lack of empathy is often identified as the central feature of the social deficit.

Second, the child fails to develop language or communication in the normal way. This symptom can include a multitude of anomalies. For example, some children with autism are functionally completely mute (see *Mutism*), whilst others are slow learning to speak, and their language development severely limited. Yet others can speak in full sentences, but nevertheless show a range of speech abnormalities, and fail to use their speech appropriately to achieve communication or to use gesture in a normal way. These abnormalities are described in detail later.

The final symptom constitutes repetitive behavior, in conjunction with a lack of normal imagination. Thus, children with autism often carry out the same action over and over again, becoming quite distressed if other people attempt to prevent them from carrying out their repetitive rituals, and their play is often devoid of any apparent creativity or imagination. During play, for example, children with autism often simply arrange objects in strict geometric patterns in the same way every day, rather than transforming objects into *pretend* or symbolic play, as normal children do even from the age of about 18 months.

Tragically, whilst the symptoms may change in form as people with autism get older, and whilst with age a considerable amount of learning may be possible, autism appears to be a lifelong condition. Some claims of 'cures' have been reported, but in none of these cases has recovery to a *normal* state been verified, and in the majority of cases individuals remain 'odd' and obviously disabled in adulthood.

2. Causes

Various causes of autism have been identified, all biological, and all of these are assumed to disturb the normal development of the central nervous system. The major causes for which there is scientific evidence are genetic, perinatal, viral, and a variety of medical conditions.

The genetic evidence centers on the higher concordance rate for autism among monozygotic (i.e., genetically identical) twins, where one has autism, than among dizygotic (i.e., genetically nonidentical) twins, where one has autism. In addition, some 2–3 percent of the siblings of children with autism also develop autism, and this is approximately 50 times higher than one would expect from chance alone. The perinatal evidence centers on the increased risk for autism produced by a range of complications during pregnancy and labor. The viral evidence centers on the statistically significant association between autism and infection by the rubella virus during pregnancy.

Finally, the range of medical conditions which can be associated with autism (and which, in those cases, are assumed to be causal) include genetic disorders (such as Fragile X Syndrome, phenylketonuria, tuberous sclerosis, neurofibromatosis, and other chromosomal anomalies); metabolic disorders (such as histidinemia, abnormalities of purine synthesis and of carbohydrate metabolism); and congenital anomaly syndromes (such as Cornelia de Lange Syndrome, Noonan Syndrome, Coffin Siris Syndrome, William's Syndrome, Biedl-Bardet Syndrome, Moebius' Syndrome, and Leber's Amaurosis).

No single cause has been identified for all cases, and theories suggest there may instead be several separate causes of autism, any one of which may affect the part of the brain that produces the condition. This view has come to be known as the 'final common pathway' hypothesis. Abnormalities have been found in various regions of the brain in different cases, but again none of these are consistent across all individuals with autism. The exception to this is the finding that the cerebellum may show specific atrophy in all cases. This new work remains to be replicated. But the clearest evidence that there is brain dysfunction in autism stems from the fact that some 30 percent of people with autism also develop epilepsy at some stage in their lives. Finally, autism has not been demonstrated to be associated with either poor parenting (contrary to early theories) or social factors (such as class or culture).

3. What are the Language Abnormalities in Autism?

Language abnormalities exist in all of the subsystems of language. In syntax, for example, there can be considerable delays in the rate of acquisition of syntactical forms, although longitudinal studies show that the order of acquisition does not differ to that found either in normal children or children with learning difficulties. Thus, children with autism who develop speech usually go through a one-word and a two-word phase, their 'mean length of utterance' (MLU) usually increases in normal ways, and the syntactical forms used seem to appear in the same order as in normal development. In phonology, intonation can sometimes be rather monotonous and 'mechanical' sounding, but otherwise is often normal, if not superior. Thus, when children with autism produce *echolalia* (echoing someone else's speech), it is often with identical intonation to the person who spoke first (see *Phonological Disorders of Language*).

In semantics, words are clearly referential, but neologisms may be present. Thus, the child may use a word that is not a conventional one, but which nevertheless has a meaning for that child. For example, one boy with autism referred to a cat as a 'milk outside.' When the origin of such neologisms is traced, they are often found to derive from incomplete learning during the first usage of the term. In the example above, the boy's mother often used to say 'Let's put the milk outside for the cat.' Kanner, the psychiatrist who first described autism in 1943, characterized such neologisms in the speech of children with autism as 'metaphorical,' although it is worth stressing that these do not conform to cases of true metaphor. Indeed, semantic abnormalities in the speech of people with autism include difficulties in understanding or creating true metaphors and other forms of figurative language (such as irony or sarcasm).

Other semantic abnormalities are seen in the production of echolalia: these may be either *immediate*, where the person repeats straight back what the other person has just said, or *delayed*, where the person repeats back a segment of conversation that was overheard some time before. In delayed echolalia, the speech echoed may be part of a television jingle, or lyrics from a song, and often testifies to excellent long-term memory in people with autism.

However, of all the language abnormalities in autism, the most severe are in the pragmatics of speech. Almost every aspect of pragmatics that has been studied in people with autism has been found to be abnormal. Thus, the range of *speech acts* that they produce is quite limited—requests being the most frequent, informatives or humorous speech acts being quite rare. They also appear not to realize how to use language in a way that is sensitive to the social context. For example, they tend to say things that are rude, not because of any wilful desire to offend, but simply because they are blind to the polite/rude distinction (e.g., one child with autism correctly noticed but then said out loud 'That woman has dyed her moustache!'). Furthermore, they often do not distinguish old and new information in a conversation, failing to take into account what the listener already knows or does not know. For example, they may repeat things they have already told the listener, or they may refer to things that the listener could not possibly know about, without explaining these. It is also rare for them to introduce their topic so that the listener can appreciate its relevance (e.g., by using phrases such as 'You know I was in France for my holidays, well...').

Another instance of the pragmatics deficit in the language of people with autism is seen in the lack of normal turn-taking in conversation. Instead, they may talk at the same time as the other person, or deliver extended monologues, or simply not reply at all when a reply is expected. This can appear as a failure to recognize the intention behind a question. For example, when asked 'Can you pass the salt?,' a person with autism may simply reply 'Yes.' Such a limited reply is not a sign of wilful rudeness, but simply due to a failure to recognize the question as a request for an object.

The pragmatics deficit is also seen in the use of a pedantic style of language that is inappropriate for the social situation. For example, one girl with autism asked 'Do you travel to work on a driver-only operated number 68 bus?' Also, many people with autism do not establish eye contact with the listener before speaking, or use eye contact to regulate any conversational turn-taking. Finally, some studies have shown that they tend to ask questions to which they already know the answers, thus violating the rules about the conventional uses of different parts of speech.

4. Relationship between the Language and the Social Abnormalities

During the 1960s and early 1970s one major theory of autism argued that the social abnormalities in this disorder were secondary to the language problems. This theory lost credibility when studies compared children with dysphasias (see *General Aspects of Developmental Language Disorders*) and children with autism. Such studies demonstrated that language disabilities did not inevitably produce social disabilities, in that children with even severe dysphasia nevertheless often showed surprisingly intact social skills and sensitivities. In contrast, late twentieth-century psychological theories suggest that language delay is an entirely independent disability which may cooccur in autism, whilst the abnormalities in pragmatic competence are an inevitable consequence of the social disability in people with autism, and are seen in all cases. One such psychological theory is elaborated in Sect. 5.

5. The Mindblindness Theory

In the early 1990s experiments demonstrated that people with autism are severely impaired in their understanding of mental states, such as beliefs and thoughts, and in their appreciation of how mental states govern behavior. This ability in normal people has been referred to as a 'theory of mind'—because of how people use their concepts of other people's mental states to explain their behavior. Attributing mental states such as thoughts, desires, intentions, etc., to other people allows the individual to understand why people do what they do, and in keeping track of both other people's mental states and their own, to mesh flexibly in social interaction.

Apart from using a theory of mind to make sense of the social world, and to participate in it, a second key function of a theory of mind in normal people is to make sense of communication, and to communicate with others. In computing the meaning and relevance of another person's speech the listener constantly takes into account the speaker's background mental state, and in making speech meaningful and relevant to a listener the speaker does the same.

Given these two functions of a theory of mind, it is clear that, if people with autism are unable to appreciate that other people have different mental states, this would severely impair their ability to understand and participate not only in social interaction, but also in communication itself. It is in this sense that the deficits they show in pragmatics are thought to be intimately entwined with their social deficits. This core inability to appreciate other people's mental states has been termed 'mindblindness.' Research is elucidating which mental states are easier to understand (e.g., for people with autism, desire seems to be easier to understand than either pretence or belief); whether this problem constitutes a case of specific developmental delay (in that some children with autism do eventually develop a theory of mind, years after it emerges in normal development); and what the origins of their mindblindness might be.

6. Treatment

Treatment in the 1990s centers on special education for children with autism, and the most effective techniques seem to include highly structured, individually tailored behavior therapy, aimed at skill-building, reducing difficult behaviors, and the facilitation of educational achievements. Other specialist therapies also play important roles, and these include speech and music therapies. Sign languages, such as Makaton or Paget-Gorman, are also used with some children with autism, if speech is particularly limited. However, none of these treatments claims any dramatic success in removing the core social abnormalities, although these may become less intrusive and disabling over time. Medical treatments exist for specific difficulties, such as epilepsy and hyperactivity, but at present there are no medical treatments which are useful in ameliorating the language or social difficulties in people with autism. Current and future research is aiming to find the links between the behavioral, psychological, and biological abnormalities in this condition, as well as seeking to develop more effective treatment and diagnostic methods.

Bibliography

Baron-Cohen S 1988 Social and pragmatic deficits in autism: Cognitive or affective? *Journal of Autism and Developmental Disorders* **18(3)**: 379–402

Baron-Cohen S 1995 *Mindblindness*. MIT Press/Bradford Books, Cambridge, MA

Baron-Cohen S, Leslie A M, Frith U 1985 Does the autistic child have a 'theory of mind?' *Cognition* **21(1)**: 37–46

Frith U 1989 *Autism: Explaining the enigma*. Blackwell, Oxford

Howlin P, Rutter M, et al. 1987 *Treatment of Autistic Children*. Wiley, Chichester

Kanner L 1943 Autistic disturbance of affective contact. *Nervous Child* **2**: 217–50

Tager-Flusberg H, Calkins S, Nolin T, Baumberger T, Anderson M, Chadwick-Dias A 1990 A longitudinal study of language acquisition in autistic and Down's Syndrome children. *Journal of Autism and Developmental Disorders* **20(1)**: 1–22

Schopler E, Mesibov G B 1987 *Neurobiological Issues in Autism*. Plenum Press, New York

Mutism

Y. Lebrun

Mutism is a condition in which there is no, or very little, oral–verbal expression, while comprehension of speech (and possibly also of written language) is normal or, at least, is at a considerably higher level than expressive speech. It is precisely the large discrepancy between the nonexistent or very scanty oral–verbal output and the normal or nearly normal receptive abilities that is characteristic of mutism.

Mutism does not necessarily mean the total absence of sounds produced with the vocal tract. Mute people may make noises either deliberately in attempts to communicate or spontaneously in reaction to various stimuli, for example, pain. But these noises are not speech sounds. Mutism thus refers to the absence of articulate speech. Also, mutism does not imply total lack of self-expression. Mute individuals may use nonvocal systems of communication. In fact, if literate, they often resort to writing.

1. Degree of Intentionality

At times, mutism is totally deliberate. When a prisoner resolves to keep his own counsel and not to answer the questions of those who have captured him, his silence is completely voluntary. Similarly, cloisterers may deliberately refrain from talking in order to commune better with God.

However, silence may also be completely unintentional. Following brain damage, an individual may be unable to express himself orally. He would like to communicate verbally but cannot because an organic lesion prevents him from speaking.

Silence, then, may be fully deliberate or, on the contrary, completely involuntary. Between these two extremes there are intermediate stages where the degree of intentionality is less easy to ascertain.

2. Functional versus Organic Mutism

In clinical practice a distinction is usually made between functional and organic mutism. The diagnostic label 'functional mutism' (or 'psychogenic mutism') is used when an individual cannot bring himself to speak under certain circumstances or in the presence of certain people, or when speech is completely suppressed, although on examination the peripheral speech organs appear normal and no central lesion can be discovered that would reasonably account for the absence of oral–verbal expression. 'Organic mutism' is spoken of when there is an organic lesion that can legitimately be made responsible for the speechlessness.

At times, organicity and functionality combine, as when a patient who, following brain damage, has severe speech difficulties, chooses to remain silent rather than to attempt painstakingly a few words.

Functional mutism is usually subdivided into selective (or elective) mutism and total (or hysterical) mutism.

3. Selective Mutism

Selective mutism denotes a condition in which the individual keeps completely silent in certain places or in the presence of certain people, while he uses speech in other places or when interacting with other people. Patients with selective mutism can use speech for communicative purposes but fail to do so in a number of circumstances where to speak would be the appropriate and expected response. Selective mutism may occur in children and in adults.

3.1 Selective Mutism in Children

In children, it often takes the form of extrafamilial mutism. The child with extrafamilial mutism speaks to his immediate relatives and possibly to a few peers, but to nobody else. Indeed, he may refrain from talking even to his parents and siblings if persons to whom he does not speak happen to be present.

3.2 School Mutism and Classroom Mutism

In some cases selective mutism is observed primarily, if not exclusively, in school. The child uses expressive speech in various places but not within the school premises. Some children with selective mutism will use speech with their schoolmates in the playground but will keep completely silent in the classroom.

3.3 Nonverbal Communication

A number of children with selective mutism are willing to use grunts, nods, and other nonverbal signs to interact with persons to whom they do not talk. Others are reluctant to use even nonverbal communication. Indeed, their faces may remain completely void as if they cannot bear to express themselves facially. These children may also avoid eye contact.

3.4 Written Language

Selectively mute children who master written language are usually prepared to communicate in writing. Indeed, some of them do their schoolwork extremely well as long as it can be done in writing. Therapy for such children therefore may be conducted in writing.

3.5 The Dynamics of Selective Mutism in Children

Selective mutism may have different causes in different children, and in any particular case several factors may be instrumental in bringing about the deviant verbal behavior.

Some children with selective mutism appear shy and restricted outside the family circle. They seem to be using their mutism to keep others at a distance, to reduce the demands of the environment, and to escape competition. In their case, silence is probably an anxiety-reducing strategy. At home, where they feel more at ease and can have a better control of the situation, they use speech actively. Indeed, they may be very talkative.

Selective mutism may also be an expression of the child's objection to being separated from his mother and sent to school. In fact, the lack of expressive speech may be a form of negativism and, at the same time, an attention-gaining device. Not infrequently, the child's reluctance to speak outside the family circle is encouraged by his parents who are unconcerned about the behavior of their offspring, or tacitly

reinforce it. Indeed, some parents are themselves taciturn or, as children, also showed selective mutism.

In addition, the family's social or geographical isolation may contribute to the child's uneasiness and aloofness when he is outside the home. The existence of a secret within the family, of something that should not be revealed to strangers, may also reinforce the child's tendency to keep silent.

3.6 Therapy for Selectively Mute Children

Selective mutism considerably hampers the child's social integration and scholastic achievement. The deviance should therefore be treated.

Essentially two types of therapeutic approach are used with selectively mute children. Some clinicians apply behavior modification techniques and others resort to psychodynamic procedures. Those who use the former approach tackle the symptom directly, and try to eliminate it gradually by means of operant conditioning strategies. In the psychodynamic approach, on the contrary, the causes of the muteness are researched and discussed, using either written language or, in the case of young children, play and drawing. Usually the parents of the patient are also given psychotherapy or, at least, psychological counseling.

3.7 Selective Mutism in Adults

Selective mutism in adults differs from selective mutism in children in that it nearly always manifests itself in relation to one individual or to a small group of individuals, not in relation to an environment. Moreover, in adults selective mutism is generally clearly deliberate. Following some disagreement or quarrel, a person decides no longer to talk to another person. The two people then cease to be 'on speaking terms.' They may write to each other, though, as written language is usually not invested with the same affective and binding value as spoken language.

4. Total Mutism

While in selective mutism the lack of expressive speech is contingent on certain places or persons, in total mutism (also called hysterical mutism), speech suppression is constant. The patient with total mutism keeps silent everywhere, he speaks to nobody. However, if literate, he may express himself in writing.

4.1 The Dynamics of Total Mutism

It is generally agreed that total mutism is a defense mechanism. Having to sustain unbearable stress, the individual retreats into a protective shell of silence. His mutism encapsulates him and enables him to withdraw from a world with which he can no longer cope. It makes a break with the environment possible and disconnects the patient from those around him.

Speech establishes a direct relation between two persons. Specifically, it commits the speaker to his listener. By keeping silent, the patient avoids this personal engagement, this consignment of himself to another person. Silence also guards the individual from disappointment, for, if he does not speak and never asks for anything, he cannot incur rejection, be denied, or turned down.

The patient may also feel that silence enables him to control himself and his environment better. He keeps his mouth shut, lest he should strike out at the others, by refraining from expressing his anger or resentment, he allows it to grow within himself and become extremely powerful. At the same time, by his silence, he denies others access to him. He thus inflicts pain on them and punishes them for whatever wrong they have been doing him.

4.2 Prognosis and Therapy of Total Mutism

If left untreated, total mutism may eventually clear up spontaneously. However, it may also persist and become a permanent component of the individual's makeup.

Persistent mutism, especially in young people, tends to hinder social integration and scholastic and professional achievement. Therefore, it is generally considered desirable to treat it. According to the case and the clinician's biases, various methods may be used. Some therapists resort to hypnosis, others to psychotherapy or psychodrama, still others to mechanical techniques that elicit reflexive coughing. This spontaneous vocal behavior is then gradually shaped into volitional voice production, production of isolated speech sounds, and, finally, connected speech.

Operant conditioning therapy is also used. It ordinarily begins with silent reactions to verbal stimuli. These responses are progressively replaced by grunts, sounds, speech sounds, and, finally, words and sentences.

If mutism occurs in an individual with underdeveloped language skills it may be necessary to give speech therapy once speech production has been deblocked.

5. Organic Mutism

Contrary to functional mutism, organic mutism is due to some physical damage to the body. It results from injury to the peripheral speech organs or to the central nervous system. If the damage is present at birth or is incurred before speech normally starts to develop, organic mutism is said to be developmental. If, on the contrary, organic damage is sustained after the acquisition of speech, mutism is said to be acquired.

6. Acquired Mutism of Peripheral Origin

Acquired mutism of peripheral origin is observed primarily in adults who have undergone laryngectomy. This operation radically modifies the anatomy of the vocal tract and, as a result, the patient has to learn to produce speech in a new way. Several techniques have been developed, the most frequently used substitutes being esophageal speech and speech with an artificial larynx.

7. Developmental Mutism of Central Origin

A number of individuals are born with cerebral lesions or suffer brain damage early in life, as a consequence of which they are prevented from acquiring the ability to speak. If they develop verbal comprehension while remaining unable to talk, they are considered to have developmental mutism of central origin.

7.1 Cerebral Palsy

Due to severe motor impairment a number of cerebral palsied individuals are unable to utter understandable words and to produce legible script. However, as their intelligence is not affected, they master language internally. They can understand spoken and written language and, if given an appropriate equipment, such as a special typewriter, they can express themselves in writing. These patients have developmental mutism of central origin (see *Developmental Dysarthrias*).

7.2 Developmental Motor Aphasia

Some children are unable to acquire speech although their speech musculature, in contradistinction to that of cerebral palsied patients, is not spastic and does not evidence involuntary, uncontrollable contractions. They may also be unable to learn to whistle or to blow their nose, or to clear their throat or puff up their cheeks deliberately. Indeed, volitional and coordinated activation of the oropharyngeal and laryngeal musculature is generally precluded.

Although it may not be age appropriate, these patients' comprehension of speech is adequate for everyday interaction. Moreover, some command of written language can usually be achieved.

The patients' scores on psychometric tests are ordinarily somewhat below the norm. This slight mental handicap may in part be due to the lack of oral–verbal expression, in particular the inability to ask questions (see *General Aspects of Developmental Language Disorders*).

This condition is sometimes referred to as 'developmental motor aphasia' or 'congenital motor aphasia' and others may even designate it as 'developmental apraxia' although, in the author's opinion, this last term is not entirely satisfactory. The Germans speak of 'Hörstummheit' (meaning audio-mutitas or hearing mutism), which stresses the fact that the absence of oral–verbal output is not due to a hearing impairment.

8. Acquired Mutism of Central Origin

This type of organic mutism may occur as a consequence of any one of a variety of neurological diseases which temporarily or durably suppress the voluntary innervation of the speech musculature. Depending on the condition that causes it, it may come about suddenly or, on the contrary, represent the final stage of a progressive dysarthria (see *Acquired Dysarthrias*).

Suppression of speech may be due to paralysis of the speech musculature, as in the opercular syndrome. The main feature of this disease is a very severe reduction of the voluntary motility of labial, oral, pharyngeal, and at times also laryngeal, muscles. Due to flaccid paralysis, the lips, tongue, and mandible can hardly be moved deliberately. As a consequence, mastication is hampered and speech is precluded.

Bulbar palsy is another condition that impairs speech movements. The disease is often progressive, with the patient being at first dysarthric and then becoming gradually speechless.

Other neurological disorders cause widespread motor impairment. If this impairment is severe and extends to the speech musculature, the patient is rendered mute. As an example, the locked-in syndrome may be quoted. This dramatic condition results from severance of the fibers connecting the motor cortex with the peripheral musculature and/or to the nuclei of cranial nerves involved in articulation. Except for a few isolated movements, such as blinking, the patient is unable to move any part of his body intentionally. In some cases, elementary communication can be achieved by having the patient use eyelid movements to answer yes–no questions.

Akinetic mutism is another condition in which voluntary movements are abolished. However, contrary to individuals with the locked-in syndrome, patients suffering from akinetic mutism are not paralyzed or else they have motor deficits that cannot completely account for the absence of movements. The pathological mechanism responsible for the patients' immobility is not yet fully understood.

Mutism can also be an accompaniment of such neurological conditions as pseudobulbar palsy, multiple sclerosis, and motor neurone disease. It may at times be observed in the initial, acute phase of speech apraxia (see *Verbal Apraxia*). Organic mutism, with or without hypokinesia, may also result from damage to the periaqueductal gray matter in the midbrain, or to the cingulate cortex of the frontal lobes.

Patients with Parkinsonism may evidence permanent or intermittent mutism. The latter form of speechlessness is sometimes called 'paradoxical mutism.'

Transitory mutism may occur after callosotomy (i.e., surgical transection of the corpus callosum in an effort to improve intractable epilepsy), as well as after surgery in the fossa posterior of the skull (especially in children). During epileptic fits without loss of consciousness or during migrainous spells the patient may be rendered temporarily mute. He understands what he is told but he cannot speak.

8.1 Anarthria and Aphemia

A number of clinicians use the term 'anarthria' to denote complete speechlessness occurring without comprehension impairment as a consequence of brain damage. In other words, they use it as a synonym of 'organic mutism of central origin.' Others speak of anarthria in severe cases of dysarthria, that is, in cases where the voluntary innervation of the speech musculature is so drastically reduced, or the speech muscles so spastic, that the patient is unable to utter words.

Still others, primarily in French-speaking countries, use the word 'anarthria,' or rather 'anarthrie,' as an equivalent of 'speech apraxia,' regardless of whether the patient is totally unable to speak or speaks with difficulty. Pierre Marie, who pioneered the use of 'anarthrie' in the French neurological literature, applied it to a variety of acquired disorders of oral–verbal expression occurring without noticeable impairment of comprehension or of writing. Accordingly, the phrase 'anarthrie de Pierre Marie' (Pierre Marie's anarthria), which is sometimes used by French authors, is ambiguous. The synonymous phrase 'pure anarthria' is no less equivocal.

The same holds true in respect of the term 'aphemia.' Paul Broca introduced the French word 'aphémie' to denote a severe disorder of oral–verbal expression without paralysis of the speech musculature and unaccompanied by comprehension, reading, or writing difficulties. The patient could be totally mute or produce a recurrent utterance whenever he attempted to speak. In fact, Broca's description resulted from the observation of a patient who could only say 'Tan,' which he would utter a few times in succession whenever he tried to express himself orally.

In the early 1990s, the term aphemia was used by some aphasiologists to refer to (acquired) organic mutism of central origin, especially when they wanted to emphasize the absence of concomitant comprehension difficulties and possibly also the preservation of written expression. Others tended to speak of aphemia when the patient had no or little verbal output and evinced no or few comprehension difficulties.

9. Therapy for Patients with Organic Mutism

Permanent organic mutism is a very incapacitating condition that makes the patient a prisoner within himself and deprives him of part of his human inheritance. Accordingly, no therapeutic effort should be spared to help the patient acquire or recover the faculty of speech. If this proves impossible, an alternative system of communication should be developed that enables the patient to express himself.

Bibliography

Kratochwill T 1981 *Selective Mutism: Implication for Research and Treatment*. Lawrence Erlbaum, Hillsdale, NJ
Lebrun Y 1990 *Mutism*. Whurr, London

Language Disorders in the Psychoses

L. C. Sanfilippo and R. E. Hoffman

1. Introduction

One of the devastating consequences of psychotic illnesses such as schizophrenia and mania is a disruption of the ability to organize intentions, beliefs, emotions, and thoughts as verbal expressions. This chapter will examine language abnormalities in psychotic patients, ranging from lower-level disturbances of word formation and syntax to higher-level disturbances in discourse organization and conversational behavior. Our hope is that a more precise differentiation of these speech and communication disturbances will provide insights into the nature of different psychotic disorders and will provide tools for improving diagnosis and treatment.

2. Defining Psychosis

The term *psychosis* refers to an impaired ability to distinguish the boundaries of what is real and unreal. Typical psychotic symptoms include delusions (i.e., false, irrational beliefs which run counter to sociocultural conventions and are impervious to disconfirmation) and perceptual abnormalities such as hallucinations. Psychotic disturbances may arise from a variety of medical conditions, including hypothyroidism or hyperthyroidism, Parkinson's disease, multiple sclerosis, Alzheimer's disease, and brain tumors. Drugs such as cocaine, cannabis, LSD, amphetamines, and alcohol can induce psychotic states, as well as medications such as steroids and anesthetics. This chapter, however, will focus on the two principal psychotic syndromes which are not due to medical conditions or drugs and which represent major challenges in psychiatry: schizophrenia and bipolar disorder.

Schizophrenia is a syndrome traditionally viewed as a disturbance in the form and content of thought. Bipolar disorder, however, is viewed as a disturbance of mood and includes periods of manic symptoms where mood is elevated or irritable. Most bipolar patients also suffer from depressive episodes as well. Beyond the traditional dichotomy of thought vs. mood disturbance, what typically distinguishes these two illnesses is the longitudinal course exhibited by these two groups of patients. Both illnesses are characterized by waxing and waning symptoms. However, patients with schizophrenia tend to exhibit a downward, deteriorating course with residual symptoms even in the absence of psychotic manifestations whereas bipolar patients often exhibit a relatively full return of function between episodes of mania and depression. When viewed on a cross-sectional basis during periods of decompensation, however, both groups of disorders can generate psychotic symptoms (e.g., delusions and hallucinations) as well as dramatic alterations in speech and language.

3. The Concept of Formal Thought Disorder

Assessment and diagnosis by a psychiatrist largely relies on conversational interactions that occur during a clinical interview. Traditionally, the term, 'formal thought disorder,' has been applied to language disturbances exhibited by psychotic persons during such interviews. The term refers to utterances which are considered to be disordered or pathological, not because of the content which is being expressed, but rather because of breakdowns in the sequential organization of content when generated as conversational speech. The term 'formal' suggests that violations of formal rules of language have occurred, although psychiatrists generally do not attempt to specify what those rules consist of. We will briefly review the current descriptive nomenclature of thought disorder. The rest of the chapter will seek to more specifically delineate particular linguistic disruptions associated with psychosis. Much of the discussion in this section derives from the widely accepted typology of formal thought disorder described by Andreasen (1979).

Looseness of association or *derailment* is the *sine qua non* of formal thought disorder and refers to utterances which seem to shift or slip from one topic to another without bridging concepts. Consider the following example produced by a schizophrenic speaker (Hoffman et al. 1982):

> *Interviewer: Tell me about where you live.*   (1)
> *Patient: I live in one place and then another place. They're black and white, you know. That's why I love Christmas and stuff because, you know, it's different colors. I used to live in Brooklyn.*

In this instance, the patient seems to attempt to respond to the interviewer's statement, referring to living in more than one place. However, even this initial reference is somewhat unclear and awkward—is she living in more than one place? The next statement, indicating that these places are 'black and white,' is even harder to interpret. Perhaps the speaker is attempting to communicate that the places are very different, 'as different as black and white.' The listener must guess the meaning. The next statement, regarding 'Christmas and stuff,' is related to the previous statement insofar as it provides another example of 'different colors.' However, the 'Christmas' statement departs entirely from the topic prompted by the interviewer's question. In short, a topical shift seems to have occurred which derails the listener. The patient finally returns obliquely to the prompt ('Tell me about where you live'), mentioning where she lived previously (rather than in the present). The effect on the listener is bewilderment.

Tangentiality refers to a less severe type of formal thought disorder. Here, the patient is unable to sustain a goal-directed conversation. Shifts in the frame of reference occur in a more gradual fashion and, at any given moment, the speaker seems to offer a coherent message. Over time, however, the speaker departs from the original frame of reference and fails in getting from a desired point in conversation to a desired goal. For example (Hoffman 1993):

> *Interviewer: Can you tell me where you live?* (2)
> *Patient: I live in Connecticut. We live in a 50-year-old Tudor house that is very much a home. The house shows my personality. It is comfortable and modest. My husband's personality is very different. He is a very closed-off person who makes people feel ill at ease.*

The patient begins by clearly attempting to respond to the question by providing information about the house where she lives. The transition from statements about the house to statements about the husband seem quite comprehensible in isolation. However, the effect is unsettling to the listener because the final topic departs clearly from the question: the listener must shift gears without warning.

Circumstantiality refers to speech that is significantly delayed in getting from its original point to its desired goal, but ultimately does so; it is often characterized by excessive detail and parenthetical commentary. An example (Hoffman and McGlashan 1997):

> *Interviewer: What are your thoughts about* (3)
> *politics?*
> *Patient: Well, I'm most interested in national politics, you know, what the President is doing. I think that a lot of our problems are up to him to solve. But I don't know then again if any human being can pull off what he's gotta do. People always promise more than they deliver. That's been my experience all along, teachers, bosses, parents. My life is just one disappointment followed by the next. It gettin' so that I just expect the worst. And that's probably gonna be the case with our new President.*

Pressured speech refers to excessive speech which is produced at a rapid rate and is difficult to interrupt. Traditionally, pressured speech is associated with mania though some patients with schizophrenia and other types of psychosis (e.g., thyrotoxicosis) can exhibit this form of speech behavior.

Flight of ideas characterizes another manifestation of formal thought disorder, more commonly associated with manic psychosis than with schizophrenia. The term refers to conversational narratives expressing topical shifts which are accompanied by pressured speech; topical shifts may be less idiosyncratic than in the case of looseness of associations and are accompanied by pressured speech. Speech deviance of this sort may arise from plays on words (such as alliteration) rather than on topical relationships. Flight of ideas is also associated with various medical conditions or substance-induced psychotic states (i.e., thyrotoxicosis, amphetamine-induced psychosis). An example:

> *Interviewer: Can you tell me why you are in* (4)
> *the hospital?*
> *Patient: I am in the hospital because I got in trouble with the police. You see, they are a forceful bunch of people who seek lawfulness, and I was breaking the law, and if the law has been violated, then someone must pay the price, and who else to pay the price but me because I broke the law. In fact, many people break the law. Have you read the newspapers recently? Everyone is breaking the law, from public officials to schoolteachers to physicians, but not everyone is ending up in the hospital, or jail. The president of the United States, well he has a tough job, and I can tell you one thing about it, ...*

Formal thought disorder is typically associated with schizophrenia, manic psychosis, or psychotic disorders due to a general medical condition. However, it may be present, albeit in milder forms, in a wide range of psychiatric disorders, such as major depressive disorder, certain personality disorders (i.e., schizotypal or borderline personality disorders), and cyclothymic disorder (Hoffman and McGlashan 1997). Of note is that topical shifts occur frequently during normal conversational speech. However, these transitions generally are signaled by speakers with comments such as, 'by the way...' or 'this may be off the topic, but...' (Hoffman et al. 1982). Jokes comprise another type of 'normal' topical shift. In these conversational scenarios the listener is also warned—either by comments ('Did you hear about...') or by a change in affective tone—that a topical shift is occurring.

Poverty of speech, or *alogia*, refers to reduced conversational output. Here, spontaneous speech is markedly diminished or absent, and responses to questions consist of only a few words. Poverty of speech can be exhibited by patients with schizophrenia, depression, Parkinson's Disease, Broca's aphasia, and various types of dementia. The most extreme form of poverty of speech is mutism, which occurs during a catatonic state. Complete mutism also can be seen in dissociative disturbances and a wide range of brain lesions (Hoffman and McGlashan 1997). *Thought blocking* is a form of poverty of speech in which the patient often indicates no recall of what he or she has just said—

typically the patient reports that his mind has gone totally blank. Consequently speech comes to an abrupt halt. Patients with thought blocking often experience marked anxiety which further disrupts their ability to speak clearly. A distinction has been made between poverty of speech, where actual language production is sparse, and *poverty of speech content*, where the patient produces a normal amount of speech but the content is only vague or repetitive and conveys little information. Poverty of speech content is often seen in schizophrenia and various aphasic syndromes.

The concept of formal thought disorder has been subcategorized into 'positive' and 'negative' types (Andreasen and Grove 1986). The former refers to derailment/looseness of associations, flight of ideas, tangentiality, circumstantiality, pressured speech, while the latter refers to poverty of speech content/alogia and thought blocking.

Other methods of categorizing thought disorder have been formulated. In a study of schizophrenic and manic speech segments using both psychiatric clinicians and linguists to judge deviance, Berenbaum and Bearch (1995) concluded that departures from social convention needs to be considered as a specific form of deviance. This category reflects the style of discourse. For instance, psychotic persons may refer to themselves in the third person, answer questions exclusively with other questions, or sermonize instead of engaging in a conversational exchange.

4. Referential Impairment and Discourse Planning Disruptions

The descriptions of formal thought disorder provided above do not consider cognitive or linguistic processes which underlie the production of conversational discourse. One concept that has been used to unpack the linguistic nature of thought disorder is 'discourse planning.' This process refers to the ability to hold a coherent message or communicative goal in mind while assembling a set of propositions which express the message and which can be understood readily by the listener. A critical requirement for this level of language processing is that the speaker take into account what the listener knows in terms of conversational conventions, shared knowledge, and previous information generated by the conversational interaction in order to ensure sufficient levels of comprehensibility of ensuing utterances.

A readily understandable class of discourse planning disturbance consists of referential failures. Take the following example (Thomas 1995):

> **Interviewer:** *You just must mean an*   (5)
> *emotional person, that's all.*
> **Patient:** *Well, not very much I mean, what if I were dead. It's a funeral age. Well I um. Now I had my toenails operated on. They got infected and I wasn't able to do it. But they would let me at my tools. Well!*

In this example, the word *they* is used twice; in the first example, *they* appears to refer to *toenails*, but in the last sentence, it is unclear what *they* refers to. The reference to *tools* is also unclear. Unclear referencing places a burden on the listener to mentally specify the 'objects' (i.e., the nouns, noun phases, and pronouns) of discourse. Empirical data has convincingly shown that vague referencing is common among thought-disordered schizophrenics (Rochester and Martin 1979; Wykes and Leff 1982). In a controlled comparison of schizophrenic and manic speech, Docherty et al. (1996a) reported that communication disturbances seen in schizophrenics were more likely to reflect information references completely unknown to the listener whereas manic subjects were more likely to use references ambiguously. Both findings indicate that referential problems are characteristic of psychotic speech.

Distinctions between schizophrenia, mania, and normal controls in the area of discourse planning also were borne out in a study by Hoffman et al. (1986). The study was based on Deese's model of textual coherence (Deese 1978, 1980), which holds that 'an extended, multisentence text will be experienced as coherent by a listener if he or she can organize the propositions expressed by the text into hierarchical form.' Schizophrenic patients were shown to be much less effective in organizing their speech into hierarchical structures (Hoffman et al. 1986). Manics, however, were able to produce complex, well-formed discourse hierarchies, but shifted from one discourse hierarchy to another (Hoffman et al. 1986). These findings demonstrated that incoherence in schizophrenic speech was marked by a failure in creating discourse structures that was not present among manic speakers. The experience of listening to the manic speaker still produces the subjective experience of 'derailment' because manic discourse 'jumps' from one discourse plan to another. However, manic speakers appeared to retain competence in generating coherent discourse; their problem seemed to be excessive levels of activation which destabilized discourse planning. In contrast, schizophrenic speakers appeared to be incompetent in generating *any* discourse structure.

Deficient discourse planning in psychotic syndromes could be due, in part, to difficulties in retaining contextual information in working memory (Docherty et al. 1996a). Working memory is a general term referring to the ability to hold information 'on-line' while using it to guide behavior. Deficits in verbal working memory have been correlated with both disturbances in discourse coherence (Serper 1993) and referential errors (Daneman 1991; Docherty et al. 1996b). It is hypothesized that if psychotic patients cannot hold in mind the context of their verbal productions, they are bound to falter in remaining goal-directed and coherent when producing conversational speech. Specific consequences of such cognitive failures would be inappropriate, vague, or erroneous referencing of information, as well as breakdowns in the hierarchial organization of sets of statements or propositions. Expanding on this notion, Barch and Berenbaum (1997), in a carefully executed study of schizophrenic subjects, tested the hypothesis that the reinforcing prior context would facilitate the retrieval of information used to generate a discourse plan. They found that presenting schizophrenics with prior context enabled them to produce more extensive, coherent speech.

Speech impairments exhibited by psychotic patients can also be examined from the perspective of formal linguistics. This view highlights formal rules which determine word selection and how words are organized as syntactic structures. These impairments will be briefly reviewed in the next two sections.

5. Language Disturbances Associated with Word Formation and Word Selection

Some psychotic patients will, on occasion, produce words that do not belong to the conventional lexicon. An example produced by a schizophrenic speaker is as follows

he still had fooch with teykrimez, I'll be (6)
willing to betcha (Chaika 1974).

Derived morphemic paraphasias represent a more common lexical disturbance in psychotic speech, in which acceptable lexical morphemes are added inappropriately or oddly to the root word (Lecours and Vanier-Clement 1976). Examples include:

attain vigoration and strength (Hoffman (7)
and Sledge 1984, 150)

stated not necessarily factuated (Vetter 1968, (8)
5; cited in Maher 1966).

Composed morphemic paraphasias represent the inappropriate binding of two lexical morphemes, a condition seen especially in schizophrenic speech (Lecours and Vanier-Clement 1976):

lie-truths (Bleuler 1991, Zifkin 1911/1950, (9)
152).

Schizophrenic patients may have difficulty with word-finding, producing speech which may have an aphasic quality as lexical elements are inserted inappropriately or oddly into syntactic frames:

He owns a store on Fifth Avenue, and that's (10)
never mentioned because that is his side-kick
(intended: *sideline*; Hoffman and Sledge 1988, 97).

Such word selection errors occur with varying degrees of severity, ranging from simple noun-noun and verb-

verb substitutions to more severe noun-verb substitutions such as the following:

fish school in their own communities (11)
(Hoffman and Sledge 1988, 97)

in which the noun, 'school,' is presumably substituted for the verb 'swim.'

Clang associations represent strings of words that are chosen because they are similar in sound, and which may even rhyme. An example of clanging is:

I'm not trying to make a noise. I'm trying (12)
to make sense. If you can make sense out of nonsense,
well, have fun. I'm trying to make sense out of
nonsense. I'm not making sense [cents] any more. I
have to make dollars (Andreasen and Black 1995,
67–68).

Disturbances in word construction and selection can occur in psychotic conditions such as schizophrenia and bipolar disorder, and may demonstrate varying levels of severity. They are more commonly detected in patients who have been seriously ill for especially long periods of time.

6. Disturbances of Syntax and Grammar

Paragrammatical segments represent speech in which word combinations or word order deviate from appropriate syntactic form. This example at least approximates grammatical English:

That's why, you know, the fact there was (13)
no stigmatism (sic) *attached to that clearly explained*
in the record why you were put back (Hoffman and
Sledge 1984, 154).

Taken in context, this segment seems to discuss consequences of being left back a grade in school. The target intention corresponds to something like the following (bracketed words need to be added in order to render the segment completely grammatical):

[It] clearly explained in the record why (13a)
you were put back...that's why, you know, there
was no [stigma] attached to the fact that I [was].

Besides the erroneous attachment of an affix to *stigma*, the relationship between (13) and (13a) reflects the exchange and reordering of phrases.

In contrast, *word salad* is an incoherent mixture of words and phrases, without regard to grammatical form, and is occasionally produced by severely impaired psychotic patients:

The honest bring-back-to-life doctors (14)
agents much take John Black out through making up
design meaning straight neutral underworld shadow
tunnel (Lorenz 1961, cited in Chaika 1977, 466).

One early study of speech samples suggested that patients in actively manic states can demonstrate disturbances of syntax and word generation similar to those found in schizophrenia (Morice and Ingram 1982). However, later studies indicated that schizophrenic speech contained more of these types of speech errors than did that of bipolar speakers (Morice and McNicol 1986; Fraser et al. 1986; Sledge et al. in press).

7. Syntactic Complexity

Studies of spontaneously produced schizophrenic speech consistently have shown diminution of syntactic complexity when compared to controls (Morice and Ingram 1982; Morice and McNicol 1986; Fraser et al. 1986). Comparing schizophrenic and non-schizophrenic speakers on the basis of syntactic complexity demonstrated a greater amount of reductions in the number and depth of embedded clauses in the former group with a reduced percentage of dependent clauses with *wh-* pronouns.

A study of written language confirmed that schizophrenic patients produce language with reduced syntactic complexity (Hoffman et al. 1985). This study utilized a writing task which controlled for the content of responses by providing a paragraph composed of very short (2–4 word) sentences describing the manufacture of aluminum. Subjects were instructed to rewrite the paragraph in a better way. Ordinarily subjects combine these very short sentences into more grammatically complex sentences with embedded clauses. Besides producing reduced sentence grammatical complexity, responses of schizophrenic patients demonstrated greater disruption in the representation of meaning of the original stimulus paragraph when undertaking complex grammatical transformations. These findings suggested that among schizophrenic patients, cognitive requirements associated with generating complex syntactic structures were excessive and disrupted the patient's ability to hold in mind the 'gist' of what they want to say or write.

Overall, reduced syntactic complexity demonstrated by schizophrenic patients suggests that their greater likelihood of producing syntactic errors arises from reduced capacity to generate well-formed syntax. These difficulties may arise from a specific impairment in linguistic capacity or a more general impairment in retention of contextual information. In support of the latter view, the aforementioned study by Barch and Berenbaum (1997) found that reinforcing context elevated syntactic complexity of schizophrenic speech.

8. Semantic Priming

There is considerable evidence suggesting that when we speak, our utterances activate words, concepts, or ideas, which in turn activate other, associated words (Collins and Loftus 1975; Neeley 1991; Paulsen et al.

1996). For instance, when we say or think to ourselves the word 'salt,' the word 'pepper' is also activated to some extent as well. The activation of semantically related words, concepts, or ideas serves to facilitate the production of additional discourse. Drawing on a semantic model of memory and language association, some researchers have proposed that schizophrenic thought disorder arises from the excessive or impaired spread of semantic associations (Manschreck et al. 1988; Spitzer et al. 1993).

A study by Paulsen et al. (1996) examined semantic associations in early-onset schizophrenics, late-onset schizophrenics, and normal controls. Subjects were administered the Animal Fluency Test to generate speech information. Subsequently, a semantic map of their verbal associations was constructed. The study demonstrated that early-onset schizophrenia, characterized by a more malignant course and outcome, was associated with more disturbed semantic organization compared to late-onset schizophrenics as well as normal control subjects.

Spitzer et al. (1993) carried out a study in which schizophrenic patients and normal controls were asked to carry out a lexical decision task on presented words (i.e., target words) that were primed by one of three types of words: (a) associated; (b) indirectly associated; or (c) nonassociated words. The lexical decision task involved seeing the prime word on a monitor, and then signaling whether the word that followed was a real word by clicking a button. Reaction times for the task were determined for each pair of words, which formed four total categories: (a) associated pair (e.g., 'hen-egg'); (b) indirectly associated (e.g., 'lemon-sweet' mediated by the word, 'sour'); (c) nonassociated pair (e.g., 'sofa-wing'); and (d) word-nonword pair—'drift-kribe' (Spitzer et al. 1993). If the target word was an associated pair, the lexical decision task ordinarily is achieved more rapidly—this phenomenon is referred to as *direct semantic priming*. The Spitzer study found that schizophrenic patients were more likely than normals to show an *indirect semantic priming effect*. These patients were more likely to be influenced by extraneous associations which could 'derail' speech.

9. Neurobiological Mechanisms

Many researchers have attempted to discern the neurobiologic underpinnings of psychotic language disturbances. Some of this work utilizes findings derived from clinical neurology. For instance, paragrammatical utterances, paraphasias, and other word generation problems demonstrated by psychotic patients at times are so severe that they resemble utterances produced by patients with Wernicke's aphasia due to organic brain lesions. These lesions involve the dominant hemisphere temporal and/or parietal lobe, suggesting that similar brain areas could be impaired in these psychotic patients. There is also good evidence that syntactic processing occurs, at least in part, in the inferior frontal lobe (Rumsey et al. 1994). Studies of brain activation have suggested that schizophrenia may be associated with disturbances of the left inferior frontal lobe (Rubin et al. 1991), which could account for the many studies demonstrating reduced syntactic complexity and syntactic errors in this group.

Neurological data provides less clear guidance as to the neuroanatomic locus of impairment of discourse level difficulties. There is some evidence that language intentions of this sort occur in prefrontal cortical areas closely associated with the supplementary motor area (Goldberg 1985; MacNeilage 1986). Numerous studies have suggested prefrontal impairment in psychosis.

There is also interest in right hemisphere abnormalities associated with schizophrenia. Several studies have related the facilitation of particular semantic associations to hemispheric laterality of brain function. The right hemisphere has been implicated in the generation of unusual or remote words in the generation of associations (Nakagawa 1991; Chiarello and Richards 1992; Abdullaev and Posner 1997; Weisbrod et al. 1998). It is possible that remote associations are excessive in schizophrenic speech (Garfield et al. 1992). The right cerebral hemisphere also has been implicated in understanding the subtle and pragmatic dimensions of conversational language (Foldi 1987). In a study by Winner and Gardner (1977), right hemisphere brain-damaged patients were shown to interpret metaphorical statements in more concrete terms, a finding commonly associated with schizophrenia. Cutting (1990) has extensively reviewed the literature of right hemispheric contributions to (a) language functions such as phonology, syntax, semantics, and pragmatics; (b) visual and auditory perception; (c) memory and attention; and (d) simple as well as complex motor movements. There is evidence to suggest that many of these areas are compromised in psychosis, implicating the right hemisphere or the differential balance of right-left hemispheric function in conditions such as bipolar disorder or schizophrenia. Lohr and Caliguri (1997) review findings of right-left hemispheric dysfunction in schizophrenia and bipolar disorder, and conduct their own study of older, psychotic patients with motor asymmetry. They contend right > left hemispheric pathology may be present in bipolar disorder, while the opposite is true in schizophrenia.

The consequence of anomalous cerebral lateralization (i.e., the inability to establish unequivocal cerebral dominance for speech) has been hypothesized by Crow (1990, 1996) to be the central genetic deficit in schizophrenia. A study by Weisbrod et al. (1998) elaborated on the hemispheric contributions to direct and indirect semantic priming effects in thought disordered and nonthought disordered schizophrenics,

as well as normals, using a lexical decision task. They demonstrated that normals and nonthought disordered schizophrenics showed no indirect priming effects in the left hemisphere but that thought-disordered schizophrenic patients did demonstrate these effects. These findings suggest that thought disorder in schizophrenic patients may arise from less focused activation of semantic networks in the left hemisphere. This study can be considered as evidence supporting Crow's anomalous lateralization hypothesis of schizophrenia; moreover, it can be taken as an extension of Spitzer's (1993) investigation showing that indirect semantic priming effects were significantly increased in schizophrenic patients.

10. Conclusion

In summary, a number of specific language and communication difficulties produced by psychotic speakers can make the job of listening much more difficult. These language disturbances may occur at many levels, ranging from word generation and syntactical sequencing of words and phrases, to producing extended discourse which reflect coherent discourse goals and a well-organized hierarchy of propositions while providing unambiguous referencing of nouns and pronouns. There is some evidence that schizophrenic speakers, when compared to manic speakers, produce more severe impairments which more often involve word generation and selection, and syntax. Similarly, schizophrenic patients seem to demonstrate more fundamental impairments in discourse planning relative to manic speakers.

These findings, considered together, suggest the following. First, language impairments demonstrated by schizophrenic patients suggest a primary disruption of capacities responsible for language production operating at different levels. Second, language impairments produced by manic speakers suggest a different mechanism: over-production of both words and speaker intentions which derail the speaker and the listener. Third, the many different types of language abnormalities produced by psychotic speakers suggest that underlying brain disturbances are not localized to a single cortical region or circuit. Instead, multiple brain regions seem to be involved to varying degrees. The extent to which language impairments in psychotic speakers reflect language-specific brain processes (either dominant hemisphere or nondominant hemisphere) versus more generalized neurocognitive impairments (involving, for instance, working memory systems) is not known. Nonetheless there has been considerable progress in better understanding the nature of language impairments in psychotic patients which holds promise in providing insights into the underlying pathophysiology of these disorders. More refined methods for classifying these impairments and corresponding brain disturbances could enhance our ability to provide more specific treatments for these patients.

Bibliography

Abdullaev Y G, Posner M I 1997 Time course of activating brain areas in generating verbal associations. *Psychological Science* **8:** 56–59

Andreasen N C 1979 Thought, language and communication disorders: I. Clinical assessment, definition of terms, and evaluation of their reliability. *Archives of General Psychiatry* **35:** 1315–21

Andreasen N C, Black D W 1995 *Introductory Textbook of Psychiatry*. American Psychiatric Press, Washington, DC

Andreasen N C, Grove W M 1986 Thought, language and communication in schizophrenia: Diagnosis and prognosis. *Schizophrenia Bulletin* **12:** 348–59

Barch D M, Berenbaum H 1997 The effect of language manipulations on negative thought disorder and discourse coherence disturbances in schizophrenia. *Psychiatry Research* **71:** 115–27

Berenbaum H, Barch D 1995 The categorization of thought disorder. *Journal of Psycholinguistic Research* **24**(5): 349–76

Bleuler E 1991 *Dementia Praecox or the Group of Schizophrenias* (Trans. by J. Zinkin, 1950). International University Press, New York

Chaika E A 1974 A linguist looks at 'schizophrenic' language. *Brain and Language* **1:** 257–76

Chaika E A 1977 Schizophrenic speech, slips of the tongue, and jargonaphasia: A reply to Fromkin and to Lecours and Vanier-Clement. *Brain and Language* **4:** 464–75

Chiarello C, Richards L 1992 Another look at categorical priming in the cerebral hemispheres. *Neuropsychologia* **30:** 381–92

Collins A M, Loftus E F 1975 The spreading activation theory of semantic processing. *Psychological Review* **82:** 407–28

Crow T 1996 Sexual selection as the mechanism of evolution of intelligence: A Darwinian theory of the origins of psychosis. *Journal of Psychopharmacology* **10:** 77–87

Crow T 1990 Temporal lobe asymmetries as the key of the etiology of schizophrenia. *Schizophrenia Bulletin* **16:** 433–43

Cutting J 1990 *The Right Cerebral Hemisphere and Psychiatric Disorders*. Oxford University Press, Oxford

Daneman M 1991 Working memory as a predictor of verbal fluency. *Journal of Psycholinguistic Research* **20:** 445–65

Deese J 1978 Thought into speech. *American Scientist* **66:** 314–21

Deese J 1980 Pauses, prosody, and the demands of production in language. In: Dechert H W, Raupach M (eds.) *Temporal Variables in Speech: Studies in Honor of Frieda Goldman-Eisler*. Mouton, The Hague

Docherty N M, DeRosa M, Andreasen N C 1996a Communication disturbances in schizophrenia and mania. *Archives of General Psychiatry* **53:** 358–64

Docherty N M, Rakfeldt J, Hawkins K A, Hoffman R E, Quinlan D M, Sledge W H 1996b Working memory, attention, and communication disturbances in schizophrenia. *Journal of Abnormal Psychology* **105:** 212–19

Foldi N C 1987 Appreciation of pragmatic interpretations of indirect commands: comparison of right and left hemisphere brain-damaged patients. *Brain and Language* **31:** 88–108

Fraser W I, King K M, Thomas P, Kendell R E 1986 The diagnosis of schizophrenia by language analysis. *British Journal of Psychiatry* **148:** 275–78

Garfield D A, Rapp C, Evens M 1992 Natural language processing in psychiatry. Artificial intelligence technology and psychopathology. *Journal of Nervous and Mental Disease* **180:** 227–37

Goldberg G 1985 Supplementary motor area: Review and hypotheses. *Behavioral and Brain Sciences* **8:** 567–88

Hoffman R E 1993 Linguistic aspects of language behavior in schizophrenia. In: Blanken G, Dittmean J, Grimm H, Marshall J C, Wallesch C W (eds.) *Linguistic Disorders and Pathologies*. Walter de Gruyter, Berlin

Hoffman R E, McGlashan T H 1997 Alterations of speech, thought, perception, and self-experience. In: Tasman A, Kay J, Lieberman J A (eds.) *Psychiatry*. W. B. Saunders Company, Philadelphia, PA

Hoffman R E, Sledge W 1984 A microgenetic model of paragrammatisms produced by a schizophrenic speaker. *Brain and Language* **21:** 147–73

Hoffman R E, Sledge W 1988 An analysis of grammatical deviance occurring in spontaneous Schizophrenic Speech. *Journal of Neurolinguistics* **3:** 89–101

Hoffman R E, Stopek S, Andreasen N C 1986 A comparative study of manic versus schizophrenic speech disorganization. *Archives of General Psychiatry* **43:** 831–38

Hoffman R E, Hogben G L, Smith H, Calhoun W F 1985 Message disruptions during syntactic processing in schizophrenia. *Journal of Communication Disorders* **18:** 183–202

Hoffman R E, Kirstein L, Stopek S, Cichetti D 1982 Apprehending schizophrenic discourse: A structural analysis of the listener's task. *Brain and Language* **15:** 207–33

Lecours A R, Vanier-Clement M V 1976 Schizophrenia and jargonaphasia: comparative description with comments on Chaika's and Fromkin's respective looks at 'schizophrenic' language. *Brain and Language* **3:** 516–65

Lohr J B, Caligiuri M P 1997 Lateralized hemispheric dysfunction in the major psychotic disorders: historical perspectives and findings from a major study of motor asymmetry in older patients. *Schizophrenia Research* **27:** 191–98

Lorenz M 1961 Problems posed by schizophrenic language. *Archives of General Psychiatry* **4:** 603–10

MacNeilage P F 1986 Bimanual coordination and the beginning of speech. In: Lindblom B, Zitterstrom R (eds.) *Precursors of Early Speech*. Stockton Press, Oslo, 189–201

Maher B A 1966 *Principles of Psychopathology*. McGraw-Hill, New York

Manschreck T C, Maher B A, Milavetz J J, Ames D, Wesstein C C, Schneyer M L 1988 Semantic priming in thought disordered schizophrenic patients. *Schizophrenia Research* **1:** 61–66

Morice R D, Ingram J C 1982 Language analysis in schizophrenia: Diagnostic implications. *Australian and New Zealand Journal of Psychiatry* **16:** 11–21

Morice R D, McNicol D 1986 Language changes in schizophrenia: A limited replication study. *Schizophrenia Bulletin* **12:** 239–51

Nakagawa A 1991 Role of anterior and posterior attention networks in hemispheric asymmetries during lexical decision tasks. *Journal of Cognitive Neuroscience* **3:** 313–21

Neely J H 1991 Semantic priming effects in visual word recognition: A selective review of current findings and theories. In: Besner D, Humphreys G W (eds.) *Basic Progress in Reading and Visual Word Recognition*. Lawrence Erlbaum, Hillsdale, NJ

Paulsen J S, Romero R, Chan A, Davis A V, Heaton R K L, Jeste D V 1996 Impairment of the semantic network in schizophrenia. *Psychiatry Research* **63**: 109–21

Rochester S, Martin J R 1979 *Crazy Talk: A Study of the Discourse of Schizophrenic Speakers*. Plenum Press, New York

Rubin P, Holm S, Friberg L, Videbach P, Andersen H S, Bendsen B B, Stromso N, Larsen J K, Lassen N A, Hemmingsen R 1991 Altered modulation of prefrontal and subcortical brain activity in newly diagnosed schizophrenia and schizophreniform disorder. *Archives of General Psychiatry* **48**: 987–95

Rumsey J M, Zametkin A J, Andreason P, Hanahan A P, Hamburger S D, Aquino T, King C, Pikus A, Cohen R M 1994 Normal activation of frontotemporal cortex in dyslexia, as measured with oxygen 15 positron emission tomography. *Archives of Neurology* **51**: 27–38

Serper M R 1993 Visual controlled information processing resources and formal thought disorder in schizophrenia and mania. *Schizophrenia Research* **9**: 59–66

Sledge W, Hoffman R, Hawkins K, Docherty N, Quinlan D, Rakfeldt J. Linguistic deviance in schizophrenia: A preliminary report. In: Spitzer M, Maher B (eds.) *Experimental Psychopathology*. Cambridge University Press, Cambridge, in press

Spitzer M, Braun U, Maier S, Hermle L, Maher B A 1993 Indirect semantic priming in schizophrenic patients. *Schizophrenia Research* **11**(1): 71–80

Thomas P 1995 Thought disorder or communication disorder: Linguistic science provides a new approach. *British Journal of Psychiatry* **166**(3): 287–90

Vetter H (ed.) 1968 *Language Behavior in Schizophrenia*. Thomas, Springfield, IL

Weisbrod M, Maier S, Harig S, Himmelsbach U, Spitzer M 1998 Lateralised semantic and indirect semantic priming effects in people with schizophrenia. *British Journal of Psychiatry* **172**: 142–46

Winner E, Gardner H 1977 The comprehension of metaphor in brain-damaged patients. *Brain* **100**: 717–29

Wykes T, Leff J 1982 Disordered speech: Differences between manics and schizophrenics. *Brain and Language* **15**: 117–24

List of Contributors

Contributors are listed in alphabetical order together with their affiliations. Titles of articles which they have written follow in alphabetical order, along with the respective page numbers. Co-authorship is indicated by *.

MASSARO, D. W. (University of California, Santa Cruz, CA, USA)
Speech Perception: 42

MATHIESON, L. (Northwick Park and St Mark's Hospitals, London, UK)
Disorders of Voice: 247

MAXIM, J. (University College London, UK)
Aging and Language: 142

MENN, L. (University of Colorado, Boulder, CO, USA)
*Acquisition of Phonemes: 106

MORRIS, R. (University of London, UK)
Language Dysfunction in Dementia: 362

MUNHALL, K. G. (Queen's University, Kingston, Canada)
*The Neurophysiology of Speech: 78

MURDOCH, B. E. (University of Queensland, Brisbane, Australia)
Acquired Childhood Aphasia: 327

OAKHILL, J. (University of Sussex, Brighton, UK)
Acquisition of Reading: 120

PETRIE, H. L. (University of Hertfordshire, Hatfield, UK)
Language Production: 97

PIZZUTO, E. (Istituto di Psicologia del CNR, Roma, Italy)
*Deafness and Sign Language: 179

RICHARDSON, S. O. (University of South Florida, Tampa, FL, USA)
Developmental Causes: 168

RINGEL, R. L. (Purdue University, West Lafayette, IN, USA)
*Acquired Causes: 165

ROBERTSON, J. (Manchester Metropolitan University, UK)
*Classification of Developmental Dyslexia and Intervention: 239

ROSENBEK, J. C. (VA Hospital, Madison, WI, USA)
Verbal Apraxia: 268

RUSTIN, L. (Michael Palin Centre for Stammering Children, London, UK)
*Disorders of Fluency: Intervention: 198

SANFILIPPO, L. C. (Yale University, New Haven, CT, USA)
*Language Disorders in the Psychoses: 400

SNOWLING, M. J. (University of York, UK)
*Disorders of Reading and Writing: 353; *Reading Difficulties*: 237

STOEL-GAMMON, C. (University of Washington, Seattle, WA, USA)
*Acquisition of Phonemes: 106; *Babbling in Hearing and Deaf Infants*: 104

TAGER-FLUSBERG, H. (Eunice Kennedy Shriver Center, Waltham, MA, USA)
Acquisition of Grammar: 112

TOGEBY, O. (University of Aarhus, Denmark)
Pragmatic Principles in Verbal Communication: 146

TRANEL, D. (University of Iowa, Iowa City, IA, USA)
*Syndromes of Aphasia: 305

VAN HOUT, A. (Catholic University of Louvain, Brussels, Belgium)
Learning Disabilities: 205

Van Lancker, D. (Carleton College, Northfield, MN, USA)
The Right Hemisphere and Verbal Communication: 365

Volterra, V. (Istituto di Psicologia del CNR, Roma, Italy)
*Deafness and Sign Language: 179

Wakita, H. J. (Panasonic Technologies Inc., Santa Barbara, CA, USA)
Acoustics of Speech: 1

Whurr, R. (National Hospital for Neurology and Neurosurgery, London, UK)
*Acquired Disorders of Language (Aphasia): Evaluation of the Effectiveness of Intervention: 384

Zhu, H. (University of Newcastle, UK)
*Sociolinguistics and Language Pathology: 149

Name Index

Subject Index